J2EE FrontEnd Technologies: A Programmer's Guide to Servlets, JavaServer Pages, and Enterprise JavaBeans

LENNART JÖRELID

Apress™

J2EE FrontEnd Technologies: A Programmer's Guide to Servlets, JavaServer Pages, and Enterprise JavaBeans

ISBN (pbk): 1-893115-96-8

Printed and bound in the United States of America 12345678910

Editorial Directors: Dan Appleman, Gary Cornell, Jason Gilmore, Karen Watterson

Marketing Manager: Stephanie Rodriguez

Technical Reviewers: Janet Traub, Steve Close, David Czarnecki

Project Manager: Carol Burbo

Developmental Editor: Valerie Perry

Copy Editors: Kim Wimpsett, Tom Gillen

Production Editor: Tory McLearn

Compositor: Susan Glinert

Indexer: Julie Kawabata

Cover Designer: Tom Debolski

Artist: Allan Rasmussen

Distributed to the book trade in the United States by Springer-Verlag New York, Inc.,175 Fifth Avenue, New York, NY, 10010

and outside the United States by Springer-Verlag GmbH & Co. KG, Tiergartenstr. 17, 69112 Heidelberg, Germany

In the United States, phone 1-800-SPRINGER, email orders@springer-ny.com, or visit http://www.springer-ny.com.

Outside the United States, fax +49 6221 345229, email orders@springer.de, or visit http://www.springer.de.

For information on translations, please contact Apress directly at 901 Grayson Street, Suite 204, Berkeley, CA 94710.

Phone 510-549-5930, fax 510-549-5939, email info@apress.com, or visit http://www.apress.com.

The source code for this book is available to readers at http://www.apress.com in the Downloads section. You will need to answer questions pertaining to this book in order to successfully download the code.

For Camilla and Lotta

Contents at a Glance

Contents

Acknowledgments

THIS BOOK HAS HAD a long and complex writing process. The specifications of all the topics covered have changed at least once during the project. Despite my constant effort to modify the text and images to reflect the changes, the many people who had a part in the book's development have accepted change with a smile.

At Apress, I would like to thank Gary Cornell, Grace Wong, and Carol Burbo for believing in the project and providing structure to the writing process. Special thanks to the technical editors Janet Traub, Steve Close, and David Czarnecki who provided invaluable assistance in the development process. Many thanks to the editors Valerie Perry, Tom Gillen, and Kim Wimpsett who read, pondered, and suggested restructuring. Their skills are what separate my scattered bursts of information from the quality structure of this book.

For an infinite patience and the ever-present warm smile despite my prolonged absence from social and worldly events, my grateful thanks go to Camilla, Lars, and Margareta. For relatives, friends, and family to whom I must have been a complete stranger during this project, I direct my most mischievous apologies.

About the Author

WITH WORKING EXPERIENCE THAT spans projects in the United States, Canada, United Kingdom, Switzerland, Sweden, and Germany, Lennart is a recognized expert, architect, and educator in the Java technology community. His key skills are in the object-oriented analysis, design, and programming of Java 2 Enterprise Edition (J2EE) systems.

Through his affiliation as Java Manager with jGuru (one of the most popular Web sites for Java developers), he has explained Java technology to thousands of programmers. Before joining jGuru.com, Lennart was Senior Java Consultant and Systems Designer for NetGuide Scandinavia in Göteborg, Sweden. His focus is server-side Java and electronic-commerce application systems. He is fluent in many programming languages, as well as most J2EE server-side technologies. Lennart has a master's degree in Engineering Physics from Chalmers University of Technology in Sweden.

Part I

Servlets

CHAPTER 1

Servlet Theory

WHENEVER A SIMPLE IDEA is elegant and powerful enough that its applications open development paths that were previously closed, the architects of that idea might truly feel their work has been a benefit to the development community. A servlet represents an idea that falls into that category, vaguely bringing back memories of the old Othello game slogan, "A minute to learn, a lifetime to master."

This chapter of the book summarizes the architecture of Java 2 Enterprise Edition (J2EE) systems where servlets take part; it also covers the programming model of servlets. Chapter 1 also provides you with a tour explaining features of the Java packages where servlet classes and support classes may be found. Finally, you'll discover how to maintain state and create a user session with a servlet.

What Are Servlets?

Servlets are pieces of business logic that may be plugged into any server process that accepts a binary or textual request stream as its only argument and produces a binary or textual response stream as a result. Most servers work this way, so there are a great number of servers, which may host and use a servlet. Figure 1-1 shows the server-side of a request/response call from an imaginary client to a Web server, which uses a servlet to communicate with a legacy system. We could actually remove the servlet from the scenario if we could modify and recompile the Server to talk to our legacy server. However, the logic of the majority of application servers encountered in daily computer usage or development is fixed in a monolithic blob of machine code, so we must use another component with a standard API to convert the incoming Request to a format understood by the back-end system. Enter Servlets.

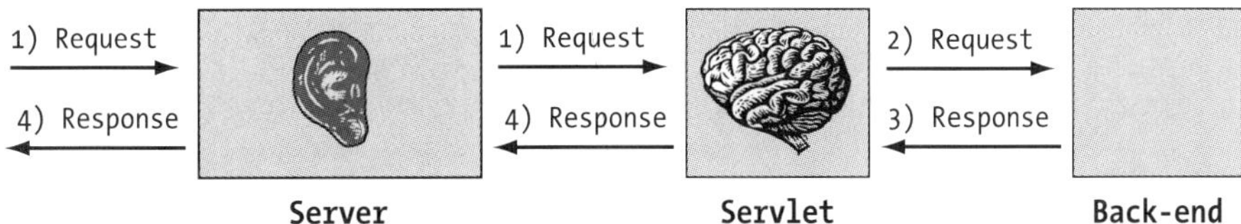

Figure 1-1. The roles of the Web server and the servlet in a roundtrip call, where a client browser receives data from a back-end legacy system

The Web server acts as a listener ("ear") that simply directs any incoming request (1) to the servlet. The servlet contains the active logic ("brains"), which reformats the incoming request to an outgoing that matches the specification of a legacy system (2). Having processed the request, the legacy system responds to the servlet (3), which reformats the data to fit the format of the client and outputs a response (4). The Web server simply relays the response (4) to the client.

Without a standardized component framework, extending the business logic of a specialized, monolithic server with your customized business logic tends to be difficult at best. If you are persistent enough to continue the learning curve, the server commonly requires you to learn a specific programming interface to create server-specific plugin modules. As an example, the popular Web servers from Netscape and Microsoft both support a custom C library that allows the developer to create business-logic plugins to each Web server. Of course, there are no similarities between the two application programming interfaces (APIs)—you must recode your plugin if you change Web servers.

In a world of binary, platform-specific servers, servlets are reusable platforms—and server-independent building blocks of business logic. The compelling idea behind servlets is the simplicity with which you may connect any existing client to any existing back-end service via the normal server of the client (frequently a Web server). To do so, follow these simple steps:

1. Create the protocol conversion between the request of the client and the request of the back-end service.

2. Wrap the conversion mapping in a servlet class.

3. Install the servlet class into the server.

If you follow the J2EE programming paradigm, you may encapsulate the legacy service in an Enterprise JavaBean (EJB) component, as shown in Figure 1-2, effectively replacing an entire legacy system structure with a Java component. EJB components are studied in Chapters 8 to 11; this chapter is devoted to the study of servlets.

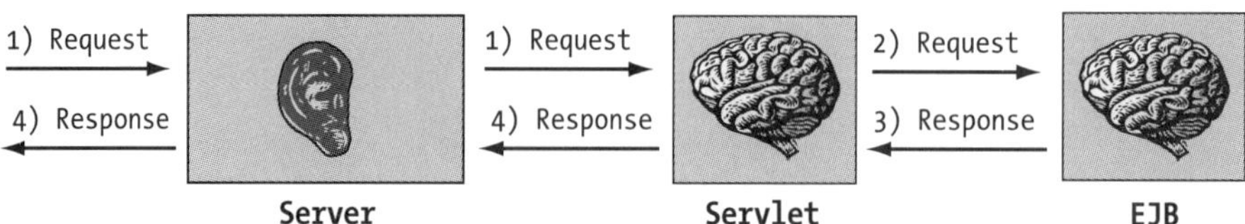

Figure 1-2. A model of a full server-side system where the servlet acts as a switchboard, delivering parsed requests from the client to the back-end legacy system, hidden behind an EJB component

The application system has only two requirements to work as a whole:

- All system nodes (client, server, and back-end) may talk to one another using streams containing binary or character data. This is a general requirement.

- The server must support the Servlet API. This requirement is less general than the preceding one. Although not a difficult implementation operation, the majority of servers supporting the Servlet API consist of Web/HTTP and Application servers. Implementing support for the Servlet API in a server is a major operation, many times more complex than implementing the servlet business functionality itself.

Thus, if you are looking to write servlets for an XYZ server that currently does not support the Servlet API, be sure to think twice before proceeding. The servlet engine implementations of most Web servers are fairly complex.

The J2EE Approach to Servlets

In the J2EE application development model, servlets are less intended for hosting business logic and more intended for conveying calls to business logic, provided in the form of EJB deployed within an EJB container. The servlet-to-EJB communication pattern is a slightly more complex one than the all-servlet solution, though, because an EJB needs more infrastructure than does a single servlet.

Small Server Systems and the J2EE Programming Model

The main argument for retaining the all-servlet solution instead of adopting the J2EE servlet development model is one of simplicity. As illustrated in Figure 1-3, introducing an extra facade tier is not an option with all smaller server-side systems for reasons of general system bulkiness without adding any desired functionality.

When connecting two existing servers using a servlet, the development project focuses on straightforward protocol conversion. Introducing an extra facade tier (frequently in the form of EJB components) adds an extra level of protocol conversion. For that reason, smaller systems frequently use only servlets to integrate two or more legacy systems.

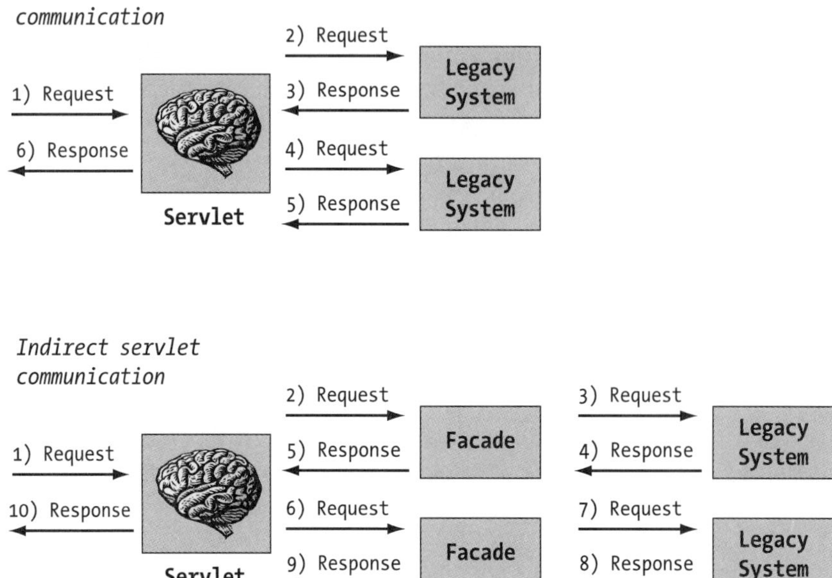

Figure 1-3. For smaller server-side systems, direct servlet communication may be advantageous because of its relative simplicity and quick development. Indirect communication may have other advantages but creates a more complex system that requires more resources in the maintainenance phase.

Large Server Systems and the J2EE Programming Model

When developing maintainable and scalable business logic, however, the most appropriate deployment technology is within EJB connected to servlets. EJB servers provide a transacted, persistent, and scalable multiuser solution for business-logic development that may be used in a number of applications.

Figure 1-4 shows the roles of the system components in an application server system.

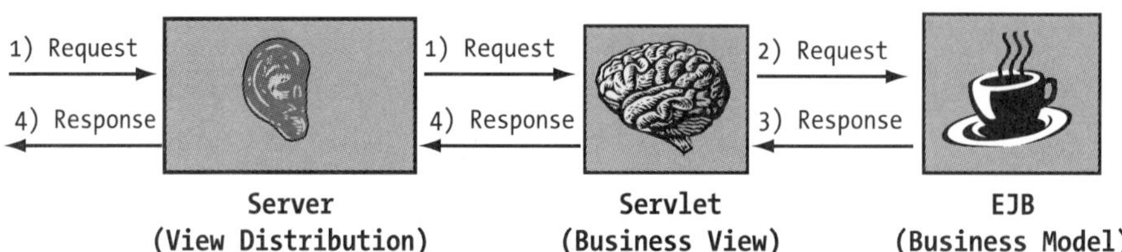

Figure 1-4. J2EE architectural model of a distributed system

In the large-scale development model of J2EE, servlets function as server-side deployment logic assisting in the creation of the view, sent back to the client for presentation to the user. The business model in the J2EE programming paradigm is deployed within the EJB tier, and the servlet tier assists in collecting data from various business models converting into a desired data protocol, understood by the client application. An example would be the conversion from the Java objects produced by the EJB tier to Extensible Markup Language (XML) or Hypertext Markup Language (HTML) transmitted by the server to the client tier for visualization.

Servlet Patterns

Static patterns describe how the classes of the Servlet API relate to each other. *Dynamic patterns* describe the order of method calls at runtime. Both types of patterns are straightforward because the Servlet API is small and to the point. This chapter covers both the static and dynamic patterns of the Servlet API.

The Java Servlet Development Kit and the J2EE Distribution

An earlier version of JavaSoft's toolkit to develop servlets was frequently referred to as the *Java Servlet Development Kit* (JSDK). The JSDK included the Servlet APIs and a small Web server (servletrunner), specially crafted to run servlets. In fact, servletrunner was specialized indeed, as it could not serve any HTML documents to a browser! Nowadays, the JSDK is included in the J2EE and is automatically installed as a part of the J2EE distribution.

Appendix A covers the configuration process for the J2EE distribution. For now, let's focus on the task at hand—understanding the different patterns of the Servlet API.

Static Patterns: a UML Blueprint of the Servlet API

The relations and associations between the classes of the Java Servlet API form the base of all static patterns used by servlets. While investigating servlet static patterns, it is useful to illustrate relations in the form of Unified Modeling Language (UML) diagrams to see the structure of the API quickly.

Most APIs evolve in an almost organic manner; when new functionality is introduced into the system, it is placed in a namespace of its own and simply added to existing functionality. The Servlet API is no exception to this rule; version 1 of the Servlet API contained two packages, whereas version 2.1 and later contains four, as shown in Figure 1-5. This book describes the Servlet API version 2.3 release.

Starting at release 2.2—in other words, Servlet API version 2.2, including JavaServer Pages (JSP) API version 1.1—four packages contain all the servlet-specific functionality. Note that the servlet classes are considered to be a standard extension to the Java platform. Therefore, the names of their packages begin with *javax*. All the packages of the Servlet API are part of the J2EE platform.

The version numbers, printed in italics beside the package symbol in Figure 1-5, correspond to the Servlet API version when the package was first introduced.

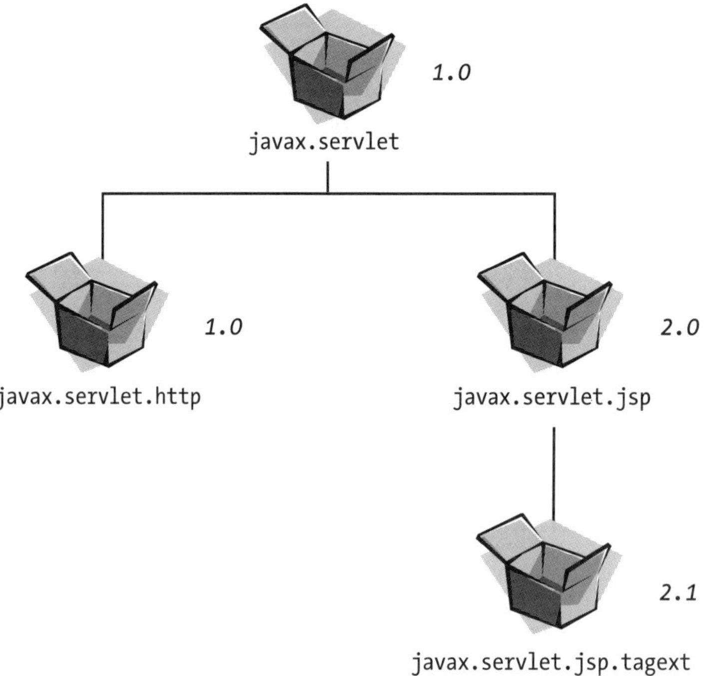

Figure 1-5. The package structure of the servlet and JSP classes in the J2EE distribution. The version numbers correspond to the Servlet API version where the package was first introduced.

The javax.servlet Package

The `javax.servlet` package contains the root interfaces and classes of the servlet hierarchy, defining life-cycle methods and basic sequence diagram structures. The servlet stream classes (`ServletInputStream` and `ServletOutputStream`) defined in the `javax.servlet` package are root classes of all specialized servlet streams in the `javax.servlet` subpackages. Thus, if implementing a servlet engine in a general server (such as a mail/SMTP or FTP server), the minimum classes and interfaces to support are the ones located in package `javax.servlet`.

The javax.servlet.http Package

The `javax.servlet.http` package contains specialized classes and interfaces for deploying servlets within Web/HTTP servers. When creating servlets to replace Common Gateway Interface (CGI) programs, the classes, utility classes, and interfaces of `javax.servlet.http` implement much of the basic data conversion methods required for handling HTTP parameters, cookies and user sessions, as well as parsing query strings and submitted HTTP POST data.

The javax.servlet.jsp Package

The `javax.servlet.jsp` package contains specialized classes and interfaces for creating JSP. JavaServer Pages permit dynamic Java code blocks to be inserted into a static view, such as a HTML or XML document, to produce a layout rendered by a Web browser. The result is an HTML document where pieces of executing the Java code can insert dynamic data into the HTML stream. As an example, JSP documents are ideal forges, molding live account data (retrieved from a legacy system) of the current user into the static HTML layout form displaying the status of all account status.

> **NOTE** *Chapters 4 and 5 cover JSP documents in depth.*

The javax.servlet.jsp.tagext Package

The `javax.servlet.jsp.tagext` package contains specialized classes and interfaces for creating custom server-side tags. When the JSP/servlet engine encounters such a custom tag, a handler method is called in a class, implemented by the developer. Alas, before sending the result to the user/browser, the JSP engine replaces all custom server-side tags with the contents produced by a method call. These tag libraries are, therefore, useful to encapsulate complex behavior.

Next, take a look at the basic class dependencies of these packages, starting slowly and comfortably.

Static Relations of Generic Servlets

By definition, any class implementing the javax.servlet.Servlet interface is regarded as a servlet. In the majority of cases, however, the developer chooses to extend the abstract class javax.servlet.GenericServlet, which implements the Servlet interface. The reason is that the GenericServlet implementation does not impose any restrictions on subclasses but minimizes the time required to implement the full functionality of the Servlet interface, by providing default (empty) implementations to all its methods.

Figure 1-6 provides a brief overview of the instances and types used by a servlet. The Servlet instance (generally implemented by a GenericServlet) acts as a simple switchboard, receiving input information from its ServletRequest and delivering output to its ServletResponse.

The ServletRequest and ServletResponse instances are not themselves communication streams and therefore handle no actual communication. Instead, they both contain a helper stream that handles the actual communication. Each communication stream may be retrieved by calling the public methods getInputStream and getOutputStream in the ServletRequest and ServletResponse instances, respectively (see Figure 1-7). Any class that obtains a reference to the ServletResponse instance may therefore print output to the resulting OutputStream using getOutputStream().write(...).

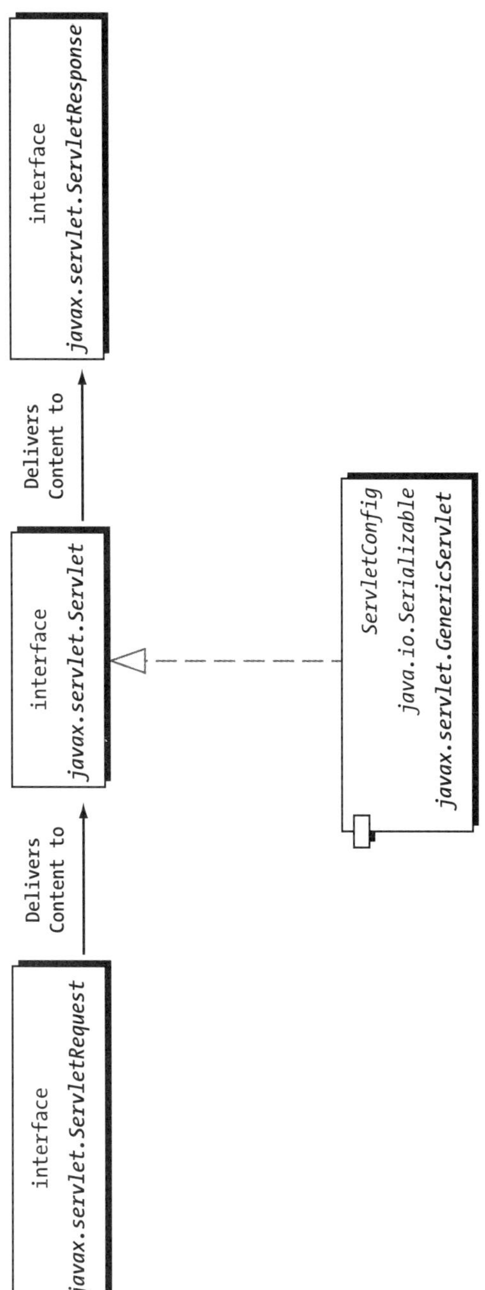

Figure 1-6. A simplified servlet runtime class pattern; no method information is shown in the figure.

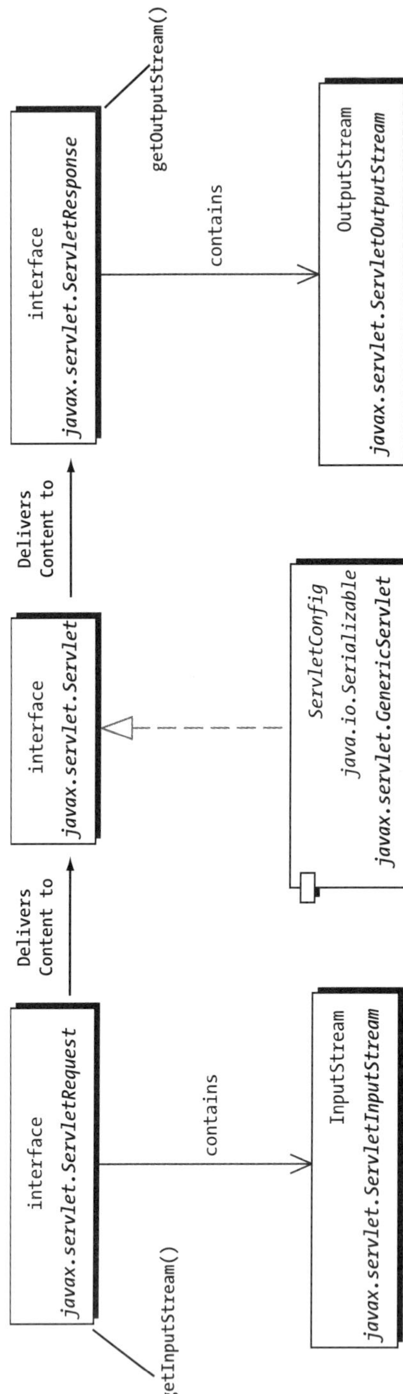

Figure 1-7. Simplified servlet runtime class pattern, showing underlying communication streams, retrieved by the calls to `getInputStream` *in the* `ServletRequest` *interface or* `getOutputStream` *in the* `ServletResponse` *interface*

Note that the ServletXXXXStream simply extends java.io.XXXXStream classes—it is as simple (or hard) to handle Java servlet communication as it is to handle the normal InputStream and OutputStream class hierarchies in Java. Note that all classes and interfaces in Figure 1-7 are abstract. Thus, it is up to the implementor of the servlet engine (such as Tomcat, Resin, IBM) to provide the actual implementation classes. As developers, don't worry about the actual implementation class—instead, treat all streams as their abstract superclass. For instance, when running the Tomcat reference servlet engine from the J2EE distribution, the class implementing the ServletRequest instance used is org.apache.tomcat.core.HttpServletRequestFacade, and the class implementing the ServletResponse is org.apache.tomcat.core.HttpServletResponseFacade.

Should you instead choose to use the Orion Application Server (OAS), the ServletRequest interface is implemented by the com.evermind.server.http.EvermindHttpServletRequest class and the ServletResponse interface by the com.evermind.server.http.EvermindHttpServletResponse class. The OAS implements its ServletInputStream interface with the class com.evermind._crb and its ServletOutputStream with the class com.evermind._crs.

Figure 1-8 shows the class diagram of the two implementations just discussed; each concrete class has gray backgrounds. The types rendered in white are part of the Servlet API framework and are all abstract.

As a contrast, take a look at the static class pattern of the Tomcat 3.0 reference implementation (see Figure 1-9). Note the different implementation classes.

Thankfully, you need not worry about such details to create working servlets—all normal servlet development requires the methods defined within the standard Servlet API. Although it may be fun to use the reflection classes provided in the standard Java API to find the details of the implementation classes, knowledge of their specific type is never required in practice.

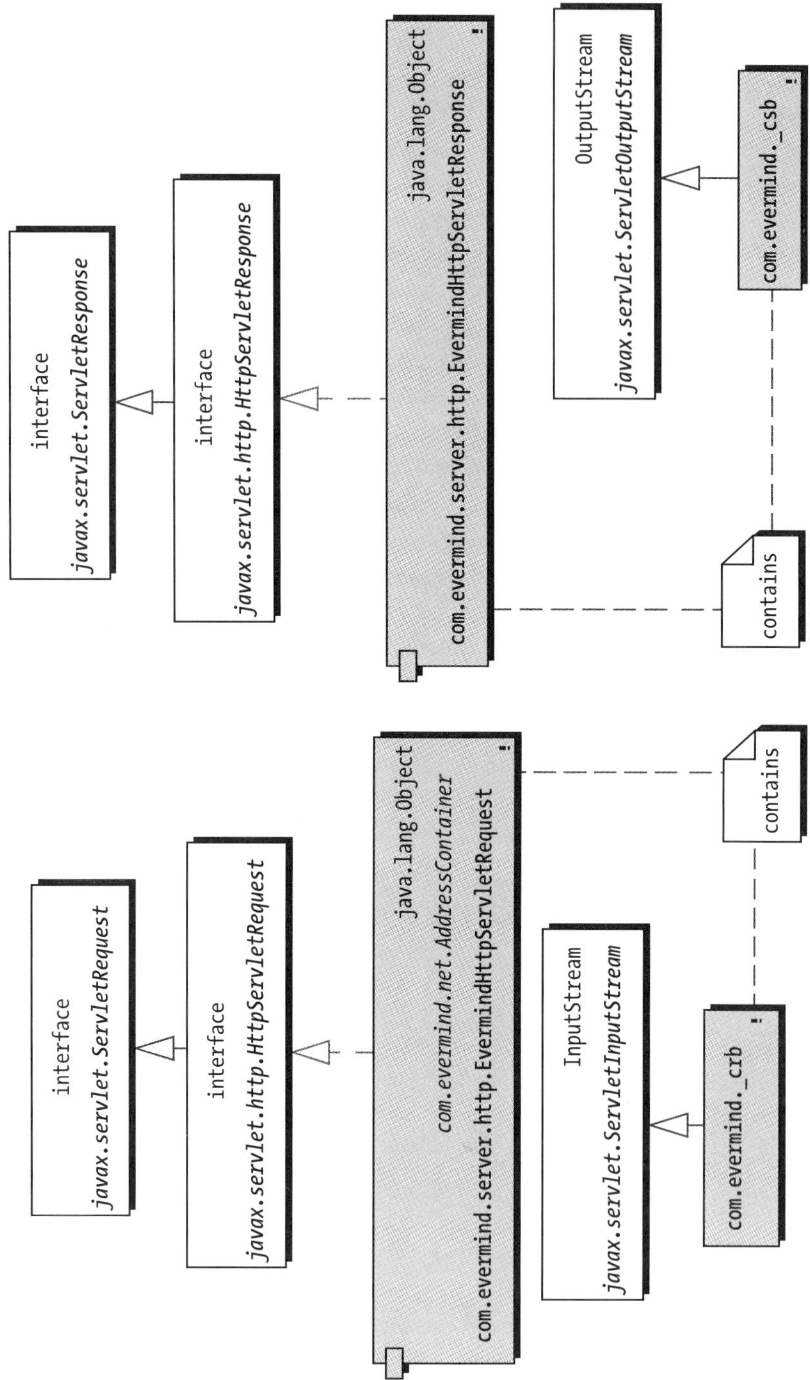

Figure 1-8. JSDK 1.0.1 implementation classes for the `ServletRequest` *and* `ServletResponse` *interfaces, including the actual communication stream implementation classes*

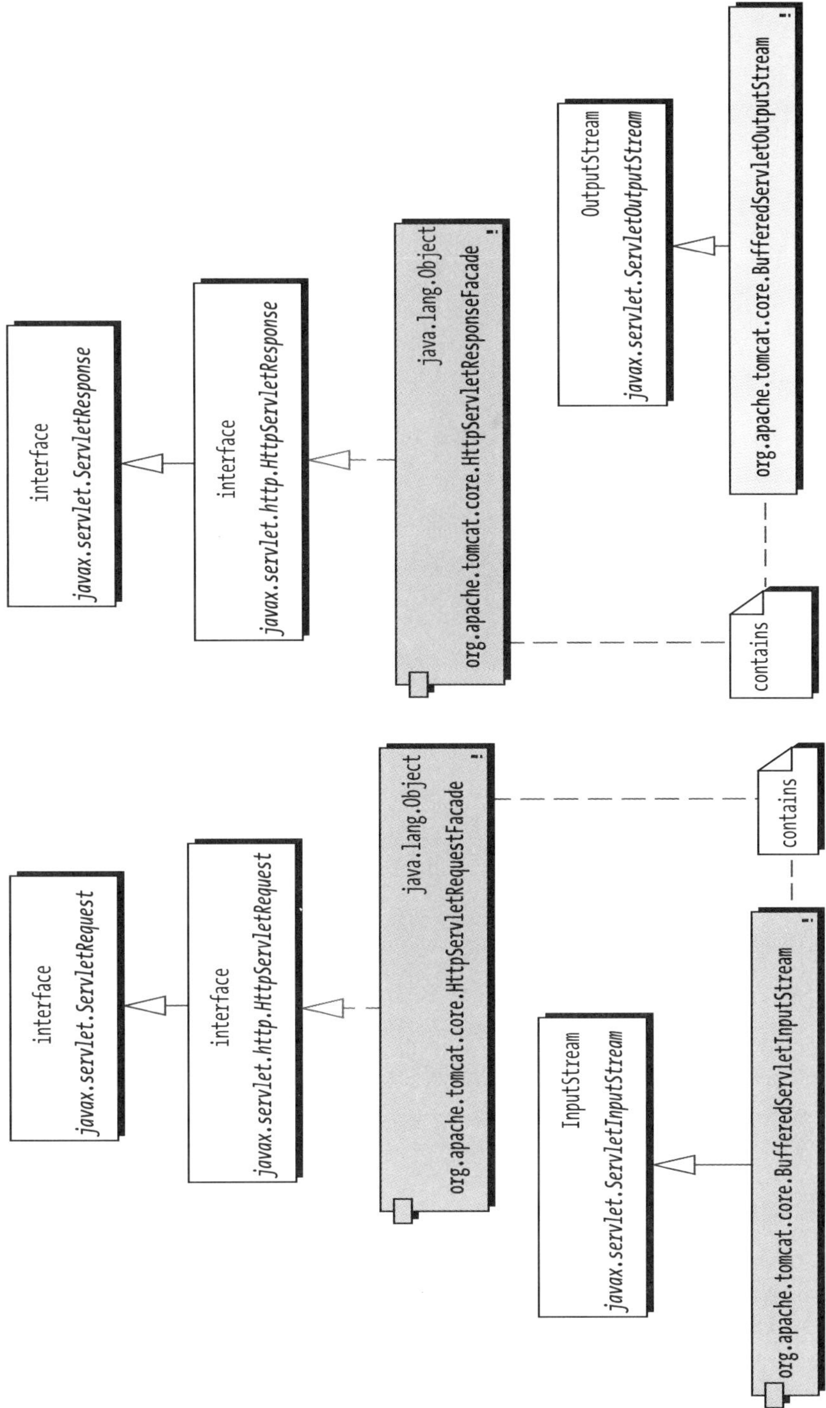

Figure 1-9. Tomcat implementation classes for the `ServletRequest` *and* `ServletResponse` *interfaces, including the actual communication stream implementation classes*

Dynamic Patterns and Use Cases of Generic Servlets

The "life cycle" of a servlet is defined by three methods, called in a particular order (see Figure 1-10). Figure 1-11 shows the three life-cycle methods of a servlet in the form of a UML state diagram.

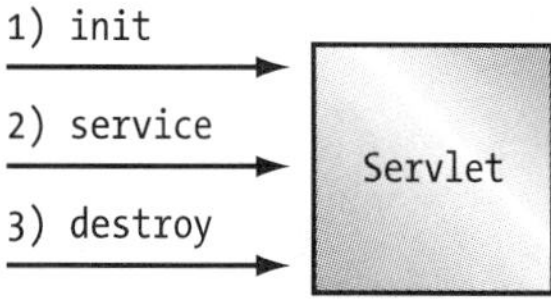

Figure 1-10. The three life-cycle methods of a servlet, along with their call order

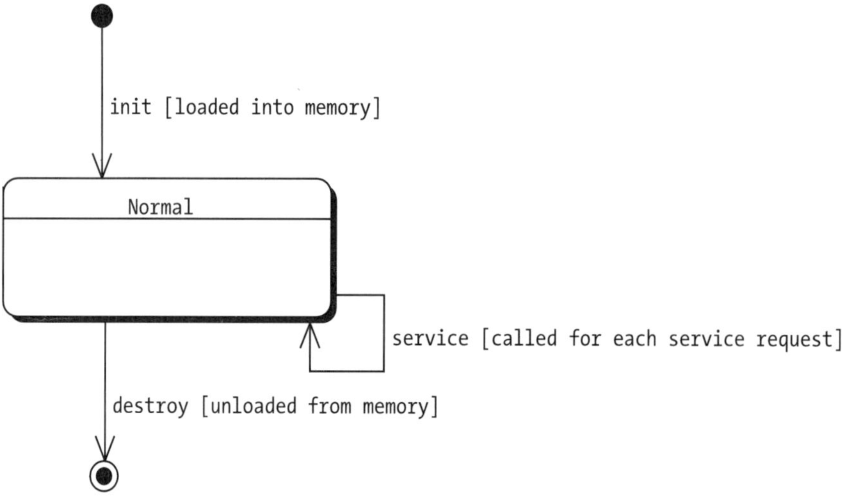

Figure 1-11. State diagram illustrating the call order of a servlet and the conditions where the state transitions are performed

The init Method

When the servlet is first loaded into memory, the `init` method is called. Similar to the `init` of applets, servlets lack constructor and main methods, instead combining them into a single `init(ServletConfig aConfig)` method. The main difference between an applet and a servlet initialization is that servlets cannot interact as easily with their load media (Web container) as applets (HTML Web page content) to read initialization parameters. The reason is that each Web server uses custom configuration tools that insert values into a J2EE configuration file, known as a *deployment descriptor*, that deliver initialization parameters to the respective servlets. It is up to the Web server implementation to provide an internal storage for the servlet initialization parameters; as shown in Figure 1-12, the Tomcat 3.0 reference implementation engine uses a `Hashtable` to store its servlet initialization parameters.

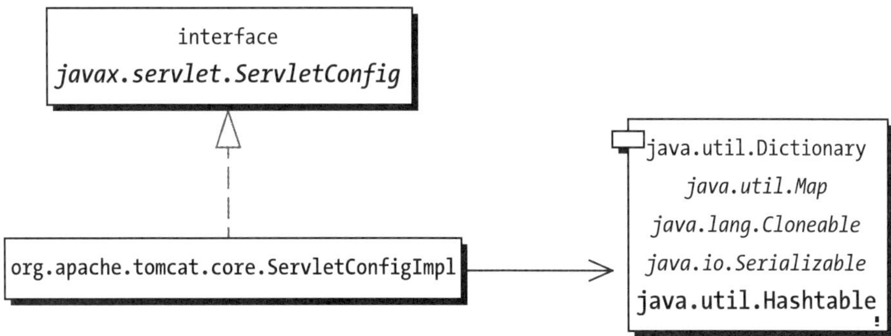

Figure 1-12. `ServletConfig` *implementation structure for the Tomcat 3.0 reference implementation servlet engine*

Applet parameters are simply delivered in a standard HTML format, whereas servlet parameter delivery requires learning the Web server's custom configuration tools to edit the deployment descriptor.

The servlet `init` method accepts a `ServletConfig` object holding all parameters required for the servlet initialization. For servlet engines that comply with the J2EE specification, these parameters are originally stored in an XML deployment descriptor document called `web.xml`. The document type definition (DTD) of `web.xml` is given by the J2EE specification. If the servlet engine is older, you may instead have to master its custom deployment and configuration tools to provide your servlets with initialization parameters.

The service Method

For each incoming service request to the servlet, the servlet engine invokes the `service` method in the servlet. The service method accepts two parameters: the incoming request stream encapsulated in a `ServletRequest` object and the outgoing response stream encapsulated in a `ServletResponse` object. Thus, the main work of a servlet consists of reading parameters and data from the incoming `ServletRequest` and writing the corresponding output on the `ServletResponse`.

The destroy Method

The `destroy` method is called by the servlet engine when the servlet is garbage-collected from memory. This method is used to clean up all resources used by the servlet, such as pooled database connections or temporary lock files. Figure 1-13 depicts the runtime collaborating objects of the servlet hierarchy.

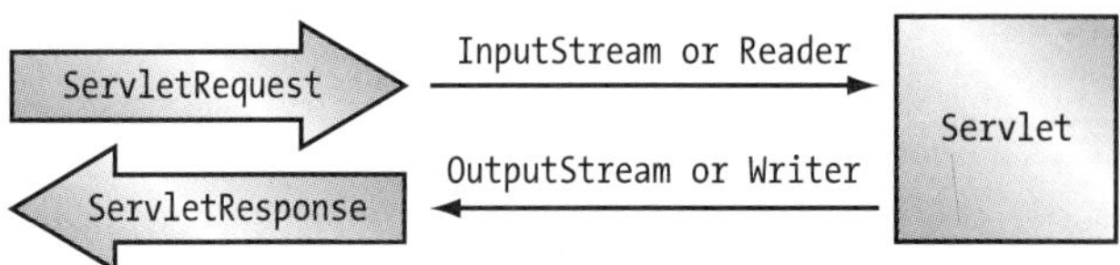

Figure 1-13. Simplified object structure of the servlet at runtime

The parameters to the service method of a servlet are the incoming `ServletRequest` encapsulating the `IntputStream/Reader` from which the servlet may read incoming commands, and the `ServletResponse` encapsulating the `OutputStream/Writer` to which the servlet may send the results of the service call.

The `ServletRequest` and `ServletResponse` instances may transmit character or textual data. A content/MIME-type string, contained within the `ServletRequest` and `ServletResponse`, implies the exact nature of the transmission. If the content type of the stream implies a binary transmission, the contained communication stream is a `ServletInputStream` or `ServletOutputStream`. If, on the other hand, the content type implies a character transmission, the contained communication stream is a `Reader` or `Writer`.

Listing 1-1 is a simple servlet that responds to all incoming requests by displaying the number of times the servlet has been called.

Listing 1-1. The `FirstServlet` code

```
package se.jguru.servlets;

// ### 1) Be sure to import the required servlet classes
import javax.servlet.*;
import java.io.*;

// ### 2)     Extending the GenericServlet class saves the
//            pain of declaring many empty method bodies.
public class FirstServlet extends GenericServlet
{
  // Variable to keep track of the number of times
  // this servlet has been called.
  private int numTimes = 0;
```

```
  // ### 3) Implement the service method to handle
  //        the request from the client.
  public void service(ServletRequest request, ServletResponse response)
  throws ServletException, IOException
  {
     // ### 4) Get the Writer of the ServletResponse
     PrintWriter out = new PrintWriter(response.getOutputStream());

     // ### 5) Write some data to the ServletResponse
     //        Call flush() to send data from the output
     //        write buffer to the output stream.
     out.println("Service method called " + numTimes++ + " times.");
     out.flush();
  }
}
```

The asterisks and comments in Listing 1-1 explain the interesting parts of the servlet Java code. With the addition of business-logic processing within the `service` method (between steps 4 and 5) and a few method implementations to oversee initialization and resource configuration, servlet classes tend to be no more complex in their structure than in Listing 1-1.

Listing 1-2 is a slightly more involved example that logs all method calls to a log file. The servlet responds to any incoming client request with the current date.

Listing 1-2. The `LoggingServlet` *code*

```
package se.jguru.servlets;

// ### 1) Be sure to import the servlet classes required
import javax.servlet.*;
import java.io.*;
import java.util.Date;

// ### 2)Extend the GenericServlet class to save the
//       pain of declaring many empty methods.
public class LoggingServlet extends GenericServlet
{
  // The log file writer
  private PrintWriter logStream;
```

```
// ### 3) The init method is called when the Servlet is loaded
//        into memory in the servlet engine.
public void init(ServletConfig conf) throws ServletException
{
    // Call the init method of our superclass
    super.init(conf);

    // Setup the logfile
    try
    {
       this.logStream = new PrintWriter(
      new FileWriter("/tmp/servlet.log"), true
      );
    }
    catch(Exception ex)
    {
        // Oops. Log to the server-specific
        // GenericServlet log file.
        this.log("Could not create logStream: " + ex);
    }

    // Use external logging
    logStream.println("init called at: " + new Date());
 }

// ### 3) Implement the Service method to log the
//        timestamp when it is called.
public void service(ServletRequest request, ServletResponse response)
throws ServletException, IOException
{
   // Use external logging
   logStream.println("service called at: " + new Date());

   // Produce a Writer from the ServletResponse
   PrintWriter out = new PrintWriter(response.getOutputStream());

   // Write some data to the ServletResponse
   // This is mainly to please the client.
   out.println("The current time is: " + new Date());
   out.flush();
}
```

```
  // ### 4) The destroy method is called when the Servlet is
  //        purged from memory in the servlet engine.
  public void destroy()
  {
     // Call the destroy method of the superclass.
     super.destroy();

     // Use external logging
     logStream.println("destroy called at: " + new Date());

     // Close the logger
     try
     {
        logStream.close();
     }
     catch(Exception ex)
     {
        this.log("Could not close logFile writer: " + ex);
     }
  }

  // ### 5) The getServletInfo method is never called in a normal
  //        Servlet lifecycle. Instead, it is a means of conveying
  //        servlet information, such as copyright information etc.
  public String getServletInfo()
  {
     return "A rather silly logging servlet\n"
          + "Copyleft Lennart Jörelid";
  }
}
```

Read the comments in Listing 1-2; they explain what task each statements performs. Note also, that the `getServletInfo` method provides a means of extracting information about the servlet in a programmatic way. However, the `getServletInfo` method is a not-yet-deprecated informational source; the same information is provided for modern servlets in their J2EE deployment descriptor file, `web.xml`.

The `destroy` method provides a school-book example of what to do when the servlet instance is garbage-collected from memory; close any open `OutputStreams`, lock files, or network connections in use by the servlet.

Having gotten a feeling for generic servlets, you'll now proceed to their `HTTPServlet` siblings, which are used more frequently because they are integrated into a J2EE Web container run within a Web server.

Static Relations of HTTP Servlets

Similar to the GenericServlet subclasses, any class extending the javax.servlet.http.HttpServlet class is regarded as an HttpServlet—a special kind of servlet intended to be used in a Web server. All classes and interfaces of package javax.servlet.http have specialized methods that handle the communication and conversion required by the HTTP protocol spoken by all Web servers. Despite their specialized nature, the static relations of HttpServlets are similar to those of GenericServlets. At a glance, the developer may simply add an extra layer of classes to the inheritance structure and add the prefix *Http* to most class/interface names.

Figure 1-14 relates the Http classes to their generic servlet siblings; note that all types in the javax.servlet.http package extend those of the javax.servlet package. Therefore, all tasks performed by a generic servlets may indeed be performed by HttpServlets.

Thus, migrating an existing GenericServlet to better fit into a Web server servlet engine is a smooth ride indeed. Import the javax.servlet.http classes and add *Http* to most class names, as indicated in the class structure previously. In fact, the communication stream classes of an HttpServlet are identical to those of the GenericServlet, as illustrated in Figure 1-15.

As indicated in Figure 1-15, the structural difference between an HttpServlet and a GenericServlet is rather small. In fact, the differences are sufficiently small that Listing 1-3 highlights the type differences between an HttpServlet and the GenericServlet presented earlier in this chapter.

Listing 1-3. The type differences between a GenericServlet *and an* HttpServlet

```
// Remember to import the relevant classes of the javax.servlet.http package,
// in addition to any other required classes
import javax.servlet.*;
import javax.servlet.http.*;

...

// Extend the HttpServlet class instead of GenericServlet
public class SimpleHttpServlet extends HttpServlet
{
    // The service method of an HttpServlet uses HttpServletRequest and
    // HttpServletResponse instead of the ServletRequest and
    // ServletResponse, respectively
    public void service(HttpServletRequest req, HttpServletResponse res)
        throws IOException
    { ... }
}
```

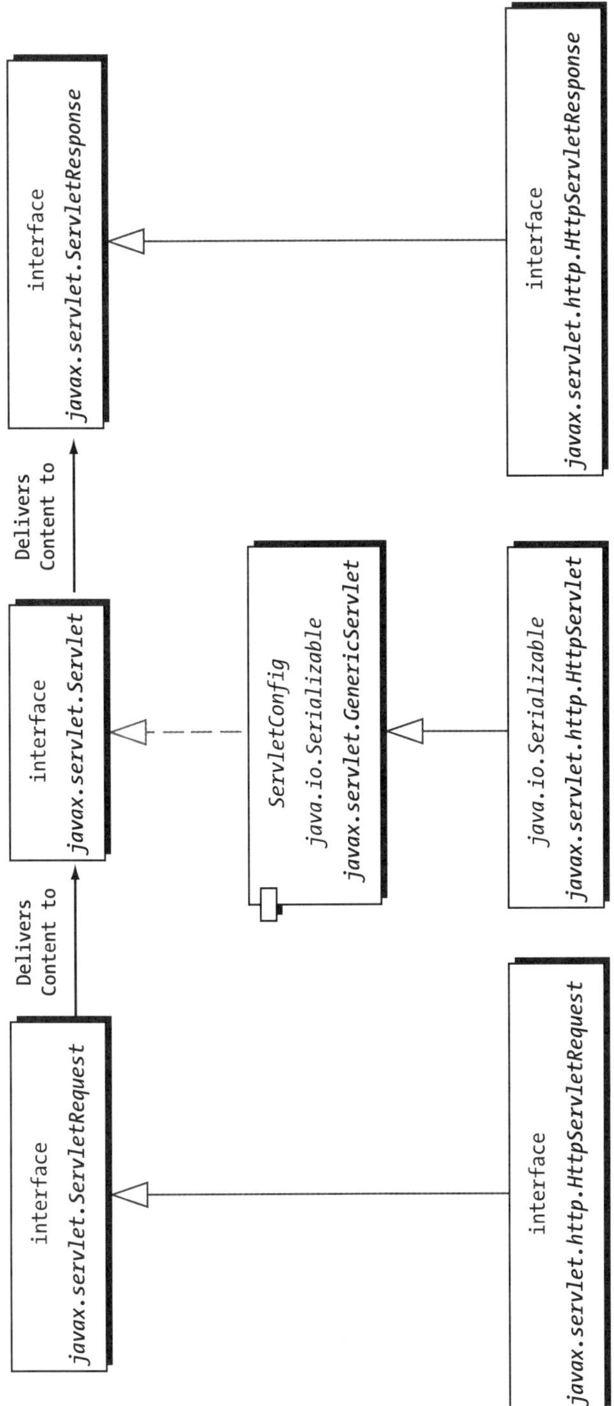

Figure 1-14. Relations between the static patterns of generic servlets and the corresponding patterns of `HttpServlets`

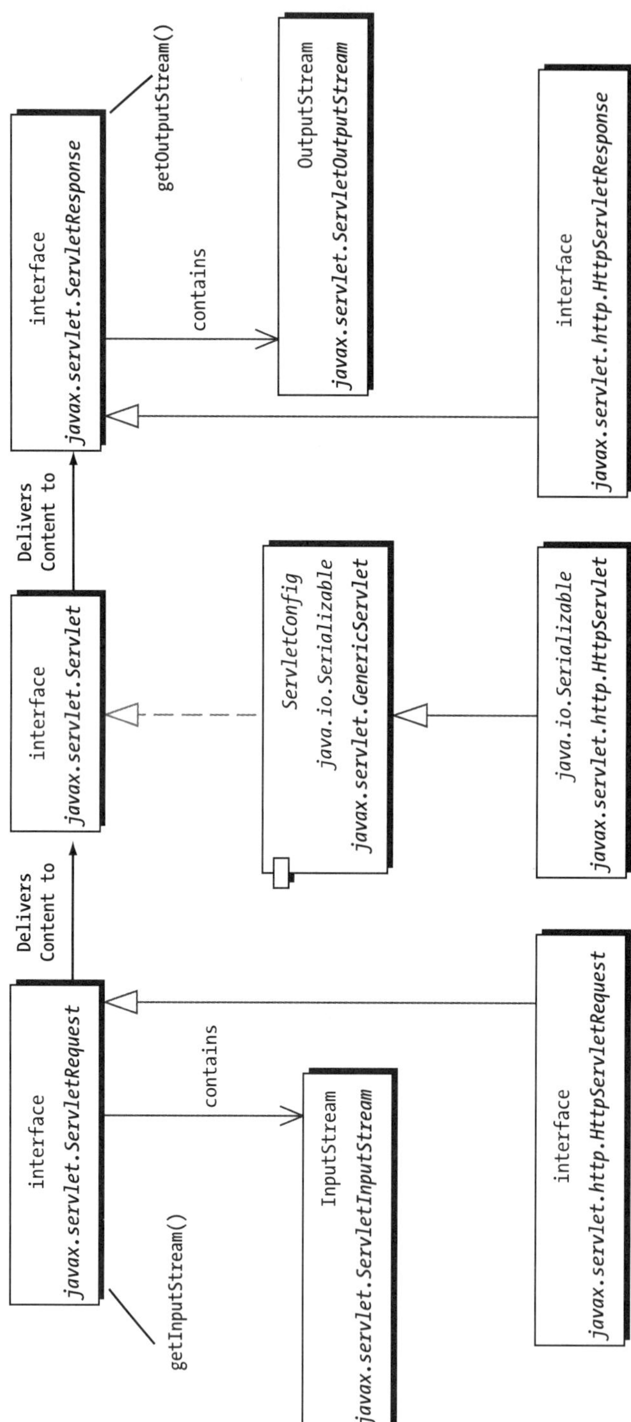

Figure 1-15. The static patterns of `HttpServlets`*, showing the inheritance from the generic servlets*

The dynamic patterns of HttpServlets are, thankfully, identical to those of the GenericServlet; you may therefore safely assume that you can apply the knowledge acquired in the "Dynamic Patterns and Use Cases of Generic Servlets" section equally to HttpServlets.

Let's proceed to a tour of the javax.servlet and javax.servlet.http packages, where types and classes are explained using small code examples. You will now investigate the methods, properties, and functions built into the Servlet API.

Touring the javax.servlet Package

This section is a condensed version of the servlet reference documentation, which highlights the important methods of the classes and interfaces presented thus far. Of course, you should start with the Servlet interface, shown in Figure 1-16, which is the root of all Servlet classes.

```
interface
javax.servlet.Servlet
-----------------------------------------------------
+init(config:ServletConfig):void
+getServletConfig():ServletConfig
+service(req:ServletRequest,res:ServletResponse):void
+getServletInfo():String
+destroy():void
```

Figure 1-16. The Servlet *interface*

The Servlet interface is simple to master because it has only the five following methods:

- public void init()
- public void service()
- public void destroy()
- public String getServletInfo()
- public ServletConfig getServletConfig()

The first three life-cycle methods were discussed earlier in this chapter in the "Dynamic Patterns and Use Cases of Generic Servlets." The two remaining types are metadata methods that describe the servlet. Here's a description of what they do:

- `public String getServletInfo()` returns a `String` with descriptive information about the servlet. This method is similar to the `getAppletInfo` method of class `java.applet.Applet`, intended to provide copyright information, for example.

- `public ServletConfig getServletConfig()` returns a `Hashtable`-like structure holding initialization parameters for the servlet. Detailed information, including code examples, on the `ServletConfig` interface are provided in the following sections.

Interface javax.servlet.ServletRequest

The `ServletRequest` interface, shown in Figure 1-17, contains methods that handle the information sent to the server from the client.
Mainly, the methods fall in one of the four following categories:

Finding properties about the computers involved in the communication. The associated methods are `String getRemoteAddr()`, `String getRemoteHost()`, `String getServerName()`, and `int getServerPort()`.

Inspecting properties about the data sent from the client to the server. These methods play the same role as metadata methods in database applications. The methods are `String getCharacterEncoding()`, `int getContentLength()`, `String getContentType()`, and `String getProtocol()`.

Obtaining a reference to the underlying `InputStream` (for binary `ServletRequests`) or `Reader` (for character `ServletRequests`). These methods are `ServletInputStream getInputStream()`, and `Reader getReader()`.

Finding attributes set by the browser client or other invoking servlets (done if one servlet invokes another servlet). Such attributes may be set in the application or request scope. These methods are `Object getAttribute()`, `Enumeration getAttributeNames()`, `String getParameter(String name)`, `Enumeration getParameterNames()`, `String[] getParameterValues(String name)`, and `void setAttribute(String key, Object value)`.

The first category of methods within the `ServletRequest` interface, finding communication attributes regarding the client and server, contains many methods. As the methods are sensibly named, understanding their use and results are

```
interface
javax.servlet.ServletRequest

+getAttribute(name:String):Object
+getAttributeNames():Enumeration
+getCharacterEncoding():String
+setCharacterEncoding(env:String):void
+getContentLength():int
+getContentType():String
+getInputStream():ServletInputStream
+getParameter(name:String):String
+getParameterNames():Enumeration
+getParameterValues(name:String):String[]
+getParameterMap():Map
+getProtocol():String
+getScheme():String
+getServerName():String
+getServerPort():int
+getReader():BufferedReader
+getRemoteAddr():String
+getRemoteHost():String
+setAttribute(name:String,o:Object):void
+removeAttribute(name:String):void
+getLocale():Locale
+getLocales():Enumeration
+isSecure():boolean
+getRequestDispatcher(path:String):RequestDispatcher
+getRealPath(path:String):String
```

Figure 1-17. The `ServletRequest` *interface*

quite simple. The quickest way to learning consists of a small code example, along with its program output, shown in Figure 1-18.

This sample program invokes some of the methods of the `ServletRequest` interface and renders the output in Listing 1-4 when viewed in a Web browser and a telnet client. Because the servlet source code does not rely on the classes and interfaces of the `javax.servlet.http` package, it is usable from any server and viewable by any client capable of contacting the server in question.

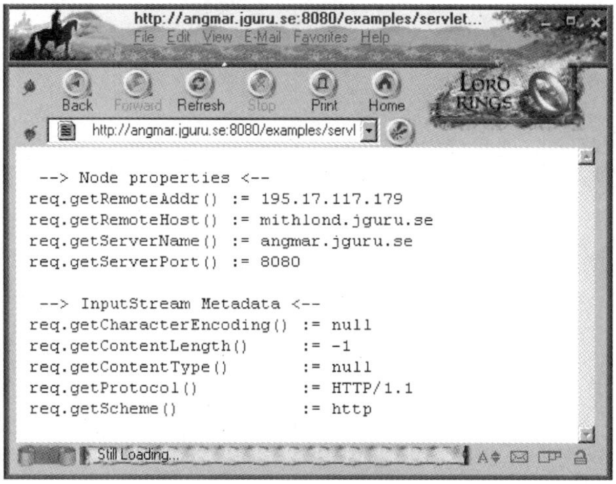

```
--> Node properties <--
req.getRemoteAddr() := 195.17.117.179
req.getRemoteHost() := mithlond.jguru.se
req.getServerName() := angmar.jguru.se
req.getServerPort() := 8080

--> InputStream Metadata <--
req.getCharacterEncoding() := null
req.getContentLength()     := -1
req.getContentType()       := null
req.getProtocol()          := HTTP/1.1
req.getScheme()            := http
```

Figure 1-18. Client output of the `RawServletRequest` *tester*

The output shown in Listing 1-4 is received by a telnet command and is similar, but not identical, to the output received from the Web browser shown in Figure 1-18. The differences in output (`getServerName` and `getProtocol`) reflect the different property sets provided to the servlet server by the Web browser and the telnet client.

Listing 1-4. Output of a raw telnet invocation of the `RawServlerRequestTester`

```
telnet> get /examples/servlet/survlut.RawServletRequestTester

--> Node properties <--
req.getRemoteAddr() := 195.17.117.179
req.getRemoteHost() := mithlond.jguru.se
req.getServerName() := 178.117.17.195
req.getServerPort() := 8080

--> InputStream Metadata <--
req.getCharacterEncoding() := null
req.getContentLength()     := -1
req.getContentType()       := null
req.getProtocol()          := null
req.getScheme()            := http
```

The code for obtaining both responses is straightforward and shows the use of the `ServletRequest` methods that investigates the properties of the communicating nodes and the underlying `InputStream's` metadata, as shown in Listing 1-5.

Listing 1-5. The `RawServletRequestTester` *code*

```
// ### 1) Note that the package name is part of the
//        fully qualified servlet URL when invoked
//        on a remote server.
//        Thus, the fully qualified name of this
//        servlet is survlut.RawServletRequestTester
package survlut;

import javax.servlet.*;
import java.io.*;
import java.util.*;

public class RawServletRequestTester extends GenericServlet
{
  public void service(ServletRequest req, ServletResponse res)
  throws ServletException, IOException
   {
       // ### 2) Get the output Writer
       PrintWriter out = res.getWriter();

       // ### 3) Find the properties of the nodes.
       out.println(" --> Node properties <--");
       out.println("req.getRemoteAddr() := " + req.getRemoteAddr() );
       out.println("req.getRemoteHost() := " + req.getRemoteHost() );
       out.println("req.getServerName() := " + req.getServerName() );
       out.println("req.getServerPort() := " + req.getServerPort() );
       out.println("");

       // ### 4) Find the InputStream metadata
       out.println(" --> InputStream Metadata <--");
      out.println("req.getCharacterEncoding() := " + req.getCharacterEncoding() );
       out.println("req.getContentLength()     := " + req.getContentLength() );
       out.println("req.getContentType()       := " + req.getContentType() );
       out.println("req.getProtocol()          := " + req.getProtocol() );
       out.println("req.getScheme()            := " + req.getScheme() );
   }
}
```

The `ServletRequest` may communicate with the client application using an `InputStream` or a `Reader`. A `Reader` is used if the data transferred consists of characters, and an `InputStream` is used otherwise (in other words, for binary data).

The `InputStream` is created and obtained using the `getInputStream` method, and the `Reader` is created and obtained using the `getReader` method. You may only create and retrieve one instance of the underlying stream; calling `getInputStream` after calling `getReader` (or vice versa) in the same service method will cause the servlet engine to throw an exception. The remaining methods, handling the attributes and parameters of a Servlet, behave similarly to a `java.util.Hashtable` structure. Some of the methods are used to share resources between servlets (resource pooling) and are therefore described in Chapter 2.

The `javax.servlet.ServletResponseWrapper` Class

Starting with the Servlet API version 2.3, the framework architects have provided developers with the means of customizing the behavior of the `ServletRequest` and `ServletResponse` instances. The purpose of the `Wrapper` classes (for example, `ServletResponseWrapper` shown in Figure 1-19 and `ServletRequestWrapper`) is to provide a convenient implementation of the respective interfaces that can be subclassed by developers wanting to override the default behavior of the `ServletResponse`. By default, all methods in the `Wrapper` classes call through to the wrapped object.

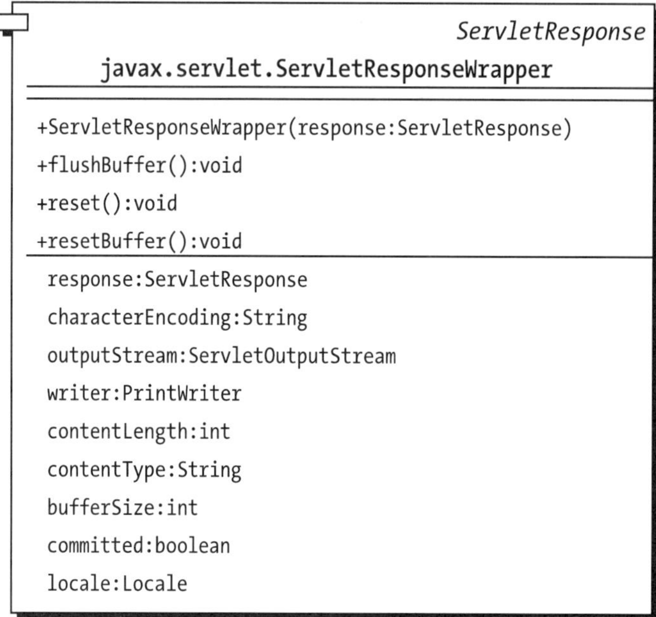

Figure 1-19. The `ServletResponseWrapper` *class*

Because the `ServletResponseWrapper` implements the `ServletResponse` interface, you may use one or the other at any time. Thus, when used in the service method of a `GenericServlet`, you may alter the behavior of any of the standard `ServletResponse` methods.

Interface javax.servlet.ServletResponse

The `ServletResponse` interface, shown in Figure 1-20, contains methods that obtain a reference to the outgoing communication stream and set the content type of the reply sent back to the client from the servlet.

```
interface
javax.servlet.ServletResponse
-----------------------------
+getCharacterEncoding():String
+getOutputStream():ServletOutputStream
+getWriter():PrintWriter
+setContentLength(len:int):void
+setContentType(type:String):void
+setBufferSize(size:int):void
+getBufferSize():int
+flushBuffer():void
+resetBuffer():void
+isCommitted():boolean
+reset():void
+setLocale(loc:Locale):void
+getLocale():Locale
```

Figure 1-20. The `ServletResponse` *interface*

These methods can be divided into the three following categories:

Retrieving character encoding information about the outgoing stream. The associated method is `getCharacterEncoding`.

Assigning content-related information to the outgoing stream. The associated methods are `setContentLength` and `setContentType`.

Obtaining a reference to the underlying output stream. The associated method is `getOutputStreamgetWriter`.

If you want to flush an image or other binary document (corresponding to a binary MIME type) over the stream of your `ServletResponse`, the `getOutputStream` method must be used to obtain a stream over which you may write binary data and information. To pass textual information, substitute the `OutputStream` for a character `Writer`.

A brief code example of how to download binary files and setting the proper content type of the outgoing `ServletResponse` is provided in Listing 1-5. First, study Figures 1-21, 1-22, and 1-23 that illustrate the output of the servlet in Listing 1-5. The simplest servlet reads the contents of a file, after which it sets the content type of the `ServletResponse`, and ships the data to the client. Start by looking at the results, while noting that three different image formats are relayed to the client browser: `jpg`, `gif`, and `png`. Therefore, the content type of the three responses must be different.

Figure 1-21. Downloading and viewing a JPG image by setting the `ServletResponse` *content type to image/jpg*

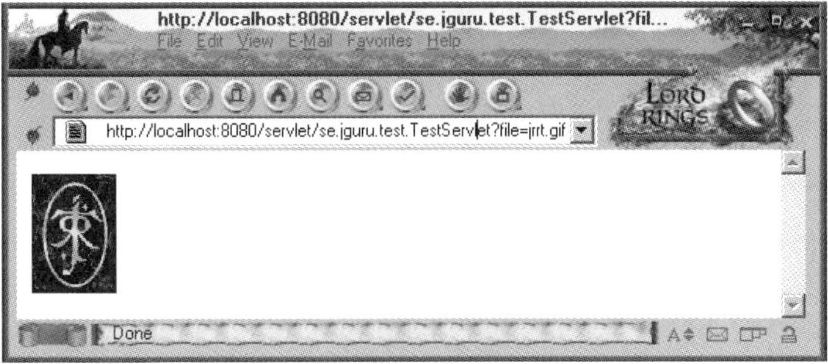

Figure 1-22. Downloading and viewing a GIF image by setting the `ServletResponse` *content type to image/gif*

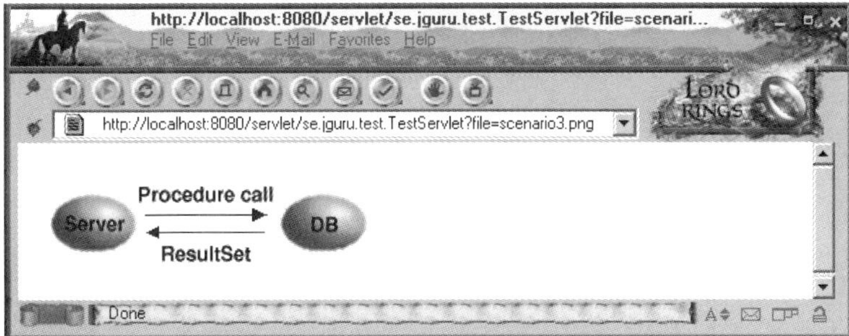

Figure 1-23. Downloading and viewing a PNG image by setting the `ServletResponse` *content type to image/png*

Figure 1-24 shows the `TestServlet` class that downloads the images. Note that the only two private instances are the MIME types Map, relating file suffices to MIME types, and the `imageDirectory` file containing the path to the directory where the images reside.

All methods of the `TestServlet`–except the `loadDefaultMimeTypes`, which is called at initialization—are called from within the `service` method. All protected methods are delegator methods intended to be overridden by subclasses of the `TestServlet` to alter behavior.

GenericServlet TestServlet
-mimeTypes:Map
-imageDirectory:File=new File("images")
#loadDefaultMimeTypes():void
+init(config:ServletConfig):void
#setContentType(response:ServletResponse,fileName:String):void
#getFileName(fileNameStart:String):String
#getImage(name:String):byte[]
#getDataFromFile(aFile:File):byte[]
+service(request:ServletRequest,response:ServletResponse):void

Figure 1-24. UML diagram of the `TestServlet` *class*

Now take a look at the relevant pieces of code producing the result shown in Figures 1-21, 1-22 and 1-23, starting with the `service` method of the `TestServlet` class. This method acts as the hub of the servlet application, calling four delegation methods, as illustrated by Figure 1-25.

The service method performs the four following tasks in order:

1. It checks the incoming `ServletRequest` parameters for the `file` parameter.

2. It calls `getFileName` to read and return the name of the image file most closely matching the parameter provided in the `file` parameter of the `ServletRequest`.

3. It sets the content type of the outgoing `ServletResponse` to the MIME type associated with the suffix of the file requested. If the file suffix is `.jpg`, the content type is set to image/jpeg, and so on. The content type map is set within the local `setContentType` method.

4. It reads all data in the image file and writes it back to the `ServletRequest`.

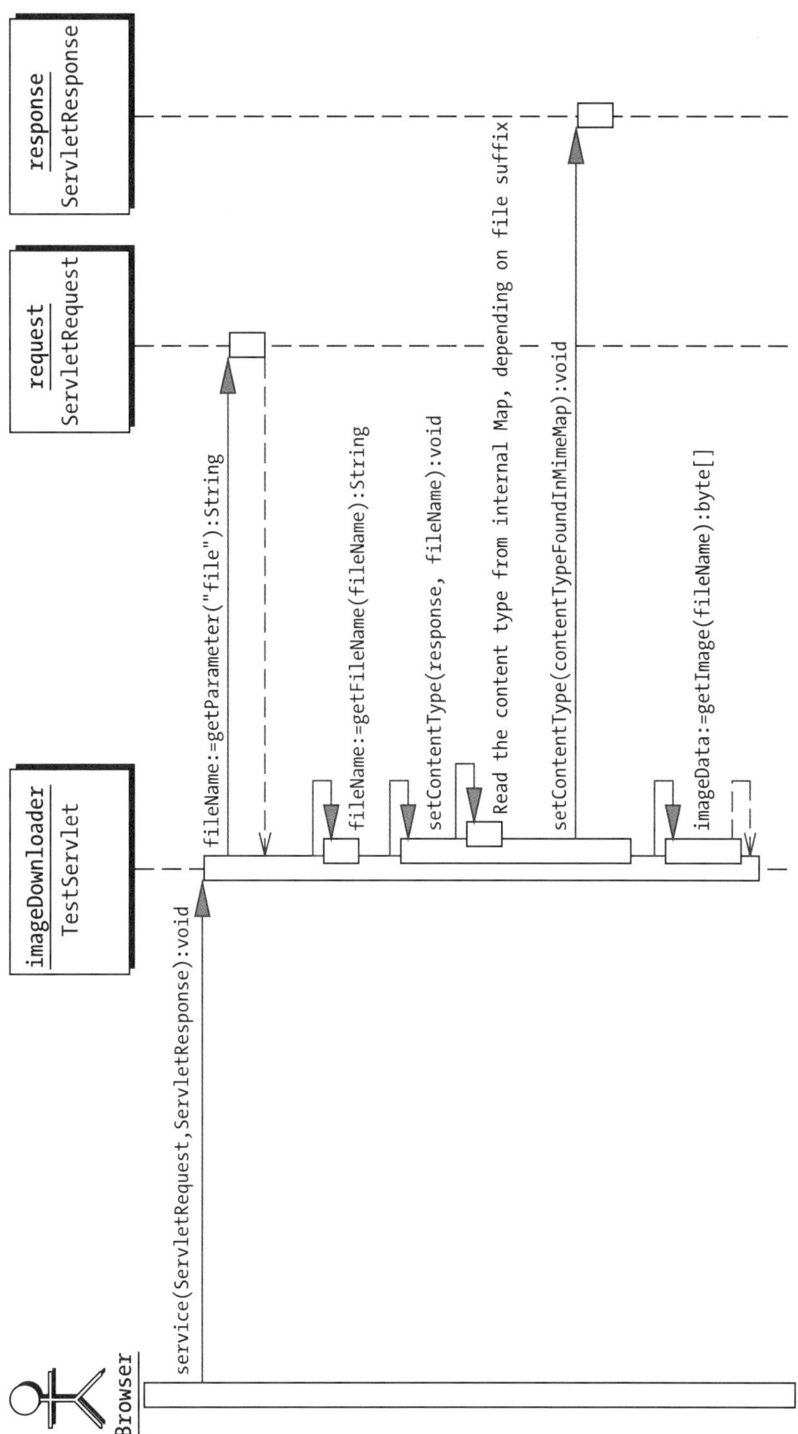

Figure 1-25. Reduced `service` *method sequence diagram*

Listing 1-5 contains the full code of the `TestServlet` program with the important constructs highlighted in bold.

Listing 1-5. The `TestServlet` *code*

```
package se.jguru.test;

import javax.servlet.*;
import java.io.*;
import java.util.*;

/**
 * TestServlet which downloads a particular image file upon
 * request by the client browser.
 *
 * @author Lennart Jörelid, lj@jguru.se
 */
public class TestServlet extends GenericServlet
{
    /**
     * Registered mime type cache, containing file suffix (key)
     * and content type (value).
     */
     private static Map mimeTypes;

    /**
     * The directory where images are stored.
     */
     private File imageDirectory = new File("images");

     /**
      * Loads default MIME keys and content type strings
      * into the mimeTypes internal Map. Override this method
      * in a subclass to alter the default Mime map.
      */
     protected void loadDefaultMimeTypes()
     {
          // Load the default recognized mime types
             // into the static array
             this.mimeTypes = Collections.synchronizedMap(new HashMap());
```

```
        this.mimeTypes.put("jpg",  "image/jpeg");
        this.mimeTypes.put("jpeg", "image/jpeg");
        this.mimeTypes.put("gif",  "image/gif");
        this.mimeTypes.put("png",  "image/png");
}

/**
 * Initialize and load all default required settings.
 */
public void init(ServletConfig config) throws ServletException
{
    super.init(config);

    // Load the default MIME keys
    this.loadDefaultMimeTypes();

    // Set the default imageDirectory, if the parameter
    // exists. Otherwise, use the default imageDirectory instance.
    String dir = config.getInitParameter("imageDirectory");
    if(dir != null) this.imageDirectory = new File(dir);
}

/**
 * Sets the content type of the outgoing ServletResponse, depending
 * on the registered MIME type of the provided fileName. The content
 * type mappings are found in the internal mimeTypes Map.
 */
protected void setContentType(ServletResponse response, String fileName)
throws ServletException
{
        // Track if we have properly set the mimetype of
        // the outgoing response stream.
        boolean mimeTypeFound = false;

        // Find the content type of the requested image
        for(Iterator it = this.mimeTypes.entrySet().iterator(); it.hasNext();)
        {
            Map.Entry current = (Map.Entry) it.next();

            // Get the key
            String fileSuffix = (String) current.getKey();
```

```
                if(fileName.toLowerCase().endsWith(fileSuffix))
                {
                        // Found a registered file type. Set the mime type
                        // of the outgoing stream.
                        response.setContentType("" + current.getValue());
                        mimeTypeFound = true;
                }
            }

            // Check sanity
            if(!mimeTypeFound)
                throw new ServletException("Could not find a registered " +
                + "mimeType for file " + fileName);
    }

    /**
     * Retrieves the full filename of a file, if one out of two conditions
     * is met:
     *
     * <ul>
     * <li>The filename exactly matches the argument (fileNameStart)
     * <li>The filename starts with the contents of argument fileNameStart.
     * </ul>
     *
     * @return the filename of an existing file, whose name starts with
     *         the fileNameStart parameter contents.
     * @exception javax.servlet.ServletException if no file was found
     */
    protected String getFileName(String fileNameStart)
    throws ServletException
    {
            // Find all files with the provided fileNameStart
            String[] allFiles = imageDirectory.list();

            // Does the exact fileName exist?
            for(int i = 0; i < allFiles.length; i++)
            {
                // Found a match?
                if(allFiles[i].toLowerCase().equalsIgnoreCase(fileNameStart))
                {
                        return allFiles[i];
                }
            }
```

```
        // No exact match found. Check all files whose
        // names start with the provided fileNameStart string.
        for(int i = 0; i < allFiles.length; i++)
        {
            if(allFiles[i].toLowerCase().startsWith(
                                fileNameStart.toLowerCase()
            ))
            {
                        // Found a partial match.
                        return allFiles[i];
            }
        }

        // Found no file at all... Complain.
        throw new ServletException("Cannot find file with [partial or " +
                    "full] name: " + fileNameStart);
}

/**
 * Reads image data from the file with the provided name.
 *
 * @param name The name of the source file
 * @exception java.io.IOException Thrown if the file could not properly
 *           be read.
 */
protected byte[] getImage(String name) throws IOException
{
      // Find a listing of all images in the image directory
      String[] allFileNames = this.imageDirectory.list();

      for(int i = 0; i < allFileNames.length; i++)
      {
                  // Names match?
                  if(allFileNames[i].equalsIgnoreCase(name))
                  {
                           // Found a match. Read all data
                           // from the file with the given
                           // filename.
                           File src = new File(
                                this.imageDirectory,
                                allFileNames[i]);
                           return getDataFromFile(src);
                  }
      }
```

```
                    // We should never wind up down here..
                    throw new IOException("File '" + name + "' not found.");
    }

    /**
     * Reads and returns all data (in the form of a byte[]) from
     * the file provided.
     *
     * @param aFile the file to read.
     * @exception java.io.IOException Thrown if any IO related
     *            exception was thrown in the read process.
     */
    protected byte[] getDataFromFile(File aFile) throws IOException
    {
        // Declare return
        byte[] content = new byte[(int) aFile.length()];

        // Read the data fully
        DataInputStream in = new DataInputStream(new FileInputStream(aFile));
        in.read(content);

        // Done.
        return content;
    }

    /**
     * Process the request, and send back the image
     * data with the proper content type.
     */
    public void service(ServletRequest request, ServletResponse response)
    throws ServletException, IOException
    {
        // Find the file name requested
        String fileName = request.getParameter("file");
        if(fileName == null)
                throw new ServletException("Cannot handle null filename");

        // Adjust for partial file name in parameter, i.e.
        // if a file has the file name "xyz.jpg", permit
        // the file parameter to be "xyz".
        fileName = this.getFileName(fileName);
```

```
            // Set the content type of the response
            this.setContentType(response, fileName);

            // Get the image with the corresponding fileName
            byte[] imageData = this.getImage(fileName);

            // Write the imageData to the response
            ServletOutputStream out = response.getOutputStream();
            out.write(imageData);
            out.flush ();
    }
}
```

The `TestServlet` provides a way of downloading images and setting their respective content types, which permits proper display by a Web browser (or another client capable of understanding HTTP). Because images are binary documents, it is imperative to use a `ServletOutputStream` retrieved from the `ServletResponse`. The `ServletOutputStream` handles binary image data well, as opposed to a `PrintWriter`.

Although the `TestServlet` class contains relatively few lines of code, its function is rather powerful because of the flexible service methods of the Servlet API. Exploring the API is a good recommendation, as it provides service classes and methods for most purposes.

The javax.servlet.http.ServletRequestWrapper Class

Starting with the Servlet API 2.3 version, the `ServletRequest` can be accessed from a `Wrapper` class, called `ServletRequestWrapper`. The `ServletRequestWrapper` UML diagram shown in Figure 1-26 reveals its many methods.

The purpose of the `Wrapper` classes are to provide a convenient implementation of the respective interfaces that can be subclassed by developers wanting to adapt the inner classes to a servlet. By default, all methods in the `Wrapper` classes call through to the wrapped object.

The constructor of the `ServletRequestWrapper` requires an existing `ServletRequest` that is later stored in an internal variable. Note that all methods from the `ServletRequest` are mirrored to the `ServletRequestWrapper`.

```
                                                   ServletRequest
        javax.servlet.ServletRequestWrapper
+ServletRequestWrapper(request:ServletRequest)
+getAttribute(name:String):Object
+getParameter(name:String):String
+getParameterValues(name:String):String[]
+setAttribute(name:String,o:Object):void
+removeAttribute(name:String):void
+getRequestDispatcher(path:String):RequestDispatcher
+getRealPath(path:String):String
 request:ServletRequest
 attributeNames:Enumeration
 characterEncoding:String
 contentLength:int
 contentType:String
 inputStream:ServletInputStream
 parameterMap:Map
 parameterNames:Enumeration
 protocol:String
 scheme:String
 serverName:String
 serverPort:int
 reader:BufferedReader
 remoteAddr:String
 remoteHost:String
 locale:Locale
 locales:Enumeration
 secure:boolean
```

Figure 1-26. The `ServletRequestWrapper` *class*

Interface javax.servlet.ServletConfig

The `ServletConfig` interface provides an API for sending initialization parameters from the Web container to a servlet. Its UML diagram, shown in Figure 1-27, reveals the simple structure of the `ServletConfig`.

```
interface
javax.servlet.ServletConfig
-----------------------------
+getServletName():String
+getServletContext():ServletContext
+getInitParameter(name:String):String
+getInitParameterNames():Enumeration
```

Figure 1-27. The `ServletConfig` *interface*

Similar to the applet paradigm, all servlets may react to configuration parameters passed to the `init` method when loading a particular `Servlet` class into memory. All parameters are passed as pairs of strings in the format `[key, value]`, so the `ServletConfig` interface mimics the behavior of the `java.util.Properties` class. ServletConfig initialization parameters correspond to the parameters sent to the newly `init`-ed applet. The parameter retrieval process and methods are exact copies of the applet brethren.

The two methods `getInitParameter` and `getInitParameterNames` provide a generic way of retrieving key/value pairs corresponding to initialization parameters. Take a look at two code snippets that show how to use these methods. Listing 1-6 shows how to use `getInitParameter`.

Listing 1-6. Example of `ServletConfig` *usage*

```
...

// The JDBC Database Connection, used to talk to the database backend.
private Connection conn;

// Open a JDBC connection using a driver class defined
// in the initialization parameters of the servlet.
public void init(ServletConfig config) throws ServletException
{
  super.init(config);

   // The JDBC driver class name, used to make a database connection
   // Use the JDBC/ODBC bridge driver as a default value.
   String driverName = "sun.jdbc.odbc.JdbcOdbcDriver";

   // Database Connection information parameters, and default values.
   String uid = "guest";
   String password = "guestPassword";
```

```
  // Load all parameters from the ServletConfig, replacing
  // the default values with specific ones.
  try
  {
    driverName = this.getInitParameter("jdbcDriver");
    uid        = this.getInitParameter("userID");
    password   = this.getInitParameter("password");
  }
  catch (Exception e)
  {
    // Log the message to the standard error stream and
    // through the GenericServlet's log method.
    String logMessage = "Exception when reading config parameters.\n" + e;
    System.err.println(logMessage);
    this.log(logMessage);
 }

  // Open a database connection using the supplied parameters, and
  // store the reference to the Connection in the private variable
  // above. This way, it may be retrieved from within the service
  // method.
  try
  {
    this.conn = DriverManager.getConnection(driverName, uid, password);
  }
  catch (Exception e)
  {
    // Log the message to the standard error stream and
    // through the GenericServlet's log method.
    String logMessage = "Exception when opening DB connection.\n" + e;
    System.err.println(logMessage);
    this.log(logMessage);
 }
}
...
```

Listing 1-7 shows how all parameters may be retrieved using the `getInitParameterNames` method. All incoming initialization parameters may be retrieved and stored for future use. In this case, the servlet is assumed to hold a private `Map` variable where all initialization parameters are stored for future use.

Listing 1-7. Getting and reading all servlet initialization parameters

```
public void init(ServletConfig config) throws ServletException
{
  super.init(config);

  // Store all initialization parameters in a Map collection.
  this.params = Collections.synchronizedMap(new TreeMap());

  // Find all initialization parameters
  for(Enumeration en = config.getInitParameterNames();
                en.hasMoreElements();
  )
  {
      String aKey = (String) en.nextElement();

      // Store the name of the initialization parameter as the
      // key of the Map, and the value of the initialization
      // parameter as the value of the Map.
      params.put(aKey, config.getInitParameter(aKey));
  }
  System.out.println("Total of " + params.size() + " parameters found.");
}
```

Retrieving initialization parameters from within the servlet is a straightforward operation. Providing the initialization parameters to the Web or Application server hosting the servlets is another matter entirely.

The last method of the `ServletConfig` interface—`getServletContext`—retrieves a handle to the server where all servlets reside. The next section thoroughly describes the `ServletContext` interface.

The ServletContext Interface

The `ServletContext` interface, illustrated in Figure 1-28, represents the context of one or many servlets, providing an interface for communicating with the servlet engine and the global attributes available to all servlets running in the same context. The methods of the `ServletContext` interface generally retrieve information about the servlet execution environment:

interface
javax.servlet.ServletContext
+getContext(uripath:String):ServletContext
+getMajorVersion():int
+getMinorVersion():int
+getMimeType(file:String):String
+getResourcePaths(path:String):Set
+getResource(path:String):URL
+getResourceAsStream(path:String):InputStream
+getRequestDispatcher(path:String):RequestDispatcher
+getNamedDispatcher(name:String):RequestDispatcher
+getServlet(name:String):Servlet
+getServlets():Enumeration
+getServletNames():Enumeration
+log(msg:String):void
+log(exception:Exception,msg:String):void
+log(message:String,throwable:Throwable):void
+getRealPath(path:String):String
+getServerInfo():String
+getInitParameter(name:String):String
+getInitParameterNames():Enumeration
+getAttribute(name:String):Object
+getAttributeNames():Enumeration
+setAttribute(name:String,object:Object):void
+removeAttribute(name:String):void
+getServletContextName():String

Figure 1-28. The `ServletContext` *interface*

There is one `ServletContext` per namespace within a running Java Virtual Machine (JVM) instance.

> **NOTE** *For those of you who do not immediately recognize the function of a namespace, think of it as a context set that contains the names of variables and methods and defines their ultimate scope of visibility. Each fully qualified class name (in other words, the class name plus all package names, such as* `java.lang.Object`*) must therefore be unique in a particular namespace. (In the J2EE, each Web application has its own namespace.)*

The `ServletContext` is an important instance where application-wide configuration information is stored. No private information should be stored in the `ServletContext`, as it is global to many servlets. If you choose to create a distributed application (running on several parallel servlet engines), the `ServletContext` of each JVM would be completely separate from all other `ServletContexts`. Because the ServletContext is unique within each JVM, you should store attributes in the `ServletContext` to identify individual node behavior and priorities—for instance, to identify the primary application servers and their load balancing priorities.

The methods of the `ServletContext` fall into the five following groups:

Obtaining information about the servlet engine itself. The associated methods are `getMajorVersion`, `getMinorVersion`, and `getServerInfo`.

Logging messages to the central log of the servlet engine log using three different signatures. The associated methods are three variants of the `log` method with different argument sets.

Handling physical resources on the servlet engine computer node. The associated methods are `getResource` and `getResourceAsStream`.

Obtaining references to other servlets (earlier versions of the Servlet API) or to a `RequestDispatcher` (current Servlet API) to be able to implement programmatic Server Side Includes (SSI) as described in Chapter 2. The associated methods are `getRequestDispatcher` (current API), and `getServlets`, `getServlet`, and `getServletNames` (earlier API).

Handling global `ServletContext` (environment) attributes. The associated methods are `getAttribute`, `setAttribute`, `removeAttribute`, and `getAttributeNames`.

Listing 1-8 shows an example of how to use the methods of the `ServletContext` interface. Before looking at the code, take a look at the results of running it, shown in Figures 1-29 through 1-32. As the methods and procedures for obtaining and using a `RequestDispatcher` have been thoroughly demonstrated already, this sample focuses on the other methods and aspects of the `ServletContext` interface.

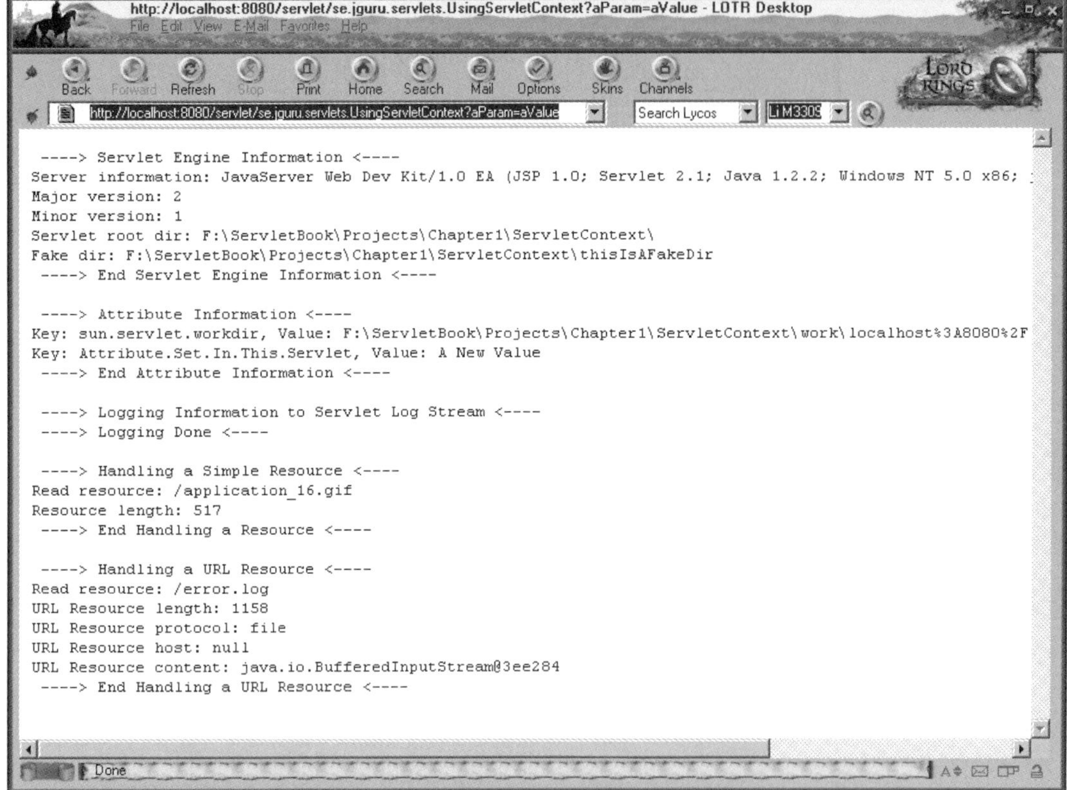

Figure 1-29. The resulting output of the `UsingServletContext` *servlet, if run inside the JSDK 1.0 with its Servlet 2.1 API. Note the difference in Figure 1-30, when the servlet is run inside a servlet 2.2 engine.*

If run in the J2EE application server, the results of the code looks slightly different because of implementation differences. Note, for instance, the result of the servlet root directory in both Figure 1-29 and 1-30.

The output from a Servlet API version 2.3–compliant engine (the Tomcat servlet engine, in this case), is rather long—it is divided into Figures 1-31 and 1-32.

Listing 1-8 shows the code that produces the output shown in Figures 1-29 to 1-32.

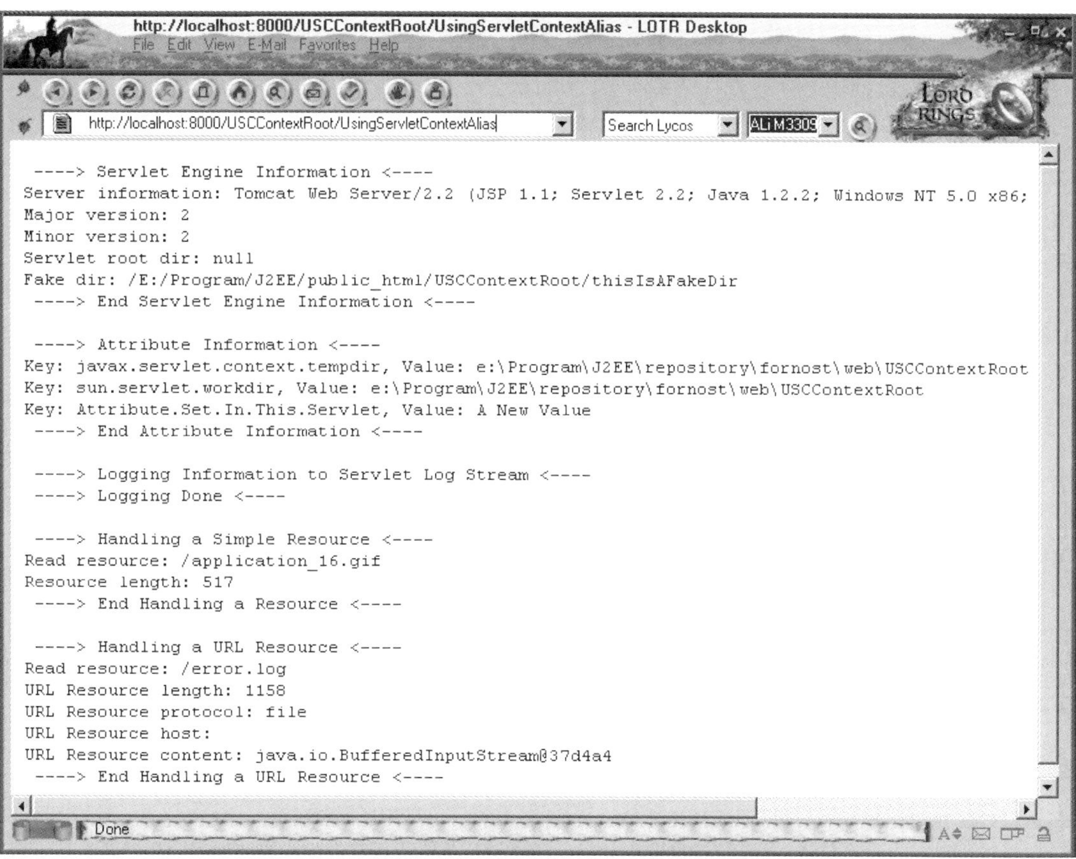

Figure 1-30. Output from the `UsingServletContext` *servlet when run inside the Tomcat servlet engine, with version 2.2 Servlet API support*

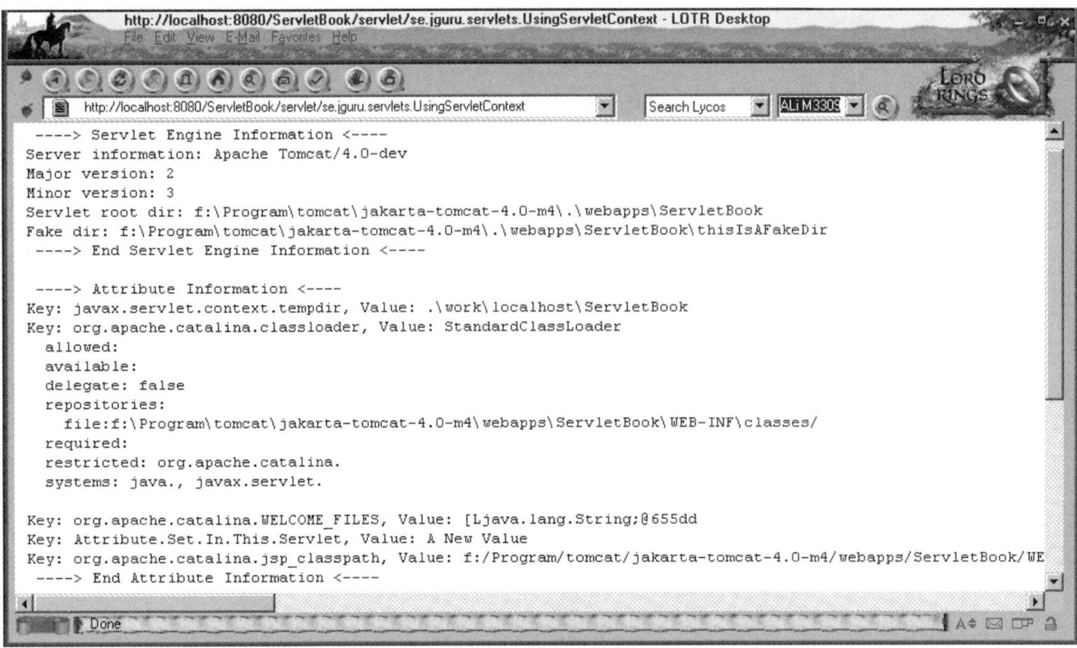

Figure 1-31. Part one of the output from the Tomcat 4.0-m4 servlet engine. Note the difference in bound attributes, where—in this version of Tomcat—the `catalina` *class loader is accessible to all servlets as it is bound to the* `ServletContext`.

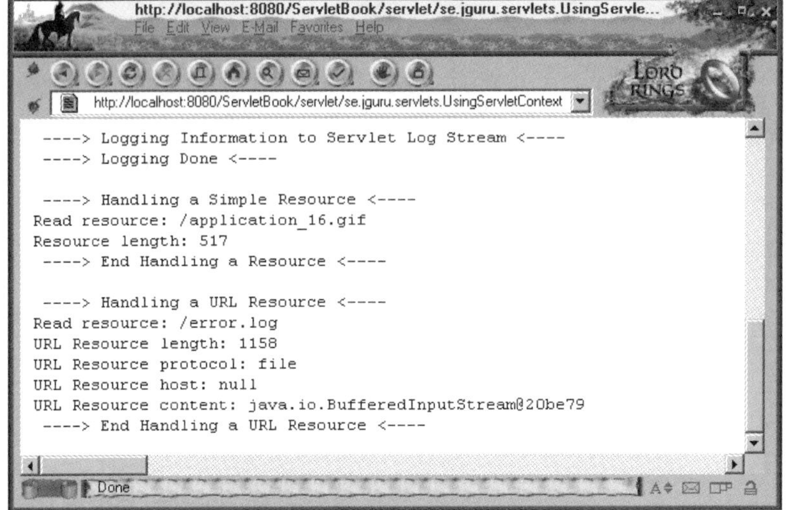

Figure 1-32. Part two of the output from the Tomcat 4.0-m4 servlet engine. This portion is similar to the two earlier versions of servlet engines shown in Figures 1-29 and 1-30.

Listing 1-8. The `UsingServletContext` *code*

```
package se.jguru.servlets;

// Import all required Java packages
import java.io.*;
import java.util.*;
import java.net.*;
import javax.servlet.*;

// Extend the GenericServlet class to avoid
// much implementation of empty methods.
public class UsingServletContext extends GenericServlet
{
    public void service(ServletRequest req, ServletResponse res)
    throws IOException, ServletException
    {
        // Get the output writer
        PrintWriter out = new PrintWriter(res.getWriter());

        // Get the ServletContext of this Servlet
        ServletContext ctx = getServletConfig().getServletContext();

        // ### 1) Get ServletContext information
        out.println("\n ----> Servlet Engine Information <----");
        out.println("Server information: " + ctx.getServerInfo() );
        out.println("Major version: " + ctx.getMajorVersion() );
        out.println("Minor version: " + ctx.getMinorVersion() );
        out.println("Servlet root dir: " + ctx.getRealPath("") );
        out.println("Fake dir: " + ctx.getRealPath("/thisIsAFakeDir") );
        out.println(" ----> End Servlet Engine Information <----");

        // ### 2) Get and Set some Attribute information
        out.println("\n ----> Attribute Information <----");
        ctx.setAttribute("Attribute.Set.In.This.Servlet", "A New Value");
        for(Enumeration en = ctx.getAttributeNames(); en.hasMoreElements();)
        {
            String attributeKey = (String) en.nextElement();
            out.println("Key: " + attributeKey + ", Value: "
                                    + ctx.getAttribute(attributeKey));
        }
        out.println(" ----> End Attribute Information <----");
```

```
// ### 3) Use the ServletContext to log
//        information to the standard
//        Servlet log stream
out.println("\n ----> Logging Information to Servlet Log Stream <----");
ctx.log("A standard Log message");
ctx.log("An exception" ,
        new IllegalArgumentException("Generated exception"));
out.println(" ----> Logging Done <----");

// ### 4) Read a physical resource from the website directories
//        Note that the path provided as an argument to the
//        getResourceAsStream method must be relative to the
//        context root.
//        Thus, it must start with "/"
out.println("\n ----> Handling a Simple Resource <----");
String resourcePath = "/application_16.gif";
DataInputStream in =
    new DataInputStream(ctx.getResourceAsStream(resourcePath));
out.println("Read resource: " + resourcePath);
out.println("Resource length: " + in.available() );
out.println(" ----> End Handling a Resource <----");

//        Note that the path provided as an argument to the
//        getResource method must be relative to the
//        context root.
//        Thus, it must start with "/"
out.println("\n ----> Handling a URL Resource <----");
resourcePath = "/error.log";
URL aURLResource = ctx.getResource(resourcePath);
InputStream is = aURLResource.openStream();
BufferedReader readMe = new BufferedReader(new InputStreamReader(is));
StringBuffer content = new StringBuffer();

while(true)
{
    // Read content from the buffer
    String aReadLine = null;
    try
    {
        aReadLine = readMe.readLine();
        if(aReadLine == null) break;
    }
```

```
            catch(IOException ex)
            {
                log("Abnormal termination of content reading", ex);
            }

            // Append
            content.append(aReadLine);
        }

        out.println("Read resource: " + resourcePath);
        out.println("URL Resource length: " + content.length() );
        out.println("URL Resource protocol: " + aURLResource.getProtocol() );
        out.println("URL Resource host: " + aURLResource.getHost() );
        out.println("URL Resource content: " + aURLResource.getContent() );
        out.println(" ----> End Handling a URL Resource <----");
    }
}
```

Listing 1-8 calls most of the methods in the `ServletContext` interface and correspondingly performs most of the actions one would do in a normal development and deployment environment.

> **NOTE** *All aspects of the* `ServletContext` *interface are common to one or more servlets. The attributes set and read in the* `ServletContext` *will be persistent until explicitly removed or the servlet engine is shut down. Thus, if you decide to run another servlet after the servlet in Listing 1-8 is run (and before rebooting the servlet engine) the attribute set to the* `ServletContext` *by the first servlet is visible to the second.*

Next, consider an example that runs a small servlet that prints out the attribute names and values of the `ServletContext`. The servlet performs the three tasks in the following order:

1. It prints out the `[attributeName]: value` pairs of the `ServletContext`.
2. It sets a new attribute with the name `aNewAttribute` and the value `A new attribute value`.
3. Again, it prints out the `[attributeName]: value` pairs of the `ServletContext`.

Note that the two listings in Figure 1-33 differ because the attribute `aNewAttribute` has been added to the `ServletContext` between the two listings.

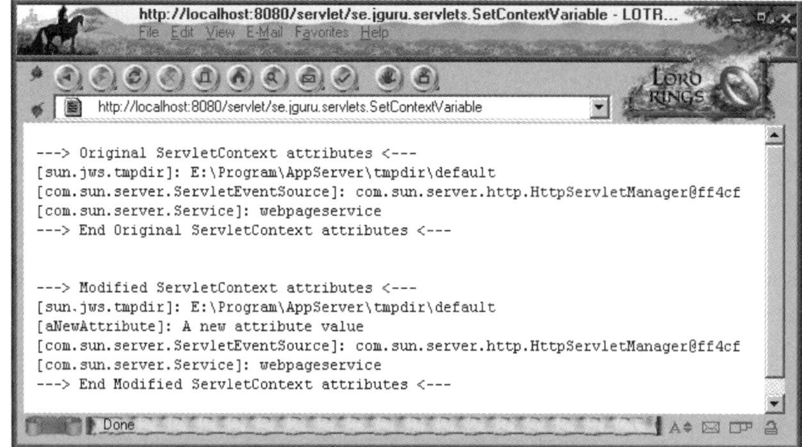

Figure 1-33. Output of the `SetContextVariable` *servlet. Note that the servlet sets a new attribute in the* `ServletContext`.

When the servlet is run again, as shown in Figure 1-34, the `aNewAttribute` still exists in the `ServletContext`. In fact, it is now global and accessible by all servlets sharing the same `ServletContext` (usually, this applies to all servlets within the same Web application).

> **CAUTION** *Be aware that all attributes bound in the ServletContext are shared by all servlets. Keep no private or secret data in such attributes.*

As illustrated by Listing 1-8 and Figures 1-33 and 1-34, `ServletContext` variables are accessible to all servlets running within the same JVM. It is therefore a good place to bind variables that are global to all servlets in a Web server. For servlets running inside a J2EE-compliant application server, however, the role of the `ServletContext` has been reduced; the J2EE Web context has taken over the role of the `ServletContext` as the holder of most globally accessible data in the Web application. For complex data types, the `ServletContext` is still used, as the J2EE Java Naming and Directory Interface (JNDI) context is somewhat limited in what types may be bound and stored there.

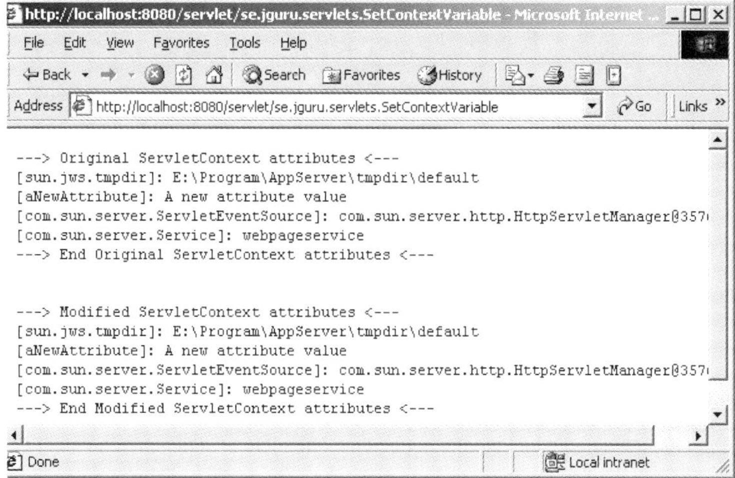

Figure 1-34. Opening a new Web browser window to connect to the same servlet engine reveals that the `aNewAttribute` *is already set from the start. All* `ServletContext` *attributes are global—shared between all servlet instances running in the servlet engine.*

The ServletContextListener Interface

The `ServletContextListener` is an interface that is implemented by all objects that must be notified when the `ServletContext` is created or destroyed (i.e., when the Web application is started or shut down). The small `ServletContextListener` interface provides only two methods, as shown in Figure 1-35.

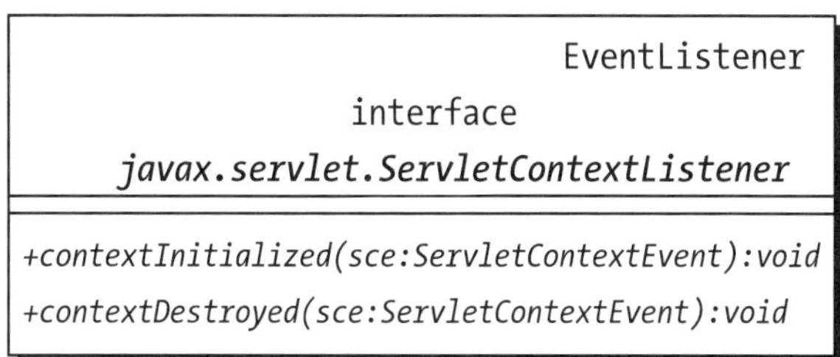

Figure 1-35. The `ServletContextListener` *interface*

Starting with Servlet API version 2.3, the way the servlet engine interacts with its surroundings has changed. The observer/observable (or generator/listener) pattern used throughout the AWT and Swing APIs has been adapted to the Servlet API as well. Figure 1-36 shows a generic `EventGenerator/EventListener` pattern, with the responsibilities of each type explained.

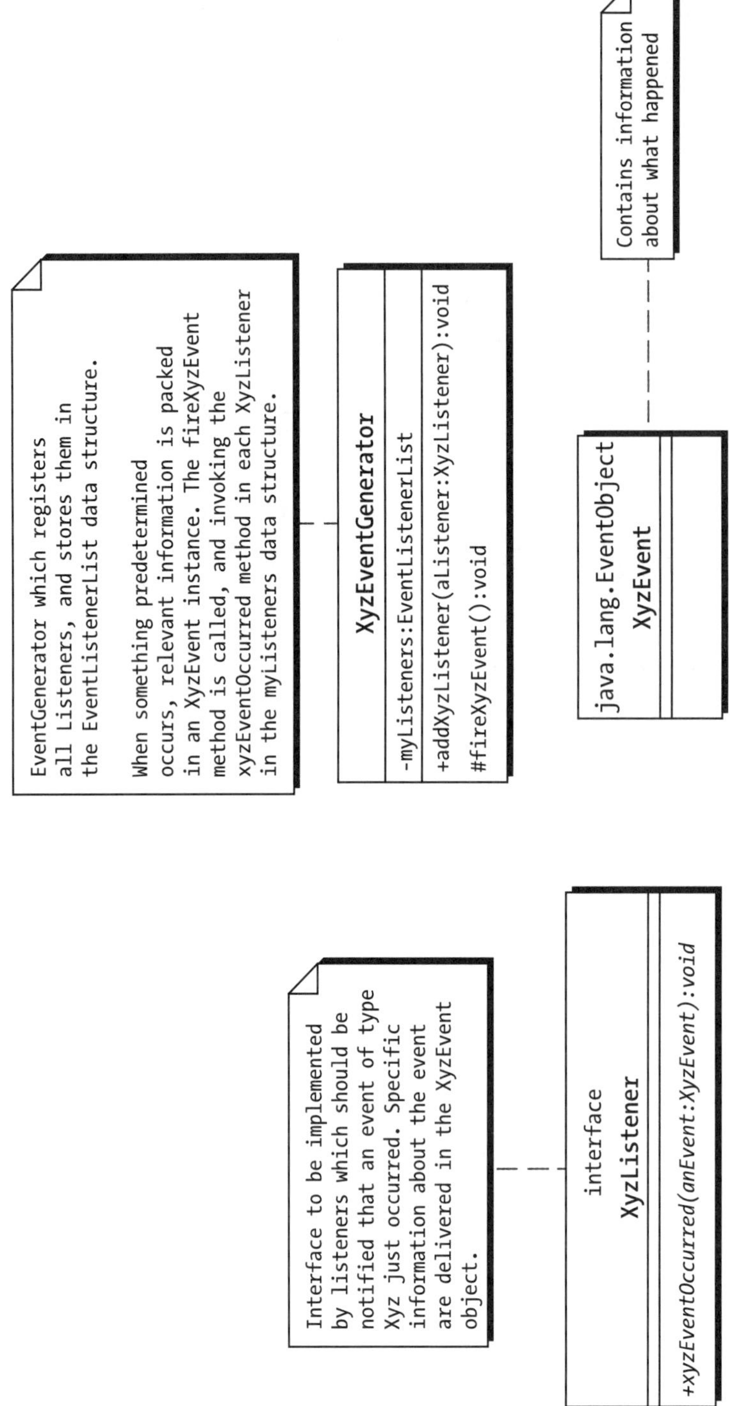

Figure 1-36. The static class pattern of the `EventGenerator/EventListener` *pattern*

Having seen the static class pattern of the `EventGenerator/EventListener` (also known as the *Observable/Observer* pattern) classes, let's take a look at the pattern's dynamic aspects. Figure 1-37 shows the UML sequence diagram of an event generation and handling.

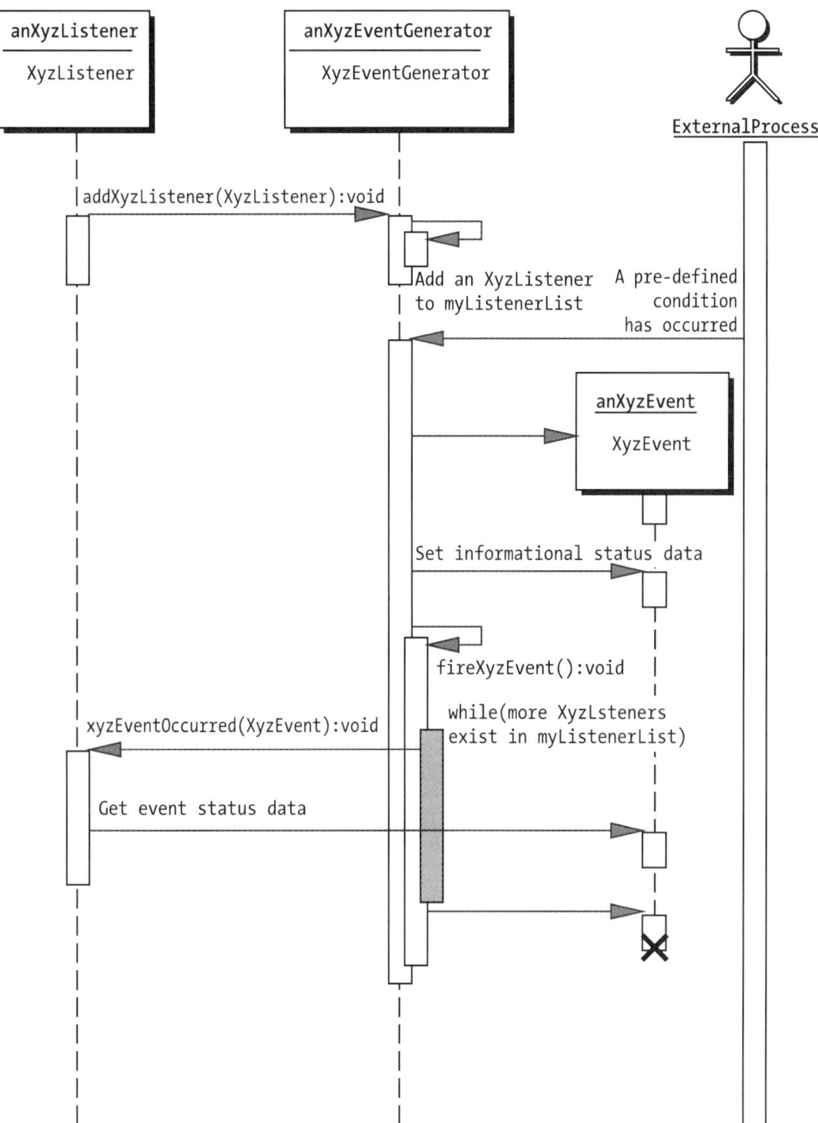

Figure 1-37. Sequence diagram of the `EventGenerator/EventListener` *pattern*

The ServletContextListener interface defines the Listener part of one such generator/listener pattern, and its methods are automatically invoked when the surrounding ServletContext is initialized or destroyed.

Objects implementing the ServletContextListener interface do so because they are required to take some specific action when the ServletContext is created or destroyed—for example, making sure a particular value is bound in the ServletContext before any other servlet is run. That way, one can make sure that particular values are available in the ServletContext when servlets requiring the information are initialized. Only highly specialized configuration classes generally need to bind such information into the ServletContext, so ServletContextListener objects are relatively rare.

Again, any instance implementing the ServletContextListener and registered in the web.xml (or equivalent configuration file) will automatically be notified by the ServletEngine when the ServletContext is created or destroyed.

The ServletContextAttributesListener Interface

Conceptually similar to the ServletContextListener interface just discussed, the ServletContextAttributesListener interface should be implemented by all objects that should receive notification when the attributes of the ServletContext interface are modified. Although ServletContextListener objects are notified of the life and death of the ServletContext, ServletContextAttributesListener objects are notified whenever an attribute is bound to or unbound from the ServletContext. The relatively small interface provides three methods to verify when attributes are added, modified, and deleted (see Figure 1-38).

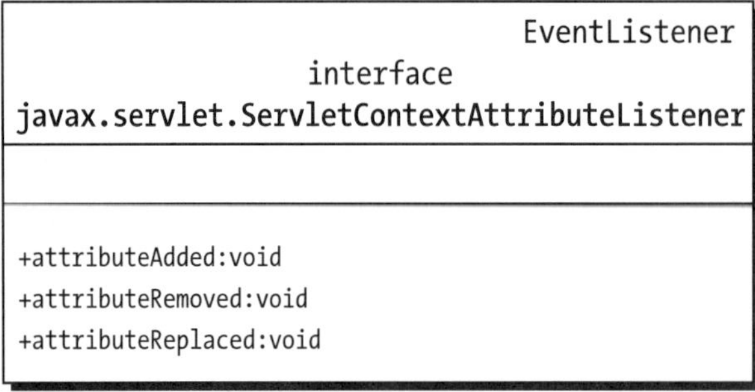

Figure 1-38. The ServletContextAttributesListener *interface*

Similar to ServletContextListeners, all ServletContextAttributesListeners must be registered in the configuration file, web.xml, to be activated.

The `ServletContextAttributesListener` was defined in the Servlet API version 2.3.

The registration section of any listener in the `web.xml` configuration file is small and straightforward. The servlet engine checks the interfaces implemented by the listener and registers it in the appropriate event dispatch queue. In the following example, the registered listener implements the `ServletContextAttributesListener` interface—so the servlet engine adds the instance to the event dispatch queue for `SevletContextAttribute` events:

```
<listener>
        <listener-class>
        se.jguru.servlets.helpers.LoggingServletContextAttributesListener
        </listener-class>
</listener>
```

The code of the `LoggingServletContextAttributesListener` class, shown in Listing 1-9, is simple—it logs the name and value of a bound attribute to the `System.out` stream.

Listing 1-9. The `LoggingServletContextAttributesListener` *class*

```
package se.jguru.servlets.helpers;

import javax.servlet.ServletContextAttributeEvent;
import javax.servlet.ServletContextAttributesListener;
import javax.servlet.ServletContextEvent;
import javax.servlet.ServletContextListener;

/**
 * Listener which logs the name and value of a bound attribute to
 * the System.out stream.
 */
public class LoggingServletContextAttributesListener
implements ServletContextAttributesListener
{
    public void attributeAdded(ServletContextAttributeEvent ev)
    {
        // Log the attribute added.
        this.log("attributeAdded", "" + ev.getName() + "=" + ev.getValue());
    }
```

```
    public void attributeRemoved(ServletContextAttributeEvent ev)
    {
        // Log the attribute removed.
        this.log("attributeRemoved", "" + ev.getName() + "=" + ev.getValue());
    }

    public void attributeReplaced(ServletContextAttributeEvent ev)
    {
        // Log the attribute replaced.
        this.log("attributeReplaced", "" + ev.getName() + "=" + ev.getValue());
    }

    protected void log(String callingMethod, String msg)
    {
        // Log to Standard.out
        System.out.println("[" + callingMethod + "]: " + msg);
    }
}
```

Essentially, for all incoming events, a log entry is generated on the `System.out` steam. The servlet invoked binds and unbinds attributes to the surrounding `ServletContext`. The relevant parts of the `service` method are provided here:

```
...
// Set some ServletContext attributes
ServletContext ctx = this.getServletContext();
ctx.setAttribute("meaningOfLife", "Around42");
ctx.setAttribute("rnd", new Random());

// Overwrite the meaningOfLife attribute
ctx.setAttribute("meaningOfLife", "Music");

// Delete the rnd Attribute
ctx.removeAttribute("rnd");
...
```

The resulting output on the log stream shows the two `ServletContext` attributes, `meaningOfLife` and `rnd`, bound and modified by the servlet code. As the `LoggingServletContextAttributesListener` class from Listing 1-9 logs all attributes bound into the `ServletContext`, the log stream also provides us with information about all default attributes bound into the `ServletContext` by the servlet engine.

Which default attributes are bound into the `ServletContext` by the servlet engine are implementation dependent and varies with the servlet engine. For example, if run in the Apache/Tomcat reference engine, the system log shows the following attribute operations, informing us that the Tomcat 4.0 engine binds two default `ServletContext` attributes, `org.apache.catalina.WELCOME_FILES` and `javax.servlet.context.tempdir`:

```
[attributeReplaced]: org.apache.catalina.WELCOME_FILES=[Ljava.lang.String;@655dd
[attributeAdded]: javax.servlet.context.tempdir=.\work\localhost\ServletBook
[attributeReplaced]: javax.servlet.context.tempdir=.\work\localhost\ServletBook
[attributeAdded]: meaningOfLife=Around42
[attributeAdded]: rnd=java.util.Random@64f6cd
[attributeReplaced]: meaningOfLife=Music
[attributeRemoved]: rnd=java.util.Random@64f6cd
```

The Orion Application Server binds no default attributes to the `ServletContext`, as shown by the following log, generated by the `LoggingServletContextAttributesListener` class:

```
[attributeAdded]: meaningOfLife=Around42
[attributeAdded]: rnd=java.util.Random@61f24
[attributeReplaced]: meaningOfLife=Music
[attributeRemoved]: rnd=java.util.Random@61f24
```

The RequestDispatcher Interface

The `RequestDispatcher` interface is used to redirect the thread of execution from the `service` method of one servlet to the `service` method of another. The two methods of the `RequestDispatcher` interface permit forwarding execution to another servlet (in other words, not returning to the original `service` method) or including the output of another service method into the currently running `service`, as shown in Figure 1-39.

interface ***javax.servlet.RequestDispatcher***
+forward(request:ServletRequest,response:ServletResponse):void *+include(request:ServletRequest,response:ServletResponse):void*

Figure 1-39. The `RequestDispatcher` *interface*

The design patterns and usage of the `RequestDispatcher` interface correspond to the "Forwarding" and "Including" design patterns described in Chapter 2. Both the forward and the include methods accept ServletRequest and ServletResponse objects as arguments. This is no coincidence, as the forward and the include methods are used to redirect the thread of execution to the service method of another servlet.

Code samples demonstrating the detailed usage of the forward and the include methods are provided in Chapter 2.

> **CAUTION** *Be careful not to obtain (or write to) the* OutputStream *of a servlet if you intend to forward the request to another servlet. Should you attempt to do so, the servlet engine throws an* IllegalStateException, *as shown in Figure 1-40.*

Figure 1-40. Client output of an internal servlet error

The code creating the error output in Figure 1-40 is provided in the following sample. Although the code sample looks logical, it contains a grave error. After obtaining the output Writer from the current servlet, an illegal forward call is made to another servlet—and the servlet engine generates an IllegalStateException:

```
public void service(ServletRequest req, ServletResponse res)
throws IOException, ServletException
{
            // Get the output writer
            PrintWriter out = new PrintWriter(res.getWriter());
            out.println("... Service method of first servlet ...");

            // Obtain a RequestDespatcher to the SetContextVariable servlet
            // and forward the request there...
            RequestDispatcher rd =
            this.getServletContext().getRequestDispatcher("/aServlet");
            rd.forward(req, res);
}
```

The Filter Interface

The Servlet 2.3 API introduced *servlet filters,* which are classes implementing the `javax.servlet.Filter` interface. A filter adds or modifies data in the request to or the response from a servlet. Much like `service` being the main workload method of all servlets, the filter performs its task in the `doFilter` method, which is the only workload method of the `Filter` interface. The `Filter` interface defines only three methods, shown in Figure 1-41.

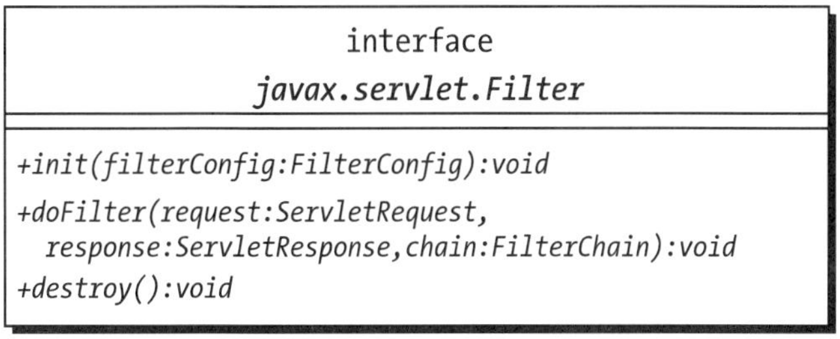

```
interface
javax.servlet.Filter
---
+init(filterConfig:FilterConfig):void
+doFilter(request:ServletRequest,
  response:ServletResponse,chain:FilterChain):void
+destroy():void
```

Figure 1-41. The `Filter` *interface*

All filters have a reference to a `FilterConfig` instance, which contains its initialization parameters from the deployment descriptor, `web.xml`. This is similar to the `ServletConfig` instance of every servlet. Also, through the `FilterConfig` interface, the filter may access the `ServletContext`, as shown in Figure 1-42.

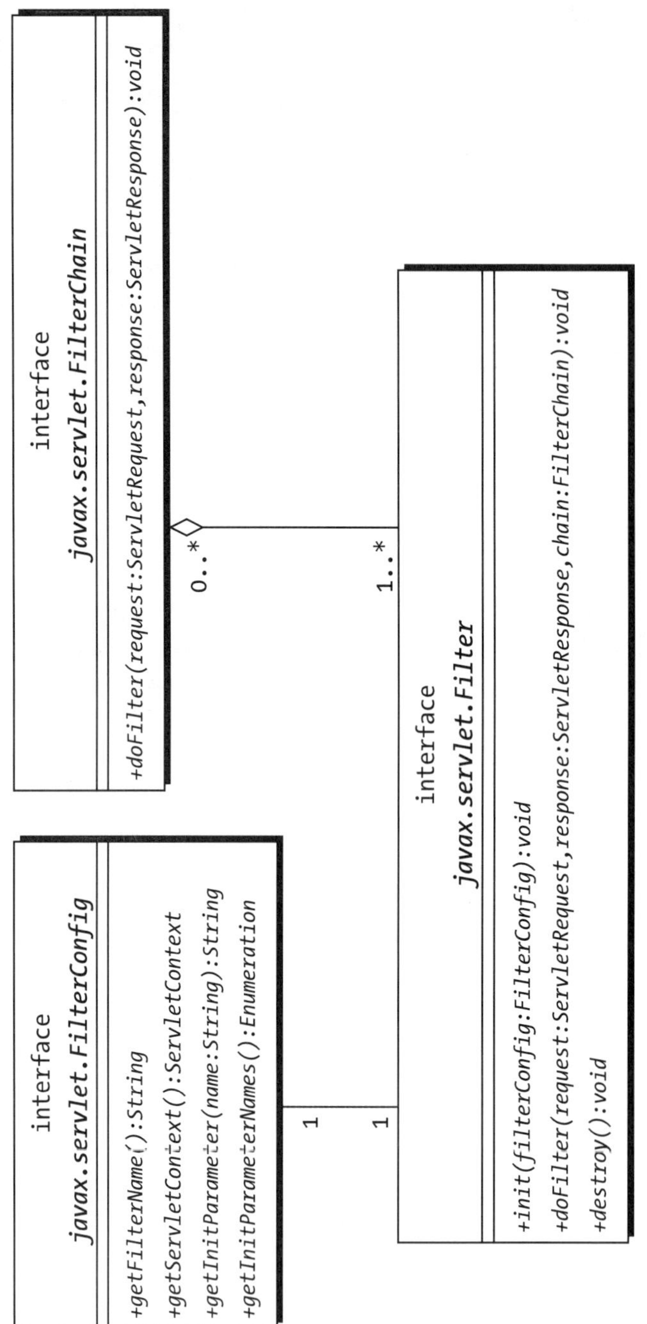

Figure 1-42. The interface structure of each filter. The `FilterConfig` *instance is supplied to the* `init` *method of the* `Filter` *instance. Using the* `FilterConfig` *reference, the filter may call JavaBean* `getter` *methods to access relevant instances, such as* `ServletContext` *and* `InitParameterNames`.

A `Filter` object behaves like a `Servlet`, since its three life-cycle methods mirror those of the Servlet interface.

- `init` is invoked once by the servlet engine when the `Filter` instance is created. The `init` method accepts a FilterConfig container object with the same function as the `ServletConfig` passed to the `init` method of a `Servlet`; it contains all initialization parameters found in the deployment descriptor, `web.xml`.

- `doFilter` contains the actual filter implementation. Similar to the `service` method of a Servlet instance, the `doFilter` method retrieves the `ServletRequest` and `ServletResponse` objects as well as the `FilterChain` to which the current filter belongs.

- `destroy` is called by the servlet engine when the Filter is unloaded from memory (i.e. scheduled for garbage collection by the JVM).

> **NOTE** *For a walkthrough and code examples of the* `Filter` *interface, refer to Chapter 2.*

The FilterConfig Interface

The `FilterConfig` interface is used to pass configuration information to a servlet filter. Starting with Servlet API version 2.3, such filters may intercept requests to or responses from servlets and modify their contents before the target servlet or other resource is invoked/handled. The `FilterConfig` interface is small, as shown in Figure 1-43.

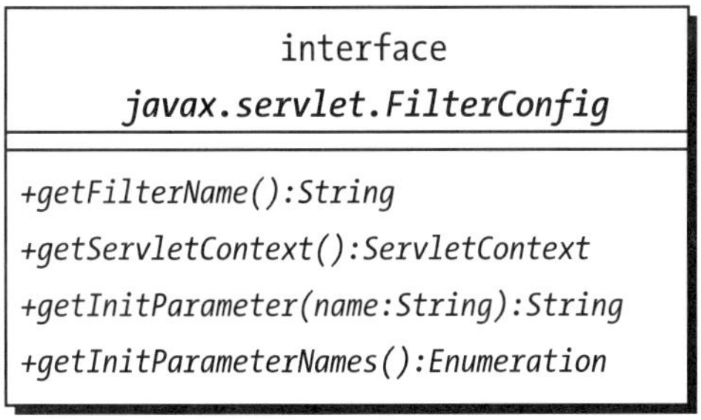

```
interface
javax.servlet.FilterConfig
-----------------------------------------
+getFilterName():String
+getServletContext():ServletContext
+getInitParameter(name:String):String
+getInitParameterNames():Enumeration
```

Figure 1-43. The `FilterConfig` *interface*

The FilterConfig interface provides similar services to a ServletConfig instance, except that it also knows the name of the filter as given in the web.xml configuration file.

All properties that may be extracted from the methods of the FilterConfig interface are read from a configuration file (such as web.xml). The following FilterConfig instantiation process is quite straightforward:

1. The configuration file is read by the servlet engine.

2. The servlet engine sends the read stream into the XML parser.

3. The XML parser creates the FilterConfig instance and sends it to the filter being created.

See Figure 1-44 for a representation of this process.

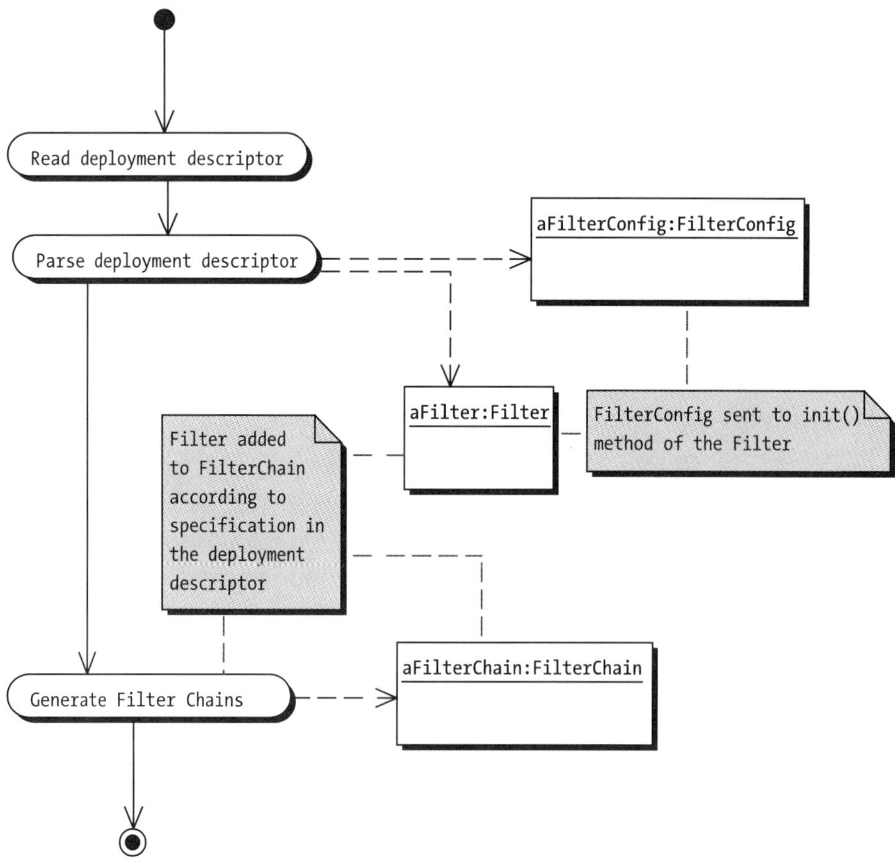

Figure 1-44. The FilterConfig *instantiation process; the* web.xml *deployment descriptor is read and parsed by the servlet engine. The values found therein provides instantiation parameters for the* FilterConfig *instance.*

The ServletInputStream Class

The `InputStream` instance used by all servlets to read data from the client browser extend the abstract `ServletInputStream` class, providing only one specialized method to read a line originating from a byte array, as shown in Figure 1-45.

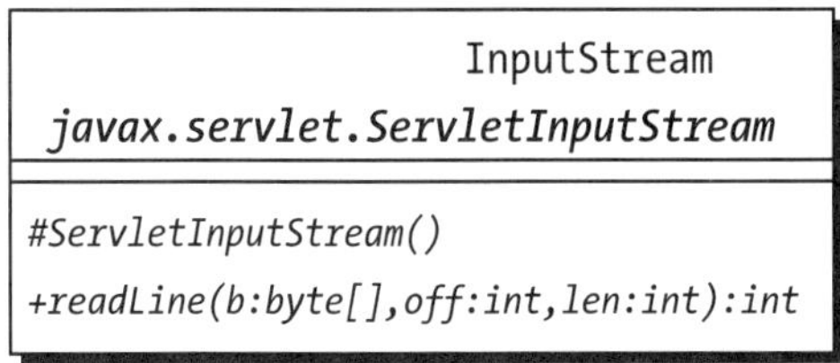

Figure 1-45. The `ServletInputStream` *class*

As the `ServletInputStream` class is abstract, the actual class used for each Web server is implementation dependent. For instance, the `ServletInputStream` instances used by two different versions of the Tomcat reference implementation engine are listed in Table 1-1.

Table 1-1. Concrete `InputStream` *Classes Used by the Apache Tomcat Reference Implementation Engine*

TOMCAT SERVER VERSION	SERVLET API VERSION SUPPORTED	ServletInputStream CLASS USED
3.*x*	2.2	`org.apache.tomcat.core.BufferedServletInputStream`
4.*x*	2.3	`org.apache.catalina.connector.http.HttpRequestStream`

The beauty of the classes of the `java.io` package is that most work similarly. If you know how to use one particular `InputStream`, you can use them all in a similar—or even identical—manner. Therefore, the walkthrough of the `ServletInputStream` is largely unnecessary; however, it is used many times throughout this book's examples.

The `ServletInputStream` itself has but one method—the overloaded `readLine` method used extensively by `BufferReader` streams in the `java.io` package. The variant defined in the `ServletInputStream` interface handles byte arrays instead of characters.

NOTE *For code examples illustrating the reading of bytes using the* `ServletInputStream` *interface, refer to Chapter 3 and Chapter 9.*

The ServletOutputStream Class

The `ServletOutputStream` class, illustrated in Figure 1-46, is an abstract `OutputStream` subtype that has been specially tailored to be used by servlets. Although the interface contains a fair amount of members (as shown in Figure 1-46), it is as simple to use as any other `OutputStream` of the `java.io` package.

```
OutputStream
javax.servlet.ServletOutputStream
-LSTRING_FILE:String="javax.servlet.LocalStrings"
-lStrings:ResourceBundle=ResourceBundle.getBundle(LSTRING_FILE)
#ServletOutputStream()
+print(s:String):void
+print(b:boolean):void
+print(c:char):void
+print(i:int):void
+print(l:long):void
+print(f:float):void
+print(d:double):void
+println():void
+println(s:String):void
+println(b:boolean):void
+println(c:char):void
+println(i:int):void
+println(l:long):void
+println(f:float):void
+println(d:double):void
```

Figure 1-46. The `ServletOutputStream` *class*

The `ServletOutputStream` is mostly similar to the `PrintStream`, although some methods have been stripped away from the `PrintStream` class to better adopt the

ServletOutputStream for servlet use. Also, the ServletOutputStream contains a ResourceBundle to provide different locales for output messages, such as debug messages.

Similar to the ServletInputStream, the ServletOutputStream is subclassed by actual servlet engine implementations. Table 1-2 lists the two versions used by the latest Tomcat reference implementations.

Table 1-2. Concrete OnputStream *classes Used by the Apache Tomcat Reference Implementation Engine*

TOMCAT SERVER VERSION	SERVLET API VERSION SUPPORTED	ServletOutputStream CLASS USED
3.*x*	2.2	org.apache.tomcat.core.BufferedServletOutputStream
4.*x*	2.3	org.apache.catalina.connector.http.HttpResponseStream

The ServletOutputStream contains variations on one single method—the print method, which sends letters and digits to the output device (usually the client browser) connected to the ServletOutputStream. For code examples involving the ServletOutputStream, refer to "The javax.servlet.ServletResponse Interface" earlier in this chapter.

The ServletException Class

The ServletException class, shown in Figure 1-47, extends java.lang.Exception with extra methods granting the power to print the stackTrace on an arbitrary OutputStream or Writer.

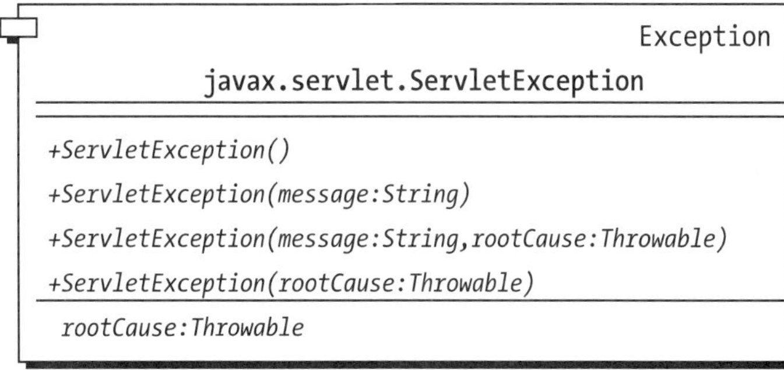

Figure 1-47. The ServletException *class*

All exceptions thrown by a servlet that should be caught by the servlet engine constitute messages from the servlet to the engine. Such messages should be wrapped within a `ServletException` instance, thrown and logged by the servlet engine.

All such `Throwables` should be assigned to the `rootCause` JavaBean property of the `ServletException`. For a code example, refer to the next section.

The UnavailableException Class

The `UnavailableException` class is thrown by a servlet container when the services of a particular servlet are unavailable for a temporary or permanent period. Figure 1-48 contains methods that reveal the nature of the unavailability.

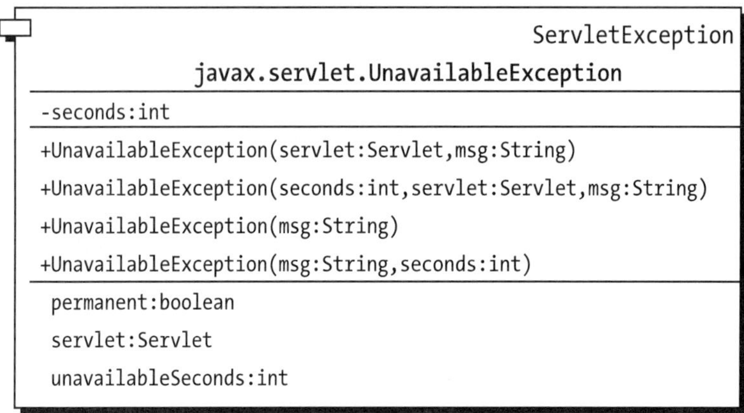

Figure 1-48. The `UnavailableException` *class*

The servlet may deem itself unavailable for service if it suffers from a system-wide malfunction, such as caused by incorrect initialization parameters, insufficient memory available, or a server needed for proper data calculations in the servlet being down.

The two JavaBean properties listed in Table 1-3 in the `UnavailableException` class assist in discovering the status of the unavailable service. The third JavaBean property, `servlet`, has been made deprecated as of the Servlet 2.2 API version and should not be used.

Table 1-3. Non-Deprecated JavaBean Properties in the `UnavailableException` *Class*

JAVABEAN PROPERTY	DESCRIPTION
`unavailableSeconds`	The number of seconds during which the servlet expects to be temporarily unavailable
`permanent`	True if the unavailability is permanent, false otherwise

Let's create a small example servlet throwing a `ServletException` with one of two different root causes, the latter of which is an `UnavailableException`. Figure 1-49 shows the output to the client browser.

Figure 1-49. Output from the `ExceptionGenerator` *servlet, when the exception generated is an arbitrary* `Exception` *type (in this case, a* `SQLException`*). Note that the* `rootCause` *JavaBean property of the* `ServletException` *is the* `Exception` *thrown by the internal servlet method call. When examining the servlet engine log, the root exception gives vital information about the actual cause of the exception.*

Just to examine the structure of the `UnavailableException` class, create and throw such an exception to be the root cause of the `ServletException` in the example. This is a rather unnatural situation, as the `UnavailableException` is a subclass of the `ServletException` class. Thus, the `UnavailableException` is usually thrown directly from a servlet to its engine. However, the unnatural situation stems from filling the purpose of the code example in Listing 1-10. Its purpose is twofold:

- It illustrates the normal way of throwing and re-throwing exceptions within a servlet.
- It illustrates the internal structure of the `UnavailableException`.

The second of the two results when running the `ExceptionGenerator` servlet is shown in Figure 1-50. This time, an `UnavailableException` is thrown as the root cause of the `ServletException`.

Figure 1-50. Result of the `ExceptionGenerator` *servlet when an* `UnavailableException` *was generated by the* `getDataFromBackend` *method call. Note the JavaBean properties of the* `UnavailableException`, *written just below its* `toString` *form in the top table.*

Figure 1-51 illustrates the creation of the `rootCause` exception and the wrapping into a `ServletException`.

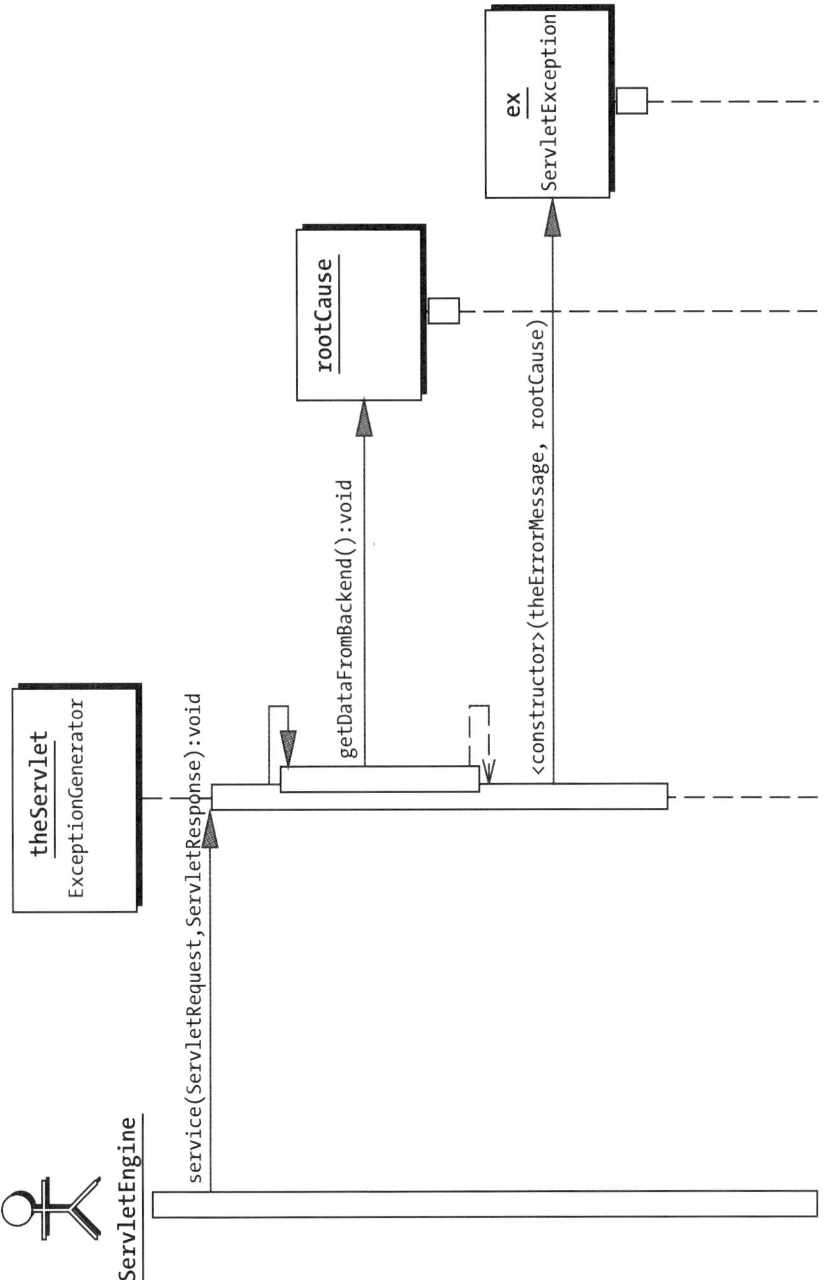

Figure 1-51. The service method of the `ExceptionGenerator` *servlet calls the* `getDataFromBackend`*, which generates an exception* (`rootCause`)*. After the return to the* `service` *method, the* `rootCause` *is wrapped within a* `ServletException` *instance, which is re-thrown to the servlet engine.*

Listing 1-10 contains the code of the `ExceptionGenerator` servlet, which is straightforward. The method calls pertaining to the exception handling in the servlet are rendered in bold.

Listing 1-10. The `ExceptionGenerator` *code*

```
package se.jguru.servlets;

import javax.servlet.*;
import java.io.*;
import java.util.*;
import java.sql.*;

/**
 * Servlet demonstrating the normal mode of encapsulating
 * application generated Exceptions as root causes within
 * ServletException instances.
 *
 * @author Lennart Jörelid, jGuru Europe AB
 */

public class ExceptionGenerator extends GenericServlet
{
    private static Random rnd = new Random();

    public void service(ServletRequest req, ServletResponse res)
    throws ServletException, IOException
    {
        // Get the output Writer
             PrintWriter out = res.getWriter();

             // Simulate digging data from a backend
             try
             {
                 getDataFromBackend();
             }
             catch(Exception sqlEx)
             {
                 // Generate the ServletException
                 ServletException ex = new ServletException("A Message", sqlEx);
```

```
            // Generate root cause message into a StringBuffer
            StringBuffer buf = new StringBuffer();
            buf.append("<td>" + ex.getRootCause());
            if(sqlEx instanceof UnavailableException)
            {
                    UnavailableException unav =
                          (UnavailableException) sqlEx;
                    buf.append("<br>Unavailability time: "
                          + unav.getUnavailableSeconds());
                    buf.append("<br>Permanent: " + unav.isPermanent());
            }

            // Write the exception and its root cause to the output stream
            out.println("<html><body><center><table border=2>");
            out.println("<tr><td>Exception generated</td>"
                          + "<td>Root cause</td></tr>");
            out.println("<tr><td>" + ex + "</td>" + buf.toString()
                          + "</td></tr>");
            out.println("</table></center></body>");

            // Re-throw the exception generated, to get the Servlet engine
            // to perform its normal error printout to the client browser.
            throw ex;
        }
    }

    /**
     * Method which throws an exception, which is either an SQLException
     * or an UnavailableException.
     *
     * Both exception types are to be used as root casuses of the
     * ServletException which is generated and handled by the servlet
     * in the service method above.
     */
    protected void getDataFromBackend() throws Exception
    {
        // Generate a random exception
        int random = Math.abs(rnd.nextInt() % 10);

        if(random < 5) throw new SQLException("Improper data generated");
        else throw new UnavailableException("Server currently unavailable", 25);
    }
}
```

The `ExceptionGenerator` servlet emulates a faulty legacy system by throwing either an `SQLException` or an `UnavailableException` from the facade method `getDataFromBackend`. When the `ExceptionGenerator` servlet receives an error, it formats the error and prints its data to the output `Writer`. This produces the topmost table seen in Figures 1-51 and 1-52. The calling servlet may therefore use the JavaBean properties of its root cause to take some specific action depending on the error thrown by a legacy accessor method.

The error printout to the bottom of Figures 1-49 and 1-50 is the default printout of a `ServletException` from the servlet engine; note the root cause exception in the browser output.

The SingleThreadModel Interface

The `SingleThreadModel` interface provides no explicit functionality, as seen in Figure 1-52. Rather, it is used as an indicator that the `service` method of a particular servlet should be executed using thread synchronization.

interface javax.servlet.SingleThreadModel

Figure 1-52. The `SingleThreadModel` *interface*

The servlet calling model is inherently multithreaded, so any call to the server will spawn a new thread in which the servlet service method will be executed. Should you desire a single-threaded service, you must indicate this to the servlet engine by implementing the `SingleThreadModel` interface as shown here:

```
import javax.servlet.*;
import java.io.*;

// This is a servlet whose service method will be single treaded
public class SingleThreadedServlet
            extends Servlet
            implements SingleThreadModel
{
            // Servlet implementation goes here
}
```

According to the specification, implementing the `SingleThreadModel` interface guarantees that no two threads will execute concurrently in the `service` method. Because the `SingleThreadModel` interface contains no methods, the implementing servlet class need not support or implement anything else but the `SingleThreadModel`. There are a few models available for achieving this, but the implementation details are left to the servlet engine.

Figure 1-53 shows two ways to implement a servlet `SingleThreadModel` interface. The *queuing call model* uses the classic mutually exclusive (mutex) lock (refer to literature on Java threads for a full explanation of mutex locks); all incoming calls are stored in a first-in-first-out (FIFO) queue and executed in due order. The *multiple servlets model* engine does not use a queue but creates a new servlet instance for each incoming call, so no two threads would execute the same service method.

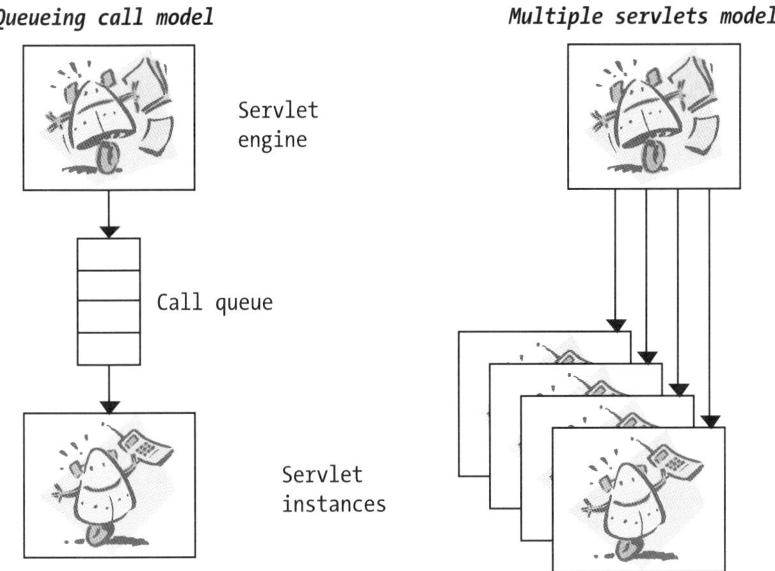

Figure 1-53. Two possible ways to solve servlet synchronization as a result of implementing `SingleThreadModel`

Your application system characteristics determine which `SingleThreadModel` implementation is the better one. The queuing call model consumes less memory than the multiple servlets model but performs poorly with regard to massive system scalability. Thus, if you are creating servlets for an embedded system, choose a servlet engine that uses the queuing call model. Should you implement servlets for an online stockbroker, choose a servlet engine using the multiple servlets model. However, avoid using single-threaded servlets at all if possible: All `SingleThreadModel` servlets have worse performance characteristics than normal, threaded servlets.

Touring the javax.servlet.http Package

It is customary to extend the `HttpServlet` class, rather than `GenericServlet`, when developing servlets for deployment within a Web server; in addition to the standard classes available to generic servlets, there are three groups of new functionality in the `javax.servlet.http` package:

- HTTP-specific methods within the interfaces `HttpServletRequest` and `HttpServletResponse`. The functionality in these interfaces includes various HTTP status code constants, HTTP header setting and reading, as well as basic client call information.

- `HttpUtils` class containing three static methods for parsing client GET and POST parameter lists (such as commonly generated by HTML forms) and obtaining the actual URL that called the servlet.

- Classes handling state within a servlet connection, transforming the inherently stateless HTTP protocol to a stateful distributed communication. These classes and interfaces are `HttpSession` with the service classes `Cookie`, `HttpSessionBindingListener`, and `HttpSessionBindingEvent`.

Let's start our tour of the `javax.servlet.http` package with the `HttpServlet` class normally extended to create a Web server servlet.

The HttpServlet Class

The only difference (on a public member view) between the `HttpServlet` and the `GenericServlet` classes is that the `HttpServlet` class defines an extra `service` method, as shown in Figure 1-54.

Although the differences between the `GenericServlet` superclass and the `HttpServlet` subclass may look minimal, they are nevertheless relevant and important. The argument list of the `HttpServlet service` method is slightly modified from the declaration in the `GenericServlet` class. Whereas the default service method requires a `ServletRequest` and `ServletResponse`, the `HttpServlet` version accepts the more specialized `HttpServletRequest` and `HttpServletResponse`, respectively.

You should derive your servlet implementation class from `HttpServlet` instead of `GenericServlet` if you intend to deploy the result in a Web server. That way, you

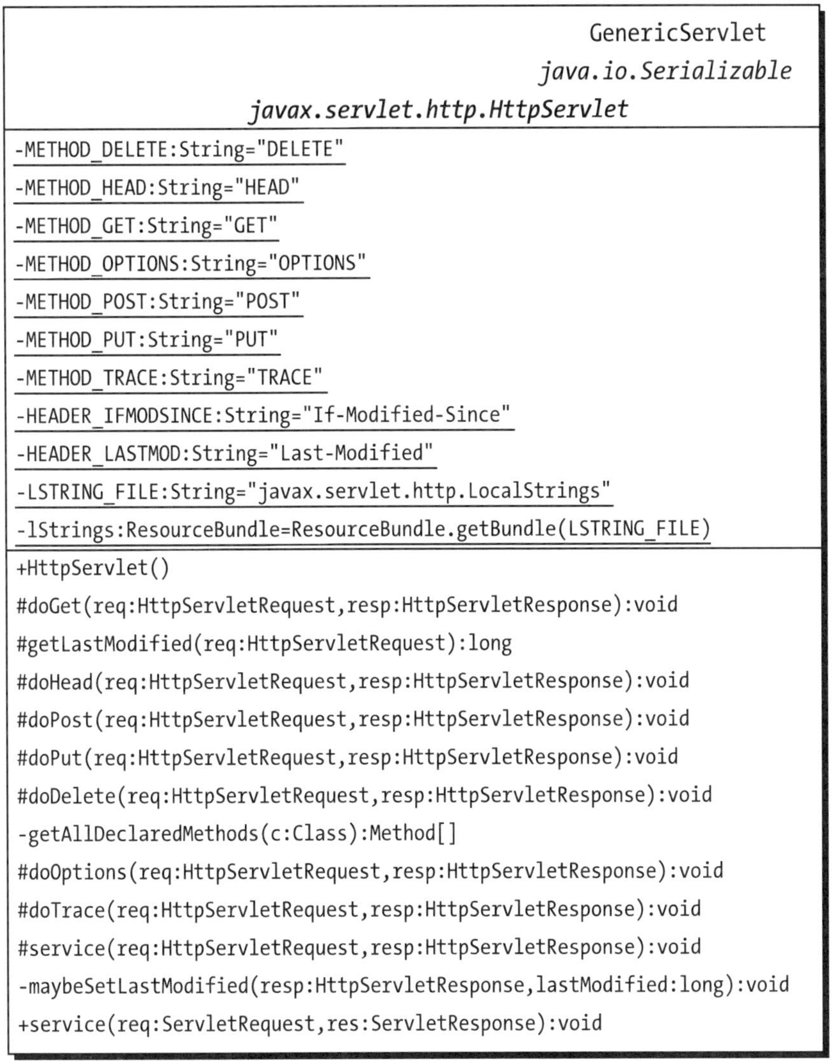

```
                                              GenericServlet
                                        java.io.Serializable
                     javax.servlet.http.HttpServlet
-METHOD_DELETE:String="DELETE"
-METHOD_HEAD:String="HEAD"
-METHOD_GET:String="GET"
-METHOD_OPTIONS:String="OPTIONS"
-METHOD_POST:String="POST"
-METHOD_PUT:String="PUT"
-METHOD_TRACE:String="TRACE"
-HEADER_IFMODSINCE:String="If-Modified-Since"
-HEADER_LASTMOD:String="Last-Modified"
-LSTRING_FILE:String="javax.servlet.http.LocalStrings"
-lStrings:ResourceBundle=ResourceBundle.getBundle(LSTRING_FILE)
+HttpServlet()
#doGet(req:HttpServletRequest,resp:HttpServletResponse):void
#getLastModified(req:HttpServletRequest):long
#doHead(req:HttpServletRequest,resp:HttpServletResponse):void
#doPost(req:HttpServletRequest,resp:HttpServletResponse):void
#doPut(req:HttpServletRequest,resp:HttpServletResponse):void
#doDelete(req:HttpServletRequest,resp:HttpServletResponse):void
-getAllDeclaredMethods(c:Class):Method[]
#doOptions(req:HttpServletRequest,resp:HttpServletResponse):void
#doTrace(req:HttpServletRequest,resp:HttpServletResponse):void
#service(req:HttpServletRequest,resp:HttpServletResponse):void
-maybeSetLastModified(resp:HttpServletResponse,lastModified:long):void
+service(req:ServletRequest,res:ServletResponse):void
```

Figure 1-54. The `HttpServlet` *class*

may use the HTTP-specific functionality of the classes and interfaces in the `javax.servlet.http` package.

The javax.servlet.http.Cookie Class

The `Cookie` class is the programming façade to a client-side HTTP cookie, which is a small textual message sent to the client for semi-persistent storage. The methods in the `Cookie` class access its JavaBean properties, as shown in Figure 1-55.

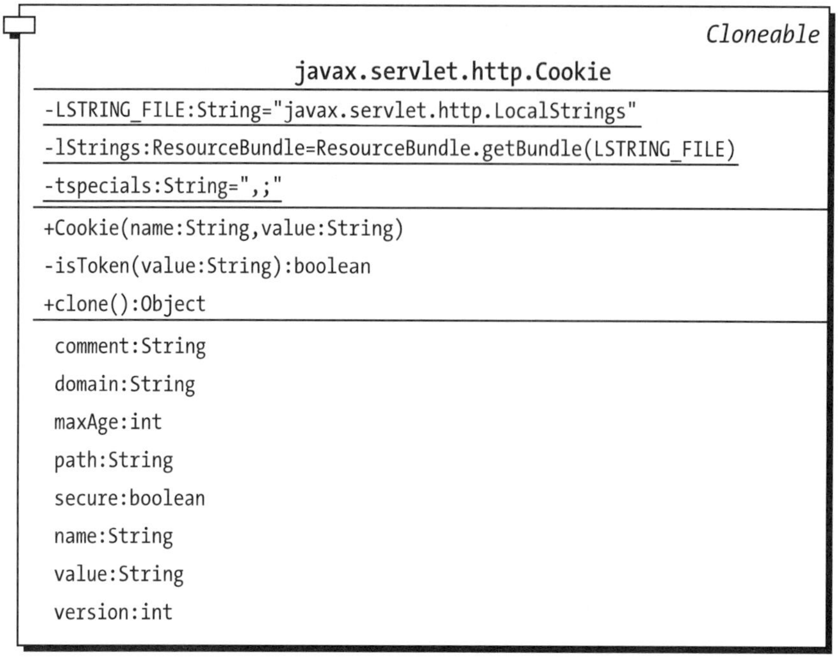

```
                                          Cloneable
              javax.servlet.http.Cookie
-LSTRING_FILE:String="javax.servlet.http.LocalStrings"
-lStrings:ResourceBundle=ResourceBundle.getBundle(LSTRING_FILE)
-tspecials:String=",;"
+Cookie(name:String,value:String)
-isToken(value:String):boolean
+clone():Object
 comment:String
 domain:String
 maxAge:int
 path:String
 secure:boolean
 name:String
 value:String
 version:int
```

Figure 1-55. The `Cookie` *class*

The (client-side) `Cookie` class encapsulates data sent from the Web server to be stored within the browser client. At each subsequent call to the same Web server, the cookie is re-sent to the Web server, permitting the server to maintain an `HttpSession` and client state. According to the HTTP specification, a browser is expected to support 20 cookies per Web server up to a limit of 300 cookies. The browser may also limit each cookie's size to 4KB; don't try to store an encyclopedia in the cookie. The `Cookie` class is simply a JavaBean property wrapper, holding a set of string and int values. For each property, the standard JavaBean getter and setter methods are available. For instance, the JavaBean property `name:String` from Figure 1-55 is provided as follows:

```
public String getName()
public void setName(String name)
private String name
```

Note that not all Web browser/server combinations may support all attributes of the `Cookie` class. The minimum property support (which must be supported by all properly working Web browsers and servers) is name and value. Let's investigate two different Web servers and their corresponding results. Now, take a look at Listing 1-11, which generates a `Cookie`.

Listing 1-11. Code snippet to create and return a `Cookie` *object*

```
//
// Metod to Create a cookie
//
private Cookie createCookie(String name, String value,
                            String comment, long maxAge)
{
   Cookie aCookie = new Cookie(name, value);
   aCookie.setComment(comment);
   aCookie.setMaxAge(maxAge);
   return aCookie;
}

...

// Create the Cookie
Cookie aCookie = createCookie("aName", "aValue", "aComment", 25);

// Add the cookie to the outgoing HttpServletResponse stream
response.addCookie(aCookie);
```

If this cookie is generated and set to the outgoing `HttpServletResponse` stream, the following result HTTP header will be generated:

```
<other HTTP Headers>
Set-Cookie: aName=aValue;Expires=Sun, 02-Mar-2000 15:59:40 GMT+02:00
<other HTTP Headers>
```

> **CAUTION** *Each Web server may handle cookies in an implementation-dependent way. Specifically, the cookie comment may not be sent to the client.*

Note that the Web server used to produce the previous output does not store the cookie comment. The exact storage format is Web server implementation dependent and may therefore take other forms if run on other Web servers. If you intend to use cookies extensively through the `javax.servlet.http.Cookie` class (generally, this is neither required nor desired), be sure to check the cookie-handling implementation of the Web server on your deployment platform.

The javax.servlet.http.HttpServletRequest Interface

The augmented HttpServletRequest interface has a large number of methods that extract information from the HTTP header of the incoming request. Such information is metadata that functions similarly to information found in the header of an electronic mail message. As shown in Figure 1-56, the HttpServletRequest interface has numerous methods that access and modify this metadata.

As is customary for the classes within the javax.servlet packages, header data is stored in and retrieved from a Hashtable-like data structure. A number of convenience methods exist to set and retrieve HTTP headers, which are typecast into specific data types, in addition to the ones for setting and retrieving strings.

Note that the incoming HttpServletRequest instance carries all incoming HTTP headers from the browser client—and the outgoing HttpServletResponse instance carries all outgoing headers transmitted back. Therefore, all getter methods are implemented in HttpServletRequest and all setter methods are all implemented in HttpServletResponse, as shown in Table 1-4.

Table 1-4. HTTP Header Methods as Declared in the HttpServletRequest *Interface*

CLASS	SETTER METHOD	GETTER METHOD	ENUMERATION GETTER METHOD
Hashtable	put(aKey, aValue)	Object value = get(aKey)	keys()
HttpServletRequest	<see HttpServletResponse>	String value = getHeader(aKey)	getHeaderNames()
HttpServletRequest	<see HttpServletResponse>	int value = getIntHeader(aKey)	
HttpServletRequest	<see HttpServletResponse>	long value = getDateHeader(aKey)	

Most of the getter methods of the HttpServletRequest interface correspond to standard properties of the HTTP protocol, as shown in Table 1-5.

Table 1-5. HTTP Protocol Properties and Their HttpServletRequest *Accessor Method*

HTTP PROPERTY	METHOD NAME
USER_AGENT	getUserAgent()
METHOD	getMethod()
QUERY_STRING	getQueryString()
REMOTE_USER	getRemoteUser()

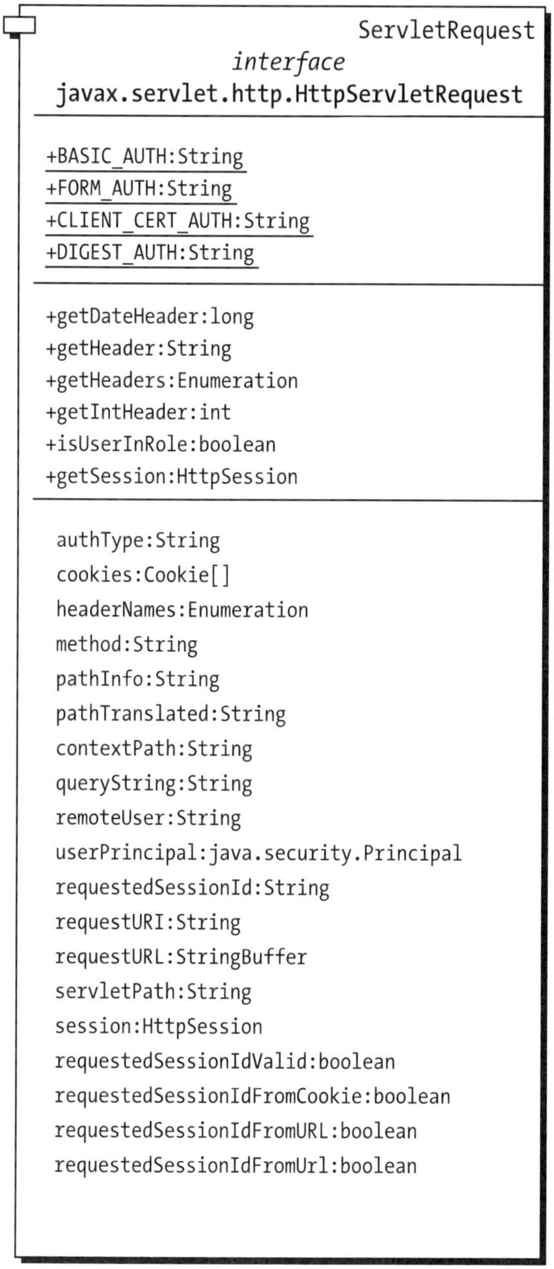

```
                              ServletRequest
                 interface
  javax.servlet.http.HttpServletRequest
---------------------------------------------
+BASIC_AUTH:String
+FORM_AUTH:String
+CLIENT_CERT_AUTH:String
+DIGEST_AUTH:String
---------------------------------------------
+getDateHeader:long
+getHeader:String
+getHeaders:Enumeration
+getIntHeader:int
+isUserInRole:boolean
+getSession:HttpSession
---------------------------------------------
 authType:String
 cookies:Cookie[]
 headerNames:Enumeration
 method:String
 pathInfo:String
 pathTranslated:String
 contextPath:String
 queryString:String
 remoteUser:String
 userPrincipal:java.security.Principal
 requestedSessionId:String
 requestURI:String
 requestURL:StringBuffer
 servletPath:String
 session:HttpSession
 requestedSessionIdValid:boolean
 requestedSessionIdFromCookie:boolean
 requestedSessionIdFromURL:boolean
 requestedSessionIdFromUrl:boolean
```

Figure 1-56. The `HttpServletRequest` *interface*

Listing 1-12 illustrates the methods of the `HttpServletRequest` interface and their usage. First, take a look at the result of the running program. The different sections of the resulting output contain results of the calls of different `HttpServletRequest` methods (see Figure 1-57).

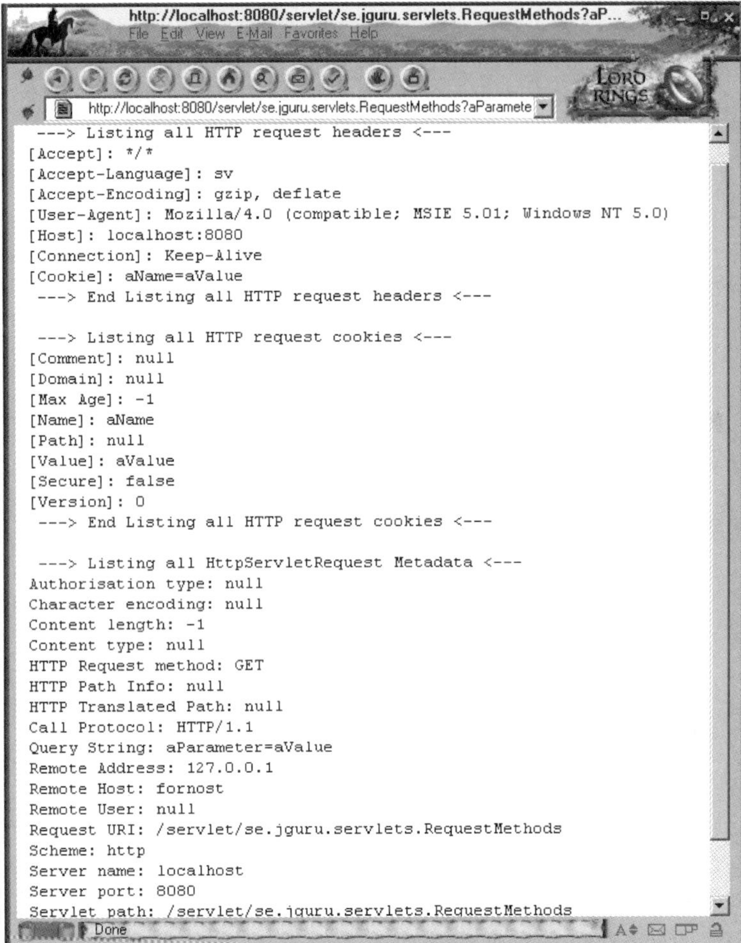

Figure 1-57. Resulting output of the `RequestMethods` *servlet*

The source code generating the output result shown in Figure 1-57, uses the metadata methods of the `HttpServletRequest` interface liberally. All relevant method calls, as well as the characteristics of an `HttpServlet` have been rendered in bold in Listing 1-12.

Listing 1-12. Code of the `RequestMethods` *class*

```
package se.jguru.servlets;

import javax.servlet.*;
import javax.servlet.http.*;
import java.io.*;
import java.util.*;

// Extend HttpServlet to avoid implementing
// lots of empty method bodies.
public class RequestMethods extends HttpServlet
{

    // Process the HTTP service request; note the difference in
    // method signatures between the GenericServlet and HttpServlet
    // classes.
    public void service(HttpServletRequest request, HttpServletResponse response)
    throws ServletException, IOException
    {
        //
        // Set a cookie if none is present on the request
        //
        if(request.getCookies().length == 0 ||
           request.getParameter("reset") != null)
        {
            Cookie aCookie = new Cookie("aName", "aValue");
            aCookie.setComment("This is a comment");
            aCookie.setMaxAge(25);
            response.addCookie(aCookie);
            return;
        }

        // Get the output writer, and set its content type
        PrintWriter out = new PrintWriter (response.getOutputStream());
        response.setContentType("text/plain");
```

```
//
// Printout all HTTP headers
//
out.println(" ---> Listing all HTTP request headers <---");
for(Enumeration en = request.getHeaderNames(); en.hasMoreElements();)
{
    // Get the header
    String aKey = (String) en.nextElement();
    out.println("[" + aKey + "]: " + request.getHeader(aKey));
}
out.println(" ---> End Listing all HTTP request headers <---");

//
// Printout all incoming Cookies
//
out.println("\n ---> Listing all HTTP request cookies <---");
Cookie[] yum = request.getCookies();
for(int i = 0; i < yum.length; i++)
{
    // Printout the Cookie
    out.println("[Comment]: " + yum[i].getComment() );
    out.println("[Domain]: "  + yum[i].getDomain() );
    out.println("[Max Age]: " + yum[i].getMaxAge() );
    out.println("[Name]: "    + yum[i].getName() );
    out.println("[Path]: "    + yum[i].getPath() );
    out.println("[Value]: "   + yum[i].getValue() );
    out.println("[Secure]: "  + yum[i].getSecure() );
    out.println("[Version]: " + yum[i].getVersion() );
}
out.println(" ---> End Listing all HTTP request cookies <---");

//
// Printout HttpServletRequest metadata
//
out.println("\n ---> Listing all HttpServletRequest Metadata <---");
out.println("Authorisation type: " + request.getAuthType() );
out.println("Character encoding: " + request.getCharacterEncoding() );
out.println("Content length: " + request.getContentLength() );
out.println("Content type: " + request.getContentType() );
out.println("HTTP Request method: " + request.getMethod() );
out.println("HTTP Path Info: " + request.getPathInfo() );
out.println("HTTP Translated Path: " + request.getPathTranslated() );
out.println("Call Protocol: " + request.getProtocol() );
out.println("Query String: " + request.getQueryString() );
```

```
        out.println("Remote Address: " + request.getRemoteAddr() );
        out.println("Remote Host: " + request.getRemoteHost() );
        out.println("Remote User: " + request.getRemoteUser() );
        out.println("Request URI: " + request.getRequestURI() );
        out.println("Scheme: " + request.getScheme() );
        out.println("Server name: " + request.getServerName() );
        out.println("Server port: " + request.getServerPort() );
        out.println("Servlet path: " + request.getServletPath() );
        out.println("Request session it from Cookie: " +
                            request.isRequestedSessionIdFromCookie() );
        out.println(" ---> End Listing all HttpServletRequest Metadata <---");

        out.close ();
    }
}
```

Apart from the handling of `Cookies` and `HttpSessions`, all method calls should be fairly trivial in the source code in Listing 1-12, as they merely acquire the underlying HTTP properties with the same name. There is quite a lot of information that may be retrieved from the metadata methods of the `HttpServletRequest`; this data may be stored to extract a fair amount of knowledge about a calling user.

The javax.servlet.http.HttpServletRequestWrapper Class

Starting with the Servlet API 2.3 version, the `HttpServletRequest` can be accessed from a `Wrapper` class, called `HttpServletRequestWrapper`. Its purpose is similar to the `ServletRequestWrapper` studied earlier in this chapter, and its method API is compliant with the `HttpServletRequest`, as shown in Figure 1-58.

The purpose of the `Wrapper` classes are to provide a convenient implementation of the respective interfaces that can be subclassed by developers wanting to adapt the inner classes to a servlet. By default, all methods in the `Wrapper` classes call through to the wrapped object.

The constructor of the `HttpServletRequestWrapper` class requires an existing `HttpServletRequest` that is later stored in an internal variable. Note that all methods from the `HttpServletRequest` are mirrored to the `HttpServletRequestWrapper`.

```
ServletRequestWrapper
HttpServletRequest
javax.servlet.http.HttpServletRequestWrapper
-----------------------------------------------
+HttpServletRequestWrapper(request:HttpServletRequest)
-_getHttpServletRequest():HttpServletRequest
+getDateHeader(name:String):long
+getHeader(name:String):String
+getHeaders(name:String):Enumeration
+getIntHeader(name:String):int
+isUserInRole(role:String):boolean
+getSession(create:boolean):HttpSession
-----------------------------------------------
authType:String
cookies:Cookie[]
headerNames:Enumeration
method:String
pathInfo:String
pathTranslated:String
contextPath:String
queryString:String
remoteUser:String
userPrincipal:java.security.Principal
requestedSessionId:String
requestURI:String
requestURL:StringBuffer
servletPath:String
session:HttpSession
requestedSessionIdValid:boolean
requestedSessionIdFromCookie:boolean
requestedSessionIdFromURL:boolean
requestedSessionIdFromUrl:boolean
```

Figure 1-58. The `HttpServletRequestWrapper` *class*

The javax.servlet.http.HttpServletResponse Interface

The `HttpServletResponse` interface, shown in Figure 1-59, groups properties and actions for outgoing messages from the Web server to the Web browser. The `HttpServletResponse` interface corresponds to the `HttpServletRequest` in that its methods set outgoing properties (whereas the methods of the `HttpServletRequest` read incoming properties).

The methods of the `HttpServletResponse` interface have several important functions, such as setting cookies and HTTP headers, as well as sending back various error codes to the browser. Most status messages of the HTTP protocol are represented as constants defined within the interface itself. The names of these constants are `SC_<Http status code>`.

Listing 1-15 is a small code snippet of the `HttpServletResponseMethods` servlet that demonstrates the setting of HTTP headers, as well as the status code redirection methods. Before studying the source code, let's first take a look at the output result of the `HttpServletResponseMethods` servlet. Because HTTP headers are not usually visible in a Web browser, you must use a raw telnet connection to see them. The error code sent back to the client browser is easier to see (Figure 1-60).

The `HttpServletResponseMethods` servlet checks the query string of the request to see if it contains the parameter "error." If so, the servlet sends back the HTTP status code 406 ("Not acceptable")—otherwise it sets a couple of nonstandard `HttpServletRequest` headers, in addition to the standard ones.

To view the set HTTP headers, you must open a raw telnet connection directly to the Web server and input the raw HTTP get command. The user's input is shown in italics in the first listing, and the response returned is shown immediately after. The three headers `Expires`, `MeaningOfLife`, and `PlainStringHeader` are visible in the bottom of the message.

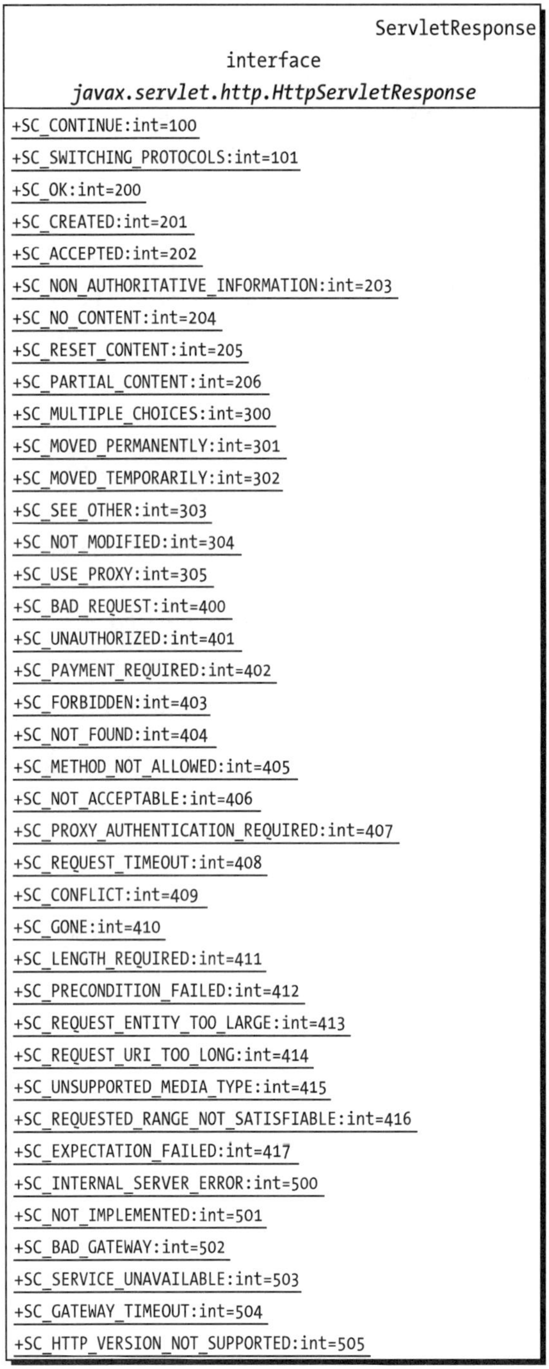

```
                                        ServletResponse
                              interface
              javax.servlet.http.HttpServletResponse
+SC_CONTINUE:int=100
+SC_SWITCHING_PROTOCOLS:int=101
+SC_OK:int=200
+SC_CREATED:int=201
+SC_ACCEPTED:int=202
+SC_NON_AUTHORITATIVE_INFORMATION:int=203
+SC_NO_CONTENT:int=204
+SC_RESET_CONTENT:int=205
+SC_PARTIAL_CONTENT:int=206
+SC_MULTIPLE_CHOICES:int=300
+SC_MOVED_PERMANENTLY:int=301
+SC_MOVED_TEMPORARILY:int=302
+SC_SEE_OTHER:int=303
+SC_NOT_MODIFIED:int=304
+SC_USE_PROXY:int=305
+SC_BAD_REQUEST:int=400
+SC_UNAUTHORIZED:int=401
+SC_PAYMENT_REQUIRED:int=402
+SC_FORBIDDEN:int=403
+SC_NOT_FOUND:int=404
+SC_METHOD_NOT_ALLOWED:int=405
+SC_NOT_ACCEPTABLE:int=406
+SC_PROXY_AUTHENTICATION_REQUIRED:int=407
+SC_REQUEST_TIMEOUT:int=408
+SC_CONFLICT:int=409
+SC_GONE:int=410
+SC_LENGTH_REQUIRED:int=411
+SC_PRECONDITION_FAILED:int=412
+SC_REQUEST_ENTITY_TOO_LARGE:int=413
+SC_REQUEST_URI_TOO_LONG:int=414
+SC_UNSUPPORTED_MEDIA_TYPE:int=415
+SC_REQUESTED_RANGE_NOT_SATISFIABLE:int=416
+SC_EXPECTATION_FAILED:int=417
+SC_INTERNAL_SERVER_ERROR:int=500
+SC_NOT_IMPLEMENTED:int=501
+SC_BAD_GATEWAY:int=502
+SC_SERVICE_UNAVAILABLE:int=503
+SC_GATEWAY_TIMEOUT:int=504
+SC_HTTP_VERSION_NOT_SUPPORTED:int=505
```

Figure 1-59 (top). The `HttpServletResponse` *interface (The figure has been divided into two halves to simplify viewing.)*

```
+addCookie(cookie:Cookie):void
+containsHeader(name:String):boolean
+encodeURL(url:String):String
+encodeRedirectURL(url:String):String
+encodeUrl(url:String):String
+encodeRedirectUrl(url:String):String
+sendError(sc:int,msg:String):void
+sendError(sc:int):void
+sendRedirect(location:String):void
+setDateHeader(name:String,date:long):void
+addDateHeader(name:String,date:long):void
+setHeader(name:String,value:String):void
+addHeader(name:String,value:String):void
+setIntHeader(name:String,value:int):void
+addIntHeader(name:String,value:int):void
+setStatus(sc:int):void
+setStatus(sc:int,sm:String):void
```

Figure 1-59 (bottom). The `HttpServletResponse` *interface (The figure has been divided into two halves to simplify viewing.)*

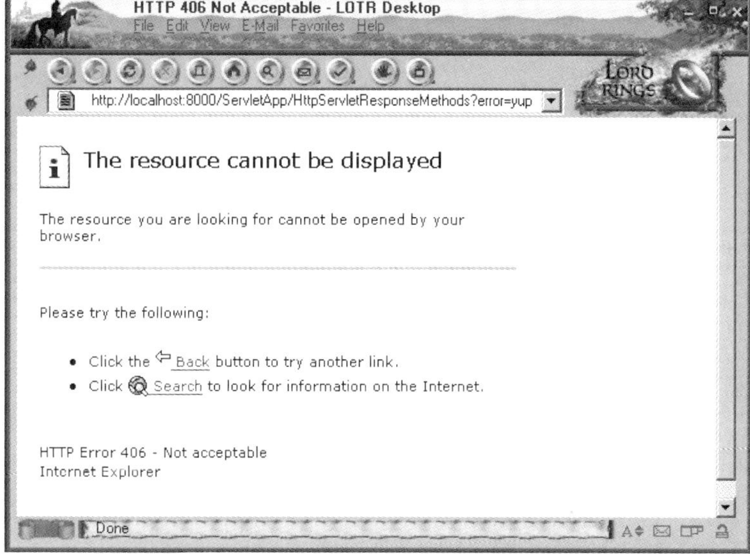

Figure 1-60. Output from the `HttpServletResponseMethods` *servlet when asked to return an error (specifically, HTTP error code 406, "Not acceptable")*

Two different Web servers (Orion and Tomcat) were called using this same telnet call (the input provided by the user is rendered in bold):

```
$ telnet localhost 80
Trying 127.0.0.1...
Connected to mordor.
Escape character is '^]'.
get /servlet/se.jguru.servlets.HttpServletResponseMethods HTTP/1.0
```

Although the call is identical, the responses differ slightly. Listing 1-14 shows the responses from the Tomcat reference implementation engine and the Orion Application Server.

Listing 1-14. Responses from two different Web application servers to the raw telnet request printed in the preceding code sample

```
HTTP/1.0 200 OK
Status: 200
Date: Tue, 26 Dec 2000 16:56:54 GMT
Servlet-Engine: Tomcat Web Server/3.1 (JSP 1.1; Servlet 2.2; Java 1.3.0;
                Windows  2000 5.0 x86; java.vendor=Sun Microsystems Inc.)
MeaningOfLife: 42
PlainStringHeader: aValue
Content-Type: text/plain
Content-Language: en
Expires: Tue, 26 Dec 2000 16:57:04 GMT
```

This is the response from Orion:

```
HTTP/1.1 200 OK
Date: Tue, 26 Dec 2000 16:52:36 GMT
Server: Orion/1.3.8
Expires: Tue, 26 Dec 2000 16:52:46 GMT
MeaningOfLife: 42
PlainStringHeader: aValue
Connection: Close
Content-Type: text/plain
```

Listing 1-15 shows the relevant part of the `service` method code producing the result.

Listing 1-15. HTTP header and status setting code snippet, assuming that the `res` *variable is the* `HttpServletResponse` *of the servlet*

```
//
// Check if a set of custom HTTP headers are set.
// If not, set them.
//
if( ! res.containsHeader("Expires") )
{
        // Set the DateHeader
        res.setDateHeader("Expires", System.currentTimeMillis() + 10000 );
}

if( ! res.containsHeader("MeaningOfLife") )
{
        // Set the intHeader
        res.setIntHeader("MeaningOfLife", 42);
}
if( ! res.containsHeader("PlainStringHeader") )
{
        // Set the string header
        res.setHeader("PlainStringHeader", "aValue");
}

…

// Check if an HTTP status code should be returned
if(req.getParameter("error") != null)
{
        res.sendError(HttpServletResponse.SC_NOT_ACCEPTABLE);

        // This line of code will never execute,
        // as the sendError method aborts further
        // execution of the service method.
        out.println("This will never get printed.");
}
```

Listing 1-15 contains all the method calls setting the HTTP headers and the error states shown in Listing 1-14 and the browser shown in Figure 1-62. All other code in this example is merely irrelevant infrastructure.

Cookies in Control of Client-Side Page Caching

Sometimes you want to avoid the browser caching a certain page. For instance, when returning results of a search in the form of a search result list, you want to avoid looking at a cached version of the result list (in other words, the results of an old query). To turn off caching, use either of the two following methods:

- **Set the header** `Cache-Control : no-cache` **of the outgoing response.** This can be done by calling `response.setHeader("Cache-Control", "no-cache");` This is part of the HTTP version 1.1 standard and requires the browser to understand HTTP/1.1.
- **Set the date header** `Expires : <timestampInMilliseconds>` **of the outoing response.** This can be done by calling `response.setDateHeader("Expires", System.currentTimeMillis() );` This is part of the HTTP version 1.0 standard and therefore requires the browser to understand only HTTP/1.0.

The javax.servlet.http.HttpServletResponseWrapper Class

Starting with the Servlet API 2.3 version, the `HttpServletResponse` can be accessed from a `Wrapper` class, called `HttpServletResponseWrapper`, shown in Figure 1-61. Its method API is compliant with the `HttpServletResponse` interface.

Recall that the purpose of the `Wrapper` classes is to provide a convenient implementation of the respective interfaces that can be subclassed by developers wanting to adapt the inner classes to a servlet. By default, all methods in the `Wrapper` classes call through to the wrapped object.

The javax.servlet.http.HttpSession Interface

`HttpSessions` are used to keep a persistent storage area for data pertaining to one particular client browser. In plain English, the `HttpSession` is used to identify a user across several HTTP calls to the server—this is generally an important aspect of all Web applications. The API of the `HttpSession` is fairly large, as shown in Figure 1-62 but simple to use.

Usually, this is done by sending a unique client-side cookie back and forth between the server and the client browser. For a detailed view on how the cookie-identity mechanism works, refer to "Maintaining State in an HTTP Connection" later in this chapter.

```
                          ServletResponseWrapper
                            HttpServletResponse
     javax.servlet.http.HttpServletResponseWrapper
---------------------------------------------------
+HttpServletResponseWrapper(response:HttpServletResponse)
-_getHttpServletResponse():HttpServletResponse
+addCookie(cookie:Cookie):void
+containsHeader(name:String):boolean
+encodeURL(url:String):String
+encodeRedirectURL(url:String):String
+encodeUrl(url:String):String
+encodeRedirectUrl(url:String):String
+sendError(sc:int,msg:String):void
+sendError(sc:int):void
+sendRedirect(location:String):void
+setDateHeader(name:String,date:long):void
+addDateHeader(name:String,date:long):void
+setHeader(name:String,value:String):void
+addHeader(name:String,value:String):void
+setIntHeader(name:String,value:int):void
+addIntHeader(name:String,value:int):void
+setStatus(sc:int):void
+setStatus(sc:int,sm:String):void
```

Figure 1-61. The `HttpServletResponseWrapper` *class*

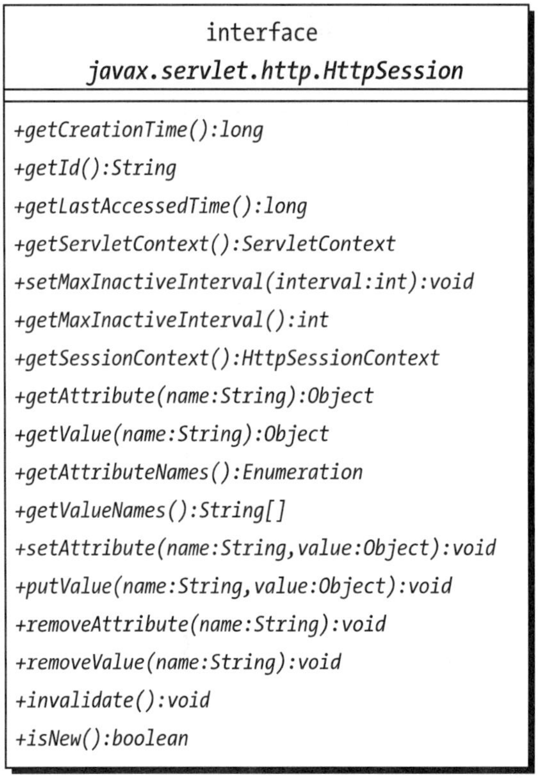

```
interface
javax.servlet.http.HttpSession
---
+getCreationTime():long
+getId():String
+getLastAccessedTime():long
+getServletContext():ServletContext
+setMaxInactiveInterval(interval:int):void
+getMaxInactiveInterval():int
+getSessionContext():HttpSessionContext
+getAttribute(name:String):Object
+getValue(name:String):Object
+getAttributeNames():Enumeration
+getValueNames():String[]
+setAttribute(name:String,value:Object):void
+putValue(name:String,value:Object):void
+removeAttribute(name:String):void
+removeValue(name:String):void
+invalidate():void
+isNew():boolean
```

Figure 1-62. The `HttpSession` *interface*

The methods of the `HttpSession` interface fall into three categories, listed in Table 1-6.

Table 1-6. Categorization of the Methods in the `HttpSession` *Interface*

CATEGORY	METHOD	DESCRIPTION
Obtaining or setting `HttpSession` parameters	`long getCreationTime();`	This retrieves the timestamp (in milliseconds since Jan. 1, 1970) when the `HttpSession` was created.
	`String getId();`	This retrieves the session identifier string—in most cases, the content of the client-side cookie used to realize the `HttpSession`.

Table 1-6. Categorization of the Methods in the `HttpSession` Interface (Continued)

CATEGORY	METHOD	DESCRIPTION
	`long getLastAccessedTime();`	This returns the last time the client sent a request associated with this session (in milliseconds since Jan. 1, 1970).
	`int getMaxInactiveInterval();`	This returns the maximum number of seconds between two client calls. If the browser does not call in the provided interval, the servlet engine will invalidate the `HttpSession`.
	`void setMaxInactiveInterval (int interval);`	This sets the session timeout length in seconds.
	`boolean isNew();`	This returns true if the `HttpSession` is generated in this call or if the client has not yet recognized the session (by transmitting a cookie, for instance).
Methods affecting `HttpSession` data	`void putValue(String key, Object value);`	This binds an object to the `HttpSession`, using the provided key. Compare this method to the `put(key, value)` of `java.util.Map`.
Deprecated since Servlet API 2.2; replaced with `setAttribute(String key, Object value);`		
	`Object getValue(String key);`	This retrieves an object from the `HttpSession`, using the provided key. Compare this method to the `get(key)` of `java.util.Map`.
Deprecated since Servlet API 2.2; replaced with `getAttribute(String key);`		
	`void removeValue(key);`	This removes an `HttpSession` key/value pair.
Deprecated since Servlet API 2.2; replaced with `removeAttribute(String key);`		
	`String[] getValueNames();`	This retrieves the names (keys) of all bound values to this `HttpSession`.
Deprecated since Servlet API 2.2; replaced with `getAttributeNames();`		

Table 1-6. Categorization of the Methods in the `HttpSession` *Interface (Continued)*

CATEGORY	METHOD	DESCRIPTION
	`void setAttribute(String key, Object value);`	This binds an object to the `HttpSession`, using the provided key. Compare this method to the `put(key, value)` of `java.util.Map`.
Since Servlet API 2.3		
	`Object getAttribute(String key);`	This retrieves an object from the `HttpSession`, using the provided key. Compare this method to the `get(key)` of `java.util.Map`.
Since Servlet API 2.3		
	`void removeAttribute(String key);`	This removes an `HttpSession` key/value pair.
Since Servlet API 2.3		
	`Enumeration getAttributeNames();`	This retrieves the attribute names (keys) of all bound values to this `HttpSession`.
Since Servlet API 2.3		
Other methods	`HttpSessionContext getSessionContext();`	This retrieves a `Map` of all existing `HttpSessions` (bound into an `HttpSessionContext` object).
Deprecated since Servlet API 2.1; no replacement.		
	`void invalidate();`	Programmatic invalidation of this `HttpSession`, and garbage collection of all bound data.

The `HttpSession` interface has gone through rather drastic redesign through the Servlet API versions. In the 2.3 revision of the Servlet API, many of its original methods are deprecated. For example, the `putValue`/`getValue` pair has been replaced by `setAttribute`/`getAttribute` to better comply with the naming standard throughout the rest of the Servlet API.

> **NOTE** *The* `HttpSessionContext` *has been deprecated since Servlet API 2.1. Its role was to collect all servlets running within a common* `Context` *and provide access to those servlets. However, for reasons of stability and system reliability, using a* `ServletContext` *is not recommended.*

Listing 1-16 illustrates the function of most `HttpSession` methods. Let's start with investigating two screenshots (shown in Figures 1-63 and 1-64) from the `HttpSessionServlet` that has been written to illustrate the methods of the `HttpSession` interface.

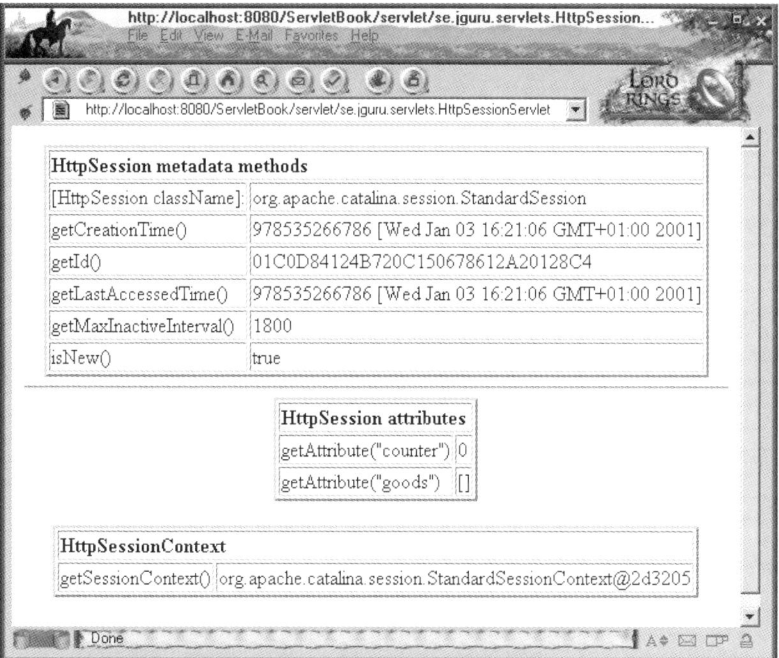

Figure 1-63. Resulting output of the `HttpSessionServlet`*, where most* `HttpSession` *methods are called. The first time an* `HttpSession` *is created, its creation time and last accessed time coincides. Also, the* `isNew` *method returns true*

The code producing the results in Figures 1-65 and 1-66 is pretty straightforward, as shown in Listing 1-16. All method calls to the `HttpSession` instance have been highlighted to facilitate locating them.

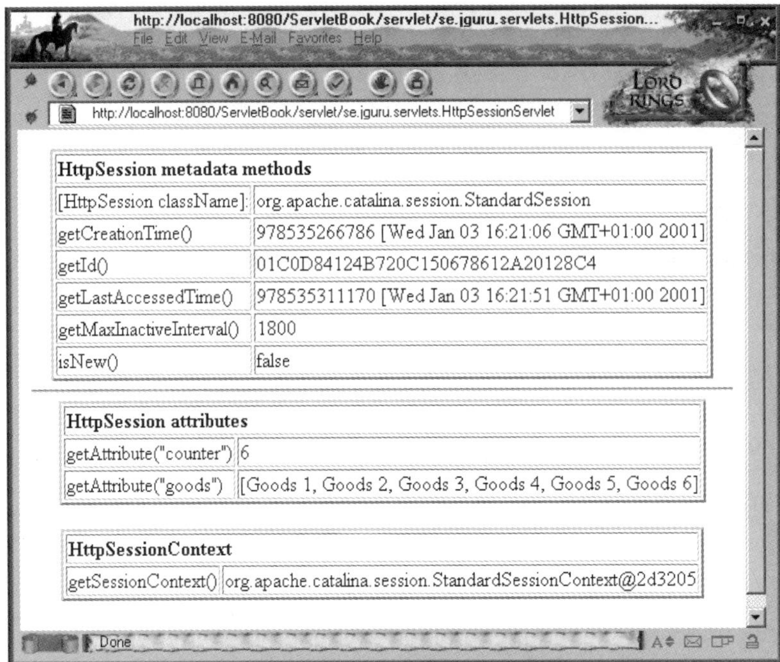

Figure 1-64. Resulting output of the `HttpSessionServlet`*, after a few reloads. Note that the* `lastAccessedTime` *and* `creationTime` *properties differ.*

Listing 1-16. The `HttpSessionServlet` *code*

```
package se.jguru.servlets;

// Lazily import all required classes
import javax.servlet.*;
import javax.servlet.http.*;
import java.io.*;
import java.util.*;

/**
 * Servlet showing the use of HttpSession methods
 */
public class HttpSessionServlet extends HttpServlet
{
```

```
public void service(HttpServletRequest req, HttpServletResponse res)
throws IOException
{
    // Get the Writer connected to the client browser.
    PrintWriter out = res.getWriter();
    out.println("<html><body><center>");

    // Get the HttpSession
    HttpSession sess = req.getSession(true);

    if(sess.isNew())
    {
        // Setup the HttpSession attributes,
        // using Servlet API 2.3 calls.
        // NOTE! If we were using an earlier
        // version of the Servlet API, the setAttribute
        // methods must be replaced by putValue methods.
        sess.setAttribute("counter", new Integer(0));
        sess.setAttribute("goods", new ArrayList());
    }

    // Call some metadata HttpSession methods
    // producing the top table in the resulting view.
    this.startTable("HttpSession metadata methods", out);
    this.printRow("[HttpSession className]:", sess.getClass().getName() ,out);
    this.printRow("getCreationTime()", "" + sess.getCreationTime()
         + " [" + new Date(sess.getCreationTime()) + "]",out);
    this.printRow("getId()", "" + sess.getId() ,out);
    this.printRow("getLastAccessedTime()", "" + sess.getLastAccessedTime()
         + " [" + new Date(sess.getLastAccessedTime()) + "]",out);
    this.printRow("getMaxInactiveInterval()",
            "" + sess.getMaxInactiveInterval() ,out);
    this.printRow("isNew()", "" + sess.isNew() ,out);
    out.println("</table><hr>");

    // Fetch all bound attributes/values of the HttpSession,
    // and print them into a HTML table.
    // NOTE! This code uses the Servlet API version 2.3—so
    // the method names are getAttributeNames and getAttribute.
    // Should an earlier version of the Servlet API be used, the
    // method names must change into getValueNames and getValue.
```

```
    this.startTable("HttpSession attributes", out);
    for(Enumeration en = sess.getAttributeNames(); en.hasMoreElements();)
    {
        String key = "" + en.nextElement();
        this.printRow("getAttribute(\"" + key + "\")",
                      "" + sess.getAttribute(key), out);
    }
    out.println("</table><br>");

    // Read, modify and re-bind the HttpSession data
    // NOTE! This code uses the Servlet API version 2.3-so
    // the method names are setAttribute and getAttribute.
    // Should an earlier version of the Servlet API be used, the
    // method names must change into setValue and getValue.
    int currentCounter = ((Integer) sess.getAttribute("counter")).intValue();
    ArrayList currentGoods = (ArrayList) sess.getAttribute("goods");
    currentGoods.add("Goods " + (currentCounter + 1));

    sess.setAttribute("counter", new Integer(currentCounter + 1));
    sess.setAttribute("goods", currentGoods);

    // Check out the HttpSessionContext
    // (deprecated since servlet API 2.1)
    this.startTable("HttpSessionContext", out);
    this.printRow("getSessionContext()", "" + sess.getSessionContext(), out);
    out.println("</table><br>");

    // Clean up
    out.println("</center></body></html>");
}

/**
 * Convenience method which embeds the method name and the
 * corresponding output into a HTML table row.
 *
 * @param methodName The name of the method invoked
 * @param output The resulting output of the invoked method
 * @param out The PrintWriter which should accept the output
 */
private void printRow(String methodName, String output, PrintWriter out)
{
    out.println(" <tr><td>" + methodName + "</td>");
    out.println("     <td>" + output + "</td></tr>");
}
```

```
    /**
     * Convenience method that outputs the start of a HTML table onto
     * the out PrintWriter.
     *
     * @param tableName The title of the newly created table
     * @param out The PrintWrter which should accept the output
     */
    private void startTable(String tableName, PrintWriter out)
    {
        out.println("<table border=2><tr><td colspan=2><b>"
                    + tableName + "</b></td></tr>");
    }
}
```

The `HttpSession` interface is vital for any kind of serious application development because the data stored in the session are the only things distinguishing one user from another. The `HttpSession` is therefore used in all forms of Web applications where users interact with legacy systems using a Web browser. As you are probably aware, such applications are currently among the most frequently developed.

Servlet API version 2.3 brought changes not only to the `HttpSession` interface, but also to the way it interacts with the servlet engine. Having used the well-working listener design pattern to describe events sent by graphical user interface (GUI) objects to their listeners, the design engineers copied the same interaction pattern to the Servlet API.

In essence, the same interaction methods used by the Swing and AWT frameworks is largely at work within the Servlet API as well—starting with version 2.3.

The javax.servlet.http.HttpSessionBindingListener Interface

An attribute (or value, depending on Servlet API version) bound to or unbound from an `HttpSession` may need to be notified about its change in state. If your attribute instance would require such notice, it must implement the `HttpSessionBindingListener` interface. Thankfully, as shown in Figure 1-65, the method API of the `HttpSessionBindingListener` is small.

As can be understood from the two method definitions in the interface, the `valueBound` method is invoked when the object is bound to an `HttpSession`—and the `valueUnbound` method is similarly called when the object is unbound (removed) from an `HttpSession`.

Usually, an object implements the `HttpSessionBindingListener` interface only in the event that it needs to perform some setup/cleanup of its internal state

EventListener
interface
javax.servlet.http.HttpSessionBindingListener
+valueBound(event:HttpSessionBindingEvent):void
+valueUnbound(event:HttpSessionBindingEvent):void

Figure 1-65. The `HttpSessionBindingListener` *interface*

variables when it is bound to a session. Examples of such activities may include creating/deleting lock files, opening/closing network or database connections, or initializing user game scores. Therefore, relatively few objects need to implement the `HttpSessionBindingListener` interface.

As is common for all listener interfaces, the `HttpSessionBindingListener` is part of a naming design pattern that includes `EventObject (HttpSessionBindingEvent)`, `Listener (HttpSessionBindingListener)`, and registration method (`addHttpSessionBindingListener`). In this particular case, the servlet engine performs the actual registration of all listeners itself—developers need not do anything more than have their bound attribute instance implement `HttpSessionBindingListener`.

For a code example involving all types in the design pattern (in other words, `HttpSessionBindingListener` and `HttpSessionBindingEvent`), refer to the next section.

The javax.servlet.http.HttpSessionBindingEvent Class

Whenever an object is bound to or unbound from the `HttpSession` using the `setAttribute/getAttribute` or `putValue/getValue` methods, an `HttpSessionBindingEvent` object is created. Should the object being bound implement the `HttpSessionBindingListener` interface, the `HttpSessionBindingEvent` is sent as an argument to one of the two methods of the `HttpSessionBindingListener`.

The `HttpSessionBindingListener` has a small set of methods, as shown in Figure 1-66.

The normal internal state of the HttpSessionBindingEvent contains three JavaBean properties:

- The name under which the object generating the event was bound to the `HttpSession`.

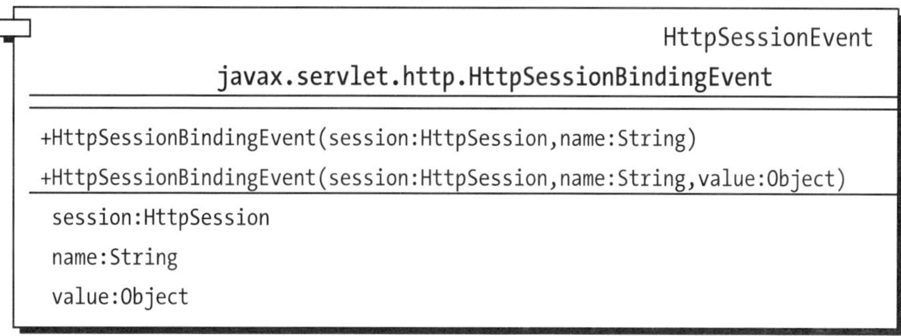

Figure 1-66. The `HttpSessionBindingEvent` *class*

- A reference to the session to which the object was bound. This reference may be used to discover other objects bound to the session, for instance.
- A reference to the event source (in other words, the object performing the actual binding or unbinding).

Because the `HttpSessionBindingEvent` is an event that notifies its listener about changes in the `HttpSession`, it is a subclass of the `HttpSessionEvent` class. For further information about the `HttpSessionEvent` class, refer to "The javax.servlet.http.HttpSessionEvent Class." Shortly, you'll take a look at a small piece of code illustrating the interaction between `HttpSessionBindingListener` and `HttpSessionBindingEvent`. Before plunging into the code, consider its results, shown in Figure 1-67.

Figure 1-67. Resulting view of the `HttpSessionBindingServlet`, *showing that a* `LoggingAttribute` *instance is bound to the* `HttpSession`. *However, the log of the* `LoggingAttribute` *itself is more interesting than the view in the Web browser.*

According to popular rumor, all software systems consist of at least two classes. Take a look at the small software system in Figure 1-68 responsible for the output in Figure 1-67.

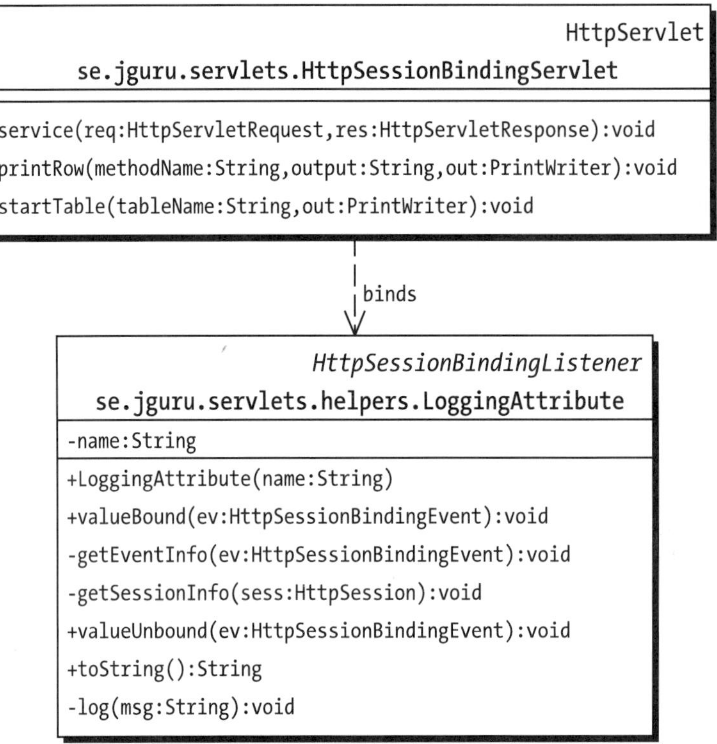

Figure 1-68. The `HttpSessionBindingServlet` *creates and binds a* `LoggingAttribute` *to its* `HttpSession`*. Because the* `LoggingAttribute` *is an* `HttpSessionBindingListener`*, the* `valueBound` *and* `valueUnbound` *methods are called.*

The relevant pieces of the code creating the output and the `System.out` log in Listing 1-17 is spread throughout two classes, the `HttpSessionBindingServlet` and the `LoggingAttribute` class. Take a look at the relevant snippets, starting with the `LoggingAttribute` class, which performs all logging seen in Listing 1-18.

Listing 1-17. The code of the `LoggingAttribute` *class*

```
/* Copyright (c) 2000 jGuru Europe AB. All rights reserved. */
package se.jguru.servlets.helpers;

import javax.servlet.http.*;
import java.util.*;

/**
 * Class logging state when bound to or unbound from the HttpSession.
 *
 * @author Lennart Jörelid, jGuru Europe
 */
public class LoggingAttribute implements HttpSessionBindingListener
{
    private String name;

    public LoggingAttribute(String name)
    {
        this.name = name;
    }

    /**
     * Method called when this object is bound to the
     * HttpSession of the web server. Automagically called
     * by the web server.
     */
    public void valueBound(HttpSessionBindingEvent ev)
    {
        // Log all relevant data.
        this.log("[ValueBound]");

        // Log data from the event object itself.
        this.getEventInfo(ev);

        // Log the HttpSession state when
        // calling this method.
        this.getSessionInfo(ev.getSession());
    }

    /**
     * Simple log method showing EventObject state on the
     * selected log stream.
     */
```

```
private void getEventInfo(HttpSessionBindingEvent ev)
{
    this.log("");
    this.log("Getting HttpSessionBindingEvent information");
    this.log("..........................................");
    this.log(". Source: " + ev.getSource() );
    this.log(". Name: "   + ev.getName() );
    this.log(". Value: "  + ev.getValue() );
    this.log("..........................................");
    this.log("End HttpSession information");
    this.log("");
}

/**
 * Simple log method showing HttpSession state on the
 * selected log stream.
 */
private void getSessionInfo(HttpSession sess)
{
    this.log("");
    this.log("Getting HttpSession information");
    this.log("..............................");
    for(Enumeration en = sess.getAttributeNames(); en.hasMoreElements();)
    {
        String key = (String) en.nextElement();
        this.log(". Key: " + key + ", type bound: "
                    + sess.getAttribute(key).getClass().getName());
        this.log(". Value: " + sess.getAttribute(key));
    }

    this.log("..............................");
    this.log("End HttpSession information");
    this.log("");
}

/**
 * Method called when this object is unbound from the
 * HttpSession of the web server. Automagically called
 * by the web server.
 */
```

```
    public void valueUnbound(HttpSessionBindingEvent ev)
    {
        this.log("[valueUnbound]");
        this.getEventInfo(ev);
        this.getSessionInfo(ev.getSession());
    }

    /**
     * Show a string representation of this instance.
     */
    public String toString()
    {
        return "[" + this.getClass().getName() + "], named: " + this.name;
    }


    /**
     * Main log method, which directs all log entries to
     * a single log stream.
     */
    private void log(String msg)
    {
        // Use System.out for simplicity.
        System.out.println(msg);
    }
}
```

From Listing 1-17, it is clear that the two main log methods, `getSessionInfo` and `getEventInfo`, are called from within the `valueBound` and the `valueUnbound` methods.

> **NOTE** *The* `valueBound` *method is called by the servlet container after the instance is bound to the* `HttpSession`*, as shown by the log in Listing 1-18. Also, the* `valueBound`*method is called after the* `LoggingAttribute` *instance is unbound from the* `HttpSession`*. In general, all* `Listeners` *instances may interact with the* `HttpSession` *when the Web server affects their state, thanks to its obtained reference to the* `HttpSession`*.*

Next, investigate the logs resulting from the calls to the `valueUnbound` and `valueBound` methods in the `LoggingAttribute` class (see Listing 1-18). Note that the `HttpSessionBindingEvent` object carries the name under which the instance was bound to the `HttpSession`, as well as the reference to the `HttpSession` to which the instance was bound. The bound instance may therefore interact with the `HttpSession` to modify its bound state—a newly bound instance may refuse to be bound under an illegal key name, for example.

Listing 1-18. Content of the `System.out` *log when the* `LoggingAttribute` *is bound to the* `HttpSession`

```
[ValueBound]

Getting HttpSessionBindingEvent information
..........................................
. Source: StandardSession[B2B415D5E17183F1B37485265213A390]
. Name: gadget
. Value: [se.jguru.servlets.helpers.LoggingAttribute], named: FirstGadget
..........................................
End HttpSession information

Getting HttpSession information
..............................
. Key: gadget, type bound: se.jguru.servlets.helpers.LoggingAttribute
. Value: [se.jguru.servlets.helpers.LoggingAttribute], named: FirstGadget
..............................
End HttpSession information
```

The corresponding log generated when the `LoggingAttribute` instance is unbound from the `HttpSession`, is seen in Listing 1-19.

Listing 1-19. `System.out` *output log generated when the* `LoggingAttribute` *is unbound*

```
[valueUnbound]

Getting HttpSessionBindingEvent information
..........................................
. Source: StandardSession[455173D231A5A186A4459325375846F3]
. Name: gadget
. Value: [se.jguru.servlets.helpers.LoggingAttribute], named: FirstGadget
..........................................
End HttpSession information

Getting HttpSession information
..............................
..............................
End HttpSession information
```

The `HttpSessionBindingServlet` is a smaller servlet simply creating and binding the `LoggingAttribute` instance. The relevant parts of its code are found in Listing 1-20.

Listing 1-20. Code binding and unbinding attributes to the `HttpSession`

```
...
    public void service(HttpServletRequest req, HttpServletResponse res)
    throws IOException
    {
        ...

        // Get the HttpSession
        HttpSession sess = req.getSession(true);

        if(sess.isNew())
        {
            sess.setAttribute("gadget", new LoggingAttribute("FirstGadget"));
        }

        ...

        // Unbind the gadget attribute
        sess.removeAttribute("gadget");
        ...
    }
...
```

Occasionally, many problems are solved by making an object aware of its binding to or unbinding from an `HttpSession`, particularly if the object requires to initialize itself according to the preferences or identity of the `HttpSession` user. The code provided in Listings 1-17 and 1-20 is all you need to make an object aware of its state with respect to the `HttpSession`.

The javax.servlet.http.HttpSessionEvent Class

The `HttpSessionEvent` is the root event object class for all events having to do with changes to the current `HttpSession` object. If you are creating an event notifying listeners that something has occurred with the `HttpSession`, you should subclass `HttpSessionEvent`, shown in Figure 1-69, which is inherently simple.

All events that notify a listener about a particular change in the `HttpSession` subclasses the `HttpSessionEvent`.

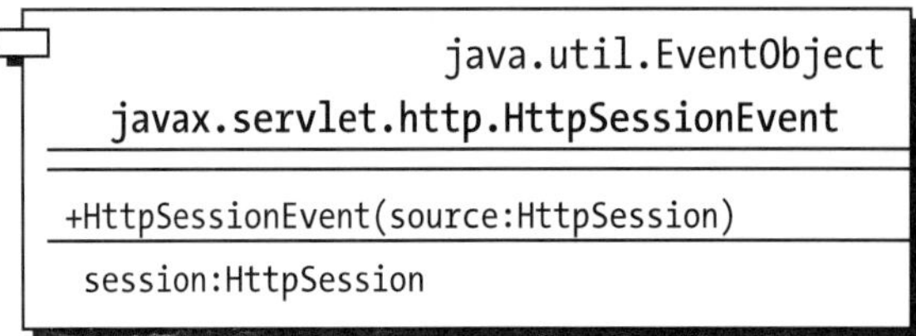

Figure 1-69. The `HttpSessionEvent` *class*

The only method available within the `HttpSessionEvent` is `getSession`. Note the JavaBean notation in Figure 1-69, where a readable JavaBean property named "session" is displayed.

The `HttpSessionEvent` has been included in the Servlet API since version 2.3, along with a redesign of most events related to the `HttpSession`.

The javax.servlet.http.HttpSessionAttributesListener Interface

The `HttpSessionAttributesListener` and the `HttpSessionBindingListener`, covered in the "The `javax.servlet.http.HttpSessionBindingListener` Interface" section may, at first, seem deceptively similar. Essentially, their functionality is similar—whenever an attribute is bound to an `HttpSession`, the `Listener` instance is notified. The `HttpSessionAttributesListener` interface provides only three methods, as shown in Figure 1-70.

Figure 1-70. The `HttpSessionAttributesListener` *interface*

The HttpSessionAttributesListener is introduced in Servlet API version 2.3 as a part of the listener pattern framework. HttpSessionBindingListener and HttpSessionAttributesListener have two differences:

- Any kind of object can implement the HttpSessionAttributesListener interface, but the HttpSessionBindingListener is solely for the object being bound to or unbound from the HttpSession.
- An HttpSessionAttributesListener is application global in the sense that it listens to all events from all HttpSessions within a Web application. It must therefore be registered within the Web application configuration file, web.xml.

The registration of the HttpSessionAttributesListener in the web.xml file is a simple matter. The specification in the web.xml DTD is straightforward; the <listener> XML container can contain only the <listener-class> element:

```
<!--
The listener element indicates the deployment properties for
a web application listener bean.
-->
<!ELEMENT listener (listener-class)>
<!--
The listener-class element declares a class in the application
must be registered as a web application listener bean.
-->
<!ELEMENT listener-class (#PCDATA)>
```

Consider a short example of an HttpSessionAttributesListener in action. As you know from reading "The javax.servlet.http.HttpSessionBindingEvent Class" earlier in this chapter, the HttpSessionBindingEven passed to each of the methods in the HttpSessionAttributesListener contains a reference to the HttpSession, as well as references to the attribute name and value.

Using the structure definition from the preceding DTD, an example of a configured Web listener class in the web.xml config file, is provided in the following listing:

```
...
    <listener>
              <listener-class>
              se.jguru.servlets.helpers.LoggingAttributeListener
               </listener-class>
    </listener>
    ...
```

The `se.jguru.servlets.helpers.LoggingAttributeListener` instance is automatically created by the servlet engine when the Web application is started (see Figure 1-71).

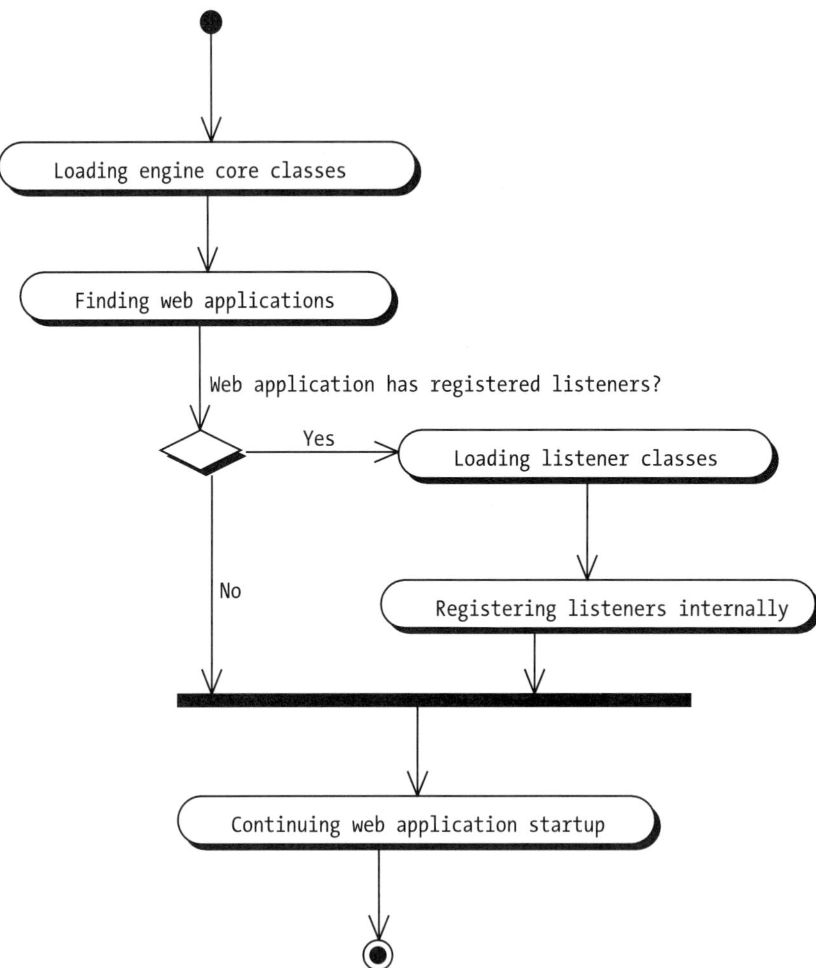

Figure 1-71. Simplified activity diagram of a starting servlet engine. Note that the `web.xml` *file contains optional listener registration entries, which, if present, will cause the servlet engine to recognize and load its listeners.*

Now, check the output of the `LoggingAttributeListener` class in Listing 1-21. The method names in brackets correspond to the method that generated the log output.

> **NOTE** *Most industrial-strength servlet engines redirect* `System.out` *to a log file. If loading and running the* `LoggingAttributeListener` *into a Web application, the output seen below is found in the main server log file.*

Listing 1-21. Output on the `System.out` *log of the* `LoggingAttributeListener` *class*

```
[attributeAdded]: Attribute named meaningOfLife added to the Session
[attributeAdded]: Attribute type: java.lang.Integer
[attributeAdded]: Attribute named newAttribute added to the Session
[attributeAdded]: Attribute type: java.lang.String
[attributeAdded]: Attribute named rnd added to the Session
[attributeAdded]: Attribute type: java.util.Random
[attributeAdded]: Attribute named today added to the Session
[attributeAdded]: Attribute type: java.util.GregorianCalendar
[attributeReplaced]: Attribute named meaningOfLife replaced in the Session
[attributeReplaced]: Attribute type: java.lang.String
[attributeRemoved]: Attribute named newAttribute removed from the Session
[attributeRemoved]: Attribute type: java.lang.String
[attributeRemoved]: Attribute named rnd removed from the Session
[attributeRemoved]: Attribute type: java.util.Random
[attributeRemoved]: Attribute named today removed from the Session
[attributeRemoved]: Attribute type: java.util.GregorianCalendar
```

Only one thing remains: taking a look at the source of the `se.jguru.servlets.helpers.LoggingAttributeListener` class responsible for the output on the log stream of the servlet engine. See Listing 1-22 for this.

Listing 1-22. The `LoggingAttributeListener` *code*

```
/* Copyright (c) 2000, 2001 jGuru Europe AB. All rights reserved. */
package se.jguru.servlets.helpers;

import javax.servlet.http.*;
import javax.servlet.*;
import java.io.*;
import java.util.*;
```

```
/**
 * Class logging state when attributes are bound
 * to or unbound from the HttpSession.
 *
 * @author Lennart Jörelid, jGuru Europe
 */
public class LoggingAttributeListener implements HttpSessionAttributesListener
{
    public void attributeAdded(HttpSessionBindingEvent ev)
    {
        // Log what attribute was added to the HttpSession
        this.log("attributeAdded", "Attribute named " + ev.getName()
                + " added to the Session");
        this.log("attributeAdded", "Attribute type: "
                + ev.getValue().getClass().getName());
    }

    public void attributeRemoved(HttpSessionBindingEvent ev)
    {
        // Log what attribute was removed from the HttpSession
        this.log("attributeRemoved", "Attribute named " + ev.getName()
                + " removed from the Session");
        this.log("attributeRemoved", "Attribute type: "
                + ev.getValue().getClass().getName());
    }

    public void attributeReplaced(HttpSessionBindingEvent ev)
    {
        // Log what attribute was replaced in the HttpSession
        this.log("attributeReplaced", "Attribute named " + ev.getName()
                + " replaced in the Session");
        this.log("attributeReplaced", "Attribute type: "
                + ev.getValue().getClass().getName());
    }

    /**
     * Main log method, which directs all log entries to
     * a single log stream.
     */
    private void log(String callingMethod, String msg)
    {
        // Use System.out for simplicity.
        System.out.println("[" + callingMethod + "]: " + msg);
    }
}
```

Finally, you can find the relevant parts of the `AttributeServlet` class that handles the `HttpSession` calls in Listing 1-23.

Listing 1-23. Relevant code parts of the `AttributeServlet` *class*

```
public class AttributeServlet extends HttpServlet
{
    public void service(HttpServletRequest req, HttpServletResponse res)
    throws ServletException, IOException
    {
        // Get the Session
        HttpSession sess = req.getSession(true);

        // Bind a few dummy objects to the session
        Object[] vals = {new Integer(42), "A new String attribute",
                new java.util.Random(), java.util.Calendar.getInstance()};
        String[] keys = {"meaningOfLife", "newAttribute", "rnd", "today"};

        for(int i = 0; i < keys.length; i++)
        {
            // Bind attributes
            sess.setAttribute(keys[i], vals[i]);
        }

        // Rebind the meaningOfLife attribute
        sess.setAttribute(keys[0], "Music and Acting");

        // Remove all bound attributes,
        // save the meaningOfLife attribute
        for(int i = 1; i < vals.length; i++)
        {
            sess.removeAttribute(keys[i]);
        }
    }
}
```

The javax.servlet.http.HttpSessionListener Interface

The `HttpSessionListener` interface is similar to the `HttpSessionAttributesListener`, but for different events. Its methods will be called when an `HttpSession` is created or destroyed—if the `HttpSessionListener` class is registered in the `web.xml` deployment descriptor of the Web application.

The UML diagram of the `HttpSessionListener` interface is small indeed, as illustrated in Figure 1-72.

```
interface
javax.servlet.http.HttpSessionListener
+sessionCreated(se:HttpSessionEvent):void
+sessionDestroyed(se:HttpSessionEvent):void
```

Figure 1-72. The `HttpSessionListener` *interface*

For a dissection of the listener registration, refer to "The javax.servlet.http.HttpSessionAtributesListener Interface" earlier in this chapter.

You can add a few lines of code to the `LoggingAttributeListener` class defined in "The javax.servlet.http.HttpSessionAtributesListener Interface" earlier in this chapter to make it implement the `HttpSessionListener` interface in addition to the `HttpSessionAttributesListener` interface. Doing so will cause the methods of the two interfaces to interact. The `LoggingAttributeListener` class now takes the form you see in Listing 1-24.

Listing 1-24. Augmented `LoggingAttributeListener` *class*

```
/* Copyright (c) 2000 jGuru Europe AB. All rights reserved. */
package se.jguru.servlets.helpers;

import javax.servlet.http.*;
import javax.servlet.*;
import java.io.*;
import java.util.*;

/**
 * Class logging state when attributes are bound
 * to or unbound from the HttpSession.
 *
 * @author Lennart Jörelid, jGuru Europe
 */
public class LoggingAttributeListener
        implements HttpSessionAttributesListener, HttpSessionListener
{
        ... code from the sample above not shown ...
```

```
    public void sessionCreated(HttpSessionEvent ev)
    {
        // Log the ID of the HttpSession just created
        this.log("sessionCreated", "Session ID: "
                + ev.getSession().getId());
    }

    public void sessionDestroyed(HttpSessionEvent ev)
    {
        // Log the ID of the HttpSession just destroyed
        this.log("sessionDestroyed", "Session ID: "
                + ev.getSession().getId());
    }
}
```

The corresponding system log has added the two following log entries, corresponding to the calls to `sessionCreated` and `sessionDestroyed` methods:

```
[sessionCreated]: Session ID: 608212A366693029A0031414C713A394
[attributeAdded]: Attribute named meaningOfLife added to the Session
...
[attributeRemoved]: Attribute named meaningOfLife removed from the Session
[attributeRemoved]: Attribute type: java.lang.String
[sessionDestroyed]: Session ID: 608212A366693029A0031414C713A394
```

From the log, it is clear that the `HttpSessionEvents` are generated before any other session events (attribute events, for instance), as well as after the last other session operation event. This is natural, because the `HttpSessionEvent` corresponds to the creation and deletion of the `HttpSession` whereas the `HttpSessionBindingEvents` correspond to objects being bound to or unbound from the `HttpSession`.

The javax.servlet.http.HttpSessionContext Interface

The `HttpSessionContext` is essentially a set containing all `HttpSession` objects in the current Web application, together with the (cookie) ID strings that uniquely identify each `HttpSession`. The UML diagram of the `HttpSessionContext`, shown in Figure 1-73, reveals a fairly simple interface.

Using the `HttpSessionContext` interface may potentially lead to rather volatile systems because components may obtain direct references to other `HttpSessions`. Its use is completely discouraged—the `HttpSessionContext` interface and all its methods are deprecated from Servlet API version 2.1.

The method calls to all methods of the `HttpSessionContext` should return constant values when run in any servlet engine whose version is greater than 2.0.

interface *javax.servlet.http.HttpSessionContext*
+getSession(sessionId:String):HttpSession
+getIds():Enumeration

Figure 1-73. The `HttpSessionContext` *interface*

> **CAUTION** `HttpSessionContext` *is a poorly designed and potentially dangerous interface. Don't use it! However, do read about it here and in other sources to understand it as fully as possible.*

The `getIds` method should return an empty `Enumeration`, and `getSession(String)` should always return null.

> **NOTE** *The* `HttpSessionContext` *interface will be completely removed from the Servlet API in a future release version. Older code referencing* `HttpSessionContext` *will ultimately raise a* `ClassNotFoundException`, *unless re-coded.*

Maintaining State in an HTTP Connection

Whenever someone mentions complex stateful applications transmitted over HTTP in the presence of a data communications specialist, (s)he gets a wild look in the eyes. There is a reason for the somewhat less-than-polite emotions for raw HTTP as a carrier of business data in today's applications. However, the HTTP protocol is good at living up to its specification—over the years, it has switched directions quite drastically from its original intent.

Now, briefly examine the original goals of HTTP and then check out some common solutions used to make HTTP accommodate state.

The Goals of HTTP, Version 1.0

The HTTP communication protocol was designed as a simple means of distributing scientific information to researchers of CERN (Swiss Atomic Research Centre). Because most information in a university is public (or, at least, non-secret), there is little need for encrypting the data in transit between the Web server and the browser. Thus, the original HTTP specification had no communication protocol security.

Moreover, if your primary need is downloading and viewing public information from a Web server on campus, there is no immediate need to create complex communication protocol structures to maintain state. With today's complex applications hosted on (multiple) Web servers, the need to maintain communication state is immediate and imperative. The HTTP protocol has been revised and amended since its inception to accommodate for better state management. The mechanism for maintaining state is a rather poor one, however, and the shortcomings of the HTTP protocol define a low level of usability in industrial-strength systems.

The solution to the security aspects of HTTP is the Secure Socket Layer (SSL) protocol, developed by Netscape. SSL encrypts socket data for transmission over open networks and introduces state mechanisms.

Because of its data encryption and decryption, SSL is rather slow compared to its insecure sibling. Therefore, SSL is generally used only to transmit secure information such as credit card data. The HTTP protocol has dealt with state information in another manner.

Maintaining State in an Unencrypted HTTP Connection

The HTTP protocol usually used to communicate between the browser client and the Web server/servlet engine has no built-in means of keeping session data. HTTP is stateless and therefore requires all data to be transmitted from the client to the server with every call. One may wonder how the server can track sessions to separate different clients from each other. The answer sounds more deliciously than it is: *cookies*.

An HTTP cookie is simply a small text string, which may be stored persistently on the client machine. Each cookie knows which server(s) it should be transmitted to—thus, if a particular servlet creates and sets a cookie into the `ServletResponse`, the cookie will be re-sent back to the server with each following request.

In principle, HTTP state is maintained by sending text back and forth between the Web browser and the Web server. The text is either appended to the returned URL (*URL rewriting*) or sent for storage on the client in the form of a small file. The text file is known as a (client-side) cookie—possibly from the association to a Chinese fortune cookie, containing a text message. For further information on the `Cookie` class, refer to "The javax.servlet.http.Cookie" earlier in this chapter.

Figure 1-74 depicts the communication process between the client browser and the Web server.

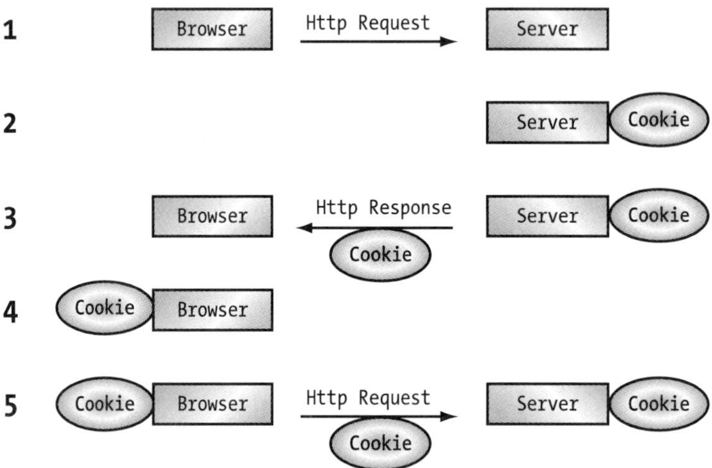

Figure 1-74. Cookie communication process between the client browser and the Web server

The five steps in the communication between the client browser and the Web server illustrated in Figure 1-76 are:

1. The browser connects to the server.
2. The server probes the incoming `HttpRequest`. If a cookie is not present, one is generated and stored in a local cookie cache.
3. The server adds a copy of the locally stored cookie to the outgoing HTTP `Response`.
4. The browser stores the cookie on its host, together with the address of the server that generated and sent it.

5. For each subsequent call to the server, the browser re-sends the cookie to the server. The server may then identify a particular user by the value of the cookie.

Many Web servers maintain a `java.util.Map` that contains the unique cookie values as keys and another `Map` file with the user's session-specific data. The structure works similar to a small relational database.

CHAPTER 2

Sharing Servlet Resources

A WEB SERVER MAY INCLUDE an application's output in its response to a calling client browser. The application and the included result are termed *server-side include* (SSI). The reasons for using SSI applications are identical to those of using a servlet in a Web server; you can use SSI when the resulting output should include dynamically generated output, such as the current time or a dynamically generated image.

If Common Gateway Interface (CGI) is an early relative of servlet technology, SSI is an earlier relative of JavaServer Pages (JSP) technology. You insert SSI directives into an otherwise plain HTML file, and the results of each SSI directive go to the client browser.

NOTE *See Chapter 4 for further information on JSP technology.*

SSI from a Scandinavian Perspective

Following the 1996 Chernobyl accident, which destroyed a Chernobyl Nuclear Power Plant reactor, the letters *SSI* made the Swedish media top 10 abbreviations with full force. SSI is the Swedish branch of the International Atomic Energy Agency (IAEA); for obvious reasons, the SSI reports were front-page news for a long time.

A few years after the Chernobyl disaster had been laid to rest in the dusty archives of news, the Web development community launched an intellectual sneak attack on the Swedish. The abbreviation SSI for server-side includes was reused to describe a design pattern for including the result of one application in the processing of another. After realizing that the abbreviation was, indeed, not the product of a joke from some governmental organization involved in radiology, the development community of Northern Europe sighed a breath of relief and started developing better Web applications.

This chapter covers the interaction between two (or more) servlets, as well as the ways that servlets share resources (such as objects or parameters) with one another. This interaction is similar to its predecessor, SSI. Before taking a closer look at the Web-related SSI, let's examine its two versions, forward and include.

What Are the Forwarding and Including Patterns?

You may use two or more servlets running in the same servlet engine to create a result that is a combination of the `service` methods of each individual servlet. This occurs when one servlet (`Servlet1`) calls the `service` method of another servlet (`Servlet2`). If execution control returns from the second servlet to the first, a dynamic pattern called *including* occurs (see Figure 2-1). If execution continues in the second servlet without returning to the first, the dynamic pattern *forwarding* occurs (see Figure 2-2). (In the figures, the thread of control is noted as a dashed box.)

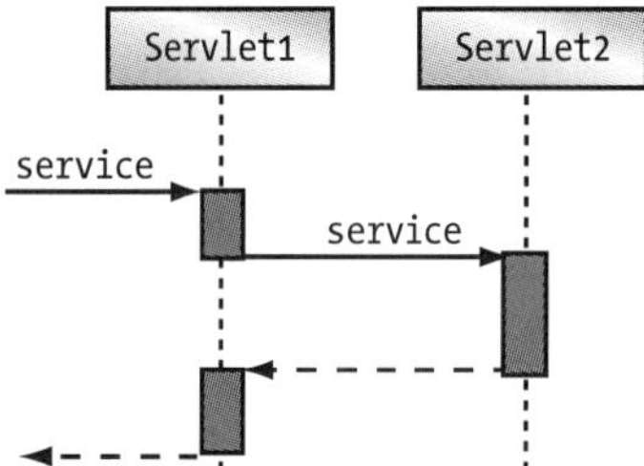

Figure 2-1. Control is returned to the `service` *method of the calling servlet in the including pattern.*

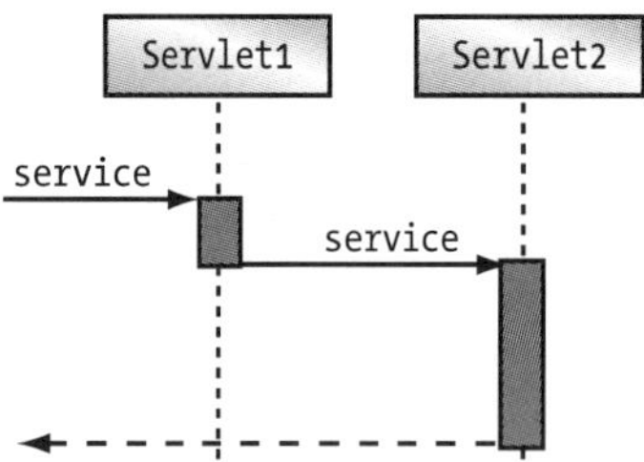

Figure 2-2. Control is not returned to the `service` *method of the calling servlet in the forwarding pattern.*

In simple terms, just as a servlet may call an arbitrary method of another object, it may call the `service` method of another servlet (`Servlet2`). If control of execution returns to the calling servlet (`Servlet1`) after executing the `service` method of `Servlet2`, the *include* pattern occurs—otherwise the *forward* pattern occurs.

Leading-Edge Patterns—in a State of Flux

As a result of the quick advancements within Web application development, the patterns for sharing resources have undergone two major changes; the first change introduced the `RequestDispatcher` architecture and the second introduced servlet filters. The Servlet API version you are using defines the preferred methods and classes involved in the including and forwarding patterns. If you have developed servlets since the 1.0 version of the API, you have likely been grinding your teeth at one or other of the changes.

The three versions of forwarding and including are as follows:

- *Direct invocation*, used by the Servlet API version 2.0 and earlier. The `ServletContext` object provides direct access to all servlet instances running within the same Web server. The programmer can manually call the `service` method of another `Servlet` instance.

- *Wrapped invocation*, used by the Servlet API version 2.1 and 2.2 where a `RequestDispatcher` instance wraps the forward or include call to the second servlet. Direct references to other servlets are banned.

- *Filtered invocation*, used by the Servlet API version 2.3 and later where proper `Filter` and `FilterChain` interfaces have been created to provide better separation between resources and any applied filter.

Take a look at the different versions of invocation forwarding and including patterns.

Direct Invocation

Up to servlet API version 2.0, the `ServletContext` instance has a reference to all servlets running within the Web server, as illustrated in Figure 2-3.

A Unified Modeling Language (UML) sequence diagram describing the call structure of the old-style forward or include is a simple matter of obtaining the reference to the target servlet and invoking the service method within it (see Figure 2-4).

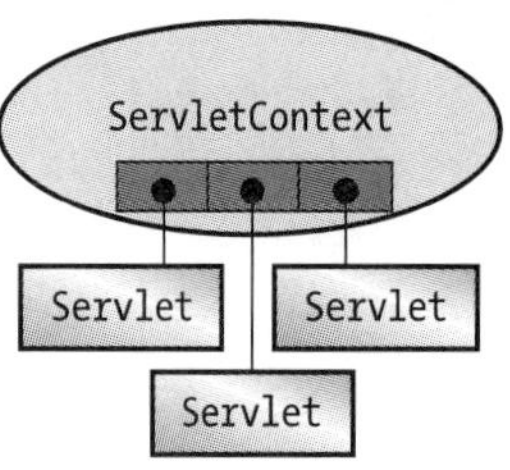

Figure 2-3. Structure of the early `ServletContext` *instance, containing references to all servlets within the running Web server. Calling methods within the* `ServletContext` *retrieves references to the enumeration and its contents.*

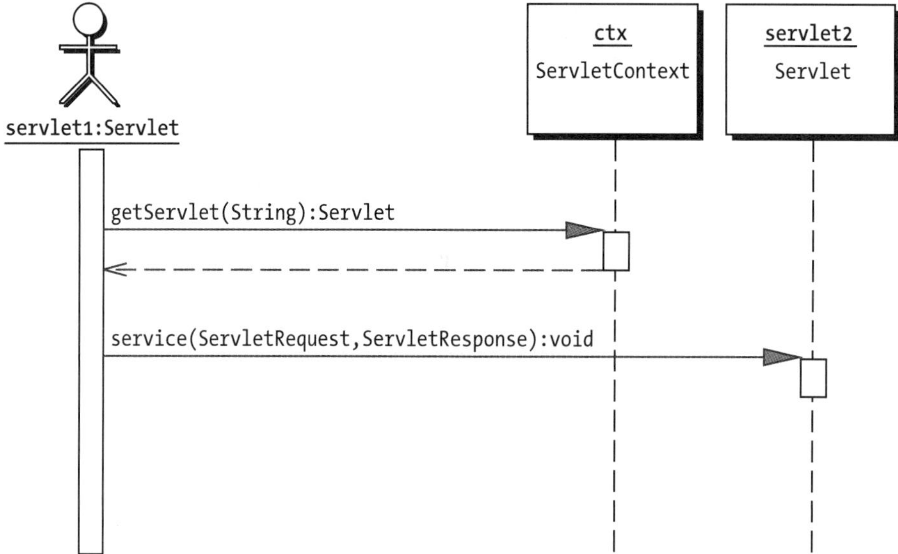

Figure 2-4. Skeleton sequence diagram for a servlet (`servlet1`*) including the* `service` *output of another servlet (*`servlet2`*). The sequence diagram shown is greatly simplified compared to the actual implementation in most Web servers.*

Table 2-1 lists three methods that control the access to the bound servlets; all of them have been deprecated in the Servlet API version 2.1 and should not be used for servlet development in later servlet API versions. If you must develop servlets using earlier Servlet APIs, they are your only chance of referencing other servlets.

Table 2-1. Pre-Servlet API 2.1 Accessor Methods

METHOD	DESCRIPTION
`Enumeration getServletNames();`	Retrieves an enumeration containing the names of each running servlet
`Servlet getServlet(String name);`	Gets a reference to the servlet bound using the name provided as an argument
`Enumeration getServlets()`	Gets an enumeration containing the direct reference to each running servlet. This method acts as a combination of the two previous methods above

Note that all of these methods are deprecated in the current version of the Servlet API and will be permanently removed in a forthcoming revision of the Servlet API. In the current Servlet API implementation, the methods are non-functional and return null or empty enumerations. The following Servlet API documentation is clear about this; the JavaDoc documentation from the standard Java 2 Enterprise Edition (J2EE) API on the method `getServletNames` serves as an example of the typical documentation for the methods in Table 2-1:

```
public java.util.Enumeration getServletNames()
Deprecated. As of Java Servlet API 2.1, with no replacement.
This method was originally defined to return an Enumeration
of all the servlet names known to this context. In this version,
this method always returns an empty Enumeration and remains
only to preserve binary compatibility. This method will be
permanently removed in a future version of the Java Servlet API.
```

You may, of course, wonder why the `getServletNames`, `getServlet`, and `getServlet(String name)` methods are deprecated. The answer is that they permit too much and may cause system instability. Observe an example of this in the skeleton code shown in Listing 2-1, which contains two servlets, `ExchangeServlet` and `EvilServlet`. The `ExchangeServlet` simply keeps an exchange rate as a static variable, and the `EvilServlet` modifies that variable using the same methods provided to permit direct invocation.

Listing 2-1. The relevant code of the `ExchangeServlet`

```
public class ExchangeServlet extends HttpServlet
{
    // The exchange rates known by this exchange servlet
    public Map myExchangeRates;

    // Setter method for the myExchangeRates variable
    public void setExchangeRates(Map rates)
    {
        if(rates == null) return;
        this.myExchangeRates = rates;
    }

    public void service(ServletRequest req, ServletResponse res)
    {
        ...
        // Get the currency exchange rate
        Integer currentRate = myExchangeRate.get(req.getParameter("currency");
        int returnedValue = originalValue * currentRate.intValue();
        ...
    }
}
```

The `EvilServlet`, on the other hand, uses the `getServlet` method to return an instance of the `ExchangeServlet` and sneakily modify its `myExchangeRates` variable. Remember that only the reference is copied, not the object to which it is pointing. After running the `EvilServlet`, the `ExchangeServlet` will most likely stop working, and the following faulty conditions will arise:

- `EvilServlet` cannot be properly garbage-collected until the `ExchangeServlet` is garbage-collected. The reason is that the `myExchangeRates` variable in the `ExchangeServlet` refers to the same object as the decoy variable in `EvilServlet`.

- `ExchangeServlet` may stop working or produce unpredictable or erroneous results because its exchange rates are replaced.

Finally, take a look at the relevant pieces of code in the `EvilServlet` shown in Listing 2-2.

Listing 2-2. The `EvilServlet` *code*

```
public class EvilServlet extends HttpServlet
{
    // Decoy Map, to be given to an ExchangeServlet instance
    Map decoy;

    public void service(ServletRequest req, ServletResponse res)
    {
        // Is the decoy Map created?
        If(decoy == null) this.createDecoy();

        // Get the Servlet I am interested in...
        for(Enumeration en = getServletContext().getServlets(); en.hasMoreElements();)
         {
              // Check that we got a servlet of the correct type
              Servlet current = (Servlet) en.nextElement();

              // Did we get an ExchangeServlet?
              if( !(current instanceof ExchangeServlet)) continue;

              // Got an ExchangeServlet. Modify its exchangeRate...
              ExchangeServlet exc = (ExchangeServlet) current;
              exc.setExchangeRates(this.decoy);
         }
    }

    public void createDecoy()
    {
         // Create and assign a spoof Map to the decoy variable
         Map m = new HashMap();
         m.put("SEK", new Integer(25));
         m.put("GBP", new Integer(1));
         m.put("USD", new Integer(30));

         // Assign
         this.decoy = m;
    }
}
```

As you can see, the `getServlets` method permits too much to a cunning developer. The method suite has therefore been deprecated; it is currently only preserved for binary compatibility with older Servlet API releases.

Wrapped Invocation

The servlet API versions 2.1 and 2.2 contained an augmented call pattern to connect servlets using the forwarding and including patterns. Direct references to running servlets from other running servlets are undesirable and potentially damaging to system stability. Furthermore, the following is true:

- Internal state variables in one servlet may be directly affected by another, which may put the system into a forbidden state. Imagine, for instance, the effect of setting an internal state variable to null or replacing one database connection with another.
- Call-level security on servlets cannot be upheld properly by the Web server unless it can control all incoming calls to the servlet in question.
- The Web server may lose the ability to properly garbage-collect resources held by a servlet containing a reference to another object.

For these and other reasons, the methods referencing running servlet instances from the `ServletContext` are deprecated and should not be used when developing servlets complying with API versions greater than 2.0. Instead, servlets created with the Servlet API 2.1 or later uses a `RequestDispatcher` instance (shown in Figure 2-5) to delegate execution to another servlet.

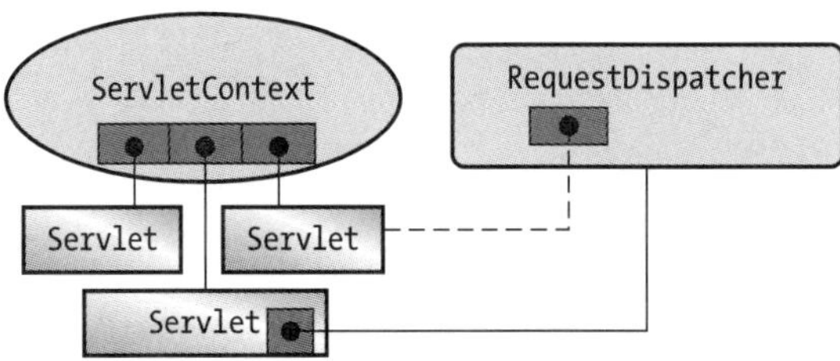

Figure 2-5. The structure of the `ServletContext` *instance contains references to all servlets within the running Web server. A servlet may call the* `getRequestDispatcher` *method of the* `ServletContext` *to retrieve a wrapper (the* `RequestDispatcher`*), which in turn calls the* `service` *method of another servlet.*

Each `RequestDispatcher` wraps precisely one servlet reference; one `getRequestDispatcher` reference is required for each servlet output that should be included in the final response. In some implementations, such as the Tomcat servlet engine implementation, the servlet whose output is included (`servlet2`) is instantiated within the call.

Figure 2-6, which describes the call structure of the `RequestDispatcher` forward or include, is a simple matter of asking the `ServletContext` for a reference to it and invoking the forward or include method within it.

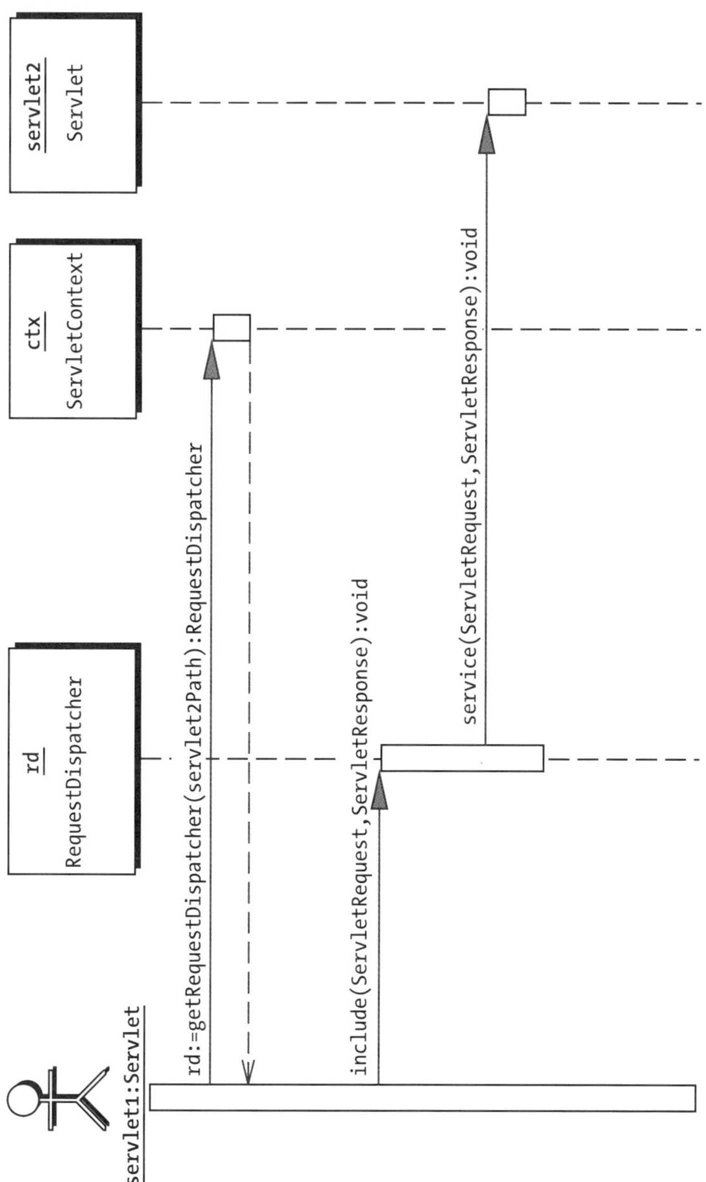

Figure 2-6. This skeleton sequence diagram for a servlet (`servlet1`) includes the service output of another servlet (`servlet2`). Note that this sequence diagram is greatly simplified compared to the actual methods called in any real-world servlet engine.

One of the advantages of wrapped invocation compared to direct invocation is that the `RequestDispatcher` may create or clean up resources as required. For example, the Tomcat reference engine creates a new instance of `servlet2` before invoking the `service` method, as shown in Figure 2-7.

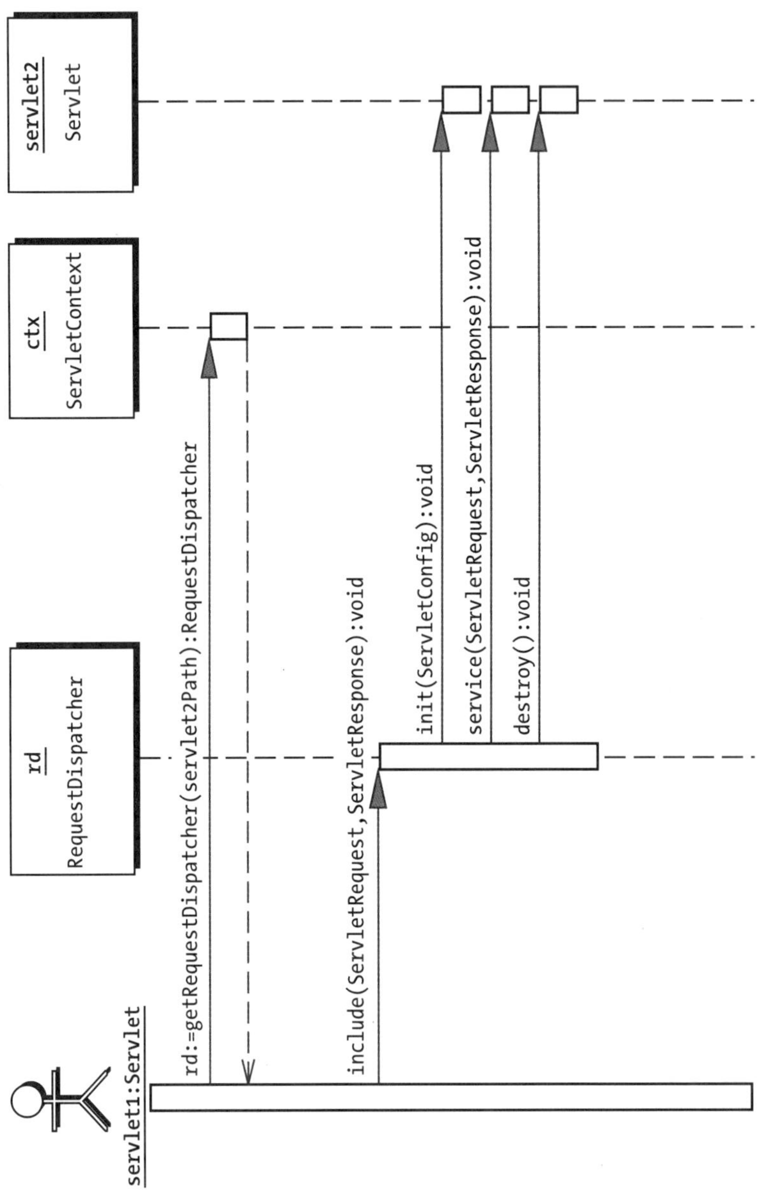

Figure 2-7. Skeleton sequence diagram of the Tomcat reference engine. The `RequestDispatcher` *instance creates a new* `servlet2` *object and invokes its three life-cycle methods. Note that this figure shows a greatly simplified version of the detailed sequence diagram in the Tomcat servlet engine.*

Table 2-2 lists the two methods of the `RequestDispatcher` interface that control the access to the bound servlets; the forward method starts the forwarding pattern, and the include method starts the including pattern.

Table 2-2. Methods of the `RequestDispatcher` *Interface*

METHOD	DESCRIPTION
`void forward(ServletRequest req, ServletResponse res);`	Forwards a request from a servlet to another resource (servlet, JSP file, or HTML file) on the server
`void include (ServletRequest req, ServletResponse res);`	Includes the content of a resource (servlet, JSP page, HTML file) in the response

Filtered Invocation

In many cases, the forwarding and including patterns are used to filter an incoming call to a servlet. Starting with servlet API version 2.3, filtering has become a standard feature of the Servlet APIs. A *servlet filter* is an object that modifies the incoming `ServletRequest` and/or the outgoing `ServletResponse`.

For example, you may use filters to add authentication control or to calculate message digests for proper verification of message integrity. Filtered invocation using `javax.servlet.Filter` and `javax.servlet.FilterChain` interfaces have these advantages over the `RequestDispatcher` approach:

- `Filter/FilterChain` is a standard servlet API interface, so all Web servers may use a filter class without having to care about implementation-specific details. Such specific details may arise as the result of poor implementation (with respect to platform independence) of the *RequestDispatcher* filter.

- `Filter/FilterChains` are associated with their targets (the JSP, HTML, servlet, or other resource to which the filter should be applied) using a standardized XML syntax. In fact, the association between filters and targets is part of the `web.xml` configuration document, standard to the J2EE platform. `RequestDispatchers` may need recompilation or modification of custom property files to filter new resources. Recompiling a filter requires access to the source code—which is not an option for purchased components.

Alas, the preferred way of filtering resources in the Servlet API version 2.3 and greater is to use `Filters` and `FilterChains`. The principal mode of operations is fairly simple; whenever a resource (such as a JSP or HTML document, servlet, and so on) is requested by a client browser, the `web.xml` configuration file is consulted to see if the document has any filters configured (see Figure 2-8).

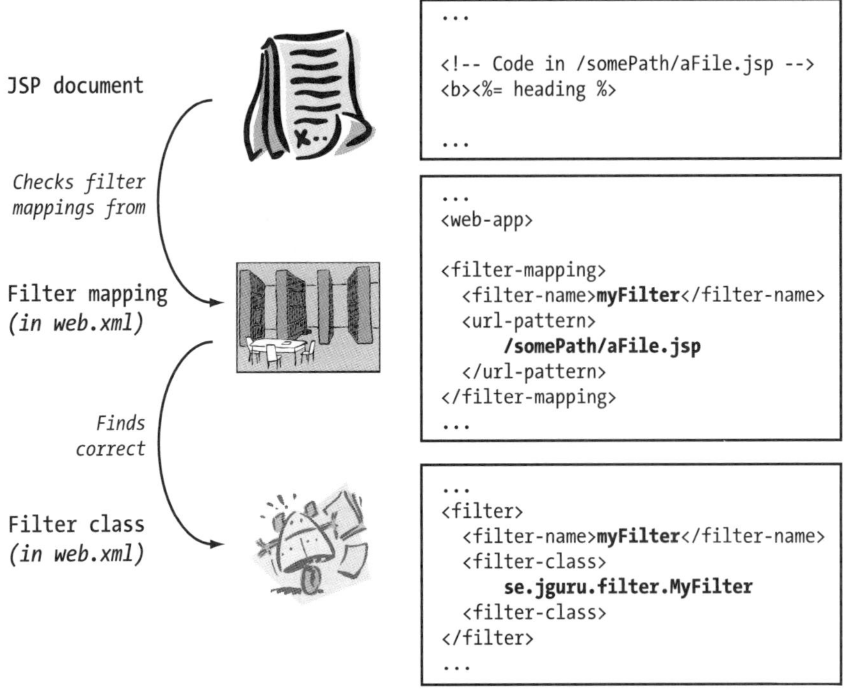

Figure 2-8. Relations and evaluation order of servlet filters. The URL of a Web resource (such as a JSP document) relates to a filter class in two lookup steps. First, the `url-pattern` *of the resource is used to find a* `filter-mapping`*. The name of the* `filter-mapping` *is later cross-referenced against the* `filter-name` *property of all filter entries. For each such filter where a match is found, the* `filter-class` *is selected for filtering.*

If a URL pattern matching the requested document has an existing filter mapping set up, the `doFilter` method of the filter class is invoked. The output of the filter is added to the result of the requested resource. The selection and registration process for servlet `Filter` instances is performed by the servlet engine in three steps, as indicated in Figure 2-8:

1. The requested URL resource is matched against all registered filter-mapping entries. Such entries are set up in the `web.xml` configuration file, and each entry maps a specific URL pattern to a logical filter name. Figure 2-8 contains a template for filter-mapping entries.

2. The filter-name entry is matched against the content of the `filter-name` tag within a filter entry in the `web.xml` file.

3. If a match is found, the `doFilter` method of the provided `filter-class` (which must implement `javax.servlet.Filter`) is invoked. This is the actual filtered invocation step.

How could an activity diagram describing runtime behavior for servlet filters look? The answer is much more complex than one might imagine because servlet filters are registered during Web application initialization and executed normally during runtime invocation. Note that the setup of the `Filter` class is implementation dependent. Most servlet engines or application servers have custom—and, in the experience of this author, rather dissimilar—internal implementations of filter handling.

Figure 2-9 shows a simplified generic activity diagram for filtering.

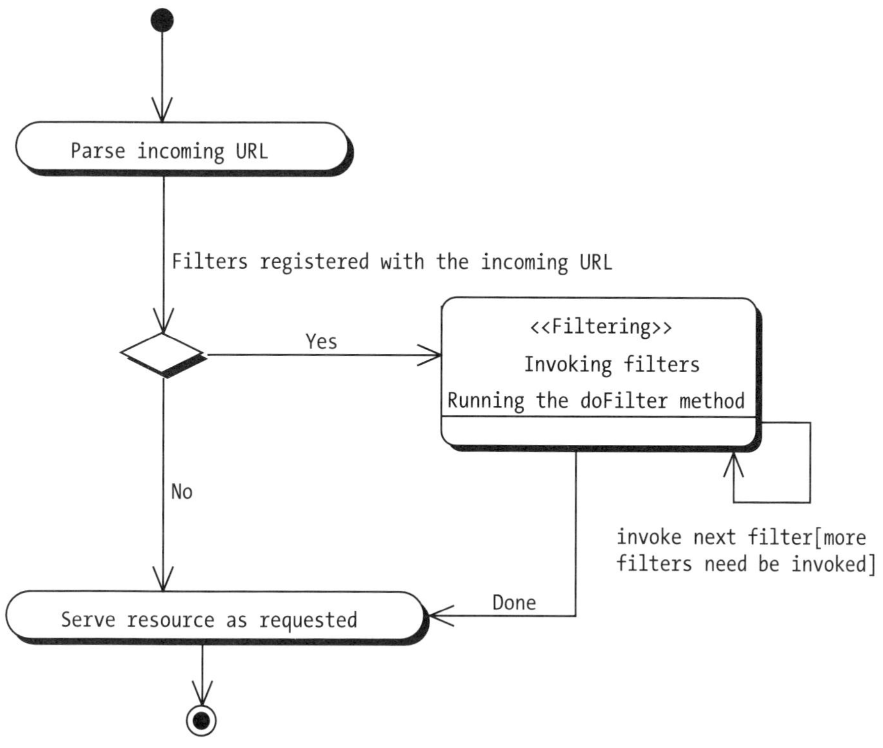

Figure 2-9. Simplified activity diagram of a filtered invocation. Registered filter classes are called whenever a URL matches a pattern provided in the `web.xml` *configuration file.*

Figure 2-9 describes the tasks performed by the servlet engine at startup, when registering all filters with their corresponding resources.

A Simplified View of Tomcat

UML diagrams describing the call structure of the filtered invocation may prove rather delicate to draw because most servlet engines have a great deal of freedom of implementation. Therefore, Figure 2-10 is considerably simplified.

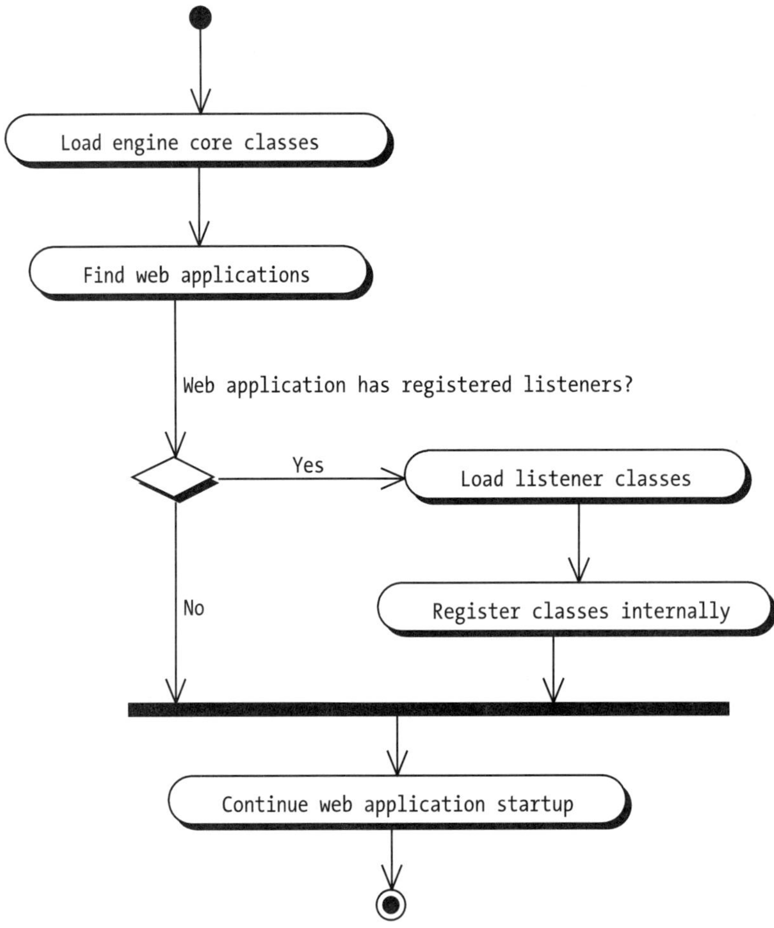

Figure 2-10. Principal activities when loading registered filter classes for a Web application

Figure 2-11 shows a much-simplified version of the filter configuration and setup process of the Tomcat 4.0 reference implementation. It shows only a portion of the classes used to create filters in Tomcat. Note that the Catalina servlet engine of the Tomcat server uses `Valve` instances to perform the actual filtering. The `FilterDef` class is the bridge between the standard `javax.servlet.Filter` instance created by the J2EE developer and the `org.apache.catalina.Valve` instance used internally by Tomcat.

The `FilterDef` instance in Figure 2-11 reads its JavaBean values—such as `filterClass`, `filterName`, `description`, and `displayName`–from the `web.xml` file as illustrated. Using the Java Reflection API, the `StandardWrapperValve` class invokes the `Filter` implementation class through its `FilterDef` instance.

Tomcat's operates on an XML formatted tree of strings, corresponding to the tree structure contained in the XML Document Type Definition (DTD) file describing the Web application. After reading the `web.xml` file to create and invoke the various `Filter` implementation classes, you should find the actual invocation of each request call pretty simple; the `doFilter` method is simply invoked for each active `Filter` instance.

Servlet Filter Examples

Filters are simple to master once you properly understand their usage and composition. In this section you'll create the following examples to illustrate servlet 2.3 API filters in action:

- `PerformanceMeter`
- `GreetingsFilter`
- `MessageDigest`

The first example is a trivial form of filter, aimed at developing and deploying a filter quickly.

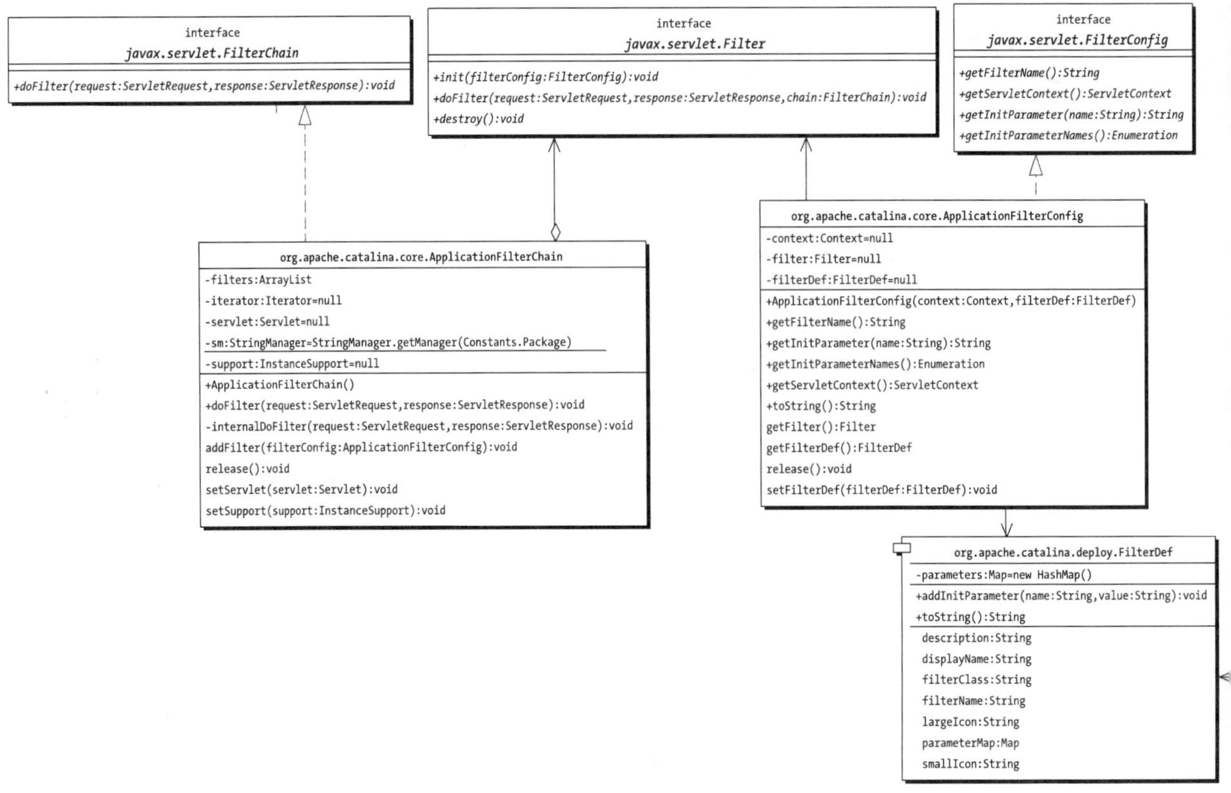

Figure 2-11. Portions of the Tomcat 4.0 (Catalina) implementation structure for `Filter` *classes. No Tomcat class implements the* `Filter` *interface directly, but the* `FilterDef` *class has a* `filterClass` *JavaBean property containing the class name of your* `Filter` *implementation.*

The PerfomanceMeter Filter

You may, at times, be interested in measuring the server roundtrip time for a specific Web application or dynamic document. Normally, "server roundtrip" is measured as the time between the entry and the exit of a particular call to a dynamic Web resource such as a JSP document communicating with a database, not counting any network latency time.

You could, of course, hard-code the measurement into a particular servlet or JSP document to measure the time elapsed for the backend calls only. However, this type of hard-coded measurement must be coded, compiled, and deployed for each call to the back-end. A better way to measure total server roundtrip is to use a filter, applied to the JSP document or servlet in question. The `PerformanceMeter` filter is a trivial form of such roundtrip measurement instrument.

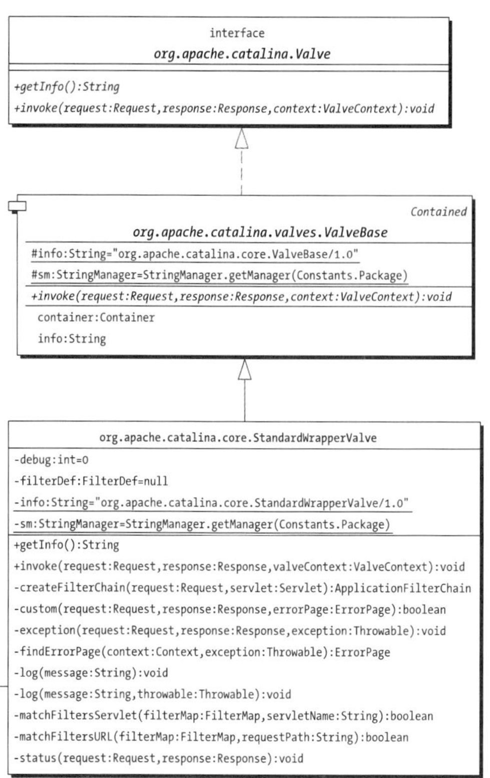

Figure 2-12 shows the output of the roundtrip measurement JSP document. Although relevant for the following example, the output generated by the filter (caught in the `System.out` output stream of the Tomcat 4.0 server) is more interesting. The filter output, when called a couple of times simply prints the server roundtrip over the JSP document called. Note that the first—longer—roundtrip over the JSP document is because of the extra time required to compile the JSP document to a servlet that is then run.

```
[PerformanceMeterFilter::doFilter]: Time for invocation: 320
[PerformanceMeterFilter::doFilter]: Time for invocation: 110
[PerformanceMeterFilter::doFilter]: Time for invocation: 120
[PerformanceMeterFilter::doFilter]: Time for invocation: 120
[PerformanceMeterFilter::doFilter]: Time for invocation: 130
[PerformanceMeterFilter::doFilter]: Time for invocation: 131
```

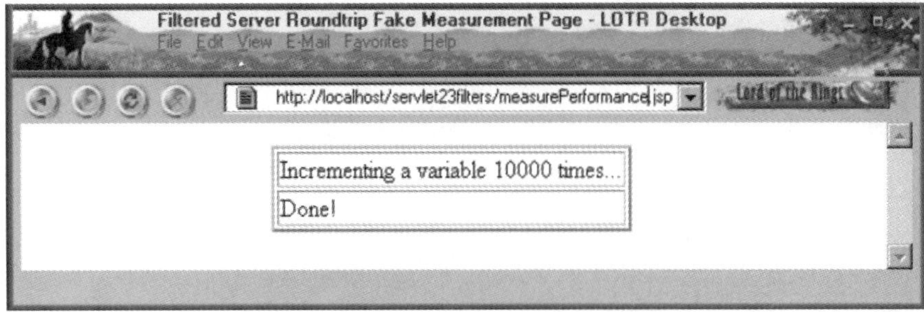

Figure 2-12. Output from the `measurePerformance.jsp` *document, which increments a variable 10,000 times to simulate the wait of a (really quick) backend system*

AbstractFilter

One utility class is required for these servlet `Filter` examples; the purpose of the `AbstractFilter` class is to prevent implementation classes from handling the `filterConfig` and the life-cycle methods—the filter implementation classes in these examples should focus on business-logic implementation only. Figure 2-13 shows the relationship between the `AbstractFilter` class and its `Filter` interface.

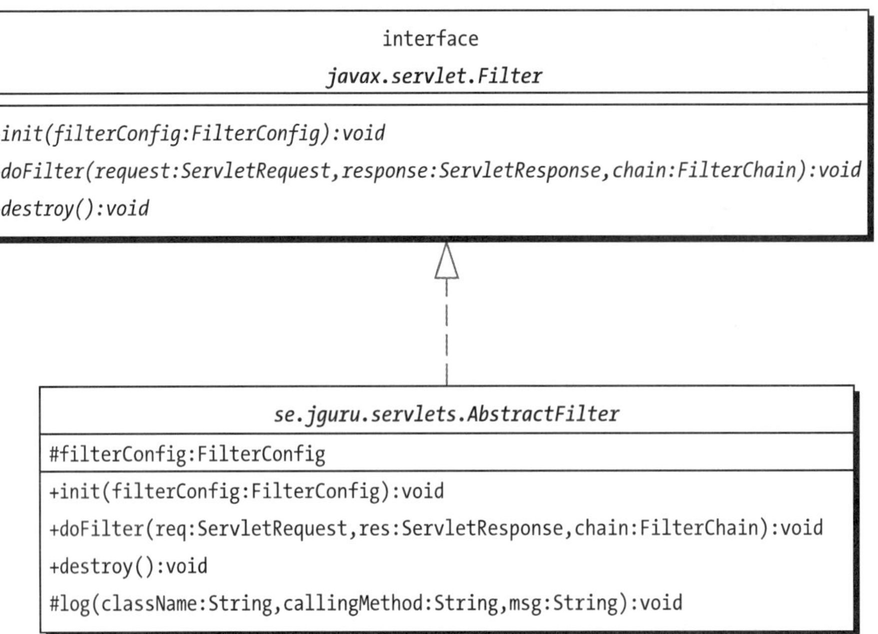

Figure 2-13. The helper class `AbstractFilter` *provides skeleton methods that implement the life-cycle methods of the* `javax.servlet.Filter` *class and a simple log method called* `log`*, which prints formatted messages to the* `System.out` *stream. Instead of implementing the* `Filter` *interface, one may therefore simply extend the* `AbstractFilter` *class.*

The only relevant code in the `AbstractFilter` class are the `init` and `log` methods. The `init` method handles the `filterConfig` to print all filter initialization parameters from the `web.xml` deployment descriptor on the `System.out` if a filter `init` parameter with the name `verbose` exists. The `log` method provides a structured printout to the `System.out` stream. The `init` and `log` methods are shown in this code sample:

```
    protected FilterConfig filterConfig;

    /**
     * Prints the contents of the FilterConfig instance
     * if the configuration parameter "verbose" is non-null.
     */
    public void init(FilterConfig filterConfig)
    {
        // Get and assign the filterConfig
        this.filtercConfig = filterConfig;

        // Check verbose mode
        if(filterConfig.getInitParameter("verbose") != null)
        {
            // Log verbosity
            this.log("AbstractFilter", "init",
                        "--> Start Verbose FilterConfig log");

            for(Enumeration en = filterConfig.getInitParameterNames();
                        en.hasMoreElements();)
            {
                String paramName = "" + en.nextElement();
                this.log("AbstractFilter", "init", "(" + paramName + "): "
                    + filterConfig.getInitParameter(paramName) );
            }

            this.log("AbstractFilter", "init",
                        "<-- End Verbose FilterConfig log");
        }
    }
…
    /**
     * Trivial log method which prints messages on the System.out
     * stream.
     */
    protected void log(String className, String callingMethod, String msg)
    {
        System.out.println("[" + className + "::" + callingMethod + "]: "
                + msg);
```

PerformanceMeasureFilter

Moving on to the actual business logic of this example, only one filter class is required, `PerformanceMeasureFilter`. It extends the `AbstractFilter` class and overloads its `doFilter` method to provide the time measurement. Figure 2-14 shows the inheritance relationship between the involved types.

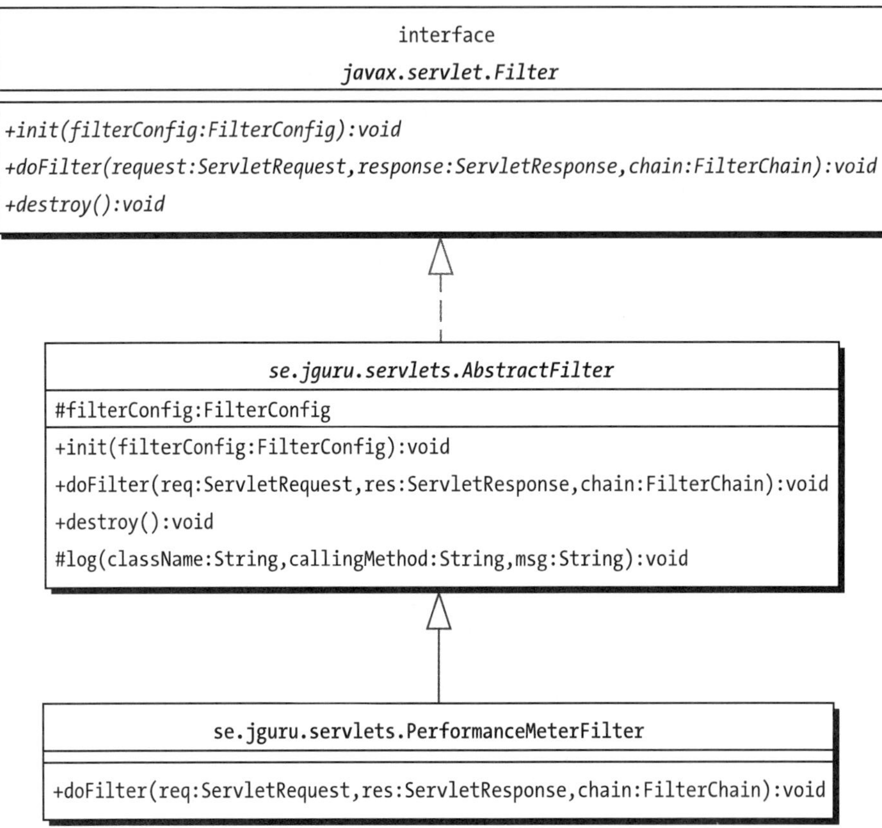

Figure 2-14. The `PerformanceMeterFilter` *extends the* `AbstractFilter` *class and provides a real implementation in its* `doFilter` *method. The filter measures the difference between a timestamp generated before calling the* `measurePerformance.jsp` *document and a timestamp generated after the return from* `measurePerformance.jsp`.

The code to create the `PerformanceMeterFilter` (see Listing 2-3) is really simple. Note the call to `chain.doFilter`, which has similar effect as the `RequestDispatcher.include` method—it may bind or modify attributes in the `HttpServletRequest` before the execution is relayed to the service method of the servlet called.

Listing 2-3. The `PerformanceMeter` *filter class*

```
/*
 * Copyright (c) 2000,2001 jGuru Europe.
 * All rights reserved.
 */

package se.jguru.servlets;

import java.util.*;
import java.io.*;
import javax.servlet.*;

/**
 * The PerformanceMeterFilter class implements a trivial
 * filtering function that measures the server roundtrip
 * time of its servlet.
 *
 * @author Lennart Jörelid, jGuru Europe AB
 */
public class PerformanceMeterFilter extends AbstractFilter
{
    /**
     * Implementation of the doFilter method in the Filter interface.
     */
    public void doFilter(final ServletRequest req, final ServletResponse res,
    FilterChain chain)
    throws IOException, ServletException
    {
        // Get the timestamp before invoking the servlet resource
        long before = System.currentTimeMillis();

        // Invoke the call to the FilterChain.
        // This includes the resource mapped to this filter in the
        // web.xml configuration file, roughly like the call to
        // rd.include(req, res), where rd is a RequestDispatcher.
        chain.doFilter(req, res);

        // Get the timestamp after invoking the servlet resource
        long after = System.currentTimeMillis();

        // Calculate and log the difference between the two timestamps.
```

```
        this.log("PerformanceMeterFilter", "doFilter",
            "Time for invocation: " + (after - before));
    }
}
```

The code in the PerformanceMeterFilter doFilter method is the simplest possible for a runtime measurement. The full measurement consists of the difference between the timestamp captured before and the timestamp generated after invoking the doFilterChain method.

measurePerformance.jsp and web.xml

Two more documents are required to make the small filter system work: the resource that the filter should be applied to (in other words, the measurePerformance.jsp document) and the web.xml configuration document for the Web container. The web.xml document presents the only slightly tricky part because it must be created according to the Web application version 2.3 DTD to be able to properly configure the servlet filter. Listing 2-4 shows the web.xml document.

Listing 2-4. The web.xml *deployment descriptor*

```
<?xml version="1.0"?>
<!DOCTYPE web-app PUBLIC
        "-//Sun Microsystems, Inc.//DTD Web Application 2.3//EN"
        "http://java.sun.com/j2ee/dtds/web-app_2_3.dtd">

<web-app>
   <filter>
      <filter-name>PerformanceMeterFilter</filter-name>
      <filter-class>se.jguru.servlets.PerformanceMeterFilter</filter-class>
   </filter>

   <filter-mapping>
      <filter-name>PerformanceMeterFilter</filter-name>
      <url-pattern>/measurePerformance.jsp</url-pattern>
   </filter-mapping>
</web-app>
```

As you can see in the web.xml document, the filter class se.jguru.servlets.PerformanceMeasureFilter is first mapped to the internal name PerformanceMeterFilter. In the <filter-mapping>...</filter-mapping> container, the PerformanceMeterFilter is applied to all URL patterns matching /measurePerformance.jsp. This document is invoked to yield the output shown in

Figure 2-15 and the corresponding response time output on the `System.out` output stream of the Tomcat server.

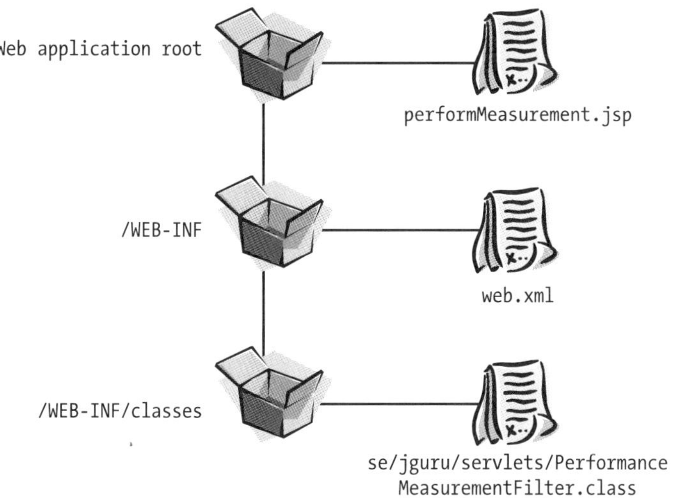

Figure 2-15. Deployment structure for the `PerformanceMeasurementFilter` *bytecode file and the filtered resource, the* `performMeasurement.jsp` *document*

You may wonder where all files in the example should be deployed. This is one of the more relevant questions for J2EE development; I have encountered more confused J2EE developers stuck with problems concerning deployment of a compiled J2EE component into the server than the actual development of one. As shown in Figure 2-15, the files must be placed in specific places.

Having managed the `PerformanceMeasurementFilter` example, you should again study the `doFilter` method of the filter implementation class. Note that the `ServletRequest` and `ServletResponse` objects are passed as arguments to the `doFilter` method—but you never used the arguments in any way. The next example shows how the filter class may modify settings for its resource by setting parameters in the `ServletRequest`.

The GreetingsFilter Example

All other things being identical to the `PerformanceMeasurementFilter` example in the previous section, you will now use the filter to set attributes in the `ServletRequest` of a JSP document named `showAttributes.jsp`. Simply create another filter that extends the `AbstractFilter` class, and re-implement its `doFilter` method to set two attributes in the `ServletRequest`. Of course, you still need to add a new configuration entry to the `web.xml` file and create a new managed resource called `showAttributes.jsp`.

The result of this five-minute hack is seen in Figure 2-16, which shows the values of the two attributes present in the `ServletRequest`.

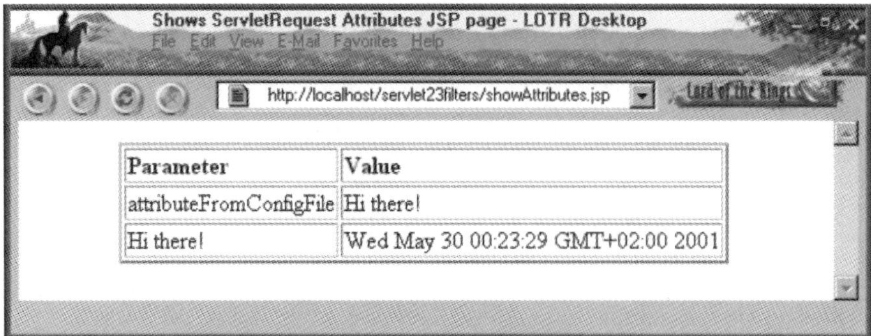

Figure 2-16. Resulting output of the `showAttributes.jsp` *document where both attributes originate from the* `GreetingsFilter`*. The* `attributeFromConfigFile` *is read from the filter configuration in the* `web.xml` *file, whereas the* `attributeFromFilter` *date is generated dynamically within the* `GreetingsFilter` *class.*

The code of the `GreetingsFilter` class, shown in Listing 2-5, is limited to the `init` and `doFilter` methods. The `greeting` parameter bound in the `FilterConfig` instance is read in the `init` method and assigned to the private variable `greeting`. The methods in the `FilterConfig` interface are similar to the ones found in the `ServletConfig` interface, and they are used in identical manners.

Listing 2-5. The `GreetingsFilter` *code*

```
/*
 * Copyright (c) 2000,2001 jGuru Europe.
 * All rights reserved.
 */

package se.jguru.servlets;

import javax.servlet.*;
import java.util.*;
import java.io.*;

/**
 * Filter which adds attributes to
 * the ServletRequest of its managed resource.
 * The filter reads a value from its filterconfig
 * parameter (which, in turn, parses the web.xml configuration
 * file to obtain its values).
 *
```

```
 * @author Lennart Jörelid, jGuru Europe AB
 */
public class GreetingsFilter extends AbstractFilter
{
    // Storage for the Greeting string.
    private String greeting;

    /**
     * Read the init parameters from the web.xml
     * deployment descriptor
     */
    public void init(FilterConfig conf)
    {
        // Call init in AbstractFilter
        super.init(conf);

        // Perform own initialization
        this.greeting = conf.getInitParameter("greeting");
        if(this.greeting == null) this.greeting = "Hello!";
    }

    public void doFilter(final ServletRequest req,
        final ServletResponse res, FilterChain chain)
    throws IOException, ServletException
    {
        // Get the values from the FilterConfig
        Date now = new Date();

        // Bind the values to the ServletRequest
        req.setAttribute("attributeFromConfigFile", this.greeting);
        req.setAttribute(this.greeting, now);

        // Invoke the call to the FilterChain
        chain.doFilter(req, res);
    }
}
```

Note that the call to `getFilterConfig().getInitParameter("greeting")` in the `init` method retrieves the value of the initialization parameter "`greeting`" from the `web.xml` file. Therefore, servlet filters may be configured using initialization parameters similar to those of normal servlets. You must provide a `web.xml` configuration file where the "`greeting`" parameter is set for the given filter—and you may simply add the text to the configuration file used in the previous example to add the new filter to the existing Web application. Listing 2-6 displays the relevant parts of the `web.xml` file.

Listing 2-6. The filter definition in the `web.xml` *configuration file*

```
<filter>
   <filter-name>GreetFilter</filter-name>
   <filter-class>se.jguru.servlets.GreetingsFilter</filter-class>
   <init-param>
      <param-name>greeting</param-name>
      <param-value>Hi there!</param-value>
   </init-param>
</filter>
<filter-mapping>
   <filter-name>GreetFilter</filter-name>
   <url-pattern>/showAttributes.jsp</url-pattern>
</filter-mapping>
```

Note that all initialization parameters are provided in the filter definition (as opposed to the filter-mapping definition), which means that a new filter definition may be created for the `se.jguru.servlets.GreetingsFilter` with another set of initialization parameters. In fact, if you choose to add another filter to the filter chain of your resource, the `doFilter` method of both filters would be called before including the JSP document.

Now modify the `web.xml` file again to include a second filter in the `FilterChain` for the `showAttributes.jsp` document. Also, include the parameter `verbose` in the two filter definitions to instruct the `init` method in the `AbstractFilter` superclass to print the `FilterConfig` instance to the `System.out`. Listing 2-7 and Figure 2-17 show the resulting `web.xml` and browser output, respectively.

Listing 2-7. The filter definitions of the modified `web.xml` *file*

```
<filter>
   <filter-name>GreetFilter</filter-name>
   <filter-class>se.jguru.servlets.GreetingsFilter</filter-class>
      <init-param>
         <param-name>greeting</param-name>
         <param-value>Hi there!</param-value>
   </init-param>
      <init-param>
         <param-name>verbose</param-name>
         <param-value>yes</param-value>
   </init-param>
</filter>
```

```
<filter>
   <filter-name>GF2</filter-name>
   <filter-class>se.jguru.servlets.GreetingsFilter</filter-class>
   <init-param>
      <param-name>greeting</param-name>
      <param-value>Hi again!</param-value>
   </init-param>
      <init-param>
         <param-name>verbose</param-name>
         <param-value>Yup!</param-value>
   </init-param>
</filter>

<filter-mapping>
   <filter-name>GreetFilter</filter-name>
   <url-pattern>/showAttributes.jsp</url-pattern>
</filter-mapping>
<filter-mapping>
   <filter-name>GF2</filter-name>
   <url-pattern>/showAttributes.jsp</url-pattern>
</filter-mapping>
```

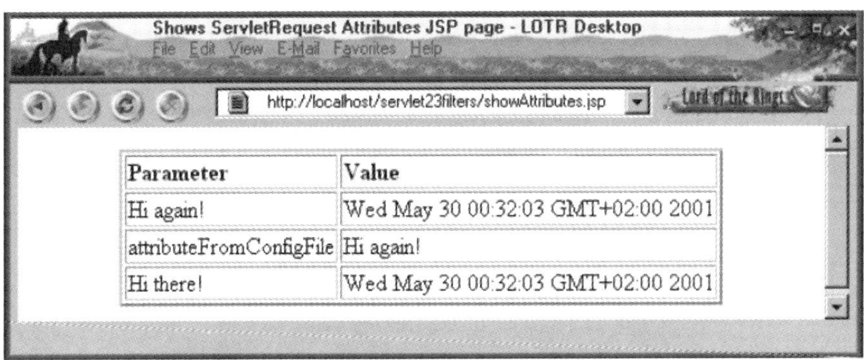

Parameter	Value
Hi again!	Wed May 30 00:32:03 GMT+02:00 2001
attributeFromConfigFile	Hi again!
Hi there!	Wed May 30 00:32:03 GMT+02:00 2001

Figure 2-17. The results of two different filters may be applied to the same document. Can you determine the order in which the filters were applied?

The `web.xml` file now defines two different filter instances; although the `GreetFilter` and the `GF2` both map to the `se.jguru.servlets.GreetingsFilter` class, the initialization parameters have different values in the two mappings. As you can see, the two filter mappings apply the two filters to the same resource, `showAttributes.jsp`. The resulting browser output, shown in Figure 2-17, proves that both filters have been applied before including the output of the `showAttributes.jsp` document.

The console output of the Tomcat server running the JSP document and the filters reveal the contents of the `FilterConfig` objects for each active filter:

```
[AbstractFilter::init]: --> Start Verbose FilterConfig log
[AbstractFilter::init]: (verbose): yes
[AbstractFilter::init]: (greeting): Hi there!
[AbstractFilter::init]: <-- End Verbose FilterConfig log
[AbstractFilter::init]: --> Start Verbose FilterConfig log
[AbstractFilter::init]: (verbose): Yup!
[AbstractFilter::init]: (greeting): Hi again!
[AbstractFilter::init]: <-- End Verbose FilterConfig log
```

Finally, you need to see the code of the `showAttributes.jsp` document. The trivial JSP document simply displays all `ServletRequest` attributes in the body of the JSP document, shown in Listing 2-8.

Listing 2-8. The `showAttributes.jsp` *document*

```
<%@ page import="java.io.*, java.util.*" %>
<html>
<head>
     <title>Shows ServletRequest Attributes JSP page</title>
</head>
  <body>
     <center>
     <table border=2>

     <tr>
          <td><b>Parameter</b></td>
          <td><b>Value</b></td>
     </tr>
     <%
          // Get the known parameters
          for(Enumeration en = request.getAttributeNames();
                         en.hasMoreElements();)
          {
               String name = "" + en.nextElement();
               String value = "" + request.getAttribute(name);
     %>
```

```
    <tr>
        <td><%= name %></td>
        <td><%= value %></td>
    </tr>
    <% } %>
    </table>
  </body>
</html>
```

The `GreetingsFilter` example shows that the servlet filters may be chained; all filters ("links in the chain") have their `doFilter` methods called in order before the result of the filtered resource is included. Now it's time to move on to a slightly more complex filter example.

The MessageDigest Filter

In this section, you'll create an example of an almost usable filter, where a digital signature (message digest) of a particular message is created and appended to a Web page. Variants of this technique are used to ensure the integrity of a message so that a receiver of a message (such as a Web page or email) may verify that the message has not been altered.

First, take a look at Figure 2-18, which shows the result of calling the `message.jsp` document.

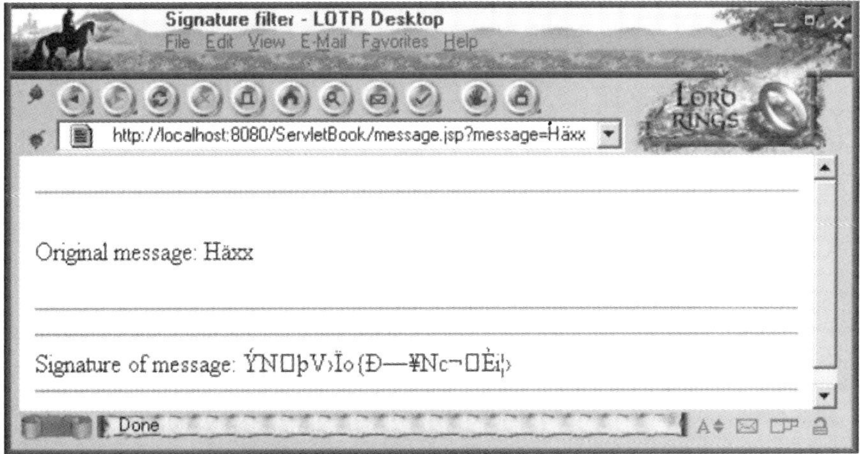

Figure 2-18. Running result of the filter acting on a JSP document. The output from the original JSP document is at the top. The result of the filter (the digital signature of the original message) is at the bottom.

The `SignatureFilter` class shown in Figure 2-19 contains the implementation performing the actual signing of data using the `java.security.MessageDigest` class. The purpose of the `SignatureFilter` is thus to create a digital signature from the message sent to its servlet and to append that signature to the actual message.

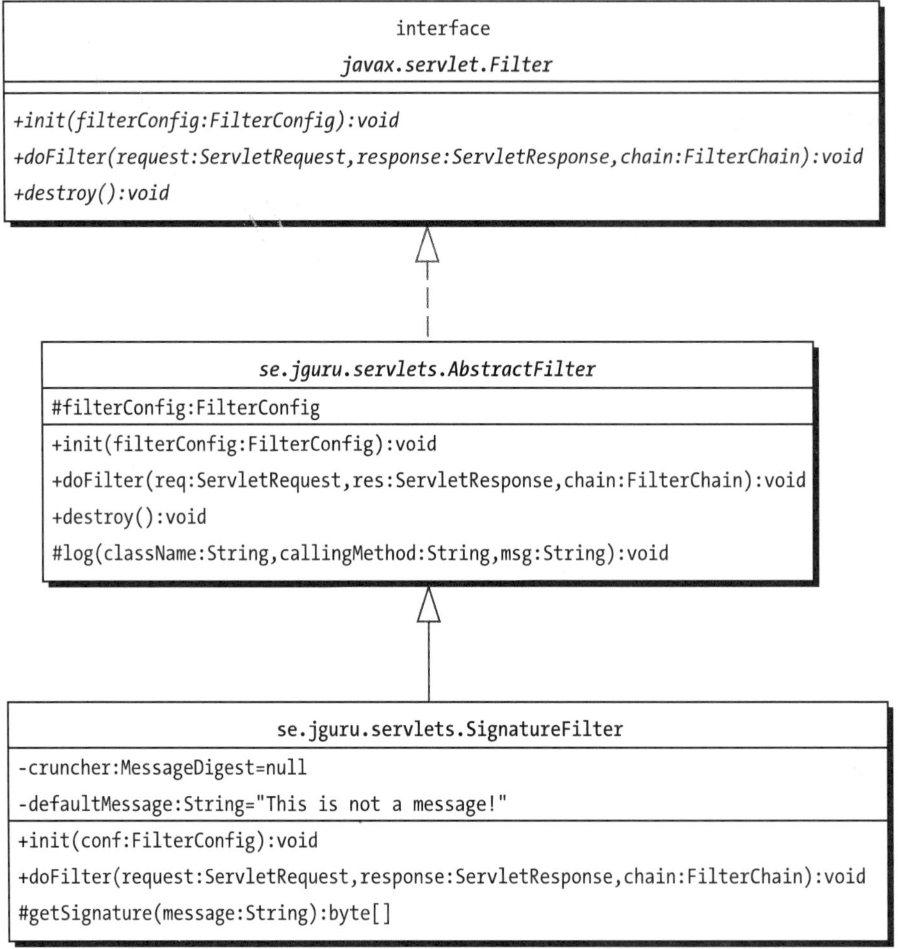

Figure 2-19. This image shows all types involved in the current example. The purpose of the `AbstractFilter` *class is simply to hide and handle the* `filterConfig` *JavaBean property. That way, the actual* `Filter` *implementation class* (`SignatureFilter`) *may focus solely on the business logic of the filtering itself.*

The effect is that the receiver of the message may verify that the message has not been modified while in transit. Although a small example and far from industrial strength, most secure message applications perform operations equivalent to the `SignatureFilter` (shown in Listing 2-9) for sending messages.

Of course, an equivalent operation must be performed on the receiving side in order to verify that the message received is intact.

Listing 2-9. The `SignatureFilter` *class*

```
package se.jguru.servlets;

import javax.servlet.*;
import javax.servlet.http.*;
import java.io.*;
import java.util.*;
import java.security.*;
import se.jguru.servlets.helpers.*;

/**
 * Simple filter implementation class, which creates a
 * digital signature from the message sent to it.
 *
 * @author Lennart Jörelid, jGuru.se
 */
public class SignatureFilter extends AbstractFilter
{
    // MessageDigest instance which performs the actual hash creation
    private MessageDigest cruncher = null;

    // The default message, if no message was sent to this filter.
    private String defaultMessage = "This is not a message!";

    /**
     * The init method creates the MessageDigest instance used
     * to create the digital signature in the filter.
     */
    public void init(FilterConfig conf)
    {
        super.init(conf);

        // Create a messageDigest using an algorithm provided
        // as an initialization parameter
        try
        {
            // Read the algorithm used in the MessageDigest
            String type = conf.getInitParameter("signatureType");
            if(type == null) type = "SHA-1";
```

```
            // Create the MessageDigest instance
            this.cruncher = MessageDigest.getInstance(type);
        }
        catch(Exception ex)
        {
            // Complain
            this.log("SignatureFilter", "init",
                "Could not create MessageDigest: " + ex);
        }
    }

    /**
     * The doFilter method creates the response from the filter.
     */
    public void doFilter(final ServletRequest request,
        final ServletResponse response, FilterChain chain)
        throws IOException, ServletException
        {
             // Get the message from the request
             String msg = request.getParameter("message");

             if (msg == null) msg = defaultMessage;
             this.log("SignatureFilter", "doFilter", "msg = " + msg);

             // Get a reference to the output stream
             OutputStream out = response.getOutputStream();

             // Allow other filters to provide their output
             GenericResponseWrapper wrapper =
             new GenericResponseWrapper((HttpServletResponse)response);
             chain.doFilter(request, response);
             out.write(wrapper.getData());

             // At the end of the resulting page, print the result of this Filter
             out.write(
              ("<HR>Signature of message: "
              + new String(this.getSignature(msg))
              + "<HR>").getBytes()
             );
             out.close();
    }
```

```
/**
 * Get the hash output from the internal cruncher instance.
 *
 * @param message The message from which to calculate the Hash.
 */
protected byte[] getSignature(String message)
{
   return cruncher.digest(message.getBytes());
}
```

As you can see in Listing 2-9, the `Filter` instance makes use of a class known as `GenericResponseWrapper`, which is a subclass of `ResponseWrapper` and an implementation of the `ServletResponse` interface. This provides an opportunity for other filters to add their output to the final result. The `web.xml` deployment descriptor defines the `message.jsp` document to be the target of the `SignatureFilter`:

```
<filter>
   <filter-name>SignatureFilter</filter-name>
   <display-name>SignatureFilter</display-name>
   <filter-class>se.jguru.servlets.SignatureFilter</filter-class>
   <init-param>
      <param-name>signatureType</param-name>
      <param-value>SHA-1</param-value>
   </init-param>
</filter>
<filter-mapping>
   <filter-name>SignatureFilter</filter-name>
   <url-pattern>/message.jsp</url-pattern>
</filter-mapping>
```

Finally, this simple file, `message.jsp`, contains the HTML and JSP code that executes the filter:

```
<HTML>
<HEAD>
     <TITLE>Signature filter</TITLE>
</HEAD>
<BODY>
     <HR>
     <P>Original message: <%= request.getParameter("message")%></P>
     <HR>
</BODY>
</HTML>
```

Servlet filters come in many shapes and levels of difficulty and sophistication; this brief walkthrough does not expose every possible trick usable in developing servlet filters; I recommend frequent browsing of the online documentation for your favourite application server for an update on sensible filter options and code tips.

Sharing Resources between Servlets—A UML Approach

You may use filtered invocation to modify the `ServletRequest` or `ServletResponse` in calls to servlets running in newer servlet engines. The vast majority of application servers are still adopting rather slowly to new standards, and the wrapped invocation method described previously is still common and appropriate for many situations. Specifically, the forwarding pattern is frequently used to realize the servlet controller—`Controller` as per the Model-View-Controller (MVC) pattern—of Web application systems.

The stage is set! Now, these three leading roles enter for the acclaimed forwarding drama:

- *GatekeeperServlet*: A filter servlet, which will check the user identity of the browser client by calling a legacy system. The actual call to the legacy system is not shown in Figure 2-20, but the return value of the call is set as an attribute in the `ServletRequest` object. The `gatekeeperServlet` will act as `Servlet1` from Figure 2-2.

- *PayServlet*: A view-producing servlet, which will create some kind of HTML view, where the userID, read from the ServletRequest, will be printed. The `payServlet` will act as `Servlet2` from Figure 2-2.

- *foundUserID*: A resource (Java object) returned by the legacy system. The resource is shared by both servlets in the call.

Figure 2-20 shows the sequence diagram of the small system.
The sequence of method calls within the scenario is as follows:

1. The browser client calls the service method of the `gatekeeperServlet`.

2. To verify that the user has properly logged on to the system, the `verifyLogin` method is called, retrieving the user ID of the caller from a legacy system (not illustrated in this sequence diagram).

3. The user ID is written as an attribute to the `ServletRequest`.

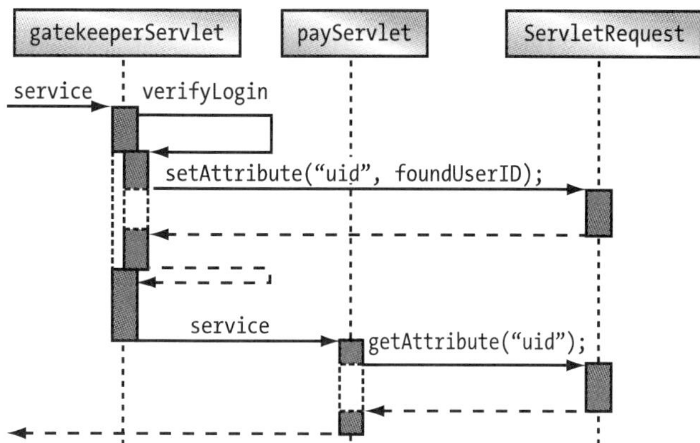

Figure 2-20. Old-style (pre Servlet API 2.3) filter example for the forwarding pattern

4. The service call is forwarded to the `payServlet` role from `gatekeeperServlet`.

5. After forwarding the service call, the `UserID` found in `gatekeeperservlet` is read from the `ServletRequest`.

Clearly, the forward pattern is used as a filter in this call scenario. On the other hand, it is also used to be able to share a resource (`foundUserId`) between the two servlets involved. Note that the resources is bound to the `ServletRequest`, which is shared by both servlets. The `ServletRequest` and `ServletResponse` are used as storage buffers for all attributes sent from one servlet to the other.

Listing 2-10 shows the relevant code for sharing the resource between the two servlets. For a full example where a "ping" service is shared, refer to "Sharing a `PingerServlet` Resource" later in this chapter. Thankfully, you need not walk through a full example to learn how resource sharing between two servlets works.

Listing 2-10. Binding a resource (`userId`) to the `ServletRequest` shared between two servlets

```
... in the service method of servlet1 ...
// Get the userId from the legacy system
String userId = verifyLogin(request.getAttribute("userID"));

// Bind the userId in the ServletRequest
// (refer to section "Using Contexts" for a walkthrough of Contexts)
request.setAttribute("userId", userId);
```

```
// Get a RequestDispatcher which is used to forward
// execution control to the second servlet
String forwardServletName = "secondServlet";
RequestDispatcher rd =
getServletConfig().getServletContext().getRequestDispatcher(forwardServletName);

// Forward to the second servlet
rd.forward(request, response);
```

In the `service` method of the second servlet, you may retrieve the bound resource (`userId`) from the `ServletRequest`. You have therefore shared the `userId` between the two servlets using the forwarding pattern:

```
... in the service method of servlet2 ...
// Get the userId from the request
String userId = request.getAttribute("userID");

// Check validity of the userId
if(userId == null)
throw new NotLoggedInException("...");

// Now, we can use the information generated in servlet1
```

The second servlet (`servlet2`) simply uses information collected by the first. Figure 2-21 shows this process.

Figure 2-22 illustrates the same scenario you saw in Figure 2-20, but the including pattern is used instead of forwarding. Note that the two servlets exchange roles—the `payServlet` becomes `Servlet1` based on Figure 2-21, and the `gatekeeperServlet` becomes `Servlet2`.

The include pattern is frequently used to join data created by several small servlets to a common result which is then sent back to the user. Such an example is provided in the "Sharing a PingerServlet Resource" section, where a small servlet (`PingerServlet`) is used as a resource by other servlets.

Including allows a servlet to use another servlet as a subroutine or resource creation device (see Figure 2-23).

As in Listing 2-10, the relevant code for including a resource between the two servlets is quite short. (For a full example where a "ping" service is shared, refer to "Sharing a `PingerServlet` Resource" later in this chapter). Listing 2-11 shows how the include pattern is used to share information.

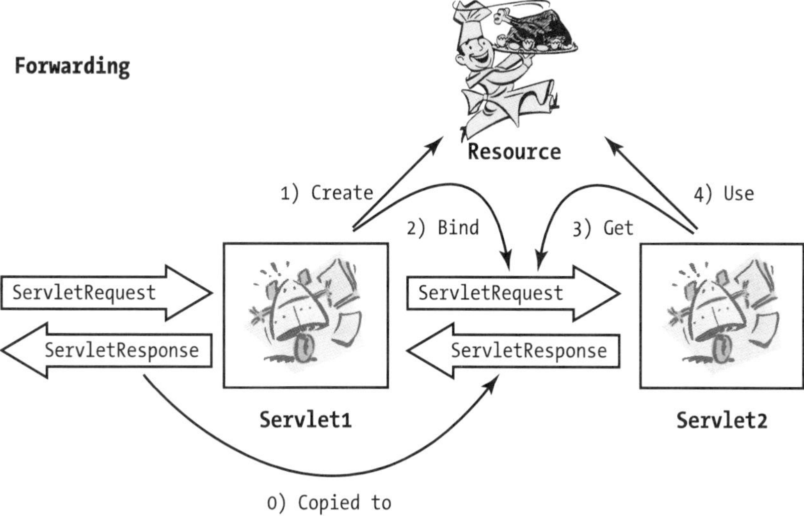

Figure 2-21. Generic view of resource sharing using the forwarding call pattern. A resource is created and bound to the `ServletRequest` *by* `Servlet1` *and later retrieved from the* `ServletRequest` *by* `Servlet2`. `Servlet2` *can then use the resource in its normal code execution.*

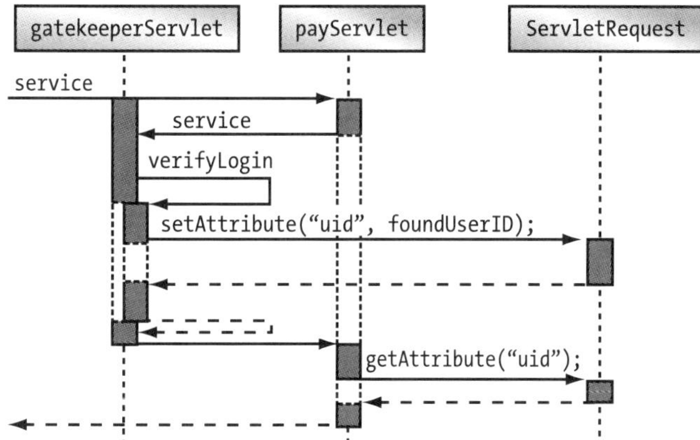

Figure 2-22. Filter example for the including pattern

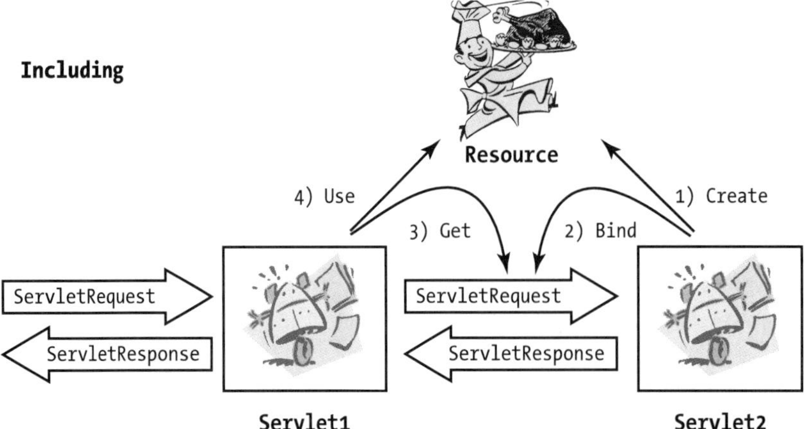

Figure 2-23. Generic view of resource sharing using the including call pattern. A resource is created and bound to the `ServletRequest` *by* `Servlet2`*, and later retrieved from the* `ServletRequest` *by* `Servlet1`*.* `Servlet1` *may later use the resource in its normal code execution.*

Listing 2-11. Code snippet illustrating using a resource (`userId`) *bound to the* `ServletRequest` *shared between two servlets*

```
... in the service method of servlet1 ...

// Get a RequestDispatcher which is used to forward
// execution control to the second servlet
String forwardServletName = "secondServlet";
RequestDispatcher rd =
   getServletConfig().getServletContext().getRequestDispatcher(
      forwardServletName
   );

// Forward to the second servlet
rd.include(request, response);

// Get the userId which has now been bound to the request
String userId = request.getAttribute("UserID");

// Check validity of the userId
if(userId == null)
throw new NotLoggedInException("...");

// Now, we can use the information (userId) generated in servlet2
```

In the `service` method of the second servlet, you may retrieve the bound resource (`userId`) from the `ServletRequest`. You have therefore shared the `userId` between the two servlets using the forwarding pattern, as shown in the following code sample:

```
... in the service method of servlet2 ...
// Get the userId from the legacy system
String userId = verifyLogin(request.getAttribute("UserID"));

// Bind the userId in the ServletRequest
// (refer to section "Using Contexts" for a walkthrough of Contexts)
request.setAttribute("userId", userId);
```

The first servlet simply includes information collected by the second servlet. The forwarding and including patterns described how two servlets may share a resource within the same client call (in other words, during a single request). However, other storage objects must be used if resources should be shared over multiple invocations or globally—for all servlets within a Web application.

> **NOTE** *In general, servlets use contexts to bind and unbind parameters.*

Using Contexts

Because all calls from client browsers to a deployed servlet spawns a new thread that uses a single servlet instance, all member attributes in a servlet are shared between all concurrent calls to a servlet. Therefore, information cannot be shared between two servlets simply by having `Servlet1` call a method in `Servlet2` and assign a value to an attribute of `Servlet2`. We must use another method to share resources that should be unique to a particular user between two servlets in a single request.

This delegation problem (which illustrates a common situation in the Servlet API) is solved by binding shared resource objects in a context shared by both servlets. All such context objects in the Servlet API have methods closely resembling the methods of `java.util.Hashtable`–and the handling of bound resources closely resemble handling the keys and values of a normal hashtable.

The developer may set and/or retrieve values from the `ServletRequest` given a specific key. The analogy with the `Hashtable` methods and usage is evident when taking a look at the API. Table 2-3 compares the different methods.

Table 2-3. Comparison of Methods in Various Contexts Accessible from a Servlet and a Hashtable.

CLASS	SETTER METHOD	GETTER METHOD	ENUMERATION GETTER METHOD
Hashtable	put(aKey, aValue)	Object value = get(aKey)	keys()
ServletRequest	setAttribute(aKey, aValue)	Object value = getAttribute(aKey)	getAttributeNames()
ServletRequest	None	String value = getParameter(aKey) or String[] values = getParameterValues(aKey)	getParameterNames()
ServletConfig	None	String value = getInitParameter(aKey)	getInitParameterNames()
ServletContext	setAttribute(aKey, aValue)	Object value = getAttribute(aKey)	getAttributeNames()
PageContext	setAttribute(aKey, aValue)	Object value = getAttribute(aKey)	getAttributeNamesInScope()
HttpSession	putAttribute(aKey, aValue)	Object value = getAttribute(aKey);	getAttributeNames ()

The purpose of the method comparison is to relate the methods used in a familiar class (`Hashtable`) to the ones provided in the context classes of the Servlet API. If you know how to use a `Hashtable`, you also know how to use the contexts of the Servlet API. As an example, consider a small piece of code that modifies and extracts data from a `Hashtable`:

```
// Get a Hashtable reference from a helper method
Hashtable hash = this.getHashtable();

// Put a value into the Hashtable
String theValue = "aValue";
hash.put("aKey",theValue);

// Get the value from the Hashtable
String readValue = (String) hash.get("aKey");
```

The similarity between the well-known `Hashtable` snippet and code doing the same thing in the `ServletContext`, is great:

```
// Get the ServletContext reference from a helper method
ServletContext sc = this.getServletContext();

// Put a value into the ServletContext
String theValue = "aValue";
sc.put("aKey",theValue);

// Get the value from the Hashtable
String readValue = (String) sc.get("aKey");
```

All the contexts of the Servlet API may be used in a similar way; simply use the correct method name from Table 2-3 instead of the `Hashtable` methods.

Sharing a PingerServlet Resource

In this section, you'll create a small standalone servlet application, which will be inserted into both the forwarding and the including patterns at a later stage. Thus, the `Pinger` servlet communicates with a legacy system (the Unix ping application, in our case) and exposes the results to the client browser. Figure 2-24 shows a call to the pinger servlet is shown in Figure 2-24.

In the example, the legacy application takes the form of the Unix command ping, which sends an Internet Control Message Protocol (ICMP) message to a remote host to receive state information. The roundtrip time is measured and collected—the `Pinger` servlet collects all roundtrip data and presents it in a simple form.

To be more specific, the Unix ping application generates output in the following form:

```
PING xyz.nowhere.se (212.91.133.14): 56 data bytes

--- xyz.nowhere.se ping statistics ---
12 packets transmitted, 12 packets received, 0% packet loss
round-trip min/avg/max = 206.0/295.3/620.2 ms
```

The `Pinger` servlet reads the last row of the stream generated by ping and extracts the three numbers displaying minimum, average, and maximum roundtrip times to the ping node. These numbers are presented on the output stream of the `Pinger` servlet. In Listing 2-12, the methods extracting attributes from the `ServletRequest` are rendered in bold.

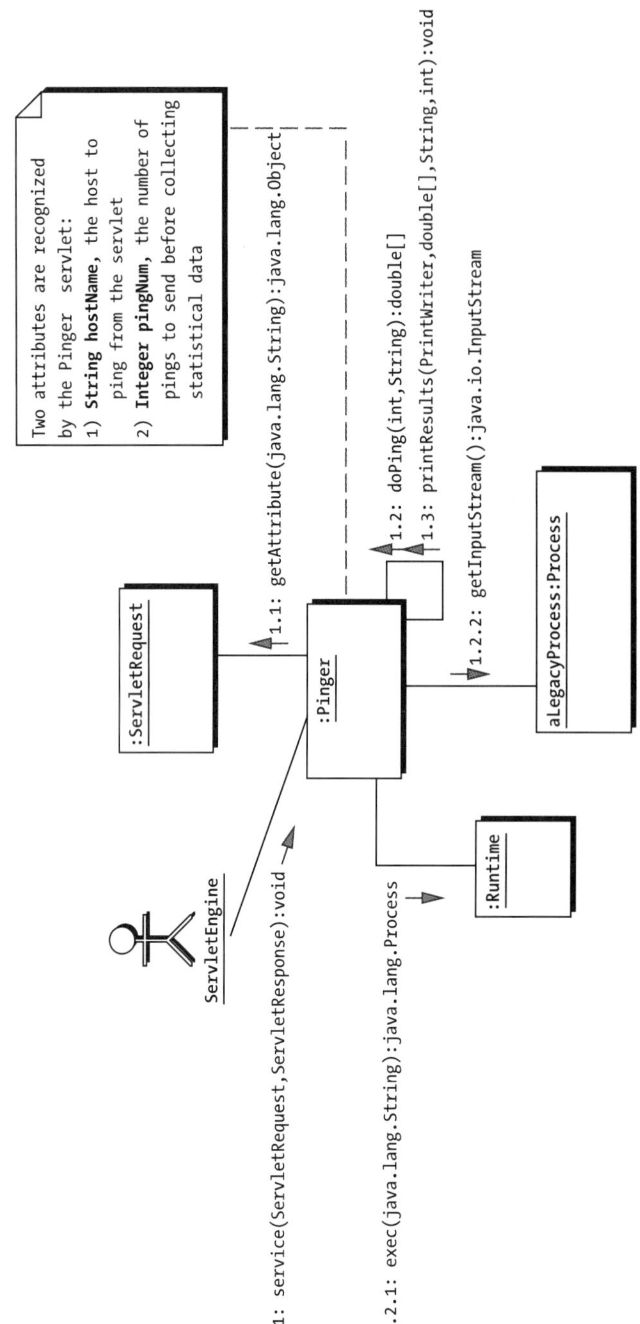

Figure 2-24. Collaboration diagram of the standalone `Pinger` *servlet, interacting with its* `ServletRequest` *and the ping process objects (*`Runtime` *and* `Process` *instances). The* `PingerServlet` *may be run as a normal, standalone servlet, as well as a shared servlet resource.*

Listing 2-12. The `PingerServlet` *class*

```
// Import all required Java packages
import java.io.*;
import java.util.*;
import javax.servlet.*;

// Extend the GenericServlet class to avoid
// implementation of many empty methods.
public class Pinger extends GenericServlet
{    // Constants for interpreting the response.
    public static final int MINIMUM = 0;
    public static final int AVERAGE = 1;
    public static final int MAXIMUM = 2;

    /**
     * Launches the legacy application (i.e. ping), to measure the
     * roundtrip time between the servlet engine node and the node
     * whose name is provided as an argument.
    *
    * @param numPings the number of roundtrip ping messages that
    *        should be sent.
    * @param node the name of the computer node to send the
    *        ping ICMP messages to.
    *
    * @return A vector of doubles, measuring the Minimum, Average
    *         and Maximum roundtrip times of the ping messages,
    *         in milliseconds.
    *         Use the constants provided in this class to access
    *         each individual element.
    */
   public double[] doPing(int numPings, String node) throws IOException
   {
        // Open the legacy Process
        //
        // The actual command executed looks similar to:
        //   '/bin/ping -q -c 5 www.apress.com'
        //
        String pingCommand = "/bin/ping -q -c " + numPings + " " + node;
        Process p = Runtime.getRuntime().exec(pingCommand);

        // Open the normal input stream of the process
        InputStreamReader isr = new InputStreamReader(p.getInputStream());
        BufferedReader in  = new BufferedReader( isr );
```

```
// Define the return object
double toReturn[] = new double[3];

// Define a dummy variable holding the line of text
// just read from the input stream of the Process.
String aReadLine = "";

// Parse the output of the Process and populate the
// toReturn double vector with the statistics obtained
// from it.
//
// Output from our process is similar to
//
//    PING xyz.nowhere.se (212.91.133.14): 56 data bytes
//
//    --- xyz.nowhere.se ping statistics ---
//    12 packets transmitted, 12 packets received, 0% packet loss
//    round-trip min/avg/max = 206.0/295.3/620.2 ms
//
// Thus, the only line we are interested in is the last one,
// which contains the statistics we require.
//
while((aReadLine = in.readLine()) != null)
{
    // If the current line contains the text
    // "round-trip", it is the desired line.

  if(aReadLine.indexOf("round-trip") != -1)
  {
        // Split the line in words, and retain only the
        // fourth word which must be further split to
        // obtain the desired statistics.

        StringTokenizer tok = new StringTokenizer(aReadLine);
        String[] words = new String[tok.countTokens()];

        for(int i = 0; tok.hasMoreTokens(); i++)
        {
            // Copy current token to the array
            words[i] = tok.nextToken();
        }
```

```
            // Split the fourth word with the '/' delimiter.
            // Assign the results to the return array.

            tok = new StringTokenizer(words[3], "/");

            for(int i = 0; tok.hasMoreTokens(); i ++)
            {
                String theTime = tok.nextToken();
                toReturn[i] = Double.valueOf(theTime).doubleValue();
            }
        }

    }

    // Log to the current console.
    System.out.println("Done pinging.");

    // Return.
    return toReturn;
}

/**
 * The service method of the Pinger servlet will extract
 * some data from the ServletRequest to control its
 * subsequent call to the legacy application.
 *
 * The parameters looked for in the ServletRequest are
 *
 *    'pingHost'  := The host which should be pinged.
 *                   Type: java.lang.String
 *
 *    'pingNum'   := The number of ICMP ping messages that
 *                   should be sent to the pingHost before
 *                   collecting the data.
 *                   Type: java.lang.Integer
 */
public void service(ServletRequest req, ServletResponse res)
throws IOException, ServletException
{
    //
   // Get the provided attributes from the
   // incoming ServletRequest
   //
```

```
        String host  = (String) req.getAttribute("pingHost");
        Integer obj  = (Integer) req.getAttribute("pingNum");
        int numPings = 5;

        // Get the writer
        PrintWriter out = new PrintWriter(res.getWriter());

        // Check arguments, and provide or leave default parameters
        //
        if (host == null) host = "www.apress.com";
        if (obj != null)  numPings = obj.intValue();

        // Execute the legacy application
        // and print the results to the ServletResponse.
        //
        double[] result = doPing(numPings, host);
        printResults(out, result, host, numPings);

        //
        // Printout all Attributes bound to the ServletRequest
        //
        out.println("\n ----> Listing All Bound Attributes <----");
        for(Enumeration en = req.getAttributeNames(); en.hasMoreElements();)
        {
           String theKey = (String) en.nextElement();
           out.println("Key: " + theKey + ", Value: "
                     + req.getAttribute(theKey));
         }

        out.println(" ----> End Listing All Bound Attributes <----");
    }

    /**
     * Print the results of the call to the legacy application on the
     * out Printwriter.
     */
    private void printResults(PrintWriter out,
                double[] results,
                String host,
                int numPings)
    {
        // Printout the statistics information
        out.println(" ---> Ping Statistics <--- ");
        out.println("Pinged host " + host + " " + numPings + " times.");
        out.println("Results:");
```

```
        out.println(" Max time: " + results[MAXIMUM]);
        out.println(" Avg time: " + results[AVERAGE]);
        out.println(" Min time: " + results[MINIMUM]);
        out.println(" ---> End Ping Statistics <--- ");
    }

    /**
     * Bonus main method, to be able to run this servlet as a standalone
     * application in addition to the normal servlet run mode.
     */
    public static void main(String args[]) throws IOException
    {
         // Define default values
         String host  = "www.apress.com";
        int numPings = 5;

        // Handle all
        for(int i = 0; i < args.length; i++)
        {
            switch(i)
            {
                case 0:
                        // This should be the name of the host to ping
                        host = args[i];
                    break;

                    case 1:
                        // This should be the number of pings to call
                        try
                        {
                            numPings = Integer.parseInt(args[i]);
                        }
                        catch(NumberFormatException ex)
                        {
                            // Display usage.
                            ex.printStackTrace();
                            showUsage();
                        }
                    break;
```

```
                default:
                    // We should never end up here
                    showUsage();
                break;
            }
        }

        // Run the Ping command and printout
        // the result.
        Pinger aPinger = new Pinger();
        double[] results = aPinger.doPing(numPings, host);

         aPinger.printResults(new PrintWriter(System.out, true),
                results, host, numPings);
    }

    private static void showUsage()
    {
        System.out.println("Usage: java Pinger [hostName [numberOfPings]]");
        System.exit(0);
    }
}
```

The `Pinger` servlet may be run as a standalone application as well as a servlet. It may also be run as a servlet by itself or as a resource called by another servlet. In the latter aspect, the `Pinger` servlet is used as `Servlet1` in the forward pattern or `Servlet2` in the include pattern. The output produced by its standalone servlet mode is something like what you see in Figure 2-25.

> **NOTE** *When running in standalone servlet mode, no attributes are set in the* `ServletRequest` *using the* `setAttribute(aKey, value)` *method. Thus, none are listed when the servlet runs.*

Now, add a client servlet that will set the attributes read by the `Pinger` servlet and then call `Pinger` using the forwarding and including patterns.

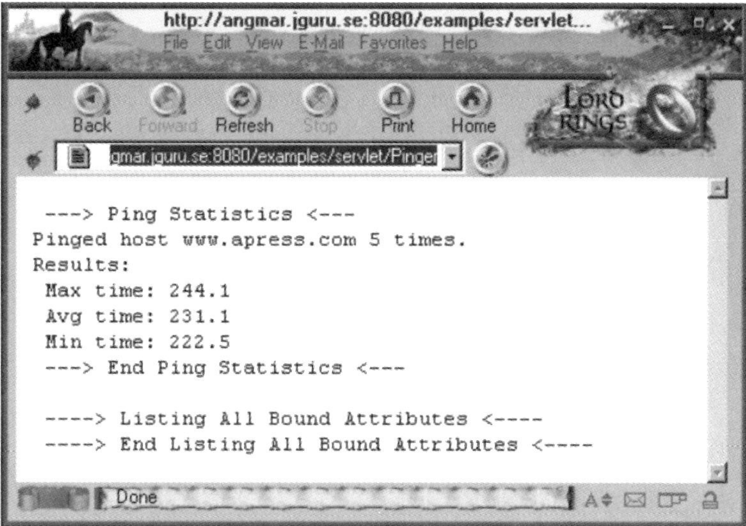

Figure 2-25. Resulting output from the `Pinger` *servlet when pinging the Apress Web server node*

Collaboration Diagrams of the Forwarding and Including Patterns

Figure 2-26 shows the two servlets in the forwarding pattern. The steps in the collaboration diagram that match the four numbered operations in Figure 2-21 are as follows:

1. Create attribute: Not illustrated in the figure but happens in the service method prior to step 2.3
2. Bind attribute: Step 2.3, using method `setAttribute(aKey, value)`
3. Get attribute: Step 2.4.1.1, using `method getAttribute(aKey)`
4. Use attribute: Not illustrated in the figure but happens somewhere in the `service` method after 2.4.1.1

Figure 2-7 shows the including pattern. The steps in the figure that match the four numbered operations in the forwarding pattern image (Figure 2-21) are as follows:

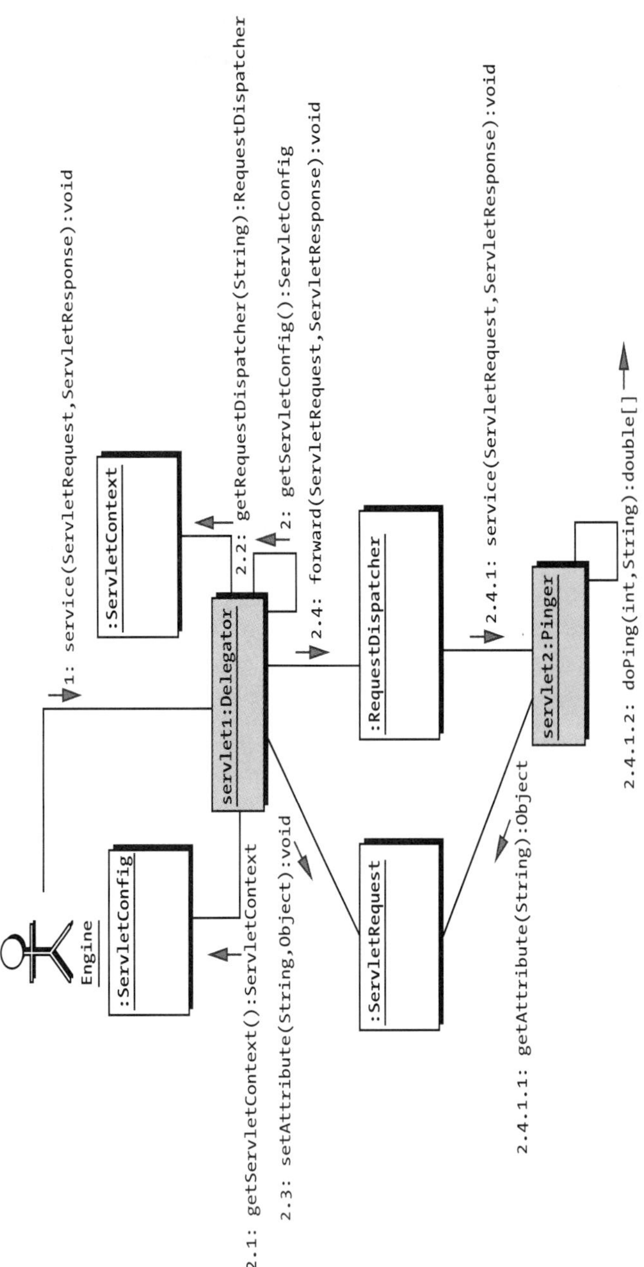

Figure 2-26. Collaboration diagram for the forwarding pattern between `servlet1` *(a* `Delegator` *servlet) and* `servlet2` *(a* `Pinger` *servlet). Both relevant resources are bound to the* `ServletRequest` *by the delegator in step 2.3 and read from the* `ServletRequest` *by the pinger in step 2.4.1.1. The attributes shared between the two servlets are* `pingHost`*, which designates the host which to ping, and* `pingNum`*, which designates the number of ICMP pings to send before returning.*

1. Create attribute: Not illustrated in the diagram but happens between steps 1.3.1 and 1.3.1.1, somewhere in the `service` method of the included servlet

2. Bind attribute: Step 1.3.1.1, using method `setAttribute(aKey, value)`

3. Get attribute: Step 1.4, using method `getAttribute(aKey)`

4. Use attribute: Not illustrated in the diagram but happens somewhere in the `service` method after 1.5

In Figure 2-27, both relevant resources are bound to the `ServletRequest` by the `Delegator` in step 2.3 and read from the `ServletRequest` by the `Pinger` in step 2.4.1.1. The attributes shared between the two servlets are `pingHost`, which designates the host which to ping, and `pingNum`, which designates the number of ICMP pings to send before returning.

Figure 2-28 shows the output of the running example. Note that the output of the `Pinger` servlet can be seen in the middle of the listing and that the `ServletContext.getAttributeNames` method found two attributes set by the servlet engine plus two attributes set by the `Delegator` servlet (`PingHost` and `PingNum`).

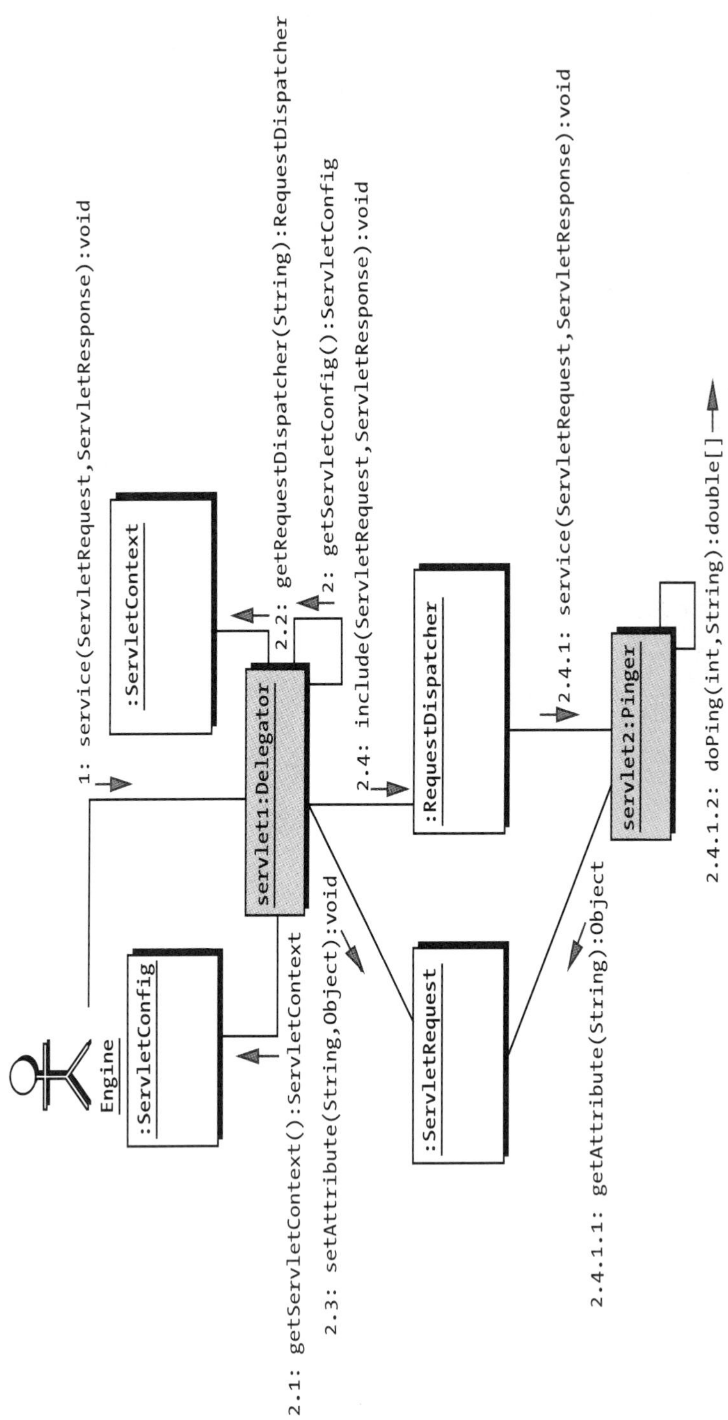

Figure 2-27. Collaboration diagram for the including pattern between `servlet1` *(a* `Delegator` *servlet) and* `servlet2` *(a* `Pinger` *servlet).*

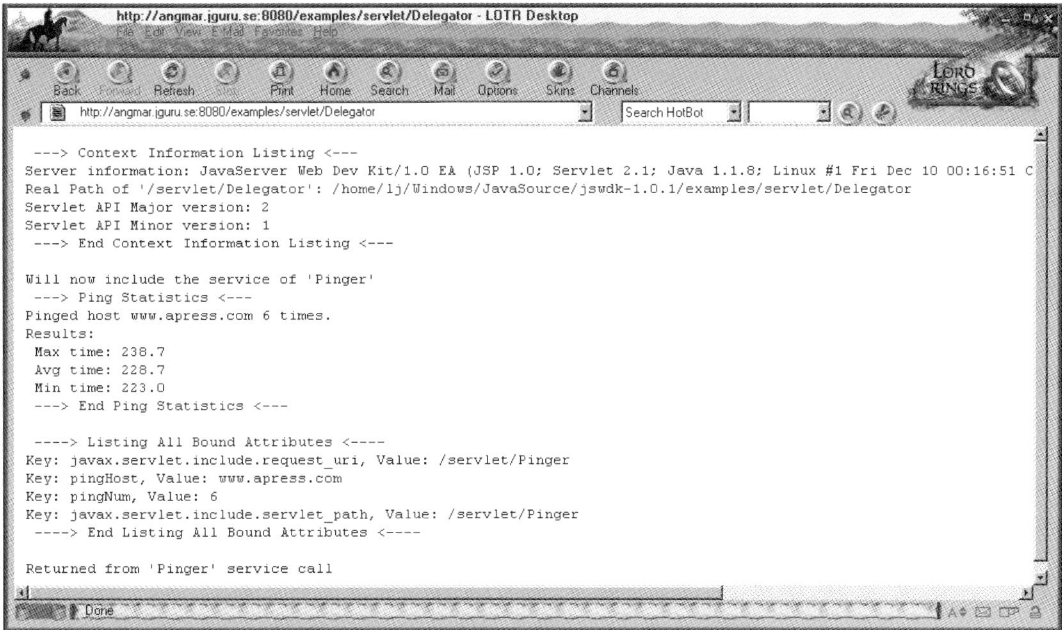

Figure 2-28. Resulting output of the `Delegator` *servlet when running the include pattern*

The source code of the `Delegator` servlet is straightforward, as shown in Listing 2-13.

Listing 2-13. The `Delegator` *servlet*

```
// Import all required packages
import javax.servlet.*;
import java.io.*;
import java.util.*;

// Extend GenericServlet to avoid implementing
// lots of empty method bodies.
public class Delegator extends GenericServlet
{
   /**
    * Service method that delegates some execution to
    * the Pinger servlet, using the Servlet API 2.1
    * call mode of the RequestDispatcher interface.
    */
```

```
public void service(ServletRequest req, ServletResponse res)
throws ServletException, IOException
{
   //
   // Create a RequestDispatcher tied to the Pinger servlet,
   // which has the local access path /servlet/Pinger.
   //
   ServletContext ctx = getServletConfig().getServletContext();
   RequestDispatcher rq = ctx.getRequestDispatcher("/servlet/Pinger");

   // Use the "Forwarding" pattern if the user supplied
   // a parameter with the key 'forward' to the service method.
   //
   if(req.getParameter("forward") != null)
   {
     // Set the attributes understood by
     // the 'Pinger' servlet
     //
     req.setAttribute("pingHost", "www.javasoft.com");
     req.setAttribute("pingNum", new Integer(10));

     // Forward the request
      rq.forward(req, res);
   }
   else
   {
     // Here, we should use the "Including" pattern to
     // retrieve data from the 'Pinger' servlet.
     //
     // Since this service method will not delegate all
     // responsibility for further execution of the
     // service method, we may open the underlying
     // Writer and print to it.
     //
      PrintWriter out = new PrintWriter(res.getWriter());

      // Print some Metadata regarding the servlet engine
     // All such data is gotten from the ServletContext
     // interface.
     //
     out.println(" ---> Context Information Listing <---");
     out.println("Server information: " + ctx.getServerInfo());
     out.println("Real Path of '/servlet/Delegator': "
         + ctx.getRealPath("/servlet/Delegator"));
```

```
            out.println("Servlet API Major version: "
                + ctx.getMajorVersion());
            out.println("Servlet API Minor version: "
                + ctx.getMinorVersion());
            out.println(" ---> End Context Information Listing <---\n");

            // Set some attributes
            req.setAttribute("pingHost", "www.apress.com");
            req.setAttribute("pingNum", new Integer(6));

            // Include the Pinger servlet
            out.println("Will now include the service of 'Pinger'");
            rq.include(req, res);
            out.println("\nReturned from 'Pinger' service call");
        }
    }
}
```

The `Delegator` servlet consists of a single `service` method call, delegating parts of its execution to the `Pinger` servlet. The first part of the service method creates the `RequestDispatcher`, pointing to the `Pinger` servlet. The same `RequestDispatcher` can be used to forward or include the servlet call to another servlet—in effect implementing the including and forwarding patterns discussed in "Sharing Resources between Servlets—a UML Approach" earlier in this chapter.

Should the servlet be called with the `ServletRequest` attribute forward (as in Figure 2-29), the `Delegator` servlet uses the `RequestDispatcher` to carry out the forwarding pattern method calls. Otherwise, the including pattern is used to get information to/from the `Pinger` `service` servlet. Before using the including pattern, the `Pinger` servlet request properties are reset so that the `Pinger` servlet checks the network statistics of `www.javasoft.com` instead of `www.apress.com`.

When you include servlet or JSP resources into a calling servlet using the `RequestDispatcher.include` method, a set of request attributes containing data from the original request are made available to the included servlet. The following section investigates these attributes.

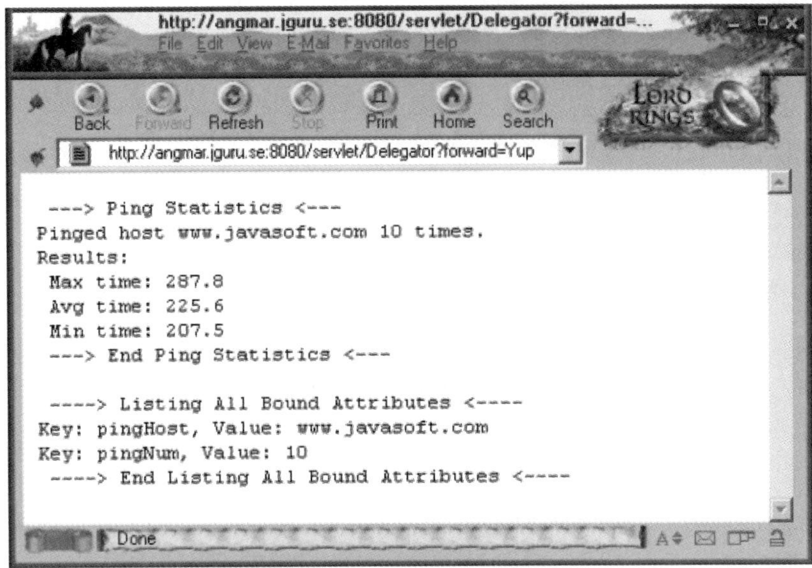

Figure 2-29. Resulting output of the `Delegator` *servlet when executing the forwarding pattern*

Finding Original Request Parameters

Suppose you use the including pattern to include a resource from a servlet called `IncludeServlet`. According to the Servlet 2.3 specification, when the code executes in the included servlet, the extra request attributes in Table 2-4 should be set.

Table 2-4. Request Attributes

ATTRIBUTE	DESCRIPTION
`javax.servlet.include.request_uri`	Request URI of the original request
`javax.servlet.include.context_path`	Context path of the original request
`javax.servlet.include.servlet_path`	Servlet path of the original servlet
`javax.servlet.include.path_info`	Path_info of the original request
`javax.servlet.include.query_string`	Query_string of the original request

Although these attributes are defined in the Servlet 2.3 specification, you are advised to verify what attributes are actually set by your Web server. As a quick example, the `IncludeServlet` logs all attributes to the response writer, `out`—Figure 2-30 shows the result.

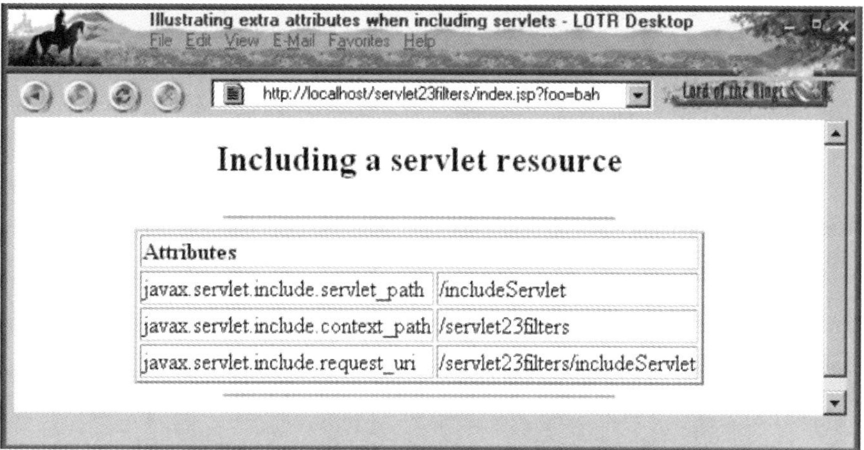

Figure 2-30. Resulting output of the `index.jsp` *documents that includes the output of the* `IncludingServlet` *using a* `RequestDispatcher`. *The table is generated in the* `service` *method of the* `IncludingServlet` *class and shows all known request attributes.*

> **NOTE** *Not all of the attributes required by the specification are present in the printout; although the query string of the original request is non-null, the* `javax.servlet.include.query_string` *attribute is not set properly. Naturally, this is a passing bug that will be corrected in the near future, but the example demonstrates that you would be wise to verify the capabilities of any Web server before trusting it.*

The source of the `IncludingServlet` is quite simple (see Listing 2-14). Note the loop over all request attributes in the `service` method. Each known request attribute, including its value, is printed in a table row by the `printTableRow` method. Those names and values are, of course, shown in the resulting output in Figure 2-30.

Listing 2-14. The `IncludeServlet` *code*

```
/*
 * Copyright (c) 2000,2001 jGuru Europe.
 * All rights reserved.
 */

package se.jguru.servlets;

import javax.servlet.http.*;
import javax.servlet.*;

import java.util.*;
import java.io.*;

public class IncludeServlet extends HttpSessionBindingServlet
{
    public void service(HttpServletRequest req, HttpServletResponse res) throws
IOException
    {
        // Get the Writer connected to the client browser.
        PrintWriter out = res.getWriter();
        out.println("<table>");

        // Start an attribute table
        this.startTable("Attributes", out);

        // Loop through all Attributes
        for(Enumeration en = req.getAttributeNames(); en.hasMoreElements();)
        {
            // Write a row containing the attribute key and value
            String name = "" + en.nextElement();
            this.printRow(name, "" + req.getAttribute(name), out);
        }
        // Finish off the table
        out.println("</table>");
    }

    private void printRow(String key, String value, PrintWriter out)
    {
        out.println(" <tr><td>" + key + "</td>");
        out.println("     <td>" + value + "</td></tr>");
    }
```

```
    private void startTable(String tableName, PrintWriter out)
    {
        out.println("<table border=2><tr><td colspan=2><b>" + tableName
        + "</b></td></tr>");
    }
}
```

The `index.jsp` document, which the browser requests in Figure 2-30, simply creates the header and the two horizontal rules. The table and its content is created in the `service` method of the `IncludingServlet` class. Listing 2-15 contains the source code.

Listing 2-15. The `index.jsp` *document*

```
<%@ page buffer="none" import="java.io.*, java.util.*" %>
<head>
<title>Illustrating extra attributes when including servlets</title>
</head>

<html>
    <body>
    <center>
    <h2>Including a servlet resource</h2>
    <hr width=50%>
<%
    // Create a RequestDispatcher, and include the output of the
    // includeServlet between the two horizontal rulers.
    RequestDispatcher rd = request.getRequestDispatcher("/includeServlet");
    rd.include(request, response);
%>
    <hr width=50%>
    </center>
    </body>
</html>
```

Concluding the walkthrough of sharing servlet resources, you're ready to move on to a chapter containing slightly longer servlet examples. Sharing resources between servlets is an important topic in real-life system design—and it is also one of the tougher topics to fully master when designing large-scale servlet applications.

CHAPTER 3

Servlet Examples

WHEN INVESTIGATING A NEW TECHNOLOGY, concise examples are often helpful. Taking a look at working and carefully crafted example code may be the only help you need, other than a brief overview and the application programming interface (API) documentation. This chapter covers three servlet examples:

- Shopping cart servlet
- Firewall HTTP tunnel to an interactive application (in other words, interacting with an application behind a firewall using HTTP tunneling)
- Binary document uploader servlet transporting a document from the client's computer to the server

Of course, the examples are thoroughly explained and illustrated with figures to facilitate understanding and raise visibility. Although not required to understand the examples, knowledge of UML diagrams and their artifacts is helpful to fully see the patterns used in the code.

Shopping Cart Servlet

In the era of electronic business and commerce (e-commerce, e-business, and similar buzzwords), most server-side development aims to expose a controlled portion of a server-side data source. Often, the contents of the exposed data sources tend to be current price lists or product descriptions intended to appeal to the user and promote online sales.

Most shopping cart servlets or server-side classes tend to simulate the interaction of a series of hashtables. The simple servlet in Figure 3-1 illustrates a fairly generic core functionality found in many shopping cart applications.

This Web page has two distinct sections, each containing static HTML and dynamic HTML. The top half of the page contains a list of all items for sale, the data for which is generated from the `Catalog` instance using the `toDefaultHTMLRepresentation` method. The bottom half of the page contains a list of all items the user has placed in the shopping cart. In this case, the HTML representation is generated by the `toDefaultHTMLRepresentation` method call in the `ShoppingCart` instance.

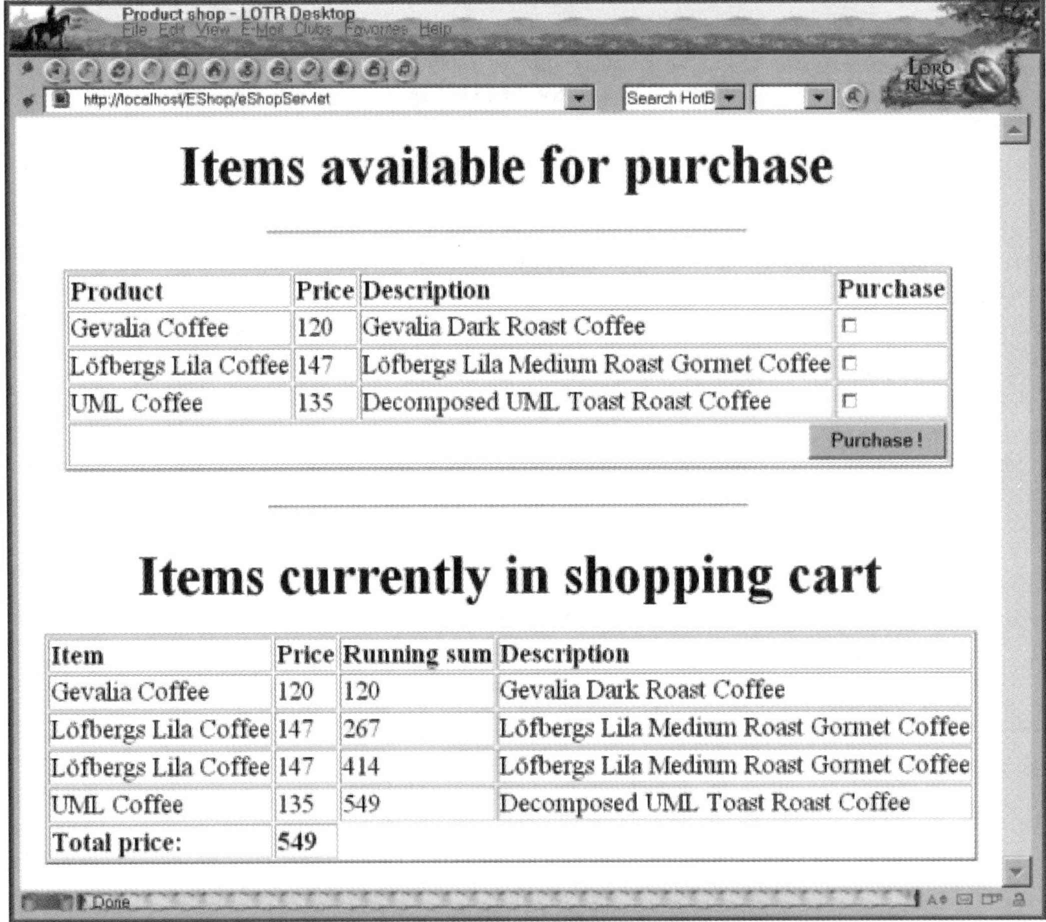

Figure 3-1. Output of the shopping cart servlet after a shopper has placed a few coffee items in the cart

Figure 3-2 illustrates which method calls within the servlet generate the different page sections.

Classes of the Shopping Cart Servlet Example

A small example, such as the simplified shopping cart application servlet shown in Figure 3-2, requires few classes and little optimization to work properly. The `ShoppingCartServlet` instance coordinates the application, which essentially consists of two wrapped `Collections`; the `Catalog` class wraps a `Map` with the catalog of products available, and the `ShoppingCart` class wraps a `List` with the products purchased by the user. Figure 3-3 shows the full class diagram of the shopping cart servlet example.

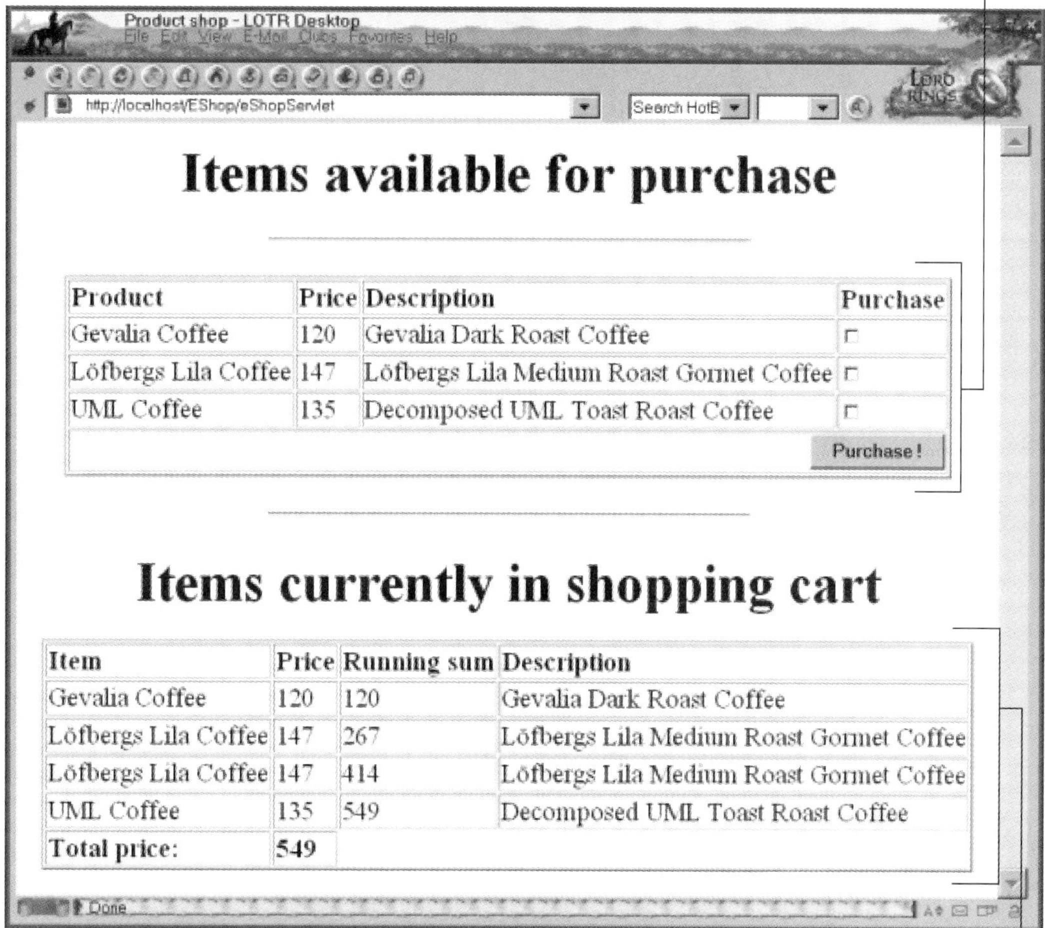

Figure 3-2. The output of the `ShoppingCartServlet` *is generated by static (hard-coded) and dynamic parts. The dynamic parts are shown with their method calls; the rest of the HTML is hard-coded into the* `ShoppingCartServlet`.

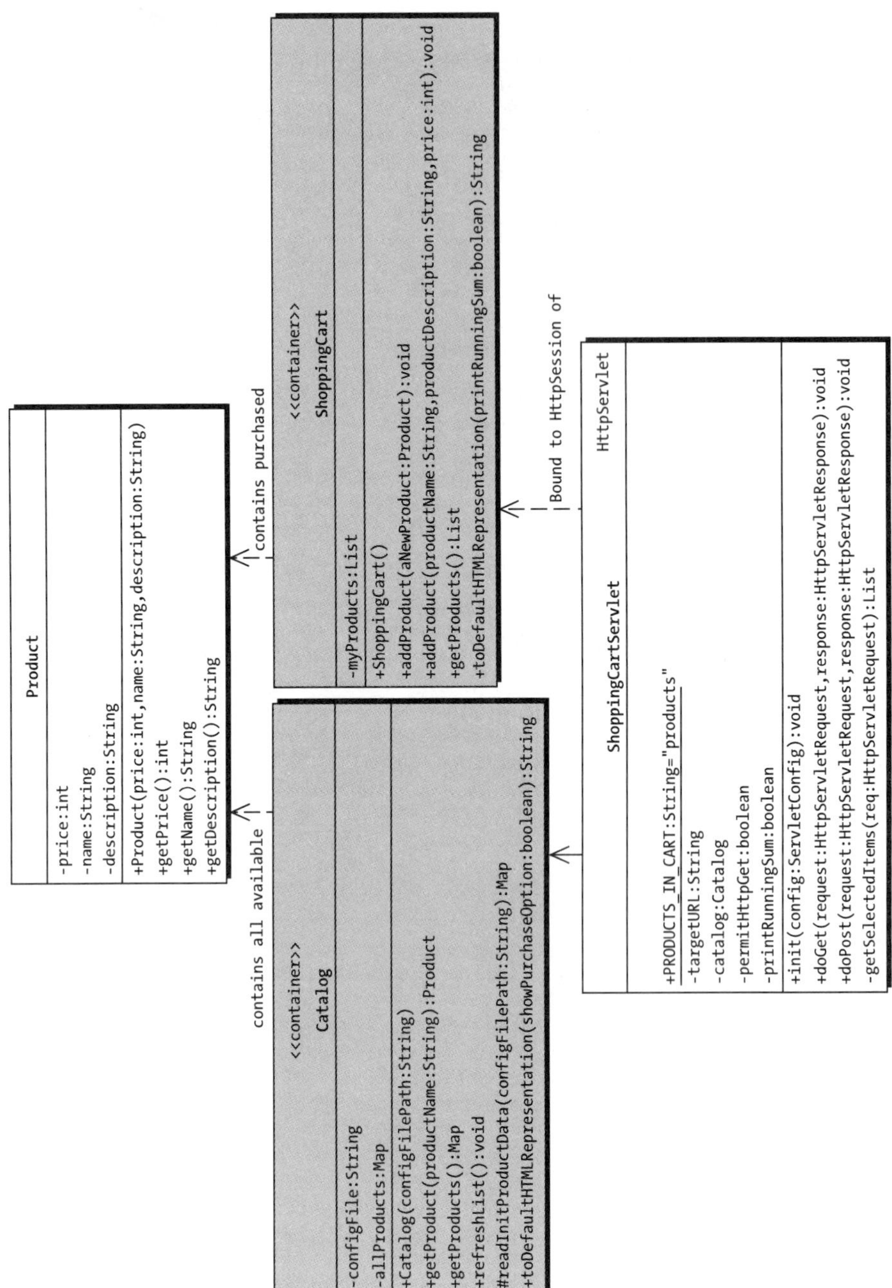

Figure 3-3. The interacting classes of the `ShoppingCartServlet` *example. The* `ShoppingCartServlet` *coordinates its* `Catalog` *instance, which contains a list of all available items in the online store, and its* `ShoppingCart` *instance, which contains all items ordered by the customer.*

Product Class

The `Product` class is a simple data container for common properties of all products. The simple e-shop you are about to design describes its products by price, description, and name. In a real-life situation, this class may hold more data members; however, the spirit of the implementation is the same.

Catalog Class

The `Catalog` class contains a `Product` template for all products available in this e-store. The `Catalog` class reads all product descriptions from a configuration file and may later present its content in a default HTML form. As an alternative, the `Catalog` instance may present the full products `Map` as well as any individual product to a caller requiring other rendering than the catalog's default HTML form, such as WML for a WAP client.

All product descriptions are read from a configuration file using the `readInitProductData` method, which is invoked from within the constructor. Thus, if you want to change the way products are read (say, by reading from a database source instead of a flat file), you have only to subclass the `Catalog` class and override the `readInitProductData` method.

ShoppingCart Class

The `ShoppingCart` class contains all products ordered by a client of the e-store. Thus, it must be bound to and read from the `HttpSession` of the current user, rather than stored as a member within the cart servlet. The `ShoppingCart` may present its content in a default HTML format, as well as in a `java.util.List` format; the former method is used by the `ShoppingCartServlet`, and the latter method may be used whenever other formatting is required.

ShoppingCartServlet Class

The `ShoppingCartServlet` class holds a global (private member) `Catalog` instance and a `ShoppingCart` instance bound to its `HttpSession` to provide a unique instance for each user. The `ShoppingCartServlet` reads four initialization parameters that control its basic operation:

- The `targetURL` attribute is the URL that should be called when a user presses the Purchase button in the catalog form.

- The `configFile` attribute is the absolute path (on the Web server node) of the product definition file, containing all product definitions of the e-store.
- The `permitHttpGet` parameter determines if the servlet should be accessible for callers using the HTTP GET command.
- The `runSum` parameter controls whether the Running Sum column should be displayed in the dynamic listing at the end of the page.

Interaction Diagrams of the Shopping Cart Servlet Example

You can start dissecting the example by investigating Figure 3-4.

init Method

The collaboration diagram of the `ShoppingCartServlet` is fairly limited in size. At the top level, the only two method calls are the `init` and `doPost` methods. The job of the `init` method is to set up the internal state of the `ShoppingCartServlet`. In this example, the servlet `init` method performs two major tasks:

- Creates a `Catalog` instance that reads product data from a flat file and creates a `HashMap` structure from the data, containing information about all products known to the system. The path and name of the flat file are provided to the servlet as a `ServletConfig` parameter.
- Reads a `ServletConfig` parameter to find the `targetURL` for the shopping cart page (shown in the browser address bar in Figure 3-1). The reason for not hard-coding this path is to allow the servlet to be moved within the virtual file system of the Web application without requiring recompilation to operate properly. Most Web servers contain facilities to create virtual filenames for deployed servlets. Specific deployment details are best provided as initialization parameters—especially during development when working with fairly inflexible Web servers.

Figure 3-5 shows the `init` method.

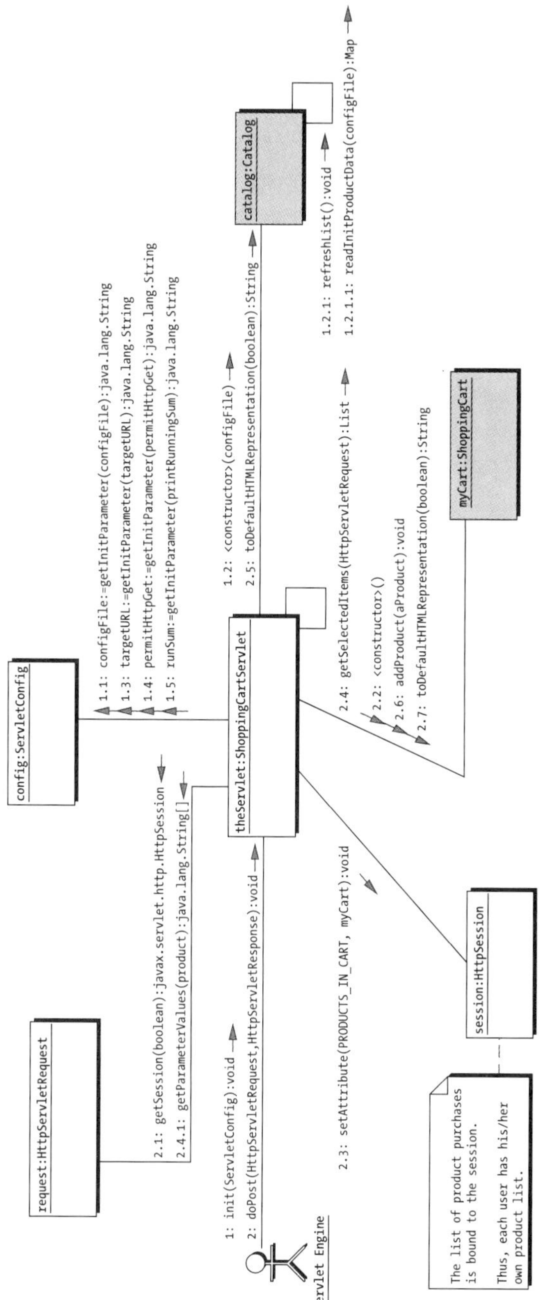

Figure 3-4. Collaboration diagram of the `ShoppingCartServlet` *instance. The call to* `init` *reads initialization parameters from the Web application configuration file,* `web.xml`. *The values read control the fundamental operation of the* `ShoppingCartServlet`. *For example, the* `configFile` `init` *parameter denotes the path of the product definition file in the remote file system.*

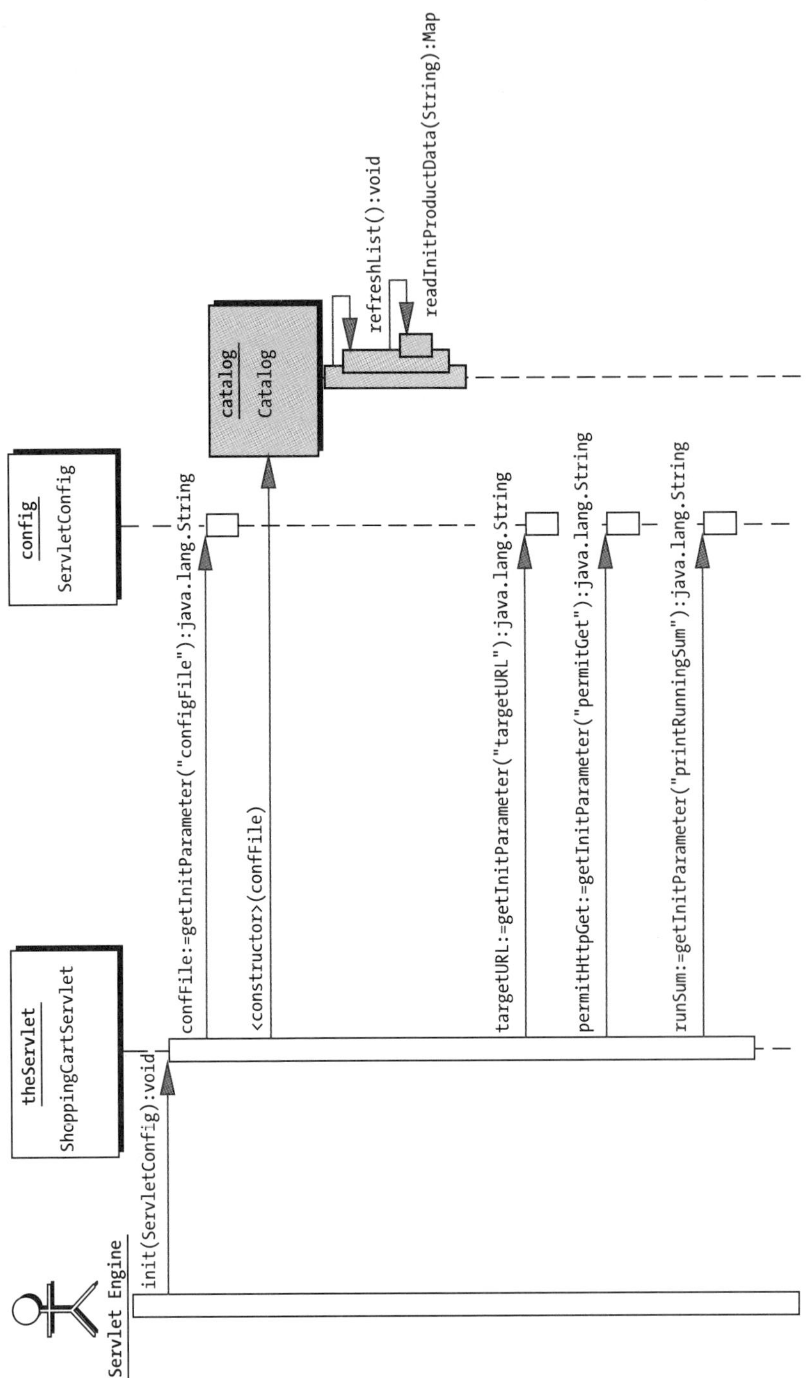

Figure 3-5. Simplified sequence diagram of the `init` *method. Type conversion method calls have been omitted from this diagram to illustrate the important method calls (that read configuration parameters) in the* `init` *method.*

It is perhaps simpler yet to take a look at the code for the `init` method, which appears in Listing 3-1.

Listing 3-1. The `init` *method of the* `ShoppingCartServlet`

```
package se.jguru.shopper;

import java.io.*;
import java.util.*;
import javax.servlet.*;
import javax.servlet.http.*;

/**
 * Class that implements a Shopping Cart servlet
 * which maps purchase details to users.
 *
 * @author Lennart Jörelid
 */
public class ShoppingCartServlet extends HttpServlet
{
    public static final String PRODUCTS_IN_CART = "products";
    private String targetURL;
    private Catalog catalog;
    private boolean permitHttpGet;
    private boolean printRunningSum;

    //
    // Initialize global variables from configuration parameters
    //
    public void init(ServletConfig config) throws ServletException
    {
        // Important! Call super.init to permit the servlet engine
        // to run its normal routines for init parameters.
        super.init(config);

        // Read all product data from
        // the configuration file
        String confFile = config.getInitParameter("configFile");
        if (confFile == null) confFile = "c:/AppServer/App/WebApp/WEB-INF/init.conf";
        this.catalog = new Catalog(confFile);
```

```
        // Define the target URL of the shopping form (i.e. the URL of this
        // servlet, where the HTTP POST call should terminate).
        String targetURL = config.getInitParameter("targetURL");
        if (targetURL == null) targetURL =
              "http://localhost/EShop/servlet/se.jguru.shopper.ShoppingCartServlet";
        this.targetURL = targetURL;

        // Should the HTTP GET method be permitted when running this servlet?
        String permitHttpGet = config.getInitParameter("permitGet");
        if (permitHttpGet == null) permitHttpGet = "false";
        this.permitHttpGet = permitHttpGet.equalsIgnoreCase("true") ? true : false;

        // Should the running sum be printed when listing the
        // contents of the ShoppingCart?
        String runSum = config.getInitParameter("printRunningSum");
        if (runSum == null) runSum = "true";
        this.printRunningSum = runSum.equalsIgnoreCase("true") ? true : false;
    }
...
```

Catalog Class

The `init` method contains all code reading initialization parameters and setting properties in the `ShoppingCartServlet` class, except the code that parses and interprets the flat file containing product data. The `readInitProductData` method of the `Catalog` class does the actual reading and parsing. The `readInitProductData` is invoked from the `Catalog` constructor. Take a look at the `Catalog` class in Listing 3-2.

Listing 3-2. The `Catalog` *class*

```
package se.jguru.shopper;

import java.util.Map;
import java.util.HashMap;
import java.util.Iterator;
import java.util.Collections;
import java.util.StringTokenizer;
import java.io.File;
import java.io.FileReader;
import java.io.BufferedReader;
import java.io.IOException;
```

```
/**
 * Catalog class which holds all available
 * Products in the online store.
 *
 * @author Lennart Jörelid
 * @stereotype container
 */
public class Catalog
{
    // The configuration file where all product data resides.
    private String configFile;

    // The Map containing all known products
    private Map allProducts;

    /**
     * Creates a new Product Catalog containing init data from
     * the provided configuration file.
     *
     * @param configFilePath Absolute path to the configuration file, containing
     *        product data on the form <product name>=<price>,<description>
     *        (i.e. Gevalia Coffee=120,Gevalia Dark Roast Coffee)
     */
    public Catalog(String configFilePath)
    {
        // Assign internal state
        this.configFile = configFilePath;

        // Refresh all products descriptions
        this.refreshList();
    }

    /**
     * Retrieves a product with the provided name from the
     * Map of all existing products - or null, should the
     * product not exist.
     */
```

```
public Product getProduct(String productName)
{
    for (Iterator it = this.allProducts.values().iterator(); it.hasNext(); )
    {
        Product current = (Product)it.next();
        if (current.getName().trim().equalsIgnoreCase(productName.trim()))
        {
            return current;
        }
    }

    // Found no matching products
    return null;
}

/** Simply retrieve all existing products */
public Map getProducts()
{
    return this.allProducts;
}

/**
 * Re-reads the allProducts Map using data from the provided configuration
 * file.
 */
public void refreshList()
{
    try
    {
        this.allProducts = this.readInitProductData(configFile);
    }
    catch (IOException ex)
    {
        System.out.println("[refreshList]: " + ex);
    }
}
```

```
/**
 * Reads product descriptions and price data from a file with the
 * provided path. Parses all configuration data and creates a HashMap
 * with the results. The HashMap contains entries of the following form:
 *
 * <pre>
 * Key          |  Value
 * -----------------------------------
 * Product name |  Product Object
 * </pre>
 *
 * <p><b>Note!</b> Should the product data or storage mode need to change
 * ("management wants the data read from a database..."), simply subclass
 * this class and override this method. The new readInitProductData(String ...)
 * method implements the new product data acquiring algorithm.</p>
 *
 * @return a Map with the parsed product data.
 */
protected Map readInitProductData(String configFilePath) throws IOException
{
    // Create the return HashMap
    HashMap data = new HashMap();

    // Connect the Reader to the product data file
    BufferedReader in = new BufferedReader(
        new FileReader(configFilePath));

    // Read all product data, which is of the form
    // productName=productPrice,productDescription
    String aReadLine = "";
    while ((aReadLine = in.readLine()) != null)
    {
        // Find the productName
        StringTokenizer tok = new StringTokenizer(aReadLine, "=", false);
        String productName = tok.nextToken();

        // Find the product data
        StringTokenizer dataTok =
                    new StringTokenizer(tok.nextToken(), ",", false);
        String productPrice = dataTok.nextToken();
        String productDescription = dataTok.nextToken();
```

```
            // Create the product holder object
            Product aProduct = new Product(
                        Integer.parseInt(productPrice),
                        productName,
                        productDescription
            );

            // Add the new product holder to the HashMap
            data.put(aProduct.getName(), aProduct);
        }
        return data;
    }

    /**
     * Returns a default HTML representation of all products in the catalog.
     * If the showPurchaseOption is true, each product is presented with
     * a checkbox and the option to order by clicking a Submit button.
     */
    public String toDefaultHTMLRepresentation(boolean showPurchaseOption)
    {
        // Create a table header
        StringBuffer toReturn = new StringBuffer("<table border=2>\n");
        toReturn.append("<tr><td><b>Product</b></td><td><b>Price</b></td><td>"
        + "<b>Description</b></td>");

       if (showPurchaseOption) toReturn.append("<td><b>Purchase</b></td></tr>\n");
       else
            toReturn.append("</tr>\n");

        // Append each product to the table
        for (Iterator it = this.allProducts.values().iterator(); it.hasNext(); )
        {
            Product current = (Product)it.next();
            toReturn.append("<tr><td>" + current.getName() + "</td><td>"
           + current.getPrice() + "</td><td>" + current.getDescription() + "</td>");

            if (showPurchaseOption)
            {
                toReturn.append("<td><input type=\"checkbox\" "
                + "name=\"product\" value=\""
                + current.getName() + "\"></td></tr>\n");
            }
            else
                toReturn.append("</tr>\n");
        }
```

```
        // Append the last, static part of the table.
        if (showPurchaseOption) toReturn.append("<tr><td colspan=4 "
                + "align=\"right\"><input type=\"submit\" value=\""
                + "Purchase !\"> </td></tr></table>");
        else
            toReturn.append("</table>");

        // Done.
        return toReturn.toString();
    }
}
```

The main portion of the `readInitProductData` method consists of basic splicing and parsing of a structured text file. The `StringTokenizer` from the `java.util` package is a good tool for splicing a stream into tokens (words) and delivering one token at a time to the caller.

Thus, the `init` method reads the four following configuration parameters:

- `targetURL`
- `configFile`
- `permitHttpGet`
- `printRunningSum`

One of which (`configFile`) is the path to the flat file containing the catalog data. All product descriptions are then read from this file, and `Product` instances are created and added to the resulting `HashMap`. The servlet is now set up for normal operation, which is achieved by calling it from a Web browser using either of the HTTP GET or HTTP POST commands.

doGet and doPost Methods

Now take a look at the `ShoppingCartServlet` itself. The execution of the `doGet` and `doPost` methods is pretty straightforward; the `doPost` method sends back a result to the client browser, but the `doGet` only does so if the `permitHttpGet` parameter is set to true. This allows for separate behavior during development and production; it is frequently a good idea to permit HTTP GET and POST during development but only HTTP POST during deployment.

There are two main reasons:

- All transmitted parameters must be encoded in the URL of a HTTP GET request. Because the maximum supported length of a URL is limited to 1,024 bytes, large parameters cannot be sent with HTTP GET. When using the POST method, all parameters are enclosed in the HTTP header section, permitting bigger arguments.

- Transmitted parameters are hidden from the user when POST is used. Thus, a user cannot manipulate transmitted parameters or bookmark a particular page when using the POST method. This behavior is preferred when manipulating semi-secure resources such as electronic commerce information, credit card numbers, and so on.

Alas, HTTP POST has the benefit of permitting longer parameter values than HTTP GET, as well as hiding those parameters from the user. Therefore, HTTP POST is the preferred way of connecting to a Web resource in distributed commerce applications. Listing 3-3 contains a `doGet` method snippet, which returns an HTTP error code if the servlet received an HTTP GET request.

> **CAUTION** *For a complete list of all the status code constants in HTTP, see the Request For Comment (RFC) specification of HTTP/1.1 at* `ftp://ftp.isi.edu/in-notes/rfc2616.txt`*, or check the symbolic constants of class* `HttpServletResponse`.

Listing 3-3. The `doGet` *returns a HTTP* `FORBIDDEN` *response unless the internal parameter* `permitHttpGet` *is true.*

```
/**
 * This servlet should not be called using the GET method.
 * Serve a standard "Forbidden" response.
 */
public void doGet(HttpServletRequest request, HttpServletResponse response)
throws ServletException, IOException
{
   // Should the GET method be permitted to execute normally?
   if(! this.permitHttpGet)
   {
       response.sendError(HttpServletResponse.SC_FORBIDDEN,
          "The product servlet cannot be contacted using HTTP GET.");
       return;
   }
```

```
        // GET method permitted
        doPost(request, response);
    }
```

Note that the second argument of the sendError method may not be presented to the browser user, as browsers display the result of error codes in an implementation-dependent way. Also, servers may transmit the error page in a custom way. For example, the default error message view rendered in Internet Explorer from the Tomcat reference implementation looks quite different from the default error view of the Orion Application Server (OAS).

Figure 3-6 shows the doGet method results. Note that the browser ignores our custom error message "The shopping cart servlet cannot be contacted using HTTP GET," and instead displays the generic Web server message, "You are not authorized to view this page."

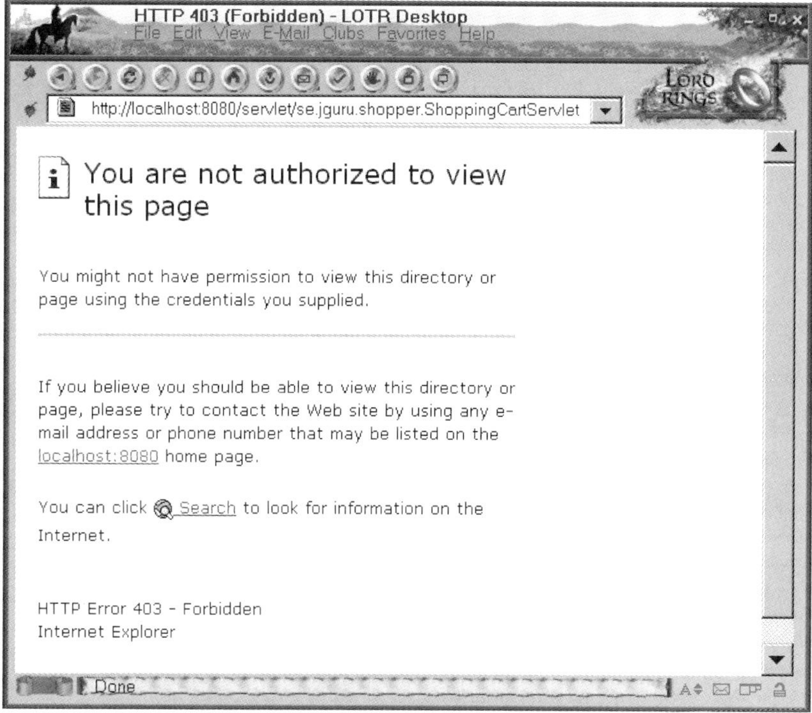

Figure 3-6. The error page generated by the Tomcat reference implementation presented by a browser after receiving the SC_FORBIDDEN *status message*

Other application servers may deliver another type of error message back to the client browser. The OAS, for instance, delivers the error message in a different form than the Tomcat reference implementation server. Figure 3-7 shows the output of the OAS.

Figure 3-7. The HTML output result of sending the forbidden status message. This time, the OAS is used, instead of the Tomcat reference implementation.

The `doPost` method, on the other hand, is the method called by the Web server when the shopping cart servlet runs in normal operation mode. The majority of the servlet code handles the request for placing a new item in the shopping cart. Figure 3-8 presents the `doPost` method.

The `doPost` method in the shopping cart servlet is a call hub, delegating its main work to private methods in the class, as well as public methods of other classes. Using this technique is generally a good idea because it prevents huge `doPost` method bodies and increases code reuse. Thus, the process flow of the `doPost` method implementation is as follows:

1. Create an empty `ShoppingCart` instance if the user session is new. Then bind the new `ShoppingCart` to the session.

2. Get shopping cart contents and add to it the products that the user transmitted as `HttpRequest` parameters.

3. Get and print the HTML representation of the catalog by calling its public method `getDefaultHTMLRepresentation()`.

4. Create the HTML that will present all items in the shopping cart by calling the `getDefaultHTMLRepresentation()` method in the `ShoppingCart` class.

5. Rebind the `ShoppingCart` to the session.

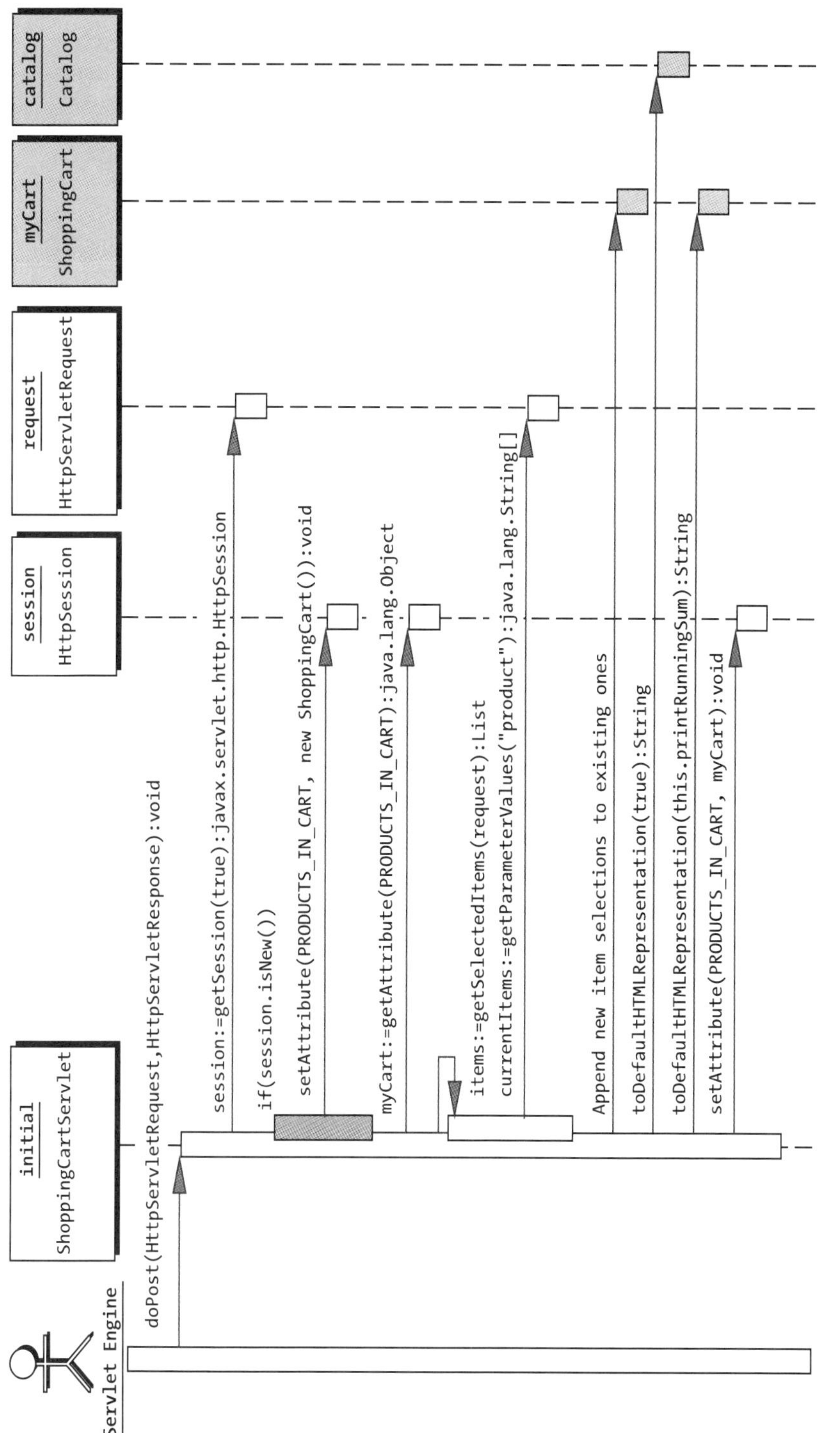

Figure 3-8. Simplified sequence diagram of the `doPost` *method call in the* `ShoppingCartServlet`

Listing 3-4 contains the code for the `doPost` method. Note that the numbers from the process flow list are marked in the comments in the code to make the code easier to follow.

Listing 3-4. The `doPost` *method*

```
/** Main servlet method, which handles the purchasing of products. */
public void doPost(HttpServletRequest request, HttpServletResponse response)
    throws ServletException, IOException
{
    // Get the output stream to write back data to the client
    PrintWriter out = response.getWriter();
    response.setContentType("text/html");

    // Output the initial html
    out.println("<html><head><title>Product shop</title></head>");
    out.println("<body><center><h1>Items available for purchase</h1>");
    out.println("<hr width=50%>");

    // ### 1) Get the session object of this user, or
    //        create one if the call is new.
    HttpSession session = request.getSession(true);
    if (session.isNew())
    {
        // Old-style putValue method should be substituted for the
        // setAttribute if running an older Servlet engine.
        //
        // session.putValue(PRODUCTS_IN_CART, new ShoppingCart());
        session.setAttribute(PRODUCTS_IN_CART,
            new ShoppingCart());
    }

    // ### 2) Check input parameters to identify new orders placed with
    //        the incoming HttpServletRequest.

    // Old-style getValue method should be substituted for the
    // getAttribute method if running an older Servlet engine.
    //
    // ShoppingCart myCatalog = (ShoppingCart)
    //    session.getValue(PRODUCTS_IN_CART);
    ShoppingCart myCart = (ShoppingCart)
       session.getAttribute(PRODUCTS_IN_CART);
    List items = this.getSelectedItems(request);
```

```
        for (int i = 0; i < items.size(); i++)
        {
            Product current = (Product)items.get(i);
            myCart.addProduct(current);
        }

        // ### 3) Create the HTML order form used to place additional orders.
        String firstPart = "<form action=\"" + this.targetURL
                + "\" method=POST >";
        out.println(firstPart
                + this.catalog.toDefaultHTMLRepresentation(true) + "</form>");

        // ### 4) Printout the current contents of the cart
        out.println("<hr width=\"50%\"><h1>Items currently "
                + "in shopping cart</h1>");
        out.println(myCart.toDefaultHTMLRepresentation(this.printRunningSum));

        // ### 5) Bind the modified cart to the session
        session.setAttribute(PRODUCTS_IN_CART, myCart);

        // Close off the page
        out.println("</center></html>");
    }
```

The Flyweight Pattern

The work of the `ShoppingCartServlet` is shared between the servlet itself and its two helper objects (the `ShoppingCart` and the `Catalog` instance). The `ShoppingCart` uses the flyweight pattern on the catalog (see, for instance, *Design Patterns* by Gamma et. al. for a thorough explanation of the flyweight pattern) to map products from the catalog to those ordered by the client. The flyweight pattern can be used because the products ordered are identical to products in stock. For each selected item, the client contains a reference to a product within the catalog. Figure 3-9 shows a sample flyweight pattern.

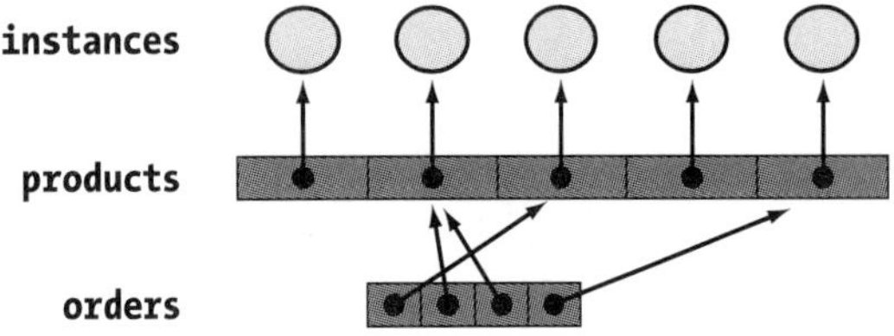

Figure 3-9. The flyweight pattern illustrated by the `orders` *collection has four references but only uses three instances from the* `products` *collection. Therefore, the memory requirements of the* `orders` *array are reduced.*

The Flyweight Pattern

Use the flyweight pattern when collections contain a large amount of identical objects. Instead of instantiating a large amount of identical template instances, create only one template instance per state and permit the collection to create multiple links to each template instance.

For instance, a word processor uses a multitude of letters to create a document. All instances of the letter *f* looks up the same font properties in the same font specification. Should each letter *f* instance create its own set of font properties, the resulting document would consume much more memory.

The `ShoppingCart` contains the individual state for each user and must therefore be bound to the `HttpSession`. The catalog instance contains all known products; instead of letting each entry in the `ShoppingCart` be a `Product` instance of its own, the flyweight pattern is used to store references. This saves much space and execution time because the number of instances required per system is greatly reduced. Note, however, that this model assumes no clients will ever be able to modify product data or delete products from the catalog.

Listing 3-5 contains the source code for the `ShoppingCart` class.

Listing 3-5. The `ShoppingCart` *class*

```
package se.jguru.shopper;

import java.util.List;
import java.util.Iterator;
import java.util.ArrayList;
import java.util.Collections;
```

```
/**
 * List wrapper containing all products held by a
 * customer shopping on our site.
 *
 * @stereotype container
 */
public class ShoppingCart
{
    // All products currently held
    private List myProducts;

    /**
     * Creates a new ShoppingCart by initializing
     * its internal state.
     */
    public ShoppingCart()
    {
        this.myProducts = Collections.synchronizedList(
            new ArrayList());
    }

    /**
     * Adds an existing Product to the list of selected
     * items in this ShoppintCart.
     *
     * @param aNewProduct the Product to add.
     */
    public void addProduct(Product aNewProduct)
    {
        this.myProducts.add(aNewProduct);
    }

    /**
     * Creates and adds an new Product to the list of selected
     * items in this ShoppintCart.
     *
     * @param aNewProduct the Product to add.
     */
   public void addProduct(String productName, String productDescription, int price)
    {
        this.myProducts.add(
            new Product(price, productName, productDescription));
    }
```

```
/**
 * Retrieves a List containing all Products currently
 * selected in this ShoppingCart.
 */
public List getProducts()
{
    return this.myProducts;
}

/**
 * Returns the default HTML representation of this ShoppingCart,
 * This representation should be used only if the caller needs
 * no custom representation of the items in this ShoppingCart.
 * If so, the getProducts method should be used to retrieve a
 * List of all existing products. The caller may then format
 * its resulting output in a customized way.
 *
 * @param printRunningSum indicates wether or not the running
 *        sum should be printed in the default HTML representation.
 *
 * @return A HTML table with the contents of this ShoppingCart.
 */
public String toDefaultHTMLRepresentation(boolean printRunningSum)
{
    int currentPrice = 0;

    // Define the StringBuffer which will be populated with the
    // default HTML representation of this ShoppingCart.
   StringBuffer buf =new StringBuffer("<table border=2><tr><td>"
          + "<b>Item</b></td><td><b>Price</b></td>");
    if (printRunningSum) buf.append("<td><b>Running sum</b></td>");
    buf.append("<td><b>Description</b></td></tr>");

    for (Iterator it = this.myProducts.iterator(); it.hasNext(); )
    {
        // Get the current product
        Product current = (Product)it.next();

        // Add the Product's price to the currentPrice counter.
        currentPrice += current.getPrice();
```

```
            // Produce an HTML table row with the current product data
            buf.append("<tr><td>" + current.getName() + "</td><td>"
            + current.getPrice() + "</td>");

            // Should the running sum be printed?
            if (printRunningSum) buf.append("<td>" + currentPrice + "</td>");

            // Finish off the table row
            buf.append("<td>" + current.getDescription() + "</td></tr>");
        }

        // Finally, print the total price
        buf.append("<tr><td><b>Total price:</b></td><td><b>"
                + currentPrice + "</b></td></tr>");

        // Finish the table
        buf.append("</table>");

        return buf.toString();
    }
}
```

getSelectedItems Method

After taking a look at the `ShoppingCart` and `Catalog` classes, as well as the `init`, `doGet`, and `doPost` methods of the `ShoppingCartServlet`, the only remaining method to complete the example walkthrough is the `getSelectedItems` method in the `ShoppingCartServlet` class. The purpose of the `getSelectedItems` method is to parse the incoming `HttpServletRequest` and generate a list containing all items selected by the user.

The code for `getSelectedItems` is fairly simple; read the parameters, parse the values, and use the results to create a product. See Listing 3-6.

Listing 3-6. The `getSelectedItems` *method*

```
    /**
     * Creates a List containing all Products corresponding to the
     * user's selections.
     */
    private synchronized List getSelectedItems(HttpServletRequest req)
    {
        // Declare return value
        List toReturn = new ArrayList();
```

```
        // Get the current orders
        String[] currentItems = req.getParameterValues("product");
        if (currentItems == null) return toReturn;

        // Find the selected item from the browser client
        for (int i = 0; i < currentItems.length; i++)
        {
            // Handle the new order - i.e. add it to the currentOrderList
            Product currentProduct = catalog.getProduct(currentItems[i]);
            if (currentProduct == null)
            {
                // This should really not happen, unless we have misconfigured
                // the system. Simply skip any processing of the null Product.
                continue;
            }

            // Found a real product. Add to the return list
            toReturn.add(currentProduct);
        }

        return toReturn;
    }
```

Again, the code for `getSelectedItems` is fairly simple. The most complex parts are the frequent comparisons of string constants. Should the list of products be very large, this code may prove to be rather inefficient.

> **NOTE** *Currently, only one item at a time is selected in the* `ShoppingCartServlet`. *Try extending the servlet to provide functionality to select an arbitrary number of products. Why not add 12 products of one type and three of another?*

Deploying the ShoppingCartServlet Code into a J2EE-Compliant Servlet Container

You have now investigated all parts of Figure 3-8. The only thing remaining is the deployment of the `ShoppingCartServlet` within a servlet container. Generally, the deployment of Web applications—the active documents of which are servlets and JavaServer Pages (JSP) documents—is fairly simple; the only problems arise when complex filtering is required.

The Web application in Figure 3-10 consists of the required servlet classes and a configuration file, named `web.xml`. You should place the files in a structure complying with the J2EE specification, where the root catalog can be named arbitrarily but the other catalogs follow a specific structure.

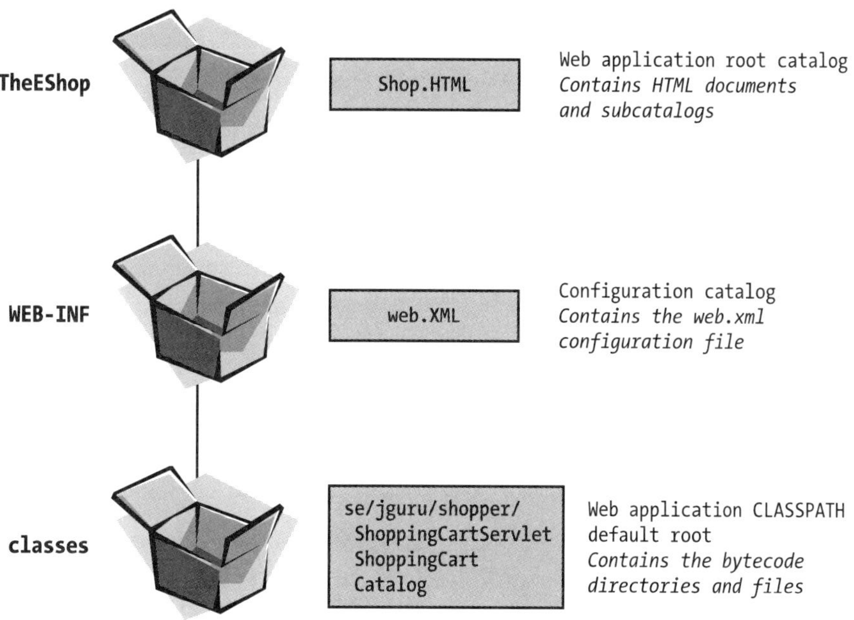

Figure 3-10. The structure of a J2EE Web application

Shown in Figure 3-10, the normal Web site file structure originates from the Web application root catalog. The `WEB-INF` subdirectory contains the configuration file `web.xml`, which defines the behavior of the Web application, as well as the classes subdirectory where unpacked bytecode files are placed. Assuming that the start page of the Web application is called `Shop.html`, Figure 3-10 contains all parts of the Web application.

The contents of the `web.xml` configuration file define the deployment descriptor of the small Web application. The structured XML document specifies the configuration settings of the current Web application (see Listing 3-7).

Listing 3-7. The `web.xml` configuration file

```
  <?xml version="1.0"?>
  <!DOCTYPE web-app PUBLIC
1    "-//Sun Microsystems, Inc.//DTD Web Application 2.3//EN"
     "http://java.sun.com/j2ee/dtds/web-app_2_3.dtd">

  <web-app>
2     <display-name>shop</display-name>
      <description>E-shop example</description>
      <servlet>
          <servlet-name>eShopServlet</servlet-name>
          <display-name>eShopServlet</display-name>
          <description>The shopping cart servlet</description>
          <servlet-class>se.jguru.shopper.ShoppingCartServlet</servlet-class>
          <init-param>
              <param-name>targetURL</param-name>
3             <param-value>http://localhost/EShop/eShopServlet</param-value>
          </init-param>
          <init-param>
              <param-name>configFile</param-name>
              <param-value>
                  /Program/Configurations/TheEShop/products.conf
              </param-value>
          </init-param>
      </servlet>
      <servlet-mapping>
          <servlet-name>eShopServlet</servlet-name>
4         <url-pattern>/eShopServlet</url-pattern>
      </servlet-mapping>
      <welcome-file-list>
5         <welcome-file>Shop.html</welcome-file>
      </welcome-file-list>
      <login-config>
          <auth-method>BASIC</auth-method>
6         <realm-name>default</realm-name>
      </login-config>
  </web-app>
```

The different parts of the `web.xml` file provide deployment information for different aspects of the Web application.

1. The first part of the `web.xml` file specifies its own document type definition (DTD) version. This part is not to be modified and may therefore simply be copied from configuration file to configuration file. Thus, when you want to deploy a Web application in your particular application or Web server, copy a `web.xml` file from an existing Web application and modify it to suit your needs.

2. The description settings for the Web application itself are usually shown in the deployment tool of the application server in which you are deploying your Web application. Figure 3-11 shows an example of a graphical user interface (GUI) assembler. Note the name and description in the figure's right pane.

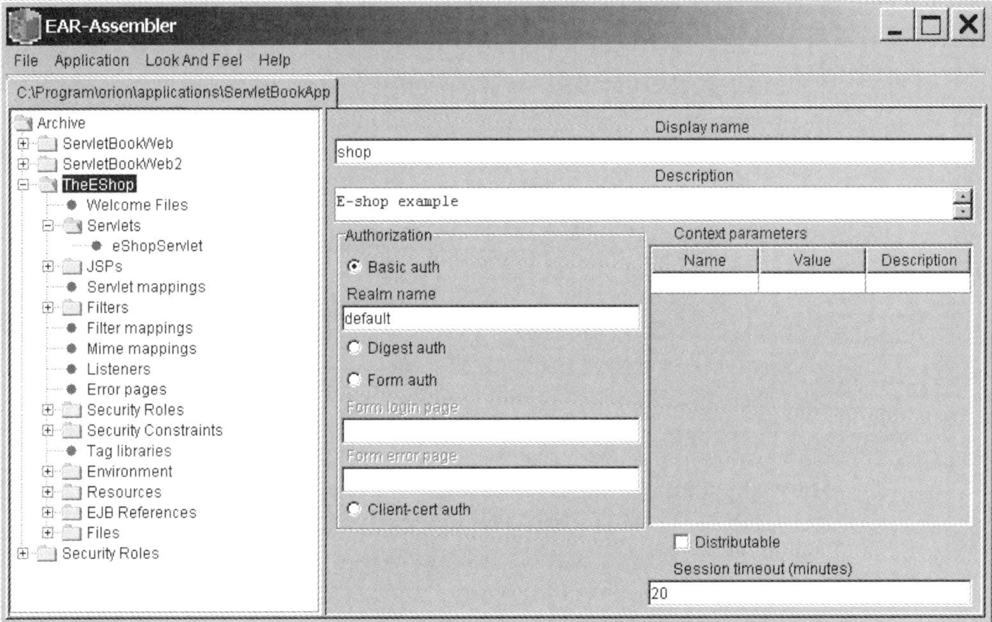

Figure 3-11. GUI administration screen of the OAS. Note the display name and description of TheEShop Web application.

The elements shown in Figure 3-11 define a set of Web applications; studying the selected Web application TheEShop, you can distinguish the graphical representations of the XML elements in the deployment descriptor from Listing 3-7. For instance, the selected pane shows the Description and Display Name properties, found in section (2) of Listing 3-7.

3. The servlet definition section of the Web-app container creates a servlet definition within the application server. Note that the `eShopServlet` servlet is mapped to the servlet class `se.jguru.shopper.ShoppingCartServlet`. Also, the initialization parameters are defined within the `<init-param>` containers.

4. The servlet-mapping container defines the URL within the Web application where the servlet should be exposed. In this case, the path `/eShopServlet` should be mapped to the `se.jguru.shopper.ShoppingCartServlet` class. Thus, when calling `http://<webserver>/<webApplicationName>/eShopServlet`, the servlet is invoked.

5. The welcome file list defines which files should be looked for in a directory if a specific file is not provided. Normally, the welcome-file entry contains `index.html`—this file is normally served when a URL terminates in a directory.
6. The login configuration defines the type of authorization required to log on to the application. In this case, no resources have been protected, so the authorization entry will not be used.

The Web application structure may now be packaged into a Web archive (`.war`) file that can be moved and deployed into an arbitrary Web application server. Although the WAR file follows the strict J2EE specification, the tools modifying the `web.xml` deployment descriptor in the WAR file are implementation dependent for each Web application server.

Thankfully, the deployment tools of most application servers are fairly straightforward to understand and manage.

Reflections on the Shopping Cart Servlet

Although it is a nice example, the shopping cart servlet has the following built-in disadvantages that make it unsuitable for industrial-strength deployment within an application system:

- **The application view and model are combined in a compilation unit**. In plain English: All the HTML is hard-coded within the servlet and its helper classes. Should the look and feel of the Web site change, most or all classes would require recoding and recompilation. This is a cumbersome operation even if the Web site is quite small. There are (at least) two possible solutions:
    - **Let the servlet read the HTML from files residing in the file system.** To change the HTML view, you would then need only to change the content of these include files without recompiling the servlets. In reality, this option poses a number of difficulties, however, and the result is barely more flexible than the first option.
    - **Recode the servlet into a JSP file,** which preserves the structure of the HTML view intact and *automatically* recompiles whenever its source changes. (Chapter 4 covers JSP.)
- **Usually, item data is kept within a database of some sort**. In general, the massive amounts of data kept in memory when caching an entire product database chews up too much valuable run-time memory on the Web server. Thus, in most live cases, the product database would be called at least once per servlet request. As the number of products and concurrent users grow, the small and simple servlet application scales poorly. There are (at least) two possible scaling solutions:

- **Cluster your Web servers to face the increasing memory demand.** This approach creates coordination problems, as internal servlet data must be shared between two (or more) different Web server JVMs. Figure 3-12 illustrates the classic problem of how to share the user's session across multiple Web servers.

  Unless the developer handles immediate propagation of information between the different Web servers (which is tricky at best), the user may be presented with different carts for each subsequent call. Thus, when a user calls one servlet to order a few goods, all other Web servers must immediately be notified of the change.

  Luckily, whenever an object is bound to the `HttpSession` of a user, an `HttpSessionBindingEvent` is generated. If a registered `HttpSessionBindingListener` exists, its `valueBound` and `valueUnbound` methods are invoked, depending on the type of event generated. Thus, within the method body of a registered `HttpSessionBindingListener`, you can notify all other Web servers of the status change of the user. Implementing this call structure may be complex, and it generates many network calls between the Web servers.

- **Use an enterprise JavaBeans (EJB) server that contains all the user and item data.** This is, by far, the better alternative. For a primer to EJB technology, refer to the EJB tutorial included in the J2EE distribution, and the pet store example on JavaSoft's Web site (`www.javasoft.com`).

As shown in Figure 3-12, the `HttpSessions` of two Web servers are not shared. Therefore, when the switch directs the second request to another Web server than the original, a new `ShoppingCart` instance is generated and bound to the `HttpSession` of the second servlet engine. The result is extremely confusing to the user; all of a sudden, the server has forgotten all his orders.

Extensions to the ShoppingCartServlet Class

That completes the shopping cart servlet example. To build on what's been covered in this chapter thus far, you might want to extend the `ShoppingCartServlet` to accommodate your own functionality. Feel free to download its code from `http://www.jguru.se/servletbook/`. Some suggestions for extensions to the small system include:

- Extend the code to accommodate for deletions of items currently within the shopping cart.
- Include a HTML start page (such as the one shown in Figure 3-13) to provide an entry point to the small application. Otherwise, no Web browser may access the `ShoppingCartServlet` when deployed with the `permitHttpGet` option switched off.

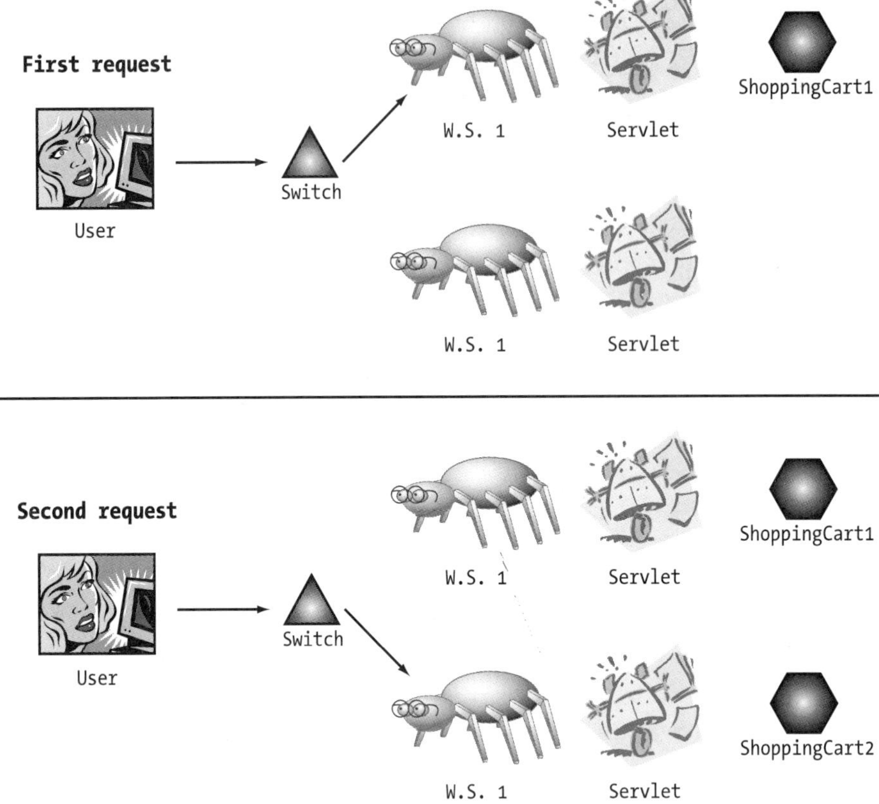

Figure 3-12. Simple call scenario illustrating two subsequent requests to a site running parallel Web servers, each running a separate instance of the `ShoppingCartServlet` *(denoted as "Servlet" in the image).*

Figure 3-13. Simple entry page to the `ShoppingCartServlet`*. When pressing the button, the* `ShoppingCartServlet` *should be invoked.*

The Servlet Mediator (HTTP Tunneling Servlet)

Many fully functional back-end applications use streams to communicate with callers. Capturing the output of such streams and relaying the content to the user is a perfect job for a servlet. In fact, the task of most servlets resembles a primitive switchboard, relaying communications from a client to a back-end server and vice versa. In this role, the servlet acts as a mediator between the (user) client and the back-end server application.

Background: A Rather Infuriating Situation

Being a consultant, I have many times found myself at a client site where a massive firewall has made it impossible to access my own mail server connected to the public Internet (see Figure 3-14). In such companies, few security officials would allow an employee or consultant direct Internet access—in fact, the job of the data security officer includes being able to say "no" in a nice enough manner to all such requests. The security officer then informs me that conversation using HTTP on ports 80 and 443 (for HTTPS) is free and open throughout the company. Not wanting to use Post Office Protocol (POP) and a phone modem to download all my mail from halfway around the world, the mail could remain unread for quite some time.

Firewalls

Although I *could* acquire a temporary email address on a free Web mail site, such as Hotmail, I prefer not to do this. Most corporations tend to be rather restrictive with respect to storing business email, potentially containing sensitive information, on a mail server outside of their own control. In general, firewalls restrict access to user services running on specified ports and/or communicating with specified protocols.

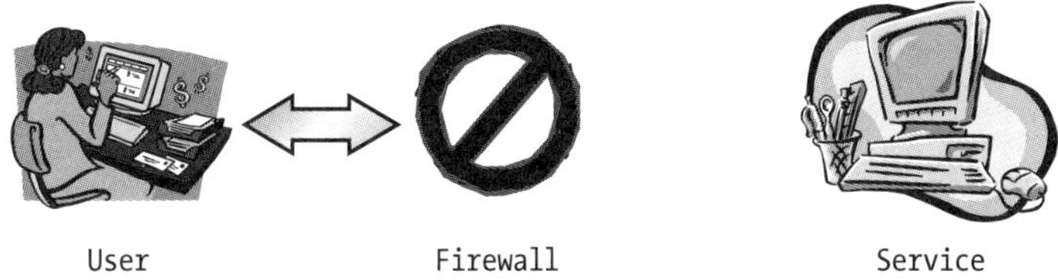

Figure 3-14. Firewall restricting user access to a service residing on the other side

Some firewalls block everything not sent as HTTP or HTTPS and that does not have the proper MIME content type identifying it as text, HTML, or images. In such a case, you could not even create an application that could communicate to the service if the service could not listen to the standard ports for the HTTP or HTTPS protocols.

In this situation, servlets may come to the rescue quickly and nicely because a servlet can tunnel commands from a Web browser to a remote process and present the results on a Web page, submitted over HTTPS (or even HTTP, for the brave and non-paranoid). This is commonly referred to as *HTTP tunneling* or *firewall tunneling* (see Figure 3-15).

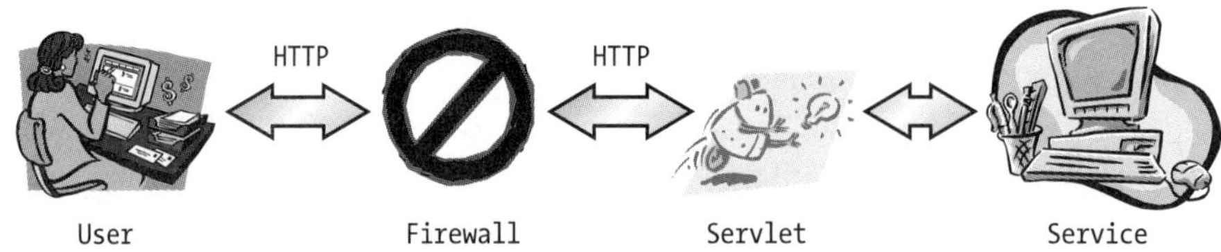

Figure 3-15. A servlet running on the Web server outside of the firewall tunnels the service communication over the HTTP protocol.

The servlet opens a new process or, alternatively, a stream connection to an existing service process running somewhere on a back-end node. Provided that the data going back and forth between the user and the service is text-oriented (such as is the case when talking to a shell), you could quite simply tunnel a service conversation over HTTP/HTML (see Figure 3-16).

Class Structure of the HTTP Tunneling Servlet

The structure of the `ExternalIntegration` servlet and support classes contains only a handful of classes, as shown in Figure 3-16. The primary classes and their respective tasks within the system are as follows:

- **ExternalIntegration**: The servlet class that accepts a request from the browser client containing a text command to the active process. It sends the command to the process and retrieves the result. It also formats the result as HTML and sends it out to the client.

- **ProcessCommunicator**: The class holding an instance of a running operative system process, as well as three streams for communicating with it. The out `PrintWriter` sends commands to the running process, and the `NonblockingStreams` reads input from the input and error streams.

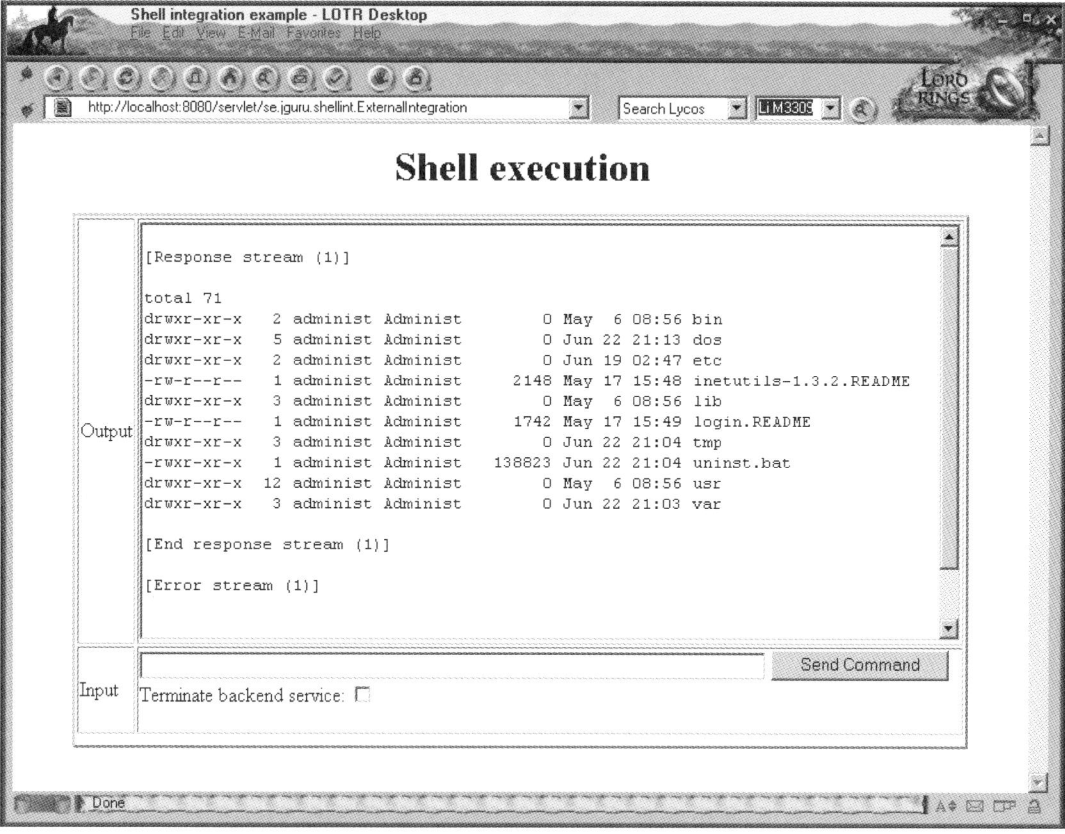

Figure 3-16. Resulting output of tunneling a bash shell over HTTP

- **NonblockingStream**: Thread class that continuously reads data from a blocking I/O stream to a `StringBuffer`, the content of which can be extracted by another thread using the `getResult` method. When no data is available from the underlying stream, the `NonblockingStream` reader thread simply halts, waiting for more data to become available.

- **Logger**: A simple interface to unify all logging within the small system.

The principal difficulty with this small system is that the back-end process cannot be closed between calls, thus creating a need for the servlet to keep the process running and its communication streams open. To this end, you need to develop a mechanism that reads data from a stream as data becomes available. However, all Java I/O streams are *blocking*, which means that the thread reading data from a stream will read all data available in the stream—and then wait until more data becomes available in the stream before continuing. Investigate this more closely by examining a simplified version of the states that the `InputStream` `read` method passes when reading data.

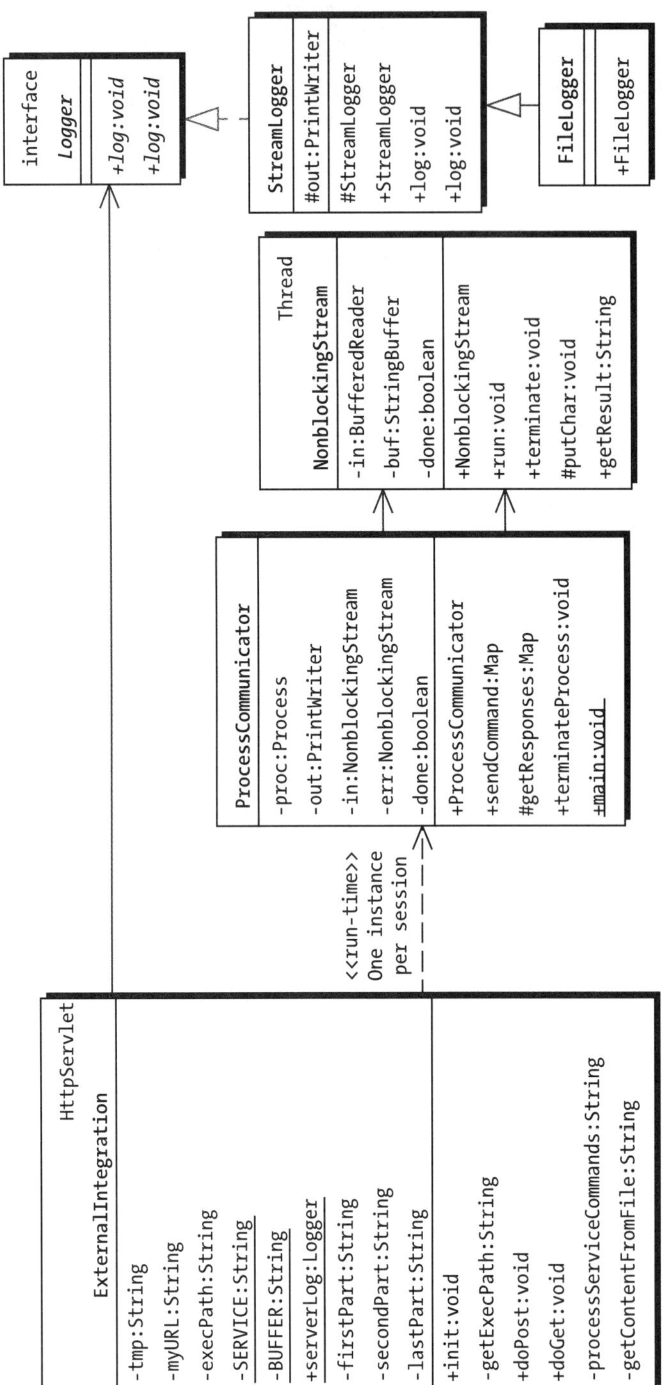

Figure 3-17. Relations of the classes in the `ExternalIntegration` *servlet example. Note that each* `ExternalIntegration` *servlet holds a* `ProcessCommunicator` *instance in its* `HttpSession`*. Therefore, all users communicate with their own process.*

The Blocking I/O Story

When an InputStream subclass reads data using any readXXX method, the real workhorse method is ultimately a read method obtaining one single byte from the stream. The workhorse method is then called repeatedly to build up more complex response types, such as the readLine method of the BufferedReader class or the various read methods of the DataInputStream class. If no data is available on the InputStream, the thread executing the read call waits for more data to become available from the stream before continuing. This is known as *blocking I/O*, as opposed to non-blocking or asynchronous I/O methods, which would simply return a value indicating that no data was currently available on the stream. If your program uses blocking I/O calls, you must take care to avoid having your program "get stuck" waiting for data to become available on a stream.

However, no non-blocking stream classes exist in the Java class libraries. In fact, the situation is far worse because there is no simple way of detecting that a stream is in a blocked state. (There is no isBlocked() method in the java.io.InputStream.) Furthermore, there is no way of detecting that a stream enters a blocked state—no event or exception is generated by the read() method as an indication of the stream state change.

These two characteristics of Java streams pose a bit of a problem for the servlet application because you cannot detect that all output from a given process command has been received. Figure 3-17 illustrates the problem with non-detectable, blocking I/O.

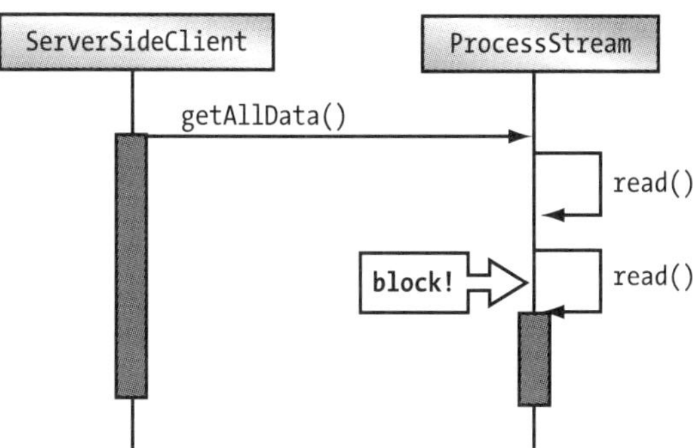

Figure 3-18. The problem with blocking I/O. The arrows indicate the method calls of a single thread. When the thread calls the read *method for the second time, the stream blocks. No data is returned to the* ServerSideClient *because the* ProcessStream *is never closed—it remains open until the process with which it communicates exits.*

A client (or servlet) tries to read data from the stream connected to the back-end process. After a few read operations complete successfully, the stream buffer is empty. Thus, the next call to `read()` blocks the stream, making the `read()` method wait for new data to arrive. Unfortunately, you cannot detect that a Java thread is blocked or is about to perform a blocking method call. Thus, the `getAllData()` method will inevitably hang. Should you implement the servlet as indicated in Figure 3-17, the call to `getAllData()` will never return until the `ProcessStream` is closed. The result is that you cannot see any output from the servlet; it appears frozen until its `ProcessCommunicator` is garbage-collected. If our back-end process is to preserve state between calls, the `ProcessCommunicator` cannot be garbage-collected, and the client browser will receive no output.

An alternative strategy is required to handle the situation. One simple option is to create a new thread that listens to each blocking I/O stream. Thus, one thread will listen to the stream and perpetually copy incoming data to a shared buffer. The main thread will read data from that buffer, thus never calling the `read()` method in the `ProcessStream`. Listing 3-8 highlights the statements granting this functionality.

Figure 3-19 shows the structure of the `NonblockingStream` class. The `ProcessStream` object encapsulates the output stream of another process. Note that the main thread call from the `ServerSideClient` instance does not need to communicate with the `ProcessStream`; it may return an empty `StringBuffer`, but it will never freeze in a deadlock situation.

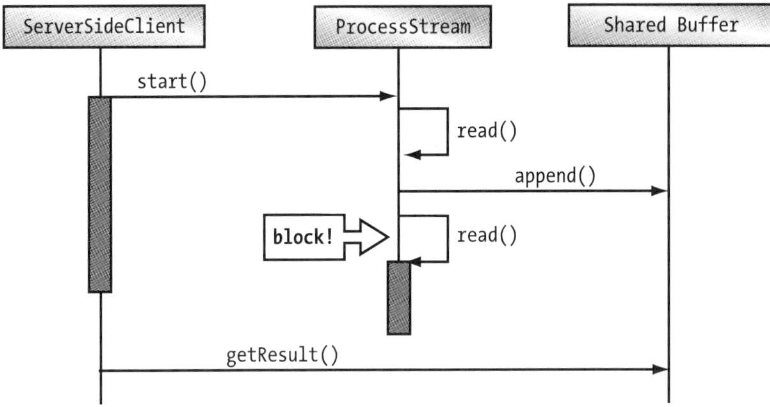

Figure 3-19. A better alternative for reading data from an open stream using blocking I/O using two separate threads. Thread 1 reads data from the stream and writes it to a shared buffer. Thread 2 reads data only from the shared buffer.

Listing 3-8. The `NonblockingStream` *class*

```
/*
 * Copyright (c) 2000 jGuru.se
 * All rights reserved.
 */

package se.jguru.shellint;

import java.io.*;
import java.util.*;

/**
 * Class to convert a normal, blocking IO stream into a
 * non-blocking stream used for continuous reading. This
 * is especially useful when reading from a stream connected
 * to an open network socket or process.
 *
 * Usage:
 * <pre>
 *     // Create the NonblockingStream from some existing stream
 *     InputStream aStream = ...
 *     NonblockingStream nbs = new NonblockingStream(aStream);
 *
 *     // Start the listening
 *     nbs.start();
 *
 *     // Send a command to the process, to which nbs
 *     // is attached through its underlying stream.
 *     ...
 *
 *     // Wait for the command to execute in the process
 *     // and for the results to be sent to nbs.
 *     Thread.sleep(500);
 *
 *     // Read the response from nbs
 *     String response = nbs.getResult();
 * </pre>
 *
 * @author Lennart Jörelid
 */
```

```
public class NonblockingStream extends Thread
{
    // Internal state
    private BufferedReader in;
    private StringBuffer buf;
    private boolean done;

    /**
     * Creates a NonblockingStream from the underlying (blocking)
     * InputStream.
     *
     * @param in the underlying blocking stream.
     */
    public NonblockingStream(InputStream in)
    {
        // The InputStream cannot be null
        if (in == null) throw new NullPointerException(
                "Cannot handle null InputStream");

        // Assign internal state
        this.in = new BufferedReader(new InputStreamReader(in));
        this.buf = new StringBuffer();
        this.done = false;
    }

    public void run()
    {
        try
        {
            // Log
            ExternalIntegration.serverLog.log("[NonblockingStream (" +
                        getName() + ") run]: Entering listen loop.");

            // This section realizes the stream reading functionality;
            // this thread (i.e. Thread.currentThread()) copies all incoming
            // characters from the stream to the shared (string)buffer buf
            // using the internal call putChar.
            while (!done)
            {
                // Read a character from the stream
                int readCharacter = in.read();
                this.putChar((char)readCharacter);
            }
        }
```

```
    catch (IOException ex)
    {
        // Log
        ExternalIntegration.serverLog.log("[NonblockingStream ("
                    + getName() + ") run]: " + ex);
    }

    // Log
    ExternalIntegration.serverLog.log("[NonblockingStream ("
                + getName() + ") run]: Closing stream.");

    try
    {
        // Kill the stream
        in.close();
    }
    catch (Exception ex)
    {
        // Log
        ExternalIntegration.serverLog.log("[NonblockingStream ("
                    + getName() + ") run]: "
                    + "Exception in closing stream: " + ex);
    }
}

/**
 * Schedules this NonblockingStream for
 * termination, which will stop this Thread
 * and close the underlying input stream.
 */
public void terminate()
{
    // Log terminate event to the standard stream
    ExternalIntegration.serverLog.log("[NonblockingStream ("
            + getName() + ") terminate]: Setting terminate flag.");

    // Set the status flag.
    this.done = true;
}
```

```
    /**
     * Appends a character to the StringBuffer.
     *
     * @param c The character to append to the
     *          internal buffer.
     */
    protected synchronized void putChar(char c)
    {
        this.buf.append(c);
    }

    /**
     * Gets the string representation of the
     * stream buffer, and clears the buffer
     * from previous content.
     *
     * @return the buffered data from the stream.
     */
    public synchronized String getResult()
    {
        ExternalIntegration.serverLog.log("[NonblockingStream ("
                + getName() + ") getResult]: Buffer length: "
                + buf.length());

        // Get all data from the shared buffer
        String toReturn = buf.toString();

        // Re-create the buffer to avoid getting data from earlier
        // commands in subsequent getResult() calls.
        this.buf = new StringBuffer();

        // Done.
        return toReturn;
    }
}
```

There are a few things worth noticing about the fairly simple `NonblockingStream` class:

- Each `NonblockingStream` instance is a thread because the `NonblockingStream` class extends `java.lang.Thread`. It should be used (in other words, created and started) as indicated in the `usage` part of the class comment.

- The internal listener thread of class `NonblockingStream` executes the `run` and `putChar` methods. The thread of the caller executes the `getResult` method to retrieve the result of a sent command. It is important that only the `putChar` method (as opposed to the whole `while` loop within the `run` method) of the listener call stack is synchronized; otherwise a deadlock would be created when another thread called `getResult` to retrieve the output of the underlying stream.

In this case, you cannot detect that all output has been sent back to the `ProcessCommunicator` from a stream connected to the running back-end process. Figure 3-20 illustrates the situation a bit further with a simplified sequence diagram of the method calling and process command execution.

Because you have no way of knowing how much time the command execution will consume (the time elapsed between calling `flush` in the `sendCommand` method and calling the `getResponses` method to collect the results in the `StringBuffer`, `buf`), you simply have to estimate.

Communicating with a Process

The `ProcessCommunicator` class communicates with an externally spawned process. The only prerequisites of a process eligible for communication with a `NonblockingStream` is that it supports the three standard streams: input, output, and error. You might want to take a look in the documentation of the `java.lang.Process` class for a better understanding of process communication from a Java perspective. Listing 3-9 contains the code for the `ProcessCommunicator`.

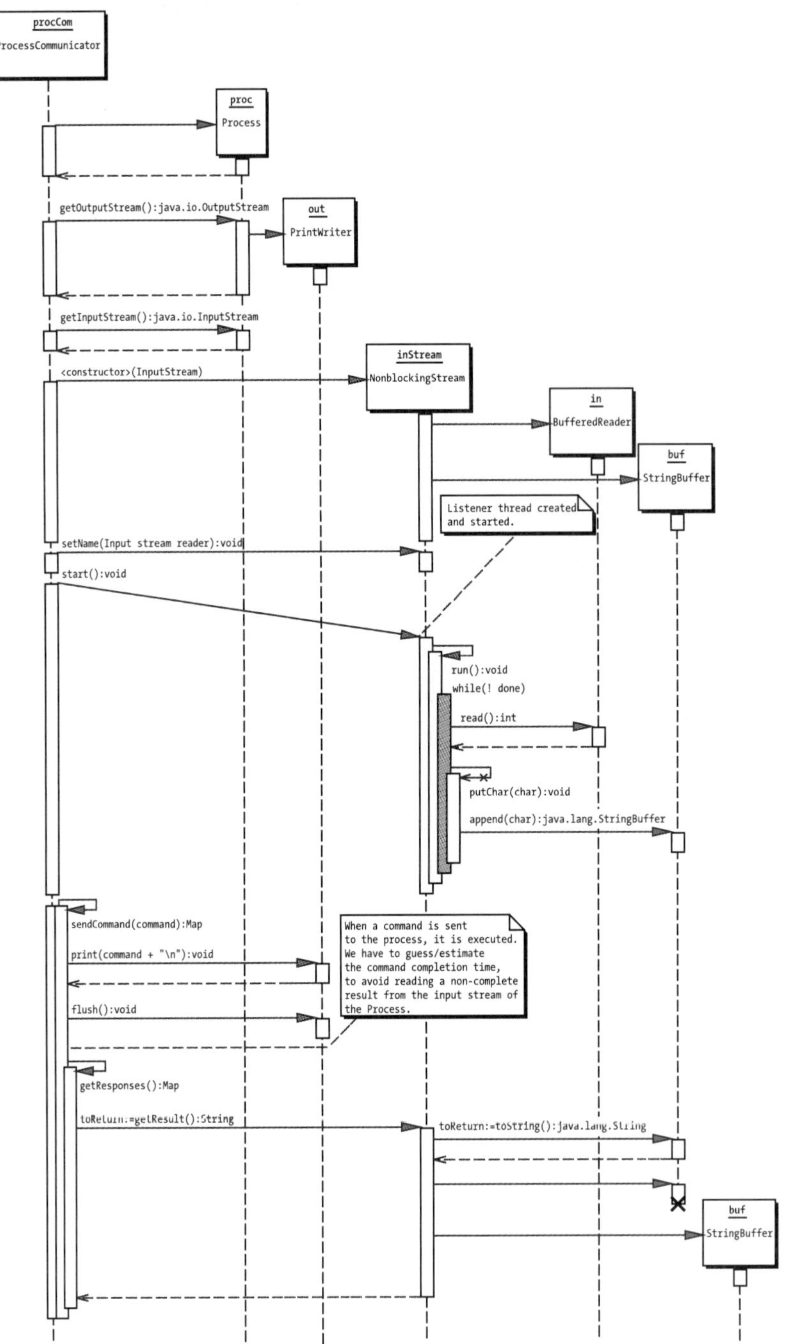

Figure 3-20. Internal interaction diagram of the `ProcessCommunicator` *instance. The* `out` *and* `in` *streams are connected to the output and input streams of the* `Process` *instance.*

Listing 3-9. The `ProcessCommunicator` *class, where all code managing the creation and start of the listener threads from the* `ProcessCommunicator`

```
/*
 * Copyright (c) 2000 jGuru.se
 * All rights reserved.
 */

package se.jguru.shellint;

import java.io.*;
import java.util.*;

/**
 * Class that communicates with an externally spawned process.
 * Usage:
 * <pre>
 *     // Create a new ProcessCommunicator
 *     ProcessCommunicator pc = new ProcessCommunicator(...);
 *
 *     // Define all commands
 *     String commands[] = {...};
 *
 *     for (int i = 0; i < commands.length; i++)
 *     {
 *         Map responses = pc.sendCommand(commands[i]);
 *
 *         // Log the responses
 *         System.out.println("[Input]: ...\n" +
 *             responses.get("INPUT") + "\n.......\n");
 *         System.out.println("[Error]: ...\n" +
 *             responses.get("ERROR") + "\n.......\n");
 *     }
 *
 *     // If applicable
 *     pc.terminateProcess();
 * </pre>
 *
 * @author Lennart Jörelid
 */
```

```
public class ProcessCommunicator
{
    // Internal state
    private Process proc;
    private PrintWriter out;
    private NonblockingStream in;
    private NonblockingStream err;
    private boolean done;

    /**
     * Creates a new ProcessCommunicator that launches the application
     * whose full path is provided as an argument. The process can
     * be communicated by using the sendCommand method.
     *
     *
     * @param application full path to an application that will be
     *        launched and communicated with.
     */
    public ProcessCommunicator(String application)
        throws FileNotFoundException, IOException
    {
        // Check sanity and create the process
        File app = new File(application);
        if (!app.isFile())
            throw new IllegalArgumentException("[ProcessCommunicator " +
                        "constructor]: Application " + application +
                        " is not a regular file.");

        // Launch process
        this.proc = Runtime.getRuntime().exec(application);

        // Tie the 3 streams to the process
        this.out = new PrintWriter(this.proc.getOutputStream());
        this.in = new NonblockingStream(this.proc.getInputStream());
        this.err = new NonblockingStream(this.proc.getErrorStream());

        // Start the NonblockingStreams
        this.in.setName("Input stream reader");
        this.err.setName("Error stream reader");
        this.in.start();
        this.err.start();
    }
```

```
/**
 * Sends a command to the process, and
 * flushes the process output stream.
 *
 * @param command the command to send to the process.
 */
public Map sendCommand(String command)
{
    // Send the command to the process
    out.print(command + "\n");
    out.flush();

    /*
    // Uncomment this section if you wish to check
    // error state with the process output stream during
    // development. In deployment, it is not required.
    boolean error = out.checkError();

    // Log
    ExternalIntegration.serverLog.log("[ProcessCommunicator " +
            "sendCommand]: Sent command '" + command + "', err: " +
            error);
    */

    try
    {
        // Sleep a little, to allow the process to finish its command
        Thread.sleep(500);
    }
    catch (Exception ex)
    {
        // Oops, log the exception
        ExternalIntegration.serverLog.log("[ProcessCommunicator " +
                    " sendCommand]: Sleep interrupted: " + ex);
    }

    return this.getResponses();
}
```

```
/**
 * Retrieves the responses from the input
 * and error streams of the current process.
 * Both responses are stored as Strings, with
 * the input stream having the key "INPUT", and
 * the error stream having the key "ERROR".
 *
 * @return all current process responses in an unmodifiable List
 */
protected Map getResponses()
{
    // Create the return Map.
    HashMap theMap = new HashMap();

    // Read the responses from the streams
    theMap.put("INPUT", in.getResult());
    theMap.put("ERROR", err.getResult());

    // Return a read-only version of the copy.
    return Collections.unmodifiableMap(theMap);
}

/**
 * Schedules the process streams for termination,
 * waits 1000 milliseconds, and destroys the process.
 */
public synchronized void terminateProcess()
{
    // Close the streams
    this.in.terminate();
    this.err.terminate();

    // Flush the output stream
    // and clean out all buffer data
    // in the input streams.
    this.out.flush();
    this.getResponses();
    this.getResponses();

    try
    {
        // Wait a little...
        wait(1000);
    }
```

```
    catch (Exception ex)
    {
        // Log
        ExternalIntegration.serverLog.log("[ProcessCommunicator " +
                    "terminateProcess]: " + ex);
    }

    // Terminate the process
    this.proc.destroy();
    this.proc = null;

    System.gc();
}


/**
 * Dummy main method, to test the integrity of this class.
 * Not used in normal running mode, and should be commented
 * out for that reason when not in development mode.
 */
public static void main(String[] args) throws Exception
{
    // Define sleep length
    int doSleep = 1000;

    // Create a new ProcessCommunicator
    ProcessCommunicator pc = new ProcessCommunicator
            ("/bin/bash");

    // Define all commands
    String commands[] = {"ls", "mount", "cd /usr", "ls"};

    for (int i = 0; i < commands.length; i++)
    {
        Map responses = pc.sendCommand(commands[i]);

        // Log the responses
        ExternalIntegration.serverLog.log("[Input]: ...\n" +
                    responses.get("INPUT") + "\n.......\n");
        ExternalIntegration.serverLog.log("[Error]: ...\n" +
                    responses.get("ERROR") + "\n.......\n");
    }
```

```
        // Shut down
        ExternalIntegration.serverLog.log("Quitting...");
        pc.terminateProcess();

        // Quit.
        System.exit(0);
    }
}
```

Note that the `Process` communicator starts two threads; one extracts data from the `Output` and the other from the `Error` stream of the `Process` to which the `ProcessCommunicator` is hooked. Examine the code and its comments of the `ProcessCommunicator` carefully if you are new to Java process communication.

Organizing Log Streams

The `Logger` interface and its two subclasses offer a unified way of logging messages to a log stream. The task coded in Listing 3-10 is simple enough task that the interface can become quite small.

Listing 3-10. The `Logger` *interface*

```
/*
 * Copyright (c) 2000 jGuru.se
 * All rights reserved.
 */

package se.jguru.shellint;

/**
 * Interface implemented by all classes being able to
 * log messages to a log stream.
 *
 * @author Lennart Jörelid
 */
public interface Logger
{
    /**
     * Logs a message to the log stream of this logger
     * and appends a linefeed character after the message.
     * Effectively calls:
     *
     * <pre> log(msg, true); </pre>
     *
```

```
     * @param msg The message to log to the standard log stream.
     */
    public void log(String msg);

    /**
     * Logs a message to the log stream of this logger.
     * Appends a linefeed character after the message only
     * if the addLineFeed parameter is set to true.
     *
     * @param msg The message to log to the standard log stream.
     * @param addLineFeed set to true if a line feed should be
     *        appended to the message before logging it to the
     *        standard log stream.
     */
    public void log(String msg, boolean addLineFeed);
}
```

StreamLogger

The `StreamLogger` implementation of the `Logger` interface allows you to send log messages through an arbitrary stream (see Listing 3-11). Because a stream may be connected to a file, network connection, external process, or memory buffer, it is a general implementation.

Listing 3-11. The `StreamLogger` *implementation of the* `Logger` *interface*

```
/*
 * Copyright (c) 2000 jGuru.se
 * All rights reserved.
 */

package se.jguru.shellint;

import java.io.*;

public class StreamLogger implements Logger
{
    // Internal state
    protected PrintWriter out;
```

```
/**
 * Constructor only for subclasses to call
 */
protected StreamLogger()
{
}

/**
 * Creates a StreamLogger connected to
 * the provided Writer.
 */
public StreamLogger(Writer logStream)
{
    // Tie the log writer to the stream
    this.out = new PrintWriter(logStream);
}

/**
 * Logs a message to the log stream of this logger
 * and appends a linefeed character after the message.
 * Effectively calls:
 *
 * <pre> log(msg, true); </pre>
 *
 * @param msg The message to log to the standard log stream.
 */
public void log(String msg)
{
    this.log(msg, true);
}

/**
 * Logs a message to the log stream of this logger.
 * Appends a linefeed character after the message only
 * if the addLineFeed parameter is set to true.
 *
 * @param msg The message to log to the standard log stream.
 * @param addLineFeed set to true if a line feed should be
 *        appended to the message before logging it to the
 *        standard log stream.
 */
```

```
    public void log(String msg, boolean addLineFeed)
    {
        if (addLineFeed) this.out.println(msg);
        else
            this.out.print(msg);

        // Flush the stream.
        this.out.flush();
    }
}
```

FileLogger

When working with server-side application development—especially in developing a large or complex system—one quickly becomes aware of the frequent lack of debugging and introspection tools. In most cases, you can stomp out problems fairly quickly if it is possible to simply log application status messages to a file separate from the standard application server log stream. Therefore, I frequently find myself using either a log framework or a small `Log` class. Frequently I choose Apache's log framework log4j, as it is a powerful and configurable open source framework. For projects where a slimmer logger is preferable, I usually create something like the `FileLogger` class, shown in Listing 3-12. The `FileLogger` is essentially a subclass of `StreamLogger` that logs messages to a specific file.

Listing 3-12. The `FileLogger` *class*

```
/*
 * Copyright (c) 2000 jGuru.se
 * All rights reserved.
 */

package se.jguru.shellint;

import java.io.*;

/**
 * Logs messages to a specified file.
 *
 * @author Lennart Jörelid
 */
```

```
public class FileLogger extends StreamLogger
{
    public FileLogger(String logFilePath)
    {
        try
        {
            // Check sanity
            File logFile = new File(logFilePath);
            if (logFile.exists() && logFile.isFile())
            {
                // Rename the existing logfile.
                boolean success = logFile.renameTo(
                    new File(logFilePath + ".old"));

                if (!success)
                    throw new IllegalArgumentException("[FileLogger " +
                    "constructor]: Could not " + "rename log file '" +
                    logFilePath + "'. Aborting.");

                // Attach to the original logfilePath name.
                logFile = new File(logFilePath);
            }

            // Create the log stream attached to the logFile
            this.out = new PrintWriter(new FileWriter(logFile));
        }
        catch (Exception ex)
        {
            // Whoops.
            System.out.println("[FileLogger constructor]: " + ex);
        }
    }
}
```

Now that you have all the service classes specified, let's take a look at the servlet masterminding the conversation with the process at one end and the user at the other end. For deployment details and init parameters, refer to "Deploying the ExternalIntegration Servlet Code into a J2EE-Compliant Servlet Engine," later in this chapter.

The ExternalIntegration Servlet

The name of this servlet (`ExternalIntegration`) stems from the fact that a process external to the servlet engine (in other words, another program) is integrated into a Web application using a servlet containing a `NonblockingStream` instance per user. Listing 3-13 shows the code of the `ExternalIntegration` servlet. The highlighted code snippets manage the actual process launched.

Listing 3-13. The `ExternalIntegration` *servlet*

```
/*
 * Copyright (c) 2000 jGuru.se
 * All rights reserved.
 */

package se.jguru.shellint;

import java.io.*;
import java.util.*;
import javax.servlet.*;
import javax.servlet.http.*;

/**
 * The ExternalIntegration servlet connects each user (unique HttpSession)
 * with a new instance of a ProcessCommunicator wrapping a specified
 * backend process. The backend process is thought to be a character-
 * oriented, terminal-like process, such as an interactive shell.
 * <br>
 *
 * The parameters accepted by the servlet are:
 * <ol>
 *  <li>logFilePath. The path of the log file.</li>
 *  <li>myURL.       The URL of this servlet.</li>
 *  <li>path.        The path to be used when locating
 *      the backend server process.</li>
 *  <li>shellName.   The application name of the backend service.</li>
 *  <li>firstPart.   The path of the HTML file to be
 *      included before any process response data.</li>
 *  <li>secondPart.  The path of the HTML part file to be
 *      included after process response data, but before the form
 *      action URL.</li>
 *  <li>lastPart.    The path of the HTML part file to be
 *      included after the form action URL.</li>
 * </ol>
 *
 * @author Lennart Jörelid
 */
```

```
public class ExternalIntegration extends HttpServlet
{
    // Internal state variables
    private String tmp;
    private String myURL;
    private String execPath;
    private static final String SERVICE = "service";
    private static final String BUFFER  = "responseBuffer";
    public static Logger serverLog      =
        new StreamLogger(new PrintWriter(System.out));

    // HTML page parts
    private String firstPart;
    private String secondPart;
    private String lastPart;

    // Standard init
    public void init(ServletConfig config) throws ServletException
    {
        super.init(config);

        // Set up the singleton logger
        String logFilePath = config.getInitParameter("logFilePath");
        if (logFilePath == null) logFilePath =
                "f:/ServletBook/Projects/Chapter3/ShellIntegration/log.txt";
        serverLog = new FileLogger(logFilePath);

        // Get the paths of the 3 page parts
        String firstPartPath = config.getInitParameter("firstPart");
        if (firstPartPath == null) firstPartPath =
                "f:/ServletBook/Projects/Chapter3/ShellIntegration/first.txt";
        this.firstPart = this.getContentFromFile(firstPartPath);

        String secondPartPath = config.getInitParameter("secondPart");
        if (secondPartPath == null) secondPartPath =
                "f:/ServletBook/Projects/Chapter3/ShellIntegration/second.txt";
        this.secondPart = this.getContentFromFile(secondPartPath);

        String lastPartPath = config.getInitParameter("lastPart");
        if (lastPartPath == null) lastPartPath =
                "f:/ServletBook/Projects/Chapter3/ShellIntegration/last.txt";
        this.lastPart = this.getContentFromFile(lastPartPath);
```

```
        this.myURL = config.getInitParameter("myURL");
        if (this.myURL == null) this.myURL = "http://localhost/tunnel/extInt";

        // Get the path of the shell
        String path = config.getInitParameter("path");
        if (path == null) path = "c:/Program/CygWin";

        // Get the shell name
        String shellName = config.getInitParameter("shellName");
        if (shellName == null) shellName = "cygwin.bat";

        try
        {
            // Find the shell execute path and launch the process
            this.execPath = this.getExecPath(path, shellName);
        }
        catch (Exception ex)
        {
            ExternalIntegration.serverLog.log(
                        "[ExternalIntegration init]: " + ex);
        }

        // Log progress.
        ExternalIntegration.serverLog.log(
                        "[ExternalIntegration init]: All done.");
    }

    /**
     * Method that retrieves the full exec path of a
     * named shell, the executable of which is located
     * somewhere within the directories of the fullPath.
     *
     * (i.e., send in the application name and the path,
     * retrieve the fully qualified execution path).
     *
     * @return the full exec path of an application in
     *         the file system.
     */
```

```
private String getExecPath(String fullPath, String appName)
    throws FileNotFoundException
{
    // Splice the fullPath into directory paths
    StringTokenizer tok = new StringTokenizer(fullPath,
            System.getProperty("path.separator"), false);
    while (tok.hasMoreTokens())
    {
        // Get the next path
        String thePath = tok.nextToken();

        // Be a bit verbose
        ExternalIntegration.serverLog.log("Scanning: " + thePath);
        File theDir = new File(thePath);
        if (!theDir.isDirectory()) continue;

        // Create a FilenameFilter for the list method
        this.tmp = appName;
        FilenameFilter flt = new FilenameFilter()
        {
            public boolean accept(File dir, String name)
            {
                if (name.equals(ExternalIntegration.this.tmp)) return true;
                return false;
            }
        };

        // List the contents of the currently processed directory.
        String[] list = theDir.list(flt);

        // Check contents of the list
        if (list.length != 0)
                    return theDir.getAbsolutePath() + "/" + appName;
    }

    throw new FileNotFoundException("" + fullPath +
            File.pathSeparator + appName);
}
```

```
/** Process the HTTP POST request */
public void doPost(HttpServletRequest req, HttpServletResponse res)
    throws ServletException, IOException
{
    // Get the HTML stream writer
    PrintWriter clout = new PrintWriter(res.getOutputStream());
    res.setContentType("text/html");

    // Get the session
    HttpSession session = req.getSession(true);
    if (session.isNew())
    {
        try
        {
            // Spawn a new service process and bind it to the session.
            ProcessCommunicator theService =
                                new ProcessCommunicator(this.execPath);
            session.putValue(SERVICE, theService);

        }
        catch (Exception ex)
        {
            // Whoops.
            ExternalIntegration.serverLog.log("[doGet]: Could not "
                                + "create processCommunicator.");
            ExternalIntegration.serverLog.log("[doGet]: " + ex);
        }
    }

    //Get the service process for this session
    ProcessCommunicator theService =
        (ProcessCommunicator)session.getValue(SERVICE);
    StringBuffer dynamicPartBuffer =new StringBuffer();

    // Find out what to do...
    if (req.getParameter("terminate") != null)
    {
        // We should terminate the service, and
        // our communication with it.
        theService.terminateProcess();
        req.getSession().invalidate();
        dynamicPartBuffer.append("\nBackend service terminated.\n");
        dynamicPartBuffer.append("Have a nice day.\n\n8)");
    }
```

```
    else
    {
        // Process the provided commands normally
        String[] cmd = req.getParameterValues("command");
        String response = this.processServiceCommands(theService, cmd);
        dynamicPartBuffer.append(response);
    }

    // All done sending and receiving commands.
    // Output the resulting page.
    clout.print(this.firstPart);
    clout.print(dynamicPartBuffer.toString());
    clout.print(this.secondPart);
    clout.print(this.myURL);
    clout.print(this.lastPart);

    ExternalIntegration.serverLog.log("[doGet]: All Done.");
    clout.flush();

}

/** Process the HTTP GET request */
public void doGet(HttpServletRequest req, HttpServletResponse res)
    throws ServletException, IOException
{
    this.doPost(req, res);
}



/**
 * Retrieves the response of the service to the commands
 * provided in the cmd[] array. All responses will be
 * presented in order and surrounded by enumerated stream
 * delimiters of the form
 *
 * <pre>
 * [<stream type> <command index>]
 * [End <stream type> <command index>]
 *
 * for instance:
 *
 * [Error stream]
 * ...
```

```
 * [End error stream]
 * </pre>
 *
 * @param theService the ProcessCommunicator that talks to the
 *        backend service.
 * @param cmd all commands sent to the backend service in this
 *        Http request.
 *
 * @return the response from the process invoked by the client.
 */
private String processServiceCommands(
    ProcessCommunicator theService, String[] cmd)
{
    // Declare the return value.
    StringBuffer buf = new StringBuffer();

    // Send all commands to the process,
    // and retrieve the responses
    Map[] responses = null;

    if (cmd != null)
    {
        // Assign a non-null value.
        responses = new Map[cmd.length];

        for (int i = 0; i < cmd.length; i++)
        {
            // Log
            ExternalIntegration.serverLog.log(
                            "[doGet]: Sending command " + cmd[i]);

            // Send the current command to the process
            // and retrieve the result.
            responses[i] = theService.sendCommand(cmd[i]);
        }
    }

    // Handle null command state
    int limit = (responses == null ? 1 : responses.length);
```

```
        // Get the responses from the sent commands
        for (int i = 0; i < limit; i++)
        {
            buf.append("[Response stream (" + (i + 1) + ")]\n\n");
            if (responses != null) buf.append(responses[i].get("INPUT") + "\n");
            else
                buf.append(" --> Command returned no response.\n\n");
            buf.append("[End response stream (" + (i + 1) + ")]\n\n");

            buf.append("[Error stream (" + (i + 1) + ")]\n\n");
            if (responses != null) buf.append(responses[i].get("ERROR") + "\n");
            else
                buf.append(" --> Command returned no errors.\n\n");
            buf.append("[End error stream (" + (i + 1) + ")]\n\n");
        }

        return buf.toString();
    }

    /** Reads all content from the file with the provided path. */
    private String getContentFromFile(String filePath)
    {
        // Define return values
        StringBuffer buf = new StringBuffer();

        try
        {
            // Create an input buffer to the file.
            File theFile = new File(filePath);
            BufferedReader fromFile = new BufferedReader(new FileReader(theFile));

            // Read all content
            for (String aLine = ""; (aLine = fromFile.readLine()) != null; )
            {
                buf.append(aLine + "\n");
            }

            // Done.
            return buf.toString();
        }
```

```
        catch (Exception ex)
        {
            ExternalIntegration.serverLog.log("[getContentsFromFile]: " + ex);
        }

        // Fool the compiler.
        return null;
    }
}
```

You may use this servlet to log in remotely on any type of computer running a servlet engine and a standard command shell. This includes remotely logging in to a Windows NT or Macintosh machine, just as users of the Unix operating system are used to doing. Because the Java `Process` stream model (in other words, all `Processes` are assumed to communicate using standard out, in, and—optionally—error streams) does not work well with the Windows standard command shell (`command.com`), I recommend installing the CygWin utilities from Cygnus labs.

If you would like to download and run the CygWin distribution, visit its distribution home page at `http://sources.redhat.com/cygwin/`.

Figures 3-21 and 3-22 show two standard Unix commands being executed on a Windows machine through the `ExternalIntegration` servlet. The results of the commands are returned in a HTML form over a HTTP connection—you could therefore use this tunnel to rid yourself of the constraints of a blocking firewall (granted, of course, that the firewall does not block the standard Web server port, 80).

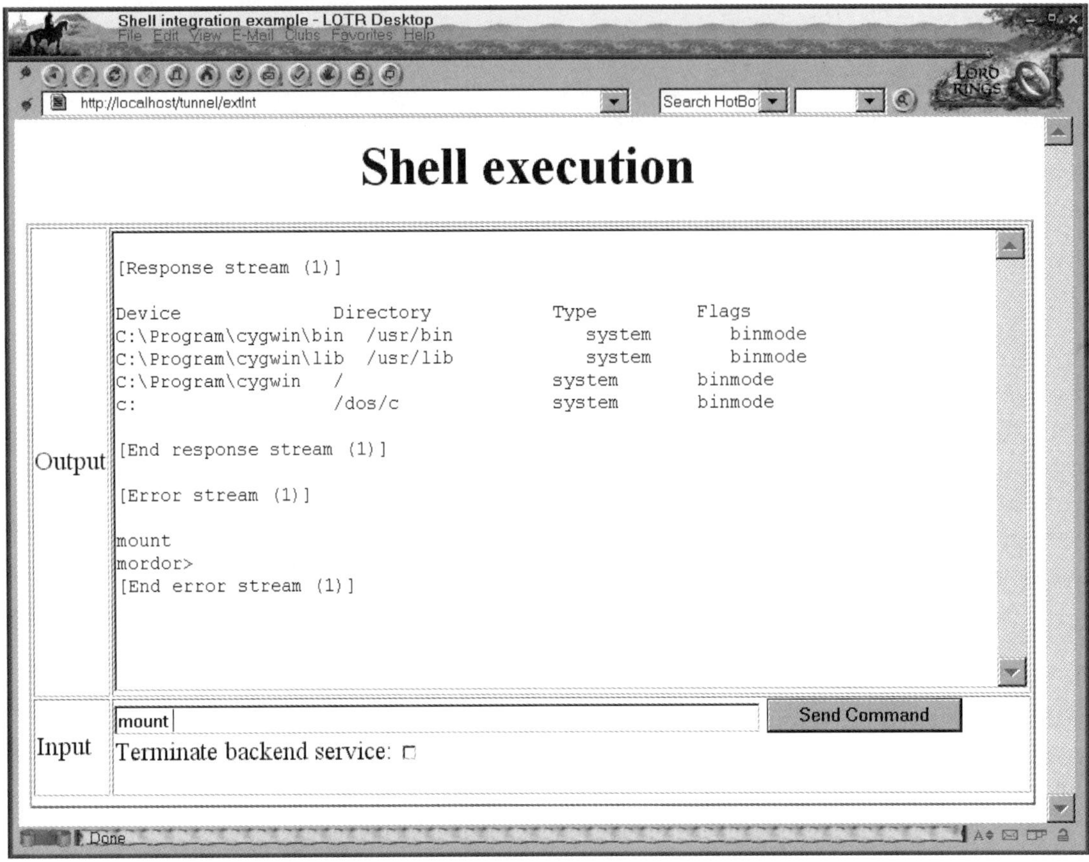

Figure 3-21. The running result from an `ExternalIntegration` *servlet executing within a servlet engine running on the Windows 2000 operating system. The* `ProcessCommunicator` *is connected to a Bourne Again Shell (bash) shell installed as a part of the CygWin release. The mount command shows all disk volumes available to the system.*

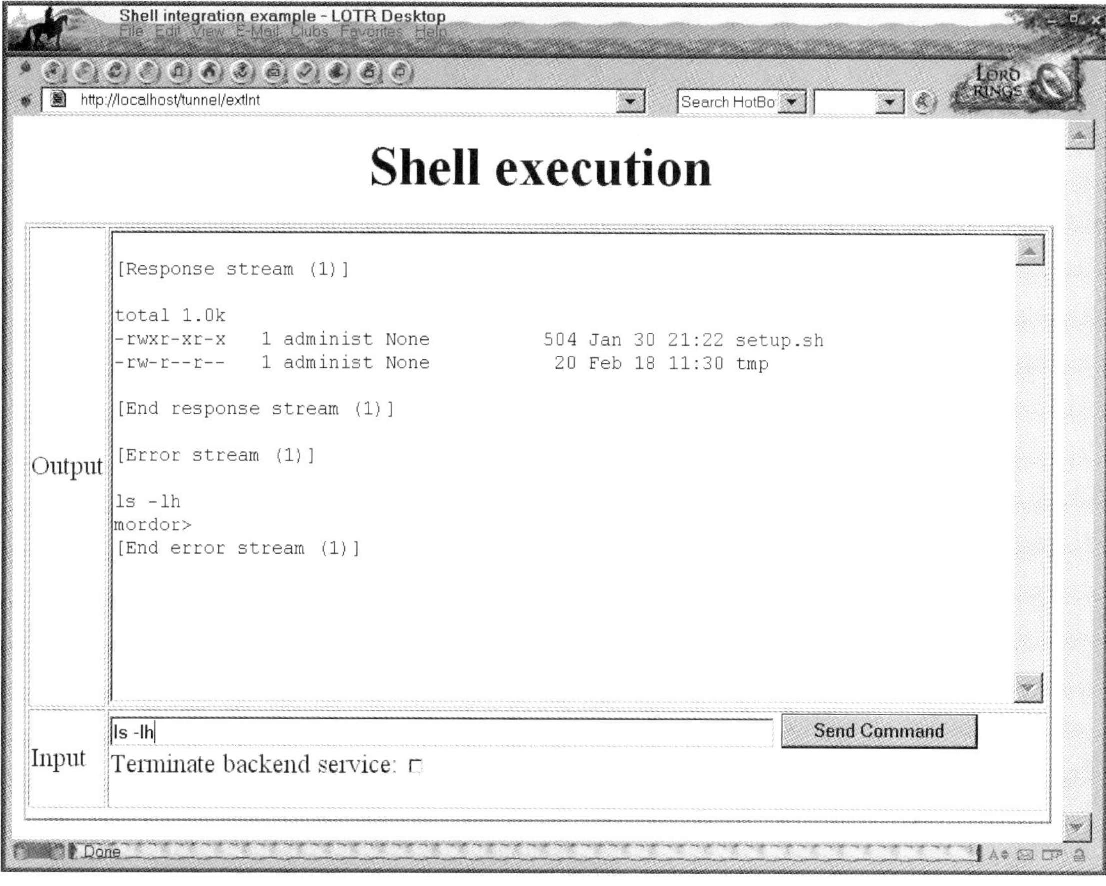

Figure 3-22. The command executed in this image is `ls`*, which lists files in a directory, in a similar way to the Windows* `dir` *command.*

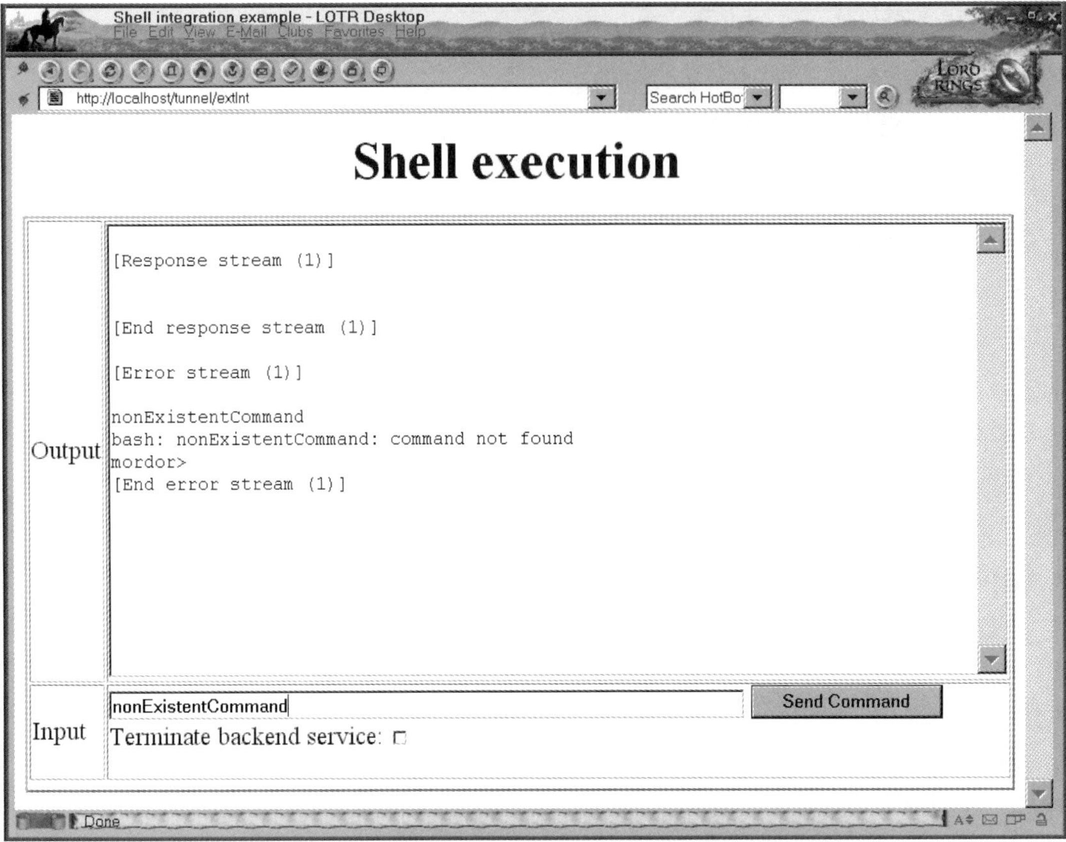

Figure 3-23. The CygWin application uses its error stream to echo the command-line prompter as well as the input parameters back to the user. When provided a non-existent command, the error stream first echoes the command given and then the error response from bash ("command not found").

Deploying the ExternalIntegration Servlet Code into a J2EE-Compliant Servlet Engine

The J2EE specification defines a common structure for the deployment of Web application resources (in other words, servlets, JSP documents, and any static resources such as image and HTML files). Our example Web application consists of a starter HTML page, the required servlet classes, and the Web application configuration file (frequently referred to as a "deployment descriptor" in J2EE literature), `web.xml`. In this case, the `web.xml` file is relevant because the `ExternalIntegration` servlet accepts a few initialization parameters.

The Web application files should be placed in a structure complying with the J2EE specification, where the root catalog can be named arbitrarily but the other catalogs follow a specific structure, as shown in Figure 3-24.

The `ExternalIntegration` servlet reads initialization parameters from its `ServletConfig` object. Those initialization parameters must be set up in the

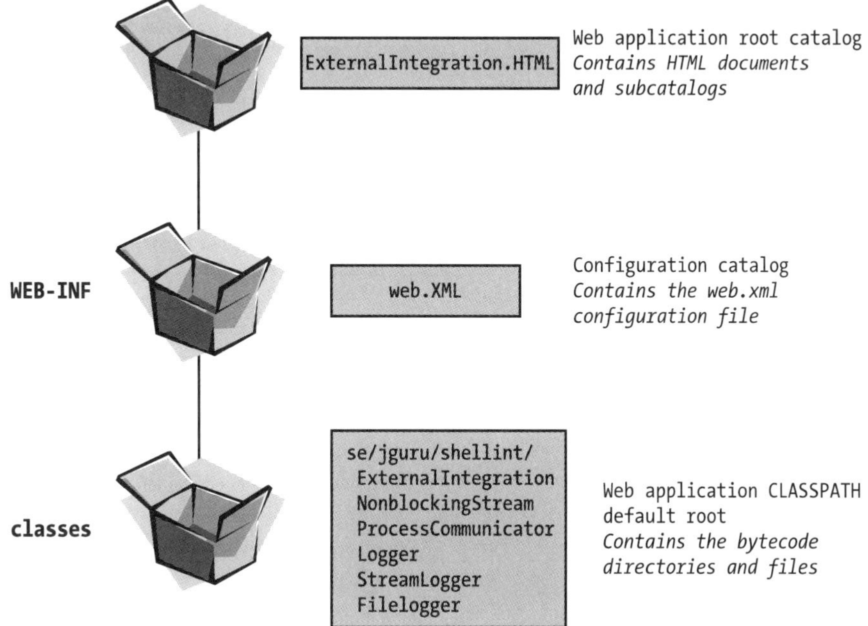

Figure 3.24. The structure of the ExternalIntegration J2EE Web application. Note that the Web site file structure originates from the Web application root catalog. The `WEB-INF` subdirectory contains the configuration file `web.xml`, which defines the behavior of the Web application, as well as the classes subdirectory where unpacked bytecode files (in other words, .class files) are placed.

`web.xml` file according to the standard J2EE servlet initialization parameter format. The initialization parameters are as follows:

- **logFilePath**—The full path to the file where the `FileLogger` will write its log, such as `c:\ProgramLogs\ExternalIntegration\log.txt`.
- **firstPart**—The full path to the file containing the first part of the HTML document that should be output to the client browser, such as `/home/applicationServer/applications/ExternalIntegration/resources/first.txt`. The "first part" of the output refers to the part of the HTML document up to the point where the servlet must output the action URL.
- **myURL**—The action URL of the presented form. This must be an URL that connects to the ExternalIntegration servlet, such as `http://myServer/tunnel/extInt`.

- **secondPart**—The full path to the file containing the second part of the HTML document that should be output to the client browser, such as `/home/applicationServer/applications/ExternalIntegration/resources/second.txt`. The "second part" of the output refers to the part of the HTML document up to the point where the servlet must output the action URL.

- **lastPart**—The full path to the file containing the last part of the HTML document that should be output to the client browser, such as `/home/applicationServer/applications/ExternalIntegration/resources/first.txt`. The "first part" of the output refers to the part of the HTML document between the action URL and the resulting output of the `ProcessCommunicator`.

- **path**—The full path to the directory where the application is found. An example would be `/bin` or `c:\Program\CygWin`.

- **shellName**—The name of the shell executable, such as bash.

Should any of the parameters be left blank, the `ExternalIntegration` servlet is understanding enough to provide a default value.

Now take a look at the example `web.xml` file in Listing 3-14. The code block sections marked in Listing 3-14 are explained after the listing.

Listing 3-14. The deployment descriptor `web.xml` *of the* `ExternalIntegration` *Web application*

```
<?xml version="1.0"?>
<!DOCTYPE web-app PUBLIC
1   "-//Sun Microsystems, Inc.//DTD Web Application 2.2//EN"
    "http://java.sun.com/j2ee/dtds/web-app_2_2.dtd">

<web-app>
    <display-name>The ExternalIntegration example</display-name>
    <description>
2       Example servlet integrating an external process
        into the servlet engine.
    </description>
    <servlet>
    <servlet-name>theExternalIntegrationServlet</servlet-name>
        <display-name>extInt</display-name>
3       <description>The ExternalIntegration servlet</description>
        <servlet-class>se.jguru.shellint.ExternalIntegration</servlet-class>
```

```
                <init-param>
                        <param-name>logFilePath</param-name>
                        <param-value>
                        /myAppServer/ServletBookApp/ExternalIntegration/log.txt
                        </param-value>
                </init-param>
                <init-param>
                        <param-name>secondPart</param-name>
                        <param-value>
                        /myAppServer/ServletBookApp/ExternalIntegration/second.txt
                        </param-value>
                </init-param>
4               <init-param>
                        <param-name>firstPart</param-name>
                        <param-value>
                        /myAppServer/ServletBookApp/ExternalIntegration/first.txt
                        </param-value>
                </init-param>
                <init-param>
                        <param-name>lastPart</param-name>
                        <param-value>
                        /myAppServer/ServletBookApp/ExternalIntegration/last.txt
                        </param-value>
                </init-param>
          <init-param>
               <param-name>myURL</param-name>
               <param-value>http://localhost/tunnel/extInt</param-value>
          </init-param>
5    </servlet>
     <servlet-mapping>
          <servlet-name>theExternalIntegrationServlet</servlet-name>
          <url-pattern>/extInt</url-pattern>
     </servlet-mapping>
     <welcome-file-list>
6         <welcome-file>ExternalIntegration.html</welcome-file>
     </welcome-file-list>
     <login-config>
7         <auth-method>BASIC</auth-method>
     </login-config>
</web-app>
```

The deployment descriptor for the Web application in Listing 3-14 has seven distinct parts:

1. The introductory metadata specifying the DTD version of the descriptor document.

2. General attributes of the WAR described by this descriptor.

3. Internal (`servlet-name`) and display names (`display-name`) of the servlet deployed and described by this WAR. The internal name is the name that will reference this servlet for all servlet-mapping and filter entries. The display name is simply the name under which the servlet should be presented in any GUI assembler tool.

4. Initialization parameters of the servlet are provided within `<init-param> ... </init-param>` containers. The structure for providing initialization parameters to a servlet running in a J2EE-compliant Web application is:

   ```
   <init-param>
          <param-name>aParameterName</param-name>
          <param-value>theValue</param-value>
   <init-param>
   ```

5. Servlet mapping, stating that any call to the application server ending in `/extInt` will invoke servlet having the name `theExternalIntegrationServlet`.

6. The structure for defining the welcome page (the document whose content will be shown to the client browser if no other document has been specified) is given in the `web.xml` file, using the following structure:

   ```
   <welcome-file-list>
            <welcome-file>ExternalIntegration.html</welcome-file>
   </welcome-file-list>
   ```

7. The login configuration is not used in this particular Web application but determines the mode of authorizing a user to the Web application. For a primer on J2EE authorization, refer to the documentation in the J2EE distribution regarding security.

You may want to package the Web application by hand; frequently that way is much quicker than any GUI-based (and application server–specific) tool. If you prefer to package the WAR file by hand, use the JAR utility. Change directory to the root directory of your Web application and create the WAR by giving the command "`jar cvf myWarFile.war .`". (Yes, the dot must be present in the command line to indicate the current directory).

Deploy the WAR file into your application server using the provided tool from the application server vendor. Normally, deploying a full WAR is quite simple; most application servers have an Import a Full JAR option. For an introduction to the J2EE standard distribution deployment tools, refer to Appendix A.

Reflections on the ExternalIntegration Servlet

The connection power provided by the ExternalIntegration servlet must be harnessed a bit to ensure security. I would, for instance, use HTTPS for transmitting any data to the remote process, as well as creating a login HTML page from which the service would be accessed. The security aspects have not been dealt with at all in the previous shopping cart example, but they are nevertheless required for safe operation.

It is, however, nice to be able to read one's email on a remote server using the terminal-based mail reader, such as Mutt (a text-based mail client for Unix operating systems; see `http://www.mutt.org/` for more information), from behind a firewall without causing any security policy problems for the client. It is also nice to be able to log in remotely on a Windows NT server.

Back-end Servlets and Legacy Application Integration

Uploading binary documents, such as images or application documents, to a legacy application is sometimes a rather tricky project. As an example, imagine you would like people to use a browser to upload Microsoft Word documents for storage in a database. Support for this kind of operation in HTML and HTTP is rather poor; although the structure for implementing it is present in HTTP/1.1, few Web servers allow for uploading with the HTTP PUT command. Even if they do, tweaking the Web server configuration to allow for secure and controlled operation is a non-trivial matter. A better and more flexible alternative is to use a servlet that processes all document uploading—especially because a servlet may process the uploaded data in some way, such as inserting it into a database.

Figure 3-25 illustrates the stages of a document upload service. The servlet accepts the document sent from the user and inserts it into a persistent storage such as a database. In many cases, however, the persistent storage is not a database but instead a message queue, file system, or transaction gateway. The persistent storage has therefore been named "Storage" to cope with general storage device types.

The user selection browser view is provided with the file upload control, as shown in the top-right table cell in Figure 3-26.

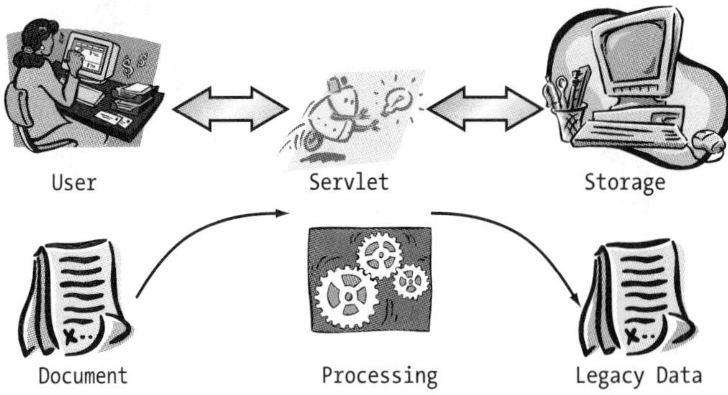

Figure 3-25. A servlet processes an uploaded document and stores it in a processed form using a back-end service. For example, image files or word processor documents are stored in a database as Binary Large Objects (BLOBs).

Figure 3-26. The form presented to the user for selecting a document to upload. After selecting a document by pressing the Browse… button, the upload itself is started by pressing the Upload Document button.

When all data is uploaded to the Web server, it is usually processed and inserted into some kind of database or other means of persistent storage. For our example, let's display the document content and its metadata when the Upload Document button is clicked. Figure 3-27 shows the resulting page when the Unix `kernel-config` file is uploaded.

Prerequisites of Document Uploading

Before sending documents to an uploader servlet, you have to make sure your favorite Web browser can support the two required aspects of client-side file uploading.

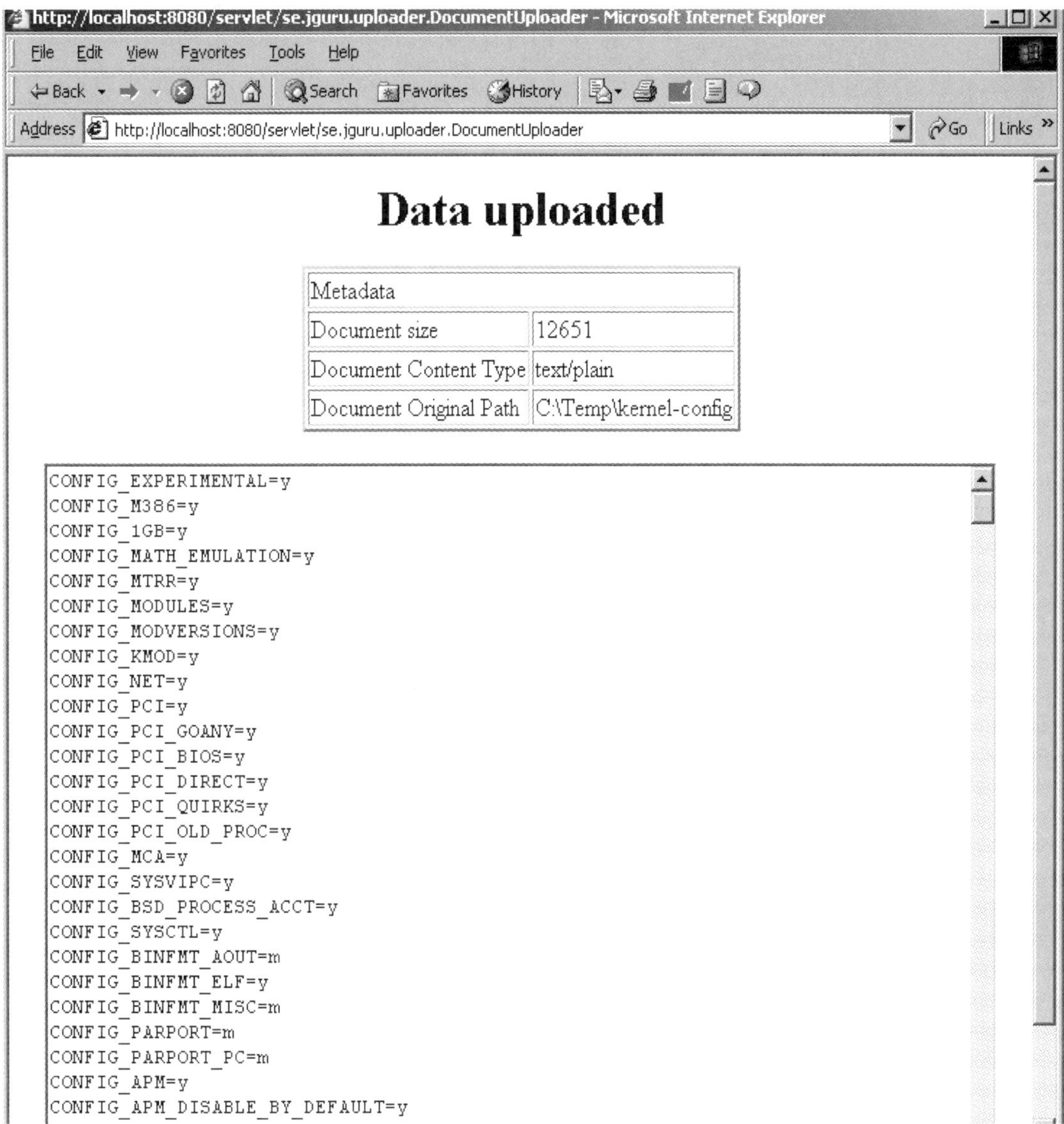

Figure 3-27. The user's view on a successful upload; the text document is shown in the bottom text area, and some document metadata is presented in the top table.

- File upload control, created with the HTML tag <INPUT type="file" … >. Today all commonly used browsers support this.
- The enctype="multipart/form-data" attribute on the <FORM> tag for submitting data from forms to the server. Today all commonly used browsers support this.

These criteria should be basic enough to permit the use of any reasonably common Web browser. However, development test browsers, such as those included in some Integrated Development Environments (IDEs), may not be sophisticated enough to manage multipart encoding of form data.

The process of uploading documents from a browser is quite simple in principle, but it still involves ensuring the correctness of a fair amount of details. The majority of the code in the `DocumentUploader` servlet deals with parsing and interpreting the results of the multipart form data. You can find the complete reference of the multipart format at `http://www.w3.org/Protocols/rfc1341/7_2_Multipart.html`. For these purposes, however, taking a look at the format of an uploaded multipart document will suffice.

A multipart-formatted document consists of several documents separated by a set of bytes or characters that act as delimiters. The structure of a multipart document is therefore simple to understand, but some parsing is required to extract the relevant uploaded data from its envelope. The business logic within the servlet simply has to separate the uploaded document from the surrounding HTTP data.

The uploaded document has this form:

```
[separator]
[metadata]
[data]
[separator]
[metadata]
[data]
...
[separator]
```

In the example shown in Listing 3-15, the separator strings are `---------------------------7d02d214100268`. Two extra hyphens are prepended to each separator and appended to the last separator in the multipart document.

Listing 3-15. The content of the full upload HTML stream, as received by the servlet

```
eparator  -----------------------------7d02d214100268
          Content-Disposition: form-data; name="document";
tadata    filename="C:\Temp\kernel-config"
          Content-Type: text/plain

          CONFIG_EXPERIMENTAL=y
          CONFIG_M386=y
          CONFIG_1GB=y
          CONFIG_MATH_EMULATION=y
          CONFIG_MTRR=y
Data      CONFIG_MODULES=y

          … a number of configuration options follows …

          CONFIG_AEDSP16_BASE=220
          CONFIG_MPU_BASE=330

eparator  -----------------------------7d02d214100268
Metadata  Content-Disposition: form-data; name="Upload!"

          Submit Query
eparator  -----------------------------7d02d214100268--
```

The document being uploaded in Listing 3-15 is a small configuration file for building a Linux kernel. The browser appends the separator character strings and metadata entries to the configuration file and encapsulates its content in the multipart document format. The data block contains the full contents of the configuration file, and the metadata appended indicates that the original file was `c:\Temp\kernel-config`.

Class Structure of the DocumentUploader Servlet

Although one could break down the `DocumentUploader` service into a multitude of classes, depending on the level of granularity you want, I have chosen to use only two classes: the servlet performing the document upload (`DocmentUploader`) and a holder class to encapsulate each uploaded document (`DocumentHolder`).

Figure 3-28 shows the `DocumentUploader`.

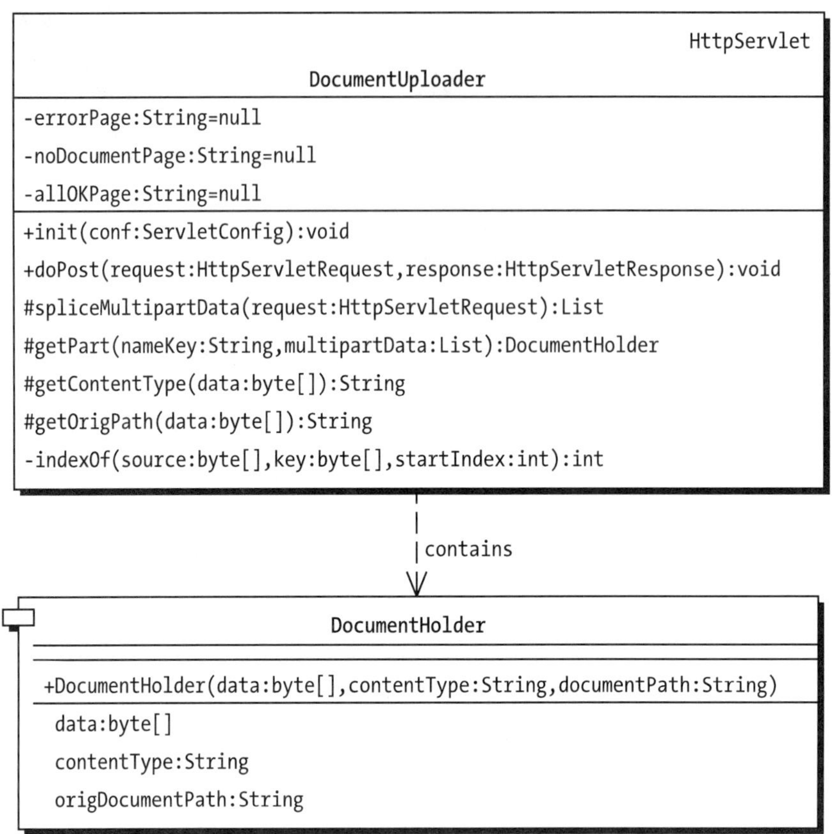

Figure 3-28. The structure of and relation between the `DocumentUploader` *servlet and its helper class,* `DocumentHolder`

DocumentHolder Class

The `DocumentHolder` class shown in Listing 3-16 is a simple data container that assigns the internal state from the constructor arguments and retrieves them again when any of its getter accessor methods are called.

Listing 3-16. The `DocumentHolder` *class*

```
/*
 * Copyright (c) 2000 jGuru Europe AB
 * All rights reserved.
 */

package se.jguru.uploader;
```

```
/**
 * Class that holds all data content and metadata that is sent
 * to a servlet using the file upload HTML control.
 *
 * @author Lennart Jörelid
 */
public class DocumentHolder
{
    // Internal state
    private byte[] data;
    private String contentType;
    private String origDocumentPath;

    /** Creates a new DocumentHolder using the provided parameters. */
    public DocumentHolder(byte[] data,
        String contentType,
        String documentPath)
    {
        // Initialize internal state
        this.data = data;
        this.contentType = contentType;
        this.origDocumentPath = documentPath;
    }

    /** @return the document data stored in this DocumentHolder. */
    public byte[] getData()
    {
        return this.data;
    }

    /**
     * @return the MIME content type of the
     *         document stored in this DocumentHolder.
     */
    public String getContentType()
    {
        return this.contentType;
    }
```

```
    /**
     * @return the original path of the document
     * stored in this DocumentHolder.
     */
    public String getOrigDocumentPath()
    {
        return this.origDocumentPath;
    }
}
```

For each uploaded document, the DocumentUploader servlet splices the incoming multipart data stream into parts and creates a DocumentHolder that contains an uploaded document and its metadata for each part. Figure 3-29 illustrates the principal calls in the doPost method that create the DocumentHolder instance.

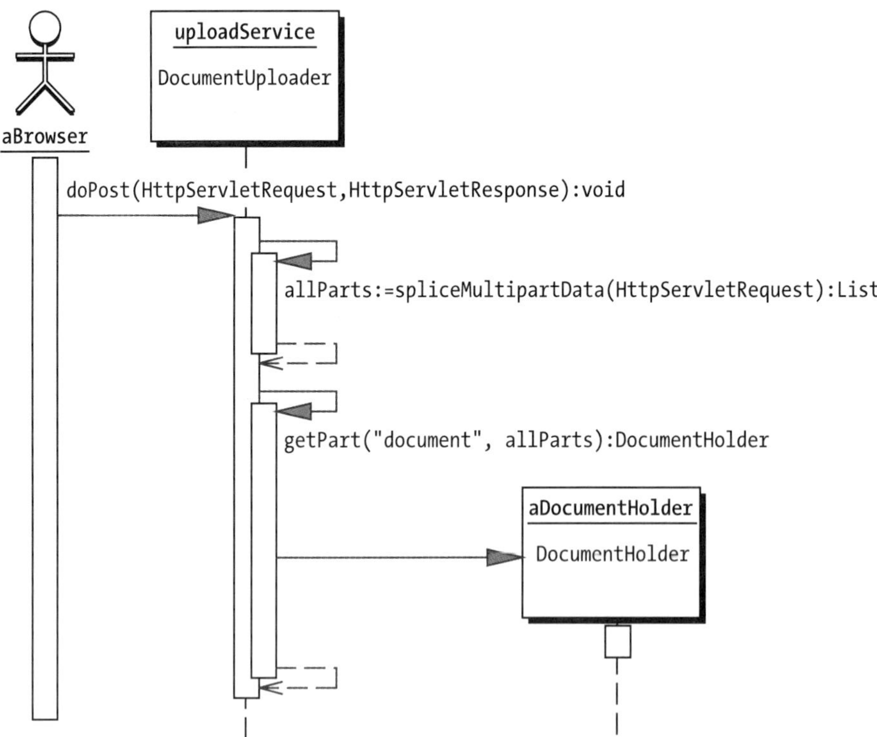

Figure 3-29. Simplified interaction diagram for a `doPost` *call to the* `DocumentUploader` *servlet, showing the calls to the* `spliceMultipartData` *and* `getPart` *methods*

doPost Method

The `doPost` method of the `DocumentUploader` servlet is rather simple. The resulting HTML view is generated within the `doPost` method. Note that the view is hard-coded into the source code of the `DocumentUploader` servlet. This is never a good solution to any industrial-strength application system. However, for the purposes of studying an example of uploading documents from the user's computer to a central server, the hard-coded view approach will be sufficient. To facilitate finding the relevant code in Listing 3-17, code related to the document uploading process (as opposed to creating the view) is rendered in bold.

Listing 3-17. The code of the `doPost` *method*

```
/**
 * Main uploader method, which will handle all types of documents.
 * Since uploaded documents may be binary in nature, we have to use
 * Stream classes, rather than Reader classes to handle the
 * uploaded document.
 */
public void doPost(HttpServletRequest request,
    HttpServletResponse response)
throws ServletException, IOException
{
    // Splice the multipart data from the request
    List allParts = this.spliceMultipartData(request);

    // Get the uploaded document.
    DocumentHolder doc = this.getPart("document", allParts);

    // Print out the parts
    response.setContentType("text/html");
    PrintWriter out = new PrintWriter(response.getOutputStream());

    // Print out to the browser.
    out.println("<html><body><center><h1>Data uploaded</h1>");
    out.println("<table border=2><tr> <td colspan=2> " +
            "Metadata</td></tr>");
    out.println("<tr><td>Document size</td><td>" +
            doc.getData().length + "</td></tr>");
    out.println("<tr><td>Document Content Type</td><td>" +
            doc.getContentType() + "</td></tr>");
    out.println("<tr><td>Document Original Path</td><td>" +
            doc.getOrigDocumentPath() + "</td></tr>");
    out.println("</table><br>");
```

```
        out.println("<textarea cols=80 rows=30>" +
                new String(doc.getData()) + "</textarea>");
        out.println("</center></body></html>");

    }
```

The complexity of the `DocumentUploader` servlet lies within the `spliceMultipartData` and `getPart` methods. Because the document is provided to you as an encapsulated stream of bytes, the only challenge is to separate the multipart/form-data encapsulation from the actual document data. This involves a fair amount of stream and byte array parsing, as well as some conversion of byte arrays to strings.

spliceMultipartData Method

Start by looking at the `spliceMultipartData` method in Listing 3-18. The important parts of the `spliceMultipartData` (the statements manipulating form and parameter data from the request) have been highlighted.

Listing 3-18. The `spliceMultipartData` *method*

```
    /**
     * Splices a multipart-encoded form-data input stream, returning
     * a List of all form parts, minus the multipart separator token.
     *
     * @param request The HttpServletRequest of the Servlet.
     * @exception if the Content-Type is not "multipart/form-data"
     */
    protected List spliceMultipartData(HttpServletRequest request)
        throws IllegalArgumentException
    {
        // Get HttpServletRequest metadata. The validity of the
        // contentLength data is crucial, as we will use it to
        // create the byte[] data holder.
        String type = request.getContentType();
        int contentLength = request.getContentLength();

        // Declare data holder variables.
        // allData will contain the data and metadata of the
        // uploaded document.
        DataInputStream in = null;
        byte[] allData = null;
```

```
// Check sanity.
if (!type.startsWith("multipart/form-data"))
throw new IllegalArgumentException
     ("Cannot parse anything but 'multipart/form-data'");

if (contentLength == 0) throw new IllegalArgumentException
     ("Null content data length. Aborting.");
try
{
    // Get the input stream from the HTTP request.
    in = new DataInputStream(request.getInputStream());
    allData = new byte[contentLength];

    // Read all raw data
    // in 1k large chunks.
    for(int bytesRead = 0;
            bytesRead != contentLength;
            bytesRead += in.read(allData, bytesRead, 1024))
    {
       // Uncomment this line if you want to monitor
       // the progress of the loading.
       // System.out.println("Got " + bytesRead + " bytes.");
    }
}
catch (Exception ex)
{
    System.out.println("Aborting splice operation: " + ex);
    return null;
}

// Find the separator key, which is included in the
// content type string. An example of such a MIME string is
//
// multipart/form-data; boundary=This_is_a_separator
//
// Isolate the text after the "=" character to find the
// multipart MIME separator.
String separator = "--" +
    type.substring(type.indexOf("=") + 1, type.length());
byte[] key = separator.getBytes();
```

```
// Declare the return value and the helper index
// List, which stores all indices in allData where
// the separator is found.
ArrayList allPieces = new ArrayList();
ArrayList indices = new ArrayList();

// Find all occurrences of the separator key within
// the source array.
for (int currentIndex = 0; currentIndex < allData.length; )
{
    int tmp = this.indexOf(allData, key, currentIndex);
    if (tmp == -1) break;

    // Append the found index to the indices List
    indices.add(new Integer(tmp));

    // Move pointer
    currentIndex += tmp + 1;
}

int startIndex = 0;
for (int i = 0; i < indices.size(); i++)
{
    //
    // Extract the part of allData between indices
    // startIndex and indices.get(i) [which holds the
    // next index of the separator].
    //
    // In short, extract the next document part of the
    // uploaded multipart document.
    //
    int separatorIndex = ((Integer)indices.get(i)).intValue();
    int partLength = separatorIndex - startIndex;
    if (partLength < 1) continue;

    // Copy the bytes from allData to part
    byte[] part = new byte[partLength];
    System.arraycopy(allData, startIndex, part, 0, part.length);

    // Add the newly extracted part to the allPieces List
    allPieces.add(part);
```

```
            // Move startIndex pointer
            startIndex = separatorIndex + key.length;
        }

        // Handle the last array index, i.e., the bytes
        // between the last found instance of the separator
        // and the end of the allData array.
        if (indices.size() != 0)
        {
            int lastSeparatorIndex = ((Integer)
                        indices.get(indices.size() - 1)).intValue();
            byte[] lastPart = new byte[
                        allData.length - lastSeparatorIndex - key.length];
            System.arraycopy(allData, lastSeparatorIndex + key.length,
                                   lastPart, 0, lastPart.length);
            allPieces.add(lastPart);
        }

        // Done.
        return allPieces;
    }
```

The `spliceMultipartData` method chops up all incoming data into chunks, just as a `StringTokenizer` or `StreamTokenizer` would. However, because the uploaded document may be binary in nature, the `spliceMultipartData` method uses byte-array representations of separators and data. The need to handle byte arrays leads to an interesting discovery—no precoded `Tokenizer` class within the standard Java API uses byte arrays as token separators. Thus, you have to create such a method for yourself.

indexOf Method

In trying to mimic the Java standard library, next implement the `indexOf` method, which is identical in usage to the `String.indexOf` method but uses byte[] arguments rather than strings. Listing 3-19 displays the `indexOf` method.

Listing 3-19. The `indexOf` *method*

```
    /**
     * Find the index of the first occurrence of key within
     * source, starting from startIndex.
     *
     * @return -1 if none found.
     */
```

```
private int indexOf(byte[] source, byte[] key, int startIndex)
{
    // Check sanity.
    if (source == null) throw new NullPointerException
            ("Cannot handle null source.");
    if (key == null) throw new NullPointerException
            ("Cannot handle null key.");
    if (startIndex >= source.length) return -1;
    if (key.length > source.length) return -1;

    // Handle insane argument
    if (startIndex < 0) startIndex = 0;

    // Start finding the desired (key) bytes within the
    // source byte array. Return the first index of a complete
    // match.
    outer :
    for (int i = startIndex; i < (source.length - key.length); i++)
    {
        // Skip as many irrelevant bytes as possible
        if (source[i] != key[0]) continue;

        // Found a match?
        for (int j = 1; j < key.length; j++)
        {
            // Still a match?
            if (source[i + j] != key[j])
            {
                i += j;
                continue outer;
            }
        }

        // Found the separator.
        // Return the index of its start
        // within source.
        return i;
    }

    // No match found.
    return -1;
}
```

getPart Method

The `spliceMultipartData` method in Figure 3-28 returns a list containing the byte arrays of each multipart. The `DocumentHolder` of the uploaded document will be created from the relevant document part using the `getPart` method as shown in Listing 3-20. The highlighted method calls shows the use of our `indexOf` method, as well as smart uses of the `System.arraycopy` method, which is helpful in manipulating byte arrays.

Listing 3-20. The `getPart` *method*

```
/**
 * Retrieves the part of a multipart uploaded data stream
 * that has the provided nameKey.
 *
 * @return The data of the multipart data container having
 *         the provided name, or <pre>null</pre> if no such
 *         multipart data exists.
 */
protected DocumentHolder getPart(String nameKey, List multipartData)
{
    // Define internal state tokens
    String tmpKey = "name=";
    byte [] key = tmpKey.getBytes();

    String endToken = "\"";
    byte[] end = endToken.getBytes();

    String newLineToken = "\n";
    byte[] newLine = newLineToken.getBytes();

    String contentTypeToken = "Content-Type";
    byte[] contentType = contentTypeToken.getBytes();

    //
    // Iterate over all multiparts to find the one whose name
    // matches the provided nameKey
    //
    for (Iterator it = multipartData.iterator(); it.hasNext(); )
    {
        // Check sanity with the extracted part.
        byte[] data = (byte[]) it.next();
        int startIndex = this.indexOf(data, key, 0);
        if (startIndex == -1) continue;
```

```
            // Extract the name of the current multipart
            startIndex += 1 + key.length;
            int endIndex = this.indexOf(data, end, startIndex);

            byte[] name = new byte[endIndex - startIndex];
            System.arraycopy(data, startIndex, name, 0, name.length);
            String tmpName = new String(name);

            // Is this the part we are looking for?
            if (tmpName.equals(nameKey))
            {
                // Find the start index of the return data
                int cntType = this.indexOf(data, contentType, endIndex);
                int nextRow = this.indexOf(data, newLine, cntType);
                nextRow = this.indexOf(data, newLine, nextRow + 1);

                // Declare and populate return data
                byte[] documentData = new byte[data.length - nextRow];
                System.arraycopy(data, nextRow, documentData,
                                 0, documentData.length);

                // This should be an uploaded document,
                // so we can safely create a DocumentHolder to
                // return.

                return new DocumentHolder (documentData,
                                 this.getContentType(data),
                                 this.getOrigPath(data));
            }
        }

        // No documents found.
        return null;
    }
```

Initialization

The only part in the `DocumentUploaderServlet` that remains to be looked at is the initialization. Examine how a `DocumentUploader` servlet ought to work and implement the initialization to match your needs.

Usually when a document is uploaded, one of three scenarios plays out:

- All upload parsing and post-upload processing went OK, and the user is redirected to a "all went OK" page.

- The uploaded multipart document contained no uploaded data document. The user is redirected to a page letting him or her know that a document is required.

- The upload parsing or the post-upload processing raised an exception of some kind, with either case resulting in the document not being uploaded properly. In this case, the user should be redirected to a "oops, try again" page with a user-friendly error message displayed.

To accommodate these outcomes, the document upload servlet must know where to redirect the user, given a certain upload status. URLs of such target Web pages make good servlet parameters. Listing 3-21 displays the initialization code.

Listing 3-21. The `init` *method and global data for the* `DocumentUploadServlet`

```
// Redirection pages, where to send the
// user after the potential document upload.
private String errorPage      = null;
private String noDocumentPage = null;
private String allOKPage      = null;

// Standard init
public void init(ServletConfig config) throws ServletException
{
    // Read the redirection parameters for pages
    // to redirect the user to after the document upload.
    this.errorPage = config.getInitParameter("ERROR_PAGE");
    this.noDocumentPage = config.getInitParameter("NO_DOCUMENT_PAGE");
    this.allOKPage = config.getInitParameter("ALL_OK_PAGE");

    // Revert to default redirection values in case
    // no parameter was provided.
    if (this.errorPage == null)
            this.errorPage = "/upload/uploadError.html";
    if (this.noDocumentPage == null)
            this.noDocumentPage = "/upload/noDocument.html";
    if (this.allOKPage == null)
            this.allOKPage = "/upload/noDocument.html";

}
```

Because you want the `DocumentUploader` servlet to be portable between different application servers and applications, all specific parameters (such as the exact URL to redirect to when an error was generated in the upload process) should be provided as initialization parameters. In general, I recommend using initialization parameters for most things specific to a particular application or server node—but be smart enough to provide default values to facilitate your own development process.

For industrial-strength software deployment, I recommend selecting a strategy regarding initialization parameters and sticking to it. If an initialization parameter is expected by a servlet but not provided by the application developer, the system may react in (at least) two ways:

- **Throw an exception that brings the servlet in question down**. This is the safe way of handling nonexistent required servlet parameters because the Web container administrator must intervene and provide a correct initialization parameter.

- **Provide a default value that permits the system to run**. This has the benefit of always enabling the system to run—and the drawback that a parameter "backdoor" left by a programmer may produce unwanted or capricious results.

The purpose of the `init` method is to read and store initialization parameters for future reference (for instance, in the `doPost` method).

Reflections on the DocumentUploader Servlet

Document uploading is perhaps one of the better ways to use servlets in normal, large-scale distributed applications. Because document uploaders, such as the servlet shown in Figure 3-30, must be able to handle binary data uploading, rather than character-based documents only, the raw servlet interface is preferable to the JSP equivalent.

> **NOTE** *Chapter 4 covers JavaServer Pages.*

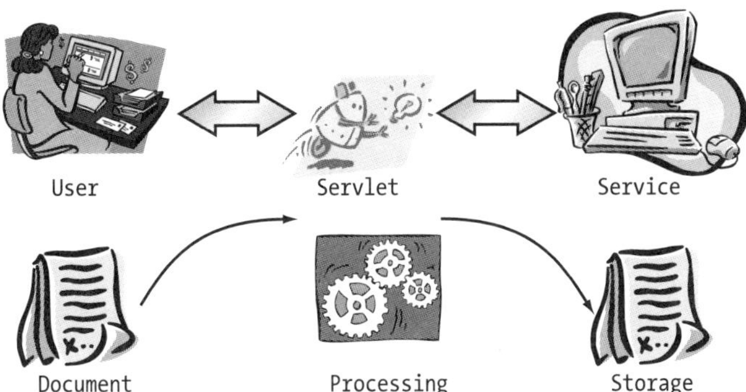

Figure 3-30. The process of uploading and displaying a document. Under normal circumstances, the `DocumentUploaderServlet` *would call upon the service of a document handler that would process the data further and would perhaps insert the processed data into a database or other persistent storage.*

Proceeding with Your Servlet Development

This sums up the pure servlet examples included in this book. The source code of all the examples, as well as upcoming updates or clarifications are online at `http://www.jguru.se/ServletBook`. Drop in for a bit of online advice on servlet development.

Java 2 Enterprise Edition
Taglib
Servlet JSP
Enterprise JavaBean
Struts

Part II

JSP

CHAPTER 4

JavaServer Pages

SERVLET TECHNOLOGY MAY BE efficient, scaleable, platform independent, and buzzword compliant—but it is far from practical when building Web applications. Servlets can become too inflexible to survive in the dynamic environment of a Web application when intimately tied to or used in generating the user interface. JavaServer Pages—JSPs for short—is a way to counter the shortcomings of servlets and bring the technology up to speed with the development process of most modern Web applications.

This chapter describes the JSP 1.2 specification, which is provided by many application servers, including the Apache Tomcat 4.0 reference implementation server. Tomcat 4.0 is a Web application server written in Java; it may be downloaded from the Tomcat project home page (`http://jakarta.apache.org/tomcat/index.html`).

Why JavaServer Pages?

When developing a server-side application, most developers want speed and manageability during the maintenance phase of the project. Indeed, the improved aspects of these issues, compared to raw servlets, are what sometimes make JSP the simpler and better alternative. At a glance, JSP looks like plain HTML documents with a few odd tags filled with Java code. This has the added benefit of providing a well-known document structure and development process for Web designers, who are generally excellent HTML hackers but poor Java programmers.

All content within a JSP is compiled to a servlet at deployment time (or first requested at runtime), and the JSP engine invokes said compiled servlet whenever an incoming request tries to access the JSP. Whenever text in the HTML portion of the JSP file is altered, the JSP engine *automatically* recompiles the JSP document to keep its associated servlet up to date.

The autocompilation process is one of the better aspects of JSP technology—anybody with HTML development skills may create or modify a JSP document, and the JSP-to-servlet compiler automatically creates, updates, and reloads a servlet that produces the same output as the JSP document. Think of this process as "the best of both worlds," combining the performance of servlets with the development simplicity of HTML. Figure 4-1 illustrates the procedure.

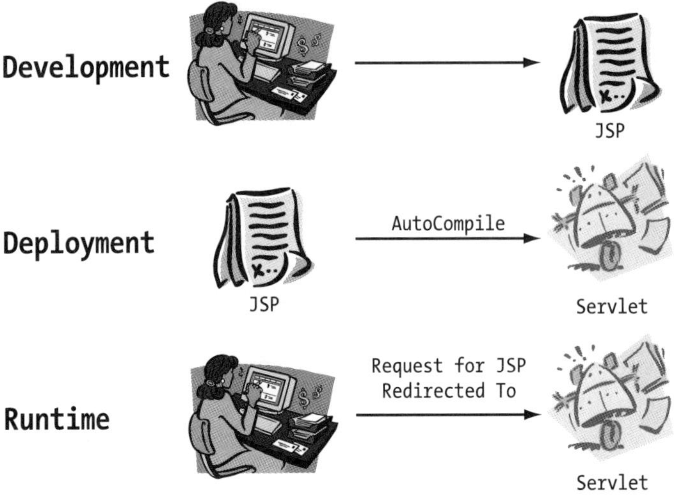

Figure 4-1. The process of JSP document generation and JSP-to-servlet compilation

The JSP specification is created with two primary output protocols in mind: HTML and XML. However, the technology is not limited to these output formats—it is fairly simple to create your own server-side tag structures to accommodate most types of back-end communication integration and result output formats.

Creating a JSP Document

During development, a developer creates a JSP document, called `firstJsp.jsp`:

```
<html>
<body>
     <h1>Simplest JSP</h1>

     <p>Current timestamp is <%= new java.util.Date() %></p>
</body>
</html>
```

Notice that the contents of `firstJsp.jsp` look like normal HTML text with the exception of the odd tag <%= ... %> containing "almost Java code." In JSP terminology, the special tag in `firstJsp.jsp` is called an *expression* tag and contains Java code that produces some form of `String` output. It is imperative that each JSP document ends with a `.jsp` file extension that is interpreted by the Web server/JSP engine as a JSP.

The first time a JSP document is requested (or during the deployment phase if you have configured your JSP engine to precompile the deployed JSP document), the JSP engine compiles a Java servlet from the JSP page. The servlet bytecode file is then stored in a cache directory; if you are using the Java 2 Enterprise Edition (J2EE) reference implementation, all compiled Java servlets are deployed in the `${J2EE_HOME}/repository/${HOSTNAME}/web` directory. Should you use the Apache Tomcat reference implementation, the cache directory is located in the `${TOMCAT_ROOT}/work/${HOSTNAME}` directory. Check the documentation of your particular JSP engine to find its cache directory. When searching this directory, the servlet byte code (`.class`) files are normally found. Note, however, that some application servers store the compiled form of the JSP document under other file suffices than `.class`.

Occasionally, you may want to keep the automatically generated Java source code for the generated servlet—it can be useful for debugging or learning purposes. Most JSP engines therefore have a configuration option telling them not to delete the generated source code file.

Listing 4-1 contains the rather chaotic servlet source code file autogenerated from the `firstJsp.jsp` page. You seldom need to be concerned with the source code of the autogenerated servlet, so every line won't be displayed. However, a few things are worth mentioning. For example, notice the last three import statements reference packages specific to the server used to compile the JSP (J2EE server in our case).

> **NOTE** *In the source code of the autogenerated servlet, most JSP compilers insert line-number comments to facilitate understanding and debugging. A comment in the form* `from=(4,28);to=(4,50)` *refers to the line and character number in the original JSP document. It is, therefore, easy to trace any errors back to the JSP source document. In simple JSP documents (such as* `firstJsp.jps`*), the whole document is inserted at once—not requiring line-number comments. For more complex JSP documents, the comments are frequent.*

Listing 4-1. Source code of the autogenerated servlet

```
import javax.servlet.*;
import javax.servlet.http.*;
import javax.servlet.jsp.*;
import javax.servlet.jsp.tagext.*;
import java.io.PrintWriter;
import java.io.IOException;
import java.io.FileInputStream;
import java.io.ObjectInputStream;
import java.util.Vector;
```

```
import org.apache.jasper.runtime.*;
import java.beans.*;
import org.apache.jasper.JasperException;


public class _0005cfirstJsp_0002ejspfirstJsp_jsp_1 extends HttpJspBase {


    static {
    }
    public _0005cfirstJsp_0002ejspfirstJsp_jsp_1( ) {
    }

    private static boolean _jspx_inited = false;

    public final void _jspx_init() throws JasperException {
    }

    public void _jspService(HttpServletRequest request,
        HttpServletResponse  response)
        throws IOException, ServletException {

        JspFactory _jspxFactory = null;
        PageContext pageContext = null;
        HttpSession session = null;
        ServletContext application = null;
        ServletConfig config = null;
        JspWriter out = null;
        Object page = this;
        String  _value = null;
        try {

            if (_jspx_inited == false) {
                _jspx_init();
                _jspx_inited = true;
            }
            _jspxFactory = JspFactory.getDefaultFactory();
            response.setContentType("text/html");
            pageContext = _jspxFactory.getPageContext(this, request, response,
               "", true, 8192, true);

            application = pageContext.getServletContext();
            config = pageContext.getServletConfig();
            session = pageContext.getSession();
            out = pageContext.getOut();
```

```
            //begin
              out.write("<html>\r \n<body>\r \n \t<h1>➥
                     Simplest JSP</h1>\r \n \r \n \t<p>Current timestamp is ");
            //end
          // begin [file="C:\\firstJsp.jsp";from=(4,28);to=(4,50)]
              out.print( new java.util.Date() );
          // end
          // begin
              out.write("</p>\r\n</body>\r\n</html>");
          // end

      } catch (Exception ex) {
          if (out.getBufferSize() != 0)
              out.clear();
          pageContext.handlePageException(ex);
      } finally {
          out.flush();
          _jspxFactory.releasePageContext(pageContext);
      }
   }
}
```

Two blocks of code appear in bold text. The topmost block contains declarations for automatically generated variables that can be accessed from Java statements in the body of the JSP document. The bold code block to the bottom of the page contains the code that generates the output to the Web browser. As you can see, when generating the servlet source code, the JSP engine reads all data from the JSP file and creates calls to `out.print` and `out.write`, which write the static data back to the browser.

The `_jspService` method in the generated code serves the same purpose for JSP documents as the `service` method for servlets; it is the method invoked for each call to the JSP document.

The *automagically* generated servlet code in Listing 4-1 is compiled to a normal servlet bytecode file following the same rules as the servlets you have been experimenting with in earlier chapters.

> **NOTE** *If you are curious about the automatically generated servlet file, a good starting point is the Apache Tomcat source code and documentation. Refer to* `http://jakarta.apache.org/tomcat/index.html` *for browsing or downloading the binaries and source.*

Finally, when calling the `firstJsp.jsp` file from a Web browser, the result is what you expected: The Java code written within the JSP expression tags has been transformed into its string output, as shown in Figure 4-2.

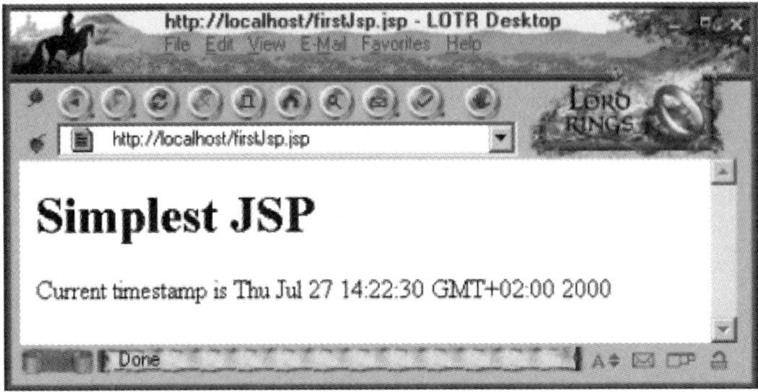

Figure 4-2. The result of calling the JSP document `firstJsp.jsp`

Altering the source code of the file `firstJsp.jsp` makes the JSP engine re-create the servlet source code file and recompiles the servlet. For example, if you edit the example JSP file to contain the following code:

```
<html>
<body>
     <h1>Simplest JSP</h1>

     <p>Current timestamp is <%= new java.util.GregorianCalendar() %></p>
</body>
</html>
```

then requesting this JSP will yield the output shown in Figure 4-3.

> **TIP** *You don't need to restart the JSP engine after modifying a JSP document. The server compares the modification timestamps on the JSP document and its autocompiled servlet cache. If the JSP document is more recent than its cache, the autocompilation process runs, and the new servlet version is used.*

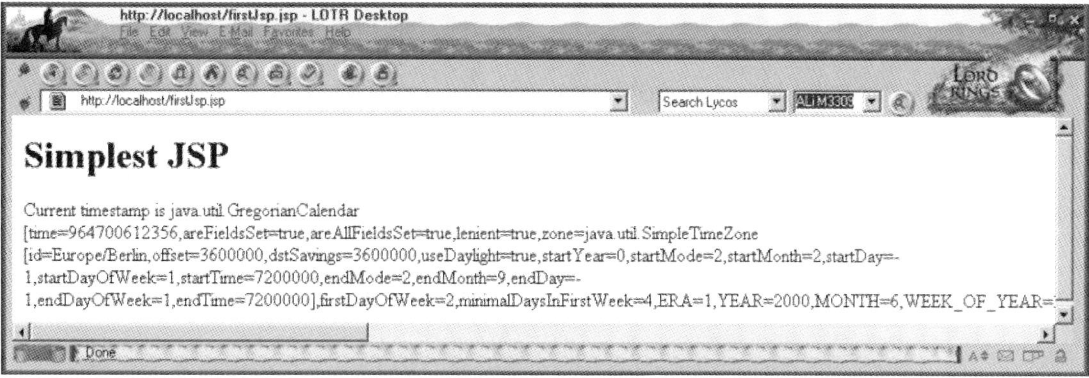

Figure 4-3. The result of calling the modified `simplestJsp.jsp` *document. The JSP engine has not been restarted between the two calls.*

JSP Patterns

JSP documents are compiled to servlets. The generated servlets therefore follow the same usage and design patterns as the servlets described in Chapters 1 and 2. However, the JSP source code documents may use additional patterns that facilitate certain frequently used tasks. These JSP-specific usage and design patterns require some extra description.

Static JSP Class Patterns

The inheritance hierarchy of the significant interfaces related to Servlets and JSP documents is fairly straightforward. All JSP documents are realized by classes implementing the `javax.servlet.jsp.JspPage` interface, which contains declarations of two life-cycle methods for all JSP documents—`jspInit()` and `jspDestroy()`.

Thus, from within a JSP document, you may call the `jspInit` method to set up custom initialization and `jspDestroy` to close or destroy any data that should be deleted when the JSP document is garbage-collected from memory.

The `service` method equivalent of the JSP document (`_jspService`), however, cannot be declared in a communication protocol neutral way. The reason is essentially that one cannot always provide a generic enough definition of the input and output streams from the JSP document. Instead, Sun's JavaSoft design engineers chose to implement the last life-cycle method, `_jspService`, in an interface extending `javax.servlet.jsp.JspPage`. For the JSP document type communicating via HTTP, the subinterface is `HttpJspPage`, which declares the method `_jspService(HttpServletRequest, HttpServletResponse)`. See Figure 4-4.

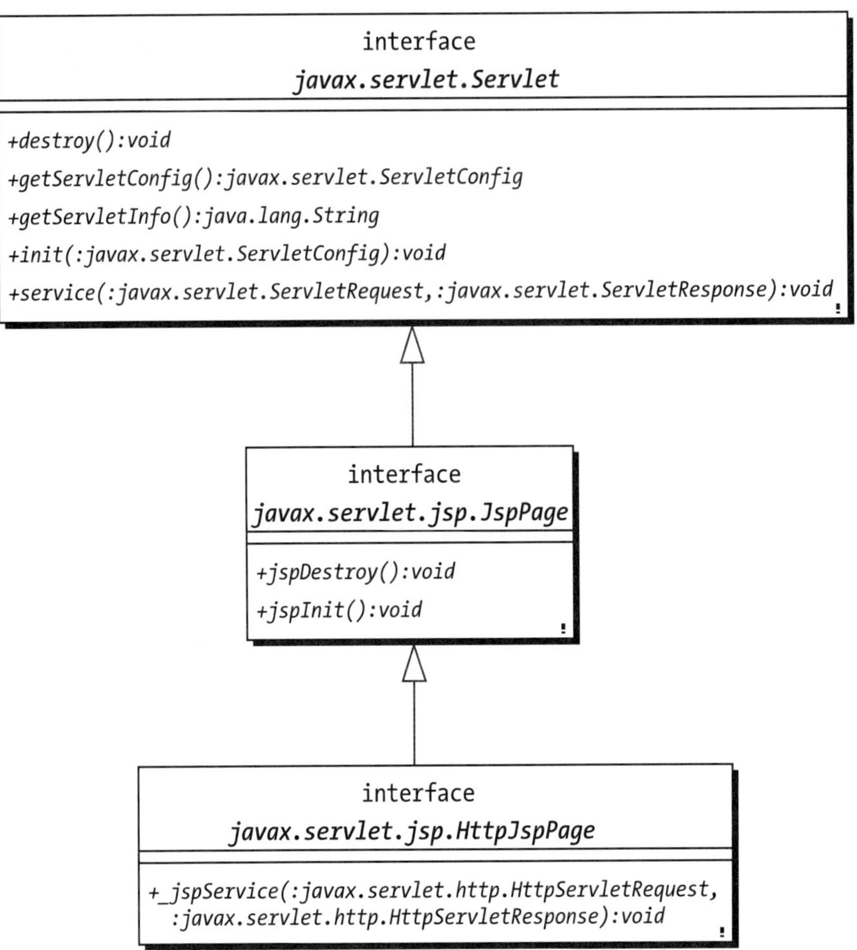

Figure 4-4. The class hierarchy of the `HttpJspPage` *class. Note that the root interface of all* `JspPage` *classes is the* `Servlet` *interface.*

Note that there may be other communication protocols besides HTTP that may be useful for JSP communications. If so, the arguments of the `_jspService` method implemented in the `HttpJspPage` interface would probably have to be replaced with something appropriate for that communication protocol.

The base class of any JSP-generated servlet must implement a series of interfaces, to facilitate most automatic code generation. The JSP document base class for the Tomcat reference implementation is `org.apache.jasper.runtime.JspBase`. Figure 4-5 illustrates the relationship between Tomcat's `HttpJspPage` base class and other relevant classes and interfaces of the servlet class hierarchy. The Tomcat JSP engine is used in the J2EE reference implementation and may therefore be of general interest as well as a working example. Be aware that the class structure shown in Figure 4-5 may not be accurate for other implementations of a JSP engine.

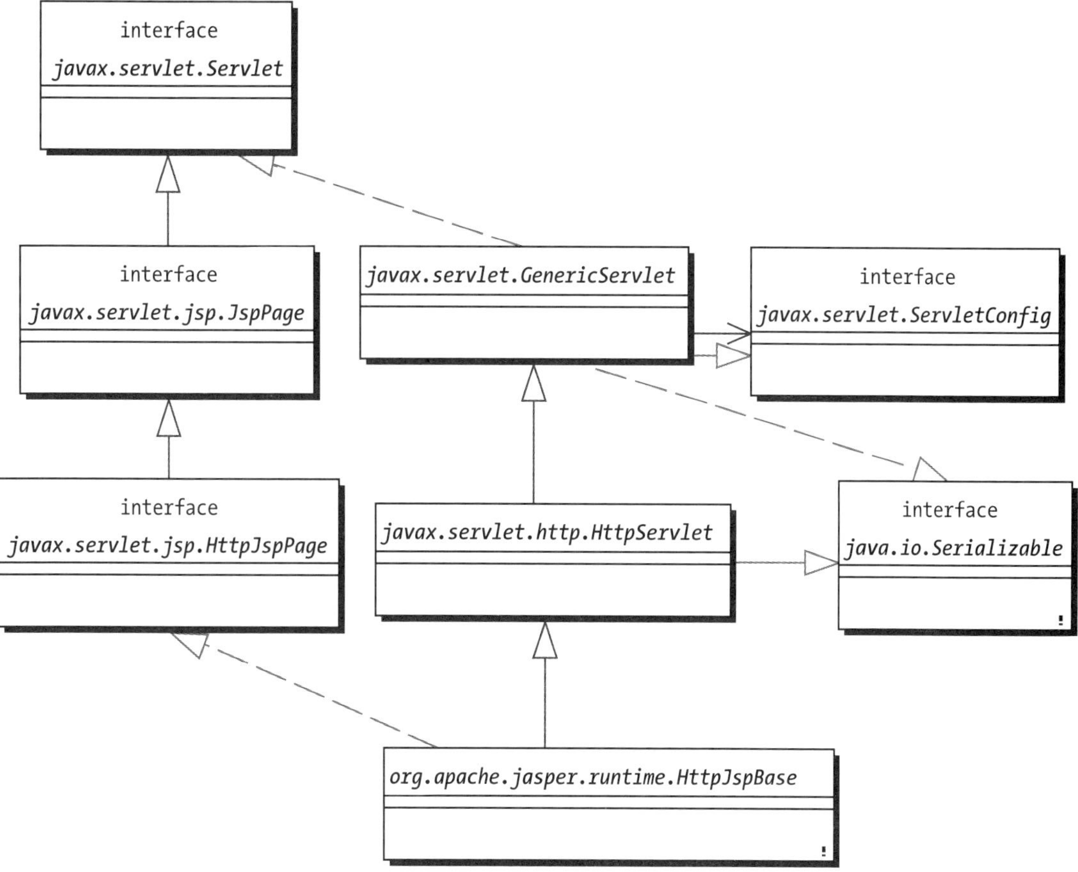

Figure 4-5. The hierarchy of the abstract `HttpJspPage` *class in the Tomcat reference engine implementation*

All automatically generated JSP servlets from the Tomcat engine extend `HttpJspBase` in the bottom of Figure 4-5. As you can see from the class hierarchy, `HttpJspBase` implements or extends quite a number of interfaces including `javax.servlet.Servlet`, `javax.servlet.http.HttpServlet`, `javax.servlet.ServletConfig`, and `javax.servlet.jsp.HttpJspPage`. Thus, all ingredients for creating a class that can handle most tasks in a JSP/servlet environment are in place.

JSP Life-Cycle Patterns

Much like the servlet life-cycle method calling pattern, JSP documents are compiled into servlet subclasses, the methods of which are called in a specific order. The life-cycle methods of a JSP document are similar to the corresponding servlet methods. See Figure 4-6.

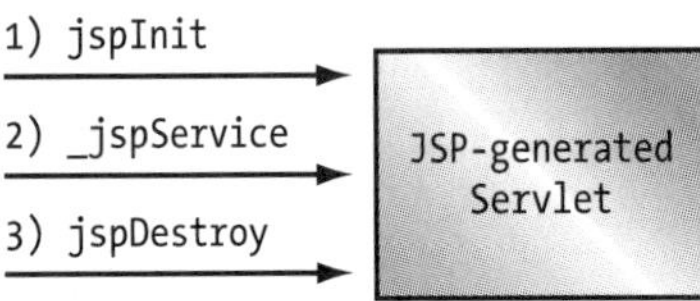

Figure 4-6. Life-cycle methods of a JSP-generated servlet, in call order

The `jspInit` method has the same significance as the `init(ServletConfig config)` method of `javax.servlet.Servlet`. It is called once per servlet class at initialization time and is mainly used for setting up class-wide parameters or any other custom initialization. The method may be declared by the user within the JSP document.

The `_jspService` method is executed once per client request and performs the same tasks as the `service(ServletRequest req, ServletResponse res)` method within a servlet. The JSP engine defines a few standard objects accessible from within the `_jspService` method, such as the standard `JspWriter`, `out`, which is connected to the response stream of the generated servlet. More on these standard object follows in the section "Automatically Created Objects (Implicit Objects)." Note that the `_jspService` method is *automagically* generated by the JSP engine originating from the text within the JSP document. It may therefore not be declared/overridden (in the JSP document) by the developer.

The `jspDestroy` method has the same significance as the `destroy()` method of `javax.servlet.Servlet`. It is called once per servlet class at destroy/garbage-collection time and mainly used for erasing or closing class-wide parameters such as lock files, threads, or network connections. The user may declare the method within the JSP document.

Automatically Created Objects (Implicit Objects)

The servlet engine running the JSP-generated servlets creates a few predefined objects that facilitate the housekeeping of objects and values specific to an application and a user session. The JSP specification refers to these objects as *implicit objects*. Implicit objects are declared and created by the JSP engine, rather than the user, but are available at all times to the JSP developer. It is illegal to give an explicit object (declared by the developer) the same name as an implicit object.

Before starting to dissect the meaning and purpose of implicit objects, let's demystify them by examining the code that generates them. Listing 4-2 shows the declaration and creation of implicit objects in a Tomcat-generated JSP servlet.

Listing 4-2. The first part of the automatically generated `_jspService` *method contains the declaration and instantiation of the implicit JSP objects.*

```
public void _jspService(HttpServletRequest request,
   HttpServletResponse  response)
...
{
     JspFactory _jspxFactory = null;
     PageContext pageContext = null;
     HttpSession session = null;
    ServletContext application = null;        Declaration
     ServletConfig config = null;
     JspWriter out = null;
     Object page = this;
     String  _value = null;

     ...
         _jspxFactory = JspFactory.getDefaultFactory();
         response.setContentType("text/html");
         pageContext = _jspxFactory.getPageContext(this, request,      Instantiation
                     response, "", true, 8192, true);

         application = pageContext.getServletContext();
         config = pageContext.getServletConfig();
         session = pageContext.getSession();
         out = pageContext.getOut();
     ...
}
```

The objects may be split into multiple categories, depending on their contract and task:

- **Factory classes that create objects for usage within the JSP-generated servlet**. The `JspFactory` class, which is responsible for creating most JSP engine–dependent objects, belongs to this category of objects.

- **Container or dictionary classes, useful for storing objects for later use and retrieving them when wanted.** The function of these classes compares quite well to any subclass of `java.util.Dictionary`, such as a normal `HashMap`. Depending on what kinds of entities the container class stores, its name and demeanor varies slightly—but the basic idea is always similar to a `HashMap`. The *application, session, request,* and *page* objects define the four scopes available to a JSP programmer and also store objects during their respective scope.

What is the significance of the different scopes? Quick answer: All bound attributes are guaranteed to exist as long as the scope dictionary object. Each scope represents a particular period of time, the length of which corresponds to a scope desired to hold attributes.

Imagine a user calling a JSP document (let's call it `JSP1`) twice. The first call is forwarded to another JSP document (`JSP2`), and the second call is handled completely by `JSP1`. The different scopes available to the JSP developer for attribute setting and getting are illustrated in Figure 4-7.

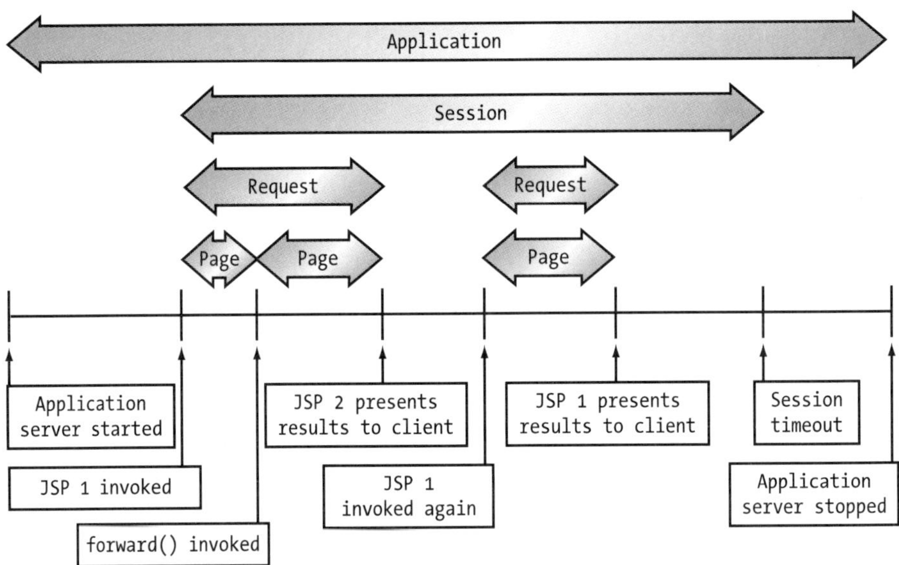

Figure 4-7. The different scopes available to the `JSP` *instance. The two calls illustrated above the timeline are assumed to be made by the same client; otherwise the session scope would not extend over the two requests.*

- *Application* scope attributes are available from when they are initially set until the application server is stopped.

- *Session* scope attributes are available from when they are initially set until the session is terminated by the user or through a `HttpSession` timeout.

- *Request* scope attributes are available from the incoming call until the results have been delivered to the calling client. Unless using the forwarding or including patterns to access data and execute code in other JSP documents, the Request scope is identical to the Page scope.
- *Page* scope attributes are available within the execution of a single JSP document only.

Next, dissect two of the key implicit object classes, `JspFactory` and `PageContext`, to better understand the capabilities of the JSP infrastructure.

JspFactory

The `JspFactory` class shown in Figure 4-8 contains methods to get/create, set/assign, and release/destroy the `PageContext` and the default `JspFactory`.

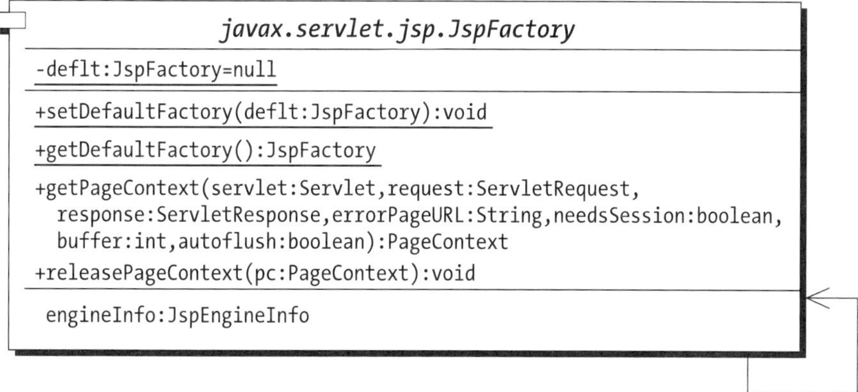

Figure 4-8. The abstract `JspFactory` *class*

The singleton `JspFactory` instance, `deflt`, is set and retrieved by the `getDefaultFactory` and `setDefaultFactory` methods. The class of the actual object is a subclass of the `JspFactory` class; in the Tomcat/Jasper reference implementation, the actual implementation class hierarchy of the `JspFactory` is `JspFactoryImpl`, as shown in Figure 4-9.

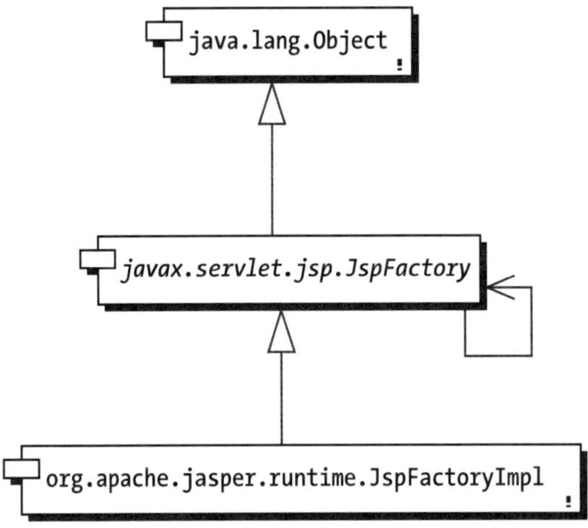

Figure 4-9. Class diagram of the `JspFactoryImpl` *class, which is the concrete implementation of the* `JspFactory` *used by Apache's Jasper engine*

> **NOTE** *Quoting the Jakarta Web site: "Jasper is the reference implementation of the JSP specification. It is packaged in Tomcat along with Catalina (the reference implementation of the servlet specification). It is a goal to have Jasper as a component that is independent of Catalina (and vice-versa). We're currently working on this."*

The `getEngineInfo()` method retrieves a `JspEngineInfo` object, containing the single method `getSpecificationVersion()`, which returns the JSP engine version, such as 1.1.

PageContext

The `PageContext` class provides a common, unified interface between the JSP engine and the JSP document. The `PageContext` contains all namespaces accessible from the JSP document, as well as some Page-scoped attributes. The `PageContext` class is abstract; the actual instance used therefore extends the `PageContext` class and implements relevant interfaces from the standard JSP class hierarchy.

As shown in Figure 4-10, the `PageContext` class defines a multitude of constants and methods. However, most of these have a common usage pattern, so the number of different method types is rather small.

```
javax.servlet.jsp.PageContext
----------------------------------------------------------------
+PAGE_SCOPE:int=1
+REQUEST_SCOPE:int=2
+SESSION_SCOPE:int=3
+APPLICATION_SCOPE:int=4
+PAGE:String="javax.servlet.jsp.jspPage"
+PAGECONTEXT:String="javax.servlet.jsp.jspPageContext"
+REQUEST:String="javax.servlet.jsp.jspRequest"
+RESPONSE:String="javax.servlet.jsp.jspResponse"
+CONFIG:String="javax.servlet.jsp.jspConfig"
+SESSION:String="javax.servlet.jsp.jspSession"
+OUT:String="javax.servlet.jsp.jspOut"
+APPLICATION:String="javax.servlet.jsp.jspApplication"
+EXCEPTION:String="javax.servlet.jsp.jspException"
----------------------------------------------------------------
+initialize(servlet:Servlet,request:ServletRequest,response:ServletResponse,
  errorPageURL:String,needsSession:boolean,bufferSize:int,
  autoFlush:boolean):void
+release():void
+setAttribute(name:String,attribute:Object):void
+setAttribute(name:String,o:Object,scope:int):void
+getAttribute(name:String):Object
+getAttribute(name:String,scope:int):Object
+findAttribute(name:String):Object
+removeAttribute(name:String):void
+removeAttribute(name:String,scope:int):void
+getAttributesScope(name:String):int
+forward(relativeUrlPath:String):void
+include(relativeUrlPath:String):void
+handlePageException(e:Exception):void
+handlePageException(t:Throwable):void
+pushBody():BodyContent
+popBody():JspWriter
----------------------------------------------------------------
 attributeNamesInScope:Enumeration[]
 out:JspWriter
 session:HttpSession
 page:Object
 request:ServletRequest
 response:ServletResponse
 exception:Exception
 servletConfig:ServletConfig
 servletContext:ServletContext
```

Figure 4-10. The abstract `PageContext` *class. Note its many constants—some of which are used to identify and access a particular scope.*

Essentially, the `PageContext` class consists of four types of methods:

- Getting and setting implicit objects: `getSession()`, `getOut()`, `getRequest()`, and `getPage()`
- Getting, setting, and removing attributes within the different scopes: `getAttribute(PageContext.APPLICATION)`, `setAttribute(PageContext.SESSION, obj)`, `removeAttribute(PageContext.PAGE)`, `findAttribute("attibuteName")`, `getAttribute(PageContext.APPLICATION)`, and `getAttributeNamesInScope(PageContext.PAGE_SCOPE)`
- Facilitating delegation of execution using the forwarding and including patterns: `forward()` and `include()`
- Methods for internal housekeeping and initialization: `release()` and `initialize()`

For most JSP applications, the most useful methods are listed in the second category in the preceding bulleted list; they handle scoped attributes.

Next, investigate the attributes bound to each of the naming scopes by running a small example JSP whose output is shown in Figure 4-11. The output presents all attributes and values bound to each of the standard four scopes in the Tomcat reference implementation. Note that the Page context (or scope) holds most of the implicit objects available to the JSP developer. This is clearly visible in the generated code. The code for this JSP document, `testPageContext.jsp`, is provided in Listing 4-3.

Listing 4-3. Code for the `testPageContext.jsp` *document*

```
<%--
        This JSP document displays all attributes
        of JSP PageContext and their scope.
--%>
<%@ page import="java.util.*" %>

<%!
        //
        // Method that returns the contents of an Enumeration
        //
        private String writeEnumeration(Enumeration en)
        {
                StringBuffer buf = new StringBuffer();
```

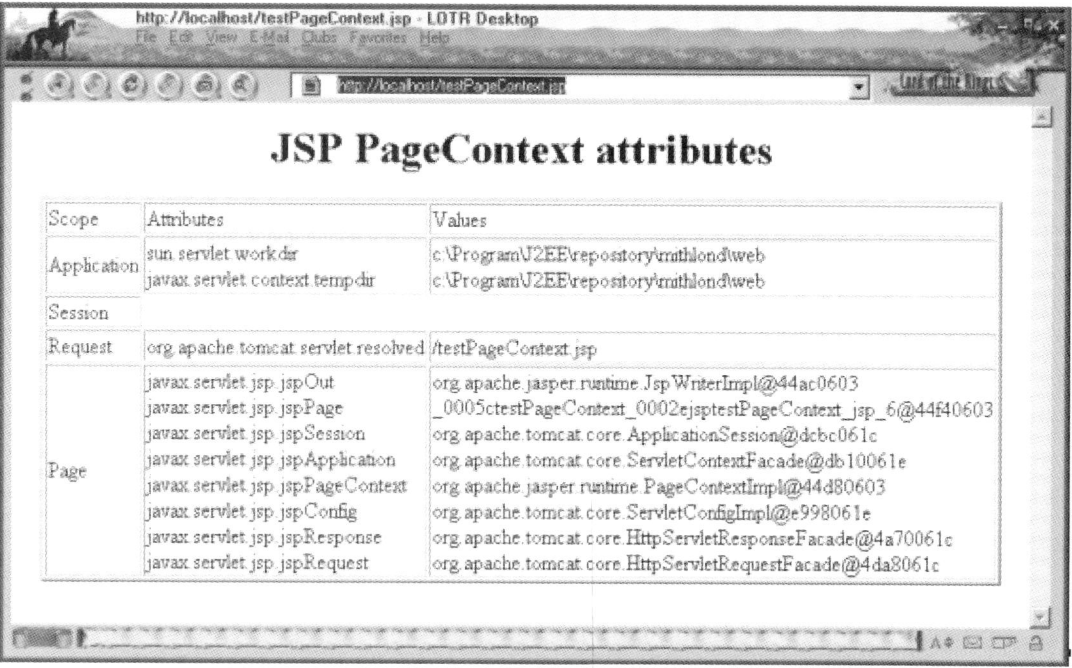

Figure 4-11. JSP document showing all bound instances in the Tomcat reference engine

```
            while(en.hasMoreElements())
            {
                    // Append to the StringBuffer
                    buf.append("" + en.nextElement() + "<br>");
            }

            // Done. Return.
            return buf.toString();
    }

    //
    // Method that finds and returns all attributes
    // of a particular JSP scope
    //
    private String getAttributeValues(Enumeration en, PageContext ctx)
    {
            StringBuffer buf = new StringBuffer();
```

```
                while(en.hasMoreElements())
                {
                    // Append the found attribute to buf
                    buf.append("" + ctx.findAttribute(
                    "" + en.nextElement()) + "<br>");
                }

                // Done.
                return buf.toString();
        }

%>

<html>
<body>
        <center><h1>JSP PageContext attributes (for Tomcat)</h1>

        <table border=2>

        <tr>
                <td><b>Scope</b></td>
                <td><b>Attributes</b></td>
                <td><b>Values</b></td>
        </tr>

        <tr>
                <td>Application</td>
                <td>
        <%= writeEnumeration( pageContext.getAttributeNamesInScope(
                PageContext.APPLICATION_SCOPE)) %>
                </td>
                <td>
        <%= getAttributeValues( pageContext.getAttributeNamesInScope(
            PageContext.APPLICATION_SCOPE), pageContext) %>
                </td>
        </tr>
```

```
        <tr>
                <td>Session</td>
                <td>
        <%= writeEnumeration( pageContext.getAttributeNamesInScope(
                PageContext.SESSION_SCOPE)) %>
                </td>
                <td>
        <%= getAttributeValues( pageContext.getAttributeNamesInScope(
            PageContext.SESSION_SCOPE), pageContext) %>
                </td>
        </tr>

        <tr>
                <td>Request</td>
                <td>
        <%= writeEnumeration( pageContext.getAttributeNamesInScope(
            PageContext.REQUEST_SCOPE)) %>
                </td>
                <td>
        <%= getAttributeValues( pageContext.getAttributeNamesInScope(
                PageContext.REQUEST_SCOPE), pageContext) %>
                </td>
        </tr>

        <tr>
                <td>Page</td>
                <td>
        <%= writeEnumeration( pageContext.getAttributeNamesInScope(
            PageContext.PAGE_SCOPE)) %>
                </td>
                <td>
        <%= getAttributeValues( pageContext.getAttributeNamesInScope(
                PageContext.PAGE_SCOPE), pageContext) %>
                </td>
        </tr>

        </table></center>

</body>
</html>
```

The details of JSP syntax will be explained in "Elements of JSP" later in this chapter, but you may already be able to get a feeling for how the autocompiler works. The preceding example's purpose is to show the contents of the different scopes in the Tomcat servlet engine reference implementation. The code actually obtaining the context, and printing the values its values to the client browser, are highlighted in bold in Listing 4-3.

> **TIP** *The* `writeEnumeration` *and* `getAttributeValues` *methods use a* `StringBuffer` *instead of a* `String`, *for reasons of performance. All Java strings are immutable, which means they are constant and cannot be modified programmatically once created. A* `StringBuffer`, *on the other hand, is the recommended implementation for a mutable string. Because the* `writeEnumeration` *and* `getAttributeValues` *methods build a resulting string by concatenating smaller string pieces, the* `StringBuffer` *is the more efficient choice of internal data type.*

Now augment the code by calling some attribute setter methods for the three relevant scopes application, session and request; the output of the `testPageContext.jsp` document changes to what you see in Figure 4-12.

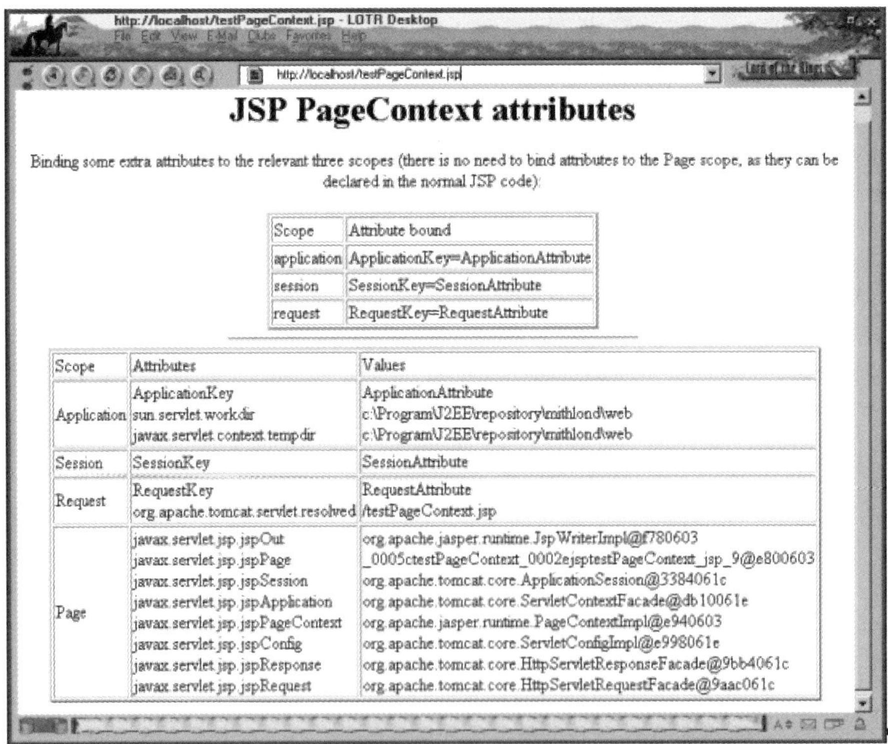

Figure 4-12. The result of the running `testPageContext.jsp` *in the Tomcat reference implementation engine*

Note that the attribute settings displayed in the preceding figure are not common to all implementations of JSP engines; it is specific to the Tomcat implementation. If the `testJspPage.jsp` document is deployed in another JSP engine, a quite different—and, after giving the matter some thought, more attractive—result is produced. See Figure 4-13.

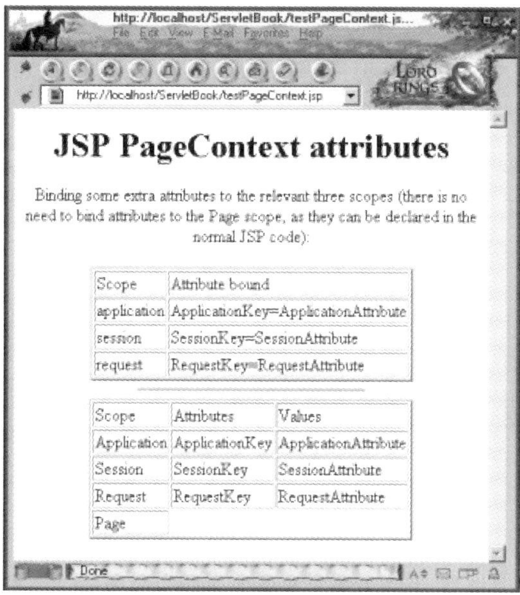

Figure 4-13. The result of the running `testPageContext.jsp` *in the Orion Server engine.*

The JSP code to bind the attributes to their respective scope is trivial. Here's the code that does it:

```
<%
   // Bind an attribute to each scope
   application.setAttribute("ApplicationKey", "ApplicationAttribute");
   session.setAttribute("SessionKey", "SessionAttribute");
   request.setAttribute("RequestKey", "RequestAttribute");
%>
```

The J2EE reference implementation's `PageContextImpl` class is a subclass of the abstract `PageContext` class, as shown in Figure 4-14. However, all methods available to the JSP developer are declared in `PageContext`.

Although the concrete classes used in a Web application server are specific per application server implementation. Thankfully, all classes and methods of the standard J2EE API are defined in superclasses or interfaces of the concrete

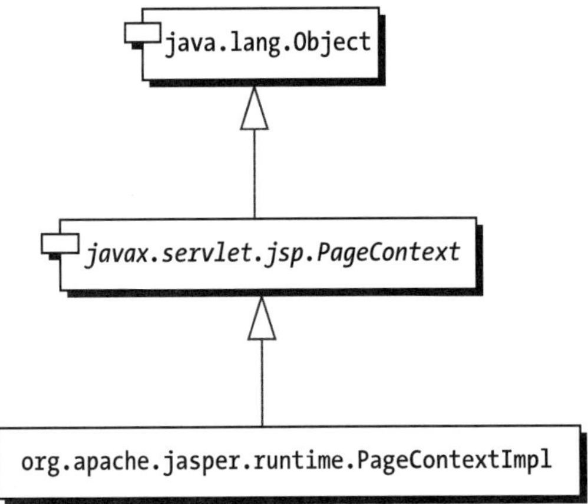

Figure 4-14. Inheritance hierarchy of the `PageContextImpl` *class that is taken from the reference implementation*

implementation classes; an example of this is shown in Figure 4-14. Therefore, developers need not worry about specific implementation classes; all useable methods are defined in the standard API.

Elements of JSP

Each JSP document may contain seven types of constructs:

- Comments
- Declarations
- Scriptlets
- Expressions
- Directives
- Actions
- Tag libraries

Although these elements will allow many, rather powerful types of statement blocks to execute, it is important to minimize the amount of Java code executed within a JSP document. This is especially important in the case of creating a system that adheres to the J2EE development model because the model dictates that the majority of code logic should be placed within Enterprise JavaBeans, which should be accessed from JSP documents.

We will study the J2EE coding platform and its front-end design using servlets and JSP documents in Chapter 5. For now, take a look at the existing JSP elements.

JSP Comments

JSP comments are purely server-side comments and are not sent with the response stream to the client browser. In fact, text between server-side comment delimiters are not included in the servlet source code generated by the JSP engine.

JSP comments reside between `<%--` and `--%>` delimiters, as shown in Listing 4-4.

Listing 4-4. Code snippet showing a JSP comment

```
<%--
                    This is a JSP comment, which
                    will continue, multi-line style
                    until terminated with the closing
                    comment delimiter.
--%>
```

JSP Declarations

Variables and methods available within the JSP document may be declared between declaration delimiters, `<%!` and `%>`. All text found between declaration delimiters is inserted into the class-level area (outside of any methods) within the automatically generated servlet. As an example, the JSP document `declarations.jsp` in Listing 4-5 declares four private members, all of which reside at the class level within the generated servlet.

Listing 4-5. JSP declaration examples

```
<%--
   This JSP document shows the declaration of
   a variable and methods, specific to this
   JSP document.
--%>

<html>
   <h1>JSP Declaration example</h1>
```

```
<%!
   //
   // Simple variable declaration
   //
   private StringBuffer buf;
%>

<p>Variable buf has been declared!</p>

<%!
   //
   // Simple method declaration
   //
   private String getBuffer()
   {
      return buf.toString();
   }
%>

<p>Method getBuffer() has been declared!</p>

<%!
   //
   // Compound declaration
   //
   private void fillBuffer()
   {
      // Fill the StringBuffer buf with
      // some data, and create it if
      // it does not currently exist.
      if(buf == null) buf = new StringBuffer();

     for(char i = 'a'; i <= 'z'; i++) buf.append(i);
   }

   private void createBuffer()
   {
      buf = new StringBuffer();
   }
%>

<p>Methods fillBuffer() and createBuffer() have been declared!</p>

</html>
```

The result of the JSP document in Listing 4-5 is fairly straightforward. Listing 4-6 contains the Java source code for the autogenerated servlet. The bold code and comments are a result of the declarations in the JSP document in the preceding listing. Notice the absence of the JSP comments, `<%-- --%>`, in the generated servlet code.

> **CAUTION** *Remember that all variables declared in a servlet are global to all users of that servlet, as each servlet request spawns a new* `Thread`*—not a new* `Servlet` *instance—that handles the user's call. JSP documents are autocompiled to servlets, so all rules that apply to servlets apply equally to JSP documents. In the multithreaded environment of a servlet, make sure not to use all declared private member variables read-only. Private members are thread-safe only if your JSP document is converted into a servlet that implements* `SingleThreadModel`.

Listing 4-6. The code of the Java servlet, automatically generated from the JSP document

```
import javax.servlet.*;
import javax.servlet.http.*;
import javax.servlet.jsp.*;
import javax.servlet.jsp.tagext.*;
import java.io.PrintWriter;
import java.io.IOException;
import java.io.FileInputStream;
import java.io.ObjectInputStream;
import java.util.Vector;
import org.apache.jasper.runtime.*;
import java.beans.*;
import org.apache.jasper.JasperException;


public class _0005cdeclarations_0002ejspdeclarations_jsp_5 extends HttpJspBase {

    // begin [file="C:\\declarations.jsp";from=(10,4);to=(16,1)]


        //
        // Simple variable declaration
        //
        private StringBuffer buf;
```

```
// end
// begin [file="C:\\declarations.jsp";from=(20,4);to=(28,1)]

  //
  // Simple method declaration
  //
  private String getBuffer()
  {
    return buf.toString();
  }

// end
// begin [file="C:\\declarations.jsp";from=(32,4);to=(52,1)]


  //
  // Compound declaration
  //
  private void fillBuffer()
  {
    // Fill the StringBuffer buf with
    // some data, and create it if
    // it does not currently exist.
    if(buf == null) buf = new StringBuffer();

   for(char i = 'a'; i <= 'z'; i++) buf.append(i);
  }

  private void createBuffer()
  {
    buf = new StringBuffer();
  }

// end

static {
}
public _0005cdeclarations_0002ejspdeclarations_jsp_5( ) {
}

private static boolean _jspx_inited = false;

public final void _jspx_init() throws JasperException {
}
```

```
public void _jspService(HttpServletRequest request,
    HttpServletResponse  response)
    throws IOException, ServletException {

    JspFactory _jspxFactory = null;
    PageContext pageContext = null;
    HttpSession session = null;
    ServletContext application = null;
    ServletConfig config = null;
    JspWriter out = null;
    Object page = this;
    String  _value = null;
    try {

        if (_jspx_inited == false) {
            _jspx_init();
            _jspx_inited = true;
        }
        _jspxFactory = JspFactory.getDefaultFactory();
        response.setContentType("text/html");
        pageContext = _jspxFactory.getPageContext(this, request, response,
                        "", true, 8192, true);

        application = pageContext.getServletContext();
        config = pageContext.getServletConfig();
        session = pageContext.getSession();
        out = pageContext.getOut();

        // begin
            out.write("\r\n\r\n<html>\r\n\t<h1>JSP Declaration➥
            example</h1>\r\n\r\n\r\n\t");
        // end
        // begin
            out.write("\r\n\r\n\t<p>Variable buf has been➥
            declared!</p>\r\n\r\n\t");
        // end
        // begin
            out.write("\r\n\r\n\t<p>Method getBuffer() has been➥
            declared!</p>\r\n\r\n\t");
        // end
        // begin
            out.write("\r\n\r\n\t<p>Methods fillBuffer() and➥
            createBuffer() have been declared!</p>\r\n\t\r\n</html>");
        // end
```

```
            } catch (Exception ex) {
                if (out.getBufferSize() != 0)
                    out.clear();
                pageContext.handlePageException(ex);
            } finally {
                out.flush();
                _jspxFactory.releasePageContext(pageContext);
            }
        }
    }
```

The result (rather silly, I admit) in the client browser is shown in Figure 4-15.

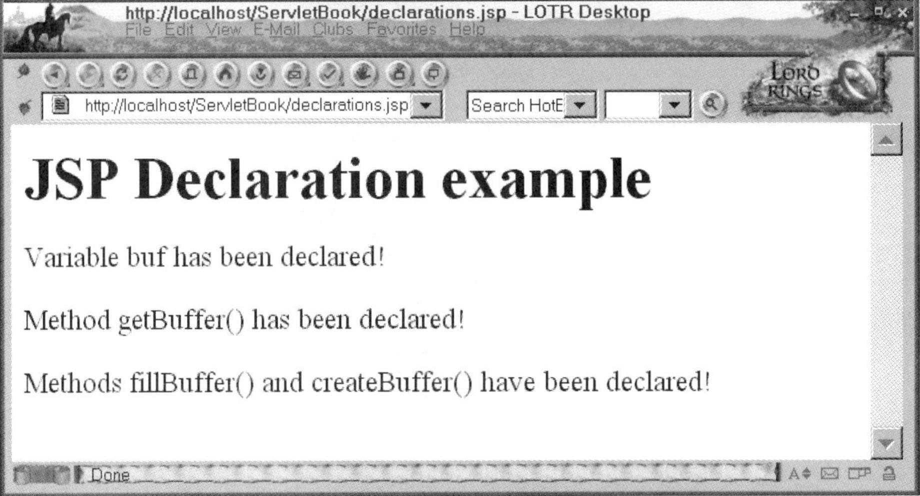

Figure 4-15. Resulting output of invoking the `declarations.jsp` *document.*

> **TIP** *Everything inside a JSP declaration container will be pasted into the class scope of the automatically generated servlet source. Therefore, all legal Java method declarations are valid in a JSP declaration.*

JSP Scriptlets

The dynamic execution and calling of Java objects bound to a JSP document is carried out via scripting elements (*scriptlets*)—in other words, embedded code, separated from the static context of the JSP document by delimiters `<%` and `%>`.

Because the default language of JSP documents is Java (although, theoretically, any language capable of producing and consuming a stream could be used), the mechanics of interpreting scriptlets involves nothing new.

Assuming you have declared the methods `createBuffer()` and `fillBuffer()` as done in Listing 4-6, you could invoke them within a scriptlet in the JSP document (see Listing 4-7).

Listing 4-7. JSP scriptlet examples

```
<%-- Invoke the methods in order. --%>

<%
   // Within a scriptlet, any
   // normal Java code is allowed.
   createBuffer();
   fillBuffer();
%>
```

The content of a scriptlet is pasted into the `_jspService` method of the autogenerated servlet, rather than at the class level (or scope) as is the case with JSP declarations. The `_jspService` snippet containing the automatically generated code from the JSP scriptlet is shown in Listing 4-8.

Listing 4-8. Scriptlet code pasted into the `_jspService` method

```
    public void _jspService(HttpServletRequest request,
        HttpServletResponse  response)
        throws IOException, ServletException {
        // ... lots of code skipped ...

        // begin [file="C:\\scriptlets.jsp";from=(58,3);to=(65,1)]
   // Within a scriptlet, any
   // normal Java code is allowed.
   createBuffer();
   fillBuffer();
        // end

        // ... more code skipped ...
}
```

As you can see, scriptlet code is inserted into and executed from within the `_jspService` method. When the JSP engine autocompiles the JSP document into a servlet, the scriptlet output is inserted into the outgoing response stream of the servlet at the place where they are located within the code. (Order is significant.)

JSP Expressions

Similar to JSP scriptlets, JSP *expressions* are inserted into the `_jspService` method and evaluated in order, as shown in Listing 4-9. JSP expressions, however, are smaller building blocks whose task solely is to output the result of an expression into the outgoing response stream of the JSP document. JSP expressions are inserted within expression tags, `<%=` and `%>`.

> **NOTE** *JSP expressions are not terminated by a semicolon (;).*

Listing 4-9. JSP scriptlet example. The scriptlet content and equivalent autogenerated code are displayed in bold.

```
<%-- Output the expression --%>

<p>The contents of buf: <%= getBuffer() %></p>

<%-- Use the scriptlet equivalent of the JSP expression above. --%>

<%
   // This scriptlet will write to the
   // standard output stream of this JSP.
   out.println("<p>The scriptlet equivalent of a JSP expression is:");
   out.print(getBuffer());
   out.println("</p>");
%>
```

The resulting, autogenerated servlet code is:

```
  // begin
      out.write("\r\n\r\n\t<p>The contents of buf: ");
  // end
  // begin [file="C:\\expressions.jsp";from=(69,28);to=(69,41)]
      out.print( getBuffer() );
  // end
  // begin
      out.write("</p>\r\n\r\n\t");
  // end
// begin [file="C:\\expressions.jsp";from=(73,3);to=(79,1)]
```

```
// This scriptlet will write to the
// standard output stream of this JSP.
out.println("<p>The scriptlet equivalent of a JSP expression is:");
out.print(getBuffer());
out.println("</p>");
        // end
```

As you can see, the effect of JSP expression tags is to place the enclosing expression as argument to an `out.print()` statement. Thus, you cannot terminate the expression with a semicolon, as it would generate a syntactic error in the generated servlet. So, if you combine our full declaration, scriptlet, and expression examples in a single JSP document, the browser view would look like Figure 4-16.

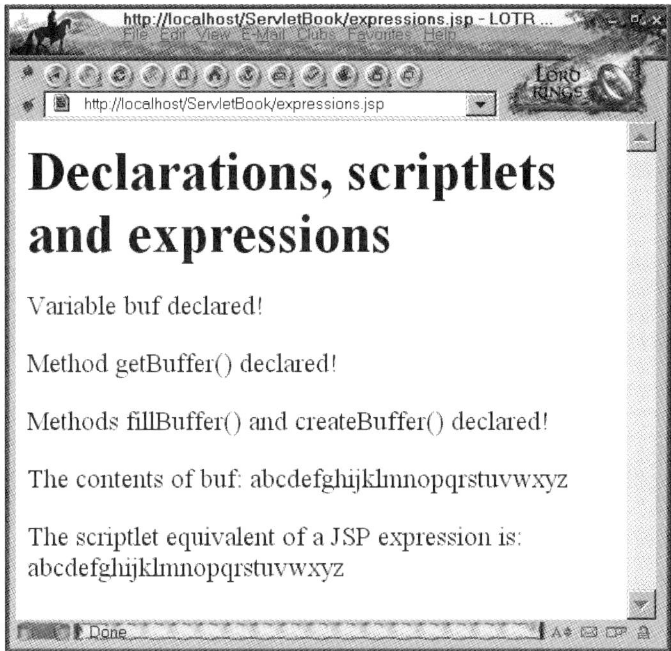

Figure 4-16. Results of the running

Listing 4-10 contains the code for the JSP document shown in Figure 4-16.

Listing 4-10. JSP code for the result shown in Figure 4-16

```
<%--
        This JSP document shows the declaration and
        usage of scriptlets, Java programmatic code
        blocks embedded in a JSP document.
--%>
```

```
<html>
        <h1>Using JSP declarations, scriptlets and expressions</h1>
        <%!

                //
                // Simple variable declaration
                //
                private StringBuffer buf;
        %>

        <p>Variable buf has been declared!</p>

        <%!
                //
                // Simple method declaration
                //
                private String getBuffer()
                {
                        return buf.toString();
                }
        %>

        <p>Method getBuffer() has been declared!</p>

        <%!

                //
                // Compound declaration
                //
                private void fillBuffer()
                {
                        // Fill the StringBuffer buf with
                        // some data, and create it if
                        // it does not currently exist.
                        if(buf == null) buf = new StringBuffer();

               for(char i = 'a'; i <= 'z'; i++) buf.append(i);
                }
```

```
                private void createBuffer()
                {

                        buf = new StringBuffer();
                }
        %>

        <p>Methods fillBuffer() and createBuffer() have been declared!</p>

        <%-- Invoke the methods in order. --%>

        <%
                // Within a scriptlet, any
                // normal Java code is allowed.

                createBuffer();

                fillBuffer();
        %>

        <%-- Output the expression --%>

        <p>The contents of buf are: <%= getBuffer() %></p>

        <%-- Use the scriptlet equivalent of the JSP expression above. --%>

        <%
           // This scriptlet will write to the
           // standard output stream of this JSP.
           out.println("<p>The scriptlet equivalent of the JSP expression is:");
           out.print(getBuffer());
           out.println("</p>");
        %>
</html>
```

JSP Directives

The JSP elements discussed up to now have all inserted their contents at class level or within the `_jspService` method of the resulting servlet. However, to use classes not located in package `java.lang`, you have to import classes from other packages—unless you want to use full package notation at all times in the code.

JSP directives handle all definitions that apply to a single JSP document only and are provided within directives delimiters, `<%@` and `%>`. Three types of directives exist:

- The JSP `<%@ page %>` directive defines attributes that apply to an entire JSP document. The page directive is explained in detail in the next section.

- The JSP `<%@ include %>` directive includes a file of text or code at the time the JSP is compiled into a servlet. The include directive is covered in "The JSP **`<%@ include %>`** Directive" section.

- The `JSP <%@ taglib %>` directive makes a set of custom-made tags accessible in the JSP document. The taglib directive is covered in its own section ("JSP `<%@ taglib %>` Directive") later in this chapter.

The JSP <%@ page %> Directive

The `<%@ page %>` directive is used for a multitude of tasks, as can be seen from its flexible syntax:

```
<%@ page options %>
```

where `options` may be one or more of these attributes: `language`, `extends`, `import`, `session`, `buffer`, `autoFlush`, `isThreadSafe`, `isErrorPage`, `isErrorPage`, `contentType`, and `infoString`. Although each attribute is simple when studied by itself, minding all attributes when developing a JSP document may prove to be more complex. We shall therefore examine each attribute in turn.

The language Attribute

The `language` attribute defines the programming language used to implement the JSP document:

```
language="language"
```

For example:

```
<%@page language="java"%>
```

Currently the only language supported is Java, so this attribute is usually omitted—but in theory, any language capable of consuming and producing streams could be used. However, this is more a theory than a reality, because the JSP specification demands that:

> *All scripting languages must support the Java Runtime Environment (JRE). All scripting languages must expose the Java technology object model to the script environment, especially implicit variables, JavaBean component properties and public methods.*

Thus, it would seem rather far-fetched to create JSP bindings in, say, a scripting language such as Python if you would have to implement full support for JRE within the Python JSP engine. Thus, at this point in time, it would appear that JSP is in reality only for use with Java.

The extends Attribute

The following attribute specifies the fully qualified name (FQN) of the superclass of the servlet this JSP is automatically complied to:

```
extends="fullyQualifiedClass"
```

For example:

```
<%@ page extends="se.jguru.xxx"%>
```

Because all JSP documents are compiled to Java classes, any JSP document could extend another to reuse its code and methods. In practice, this is seldom used, as the JSP include directive provides a delegation reuse of code, and the class that a JSP generated servlet must extend has to implement `javax.servlet.Servlet`. Nevertheless, reuse through inheritance is a powerful mechanism and may be used in JSP documents just like in other system development.

The import Attribute

This attribute adds the corresponding `import` statements to the generated servlet file and thus makes the classes or packages available:

```
import="{fullyQualifiedClass | fullyQualifiedPackage.*}, …"
```

For example:

```
<%@ page import="java.util.*, java.beans.Beans"%>
```

which is equivalent to:

```
<%@ page import="java.util.*" %>
<%@ page import= "java.beans.Beans" %>
```

In addition to the imports of the developer, the following import statements are automatically added to all generated servlets:

- `java.lang.*`
- `javax.servlet.*`
- `javax.servlet.http.*`
- `javax.servlet.jsp.*`

The session Attribute

The `session` attribute determines whether the JSP document will be part of an HTTP session, effectively creating the equivalent of a `request.getSession()` call within the generated servlet. The `session` attribute defaults to `true`, as indicated by the highlighted value:

```
session="true|false"
```

For example:

```
<%@ page session="false"%>
```

The buffer Attribute

The `buffer` attribute sets the size of the JSP writer buffer, which sends output from the generated servlet to the client. The default value, according to the JSP syntax specification, is at least 8kb (the default):

```
buffer="none|8kb|bufferSizekb"
```

For example:

```
<%@ page buffer="12kb"%>
```

Setting the `buffer` attribute to `none` turns off buffering of the response stream. This generally reduces the performance of the servlet engine because all `out.println("")` statements are sent immediately over the Internet to the client browser.

In contrast, if using a buffered output, the resulting output is written to a network buffer and sent to the client browser using only one TCP connection. In general, buffered output greatly enhances performance.

The autoFlush Attribute

The `autoFlush` attribute determines whether the output buffer should be autoflushing, (flushed automatically when the buffer is full):

```
autoFlush="true|false"
```

For example:

```
<%@ page autoFlush="true"%>
```

The default is `true` and may not be set to `false` if the output is not buffered (in other words, when `buffer="none"` has been specified).

The isThreadSafe Attribute

The `isThreadSafe` attribute determines whether the JSP document `_jspService` method is thread safe and therefore can be called concurrently:

```
isThreadSafe="true|false"
```

For example:

```
<%@ page isThreadSafe="false"%>
```

By default, the JSP document is declared thread safe, and it is up to the programmer to synchronize its internal state. If any access to the `SessionContext` or `HttpSession` of the generated servlet is made, the programmer cannot rely on the `isThreadSafe` attribute to save him or her from concurrent thread access—in such cases the programmer has to synchronize the external states.

The thread-safe switch simply makes the autogenerated servlet implement the `SingleThreadModel` interface; all properties of single-threaded servlets discussed in Chapter 1 apply. Setting the `isThreadSafe` property to `true` is, therefore, generally a poor design choice. The `isTheadSafe` property defaults to `true`.

The info Attribute

The `info` attribute, generates a `getServletInfo()` method, which returns the `infoString` value:

```
info="infoString"
```

For example:

```
<%@ page info="This servlet was generated by Lennart."%>
```

The isErrorPage Attribute

The `isErrorPage` attribute indicates whether this JSP document is used as an error page, which will be shown to the client whenever an exception was raised within the generated servlet of another JSP document:

```
isErrorPage="true|false"
```

For example:

```
<%@ page isErrorPage="true"%>
```

A JSP document having the `isErrorPage` property set to `true` will have a declaration within its `_jspService` method identical to the following statement:

```
Throwable exception = (Throwable) request.getAttribute(
        "javax.servlet.jsp.jspException");
```

It is assumed that an exception thrown within another JSP page is bound to the request under the key `javax.servlet.jsp.jspException`. The bound exception may be handled by a JSP document that has its `isErrorPage` property set to `true`.

The `isErrorPage` property defaults to `false`.

The errorPage Attribute

The `errorPage` attribute provides a URL to another JSP document to which the execution should be redirected whenever an exception is thrown (but not caught) within this JSP document:

```
errorPage="URLrelativeToThisDocument"
```

For example:

```
<%@ page errorPage="/error.jsp"%>
```

It is generally preferable to let the JSP engine handle exceptions thrown within a JSP document, compared to inserting `try/catch` blocks in the JSP code. For an example of the `errorPage/isErrorPage` attributes and exception-handling mechanism, refer to the `errorGenerator.jsp` example in the section "The errorGenerator.jsp Document."

The contentType Attribute

The `contentType` attribute indicates the content type set with the outgoing HTTP response stream from the generated servlet:

```
contentType="mimetype [; charset]"
```

For example:

```
<%@ page contentType="text/html; charset=ISO-8859-1"%>
```

The default MIME type is `text/html` and the default character set is `ISO-8859-1` as indicated in the example previously, but a JSP document may transmit any MIME type data to the client, such as `image/gif`.

JSP Directive Examples

Given the many attributes and combinations possible for the JSP page directive, a few examples are in order. First, study the `<%@ page %>` directive's frequently used `import` attribute. You see the output from the JSP generated servlet in Figure 4-17.

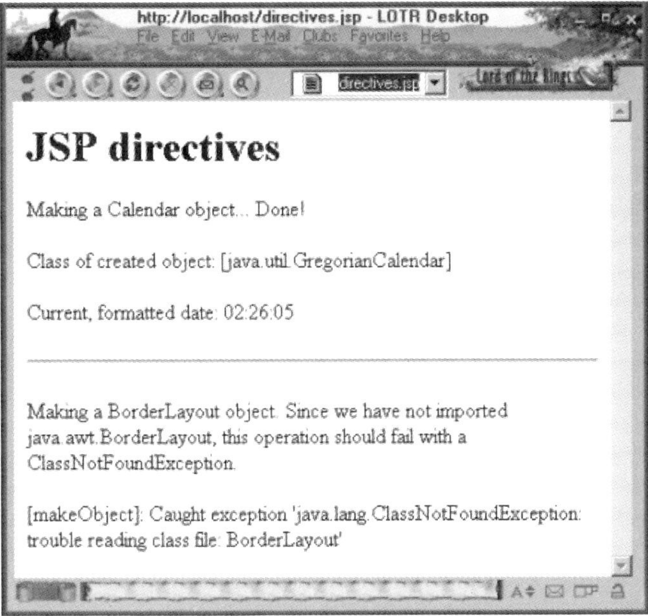

Figure 4-17. The resulting output of the JSP directives example

The following page directive imports the required classes for the output in Figure 4-17:

```
<%@ page import="java.util.*, java.text.*, java.beans.*" %>
```

This page directive results in the following code being added to the automatically generated servlet:

```
import java.util.*;
import java.text.*;
import java.beans.*;
```

The tricky part of the previous example is the `makeObject` method that uses the `Beans.instantiate()` method to dynamically create instances from classes. Although the `Class.newInstance()` method may be more flexible in performing the same task, currently ignore the finer details of dynamic object creation, as the `makeObject` method in Listing 4-11 is sufficient for this example.

Listing 4-11. The `makeObject` method, with the actual object creation rendered in bold

```
<%!
   // Declare a dynamic constructor method
   private Object makeObject(String className)
   {
      try
      {
         System.out.println("Trying to instantiate: " + className);
         return Beans.instantiate(getClassLoader(), className);
      }
      catch(Exception ex)
      {
         return "[makeObject]: Caught exception '" + ex + "'";
      }
   }

   private SimpleDateFormat sdf = new SimpleDateFormat("hh:mm:ss");
%>
```

The `makeObject` method returns an instance of whatever fully qualified class was sent as a string argument to it—or a `String` with an error message letting us know why the desired instance could not be created.

The rest of the JSP document instantiates a `GregorianCalendar` object and uses its methods in conjunction with the `SimpleDateFormat sdf` above to display the current time. When done, the servlet tries to instantiate a `BorderLayout` object that fails because the `java.awt.BorderLayout` class has not been imported. See Listing 4-12.

Listing 4-12. The `makeObject` *method used to create instances. Methods producing introspective output shown in Figure 4-17 are rendered in bold.*

```
<%--
   Make sure we import all classes from a few packages, namely
   java.util and java.text. These classes are required to display
   a Calendar instance, formatted using a SimpleDateFormat instance.
--%>

<%@ page import="java.util.*, java.text.*, java.beans.*" %>

<p>Making a Calendar object...
<%
   // Create a Calendar instance
   Object obj = makeObject("java.util.GregorianCalendar");
   Calendar now = (Calendar) obj;
%>
Done!</p>

<p>Class of created object: [<%= obj.getClass().getName() %>]</p>
<p>Current, formatted date: <%= sdf.format(now.getTime()) %></p>

<hr>
<p>Making a BorderLayout object. Since we have not imported
   java.awt.BorderLayout,
   this operation should fail with a ClassNotFoundException.</p>

<%
   // Try to create a BorderLayout instance
   // This should not work, since we have not
   // imported the class.
   Object bl = makeObject("BorderLayout");
   if(bl instanceof String) out.println("" + bl);
%>
```

Now create a new `<%@ page %>` directive example that illustrates the smooth exception handling built into the JSP engine. Such exception handling is controlled by the page directive attributes `errorPage` and `isErrorPage`, where two JSP pages work together roughly similar to a `try/catch`. The result retrieved when calling the JSP document that generates an error appears in Figure 4-18.

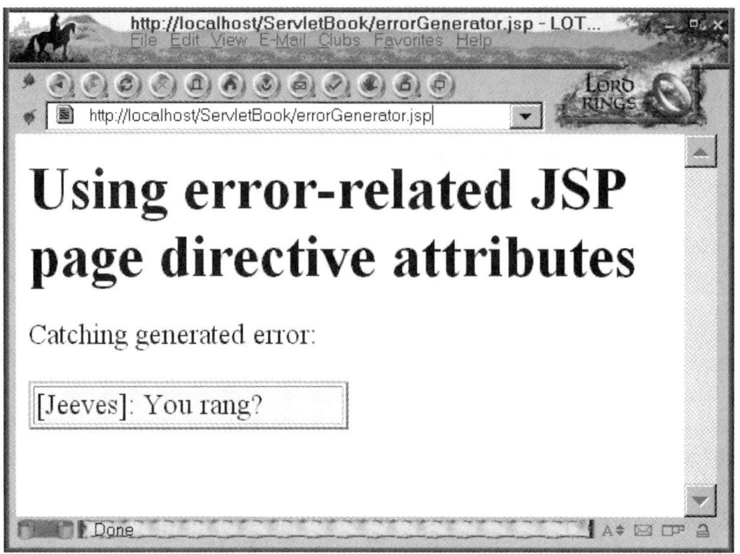

Figure 4-18. The resulting output of the `errorGenerator.jsp/errorPage.jsp` *document combination*

The errorGenerator.jsp Document

The first JSP document called is `errorGenerator.jsp` (see Listing 4-13). Its only function is to declare a method that generates and throws an exception. This exception will be caught and handled by the `errorPage.jsp` document, roughly in the same manner as a `catch` clause after a `try` block. Notice that the page directive line within the `errorGenerator.jsp` file includes the `errorPage` option, which will redirect the execution to the `errorPage.jsp` document whenever an unhandled exception is raised.

Listing 4-13. Code of the `errorGenerator.jsp` *document. The code producing the error is bold.*

```
<%--
   This JSP document shows the use
   of JSP page directives.
--%>
<%@ page import="java.util.*" errorPage="errorPage.jsp" %>

<html>
   <h1> Using error-related JSP page directive attributes </h1>
```

```
<%!
   // Declare a method which throws an exception
   private void talkToJeeves() throws IllegalArgumentException
   {
      // No chance of avoiding this exception ... :)
      throw new IllegalArgumentException("[Jeeves]: You rang?");
   }
%>

<p>Generate an error...</p>
<%
   // Talk to Jeeves...
   this.talkToJeeves();
%>

   <p>Done!</p>
</html>
```

The relevant parts of the servlet, generated from the `errorGenerator.jsp` document:

```
// ... lots of statements ...
public void _jspService(HttpServletRequest request,
       HttpServletResponse  response)
       throws IOException, ServletException
{
     PageContext pageContext = null;
     try
     {
          pageContext = _jspxFactory.getPageContext(this, request,
          response,"errorPage.jsp", true, 8192, true);

     ... statements ...

          // begin [file="C:\\errorGenerator.jsp";from=(20,3);to=(23,1)]
          // Talk a little to Jeeves...
               this.talkToJeeves();
          // end

     }
```

```
        catch (Exception ex)
        {
            if (out.getBufferSize() != 0)
                out.clear();
            pageContext.handlePageException(ex);
        }
        finally
        {
            out.flush();
            _jspxFactory.releasePageContext(pageContext);
        }
}
```

Tracing the call structure a little, because the servlet waters may be a trifle muddy, you find the following process:

1. The `pageContext` is initialized within the `_jspService` method. The error page from the JSP page directive is passed as an argument to said `pageContext` constructor.

2. The `talkToJeeves` method is called a little later, raising an `IllegalArgumentException`.

3. The exception is caught in the local catch clause, and the thrown exception is passed as an argument to the `handlePageException` method of the `pageContext`. This method essentially performs two tasks:

    a. Binds the exception object as an attribute to the `HttpRequest`.

    b. Performs an HTTP redirect according to the servlet forwarding pattern discussed in Chapter 3. Thus, the execution is redirected to the servlet generated from the JSP document `errorPage.jsp`.

Listing 4-14 contains the source code of the corresponding JSP document `errorPage.jsp`.

Listing 4-14. The `errorPage.jsp` *document*

```
<%--
    This JSP document shows the use
    of the error-related JSP page directives.
--%>
<%@ page import="java.util.*" isErrorPage="true" %>
```

```
<html>
     <h1> Using the error-related page directives</h1>
     <p>Catching generated error:</p>

     <table border=2 width=50% bgcolor="#FFFFCC">
          <tr><td>
               <%= exception.getMessage() %>
          </td></tr>
     </table>

</html>
```

Note that the isErrorPage="true" option has generated an extra object, called exception. The exception object contains whatever Throwable was sent to this document, in this case an IllegalArgumentException generated by the talkToJeeves method.

The relevant parts of the generated servlet for errorPage.jsp appear in Listing 4-15, where the error-catching and error-handling statements have been rendered in bold.

Listing 4-15. The code of the autogenerated servlet

```
... lots of irrelevant stuff skipped ...

    public void _jspService(HttpServletRequest request,
                    HttpServletResponse  response)
                    throws IOException, ServletException {

        Throwable exception = (Throwable)
          request.getAttribute("javax.servlet.jsp.jspException");

            // begin [file="C:\\errorPage.jsp";from=(13,5);to=(13,29)]
                out.print( exception.getMessage() );
            // end
    }
}
```

As you can seen, the isErrorPage="true" option in the JSP <%@ page %> directive created an extra object, called exception, which gets its value from the request attribute "javax.servlet.jsp.jspException". You may therefore safely assume that the handlePageContext method bound the exception generated in the errorGenerate.jsp using that very name (javax.servlet.jsp.jspException). The developer should therefore not use that string as a key when binding attributes to the HttpRequest.

The JSP <%@ include %> Directive

Typically, a large portion of all HTML included in a resulting document is constant for all Web pages in an entire Web application. Such template content may include header or footer sections, navigational frame content, and so on. It is desirable to place all template content in separate documents to facilitate maintenance of the template content. Somehow, the template content must be included into the actual data of each application page, and there are two different ways of including the data in a JSP document:

- *Static* inclusion is the equivalent of pasting text from another document into the current JSP document before generating the JSP delegation servlet.
- *Dynamic* inclusion is the equivalent of reading text from another document into the current JSP document each time that the `_jspService` method is called.

The `<%@ include %>` directive is used for *static* inclusion of a document. Its syntax is:

```
<%@ include file="relativeURLtoFile" %>
```

For example:

```
<%@ include file="/includeFiles/methods.inc"%>
```

The `<%@ include %>` directive is probably simplest to explain using an example. Now create a small system of two JSP files, where one includes all statements from the other using the JSP include directive. Figure 4-19 displays the result of running the first JSP document, `includes.jsp`. The output contains all `ServletContext` attributes of the generated servlet.

Listing 4-16 contains the source code of the `includes.jsp` file, with all statements pertaining to the include and method usage have been rendered in bold.

Listing 4-16. The `includes.jsp` *source code*

```
<%--
     This JSP document shows the use
     of JSP include directive.
--%>
<%@ page import="java.util.*" %>
<%@ include file="/includeFiles/methods.inc" %>
```

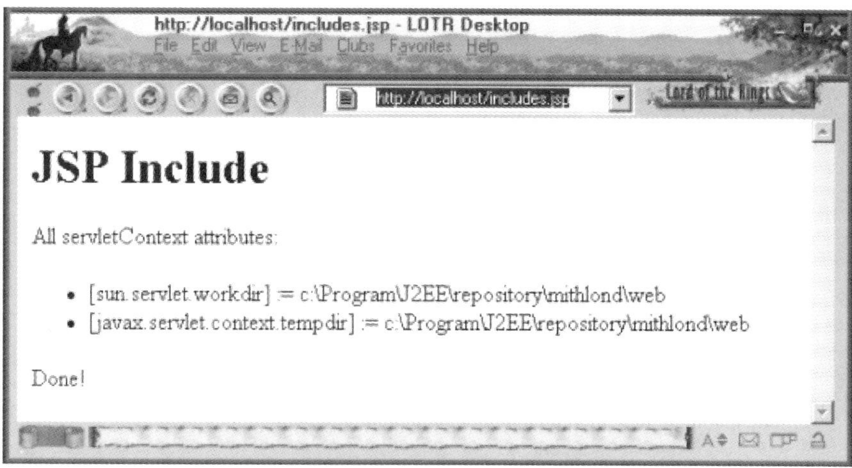

Figure 4-19. The output of the running `includes.jsp` *document. Note that the actual content of the document is included from the file* `/includeFiles/methods.inc`.

```
<html>
    <h1>JSP Include </h1>
    <p>All servletContext attributes:</p>

    <ul>
<%
    for(Iterator it = getServletContextAttributeKeys().iterator();
        it.hasNext();)
    {
        String aKey = (String) it.next();
%>
    <li> [<%= aKey %>] :=
        <%= this.getServletContext().getAttribute(aKey) %>
<%  } %>

    </ul>
    <p>Done!</p>
</html>
```

The include directive in Listing 4-17 includes all resources from the file with the relative path `/includeFiles/methods.inc`. The content of that included file is simply a method declaration generating a `List` containing all `ServletContext` attribute key names.

Listing 4-17. The `methods.inc` *file*

```
<%!

private List getServletContextAttributeKeys()
{
          // Get the context
          ServletContext ctx = this.getServletContext();

          // Declare return v.alue
          List toReturn = Collections.synchronizedList(new ArrayList());

          // Get all the names
          for(Enumeration en = ctx.getAttributeNames(); en.hasMoreElements(); )
          {
                    // Append the attribute name
                    toReturn.add(en.nextElement());
          }

          // Done.
          return toReturn;
}

%>
```

The method `getServletContextAttributeKeys` is called within the `_jspService` body of the `includes.jsp` servlet, and its results are looped through to get all parameter names and values present within the running `ServletContext`. These are then printed to the standard output stream to the client.

The interesting part, as you take a look at the generated servlet code for the `includes.jsp` file, is that the inclusion is static; in other words, the contents of `methods.inc` is simply pasted into the servlet source code file. See Listing 4-18.

Listing 4-18. The autogenerated servlet from the `includes.jsp` *document. Note the section from the* `methods.inc` *that has been pasted into the source code.*

```
import javax.servlet.*;
import javax.servlet.http.*;
import javax.servlet.jsp.*;
import javax.servlet.jsp.tagext.*;
import java.io.PrintWriter;
import java.io.IOException;
import java.io.FileInputStream;
import java.io.ObjectInputStream;
```

```
import java.util.Vector;
import org.apache.jasper.runtime.*;
import java.beans.*;
import org.apache.jasper.JasperException;
import java.util.*;


public class _0005cincludes_0002ejspincludes_jsp_0 extends HttpJspBase {
    // begin [file="C:\\includeFiles\\methods.inc";from=(0,3);to=(21,0)]

    private List getServletContextAttributeKeys()
    {
        // Get the context
        ServletContext ctx = this.getServletContext();

        // Declare return value
        List toReturn = Collections.synchronizedList(new ArrayList());

        // Get all the names
        for(Enumeration en = ctx.getAttributeNames();
            en.hasMoreElements(); )
        {
            // Append the attribute name
            toReturn.add(en.nextElement());
        }

        // Done.
        return toReturn;
    }
    // end

    static {
    }
    public _0005cincludes_0002ejspincludes_jsp_0( ) {
    }

    private static boolean _jspx_inited = false;

    public final void _jspx_init() throws JasperException {
    }

    public void _jspService(HttpServletRequest request,
        HttpServletResponse  response)
        throws IOException, ServletException
```

```
{
    JspFactory _jspxFactory = null;
    PageContext pageContext = null;
    HttpSession session = null;
    ServletContext application = null;
    ServletConfig config = null;
    JspWriter out = null;
    Object page = this;
    String  _value = null;
    try
    {
        if (_jspx_inited == false)
        {
            _jspx_init();
            _jspx_inited = true;
        }
        _jspxFactory = JspFactory.getDefaultFactory();
        response.setContentType("text/html");
        pageContext = _jspxFactory.getPageContext(this, request, response,
                             "", true, 8192, true);

        application = pageContext.getServletContext();
        config = pageContext.getServletConfig();
        session = pageContext.getSession();
        out = pageContext.getOut();

        // begin
            out.write("\r\n");
        // end
        // begin
            out.write("\r\n");
        // end
        // begin
            out.write("\r\n\r\n<html>\r\n\t<h1>JSP➥
             Include</h1>\r\n\r\n\r\n\t<p>All servletContext➥
             attributes:</p>\r\n\t<ul>\r\n\t\t\r\n\t\t");
        // end
        // begin [file="C:\\includes.jsp";from=(14,4);to=(18,2)]

            for(Iterator it = getServletContextAttributeKeys().iterator();
                        it.hasNext();)
            {
              String aKey = (String) it.next();
```

```
                // end
                // begin
                   out.write("\r\n\t\r\n\t\t<li> [");
                // end
                // begin [file="C:\\includes.jsp";from=(20,11);to=(20,17)]
                   out.print( aKey );
                // end
                // begin
                   out.write("] := ");
                // end
                // begin [file="C:\\includes.jsp";from=(20,27);to=(20,72)]
                   out.print( this.getServletContext().getAttribute(aKey) );
                // end
                // begin
                   out.write("\r\n\r\n\t\t");
                // end
                // begin [file="C:\\includes.jsp";from=(22,4);to=(22,7)]
                   }
                // end
                // begin
                out.write("\r\n\t\t\t\r\n\t</ul>\r\n\r\n\t<p>➥
                Done!</p>\r\n\t\t\r\n</html>");
                // end
            }
            catch (Exception ex)
            {
                if (out.getBufferSize() != 0)
                out.clear();
                pageContext.handlePageException(ex);
            }
            finally
            {
                out.flush();
                _jspxFactory.releasePageContext(pageContext);
            }
        }
}
```

The topmost bold area is simply the included data from the `methods.inc` file, and the second bold area of the generated servlet is the usage and results printout to the client. An important question must be raised after seeing the results of the include directive: What happens if the included file is altered? Will the `includes.jsp` *automagically* be regenerated with the new contents? The answer is "no." Once the included file is pasted into the resulting servlet using the JSP include directive, one would have to recompile the JSP document before any change would be seen. This is easily accomplished using tools such as `touch`, which changes the modification timestamp of the JSP file, causing it to be recompiled by the JSP/servlet engine.

In other words: You need to make a change to the enclosing JSP document (which contains the include directive) to see changes in the included document.

After the recompilation and following automatic redeployment, the included template content modification is visible on the JSP document result.

After modification of the `methods.inc` file, but before modifying `includes.jsp`, the output looks as shown in Figure 4-20.

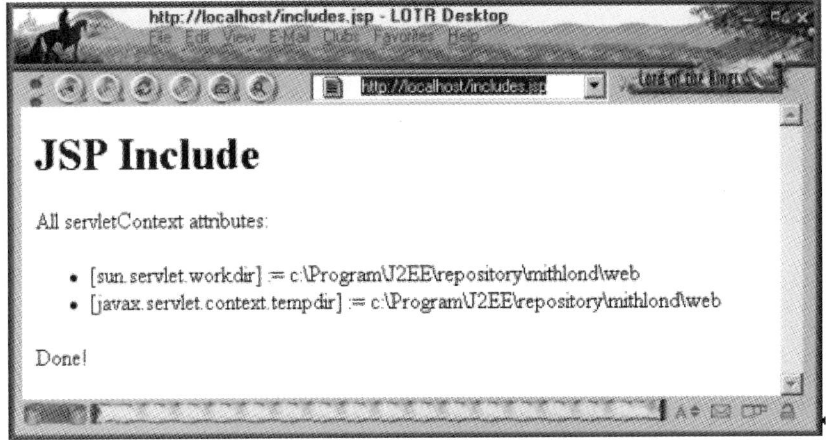

Figure 4-20. The resulting output of the `includes.jsp` *document after modifying the included method template file but before forcing a recompilation of the* `includes.jsp` *document itself*

After forcing a recompilation of the `includes.jsp` file, the resulting output alters to what you see in Figure 4-21.

The modification done to the file `methods.inc` file is rather small and has been highlighted in bold in Listing 4-19.

Listing 4-19. The modified `methods.inc` *file.*

```
<%!

private List getServletContextAttributeKeys()
{
    // Get the context
    ServletContext ctx = this.getServletContext();
```

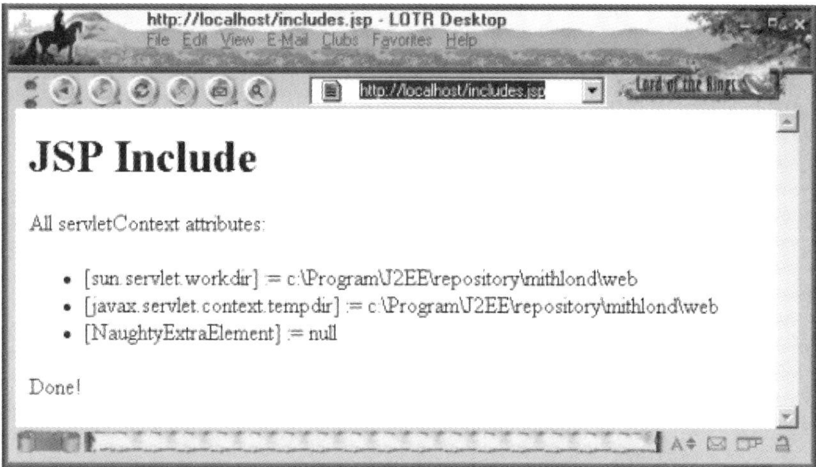

Figure 4-21. The resulting output of the `includes.jsp` *document after a modification to the* `methods.inc` *include file, and a following recompilation*

```
        // Declare return value
        List toReturn = Collections.synchronizedList(new ArrayList());

        // Get all the names
        for(Enumeration en = ctx.getAttributeNames(); en.hasMoreElements(); )
        {
            // Append the attribute name
            toReturn.add(en.nextElement());
        }

        // Add an extra element.... :)
        toReturn.add("NaughtyExtraElement");

        // Done.
        return toReturn;
}
```

TIP *When using the* `<%@ include %>` *directive, all text in the included files will be part of the JSP compilation. In the* `_jspService` *method of the including JSP document, one can therefore use Java methods, variables, or programming constructs defined in the included file. This is impossible if using the JSP include action; as a result I usually rely completely on the JSP* `<%@ include %>` *directive.*

JSP <%@ taglib %> Directive

A *tag library* (or *taglib* for short) is a file defining new sets of JSP tags in addition to the standard ones available from the JSP specification. A `<%@ taglib %>` directive includes the contents of a tag library file, thus making the custom tags defined there available to the JSP document. The taglib directive must be located before actually using the custom-defined tags within the JSP document.

The `<%@ taglib %>` directive is used for static inclusion of a tag library document. Its syntax is:

```
<%@ taglib uri="relativeURLtoFile" prefix="aPrefix" %>
```

For example:

```
<%@ taglib uri="/tagLibs/accounting.tgl" prefix="accounting" %>
```

The tag library resides in its own namespace, defined by the prefix string. Thus, if the tag library with the prefix `accounting` defines a tag called `calculateSalary`, the usage within a JSP document would be:

```
<%@ taglib uri="/taglibs/accounting.tgl" prefix="accounting" %>
...
<accounting:calculateSalary>
...
</accounting:calculateSalary>
```

As always in XML and HTML, tags may use attributes. It is up to the developer to decide if an attribute should be defined as optional or mandatory. For instance, if the `calculateSalary` tag should accept a person attribute, it could be rendered as follows:

```
<%@ taglib uri="/taglibs/accounting.tgl" prefix="accounting" %>
...
<accounting:calculateSalary person="Camilla Bexner">
...
</accounting:calculateSalary>
```

The tags defined within a tag library file may be either *standalone* or *container tags*; where the container tags optionally may contain text (known as the *body* of a tag). The `calculateSalary` tag is an example of a custom container tag. The following example illustrates the use of a custom standalone tag. Note that the standalone tag is terminated with a `/>` character combination:

```
<%@ taglib uri="/taglibs/accounting.tgl" prefix="accounting" %>
...
<accounting:createChaos where="engineering" how="annualReorganization" />
```

Custom tags may accept mandatory or optional attributes. The `where` and `how` in the preceding JSP code snippet are examples of attributes to the `createChaos` tag. Creating JSP tag libraries and implementing tag handler classes is non-trivial but useful to encapsulate complex server-side behavior within a custom tag. That's all we'll say about the taglib directive for now. The next chapter discusses most aspects of JSP tag libraries.

> **TIP** *The prefixes* `jsp:`, `jspx:`, `java:`, `javax:`, `servlet:`, `sun:`, *and* `sunw:` *are reserved. Refer to Table JSP.2-4 in the JSP specification document for information regarding the reserved prefixes.*

JSP Actions

JSP *actions* output something to the response stream of the generated JSP servlet. JSP actions look like XML tags and are a user-friendly way to create the equivalent of a series of Java statements within a scriptlet. Indeed, one may regard JSP actions as a constraint similar to encapsulation, preventing programmatic errors in a series of scriptlet statements.

Here's an example of a JSP action:

```
<%-- This is a counter object bound to the JSP Session --%>
<jsp:useBean id="theCounter" class="se.jguru.utils.Counter" >
```

The JSP specification defines a set of six *standard JSP actions* always available to the JSP developer (regardless of the JSP API version and JSP engine that you are using):

- `<jsp:include>`
- `<jsp:forward>`
- `<jsp:usebean>`
- `<jsp:setProperty>`
- `<jsp:getProperty>`
- `<jsp:plugin>`

In addition, the JSP developer may define custom actions in a tag library. The standard JSP actions can be grouped into three categories of actions that perform the following tasks:

- Implementing a particular servlet pattern. Refer to Chapter 2 for a discussion on each pattern. For example, `<jsp:include>` and `<jsp:forward>`.
- Creating a bound attribute and read or write its JavaBean properties. For example: `<jsp:useBean>`, `<jsp:setProperty>`, and `<jsp:getProperty>`.
- Controlling the downloading and executing of a particular browser plugin (a program downloaded to and executed within a calling client browser, such as an applet or ActiveX control). For example: `<jsp:plugin>`.

Each of these categories of JSP actions is discussed in the following sections.

JSP Actions Implementing Servlet Patterns

The two patterns, forwarding and including, are slightly simplified when using JSP actions. In both cases, the encapsulation of Java code within the JSP action tag provides more robust code than the servlet equivalent—at least if one assumes that the number of errors introduced in the code is proportional to the amount of code typed. Using JSP action tags to achieve forwarding or including is therefore preferable to the Java code equivalent.

The <jsp:include> Action

The JSP *include action* (`<jsp:include>`) differs from the JSP *include directive* (`<%@ include file="someFile.jsp" %>`) in that it implements a dynamic text inclusion, rather than a static one. Also, the text returned by the JSP include action is pasted into the contents of the `_jspService` method when called. It is therefore impossible to declare methods or other Java programmatic constructs within a document included using a JSP include action. A document included with the `<jsp:include>` action may therefore generally contain only static text, such as HTML or XML.

The `<jsp:include>` action may be written as a standalone tag or as a container with a body. Start by taking a look at the following standalone version, and move on to the container syntax shortly:

```
<jsp:include page="relativeURLtoFile" flush="true" />
```

For example:

```
<jsp:include page="/includeFiles/plaintext.txt" />
```

The two attributes accepted by the `<jsp:include>`action are as follows:

- Page: The path to the document that is to be included by the include action.
- Flush: Optional attribute indicating that the output buffer should be flushed immediately. The default value is `false`.

The simplest example possible using an include action is outputting the contents of another file within the calling JSP document. Such an example JSP document has the output you see in Figure 4-22.

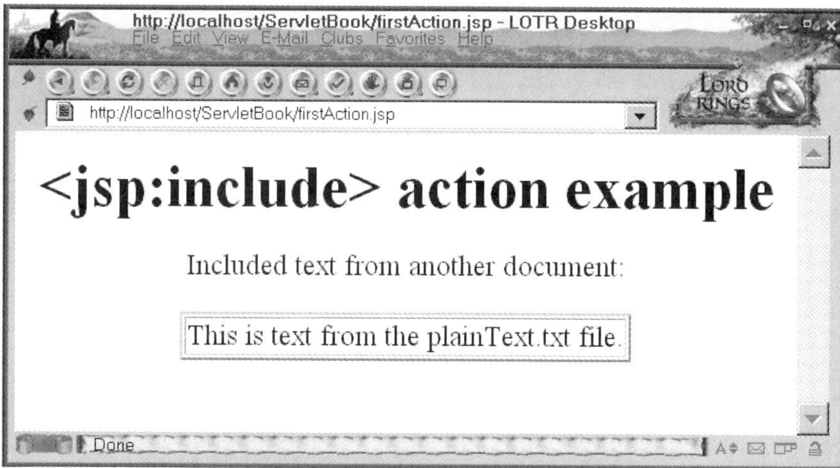

Figure 4-22. Resulting output of the `firstAction.jsp`*document*

The JSP document itself is straightforward; the relevant piece of code is the `<jsp:include>` action tag (shown in bold in Listing 4-20).

Listing 4-20. The `firstAction.jsp` *document*

```
<%--
  This JSP document shows the use
  of a <jsp:include> action.
--%>

<html>
<body>
  <center><h1>&lt;jsp:include> action example</h1>

  <p>Included text from another document:</p>
    <table border=2>
      <tr><td>
        <jsp:include page="/includeFiles/plainText.txt"
          flush="true" />
      </td></tr>
    </table>
</body>
</html>
```

The contents of file `/includeFiles/plainText.txt` is simply:

```
This text is from the plainText.txt file.
```

The interesting part of the automatically generated servlet for the Tomcat reference implementation engine lets you know that the include action provides dynamic inclusion which is performed each time the `_jspService` method is called. Shown in Listing 4-21, the `pageContext.include` statement opens a `FileInputStream` (or –`Reader`) to include the contents of the file with the given name. Thus, changes in the file `/includeFiles/plaintext.txt` will be visible immediately when calling the document that included it.

Listing 4-21. File including section of the servlet generated from the `firstAction.jsp` *document*

```
... Lots of irrelevant stuff skipped ...

  public void _jspService( ... )
  {
    ...
      // begin [file="C:\\firstAction.jsp";from=(13,2);to=(13,65)]
      {
        String _jspx_qStr = "";
        out.flush();
        pageContext.include("/includeFiles/plainText.txt" +
                              _jspx_qStr);
      }
      // end


    ...

  }
```

A small change in the file `plainText.txt` will be shown immediately after the alteration—without requiring any changes to the JSP document that forces a recompilation. Thus, the `<jsp:include>` action is commonly used for including plain HTML template sections, such as a footer. The result of modifying the `plaintext.txt` (but not the `firstAction.jsp`) document is shown in Figure 4-23.

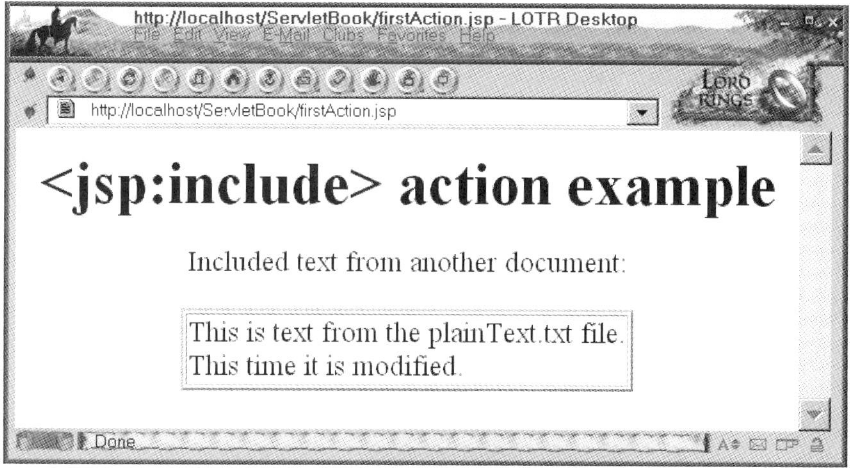

Figure 4-23. The resulting output after changing the included file by appending "This time it is modified." We are not required to force a recompilation of the JSP document for the change to be visible.

The second form of the <jsp:include> tag permits sending parameters to the included document. This is relevant if the document included maps to a servlet or other JSP document. Parameters passed to the included document are HttpServletRequest parameters and may be treated as such by the included document.

To supply parameters to the included document, one must create <jsp:param /> tags within the body of the jsp:include action *container*:

```
<jsp:include page="relativeURLtoFile" flush="true">
     <jsp:param name="name" value="value" />
...
</jsp:include>
```

The easiest way to learn most enterprise coding patterns is simply showing an example of it. The alternate container tag syntax of the <jsp:include> action is no exception. Our simple example devised to illustrate the use of the include parameters consists of two JSP documents—a "client" document that includes a "service" document.

The service JSP is called printRequestArguments.jsp and prints out a small table with all request parameter names and values. Before showing the full results of the JSP document using the jsp:include action to import the results of another document, look at a standalone invocation of the printRequestArguments.jsp document. The standalone invocation screenshot is provided to show the output of the "service" JSP document only. Note that the JSP document was called using the HTTP GET method (because you can see its URL query string parameters) in Figure 4-24.

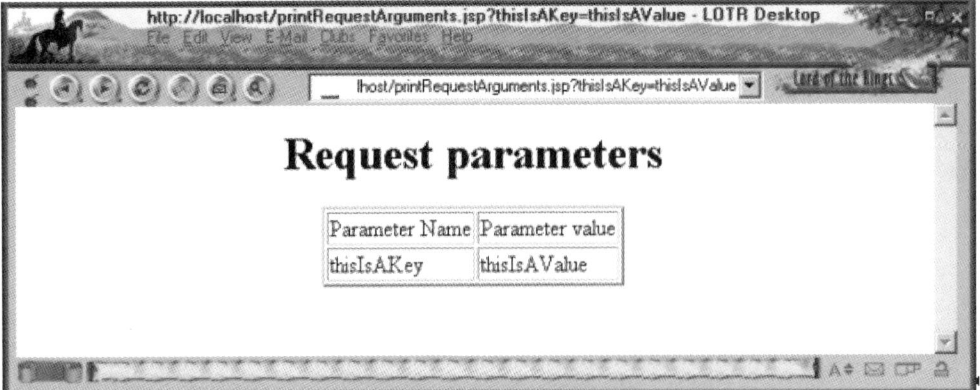

Figure 4-24. The resulting output of the printRequestArguments.jsp *document when invoked standalone. Note that the query string provide the parameter key name and attribute value, as is customary to a HTTP GET method request.*

The client JSP, called `secondAction.jsp`, includes all services from the `printRequestArguments.jsp` document with the `<jsp:include>` action. The `secondAction.jsp` document adds a couple of request parameters to the existing ones, as you can see in Listing 4-22.

Listing 4-22. The `secondAction.jsp` *document. The statements adding extra parameters to the include statement are in bold.*

```
<%--
   This JSP document shows the use
   of JSP actions.
--%>



<html>
<body>
   <center><h1> &lt;jsp:include> action example
   using request parameters</h1>

   <p>Included text from another document using request parameters</p>
   <table border=2>
      <tr><td>

      <jsp:include page="/printRequestArguments.jsp" flush="true">
         <jsp:param name="paramOne" value="valueOne" />
         <jsp:param name="paramTwo" value="valueTwo" />
         <jsp:param name="dateParam" value="<%= new java.util.Date() %>" />
      </jsp:include>

      </td></tr>
   </table>
   </center>
</body>
</html>
```

Figure 4-25 shows the result of the code in Listing 4-22. Note that the order in which the request parameters are presented is not the same as the order in which they were provided. This is in line with the `HttpServletRequest` parameter specification, which specifically states that the order of provided parameters may not be preserved.

Note that although you may pass any type of argument to the included document's `HttpServletRequest`, it may be a good point to check the type of the arriving parameter. The reference implementation converts all objects to strings

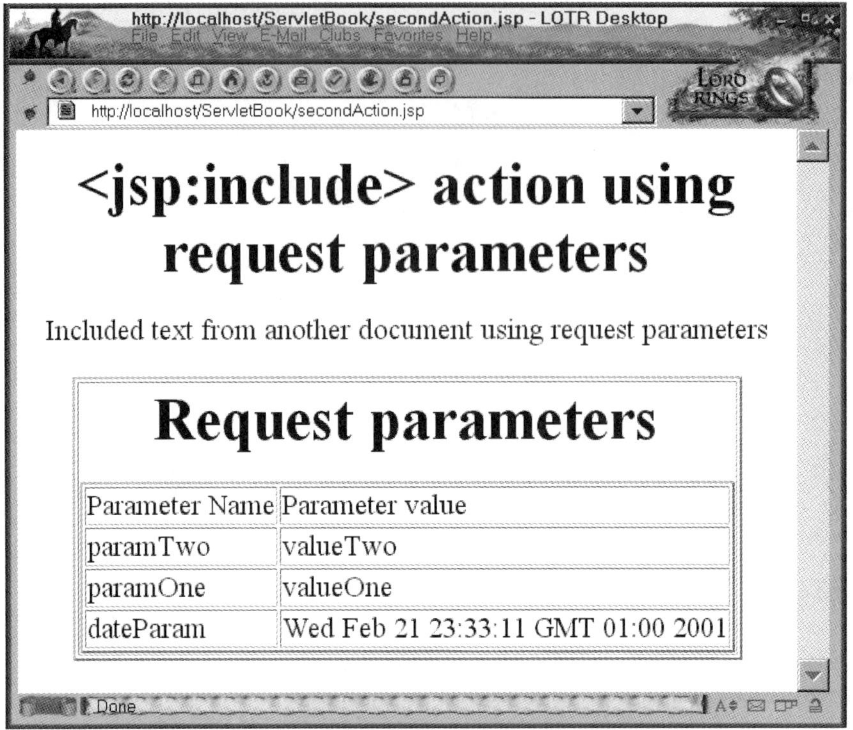

Figure 4-25. The resulting output of the `secondAction.jsp` *document that sets three request parameters and includes the resulting output from the* `printRequestArguments.jsp` *document*

before sending the parameters, as can be seen in the following servlet code snippet. Be sure to check the behavior of your chosen JSP engine:

```
// begin [file="C:\\secondAction.jsp";from=(14,2);to=(18,16)]
{
        String _jspx_qStr = "";
        out.flush();
        _jspx_qStr = _jspx_qStr + "?paramOne=" + "valueOne";
        _jspx_qStr = _jspx_qStr + "&dateParam=" +  new java.util.Date() ;
        _jspx_qStr = _jspx_qStr + "&paramTwo=" + "valueTwo";
        pageContext.include("/printRequestArguments.jsp" + _jspx_qStr);
}
// end
```

In this case, the included document is called using the HTTP GET method. One side effect of such behavior is that binary parameters cannot be used because the maximum allowed length of a standard HTTP URL is 1024 characters.

> **TIP** *The* `jsp:include` *action may—especially if including the output of a servlet or other JSP document—be regarded as a method call where the return value is a* `String` *containing the resulting* `Stream` *from the included document. Your Web application may therefore benefit from dividing JSP documents into smaller chunks included into frame or parent JSP documents. This technique is particularly powerful if the behavior of each chunk is controlled by or depends on the parameters provided.*

The <jsp:forward> Action

The `<jsp:forward>` action is similar to the `<jsp:include>` action in almost all syntactic aspects, although the semantics of JSP forward actions corresponds to the forwarding pattern. The only difference is that the forward action cannot accept the flush attribute (which is mandatory with the `<jsp:include>` action tag). Thus, the simplest way of regarding the `<jsp:forward>` action is to use it like variant of the `<jsp:include>` action, which immediately terminates the evaluation in its JSP document.

Thus, the two permissible syntax styles of the `<jsp:forward>` tag are:

```
<jsp:forward page="relativeURLtoFile" />
```

and

```
<jsp:forward page="relativeURLtoFile" >
        <jsp:param name="name" value="value" />
...
</jsp:forward>
```

When a `<jsp:forward>` tag is encountered by the servlet engine during the compilation of a JSP document, the autocompiler will generate statements that ignore any existing buffered content in the output response stream. The JSP engine will therefore delete all generated buffered contents from a JSP document when forwarding the request to another JSP document. Listing 4-23 shows the generated output—without any trace of the text before or after the forward action.

Listing 4-23. The `forwardAction.jsp` document. The JSP actions generating the forward statements have been rendered in bold.

```
<%--
   This JSP document shows the use
   of the <jsp:forward> action.
--%>
<html>
<body>
   <p>This is text before the forward statement.</p>

   <jsp:forward page="/printRequestArguments.jsp">
      <jsp:param name="paramOne" value="valueOne" />
      <jsp:param name="paramTwo" value="valueTwo" />
      <jsp:param name="dateParam" value="<%= new java.util.Date() %>" />
   </jsp:forward>

   <p>This is text after the forward statement.</p>
</body>
</html>
```

The resulting output has no text originating from the `forwardAction.jsp` document; instead the view is generated completely from the `printRequestArguments.jsp` document. However, the extra request arguments appended to the `HttpServletRequest` are delivered to the target JSP document before executing its `_jspService` method.

Listing 4-24 displays the relevant part of the autogenerated servlet. Note that the out `JspWriter` is cleared before the forwarding pattern is applied and that the `_jspService` method is forced to return immediately after the call to `pageContext.forward()`.

Listing 4-24. The code of the autocompiled servlet, resulting from the forward action

```
// begin [file="C:\\forwardAction.jsp";from=(11,2);to=(15,16)]
         if (true) {
                  out.clear();
                  String _jspx_qfStr = "";
                  _jspx_qfStr = _jspx_qfStr + "?paramOne=" + "valueOne";
                  _jspx_qfStr = _jspx_qfStr + "&dateParam=" + new java.util.Date() ;
                  _jspx_qfStr = _jspx_qfStr + "&paramTwo=" + "valueTwo";
                  pageContext.forward("/printRequestArguments.jsp" + _jspx_qfStr);
                  return;

         }
// end
```

Figure 4-26 displays the resulting output of the forwarding page.

Parameter Name	Parameter value
paramOne	valueOne
dateParam	Tue Aug 01 21:13:28 PDT 2000
paramTwo	valueTwo

Figure 4-26. This is the `forwardAction.jsp` *document. Note that the result closely resembles the standalone call to the* `printRequestArguments.jsp` *document. In fact, the only difference is the request parameters added by the* `forwardAction.jsp` *document—exactly like a forward action described in Chapter 2 is supposed to work.*

JSP Actions Managing JavaBean Objects

The JavaBean design pattern is the preferred data container structure in the Java API. The JSP API has good support for talking to JavaBean objects. Also, JavaBeans may be handled in a smart manner by JSP actions. The three primary JSP actions (`<jsp:useBean>`, `<jsp:getProperty>`, and `<jsp:setProperty>`), which manage bound JavaBean objects, provide a simpler and less error-prone version of several frequently used series of Java method calls.

The usage patterns for the JavaBean-handling JSP actions are similar to the patterns for binding and unbinding attributes to a `HttpSession`–which, in turn, implies employment of a `HashMap` look-alike usage pattern.

Table 4-1 lists the three primary JSP actions for managing bound attributes and properties map directly to the servlet API.

Table 4-1. JSP Actions-Managing JavaBean Properties of a JSP Document

JSP ACTION	SERVLET METHOD EQUIVALENT

<jsp:useBean id= "aKey" class="Type"
scope=”session”/>
	if(session.getValue("aKey") == null)
	session.putValue("aKey", new Type());
	Type aKey = (Type) session.getValue("aKey");

<jsp:getProperty name="aKey" property="aPropertyName /">	((Type) Session.getValue("aKey")).getAPropertyName();
<jsp:setProperty name=“aKey” property="aPropertyName" value= "aValue">	((Type) session.getValue("aKey")).setAPropertyName(aValue);

What Are JavaBeans...Really?

Before venturing any further, it is important to understand what JavaBeans are. Have no fear; the JavaBean design pattern is a simple one, easily used and understood by all developers. See Figure 4-27.

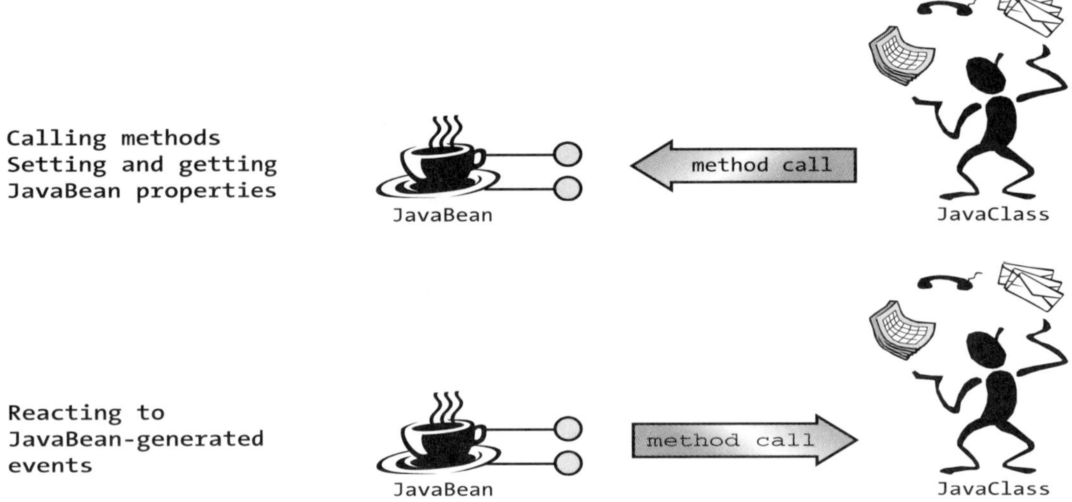

Figure 4-27. The JavaBean as a component either receiving events from an event generator object or sending events to a registered eventlistener instance

JavaBeans vs. Enterprise JavaBeans

The term *JavaBeans* denote a class adhering to a particular design pattern that permits automatic code builder tools to introspect the class presenting its settable and gettable properties. The term *Enterprise JavaBeans* denotes a server-side component in the distributed component model for the J2EE, complying with the Enterprise JavaBeans specification. Chapters 8 to 11 examine the interaction between JSP documents and Enterprise JavaBeans.

JSP developers need to be concerned with the following four facts about JavaBeans:

- A JavaBean is a Java class (or component) composed of one or more Java objects. The JavaBean component communicates with the surrounding code/environment through the use of public methods and generated events. If the public methods of the component adhere to a certain naming pattern, they are called *JavaBean properties.*

- A *simple readable* JavaBean property of name `name` and type `Type` is considered present in a JavaBean component or class if it exposes a public method with this exact signature:

  ```
  public Type getName();
  // For example:
  public String getCorporateName();
  ```

  Similarly, a *simple writeable* JavaBean property of name `name` and type `Type` is considered present in a JavaBean component or class if it exposes a public method with this exact signature:

  ```
  public void setName(Type aNewName);
  ```

  where the name of the method argument, `aNewName`, is arbitrary and therefore not part of the naming pattern.

  For example:

  ```
  public void setCorporateName (String name);
  ```

- An *indexed readable* JavaBean property of name `name` and type `Type[]` is considered present in a JavaBean component or class if it exposes public methods with these exact signatures:

```
public Type[] getName(); //gets the entire array at once
public Type getName(int index);
      //gets a single array element specified by the index
```

For example:

```
public Employee[] getEmployees();
public Employee getEmployees(int idNumber);
```

Similarly, an *indexed writable* JavaBean property of name `name` and type `Type[]` is considered present in a JavaBean component or class if it exposes public methods with these exact signatures:

```
public void setName(Type[] aNewName); //sets the entire array at once
public void setName(int index, Type aNewName); //sets a single array element
  specified by the index
```

where the names of the method arguments, `aNewName`, are arbitrary and therefore not part of the naming pattern.

For example:

```
public void setEmployees(Employees[] allEmployees);
public void setEmployees(int idNumber, Employee aNewEmployee);
```

- A JavaBean may generate events that classes external to the JavaBean component can receive and react upon. If a JavaBean should be able to generate such events, it must provide one or more `EventListener` interfaces, implemented by all classes capable of receiving notification whenever an event was generated within the JavaBean. The naming patterns of such `EventListener` definitions are tied to the `EventObjects` generated:

```
public class XYZEvent extends java.util.EventObject { ... }

public interface XYZListener
{
          // Definition of all listener methods ...
          public void somethingHappened(XYZEvent event);
}

public class SomeListenerClass implements XYZListener
{
          // Implement the listener method
           public void somethingHappened(XYZEvent event) { ... }
}
```

Moreover, the naming patterns for the `EventListener` registration on the events generated within the JavaBean component are:

```
public void add<ListenerType>(<ListenerType> listener);
public void remove<ListenerType>(<ListenerType> listener);
```

NOTE *For a full definition of JavaBeans, visit the JavaBeans section on JavaSoft's Web site (*`http://www.javasoft.com`*).*

Although a small subset of the full JavaBean specification, the previous definitions are really all you need to know to be able to deduct a fair amount of knowledge on JavaBeans and their use. Utility classes in the u package handle instantiation, introspection, and other housekeeping issues regarding JavaBeans, to a large extent hiding system complexity from the developer.

Doubtlessly, the question of relevance appears: what significance has the JavaBean specification on the JSP document actions? Here's a quick answer: The requirements on the class defining JavaBean objects handled by the JSP actions are dictated by the first three definitions previously.

JSP Standard Actions and the JavaBean Design Pattern

As the JSP Standard Actions use the JavaBean design pattern to investigate existing properties and find any accessor methods. If you want to use standard JSP actions on your class, it is important not to deviate from the standard JavaBean naming pattern—otherwise, the behavior of the JSP or servlet engine may be undetermined.

Suppose you would like to use a JavaBean of type `Type`—what requirements must class `Type` adhere to? The answer is simple; the `Type` class must adhere to two requirements:

- `Type` must have a public, no-argument constructor, in other words, `public Type() { … }`. That constructor is used by the `<jsp:useBean>` action.
- All methods accessible by the `<jsp:getProperty>`action must be simple, readable JavaBean properties. Likewise, all methods accessible by the `<jsp:setProperty>` action must be simple, writeable JavaBean properties.

Now take a closer look at the three JSP actions handling bound JavaBean components:

```
<jsp:useBean>
<jsp:getProperty>
<jsp:setProperty>
```

The <jsp:useBean> Action

The `<jsp:useBean>` action retrieves or instantiates JavaBean objects and binds them to one of four possible JSP scopes (application, session, request, or page). An alternate usage is accessing objects created in other JSP documents (in other words, an object alias).

The `<jsp:useBean>` tag syntax is:

```
<jsp:useBean id="anId" scope="aScope" typeDef />
```

and

```
<jsp:useBean id="anId" scope="aScope" typeDef >
    ... body ...
</jsp:useBean>
```

where the following is true:

- `anID` denotes the variable name of the JavaBean. You can use this variable name in expressions or scriptlets in the same JSP document. Note that this variable name is case-sensitive and must follow the normal Java variable naming conventions.

- `aScope` defines the scope of the bean and may be one of the four relevant scopes for a JSP bound JavaBean object: application, session, request, or page.

- `typeDef` defines the type of the JavaBean bound object. There are four allowed combinations of the attributes `class`, `type`, and `beanName`, because `class` and `beanName` are mutually exclusive.

  - `class` simply denotes the fully qualified package and class name of the JavaBean, such as `se.jguru.utils.Counter`.

  - `beanName` works identical to the `class` attribute, but the fully qualified class name may refer to a serialized class descriptor. Refer to the `java.beans.Beans.instantiate` method for full description of the handling of serialized beans. The `beanName` attribute is a bit more flexible than the `class` attribute because it can use the results of JSP expressions.

- `type` is the class type desired. It must be a superclass of the *class* or `beanName` provided, or an interface implemented by the bean. If the `type` is unrelated to the class or beanName, a `ClassCastException` is thrown. You need only provide a type attribute if you want the bean to be treated as a superclass or implemented interface to facilitate using polymorphism in the JSP document. Refer to the following examples to see the `jsp:useBean` where an `ArrayList` instance is assigned to a `List` variable using the `type` attribute.

The simple way of looking at a `<jsp:useBean>` action is that it completely replaces a Java variable declaration and instantiation. Suppose you would like to create an object of class `ArrayList`, treat it as a `List`, and bind it to the JSP session scope. Your Java code would be:

```
<%
        List items = new ArrayList();
        // or, alternatively
        // List items = Beans.instantiate("java.util.ArrayList",
        //                                     getClassLoader());
        // Now, bind the items List to the session
        session.setAttribute("items", items);
%>
```

The `<jsp:useBean>` action generating the same code would be:

```
<jsp:useBean  id="items"
   scope="session"
   type="java.util.List"
   class="java.util.ArrayList" />

<%-- or, alternatively --%>

<jsp:useBean  id="items"
   scope="session"
   type="java.util.List"
   beanName="java.util.ArrayList" />
```

The body (or block of statements) within the `<jsp:useBean>` action container tag (shown in bold in the snippet on the next page) is only executed if the JavaBean was *instantiated* by the `<jsp:useBean>` action—not if the JavaBean was simply *retrieved from the given scope*. Thus, Listing 4-25 could be a compound creation and assignment of JavaBean properties.

Listing 4-25. Snippet showing the `<jsp:useBean>` tag. The highlighted `setProperty` action will only be taken if the bean was created, not if it was retrieved.

```
<jsp:useBean  id="shoppingBag"
   scope="session"
   class="se.jguru.utils.ShopBagBean">

<%--
   The <jsp:setProperty> action and the scriptlet below
   will only be called if the shoppingBag JavaBean
   was just instantiated.
--%>
<jsp:setProperty name="shoppingBag" property="Name"
   value="<%= getUserName() %>" />

<%
   // Call some non-JavaBean method within
   // the shoppingBag object.
   shoppingBag.doSomething();
%>

</jsp:useBean>
```

The <jsp:getPropery> Action

The `<jsp:getProperty>` action prints the results of a JavaBean property method, converted to a string, onto the `out JspWriter`. The string conversion is done using the standard `toString()` method defined in `java.lang.Object`, unless the result is a primitive type. In the latter case, the conversion to `String` is done directly.

The `<jsp:getProperty>` tag syntax is:

```
<jsp:getProperty name="aName" property="aProperty" />
```

where

- `name` indicates the object variable to call.
- `property` is the name of the readable JavaBean property—in other words, the JavaBean getter method to invoke.

As an example, the `<jsp:getProperty>`action:

```
<jsp:getProperty name="theCounter" property="currentValue" />
```

would render this JSP Java code:

```
// begin [file="C:\\counterBeanPage.jsp";from=(21,22);to=(21,83)]
out.print(JspRuntimeLibrary.toString(
   theCounter.getCurrentValue())
);
// end
```

Apart from the housekeeping calls to `out.print` and `JspRuntimeLibrary.toString()`, the code generated originating from the `<jsp:getProperty>` action is `theCounter.getCurrentValue()` as would be expected from the JavaBean property pattern described previously. The `JspRuntimeLibrary.toString()` part of the call is implementation- and JSP engine-dependent and makes sure all data gets properly converted to a `String`.

The <jsp:setProperty> Action

The `<jsp:setProperty>` action assigns a new value to a JavaBean property by creating a call to its corresponding setter method, converted to a `String`, onto the `out JspWriter`. The string conversion is done using the standard `toString()` method if the argument is an object or directly if the argument is a primitive.

The `<jsp:setProperty>` tag syntax is:

```
<jsp:setProperty name="aName" property="propExpr" valueOption />
```

where

- `name` indicates the object variable in which to call the `setXXX` method supplied in the property field. Note that the value for `name` must match the value of `id` in the `<jsp:useBean>` tag.

- `property` is either the name of the writeable bean property (in other words, a JavaBean setter method having the name `setProperty(Type obj)`) or * to indicate that the JSP engine should set *all* bean properties whose names exist as `ServletRequest` parameters. In the latter case, the JSP engine will loop through all `ServletRequest` parameter names, setting only the writeable JavaBean properties if the `ServletRequest` parameter is non-empty.

- `param=”paramName”` indicates the name of the `ServletRequest` parameter that contains the value that should be used when setting the value of the JavaBean property.

- value="aValue" directly provides the value that should be used when setting the value of the JavaBean property. The value can be a string or JSP expression. If the parameter has an empty or null value, the corresponding bean property is not set. Frequently, one must compensate for the potential null value by manually investigating incoming HttpRequest parameters.

Request Parameter Types and JavaBean Writeable Properties

All incoming Http request parameters are of type String or String[]. Several parameters may have the same name (but different values). If so, the type of the particular parameter is String[], otherwise String.

As an example, this <jsp:setProperty> tag:

```
<jsp:setProperty name="theCounter" property="*" />
```

would render the Tomcat/J2EE JSP Java code:

```
// begin [file="C:\\counterBeanPage.jsp";from=(7,0);to=(7,50)]
 JspRuntimeLibrary.introspect(theCounter, request);
// end
```

The preceding approach performs a multitude of Java method calls, roughly sketched in the next example.

A Counter JavaBean Example

This simple example, shown in Figure 4-28, uses all three bean-related JSP actions, (<jsp:useBean>, <jsp:getProperty>, and <jsp:setProperty>) and illustrates the interaction between two classes:

- The autogenerated servlet class, counterJspPage
- The Counter JavaBean class

The counterJspPage class uses a Counter object (with the variable name theCounter) to keep track of the number of times the page has been requested (by a particular user). The `Counter` object must therefore be bound to the session of a particular user (lest we dare run the risk of confusing counters belonging to different users).

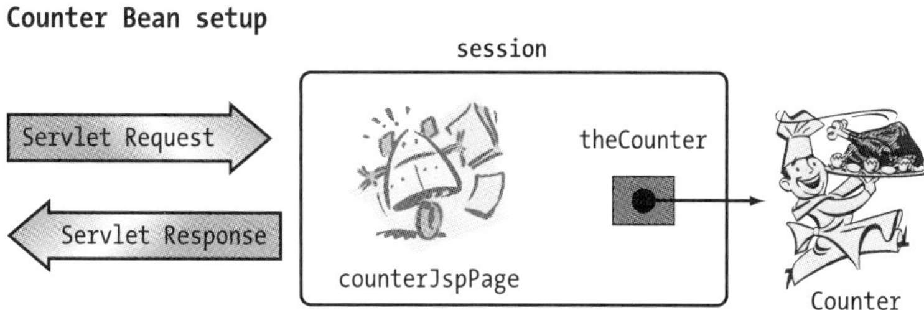

Figure 4-28. Structure of the relation between the `counterJspPage.jsp` *document and its counter JavaBean object*

The `Counter` class exposes two JavaBean properties:

- `int currentValue`, which is a read-only property. Thus, the method to call in the `Counter` class must have the signature public `int getValue()`, according to the JavaBean specification. When calling this method, the internal counter value is incremented and returned.

- `String reset`, which is a write-only property. Thus, the method to call in the `Counter` class must have the signature `public void setReset(String aNewValue)`, according to the JavaBean specification. When calling this method, the internal counter value is reset to 0. This property might be regarded as rather ill-designed, but the relevance of its existence will be revealed shortly.

The result of running the `counterJspPage.jsp` document is shown below in a series of figures. When the page is initially requested the page displays saying the "Current value" for the counter is 1. When clicking on the Increase Value button, the `counterJspPage.jsp` document is called again, and the counter is incremented. If the Reset Counter check box is selected and then the user clicks the button, the counter value will be reset once again to 0.

Assuming you have hit the button three times after initially requesting the page, the browser looks like Figure 4-29.

After pressing the Increase Value button again, the page looks like Figure 4-30.

Selecting the Reset Counter check box shown in Figures 4-29 and 4-30 and then clicking the Increase Value button again, the page looks like Figure 4-31.

Note that the counter has been reset to 0 and incremented to 1 to reflect the page's initial state.

Figure 4-29. The view of the `counterJspPage.jsp` *document assuming you have submitted the form three times*

Figure 4-30. The counter is increased as expected. Note that the Reset Counter check box has been selected.

Figure 4-31. The resulting view after submiting

The `Counter` class code displayed in Listing 4-26 is simple.

Listing 4-26. The `Counter` *class*

```
public class Counter
{
   // Internal state
   private int ctr;

   public Counter()
   {
      // Assign internal state
      this.ctr = 0;
   }

   public int getCurrentValue()
   {
          // Bump counter
          this.ctr++;

          //return
          return this.ctr;
   }
```

```
    public void setReset(String val)
    {
            // Reset the counter value
            this.ctr = 0;
    }
}
```

The two available methods in the `Counter` class (`getCurrentValue` and `setReset`) are JavaBean property methods, according to the JavaBean naming convention pattern discussed earlier. The two properties exposed by the `Counter` class are used within the JSP document to display or bind values from the HTML `<FORM>` to `theCounter` bean.

Listing 4-27 displays the `counterJspPage.jsp`. document

Listing 4-27. The `counterJspPage.jsp` *code. The* `<jsp:setProperty>` *and* `<jsp:getProperty>` *actions invoking the methods in the* `Counter` *class have been rendered in bold.*

```
<HTML>
<HEAD>

<%--
    Create a Counter object and bind it to the session of the
    Current user. This JSP action performs the equivalent of
    The following java statements:

    Counter theCounter = (Counter) session.getValue("theCounter");
    if(theCounter == null)
    {
       session.setAttribute("theCounter", new Counter());
       theCounter = session.getAttribute("theCounter");
    }
--%>
<jsp:useBean id="theCounter" class="Counter" scope="session" />

<%--
    Read all parameters from the incoming HttpServletRequest stream,
    And call all setter methods in theCounter object where the
    Property name matches the HttpServletRequest parameter.

    This JSP Action performs the equivalent of the Java
    statements below.
    (Note that classes Introspector and PropertyDescriptor are
    Found in package java.beans, and class Method is found in
    The java.lang.reflect package).
```

```
    // Get all properties within the bean
    Counter theCounter = (Counter) session.getAttribute("theCounter");
    PropertyDescriptor[] allProperties =
       Introspector.getBeanInfo().getPropertyDescriptors();

    for(Enumeration en = request.getParameterNames();
         en.hasMoreElements; )
    {
       // Loop through all Properties in the bean
       for(int j = 0; j < allProperties.length; j++)
       {
          // Property writeable?
          if(allProperties[j].getWriteMethod() == null) continue;

          // Request parameter name matches existing
          // property within the bound JavaBean?
          String readParameter = (String) en.nextElement();
          if(allProperties[j].getName().equals(readParameter))
          {
             // Get the method to invoke
             Method setterMethod =
                allProperties[j].getWriteMethod();

             // Create the argument array to the Method
             Object[] args = new Object[1];
             args[0] =  session.getParameter(readParameter);

             // Finally, invoke the setter method to set
             // the desired property.
             setterMethod.invoke(theCounter, args);
          }
       }
    }
--%>
<jsp:setProperty name="theCounter" property="*" />

    <TITLE> counterJspPage </TITLE>
</HEAD>

<BODY>
<center><H1> Counter JSP</H1>
```

```
<hr>
<FORM method="post" action="http://TheServer/theWebApp/counterJspPage.jsp" >
<table border=2>
<tr>

<%--
   Now, extract the currentValue property from the bound
   Counter object. This is the equivalent of calling

   Counter theCounter = (Counter) session.getAttribute("theCounter");
   String counterValue = theCounter.getCurrentValue();
--%>

   <td>Current value: <jsp:getProperty name="theCounter" property="currentValue" />
   </td>
</tr>
<tr>

<%--
   Make the form reset checkbox have the name "reset",
   So that it will be associated with the reset property
   In the bound Counter object.

   Thus, when calling this JSP document again, the
   HttpServletRequest has a bound parameter "reset" which
   will cause the <jsp:setProperty ... /> action above
   to call the public void setReset(String str) method
   in the Counter class.

--%>

   <td>Reset counter? <input type="checkbox" name="reset">
   </td>
</tr>
<tr>
   <td>
   <INPUT TYPE="SUBMIT" NAME="Submit" VALUE="Increase value!">
   </td>
</tr>
</table>
</FORM>

</center>
</BODY>
</HTML>
```

Comparing the equivalent Java statements of the JSP actions in Listing 4-27 (they are listed within the comments immediately before the action statements themselves) with the action statements themselves, it is clear that the reduction in typing will provide a quicker and more stable solution than coding everything by hand within a servlet.

The <jsp:plugin> Action

The last of the standard JSP actions is the `<jsp:plugin>`tag, which creates a piece of HTML code that makes a browser download a plugin application. Depending on the Web browser, the plugin action creates either an `<EMBED>` or `<OBJECT>` HTML container describing the required download information.

The `<jsp:plugin>` tag syntax is:

```
<jsp:plugin type="""bean|applet" code="classFileName" codebase="aURL" HTMLparams >
     <jsp:params>
          <jsp:param name="name" value="value" />
     </jsp:params>
     <jsp:fallback> FallbackData </jsp:fallback>
</jsp:plugin>
```

where

- `type` indicates the type of plugin that should be downloaded and may have the value `bean` or `applet`. Note that you must specify either `bean` or `applet` as this attribute does not have a default value.
- `code` indicates the code to run for the plugin, in other words, the class name. Note that you must include the `.class` extension in the filename, and it must be located in the directory specified in the `codebase` attribute.
- `codebase` indicates the URL where `code` can be found.
- `HTMLparams` behave identically to parameters defined in the HTML specification, but only a limited set of HTML parameters may be used within the `<jsp:plugin>` tag. All parameters should therefore be given on the form `paramName="paramValue"`. The actual parameters are:
    - Parameters directly found in the HTML specification: `height`, `width`, `hspace`, `vspace`, `align`, `archive`, `name`, `title`

- Parameters specific to the <jsp:plugin> action: `jreversion` (defines minimum JRE version for the plugin to work), `nspluginurl` (defines a URL where Netscape Navigator compatible browsers may download the plugin), and `iepluginurl` (defines a URL where Internet Explorer compatible browsers may download the plugin)

Listing 4-28 shows an example of the `<jsp:plugin>` action.

Listing 4-28. A full `<jsp:plugin>` *section of a JSP document.*

```
<jsp:plugin
   type="applet"
   code="SillyApplet"
   codebase="/"
   width="400" height="100">

   <jsp:params>
      <jsp:param name="msg0"
         value="Andy Rooney: 'Computers make it easier to do a lot
            of things, but most of the things they make it easier
            to do don't need to be done.'" />
      <jsp:param name="msg1"
         value="Therapy is expensive, popping bubble wrap is cheap!" />
      <jsp:param name="msg2"
         value="Spouse, n.: 'Someone who'll stand by you through all
            the trouble you wouldn't have had if you'd stayed single.'" />
      <jsp:param name="msg3"
         value="Unknown: 'After all is said and done, a lot more
            will be said than done.'" />
      <jsp:param name="msg4"
         value="The decision is maybe and that's final!" />
   </jsp:params>

   <jsp:fallback><b>Note:</b> Could not launch the applet!</jsp:fallback>
</jsp:plugin>
```

This code renders autogenerated servlet code creating the HTML seen in Listing 4-29. The HTML code launches the provided applet ("SillyApplet") in the Java plugin, which is downloaded from the `codebase` location of the Java plugin, in other words, `http://java.sun.com/products/plugin/1.2.2/jinstall-1_2_2-win.cab#Version=1,2,2,0` unless it is already installed.

Listing 4-29. Launching SillyApplet

```
<OBJECT
     classid="clsid:8AD9C840-044E-11D1-B3E9-00805F499D93"
     width="400"
     height="100"
     codebase="http://java.sun.com/products/plugin/1.2.2/➥
jinstall-1_2_2-win.cab#Version=1,2,2,0">

     <PARAM name="java_code" value="SillyApplet">
     <PARAM name="java_codebase" value="/">
     <PARAM name="type" value="application/x-java-applet;">
     <PARAM name="msg1"
          value="Therapy is expensive, popping bubble wrap is cheap!">
     <PARAM name="msg0"
          value="Andy Rooney: 'Computers make it easier to do a lot of
               things, but most of the things they make it easier to
               do don't need to be done.'">
     <PARAM name="msg4" value="The decision is maybe and that's final!">
     <PARAM name="msg3"
          value="Unknown: 'After all is said and done, a lot more
               will be said than done.'">
     <PARAM name="msg2"
          value="Spouse, n.: 'Someone who'll stand by you through all
          the trouble you wouldn't have had if you'd stayed single.'">

<COMMENT>
<EMBED
     type="application/x-java-applet;"
     width="400"
     height="100"
     pluginspage="http://java.sun.com/products/plugin/"
     java_code="SillyApplet"
     java_codebase="/"

     msg1="Therapy is expensive, popping bubble wrap is cheap!"
     msg0="Andy Rooney: 'Computers make it easier to do a lot of
          things, but most of the things they make it easier to
          do don't need to be done.'"
     msg4="The decision is maybe and that's final!"
     msg3="Unknown: 'After all is said and done, a lot more
          will be said than done.'"
     msg2="Spouse, n.: 'Someone who'll stand by you through all
          the trouble you wouldn't have had if you'd stayed single.'" >
<NOEMBED>
```

```
</COMMENT>
<b>Note:</b> Could not launch the applet!
</NOEMBED></EMBED>
</OBJECT>
```

If the Java plugin is not installed on the browser, a dialog box similar to the one shown in Figure 4-32 will appear to notify the user about the imminent component download and install.

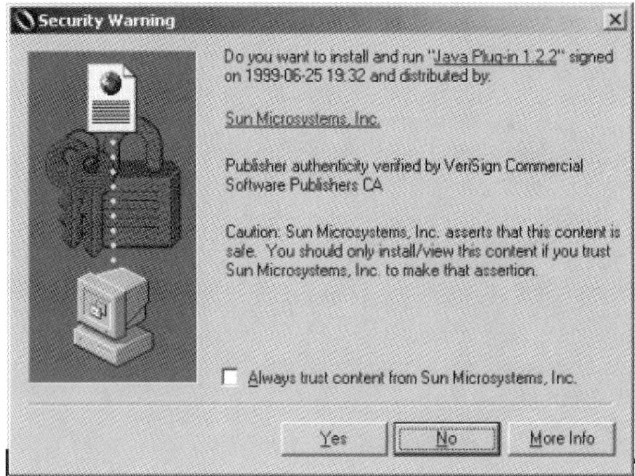

Figure 4-32. The security warning dialog shown by the browser before downloading and installing the Java plugin

Should the user choose to deny the browser the authority to download and install the Java plugin, the `<jsp:fallback>` text is shown instead of the applet, as shown in Figure 4-33. This also happens if the user has denied the browser authority to run ActiveX objects in the Windows environment.

Should the user choose to download and install the Java plugin, the download and install dialog is shown, after which the applet is launched. The benefit of this procedure is that a modern Java Virtual Machine is used to run applets in the client browser. The drawback is that the Java plugin is roughly 7.2MB in size—it therefore takes far too long to download and install it over a 28.8kbs modem line. See Figure 4-34.

The running applet, when run inside the Java plugin appears as in Figure 4-35.

This concludes a walkthrough of the standard actions defined in the JSP specification. However, the JSP specification includes a controlled way of creating custom server-side tags. This technology is known as Tag Library Definitions (TLD) and will be thoroughly investigated in the following chapter.

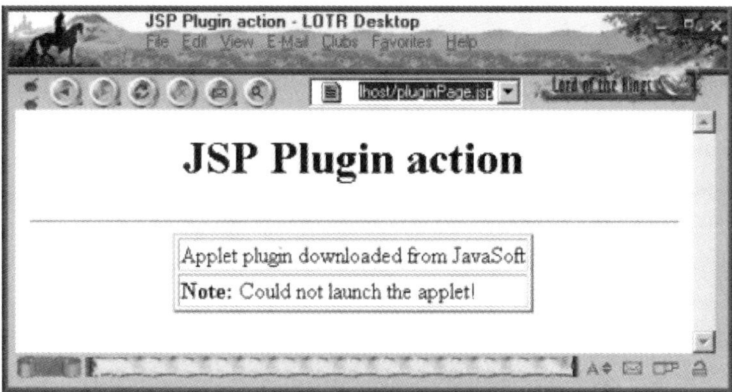

Figure 4-33. If the user has configured the browser not to accept Java content or ActiveX objects, the `<jsp:fallback>` *text is shown.*

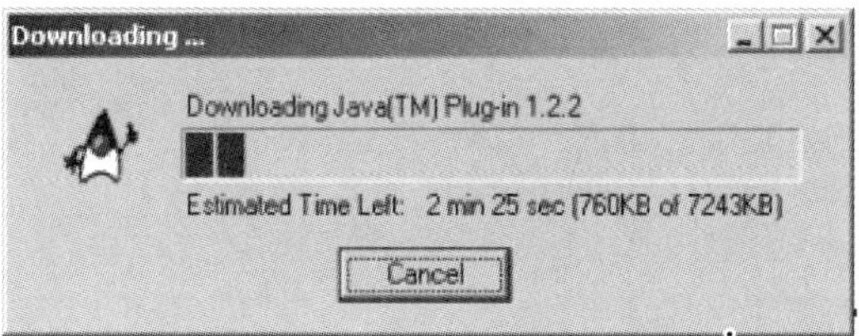

Figure 4-34. The download control shown by the client browser when downloading the Java plugin. Note its total size.

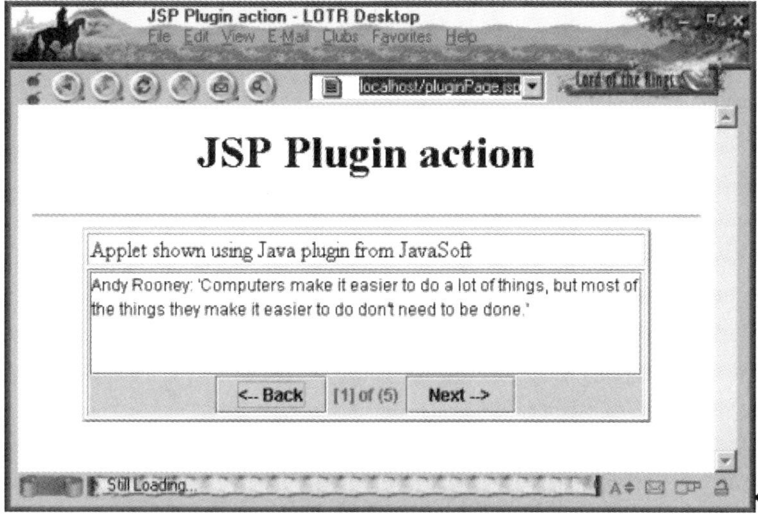

Figure 4-35. When downloaded and installed, the Java plugin provides Java 2 support for the browser. This figure is a running `javax.swing.JApplet`, *which requires the Java 2 Swing classes to work properly.*

CHAPTER 5

JSP Tag Libraries

THE TERM *TAG* IS CENTRAL to markup languages such as HTML and XML. A markup document grants meaning to text by surrounding or preceding it with a set of characters collectively called a *tag*. In HTML and XML documents, tags have the form `<text>` where *text* defines the meaning of the tag. For instance, a HTML first-level header may be created simply by surrounding the text with header tags: (`<h1>This is a first-level header</h1>`). JSP technology provides a standard mechanism whereby a programmer can create his/her own server-side tags. These *JSP tags* are evaluated on the server, and their results are sent back to the client browser.

This chapter describes how to create, use, and structure JSP tag libraries for the three existing types of JSP tags: standalone, iterative, and body content tags.

Describing Tags

Tags are displayed by a rendering engine on the client, which converts the cryptic text to a layout presented to the user. All HTML browsers contain a rendering engine—even the text-only browser Lynx highlights text made "bold" by a HTML tag pair. One may, therefore, regard the tag as an encapsulation of client-side rendering information; it is much simpler for the HTML author to include a tag than a full specification of what the client-side rendering engine should do with the text.

Pondering the situation a minute, you may quickly realize that the same principle holds true for encapsulating server-side information. Many server-side documents contain complex data manipulation instructions; hiding the complexity behind a simpler construct makės for a simpler overview of the document. Figure 5-1 illustrates two ways of inserting a string of characters into a JavaServer Pages (JSP) document; although both versions perform the same task, the custom tag hides most of the complexity (or, more to the point, the code mass) shown in the code block. In general, it is simpler to quickly get an overview of a JSP document containing several custom tags than multiple code blocks.

Of course, there has to be a catch to the beautiful story of the custom JSP tag. You may rightfully wonder where the information logic invoked by the custom tag illustrated in Figure 5-1 is placed. If it's not in the JSP document, then where is it? The simple answer is that you may create *libraries* of tag handler classes, which must be placed in the classpath of the Web application to be usable. Frequently, one copies such a tag library—in the form of a JAR file—to the `WEB-INF/lib` directory of the Web

```
Code block              <%
(Unencapsulated)           // This block will output a length of
                           // concatenated characters to the output
                           // stream out (connected to the response
                           // output writer).

                           StringBuffer buf = new StringBuffer();
                           for(char i ='a'; i < stopChar; i++)
                           {
                              // Printout the character with the
                              // provided index in the alphabet
                              buf.appendix(i);
                           }

                           // Print.
                           out.println(buf.toString());
                        %>
```

```
Custom Tag              <homeMadeTags:printChars stopChar="m" />
(Encapsulated)
```

Figure 5-1. Compare the two ways to specify printing a set of characters to the browser. If both ways accomplished the same thing, which notation would be simplest?

application. Using custom tags ensures low-impact portability between Web applications because the full functionality of a set of custom JSP tags resides in the JAR file. As an alternative, the bytecode files of the tag handler classes may be placed in the classpath of the Web application.

As a conclusion, there are several good reasons to use custom JSP tags in JSP documents, instead of raw code blocks:

- **Simplicity**. Custom JSP tags have better encapsulation and expose only the most relevant information. Reducing information clutter improves efficiency in learning and usage.

- **Protection**. Custom JSP tags hide the code statements; an information editor altering the text of a JSP document may accidentally modify text within a block of code—with disastrous effects on the Web application. Custom tags prevent such accidental modification.

- **Portability**. Custom JSP tags grant portability because their functionality (normally placed within an archive) may be moved between Web applications and/or Web application servers in a simple manner.

- **Familiarity**. Custom tags are well-known building blocks to information architects and HTML hackers—Java code is generally not. Presenting another building block that looks similar to a normal tag is likely not to summon a storm of protests; adding "strange code" in JSP documents may.

What Is a Custom Action?

You may have heard the phrase *custom action*, which is another name for a JSP custom tag. Because custom JSP tags look similar to a standard JSP action, it is plain to see how the nickname arose.

Having seen an example of a custom tag in Figure 5-1, let us now investigate how to describe custom JSP tags in general.

There are two custom JSP tag types: *empty actions*, which are standalone and contain no bodies, and *non-empty actions*, which are containers that have a body (see Figure 5-2). Of course, the body of a non-empty tag may be completely empty—but it must exist for a non-empty tag. To facilitate things, the terminology used within this book is the same as used within the Tag Library API (in other words, `package javax.servlet.jsp.tagext`).

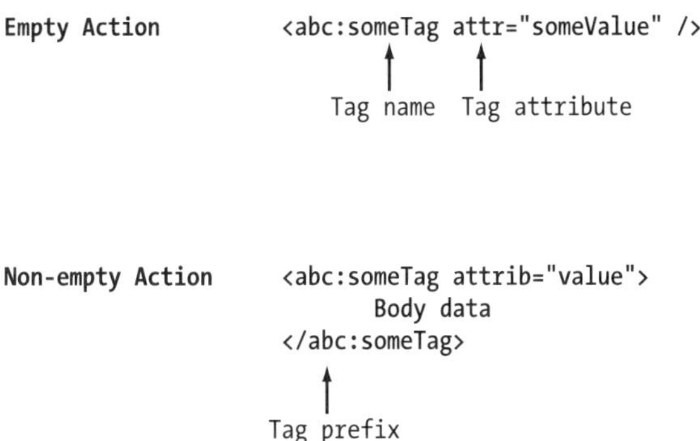

Figure 5-2. The definitions pertaining to the structure of empty (standalone) and non-empty (container) JSP tags. The definitions in this image (that follows the JSP 1.2 specification terms) will be used throughout this chapter.

Now investigate how to create powerful, platform-independent, and reusable custom JSP actions. In fact, creating a tag library is one of the better uses of encapsulation to guide developers in creating reusable JSP custom tags. In turn, custom tags reduce the amount of errors generated by JSP developers in server-side documents.

The JSP tag library system has four parts:

- *The tag handler class* implements the life-cycle methods required for all tag handlers by the JSP specification. The methods of the tag handler perform whatever custom behavior the developer has created. The tag handler class must be deployed into the classpath of the Web application which uses it; normally the tag handler classes are deployed into the `WEB-INF/classes` directory or packaged into a JAR file in the `WEB-INF/lib` directory.

- *The tag library descriptor* (TLD) document contains XML definitions mapping tag handler classes to logical tag names. Such logical names are the equivalent of an internal servlet name in the `web.xml` configuration document and must be unique within each TLD. The TLD document may have any name but is frequently called `taglib.tld`. In the JSP 1.1 specification, the TLD file must be placed in the `META-INF` directory and named `taglib.tld`, but the JSP 1.2 specification permits arbitrary placement and name.

- *The web.xml* configuration document may define several taglib constructs. Each taglib construct maps a TLD document to a logical Uniform Resource Identifier (URI) that must be unique within the Web application.

- The JSP document may contain one or more *JSP TLD directives* that map a URI defined in the `web.xml` to a unique prefix string for use within the document. This mapping is generally convenient because URIs may be rather long and awkward to type repeatedly within the JSP document; a prefix may be shorter and, consequently, more convenient.

XML in the J2EE World

Configuration settings used by Java 2 Enterprise Edition (J2EE) components and servers are frequently XML-formatted documents. XML documents, like HTML, are markup documents containing a set of tags that are defined in a document type definition (DTD). The DTD document is used as a template that defines an XML data tree, such as which tags are permitted within other tags. Although most of the XML examples within this book are explained in detail, you may want to visit `http://www.xml.org` for more information on XML.

Figure 5-3 shows a skeleton content version of the four files mentioned in the preceding bulleted list. A JSP document containing a particular `<%@ taglib ... %>` directive uses the `uri` attribute of the taglib directive to locate the archive containing the TLD file. Unless the `uri` is a hyperlink to an actual TLD document, the hyperlink contains a logical name for the TLD file. The `web.xml` configuration document is consulted to find the physical location of the TLD file requested. Using the definitions in the TLD file, a tag handler class is located. Moreover, the taglib directive defines a prefix (“`apress`” in the image) used in the JSP file to identify all tags from a particular TLD—when that prefix is encountered in a custom tag in a JSP document, the JSP engine knows which TLD to query for a tag definition. The class is resolved and instantiated to enable a method call to its life-cycle method.

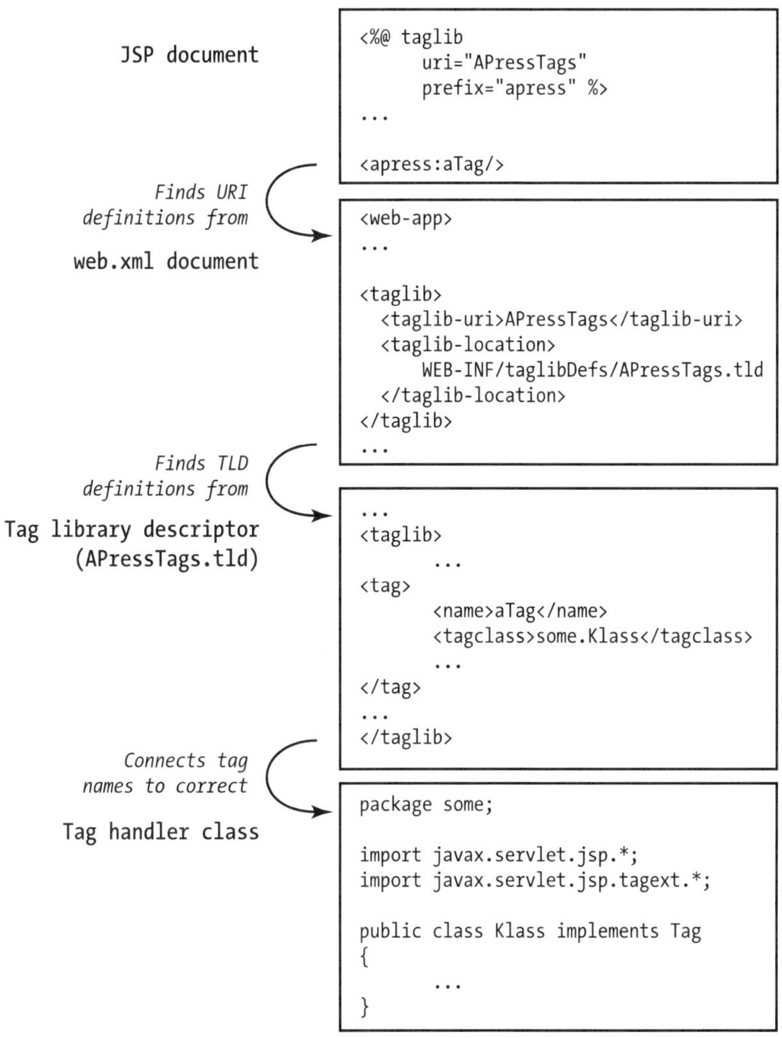

Figure 5-3. The tag handler class, TLD, `web.xml` *document, and JSP document work together. The JSP engine creates an instance of the correct tag handler class and invokes a set of methods within it whenever a particular tag is found within the JSP document. This figure shows the conversion between the name and prefix of the custom JSP tag and the tag handler class.*

The taglib directive may use four different URI attribute types to locate the TLD file. Those attributes may contain the following items:

- URL to a Web server from which the TLD file may be downloaded. An example of such a taglib URI is `<%@ taglib uri="http://www.apress.com/servletbook/tlds/examples.tld" prefix="dummy" %>`.
- An absolute local Web application path, which originates from the root of the local Web application. Such URI attributes must start with a forward slash (/); an example is `<%@ taglib uri="/some/path/theExamples.tld" prefix="examples" %>`.
- Relative local Web application path, which originates from the directory where the JSP document resides. Such URI attributes may neither start with a forward slash nor a `http://` prefix. An example of a relative address taglib directive is `<%@ taglib uri="aDir/theExamples.tld" prefix="moreExamples" %>`.
- Arbitrary string, provided that the string is defined as a `<taglib-uri>` in the `web.xml` configuration file. Note that the `uri` attribute in the taglib directive must match the `web.xml` definition exactly, as in `<%@ taglib uri="accountingTags" prefix="accTags" %>`, providing that the `web.xml` file contains a taglib entry with the `taglib-uri` entry being `<taglib-uri>accounting Tags</taglib-uri>`.

The first of these options, loading the TLD document directly from a URL address somewhere on the Web, is considerably slower and more unpredictable than the other three options that loads the TLD from a file in the local file system. For industrial-strength systems, therefore, the second and fourth are used more frequently.

The JSP definition is quite liberal regarding the deployment placement of most documents described previously. Apart from the `web.xml` document that must be placed in the `WEB-INF` directory, all other documents may be placed arbitrarily. As the tag handler classes must reside in the `CLASSPATH` to be loaded by the Java Virtual Machine (JVM) running the servlet engine, they are frequently found in `WEB-INF/classes` or packaged in a JAR file in `WEB-INF/lib`.

You can see an example of a simple JAR file structure containing a full tag library in Figure 5-4. The `FirstTag.class` is a compiled tag handler class, which is invoked whenever a particular tag is found within the JSP document. Although it may be good practice to place TLD files in the `META-INF` directory, the JSP specification permits placing the TLD file in an arbitrary directory.

```
META-INF/
META-INF/MANIFEST.MF
META-INF/taglib.tld
se/jguru/tags/FirstTag.class
```

Figure 5-4. The content of a JAR file containing a tag library definition (`taglib.tld`) and the tag handler class (`FirstTag.class`). In addition to the two files previously, the normal `MANIFEST.MF` file of a JAR is present. This structure is compliant with the JSP 1.1 deployment requirement because the TLD file is named `taglib.tld` and placed in the `META-INF` directory.

When developing an industrial-strength library of custom tag handler classes, you should strive for providing a tag handler class name that would let the developer realize what function the tag performs. In the example shown in Figure 5-4, however, the main concern is to grant understanding for the deployment of all files being part of the custom JSP tag system, so we have relaxed the demand for usability in this example.

The Life Cycle of a Tag Handler Class

JSP tag handler classes behave much like servlets; they have a strict life cycle where methods are called in a specific order. The life cycle of JSP tag handlers is more difficult to grasp because the methods are found in four different interfaces/classes:

- The `Tag` interface defines life-cycle methods common to all tag handler classes. These life cycle methods define methods `doStartTag` and `doEndTag` that are called by the JSP engine to start and stop the evaluation of a tag. Also, the `Tag` interface defines JavaBean accessor methods to get and set `pageContext` and parent variables. The `Tag` interface should be implemented for empty tags.

- The `IterationTag` interface extends the `Tag` interface and provides an extra method (`doAfterBody`), which may be called repeatedly by the JSP engine when iterating over the body of the `IteratorTag`. Use the `IterationTag` to create a JSP custom tag that requires body iteration. `IterationTag`s are frequently used when generating HTML or XML lists that should be output to the client.

- The `BodyTag` interface extends the `Tag` interface and provides additional methods for non-empty tags only. The JSP tag handler class should implement the `BodyTag` interface if you want to manipulate the body content of the JSP tag.

- The tag handler implementation class provides implementations for the standard `Tag` life-cycle methods in addition to standard methods for setting (and getting) JavaBean properties. Such properties are automatically set by the JSP engine if the TLD file defines attributes for a tag. You'll learn more about tag attributes in sections "The Ideal Life Cycle for an Empty Tag with Attributes," "The Ideal Life Cycle for an IterationTag with Attributes," and "Tag Definitions."

The life cycle of a tag differs slightly depending on its type; empty tags without any attributes have a simpler life cycle than non-empty container tags with many attributes. Let's take a look at each type in turn to investigate the effect on tag life cycle that different constructs have.

Tag Interface

Figure 5-5 shows the life cycle of a handler class implementing the `javax.servlet.jsp.tagext.Tag` interface. During initialization, the tag handler class is created and configured, where all its JavaBean setter methods are called with the values provided in the TLD configuration document (`taglib.tld`, for instance). JavaBean setter methods are represented with the message "setXXX()". During runtime, the `doStartTag` and `doEndTag` methods are called and the actual processing of the tag is done. The four states of a tag handler class are:

- **Created**. This is the state entered after the default (parameterless) constructor is invoked. All internal variables in the tag handler instance just created have their default values, as set programmatically in the constructor. The created state is transient, in the sense that the tag handlers need additional setup methods called to be properly configured.

- **Configured**. Having created the tag handler instance, the JSP engine must configure it according to the directions found in the TLD configuration file. Configuration is performed by calling the default setter methods of a JSP engine, as well as any setter methods for JavaBean properties defined for the tag in the TLD configuration file.

- **Executing**. In runtime, the JSP engine invokes the `doStartTag` and `doEndTag` methods in the tag handler class. The return value of the `doStartTag` method indicates whether the body text (if existent) should be included in the JSP output. The `doStartTag` method is called before and the `doEndTag` after including the body text in the output, if applicable.

- **Undefined**. Having being released to an instance pool, the tag handler instance is set in an undefined state and cannot be used before again being properly configured by calls to `setParent`, `setPageContext`, and the declared JavaBean property setter methods. The JSP engine guarantees that the release method will be called in a tag handler before garbage collection sets in.

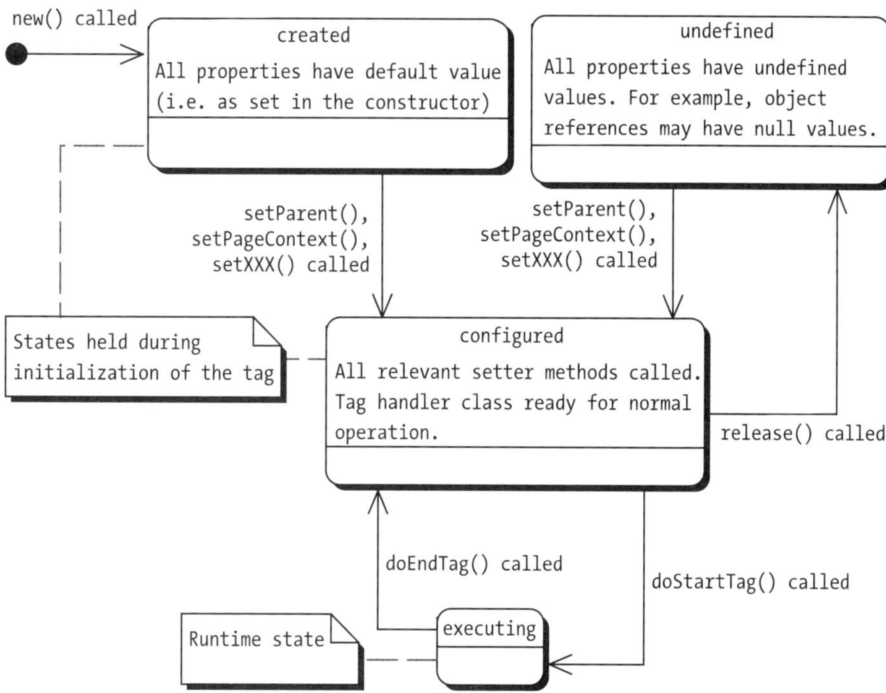

Figure 5-5. The life cycle for empty tags, where the tag handler class implements the `javax.servlet.jsp.tagext.Tag` *interface*

The Ideal Life Cycle for an Empty Tag without Attributes

State diagrams are wonderful for visualizing all possible scenarios for a particular instance. However, the simplicity of code may occasionally be lost in the wonderful box-and-line landscape of the Unified Modeling Language (UML). The ideal life cycle of a tag handler for a standalone tag without attributes is rather simple (see Figure 5-6).

The two first method calls provide the tag handler instance with references to the `PageContext` of the JSP document and the handler instance of a tag container being the parent of `theTagHandler`. A tag handler class is a parent of another if its JSP tag contains the second tag. In the following example, calling

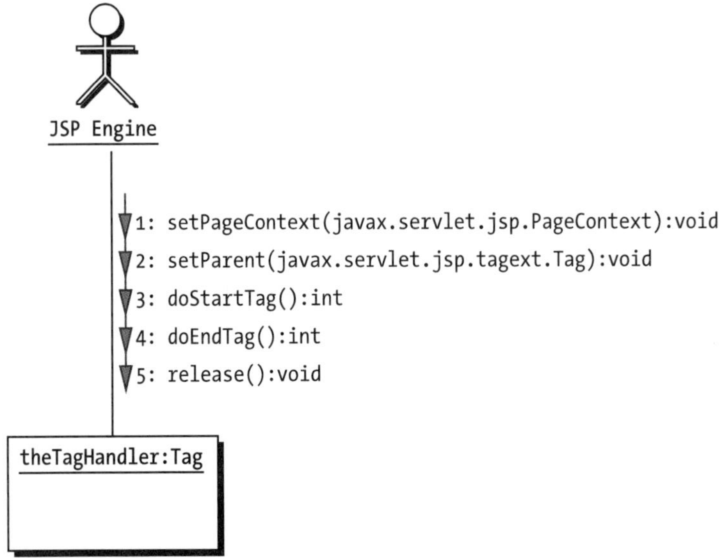

Figure 5-6. The life cycle of a standalone tag without any attributes, drawn as a UML collaboration diagram

`getParent` in the handler instance for `theChildTag` would return a reference to the handler instance for `theParentTag`:

```
<x:theParentTag>
        <!-- This is the body of theParentTag -->
        <x:theChildTag />
</x:theParentTag>
```

Methods 3 and 4, `doStartTag` and `doEndTag` from in Figure 5-6 are called when the JSP engine encounters the tag start and end respectively. For empty tags, there is no real difference between the two—but for non-empty tags the difference is obvious.

When done processing, the JSP engine calls the `release` method. This method has the same purpose as the `finalize` method of `java.lang.Object` in that it provides a standard place where the developer may free all objects held during the tag evaluation. Also, in the `release` method, the internal state of the tag handler instance is released, as shown in Figure 5-6.

The Ideal Life Cycle for an Empty Tag with Attributes

The typical life cycle of a tag handler for an empty tag accepting attributes differs slightly from the life cycle of an empty tag lacking attributes. In the case illustrated in Figure 5-7, the tag descriptor for the tag handler `attributeTag` has declared that the tag has an attribute (in other words, a JavaBean property) called `output`. The state chart diagram in Figure 5-7 is identical for empty tags with and without attributes.

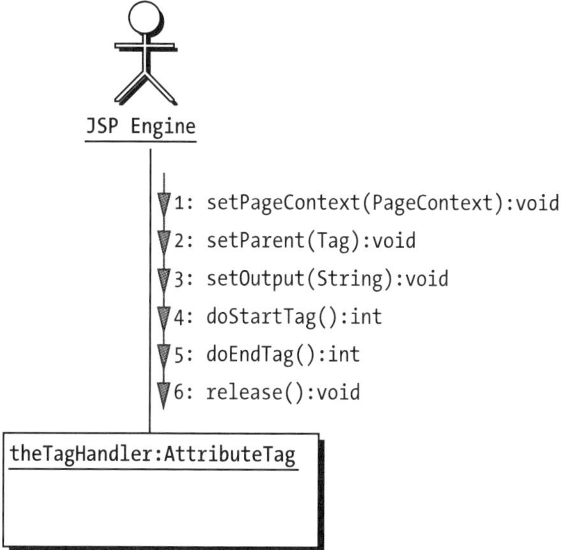

Figure 5-7. The life cycle of a standalone tag accepting one attribute (in other words, JavaBean property), drawn as a UML collaboration diagram. Note that the only difference between the two life cycles described in Figures 5-6 and 5-7 is the call to the `setOutput` *method, corresponding to setting a JavaBean property.*

Thus, between the `setParent` and the `doTagStartTag` methods, the JSP engine calls all JavaBean setter methods (in our case, `setOutput`) to initialize the state of the handler. Should any other JavaBean properties be declared in the tag library descriptor, the corresponding setter methods are invoked accordingly. Such setter methods are only invoked if an attribute is actually supplied within the JSP document, for example:

```
<!-- Setter method invoked. -->
<x:someTagName output="Some output" />

<!-- Setter method not invoked. -->
<x:someTagName />
```

From Figure 5-7 and the preceding listing, it is assumed that the tag `<x:someTagName />` name will invoke the life-cycle method calls on an instance of the `AttributeTag` class. However, the TLD linking the two for usage in the previous code snippet is not provided here; the syntax of the TLD file will be discussed in "Tag Library Descriptors," later in this chapter.

Having dealt with tag handlers implementing the `Tag` interface that may or may not have registered attributes, proceed to study the life cycle for tag handlers that implement the `IterationTag` interface.

IterationTag Interface

The life cycle of a handler class implementing the `javax.servlet.jsp.tagext.IterationTag` interface is similar to the life cycle for tag handlers implementing the `Tag` interface. As shown in Figure 5-8, the initialization states of the `Tag` implementation class depend on the exact type of tag. The five states of an `IterationHandler` class are as follows:

- **Created.** This is the state entered after the default (parameterless) constructor is invoked. All internal variables in the tag handler instance just created have their default values, as set programmatically in the constructor. The created state is transient, in the sense that the tag handlers need additional setup methods called to be properly configured.

- **Configured.** Having created the tag handler instance, the JSP engine must configure it according to the directions found in the TLD configuration file. Configuration is performed by calling the default setter methods of a JSP engine, as well as any setter methods for JavaBean properties defined for the tag in the TLD configuration file.

- **Executing.** In runtime, the JSP engine invokes the `doStartTag` and `doEndTag` methods in the tag handler class. The return value of the `doStartTag` method indicates whether the body text (if existent) should be included in the JSP output. The `doStartTag` method is called before and the `doEndTag` after including the body text in the output, if applicable.

- **Undefined.** Having being released to an instance pool, the tag handler instance is set in an undefined state and cannot be used before again being properly configured by calls to `setParent`, `setPageContext`, and the declared JavaBean property setter methods. The JSP engine guarantees that the release method will be called in a tag handler before garbage collection sets in.

- **Evaluating body.** If the `doStartTag` method invoked in the configured state returned `Tag.EVAL_BODY_INCLUDE`, the body of the non-empty tag is evaluated. Having evaluated the body, the `doAfterBody` method is called—and the `IterationTag` will keep evaluating the body as long as the `doAfterBody` returns `IteratorTag.EVAL_BODY_AGAIN`. When done iterating, the `doAfterBody` method should return `Tag.SKIP_BODY`.

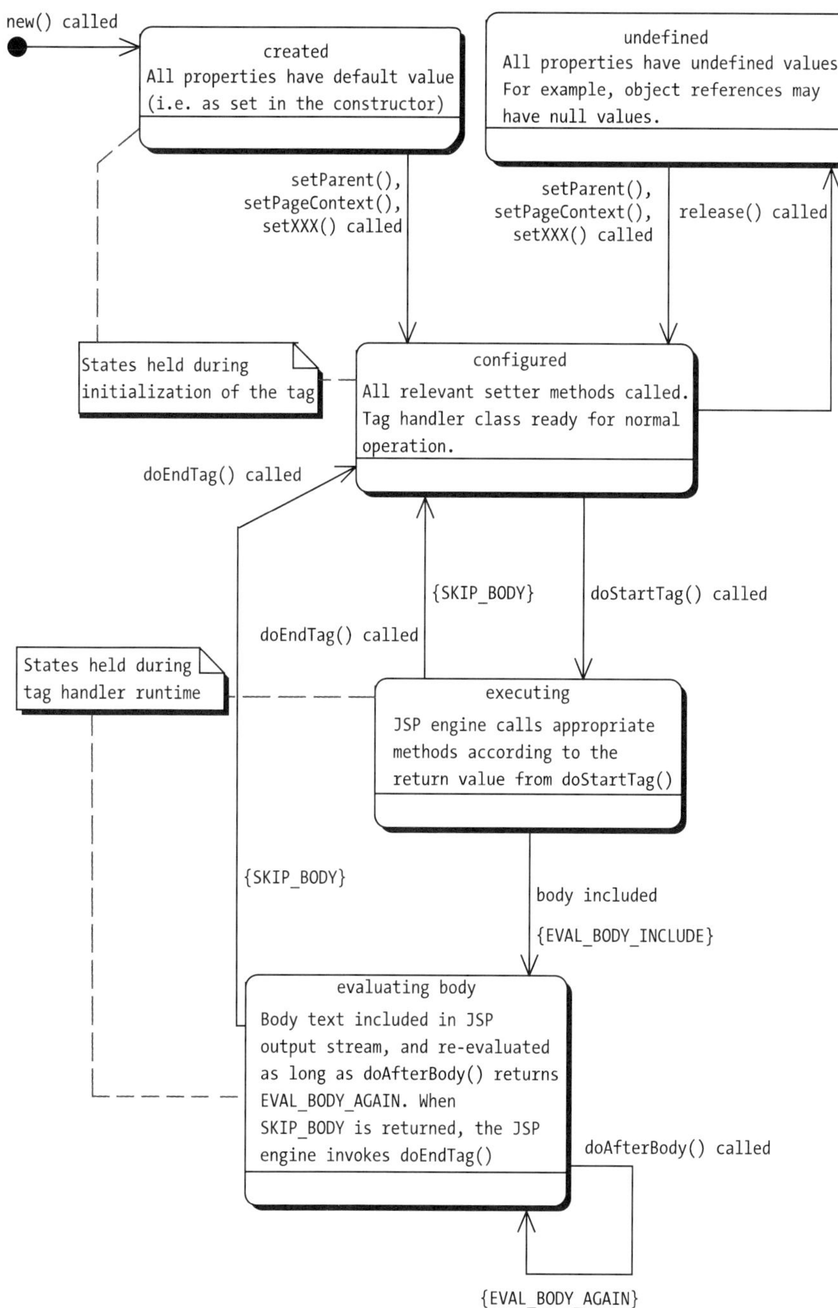

Figure 5-8. The five states of the `IterationTag` *handler class shown with the return values required to enter a given state. As shown, the evaluating body state will be preserved as long as the* `doAfterBody` *method returns* `IterationTag.EVAL_BODY_AGAIN`*. The main purpose of* `IterationTags` *is to simplify generating lists of output in the JSP view.*

The Ideal Life Cycle for an IterationTag without Attributes

The ideal life cycle of a tag handler for a non-empty tag (implementing the `IterationTag` interface) without attributes is rather simple (see Figure 5-9).

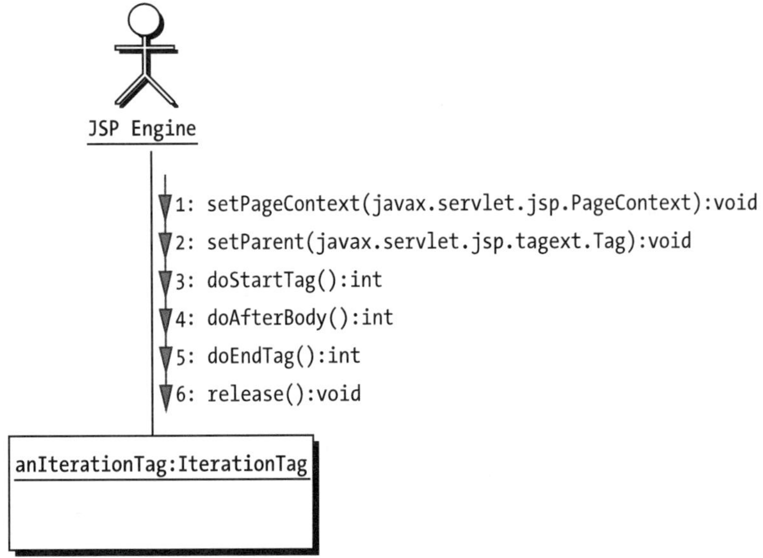

Figure 5-9. The life cycle of an `IterationTag` *without any declared attributes, drawn as a UML collaboration diagram. If you compare the ideal lifecycle to the one drawn for tag handler classes implementing the* `Tag` *interface, the* `doAfterBody` *method is added for* `IterationTags`.

Identical to the case of an empty custom JSP tag whose handler implements the `Tag` interface, the two first method calls provide the `IterationTag` handler instance with references to the `PageContext` of the JSP document and its parent. Methods 3 and 5 (`doStartTag` and `doEndTag` from Figure 5-9) are called when the JSP engine encounters the opening tag of the `IterationTag` and when the last iteration is just performed, respectively.

The major difference between tag handler classes that implement the `Tag` and `IterationTag` interfaces is, of course, the call to `doAfterBody` that is performed once after every evaluation of the body content. The return value of the `doAfterBody` method defines if the `IterationTag` will continue looping (`IterationTag.EVAL_BODY_AGAIN` is returned) or not (`Tag.SKIP_BODY` is returned).

When done iterating over the body text, the JSP engine calls the `release` method in the tag handler class, in an identical manner to the `Tag` handler.

The Ideal Life Cycle for an IterationTag with Attributes

As can be expected, the only difference between the ideal life cycles of `IterationTags` with and without attributes is that the JSP engine will attempt to call all setter methods for non-null JavaBean properties (see Figure 5-10).

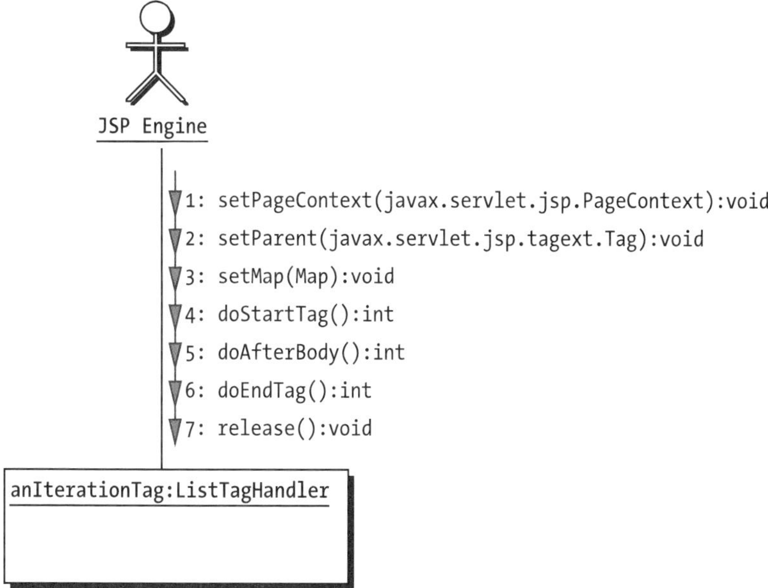

Figure 5-10. The life cycle of an `IterationTag` *with one declared attribute (the JavaBean property* `map` *of type* `Map`*), drawn as a UML collaboration diagram*

Identical to the case for a handler class implementing the `Tag` interface, all registered attributes for the `IterationTag` are set before the JSP engine calls the `doTagStartTag` method. The setter method, `setOutput`, is invoked to make the handler class do a state transition from *created* to *configured*, as shown in Figure 5-8. Of course, the setter methods are only invoked if an attribute is actually supplied within the JSP document. Assuming that the `someIterationTagName` is mapped to the `ListTagHandler` class shown in Figure 5-10, only the first of the two following code snippets will cause the JSP engine to call the `setMap` method:

```
<!-- Setter method invoked. -->
<x:someIterationTagName map="<%= aMap %>" />

<!-- Setter method not invoked. -->
<x: someIterationTagName />
```

The last subinterface to the `Tag` class is the `BodyTag` interface, which adds functionality that provides control over the body content.

BodyTag Interface

The life cycle of a handler class implementing the `javax.servlet.jsp.tagext.BodyTag` interface is similar to the life cycle for tag handlers implementing the `IterationTag` interface. As shown in Figure 5-11, the initialization states of the `BodyTag` handler are as follows:

- **Created.** This is the state entered after the default (parameterless) constructor is invoked. All internal variables in the tag handler instance just created have their default values, as set programmatically in the constructor. The created state is transient, in the sense that the tag handlers need additional setup methods called to be properly configured.

- **Configured.** Having created the tag handler instance, the JSP engine must configure it according to the directions found in the TLD configuration file. Configuration is performed by calling the default setter methods of a JSP engine, as well as any setter methods for JavaBean properties defined for the tag in the TLD configuration file.

- **Executing.** In runtime, the JSP engine invokes the `doStartTag` and `doEndTag` methods in the tag handler class. The return value of the `doStartTag` method indicates whether or not the body text (if existent) should be included in the JSP output. The `doStartTag` method is called before and the `doEndTag` after including the body text in the output, if applicable.

- **Undefined.** Having being released to an instance pool, the tag handler instance is set in an undefined state and cannot be used before again being properly configured by calls to `setParent`, `setPageContext`, and the declared JavaBean property setter methods. The JSP engine guarantees that the release method will be called in a tag handler before garbage collection sets in.

- **Setting body content**. If the `doStartTag` method returns `BodyTag.EVAL_BODY_BUFFERED`, the tag handler class proceeds to creating a buffer containing the body content of the tag, encapsulated in a `javax.servlet.jsp.tagext.BodyContent` object. The `BodyTag` handler class may then modify the buffered contents of the `BodyContent` and output the result to the JSP document, replacing the original body text. The `setBodyContent` method is not to be overridden by developers.

- **Preparing body**. The `doInitBody` method is called after the body content is set but before evaluation of the tag body has started. Thus, you may modify the buffered body text as retrieved from the JSP custom tag before starting to iterate and evaluate in the *Evaluating body* state.

- **Evaluating body**. If the `doStartTag` method invoked in the configured state returned `Tag.EVAL_BODY_INCLUDE`, the body of the non-empty tag is evaluated. Having evaluated the body, the `doAfterBody` method is called—and the `IterationTag` will keep evaluating the body as long as the `doAfterBody` returns `IteratorTag.EVAL_BODY_AGAIN`. When done iterating, the doAfterBody method should return `Tag.SKIP_BODY`.

For a non-empty tag, the state diagram and typical life cycle of its handler class differs from what has been described for `IterationTags` earlier in this chapter. Two new methods, `setBodyContent` and `doInitBody` are introduced; you are wise to leave the `setBodyContent` method as is, and focus on providing your own implementation for the `doInitBody` method only. The three methods `setBodyContent`, `doInitBody`, and `doAfterBody` are defined in the `BodyTag` interface, and the respective methods are called in order by the JSP engine.

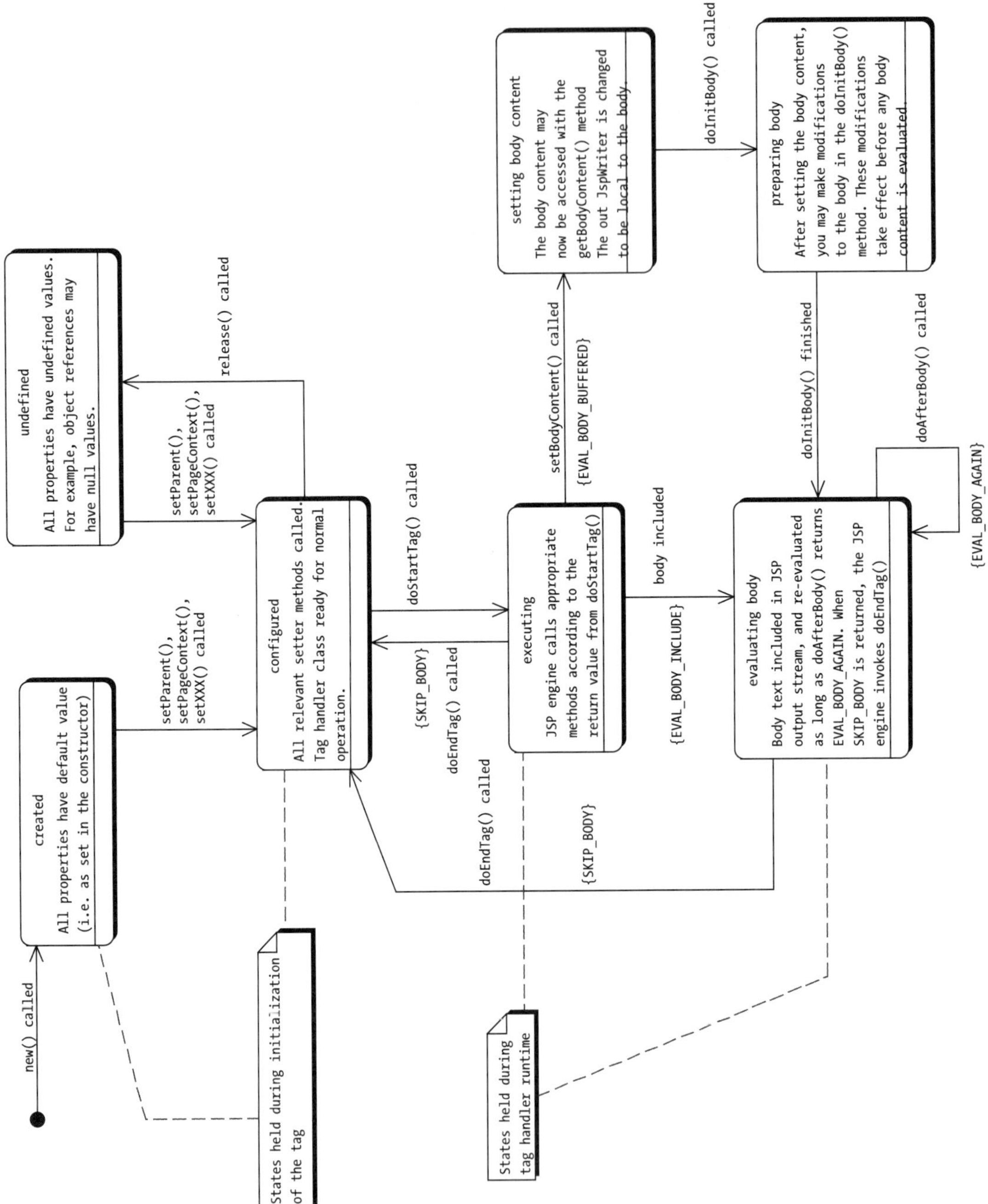

Figure 5-11. The seven states of the `BodyTag` *handler class illustrated with the return values required to enter a given state. The state of the tag handler class is largely controlled by the return value from the* `doEndTag` *of the executing state. The* `BodyTag` *handler class may either skip the body, evaluate identical to an* `IterationTag`*, or create a buffer containing the tag body content usable for further evaluation.*

As shown in Figure 5-12, some methods in the life-cycle pattern return integers. Take a look at Table 5-1 to see which values are legal to return and what effect the return value has on further JSP evaluation.

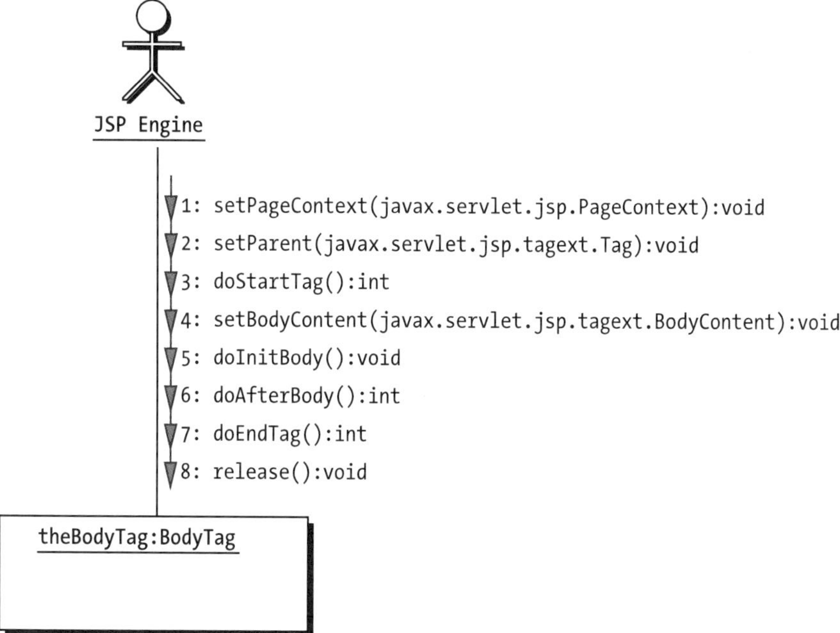

Figure 5-12. The life cycle of a body tag without any attributes, drawn as a UML collaboration diagram

Table 5-1. Values Returned from Lifecycle Methods of the BodyTag *Interface*

METHOD NAME	RETURN VALUE	EFFECT
doStartTag	Tag.EVAL_BODY_INCLUDE	The body contents of the container tag are evaluated into the existing out stream (in other words, unbuffered). This value is illegal if the tag handler class implements BodyTag; such tag handler classes must instead return BodyTag.EVAL_BODY_BUFFERED.
	BodyTag.EVAL_BODY_BUFFERED	A new BodyContent object (which contains a buffered copy of the original tag body content) is created and readied for evaluation. Note that BodyTag.EVAL_BODY_BUFFERED only is a legal return value from the doAfterBody method if the tag handler class implements BodyTag.
	BodyTag.EVAL_BODY_TAG	Deprecated in the JSP 1.2 specification; use BodyTag.EVAL_BODY_BUFFERED instead.
	Tag.SKIP_BODY	The body content of the non-empty tag is skipped and not evaluated. This value must be returned by empty tags (in other words, non-container tags).
doAfterBody	BodyTag.EVAL_BODY_TAG	Deprecated in the JSP 1.2 specification; use IterationTag.EVAL_BODY_AGAIN instead.

Table 5-1. Values Returned from Lifecycle Methods of the `BodyTag` *Interface (Continued)*

METHOD NAME	RETURN VALUE	EFFECT
	`IterationTag.EVAL_BODY_AGAIN`	Return this value to re-evaluate the body content of the `IterationTag` or `BodyTag`. For backwards compatibility with the JSP 1.1 version, the value of (the deprecated) `BodyTag.EVAL_BODY_TAG` is identical to `IterationTag.EVAL_BODY_AGAIN`.
	`Tag.SKIP_BODY`	Return this value to quit re-evaluation of the `IterationTag` or `BodyTag` and proceed with the JSP output generation.
`doEndTag`	`Tag.EVAL_PAGE`	Further contents of the JSP document are evaluated normally.
	`Tag.SKIP_PAGE`	No more JSP document content is evaluated; effectively returns from the `service` method of the generated servlet. Use this method to skip any output to the client browser after this tag.

Figure 5-13 provides a more detailed activity flow and state chart for custom tag evaluation.

The activity states from the flow diagram in Figure 5-13 represent activities performed by the JSP engine. The first activity state "Finding taglib definitions for tag" is completely handled by the JSP engine. The activities include reading metadata class definitions, instantiating metadata objects and calling methods within them to create the proper Java code placed within the servlet.

In the second activity state, "Evaluating body content," the JSP engine performs normal variable substitution in the body content of the current `IterationTag` or `BodyTag`. When done substituting within the current iteration over the tag body, the method `doAfterBody` is called. As indicated in Figure 5-13, the iteration and substitution continues as long as the `doAfterBody` method returns `IterationTag.EVAL_BODY_AGAIN`. Iteration over the tag body is aborted when the `doAfterBody` method returns `Tag.SKIP_BODY`; the JSP engine then proceeds to invoke the `doEndTag` method.

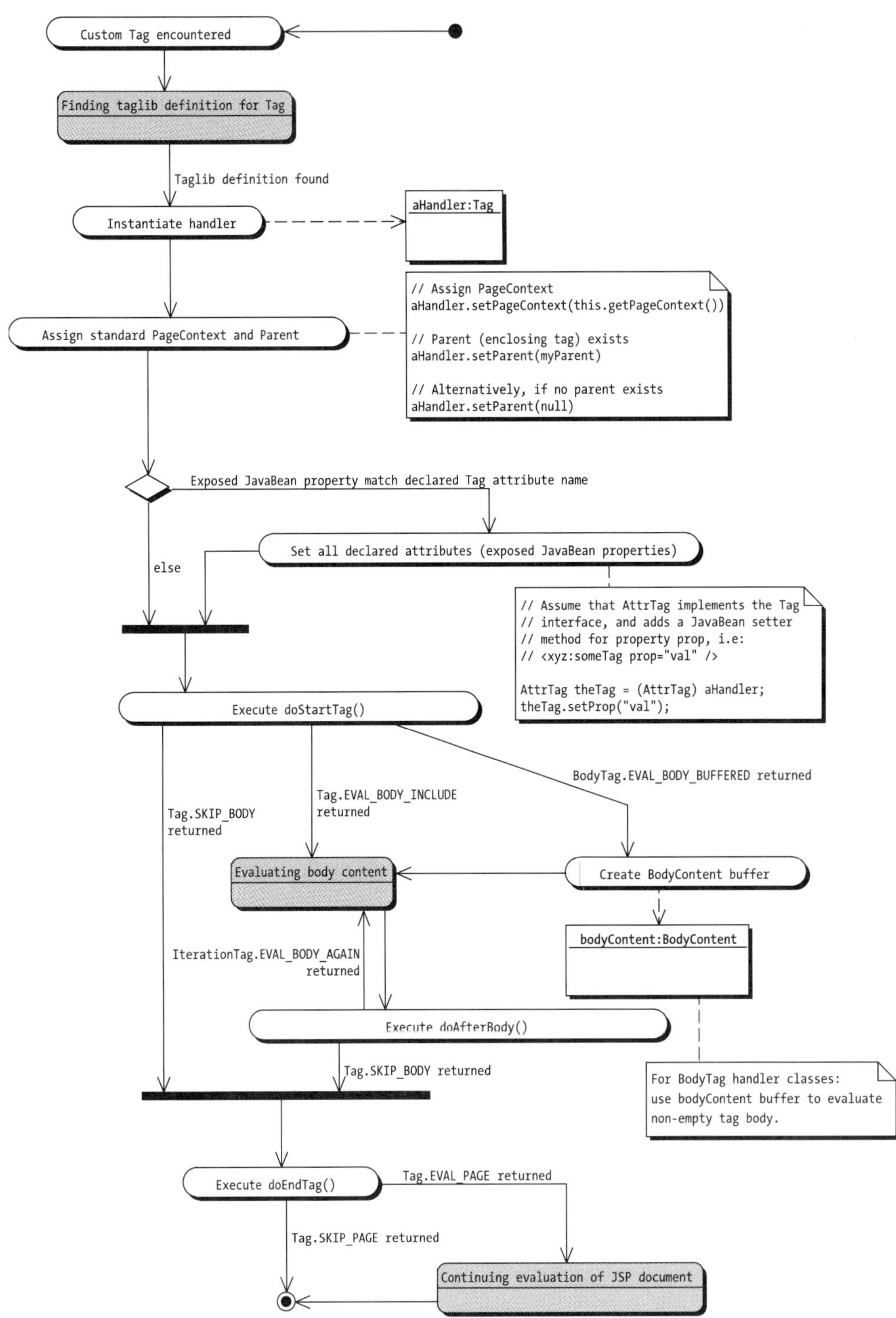

Figure 5-13. UML activity flow and state chart diagram for the life-cycle method of a tag handler class

The most common value returned by `doEndTag` is `Tag.EVAL_PAGE`, which instructs the JSP engine to keep parsing and evaluating the rest of the JSP document, found after the tag just evaluated. If, on the other hand, `Tag.SKIP_PAGE` is returned, the execution of the JSP document is aborted.

Before plunging into the details and principles of creating customized tag libraries, start with a small, warm-up example.

The firstTag.jsp Example

The objective of the `firstTag.jsp` example shown in Figure 5-14 is to create an empty custom JSP tag without any attributes that prints, "This is the First Tag." to the standard `JspWriter`.

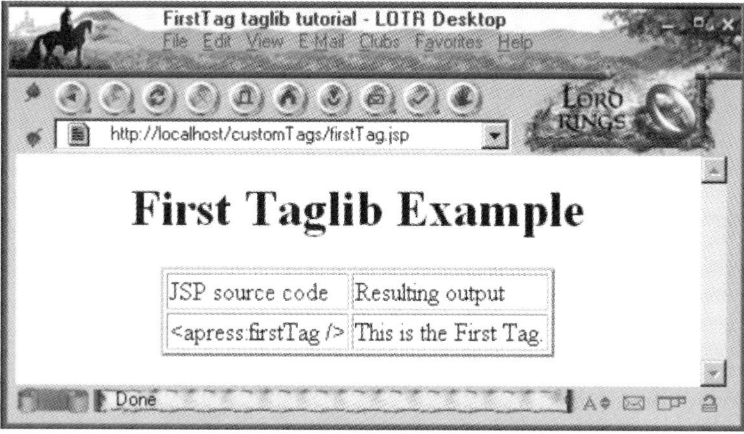

Figure 5-14. The output result of the `firstTag.jsp` *document*

Study the four documents involved in the process:

- `firstTag.jsp` contains the view and the JSP taglib directive.
- `WEB-INF/web.xml` contains the mapping between the URI provided in the `firstTag.jsp` document and the taglib definition file.
- `WEB-INF/taglibs/APressTags` contains the tag library definitions.
- `WEB-INF/classes/se/jguru/tags/FirstTag.class` contains the compiled bytecode for the tag handler class.

The JSP document is the origin of all tag library activity, and its relevant parts are shown in Listing 5-1. Note that the taglib directive pinpoints a JAR file, and identifies the tags defined within using the prefix "apress".

Listing 5-1. firstTag.jsp

```
<%--
        Include all tags defined in the Tag Library identified by the
        URI APressServletBookTags. To distinguish them from
        tags defined in other places, we identify them with the name "apress".
--%>
<%@ taglib uri="APressServletBookTags" prefix="apress" %>

<HTML>

...

<tr>
        <td>
<%--
        Output the HTML equivalent of the tag to invoke.
        This is done only for viewing purposes; to identify
        on the client view what is being invoked within
        the JSP document.
--%>
        &lt;apress:FirstTag/&gt;
        </td>

        <td>
<%--
        Invoke the handler class for the tag FirstTag, defined
        In the taglib having the prefix apress.
--%>
        <apress:firstTag />
        </td>

...
```

The JSP document uses the <apress:firstTag /> tag and provides a URI for the prefix apress. The next document in the definition chain that leads to the Tag implementation is the web.xml descriptor document, as shown in Figure 5-3 previously.

Including a TLD Archive

If your custom tag libraries are distributed in a JAR file, you are recommended to name the TLD file `taglib.tld` and place it in the directory `META-INF` within the JAR. When packaging your custom tag handler classes in a JAR file, you may skip providing a mapping in the `web.xml` configuration file.

The JSP file would pinpoint the tag library definition file in the following way:

```
<%--
        Include all tags defined within the META-INF/taglib.tld file of
        The JAR file /taglibs/APressTags.jar. To distinguish them from
        tags defined in other places, we identify them with the name "apt".
--%>
<%@ taglib uri="/taglibs/APressTags.jar" prefix="apt" %>
...
<%--
        Invoke the handler class for the tag firstTag, defined
        In the taglib having the prefix dummy.
--%>
        <apt:FirstTag />
...
```

All other properties of the JSP custom tags (such as attributes and validators) apply identically to tags deployed outside of a JAR file.

The web.xml Configuration File

When the JSP file has defined a taglib URI that cannot be found as a file in the Web application's file system, the `web.xml` configuration file is consulted. The `web.xml` file may contain several tag library mappings, similar to Listing 5-2, that map a taglib URI defined in the JSP page to a TLD file.

Listing 5-2. The `web.xml` deployment descriptor

```
<?xml version="1.0" encoding="ISO-8859-1"?>
<!DOCTYPE web-app
    PUBLIC "-//Sun Microsystems, Inc.//DTD Web Application 2.3//EN"
    "http://java.sun.com/j2ee/dtds/web-app_2_3.dtd">
```

```
<web-app>
    <taglib>
        <taglib-uri>
        APressServletBookTags
        </taglib-uri>
        <taglib-location>
           /WEB-INF/taglibs/ApressTagLibs.tld
        </taglib-location>
    </taglib>
</web-app>
```

The URI "APressServletBookTags" in the JSP taglib directive is mapped to the taglib definition file `/WEB-INF/taglibs/ApressTagLibs.tld`. That tag library definition file is consulted to find the tag handler classes used for each found custom JSP tag.

> **NOTE** *The Tomcat reference implementation engine uses the default name* `taglib.tld` *to identify a taglib definition file, unless another name is specified.*

The Tag Library Definition File

The TLD file contains all mappings between custom JSP tags and tag handler classes. The TLD may either be referenced directly from the URI attribute of the `<%@ taglib %>` directive, or by using a logical name (`<taglib-uri>`) defined in the `web.xml` configuration file.

In this example, the TLD (`/WEB-INF/taglibs/ApressTagLibs.tld`) is defined in the `web.xml` file. See Listing 5-3.

Listing 5-3. The taglib definition file, `ApressTagLibs.tld`

```
<?xml version="1.0" encoding="ISO-8859-1"?>
<!DOCTYPE taglib PUBLIC
   "-//Sun Microsystems, Inc.//DTD JSP Tag Library 1.2//EN"
   "http://java.sun.com/dtd/web-jsptaglibrary_1_2.dtd">

<taglib>
     <tlib-version>1.2</tlib-version>
     <jsp-version>1.2</jsp-version>
```

```
    <short-name>
        J2EE frontend technologies; servlets, JSPs and
        EJBs tutorial tag library
    </short-name>
    <uri>http://localhost/taglib/tagz.jar</uri>
    <description>Sample Tutorial Tag Library</description>
    <tag>
            <name>FirstTag</name>
            <tag-class>se.jguru.tags.FirstTag</tag-class>
            <body-content>empty</body-content>
            <description>The first tutorial tag</description>
    </tag>
</taglib>
```

Note that the DOCTYPE element provides the version specification for this taglib (JSP tag library 1.2) and that the versions required by the tag handlers of this TLD are included in the `<tlib-version>` and `<jsp-version>` tags.

The taglib.tld file contains three sections:

- Standard XML header, defining this document to adhere to the XML JSP Tag Library 1.2 DTD. If you are interested in taking a closer peek at this DTD, it can be downloaded from the URI provided in the header.

- Tag library container tag (`<taglib>`), which contains:

  - Metadata section providing information about the tag library itself, rather than any of its defined tags.

  - A `<tag>` definition linking this custom tag called FirstTag (which is empty and has no body content) to the tag handler class se.jguru.tags.FirstTag. Thus, whenever this tag library is used and a FirstTag tag is encountered by the JSP engine, an instance of se.jguru.tags.FirstTag is created and life-cycle methods are invoked in that instance to produce any desired output.

TIP *If you are deploying your tag handler classes into a JAR file, be sure to use the name* taglib.tld *for the TLD file, as some commercial implementations of Web containers will start searching for the TLD assuming its Web application path to be* META-INF/taglib.tld. *For convenience, the JAR file should be placed in* WEB-INF/lib. *That way, all tag handler classes will always be included in the Web application classpath.*

Tag library definition files will be discussed in greater detail in "Tag Library Descriptors," later in this chapter.

The TLD File for JSP version 1.1

Should you be using a JSP engine that does not support version 1.2, you must create a TLD file complying with JSP version 1.1. Refer to "Tag Libraries in JSP 1.1," later in this chapter, for information on TLD under JSP version 1.1.

Having defined a mapping between the tag handler class and the tag name, you must now examine the Tag handler class for the `FirstTag` custom JSP tag.

The Tag Handler Class

The last part of the four-file system is the handler class, `se.jguru.tags.FirstTag`, which is a JavaBean with the structure you see in Figure 5-15.

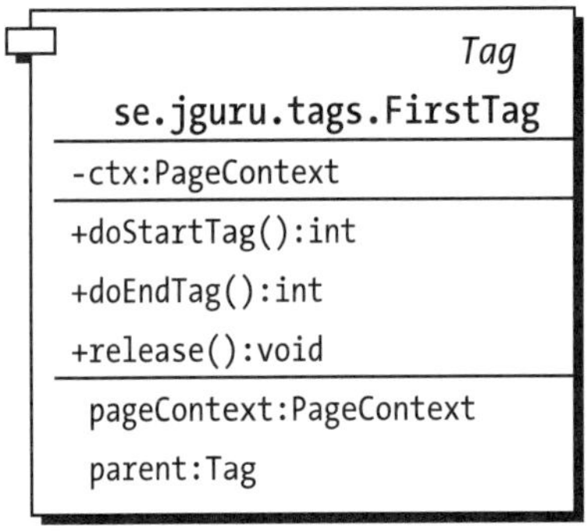

Tag
se.jguru.tags.FirstTag
-ctx:PageContext
+doStartTag():int
+doEndTag():int
+release():void
pageContext:PageContext
parent:Tag

Figure 5-15. The UML diagram of the tag handler class `FirstTag`

The `FirstTag` class is a tag handler because it implements the interface `javax.servlet.jsp.tagext.Tag`, which contains the life-cycle methods of a tag handler class. These methods are *automagically* called in a certain order by the JSP engine whenever a custom tag is encountered, as shown in Figure 5-15.

Taking a quick peek at a pseudo-code compilation of the relevant parts of the generated JSP servlet reveals the order in which these methods are called (see Listing 5-4). Note that the variable name has been abbreviated (to `theTag`) and the absolute class name `se.jguru.tags.FirstTag` has been abbreviated to `FirstTag`, for purposes of readability. In Listing 5-4 the `Tag` life-cycle methods have been highlighted in bold.

Listing 5-4. The generated servlet code for a JSP document containing the `<apress:firstTag />` *tag*

```
// begin
/* ----  dummy:firstTag ---- */
    FirstTag theTag = new FirstTag();
    theTag.setPageContext(pageContext);
    theTag.setParent(null);

    try
    {
        int eval = theTag.doStartTag();
        if (eval == BodyTag.EVAL_BODY_BUFFERED)
            throw new JspTagException("Since tag handler class "
            + "se.jguru.tags.FirstTag does not implement BodyTag, it can't
            + "return BodyTag.EVAL_BODY_TAG");
        if (eval != Tag.SKIP_BODY)
        {
            do {
                    // end
                    // begin
            } while (false);
        }
        if (theTag.doEndTag() == Tag.SKIP_PAGE)
            return;
    }
    finally
    {
        theTag.release();
    }
// end
```

The JSP 1.1 Code Equivalent

If you are using a JSP 1.1-compliant engine, the code generated by the JSP engine to call the life-cycle methods of the `FirstTag` handler class becomes slightly different than the 1.2 equivalent. Refer to "Tag Libraries in JSP 1.1," later in this chapter, for a discussion of JSP 1.1-compliant tag library definition files.

You may simplify the pseudo-code further to reveal the principal life cycle of a tag handler class for an empty tag without attributes. See Listing 5-5.

Listing 5-5. Servlet code for invoking a JSP 1.1-style taglib tag

```
// ### 1)          Create the tag instance, and set its internal
//                     handler objects, which allow communication with
//                     the pageContext and any enclosing(parent) tags,
//                     should this tag be placed within another.
FirstTag theTag = new FirstTag();
theTag.setPageContext(pageContext);
theTag.setParent(null);

// ### 2)          Call the doStartTag() method in the handler class.
//                     (For non-empty tags, this method is called prior
//                     to evaluating any body content).
theTag.doStartTag();

// ### 3)          Call the doEndTag() method in the handler class.
//                   (For non-empty tags, this method is called after
//                    evaluating the body content).
theTag.doEndTag();

// ### 4)          Call the release() method to free up any used resources
/                      after the tag has been completely processed.
theTag.release();
```

Thus, you can see that the JSP engine calls most of the available methods of the tag handler class. Most of those methods are defined in the interface `javax.servlet.jsp.tagext.Tag`, which must be implemented by all tag handler classes. A better walkthrough of the `java.servlet.jsp.tagext` package and its interfaces and classes will be done in "Touring the javax.servlet.jsp.tagext Package," later in this chapter. Listing 5-6 provides the complete code of the tag handler.

Listing 5-6. The `FirstTag` *implementation class. Life-cycle methods are highlighted in bold.*

```
/*
 * Copyright (c) 2000 jGuru Europe AB
 * All rights reserved.
 */

package se.jguru.tags;
```

```
import javax.servlet.jsp.*;
import javax.servlet.jsp.tagext.*;

/**
 * Tag handler class which simply replaces the
 * occurrence of the tag with the text "This is
 * the First Tag.".
 *
 * This tag is empty (i.e. it does not have a
 * body or body content).
 */
public class FirstTag implements Tag
{
    // Internal state
    private PageContext ctx;
    private Tag parent;

    /**
     * Method called by the JSP engine before the tag body is
     * evaluated. Since this is a standalone tag, simply return
     * Tag.SKIP_BODY to indicate that we will not evaluate any
     * body content.
     */
    public int doStartTag() throws JspException
    {
        // Do not do anything when the tag starts.
        return SKIP_BODY;
    }

    /**
     * Method called by the JSP engine after any body evaluation
     * has taken place.
     */
    public int doEndTag() throws JspException
    {
        try
        {
            // Get the JspWriter connected to the
            // client browser output. This is received from
            // the pageContext, ctx.
            JspWriter outWriter = ctx.getOut();
```

```
            // Write something to the JspWriter.
            outWriter.write("This is the First Tag.");
        }
        catch(Exception ex)
        {
            throw new JspException("[doEndTag]: " + ex);
        }

        // Tell the JSP engine to continue evaluating the
        // rest of the JSP page, rather than aborting all
        // evaluation here.
        return EVAL_PAGE;
    }

    /**
     * Since this handler has allocated no resources, we don't need
     * to release any when the JSP engine is done with the tag.
     */
    public void release() {}

    /**
     * Method called by the JSP engine before any evaluation
     * has taken place. The purpose of it is to provide a handle
     * to the PageContext of the running page to the tag.
     */
    public void setPageContext(PageContext context)
    {
        this.ctx = context;
    }

    /**
     * Method called by the JSP engine before any evaluation
     * has taken place. The purpose of it is to provide a handle
     * to the parent (enclosing) tag handler of this tag handler.
     */
    public void setParent(final Tag parent)
    {
        this.parent = parent;
    }
```

```
    /**
     * Method returning the parent Tag handler class of this one.
     */
    public Tag getParent()
    {
        return this.parent;
    }
}
```

The code of the JSP-compiled servlet in Listing 5-6, shows the two relevant evaluation methods of this tag handler: `doStartTag` and `doEndTag`. The former is called before and the latter after any body content of the tag is evaluated—but because the `firstTag` has no body content, you need not do anything special to the `out JspWriter` here. To tell the JSP engine to skip any evaluation of body content, you return `Tag.SKIP_BODY` from the method.

The latter of the two methods, `doEndTag`, is called after any evaluation of body content. In this case, you obtain a reference to the `out JspWriter` connected to the `HttpResponse` of the generated servlet. After this, you are able to write any content to the client from within the handler class—in our case the static string "This is the First Tag." is printed to the output stream.

Tag Library Descriptors

The TLD file is a document that maps tag handler classes to tag names and provides metadata about the tag library itself and all tags defined within it. The TLD is an XML document—so the document structure is defined within the DTD provided in the XML header ("`http://java.sun.com/dtd/web-jsptaglibrary_1_2.dtd`"). An XML visualization of the TLD DTD may give greater understanding.

The TLD DTD 1.2 specification, illustrated in Figure 5-16, requires the following information to be present in the TLD file:

- XML version definition (`<?xml version="1.0" encoding="ISO-8859-1" ?>`).
- DTD telling the JSP engine what tag library definition structure is used in this TLD. For example, the 1.2 specification has the following structure: `<!DOCTYPE taglib PUBLIC "-//Sun Microsystems, Inc.//DTD JSP Tag Library 1.1//EN" "http://java.sun.com/j2ee/dtds/web-jsptaglibrary_1_1.dtd">`.
- `<taglib>` container tag, declaring a tag library definition. This is a container that encloses all real specifications in the TLD file.

- Tag library metadata, containing version information and other data common to the entire tag library. Referring to the TLD file listing below, the taglib metadata elements provided are `<tlib-version>`, `<jsp-version>`, `<short-name>`, and `<description>`.

- Tag definitions for all custom tags defined within this tag library. The TLD file in Listing 5-7 defines one empty custom JSP tag, `FirstTag`. The `Tag` definition is a container XML element; its children defines all aspects of the custom JSP tag, according to the DTD illustrated in Figure 5-16.

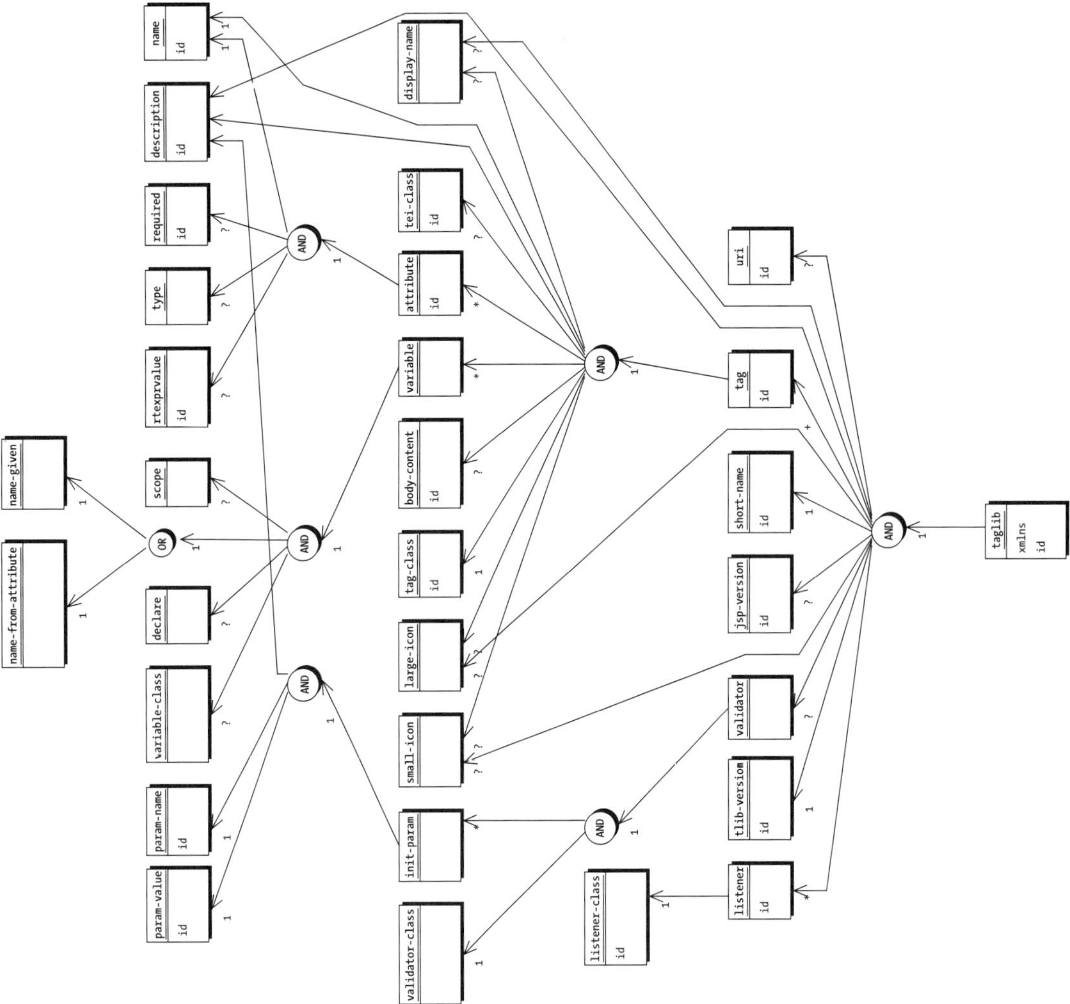

Figure 5-16. The TLD DTD 1.2 specification for the tag library definition file

Listing 5-7 shows what a typical `.tld` *file looks like.*

Listing 5-7 shows what a typical `.tld` file looks like.

Listing 5-7. A typical `.tld` file

```
<?xml version="1.0" encoding="ISO-8859-1"?>
<!DOCTYPE taglib PUBLIC
   "-//Sun Microsystems, Inc.//DTD JSP Tag Library 1.2//EN"
   "http://java.sun.com/dtd/web-jsptaglibrary_1_2.dtd">

<taglib>
            <tlib-version>1.2</tlib-version>
            <jsp-version>1.2</jsp-version>
            <short-name>APress tutorial tags</short-name>
            <description>Sample Tutorial Tag Library</description>

            <tag>
               <name>FirstTag</name>
               <tag-class>se.jguru.tags.FirstTag</tag-class>
               <body-content>empty</body-content>
               <description>The first tutorial tag</description>
            </tag>
</taglib>
```

Figure 5-16 shows all elements permitted within a Tag Library Descriptor XML container. All XML documents use data found within their DTD to define permitted XML elements. Understanding the tag library XML DTD is the best way to realize the possibilities of the XML DTD, so take a peek at a fully populated TLD document and correlate its contents with the Taglib DTD, starting with TLD metadata.

Tag Library Metadata

All tag libraries contain a set of metadata information tags, some of which are required. Listing 5-8 is an excerpt from a taglib definition containing fully populated metadata entries.

Listing 5-8. Excerpt from a taglib definition

```
<!--
     Mandatory Metadata Container Tags
     --------------------------------

     tlib-versionTag Library version of this tag library, given
          in Dewey decimal notation (i.e: 1.25-1.6) A regular
          expression of the Dewey decimal otation is [0-9]*{ "."[0-9] }0..3,
          which denotes a maximum of 3 dots.
          Example: 1.2
     jsp-versionMinimum JSP version required for this tag
          library to function, given in Dewey decimal noration.
          Example: 1.2
     short-nameFreetext description of this tag library, which
          may be used by builder tools to generate a default taglib prefix.
          According to the DTD, one should not use white space, and not
          start with digits or underscore.

     Optional Metadata Container Tags
     --------------------------------

     uri          Unique identifier of this tag library
     display-name Human-readable name intended for use by
                  taglib construction tools
     description  Human-readable string describing the "use" of this taglib
     small-icon   Filename of an icon image for use by taglib construction tools
     large-icon   Filename of an icon image for use by taglib construction tools
     validator    Classname of a validator class which performs runtime
                  validation on the <%@ taglib ...%> directives connected
                  to this tag library definition.
     listener     Classname of an event listener to this Tag.
-->
     <tlib-version>1.2</tlib-version>
     <jsp-version>1.2</jsp-version>
     <short-name>APress custom IterationTag</short-name>
     <uri>taglib/apressTags.tld</uri>
     <description>Sample Tutorial Tag Library</description>
     <!-- Mandatory Custom Tag definitions go here -->

</taglib>
```

An XML element definition corresponds to a container tag in Listing 5-8. Thus, reading from the taglib DTD, you find the following <taglib> element definition:

```
<!ELEMENT taglib (tlib-version, jsp-version, short-name, uri?, display-name?,
small-icon?, large-icon?, description?, validator?, listener*, tag+) >
```

Interpreting XML DTD Entries

The <taglib> element may contain a well-defined series of child elements, the names of which are given within the parentheses. Let's originate from the taglib XML element definition:

```
<!ELEMENT taglib (tlib-version, jsp-version, short-name, uri?,
   display-name?, small-icon?, large-icon?, description?,
   validator?, listener*, tag+) >
```

The XML DTD defines the four meanings listed in Table 5-2 to the child elements of an XML container, depending on the character appended to the child element name.

Table 5-2. Character Definitions

CHARACTER APPENDED	CARDINALITY	STATUS	DESCRIPTION
<none>	1	Mandatory	A mandatory element must occur exactly once within its parent. The <tlib-version> element is mandatory within its <taglib> parent.
?	0..1	Optional	An optional element may occur exactly once within its parent. The <display-name> element is mandatory within its <taglib> parent.

Table 5-2. Character Definitions (Continued)

CHARACTER APPENDED	CARDINALITY	STATUS	DESCRIPTION
*	0..n	Optional, list	An optional list element may occur several times within its parent. The <listener> element is an optional list within its <taglib> parent.
+	1..n	Mandatory, list	A mandatory list element must occur at least once within its parent. The <tag> element is a mandatory list within its <taglib> parent.

Figure 5-16 shows the element specification of the TLD DTD. The element cardinalities are implied in Figure 5-16 by printing the character from the Character Appended column in the preceding table. Can you find the two mandatory child elements of the `<tag>` element?

Before taking a look at the `<tag>` element definitions in detail, study the optional `<validator>` element a little closer. The functionality provided by a tag library validator instance is powerful; it may be beneficial—especially in larger projects.

The <validator> Element

Each tag library may contain one (optional) tag library validator object. The purpose of the validator is to verify that the `<@% taglib … %>` directive is well-formed and potentially perform a custom validation on the JSP document. The `<validator>` element is new to JSP version 1.2, with no corresponding TLD 1.1 equivalent.

The tag library validator instance must extend the class `javax.servlet.jsp.tagext.TagLibraryValidator`, which is shown in Figure 5-17. The developer must override at least one method—`validate`. Frequently, one makes use of initialization parameters sent to the validator from the TLD file. If so, the `setInitParameters` and `getInitParameters` methods are also of interest to the development. The JSP container will invoke the `setInitParameters` method before calling validate, ensuring that all `init` parameters will be available during validation.

The TLD DTD specifies that the `<validator>` element has the following structure:

```
<!ELEMENT validator (validator-class, init-param*, description?) >
```

```
                                              java.lang.Object
        javax.servlet.jsp.tagext.TagLibraryValidator
--------------------------------------------------------------------
+TagLibraryValidator()
+release():void
+validate(:String,:String,:javax.servlet.jsp.tagext.PageData):String
--------------------------------------------------------------------
 initParameters:java.util.Map
```

Figure 5-17. The `TagLibraryValidator` *class encapsulates a minimalistic but powerful functionality. The only two methods requiring the attention of a developer are* `release` *and* `validate`*. The JavaBean setter and getter for the* `initParameters` *JavaBean property are merely convenience methods, which do not require overriding on the part of the developer.*

Listing 5-9 is a sample validator specification from a TLD file.

Listing 5-9. A validator definition

```
<taglib>
      ...
<!--
      Mandatory Validator Container Tags
      ---------------------------------
      validator-class     The class which should be instantiated to
            obtain the tag library validator.

      Optional Validator Container Tags
      ---------------------------------
      init-param     An initialization parameter specification
            to the Validator instance. All parameters defined in
            the TLD file will be parsed and inserted into a Map which
            may be retrieved with the getInitParameters(); method.
      -->
      <validator>
            <validator-class>
               se.jguru.tags.BasicTagLibValidator
            </validator-class>
            <init-param>
                  <param-name>logFileName</param-name>
                  <param-value>validatorLog.txt</param-value>
            </init-param>
```

```
        <init-param>
            <param-name>dateFormat</param-name>
            <param-value>-hh:mm:ss.SSSS-</param-value>
        </init-param>
    </validator>
    ...
</taglib>
```

The simplest way to understand the function and use of a TagLibraryValidator subclass is to show a simple example of its use. Therefore, take a look at the three entries that join forces to create a validator service:

- JSP file contains the <@% taglib ... %> directive. Let's assume that the taglib directive is <%@ taglib uri="apressTags" prefix="apt" %>.
- TLD file contains the <validator> specification. Let's use the previous TLD snippet as a point of origin in this small example.
- javax.servlet.jsp.tagext.TagLibraryValidator subclass contains the validation definition. According to the previous TLD file, you will use a validator class called se.jguru.tags.BasicTagLibValidator (see Figure 5-18).

```
TagLibraryValidator
se.jguru.tags.BasicTagLibValidator
-------------------------------------------------------
-logOut:PrintWriter
+DEFAULT_LOGFILE_NAME:String="BasicTLV_logfile.txt"
-sdf:SimpleDateFormat
-------------------------------------------------------
+BasicTagLibValidator()
+release():void
-openLogFile():void
-log(msg:String):void
+validate(prefix:String,uri:String,page:PageData):String
-------------------------------------------------------
 initParameters:Map
```

Figure 5-18. The taglib validator class of this small example. Besides overriding the validate *and* release *methods, the* BasicTagLibValidator *may log data to a log file—and the* logOut Writer *is connected to the log file.*

Listing 5-10 provides the resulting output to the log file. Note that the output in the topmost section, where the initialization parameters names and values are printed, correspond perfectly to the values provided in the TLD file in Listing 5-9. Note also, that the *prefix* and *uri* printouts are read from the `<@% taglib ... %>` directive in the JSP document. The `PageData` output is simply the XML version of the JSP document, which is sent to the validator as an argument to the `validate` method.

Listing 5-10. Log file excerpt

```
[-02:04:38.0739-]: Log file opened. Validator in normal operational mode.

[-02:04:38.0739-]:  -- Printing all init parameters
[-02:04:38.0759-]:  [dateFormat]: -hh:mm:ss.SSSS-
[-02:04:38.0759-]:  [logFileName]: validatorLog.txt
[-02:04:38.0759-]:  -- All init parameters printed.

[-02:04:38.0819-]:  prefix: apt
[-02:04:38.0819-]:  uri: apressTags

[-02:04:38.0819-]:  --> Begin PageData
[-02:04:38.0819-]: (1): <jsp:root
[-02:04:38.0819-]: (2):   xmlns:jsp="http://java.sun.com/JSP/Page"
[-02:04:38.0819-]: (3):   version="1.2"
[-02:04:38.0819-]: (4):   xmlns:apt="apressTags"
[-02:04:38.0819-]: (5): >
[-02:04:38.0829-]: (6): <jsp:text><![CDATA[
[-02:04:38.0829-]: (7):
[-02:04:38.0829-]: (8): <html>
[-02:04:38.0829-]: (9):         <head>
[-02:04:38.0829-]: (10):        <title>AnotherBody Tag Sample</title>
[-02:04:38.0829-]: (11):        </head>
[-02:04:38.0829-]: (12):
[-02:04:38.0829-]: (13):        <body>
[-02:04:38.0829-]: (14):        <center>
[-02:04:38.0829-]: (15):
[-02:04:38.0829-]: (16):        <h1>Body Tag Example</h1>
[-02:04:38.0829-]: (17):
[-02:04:38.0829-]: (18):        <table border=2>
[-02:04:38.0829-]: (19):        <tr>
[-02:04:38.0829-]: (20):                <td>JSP source code</td>
[-02:04:38.0829-]: (21):                <td>Resulting output</td>
[-02:04:38.0839-]: (22):        </tr>
[-02:04:38.0839-]: (23):
[-02:04:38.0859-]: (24):        <tr>
[-02:04:38.0859-]: (25):                <td>&lt;apt:SimpleBodyTag>This is a
                                body text.&lt;/apt:SimpleBodyTag></td>
```

```
[-02:04:38.0859-]: (26):                  <td>]]>
[-02:04:38.0879-]: (27): </jsp:text>
[-02:04:38.0879-]: (28): <apt:SimpleBodyTag><jsp:text><![CDATA[
[-02:04:38.0879-]: (29): This is a body text.]]>
[-02:04:38.0899-]: (30): </jsp:text>
[-02:04:38.0899-]: (31): </apt:SimpleBodyTag>
[-02:04:38.0899-]: (32): <jsp:text><![CDATA[
[-02:04:38.0919-]: (33): </td>
[-02:04:38.0919-]: (34):         </tr>
[-02:04:38.0919-]: (35):
[-02:04:38.0919-]: (36):         </table>
[-02:04:38.0919-]: (37):
[-02:04:38.0919-]: (38):         </center>
[-02:04:38.0919-]: (39):         </body>
[-02:04:38.0919-]: (40): </html>]]>
[-02:04:38.0919-]: (41): </jsp:text>
[-02:04:38.0929-]: (42): </jsp:root>
[-02:04:38.0929-]:  <-- End PageData
```

The full source code of the `BasicTagLibValidator` shows that the `validate` method has access to the initialization parameters, as well as a `PageData` object that encapsulates the XML version of the JSP document. The `PageData` class has one single method of interest, `getInputStream`, which returns an `InputStream` connected to the XML stream of the document. The developer may therefore validate documents originating from the data found in the JSP file, the taglib directive, or the initialization parameters.

In Listing 5-11, the `TagLibraryValidator`-specific method calls appear in bold text.

Listing 5-11. The `BasicTagLibValidator` *class*

```
/*
 * Copyright (c) 2000,2001 jGuru Europe.
 * All rights reserved.
 */

package se.jguru.tags;

import javax.servlet.jsp.tagext.*;
import javax.servlet.jsp.*;
import java.util.*;
import java.io.*;
import java.text.SimpleDateFormat;
```

```
public class BasicTagLibValidator extends TagLibraryValidator
{
    // Writer to a log file where the log messages will go.
    private PrintWriter logOut;

    // Define the default logfile name
    public static final String DEFAULT_LOGFILE_NAME = "BasicTLV_logfile.txt";

    // The simple date format of the log messages
    private SimpleDateFormat sdf;

    public BasicTagLibValidator()
    {
        // Call the constructor of our superclass
        super();
    }

    /**
     * Free up all held resources; i.e. close the log file.
     */
    public void release()
    {
        // Close the logFile
        try
        {
            this.logOut.close();
        }
        catch (Exception ex)
        {
            // Whoops.
            System.err.println("[BasicTagLibValidator::release]: "
            + "Could not close the log file Writer: " + ex);
        }

        // Call the release of our superclass
        // to continue the release of the state
        // in this validator.
        super.release();
    }
```

```
public void setInitParameters(Map params)
{
    // Proceed with the normal setInitParameters
    super.setInitParameters(params);

    // Setup the log file...
    this.openLogFile();
}

private void openLogFile()
{
    // Don't redo the openLogFile tasks
    // if the log file is already open.
    if (this.logOut != null)
    {
        // Log the attempt.
        this.log("Log file already opened.");

        // Bail out.
        return;
    }

    // Get the configuration parameters
    Map params = this.getInitParameters();

    // Get the log file name
    String logFileName = "" + params.get("logFileName");
    if (logFileName == null || logFileName.equals(""))
        logFileName = DEFAULT_LOGFILE_NAME;

    // LogFile exists?
    File logfile = new File(logFileName);
    if (logfile.exists())
        logfile.renameTo(
            new File(logfile.getName() + ".old"));

    // Open the logfile Writer
    try
    {
        this.logOut = new PrintWriter(
            new FileWriter(logfile));
    }
```

```
    catch (IOException ex)
    {
        // Whoops...
        System.out.println("Could not open the logging Writer: " + ex);
    }

    // Get the format string for the simple date format
    String sdfString = "" + params.get("dateFormat");
    if (sdfString == null || sdfString.equals(""))
            sdfString = "hh:mm:ss.SSSS";

    // Create the internal log format
    this.sdf = new SimpleDateFormat(sdfString);

    // Done.
    this.log("Log file opened. Validator in normal operational mode.");
    this.log(" -- Printing all init parameters");
    for (Iterator it = params.keySet().iterator(); it.hasNext(); )
    {
        // Get the current key
        Object key = it.next();

        // Log the key/value pair
        this.log(" [" + key + "]: " + params.get(key));
    }

    // Done.
    this.log(" -- All init parameters printed.");
}

/**
 * Private logging method, which writes a log message
 * to the standard log stream of this validator, i.e.
 * logOut.
 */
private void log(String msg)
{
    // Check sanity
    if (this.logOut == null) this.openLogFile();
    if (msg == null || msg.equals("")) return;

    // Get the current timestamp
    Date now = new Date();
```

```
        // Potentially sane. Log.
        String completeMessage = "[" + this.sdf.format(now) + "]: " + msg;
        this.logOut.println(completeMessage);
        this.logOut.flush();
    }

    /**
     * Validate a JSP page. This will get invoked once per directive in the
     * JSP page. This method will return a null String if the page passed
     * through is valid; otherwise an error message.
     */
    public String validate(String prefix, String uri, PageData page)
    {
        // Log
        this.log(" prefix: " + prefix);
        this.log(" uri: " + uri);

        // Get the content of the JSP document from the PageData argument
        LineNumberReader lnr = new LineNumberReader(
            new InputStreamReader(page.getInputStream()));
        String aReadLine = "";

        // Output the content of the PageData
        this.log(" --> Begin PageData");
        try
        {
            while ((aReadLine = lnr.readLine()) != null)
            {
                // Output the current line
                this.log("(" + lnr.getLineNumber() + "): " + aReadLine);
            }
        }
        catch (IOException ex)
        {
            this.log("Error reading PageData: " + ex);
        }
        this.log(" <-- End PageData");

        // If something displeases us, return a String with an
        // error message. If all went well, return null.
        return null;
        // Or: return "This is an error message from the validator.";
    }
}
```

A TagLibraryValidator instance is global for all directives referring to a particular TLD file. Its fully qualified class is defined as an XML element in the TLD file, as seen in Listing 5-11.

Having taken a look at the metadata structure of tag libraries, now turn your attention to the tag definitions themselves.

Tag Definitions

Each <tag> element defined in the TLD file maps a handler class to a tag name. Each <tag> element is a container, grouping tag metadata and possibly attribute definitions (contained in <attribute> elements) for all attributes known (in other words, automatically set by the tag handler instance). All <tag> definition elements must be contained within their <taglib> parent. The <tag> elements in Listing 5-12 are therefore assumed to be contained in a <taglib> parent.

Listing 5-12 builds on Listing 5-8. Because you did not actually create any <tag> containers, the TLD file does not currently define any custom actions. However, the comment `<!-- Mandatory Custom Tag definitions go here -->` indicates that more information is to be inserted into the TLD file. Create a <tag> entry that defines a new tag called FirstTag. The comments within the code listing explain the effect of each entry.

Listing 5-12. The tag definition section of the TLD file

```
<!--
        All tag metadata and attribute definitions must be contained
        within the tag element, and each tag element must in turn
        be contained within the taglib parent element.
-->

<tag>

    <!--
        Mandatory metadata container tags
        --------------------------------

        name       := The (unique) name of the tag, found in the action
                      tag name of the JSP action. (i.e: For the JSP action
                      <x:someName />, the name attribute is someName ).

        tag-class  := Fully qualified class name of the Tag handlerclass
                      of this tag. The handler must implement interface
                      javax.servlet.jsp.tagext.Tag
```

```
    -->
                <name>FirstTag</name>
                <tag-class>se.jguru.tags.FirstTag</tag-class>

<!--
    Optional metadata container tags
    --------------------------------
    tei-class    The Tag Extra Information class is a fully
                 qualified class name to a class which contains
                 metadata describing the attributes of a
                 tag. The teiclass must implement
                 javax.servlet.jsp.tagext.TagExtraInfo

    body-content     Defines whether or not the tag should
                 be used in standalone or container mode.
                 3 different values are permitted:
                     a) JSP. This (default) value indicates
                        that the body of the tag contains normal
                        JSP data.
                     b) empty. This value Indicates that the
                        tag cannot have any body content (i.e.
                        the tag Is empty).
                     c) tagdependent. This value indicates that
                        the body of the tag contains statements
                        in some language other than JSP. An example
                        could be SQL statements for execution within
                        a DB.
    display-name  Human-readable name intended for use by tag
                  construction tools
    small-icon    Filename of a 16x16 icon image for use by tag
                  construction tools
    large-icon    Filename of a 32x32 icon image for use by tag
                  construction tools
    description   Human-readable string describing the "use" of this tag
    variable      Provides information about any scripting variables declared
                  by this tag. If variable definitions are present, the tag
                  must have a TagExtraInfo companion class, defined in the
                 <tei-class> element.
    attribute    Each tag element may contain 0 or more attribute
                 definitions, specifying all the attributes which should be
                 recognized by the tag in question. All attributes definitions
                 are XML containers, which fully defines the attribute as a
                 Java object. Tag attributes are covered in detail shortly.
    example      Human-readable string providing an example of
                 this tag used
```

```
-->

<tag>
      <name>FirstTag</name>
      <tag-class>se.jguru.tags.FirstTag</tag-class>
      <body-content>empty</body-content>
      <description>The first tutorial tag</description>

            <!-- Attribute definitions go here. -->
</tag>
```

The tag defined in Listing 5-12 is an empty tag; its definition elements are seen in the last part of the definition file. A graphical listing of the element nodes introduced in the <tag> element reveals the structure (see Figure 5-19).

This is the XML definition for the tag element:

```
<!ELEMENT tag (name, tag-class, tei-class?, body-content?, display-name?,
  small-icon?, large-icon?, description?, variable*, attribute*, example?) >
```

Note that the order of the elements within their parent container could be—but rarely is—irrelevant. Some well-known XML processors do not create a full-dependency tree like a regular compiler—the programmer must therefore still pay close attention to the element order, rather than simply focus on the content. Undoubtedly, this situation will improve in the future, but the current state of XML parsers is such that the development community is required to mind yet another formatting detail of the taglib configuration.

The element order within the <tag> element container is clear from the element definition. Although it may be trivial to deduct the required element order from a look at the element definition, it certainly is cumbersome to constantly keep an eye at the tag definition at all times while generating a TLD file. In fact, one of the better uses of integrated development environments is the sanity checking and automatic re-ordering of XML tags to comply with the DTD in question. If you find yourself getting frequent XML parse exceptions, I recommend finding a development environment that has tools for strict generation and parsing of XML files.

As shown in the preceding element tag definition (and in Figure 5-18), the only two indexed (list) subelements of <tag> are attribute and variable. The former defines an attribute known to the JSP custom tag, and the latter defines a variable declared for use by other tags in the JSP page. Take a look at each in turn.

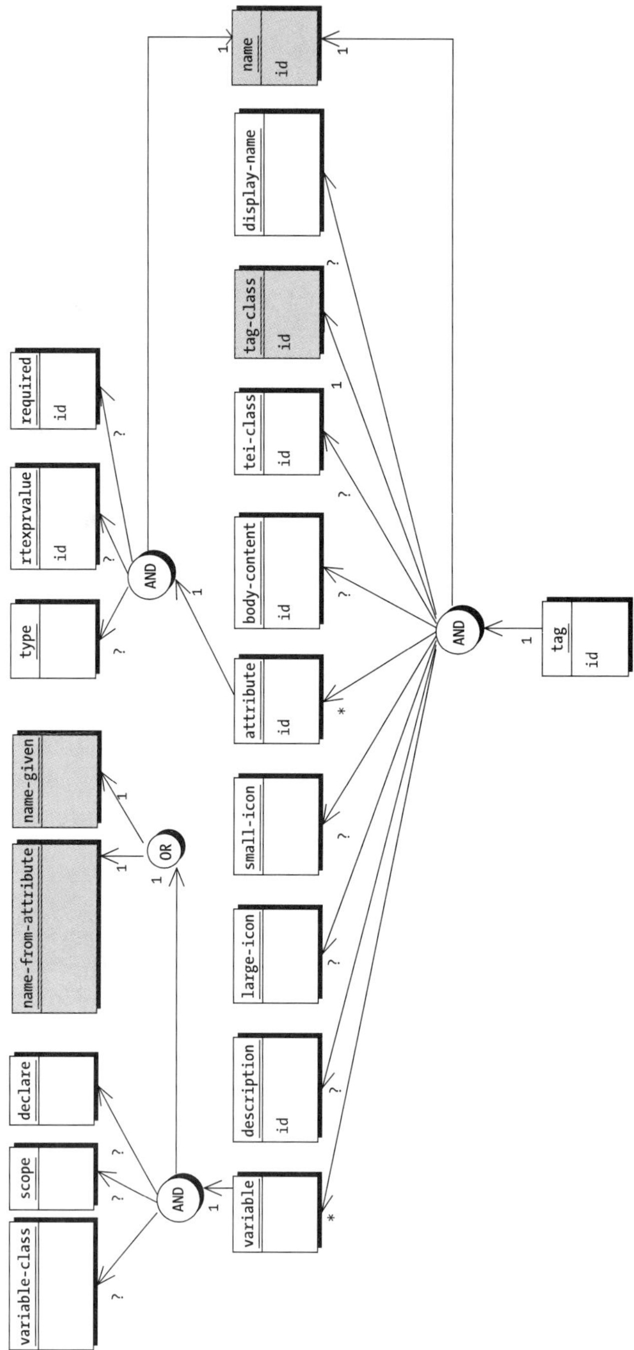

Figure 5-19. The XML structure of the tag element. All mandatory elements have been shaded. Although a detailed description for all elements in the image hasn't been given, you can see that all the elements are subelements to the `<tag>` *container.*

The <attribute> Element

The `<attribute>` element, where attributes of a JSP custom action are defined. The `<attribute>` element definition is small and simple to understand, as shown here and in Figure 5-20:

```
<!ELEMENT attribute (name, required? , rtexprvalue?, type?, description?) >
```

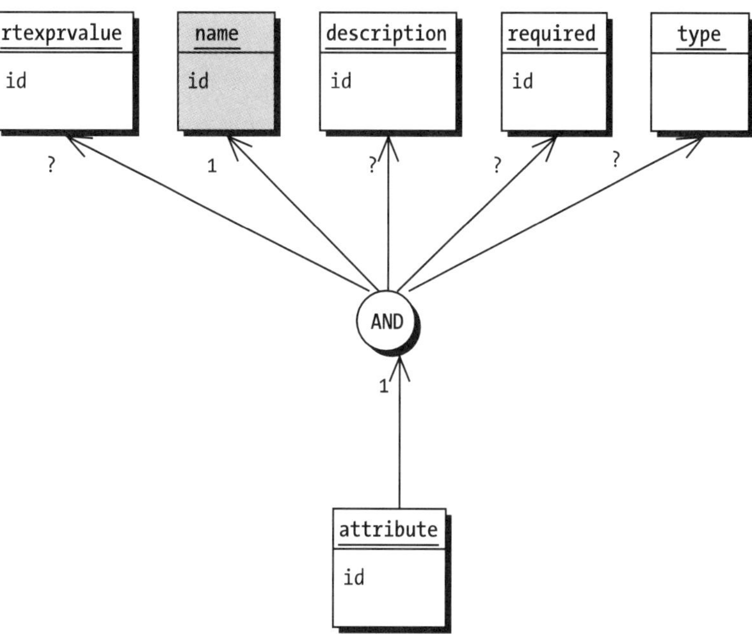

Figure 5-20. Visual representation of the `<attribute>` *element. Note that the only mandatory subelement of the attribute tag is* `<name>`*. If you choose to use types other than the default* (`java.lang.String`)*, the* `<type>` *element must be defined as well.*

Attribute definitions are straightforward; all properties in the attribute definition amounts to providing a Java code snippet that declares a variable. All elements of the attribute container are explained in the comments of the `taglib.tld` excerpt shown in Listing 5-13.

Listing 5-13. The tag attribute specification

```
<!--
      All tag attribute metadata and must be contained
      within the tag container.
-->
<attribute>

      <!--
            Mandatory metadata container tags
            --------------------------------

        name       The name of the attribute, found in the action tag name of the
                   JSP action.
                   (i.e: The JSP action <x:someName someKey="apa" />
                    has the attribute name someKey).

      -->

      <name>allClients</name>

      <!--
            Optional metadata container tags
            -------------------------------

        required       Indicates whether or not this attribute is mandatory.
                       If this value is false or no, a default value must be
                       defined in the code of the Tag handler class.
                       Default value: false.
                       Legal values are { yes | true | no | false }
        rtexprvalue    Indicates whether or not the value of this attribute
                       can be calculated during runtime as a JSP expression,
                       as opposed to a static (pre-defined) value set during
                       compilation.
                       Default value: false.
                       Legal values are { yes | true | no | false }
        type           The type of the attribute, expressed as a fully
                       qualifiedclass, such as java.util.Map.
                       Default value: java.lang.String.
        description    Human-readable string describing the purpose of
                       this attribute
```

```
        -->
        <required>yes</required>
        <rtexprvalue>yes</rtexprvalue>
        <type>java.util.List</type>
        <description>The List of all Clients</description>

</attribute>
```

As shown in Listing 5-13, the definition of an attribute to a custom `Tag` implementation class is straightforward.

Java Code for a JSP Custom Tag Attribute

It seems tragic that it is much simpler to understand the generated Java code deriving from a TLD attribute than the TLD attribute definition itself. In other words, the TLD definition does a great job of making a rather simple task a good deal more complex. For instance, the XML definition:

```
<attribute>
    <name>map</name>
    <required>false</required>
    <rtexprvalue>true</rtexprvalue>
    <type>java.util.Map</type>
</attribute>
```

and the JSP document:

```
<apt:ListTag map="<%= aMap %>"></apt:ListTag>
```

creates the Java call:

```
listTagInstance.setMap( aMap );
```

It would appear that the TLD definition is more complex (and involves more typing than) the JSP document and the corresponding generated Java code.

The remaining optional list element of the `<tag>` container is the `<variable>` container element that defines scripting variables declared by the custom JSP action.

The <variable> Element

JSP custom tags may define variables that may be accessed from the JSP document or other custom tags. This mechanism is useful to share information from a custom JSP parent tag to its contained children. That way, the child custom action needs not know about the existence of its parent at all, which permits complete separation of the two handler classes. The `<variable>` element definition is small, as shown in the following definition and in Figure 5-21:

```
<!ELEMENT variable ( (name-given | name-from-attribute), variable-class?,
  declare?, scope?, description?) >
```

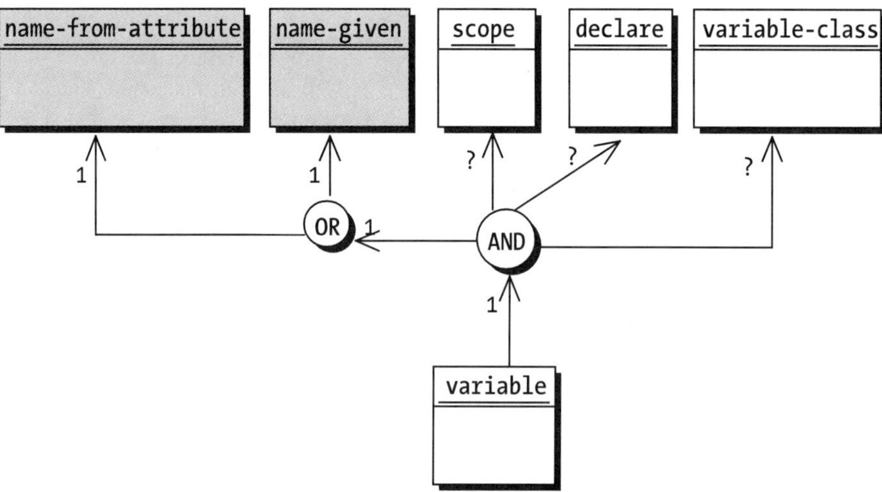

Figure 5-21. Visualization of the variable container element of the TLD 1.2 DTD. Mandatory elements are shaded; note that each variable must include either a `<name-given>` *or a* `<name-from-attribute>` *container element.*

It is easy to get confused by the naming element dualism of the `<variable>` container, but it's a simple process to understand the vision of the TLD DTD design engineers. Each variable may be named in either of two ways:

- The script variable name is assigned by the Web application deployment engineer, who provides a `<name-given>` attribute in the TLD file.
- The script variable name is provided as a translation-time value of an attribute. The name of the attribute is given in the `<name-from-attribute>` element.

Listing 5-14 contains a full description of the variable element in the TLD.

Listing 5-14. A variable element definition

```
<!--
      All tag variable metadata and must be contained
      within the tag container.
-->
<variable>

      <!--
            Mandatory metadata container elements
            --------------------------------
            name-given       Name of the scripting variable. Either a
                             name-given or a name-from-attribute element
                             must be supplied to the variable - but both
                             cannot be used at the same time.
            name-from-attribute     Name of the attribute whose value
                             is the name of this scripting variable. Either
                             a name-given or a name-from-attribute element
                             must be supplied to the variable - but both
                             cannot be used at the same time.
      -->
      <name-given>firstName</name-given>

      <!--
            Optional metadata container tags
            -------------------------------

            variable-class    Class name of the variable declared. Defaults
                              to String if not provided.
            declare           true if the variable should be declared (as
                              opposed to simply used) by the JSP container,
                              false otherwise. The default value is true.
            scope             One of three values indicating which scope the
                              declared element should have. The values are
                              VariableInfo.AT_BEGIN, VariableInfo.AT_END and
                              VariableInfo.NESTED. Refer to the section
                              "Class javax.servlet.jsp.tagext.VariableInfo"
                              for a detailed walkthrough on variable scoping,
                              and to the sidebar below for the associated code.
            description       Human-readable description of this variable.
```

```
        -->
        <variable-class>String</variable-class>
        <declare>true</declare>
        <scope>AT_BEGIN</scope>
        <description>The first name of the current client</description>
</variable>
```

Listing 5-14 defines the variable `String firstName` with a visibility scope starting from the opening tag delimiter.

Java Code for the <variable> Element

The code generated for a `<variable>` definition in a custom JSP page is a small matter; the following snippet was generated by the Tomcat4.0-b5 Web container. Paths and variable names have been abbreviated for readability; the Catalina engine of Tomcat has an affinity for always using the fully qualified class path for all type definitions and variables. Although this is good indeed for system stability, the autogenerated code is somewhat tricky to read unedited.

The code pertaining to the variable definition is bolded in the following snippet. Note that the variable has nested scope (in other words, it is accessible only within the body of the tag) because it is declared between the `doStartTag` and `doEndTag` method calls). The visibility of a script variable is indicated by one of three constants, defined in the `javax.servlet.jsp.tagext.VariableInfo` class. When the variable is nested within the body of the enclosing custom JSP tag, its corresponding `VariableInfo` constant is `VariableInfo.NESTED`. Refer to "Class javax.servlet.jsp.tagext.VariableInfo," later in this chapter, for more information about the `VariableInfo` class.

```
/* ----  apt:VariableTag ---- */
VariableDefinitionTag vt = new VariableDefinitionTag();
vt.setPageContext(pageContext);
vt.setParent(null);
try
{
   int startResult = vt.doStartTag();
   if (startResult == BodyTag.EVAL_BODY_BUFFERED)
      throw new JspTagException("Since tag handler class VariableDefinitionTag "
      + "does not implement BodyTag, it can't return BodyTag.EVAL_BODY_TAG");
```

```
    if (startResult != Tag.SKIP_BODY)
    {
       do
       {
          String foo = null;
          foo = (String) pageContext.findAttribute("foo");
       } while (vt.doAfterBody() == BodyTag.EVAL_BODY_AGAIN);
    }
    if (vt.doEndTag() == Tag.SKIP_PAGE)
       return;
}
finally
{
    vt.release();
}
```

Note that the value of the variable is retrieved from an attribute bound in the `pageContext` with the same name as the `<variable>` element.

When altering the scope of a declared variable, such as in `<scope>AT_BEGIN</scope>`, the declaration is done in another place; but all other aspects of the invocation is identical to the `<scope>NESTED</scope>` case illustrated in the previous code snippet. Taking a look at a piece of the resulting JSP code, generated by the Tomcat-4.0 engine, you see two alterations: the variable is declared in another place, and it is initialized in two places. This rather odd behavior is done to permit `IterationTags` and `BodyTags` to modify and re-read the value of the variable with each iteration.

```
try
{
    String foo = null;
    int startResult = vt.doStartTag();
    foo = (String) pageContext.findAttribute("foo");

    if (startResult == BodyTag.EVAL_BODY_BUFFERED)
      throw new JspTagException("Since tag handler class VariableDefinitionTag "
      + "does not implement BodyTag, it can't return BodyTag.EVAL_BODY_TAG");

    if (startResult != Tag.SKIP_BODY)
    {
       do
       {
          foo = (String) pageContext.findAttribute("foo");
       } while (vt.doAfterBody() == BodyTag.EVAL_BODY_AGAIN);
```

Using the `<scope>AT_END</scope>` setting for declaring a variable alters the code produced by the JSP compiler yet again, placing the final assignment of the `foo` variable after the `while` statement marking the end of the tag body, as shown in the previous code snippet. Feel free to verify the code generated by your favorite Web container.

Of course, the full XML DTD can be found and downloaded using a regular Web browser, after navigating to `http://java.sun.com/dtd/web-jsptaglibrary_1_2.dtd`.

> **NOTE** *Chapter 6 provides some thorough examples of creating new Tag libraries.*

For those of you still using the 1.1 TLD specification, take a brief look at the 1.1 TLD file.

Tag Libraries in JSP 1.1

The TLD specification version 1.1 contains most options found in version 1.2, but it lacks many descriptor elements of JSP 1.2. In fact, the full XML DTD of the TLD for JSP 1.1 is a lot simpler than the corresponding for 1.2. Figure 5-22 shows the DTD for the TLD document version 1.1.

The difference between TLD DTD versions 1.2 and 1.1 is rather big; apart from the obvious alteration of the `DOCTYPE` element at the TLD document top, and the values of the `<tlibversion>` and `<jspversion>` elements, more subtle differences occur frequently in the document. The 1.1 versions of the TLD DTD uses concatenated element names (for example, `jspversion`), but the 1.2 TLD DTD uses hyphens to separate word parts from one another (for example, `jsp-version`).

Also, some element names in the JSP 1.1 TLD have been altered in the JSP 1.2 release. For instance, the `<info>` element has been renamed `<description>` in the JSP 1.2 TLD DTD. For a full listing of the changes between the 1.1 and 1.2 TLD DTDs, refer to the JSP specification, section "Changes."

To illustrate the differences between the TLD versions, the `FirstTag` custom action discussed in "The Tag Library Definition File" earlier in this chapter is re-created in Listing 5-15 TLD version 1.1.

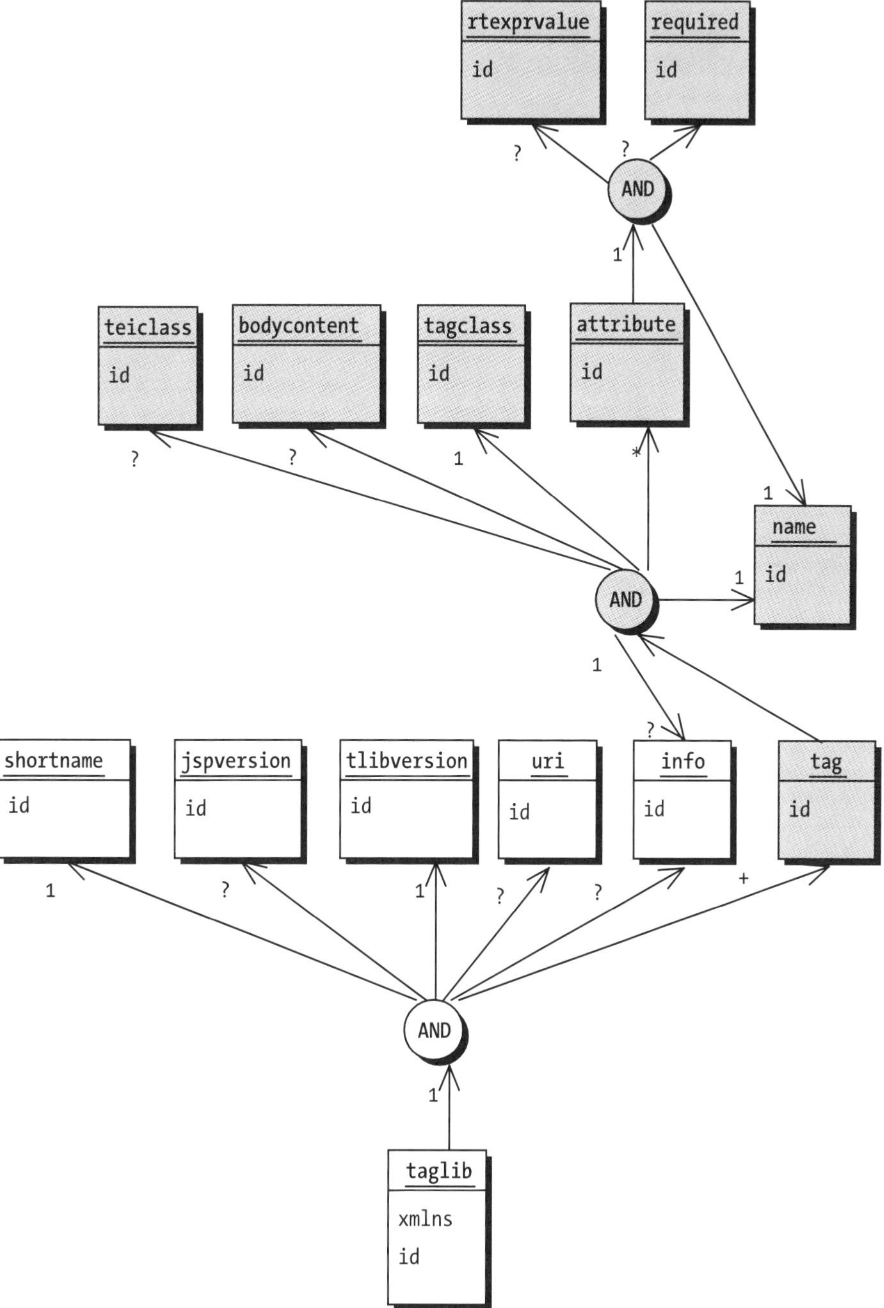

Figure 5-22. Visualization of the TLD DTD for the JSP 1.1 specification. All elements pertaining to a tag definition has been shaded. Note that several of the elements from the TLD DTD version 1.2 are missing or spelled differently. For instance, the `<info>` *element corresponds to the description element of TLD DTD version 1.2.*

Listing 5-15. The TLD document

```
<?xml version="1.0" encoding="ISO-8859-1" ?>
<!DOCTYPE taglib PUBLIC
   "-//Sun Microsystems, Inc.//DTD JSP Tag Library 1.1//EN"
   "http://java.sun.com/j2ee/dtds/web-jsptaglibrary_1_1.dtd">

<taglib>
        <tlibversion>1.0</tlibversion>
        <jspversion>1.1</jspversion>
        <shortname>
                J2EE frontend technologies; servlets, JSPs and
                EJBs tutorial tag library
        </shortname>
        <uri>http://localhost/taglib/tagz.jar</uri>
        <info>Sample Tutorial Tag Library</info>

        <tag>
                <name>FirstTag</name>
                <tagclass>se.jguru.tags.FirstTag</tagclass>
                <bodycontent>empty</bodycontent>
                <info>The first tutorial tag</info>
        </tag>
</taglib>
```

The XML `<tag>` element definition from the TLD DTD version 1.1 (shown in the code line below) is smaller than its 1.2 counterpart. Note that the only two mandatory subelements are `<name>` and `<tagclass>`:

```
<!ELEMENT tag (name, tagclass, teiclass?, bodycontent?, info?, attribute*)>
```

A graphical illustration of the tag element shows the simplicity even better (see Figure 5-23).

The code generated by the JSP engine to call the life-cycle methods of the `FirstTag` handler class becomes slightly different than the 1.2 equivalent. The only significant difference is that the named constant in one boolean expression is declared deprecated in 1.2, as shown here:

```
if (eval == BodyTag.EVAL_BODY_TAG)
throw new JspTagException("Since tag handler class se.jguru.tags.FirstTag "
+ "does not implement BodyTag, it can't return BodyTag.EVAL_BODY_TAG");
```

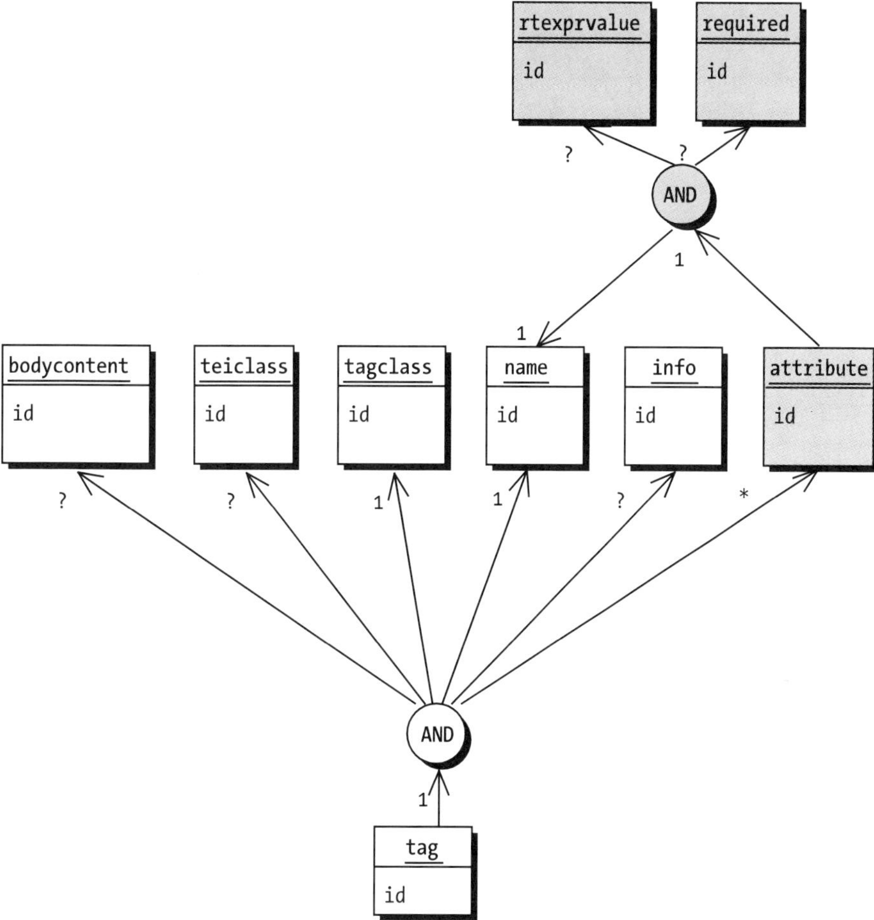

Figure 5-23. XML structure of the `<tag>` *element in the JSP 1.1 version of the TLD DTD*

Thus, although the JSP 1.2 specification may have altered quite a lot with regards to specification files and DTDs, the autogenerated code compiled to a servlet is practically the same between the two revisions.

Touring the javax.servlet.jsp.tagext Package

All classes for implementing the functionality of JSP custom tags are found in the `javax.servlet.jsp.tagext` package. The package contains two types of classes:

- Required interfaces of tag handler classes and their abstract implementation classes. Tags are separated into two categories, corresponding to the three tag handler interfaces (`javax.servlet.jsp.tagext.Tag`, `javax.servlet.jsp.tagext.IterationTag`, and `javax.servlet.jsp.tagext.BodyTag`) with their corresponding helper classes (`TagSupport` and `BodyTagSupport`).

- Metadata classes describing tag handlers, their required and optional attributes, and the operation of the tag. The information provided by the metaclasses includes: optional or mandatory body content, required parent tag, and any attributes required or variables declared.

The tagext metadata classes are numerous but well-designed, where each class encapsulates specific information about the tag. The main task of these metadata classes is encapsulating information from the TLD file and exposing it to the JSP engine. This metadata information allows the JSP engine to create the Java code of the autogenerated servlet and permits the developer to provide specifications to the JSP engine. Such specifications include valid value ranges for attributes, parameters, and so on.

Standalone tags are handled by a class implementing the `javax.servlet.jsp.tagext.Tag` interface. Body tags (possibly containing text) are handled by a class implementing the `javax.servlet.jsp.tagext.BodyTag` interface if the body content of the tag container should be modified during runtime or the `javax.servlet.jsp.tagext.IterationTag` interface otherwise.

All three interfaces are implemented by a related support class with empty method bodies, similar in construction to the `Adapter` classes of the `java.awt.event` package. Thus, when implementing a tag handler class, the developer may choose to implement the proper interface or extend its support class (which is frequently done, because it facilitates and speeds up the development). Note that both the `IterationTag` and the `BodyTag` interfaces extends the `Tag` interface, thus providing additional sets of methods that may operate on the body content of a container tag.

These three interfaces contain life cycle method definitions of all non-tag specific methods called by the JSP engine when it executes the code defined for a particular tag. Put simpler, the JSP engine will call only the methods defined in the three interfaces in Figure 5-24, plus any methods implied by descriptor entries in the TLD file. Although not complex in nature, the indirect calling convention of the `Tag`, `IterationTag` and `BodyTag` methods make these classes worthwhile to study.

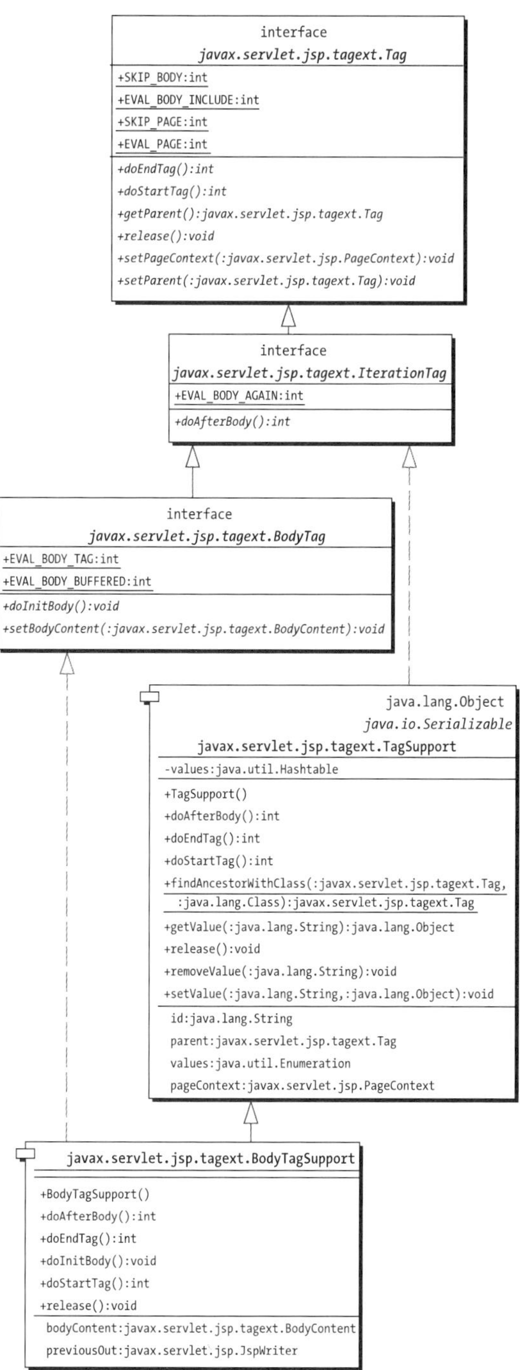

Figure 5-24. Structure of the tag specification interfaces (`Tag`, `IterationTag` *and* `BodyTag`*) and their implementation class counterparts (*`TagSupport` *and* `BodyTagSupport`*). Note that both the* `Tag` *and* `IterationTag` *interfaces are implemented by the* `TagSupport` *class.*

Interface javax.servlet.jsp.tagext.Tag

The `Tag` interface contains methods and constants defining the life cycle of a tag handler class (see Figure 5-25).

interface *javax.servlet.jsp.tagext.Tag*
+SKIP_BODY:int
+EVAL_BODY_INCLUDE:int
+SKIP_PAGE:int
+EVAL_PAGE:int
+doEndTag():int
+doStartTag():int
+getParent():javax.servlet.jsp.tagext.Tag
+release():void
+setPageContext(:javax.servlet.jsp.PageContext):void
+setParent(:javax.servlet.jsp.tagext.Tag):void

Figure 5-25. The `Tag` *interface*

Mainly, the methods fall in one of the two following categories:

- JavaBean property setter methods, called by the JSP engine to set the state of the tag handler instance. The corresponding JavaBean getter method is generally called from within the tag handler. The methods are `setParent(Tag t)` and `setPageContext(PageContext obj)`.

- Life-cycle methods called by the JSP engine at specific points in the execution of the tag handler. The methods are `doEndTag`,`doStartTag`, `release`.

Being root interface of all tag handler classes, the `Tag` interface defines the primary life-cycle methods called by the JSP engine when executing the methods belonging to a custom tag, as defined previously.

The JSP engine is responsible for completely setting up all internal data (by calling the JavaBean `setXXX` setter methods) prior to evaluating any tag content. This content is evaluated by calling the `doStartTag` and `doEndTag` methods.

Class *javax.servlet.jsp.tagext.TagSupport*

`TagSupport` is an `Adapter` class implementing an abstract infrastructure that supports all methods in the `Tag` interface, as shown in Figure 5-26. Thus, its main development benefit is reducing the amount of specific code that the developer must create.

```
                                    java.lang.Object
                  javax.servlet.jsp.tagext.IterationTag
                                  java.io.Serializable
           javax.servlet.jsp.tagext.TagSupport
-------------------------------------------------------
-values:java.util.Hashtable
-------------------------------------------------------
+TagSupport()
+doAfterBody():int
+doEndTag():int
+doStartTag():int
+findAncestorWithClass(:javax.servlet.jsp.tagext.Tag,
  :java.lang.Class):javax.servlet.jsp.tagext.Tag
+getValue(:java.lang.String):java.lang.Object
+release():void
+removeValue(:java.lang.String):void
+setValue(:java.lang.String,:java.lang.Object):void
-------------------------------------------------------
 id:java.lang.String
 parent:javax.servlet.jsp.tagext.Tag
 values:java.util.Enumeration
 pageContext:javax.servlet.jsp.PageContext
```

Figure 5-26. The `TagSupport` *class*

Tag-wide values, which should be accessible from all parts and methods, are stored within the `values` hashtable and retrieved using the `getValue`, `getValues`, `setValue`, and `setValues` methods.

Most methods of the `TagSupport` class are quite self-explanatory, given their good-fashioned naming convention. The only method that deserves some special attention within the `TagSupport` class is `findAncenstorWithClass`, which locates the closest enclosing tag handler of the particular class provided. Take a look at Listing 5-16, which illustrates the use of the `findAncestorWithClass` method.

Listing 5-16. The `findAncestorWithClass` *method*

```
// Let us assume that the JSP document has a structure like so:
//
//       <xyz:parentTag >
//             <xyz:firstChildTag >
//                     <xyz:innerChildTag />
//             </ xyz:firstChildTag >
//      </ xyz:parentTag >
//
// A nice way to access a reference to either of the enclosing tags
// from within the methods of the innerChildTag handler class is:

public void someMethodInInnerChildTagHandler()
{
        // Get a reference to the handler class of parentTag
        ParentTagHandler myParent = (ParentTagHandler) findAncestorWithClass(
                this, ParentTagHandler.class);

        // Check sanity
        if(myParent == null) throw new JspException("The innerChildTag must" +
                "be contained within a parentTag.");

        // Get a reference to the handler class of firstChildTag
        Child1TagHandler bigSister = (Child1TagHandler) findAncestorWithClass(
                this, Child1TagHandler.class);

        // Check sanity
        if(bigSister == null) throw new JspException("The innerChildTag must"
                + "be contained within a firstChildTag.");

        // Call some methods within the handler instances.
        ...
}
```

As shown in Listing 5-16, the `findAncestorWithClass` method may be used to obtain a reference to an enclosing parent having a particular type. This is useful to avoid type mismatches and corresponding exceptions when calling the parent from the child.

Interface javax.servlet.jsp.tagext.IterationTag

The `IterationTag` interface extends the `Tag` interface and defines an additional life-cycle method called by the Web container at the end of the `IterationTag` body evaluation. The `IterationTag` interface introduces but one new method, `doAfterBody`, as shown in Figure 5-27.

javax.servlet.jsp.tagext.Tag interface *javax.servlet.jsp.tagext.IterationTag*
+EVAL_BODY_AGAIN:int
+doAfterBody():int

Figure 5-27. The `IterationTag` *interface*

The `doAfterBody` method is called once after each pass through the body text. As long as the `doAfterBody` method returns `BodyTag.EVAL_BODY_AGAIN`, the iteration over the body text continues.

In practice, it is uncommon to implement the IterationTag interface directly; most tag handler classes requiring the functionality of the IterationTag would instead extend the `TagSupport` class (see "Class javax.servlet.jsp.tagext.TagSupport" later in this chapter).

Interface javax.servlet.jsp.tagext.BodyTag

The `BodyTag` interface extends the `IterationTag` interface, defining additional life-cycle methods that facilitate modifying the body text contained in the tag, as shown in Figure 5-28.

When the JSP engine generates the servlet, the calling order of the methods will always be:

1. The JSP engine creates a `BodyContent` object from the text in the container body and calls `setBodyContent` using the newly created object. Using methods within the `BodyContent`, the text may be retrieved or sent to the `JspWriter` of the enclosing tag handler.

2. `doInitBody` is called once, prior to first pass through the body text.

3. doAfterBody (defined in the IterationTag interface) is called once after each pass through the body text. As long as the doAfterBody method returns BodyTag.EVAL_BODY_AGAIN, the iteration over the body text continues.

javax.servlet.jsp.tagext.IterationTag interface *javax.servlet.jsp.tagext.BodyTag*
+EVAL_BODY_TAG:int +EVAL_BODY_BUFFERED:int
+doInitBody():void *+setBodyContent(:javax.servlet.jsp.tagext.BodyContent):void*

Figure 5-28. The BodyTag *interface*

In practice, it is uncommon to implement the BodyTag interface directly; most tag handler classes requiring the functionality of the BodyTag would instead extend the BodyTagSupport class (refer to the following section for a walkthrough of the BodyTag class).

> **NOTE** *Refer to Chapter 6 for examples of extending the BodyTag class.*

Class javax.servlet.jsp.tagext.BodyTagSupport

Similar to the TagSupport class, the main benefit of extending from BodyTagSupport instead of directly implementing the BodyTagSupport interface is that the amount of trivial code one needs to create is somewhat reduced. Figure 5-29 shows the BodyTagSupport class.

Note that the added convenience JavaBean properties bodyContent and previousOut may simplify the development further. The getBodyContent method returns a reference to information about the body text, and the getPreviousOut method returns a reference to the out JspWriter of the enclosing context or tag. Normally, you need to use the previousOut to write text to the JSP document—which, in turn, is connected to the client browser.

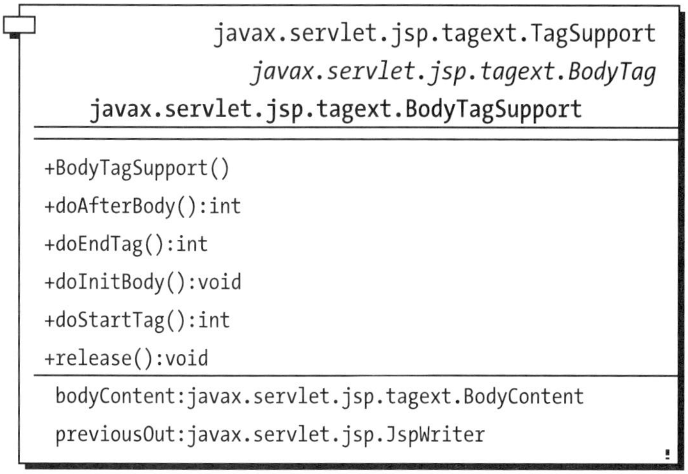

```
javax.servlet.jsp.tagext.TagSupport
javax.servlet.jsp.tagext.BodyTag
javax.servlet.jsp.tagext.BodyTagSupport
+BodyTagSupport()
+doAfterBody():int
+doEndTag():int
+doInitBody():void
+doStartTag():int
+release():void
bodyContent:javax.servlet.jsp.tagext.BodyContent
previousOut:javax.servlet.jsp.JspWriter
```

Figure 5-29. The `BodyTagSupport` *class*

Interface javax.servlet.jsp.tagext.TryCatchFinally

The `TryCatchFinally` interface shown in Figure 5-30 declares two methods, `doCatch` and `doFinally`, which are called from within automatically generated `catch` and `finally` blocks, respectively.

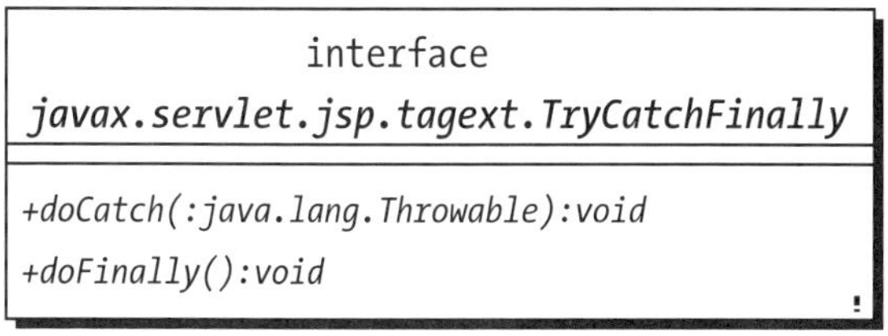

```
interface
javax.servlet.jsp.tagext.TryCatchFinally
+doCatch(:java.lang.Throwable):void
+doFinally():void
```

Figure 5-30. The `TryCatchFinally` *interface*

Thus far, the assumption has been that all code execution would progress according to plan. If the code of a tag handler class throws an exception during its execution, a somewhat tricky situation arises. How can the programmer handle the conditional execution that takes place in the `catch` and `finally` blocks following a `try` block? The simple answer is that such coding has been left up to the programmer before JSP version 1.2.

Although it is a simple task to encapsulate all text of a JSP document in a catch-all `try` block, it is not recommended, as the JSP document becomes burdened with a mandatory `<% try { %> ... <% } catch(Exception ex) { // Handler goes here } %>` scriptlet. The JSP document content should replace the ... for this pattern to work. Apart from making the document quite unreadable, the potential for errors in the JSP document using this structure is quite high.

The better alternative is to let your tag handler class implement the `TryCatchFinally` interface, having the two methods `doCatch` and `doFinally` as described in Table 5-3.

Table 5-3. The Function of Methods `doCatch` *and* `doFinally`

METHOD	DECLARATION
Handler method invoked from within the mandatory `catch` of the JSP body	`void doCatch(Throwable t)` throws `Throwable.`
Handler method invoked from within the `finally` block of the JSP body (in other words, this method is always invoked)	`void doFinally()`

> **NOTE** *It is important that the* `doFinally` *method does not throw any exceptions because these cannot normally be handled by the autogenerated Java class.*

Java Code Generated from a TryCatchFinally

The stereotypical implementation of the JSP-generated code for a tag handler class implementing the `TryCatchFinally` interface reveals little new functionality. Note, however, the calls to the `doCatch(Throwable)` and `doFinally()` methods, which are inserted into the `catch` and `finally` blocks.

For improved readability, the `doCatch` and `doFinally` methods in the following listing appear in bold, and the full type paths converted into simple ones:

```
 /* ----  apt:VariableTag ---- */
VariableDefinitionTag vt = new VariableDefinitionTag();
vt.setPageContext(pageContext);
vt.setParent(null);
```

```
try
{
   int startTagResult = vt.doStartTag();
   if (startTagResult == BodyTag.EVAL_BODY_BUFFERED)
      throw new JspTagException("Since tag handler class VariableDefinitionTag "
      + "does not implement BodyTag, it can't return BodyTag.EVAL_BODY_TAG");
   if (startTagResult != Tag.SKIP_BODY)
   {
      do
      {
      } while (vt.doAfterBody() == BodyTag.EVAL_BODY_AGAIN);
   }
   if (vt.doEndTag() == Tag.SKIP_PAGE) return;
}
catch (Throwable t)
{
   vt.doCatch(t);
}
finally
{
   vt.doFinally();
   vt.release();
}
String foo = null;
foo = (String) pageContext.findAttribute("foo");
```

Extra bonus: The `VariableDefinitionTag` defines one variable, named `foo` of type `String`. From the previous code, can you determine the value of its `<scope>` element in the TLD?

Class javax.servlet.jsp.tagext.BodyContent

Non-empty tags, which enclose text between their opening and closing tag delimiters, may manipulate the enclosed text and optionally react to its content. The `javax.servlet.jsp.tagext.BodyContent` class, shown in Figure 5-31, encapsulates a buffer that holds the body text content and also contains the methods used to interact with the body text.

At construction time, the `BodyContent` instance is given a `JspWriter` object argument; this object should be the `JspWriter` connected to the browser output. One may thereafter get a reference to the contained `JspWriter` by calling the `getEnclosingWriter` method.

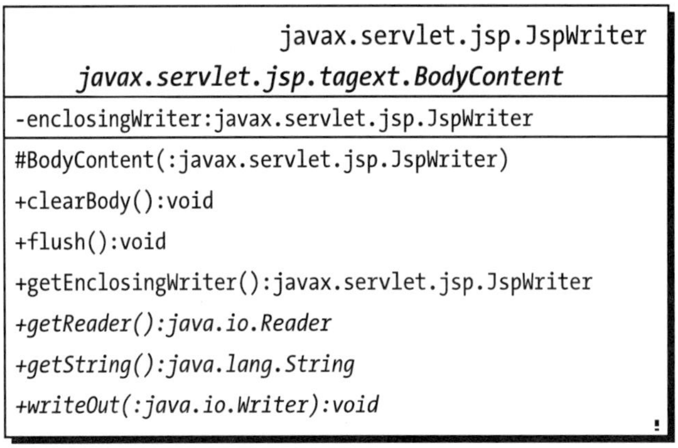

javax.servlet.jsp.JspWriter *javax.servlet.jsp.tagext.BodyContent*
-enclosingWriter:javax.servlet.jsp.JspWriter
#BodyContent(:javax.servlet.jsp.JspWriter) +clearBody():void +flush():void +getEnclosingWriter():javax.servlet.jsp.JspWriter *+getReader():java.io.Reader* *+getString():java.lang.String* *+writeOut(:java.io.Writer):void*

Figure 5-31. The BodyContent interface

The `BodyContent` class extends `JspWriter`, so you may regard it as a local wrapper containing extra convenience methods that extracts the buffered contents from the wrapped writer. The methods can be divided into the two following logical groups:

- Retrieving a representation of the `BodyContent` string. If you wish to retrieve a String representation, use the `getString` method. Should you prefer a Reader representation, use the `getReader` method.

- Writing data to the `JspWriter` of the enclosing JSP page. This `JspWriter` is obtained by calling the `getEnclosingWriter` method. The methods are `writeOut(Writer out)`, `clearBody()`, and `flush()`.

The usage of the `BodyContent` and `BodyTagSupport` classes is simplest demonstrated with an example. You'll develop a custom JSP action called `SimpleBodyTag` and a JSP page called `simpleBodyTag.jsp`. The purpose of the `SimpleBodyTag` handler is to provide information about the text that was enclosed inside it. You can see the resulting output of running the `simpleBodyTag.jsp` page in Figure 5-32.

The relevant source code of the JSP document, which produced the output in Figure 5-32, is rather minimalistic. Note that the content of the leftmost cell simply illustrates the code in the JSP document and does not perform any actual server-side code invocations. The relevant code of the `simpleBodyTag.jsp` document is provided here, and the custom JSP action appears in bold text:

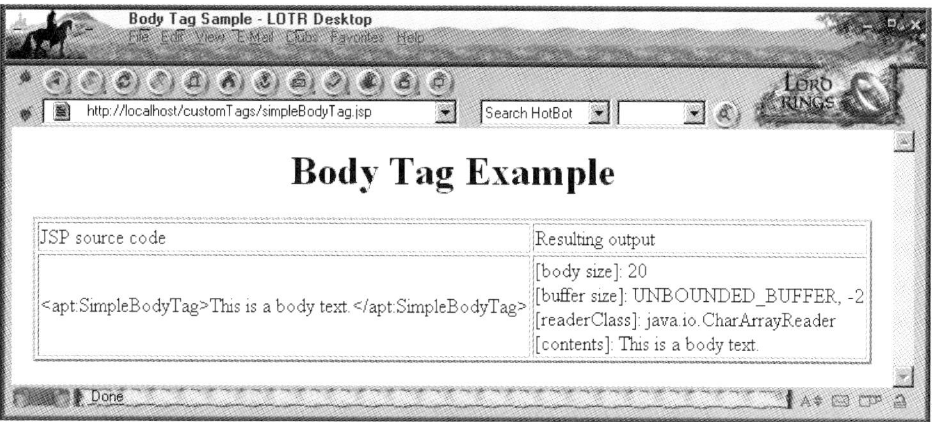

Figure 5-32. The resulting output of the `SimpleBodyTag` *example custom JSP action. Only the output in the table cell to the bottom right originate from the* `SimpleBodyTag` *handler; all other output comes from the JSP document,* `simpleBodyTag.jsp`.

```
<%@ taglib uri="apressTags" prefix="apt" %>
...
<tr>
<td>&lt;apt:SimpleBodyTag>This is a body text.&lt;/apt:SimpleBodyTag></td>
<td><apt:SimpleBodyTag>This is a body text.</apt:SimpleBodyTag></td>
</tr>
...
```

The JSP-to-servlet compiler generated the code in Listing 5-17 for the JSP document in the preceding snippet. Again, as the code generated may be less than perfectly simple to read for humans; its variable names, class paths, and indentation have been cleaned up for easier reading. The bold code in Listing 5-17 corresponds to the execution of the tag body. Note that the body content from the JSP document has been converted into the `out.write("This is a body text.");` statement.

Listing 5-17. The autogenerated code for the `SimpleBodyTag`

```
/* ----  apt:SimpleBodyTag ---- */
SimpleBodyTag sbt = new SimpleBodyTag();
sbt.setPageContext(pageContext);
sbt.setParent(null);
```

```
try
{
   int startResult = sbt.doStartTag();
   if (startResult != Tag.SKIP_BODY)
   {
      try
      {
         if (startResult != Tag.EVAL_BODY_INCLUDE)
         {
            out = pageContext.pushBody();
            sbt.setBodyContent((BodyContent) out);
         }
         sbt.doInitBody();
         do
         {
            out.write("This is a body text.");
         } while (sbt.doAfterBody() == BodyTag.EVAL_BODY_AGAIN);
      }
      finally
      {
         if (startResult != Tag.EVAL_BODY_INCLUDE)
         out = pageContext.popBody();
      }
   }
   if (sbt.doEndTag() == Tag.SKIP_PAGE) return;
}
finally
{
   sbt.release();
}
// end
```

The full code of the `SimpleBodyTag` handler class is smaller one than might think, as simply extending the `BodyTagSupport` class can perform powerful tasks without large amounts of custom code. In this case, the only custom code of the `SimpleBodyTag` has been supplied in the `doAfterBody` method. The simple UML diagram of the tag handler class is shown in Figure 5-33.

BodyTagSupport se.jguru.tags.SimpleBodyTag
+doAfterBody():int

Figure 5-33. The structure of the `SimpleBodyTag` *handler class is minimalistic—only the* `doAfterBody` *method needs be overridden from the* `BodyTagSupport` *superclass. All other methods are run with the default behaviour from* `BodyTagSupport`.

Listing 5-18 displays the full code for the `SimpleBodyTag` handler class.

Listing 5-18. The `SimpleBodyTag` *handler class*

```
/*
 * Copyright (c) 2000 jGuru.se
 * All rights reserved.
 */

package se.jguru.tags;

import java.util.*;
import javax.servlet.jsp.*;
import javax.servlet.jsp.tagext.*;

public class SimpleBodyTag extends BodyTagSupport
{
    /**
     * Method which prints out some status messages regarding its
     * body contents. Therefore, the BodyTagSupport
     * class is used as a superclass of this Tag handler.
     */
    public int doAfterBody() throws JspException
    {
        // Get the BodyContent.
        BodyContent bc = this.getBodyContent();

        // Get the body content as a string.
        String bodyAsString = bc.getString();

        // Get the JspWriter connected to the JSP document
        JspWriter out = this.getPreviousOut();
```

```
            // Find out some Reader metadata
            int bufferSize = bc.getBufferSize();
            String strBufSize = "UNKNOWN, size=" + bufferSize;
            if (bufferSize == out.DEFAULT_BUFFER)
                    strBufSize = "DEFAULT_BUFFER, " + bufferSize;
            if (bufferSize == out.NO_BUFFER)
                    strBufSize = "NO_BUFFER, " + bufferSize;
            if (bufferSize == out.UNBOUNDED_BUFFER)
                    strBufSize = "UNBOUNDED_BUFFER, " + bufferSize;

            // Get the fully qualified class name of the BodyContent reader
            String readerClass = bc.getReader().getClass().getName();

            // Clear the original body content from the JSP document.
            // If we do not, the tag body from the JSP document will
            // be written to the client browser. However, our intention
            // is to output onlyprocessed text with metadata about
            // the body text. We must therefore clear the original body,
            // and create a new one.
            bc.clearBody();

            // Now, generate the new body content of this tag.
            try
            {
                out.println("[body size]: " + bodyAsString.length() + "<br>");
                out.println("[buffer size]: " + strBufSize + "<br>");
                out.println("[readerClass]: " + readerClass + "<br>");
                out.println("[contents]: " + bodyAsString + "<br>");
            }
            catch (Exception ex)
            {
                System.out.println("Whoops! " + ex);
            }

            // Done.
            return Tag.SKIP_BODY;
        }
}
```

The doAfterBody method of Listing 5-18 prints metadata corresponding to the BodyContent held by the tag. The explanation of each individual statement in Listing 5-18 can be found in its comments.

Class javax.servlet.jsp.tagext.TagExtraInfo

The TagExtraInfo class shown in Figure 5-34, is used as a superclass from which descriptions about tag handlers are derived.

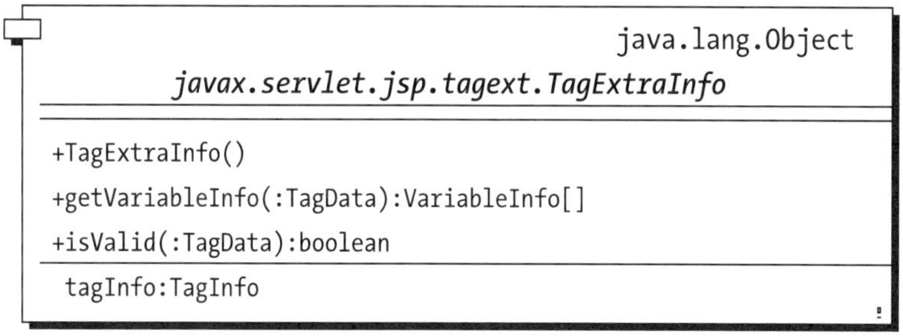

```
java.lang.Object
javax.servlet.jsp.tagext.TagExtraInfo
---
+TagExtraInfo()
+getVariableInfo(:TagData):VariableInfo[]
+isValid(:TagData):boolean
---
tagInfo:TagInfo
```

Figure 5-34. The TagExtraInfo *class*

The extra information about a tag handler provided by the TagExtraInfo class is required for proper operation in two situations:

- When your tag handler defines scripting variables (in other words, variables existing within the boundaries of a container tag or from the tag onwards within the JSP document). Type information about scripting variables is given through the method public VariableInfo[] getVariableInfo(TagData data), where the JSP engine encapsulates attribute metadata information in the TagData object and passes it as a method argument. The return array contains information and about all variables/attributes created or modified by the tag handler.

- When you want to perform validation checking of attributes, provided within a JSP tag. Such validation is achieved by the method public boolean isValid(TagData data).

Both these methods return or handle arguments that encapsulate attribute or data information in a similar manner. Their specific details are described in the following sections on TagData and VariableInfo, respectively.

In addition, the TagExtraInfo class contains a TagInfo object, which contains information about the attributes declared in the TLD file. This TagInfo object can be retrieved from the TagExtraInfo class by calling public TagInfo getTagInfo().

Class javax.servlet.jsp.tagext.TagInfo

The TagInfo class, shown in Figure 5-35, is used to retrieve runtime metadata about the attributes of a tag handler class.

```
                                                    java.lang.Object
              javax.servlet.jsp.tagext.TagInfo
+BODY_CONTENT_JSP:java.lang.String
+BODY_CONTENT_TAG_DEPENDENT:java.lang.String
+BODY_CONTENT_EMPTY:java.lang.String
-attributeInfo:javax.servlet.jsp.tagext.TagAttributeInfo[]
-tagVariableInfo:javax.servlet.jsp.tagext.TagVariableInfo[]
+TagInfo(:java.lang.String,:java.lang.String,:java.lang.String,
  :java.lang.String,:javax.servlet.jsp.tagext.TagLibraryInfo,
  :javax.servlet.jsp.tagext.TagExtraInfo,
  :javax.servlet.jsp.tagext.TagAttributeInfo[])
+TagInfo(:java.lang.String,:java.lang.String,:java.lang.String,
  :java.lang.String,:javax.servlet.jsp.tagext.TagLibraryInfo,
  :javax.servlet.jsp.tagext.TagExtraInfo,
  :javax.servlet.jsp.tagext.TagAttributeInfo[],:java.lang.String,
  :java.lang.String,:java.lang.String,
  :javax.servlet.jsp.tagext.TagVariableInfo[])
+getVariableInfo(:javax.servlet.jsp.tagext.TagData)
  :javax.servlet.jsp.tagext.VariableInfo[]
+isValid(:javax.servlet.jsp.tagext.TagData):boolean
+toString():java.lang.String
 attributes:javax.servlet.jsp.tagext.TagAttributeInfo[]
 bodyContent:java.lang.String
 displayName:java.lang.String
 infoString:java.lang.String
 largeIcon:java.lang.String
 smallIcon:java.lang.String
 tagClassName:java.lang.String
 tagExtraInfo:javax.servlet.jsp.tagext.TagExtraInfo
 tagLibrary:javax.servlet.jsp.tagext.TagLibraryInfo
 tagName:java.lang.String
 tagVariableInfos:javax.servlet.jsp.tagext.TagVariableInfo[]
```

Figure 5-35. The TagInfo *class*

The metadata retrieved from calling methods in the `TagInfo` class is interpreted form the TLD file. The methods of the `javax.servlet.jsp.tagext.TagInfo` are of three main types:

- Methods that return a string form of the data found in the `taglib.tld`. The methods are `getAttributes`, `getTagName`, `getBodyContent`, and `getTagClassName`.
- Methods that return containers holding metadata describing other JSP entities. The methods are `getTagExtraInfo` and `getTagLibrary`.
- Methods that return runtime information from parsing the JSP document. The method is `getVariableInfo`.

The `toString` method of a `TagInfo` object returns a `String`, which provides some information about the contents of a `TagInfo` object.

Listing 5-19 is the output result of calling the `toString` method on a `TagInfo` instance. Compare the output in the listing with the provided information in the `taglib.tld` file. Can you find any discrepancies?

Listing 5-19. Printout of a `TagInfo.toString()` *call*

```
name = printTypeTree
class = se.jguru.tags.PrintTypeTreeTag
body = JSP
info = Tag iterating over a Map of instances, exposing each instance using its
target JavaBean property.
attributes = { name = allTargets type = null reqTime = true required = true}
```

The relevant parts of the TLD file which was used as the source for the listing in 5-19, is reprinted in Listing 5-20.

Listing 5-20. The tag definition in the TLD file

```
<tag>
        <name>printTypeTree</name>
        <tag-class>se.jguru.tags.PrintTypeTreeTag</tag-class>
        <tei-class>se.jguru.tags.PrintTypeTreeExtraInfo</tei-class>
        <body-content>JSP</body-content>
        <description>Tag iterating over a Map of instances,
                exposing each instance using its target JavaBean
                property.</ description>
```

```
        <attribute>
                <name>allTargets</name>
                <required>yes</required>
                <rtexprvalue>yes</rtexprvalue>
        </attribute>
</tag>
```

As you can see, the TagInfo class simply contains the parsed version of the TLD file.

Class javax.servlet.jsp.tagext.TagData

TagData objects contain metadata information describing attribute names and values used by tags (see Figure 5-36).

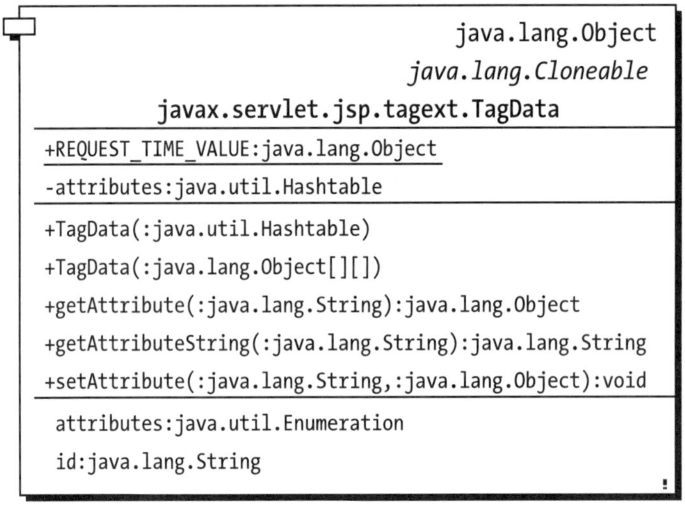

```
                                        java.lang.Object
                                      java.lang.Cloneable
           javax.servlet.jsp.tagext.TagData
+REQUEST_TIME_VALUE:java.lang.Object
-attributes:java.util.Hashtable
+TagData(:java.util.Hashtable)
+TagData(:java.lang.Object[][])
+getAttribute(:java.lang.String):java.lang.Object
+getAttributeString(:java.lang.String):java.lang.String
+setAttribute(:java.lang.String,:java.lang.Object):void
 attributes:java.util.Enumeration
 id:java.lang.String
```

Figure 5-36. The TagData *class*

The TagData instance vaguely mimics the behavior of a Hashtable from which data may be retrieved using the getAttribute methods. TagData instances are created and populated by the JSP engine for your convenience.

If the scripting variable described by a particular TagData object has not yet been given a value (such as, for instance, is the case with runtime variables being set by the Tag handler), the scripting variable has the value TagData.REQUEST_TIME_VALUE. This value simply distinguishes variables having been set from those not yet given a value.

The three relevant getter methods of the TagData class are:

- `public Object getAttribute(String attributeName)` is a normal hashtable getter method, which retrieves the value of the attribute with the provided name.
- `public String getAttributeString(String attributeName)` is a normal hashtable getter method, which retrieves the value of the attribute with the provided name. The difference between the `getAttributeString` and the `getAttribute` methods is simply that the former will typecast the results to a string.
- `public String getId()` returns the identifier of the tag (in other words, its `id` attribute value).

Class javax.servlet.jsp.tagext.VariableInfo

Each `VariableInfo` instance contains information about a scripting variable created or modified by a tag handler. All methods in this class, shown in 5-37, are getter JavaBean methods that return information about a declared variable.

```
java.lang.Object
javax.servlet.jsp.tagext.VariableInfo
+NESTED:int
+AT_BEGIN:int
+AT_END:int
+VariableInfo(:java.lang.String,:java.lang.String,:boolean,:int)
className:java.lang.String
declare:boolean
scope:int
varName:java.lang.String
```

Figure 5-37. The `VariableInfo` *class*

The following methods of the `VariableInfo` class have simple modes of operation:

- `public String getVarName()` returns the name of the variable described. Say that a `VariableInfo` instance `obj` describes a variable that was declared with the statement `String aCuteString;`. The call to `obj.getVarName()` would return the value `"aCuteString"` describing the variable name.

- `public String getClassName()` returns the name of the class of the variable. Say that a `VariableInfo` instance `obj` describes a variable that was declared with the statement `String aCuteString;`. The call to `obj.getClassName()` would return the value "`java.lang.String`" describing the class name of the declared variable.

- `public String getDeclare()` returns `true` if the variable is declared by the tag handler class for which this `VariableInfo` object is provided.

- `public int getScope()` returns one of the constants defined in the `VariableInfo` class and reveals which scope the declared variable will have in the JSP document.

- `VariableInfo.NESTED` denotes that the variable exists only between the start and end tag delimiters of the tag whose variable is described by the `VariableInfo` object.

- `VariableInfo.AT_BEGIN` indicates that the variable is defined from the start tag delimiter to the end of the JSP document.

- `VariableInfo.AT_END` indicates that the variable is defined from the end tag delimiter to the end of the JSP document.

Figure 5-38 depicts the areas of the JSP document where a declared variable will be visible. Of course, the variable must be declared by a tag handler class; examples of classes declaring variables will be provided in the next chapter.

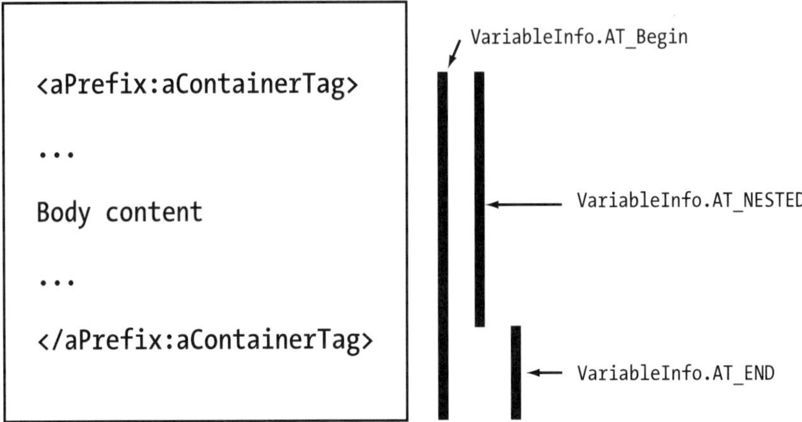

Figure 5-38. The different declaration scopes of a declared variable

Class javax.servlet.jsp.tagext.TagAttributeInfo

The `TagAttributeInfo` class, shown in Figure 5-39, is a simple storage class for parsed data, and its methods retrieve information about attributes of a tag handler, as defined in the `taglib.tld` file.

```
                                              java.lang.Object
              javax.servlet.jsp.tagext.TagAttributeInfo
+ID:String
-type:String
-reqTime:boolean
+TagAttributeInfo(:String,:boolean,:String,:boolean)
+canBeRequestTime():boolean
+getIdAttribute(:TagAttributeInfo[]):TagAttributeInfo
+toString():String
 name:String
 typeName:String
 required:boolean
```

Figure 5-39. The `TagAttributeInfo` *class*

The methods fall in the two following categories:

- Methods returning parsed and interpreted values from the attribute definitions provided in the `taglib.tld` file. The methods are `canBeRequestTime`, `getName`, `getTypeName`, `isRequired`, and `toString`.
- Static convenience method that returns the `TagAttributeInfo` object for the `id` attribute, corresponding to the variable name within the generated servlet. The method is `getIdAttribute(TagAttributeInfo a[])`.

Class javax.servlet.jsp.tagext.TagLibraryInfo

The `TagLibraryInfo` class shown in Figure 5-40 is a simple storage class for parsed data, and its methods retrieve data provided in the taglib descriptor file.

All methods are JavaBean getter methods, which return the data in the variable with the same name. For instance, the `getShortName` method returns the value kept within the `shortname` variable.

```
                                   java.lang.Object
          javax.servlet.jsp.tagext.TagLibraryInfo
#prefix:java.lang.String
#uri:java.lang.String
#tags:javax.servlet.jsp.tagext.TagInfo[]
#tlibversion:java.lang.String
#jspversion:java.lang.String
#shortname:java.lang.String
#urn:java.lang.String
#info:java.lang.String
#TagLibraryInfo(:java.lang.String,:java.lang.String)
+getInfoString():java.lang.String
+getPrefixString():java.lang.String
+getReliableURN():java.lang.String
+getRequiredVersion():java.lang.String
+getShortName():java.lang.String
+getTag(:java.lang.String):javax.servlet.jsp.tagext.TagInfo
+getTags():javax.servlet.jsp.tagext.TagInfo[]
+getURI():java.lang.String
```

Figure 5-40. The `TagLibraryInfo` *class*

The need to manually extract data from the `TagLibraryInfo` class is rather limited, as it is mainly intended to be used by the JSP engine in its metadata extraction.

Class javax.servlet.jsp.tagext.TagLibraryValidator

As the developer of a tag library, you may want to make sure that the `<@% taglib ... %>` directive is printed in a proper way. Before JSP version 1.2, there was no simple way of performing such validation—the `TagLibraryValidator` class, shown in Figure 5-41, has been added to the JSP version 1.2 class library to provide a simple way of validating a `TagLib` directive within a JSP document.

A `TagLibraryValidator` instance is global for all directives referring to a particular TLD file. Its fully qualified class is defined as an XML element in the TLD file, as seen in earlier "The <validator> Element" section.

The four methods in the class fall in the two following categories:

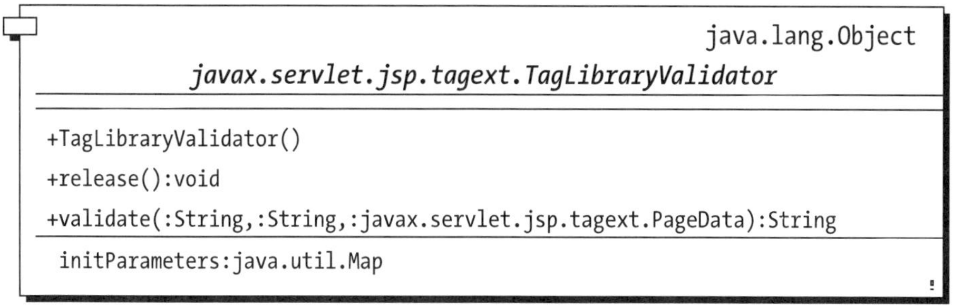

```
                                        java.lang.Object
         javax.servlet.jsp.tagext.TagLibraryValidator
-----------------------------------------------------------------
+TagLibraryValidator()
+release():void
+validate(:String,:String,:javax.servlet.jsp.tagext.PageData):String
-----------------------------------------------------------------
 initParameters:java.util.Map
```

Figure 5-41. The `TagLibraryValidator` *class*

- Methods manipulating the initialization parameters and state (instance variables) of the `TagLibraryValidator` instance. (All parameters are provided in the TLD file). These methods are `setInitParameter(Map aMap)`; `Map getInitParameters()`; and `release()`.
- Methods handling life-cycle validation for the `TagLibraryValidator` instance. This method is `validate(String prefix, String uri, PageData page)`.

Any non-null result from the `validate` method is regarded as an error message by the JSP engine. If the validate method returns a non-null string, it is wrapped in an `Exception` object and thrown by the JSP engine. Be sure to return `null` from the validate method to indicate successful validation. If running the Tomcat-4.0 reference implementation, the root exception prints the following message:

```
org.apache.jasper.JasperException: TagLibraryValidator in APress
   tutorial TagLib - invalid page: This is an error message from
   the validator.
```

The last part of the message ("This is an error message from the validator") is the string that was returned from the `validate` method, and the ("APress tutorial TagLib") is the short name (content of the `<short-name>` element) of the TLD file.

The Role of JSP Tag Libraries in Middle-Tier System Development

JSP taglib definitions are indeed flexible and powerful to use in the development of server-side customized JSP functionality. The massive increase in complexity to plan, create, and implement JSP tag libraries compared using the standard JSP functionality is evident to most developers investigating taglib functionality for the first time. Thus, the relevancy and major benefit of taglibs require a bit of evaluating.

Many server-side systems have front-end functionality that mimics the Model View Controller (MVC) design pattern to divide the separate functionalities of the server. Thus, the middleware front ends commonly use either of the design patterns (view or controller) illustrated in Figure 5-42.

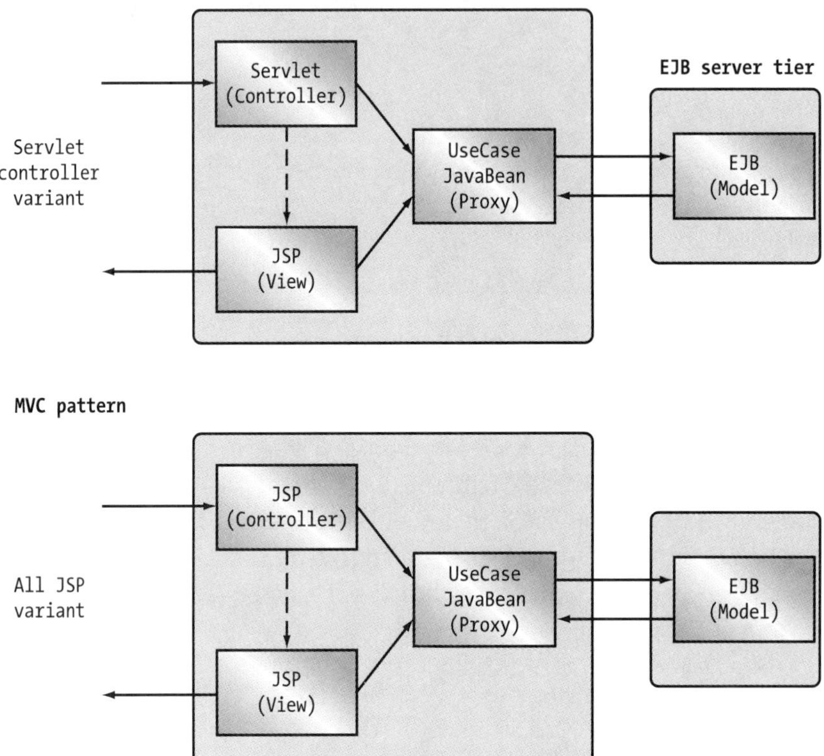

Figure 5-42. Frequently used system-wide design pattern for collaborating components or class clusters when developing a Web application system

Briefly consider the functionalities and call order of the two front-end entities (in other words, the controller and view of the MVC design pattern). The tasks of the three objects in the pattern are:

- *Controller* reacts to the input and commands sent by the user. Any capture of user-supplied data or command parameters is handled by the controller servlet. When finished in reading all data provided by the user, the controller servlet updates the model to incorporate the commands from the user.

- *Model* holds the business object state and behavior. All system entities should be held and manipulated within an application server. Figure 5-42 illustrates the standard J2EE model that assumes an enterprise JavaBeans (EJB) server as the application server. An application server of some type should always be used, unless the system is sufficiently small that the model can be included in the controller or view. Such design is recommended only for the smallest of systems. The dynamic data required by the view is read from the model and sent to the view encapsulated within a JavaBean instance.

- *View* defines non-dynamic HTML code areas and joins it with the dynamic data extracted from the model. The actual joining is performed by calling JavaBean getter property methods in the value object, holding model data.

The joining of dynamic and static data presents a fundamental problem, as two professional roles must work together to create the final result. The developer is responsible for the dynamic data, and the Web designer/content manager is responsible for the static data of the view. The system code must be shielded from improper modifications (such as tampering with the JSP tag syntax) by mistake—enforcing data encapsulation in the server tier reduces the risk of having somebody corrupting the JSP document.

Tag library definitions and customized server-side tags provide a good way of encapsulating the data from the model. In general, more encapsulated and data-wise hidden modes of operations tend to be more stable in the long run. Also, simpler models and modes of usage tend to have a rewarding quality about themselves.

The Apache framework Struts uses the model illustrated in Figure 5-42. Refer to `http://jakarta.apache.org/struts/` for a reference to the Struts architecture—or the next chapter for a walkthrough.

CHAPTER 6

JSP Examples

THE MORE ABSTRACT A TECHNOLOGY gets, the more difficult it can be to determine its usefulness. In many cases, however, using a particular set of Java APIs simply requires understanding the order and name of the life-cycle methods to invoke.

Because new technologies are quickest taught by example, this chapter is a walkthrough of the JSP and TLD technologies that were introduced in the last two chapters. To focus on the J2EE platform, the examples in this chapter include a deployment settings section, "Deploying the JSP Document in a J2EE Server," which guides you to a fast deployment of the documents within a J2EE-compliant Web application server. Now let's get started.

Using JSP Standard Objects

To warm up, start by creating a JSP document that investigates properties and parameters sent into it by the browser client, as well as standard JSP engine objects such as the content of the Session scope table. The JSP version of the servlet introspector (which you encountered in bits and pieces in Chapter 2 and 3) contains significantly more HTML layout code and a little less Java code. The JSP document that produces the resulting view is called `inspector.jsp`. To demonstrate the power of the J2EE deployment descriptors, you'll create two separate JSP mappings for the `inspector.jsp` file: `showMethodNames` and `showUserFriendlyNames`. The two mappings contain initialization parameter settings that alter the way in which data is presented to the user. Shortly, you'll take a look at the first of the two resulting outputs that has been split into three separate figures due to their length.

Moreover, the example will be run on two different application servers: the Tomcat 4.0 application server and the Orion Application Server (OAS) version 1.4.7 from Ironflare AB. If you compare the resulting outputs, you'll note some of the implementation differences between these two servers. But here is a picture of the J2EE specification in a nutshell: two servers that are internally completely different may deploy and run a single (Web) application in an almost identical manner.

The Class Names and Engine Info Sections

A healthy level of paranoia is required to attain "star" developer status; you must know better than to trust the specification or the vendor documentation for a particular server, because responses are handled slightly differently in different application servers. As you will see, this is also true for the two application servers chosen for this example. An experienced J2EE server-side developer knows better than to trust product documentations implicitly, just as any experienced Java developer regards the level of portability of a Java application in different virtual machines. In short, you are wise to follow the almost-Java principle: "Code once, test everywhere."

First, you'll take a look at Figure 6-1, 6-2, and 6-3, which illustrate the output of the JSP document. Then you'll look at its code.

> **NOTE** *At the time of writing, the Servlet 2.3 API is being implemented and deployed (rather than being fully deployed already) in most Web application servers, including the OAS. By the time this book is published, support is likely to have been augmented in all application servers; be sure to check your application server documentation.*

Figure 6-1. The implementation class names of some significant classes in the Orion Application Server servlet engine. Note that the JSP engine information (retrieved with the call to `JspFactory.getDefaultFactory().getEngineInfo().getSpecificationVersion();`*) does not compile in this version of the Orion Application Server.*

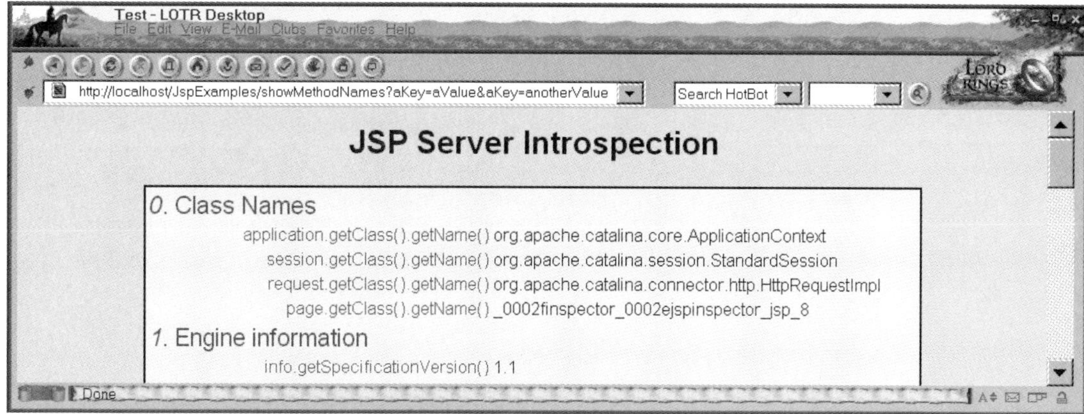

Figure 6-2. The implementation class names of the Tomcat 4.0 servlet engine are quite different from those of the Orion Application Server, as seen in Figure 6-1.

The "0. Class Names" part of Figure 6-1 and 6-2 reveals shallow type information of the four scope objects, as well as the JSP version supported by the JSP engine. This information is provided to show that different Web application servers implement the required standard interfaces in potentially different ways. Of course, developers do not need to learn the exact types of the implementation classes for any given application server; they may simply use the superclasses or superinterfaces that are part of the standard J2EE API.

Comparing the responses of the OAS and Tomcat, the most surprising piece of information is that the OAS version 1.4.7 engine does not yet implement the `JspFactory.getDefaultFactory().getEngineInfo().getSpecificationVersion();` method. Then again, how often do your JSP documents query the JSP engine for version information and react in different ways depending on the result? This piece of information potentially has great significance, but the real-life systems that this author has had the pleasure of working with have never accessed this particular piece of information because it has not been available as a standard call until the Servlet API version 2.3.

The Request object provides a more interesting comparison between the differences of our two chosen Web application servers. Onward!

The Request Object

The information in the former section may have been of a less important nature (you will rarely if ever need to use anything but the standard J2EE classes), but the content of the Request object is far more important and frequently used. There is no room for errors when handling the data of a user request. If run in the Orion Application Server, the information from the Request object becomes what you see in Figure 6-3. For comparison, the Request metadata from the Tomcat reference implementation engine is shown in Figure 6-4.

> **NOTE** *The servlet path and request URI all reflect the existing mapping between the JSP document (*`inspector.jsp`*) and its alias (*`showMethodNames`*) which is set up in the* `web.xml` *configuration document. (Refer to "Deploying the JSP Document in a J233 Server" later in this chapter for detailed information about the deployment descriptor.)*

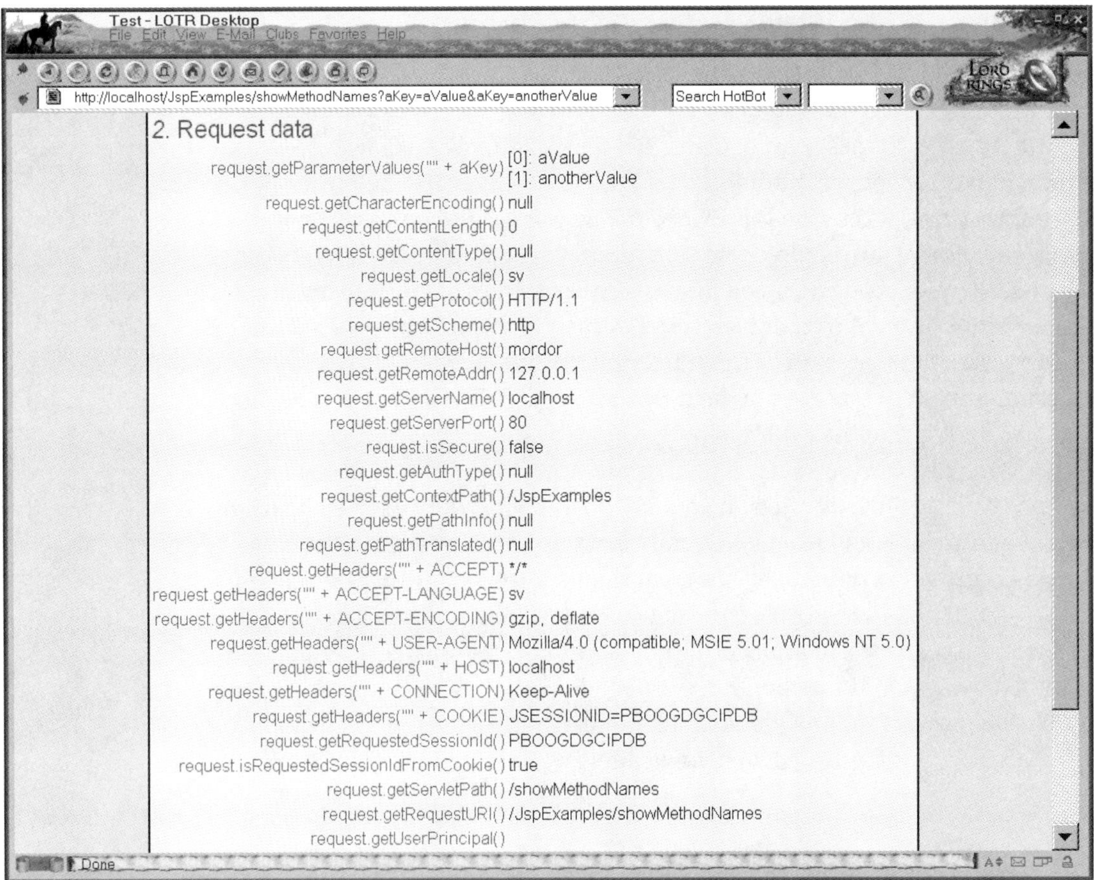

Figure 6-3. Data gathered from the request object, when the `inspector.jsp` *file is run in OAS*

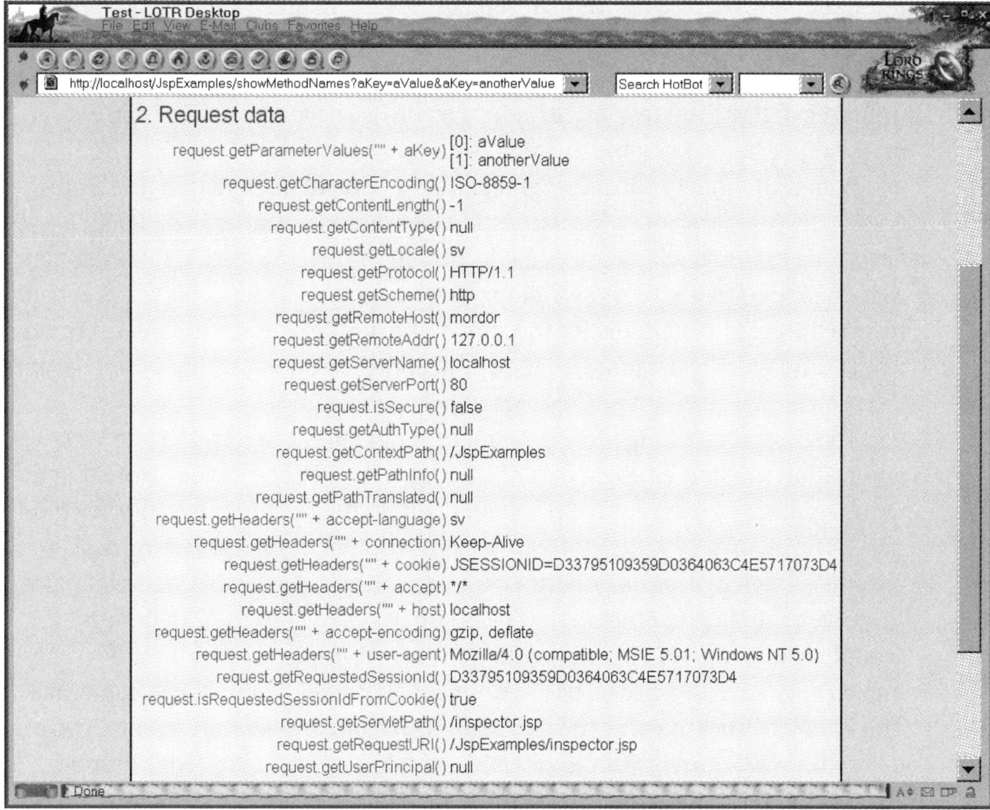

Figure 6-4. Data gathered from the Request object, when the `inspector.jsp` *file is run in the Tomcat 4.0 reference engine*

> **NOTE** *The servlet path and request URI all reflect the actual name and path of the JSP document (*`inspector.jsp`*), and not its alias (*`showMethodNames`*) which is set up in the* `web.xml` *configuration document. (Refer to "Deploying the JSP Document in a J233 Server" later in this chapter for detailed information about the deployment descriptor.)*

The binary world of application servers has its twists and surprises for most developers. Although both Web application servers properly handle the most important data gathered from the request (such as parameters and headers), there are significant differences in the presentation of less frequently used request data. Whereas the Tomcat server finds the character encoding to be ISO-8859-1, the OAS simply disregards that value. Also, the Tomcat reference implementation correctly presents the content length of the request as –1 (which indicates that the request length is "unknown"). The Orion Application Server, on the other hand, presents the request length as 0.

Both the Orion Application Server and the Tomcat reference engine store the session ID cookie as an HTTP request header using the name JSESSIONID, according to the specification. Such information can be valuable to developers, as in this case, where we know that the user's browser must be able to accept and resend the cookie unaltered for the server to maintain the session. All users who want to maintain a session with the application servers must, therefore, permit the browser to use client-side cookies.

The most interesting part of the request data presented by the two Web application servers is the last part of data from the Request object. Note that the Orion Application Server uses the actual URI, as the documentation of method `javax.servlet.http.HttpServletRequest.getRequestURI()` states. The Tomcat reference implementation, on the other hand, uses the translated servlet path.

Given the speed of the server development to achieve J2EE standards compliance, it isn't very surprising that the server implementations differ. These implementation differences cause the output of JSP documents to differ somewhat. The moral: be sure to verify the exact results of your application server if you are depending on them for your application development—it is unwise to trust application server documentation.

Now move along to study some data from the `HttpSession` object, received from the two Web application servers.

The HttpSession Object

The `HttpSession` instance is one of the most important and frequently used objects in a servlet/JSP engine. If any interface should be implemented to work identically across Web application server types, the `HttpSession` is a strong candidate.

Now take a look at the third (and last!) of the data sections presented in this example, starting with the result from the Orion Application Server as shown in Figure 6-5.

All values, save the default session timeout, work in an identical manner in the Tomcat reference implementation engine. (See Figure 6-6.)

After taking a look at the resulting output of a JSP document, you should study the code of the JSP document to see how the output was generated.

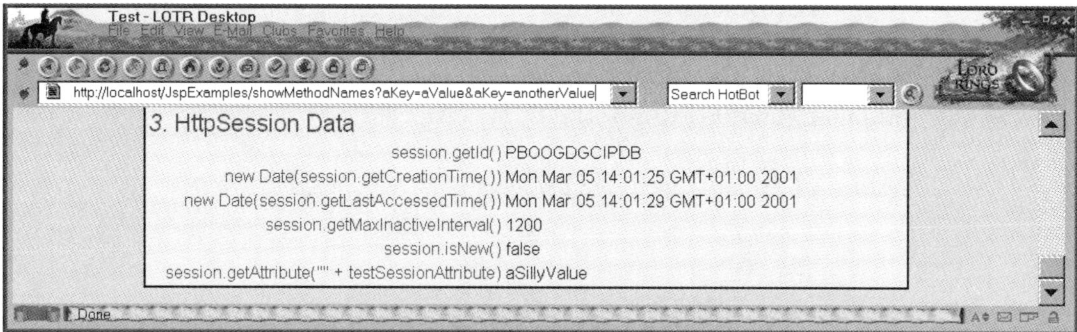

Figure 6-5. The `HttpSession` *instance of the Orion Application Server has a default timeout of 1,200 seconds (= 20 minutes).*

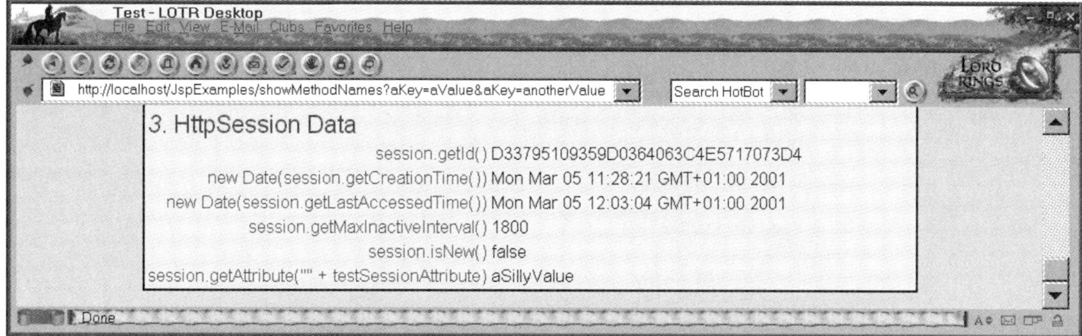

Figure 6-6. The `HttpSession` *instance of the Tomcat reference implementation engine has a default timeout of 1,800 seconds (= 30 minutes).*

The JSP Document

The output in Figure 6-6 is produced solely from the JSP document using the standard scope objects for reference points. Thus, all the code is encapsulated within the JSP document. This is normally unwise; most application business logic should be placed in a J2EE application communicating with the JSP document. This example studies only certain aspects of the Web application server, so we need not involve the application server at all.

The JSP document (`inspector.jsp`) is capable of serving its data in two different forms. If invoked using its alias `showMethodNames`, the left column contains the method name used to produce the results in the right column. If, on the other hand, the JSP document is invoked using its other alias (`showUserFriendlyNames`), the data in the left column contains a user-friendly description of the data presented in the right column.

Before investigating the JSP document in depth, examine the patterns used to achieve the result. Start by investigating a single row within the HttpSession section. (See Listing 6-1.) The methods getting the data shown in the resulting output of Figure 6-1 to 6-6 is bolded in Listing 6-1.

Listing 6-1. Pattern used to extract data in the HttpSession section

```
<tr>
    <%!--
        This is a definition cell; use the predefined style îdef-
        from the Cascading Style Sheet used by this JSP document.
    --%>
    <td class="def">
        <%= get("Is New?") %>
    </td>

    <%!--
        This is an explanation cell; use the predefined style îexpl-
        from the Cascading Style Sheet used by this JSP document.
    --%>
    <td class="expl">
        <%= session.isNew() %>
    </td>
</tr>
```

The CSS `class` attributes contain view formatting information for the cells, and are not part of the Java compilation or interpretation of the JSP document. However, the first of the two table cells in the row contains a JavaBean property name (`isNew`), and the next cell displays the current property value. The JavaBean property name may be presented as the method name used to retrieve its value or as a user-friendly static text describing the property. As indicated in the pattern above, the method `String get(String aKeyName)` is used to retrieve the property name. The implementation of the get method is pretty simple: if a Boolean variable called useMethodNames is true, the method name of the particular user-friendly description is returned. Otherwise, the description itself is returned.

The get method is required to be able to present the data in the left column in two different ways. Now take a look at a slightly simplified version of its code (Listing 6-2.) To simplify the listing and reduce irrelevant code bloat, a couple of method calls logging variable status are not present in this version of the get method.

Listing 6-2. The get and set methods permit switching between user-friendly and fully qualified Java.

```
// Method that returns the proper key
private String get(String userFriendlyDescription)
     {
          // Should we use full method names?
          if(useMethodNames)
          {
               return displayData.get(userFriendlyDescription);
          }

          // Simply return the userFriendlyDescription itself
          return userFriendlyDescription;
     }
```

Each row in the tables that contain simple property getter methods follow the pattern just described. However, for iterative/indexed properties, the pattern differs slightly, as shown in Listing 6-3. Again, the code that actually produces the output shown in Figures 6-1 to 6-6 is bolded.

Listing 6-3. Standard pattern for showing the values of a Vector variable in Figures 6-1 to 6-6

```
<%--
     Loop through all request headers.
     Output the key and value of each of them.
--%>
<%
     Enumeration en = request.getHeaderNames();
     if(!en.hasMoreElements())
          out.write("<tr><td class=\"def\">No Headers found. </td>
                    <td></td></tr>");
     else
     {
          while(en.hasMoreElements())
          {
               // Define variables
               Object key = en.nextElement();
               Enumeration vals = request.getHeaders("" + key);
%>
```

```
        <tr>
            <td class="def">
                <%= (useMethodNames
                  ? "request.getParameterValues(\"\" + " + key + ")"
                  : "Parameter: " + key) %>
            </td>

            <td class="expl">
                <%
                    while(vals.hasMoreElements()) {
                    out.println("" + vals.nextElement() + "<br>");
                    }
                %>
            </td>
<%
            } // End while
        } // End else
%>
```

> **TIP** *The ("" + instance) in this code is a quick way to convert instance to a String, using the* `public String toString()` *method. The* `toString()` *method is defined in* `java.lang`*.Object, so any type of object may be converted to a String.*

The main difference between these two patterns is that the latter pattern writes all values for each key to the output `JspWriter`. These two patterns are the only code patterns used in the JSP document. Because the standard objects (application, page, request, and session) are already defined for us by the JSP-to-servlet compiler, this example is a straightforward matter of finding the proper method names to call to expose the requested properties. However, the document itself (shown in Listing 6-4) is rather large, due to the excessive amount of HTML/formatting commands.

Listing 6-4. Source of the `inspector.jsp` *document*

```
<%-- import all required classes --%>
<%@ page import="java.util.*,java.io.*" %>

<%!
    // Declare a Map containing the data to display
    private Map displayData;
```

```
// Switch to control if all keys displayed in this
// document should be
// true)      method names, or
// false)     user-friendly descriptions
boolean useMethodNames = true;

// Method that returns the proper key
private String get(String aKeyName)
{
     // Should we use full method names?
     if(useMethodNames)
     {
          String got = "" + displayData.get(aKeyName);
          System.out.println("[get]: got: " + got);
          return got;
     }

     // Simply return the keyName itself
     return aKeyName;
}

public void jspInit()
{
     // Get the init parameter useMethodNames to decide whether
     // or not this JSP document should present method names or
     // user friendly names in the left column of the resulting
     // output.
     String str = getServletConfig().getInitParameter("useMethodNames");
     if(str != null) useMethodNames = str.trim().equalsIgnoreCase("true");

     // Log the results ?
     // System.out.println("[jspInit()] Got str: " + str + ", made bool: "
                          + useMethodNames);

     // Create the displayData Map
     displayData = Collections.synchronizedMap(new TreeMap());

     // Populate the displayData Map
     displayData.put("application",
                    "application.getClass().getName()");
     displayData.put("session", "session.getClass().getName()");
     displayData.put("request",  "request.getClass().getName()");
     displayData.put("page",     "page.getClass().getName()");
```

```
            // Put the Jsp Engine information into the displayData Map
            displayData.put("Jsp Engine Info", "info.getSpecificationVersion()");

            // Put the Request data into the displayData Map
            displayData.put("Parameter", "request.getParameterValues(");
            displayData.put("Character Encoding",
                            "request.getCharacterEncoding()");
            displayData.put("Content Length", "request.getContentLength()");
            displayData.put("Content Type",   "request.getContentType()");
            displayData.put("Locale",         "request.getLocale()");
            displayData.put("Protocol",       "request.getProtocol()");
            displayData.put("Scheme",         "request.getScheme()");
            displayData.put("Remote Host",    "request.getRemoteHost()");
            displayData.put("Remote Address", "request.getRemoteAddr()");
            displayData.put("Server Name",    "request.getServerName()");
            displayData.put("Server Port",    "request.getServerPort()");
            displayData.put("Server Name",    "request.getServerName()");
            displayData.put("Secure",         "request.isSecure()");
            displayData.put("Auth Type",      "request.getAuthType()");
            displayData.put("Context Path",   "request.getContextPath()");
            displayData.put("Path Info",      "request.getPathInfo()");
            displayData.put("Path Translated","request.getPathTranslated()");
            displayData.put("Requested Session Id",
                            "request.getRequestedSessionId()");
            displayData.put("Using Cookie?",
                            "request.isRequestedSessionIdFromCookie()");
            displayData.put("Servlet Path",   "request.getServletPath()");
            displayData.put("Request URI",    "request.getRequestURI()");
            displayData.put("User Principal", "request.getUserPrincipal()");

            // Put the session data into the displayData Map
            displayData.put("Id",             "session.getId()");
            displayData.put("Creation Time",  "new Date(session.getCreationTime())");
            displayData.put("Last Accessed Time",
                            "new Date(session.getLastAccessedTime())");
            displayData.put("New Session?",   "session.isNew()");
            displayData.put("Max Inactive
                            Interval","session.getMaxInactiveInterval()");

        }
%>
```

```
<%
     // Get the JspEngineInfo
     JspEngineInfo info = JspFactory.getDefaultFactory().getEngineInfo();
%>

<html>
<head>
     <title>Test </title>
     <style type="text/css" ref>
          @import url(style.css);
     </style>
</head>
<body>
<center>

     <h1>JSP Server Introspection</h1>


     <table border="0" bgcolor="#000000" cellspacing="1">
     <tr><td>
          <table border="0" bgcolor="#eeffaa">

          <tr>
          <td class="header" colspan="2">
               <i class="header">0</i>. Class Names
          </td>
          </tr>

          <tr>
          <td class="def">
               <%= get("application") %>
          </td>

          <td class="expl">
               <%--     Note how small the ratio Java code to HTML
                    is in this document. That may prove a blessing to
                    HTML hackers, but is less of an advantage to the
                    normal Java developer. --%>
               <%= application.getClass().getName() %>
          </td>
          </tr>
```

```
<tr>
<td class="def">
     <%= get("session") %>
</td>

<td class="expl">
     <%= session.getClass().getName() %>
</td>
</tr>

<tr>
<td class="def">
     <%= get("request") %>
</td>

<td class="expl">
     <%= request.getClass().getName() %>
</td>
</tr>

<tr>
<td class="def">
     <%= get("page") %>
</td>

<td class="expl">
     <%= page.getClass().getName() %>
</td>
</tr>

<tr>
<td class="header" colspan="2">
     <i class="header">1</i>. Engine information
</td>
</tr>

<tr>
<td class="def">
     <%= get("Jsp Engine Info") %>
</td>

<td class="expl">
     <%= info.getSpecificationVersion() %>
</td>
</tr>
```

```
<tr>
<td class="header" colspan="2">
     <i class="header">2</i>. Request data
</td>
</tr>

<%--
     Loop through all request parameters.
     Output the key and value of them all.
--%>
<%
     for(Enumeration en = request.getParameterNames();
          en.hasMoreElements(); )
     {
          // Define variables
          Object key = en.nextElement();
          String[] vals = request.getParameterValues("" + key);
%>

<tr>
<td class="def">
     <%= (useMethodNames
         ? "request.getParameterValues(\"\" + " + key + ")"
         : "Parameter: " + key) %>
</td>

<td class="expl">
     <%
          for(int j = 0; j < vals.length; j++)
          {
               out.println("[" + j + "]: " + vals[j] + "<br>");
          }
     %>
<%
     } // End for
%>
</tr>

<tr>
<td class="def">
     <%= get("Character Encoding") %>
</td>
```

```
<td class="expl">
     <%= request.getCharacterEncoding() %>
</td>
</tr>

<tr>
<td class="def">
     <%= get("Content Length") %>
</td>

<td class="expl">
     <%= request.getContentLength() %>
</td>
</tr>

<tr>
<td class="def">
     <%= get("Content Type") %>
</td>

<td class="expl">
     <%= request.getContentType() %>
</td>
</tr>

<tr>
<td class="def">
     <%= get("Locale") %>
</td>

<td class="expl">
     <%= request.getLocale() %>
</td>
</tr>

<tr>
<td class="def">
     <%= get("Protocol") %>
</td>

<td class="expl">
     <%= request.getProtocol() %>
</td>
</tr>
```

```
<tr>
<td class="def">
     <%= get("Scheme") %>
</td>

<td class="expl">
     <%= request.getScheme() %>
</td>
</tr>

<tr>
<td class="def">
     <%= get("Remote Host") %>
</td>

<td class="expl">
     <%= request.getRemoteHost() %>
</td>
</tr>

<tr>
<td class="def">
     <%= get("Remote Address") %>
</td>

<td class="expl">
     <%= request.getRemoteAddr() %>
</td>
</tr>


<tr>
<td class="def">
     <%= get("Server Name") %>
</td>

<td class="expl">
     <%= request.getServerName() %>
</td>
</tr>

<tr>
<td class="def">
     <%= get("Server Port") %>
</td>
```

```
<td class="expl">
     <%= request.getServerPort() %>
</td>
</tr>

<tr>
<td class="def">
     <%= get("Secure") %>
</td>

<td class="expl">
     <%= request.isSecure() %>
</td>
</tr>


<tr>
<td class="def">
     <%= get("Auth Type") %>
</td>

<td class="expl">
     <%= request.getAuthType() %>
</td>
</tr>

<tr>
<td class="def">
     <%= get("Context Path") %>
</td>

<td class="expl">
     <%= request.getContextPath() %>
</td>

<tr>
<td class="def">
     <%= get("Path Info") %>
</td>

<td class="expl">
     <%= request.getPathInfo() %>
</td>
```

```
<tr>
<td class="def">
     <%= get("Path Translated") %>
</td>

<td class="expl">
     <%= request.getPathTranslated() %>
</td>

</tr>

<%--
     Loop through all request headers.
     Output the key and value of them all.
--%>
<%
     Enumeration en = request.getHeaderNames();
     if(!en.hasMoreElements())
          out.write("<tr><td class=\"def\"> "
          + "No Headers found.</td><td></td></tr>");
     else {
     while(en.hasMoreElements())
     {
          // Define variables
          Object key = en.nextElement();
          Enumeration vals = request.getHeaders("" + key);
%>

<tr>
<td class="def">
     <%= (useMethodNames
          ? "request.getHeaders(\"\" + " + key + ")"
          : "Header: " + key) %>
</td>

<td class="expl">
     <%
          while(vals.hasMoreElements())
          {
               out.println("" + vals.nextElement() + "<br>");
          }
     %>
</td>
<%
     } // End while
%>
```

```
</tr>
<%
} // End else
%>

<tr>
<td class="def">
     <%= get("Requested Session Id") %>
</td>

<td class="expl">
     <%= request.getRequestedSessionId() %>
</td>
</tr>

<tr>
<td class="def">
     <%= get("Using Cookie?") %>
</td>

<td class="expl">
     <%= request.isRequestedSessionIdFromCookie() %>
</td>
</tr>

<tr>
<td class="def">
     <%= get("Servlet Path") %>
</td>

<td class="expl">
     <%= request.getServletPath() %>
</td>
</tr>

<tr>
<td class="def">
     <%= get("Request URI") %>
</td>

<td class="expl">
     <%= request.getRequestURI() %>
</td>
</tr>
```

```
<tr>
<td class="def">
    <%= get("User Principal") %>
</td>

<td class="expl">
    <%= request.getUserPrincipal() %>
</td>
</tr>

<tr>
<td class="header" colspan="2">
    <i class="header">3</i>. HttpSession Data
</td>
</tr>

<tr>
<td class="def">
    <%= get("Id") %>
</td>

<td class="expl">
    <%= session.getId() %>
</td>
</tr>

<tr>
<td class="def">
    <%= get("Creation Time") %>
</td>

<td class="expl">
    <%= new Date(session.getCreationTime()) %>
</td>
</tr>

<tr>
<td class="def">
    <%= get("Last Accessed Time") %>
</td>

<td class="expl">
    <%= new Date(session.getLastAccessedTime()) %>
</td>
</tr>
```

```
<tr>
<td class="def">
     <%= get("Max Inactive Interval") %>
</td>

<td class="expl">
     <%= session.getMaxInactiveInterval() %>
</td>
</tr>

<tr>
<td class="def">
     <%= get("New Session?") %>
</td>

<td class="expl">
     <%= session.isNew() %>
</td>
</tr>
<%--
     Loop through all session attributes.
     Output the key and value of them all.
--%>
<%
     session.setAttribute("testSessionAttribute", "aSillyValue");

     en = session.getAttributeNames();
     if(!en.hasMoreElements())
          out.write("<tr><td class=\"def\">"
          + "No Attributes found.</td><td></td></tr>");
     else {
     while(en.hasMoreElements())
     {
          // Define variables
          Object key = en.nextElement();
          Object val = session.getAttribute("" + key);
%>

<tr>
<td class="def">
     <%= (useMethodNames
          ? "session.getAttribute(\"\" + " + key + ")"
          : "Attribute: " + key) %>
</td>
```

```
        <td class="expl">
            <%= val %>
        </td>
        <%
            } // End while
            } // End else
        %>
        </tr>

        </table>
    </td></tr>
    </table>


</center>
</body>
</html>
```

Deploying the JSP Document in a J2EE Server

One of the benefits of JSP technology is that you aren't required to create complex deployment descriptors to deploy, autocompile, and run a JSP document in a J2EE server. We could, quite frankly, completely disregard the J2EE Web application descriptor for all JSP documents—especially if they are trivial documents simply presenting a view.

What is gained from performing a full J2EE deployment with a JSP document? The simple answer is *flexibility*. A properly deployed servlet or JSP document may accept two different initialization parameter settings for two different servlet or JSP mappings (J2EE aliases). A single document may therefore behave quite differently in a Web application server if called under two different URLs. This is an example of runtime flexibility that cannot be provided unless one uses J2EE mappings for JSP documents, as provided in the `web.xml` configuration document.

The structure of the deployed document and its deployment descriptor deserves a bit of elaboration. A J2EE Web application has a simple structure, as seen in Figure 6-7. Apart from a CSS style document, the only two files in the J2EE application are `inspector.jsp` and `web.xml`.

The structure of the `web.xml` document is given by the Web-application document type definition (DTD), which may be downloaded from `http://java.sun.com/j2ee/dtds/web-app_2_3.dtd`. (For examples of `web.xml` files, refer to Chapter 3.) The deployment descriptor in Figure 6-7 deploys a minimalist Web application, containing two servlet mappings referring to one

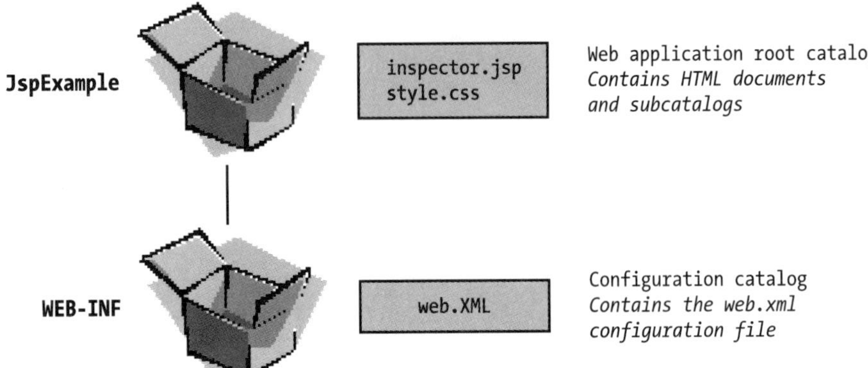

Figure 6-7. Minimalist deployment structure of a J2EE Web application

defined JSP document. Its code is shown in Listing 6-5, in which the JSP definition specifications have been bolded.

Listing 6-5. The `web.xml` *deployment descriptor*

```
<?xml version="1.0"?>
<!DOCTYPE web-app PUBLIC
         "-//Sun Microsystems, Inc.//DTD Web Application 2.3//EN"
         "http://java.sun.com/j2ee/dtds/web-app_2_3.dtd">

<web-app>
     <display-name>ServletBookWeb</display-name>
     <servlet>
          <servlet-name>inspectJspEngine</servlet-name>
          <display-name>inspectJspEngine</display-name>
          <description>
                    Runs inspector.jsp displaying user
                    friendly aliases for each method invoked.
          </description>
          <jsp-file>/inspector.jsp</jsp-file>
          <init-param>
               <param-name>useMethodNames</param-name>
               <param-value>false</param-value>
          </init-param>
     </servlet>
```

```
    <servlet>
        <servlet-name>inspectUsingMethodNames</servlet-name>
        <display-name>inspectUsingMethodNames</display-name>
        <description>
                Runs inspector.jsp displaying method
                names for each method invoked.
        </description>
        <jsp-file>/inspector.jsp</jsp-file>
        <init-param>
            <param-name>useMethodNames</param-name>
            <param-value>true</param-value>
        </init-param>
    </servlet>
    <servlet-mapping>
        <servlet-name>inspectJspEngine</servlet-name>
        <url-pattern>/showUserFriendlyNames</url-pattern>
    </servlet-mapping>
    <servlet-mapping>
        <servlet-name>inspectUsingMethodNames</servlet-name>
        <url-pattern>/showMethodNames</url-pattern>
    </servlet-mapping>
</web-app>
```

The `web.xml` deployment descriptor provides two servlet mappings (URLs `/showUserFriendlyNames` and `/showMethodNames`) to the same JSP document, `inspector.jsp`. The difference between the two mappings lies in the different initialization parameters; the environment parameter useMethodNames is set to `true` for the `/showMethodNames` mapping, and `false` for the `/showUserFriendlyNames` mapping.

So far, all of the figures in this example have invoked the `inspector.jsp` document using its servlet mapping inspectJspEngine (that is, the URL `/showMethodNames`). However, the `inspector.jsp` document may be invoked with another mapping (`/showUserFriendlyNames`) that displays user-friendly inspection keys instead of programmatic method names. The `/showMethodNames` may be helpful to programmers, but a display of method names will certainly not make a curious normal user any wiser.

The output of the `/showUserFriendlyNames` servlet mapping is quite similar to the previous `/showMethodNames` mapping: all values displayed in the right column are identical, but all keys displayed in the left column have changed to a user-friendly text instead of the method names seen in Figures 6-2 to 6-6. Figure 6-8 displays a partial listing of this servlet mapping.

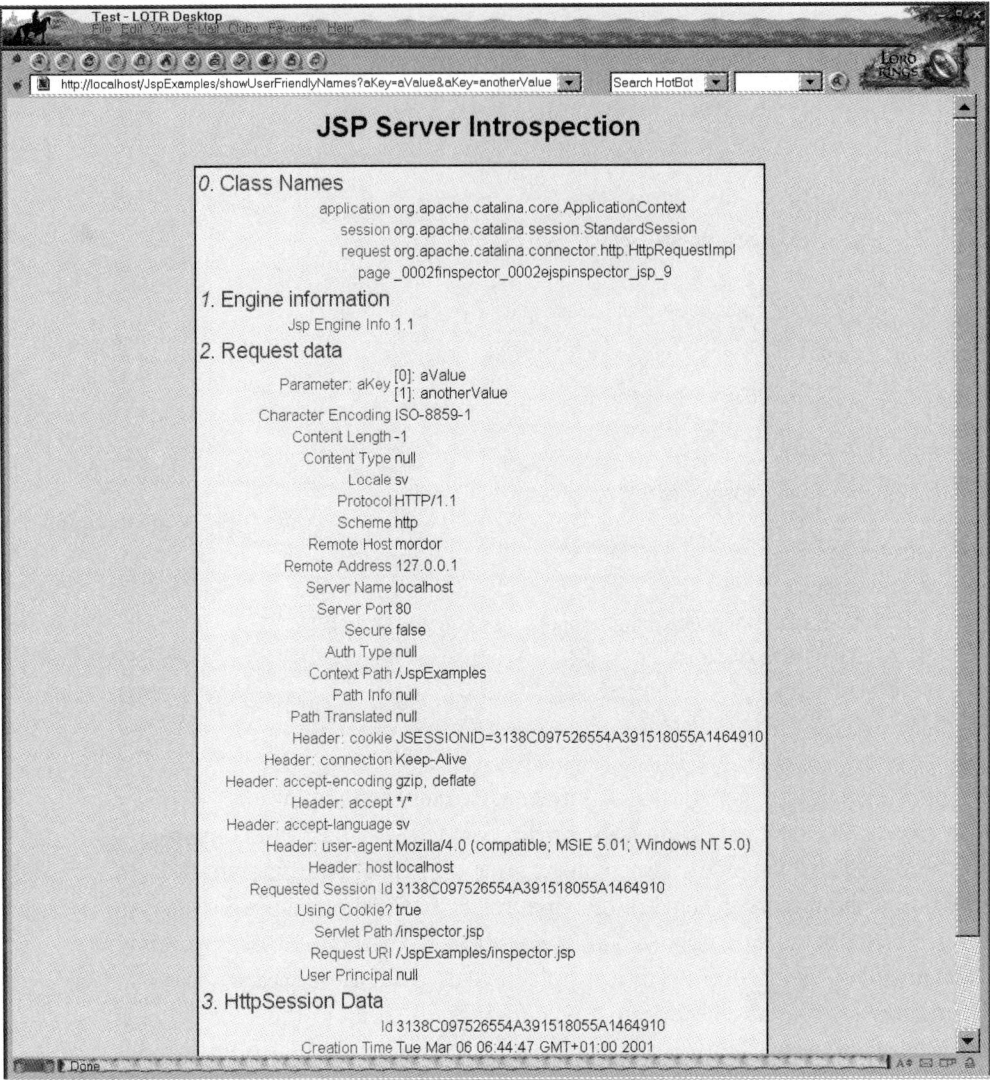

Figure 6-8. The `/showUserFriendlyNames` *servlet mapping calls the* `inspector.jsp` *document, just as does the* `/showMethodNames mapping`*. However, the* `/showUserFriendlyNames` *mapping has replaced all method names from the* `/showMethodNames` *with a user-friendly text.*

Reflections on the Standard JSP Objects

Where should business logic be placed in a distributed system, such as a Web application? Sometimes, the art of distributing business logic properly in the system is a bit like a medieval dance—for every two steps forward, you must take at least one step back. The choices you make for deployment inevitably tend to reduce system flexibility at a larger scale, either by reducing the options available to the system as a whole or by making the system more complex (which reduces the number of people who will understand it). For Web applications in general and this example in particular, distributing the business logic is a delicate and important issue.

This example reflects one of the more drastic choices: placing all business logic (Java code) in the JSP document. Chapter 3 contains similar introspective code that runs within a servlet, rather than a JSP document. The result is a rather compact yet unmanageable system. The JSP document in this example becomes extremely bloated due to the repetition of HTML formatting tags, but the business logic remains simple.

Whenever you want to alter the layout or business logic flow of the system, you are required to recompile several documents. Moreover, error tracing is a real nightmare in a system of combined JSP and servlet documents in which code is distributed throughout the system documents. The business logic should—as much as possible—be kept away from the JSP (view) document. The Apache Struts framework is a good example of a structure that strives to separate the business logic from the view.

Both servlet and JSP technology have advantages for certain tasks, but neither servlets nor JSP documents alone can provide an acceptable solution for encapsulating server-side business logic. Most systems use servlets for system controllers and JSP documents to implement the view. This is generally known as the "MVC model 2" (or simply "Model 2") pattern.

> **NOTE** *Refer to Chapter 7 for a walkthrough of the Struts framework and Model 2.*

Custom JSP Tags-Nesting and Looping

The custom-made server-side tag specification provides a set of powerful scripting constructs that behave similar to scripting macros. Macros are mainly used in scripting languages that need controlled execution flow—in other words, programming constructs such as iteration and selection. You would use macros instead of the pure programming constructs simply to facilitate reading and increase encapsulation. This example shows how you may reduce the amount of Java code in the view document by using JSP tags roughly as macros.

You will create two custom JSP tags that need to collaborate to produce the resulting output; a parent tag defines scripting variables that are used by the contained child tag. You will therefore study a very common concept that inevitably arises in the JSP world: nested custom tags that use iteration to print the elements in a collection. Having that in mind, you will have two JSP tags loop over a set of prominent classes in the JSP engine and display their introspection information (that is, inheritance trees and type information). Figure 6-9 displays the result of the collaborating tags presented in the output view.

Running the same JSP document in another application server yields rather different results regarding the internal class structure. For example, Figure 6-10 shows the output when running with Evermind's OAS.

Classes of the JSP Class Inspector Example

The JSP document has four main helper objects:

- **`HashMap`** stores the objects and their user-friendly display names. The display name is stored as the `HashMap` entry's key, and the object itself is stored as the entry's value.

- **`PrintTypeTreeTag`** is our looping tag. It iterates through the `HashMap`, exposing each entry in turn. The entry's key is exposed as a scripting variable, `targetName`, which can be printed using a JSP expression (such as `<%= targetName %>`). The `PrintTypeTreeTag` requires assistance from a `TagExtraInfo` class because it defines a scripting variable.

- The **`TagExtraInfo`** class contains variable definition specifications and optional translation-time validation of the tag attributes. The `PrintTypeTreeExtraInfo` tag contains data that assists the JSP engine in creating the Java code corresponding to a variable declaration and optional data validation. When the JSP engine executes the code of a `TagExtraInfo` class, it outputs text into the source code of an intermediate Java class. The intermediate Java class is what gets compiled into a servlet, and the result of the `TagExtraInfo` class is a variable declaration (that is, something like `String aString = "ThisIsADefaultValue";`).

- For each object instance in the `HashMap`, **`DisplayClassTag`** performs introspection and displays class names of all superclasses and implemented interfaces of the object. The `DisplayClassTag` reads the object to be introspected from the `PrintTypeTreeTag` handler, so the tag displaying the value of the scripting variable (`<%= targetName %>`) must be contained within the body of the `PrintTypeTree` tag.

Figure 6-11 sums up the mechanics of each of these objects.

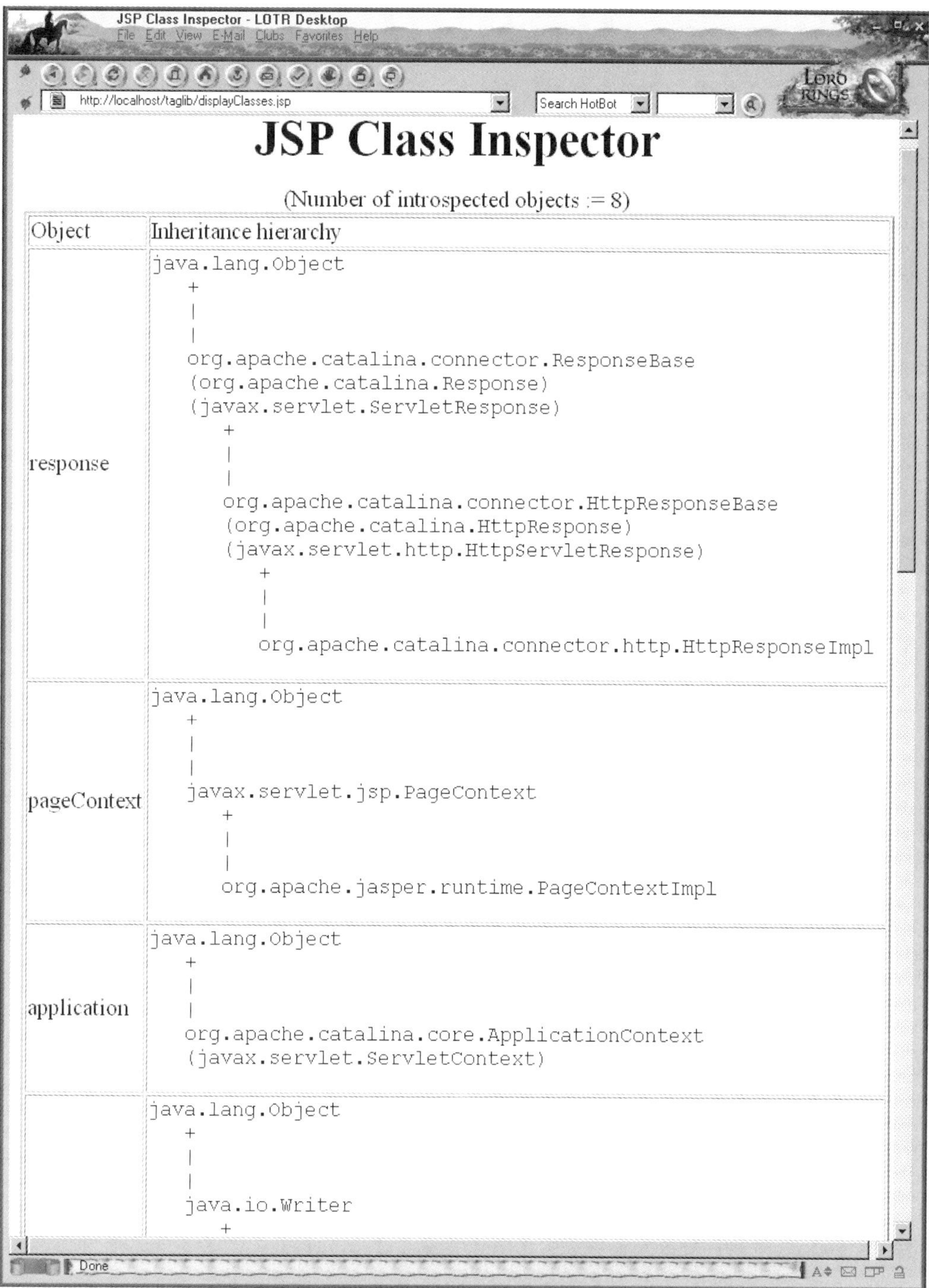

Figure 6-9. The introspected class information of a few of the prominent servlet and JSP classes. Interfaces types are shown in parenthesis; class types are not. The classes and interfaces are specific to the Tomcat 4.0 Web application server.

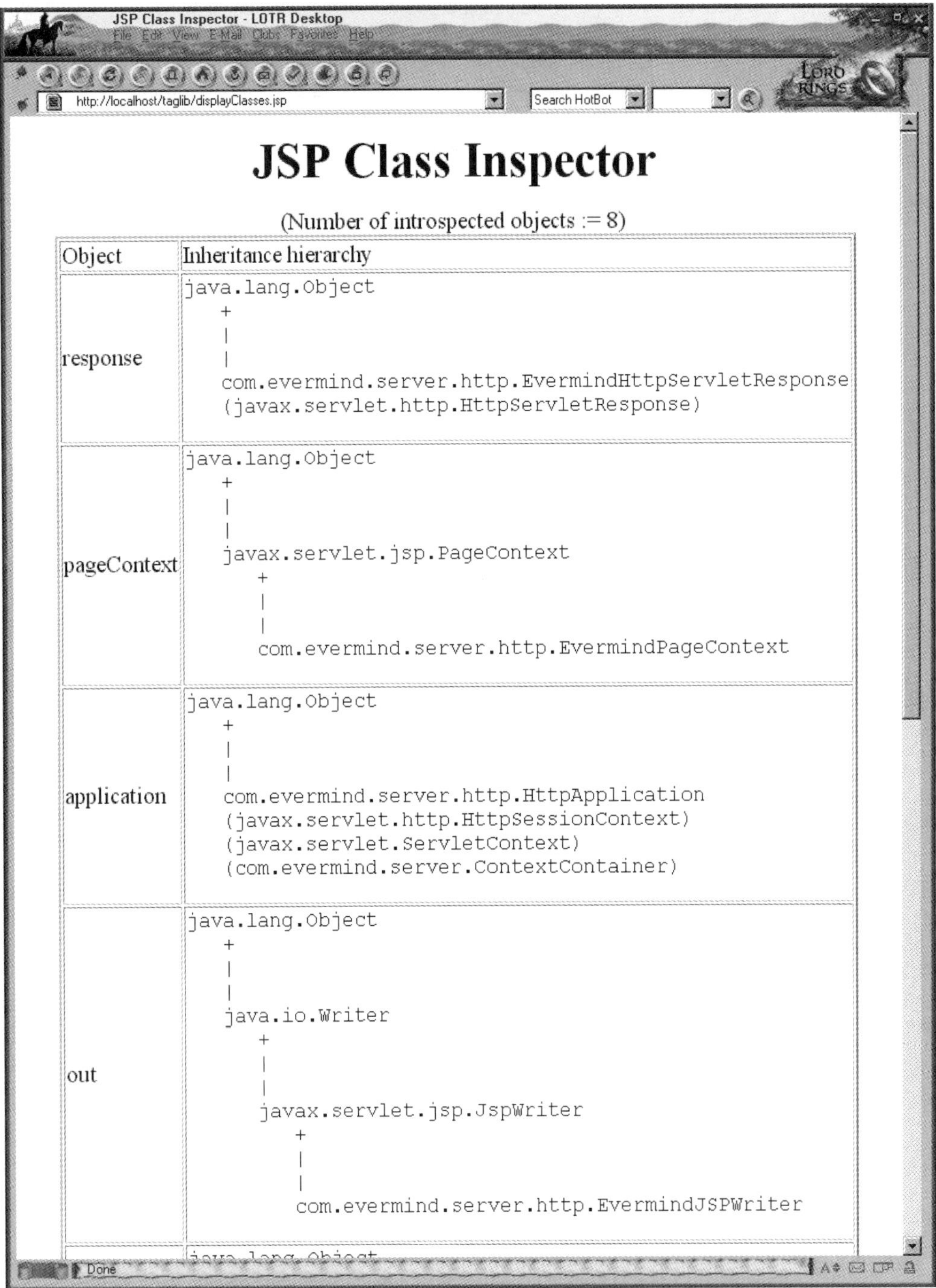

Figure 6-10. The same tag library example as shown in Figure 6-9. This time, the application server is OAS version 1.4.7. Note the difference in types used from the Tomcat reference implementation server.

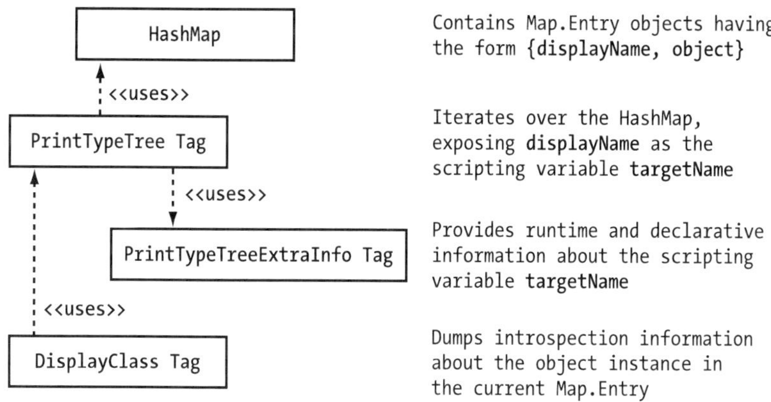
HashMap
Contains Map.Entry objects having the form {displayName, object}
<<uses>>
PrintTypeTree Tag
Iterates over the HashMap, exposing displayName as the scripting variable targetName
<<uses>>
PrintTypeTreeExtraInfo Tag
Provides runtime and declarative information about the scripting variable targetName
<<uses>>
DisplayClass Tag
Dumps introspection information about the object instance in the current Map.Entry

Figure 6-11. The runtime dependencies, or roles of the different classes. Despite the limited amount of classes involved, JSP systems with collaborating custom tags have a tendency to befuddle the programmer looking for a clean execution flow line.

The UML class diagram in Figure 6-12 reveals the public API of the two direct tag classes (`PrintTypeTreeTag` and `DisplayClassTag`), and their dependencies on the standard extension classes of package `javax.servlet.jsp.tagext`.

The inner structure of the tag handler classes reveals a set of operational fields and methods, as well as some controlling the execution flow. The `PrintTypeTreeTag` class wraps the `allTargets` map, and its corresponding helper objects (the `Iterator it` and `Map.Entry currentTarget`). Although the iterator is used in the `doInitBody()` as well as in the `doAfterBody()` methods (to advance in the `allTargets` map and mark its next `Map.Entry`), the `currentTarget Map.Entry` is used only within the evaluation of the `PrintTypeTreeTag` body.

You may think of the `DisplayClassTag` handler as a dependent subtype of the `PrintTypeTreeTag`. Indeed, the `DisplayClassTag` essentially performs class introspection within the method `dumpClassInfo()` (called from within the `doEndTag()`) and outputs the result to the view.

The `TagExtraInfo` class, `PrintTypeTreeExtraInfo`, is statically related only to its superclass, `TagExtraInfo`. The dynamic relationship of the JSP Class Dumper is nontrivial, and therefore deserves its own section, which is next.

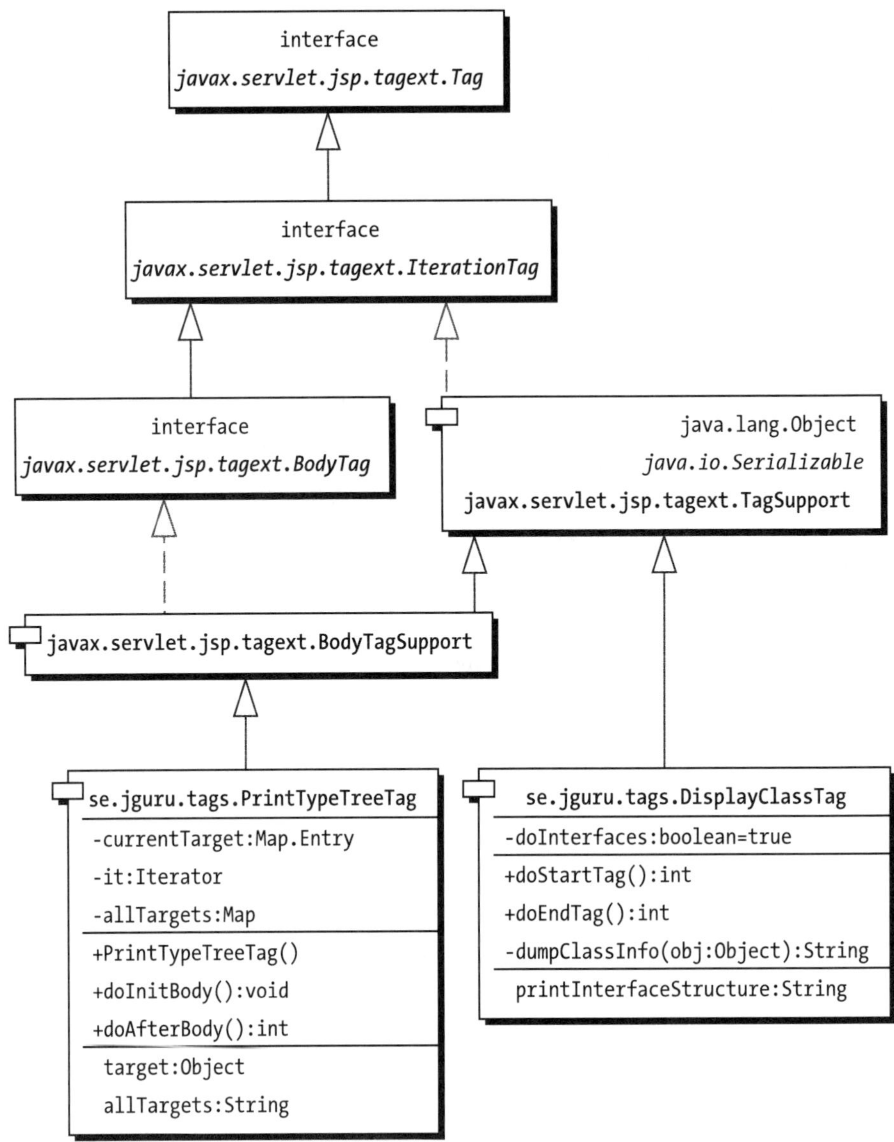

Figure 6-12. Static class relations between the JSP tag handler classes used in this example and their superclasses in the `javax.servlet.jsp.tagext` *package*

Dynamic Call Structure of the JSP Class Dumper

The biggest problem with visualizing the dynamic call structure of a complex JSP document with embedded custom tags is that only relatively few method calls are generated by the developer. The automatic servlet-to-JSP compiler generates the majority of the calls, which reduces the visibility of the dynamic call structure. Thus, it is often a good idea to keep the generated servlet code—at least in the beginning of working with a new application server—to verify that the code being generated has the desired and expected structure.

To be able to understand the dynamic call structure of the involved classes, first look at the JSP document that contains our custom tags, `<xyz:printTypeTree>` and `<xyz:showHierarchy>`. (See Listing 6-6 in which the population of the hashtable instance as well as the custom JSP tags have been bolded.)

Listing 6-6. The `displayClasses.jsp` *document*

```
<%@ taglib uri="/taglibs/tagz.jar" prefix="xyz" %>
<%@ page import="java.util.*"%>
<html>
    <head>
    <title>JSP Class Introspector </title>
    </head>

    <body>
    <center>

    <h1>JSP Class Introspector</h1>


    <jsp:useBean id="objs" class="java.util.HashMap">
    <%
        // Populate the HashMap with
        // a few objects worth introspecting.
        // Each Map.Entry holds the displayName

        // as the key and the instance as the value.
        objs.put("request", request);
        objs.put("response", response);
        objs.put("out", out);

        objs.put("application", application);
        objs.put("session", session);
        objs.put("page", page);
```

```
            objs.put("JspFactory", JspFactory.getDefaultFactory());
            objs.put("pageContext", pageContext);
        %>
        </jsp:useBean>

        (Number of introspected objects := <%= objs.size() %>)

        <table border=2>
        <tr>
            <td>Object</td>
            <td>Inheritance hierarchy</td>
        </tr>


        <xyz:printTypeTree allTargets="objs">
            <tr>

<%--
        The targetName variable is defined by the printTypeTree tag,
        which retrieves its specification from the PrintTypeTreeTagExtraInfo
        helper class.
--%>

                <td> <%= targetName %></td>
                <td> <pre><xyz:showHierarchy /></pre></td>


            </tr>
        </xyz:printTypeTree>

        </table>

        </center>
        </body>
</html>
```

In this case, the autocompiler of the Tomcat reference implementation server generates the final call structure shown in the collaboration diagram in Figure 6-13. Although the call order and mode is defined by the J2EE standard, I recommend verifying that your Web application server follows the same patterns (that is, that it conforms to the J2EE specification).

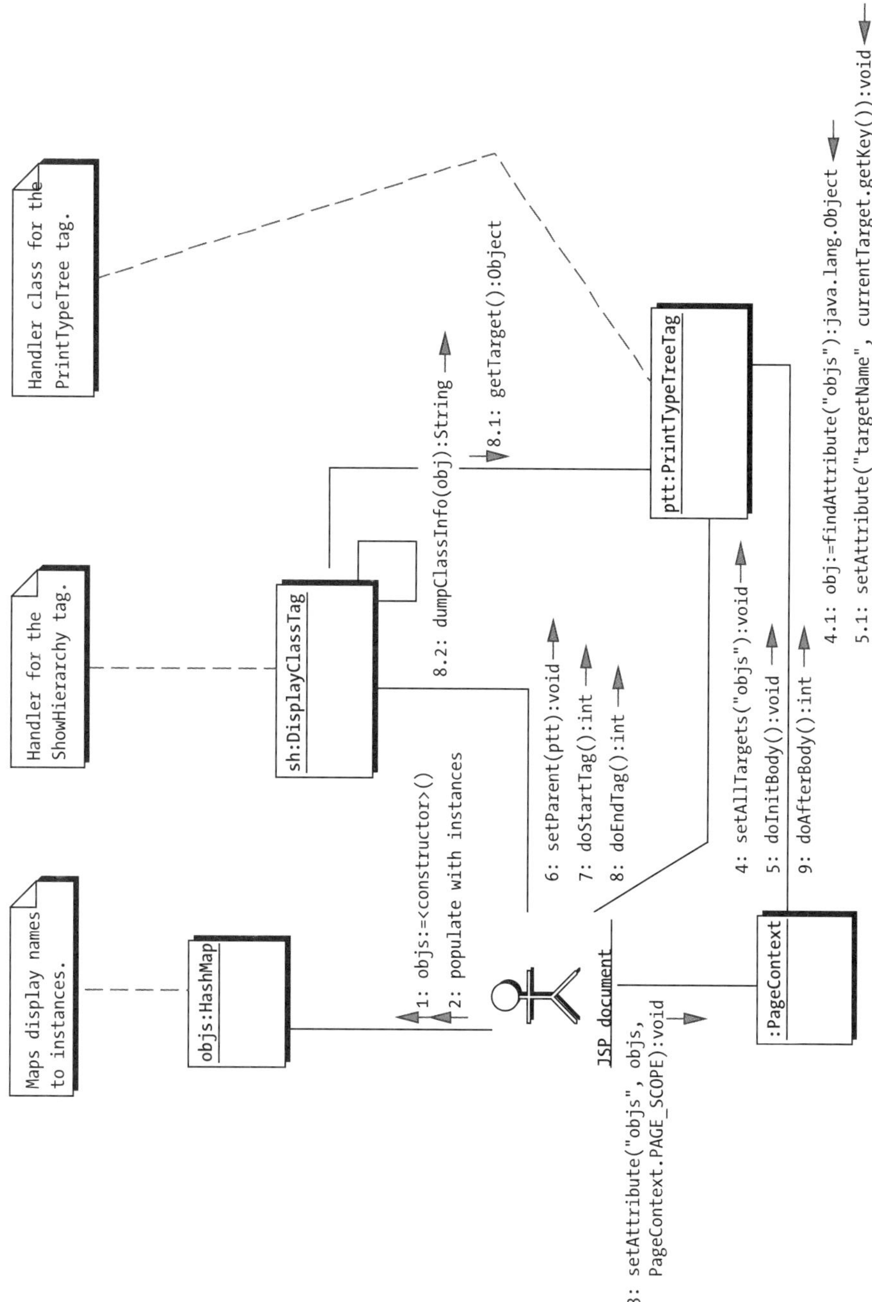

Figure 6-13. Interaction diagram of the objects in the running system

In Figure 6-13, the TagExtraInfo instance has been left out because it merely contains variable declaration information; the information it contains is already consumed by the JSP engine when the JSP document is compiled into the servlet bytecode. All other objects presented in this example exist at runtime, as indicated in the collaboration diagram.

The servlet generated by the JSP document compiler performs nine major method calls. Calls 1-3 assemble the HashMap with the display names and their corresponding object instances. Calls 1 and 3 are automatically generated by the JSP-to-servlet compiler, but the population calls (represented by call 2 in Figure 6-13) are made by the developer.

Calls 4 and 5 set up and populate the PrintTypeTreeTag. The JSP-to-servlet compiler generates both of these calls, but the developer implements all of the methods. Visibility and control are therefore rather good regarding the subcalls 4.1 and 5.1 from within doInitBody and doAfterBody, respectively.

Calls 6 and 7 are initiated by the JSP-to-servlet compiler, and they properly set up the DisplayClassTag instance. The first call notifies the DisplayClassTag of its parent, and the second verifies that the parent is indeed of type PrintTypeTreeTag. Normally, only the latter method is overridden by the developer.

Call 8 constitutes the main work method of the iteration, as it generates the class hierarchy listing of the instance within the current Map.Entry.

Call 9 advances the HashMap iterator, and starts another loop from call 6.

Alternatively, the collaboration diagram from Figure 6-13 may be rendered as a sequence diagram. This equivalent sequence diagram is shown in Figure 6-14.

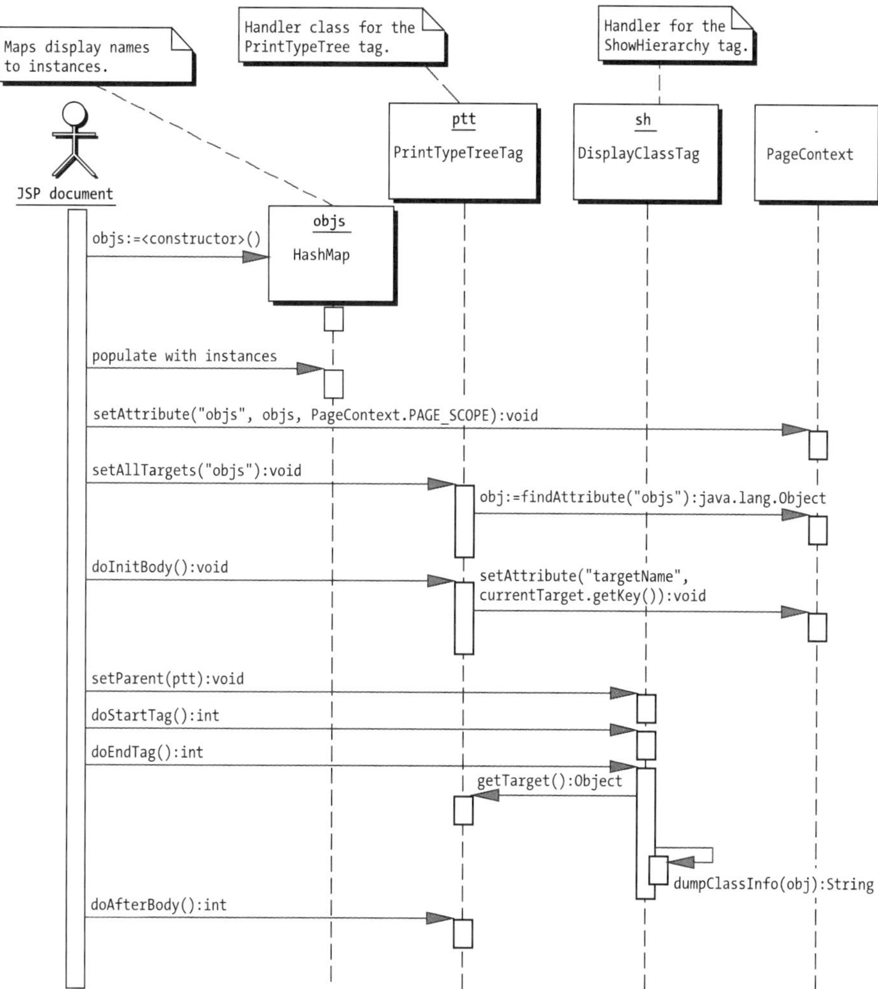

Figure 6-14. Sequence diagram containing the same information as the collaboration diagram from Figure 6-13

Tag Library Definition

The tag library definition document `taglib.tld` for the two tag handlers defines all classes used to realize the interaction diagrams from Figure 6-13 and 6-14.The tag library definition file is shown in Listing 6-7. The mapping between a tag name and its implementation class is bolded.

Listing 6-7. The `taglib.tld` *document*

```
<?xml version="1.0" encoding="ISO-8859-1" ?>
<!DOCTYPE taglib PUBLIC
        "-//Sun Microsystems, Inc.//DTD JSP Tag Library 1.1//EN"
        "http://java.sun.com/j2ee/dtds/web-jsptaglibrary_1_1.dtd">

<taglib>
    <tlibversion>1.0</tlibversion>
    <jspversion>1.1</jspversion>
    <shortname>JSP Book</shortname>
    <uri>http://localhost/taglib/tagz.jar</uri>
    <info>Tutorial Tag Library</info>

    <tag>
    <!--
         The showHierarchy parent tag loops over a
         collection of objects,  and exposes them
         to Introspection by Its child tag, printTypeTree.
    -->
        <name>showHierarchy</name>
        <tagclass>se.jguru.tags.DisplayClassTag</tagclass>
        <bodycontent>empty</bodycontent>
        <info>Tag displaying superclass inheritance tree</info>

        <attribute>
            <!--
                If the printInterfaceStructure variable is set
                to false, no Interface types will be printed
                on the resulting view
            -->
            <name>printInterfaceStructure</name>
            <required>no</required>
            <rtexprvalue>no</rtexprvalue>
        </attribute>
    </tag>

    <tag>
    <!--
        Tag printing introspection information (inheritance tree)
        for an Object exposed by its parent (the showHierarchy Tag
        defined above).
```

```
    -->
        <name>printTypeTree</name>
        <tagclass>se.jguru.tags.PrintTypeTreeTag</tagclass>
        <teiclass>se.jguru.tags.PrintTypeTreeExtraInfo</teiclass>
        <bodycontent>JSP</bodycontent>
        <info>Tag iterating over a Map of instances,
            exposing each instance using its target JavaBean
            property.</info>

        <attribute>
            <!--
                The allTargets variable contains the name of the
                collection which contains all objects that should
                be Introspected.
            -->
            <name>allTargets</name>
            <required>yes</required>
            <rtexprvalue>yes</rtexprvalue>
        </attribute>

    </tag>
```

You can see the bindings between tag names and handler classes, noting that the printTypeTree tag has an associated TagExtraInfo class, se.juru.tags.PrintTypeTreeExtraInfo, the main task of which is to assist in the declaration of the targetName scripting variable. Whereas the showHierarchy tag is a standalone tag (because its <bodycontent> attribute has the value empty), the printTypeTree tag contains JSP code.

Note that the system of tags in the above JSP document has the following three aspects, which in combination makes the system a trifle complex to create:

- The printTypeTree tag iterates over a collection.
- The printTypeTree tag defines a scripting variable (targetName).
- The showHierarchy tag retrieves the target from its parent (the printTypeTree tag), and must therefore check that it indeed has such a parent.

The Tag Handler Classes

Take a look at the code in the tag handler classes of the example. (See Listing 6-8.) The PrintTypeTreeTag class handles the outermost (parent) iterator tag. The code pertaining to the iteration loop in the `PrintTypeTreeTag` class has been bolded in Listing 6-8.

Listing 6-8. The `PrintTypeTreeTag` *class*

```
/*
 * Copyright (c) 2000 jGuru.se
 * All rights reserved.
 */

package se.jguru.tags;

import java.io.*;
import java.util.*;
import javax.servlet.jsp.*;
import javax.servlet.jsp.tagext.*;

/**
 * Tag handler class for the printTypeTree tag.
 * This tag handler will loop through a collection
 * ("allTargets") and display type information about each entry.
 * Each entry in the allTargets Map must be of the form
 * <tt>displayName := instance</tt>, where <tt>displayName</tt>
 * is the user-friendly name displayed in the view of the object
 * to be introspected, and <tt>instance</tt> is the actual name
 * of the object tobe introspected.
 *
 * @author Lennart Jörelid
 */
public class PrintTypeTreeTag extends BodyTagSupport
{
    // Custom JavaBean properties
    private Map.Entry currentTarget;
    private Map allTargets;
    private Iterator it;

    /** Default constructor. */
    public PrintTypeTreeTag()
    {
        super();
    }
```

```
/**
 * Method called by the JSP engine before the
 * tag body is evaluated.
 */
public void doInitBody() throws JspException
{
    // Check sanity
    if (allTargets == null) return;
    else
    {
        // Sane. Generate the iterator looping over
        // all elements in the internal Collection.
        this.it = allTargets.entrySet().iterator();

        // Does the Collection contain any objects?
        // If not, skip all body evaluation.
        if (!it.hasNext()) return;
        else
        {
            // All is well. Ready the first object
            // in the collection for introspection,
            // by assigning its reference to the
            // currentTarget variable, corresponding
            // to the target JavaBean property.
            this.currentTarget = (Map.Entry) it.next();

            // Also, store the display name of the
            // current entry in the variable called
            // "targetName". This is defined within
            // the TagExtraInfo class (called PrintTypeTreeExtraInfo)
            // related to this tag handler class.
            this.pageContext.setAttribute
                ("targetName", currentTarget.getKey());
        }
    }
}

/**
 * Method called by the JSP engine after the
 * tag body is evaluated. It advances the Iterator and starts another loop.
 */
```

```
public int doAfterBody() throws JspException
{
    // Get the body content as a String, with all
    // contained JSP tags evaluated.
    BodyContent body = this.getBodyContent();
    String content = body.getString();

    try
    {
        // Printout the current body content onto the JSP view
        body.getEnclosingWriter().println(content);
    }
    catch(Exception ex)
    {
        Logger log = Logger.getInstance();
        log.log("Whoops: " + ex);
    }

    // Clear the body for the next iteration
    body.clearBody();

    // Should we iterate once again?
    if (it == null || !(it.hasNext())) return BodyTag.SKIP_BODY;

    // More objects left in the Collection.
    // Move to the next one, and iterate.
    this.currentTarget = (Map.Entry) it.next();

    // Also, store the display name of the
    // current entry in the variable called
    // "targetName". This is defined within
    // the TagExtraInfo class (called PrintTypeTreeExtraInfo)
    // related to this tag handler class.
    this.pageContext.setAttribute
      ("targetName", currentTarget.getKey());

    // Return BodyTag.EVAL_BODY_TAG  to Indicate that we should Iterate again
    return BodyTag.EVAL_BODY_TAG;
}

///////
```

```
    /**
     * Setter method for the allTargets JavaBean property.
     * The mapName parameter indicates which attribute name
     * to use to extract the allTargets Map from the pageContext.
     */
    public void setAllTargets(String mapName)
    {
        // Read the attribute from the pageContext
        if (mapName == null || mapName.equals("")) return;

        Object obj = pageContext.findAttribute(mapName);

        // Check sanity.
        if(obj == null)
        {
            System.out.println("[setAllTargets]: Not good. "
               + "obj is NULL for mapName = " + mapName);
        }
        if (!(obj instanceof Map)) return;

        // Sane.
        this.allTargets = (Map) obj;
    }
}
```

As indicated in Listing 6-8, the `PrintTypeTreeTag` handler essentially performs three tasks:

- In the `setAllTargets()` method, the `HashMap` is read from the `pageContext` and assigned to the internal `allTargets` variable.
- The Iterator, `it`, is created and advanced for the first time in the `doInitBody()` method. The `Map.Entry` instance, `currentTarget`, is assigned for the first time by the value retrieved from the iterator.
- In the `doAfterBody()` method, the Iterator is advanced. If a `Map.Entry` object is retrieved, the body is cleared and re-evaluated, otherwise the flow of control is returned to the JSP-generated servlet.

The `DisplayClassTag` handler class, shown in Listing 6-9, performs introspection of a class, to find its superclasses and implemented interfaces. The introspection process is continued up to the root class `java.lang.Object`. The code specific to a tag handler class is rendered in boldface in Listing 6-9. (Note that the `DisplayClassTag` verifies that it has a parent with the type `PrintTypeTreeTag`.) This technique is very useful to avoid type casting problems and `NullPointerExceptions`, due to a nonexistent or incorrect parent tag.

Listing 6-9. The `DisplayClassTag` class

```
/*
 * Copyright (c) 2000 jGuru Europe AB
 * All rights reserved.
 */

package se.jguru.tags;

import javax.servlet.jsp.*;
import javax.servlet.jsp.tagext.*;
import java.util.*;

/**
 * Tag handler class which displays the superclass and
 * interface structure of a given target instance.
 */
public class DisplayClassTag extends TagSupport
{
    // Internal state
    private boolean doInterfaces = true;

    /**
     * Check that this tag is placed properly within the container
     * body of a tag handled by a PrintTypeTreeTag handler.
     */
    public int doStartTag() throws JspException
    {
        // Check that this tag is really embedded within
        // a <xyz:printTypeTree> ... </xyz:printTypeTree>
        // container.
        //
        // Remember, this Tag cannot live outside of its
        // container parent.
        Tag enclosingParent = TagSupport.findAncestorWithClass(
               this, PrintTypeTreeTag.class );

        if ( enclosingParent == null )
            throw new JspException( "DisplayClass tag must be placed "
               + "inside a PrintTypeTree tag." );
```

```
        // Do not do anything when the tag starts.
        return SKIP_BODY;
    }

    /**
     * Method called by the JSP engine after any body
     * evaluation has taken place.
     */
    public int doEndTag() throws JspException
    {
        try
        {
            // Get the target (instance to be introspected) from the parent
            Object target =
               ((PrintTypeTreeTag ) getParent()).getTarget();

            // Print the class hierarcy to the enclosing out
            // JspWriter of the JSP page.
            JspWriter out = pageContext.getOut();
            out.write(dumpClassInfo(target ));
        }
        catch ( Exception ex )
        {
            throw new JspException( "[doEndTag)]: " + ex );
        }

        // Tell the JSP engine to continue evaluating the
        // rest of the JSP page, rather than aborting all
        // evaluation here.
        return EVAL_PAGE;
    }

    ////////////////////////////////////////////////
    /**
     * Setter method for the JavaBean property printInterfaceStructure.
     * When this attribute is true, interfaces types in addition to
     * class types will be logged to the view.
     */
    public void setPrintInterfaceStructure( String doInterfaces )
    {
        this.doInterfaces = (doInterfaces.trim().equalsIgnoreCase("true"));
    }
```

```
/**
 * Worker method which returns a String containing the fully
 * formatted display of superclass information as well as
 * interface information of the obj instance. Interface
 * information will only be dumped if the printInterfaceStructure
 * JavaBean property is set to <code>true</code>.
 */
private String dumpClassInfo( Object obj )
{
    StringBuffer buf = new StringBuffer();

    // Get the class information and store it
    // within the buffer above.
    ArrayList allClasses  = new ArrayList();
    HashMap allInterfaces = new HashMap();
    Class current         = obj.getClass();

    while ( current != null )
    {
        // Get the name of the current class
        String name = current.getName();
        allClasses.add( name );

        // Get all the interfaces implemented by
        // the current class.
        allInterfaces.put( name, current.getInterfaces() );

        // Move the current pointer
        current = current.getSuperclass();
    }

    // Got all class and interface types of the obj
    // instance. Concatenate and print them in the
    // reverse order (i.e. where java.lang.Object is topmost) onto the
    // view buffer.
    String extender = "";
    Object[] classes = allClasses.toArray();

    for ( int i = classes.length - 1; i >= 0; i-- )
    {
        // Print the Class name
        buf.append( extender + classes[ i ] + "\n" );
```

```
            // Printout all interfaces implemented by
            // the current class.
            if ( doInterfaces )
            {
                Class[] ifs = (Class[])
                    allInterfaces.get((String)classes[i]);

                for ( int j = 0; j < ifs.length; j++ )
                {
                    buf.append( extender + "(" + ifs[ j ].getName() +
                         ")\n" );
                }
            }

            // Print the inheritance indicator, unless
            // we are already at the Object class.
            if ( i != 0 )
            {
                extender += "    ";
                buf.append( extender + "+\n" );
                buf.append( extender + "|\n" );
                buf.append( extender + "|\n" );
            }
        }

        // Done creating the inheritance hierarchy.
        return buf.toString();
    }
}
```

The `DisplayClassTag` handler performs two tasks:

- In the `doStartTag()`, the `DisplayClassTag` makes sure that it is contained within a `<xyz:printTypeTree>` tag body.
- In the `doEndTag()`, the `dumpClassInfo()` method is called to output the class hierarchy to the view.

The `PrintTypeTreeTagExtraInfo` class relates to its superclass, `TagExtraInfo`, by inheritance, as shown in Figure 6-15. The few public methods of the `TagExtraInfo` are implemented, along with a few introspection methods which assist in creating a log file that will assist in evaluating the call order of the `TagExtraInfo`.

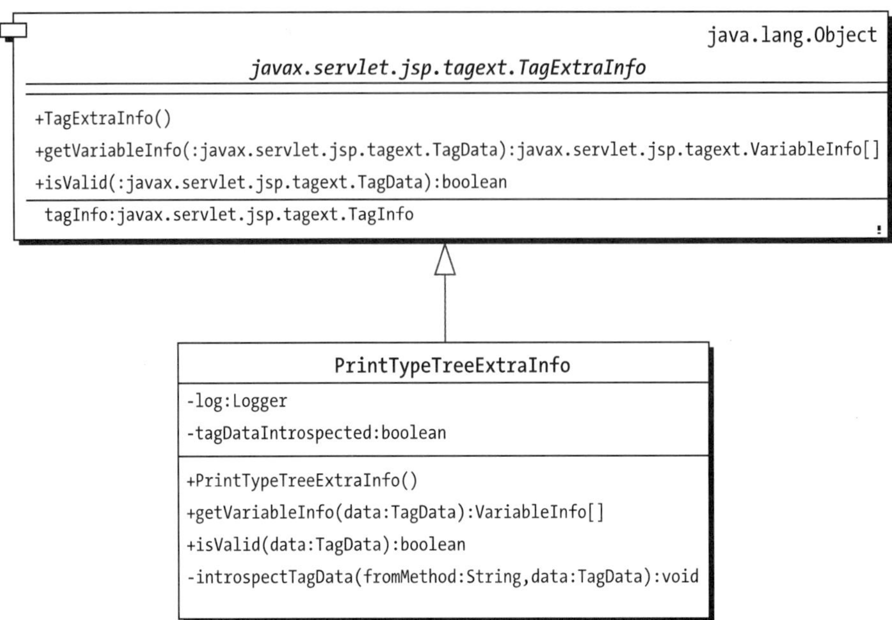

Figure 6-15. The inheritance structure of the `PrintTypeTreeExtraInfo` *class*

When the JSP-to-servlet compiler should declare and define a variable, it requires type declaration information. Specifically, a Java variable declaration has the following form:

```
java.lang.String targetName = null;
```

The `getVariableInfo()` method returns the information required by the JSP-to-Servlet compiler, packaged within a `VariableInfo` object. The type name and variable name occupies the first two arguments of the `VariableInfo` constructor, and are retrieved by the `getVarName()` and `getClassName()` methods. The latter two arguments in the constructor define whether the variable should be declared (in some languages, special syntax is required at declaration time) and what scope the variable should have.

The scope of the declared variable, `targetName` has three possibilities:

- The variable may be present only within the body of the tag (that is, from the invocation of the `doInitBody()` until the invocation of the `doAfterBody()`). Select this mode of operations with the value `VariableInfo.NESTED`.

- The variable may be in scope from the start of the body until the end of the JSP document. Select this mode of operations with the value `VariableInfo.AT_BEGIN`.

- The variable may be in scope from the end of the body until the end of the JSP document. Select this mode of operations with the value `VariableInfo.AT_END`.

Scripting variable scopes are best illustrated with a brief example. Figure 6-16 shows a skeleton of a JSP document that contains the opening and closing delimiters of a custom JSP tag called `aBodyTag`. The `aBodyTag` tag has a body and defines a scripting variable, whose name is irrelevant. We are only interested in its declaration scope. Figure 6-16 shows three possible scopes of the variable defined by the `aBodyTag` custom JSP tag, related to the opening and closing delimiters of the `aBodyTag`. The shaded lines mark areas within the JSP document where it is legal to access the variable (say, by calling `<%= theVariableName %>`).

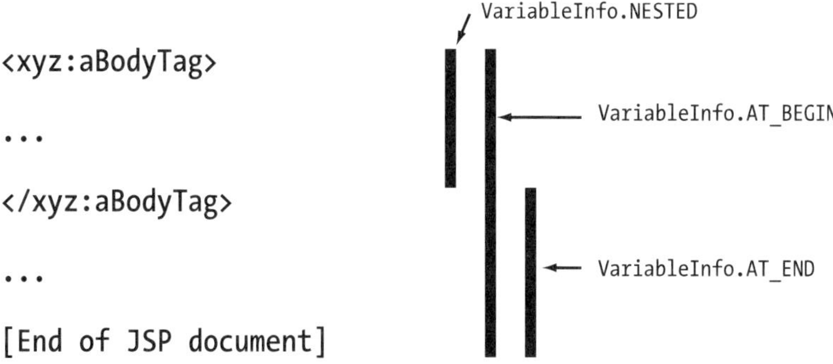

Figure 6-16. The declaration scope of a scripting variable, as given by its three possible `VariableInfo` *configuration parameters*

The `PrintTypeTreeExtraInfo` class has been tweaked slightly away from the bare-bone declarations of a normal implementation, as we want to log messages to verify the call order of its methods. Several log calls have therefore been inserted into the normal code. Normally, a `TagExtraInfo` class is simply used to define scripting variables.

Such variables are declared in the `getVariableInfo()` method, and they may be used in the running JSP document. (See Listing 6-10.)

Listing 6-10. The `PrintTypeTreeExtraInfo` *class. The statements pertaining to variable information are bolded.*

```
/*
 * Copyright (c) 2000 jGuru.se
 * All rights reserved.
 */

package se.jguru.tags;

import java.lang.reflect.*;
import java.util.*;
import javax.servlet.jsp.*;
import javax.servlet.jsp.tagext.*;

/**
 * Extra information about variables declared in the JSP document
 * by the PrintTypeTreeTag handler class.
 */
public class PrintTypeTreeTagExtraInfo extends TagExtraInfo
{
    // Internal state
    private Logger log;
    private boolean tagDataIntrospected;

    public PrintTypeTreeTagExtraInfo()
    {
        // Define internal state
        log = Logger.getInstance();
    }

    /**
     * Define the syntax for the variables defined by the PrintTypeTreeTag.
     * The JSP-to-Servlet compiler uses each VariableInfo instance to
     * declare the variable.
     *
     * @return declaration information for all variables declared by the
     *             PrintTypeTreeTag handler class.
     */
    public VariableInfo[] getVariableInfo(TagData data)
    {
        log.log("-> getVariableInfo called. TagData hashCode := "
                + data.hashCode());
        introspectTagData("getVariableInfo", data);
```

```
        // Create the VariableInfo for the targetName
        // String, which contains the variable name
        // retrieved from the HashMap submitted to the
        // PrintTypeTreeTag using the setAllTargets
        // JavaBean setter method.
        VariableInfo targetNameInfo = new VariableInfo("targetName",
                    "java.lang.String", true, VariableInfo.NESTED);

        // Create the return value.
        VariableInfo[] toReturn = { targetNameInfo };

        return toReturn;
    }

    /**
     * Permits run-time validation for each scripting variable
     * during runtime.
     *
     * @param data contains a HashMap which maps tag attribute names to
     *        their respective values. (i.e. 'key=value' maps for tag
     *        attributes; given the tag <x:y attrib="value" />, the TagData
     *        instance will return value if the getAttribute("key")
     *        method is called.
     */
    public boolean isValid(TagData data)
    {
        // Inspect the internal state of the TagData
        // argument to this method.
        log.log("-> isValid called. TagData hashCode := " +
                    data.hashCode());
        introspectTagData("isValid", data);

        return true;
    }
    /**
     * Metadata information method which prints a trace of the TagData
     * sent to this TagExtraInfo class. Remember, TagData Is constructed from
     * the attributes sent to of a JSP tag.
     *
     * @param fromMethod a String containing the method from which this
     *            instrospection method was called.
     * @param data the TagData instance to introspect.
     */
```

```
private void introspectTagData(String fromMethod, TagData data)
{
    if(this.tagDataIntrospected)
    {
        // Simply print the name of the caller method
        log.log(" introspectTagData called from " + fromMethod);
        return;
    }

    //
    // Log information from this tag.
    //
    // Note that the data extracted here reflects
    // only what has been provided in the taglib.tld definition file        //
    TagInfo theInfo = this.getTagInfo();

    log.log("\n --- Introspecting tag data. Caller method := "
                + fromMethod);
    log.log("");
    log.log("[ Tag name ] := " + theInfo.getTagName());
    log.log("[ Tag classname ] := " + theInfo.getTagClassName());
    log.log("[ bodyContent ] := " + theInfo.getBodyContent());
    log.log("[ infoString ] := " + theInfo.getInfoString());

    //
    // Log TagAttributeInfo from the attributes of this Tag
    //
    TagAttributeInfo[] tai = theInfo.getAttributes();
    if(tai == null)
    {
        // Log.
        log.log(" -> [ Null TagAttributeInfo ]");
    }
    else
    {
        for(int i = 0; i < tai.length; i++)
        {
            // Printout all relevant TagAttributeInfo data
            TagAttributeInfo current = tai[i];

            // Get the name of the current attribute
            String theName = current.getName();
```

```
            log.log(" ---> Attribute [" + theName + "] := " +
                data.getAttribute(theName));
            log.log("      [ attributeString ] := " +
                data.getAttributeString(theName));
            log.log("      [ request possible ] := " +
                current.canBeRequestTime());
            log.log("      [ required ] := " + current.isRequired());

            // Get the tag data class
            log.log("      [ attributeClass ] := " +
                data.getAttribute(theName).getClass().getName());
        }
    }


    // Break the log slightly for visibility.
    log.log(" --- Done Introspecting tag data\n");
  }
}
```

Listing 6-11 displays the code in the generated servlet that realizes the scripting variable as declared in Listing 6-10, but for the reference implementation of J2EE. Note how the `targetName` variable is forced to the specified scope because it is declared within the do/while loop that realizes the body of the tag handler class. The assignment statement has been bolded in Listing 6-11.

Listing 6-11. Source code snippet from the autogenerated servlet

```
...

theTagHandler.doStartTag();

...

theTagHandler.doInitBody();

do {
     java.lang.String targetName = null;
     targetName = (java.lang.String)pageContext.getAttribute("targetName");
...

} while (theTagHandler.doAfterBody() == BodyTag.EVAL_BODY_TAG);

...

theTagHandler.doEndTag ();
```

The code in Listing 6-11 is a cleaned-up version of the servlet that is autogenerated by the J2EE reference implementation server; full Java paths have been skipped to improve readability and irrelevant code has been skipped. However, it is clear from the code in Listing 6-11 how the life-cycle methods are called and what scope the scripting variable `targetName` has.

Log File Contents

The application log file contains the log messages from the `PrintTypeTreeTagExtraInfo` class and the contents of its internal variables. This verifies that the `TagData` object, passed as a parameter to the `isValid()` and `getVariableInfo()` methods, does indeed contain the values of each of the attributes passed to the tag.

> **TIP** *The* `isValid()` *method hosts attribute validation logic (that is, logic that's intended to assert that an attribute indeed has a permitted value). Although they are not used in this example, the implications of tags supporting runtime attribute validation should be evident. For instance, imagine that we create a scientific Web application that should calculate something originating from temperature data. Because most scientific applications use the Kelvin scale, containing only positive temperatures, a* `KelvinTemperature` *JSP tag could accept only positive temperature attributes, and complain otherwise.*

Therefore, you may learn that the only attribute defined and provided by the `PrintTypeTreeTag` handler class is the equivalent of

```
String allTargets = "objs";
```

The log in Listing 6-12 presents the order in which the JSP engine calls the methods in the `TagExtraInfo` class. All data required to create a scripting variable in the JSP document is present in the log below. Comparing the log output with the code in Listing 6-10 yields the call order of the JSP engine.

Listing 6-12. Contents of the log file

```
-> isValid called. TagData hashCode := 4358817

 --- Introspecting tag data. Caller method := isValid

[ Tag name ] := printTypeTree
[ Tag classname ] := se.jguru.tags.PrintTypeTreeTag
[ bodyContent ] := JSP
[ infoString ] := Tag iterating over a Map of instances,
                  exposing each instance using its target JavaBean
                  property.
 ---> Attribute [allTargets] := objs
      [ attributeString ] := objs
      [ request possible ] := true
      [ required ] := true
      [ attributeClass ] := java.lang.String
 --- Done Introspecting tag data

-> getVariableInfo called. TagData hashCode := 4358817
 introspectTagData called from getVariableInfo
```

Although logging can be fun or informative for development purposes, it reduces the overall performance of the Web application. All excessive logging (short of error logging) should therefore be switched off in the running Web application server.

Reflections on the JSP Class Inspector Example

The class dumper example is fairly tricky because it involves tag library iteration, cooperating tags, scripting variable declaration, and a little introspection. Although each problem—if seen as a single item—is far from complex, the sheer volume of trivial problems contributes to the overall complexity.

A good and nontrivial complement to the example above is to make the class introspection extensible by allowing the user to input the fully qualified class name of a class that should be loaded into memory using `Class.forName()` and then introspected as done above.

> **CAUTION** *Tomcat version 3.2 does not properly handle attributes computed at runtime or attribute type conversion. To be safe, use only String variables.*

The If-Then-Else Custom JSP Tag Example

This example begins with an experiment in empathy. Imagine that you are a newly employed art director with very little understanding of programming, but a firm grasp of HTML and the inner magic of image construction in Photoshop or GIMP. You've just been assigned the task of updating the HTML of an existing view document in the corporate Web site. You are to incorporate some "important changes" and modify the behavior of a few buttons. In passing, a senior programmer hastily informs you that you should be careful not to damage the business logic in the view documents. A microsecond later, the programmer has vanished into a room for an important meeting with a corporate VIP. The secretary informs you that the meeting will continue until a business negotiation has been settled, and hints that it will take no less than nine hours.

Gathering courage, you open the view document only to find the following code:

```
<% if( theButtonLabel.equals(requiredLabel)) { %>
<input type="submit" value="Go to Corporate Home">
<% }
else
{
%>
<input type="reset" value="Clear form">
<% } %>
```

What are the odds that the company will have a broken Web site roughly two hours into the business meeting?

The example in this section shows you how to use JSP tags to create a simpler and neater JSP view without any "strange" embedded Java code. Conditional logic is a common construct in most programming languages. Indeed, you would often like to include text into the output of a JSP document depending on the state of a conditional variable. An easy way of achieving such behavior is to embellish the JSP document with normal Java If-Then-Else statements. However, in most cases, the people creating and maintaining the JSP documents are content managers and information architects who are not programmers. A simple typing mistake can cause a compile error when trying to access the JSP document from a Web browser, thus causing a server internal error (HTTP error code 500) displayed in the browser that's enough to frighten most users.

Instead of embedding Java code in the JSP view, a better option is to create three cooperating custom JSP tags that realize the standard if-then-else pattern. (For more details, see "Classes of the If-Then-Else Custom JSP Tags Example" later in this chapter.) This way, no Java code has to be embedded within the HTML code, and the document will seem less complex to nonprogrammers. The reactions I've seen from the content managers of a few projects were rather positive; although the document contained a few strange tags, at least it held no incomprehensible programming mumbo-jumbo.

A fairly complex selection in a JSP document could look as simple as the following code snippet:

```
<logic:if  condition='<%= condition %>' logFile="IfThenElseLog.txt" >

<logic:then>
The condition is true. This is the THEN body.
</logic:then>

<logic:else>
The condition is false. This is the ELSE body.
</logic:else>
</logic:if>
```

To illustrate the effects of the conditional logic tags, a small JSP document has been created to contain a conditional switch that gathers its boolean condition from the `condition` HTTP parameter. If the condition parameter contains the string "true", the condition evaluates to boolean `true`, and the body of the `ThenTag` is included as shown in Figure 6-17.

Figure 6-17. The output of the `ifThenElse.jsp` *document when the condition is* `true`

Otherwise, the body of the `ElseTag` is included as shown in Figure 6-18.

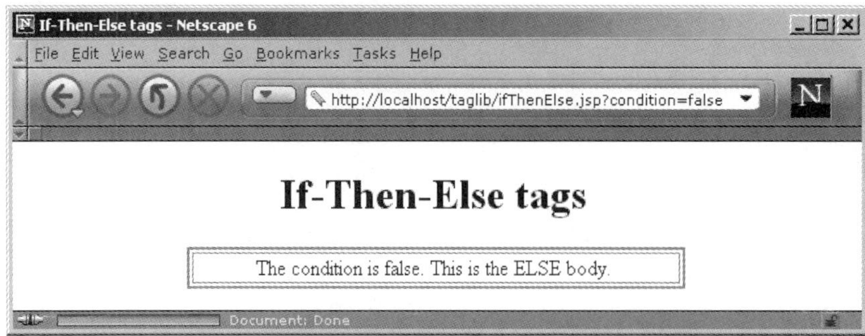

Figure 6-18. The output of the `ifThenElse.jsp` *document when the condition is* `false`

Classes of the If-Then-Else Custom JSP Tags Example

The JSP document contains three custom defined tags:

- <logic:if>
- <logic:then>
- <logic:else>

They're handled, respectively, by these three tag handler classes (shown in Figure 6-19):

- `IfTag`
- `ThenTag`
- `ElseTag`

All tag handler classes of this example implement simple body evaluate-and-include or exclude functionality. Thus, all tag handler classes extend the `TagSupport` class, rather than the `BodyTagSupport` class, which should be extended in a custom tag only if the tag alters the body content of its tag.

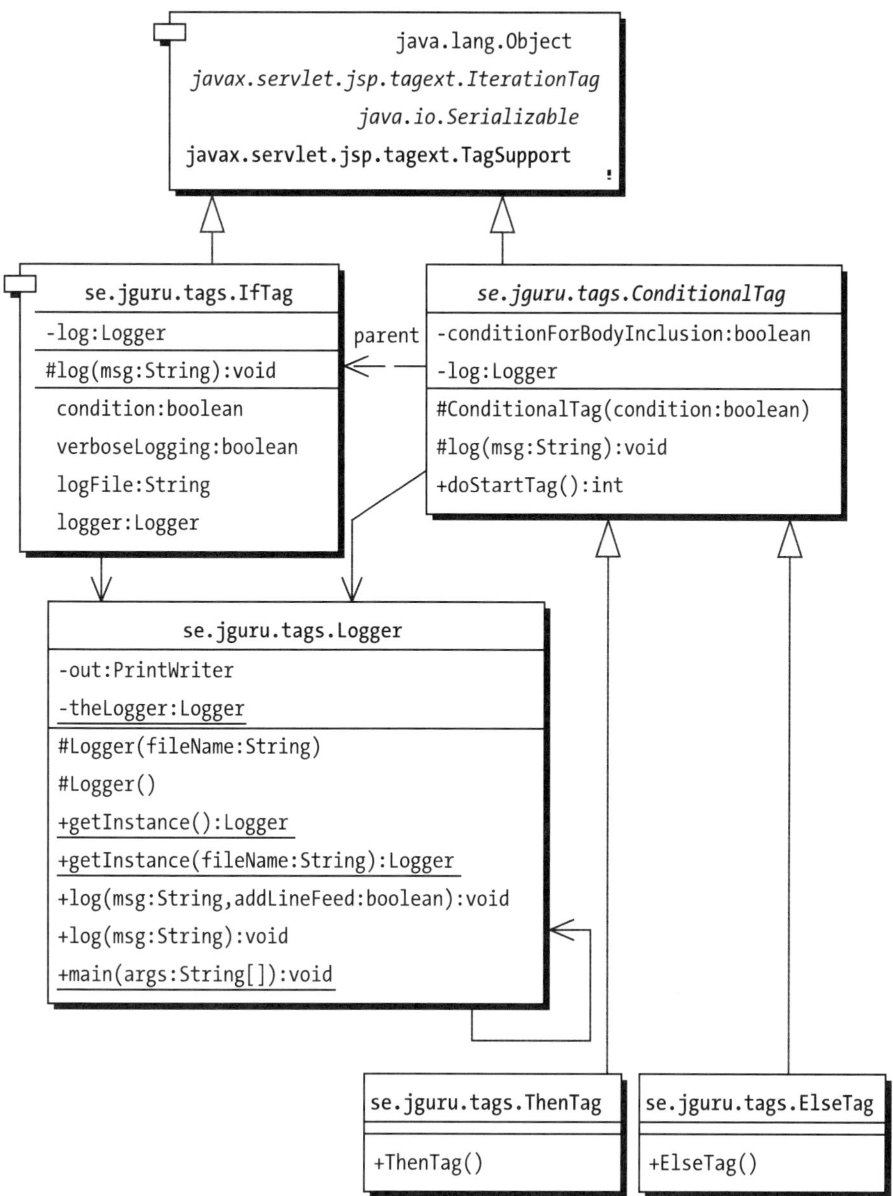

Figure 6-19. UML diagram of all classes in the If-Then-Else tag system. The actual implementation of both the `ThenTag` *and* `ElseTag` *classes reside in their common ancestor,* `ConditionalTag`*. The logger enables us to log messages, generated during runtime, for later study.*

This small system of collaborating tags is quite simple to understand, and the responsibilities are clear and simple. The five classes in this system are as follows:

- The **IfTag** handler class contains a boolean variable, `condition`, that's set as an attribute in the JSP page. This variable manifests itself as a readable and writeable JavaBean property, as indicated in the class diagram in Figure 6-18. Also, logging facilities are contained within the `IfTag` in the form of a `Logger` instance, which logs messages to a common log file (or to the `System.out` if no `logFile` is set). The `verboseLogging` attribute controls if any log messages should be written to the log file. Providing such development/runtime switches can greatly enhance system performance because all debug logging can be switched off in the running system.

- The abstract **ConditionalTag** handler class contains a boolean variable, `conditionForBodyInclusion`, set at construction time from an argument to the constructor. If the condition from the parent tag handler (`IfTag`) equals the `conditionForBodyInclusion`, the body of the `ConditionaltTag` handler output is included in the JSP `out` stream, and otherwise not.

- The **ThenTag** handler class sets its `conditionForBodyInclusion` to true, thus including its body in the JSP `out` stream if the condition in the `IfTag` handler class is true.

- The **ElseTag** handler class sets its `conditionForBodyInclusion` to false, thus including its body in the JSP `out` stream if the condition in the `IfTag` handler class is false.

- Aside from the tag handler classes, a small helper class assists in writing messages to the log stream. The **Logger** class encapsulates a `PrintWriter` that may be set up to log messages onto a given writer or to `System.out` if no writer is supplied. Logging is invoked by calling the `logWriter.log(String msg)` method.

Dynamic Call Structure of the If-Then-Else Tags Example

Although deceptively simple in functionality and static class structure, the small system does contain a hidden difficulty that manifests itself only in the dynamic call structure. A portion of the JSP specification is left to the implementers of the JSP engine, resulting in a potential race condition in setting JavaBean properties. For now, imagine yourself ignorant of any such difficulties, and carry on with the example. In due time, this race condition will be revealed.

What Is a Race Condition?

Imagine that two threads, T1 and T2, call a method in an object. A *race condition* exists if any output or system state variable depends on the order of invocation. In plain English, if your system will find itself in a certain state if T1 invokes a specific method before T2 does, and another state if T2 invokes the method before T1, the system contains a built-in race condition.

Now return to the JSP document (shown in Listing 6-13) and examine it in detail. The numbers in the margin correspond to the numbered method calls in the collaboration diagram in Figure 6-20, and are provided to facilitate call tracking.

Listing 6-13. The `ifThenElse.jsp` *document*

```
<%@ taglib uri="/WEB-INF/lib/tagz.jar" prefix="logic" %>
<%
     // Define the condidional variable
     String str = request.getParameter("condition");
     boolean condition = false;

     if(str != null) condition = (str.equalsIgnoreCase("true"));
%>
<html>
     <head>
     <title>If-Then-Else tags</title>
     </head>

     <body>
     <center>

     <h1>If-Then-Else tags</h1>

     <table width="60%" border="2">
<!--
     Uncomment this If you wish to see the state variables
     printed In your JSP view document.
          <tr>
          <td>
          Got request parameter "condition": <%= (str != null) %>.
          </td>
          </tr>
```

```
                <tr>
                <td>
                    Conditional: <%= condition %>.
                </td>
                </tr>


-->


                <tr>
                <td align="center">
3, 4, 5             <logic:if condition='<%= condition %>' verboseLogging="true" >


6, 7                <logic:then>
                                  The condition is true. This is the
                                  THEN body.


                    </logic:then>
6, 7                <logic:else>
                                  The condition is false. This is the ELSE body.
                    </logic:else>
                    </logic:if>
                </td>
                </tr>
            </table>

            </center>
            </body>
</html>
```

The skeleton collaboration diagram of the If-Then-Else tags example is illustrated in Figure 6-20. Although the diagram contains only the `IfTag` and `ThenTag` handler classes, the `ElseTag` handler class has an interaction pattern that's almost identical to the `ThenTag` handler class. In fact, the only difference between the `ThenTag` and `ElseTag` handler classes is that the argument to the `super()` constructor call has different values. The `ThenTag` constructor calls its superclass with the argument set to `true`, whereas the value of the `ElseTag` constructor is `false`.

As described in the following paragraphs, methods 1 through 5 are called to configure the internal state of the tag handler instances, and these methods correspond to the JavaBean properties known to the `IfTag` instance and the

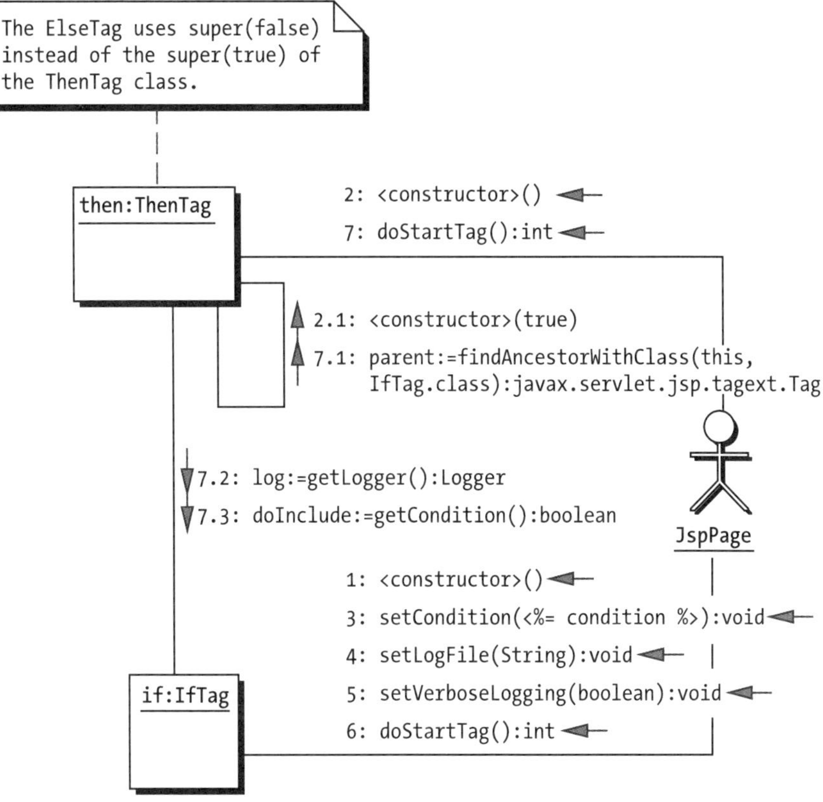

Figure 6-20. Interaction diagram displaying the order of method calls in the system. Of course, all "JSP page" calls are performed by the servlet engine of the Web application server, and therefore hidden from direct view by the programmer. We simply define the handler methods invoked by the engine.

`ThenTag` instance. Methods 6 and 7, on the other hand, are the main entry points to the runtime evaluation of the conditional tag system. In greater detail:

Calls 1 and 2 create the tag handler class instances. Note that the call 2.1 (`super(true);`) populates the internal condition of the `ThenTag`.

Call 3 sets the internal variable, `condition`, of the parent `IfTag`. Note that this variable is set in the JSP in an expression tag. Thus, any variable or Java expression within the JSP that evaluates to a boolean can be used to populate the attribute in the `IfTag` with the `setCondition()` method.

Calls 4 and 5 populate the internal state variables that correspond to the JavaBean attributes `verboseLogging` and `logFile`. These attributes control the logging principles of the system.

Calls 6 and 7 start the conditional evaluation, and include the body of the `ThenTag` if the parent condition equals the condition held in `this.doInclude()`.

The sequence diagram in Figure 6-21 shows how the `doStartTag()` method of the `ThenTag` and `ElseTag` classes work as a tag pair. First, the `ThenTag` verifies that it is contained within an `if` tag. If not, an exception is thrown to notify the developer of the mistake. Having made sure that it resides in the right place, the tag proceeds in asking its superclass about the condition from the JSP document. A `ThenTag` always includes its body if `condition` is `true`, and skips its body if `condition` is `false`, whereas an `ElseTag` always skips its body if `condition` is `true`, and includes it if `condition` is `false`. If the logger instance does not exist, the tag proceeds to create one and log a message to its stream.

Tag Library Definition

The tag library definition document for the three collaborating tag handlers is found in the `taglib.tld` file you see in Listing 6-14, in which the mapping between tag names and implementation classes have been bolded.

Listing 6-14. The `taglib.tld` *file*

```
<?xml version="1.0" encoding="ISO-8859-1" ?>
<!DOCTYPE taglib PUBLIC
   "-//Sun Microsystems, Inc.//DTD JSP Tag Library 1.1//EN"
   "http://java.sun.com/j2ee/dtds/web-jsptaglibrary_1_1.dtd">

<taglib>
     <tlibversion>1.0</tlibversion>
     <jspversion>1.1</jspversion>
     <shortname>JSP Book</shortname>
     <uri>http://localhost/taglib/tagz.jar</uri>
     <info>Tutorial Tag Library</info>
     <tag>
          <name>if</name>
          <tagclass>se.jguru.tags.IfTag</tagclass>
          <bodycontent>JSP</bodycontent>
          <info>Handler class for an IF statement</info>

          <attribute>
               <name>condition</name>
               <required>yes</required>
               <rtexprvalue>yes</rtexprvalue>
          </attribute>
```

```
        <attribute>
            <name>verboseLogging</name>
            <required>no</required>
            <rtexprvalue>yes</rtexprvalue>
        </attribute>

        <attribute>
            <name>logFile</name>
            <required>no</required>
            <rtexprvalue>yes</rtexprvalue>
        </attribute>

    </tag>

    <tag>
        <name>then</name>
        <tagclass>se.jguru.tags.ThenTag</tagclass>
        <bodycontent>JSP</bodycontent>
        <info>Handler class for the THEN part of a if/then/else
            statement.</info>

    </tag>

    <tag>
        <name>else</name>
        <tagclass>se.jguru.tags.ElseTag</tagclass>
        <bodycontent>JSP</bodycontent>
        <info>Handler class for the ELSE part of a if/then/else
            statement.</info>
    </tag>

</taglib>
```

The tag library definition file binds tag names to handler classes. Note that the enclosing `IfTag` defines the level of verbosity for logging purposes. Therefore, the system either runs in development mode (verbose logging switched on) or production mode (no verbose logging for optimum performance).

Note also that all the tag's `<bodycontent>` definitions must have the value JSP to indicate that their body may be `evaluated` and written to the standard `JspWriter`.

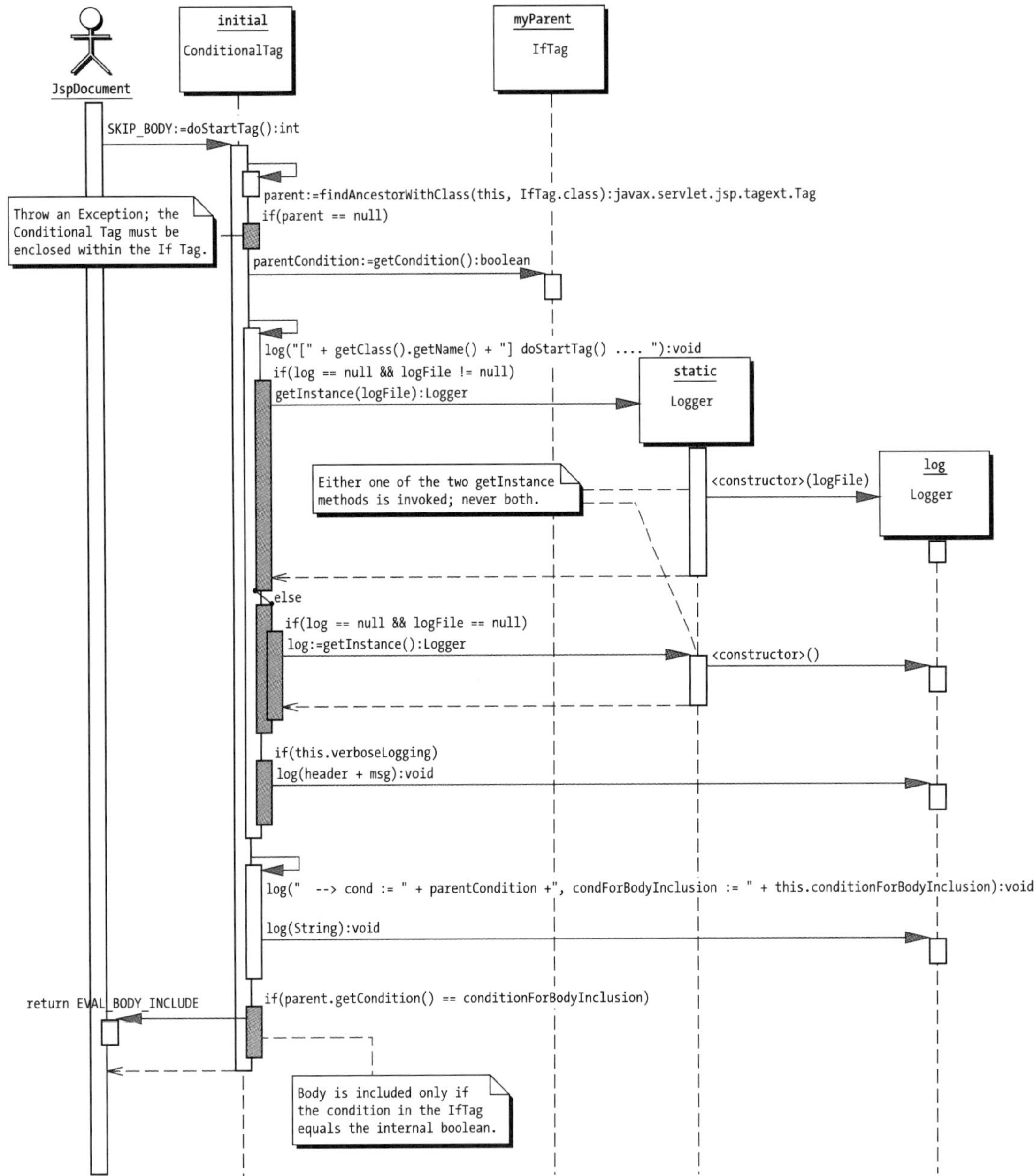

Figure 6-21. The implementation of the `doStartTag()` *method, shown as a sequence diagram*

The Tag Handler Classes

The tag handler classes of this example are much more straightforward than the corresponding classes in the example you saw earlier in this chapter in the section "Custom JSP Tags—Nesting and Looping." First look at the handler class of the `IfTag` in Listing 6-15. (You'll see the source code for the `ThenTag` and `ElseTag` later in this section.)

Listing 6-15. The `IfTag` class, with the tag specific and relevant log statements in bold

```
/*
 * Copyright (c) 2000 jGuru Europe AB.
 * All rights reserved.
 */

package se.jguru.tags;

import javax.servlet.jsp.tagext.BodyTag;
import javax.servlet.jsp.tagext.TagSupport;
import javax.servlet.jsp.JspException;

/**
 * The IfTag handler encapsulates the boolean condition of an if statement,
 * and acts as a parent handler for the Then and Else tags.
 */
public class IfTag extends TagSupport
{
    // Internal state to store the set condition of the If tag
    private boolean condition;

    // The common instance logger which should be used for logging.
    private Logger log;

    // Log file path
    private String logFile;

    // Should the Logger be verbose?
    private boolean verboseLogging;
```

```
/**
 * Setter method for the boolean condition, converted from the string
 * condition argument to this method.
 */
public void setCondition( boolean condition )
{
    this.condition = condition;

    // Log to system out (not to disrupt standard logger creation)
    System.out.println( "(" + this.getClass().getName() +
            "): Condition := " + this.condition + ", [orig:" +
            condition + "]" );
}

/** Getter method for the boolean condition. */
public boolean getCondition()
{
    return this.condition;
}

/**
 * Logs the message to the provided log file or to
 * System.out if no log file has been specified.
 */
protected void log( String msg )
{
    // Check sanity
    if ( log == null )
    {
        // Create a Logger connected to System.out
        log = Logger.getInstance();

        // Log internal state
        this.log( "Created default logger.");
        this.log( "verboseLogging = " + verboseLogging );
    }

    // Log only if we are running in verbose mode.
    if ( this.verboseLogging )
    {
        // Create log header
        String header = "[" + this.getClass().getName() + "] : ";
        log.log( header + msg );
    }
}
```

```
    /**
     * Flag set to invoke verbose logging.
     * @param doVerboseLogging Set to true to invoke verbose
     *          logging in the Logger.
     */
    public void setVerboseLogging( boolean doVerboseLogging )
    {
        this.verboseLogging = doVerboseLogging;
    }

    /** Log file path of the logger used if verbose logging is set. */
    public void setLogFile( String fullPath )
    {
        // Check sanity
        if ( fullPath == null || fullPath.equals( "" ) ) return;
        this.logFile = fullPath;
    }

    /** @return the internal logger instance. */
    public Logger getLogger()
    {
        log("Creating logger");
        return this.log;
    }
}
```

The `IfTag` handler class controls log settings for the If-Then-Else tag collective, by defining and using the two following attributes:

- **`verboseLogging`** indicates whether logging should be echoed to the standard log stream at all. Should `verboseLogging` be set to `false`, no message is echoed to the log stream.

- **`logFile`** is the full path of the log file to use for the logging. In case this attribute is `null`, the log is directed to the standard output stream.

Note that you may have to resolve a hidden race condition in which creating tag handler classes whose internal state depends on set JavaBean attributes. (Recall that a race condition occurs when the order in which methods are called or instructions are executed alters the final result of the execution.) The order in which the attribute setter methods are called depends on implementation and may vary from server to server. Let us for a moment imagine that the `setCondition(boolean condition)` method would have been declared as follows:

```
    public void setCondition( boolean condition )
    {
        this.condition = condition;

        // Log condition
        this.log( "Condition := " + this.condition +
                  ", [orig:" + condition + "]" );
    }
```

Also, imagine the following IfTag realization within the JSP document:

```
<logic:if
    condition='<%= condition %>'
    verboseLogging="true"
    logFile="IfThen.txt">
```

The IfTag handler now includes a race condition, and the two possible results are as follows:

- The IfTag handler calls the setLogFile method before calling the setCondition. The call to setLogFile contains a call to Logger.getInstance(filename), which constructs the singleton Logger and connects it to the file of choice.

- The setCondition method is called *before* setLogFile. When the log method is called, a default Logger is constructed and connected to System.out.

You may ask "Well, why don't you simply remove the construction of the log instance from the log method?" The answer is because it's impossible. The logFile attribute has the following characteristics:

- **optional**, which means that we cannot be certain that the setLogFile method is called at all, and

- **calculated at runtime**, which means that we cannot use some clever initialization method to set up the value of logFile.

Take a look at Listing 6-16, which provides two examples of the opening delimiter and parameters of an If tag. The two If tags illustrate the race condition problems involved, due to the different attributes provided to the If tag. The attributes are in boldface in Listing 6-16.

Listing 6-16. The code of an imaginary JSP file, using the If-Then-Else tags in two different ways

```
<%--
     Verbose logging, to a file whose name is calculated at runtime
--%>
<logic:if
     condition='<%= condition %>'
     verboseLogging="true"
     logFile='<%= request.getParameter("logFile") == null ?
                    standardLog.txt– : request.getParameter("logFile")%>'
     >

<%--
     Verbose logging, to System.out
     Note that no logFile attribute is supplied.
--%>
<logic:if
     condition='<%= condition %>'
     verboseLogging="true" >
```

Of course, there are better ways to handle logging from JSP documents and servlets. (A grand example of good logging procedures is the log4j framework from Apache.) This example, however, is designed to illustrate the possible race condition that results from the fact that we cannot be certain about the call order of setter methods in the JSP document; it's not meant to provide a walkthrough of a logging framework.

Before you can introduce the leaf classes—`ThenTag` and `ElseTag`–you need to define the abstract `ConditionalTag` class that encapsulates all common behavior of the `IfTag` and `ElseTag` handler classes. See Listing 6-17.

Listing 6-17. The `ConditionalTag` *class. The* `TagHandler` *specific calls are bolded.*

```
/*
 * Copyright (c) 2000 jGuru Europe AB.
 * All rights reserved.
 */

package se.jguru.tags;

import javax.servlet.jsp.*;
import javax.servlet.jsp.tagext.*;
import java.io.*;
```

```
/**
 * Tag handler class implementing a conditional; evaluates its
 * body only if the condition within its parent is equal to the
 * internal boolean condition.
 */
public abstract class ConditionalTag extends TagSupport
{
    // Contains the state required to include the body
    // of this conditional tag
    private boolean conditionForBodyInclusion;

    // The logger of the conditional tag.
    private Logger log;

    /**
     * Creates a new ConditionalTag instance, with the
     * provided condition for including its body.
     */
    protected ConditionalTag( boolean condition )
    {
        this.conditionForBodyInclusion = condition;
    }

    /**
     * Logs the message to the provided log file or to
     * System.out if no log file has been specified.
     */
    protected void log( String msg )
    {
        // Create log header to indicate in which
        // class the call originated
        String header = "[" + this.getClass().getName() + "] : ";

        // Log the message
        log.log( header + msg );
    }

    /**
     * Makes sure that this conditionalTag is contained within an IfTag,
     * and checks the condition in the IfTag. If that condition is equal
     * to the value of the conditionForBodyInclusion within this instance,
     * the body is included (by returning EVAL_BODY_INCLUDE) otherwise not.
     */
```

```
    public int doStartTag() throws JspException
    {
        // Verify that the parent of this ThenTag
        // is an IfTag instance.
        Tag parent = this.findAncestorWithClass( this, IfTag.class );
        if ( parent == null )
            throw new JspException( "Then/Else tag must be " +
                         "enclosed within an IfTag." );

        // Sane. Proceed.
        IfTag myParent          = ( IfTag )parent;
        boolean parentCondition = myParent.getCondition();
        boolean doInclude       =
               ( parentCondition == this.conditionForBodyInclusion );

        // Get the logger
        this.log = myParent.getLogger();

        // Log state.
        this.log( " doStartTag() .... " );
        this.log( "  --> cond := " + parentCondition +
          ", condForBodyInclusion := " + this.conditionForBodyInclusion );

        // Include or exclude body
        if ( doInclude )
        {
            return EVAL_BODY_INCLUDE;
        }
        return SKIP_BODY;
    }
}
```

Note that all of the work is done in the `doStartTag()` method, which contains three tasks:

1. You make sure that the `ConditionalTag` is enclosed within an `IfTag`, and obtain a reference to it.

2. The internal boolean condition is matched against the boolean condition from the parent `IfTag`.

3. After having logged some internal state to the logger, you include the body of the current `ConditionalTag` if the expression from step 2 evaluates to `true`. If the evaluation results in a false condition, the body is skipped.

The ThenTag and ElseTag classes are very small because most of their functionality is defined in their common superclass, ConditionalTag. The ThenTag handler class, shown in Listing 6-18, has only one significant method call, the bolded super(true); of its constructor, which defines the condition for including the body of the ThenTag.

Listing 6-18. The ThenTag *class*

```
/*
 * Copyright (c) 2000 jGuru Europe AB.
 * All rights reserved.
 */

package se.jguru.tags;

/**
 * Tag handler for the ThenTtag, which includes its
 * body if the condition in the enclosing IfTtag evaluates
 * to true.
 *
 * @author Lennart Jörelid
 */
public class ThenTag extends ConditionalTag
{
    public ThenTag()
    {
        super(true);
    }
}
```

The structure of the ElseTag is left as an exercise to the reader.

The calls to the log method produced the contents of the log file. Although they could be tailored to reveal more detail than the application currently is designed to do, the purpose of logging in this example is to show a way to display internal state to the developer. When a development environment is tailored to a particular JSP/servlet engine, one can often debug JSP documents and/or servlets inside the running server.

However, debugging JSP in a running J2EE server using the visualization power of an integrated development environment requires much more knowledge of a Web application server than is exposed by the J2EE specification. You will therefore have to purchase a bundled server and development environment if you wish to use enterprise debugging of running instances within specific Web application servers.

TIP *In my experience with developing large-scale enterprise systems, the debugger is generally a blunt and rather poor tool for quickly finding information about what went wrong. Even something as crude as* `System.out.println` *is often much more effective in stomping out bugs than a debugger because you can control precisely what information is presented to you during system execution. Therefore, if you wish to effectively rid the system of errors, I would recommend learning a decent logging framework before starting humongous debugging sessions on an enterprise development system.*

For those developers not wishing to alter their development environment to the one matching the Web server, the best state check of the system is often to log internal state to a common log (like we do in this example) in which entries reveal what is needed to understand system operation during development.

The log of the conditional custom JSP tags example reveals this (not surprising) call order of the `doStartTag()` methods.

```
[se.jguru.tags.IfTag] : Creating logger
[se.jguru.tags.ThenTag] doStartTag() ....
  --> cond := false, condForBodyInclusion := true
[se.jguru.tags.IfTag] : Creating logger
[se.jguru.tags.ElseTag] doStartTag() ....
  --> cond := false, condForBodyInclusion := false
```

The log output is generated by the calls to the `Logger.log()` method. Do examine the source code of the `IfTag` (Listing 6-15) and `ConditionalTag` (Listing 6-17) handler classes to see what variables are logged and where.

Reflections on the Conditional If-Then-Else Custom JSP Tags Example

Although a fairly straightforward example, the custom If-Then-Else tags example illustrates the importance of realizing two things:

- Which superclass to use when implementing tag handler classes. For simpler include-or-exclude-only handlers, use `TagSupport`. Use `BodyTagSupport` only if you need to:
  - iterate over the body of the tag, and

    - alter/modify the body content.

- The implied race condition/implementation dependency regarding the order of setting JavaBean properties.

To realize what differences exist between the `TagSupport` and the `BodyTagSupport` classes, try altering the above example making the `IfTag` extend `BodyTagSupport` instead of `TagSupport`. Try finding out what you have to do to make the newly created `BodyTagSupport` subclass work just like the `IfTag` does.

Another interesting task is to log to `System.out`, for example, when each JavaBean setter method is called. This reveals the call order of the JSP-to-servlet compiler. Try to find patterns to understand how your servlet engine works.

Part III
Struts

CHAPTER 7

The Apache Struts Framework Walkthrough

SYSTEM ARCHITECTURE IS A TOPIC much debated when building Web application systems; most J2EE architects and developers have their own household rules, frequently collected over a series of development projects. Every customer stresses that it is important to plan ahead, develop for reusability, create a robust system that will withstand changes of requirements and specifications—and, of course, be buzzword compliant.

This chapter describes a framework that can be used to ensure that the final product meets a series of demands. The framework is called Struts and is developed by the Apache Software Foundation as an attempt to cope with rapidly changing application specifications for J2EE Web applications. When you use the Struts framework to build your Web application, you benefit from a number of powerful built-in features:

- Built-in configurable support for internationalization and personalization
- Full separation of application flow (controller), business objects (model) and presentation documents (view)
- Powerful Web application structure, permitting you to focus your development on the application rather than on flow logic
- Simplified handling of user-provided form data

Overview of the Struts Architecture

The Struts project from the Apache Software Foundation (`http://jakarta.apache.org/struts/index.html`) is an attempt at creating a common systems architecture for the Web server tier of a Web application. The architecture and thoughts behind the Struts framework serve as an interesting point of reference to discuss front-end Web application architecture. At this writing, Struts is released in version 1.0.

The Model-2 Pattern

The overall architecture of Struts is a distributed variant of the MVC (model-view-controller) pattern, often referred to as *Model-2*. Before taking a closer look at the Struts framework itself, let's first view a simplified illustration of the architecture of a generic Web application. The well-known MVC pattern is used by the Web server tier in a J2EE-compliant application server, as shown in Figure 7-1.

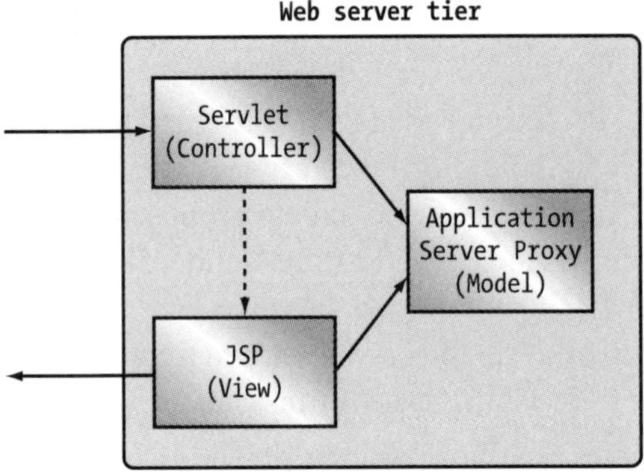

Figure 7-1. The MVC Model-2 pattern as used in a Web application tier. Note that both a servlet and a JSP document collaborate with a model to produce the output. The "Application Server Proxy" is frequently a JavaBean instance (that is, a normal Java class having methods following the JavaBean naming pattern).

The Struts framework uses more classes than the minimalist view shown in Figure 7-1. In fact, the class clutter of the Struts framework makes it a little difficult—at least at a first glance—to see where settings and flow control reside. Like most frameworks, however, Struts is pretty simple once you have grasped its design and call patterns. Let's first study the Struts deployment to see where everything is located, and then take a look at each part in turn. For each building block, we will modify the generic MVC pattern in small steps until we can clearly see the patterns and usefulness of the Struts framework.

Struts Parts and Deployment

Who said that strength in numbers is always a good thing? One of the most obvious downsides of the Struts framework compared to an ordinary servlet/JSP solution is that the functionality of your application is spread out over a larger number of files. Deploying Struts into an empty Web application directory structure is a rather straightforward matter: simply copy five definition files and a template configuration file into your Web application to include the Struts framework functionality.

Figure 7-2 illustrates the layout of a minimal Struts deployment; however, most of the files required for normal operation (that is, when using the Struts framework functionality optimally) are not illustrated. For now, you are shielded from the Struts class clutter; more files will be added when we explain the functionality of the Struts building blocks as required in the walkthrough.

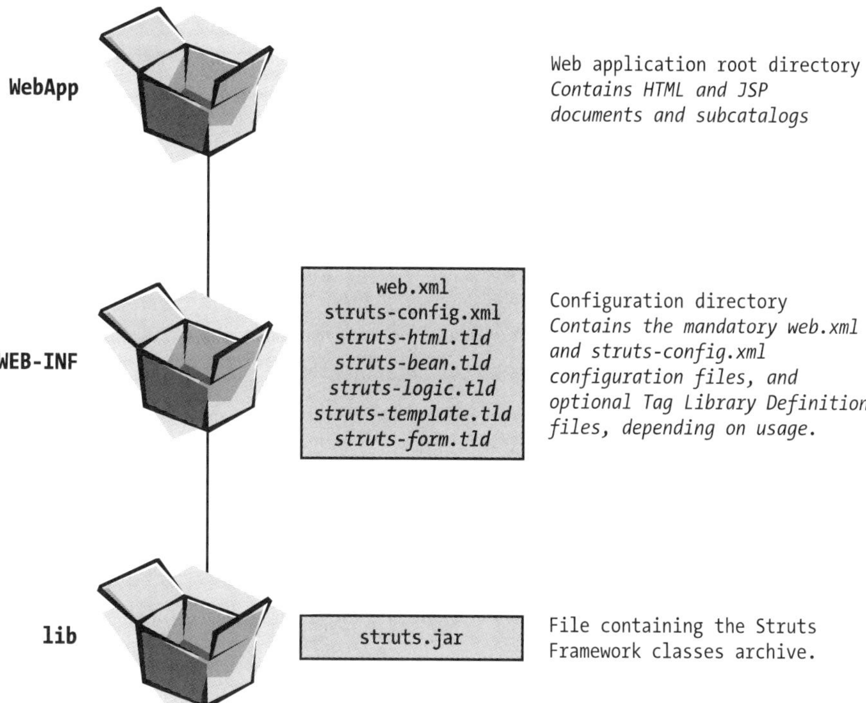

Figure 7-2. The minimal deployment of a Struts Web application. Note that the files containing the actual implementation of a Web application are not shown in this figure. More files will appear in the `WEB-INF/classes` *directory as we start investigating a Struts Web application.*

The conversion of a standard Web application to a Struts-enabled one is a significant operation. Just creating the structure shown in Figure 7-2 changes nothing at all in the behavior of the Web application. You must also alter all of the application's HTML and JSP files to provide the desired Struts functionality.

Table 7-1 provides a quick overview of the components illustrated in Figure 7-2.

Table 7-1. Struts Framework Configuration Files Overview

FILE	DESCRIPTION
`/WEB-INF/lib/struts.jar`	The Struts framework binary distribution. The JAR file is roughly 304KB in size.
`/WEB-INF/web.xml`	Standard web application deployment descriptor, which must contain a servlet definition for the Struts `ActionServlet`. (The `ActionServlet` instance is the controller of the Struts Web application. Refer to the Controller section for an in-depth look at the `ActionServlet`.)
`/WEB-INF/struts-config.xml`	Configuration file for the Struts part of the application. This file is central for configuring actions that control the execution flow for the Web application. (Refer to the section "Struts Controller Components" for an in-depth look at this file.)
`/WEB-INF/struts-bean.tld`	Tag Library Definition (TLD) file for tag handler classes manipulating JavaBean model elements in the Struts framework.
`/WEB-INF/struts-html.tld`	TLD file for tag handler classes manipulating HTML view element output in the Struts framework.
`/WEB-INF/struts-form.tld`	TLD file for tag handler classes manipulating `ActionForm` JavaBean Model elements in the Struts Framework. (Refer to the section "Struts Controller Components" for an in-depth look at the power of this TLD.)
`/WEB-INF/struts-template.tld`	TLD file for tag handler classes that dynamically joins content from several files to build a resulting view.
`/WEB-INF/struts-logic.tld`	TLD file for tag handler classes manipulating flow logic control elements in the Struts framework. (Refer to the section "Struts Controller Components" for an in-depth look at the power of this TLD.)

The file structure presented in Figure 7-2 contains no Web application; it is simply the bare-bones framework required to install Struts into your application server. To actually develop a fully Struts-enabled Web application, you need at least one (but preferably four) more files:

- The JSP file(s) to present the view to the user
- An instance of the Struts `Action` class that provides the controller flow execution logic (that is, selects the proper view to which the execution should be redirected)

- An `ActionForm` JavaBean instance that encapsulates HTML form data (This is the model of the MVC pattern illustrated in Figure 7-1.)
- A `PropertyResourceBundle` file that contains a locale-specific set of static strings in the form `<key>=<value>`

Extend Figure 7-2 by adding these four files without actually explaining the function of the `Action` and `ActionForm` classes. (Their function will be explained shortly.) Figure 7-3 shows the Web application including the newly added files, which have been shaded for easier identification. All files are placed in their standard deployment directories. The small example that will be used is a login page and a page displaying feedback to the user.

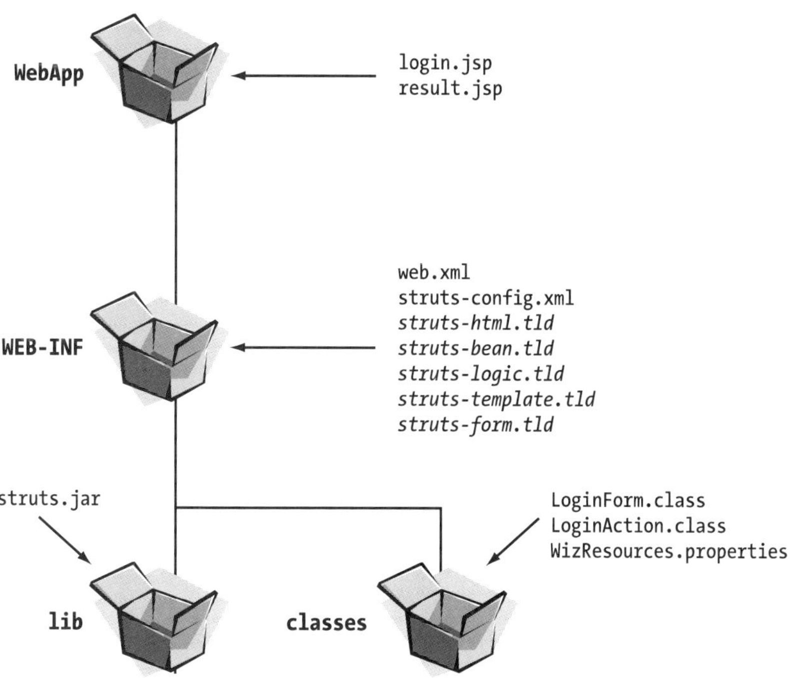

Figure 7-3. Deployment of a small—but real—Struts application

The MVC pattern is enforced throughout the Struts framework. In Figure 7-4, the model is presented as a `LoginForm` instance, the view consists of the `login.jsp`, `result.jsp`, and `Resources.properties` files, and the controller is the `LoginAction` instance. Table 7-2 summarizes the sections of a deployed Struts application.

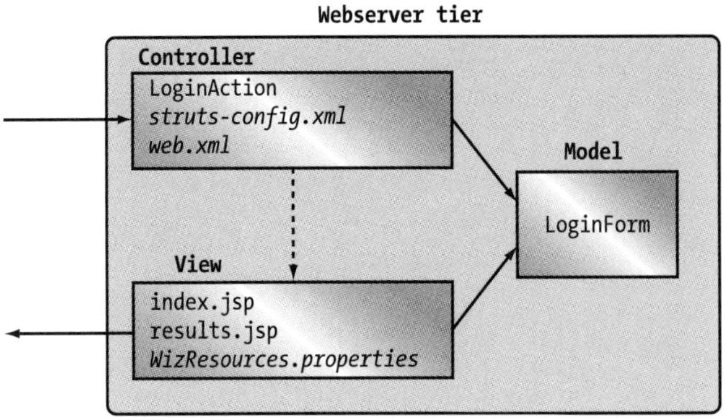

Figure 7-4. The MVC pattern is clearly visible in the structure; the `LoginForm` *class constitutes the model, and the* `LoginAction`, `struts-config.xml`, *the* `web.xml` *documents define the controller, and the combination of the documents* `WizResources.properties`, `index.jsp`, *and* `results.jsp` *creates the view.*

Table 7-2. The Files of the Struts Application, Grouped by Function

STRUTS SECTION	EXAMPLE FILES IN SECTION
Struts configuration or deployment descriptor files	/WEB-INF/struts-config.xml
	/WEB-INF/struts-html.tld
	/WEB-INF/struts-bean.tld
	/WEB-INF/struts-logic.tld
	/WEB-INF/struts-template.tld
	/WEB-INF/struts-form.tld
Model	/WEB-INF/classes/LoginForm.class
View	/index.jsp
	/results.jsp
Controller	/WEB-INF/classes/LoginAction.class
Struts framework binaries	/WEB-INF/lib/struts.jar
ResourceBundle files	/WEB-INF/classes/WizResources.properties

The two deployment descriptor documents of a Struts-enabled Web application are `web.xml` and `struts-config.xml`. We'll examine each of them in turn.

web.xml

When learning something new, it's always helpful to start by building on something that's already understood. Therefore, let's start by taking a look at the web.xml document to configure the Struts ActionServlet and tag libraries. The details of some parameters will be skipped in this walkthrough, as you'll want to focus on the main issues at hand and leave archaic configuration options for your own excursions into the Struts reference.

Listing 7-1 contains the minimal web.xml deployment descriptor for a Struts-enabled application.

Listing 7-1. The Struts-related definitions are bolded in the web.xml *listing.*

```
<?xml version="1.0" encoding="ISO-8859-1"?>

<!DOCTYPE web-app
  PUBLIC "-//Sun Microsystems, Inc.//DTD Web Application 2.2//EN"
  "http://java.sun.com/j2ee/dtds/web-app_2_2.dtd">

<web-app>

  <!-- Action Servlet Configuration -->
  <servlet>
    <servlet-name>wizAction</servlet-name>
    <servlet-class>org.apache.struts.action.ActionServlet</servlet-class>
    <init-param>
      <param-name>application</param-name>
      <param-value>se.jguru.wizard.WizResources</param-value>
    </init-param>
    <init-param>
      <param-name>config</param-name>
      <param-value>/WEB-INF/struts-config.xml</param-value>
    </init-param>
    <init-param>
      <param-name>debug</param-name>
      <param-value>2</param-value>
    </init-param>
    <init-param>
      <param-name>detail</param-name>
      <param-value>2</param-value>
    </init-param>
```

```
    <init-param>
      <param-name>validate</param-name>
      <param-value>true</param-value>
    </init-param>
    <load-on-startup>2</load-on-startup>
  </servlet>


  <!-- Action Servlet Mapping -->
  <servlet-mapping>
    <servlet-name>wizAction</servlet-name>
    <url-pattern>/run/*</url-pattern>
  </servlet-mapping>


  <!-- The Welcome File List -->
  <welcome-file-list>
    <welcome-file>index.jsp</welcome-file>
  </welcome-file-list>

  <!-- Struts Tag Library Descriptors -->
  <taglib>
    <taglib-uri>/WEB-INF/struts-bean.tld</taglib-uri>
    <taglib-location>/WEB-INF/struts-bean.tld</taglib-location>
  </taglib>

  <taglib>
    <taglib-uri>/WEB-INF/struts-html.tld</taglib-uri>
    <taglib-location>/WEB-INF/struts-html.tld</taglib-location>
  </taglib>

  <taglib>
    <taglib-uri>/WEB-INF/struts-logic.tld</taglib-uri>
    <taglib-location>/WEB-INF/struts-logic.tld</taglib-location>
  </taglib>

</web-app>
```

It's important to note the following points about the `web.xml` deployment descriptor document:

- The `ActionServlet` class is `org.apache.struts.action.ActionServlet`. You may, of course, subclass this type to provide your own custom implementation of the `ActionServlet`. (The `ActionServlet` class is covered in its own section later in this chapter.)

- The resource property file for this Web application is found in the `se.jguru.wizard.WizResources` resource bundle. This generally refers to a `PropertyResourceBundle` file `/WEB-INF/classes/se/jguru/wizard/WizResources.properties`. (Static string resources are explained in more detail in the section "JSPs and Tag Libraries" later in this chapter.)

- The `ActionServlet` configuration file is `/WEB-INF/struts-config.xml` as indicated by the `config` parameter. (This is assumed throughout this walkthrough.) You could, of course, use any XML document name as the configuration document for the Struts framework.

- The `ActionServlet` is mapped to the URL `/run/*`, so it will be invoked for each call to the Web application that includes the path `/run/`. This is known as *prefix mapping*. As a contrast, the default Struts configuration maps all documents ending with the `.do` extension to the `ActionServlet`. Because the default configuration reacts to document suffices, it is known as a *suffix mapping*.

NOTE *If you use Struts custom tags to generate the HTML in the view, the correct URL to invoke the* `ActionServlet` *is autogenerated. (You'll find more information on the custom tags of Struts in the section "JSPs and Tag Libraries" later in this chapter.)*

- Because many of the HTML elements in a Struts-enabled Web application are likely to be produced by the Struts custom tags, the Web administrator of the application has defined a new welcome page, the document that's shown to a user if the URL ends in a directory. Normally, the welcome page is `index.html`, but, in this dynamic Web application, it's been changed to `index.jsp`. (The section "JSPs and Tag Libraries" contains more information on the custom tags of Struts.)

- The Struts TLD files are specified in the `web.xml` file to load all required tag libraries into the Web application.

struts-config.xml

The Struts configuration document, `struts-config.xml`, has a rather small document type definition (DTD), which makes its topmost structure easy to view. Figure 7-4 shows a Unified Modeling Language (UML) visualization of the DTD that specifies the `struts-config.xml` document just shown. A Struts configuration document has a `struts-config` root container tag that may contain only four subtag types, as illustrated in Figure 7-5.

The Help Documents of Struts

The Struts distribution contains a small set of help files that, in most cases, provide adequate information to get started with most Struts-related tasks. The help files are as follows:

- `<Struts-Home>/README` serves as a point of origin in the newly installed (or, at least, unpacked) Struts distribution. The README file contains information about what has been unpacked, as well as pointers to sources of information in the distribution and on the Web site of the Struts project.
- `<Struts-Home>/INSTALL` contains additional Struts framework installation instructions for a few common application servers.
- `<Struts-Home>/LICENSE` contains the license agreement for the Struts framework.
- `<Struts-Home>/INSTALL` contains instructions that simplify the installation of the Struts framework into several well-known application servers.
- `<Struts-Home>/webapp/struts-documentation.war` is a Web application that unpacks and installs into the Struts User Guide and the full JavaDoc structure for the Struts framework classes.

Although the DTD root level is deceptively simple, each subtype has a rather complex structure that contains several optional attributes. The Struts documentation (downloaded and installed with the Struts distribution) provides valuable help on the details of each attribute.

The tags of the `struts-config.xml` are explained in their respective sections. For now, examine the controller, the model, and the view components in detail.

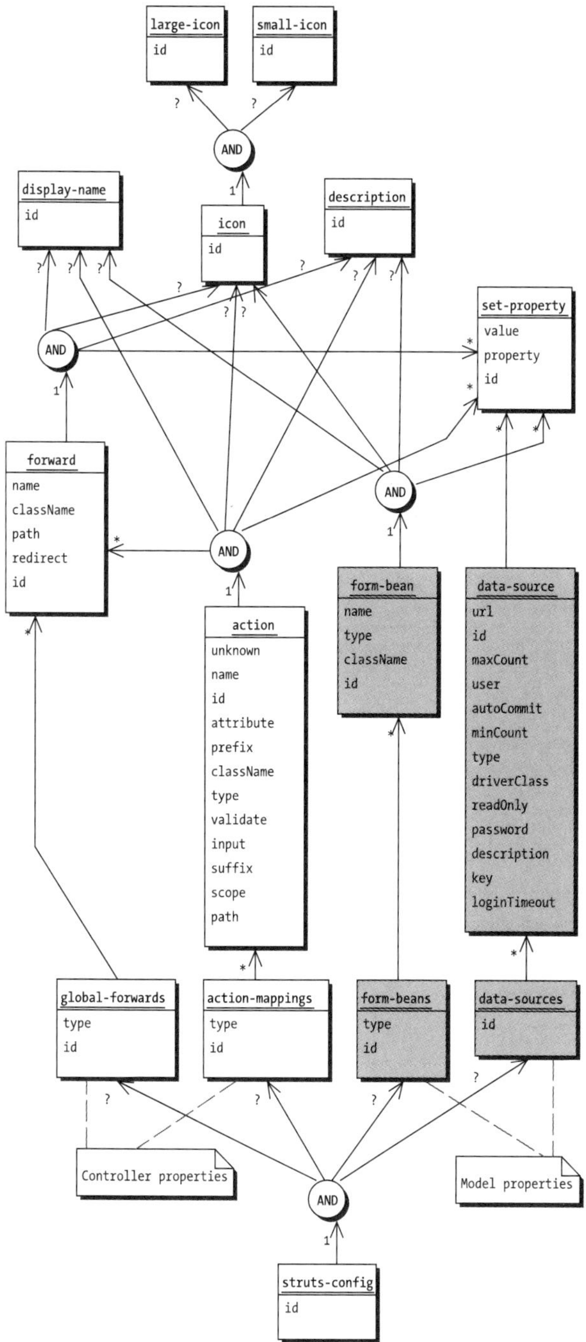

Figure 7-5. The DTD of the `struts-config.xml` *file is straightforward to interpret. The two top-most XML element containers are shaded to indicate their configuration control extent. The* `global-forwards` *and* `action-mappings` *sections that provide configuration information to the Struts controller have white backgrounds in the figure, and the* `form-beans` *and* `data-sources` *tags that provide configuration information to the Struts model have shaded backgrounds.*

Struts Controller Components

The ActionServlet

In the Struts naming terminology, the controller servlet is called `ActionServlet`. At initialization time (when the servlet is loaded into memory and its init method is called), the `ActionServlet` reads and parses a configuration file (`/WEB-INF/struts-config.xml`) to create its registered `ActionMappings` containing definitions to create the `ActionMapping` instances of the `ActionServlet`. An `ActionMapping` is something similar to a HashMap entry, linking an incoming HTTP request URL to execution flow logic objects, known as `Action` instances. (The difference between business logic and flow logic is that the former implements business entities and application logic, whereas the latter controls execution flow.)

The `Action` instance is responsible for finding an `ActionForward` instance that uniquely identifies an internal or external view (such as an HTML, JSP, or XML document) to which the execution will be forwarded. Assisting the `Action` instance in selecting the target `ActionForward` is an optional `ActionForm`, a JavaBean model instance that wraps data entered into a client-side HTML form by the user.

Table 7-3 contains the definitions.

Table 7-3. Important Struts Classes and Their Functions

TYPE	DESCRIPTION
`org.apache.struts.action.ActionServlet`	Controller servlet class; receives the incoming HTTP request, and finds the associated `ActionMapping` from the specifications in the config.xml file. Creates and populates an `ActionForm` instance if required
`org.apache.struts.action.ActionMapping`	Container class that relates a particular HTTP URI (String) to a unique Action instance
`org.apache.struts.action.ActionMappings`	Collection class that contains all known `ActionMappings` of a particular `ActionServlet`
`org.apache.struts.action.ActionForm`	Simple JavaBean property container that encapsulates incoming data from an HTML form

Table 7-3. Important Struts Classes and Their Functions (Continued)

TYPE	DESCRIPTION
`org.apache.struts.action.Action`	Flow execution logic responsible for finding a particular `ActionForward` (redirection target) using the data in the `(Http)ServletRequest` and optional `ActionForm`
`org.apache.struts.action.ActionForward`	Contains the internal (forward) or external (redirect) URI selected by the `Action` instance as the view which should be redirected to
`org.apache.struts.action.ActionForwards`	Contains all known `ActionForward` instances of a particular Action instance

Before venturing further into the dark forest of terminology, consider the currently known state of affairs depicted in Figure 7-6.

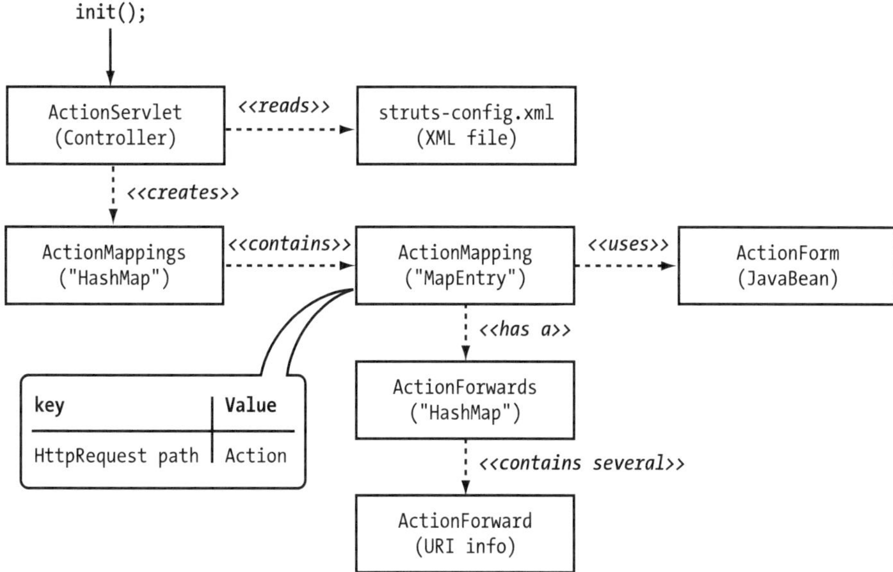

Figure 7-6. Simplified diagram of the setup of the Struts system in the `init()` *method*

The `ActionServlet` instance reads its configuration XML document and creates an `ActionMapping` instance for each found entry. Each `ActionMapping` represents a potential business flow use case (that is, a redirection to a particular JSP if the incoming HTTP request matches a given string pattern).

The `Action` instance contains a reference to the `ActionServlet` controller and may therefore set or get attributes in any of the standard contexts used by the `ActionServlet` (Application, Session, Request, and Page). Again, the `Action` instance represents flow logic; its function is similar to an event listener. Whenever the incoming HTTP request URI matches the key of a particular `ActionMapping`, the `perform()` method is invoked in the Action instance belonging to the `ActionMapping` in question. The Action instance is shared between multiple users and therefore may not use object-wide or static variables to store session or individual user state; all such data must be stored in either the `HttpSession` or `HttpServletRequest` scopes of the `ActionServlet`.

Actions and struts-config.xml

An Action instance is created from the `struts-config.xml` file, which contains entries of the form presented in Figure 7-7. All Action objects are created at initialization time by the `ActionServlet` according to the instructions in the `struts-config.xml` file. Note that the DTD presented in Figure 7-7 is a subset of the full `struts-config.xml` DTD shown in Figure 7-6.

Now take a look at the parts of the `struts-config.xml` configuration file that define a new `ActionMapping` for our `index.jsp`, in compliance with the DTD snippet shown in Figure 7-7. `ActionMappings` represent all possible "next page" destinations for when the client-side HTTP form is submitted.

Listing 7-2 shows the configuration document `struts-config.xml` for a wizard-like application that will be generated as you progress through this chapter.

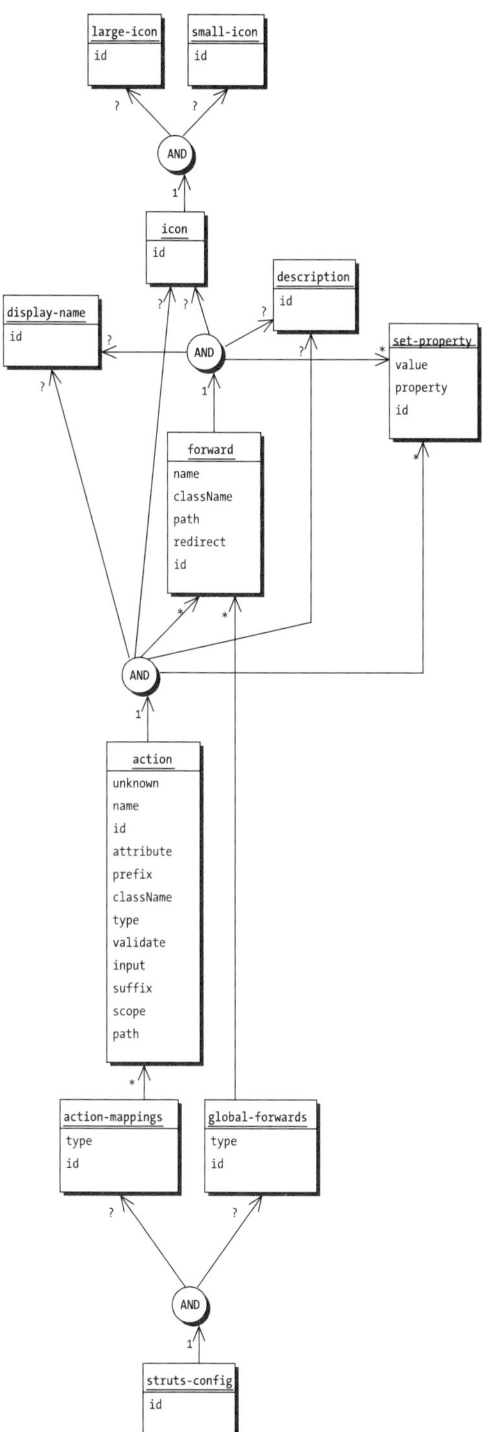

Figure 7-7. The `action-mapping` *and* `global-forwards` *substructure of the* `struts-config.xml` *DTD*

Listing 7-2. The `struts-config.xml` *document*

```
<struts-config>
<!-- ---------- Global Forward Definitions ---------- -->
<global-forwards>
            <forward  name="failure" path="/errorPage.jsp" />
            <forward  name="next" path="/wiz1.jsp" />
</global-forwards>

<!-- ---------- Action Mapping Definitions ---------- -->

 <action-mappings>
            <action
                          path="/login"
                          type="se.jguru.wizard.LoginAction"
                          name="loginForm"
                          scope="request">
            <forward name="success" path="/results.jsp" />
            </action>
<action-mappings>

... more configuration settings go here ...

</struts-config>
```

The `<action>` element definition in Listing 7-2 connects the incoming relative Web path `/login` to an action handler of the type `se.jguru.wizard.LoginAction`. If the `LoginAction` controller returns an `ActionForward` instance having the key "`success`", the resulting view presented to the user will be contained in the file `/results.jsp` (relative to the Web application root). Also, the incoming `HttpServletRequest` will contain HTML form data that will be inserted into a (newly created) instance of the `ActionForm` that has the name `loginForm`. The actual type of the `loginForm` is defined in another section in the `struts-config.xml` file, which will be presented in the upcoming section "Struts Model Components."

In addition to the ActionMappings provided, the `struts-config.xml` file defines two global forwards. A global forward is used if a local one (defined as a `<forward>` tag within the `<action>` container element tag) cannot be found.

The `<action-mappings>` element may contain many `<action>` definitions that, in turn, may contain several `<ActionForward>` definitions. Look at the Java code for a minute to discuss the concrete `Action` class implementation `se.jguru.wizard.LoginAction`. The `LoginAction` qualified class path is given as the concrete `Action` class in the `<ActionMapping>` defined above. What, you may ask, are the constraints of that class?

The Action Controller

The Action controller is a class that extends the `Action` class to provide—at the least—a `perform()` method handling the incoming request and returning an `ActionMapping` telling the application which view document the Action servlet should use as the "next" document. Frequently, the custom Action controller instance simply extends `org.apache.struts.action.Action` and provides an implementation to the `perform()` method. Because most relevant methods in the `Action` class are declared with protected access scope, you may override their functionality to provide your custom implementation. It is rather uncommon to override anything but the `perform()` method; the most common type of Action implementation class inherits the `Action` class directly. (See Figure 7-8.)

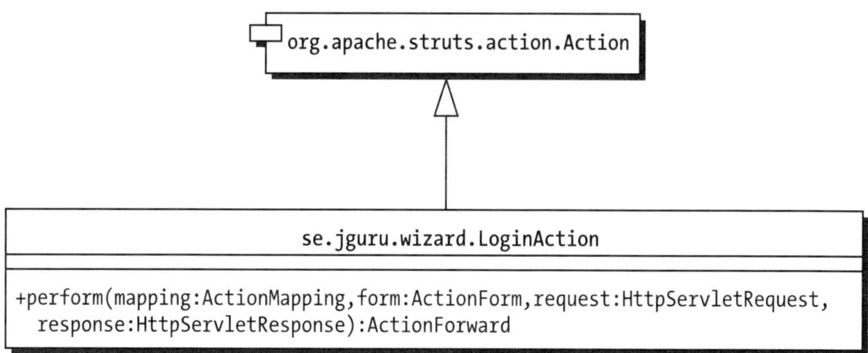

Figure 7-8. Inheritance structure of the `LoginAction` *class*

The only method of the `LoginAction` class is `perform()`, which returns an `ActionForward` instance containing the address of the view to forward the request to. In addition to the instances passed as arguments to the `perform()` method, the `Action` class contains a protected instance variable, called `servlet`, that is a reference to the `ActionServlet` called. Via that reference, all public methods of the `ActionServlet` are accessible from the `LoginAction`.

Although the small `perform()` method is quickly generated, the Struts framework permits very complex determination algorithms for retrieving the view address. We'll start with the simple example shown in Listing 7-3 and move on to more complex ones.

Listing 7-3. An example `perform()` *method*

```
public ActionForward perform(ActionMapping mapping,
    ActionForm form,
    HttpServletRequest request,
    HttpServletResponse response)
    throws IOException, ServletException
    {
        // This is a very simple perform method which will
        // return either the ActionMapping associated with the
        // key "success" or the key "failure".
        // The views (as defined In struts-config.xml) are :
        //        /result.jsp for the "success" mapping.
        //        /errorPage.jsp for the "failure" mapping.
        if(request.getParameterValues("someValue")[0] != null)
                return mapping.findForward("success");
        else return mapping.findForward("failure");
    }
```

The UML class diagram in Figure 7-9 illustrates the associations between the classes related to the Action instance.

Note in Figure 7-9 the cardinalities of each type. In some cases, such as the association between the `ActionForwards` and `ActionForward` classes, the contained element is stored within a collection or map inside its parent. Few UML tools are capable of discovering this hidden one-to-many association, and the relation won't therefore be discovered by a normal UML tool import process.

Of course, the class structures in Figures 7-8 and 7-9 are quite simplified. By comparison, Figure 7-10 shows the full UML diagram of the three Struts framework classes `ActionMapping`, `ActionMappings`, and `ActionServlet`.

Although the number of methods in Figure 7-10 may appear overwhelming at first sight, the naming patterns assist in quickly grouping the methods into stereotypes (sets of methods with similar properties) that may be treated as a single method with variations. As you can see, the Struts framework is rich in implementation detail, yet it is still fairly simple to understand and use. Note that all of the methods and data of the `ActionServlet` class are protected. You may therefore alter the behavior of any internal `ActionServlet` method by overriding it in an `ActionServlet` subclass.

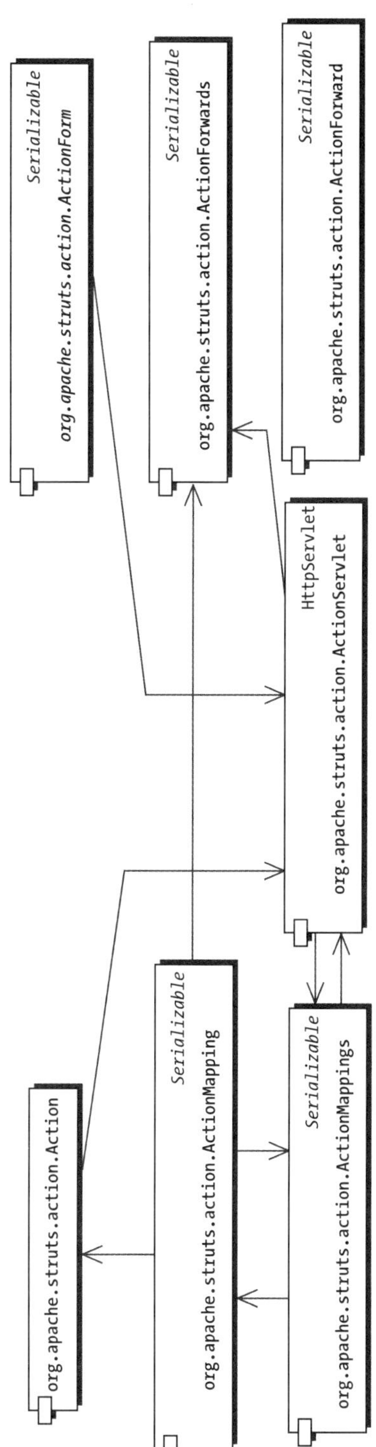

Figure 7-9. UML diagram of some of the `ActionServlet`*-related classes*

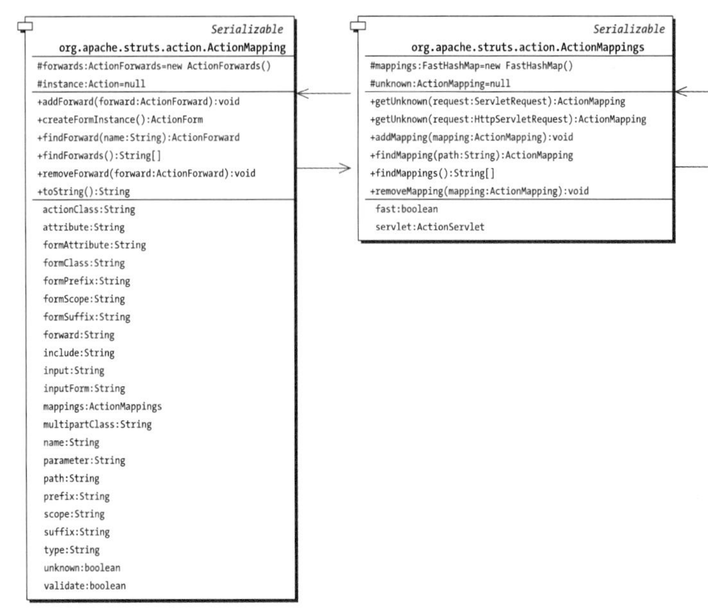

Figure 7-10. The full structure of three of the Struts framework classes

```
                                                              HttpServlet
                    org.apache.struts.action.ActionServlet
#actions:FastHashMap=new FastHashMap()
#application:MessageResources=null
#config:String="/WEB-INF/struts-config.xml"
#content:String="text/html"
#dataSources:FastHashMap=new FastHashMap()
#defaultLocale:Locale=Locale.getDefault()
#factoryClass:String=null
#formBeans:ActionFormBeans=new ActionFormBeans()
#forwards:ActionForwards=new ActionForwards()
#internal:MessageResources=null
#internalName:String="org.apache.struts.action.ActionResources"
#locale:boolean=true
#mappings:ActionMappings=new ActionMappings()
#nocache:boolean=false
#registrations:String[]={       "-//Apache Software Foundation//DTD Struts Configuration 1.0//EN",
        "/org/apache/struts/resources/struts-config_1_0.dtd",
        "-//Sun Microsystems, Inc.//DTD Web Application 2.2//EN",
        "/org/apache/struts/resources/web-app_2_2.dtd",
        "-//Sun Microsystems, Inc.//DTD Web Application 2.3//EN",
        "/org/apache/struts/resources/web-app_2_3.dtd"    }
#servletMapping:String=null
#servletName:String=null
#validate:boolean=true
#validating:boolean=true
+destroy():void
+init():void
+doGet(request:HttpServletRequest,response:HttpServletResponse):void
+doPost(request:HttpServletRequest,response:HttpServletResponse):void
+addDataSource(key:String,dataSource:DataSource):void
+addFormBean(formBean:ActionFormBean):void
+addForward(forward:ActionForward):void
+addMapping(mapping:ActionMapping):void
+addServletMapping(servletName:String,urlPattern:String):void
+findDataSource(key:String):DataSource
+findFormBean(name:String):ActionFormBean
+findForward(name:String):ActionForward
+findMapping(path:String):ActionMapping
+log(message:String,level:int):void
+reload():void
+removeFormBean(formBean:ActionFormBean):void
+removeForward(forward:ActionForward):void
+removeMapping(mapping:ActionMapping):void
#destroyActions():void
#destroyApplication():void
#destroyDataSources():void
#destroyInternal():void
#initActions():void
#initApplication():void
#initDataSources():void
#initDebug():void
#initDigester(detail:int):Digester
#initDigesterOld(detail:int):Digester
#initInternal():void
#initMapping():void
#initOther():void
#initServlet():void
#initUpload():void
#process(request:HttpServletRequest,response:HttpServletResponse):void
#processActionCreate(mapping:ActionMapping,request:HttpServletRequest):Action
#processActionForm(mapping:ActionMapping,request:HttpServletRequest):ActionForm
#processActionForward(forward:ActionForward,mapping:ActionMapping,
  formInstance:ActionForm,request:HttpServletRequest,
  response:HttpServletResponse):void
#processActionPerform(action:Action,mapping:ActionMapping,
  formInstance:ActionForm,request:HttpServletRequest,
  response:HttpServletResponse):ActionForward
#processContent(response:HttpServletResponse):void
#processForward(mapping:ActionMapping,request:HttpServletRequest,response:HttpServletResponse):boolean
#processInclude(mapping:ActionMapping,request:HttpServletRequest,response:HttpServletResponse):boolean
#processLocale(request:HttpServletRequest):void
#processMapping(path:String,request:HttpServletRequest):ActionMapping
#processNoCache(response:HttpServletResponse):void
#processPath(request:HttpServletRequest):String
#processPreprocess(request:HttpServletRequest,response:HttpServletResponse):boolean
#processPopulate(formInstance:ActionForm,mapping:ActionMapping,request:HttpServletRequest):void
#processValidate(mapping:ActionMapping,formInstance:ActionForm,request:HttpServletRequest,response:HttpServletResponse):boolean
 bufferSize:int
 debug:int
 formBeanClass:String
 forwardClass:String
 mappingClass:String
 maxFileSize:String
 multipartClass:String
 resources:MessageResources
 tempDir:String
```

At first glance, Figure 7-10 may suggest that the Struts framework is large and cumbersome to learn. However, in reality, the amount of code that has to be understood and implemented by the programmer is quite small, especially when you consider that the Struts framework, once mastered, may be reused for all types of Web application development. Also, the framework will simply coexist with any "ordinary" Web application that has not been modified to use the Struts framework.

Web application migration to the Struts framework architecture is greatly simplified by two properties of Struts:

- The minimum code to create a running, Struts-compliant, Web application is quickly manufactured. In fact, all you need to do to run the Struts framework is provide a working `struts-config.xml` document and an `ActionServlet` definition in the `web.xml` deployment descriptor.
- You do not have to convert all pieces of your Web application to the Struts framework before being able to redeploy it. Simply migrate one JSP at a time.

An important part of the migration to the Struts-Aware Web application is understanding its model components, such as `ActionForms` and other JavaBeans. Therefore, let's take a look at the model component of the Struts framework.

Struts Model Components

ActionForms

An `ActionForm` instance is a JavaBean that contains data submitted from an HTML form. The JavaBean paradigm, along with some Java introspection, is used to generate Struts model instances in two steps:

1. Each action defined in the `struts-config.xml` file may accept a form attribute, which is mapped to a `<form-bean>` element. The type of the `<form-bean>` container element is considered a fully qualified class name of a subclass to the class `org.apache.struts.action.ActionForm` and is instantiated to act as a data container for HTML form data.
2. The `ActionServlet` populates the `ActionForm` instance by examining all incoming `ServletRequest` parameters. Whenever a JavaBean having the same name as a `ServletRequest` parameter name is found in the `ActionForm`, its setter method is invoked with the corresponding parameter's value as the argument.

The ActionForm instance is submitted as an argument to the perform() method of the Action implementation class. Thus, any data that the user entered into forms may be accessed in the perform() method of the Action controller instance.

Create the small example ActionForm class shown in Listing 7-4 to illustrate the procedure described at the very beginning of this section. Although it has a rather bulky body, its four methods simply set and get the two strings containing a user ID and a password. Of course, the LoginForm class may be used as a model for a dynamic Web application that permits users to authenticate themselves.

Listing 7-4. The LoginForm *class*

```
/* Copyright (c) 2000 jGuru Europe.
 All rights reserved. */

package se.jguru.wizard;

import org.apache.struts.action.ActionForm;

/**
 * DataContainer for data from the HTML login form
 * in this Web Application.
 */
public class LoginForm extends ActionForm
{
    // Define interal state
    protected String userId;
    protected String password;

    public void setUserId(String userId)
    {
        this.userId = userId;
    }

    public String getUserId()
    {
        return this.userId;
    }

    public void setPassword(String plaintextPasswd)
    {
        this.password = plaintextPasswd;
    }
```

```
    public String getPassword()
    {
        return this.password;
    }
}
```

Indeed, the UML diagram in Figure 7-11 (using JavaBean notation) of the `LoginForm` class and its superclass `ActionForm` shows that the `LoginForm` class simply contains all JavaBean properties that should be set with the values that match the form field names in the HTML form on `login.jsp`. Although no other code is required in simple `ActionForm` implementations, one may need to validate the data entered by a user before starting to process it in the `ActionServlet` controller. The `ActionForm` class itself may perform data validation.

Figure 7-11. The `ActionForm` *superclass and its implementation,* `LoginForm`. *Note the simplicity of the* `LoginForm` *subclass: merely define JavaBean properties (that is, getter and setter methods) for all form data, and use the built-in power of the Struts framework.*

ActionForm data validation is done in the validate method. If you wish a particular ActionForm subclass to validate its data, simply override the method:

```
public ActionErrors validate(ActionMapping, ServletRequest);
```

The validate method is called automagically by the Struts framework before it invokes the perform method in the Action class. Any ActionErrors instances returned by the validate method may be used by the Action implementation class in its code execution. If no malformed data was entered, the validate method should simply return null or an empty ActionErrors instance.

The ActionForm instance is supplied as an argument to the perform method fully populated and ready to have its data used by the Action controller implementation.

Take another look at the perform method of the LoginAction class, this time augmented with the usage pattern of the LoginForm instance, as shown in Listing 7-5.

Listing 7-5. The perform() *method using a* LoginForm *instance to read data from the user*

```
public ActionForward perform(ActionMapping mapping,
    ActionForm form,
    HttpServletRequest request,
    HttpServletResponse response)
    throws IOException, ServletException
    {
        // Typecast the ActionForm to the proper type,
        // and get the data entered into it.
        LoginForm theForm = (LoginForm) form;

        // Simply write the form data to the console to
        // view the contents of ActionForm
        System.out.println("Got form: " + theForm.getUserId()
                + ":" + theForm.getPassword());

        // Forward to different views depending on the
        // data submitted In the LoginForm.
        if(theForm.getUserId().equalsIgnoreCase("duke"))
                return mapping.findForward("failure");
        else mapping.findForward("success");
    }
```

Of course, other model instances may be used when running a Web application in the Struts framework. You can always access the ActionServlet, HttpServletRequest, HttpSession, HttpServletResponse, and other instances such as ActionMappings and

ActionForwards within the perform method. It is therefore a simple matter to retrieve any bound JavaBean or other model objects from any such model object container.

To use an ActionForm subclass (such as the se.jguru.wizard.LoginForm presented above), you must define it in the struts-config.xml document. The TLD tags pertaining to ActionForm instances are pretty straightforward. To add a particular ActionForm to an <action>, you simply need to follow these two steps:

1. Define a <form-bean> element, which contains the type and logical name for the ActionForm class.

2. Define a name attribute for the <action> element that should use the <form-bean>. The name attribute of the <action> element must be identical to the logical name of an existing <form-bean>.

Augment the struts-config.xml file from Listing 7-2 to include a <form-bean> element as shown in Listing 7-6. The <form-bean> element should be used by the only defined action in the struts-config.xml file (invoked from the action path /login). All XML code pertaining to the <form-bean> declaration is shown in boldface to distinguish it from XML tags configuring the controller. Note, again, that the name attributes of the <form-bean> and <action> tags must be identical.

Listing 7-6. The modified struts-config.xml, *with the form configuration properties in bold*

```
<struts-config>
<!-- ---------- Form Bean Definitions ---------- -->
<form-beans>
            <form-bean name="loginForm" type="se.jguru.wizard.LoginForm"/>
</form-beans>

<!-- ---------- Global Forward Definitions ---------- -->
<global-forwards>
            <forward  name="failure" path="/errorPage.jsp" />
            <forward  name="next" path="/wiz1.jsp" />
</global-forwards>

<!-- ---------- Action Mapping Definitions ---------- -->
<action-mappings>
            <action
                        path="/login"
                        type="se.jguru.wizard.LoginAction"
                        name="loginForm"
                        scope="request">
            <forward name="success" path="/results.jsp" />
            </action>
```

```
</action-mappings>
... more configuration settings go here ...
</struts-config>
```

If you want to alter the behavior of a particular `ActionForm` without recompiling the `Action` class (that typecasts the `ActionForm` instance to the correct type), you may simply subclass an existing `ActionForm` instance, modify the `<form-bean>` element in the `struts-config.xml` file, and restart your Web application server. Should you want to store the password in the `LoginForm` as a `MessageDigest` hash rather than in plain text, you could provide a subclass called `HashedPasswdLoginForm` that overrides the `setPassword` method. See Figure 7-12.

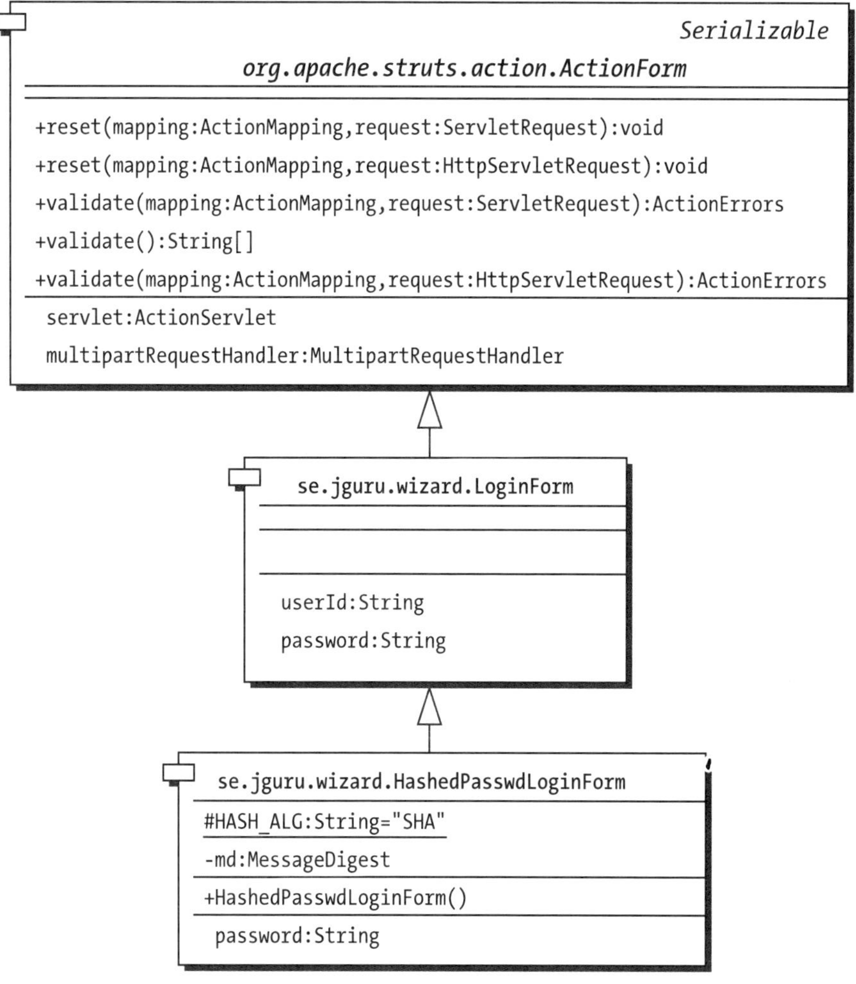

Figure 7-12. Subclassing an existing `ActionForm` *class to alter its behavior. In this case, the* `HashedPasswdLoginForm` *stores the password JavaBean property as a* `MessageDigest` *hash rather than a plain-text password.*

Although the code of the `HashedPasswdLoginForm` is simple, you should note that the storage format of the password (whether hashed or not) is an internal implementation detail of the Web application. It is still transmitted from the browser to the Web server in plain text, and can still be read as a plain-text password from the proper request attribute. Still, the class is a useful representation of an internal password storage. Take a look at its code in Listing 7-7.

Listing 7-7. The `HashedPasswdLoginForm` *class*

```
/*
 * Copyright (c) 2000 jGuru Europe.
 * All rights reserved.
 */

package se.jguru.wizard;

import java.security.MessageDigest;
import java.security.NoSuchAlgorithmException;

/**
 * MessageDigest version of the LoginForm, which stores
 * the retrieved plain text password as a MessageDigest hash
 * encapsulated within a Unicode armour, to facilitate
 * handling.
 */
public class HashedPasswdLoginForm extends LoginForm
{
    // Default MessageDigest algorithm - refer to the J2SE JavaDoc
    // for a walkthrough of standard encryption algorithms, their
    // usefulness and abbreviations.
    protected static String HASH_ALG = "SHA";

    // Declare internal state
    private MessageDigest md;

    /**
     * Create a new HashedPasswordLoginForm instance which contains
     * a MessageDigest instance wich stores a hashed string from the
     * password submitted in the setPassword method.
     */
```

```
public HashedPasswdLoginForm()
{
    try
    {
        // Create the MessageDigest instance
        this.md = MessageDigest.getInstance(this.HASH_ALG);
    }
    catch(NoSuchAlgorithmException ex)
    {
        try
        {
            // Use a standard algorithm (defined in the
            // standard Java 2 SDK).
            this.md = MessageDigest.getInstance("SHA");
        }
        catch(Exception ex2)
        {
            System.out.println("Insane state. Could not find "
                    + "standard SHA algorithm: " + ex2);
        }
    }
}

/**
 * Sets a hashed password if the MessageDigest instance of this
 * object is non-null. Otherwise, default to plain text password.
 *
 * @param plaintextPasswd The plain text password sent by the browser
 */
public void setPassword(String plaintextPasswd)
{
    // Return the normal plain text password
    if(this.md == null)
    {
        this.password = plaintextPasswd;
        return;
    }

    // The local MessageDigest is not null. Let us
    // create a hashed password.
    byte[] plainPasswd = plaintextPasswd.getBytes();
    byte[] hashedPassword = md.digest(plainPasswd);
```

```
            // Convert to a String, and assign to internal state.
            // This may be a potentially harmful operation, since
            // some unprintable characters may arise. In this small
            // demo, however, we should focus on the method rather
            // than the means.
            this.password = new String(hashedPassword);
        }
}
```

Now you need to modify the `struts-config.xml` document to use our new implementation of `HashedPasswdLoginForm` instead of the old `LoginForm`. The bolded attribute is the only required change in the configuration.

```
<struts-config>
<!-- ---------- Form Bean Definitions ---------- -->
     <form-beans>
     <form-bean
          name="loginForm"
          type="se.jguru.wizard.HashedPasswdLoginForm"/>
     </form-beans>
... more configuration ...
```

After studying the Struts `ActionForm` model components, proceed to make something visible to the user. To do so, you need to understand the Struts JSP view and tag libraries before proceeding to the interaction diagrams and dynamic aspects of a Struts Web application.

Struts View Components

JSPs and Tag Libraries

The two main parts of the view in the Struts framework are:

- The JSP document itself which, in most cases, contains mostly HTML or XML code, and
- The Struts TLDs found in the WEB-INF directory. The implementation classes of the `.tld` files are found in the `org.apache.struts.taglib` package and its four subpackages. (See Table 7-4.)

JSP technology was explained in Chapter 4, but the Struts TLDs are pretty extensive. Even more puzzling is that, at a glance, the Struts TLDs seem to mimic some of the most commonly used HTML tags. Although it may seem that we are reinventing the wheel, you are advised to learn and use the Struts TLD elements because they will hide some complexities of cross-browser dynamic Web page design. The reason why becomes apparent when you consider the needs of a modern Web application.

HTML is completely static: it supports neither internationalization nor localization. Fundamentally, this is true also for static text provided in JSP documents. However, any JSP document may use `java.text.ResourceBundle` and related classes to implement an internationalized (or personalized) version of the site. However, in doing so, one fills the JSP document with Java code that renders it more or less unreadable to HTML content developers. In the Struts framework, a series of tag libraries encapsulate—among other things—all the code required to provide internationalization and localization within the Struts JSP tags. Alas, one benefit of the Struts framework is that you may use tags similar to those found in the HTML specification, but achieve a fully internationalized site with deployment time integrity verification almost for free.

Moreover, added Struts-specific functionality includes automagic generation of utility client-side JavaScript snippets to achieve things such as setting focus to a particular field of an HTML form. The tag library provided by the Struts framework contains quite a number of tags. For full documentation on each tag, refer to the Struts reference documentation provided in the Struts distribution. (You may also find a copy of the documentation at `http://jakarta.apache.org/struts/index.html`.) At a glance, the Struts tag library looks pretty diversified, but the tags are nicely ordered in the four logical groups explained in Table 7-4.

Table 7-4. The Four Logical Groups of Custom JSP Tags Present in the Struts Framework

TAG GROUP	PACKAGE	DESCRIPTION
Bean Tags	`org.apache.struts.taglib.bean`	Tags for defining and accessing JavaBeans and JavaBean properties. JavaBeans may be created from data in Request parameters or cookies and HTTP headers.
HTML Tags	`org.apache.struts.taglib.html`	Tags used to generate HTML, specializing on the creation of HTML forms

Table 7-4. The Four Logical Groups of Custom JSP Tags Present in the Struts Framework (Continued)

TAG GROUP	PACKAGE	DESCRIPTION
Logic Tags	`org.apache.struts.taglib.logic`	Tags useful for managing conditional generation of HTML output, iteration over collections, and application flow management
Template Tags	`org.apache.struts.taglib.template`	Tags used to create dynamic JSP templates for pages that share a common structure. These tags provide functionality similar to that of standard JSP include directives. However, the Struts templates use dynamic inclusion rather than the static one used by the JSP include directive.

The output of most of the Struts tags is plain HTML; using the Struts tags instead of HTML tags grants runtime and deployment time validation. All classes, documents, resources, and entities referred to in a Struts-aware JSP document must be present to permit proper deployment of the Struts application. The classes and resources must be placed in the CLASSPATH of the Web application, whereas the configuration files are normally placed in the WEB-INF directory.

The Struts Wizard Example

By far, the quickest way to learn the Struts framework is to create a small example. You will create a wizard-like survey application that collects user information in a form, distributed over a couple of JSP documents. To make this example more like a real-life application, you will also add a login screen to the example. Because you would want the login screen as the welcome file in the Web application, call it `index.jsp`. The files used to produce the output in Figure 7-14 are placed in a Web application as shown in Figure 7-13.

So what do all these files do in the application? The quick answer is that most of them are read and parsed during initialization time (when the Web container

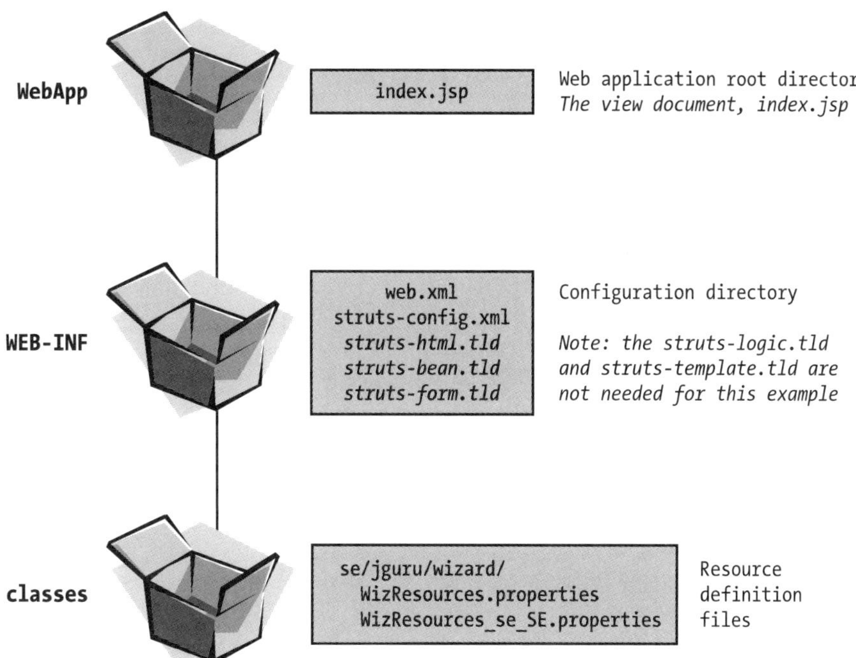

Figure 7-13. Deployment structure of the files required to produce the view of the `index.jsp` *page. For clarity, the* `WEB-INF/lib/struts.jar` *file has been omitted.*

calls the `init()` and `jspInit()` methods of the components). In fact, only the `index.jsp` file is accessed during runtime to provide the view for the client browser. All the other files contain configuration information and are accessed during system initialization. Here's a quick explanation:

- `web.xml` provides general Web application configuration. The `ActionServlet` is mapped here.

- `struts-config.xml` provides configuration settings for the Struts framework. It is read and parsed during initialization time, and defines all known actions for the `ActionServlet`.

- The properties files contain localized resources, and are read during initialization time to provide internationalization for the Struts-aware Web application.

Examine a simplified version of the login page shown in Figure 7-14. Although it may look like static HTML page, the Struts framework will shortly transform the login page into a fully internationalized view.

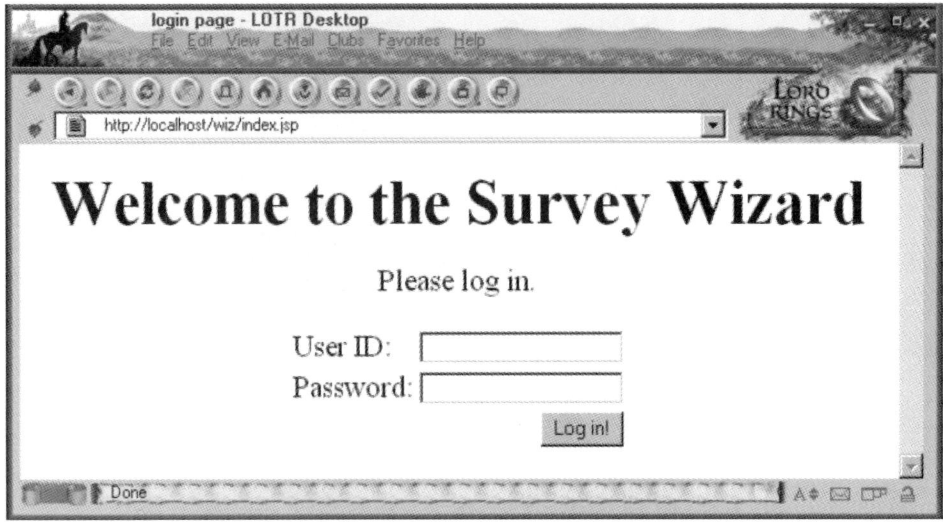

Figure 7-14. The `index.jsp` *page of the survey wizard. Although humble in appearance, the survey wizard is fully internationalized and uses property resource files to read the text for all of its labels.*

If the login page contained only static HTML, the login page's form HTML could have been generated using the code snippet in Listing 7-8.

Listing 7-8. Static HTML equivalent version of the document shown in Figure 7-14

```
<form action="someaction" method="post">
<table border="0">
<tr
   <td>User ID:</td>
   <td><Input type="text" name="userId"></td>
</tr>
<tr>
   <td>Password:</td>
   <td><Input type="password" name="password"></td>
</tr>
<tr>
   <td colspan="2"><Input type="submit" name="Log In!"></td>
</tr>
</table>
</form>
```

The Struts framework provides internationalization and localization properties to the Web application in a very simple manner. Simply include all resource strings in a `PropertyResourceBundle` file. It is a common practice to name the resource bundle with the following naming convention:

```
<locale>.properties
```

For example, `SomeResourceFile_en_US.properties` provides resource static text strings for an American English locale, and `SomeResourceFile_fr_FR.properties` contains French resource strings. The default `PropertyResourceBundle` (used when no property file implies a locale with a better fit than the default) has no locale specification (that is, `SomeResourceFile.properties`). Let's look at a portion of the resource bundle file in our wizard survey application, `WizResources.properties`:

```
login.uidLabel=User ID:
login.passwordLabel=Password:
login.submitbuttonLabel=Log in!
```

Wouldn't it be nice if the resource strings within the `PropertyResourceBundle` file could be printed in the HTML document at the locations where the static text is found in the code snippet?

Thanks to the Struts framework, it can be done, and in a simple way. Listing 7-9 shows the equivalent JSP snippet in the Struts framework. The Struts custom JSP tags that insert string resources from the `WizResources.properties` file are in bold type.

Listing 7-9. Source for the Struts-enabled document in Figure 7-14

```
<form action="someaction" method="post">

<table border="0">
     <tr>
          <td><bean:message key="login.uidLabel"/></td>
          <td><input type="text" size="20"></td>
     </tr>
     <tr>
          <td><bean:message key="login.passwordLabel"/></td>
          <td><input type="password" size="20" ></td>
     </tr>
     <tr>
          <td colspan="2" align="right">
          <input type="submit" value="<bean:message
               key="login.submitbuttonLabel"/>"></td>
     </tr>
</table>
</form>
```

The key attributes of the <bean:message> tags have identical values to the keys within the PropertyResourceBundle file. At runtime, the Struts framework may substitute the custom JSP tags for the PropertyResourceBundle values. If you would like to provide PropertyResourceBundle entries for another locale (say Sweden, which has the locale definition string "se_SE"), simply add another PropertyResourceBundle file with the locale definition string inserted into its name, as indicated in Figure 7-15. Assuming that you provided the following resource strings, the new locale strings appear in the JSP output after restarting the Web server.

```
login.uidLabel=Användarnamn:
login.passwordLabel=Lösenord:
login.submitbuttonLabel=Logga in!
```

On Forms and Localized Messages

Although the localized messages presented here exist within a HTML form, you may provide a <bean:message> tag anywhere in the JSP document. The custom JSP tag is not tied to a <form>.

Figure 7-15 renders the resulting output when running the example in a Web browser using a Swedish locale.

Figure 7-15. The index.jsp *for our survey wizard when run in a Swedish locale*

The form's static text ("Användarnamn", "Lösenord", and "Logga in!") are explained in the preceding JSP code snippet, but the two heading lines are not. However, the code to insert localized strings in a JSP page is identical. How would you create the locale-sensitive header and subheader?

Of course, the preceding explanation isn't complete. For instance, how did the JSP document know about the `<bean:message … />` tag? The simple answer is that we must create a JSP taglib directive to tell the document about the standard Struts tag library definitions, where the `<bean:message>` tag is defined. Two of the four standard Struts tag libraries are included with the following code block:

```
<%@ page language="java" %>
<%@ taglib uri="/WEB-INF/struts-bean.tld" prefix="bean" %>
<%@ taglib uri="/WEB-INF/struts-html.tld" prefix="html" %>
```

This JSP document obviously relies on the TLD files for the two tag libraries `struts-bean` and `struts-html` being located in the `<applicationHome>/WEB-INF/` directory. These tag libraries, in turn, assume that the `struts.jar` library resides in the `<applicationHome>/WEB-INF/lib` directory, and that a `struts-config.xml` document can be found in the `<applicationHome>/WEB-INF/` directory. Refer to Figure 7-13 for an illustration of the deployment structure.

Moving along to the actual wizard pages of this Struts example, you'll use Struts' capabilities to incrementally populate parts of an `ActionForm` JavaBean by collecting one wizard screen of data at a time until all required data is stored within the model. The wizard has four steps, three of which collect data from the user. Before diving into the code, however, let's look at the wizard's view, step by step.

The survey wizard starts with a form page asking the user a couple of questions, as shown in Figure 7-16. Behind the scenes, the page uses `struts-bean.tld` tags to generate all HTML controls and the `struts-bean.tld` tags to read all locale-dependent strings from a `PropertyResourceBundle` configuration file. When the user has entered all required data into the form, he or she clicks on the Next button to display the next wizard form.

Step 2 of the wizard (see Figure 7-17) gathers first and last names and the nationality of the user. Here, you use another set of HTML controls (the textbox and select/option controls) generated from Struts tags. The data gathered from the user in this step is combined with preexisting data in the SurveyForm JavaBean, which eventually will contain the data entered in step 3 in the survey wizard as well.

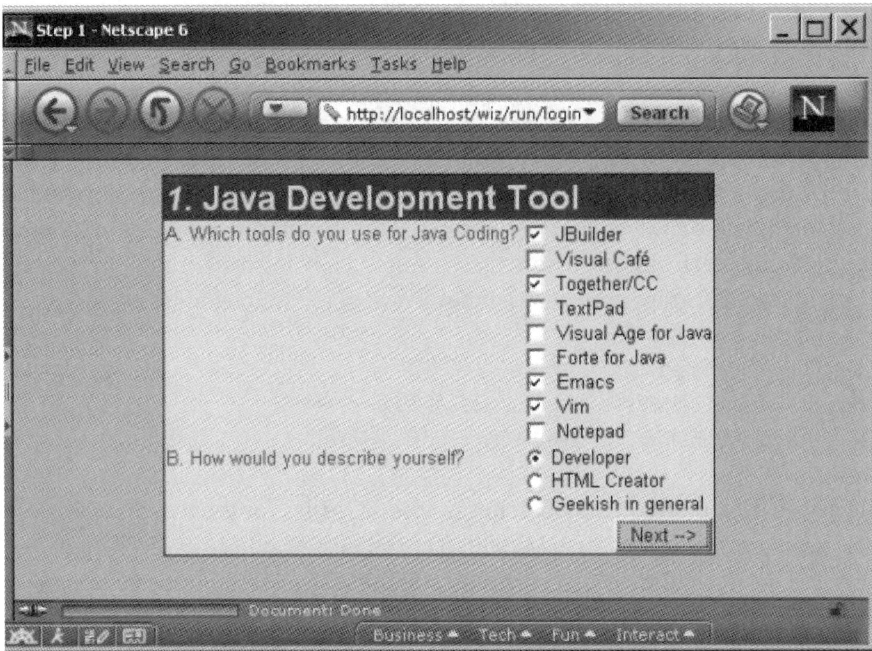

Figure 7-16. Step 1 of the survey wizard, `wiz1.jsp`

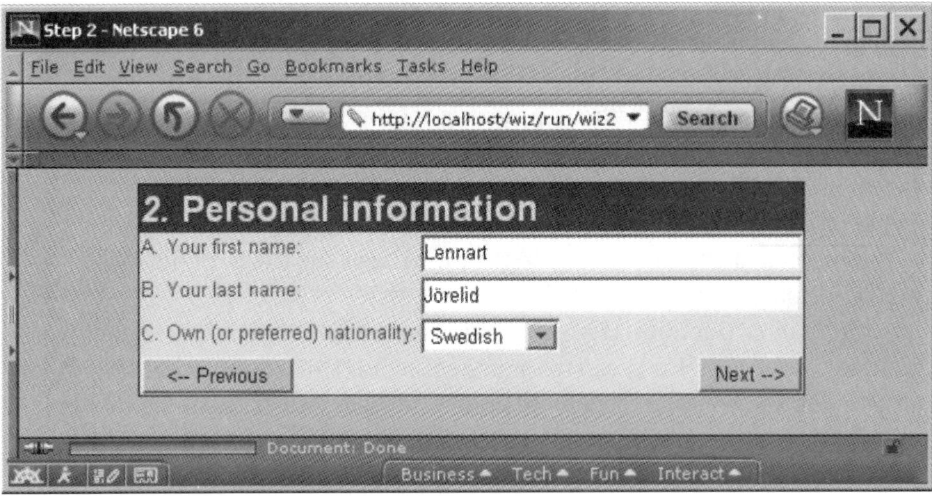

Figure 7-17. Step 2 of the survey wizard, `wiz2.jsp`

The Joys of Navigation

The user may navigate the wizard pages by clicking on the Previous and Next buttons. HTML controls created with the Struts custom tags will be initialized with the data available in a Struts `ActionForm`. In this case, whenever a user clicks on a Previous button to return to a form page previously visited, all HTML controls default to their state set by the user on the last visit. This is a great feature when developing Web-based wizards and other documents that communicate with HTML form data.

Step 3 of the survey wizard (Figure 7-18) permits the user to enter a general description of himself/herself in a text area control. Thus, you will use another Struts custom tag, defined in the Struts framework, to generate the HTML required to create the text area. When the user finally clicks on the Finish button, the last step of the survey wizard (a simple "Thank you" page) is displayed.

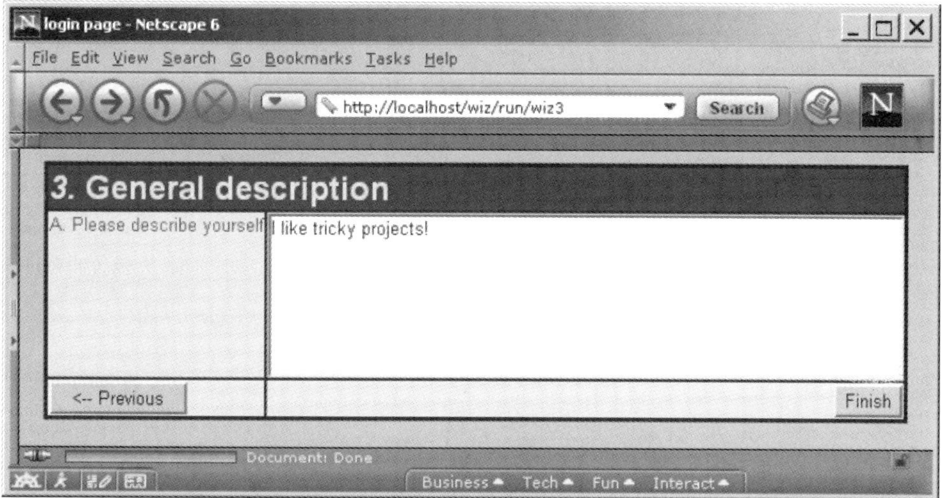

Figure 7-18. Step 3 of the survey wizard, `wiz3.jsp`

The final page of the survey wizard (Figure 7-19) simply displays a "Thank you" message to the user. In a real Web application, this page would probably echo back all data entered in the survey wizard and present a few links to allow the user to navigate to other relevant pages. At this stage though, it is important not to get lost in the myriad of details surrounding form layout. The purpose of this example is to introduce you to the Struts framework—not the finer details of HTML hacking, usability engineering, or art design.

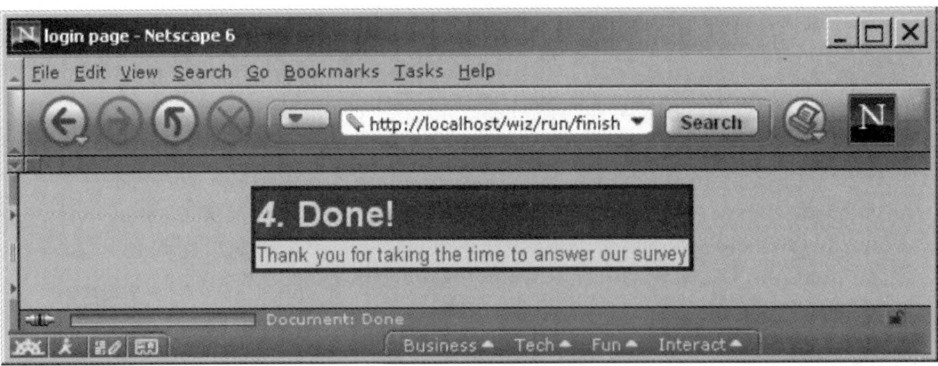

Figure 7-19. The final page of the wizard, `finished.jsp`

To verify that the Web application holds all of the data that you expect it to, simply click on the Next and Forward buttons a few times. This will let you know if the data seen in the controls is really the data you entered the last time that you visited the page.

Now that you have seen the user's view of the survey wizard, take a look at the different pieces of code that must be pieced together to generate the desired result. Starting with the model of the survey wizard, let's take a look at the Java classes that are used to realize the `ActionForm` instance, `SurveyForm`.

The `SurveyForm` Model

The model of the survey wizard is simple indeed; the JavaBean class `se.jguru.wizard.SurveyForm` contains only readable and writable JavaBean properties. The UML diagram in Figure 7-20 shows the JavaBean properties held by the class.

The JavaBean properties fall in one of two categories:

- Simple single-valued properties (such as description and nationality), which have a setter and getter method, as well as a variable in which the property value is stored between the calls to the setter and the getter method.
- Indexed (or multivalued) properties, which normally have two setter methods and two getter methods in addition to the variable. One set of methods sets or gets the whole array, whereas the other sets or gets an individual element.

Check out the corresponding code of the `SurveyForm` class, as shown in Listing 7-10.

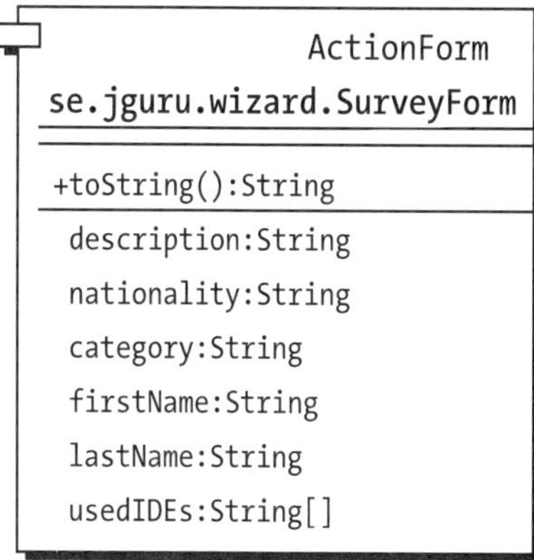

Figure 7-20. The `se.jguru.wizard.SurveyForm` class

Listing 7-10. The `SurveyForm` *class*

```
/*
 * Copyright (c) 2001 jGuru Europe.
 * All rights reserved.
 */

package se.jguru.wizard;

import org.apache.struts.action.ActionForm;
import org.apache.struts.action.ActionMapping;

import javax.servlet.http.HttpServletRequest;

/**
 * Model ActionForm JavaBean which will gradually be populated
 * by the  data collected in the 3 wizard steps. Note that not all of the
 * data will be populated at once, since different wizard
 * steps will populate different properties.
 */
public class SurveyForm extends ActionForm
{
    private String firstName;

    private String lastName;

    private String nationality;
```

```
private String[] usedIDEs;

private String category;

private String description;

public String getDescription()
{
    return description;
}

public void setDescription(String description)
{
    this.description = description;
}

public String getNationality()
{
    return nationality;
}

public void setNationality(String nationality)
{
    this.nationality = nationality;
}

public String getCategory()
{
    return category;
}

public void setCategory(String category)
{
    this.category = category;
}

public String getFirstName()
{
    return firstName;
}
```

```
    public void setFirstName(String firstName)
    {
        this.firstName = firstName;
    }

    public String getLastName()
    {
            return lastName;
    }

    public void setLastName(String lastName)
    {
            this.lastName = lastName;
    }

    public String[] getUsedIDEs(){
    {
            return usedIDEs;
    }

    public void setUsedIDEs(String[] usedIDEs)
    {
            this.usedIDEs = usedIDEs;
    }

    public String toString()
    {
        return "Form: " + getDescription() + ", " + getNationality() + ", "
            + getCategory() + ", " + getFirstName() + ", " + getLastName();
    }
}
```

The code in Listing 7-10 is actually simple enough that commenting often reduces readability; it has therefore been left in a rather raw state. For larger systems with bigger or more complex forms, the need for commenting each class increases quickly.

The purpose of the survey wizard Web application is to collect data that corresponds to the JavaBean properties of the `SurveyForm` class. Before being able to tie the model class into the view documents, you need to set up and configure the controller classes. Let's take a look at them.

The SurveyWizardAction Controller

Most well-written and frequently used frameworks require only small additions of custom code to be completely functional. Such is the case with the Struts framework with respect to the class that must be implemented to define the tasks of a listener. The `se.jguru.wizard.SurveyWizardAction` class implements the required `perform` method in a rather simple manner: by gathering its required information from the framework support classes instead of hard-coding or generating it from scratch.

The immediate superclass of the `SurveyWizardAction` is the `Action` controller class of the Struts framework, as seen in Figure 7-21.

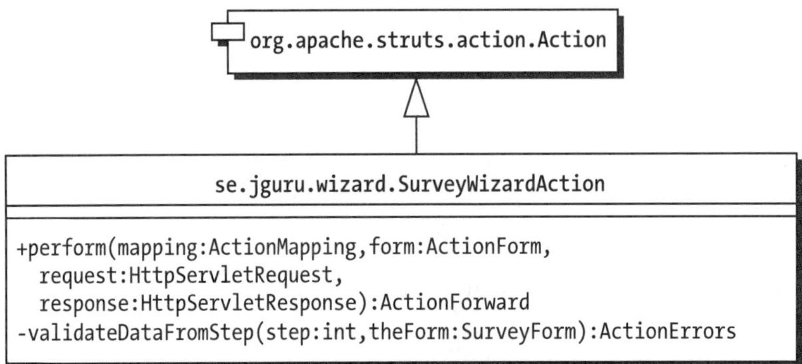

Figure 7-21. The structure and inheritance hierarchy of the `SurveyWizardAction` *class. The only mandatory operation in a Struts-compatible* `Action` *class is the* `perform` *method, which implements all required controller functionality. We have added a small helper method (*`validateDataFromStep`*) to assist in validating any data provided in the* `ActionForm` *of the application.*

The primary function of the `perform` method is to choose an `ActionForward` object that contains forwarding information (that is, URL redirect or an internal forward) from the information contained in the arguments to the `perform` method, as well as any globally known parameters. The classes supporting the `Action` instance assist in providing data that is used to select the proper `ActionMapping`. For instance, the localized `ResourceBundle` strings are retrieved from a `MessageResources` object. Frequently, one requires assistance from several objects that contain important data.

Figure 7-22 illustrates the most frequently used Struts support classes that contain data required for proper view selection. (Or course, standard J2EE classes such as `HttpServletRequest` and `HttpServletResponse` have been omitted from the image.)

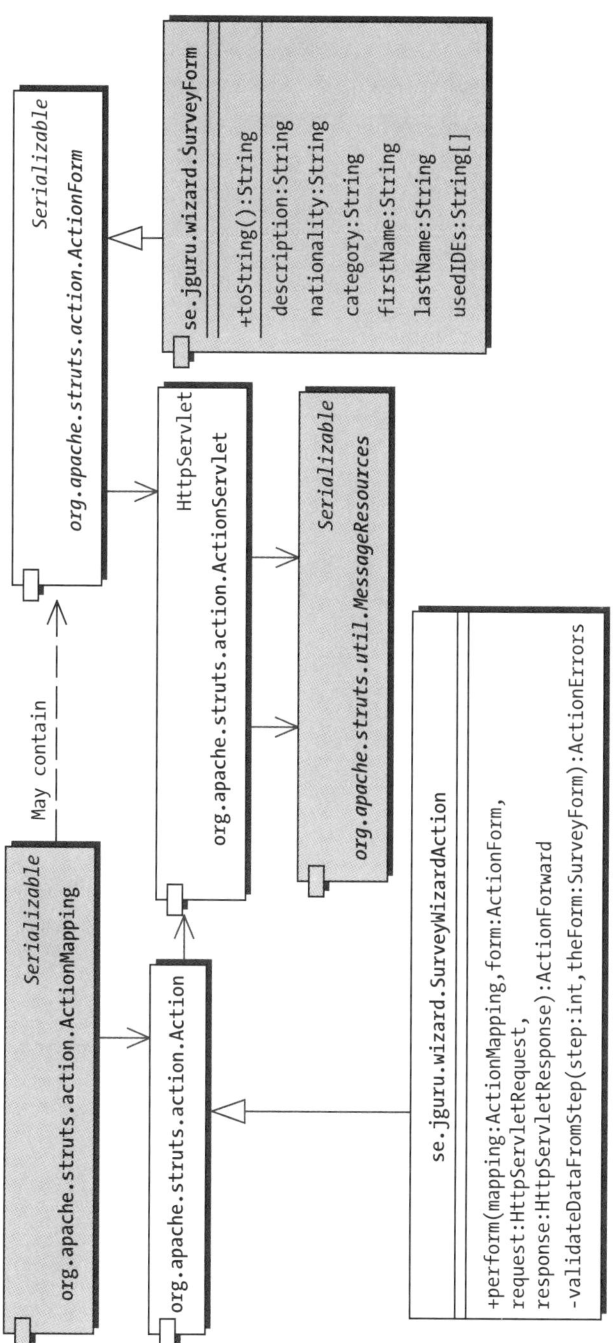

Figure 7-22. The most frequently used support objects in an `Action` *subclass are shaded. The association arrows indicate which object actually contains a reference to the desired support instance. Alas, if you want to reach the associated* `MessageResources` *instance, your concrete action must call the* `getMessages` *method which delegates the lookup to the* `ActionServlet`.

The job of the action is to select or create the `ActionForward` instance that points to the view that should be displayed to the user. Any `Action` subclass may dynamically create a new `ActionForward` instance simply by invoking a constructor, but one normally finds an `ActionForward` defined in the current `ActionMapping` (which is set up in the `struts-config.xml` file).

Take a look at the `perform` method of the `SurveyWizardAction`. The shaded support instances in Figure 7-22 are shown in bold in Listing 7-11.

Listing 7-11. The `SurveyWizardAction` *class*

```
/*
 * Copyright (c) 2000,2001 jGuru Europe.
 * All rights reserved.
 */

package se.jguru.wizard;

import org.apache.struts.action.Action;
import org.apache.struts.action.ActionForm;
import org.apache.struts.action.ActionForward;
import org.apache.struts.action.ActionError;
import org.apache.struts.action.ActionErrors;
import org.apache.struts.action.ActionMapping;
import org.apache.struts.util.MessageResources;

import java.io.IOException;
import java.util.Locale;
import javax.servlet.ServletException;
import javax.servlet.http.HttpServletRequest;
import javax.servlet.http.HttpServletResponse;

/**
 * The SurveyWizardAction class is the sole Action implementation
 * for the entire SurveyWizard web application.
 */
public class SurveyWizardAction extends Action
{
    public ActionForward perform(ActionMapping mapping,
    ActionForm form,
    HttpServletRequest request,
    HttpServletResponse response)
    throws IOException, ServletException
```

```
{
    // Get or create instances we will need to
    // process the current request.
    Locale locale = getLocale(request);
    MessageResources messages = getResources();

    // Find out which button the user pressed.
    String buttonPressedLabel  = request.getParameter("submit").trim();
    String nextButtonText      = messages.getMessage(locale,"wiz.nextLabel");
    String finishButtonText    = messages.getMessage(locale,"wiz.finishLabel");
    String previousButtonText  = messages.getMessage(locale,"wiz.previousLabel");
    String returnFromErrorsButtonText   =
            messages.getMessage(locale,"wizError.returnLabel");
    boolean nextButtonPressed   =
            buttonPressedLabel.equalsIgnoreCase(nextButtonText);
    boolean finishButtonPressed =
            buttonPressedLabel.equalsIgnoreCase(finishButtonText);
    boolean returnFromErrorsButtonPressed =
            buttonPressedLabel.equalsIgnoreCase(returnFromErrorsButtonText);

    /*
    // Log information for visualization and debugging purposes.
    System.out.println("messages := " + messages);
    System.out.println("Locale := " + locale);
    System.out.println("nextButtonText := " + nextButtonText);
    System.out.println("nextButtonPressed := " + nextButtonPressed);
    System.out.println("finishButtonPressed := " + finishButtonPressed);
    System.out.println("returnFromErrorsButtonPressed := " +
            returnFromErrorsButtonPressed);
    System.out.println("request.getParameter(\"submit\").trim(): " +
            request.getParameter("submit").trim());
    */

    // Keep track of the survey wizard phase (i.e. step just completed).
    int step = 0;
    try
    {
        step = Integer.parseInt(request.getParameter("phase"));
    }
    catch(Exception ex)
    {
        // Whoops
        System.out.println("Could not get the step: " + ex);
    }
```

```
// Typecast the ActionForm parameter to the proper type.
SurveyForm theForm = (SurveyForm) form;

// Check any errors from the data in the form.
ActionErrors errors = this.validateDataFromStep(step, theForm);

// Did any errors occur?
if(errors != null) System.out.println("errors: [empty="
        + errors.empty() + "], [size=" + errors.size() + "]");

// If the data entered into the HTML form was not accepted, complain.
if (errors != null && !errors.empty())
{
    // Save the generated errors in the request, so that the
    // error page may acquire them and print them.
    saveErrors(request, errors);

    // Also, save the originating URL, so we may jump back to it.
    String origUrl = "/wiz" + step;
    request.setAttribute("wiz.originalURL", origUrl);

    // Forward to the error page.
    return mapping.findForward("failure");
}

// All went well... simply move on to the target
// corresponding to the button pressed.
if(nextButtonPressed)
{
    // Find the appropriate mapping
    ActionForward theMapping = mapping.findForward("next");

    // Print verbose output so that we may verify the correlation
    // between the struts-config.xml document and actual
    // operation.
    System.out.println("mapping.findForward(\"next\") := "
        + mapping.findForward("next")
        + ", path := " + theMapping.getPath() + ", name := "
        + theMapping.getName());

    // Done. Return.
    return theMapping;
}
```

```
    // Are we at the end of the Wizard?
    if(finishButtonPressed)
    {
        // Print a verbose output so that we may verify the correlation
        // between the struts-config.xml document and actual
        // operation.
        System.out.println("mapping.findForward(\"finish\") := "
            + mapping.findForward("finish"));

        // Done.
        return mapping.findForward("finish");
    }

    if(returnFromErrorsButtonPressed)
    {
        // We are returning from the error page.
        // In this case, we need to go to the previous
        // document, i.e. the mapping from the config.
        return mapping.findForward("backFromErrorPage");
    }

    // It seems that the user has pressed the "Previous" button.
    ActionForward theMapping = mapping.findForward("previous");

    // Print a verbose output so that we may verify the correlation
    // between the Struts configuration XML document and actual
    // operation.
    if(theMapping != null)
    {
        System.out.println("mapping.findForward(\"previous\") := "
            + mapping.findForward("previous")
            + ", path := " + theMapping.getPath() + ", name := "
            + theMapping.getName());

            // Done. Return.
            return theMapping;
    }

    // We should never wind up here...
    return mapping.findForward("failure");
}
```

```
/**
 * Validates data from the SurveyForm of this Action at the wizard step
 * provided as an argument.
 *
 * @param step the step of the wizard (1 - 3)
 * @param theForm The SurveyForm instance that collects the data from the
 *                survey wizard.
 *
 * @return A populated ActionErrors collection if anything went wrong,
 *         or null if all data was found correct at the given step.
 */
private ActionErrors validateDataFromStep(int step, SurveyForm theForm)
{
    // We require the application messages to generate locale-specific
    // error messages to the User.
    MessageResources msg = getResources();

    // Declare the ActionErrors collection to return.
    ActionErrors toReturn = null;

    // Different steps require different validation procedures.
    switch(step)
    {
    case 1:
        // This is step one of the survey wizard. At this point,
        // we only require that the user fill in the description of
        // himself/herself.
        if(theForm.getCategory() == null || theForm.getCategory().equals(""))
         {
         // We must have a proper Category for this step.
            // It appears that we do not. Complain.
            // Let's create an ActionError from the Application message with the
            // key wiz.defaultErrorMessage (found in the global resource property
            // messages file). That particular message accepts a parameter
            // - which is given as the second argument to the ActionError
            // constructor.
            ActionError theError = new ActionError("wiz.defaultErrorMessage",
                "Category", new Integer(1));

            // Put the ActionError in the toReturn collection
            toReturn = new ActionErrors();
            toReturn.add(ActionErrors.GLOBAL_ERROR, theError);
         }
    break;
```

```
case 2:
    // This is step two of the survey wizard. At this point,
    // we require that the user fill in his/her first and last names.
    String firstName = theForm.getFirstName();
    String lastName = theForm.getLastName();

    // Check sanity
    if(firstName != null && lastName != null)
    {
        if(!firstName.equals("") && !lastName.equals(""))
        {
            // This is an accepted result. Return null.
            return null;
        }
    }

    // Something is wrong. Create the ActionErrors collection
    // and continue.
    toReturn = new ActionErrors();

    // Check what was wrong, and add appropriate ActionError objects
    // to the outgoing ActionErrors Collection
    if(firstName == null) toReturn.add(ActionErrors.GLOBAL_ERROR,
        new ActionError("wiz.defaultNullErrorMessage", "First Name"));
    if(lastName == null) toReturn.add(ActionErrors.GLOBAL_ERROR,
        new ActionError("wiz.defaultNullErrorMessage", "Last Name"));
    if(lastName.equals("")) toReturn.add(ActionErrors.GLOBAL_ERROR,
        new ActionError("wiz.defaultEmptyErrorMessage", "Last Name"));
    if(lastName.equals("")) toReturn.add(ActionErrors.GLOBAL_ERROR,
        new ActionError("wiz.defaultEmptyErrorMessage", "First Name"));
break;
case 3:
    // The information from step 3 is completely optional, so we will
    // not complain if theForm.getDescription() returns null or empty
    // values. Simply return.
    break;

default:
    // Simply permit the action to continue executing without
    // generating any excepions.
    break;
}
```

```
        // Done. Return.
        return toReturn;
    }
}
```

The code comments provide a description of each section in the `perform` method. Because this particular `perform` method is close to that of a normal running Web application, I'll be a bit more thorough explaining its execution flow. The main steps of the `perform` method are as follows:

1. Create or get all support objects containing data required to determine the view we should redirect to.

2. Find the actual button clicked, to fully understand what the user wants to do. This is determined from its label, as provided in the application message resources (that is, the resource strings in the properties files). In this survey wizard, we provide relatively few options, and we may encapsulate all information about the button clicked in the `perform` method itself. For larger applications, it is advisable to place such logic in a separate method to reduce code clutter and increase visibility in the `perform` method.

3. Typecast the `ActionForm` parameter (from the perform method declaration) to the `SurveyActionForm` it really is, and call the `validateDataFromStep` method to validate all data provided in the current step. All runtime errors are copied into an `ActionErrors` collection, which may contain multiple `ActionError` objects. In this way, the user may receive a message containing all data-entry mistakes at once, rather than spread out over several form submittals.

4. If any errors were generated in the process, redirect to the mapping "failure," which takes us to an error page. The `ActionErrors` collection from step 3 is bound to the `HttpServletRequest` before the actual redirection, so we may access it in the error page. Also, the button on the error page must know which action it should take to return to the proper step of the wizard to allow the user to fix the data. The name of the Struts action is bound to the request under the key `wiz.originalUrl`.

5. If no errors were generated in the process, redirect to the mapping corresponding to the button pressed (Next, Previous, or Finish). The targets of these button actions are defined in the `struts-config.xml` file.

To fully understand the actions taken in the `perform` method, you need to know the data contained in the `struts-config.xml` document and the application's resource bundle file. The former holds all of the `ActionMappings` of the application, and the latter presents all of the resource strings used in the application. Note that the application properties file contains data that is used by the view as well as the controller.

Keep in mind that the Next `ActionForward` is used whenever the Next submit button is clicked on a form, and the Previous `ActionForward` is used when the Previous button is clicked. Next, look at Listing 7-12, which contains the structure and content of the `struts-config.xml`.

Listing 7-12. The `struts-config.xml` *document*

```
<?xml version="1.0" encoding="ISO-8859-1" ?>

<!DOCTYPE struts-config PUBLIC
        "-//Apache Software Foundation//DTD Struts Configuration 1.0//EN"
        "http://jakarta.apache.org/struts/dtds/struts-config_1_0.dtd">

<struts-config>

    <!-- .................... Form Bean Definitions ................... -->
    <form-beans>
        <!-- Login form bean -->
        <form-bean name="loginForm" type="se.jguru.wizard.LoginForm"/>
        <form-bean name="surveyForm" type="se.jguru.wizard.SurveyForm" />
    </form-beans>


    <!-- .................... Global Forward Definitions ................... -->
    <global-forwards>
        <forward  name="gologin"      path="/login.jsp"     redirect="false"/>
        <forward  name="failure"      path="/wizError.jsp" />
        <forward  name="next"         path="/wiz1.jsp" />
    </global-forwards>

    <!-- .................... Action Mapping Definitions ................... -->
    <action-mappings>
        <action
            path="/login"
            type="se.jguru.wizard.LoginAction"
            name="loginForm"
            scope="request">
            <forward name="success" path="/wiz1.jsp" />
        </action>
```

```
        <action
            path="/wiz1"
            type="se.jguru.wizard.SurveyWizardAction"
            name="surveyForm"
            scope="session">
            <forward name=" backFromErrorPage " path="/wiz1.jsp" />
            <forward name="backFromErrorPage" path="/wiz1.jsp" />
        </action>
        <action
            path="/wiz2"
            type="se.jguru.wizard.SurveyWizardAction"
            name="surveyForm"
            scope="session">
            <forward name="next" path="/wiz2.jsp" />
            <forward name="backFromErrorPage" path="/wiz2.jsp" />
        </action>
        <action
            path="/wiz3"
            type="se.jguru.wizard.SurveyWizardAction"
            name="surveyForm"
            scope="session">
            <forward name="next" path="/wiz3.jsp" />
            <forward name="previous" path="/wiz1.jsp" />
            <forward name="backFromErrorPage" path="/wiz3.jsp" />
        </action>
        <action
            path="/finish"
            type="se.jguru.wizard.SurveyWizardAction"
            name="surveyForm"
            scope="session">
            <forward name="finish" path="/finished.jsp" />
            <forward name="previous" path="/wiz2.jsp" />
        </action>
    </action-mappings>

</struts-config>
```

Phew! This is indeed a mouthful of controller instructions. Study one of the action mappings in detail simply to understand its structure a little better. The action defined for step 3 of the wizard is repeated here and will suffice for this study:

```
<action
   path="/wiz3"
   type="se.jguru.wizard.SurveyWizardAction"
   name="surveyForm"
   scope="session">
```

The opening `<action>` tag contains the four following attributes that define its general behavior (each of which is explained in the following sections):

- `path`
- `type`
- `name`
- `scope`

path Attribute

The `path` attribute defines its so-called *action path* (a virtual path to which the action is mapped) relative to the Web application of which it is part. In this case, given the Web application root `/someApp` and an `ActionServlet` mapping of `/run/*`, the path `/wiz3` corresponds to the URL `http://<serverName>/someApp/run/wiz3`.

Changing the ActionServlet Mapping

All path crunching will be automagically generated and handled by the Struts framework, so if you decide to change, say, the `ActionServlet` `<servlet-mapping>` within the `web.xml` configuration file to `*.exec`, the (virtual) action URL will change to `http://<serverName>/someApp/wiz3.exec`. You need only reboot the Web application server running your Struts-aware Web application to reload the resources required. None of your other documents need changing in any way. (This behavior is documented in screenshots, provided later in this example.)

type Attribute

The second attribute to the `<action>` tag is `type`, which defines the concrete class of the `Action` instance whose `perform` method should be invoked to handle this action. All required type classes are loaded and instantiated at initialization time, so a type error in an action mapping will result in the Struts application not starting properly.

In fact, some Web application servers (such as the Apache Tomcat reference implementation server) will close the Web application, presenting only a "not running" HTML error page to the client browser. You may therefore be assured that any type classes required by a Struts-enabled Web application are properly loaded when it is running.

name Attribute

The third attribute, `name`, defines a logical name for the `ActionForm` used by the action being defined. The logical name is resolved against an actual implementation class name in the `<form-beans> … </form-beans>` definition section of `struts-config.xml`. Whenever a name attribute is provided, look for an entry in the `<form-beans>` section in which the name matches the value of your `<action>` attribute name. In this particular case, the entry

```
<form-bean name="surveyForm" type="se.jguru.wizard.SurveyForm" />
```

indicates that the form used for the `wiz3` action is of type `se.jguru.wizard.SurveyWizardAction`.

scope Attribute

Finally, the fourth attribute, `scope`, defines the scope where the `ActionForm` should be bound and queried for. The default attribute is `request` (which, far from surprising, indicates that the form bean should be bound to the request scope), but, in our case, we need the form bound to the session scope because it must persist over several requests.

ActionForward Definitions

All `ActionForward` definitions are placed inside the `<action>` container tag. Normally, an `ActionForward` definition contains a logical name and a relative path definition. If the path is to be interpreted absolutely (which will happen if an HTTP redirect command is sent to the browser), the `ActionForward` will contain a `redirect="true"` attribute. Most frequently, though, `ActionForward` entries contain relative paths to targets within the existing Web application.

When executing the `perform` method of the `Action` class, you redirect to a particular `ActionForward` path by returning its corresponding `ActionForward` instance. All `ActionForward` instances are found in the `ActionForwards` collection, which is available in the `Action` class; forwarding to the `/wiz3.jsp` view is achieved in the `SurveyWizardAction.java` file by the following statement:

```
return mapping.findForward("next");.
```

If a particular mapping—say "foo"—is not found locally (that is, defined as a `<forward name="foo"... >` within the current `<action>` container element), the `<global-mappings>` tag is searched for an element with the name "foo" (that is, `<forward name="foo"... >`). In that aspect, global `ActionMappings` are inherited to each action, similar to properties inherited by a subclass from a superclass. Simply regard the global forwards as accessible from all action paths.

As an example, the action in the following code snippet has four `ActionMappings`, because it knows four `ActionForwards`. The forwards named "next", "previous", and "backFromErrorPage" are local to the current action, and the "gologin" `ActionForward` is known because it is global, inherited to all actions from the `<global-forwards>` collection.

```
<global-forwards>
     <forward  name="gologin" path="/index.jsp" redirect="false"/>
</global-forwards>
<action ... >
     <forward name="next" path="/wiz3.jsp" />
     <forward name="previous" path="/wiz1.jsp" />
     <forward name="backFromErrorPage" path="/wiz3.jsp" />
</action>
```

messages Instance

The remaining item to be resolved is the `messages` instance of a `MessageResource` used in the `perform` method of the `SurveyWizardAction` class in Listing 7-11. First of all, you may wonder where it is defined. When browsing through `struts-config.xml`, there is no trace of a `PropertyResourceBundle` resource file configuration.

The answer is that the `ActionServlet` configuration (found in the `/WEB-INF/web.xml` file) contains the fully qualified path to the property resource bundle file containing all resources. The `ActionServlet` reads all resources at initialization, so changes in the resource configuration file require the application server to be rebooted to take effect.

For a sample `ActionServlet` configuration file (`web.xml`), refer to the sections "`web.xml`" and "`struts-config.xml`" earlier in this chapter. The element you are looking for is the application initialization parameter, which appears in bold text in the following snippet:

```
  <!-- Action Servlet Configuration -->
  <servlet>
    <servlet-name>wizAction</servlet-name>
    <servlet-class>org.apache.struts.action.ActionServlet</servlet-class>
    <init-param>
      <param-name>application</param-name>
      <param-value>se.jguru.wizard.WizResources</param-value>
    </init-param>
...
```

The content of the messages file, named `WizResources.properties` for the default English locale and found in the `WEB-INF/classes/se/jguru/wizard` directory, appears in Listing 7-13.

Listing 7-13. `WizResources.properties`

```
login.welcomeLabel=Welcome to the Survey Wizard
login.subwelcomeLabel=Please log in.
login.uidLabel=User ID:
login.passwordLabel=Password:
login.submitbuttonLabel=Log in!
logon.illegalUid=User ID foo illegal in this application due to complete geekness.
button.cancel=Cancel
button.confirm=Confirm
button.reset=Reset
button.save=Save
wiz.nextLabel=Next -->
wiz.previousLabel=<-- Previous
wiz.finishLabel=Finish
wiz.defaultErrorMessage=You must give {0} information in step {1} of the survey wizard.
wiz.defaultNullErrorMessage=You must provide information about <i>{0}</i>.
wiz.defaultEmptyErrorMessage=You must provide {0} information.
wiz1.title=Java Development Tool
wiz1.q1=Which tools do you use for Java Coding?
wiz1.a1=JBuilder,Visual Café,Together/CC,TextPad,Visual Age for Java,
        Forte for Java,Emacs,Vim,Notepad
wiz1.q2=How would you describe yourself?
wiz1.a2Dev=Developer
wiz1.a2Htm=HTML Creator
wiz1.a2Gee=Geekish in general
wiz1.illegalCategory=You must select a description category for yourself!
wiz2.title=Personal information
wiz2.country1=Swedish
```

```
wiz2.country2=Norwegian
wiz2.q1=Your first name:
wiz2.q2=Your last name:
wiz2.q3=Own (or preferred) nationality:
wiz3.title=General description
wiz3.q1=Please describe yourself
wiz4.title=Done!
wiz4.thankyou=Thank you for taking the time to answer our survey
wizError.title=An error occurred.
wizError.returnLabel=Return to the original form.
errors.header=The current errors are: <ol>
errors.footer=</ol>Done reporting errors.
```

A message resource bundle works like a HashMap, so the controller or view documents may query the `messages` instance in the `Action` class for a specific key to retrieve its corresponding value. For example, in the `perform` method, a call to

```
Locale locale = … // Get a desired locale
messages.getMessage(locale,"wiz.nextLabel");
```

retrieves the value for the key `wiz.nextLabel` using the locale provided as an argument. If the locale indicates that the default message resources file should be used as source for the application messages, the value returned from the `getMessage()` method is "Next-->" (that is, the button label specified in the `WizResource.properties` file for the wizard survey application).

Move on to the application view, which renders the output of our Web application.

The View and JSP Documents

The view documents of our Struts application has three main components:

- Several JSP documents,
- Struts custom tags, and
- The `MessageResources` used by the application.

The JSP documents must include all required Struts TLDs to make the required custom tags available for access. Some of the custom tags make use of the message resources, defined in the `WizResources.properties` file presented in Listing 7-13.

The views of the wizard are deployed in four files:

- `wiz1.jsp`
- `wiz2.jsp`
- `wiz3.jsp`
- `finished.jsp`

In addition to the actual view files, a `wizError.jsp` document serves as the common error page of the wizard Web application.

Study the full code of the `wiz1.jsp` document that displays step 1 of the survey wizard. (See Figure 7-23.) All other JSP documents have similar structure to the `wiz1.jsp` document, and so we may compare all the JSP view documents with `wiz1.jsp` to discover differences and new Struts tags. The alternative—studying the full JSP source for each individual JSP document—takes longer and doesn't provide any added understanding or value. (That's a programmer's way of saying "work smarter, not harder.")

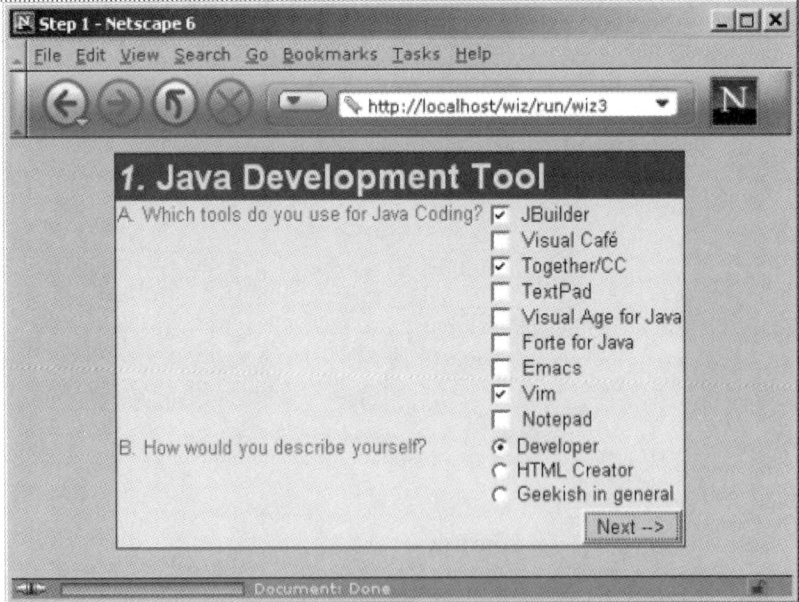

Figure 7-23. Step 1 of the wizard, which contains four visible HTML tags (all mapped from Struts custom taglib tags). The checkboxes are generated by the Struts multibox tag, the radio buttons by the Struts radio tag, the button by the Struts button tag, and the form in which they all reside by the Struts form tag.

Step 1 of the wizard makes use of several Struts tags, which are deployed in the Struts taglib archive file (`struts.jar`). These taglibs must, of course, be imported by a Struts taglib directive. Therefore, the first lines of code in `wiz1.jsp` are the three following import directives:

```
<%--
                Import required classes and Tag Libraries.
--%>
<%@ page import="java.util.*, java.io.*" %>
<%@ taglib uri="/WEB-INF/struts-bean.tld" prefix="bean" %>
<%@ taglib uri="/WEB-INF/struts-html.tld" prefix="html" %>
```

Note that the two taglib definition files—`struts-bean.tld` and `struts-html.tld`—are found in the `struts.jar` archive (which is deployed in the `/WEB-INF/lib` directory as shown in the previous "Struts Parts and Deployment" section).

Bean Tags

The `struts-bean.tld` contains tags that assist in accessing, reading, and writing JavaBean properties from classes bound to any of the available scopes of a Web application. The Struts framework contains the 11 bean tags listed in Table 7-5. (For a detailed description of each tag, refer to the Struts reference documentation that is installed along with the Struts framework itself).

Table 7-5. Custom JSP Tag Names and Descriptions for the Struts Bean Tags

TAG NAME	DESCRIPTION
`cookie`	Defines a scripting variable based on the value(s) of the specified request cookie
`define`	Defines a scripting variable based on the value(s) of the specified bean property
`header`	Defines a scripting variable based on the value(s) of the specified request header
`include`	Loads the response from a dynamic application request and makes it available as a bean
`message`	Renders an internationalized message string to the response object
`page`	Exposes a specified item from the page context as a bean
`parameter`	Defines a scripting variable based on the value(s) of the specified request parameter(s)

Table 7-5. Custom JSP Tag Names and Descriptions for the Struts Bean Tags (Continued)

TAG NAME	DESCRIPTION
`resource`	Loads a Web application resource and makes it available as a bean
`size`	Defines a bean containing the number of elements in an array, collection, or map
`struts`	Exposes a named Struts internal configuration object as a bean
`write`	Renders the value of the specified bean property to the current `JspWriter`

The `struts-html.tld` file contains tags that deal with generating HTML tags that the Struts-aware application checks for validity and sanity. One may therefore consider the Struts framework as providing a validating and unified set of tags that complement—or, in some cases, completely replace—the need to use normal HTML tags in the creation of Struts view documents. This example has been designed so that several (but not all) of the 23 HTML tags are used, therefore showing the use of some of the more frequently used tags.

HTML Tags

Table 7-6 contains the short descriptions of all available Struts HTML tags in the reference documentation. For detailed documentation on each element, refer to the Struts reference documentation that is installed along with the Struts framework.

Table 7-6. Custom JSP Tags of the `struts-html.tld` *TLD File*

TAG NAME	DESCRIPTION
`base`	Renders a `<base>` element
`button`	Renders a button input field
`cancel`	Renders a Cancel button
`checkbox`	Renders a Checkbox input field
`errors`	Conditionally displays a set of accumulated error messages
`file`	Renders a file Select input field
`form`	Defines a `<form>` element
`hidden`	Renders a hidden field
`html`	Renders an `<html>` element

Table 7-6. Custom JSP Tags of the `struts-html.tld` *TLD File (Continued)*

TAG NAME	DESCRIPTION
image	Renders an input tag of type "image"
img	Renders an HTML <img> tag
link	Renders an HTML anchor or hyperlink
multibox	Renders a Checkbox input field corresponding to an element in a value array
option	Renders a Select option
options	Renders a group of Select options
password	Renders a Password input field
radio	Renders a radio button input field
reset	Renders a Reset button input field
rewrite	Renders an URI
select	Renders a <select> element
submit	Renders a Submit button
text	Renders an input field of type "text"
textarea	Renders a text area

wiz1.jsp in Detail

Having taken a quick look at some of the custom tags that are standard in the Struts framework, you can now start looking at the source code of the JSP documents that present the view of our survey wizard application.

The beginning of the `wiz1.jsp` document looks almost like a normal HTML document, but it contains two custom Struts tags (shown in bold text in the following code snippet):

```
<html:html locale="true">
  <head>
    <title>Step 1</title>
    <html:base/>
    <style type="text/css" ref>
      @import url(style.css);
    </style>
  </head>
```

To see the effect of the Struts custom tags, compare the preceding snippet of JSP code with the corresponding HTML that is actually sent to the browser to generate the screen shown in Figure 7-23.

```
<html lang="sv">
  <head>
    <title>Step 1</title>
    <base href="http://localhost/wiz/wiz1.jsp">
    <style type="text/css" ref>
      @import url(style.css);
    </style>
  </head>
```

As you can see, the `<html:html>` tag creates the standard opening tag for the HTML document, including a `lang` attribute that specifies the locale. Because the computer that ran this example was configured to run with a Swedish locale, the `lang` attribute of the resulting HTML code was set to `sv`. If the Web server node uses another locale, the `lang` attribute will be different than the one seen in the second listing.

The `<html:base/>` tag inserts a `<base href=...>` tag that defines a reference in the HTML structure. That reference will be used as a base for the browser if it needs to create relative URLs to other local resources. The `href` attribute automatically points to the actual view document.

Moving on to the `<body>` section of the `wiz1.jsp` document, you encounter more Struts custom tags. First, you'll print the source of the JSP document, including the Struts custom tags. Later, we'll compare this document to the resulting output created by the Struts `ActionServlet` and sent to the browser. All Struts-specific tags in the document are shown in Listing 7-14 in bold text.

Listing 7-14. The body section of the `wiz1.jsp` *document*

```
<%--
     Include all common utility methods.
--%>
<%@ include file="methods.include" %>
...
<body bgcolor="white">
   <center>
      <html:form action="/wiz2" focus="submit">
      <html:hidden property="phase" value="1" />
      <table border="0" bgcolor="#0000ff" cellpadding="1">
```

```
        <tr><td>
           <table border="0" bgcolor="#ddddff" cellspacing="0">
              <tr>
                  <td colspan="2" class="wizHeader">
                <h1><i>1.</i> <bean:message key="wiz1.title"/><html:errors/></h1>
                 </td>
              </tr>
              <tr>
                 <td class="question">
                    A. <bean:message key="wiz1.q1"/>
                 </td>

                 <td class="answer">
<%
        String[] ides = spliceBundleMessage("se.jguru.wizard.WizResources",
                "wiz1.a1", ",");

        for(int i = 0; i < ides.length; i++)
        {
%>
        <html:multibox property="usedIDEs"><%= ides[i] %></html:multibox>
                <%= ides[i] %></br>
<% } %>
                 </td>
              </tr>



              <tr>
                  <td class="question">
                    B. <bean:message key="wiz1.q2"/>
                 </td>

                 <td class="answer">
                    <html:radio property="category" value="developer">
                    <bean:message key="wiz1.a2Dev"/></html:radio><br>
                    <html:radio property="category" value="html">
                    <bean:message key="wiz1.a2Htm"/></html:radio><br>
                    <html:radio property="category" value="geekInGeneral">
                    <bean:message key="wiz1.a2Gee"/></html:radio>
                 </td>
              </tr>
```

```
                <tr>
                    <td colspan="2" align="right">
                      <html:submit><bean:message key="wiz.nextLabel"/></html:submit>
                    </td>
                </tr>
            </table>
        </td></tr>
    </table>
</html:form>

</body>
</html:html>
```

The source in the `<body>` section contains a fair amount of Struts-specific tags, namely the `form`, `hidden`, `multibox`, `radio`, and `submit` tags from `struts-html.tld`, and the `message` tag from `struts-bean.tld`.

The tag

```
<bean:message key="<key>"/>
```

simply inserts a value from the application's resource bundle into the JSP document at the place it is defined. Similar to a HashMap, you must specify the key whose value you wish to retrieve. In the case of a message resource bundle, though, the value is qualified not only by a key but also by locale.

The `wiz1.jsp` document imports a helper JSP document (with the `<%@ import ... %>` JSP directive) that declares one method, `spliceResourceBundle`. This method manually reads and parses the value of a resource, given its key as an argument.

The parsing is used to find the names of all the Integrated Development Environments (IDEs) that are presented in the first step of the wizard. We could, of course, present an individual `key=value` pair for each IDE in the `WizResources.properties` file, but that wouldn't be efficient. (How could we keep track of newly added IDEs with arbitrary resource key strings?) Instead, the `spliceResourceBundle` method (shown in Listing 7-15) has been provided to illustrate how the `ResourceBundle` of the application may be accessed manually from within the Struts-aware application:

Listing 7-15. The `methods.include` *document*

```
<%--
        This JSP document (methods.include) contains resource
        method definitions to be used in other JSP documents.
--%>
<%!
        private String[] spliceBundleMessage(String bundleType,
                String message, String delimiter)
        {
                // Get the ResourceBundle from the resourceBundleFileName
                ResourceBundle bundle =
                     ResourceBundle.getBundle(bundleType, Locale.getDefault());

                // Get the desired message from the ResourceBundle
                String messageValue = bundle.getString(message);

                // Create a splicing StringTokenizer
                StringTokenizer tok = new StringTokenizer(messageValue, delimiter);

                // Declare the return value
                String[] toReturn = new String[tok.countTokens()];

                // Populate the return String[]
                for(int i = 0; i < toReturn.length; i++)
                {
                        toReturn[i] = tok.nextToken();
                }

                // Return the fully populated String[]
                return toReturn;
        }
%>
```

To study the result of the Struts HTML tags, compare the `wiz1.jsp` source with the actual HTML output sent to the browser. Understanding the purpose of each custom tag is important, and fortunately rather simple. In Listing 7-16, code or text that has originated from custom Struts tags is shown in bold type.

Why Are Some Checkbox Elements Checked?

The Struts framework dynamically produces HTML before sending it out to the client browser. Some of the checkboxes are set in the checked state according to the HTML code in Listing 7-16. This setting originates from the internal state of Struts; the internal state of the framework is translated to this particular HTML syntax before any result is sent to the client browser. This is why the state of the `SurveyForm` model is preserved over multiple calls.

Listing 7-16. The resulting HTML sent to the client browser by the Struts application

```
<body bgcolor="white">
        <center>
        <form name="surveyForm" method="POST" action="/wiz/run/wiz2">
        <input type="hidden" name="phase" value="1">
        <table border="0" bgcolor="#0000ff" cellpadding="1">
        <tr><td>
        <table border="0" bgcolor="#ddddff" cellspacing="0">
        <tr>
                <td colspan="2" class="wizHeader">
                <h1><i>1.</i> Java Development Tool</h1>
                </td>
        </tr>
        <tr>
                <td class="question">
                A. Which tools do you use for Java Coding?
                </td>

                <td class="answer">


        <input type="checkbox" name="usedIDEs"
                value="JBuilder" checked>JBuilder</br>
        <input type="checkbox" name="usedIDEs"
                value="Visual Café">Visual Café</br>
        <input type="checkbox" name="usedIDEs"
                value="Together/CC" checked>Together/CC</br>
        <input type="checkbox" name="usedIDEs"
                value="TextPad">TextPad</br>
        <input type="checkbox" name="usedIDEs"
                value="Visual Age for Java">Visual Age for Java</br>
```

```
        <input type="checkbox" name="usedIDEs"
                value="Forte for Java">Forte for Java</br>
        <input type="checkbox" name="usedIDEs"
                value="Emacs">Emacs</br>
        <input type="checkbox" name="usedIDEs"
                value="Vim" checked>Vim</br>
        <input type="checkbox" name="usedIDEs"
                value="Notepad">Notepad</br>
        </td>
        </tr>

        <tr>
                <td class="question">B. How would you describe yourself?
                </td>

                <td class="answer">
                        <input type="radio" name="category"
                        value="developer" checked>Developer<br>

                        <input type="radio" name="category"
                        value="html">HTML Creator<br>

                        <input type="radio" name="category"
                        value="geekInGeneral">Geekish in general
                </td>
        </tr>

        <tr>
                <td colspan="2" align="right">
                <input type="submit" name="submit" value="Next -->">
        </tr>

        </table>
        </td></tr>
        </table>
        </form>
<script language="JavaScript" type="text/javascript">
  <!--
    document.surveyForm.submit.focus()
  // -->
</script>


</body>
</html>
```

As you can see in the HTML code produced by the Stuts framework, the Struts tags insert information pertaining to the internal state of its model. This information is not provided in the JSP document source. As an example, the `action` attribute of the `<html:form>` is replaced with the Web application name and the proper action prefix, in addition to the given attribute value.

Note that some of the Struts tags give rise to a combination of server-side and client-side code; the `<html:form>` tag accepts an attribute (`focus`) that generates a client-side JavaScript requesting focus for a form element whose name is provided as a value to the form attribute. The client-side JavaScript is found immediately after the HTML `</form>` tag in the resulting output. Can you see the correlation between the Struts custom JSP tag and the generated JavaScript? Although the JavaScript is tiny, it is functional and convenient. One of the greater strengths of the Struts framework is that its custom tags encapsulate all data—including any client-side scripts that may be needed—that is concerned with a specific element, such as a pushbutton or form.

I encourage you to examine the Struts reference documentation for specific details on all options and attributes available to the Struts tags. In traditional Apache style, the documentation is precise and provided in the form of a Web application in the Struts distribution.

wiz2.jsp

Let's move on to the second step of the survey wizard, `wiz2.jsp`, which collects some personal information from the user. (See Figure 7-24.)

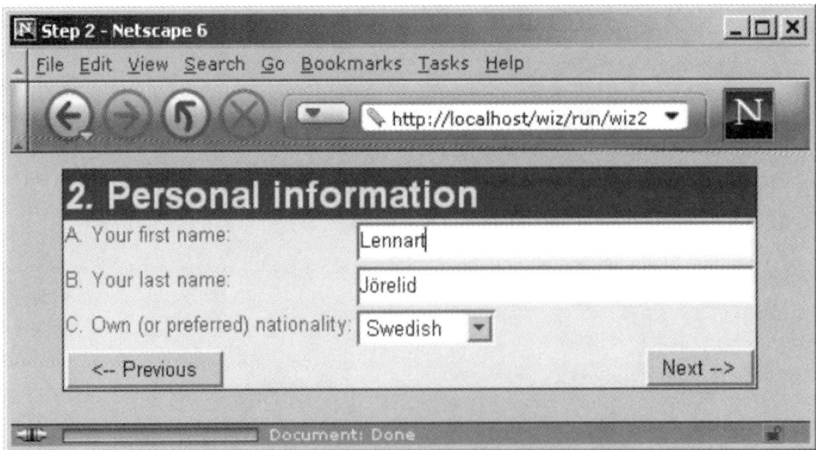

Figure 7-24. Step 2 of the survey wizard, `wiz2.jsp`

This time, use textbox and select/option input HTML controls, which are generated by the `<html:text>` and `<html:select>` tags.

Comparing two code snippets from the `wiz2.jsp` document illustrates quite well how the two Struts tags generate the resulting HTML code that is sent to the browser. Start with the upper-most text field control, and highlight all Struts custom tags, as shown here:

```
<tr>
   <td class="question">
      A. <bean:message key="wiz2.q1"/>
   </td>

   <td class="answer">
      <html:text styleClass="answer" property="firstName" size="20" />
   </td>
</tr>
```

Note that the question text is read from the `WizResources.properties` file using the `<bean:message>` tag. In this way, locale independence is preserved throughout the Web application. The `<html:text … />` tag produces an HTML form `<input>` tag of type `text` with the `name` attribute identical to the property attribute value. Let's look at the resulting HTML output sent to the browser; the text generated by the Struts tags is highlighted in bold type:

```
<tr>
   <td class="question">
      A. Your first name:
   </td>

   <td class="answer">
      <input type="text" name="firstName" size="20" value="" class="answer">
   </td>
</tr>
```

Some properties of the Struts custom JSP tags are copied directly to the generated HTML, whereas others are first validated against data in the `struts-config.xml` file or existing classes in the Struts-aware Web application. After some practice, you're likely to find that most Struts tags behave in a similar manner; the initial difficulties of creating a Struts-aware view document will quickly be replaced by the delight of using the powerful Struts custom JSP tags. For instance, because the `wiz2` action contains an `ActionForm` (`SurveyForm` in our example), the Struts framework verifies that the values of the `property` attributes in the JSP match the JavaBean property names in the `ActionForm`.

The dropdown (combobox) HTML control is produced by a combination of an enclosing `<select>...</select>` container and several contained `<option>` tags. Struts' custom tags producing a combobox HTML control are similar. Note in the following code snippet that the `<html:option ... />` tags have two forms: the first one uses a hard-coded value provided in the body of the tag, and the second uses a value from the `WizResources.properties` file.

```
<tr>
  <td class="question">C. <bean:message key="wiz2.q3"/>
  </td>

  <td class="answer">
    <html:select property="nationality">
      <html:option value="Swedish">Swedish</html:option>
      <html:option value="Norwegian" key="wiz2.country" />
    </html:select>
  </td>
</tr>
```

Of course, the application message resources (found in the `WizResource.properties` file) contain a key=value pair, `wiz2.country=Norwegian`. Can you see the connection between the attribute `wiz2.country` and the value in the resulting HTML output?

wiz3.jsp

When finished with step 2, the user clicks on the Next button, and is routed to step 3 of this short wizard, `wiz3.jsp`. This step is optional in the sense that the user is not required to fill in a value in the text area HTML control. When run in a browser, the view looks like Figure 7-25.

The text area control shown in Figure 7-25 is generated with the Struts custom tag `<html:textarea>`. The relevant part of the `wiz3.jsp` document is shown here:

```
<td class="answer">
  <html:textarea styleClass="answer" property="description" cols="40" rows="5"/>
</td>
```

The corresponding HTML output that is sent to the browser client is quite straightforward:

```
<td class="answer">
  <textarea name="description" cols="40" rows="5" class="answer"></textarea>
</td>
```

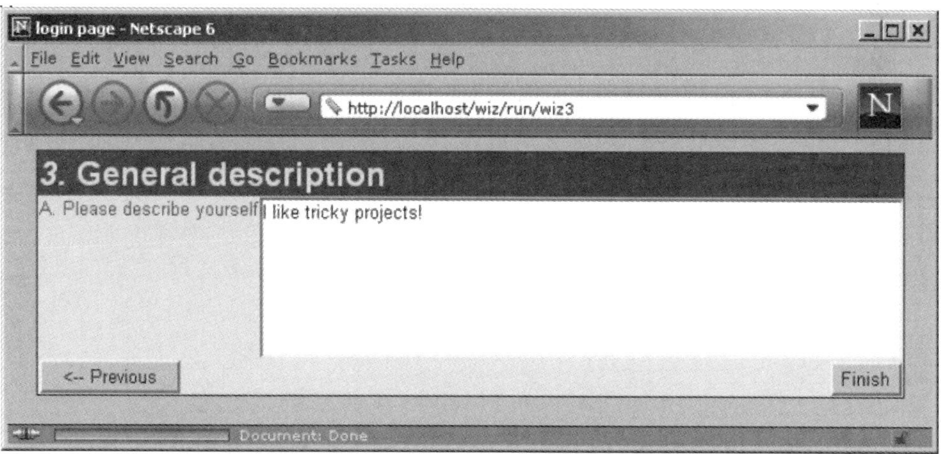

Figure 7-25. Step 3 of the wizard, `wiz3.jsp`*, presents a HTML text area control, enabling the user to enter a general description of him/herself.*

Note that the attribute `styleClass` is converted to the HTML attribute class, which controls the CSS (cascading style sheet) class used to render the text area control. Although CSS technology is certainly important in creating nice-looking HTML pages, our focus is the Struts framework. (For a tutorial on CSS, refer to `http://www.w3.org/Style/CSS/`.

finished.jsp

The final confirmation page of the wizard, `finished.jsp`, contains a simple "Thank you" message and an image. (See Figure 7-26). The only new Struts tag is `<html:img />`, which generates an HTML `<img>` tag.

The relevant piece of code in `finished.jsp` is small indeed. It is quite common to present all data collected in the steps of the wizard in the final verification screen, but for these purposes this is irrelevant. Instead, provide the relevant code of the `finished.jsp` document that generates the HTML `<img>` tag:

```
<html:img border="1" page="/images/struts-power.gif"/>
```

The resulting HTML output sent back to the browser simply copies the Web application name into the `src` attribute of the image tag and appends the path of the image:

```
<img src="/wiz/images/struts-power.gif" border="1">
```

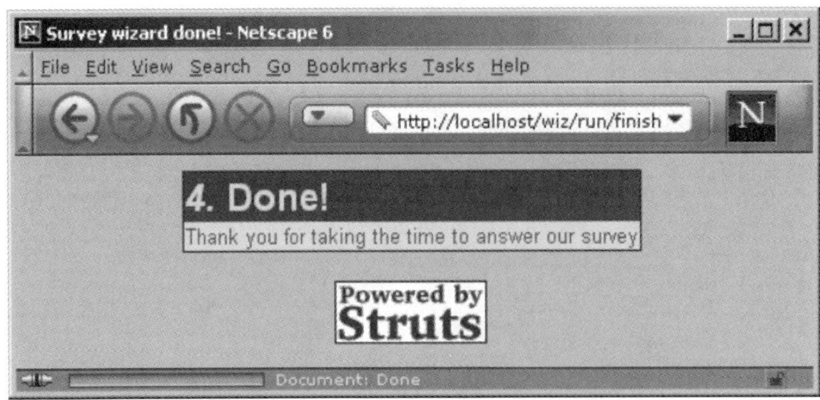

Figure 7-26. The final confirmation page of the SurveyWizard, `finished.jsp`

Having completed the steps through the wizard, you must now consider the potential for user errors. So far, we've given little thought to inputs that contain errors or that are absent in mandatory fields. We must now study the error-handling capabilities of Struts.

Error Handling in the Survey Wizard Application

Up to now, you have included error code, but you haven't generated any errors. What happens if an error is generated during the progress of our wizard application? Let's say that the user forgets to fill in the last-name field in step 2. (See Figure 7-27.)

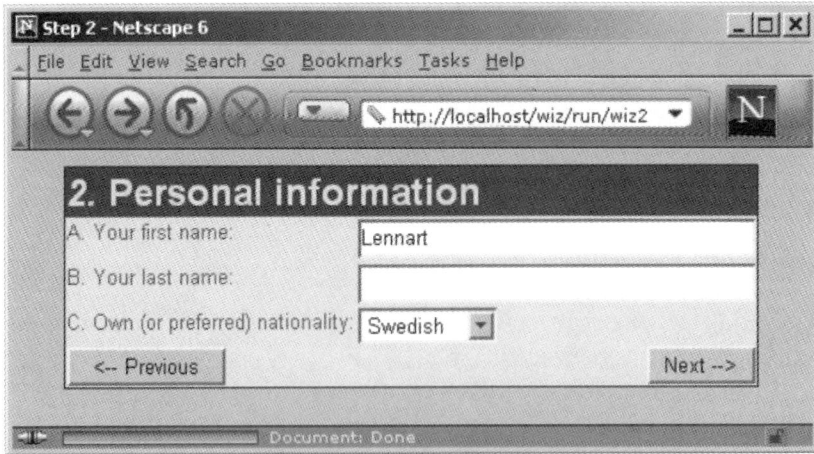

Figure 7-27. The user must provide his/her last name in the survey wizard. If no last name is provided when the Next button is clicked on, the user is redirected to the error page.

The error page of the application, `wizError.jsp`, displays the error that was generated by the calling document, and provides a button to return the user to the page where the error occurred. See Figure 7-28.

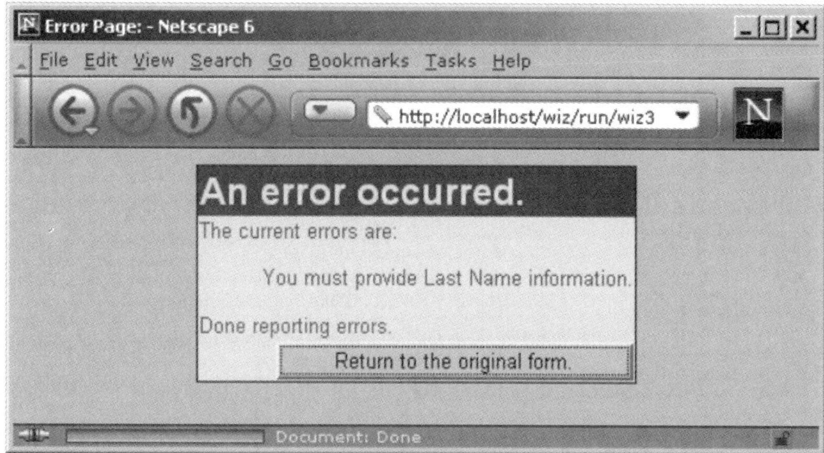

Figure 7-28. The error page, `wizError.jsp`, *displays the error text and a button to return to the original form and correct the erroneous input data.*

The relevant code of `wizError.jsp`, shown in Listing 7-17, displays the error text. This includes the header and footer text defined in the `WizResources.properties` file using the keys `errors.header` and `errors.footer`.

Listing 7-17. The `wizError.jsp` *document, with the Struts-specific JSP custom tags highlighted in bold text*

```
<html:form
   action='<%= "" + request.getAttribute("wiz.originalURL") %>' focus="submit">
        <html:hidden property="phase" value="0" />
        <table border="0" bgcolor="#0000ff" cellpadding="1">
        <tr><td>
        <table border="0" bgcolor="#ddddff" cellspacing="0">
        <tr>
                <td colspan="2" class="wizHeader">
                <h1><bean:message key="wizError.title"/></h1>
                </td>
        </tr>
        <tr>
                <td class="question">
                <html:errors/>
                </td>
        </tr>
```

```
<tr>
        <td colspan="2" align="right">
        <html:submit>
           <bean:message key="wizError.returnLabel"/>
        </html:submit>
</tr>


</table>
</td></tr>
</table>
</html:form>
```

Note that the only required Struts tag to show all error messages is `<html:errors/>`. Error handling in the Struts framework is quite pleasant, as all application-level errors may be caught and handled in the perform method.

Reflections on the Struts Framework Walkthrough Example

The Struts framework is neither a silver bullet that solves all problems regarding Web application development, nor is it a useless vaporware product that should best be left to the dusty archives. Many tasks that are needed in a large Web application are simplified (or even included) in the standard Struts framework functionality. Programmers must learn enough about the Struts framework to use its powerful advantages without having to suffer from its drawbacks; for instance, the difficulty of reading and understanding all the Struts configuration files drastically limits the number of available programmers.

Recall that you may change the `<servlet-mapping>` for the `ActionServlet` to alter all virtual URLs used by the Struts-aware Web application. Let's alter the mapping for the `ActionServlet` from `/run/*` to `*.exec`. This is done in the `web.xml` configuration file, and the relevant snippet is:

```
<!-- Action Servlet Mapping -->
<servlet-mapping>
  <servlet-name>wizAction</servlet-name>
  <url-pattern>/run/*</url-pattern>
</servlet-mapping>
```

Change the value of the `<url-pattern>` element to `*.exec` and restart the Web application. Lo and behold, all required application links are altered and the system works. Figures 7-29 through 7-32 are your proof.

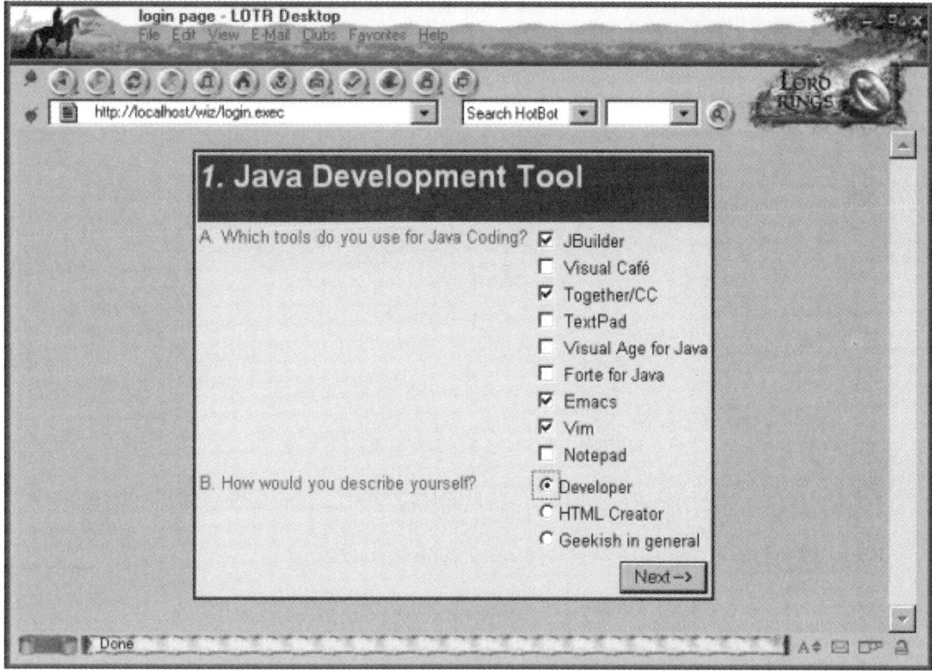

Figure 7-29. Step 1 of the survey wizard. Note the URL used.

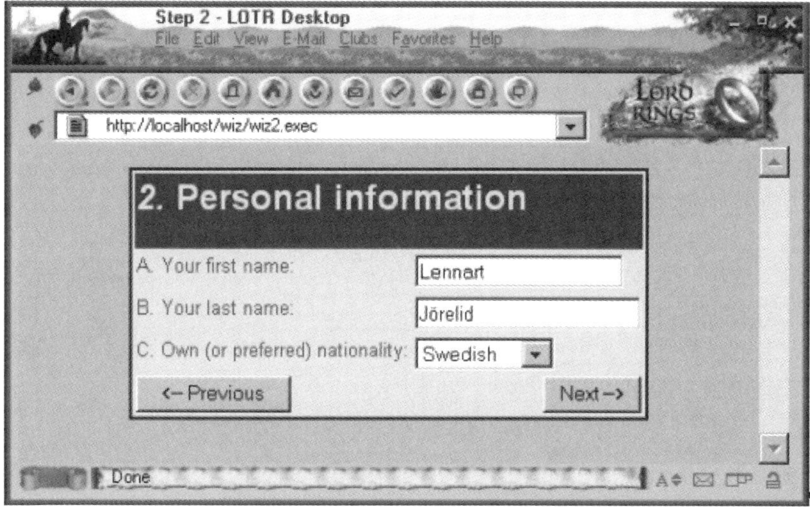

Figure 7-30. Step 2 of the survey wizard. Note the URL.

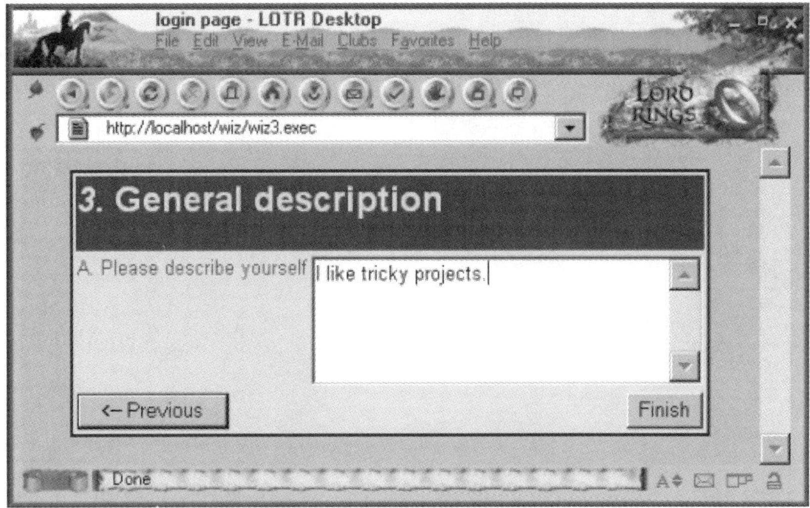

Figure 7-31. Step 3 of the survey wizard. Note the URL.

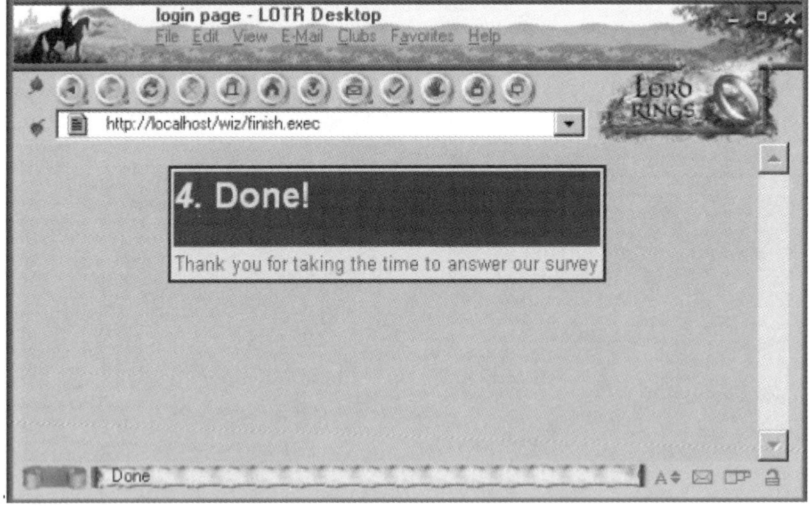

Figure 7-32. Step 4 of the survey wizard. Note the URL.

The Struts framework is a powerful way of building self-validating and internationalized Web applications. I recommend that you take a thorough look at it. After an initial time period of fumbling around, the steep learning curve starts paying off in well-constructed Web applications. I suggest you visit the Struts Web site at `http://jakarta.apache.org/struts/index.html` to learn more about the Struts framework and download its distribution files.

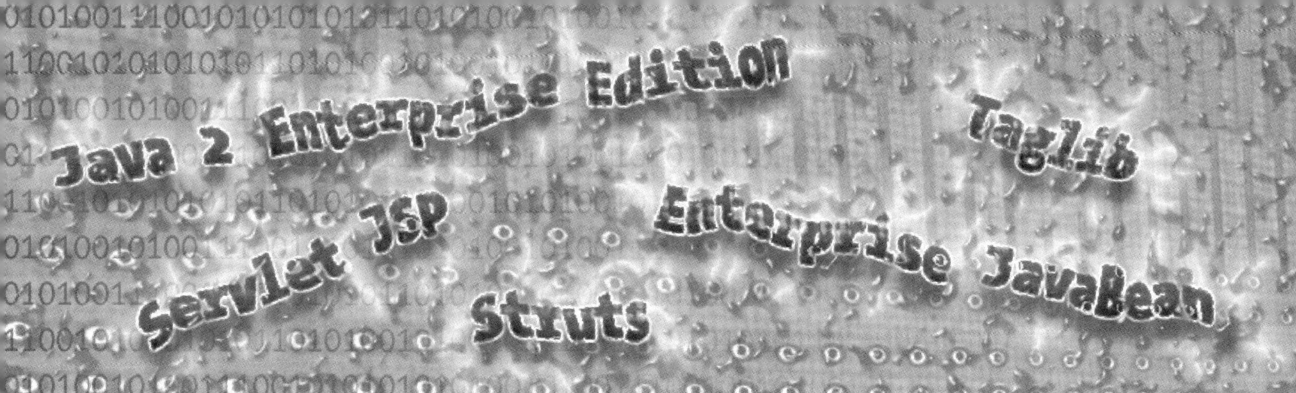
Java 2 Enterprise Edition
Taglib
Servlet JSP
Enterprise JavaBean
Struts

Part IV

EJB

CHAPTER 8

Integrating with the Business Tier

ALL VIEW AND CONTROLLER SERVLETS and JSP documents require some form of support from business entities; data that should be presented in the view tends to be a controlled and limited version of the corporate business database. In the case of a financial institution such as a bank, a normal view could be the account balance of a logged-in customer. Very few systems generate such business data solely in the Web application; the majority of Web applications present data read from enterprise information systems (EIS) and laundered in a business logic tier. Most industrial-grade Web applications are designed according to the J2EE paradigm; they therefore require support from both enterprise JavaBeans (EJB)—which contain the business logic—and from large databases that constitute the EIS tier.

Although direct integration between the Web application and business tier is a necessity, it presents the developers with a distinct set of nontrivial problems caused partly by the immaturity of the J2EE platform specification and partly by the difficult learning curve for business logic encapsulated in EJB. This chapter explains how to circumvent problems of a technological nature when creating and communicating with EJB components, and what types of problems must be solved outside of the current J2EE specification.

Reviewing the Structure of a J2EE Application

Before plunging into the technological delicacies of EJB creation and integration, we should refresh our memories regarding the structure of the J2EE application and the role of the Web application within it. Figure 8-1 shows the basic structure of a J2EE application.

So far, this book has dealt with the creation of proper Web applications, that is, the servlet and JSP technologies that are deployed in Tier 1. In this chapter, we'll investigate how to create and interact with the business EJBs from Tier 2.

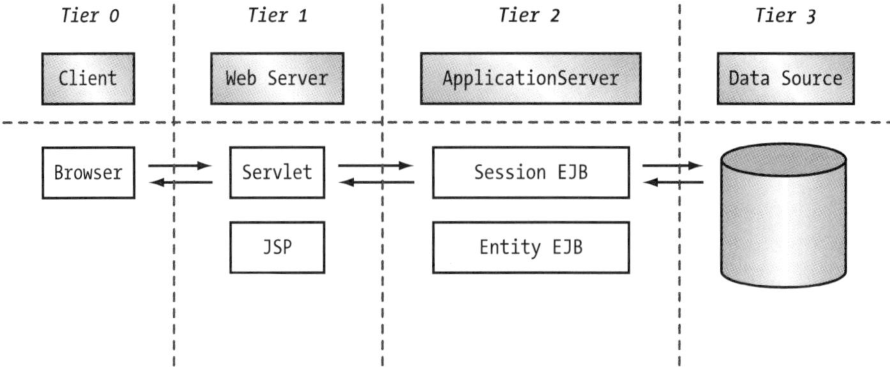

Figure 8-1. Principal structure of a J2EE application, including the Web server, application server, and data source. Used technologies are displayed below the dashed line; normal application designations are displayed above it.

Advantages of Using a Separate Business Logic Layer

Why should we use a business logic tier at all? You may argue that we could connect directly to the data source (frequently a relational database) from the Web application tier. You may even convince your management department that this approach is best for your particular system development project.

In fact, depending on system properties, development specification goals, and runtime demands, you may be correct that we could connect directly from a servlet controller to a relational database, read its data, and populate the outgoing JSP view. Some enterprise applications have requirements that are incredibly difficult to provide in a Web application tier only.

Let's illustrate one of these problems by sketching a normal deployment situation for a large-scale enterprise application that employs clustering/mirroring to enhance the performance of the Web application tier. Figure 8-2 provides an example. In it, the switch picks a Web server out of several identical servers that should handle the request from the user. Each Web server has its own container, with its own HttpSession containing session-specific data. Unless we implement a distribution protocol that makes all HttpSessions contain identical data (unless the Web server supports clustering, which performs just that, this is much more complex than it may seem at first sight), we cannot use the HttpSession to bind session-wide data in the enterprise application. Session-wide data must therefore be bound elsewhere—namely in the business logic tier.

Taking a look at the setup in Figure 8-2, one realizes that session-scoped business logic must be bound in the business logic tier to be accessible by all

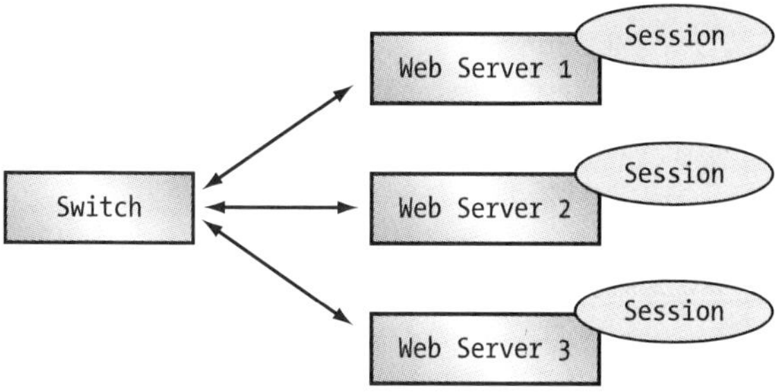

Figure 8-2. Principal sketch of a clustered Web application server tier

Web servers. Figure 8-3 shows the normal setup of clustered application servers talking to clustered Web servers.

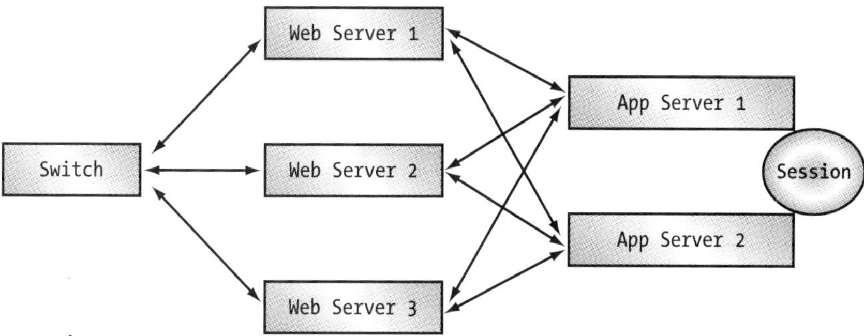

Figure 8-3. Application servers, as opposed to Web servers, implement session data sharing protocols to share session data between multiple nodes in a cluster.

Because application servers generally contain more functionality that cares for data integrity and data security than do Web servers, one prefers to leave all data manipulation operations to the application servers. Application servers provide functionality for the following desirable and tricky-to-implement features for all EJB objects running within them:

- **Life-cycle management:** EJBs running inside an application server have a well-defined and strictly enforced life cycle that ensures that any EJBs created in the application server may potentially be saved to and read from persistent storage in a controlled manner. In short, 20 EJB instances—if coded properly—may well be able to handle 200 concurrent users due to resource pooling. Although business object resource pools are quite difficult to code by hand, they are powerful runtime assistants.

- **Resource pooling:** Although only specified in a standard format for relational database connection pooling, the J2EE standard is quickly moving towards integrating arbitrary resource pools into the enterprise model. Many real-life EIS are (large!) relational databases, but it is still likely that systems need to interact with "database-ish" systems that may behave similarly to a database but that do not use SQL or the table data structure. However, being able to pool relational database connections is a powerful feature that requires quite some time to implement by hand in a Web application.

- **Security:** The J2EE application server model contains a crude but easy-to-handle role-based security model. This model can enforce that only authorized clients can invoke a particular method in an EJB.

- **Transactions:** Application servers automagically manage transactions for enterprise applications. Although this functionality may be written by hand and deployed in the Web server tier, transaction control in a distributed environment is far from a trivial matter. It is by far more convenient to leave this to a framework, rather than create it from scratch.

So, how do the inhabitants of the business logic tier look? Let's take a closer look at EJBs and EJB technology.

EJBs and EJB Technology

Simply put, an EJB is a distributed business logic component. It is distributed in the sense that it looks and behaves as a local object while behind the scenes it may be created and deployed on a remote server. It is a component in the sense that several classes collaborate to make its services available to the application system. EJB technology models business logic, as opposed to view or controller code that is handled by servlets or JSP documents.

Enterprise JavaBean technology is the answer to a "what if" vision: "What if you could use the simpler paradigm for developing a single-user/one machine program and pour that code into a server that would automagically make it distributed in a secure manner"? EJB technology is close to realizing that "get something for nothing" vision.

The three main types of EJB are:

- **Entity Enterprise JavaBeans (E-EJB):** E-EJBs represent an encapsulation of persistent data and may therefore be created or looked up (using so-called "finder" methods) in a persistent storage. If the application server is responsible for synchronizing the E-EJB state with the persistent storage, the E-EJB is said to use CMP (container-managed persistence), and if the developer is responsible for synchronizing the two states, the E-EJB uses BMP (bean-managed persistence).

- **Message-driven EJBs (M-EJB):** M-EJBs are crafted specifically to receive messages from asynchronous message queues, compliant with the Java Message Service (JMS) specification. M-EJBs are new to the EJB specification 2.0, and differ from session and Entity EJBs in their structure, due to their specialized nature.

- **Session Enterprise JavaBeans (S-EJB):** S-EJBs have no persistent state. A session EJB exists just as long as it is needed; normally, a relative few session EJBs handle many user calls. Session EJB components may be *stateful* (associated with a specific user session) or *stateless* (impersonal, not associated with a user session). Only the EJB client can create and use session EJB components.

Enterprise JavaBeans use similar patterns during deployment and runtime: the structure of session and entity beans is almost identical from the client's point of view. As shown in Figure 8-4, a session or Entity EJB has at least six parts (M-EJB are slightly simpler), three that you create and three that the EJB application server creates. The classes created by the developer have a white background, whereas the classes that the EJB application server generates as part of the deployment process have patterned backgrounds.

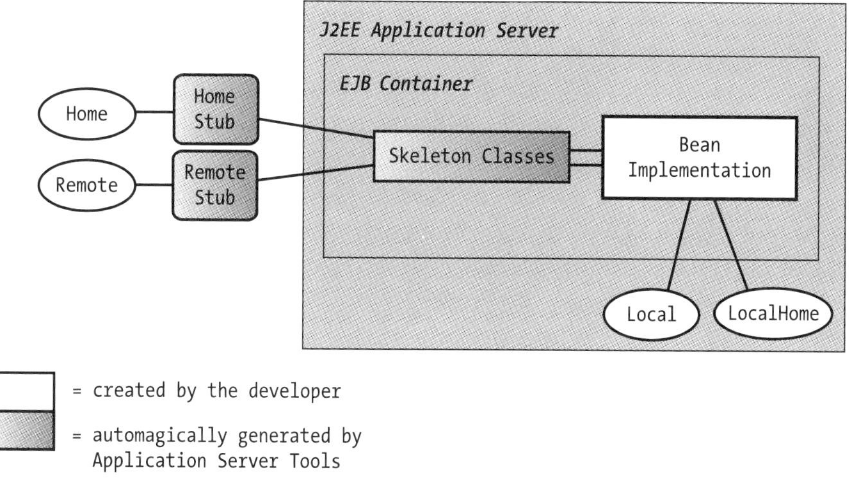

Figure 8-4. Structure of session and Entity EJB constructs

As shown in Figure 8-4, both S-EJB and E-EJB consist of a minimum of three types implemented by the developer:

- Home and/or LocalHome interface
- Remote and/or Local (Business) interfaces
- Bean implementation class

Starting with the EJB 2.0 specification, an EJB component may provide LocalHome and Local interfaces that have the same function as the Home and Remote interfaces, but lack any stub and skeleton classes. Thus, EJB components that use Local/LocalHome interfaces cannot be networked.

E-EJB components may implement a Primary Key class in addition to the five types just discussed. The Tie classes (stub and skeleton classes) are automatically generated by the EJB application server as part of the deployment process.

The eight different parts of the EJB component collaborate to create a distributed object. The first five of these (white backgrounds in Figure 8-4) define the interaction between the client and server parts of the EJB component. They must therefore be created by the developer. All code in the standard classes are independent of a EJB server, so the compiled code of any EJB component can be redeployed in a new EJB application server without any recompilation.

The last three objects required to make the EJB component work properly (striped backgrounds in Figure 8-4) can be automatically generated by the EJB application server, originating from the specification code in the Home, Remote, and Bean objects in addition to configuration settings read from EJB deployment descriptors. Encapsulated within the automatically generated classes are communication classes that enable transparent remote communication between the client (Remote and Home interfaces) and server (Bean implementation class).

Here's a definition of the roles of each of the eight objects in Figure 8-4:

- **Remote interface:** This interface contains the business methods of the EJB; this is where you declare the API that you want to use with the EJB. If you imagine a standard "Hello World" application crafted with EJB technology, the Remote interface contains the `public String sayHello()...` method which would return the "Hello World" string.

- **Local interface:** This interface is identical to the Remote interface in function and business method structure, but it lacks support for remote operation over a network. Local interfaces are used by EJB clients deployed within the same J2EE server in the same way as Remote interfaces, but without the cumbersome networking classes. Performance of EJB components using Local interfaces is therefore better than the corresponding components using Remote interfaces.

- **Home interface:** This interface declares factory methods that are used to create a reference to the Remote business interface aspect of an EJB. The Home interface may contain `create` (and, in the case of E-EJB, `find`) methods that either create a new EJB instance or find an already created EJB instance in a persistent storage. `create` methods must return an instance of the Remote interface; they work roughly like a constructor.

- **LocalHome interface:** This interface is identical to the Home interface in function and business method structure, but it lacks support for remote operation over a network. LocalHome interfaces are used by EJB clients deployed within the same J2EE server in the same way as Home interfaces, but without the cumbersome networking classes. Performance of EJB components using LocalHome interfaces is therefore better than the corresponding components using Home interfaces.

- **Bean implementation:** This class mirrors methods in the Home and Remote interfaces and is where you provide the implementation bodies of the methods declared in the Home and Remote interfaces. However, it is important to realize that the Bean implementation is not a skeleton class itself (that is, it does not directly implement the Home and Remote interfaces). Instead, the Bean implementation class does provide the actual business logic to the methods defined in the Home and Remote interfaces.

- **Home stub:** The actual implementation of the home interface, which accepts a method call, serializes all incoming arguments and transmits them to the corresponding skeleton class on the server node. Similarly, when receiving a serialized return response from the server, the Home stub de-serializes any received instances and answers the Home interface. The Home stub is the class enabling the Home interface to talk to its actual implementation on the server side. All communication that takes place between the Home interface and its Bean class implementation is hidden from the developer.

- **Remote stub:** Similar in deployment and operation to the Home stub, the Remote stub manages communication between the Remote interface and its business method implementations residing in the Bean implementation class on the server node. All network communication is transparent; a client developer does not even need to know that the Remote stub class even exists.

- **Skeleton classes:** These classes implement JRMP (Java Remote Method Protocol) skeleton classes for distributed communication with the home and remote instances. These automatically generated objects implement the Home and Remote interface of the EJB component and delegate any incoming method call to the Bean implementation class.

Aside from the first three Java classes or interfaces described in the preceding list, a deployment descriptor is needed to properly generate the stubs and skeletons that are required for proper communication with the server. Herein lies the trickiest part of EJB development; although the EJB development itself is trivial, deployment descriptor construction is not. You may initially feel that Java is a familiar and simple language, but yet another XML descriptor containing mandatory data structures for proper deployment poses a bigger problem. If you feel that this is the case, fear not! XML descriptors are simple in nature; although their structure may be required knowledge to get even the most trivial example working in a distributed environment, one can safely copy an existing deployment descriptor and modify it to suit one's needs.

Required Imports for EJB Development

EJB root classes and interfaces reside in the J2EE package `javax.ejb`. Required support classes assisting in the lookup and typecasting of the EJB Home interface are found in packages `javax.naming`, `java.rmi`, and `javax.rmi`. All you need to do to develop EJB components is install the J2EE distribution (which requires that you already have the J2SE distribution installed).

Figure 8-5 illustrates the required packages and their responsibilities.

Having investigated the parts of an EJB component, we should develop a small example EJB application to get a feeling for how it is done. Onwards!

The EJB Development Process

Different EJB types have slightly different needs, so you may need to slightly modify some steps of the development process to suit your particular requirements. However, the absolute majority of the development process remains unaltered for all types of EJB. Let's show the process by creating a simple stateless Session EJB component, in the form of *palindrome server.*

> **NOTE** *A palindrome is a word, phrase, verse, or sentence that reads the same backward or forward, such as "Eve", "Anna", "Go hang a salami; I'm a lasagna hog", or "Lisa Bonet ate no basil".*

The goal of the EJB development is a deployable JAR file that can be installed into an application server that supports your EJB specification. The process for

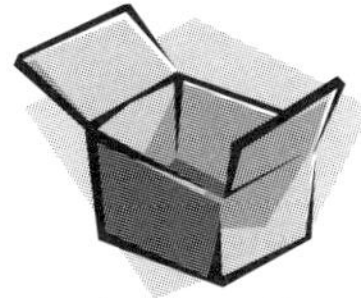
javax.ejb
Superclasses and superinterfaces
for EJB Remote, Home and
Implementaion objects

javax.naming
Java Naming and Directory Interface
(JNDI) classes required to locate
the EJB Home

java.rmi
RemoteException required for all
objects and methods which should
be executed on a remote machine

javax.rmi
PortableRemoteObject
required to typecast
the EJB ome to its
actual type

Figure 8-5. Packages required for EJB development. Note that all required types are found either in the J2EE installation or, in the case of the `javax.naming` *and* `java.rmi` *packages, the J2SE installation.*

developing the EJB server component has six steps, and there's one extra step for developing the EJB client component (proxy):

1. Define the Remote interface (that is, define what the component should do).

2. Define the create methods of the Home interface. (Define how the component should be created.)

3. Define the finder methods of the Home interface. (Define how the component should be retrieved from persistent storage.) This step is required only for Entity EJBs.

4. Implement the methods in the Bean implementation class. (Define how the component should implement its API.) Compile Java classes for Home, Remote, and Bean Implementation.

5. Create the standard J2EE deployment descriptor for the EJB component in the META-INF subdirectory from the compilation root. Compile and package all classes (from steps 2, 3, and 4) and the standard J2EE deployment descriptor in a JAR archive (called a *standard* EJB JAR) to create an unfinished but completely portable EJB component. If you know which application server your EJB component should be deployed in, you may also create and include any custom deployment descriptors in the JAR. In this case, the JAR is called *customized.*

6. If you are deploying your EJB component to an application server, you must run a custom application server deployment tool, which generates the stub and skeleton classes that are required for proper operation in the application server. Frequently, these EJB stub compilers require a customized JAR and produce a *deployable* JAR, containing all EJB stubs and skeletons required for deployment in the application server.

7. Create an application client or standard JavaBean proxy class that creates and communicates with the EJB component. An application client is a standalone Java application that communicates with the EJB deployed in the application server. A JavaBean proxy is an EJB client that is deployed in the Web container of an application server. The JavaBean proxy encapsulates the EJB component and exposes its results to servlets or JSP documents running in the Web application.

Most EJB server objects may be run inside an application server connected to a JavaBean that talks to the Web application, or from a standalone client that is run by invoking its `main()` method. Similar to classes that double as applications and applets, the JavaBean instances that communicate with EJB server may be developed to run either inside an application server or as a standalone client. Although it is possible, EJB bean developers rarely use classes doubling as clients and servers because the code bloat and complex deployment descriptors generally outweigh the benefits.

Before examining any code, let's look at the result of the running Web application that uses our palindrome EJB server. (See Figure 8-6.)

Having seen the result of running this small example, let's proceed to study the structure of its classes.

Step 1—Define the Remote Interface

The remote interface of the palindrome server is small indeed, as shown by its UML diagram in Figure 8-7. However, an important condition must be observed when

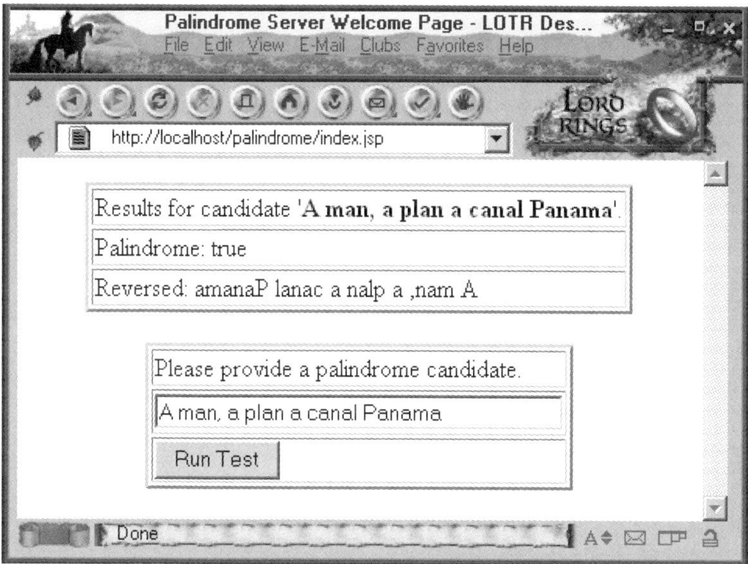

Figure 8-6. The result of the running Web application communicating with the EJB palindrome server

developing a Remote interface; the interface must extend `javax.ejb.EjbObject`, which is the superinterface of all Remote EJB interfaces.

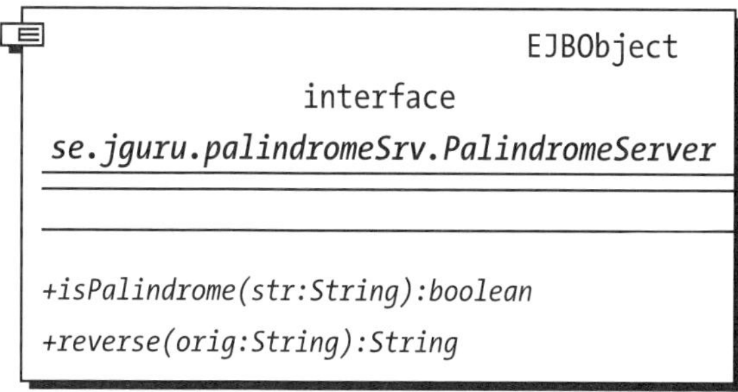

Figure 8-7. The PalindromeServer remote interface

`EjbObject`, in turn, extends `java.rmi.Remote`, so all instances of an EJB object may be distributed objects. As a consequence, all methods in the Remote interface must be declared to throw `java.rmi.RemoteException`.

In Listing 8-1, the EJB-specific code has been rendered in bold text.

Listing 8-1. Remote interface (PalindromeServer)

```
/*
 * Copyright (c) 2000,2001 jGuru Europe.
 * All rights reserved.
 */

package se.jguru.palindromeSrv;

import javax.ejb.EJBObject;
import javax.ejb.EJBException;
import java.rmi.RemoteException;

/**
 * The PalindromeServer interface is the business interface of
 * the EJB component residing on the application server node.
 */
public interface PalindromeServer extends EJBObject
{
    /**
     * Method that investigates if a particular string is
     * a palindrome. Whitespace will first be removed from
     * the string (i.e. whitespace characters will not be
     * taken into consideration). Null values are not considered
     * palindromes, but empty Strings are.
     *
     * @param str A string which should be checked for
     *        palindrome property (i.e. reversability).
     *
     * @return true if str is a palindrome.
     */
    public boolean isPalindrome(String str) throws RemoteException;

    /**
     * Reverses a string.
     *
     * @param orig the original string (which should be returned, in reverse).
     *
     * @return A reversed copy of the original string (parameter orig).
     */
    public String reverse(String orig) throws RemoteException;
}
```

The simple structure of the `PalindromeServer` interface, illustrated in Figure 8-8, shows what methods are to be implemented in the deployment process by the application server. None of the methods in the `EJBObject` interface should be implemented by the developer (but all may, of course, be used by the developer).

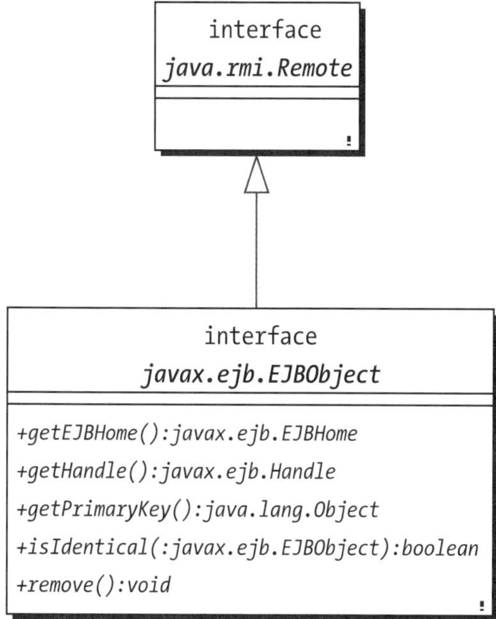

Figure 8-8. The inheritance structure of the EJBObject interface

Staying for a while longer in the simple part of the EJB development process, we move on to develop the Home interface.

Step 2—Define the Create Methods of the Home Interface

Following the swift definition of the Remote interface comes the equally simple task of defining the create methods of the Home interface. (See Figure 8-9.) Because our palindrome EJB server contains no specific state, a default create method (corresponding to a default constructor) will suffice.

Note that the Home interface of an EJB component must extend `javax.ejb.EJBHome`, which, in turn, extends `java.rmi.Remote`. Similar to the Remote interface, all methods in the Home interface must therefore throw `java.rmi.RemoteException`.

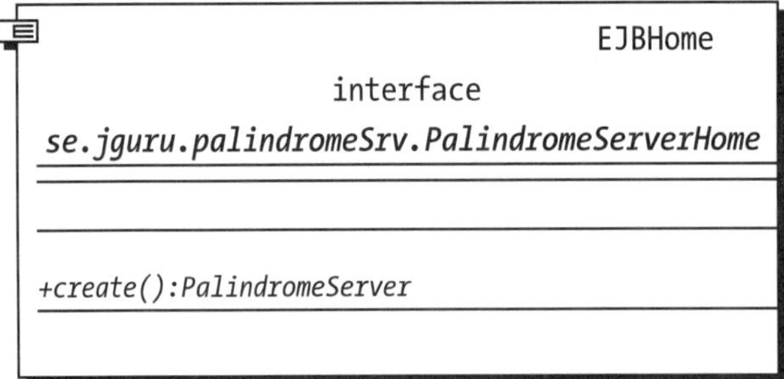

Figure 8-9. The `PalindromeServerHome` *interface*

In addition, all create methods of the Home interface must be declared to throw `CreateException`. If errors occur in the construction process, `CreateExceptions` may be thrown from within the create method. (See Listing 8-2. Again, relevant pieces of the Home interface code are rendered in bold text.)

Listing 8-2. The `PalindromeServerHome` *interface*

```
/*
 * Copyright (c) 2000,2001 jGuru Europe.
 * All rights reserved.
 */

package se.jguru.palindromeSrv;

import javax.ejb.EJBHome;
import javax.ejb.CreateException;
import java.rmi.RemoteException;

/**
 * The home interface is responsible for declaring the factory methods
 * which will create the PalindromeServer instances.
 */
public interface PalindromeServerHome extends EJBHome
{
    /**
     * The palindrome server needs no special constructor arguments;
     * a default create method will suffice.
     */
    public PalindromeServer create() throws CreateException, RemoteException;
}
```

The simple structure of the `PalindromeServerHome` interface shows what factory methods are available in the EJB component.

The EJB Home interface defines four methods that are automatically implemented by the application server deployment tools at deploy time. (See Figure 8-10.) All methods may be used by the developer at runtime, but they should not be overridden or implemented by the developer.

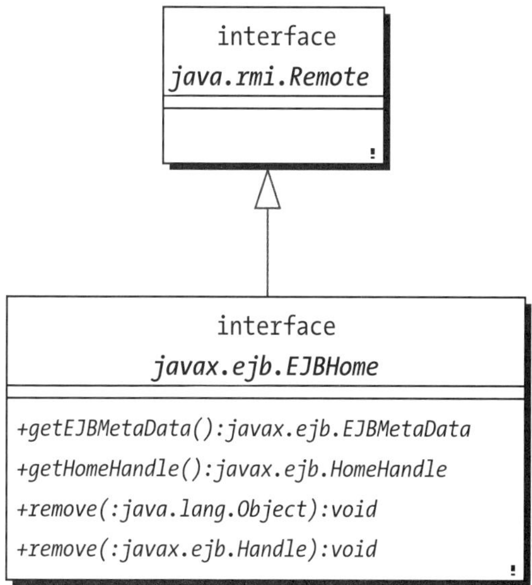

Figure 8-10. The EJBHome inheritance structure

When the `create` method API of the Home interface has been defined fully by the developer, it is time to proceed to the next step of the EJB component development; defining the `finder` methods of the Home API.

Step 3—Declare the Finder Methods of the Home Interface

Because we are developing a Session EJB, we don't need to save our state in a persistent storage such as a database. Finder methods are required only to read and repopulate data from a database into an Entity EJB. We may therefore skip step 3 of the EJB development process. (Writing `finder` methods is required only for developing E-EJB components.)

Although the two interfaces of the EJB component are defined, we still need to define the implementation class and provide method body implementations for all methods in the Home and Remote interfaces. This is done in step 4 of the EJB component creation process.

Step 4—Implement the Bean Class

We have already defined our API to the Remote and Home interfaces of the EJB component, but we haven't implemented any method bodies to provide an explanation of how the API should perform its operations. In addition to defining the Home and Remote methods of the bean, an EJB Bean implementation class needs life-cycle methods and a context object that is a handle to the surrounding EJB container. Thus, the implementation class must contain more methods and variables than are defined in the Remote and Home interfaces, as is shown in Figure 8-11.

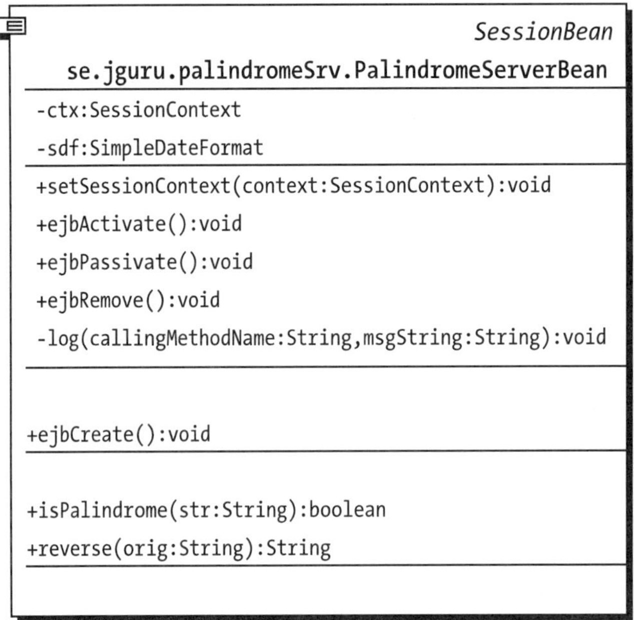

Figure 8-11. The Bean implementation class contains several kinds of members.

Figure 8-11 shows the members of the Session EJB UML diagram, grouped into five categories separated with lines. The five categories are, in order, private members, public members (that is, public methods), home factory methods (as declared in the Home interface), remote business methods (as declared in the Remote interface), and EJB environment references.

The top-most section contains variable members, both of which are private in this example. The `SessionContext` variable holds a reference to the EJB container in which the bean is run, and the `sdf` object is used to format timestamps for log messages.

The second section contains the methods that aren't defined in a Home or Remote interface. There are two categories of methods here; the `setSessionContext` and all methods starting with `ejb` are part of the EJB life cycle and will, for now, be ignored. (The EJB life cycle is detailed in the section "The EJB Life Cycle" later in this chapter.) The last method in this section, `log`, provides an interface to the system log. In this development walkthrough, we focus on the business logic methods of the EJB component, and simply leave all life-cycle methods empty, except for the `ejbCreate()`.

The third section contains the implementation of the methods declared in the Home interface of the EJB component. "Wait a minute," you may be saying. "The method declared in the Home interface had the signature `public PalindromeServer create()`, not `public void ejbCreate()`, as is the case in this Bean implementation class." This is correct; the Bean implementation class does not implement the Home interface per se, but it does provide a mirror of the methods implemented in the Home interface.

Remember, the skeleton class actually implementing the Home interface is generated automatically by the application server at deployment time. (Refer to Figure 6-4 for a deployment schematic of an EJB component.) Our skeleton class delegates each incoming call to a corresponding method in the Bean implementation class; the name of each corresponding method is `ejbCreate`, and its types and number of arguments are identical to the `create` method declared in the Home interface.

The fourth section contains the implementation of the methods declared in the Remote interface of the EJB component. Note that the methods are identical to their declaration, with the exception of what errors may be thrown by the method. The skeleton class encapsulates some error handling for us, so the implementation methods defined in the Bean implementation class contain no trace of their inherent distributed nature. This means that you may develop code as if the EJB component were completely run inside the local JVM, and simply have the application server handle all matters having to do with the distributed nature of the EJB component.

The fifth section contains the EJB environment references. Because we do not use any such references in this tutorial EJB component, section five is empty.

What Is Done in the Skeleton Class?

To clear some of the confusion about the automatically generated skeleton class running on the application server node, simply imagine that it delegates all calls to the EJB implementation class. For instance, when a client calls the `create()` method in the Home interface, the call terminates in the automatically generated skeleton class on the EJB server node.

Imagine that a part of the skeleton class has the following structure:

```
public class Skeleton_PalindromeServer implements PalindromeServerHome
{
    private PalindromeServerBean delegate;
    ...
    public PalindromeServer create() throws RemoteException,
        CreateException, EJBException
    {
        // Create the delegate
        this.delegate = new PalindromeServer();

        // Check sanity
        if(...) throw new RemoteException(...);
        if(...) throw new EJBException(...);

        // All seems to have gone well. Delegate the call, to
        // populate the state of the delegate.
        this.delegate.ejbCreate();
    }
}
```

All methods in the automatically generated skeleton class delegate their execution to the Bean implementation object.

The only thing remaining in step 4 is to examine the generated code of the Bean implementation class. Note that the Bean implementation class has to comply with three rules of EJB creation:

- The implementation class has to implement the interface pertaining to the bean type being created (that is, `javax.ejb.SessionBean`, `javax.ejb.EntityBean` or `javax.ejb.MessageDrivenBean`).

- The implementation class should not implement the Home or Remote interface directly. This is instead the task of the automatically generated skeleton classes.

- All `create` methods must be declared to throw `CreateException`, and `find` methods `FinderException`. If you are using an application server that is compliant with the EJB 1.0 (or earlier) specification, all methods in the Bean class may also throw `RemoteException`. This has been deprecated since EJB specification 1.1.

The pieces of code in Listing 8-3 that provide the compliance with the preceding rules appear in bold text.

Listing 8-3. The `PalindromeServerBean` *class*

```
/*
 * Copyright (c) 2000,2001 jGuru Europe.
 * All rights reserved.
 */

package se.jguru.palindromeSrv;

import javax.ejb.SessionBean;
import javax.ejb.SessionContext;
import java.rmi.RemoteException;
import javax.ejb.EJBException;
import javax.ejb.CreateException;

import java.text.SimpleDateFormat;
import java.util.Date;

/**
 * The PalindromeServerBean class that provide method implementations
 * for methods in the Home and Remote interfaces.
 *
 * @author Lennart Jörelid
 */
public class PalindromeServerBean implements SessionBean
{
    //
    // Session Context pattern
    //
```

```
// Handle to the EJB Container
private SessionContext ctx;

public void setSessionContext(SessionContext context)
{
    ctx = context;
}

//
// End Session Context pattern
//

// Create a formatter for logging timestamps
private SimpleDateFormat sdf;

//
// EJB Life Cycle methods
//

public void ejbActivate()
{
    this.log("ejbActivate", "--");
}

public void ejbPassivate()
{
    this.log("ejbPassivate", "--");
}

public void ejbRemove()
{
    this.log("ejbRemove", "--");
}

public void ejbCreate() throws CreateException
{
    // Create the SimpleDateFormat for the log
    this.sdf = new SimpleDateFormat("kk.mm:ss,SSS");

    // Log that we ran ejbCreate
    this.log("ejbCreate", "--");
}
```

```
//
// End EJB lifecycle methods
//

//
// Remote Business methods
//

/**
 * Method that investigates if a particular string is
 * a palindrome. Whitespace will first be removed from
 * the string (i.e. whitespace characters will not be
 * taken into consideration). Null values are not considered
 * palindromes, but empty Strings are.
 *
 * @param str A string which should be checked for
 *        palindrome property (i.e. reversability).
 *
 * @return true if str is a palindrome.
 */
public boolean isPalindrome(String str)
{
    // Check the special cases. Null values are not considered
    // palindromes, but empty Strings are.
    if (str == null) return false;
    if (str.equals("")) return true;

    // Define a Stringbuffer which contains a laundered
    // version of the str argument.
    StringBuffer laundered = new StringBuffer();

    // Wash out all whitespace from the str argument
    for (int i = 0; i < str.trim().length(); i++)
    {
        // Get the current char
        char current = str.charAt(i);

        // Is the current char considered whitespace?
        if (!Character.isJavaLetterOrDigit(current)) continue;
        // if(whitespace.indexOf("" + current) != -1) continue;

        // No. Copy it.
        laundered.append(current);
    }
```

```
        // Ignore case when determining a palindrome
        String lowerCaseStr = laundered.toString().toLowerCase();
        String reversed = this.reverse(lowerCaseStr);

        // Check palindrome status, and return.
        return lowerCaseStr.equals(reversed);
    }

    /**
     * Reverses a string.
     *
     * @param orig the original string (which should be returned, in reverse).
     *
     * @return A reversed copy of the original string (parameter orig).
     */
    public String reverse(String orig)
    {
        // Handle null and empty argument strings.
        if (orig == null) return null;
        if (orig.equals("")) return "";

        // Define the StringBuffer with which to work
        StringBuffer buf = new StringBuffer();

        for (int i = 0; i < orig.length(); i++)
        {
            // Copy the character to the outgoing buffer
            buf.append(orig.charAt(orig.length() - i - 1));
        }

        // Done.
        return buf.toString();
    }

    //
    // End Remote Business methods
    //

    //
    // Internal helper methods
    //
```

```
    private void log(String callingMethodName, String msgString)
    {
        // Get a Timestamp
        Date now = new Date();

        // Join the Resulting message string
        String msg = "<" + sdf.format(now) + "> [PalindromeServerBean::"
        + callingMethodName + "]: " + msgString;

        // Print to System.out
        System.out.println(msg);
    }

    //
    // End Internal helper methods
    //
}
```

Although a great level of detailed knowledge is required to control all parts of the EJB life cycle, implementing its business methods is quite simple, as can be seen in the code in Listing 8-3. Simply provide an implementation that is identical to the one of a local class, comply with the rules for an EJB implementation class, and leave the distribution to the application server.

The small UML diagram for the Bean implementation class reveals all its dependencies. (See Figure 8-12.)

Now that the three types of an EJB component have been implemented and the classes compiled, we should only have to run the deployment tool of our EJB application server of choice to generate the required skeleton and stub classes, right? Wrong. The deployment tool requires instructions on how the stub and skeleton classes should be generated, and these instructions are provided in the form of at least two configuration files (that is, deployment descriptors). Alas, we need to create EJB deployment descriptors before deployment is possible.

Step 5—Create the Deployment Descriptors

The standard J2EE EJB deployment descriptor is a file with the name `ejb-jar.xml`, placed in a directory called `META-INF`. It defines how the application server should treat the EJB component during deployment and runtime, providing a description for how the application server should generate the stub and skeleton files. The EJB deployment descriptor is similar in function to the Web application deployment descriptor, `web.xml`.

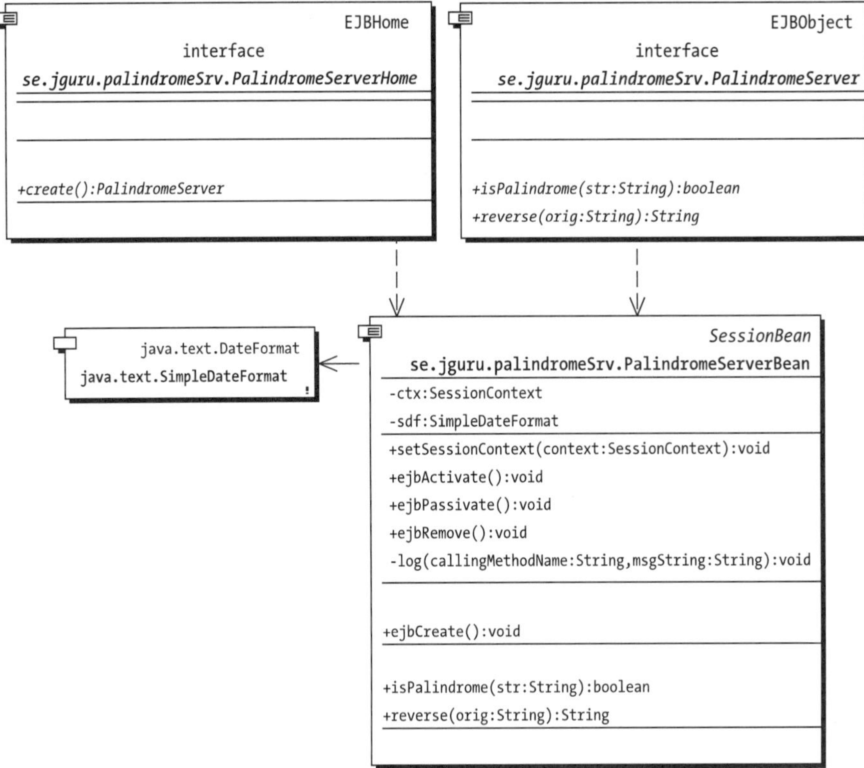

Figure 8-12. Relations of the `PalindromeServerBean` *implementation class. Aside from its natural dependency on the Home and Remote interfaces, the* `PalindromeServerBean` *has a* `java.text.SimpleDateFormat` *object that assists in formatting a timestamp for the internal log method.*

The deployment descriptor of our Session bean is pretty small and understandable, but a full deployment descriptor reference is provided in the section "EJB Deployment Descriptors" later in this chapter. With the understanding that we will provide details of all nodes and attributes in the XML deployment descriptor, examine the `ejb-jar.xml` deployment descriptor of the `PalindromeServer` EJB component. (See Listing 8-4.)

Listing 8-4. The `ejb-jar.xml` *standard J2EE deployment descriptor*

```
<?xml version="1.0"?>
<!DOCTYPE ejb-jar PUBLIC
   "-//Sun Microsystems, Inc.//DTD Enterprise JavaBeans 2.0//EN"
   "http://java.sun.com/dtd/ejb-jar_2_0.dtd">
```

```
<ejb-jar>
   <!-- Generic descriptions for the EJB JAR as a whole -->
   <description>This is the palindrome server</description>
   <display-name>PalindromeServerBean</display-name>

   <enterprise-beans>
      <session>

      <!-- Common definitions for this session EJB -->
      <description>This is the PalindromeServer Bean</description>
      <display-name>se.jguru.palindromeSrv.PalindromeServer</display-name>
      <ejb-name>se.jguru.palindromeSrv.PalindromeServer</ejb-name>
      <home>se.jguru.palindromeSrv.PalindromeServerHome</home>
      <remote>se.jguru.palindromeSrv.PalindromeServer</remote>
      <ejb-class>se.jguru.palindromeSrv.PalindromeServerBean</ejb-class>
      <session-type>Stateful</session-type>
      <transaction-type>Container</transaction-type>

      <!-- Security definition, for a security role reference called
           standardUser. StandardUser refers to an actual security role called
           standardUserRole, which is defined in the assembly descriptor below.
      -->
      <security-role-ref>
         <role-name>standardUser</role-name>
         <description>
            The standard User Role of the palindromeServer
         </description>
         <role-link>standardUserRole</role-link>
      </security-role-ref>
      </session>
   </enterprise-beans>

   <!--  The Assembly descriptor section of the ejb-jar.xml maps security roles to
         permissions. EJB permissions grant the ability to execute a given method
         potentially with a given set of arguments.
   -->
   <assembly-descriptor>

      <!-- Define a security role called standardUserRole for this EJB -->
      <security-role>
         <description>Standard Application User</description>
         <role-name>standardUserRole</role-name>
      </security-role>
```

```
    <!-- Each method-permission section grants one or more security roles
         method execution privileges for a set of methods in an EJB.
         In this case, the standardUserRole is granted execute privileges
         to all methods in the Home and Remote interfaces of the EJB with
         the name se.jguru.palindromeSrv.PalindromeServer
    -->
    <method-permission>
      <description>palindromeServerUserPermission</description>
      <role-name>standardUserRole</role-name>
      <method>
        <ejb-name>se.jguru.palindromeSrv.PalindromeServer</ejb-name>
        <method-name>*</method-name>
      </method>
    </method-permission>

    <!-- Each container-transaction defines the transactional settings for a
         set of methods in an EJB component. In this case, all methods in the
         se.jguru.palindromeSrv.PalindromeServer must execute within a
         transaction. -->
    <container-transaction>
      <description>Standard transaction type</description>
      <method>
        <ejb-name>se.jguru.palindromeSrv.PalindromeServer</ejb-name>
        <method-name>*</method-name>
      </method>
      <trans-attribute>Required</trans-attribute>
    </container-transaction>
  </assembly-descriptor>
</ejb-jar>
```

The deployment descriptor contains four primary sections:

- **General archive metadata** contains descriptive information about the `ejb-jar` archive itself. This section contains two entries: a description and a display name (the name under which the entire archive is shown in GUI administration tools).

- **Enterprise beans metadata** contains one or more bean deployment descriptors (in this case a single session bean descriptor for the `PalindromeServer` session bean). After the Session EJB has been given a description and a display name of its own, the following six important properties are defined:

    - `<ejb-name>` has the same function as a primary key in a database: it uniquely identifies an EJB component within the `ejb-jar.xml` descriptor. This value can be chosen arbitrarily, although it is recommended that you select a name that illustrates which type or function the EJB behind it plays. In this case, the qualified type name of the Remote interface has been chosen.

    - `<home>` contains the fully qualified type name (that is, including all packages) of the Session bean's Home interface. This interface must extend `javax.ejb.EJBHome` directly or indirectly.

    - `<remote>` contains the fully qualified type name of the Session bean's Remote interface. This interface must extend `javax.ejb.EJBObject` directly or indirectly.

    - `<ejb-class>` contains the fully qualified type name of the Session bean's implementation class. As we are deploying a Session EJB, this class must implement `javax.ejb.SessionBean` directly or indirectly. For Entity EJB components, the `<ejb-class>` must extend `javax.ejb.EntityBean` and for MessageDriven EJB components, `javax.ejb.MessageDrivenBean`.

    - `<session-type>` defines whether or not the EJB is stateful or stateless. The deployment descriptor above defines a stateful bean, thus associating a separate EJB state with each user.

    - `<transaction-type>` defines whether the EJB container or the bean itself should manage the transactions of the EJB component. When you leave the EJB transaction management to the container (as is done in this case) it is illegal to start, commit, or rollback a transaction from within the bean.

- **security role reference definition**, contained in the last part of the `<session>...</session>` element, maps a J2EE principal from the application server to a security role defined in the assembly descriptor section.

- **Assembly descriptor metadata** contains three types of definitions:

    - **Security role definitions and descriptions**: A security role is simply a name to which method execution and access privileges can be tied.

    - **Method permission definitions**: These relate a set of method access privileges to one or more defined security roles. In our deployment descriptor above, users belonging to the `standardUsers` security role may access all methods in the Home and Remote interfaces.

- **Container transaction specifications**: These provide information about how the container in which the EJB component is deployed should handle transaction isolation in the call thread. In this case, all methods in the Home and Remote interfaces must be run within a transaction.

Although the standard J2EE deployment descriptor may seem quite a mouthful, we're still missing some important data that is required for the deployment of the EJB component into an application server. How does, for instance, an EJB security role correlate to a logged-in user of an application server? This and other issues are addressed in a custom way, specific to each application server. Frequently, the custom deployment document takes the form of another deployment descriptor, specific to a particular application server. As an example, the WebLogic Application Server has a deployment descriptor called `weblogic-ejb-jar.xml`, the Orion Application Server has a deployment descriptor called `orion-ejb-jar.xml`, the Inprise Application Server has a deployment descriptor called `ejb-inprise.xml`, and so forth.

The combined data in the standard and custom deployment descriptors provide enough information for the application server to create and compile the code for the stub and skeleton classes from Figure 8-4. Therefore, take a look at an example custom deployment descriptor from the Orion Application Server. (See Listing 8-5.)

Listing 8-5. The custom deployment descriptor `orion-ejb-jar.xml` *for the Orion Application Server*

```
<?xml version="1.0"?>
<!DOCTYPE orion-ejb-jar PUBLIC
   "-//Evermind//DTD Enterprise JavaBeans 1.1 runtime//EN"
   "http://www.orionserver.com/dtds/orion-ejb-jar.dtd">

<orion-ejb-jar deployment-version="1.5.2" deployment-time="e81403c711">
   <enterprise-beans>

      <session-deployment
         name="se.jguru.palindromeSrv.PalindromeServer"
         location="se.jguru.palindromeSrv.PalindromeServer"
         wrapper="PalindromeServerHome_StatefulSessionHomeWrapper19"
         max-tx-retries="3"
         timeout="1800"
         persistence-filename="se.jguru.palindromeSrv.PalindromeServer" />
   </enterprise-beans>
```

```
    <assembly-descriptor>
        <security-role-mapping name="standardUserRole">
            <group name="defaultApplicationUsers" />
        </security-role-mapping>

        <default-method-access>
            <security-role-mapping name="&lt;default-ejb-caller-role&gt;">
            </security-role-mapping>
        </default-method-access>
    </assembly-descriptor>
</orion-ejb-jar>
```

The custom deployment descriptor for the Orion Application Server contains two primary sections:

- `<enterprise-beans>` contains a `<session-deployment>` tag, which defines the concrete deployment values for a session EJB bean. The `<session-deployment>`, in turn, defines the custom deployment properties for a bean whose `<ejb-name>` (from the `ejb-jar.xml`, remember?) matches the given `name` attribute. The only really important setting is the `location` attribute, which provides the Java Naming and Directory Interface (JNDI) registry key where the bean is bound. This string is required for the EJB client to find the `PalindromeServer`; it is described in "Step 7—Create a JavaBean Proxy" later in this chapter.

- `<security-role-mapping>` associates the `standardUserRole`, defined in the standard J2EE deployment descriptor, `ejb-jar.xml`, with all members of the group `defaultApplicationUsers`. The Orion Application Server uses other deployment descriptors to define users and groups, and we investigate these in further detail in Chapter 9.

The `orion-ejb-jar.xml` file serves as a good illustration of what type of information is commonly provided in a custom EJB deployment descriptor. Concrete JNDI registry keys are matters outside of the J2EE specification as are concrete security properties such as user IDs and passwords.

Figure 8-13 illustrates the development process for our EJB JAR. When the EJB component classes (including any nonstandard classes used by the Home, Remote, and Bean classes) are compiled and packaged along with the standard J2EE deployment descriptor `ejb-jar.xml`, we have a standard JAR file that is completely portable between application servers. However, for all its portability, the standard JAR is utterly useless because it cannot be deployed into an application server.

When adding the application server-specific deployment descriptor (frequently in the form of another XML document) to the standard J2EE JAR, a customized

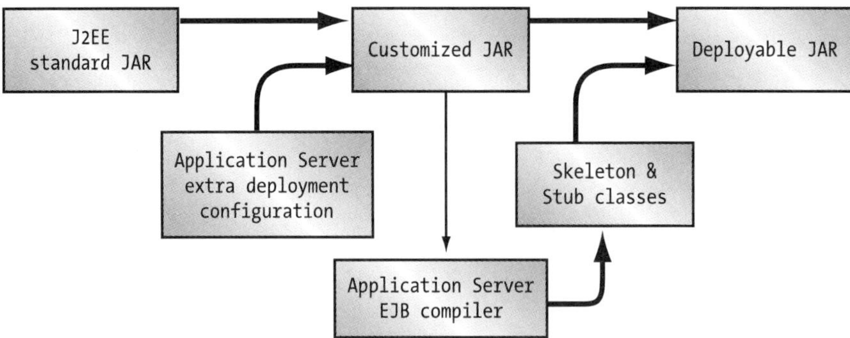

Figure 8-13. The packaging process of an EJB component may involve up to three different JAR files, two deployment descriptors, and the attention of an application server-specific EJB stub compiler. Most application servers have nondestructive extra deployment configurations, so you can generally create a JAR that may be customized for several different application servers.

JAR is produced. All J2EE-compliant application servers can use a J2EE standard JAR file as an origin when creating customized JAR archives.

The customized JAR is still portable between application servers, although it carries the extra deadweight of an extra deployment descriptor. Although much closer to deployment, a customized JAR cannot directly be deployed into an application server. First, we need to generate all stub and skeleton files for the application server using a custom EJB compiler tool.

Step 6—Compile and Package Classes and Deployment Descriptors

From step 5, we have created a customized EJB JAR, which can be used by the application server EJB compiler to create a deployable JAR. Simply package the deployment descriptors (`ejb-jar.xml`) in a directory called `/META-INF`, and the fully qualified class package directly under the root. Refer to your application server's documentation to find where the custom deployment descriptor should go in the archive. Frequently, the custom deployment descriptor is placed alongside the standard J2EE one, as shown in Figure 8-14. Generally, the structure packaged into the customized JAR file looks like that shown in Figure 8-14.

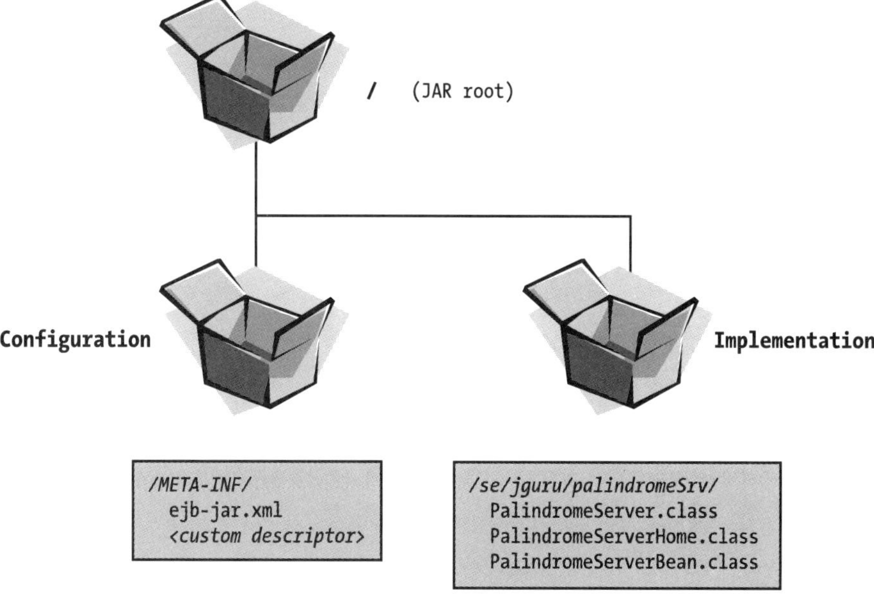

Figure 8-14. The internal structure of the packaged JAR file. The actual EJB implementation classes are found in the `se.jguru.palindromeSrv` *package, and the deployment descriptor* `ejb-jar.xml` *is found in the* `META-INF` *directory.*

> **NOTE** *The Orion Application Server has a slightly different deployment structure, which will be explored in Chapter 9. As a result, the J2EE standard JAR is directly deployable in the Orion Application Server—both in packed and unpacked form.*

In general, the EJB deployment process into an application server is a simple three-step approach. Actually, one of the more complex parts of the process is realizing that three different JAR files are involved in the process of deploying an EJB into an application server, as illustrated in Figure 8-13.

Let's follow this small procedure for another commercial application server, the Inprise Application Server. The procedure is fairly generic for most application servers (although, of course, the corresponding form and data in the extra deployment descriptor information varies from application server to application server). The additional configuration file required by the Inprise Application Server is called `ejb-inprise.xml` but its content is similar to the content in the `orion-ejb-jar.xml` deployment descriptor.

Shown in Figure 8-15, the customized JAR file is quite similar to the J2EE standard JAR file; the only difference is the existence of the `ejb-inprise.xml` in the

META-INF directory. Most other application servers modify the customized JAR in a similar way. Remember, however, that the difference between the J2EE standard JAR file and the customized JAR is nonstandard; different application servers have different formats and data in their extra deployment descriptor.

ejb-inprise.xml	XML Document	456	meta-inf\
ejb-jar.xml	XML Document	1 447	meta-inf\
Manifest.mf	MF File	262	meta-inf\
PalindromeServer.class	CLASS File	364	se\jguru\palindromeSrv\
PalindromeServerBean.class	CLASS File	2 146	se\jguru\palindromeSrv\
PalindromeServerHome.class	CLASS File	348	se\jguru\palindromeSrv\

Figure 8-15. Contents of the customized JAR file. The only difference from the original, standard J2EE JAR is the `ejb-inprise.xml` *file in the* `/META-INF` *directory. This particular customized JAR can therefore be reused in another application server's deployment process.*

NOTE *Although a bit exotic, one may as a consequence create a deployed JAR that may run on different application servers.*

After running the deployment wizard of the Inprise Application Server, the contents of the deployable JAR file is seen in Figure 8-16. If you are familiar with CORBA programming, the skeleton and stub class names are well known. The Inprise Application Server uses the CORBA paradigm to communicate between the EJB server component and the EJB remote interface. The EJB component model may communicate freely over IIOP (Internet Inter-ORB Protocol), which is the standard communication protocol for CORBA. Without getting bogged down in communication technicalities, we can clearly see that the deployment tool has created many classes that assist in the communication between client and server.

The skeleton and stub files generated by the deployment tools of the application server are accompanied by several other files that keep track of internal state in the EJB component. Thankfully, we need not bother with creating or modifying all communication assistance classes; the application server generates them as part of the deployment process.

Although packaging compiled classes and a deployment descriptor is a small step in itself, the full deployment process for an EJB component can get rather complex. Remember, two separate entities (an information specification file and a deployment tool) are required to transform the standardized J2EE EJB

ejb-inprise.xml	XML Document	1 021	meta-inf\
ejb-jar.xml	XML Document	1 346	meta-inf\
Manifest.mf	MF File	244	meta-inf\
_LegacyFacade_Stub.class	CLASS File	3 599	se\jguru\webdb\proxy\
_LegacyFacadeHome_Stub.class	CLASS File	3 947	se\jguru\webdb\proxy\
LegacyFacade.class	CLASS File	524	se\jguru\webdb\proxy\
LegacyFacadeBean.class	CLASS File	4 764	se\jguru\webdb\proxy\
LegacyFacadeHelper.class	CLASS File	4 587	se\jguru\webdb\proxy\
LegacyFacadeHolder.class	CLASS File	967	se\jguru\webdb\proxy\
LegacyFacadeHome.class	CLASS File	302	se\jguru\webdb\proxy\
LegacyFacadeHomeHelper.class	CLASS File	4 663	se\jguru\webdb\proxy\
LegacyFacadeHomeHolder.class	CLASS File	995	se\jguru\webdb\proxy\
LegacyFacadeHomeOperations.class	CLASS File	357	se\jguru\webdb\proxy\
LegacyFacadeHomePOA.class	CLASS File	3 871	se\jguru\webdb\proxy\
LegacyFacadeHomePOAInvokeHand...	CLASS File	3 106	se\jguru\webdb\proxy\
LegacyFacadeHomePOATie.class	CLASS File	1 660	se\jguru\webdb\proxy\
LegacyFacadeOperations.class	CLASS File	321	se\jguru\webdb\proxy\
LegacyFacadePOA.class	CLASS File	3 662	se\jguru\webdb\proxy\
LegacyFacadePOAInvokeHandler.class	CLASS File	3 187	se\jguru\webdb\proxy\
LegacyFacadePOATie.class	CLASS File	1 678	se\jguru\webdb\proxy\

Figure 8-16. An example of the contents of a deployable JAR file

JAR into a deployable JAR that may be used by an application server. Consult your application server documentation for an exact reference regarding its required extra deployment descriptor and tool.

When the compiled classes and descriptors are packaged in the JAR file, we could start using it directly from within a JSP document. However, this is not particularly smooth because we would have to deal with its rather complex runtime patterns directly within the JSP document code. To avoid large amounts of Java code in the JSP document, we will use a JavaBean proxy encapsulating the reference to the EJB Home and Remote objects within the JSP document.

Let us, therefore, take a look at the needs of the JavaBean proxy.

Step 7—Create a JavaBean Proxy

When you develop a Web application, it is highly recommended that you hide as much complexity as possible inside what looks and behaves like a standard JavaBean model component. A JavaBean proxy object is a perfect way to provide such encapsulation; it behaves just like a normal JavaBean so it may be accessed and manipulated using the standard `<jsp:useBean>` tags. The internal code in the JavaBean proxy hides the Java programming statements that are required to look up and access the EJB Remote interface, and it presents a clean JavaBean API to the JSP developer.

In principle, the JavaBean proxy acts as a mediator between the JSP document and the EJB model. You may well imagine that the JavaBean proxy object works like a salesperson: keeping a smooth and easy-going conversation with the client while taking care not to reveal any of the complex technological stuff. Figure 8-17 shows the principal pattern of the JavaBean proxy: being referenced from the JSP view document, the JavaBean proxy delegates most or all incoming invocation methods to its contained EJB remote instance.

```
                                                   Serializable
        se.jguru.palindromeClient.PalindromeJavaBean
------------------------------------------------------------------
#svr:PalindromeServer
#palindromeCandidate:String
#JNDI_LOOKUP:String="java:comp/env/palindromeServerHome"
------------------------------------------------------------------
+PalindromeJavaBean(props:Properties)
+PalindromeJavaBean()
+setPalindromeCandidate(aCandidate:String):void
+isPalindrome():boolean
+getReverse():String
-log(callingMethod:String,msg:String):void
+main(args:String[]):void
------------------------------------------------------------------
 palindromeCandidate:String
 palindrome:boolean
 reverse:String
```

Figure 8-17. The principal function of the JavaBean proxy is to hide all complex EJB lookup and method invocation code, presenting a simple JavaBean calling API that may be handled by the bean-handling tags of the JSP standard. Tags such as `<jsp:useBean />`, `<jsp:setProperty />`, *and* `<jsp:setProperty />` *are much cleaner and simpler to embed in a JSP view document than a lot of Java code between* <% *and* %> *tags.*

All methods within JavaBean proxies have principally the same structure. They delegate the method call to their contained EJB member; in the general case, a JavaBean proxy class has the structure shown in Listing 8-6.

Listing 8-6. Structure of a JavaBean proxy class

```
public class XXXXClient
{
   // Declare the delegate instance (i.e. the EJB Remote object)
   private XXXXXServer delegate;
```

```
    public XXXXClient()
    {
        // Find the delegate
    }

    // A template JavaBean setter method
    // that sets its property in the delegate
    public void setPropertyName(PropertyType arg)
    {
        // Check sanity
        try
        {
            this.delegate.setPropertyName(arg);
        }
        catch(XXXException ex)
        {
            // Handle the exception
        }
    }

    // A template JavaBean getter method
    // that retrieves its property from the delegate
    public PropertyType getPropertyName()
    {
        // Check sanity
        if(this.delegate == null)
        { // Handle exception }

        // Sane. Proceed.
        return this.delegate.getPropertyName();
    }
}
```

In most cases, one performs a rather limited amount of processing in the JavaBean proxy, as it is mainly thought of as a mediator between the JSP view and the EJB model. However, all forms of argument repackaging and exception state handling should be present in the JavaBean proxy. Therefore, large portions of the JavaBean proxy can be created more or less on routine. The patterns illustrated in Listing 8-6 look like templates for the Delegator pattern (where all calls are mirrored to or from a delegate).

Enough talk, recruits! The actual code of the JavaBean proxy awaits your discovery in Listing 8-7.

Listing 8-7. The `PalindromeJavaBean` *class*

```
/*
 * Copyright (c) 2000,2001 jGuru Europe.
 * All rights reserved.
 */

package se.jguru.palindromeClient;

import se.jguru.palindromeSrv.PalindromeServer;
import se.jguru.palindromeSrv.PalindromeServerHome;

import javax.naming.Context;
import javax.naming.InitialContext;
import javax.naming.NamingException;

import javax.rmi.PortableRemoteObject;
import java.rmi.RemoteException;

import javax.ejb.CreateException;
import java.io.Serializable;

import java.util.Properties;

/**
 * A useable JavaBean that is simple to use from within a JSP document,
 * or as a standalone EJB client. All getter methods delegate their
 * invocation to the internal EJB Remote object (the PalindromeServer
 * instance), and catch all potential errors pertaining to network errors
 * or invocation misfortunes.
 */
public class PalindromeJavaBean implements Serializable
{
    // The internal PalindromeServer instance
    protected PalindromeServer svr;

    // The internal string which should be checked for
    // palindrome status.
    protected String palindromeCandidate;

    // The string used for JNDI lookup against the
    // PalindromeServer Home interface.
    protected static final String JNDI_LOOKUP = "java:comp/env/palindromeServerHome";
```

```
/**
 * Create a default PalindromeServerJavaBean, which
 * instantiates the PalindromeServer for further calls.
 */
public PalindromeJavaBean()
{
    try
    {
        //
        // Get an initial context
        //
        this.log("<constructor>", "Getting initial context");
        Context ctx = new InitialContext();

        // Log the context retrieved.
        this.log("<constructor>", "Got Context of type "
            + ctx.getClass().getName());

        // Lookup our PalindromeServerHome in the JNDI registry
        Object obj = ctx.lookup(JNDI_LOOKUP);
        this.log("<constructor>", "Got PalindromeServerHome of type "
            + obj.getClass().getName());

        // Typecast to a PalindromeServerHome.
        PalindromeServerHome home = (PalindromeServerHome)
            PortableRemoteObject.narrow(obj, PalindromeServerHome.class);

        // Create our PalindromeServer instance
        this.svr = home.create();
    }
    catch (NamingException ex)
    {
        // Whoops - could not find the name
        this.log("<constructor>", "Could not localize the "
            + "PalindromeServer. (" + ex + ")");
    }
    catch (CreateException ex)
    {
        // Internal error in the creation process
       this.log("<constructor>", "Could not create Palindrome server: " + ex);
    }
    catch (RemoteException ex)
    {
        this.log("<constructor>", "Could not reach the server: " + ex);
    }
```

```
    // Finally, log the existence of a server (or null if the Lookup
    // and creation process failed).
    this.log("<constructor>", "server := " + svr);
}

/**
 * JavaBean setter method that sets the palindrome
 * candidate string which is used as a source
 * for both JavaBean getter methods below.
 */
public void setPalindromeCandidate(String aCandidate)
{
    // Simply set the candidate
    this.palindromeCandidate = aCandidate;
}

/** Returns true if the palindromeCandidate is a palindrome. */
public boolean isPalindrome()
{
    try
    {
        // Invoke the method in the remote server
        return this.svr.isPalindrome(this.palindromeCandidate);
    }
    catch (RemoteException ex)
    {
        this.log("isPalindrome", "No connection to server EJB: " + ex);
    }

    // Return displeasure indicator
    return false;
}

/** Returns the palindromeCandidate in reverse. */
public String getReverse()
{
    try
    {
        // Reverse the current palindrome candidate.
        return this.svr.reverse(this.palindromeCandidate);
    }
    catch (RemoteException ex)
    {
        this.log("getReverse", "No connection to server EJB: " + ex);
    }
```

```
        // Return displeasure indicator
        return "No palindromeCandidate set";
    }

    /**
     * Internal log method which prints a well-formatted
     * logging message to the Standard output stream.
     *
     * @param callingMethod The name of the calling method
     */
    private void log(String callingMethod, String msg)
    {
        // Log to standard out.
        System.out.println("[PalindromeJavaBean::" + callingMethod + "]: " + msg);
    }
}
```

All methods but the constructor of the `PalindromeJavaBean` class are fairly simple to understand, but the constructor that contains all the code required to connect to the `PalindromeServer` EJB is more complex. Let us therefore study the statements establishing the connection in detail.

The JNDI, which functions similarly to a HashMap, is used to bind and look up all EJB Home instances. The first statements in the constructor shown in Listing 8-8 simply create a new `InitialContext`, which is the root JNDI directory available to the application. This form of the `InitialContext` constructor may only be used by components deployed within a J2EE application server.

Listing 8-8. Creating a new `InitialContext`

```
            //
            // Get an initial context
            //
            this.log("<constructor>", "Getting initial context");
            Context ctx = new InitialContext();

           // Log the context retrieved.
            this.log("<constructor>", "Got Context of type "
                + ctx.getClass().getName());
```

Having created a reference to the context of the application server, we may use the lookup method shown in the following example to access the bound Home interface of the EJB component. The returned object may be an instance of the Home interface, but it may also be a CORBA holder object or some other container or stream factory. Therefore, normal Java typecasting cannot be used directly on the return object, `obj`. Instead, the `javax.rmi.PortableRemoteObject.narrow` method is used to typecast the EJB Home instance to its correct type.

```
// Lookup our PalindromeServerHome in the JNDI registry
Object obj = ctx.lookup(JNDI_LOOKUP);
this.log("<constructor>", "Got PalindromeServerHome of type "
    + obj.getClass().getName());

// Typecast to a PalindromeServerHome.
PalindromeServerHome home = (PalindromeServerHome)
    PortableRemoteObject.narrow(obj, PalindromeServerHome.class);
```

The last step of the EJB setup in the `PalindromeJavaBean` constructor is creating the actual `PalindromeServer` remote instance by running the `create()` factory method of the Home interface. This is trivial, but it extracts the EJB server reference that will be used throughout the `PalindromeJavaBean` proxy to communicate with the EJB server:

```
// Create our PalindromeServer instance
this.svr = home.create();
```

Alas, the JavaBean proxy instance is simply an adapter between the JSP document and the `PalindromeServer` EJB object; all its methods save the `setPallindromeCandidate` method mirror the methods of the `PalindromeServer` EJB remote interface. All methods used in a JavaBean proxy should adhere to the standard JavaBean design pattern because they should be simple to access from JSP `useBean`, `setProperty`, and `getProperty` tags. Also, all JavaBean proxy methods should handle the exceptions (such as `RemoteException`) that may be thrown by an EJB server instance.

The JSP view document of the application that uses the JavaBean proxy is rather small and straightforward. The relevant code snippets (manipulating the JavaBean proxy) in the JSP document appear in bold text in Listing 8-9.

Listing 8-9. The JSP view document using the `PalindromeJavaBean`

```
<%--
    Create a JavaBean handling our palindrome server
    or set all possible JavaBean properties in it.
--%>
<jsp:useBean
    id="palindromeBean"
    scope="session"
    class="se.jguru.palindromeClient.PalindromeJavaBean" />
<jsp:setProperty name="palindromeBean" property="*" />
<%
    // Check sanity. Did the user enter a palindrome candidate?
    String candidate = request.getParameter("palindromeCandidate");
    if(candidate == null) candidate = "No palindrome candidate provided";
%>

<html>
<head>
    <title>Palindrome Server Welcome Page</title>
</head>
  <body>
    <center>
    <table border=2>
    <tr><td>Results for candidate '<b><%= candidate %></b>'.</td></tr>
    <tr><td>Palindrome:
        <jsp:getProperty name="palindromeBean" property="palindrome" />
    </td></tr>
    <tr><td>Reversed:
        <jsp:getProperty name="palindromeBean" property="reverse" />
    </td></tr>
    </table>


    <form action="http://localhost/palindrome/index.jsp" method=post>
    <table border=2>

    <tr><td>Please provide a palindrome candidate.</td></tr>
    <tr><td><input type=text name="palindromeCandidate"></td></tr>
    <tr><td><input type=submit value="Run Test"></td></tr>
    </table>
    </form>
  </body>
</html>
```

Note that the JSP view document uses only standard JSP tags to handle the JavaBean proxy. Apart from a few request argument parameters, there is no trace in the view document of the EJB component being used within it; the JavaBean proxy catches any exceptions raised by the `PalindromeServer` EJB component. When the JSP document is deployed in a J2EE Web container, the resulting output from Figure 8-6 is shown.

> **NOTE** *See Chapters 4 and 11 for examples of deploying the Web application.*

All documents regarding the EJB development and the JavaBean proxy are thereby walked through, but the JavaBean proxy has several implied requirements that constrain it to deployment and execution within an application server. We will now study how to augment its code to execute it as a Java application.

A Standalone PalindromeJavaBean Client

When the `PalindromeJavaBean` proxy is run from within a Web container in the same application server as the `PalindromeServer`, it operates fine. However, should we want to connect to the `PalindromeServer` from a Java application simply by adding a main method to the `PalindromeJavaBean` class, the EJB connection to the application server fails, throwing several "disaster-class" exceptions. This happens for several reasons; we need to modify the JavaBean proxy to work both inside a running J2EE Web container and as a standalone application. The UML of the modified `PalindromeJavaBean` is shown in Figure 8-18.

We have provided—in addition to the actual business methods exposed by the JavaBean proxy—a `main` method that provides a simple unit test. This is a frequent way of providing a standalone functional verification of a proxy class, but, in the case of proxies containing EJB references, the standalone verification is slightly trickier than a normal Java class. This is because the calls that make the JNDI context (where the Home interface of the EJB server is bound) accessible are simpler when run from within the application server than as a standalone client.

In Listing 8-10, study the parts of the `PalindromeJavaBean` that needs modification to work properly when run as a standalone application, starting with the main method.

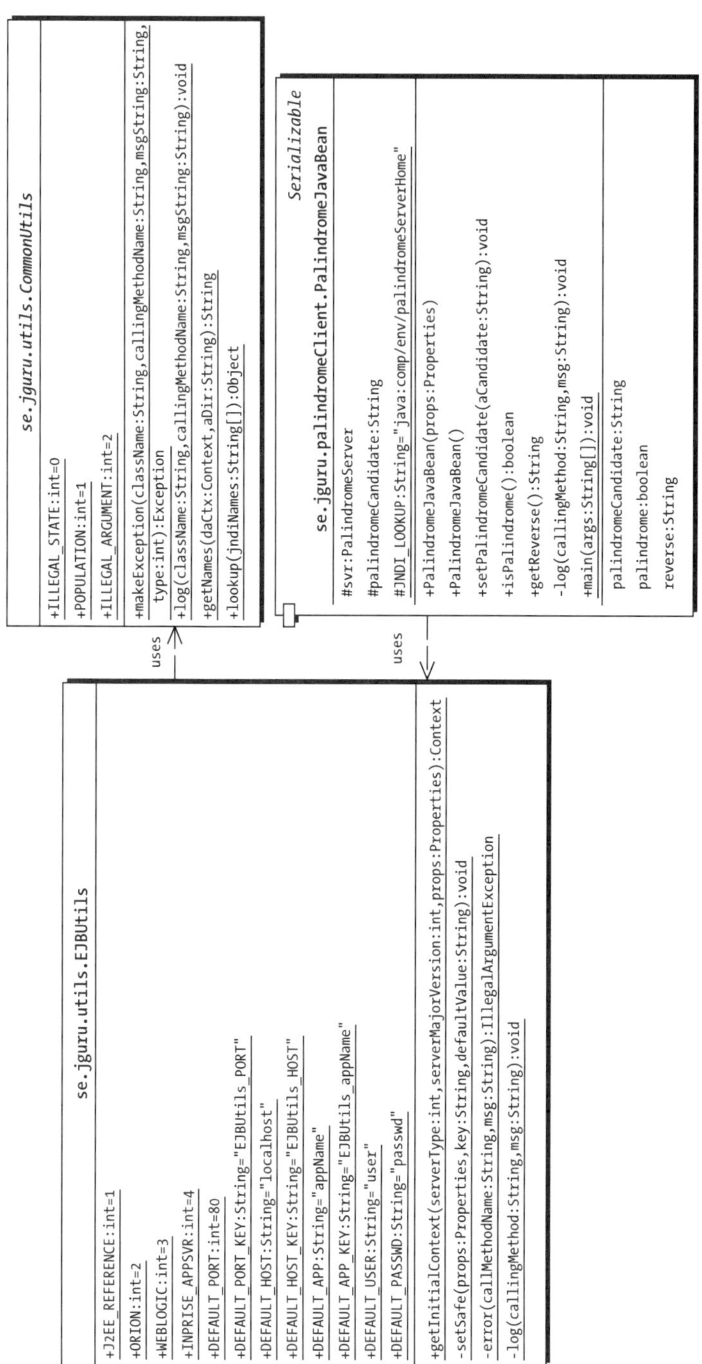

Figure 8-18. The UML diagram of the `PalindromeJavaBean` *shows only two modifications from the former version; an additional constructor and the required main method of an application. However, the standalone version of the* `PalindromeJavaBean` *uses the helper classes* `EJBUtils` *and* `CommonUtils`.

Listing 8-10. The main method of the `PalindromeJavaBean` *class*

```
public static void main(String[] args) throws Exception
    {
        // Compile the connection Properties required for standalone operation.
        // Compile the JNDI connection properties
        Properties props = new Properties();
        props.setProperty(EJBUtils.DEFAULT_HOST_KEY, "localhost");
        props.setProperty(Context.SECURITY_PRINCIPAL, "obiWan");
        props.setProperty(Context.SECURITY_CREDENTIALS, "useTheSource");
        props.setProperty(EJBUtils.DEFAULT_APP_KEY, "PalindromeServerApp");

         // Create the standalone JavaBean instance
        PalindromeJavaBean pjb = new PalindromeJavaBean(props);

        // Run a few palindrome candidate tests
        pjb.setPalindromeCandidate("MonaLisa");
        System.out.println("MonaLisa is palindrome: " + pjb.isPalindrome());
        System.out.println("MonaLisa reversed: " + pjb.getReverse());

        pjb.setPalindromeCandidate("Ab ba");
        System.out.println("Ab ba is palindrome: " + pjb.isPalindrome());
        System.out.println("Ab ba reversed: " + pjb.getReverse());
    }
```

This main method has three distinct parts:

- Connection information is collected into a Properties instance. This information will be used when connecting to the JNDI context of the application server.
- The `PalindromeJavaBean` instance is created, using the connection properties just collected. Behind the scenes, the constructor uses the `EJBUtils` class to establish the connection to the `InitialContext`.
- The main method runs two test examples of palindromes; the first is not a palindrome, but the second is. The whole main method can be seen as a unit test for the `PalindromeJavaBean` class.

The second part that has been altered in the `PalindromeJavaBean` class is the two constructors. Having two of them accomplishes usage transparency; if the `PalindromeJavaBean` is instantiated from a JSP document with a `useBean` JSP action, the parameter-less constructor is called. A standalone client, on the other hand, uses the constructor with a properties parameter.

The three lines of code that have been altered in the main constructor appear in bold text in Listing 8-11.

Listing 8-11. The `PalindromeJavaBean` *constructor*

```
/**
 * Create a default PalindromeJavaBean, which
 * instantiates the PalindromeServer for further calls.
 *
 * @param props The InitialContext connection Properties, which
 *              should be non-null only if running as a standlone
 *              client. Should the props parameter be null, the
 *              parameterless InitialContext constructor is used.
 */
public PalindromeJavaBean(Properties props)
{
    try
    {
        //
        // Get an initial context, and use the correct
        // form of the InitialContext depending on if
        // we are running in standalone mode or not.
        //
        // The parameterless constructor assumes that
        // we are running as part of the application
        // server the JNDI registry of which should be
        // used for the lookup.
        //
        // The constructor accepting a Properties object
        // can be run from a standalone client.
        //
        Context ctx = null;
        this.log("<constructor>", "Getting initial context");
        if(props !=null)
          ctx =EJBUtils.getInitialContext(EJBUtils.ORION,1,props);
        else
        {
            //Log
            this.log("<constructor>", "Running inside application server");

            // Get the InitialContext
            ctx = new InitialContext();
        }
```

```
            // Log the context retrieved.
            this.log("<constructor>", "Got Context of type "
                + ctx.getClass().getName());

            // Lookup our PalindromeServerHome in the JNDI registry
            Object obj = ctx.lookup(JNDI_LOOKUP);
            this.log("<constructor>", "Got PalindromeServerHome of type "
                + obj.getClass().getName());

            // Typecast to a PalindromeServerHome.
            PalindromeServerHome home = (PalindromeServerHome)
                PortableRemoteObject.narrow(obj, PalindromeServerHome.class);

            // Create our PalindromeServer instance
            this.svr = home.create();
        }
        catch (NamingException ex)
        {
            // Whoops - could not find the name
            this.log("<constructor>", "Could not localize the "
                + "PalindromeServer. (" + ex + ")");
        }
        catch (CreateException ex)
        {
            // Internal error in the creation process
           this.log("<constructor>", "Could not create Palindrome server: " + ex);
        }
        catch (RemoteException ex)
        {
            this.log("<constructor>", "Could not reach the server: " + ex);
        }

        // Finally, log the existence of a server (or null if the Lookup
        // and creation process failed).
        this.log("<constructor>", "server := " + svr);
    }

    /**
     * This constructor is used by JSP documents, and should therefore
     * be parameterless.
     */
    public PalindromeJavaBean()
    {
        // Cascade
        this(null);
    }
```

It would appear that the code of the standalone client is nearly identical to that of the Web client. This is almost true, but the static factory method `EJBUtils.getInitialContext` encapsulates some nontrivial complexity. Two issues must be revealed to be able to deploy this Enterprise JavaBean component: the EJBUtils class must be defined, and a basic level of JNDI knowledge must be attained. Let's start with the JNDI.

Basic JNDI-ology from a Programmer's Perspective

At a minimum, four properties are required for a standalone client to connect to the application server and retrieve a reference to its context:

- **User ID**: The application server security manager generally requires that any user performs a valid authorization before returning a reference to its context. The authorization may be done in one of several possible modes, but the most frequent is plain user ID/password. The user ID should be set in the Properties object using the key `Context.SECURITY_PRINCIPAL`.

- **Password**: The sibling of the user ID, a plain-text password is required for proper authorization if plain-text authorization is used. The password should be set in the Properties object using the key `Context.SECURITY_CREDENTIALS`.

- **InitialContext factory class**: Although the `InitialContext` object is created with a call to a constructor, the `InitialContext` class uses a delegate pattern to an actual connection factory implementation object. That connection factory class is instantiated to create an actual connection to the context. The `InitialContext` factory should be set in the Properties object using the key `Context.INITIAL_CONTEXT_FACTORY`.

- **JNDI URL**: The `InitialContext` implementation class requires a specially formed string to connect to a particular application server. This string is known as a JNDI URL, and it functions in the same manner as a JDBC URL used by a JDBC driver. The JNDI URL should be packed in the properties using the key `Context.PROVIDER_URL`.

These properties are packed within a Properties instance that is supplied to the constructor of the `InitialContext` class.

Listing 8-12 displays a short code snippet that creates a standalone `InitialContext` that is ready for use with either the Orion Application Server or the BEA WebLogic Server. Note that the two variables—`runningOrionServer` and `runningWeblogicServer`–are assumed to be boolean and defined elsewhere. Also, the `InitialContext` constructor may throw a `NamingException`, so the actual code performing the lookup must try/catch a `NamingException`.

Listing 8-12. Creating a reference to the `InitialContext` *for a standalone EJB client*

```
// Create the Properties instance required for connection
Properties props = new Properties();

// Set UserID and Password
props.setProperty(Context.SECURITY_PRINCIPAL, "theUserID");
props.setProperty(Context.SECURITY_CREDENTIALS, "thePassword");

// Check which application server we are running
// (the variable is assumed to have been defined
// before this usage).
if(runningOrionServer)
{
   props.setProperty(Context.INITIAL_CONTEXT_FACTORY,
      "com.evermind.server.ApplicationClientInitialContextFactory");

   props.setProperty(Context.PROVIDER_URL,
      "ormi://localhost/ServletBookApp");
}

if(runningWeblogicServer)
{
   props.setProperty(Context.INITIAL_CONTEXT_FACTORY,
       "weblogic.jndi.WLInitialContextFactory");

   props.setProperty(Context.PROVIDER_URL,
      "t3://localhost:80");
}

// Done setting InitialContextFactory properties.
// Create the InitialContext
Context ctx = new InitialContext(props);
```

The `EJBUtils` class encapsulates all the property settings for some J2EE application servers. (See Figure 8-19.) Additionally, this class makes sure that all required properties are set to a value. This way, you may change the application server with minimal impact on the standalone EJB client or JavaBean proxy. With the code of the `EJBUtils` class, the JavaBean proxy is completed.

The code of the `EJBUtils` class is pretty straightforward. (See Listing 8-13.) Note that the `setSafe` method assigns a new value to the provided key only if the value is non-null and non-empty. The workhorse method is the `getInitialContext(int serverType, int serverMajorVersion, Properties props)` method that uses any properties found in the props argument, setting the hard-coded default values provided only if no other value is found for the same key.

```
se.jguru.utils.EJBUtils
+J2EE_REFERENCE:int=1
+ORION:int=2
+WEBLOGIC:int=3
+INPRISE_APPSVR:int=4
+DEFAULT_PORT:int=80
+DEFAULT_PORT_KEY:String="EJBUtils_PORT"
+DEFAULT_HOST:String="localhost"
+DEFAULT_HOST_KEY:String="EJBUtils_HOST"
+DEFAULT_APP:String="appName"
+DEFAULT_APP_KEY:String="EJBUtils_appName"
+DEFAULT_USER:String="user"
+DEFAULT_PASSWD:String="passwd"
+getInitialContext(serverType:int,serverMajorVersion:int,props:Properties):Context
-setSafe(props:Properties,key:String,defaultValue:String):void
-error(callMethodName:String,msg:String):IllegalArgumentException
-log(callingMethod:String,msg:String):void

uses

se.jguru.utils.CommonUtils
+ILLEGAL_STATE:int=0
+POPULATION:int=1
+ILLEGAL_ARGUMENT:int=2
+makeException(className:String,callingMethodName:String,
  msgString:String,type:int):Exception
+log(className:String,callingMethodName:String,
  msgString:String):void
+getNames(daCtx:Context,aDir:String):String
+lookup(jndiNames:String[]):Object
```

Figure 8-19. Class structure of the `EJBUtils` *class, and its associated* `CommonUtils` *instance. The* `getInitialContext()` *method returns a context properly set up for a particular server type, passed as an* `int` *argument to the* `getInitialContext`.

Listing 8-13. The `EJBUtils` *class*

```
package se.jguru.utils;

import javax.naming.*;
import java.util.*;
import java.text.SimpleDateFormat;

/**
 * EJB utility class useable by all EJB instances in the
 * system. The purpose of this is to hide the complexities
 * of JNDI property settings (InitialContext factory class,
 * etc. for standalone EJB clients,
 * as well as hide any dissimilarities WRT
 *
 * @author Lennart Jörelid, jGuru
 */
public class EJBUtils
{
    // Defined (known) application server types
    public final static int J2EE_REFERENCE = 1;
    public final static int ORION = 2;
    public final static int WEBLOGIC = 3;
    public final static int INPRISE_APPSVR = 4;

    // Default keys and values of frequently used building blocks
    // for constructing the PROVIDER_URL.
    public static final int DEFAULT_PORT = 80;
    public static final String DEFAULT_PORT_KEY = "EJBUtils_PORT";

    public static final String DEFAULT_HOST = "localhost";
    public static final String DEFAULT_HOST_KEY = "EJBUtils_HOST";

    public static final String DEFAULT_APP = "appName";
    public static final String DEFAULT_APP_KEY = "EJBUtils_appName";

    public static final String DEFAULT_USER = "user";
    public static final String DEFAULT_PASSWD = "passwd";
```

```
/**
 * Retrieves the initial context for a particular
 * Application server as indicated.
 *
 * @param serverType Constant indicating which server is used;
 *          determines default property values in the props argument (unless
 *          provided by the client).
 * @param props Populated with properties to indicate the application
 *          server node name and port number. If <code>null</code> is provided,
 *          the call is assumed to come from within the running application
 *          server, as opposed to from a standalone client.
 *
 * @exception java.lang.IllegalArgumentException Thrown if the server
 *            type/majorVersion combination is not supported, or the
 *            properties for connecting were malformed.
 * @exception javax.naming.NamingException Thrown if a Naming
 *            exception was encountered.
 */
public static Context getInitialContext(int serverType, int serverMajorVersion,
Properties props)
throws IllegalArgumentException, NamingException
{
    // Running within an application server?
    if (props == null) return new InitialContext();

    // Declare the Context to return
    Context initContext = null;

    // Add the default SECURITY_PRINCIPAL and SECURITY_CREDENTIALS
    // if they are not already provided in the Properties
    setSafe(props, Context.SECURITY_PRINCIPAL, DEFAULT_USER);
    setSafe(props, Context.SECURITY_CREDENTIALS, DEFAULT_PASSWD);

    // Add the default PORT, HOST and APP_NAME
    setSafe(props, DEFAULT_HOST_KEY, DEFAULT_HOST);
    setSafe(props, DEFAULT_PORT_KEY, "" + DEFAULT_PORT);
    setSafe(props, DEFAULT_APP_KEY, DEFAULT_APP);

    switch (serverType)
    {
```

```
case ORION:
    {
        // The Orion application server creates its provider
        // URL originating from two properties:
        //
        // 1) hostname
        // 2) application name
        String jndiUrl = "ormi://"
        + props.getProperty(DEFAULT_HOST_KEY)
        + "/" + props.getProperty(DEFAULT_APP_KEY);

        // We are potentially running as a standalone client
        // Populate props.
        setSafe(props, Context.INITIAL_CONTEXT_FACTORY,
        "com.evermind.server.ApplicationClientInitialContextFactory");
        setSafe(props, Context.PROVIDER_URL, jndiUrl);

        // Done.
        break;
    }

case WEBLOGIC:
    {
        // The weblogic application server creates its
        // provider URL originating from two properties:
        // hostname and port.
        String providerUrl = "t3://" + props.getProperty(DEFAULT_HOST_KEY)
        + ":" + props.getProperty(DEFAULT_PORT_KEY);

        // Populate props.
        setSafe(props, Context.INITIAL_CONTEXT_FACTORY,
        "weblogic.jndi.WLInitialContextFactory");
        setSafe(props, Context.PROVIDER_URL, providerUrl);

        // Done.
        break;
    }
```

```
        case INPRISE_APPSVR:
            {
                // Populate props.
                setSafe(props, javax.naming.Context.INITIAL_CONTEXT_FACTORY,
                "com.inprise.j2ee.jndi.CtxFactory");
                setSafe(props, javax.naming.Context.URL_PKG_PREFIXES,
                "com.inprise.j2ee");

                // Done.
                break;
            }


        default:
            // Server configuration not supported.
            // Complain.
            throw new java.lang.UnsupportedOperationException("Could "
            + "not support server type : " + serverType
            + "at this time.");
    }

    // Log the contents of Props
    log("getInitialContext",
        "Creating initialContext using settings: " + props);

    // Create and return the InitialContext
    return new InitialContext(props);
}



/**
 * Convenience method to make sure a certain key within a Properties instance
 * has a value - either its existing value or the defaultValue provided.
 *
 * @param props The Properties which to populate
 * @param key   The key that should be verified
 * @param defaultValue The value assigned to the property key, unless
 *              an existing value can be found.
 */
```

```
    private static void setSafe(Properties props, String key, String defaultValue)
    throws IllegalArgumentException
    {
        // Check sanity
        if (key == null || key.equals(""))
            throw error("setSafe", "Cannot handle null key.");

        if (defaultValue == null || defaultValue.equals(""))
            throw error("setSafe", "Cannot handle null defaultValue.");

        if (props == null)
            throw error("setSafe", "Cannot handle null Properties.");

        // Sane. Proceed.
        props.setProperty(key, props.getProperty(key, defaultValue));
    }

    /** Local wrapper of the CommonUtils.makeException method */
    private static IllegalArgumentException error(String callMethodName,
              String msg)
    {
        return (IllegalArgumentException) CommonUtils.makeException("EJBUtils",
            callMethodName, msg, CommonUtils.ILLEGAL_ARGUMENT);
    }

    /** Logs a timestamped message to the standard out stream */
    private static void log(String callingMethod, String msg)
    {
        // Delegate to the CommonUtils log method
        CommonUtils.log("EJBUtils", callingMethod, msg);
    }
}
```

Having taken a not-so-brief walk through the full creation, design, and deployment of an EJB component within an application server, we must investigate in greater detail these specific conditions for EJB components:

- Developing session EJBs
- Developing Entity EJBs

Developing Session EJBs

The development process described in sections "Step 1—Define the Remote Interface" to "Step 7—Create a JavaBean Proxy" applies well to Session EJB components. Session EJB components are generally used as facades that encapsulate business logic. Session EJB components are frequently stateless, relaying their calls to stateful Entity EJB components that contain all business logic extracted from the legacy system.

Figure 8-20 shows a common structure for all EJB components deployed within the EJB container of the J2EE application server. Session EJB components act as coordinator facades that accept either remote calls from application clients through their Home/Remote interface or local calls from components deployed in the same J2EE application server (frequently servlets or JavaBean proxies).

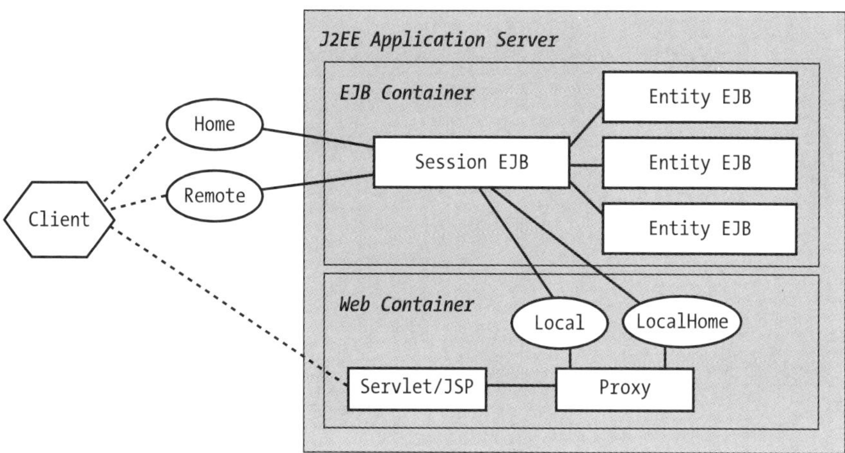

Figure 8-20. A client may communicate with the Session EJB components using remote calls (EJB application client) or local calls (Web client).

If modifying (as opposed to only reading) legacy data is required, Entity EJB components must be used for the legacy communication. The role played by session EJB components involves coordination of all the legacy data read from Entity EJB components. It is not uncommon for business methods of session EJBs to look like that shown in Listing 8-14.

Listing 8-14. The `getAccountInfo()` *business method*

```
public AccountInformation getAccountInfo(Customer aBankCustomer)
throws NoSuchCustomerException
{
   // Define the return value
   AccountInformation toReturn = new AccountInformation();

   // Get the accounts held by the customer. This method may
   // throw NoSuchCustomerException if the given customer was not found.
   List allAccounts = accountEntity.getAccounts(aBankCustomer);

   // Get the recent transaction information for all Accounts
   TransactionInfo[] ti = new TransactionInfo[allAccounts.size()];
   for(int i = 0; i < ti.length; i++)
   {
      // Get the current account
      Account current = (Account) allAccounts.get(i);
      ti[i] = transactionEntity.getRecentTransaction(aBankCustomer, current);
   }

   // Populate the AccountInformation value object
   toReturn.setTransactionInfo(ti);
   toReturn.setAccounts(allAccounts);

   // Done.
   return toReturn;
}
```

> **NOTE** *Remember that all objects that should be returned from an EJB business method must implement the Serializable interface to be sent over the network to the client. This is not required for return values of Local interfaces. Therefore, you should use Local/LocalHome whenever possible, and Remote/Home only when strictly necessary.*

Developing Entity EJBs

The development process described earlier in this chapter under "The EJB Development Process" uses a Session EJB component as an example, and is therefore a little thin regarding description of the issues that are specific to Entity

EJB components. Therefore, I'll highlight these issues by providing a small but complete EJB development process for an Entity EJB component.

For starters, EJB components are thought to communicate with a data source (persistent storage for the bean state), so they are used as an object encapsulation of legacy data as shown in Figure 8-21—not as containers of vast amounts of business logic, as is customary for session EJB components.

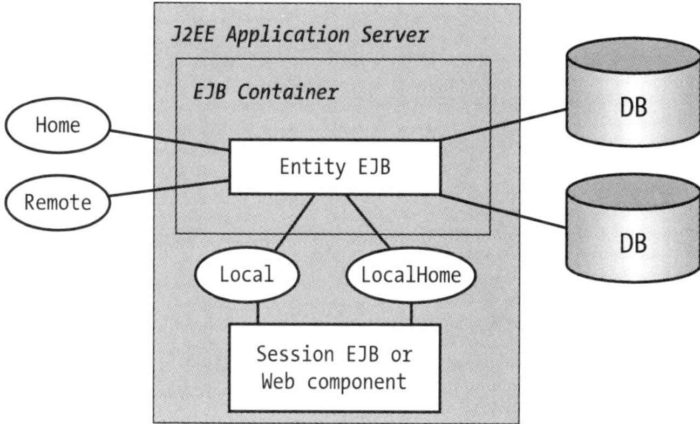

Figure 8-21. The Entity EJB component encapsulates legacy data from one or more data sources, represented by relational databases in this image.

Entity EJB components correspond to a logical view of a data source. (A *logical view* is any kind of result that may be obtained from a SELECT statement in a database (or a database look-alike, such as a transaction gateway.) In simpler cases, the logical view corresponds to a single table in a relational database schema.

Primary Keys

Whether simpler or more complex logical views are encapsulated by the Entity EJB component, a primary key is needed in addition to the business interfaces and the implementation class. The primary key is used to uniquely find the state of the Entity EJB object within its persistent storage, similar to the primary key column of the table in a database. In short, the primary key must contain a unique value that may be used to locate the state of the Entity EJB component in the data source.

Types of Entity EJBs

There are two major types of Entity EJBs: the Entity EJB components managing their internal state synchronization with the data source in the code of the Bean implementation class (referred to as *bean-managed persistence*, or *BMP*), and Entity EJB components delegating their persistence management to the EJB container (which is known as *container-managed persistence*, or *CMP*). The internal state of an Entity EJB component is kept synchronized with the data source by storing the values of given internal member variables to the data source whenever the members are altered. Consequently, the values of the internal EJB state are overwritten with data from the data source if it is altered. See Figure 8-22.

Bean-Managed Persistence (BMP)

Entity EJB components using bean-managed persistence simply contain JDBC statements to read and write data to the contained data source in the appropriate life-cycle methods of the Entity EJB. All Bean implementation classes of an Entity EJB component must implement the `javax.ejb.EntityBean` interface, which defines the life-cycle methods of an Entity EJB component. For instance, the `ejbStore()` method is invoked by the EJB container when it has been notified that the state of the EJB component should be saved to persistent storage. For detailed information about the EJB life cycle, refer to "The Life Cycle of Entity EJB Components" later in this chapter.

Container-Managed Persistence (CMP)

Entity EJBs using container-managed persistence have a very different way of communicating with their data source, as all such calls are delegated to the EJB container. We will study a small example of an Entity bean using CMP to illustrate the development process for Entity EJB components. Our `DemoEntity` component is a trivial Entity EJB that contains a first name and a last name, in addition to an integer primary key field. This example involves the following six steps:

- Defining the remote interface
- Defining the `create` methods of the Home interface
- Declaring the `finder` methods of the Home interface
- Implementing the bean class

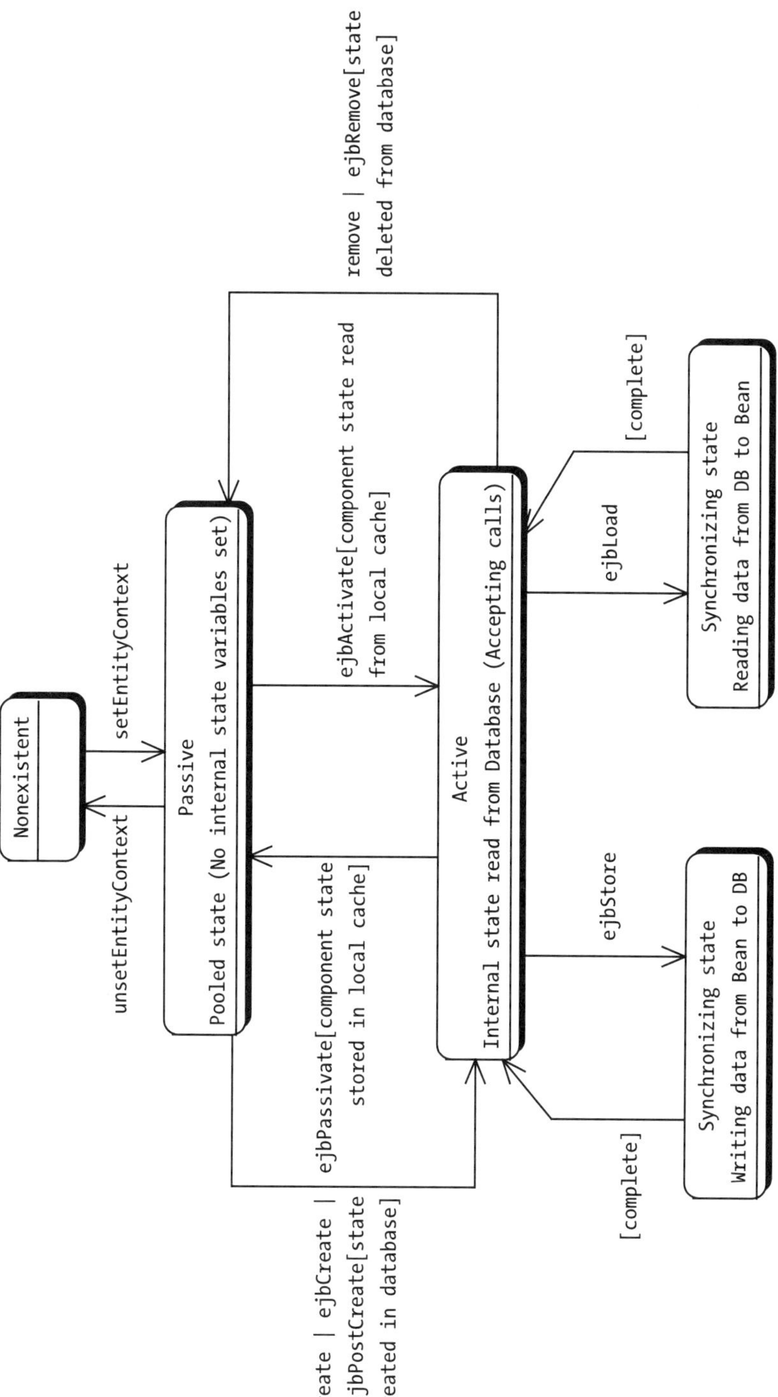

Figure 8-22. Entity EJB state transition diagram

- Creating the deployment descriptor
- Compiling the EJB classes

Step 1—Define the Remote Interface

This step is trivial in our case, as we must manage each JavaBean property through its two public accessor methods. Therefore, the API of the `DemoEntity` remote interface contains six methods, as shown in Figure 8-23.

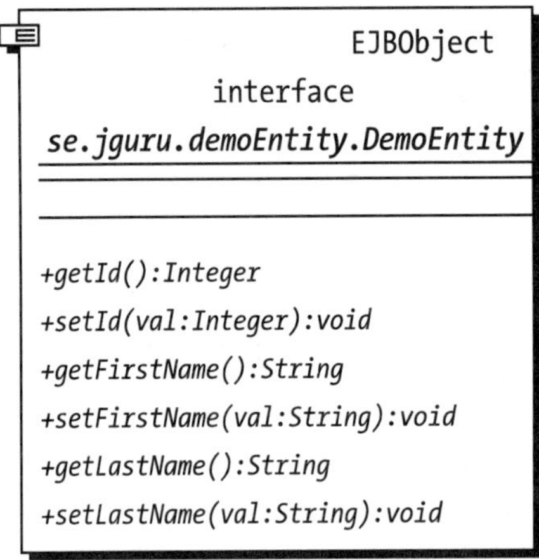

Figure 8-23. The Remote interface of the `DemoEntity` *Entity EJB component*

The code of the remote interface of the `DemoEntity` EJB component (shown in Listing 8-15) is trivial, containing only the definitions of standard JavaBean setters and getters. The Id JavaBean property is the primary key property of the entity bean; the others are properties read from or written to the database.

Listing 8-15. Remote interface of the `DemoEntity` *EJB component*

```
package se.jguru.demoEntity;

import javax.ejb.EJBObject;
import javax.ejb.EJBException;
import java.rmi.RemoteException;

public interface DemoEntity extends EJBObject
{
```

```
    public Integer getId() throws RemoteException;
    public void setId(Integer val) throws RemoteException; // Primary key

    public String getFirstName() throws RemoteException;
    public void setFirstName(String val) throws RemoteException;

    public String getLastName() throws RemoteException;
    public void setLastName(String val) throws RemoteException;
}
```

As the remote interface of the Entity EJB component is trivial, it has been left completely without commenting. Indeed, the Home interface contains much more depth and implications than its Remote counterpart.

Step 2—Define the Create Methods of the Home Interface

Naming the Home interface of the `DemoEntity` EJB component `DemoEntityHome`, we may supply as many `create` methods as we see fit. However, because all `create` methods can be regarded as a constructor, they must all populate the internal state of the legacy data source as well as the entity instance itself. Therefore, it is logical to define `create` methods that set all properties in the entity bean component—so the number and types of parameters to the `create` methods are trivial to extract.

In this case, we will define a single `create` method that accepts two arguments that correspond to the `firstName` and `lastName` properties of the EJB component. Thus, we may define a skeleton `DemoEntityHome` class with the single `create` method, like this:

```
public DemoEntity create(String firstName, String lastName)
throws CreateException, RemoteException;
```

Of course, if you have default values that could be assigned to the properties of the Entity EJB at creation time, you could have defined additional `create` methods. Remember, however, that the `create` methods defined in the Home (or LocalHome) interface should be regarded as constructors; they must fully populate the state of the entity instance and its logical view in the data source.

> **NOTE** *All* `create` *methods declared in the Home interface may throw a* `CreateException` *if anything goes wrong during the execution of the* `create` *method. In addition, all* `create` *methods defined in the Home interface may throw* `RemoteExceptions` *due to their networked nature. This is not true for LocalHome implementations, which must only throw* `CreateException`.

Step 3—Declare the Finder Methods of the Home Interface

A `finder` method of an Entity EJB component retrieves one or more entities from the data source, given the provided search criteria. `Finder` methods behave like SELECT statements in relational databases: they select data from a set of tables and form a logical view from the retrieved data. The logical view of any SELECT statement generated is then used to populate the internal state of the Entity EJB component.

All Entity EJB components are required to support a `finder` method called `findByPrimaryKey`, which finds a unique entity component from its primary key. Note that the return type of the `findByPrimaryKey` method is an instance of type `DemoEntity`. You may, of course, define as many `finder` methods as you like in the Home interface; each `finder` method will be specified in the deployment descriptor of the entity bean (for CMP Entity EJBs) or the Bean implementation class (for BMP Entity EJBs).

It is customary for all `finder` methods to have a name of the form `findByXXXX`, where XXXX is the criteria used to pinpoint the Remote instance(s) that should be returned by the finder. Should a `finder` method be able to return multiple instances, the return type of the finder should be a `java.util.Collection` rather than a single instance of the Remote instance of the Entity EJB component. If you encounter a finder method returning a `java.util.Enumeration` instead of a collection, the EJB adheres to the 1.0 EJB specification. Simply update the type returned to collection and carry on. The full Home interface of the `DemoEntity` EJB component is shown in Figure 8-24.

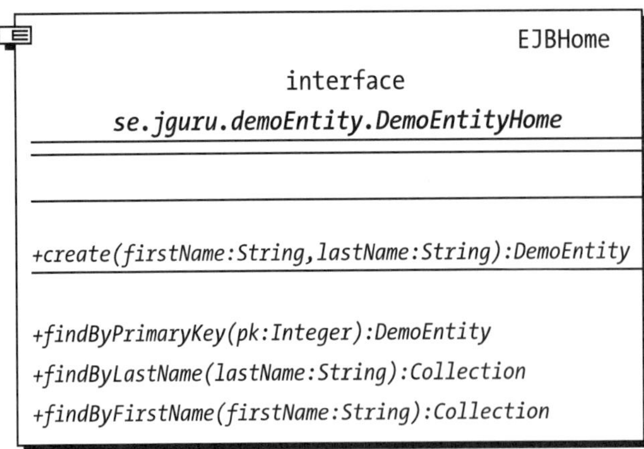

Figure 8-24. The Home interface of the `DemoEntity` *EJB component*

As indicated in Figure 8-24, the `findByLastName` and `findByFirstName` methods may return multiple instances of the `DemoEntity` interface, reflecting that many `DemoEntity` objects may have a particular first or last name.

Having defined the `DemoEntityHome` interface, we should move on to the next step—defining the `DemoEntityBean` implementation class.

Step 4—Implement the Bean Class

Voilà! The time for the real implementation of the Entity EJB component has come. Be aware that the Bean implementation class of Entity EJB components is not the only file wherein code is created—especially for CMP Entity EJBs, such as the `DemoEntity` EJB component used as an example in this section. CMP beans delegate much of their code generation and creation to the EJB container, so we must provide instructions to the EJB container about how the code should be created. The standard deployment descriptor of EJB components, `ejb-jar.xml`, contains these instructions.

We shall examine the standard J2EE descriptor of the `DemoEntity` EJB component in the next section, "Step 5—Create the Deployment Descriptors." For now, let's study the code of the `DemoEntityBean` implementation class, whose UML diagram is shown in Figure 8-25.

For CMP Entity EJBs, the `finder` methods are completely defined by the EJB compiler tool in the application server. Finders are not defined in the Bean implementation class at all for CMP Entity beans, but, for BMP Entity EJBs, the `finder` methods are simply defined as another method in the class. For CMP Entity EJBs, the deployment descriptor provides enough information that the EJB compiler should be able to define the complete code for all `finder` methods in the EJB component.

But enough talk. The code of the Bean implementation class in the `DemoEntityBean` component is shown in Listing 8-16.

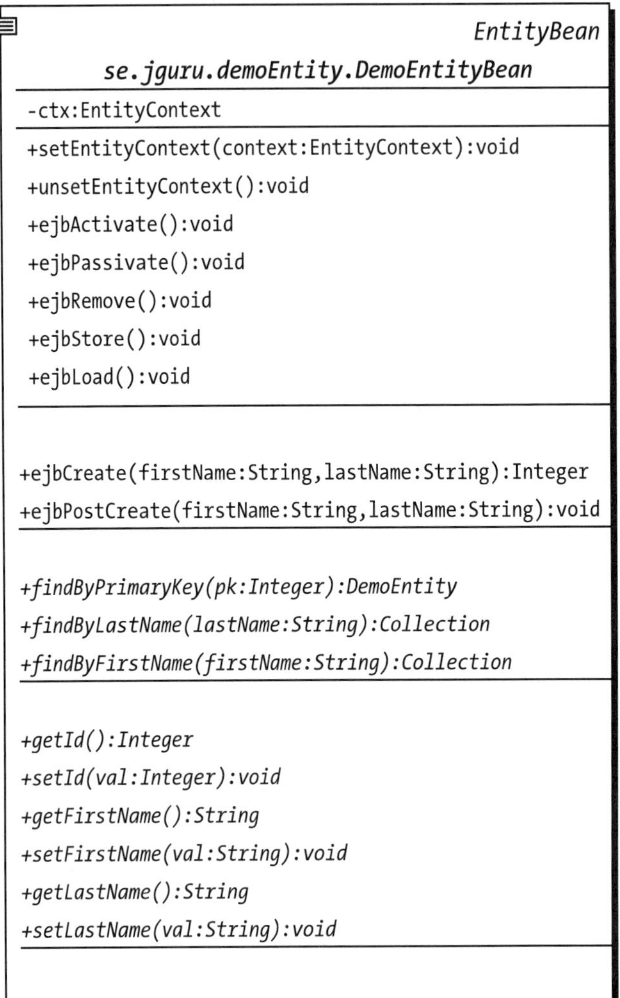

Figure 8-25. The UML diagram of the `DemoEntityBean` *implementation class is partitioned into sections to group the members into categories. The non-empty sections, from the bottom up, are remote business methods, finders,* `create` *methods, other method members, and internal state variables. Note that a CMP entity bean has very few internal state members.*

Listing 8-16. Bean implementation class in the `DemoEntityBean` *component*

```
package se.jguru.demoEntity;

import javax.ejb.*;
import java.rmi.*;

public abstract class DemoEntityBean implements EntityBean
{
    //
    // Abstract CMP method stubs (DataSource setter and getter
    // methods). The application server deployment tools provide
    // the implementation classes for these methods.
    //
    public abstract Integer getId();
    public abstract void setId(Integer val); // Primary key

    public abstract String getFirstName();
    public abstract void setFirstName(String val);

    public abstract String getLastName();
    public abstract void setLastName(String val);

    //
    // End Abstract CMP methods.
    //

    //
    // EntityContext pattern
    //

    private EntityContext ctx;

    public void setEntityContext(EntityContext context) { ctx = context; }
    public void unsetEntityContext() { ctx = null; }

    //
    // End EntityContext pattern
    //

    //
    // Lifecycle methods
    //
```

```
public void ejbActivate()
{
}

public void ejbPassivate()
{
}

public void ejbRemove()
{
}

public void ejbStore()
{
}

public void ejbLoad()
{
}

//
// Create methods defined in the Home interface (part of the
// lifecycle methods, but defined in the DemoEntityHome interface).
//

public Integer ejbCreate(String firstName, String lastName)
    throws CreateException
{
    // Assign the internal state of this object.
    this.setFirstName(firstName);
    this.setLastName(lastName);

    // Since this is a CMP bean, the ejbCreate methods
    // must return null - only BMP beans should return
    // their primary keys from the ejbCreate methods.
    return null;
}
```

```
    public void ejbPostCreate(String firstName, String lastName)
        throws CreateException
    {
        // The ejbPostCreate method is invoked immediately after the
        // ejbCreate method. Thus, this is the place to find dependents
        // in the DataSource - originating from the newly read properties
        // in this instance.
    }
}
```

The methods of the `DemoEntityBean` class fall into one out of four categories:

- **`EntityContext` pattern** members include the `setEntityContext` and `unsetEntityContext` methods as well as the `ctx` member. The `EntityContext` provides a reference to a well-defined part of the EJB container whose methods may be called from within the Bean implementation class. Your entity beans rarely require anything other than the implementation provided in the above code, so simply copy it into your CMP or BMP entity beans.

- **Abstract business methods** are frequently trivial setters and getters (which must be declared abstract in the case of a CMP entity bean) when defining Entity EJB components. Normally, these business methods may be used to access the persistent, internal state of the EJB component. The EJB container provides the implementations of these methods for CMP entity Beans when running the proprietary EJB compiler tools for the specific application server.

- **Life-cycle methods** are defined in the `javax.ejb.EntityBean` interface that must be implemented by all EJB bean classes. These methods are invoked by the EJB container when the Entity EJB undergoes a state change.

- **`Create` and `finder` methods** are part of the life-cycle methods. However, they define the ways in which an EJB client can obtain a reference to a Remote instance of the EJB component (that is, a `DemoEntity` instance)—either by creating a new persistent state or by retrieving and objectifying an existing persistent state from the data source.

Although the Bean implementation class represents a significant part of the code generation in an EJB component, the settings provided in the deployment descriptor are equally significant for the stub and skeleton code generation of an Entity EJB component. In principle, the more tasks that you delegate to the EJB container, the greater the task to configure its deployment descriptor, `ejb-jar.xml`.

This is the malicious syndrome of Entity EJB components: the Java code generated is only a small part of the entire source required to deploy an Entity

EJB component. XML code cannot be compiled and understood in the same simple way as Java code, but it does play an integral role for each EJB component.

Step 5—Create the Deployment Descriptor

An Entity EJB component normally has at least two deployment descriptors. The standard `ejb-jar.xml` descriptor provides most configuration settings, but because the J2EE standard does not encompass everything that is required to deploy an EJB component, custom deployment descriptors are frequently required for the full deployment of an Entity EJB component.

The deployment descriptor of BMP and CMP Entity EJBs are quite different; the most complex of the two is the CMP entity descriptor. Thankfully (at least for the general understanding of EJB components and EJB technology), we have taken a CMP Entity EJB as this example, so the deployment descriptor of that component definitely won't be simpler than a deployment descriptor of a BMP entity component.

Thus, we will provide a nontrivial deployment descriptor for the example Entity EJB component. The standard deployment descriptor, `ejb-jar.xml`, for the `DemoEntity` EJB is quite simple, as shown in Listing 8-17.

Listing 8-17. The `ejb-jar.xml` *standard deployment descriptor*

```
<?xml version="1.0"?>

<!DOCTYPE ejb-jar PUBLIC
   '-//Sun Microsystems, Inc.//DTD Enterprise JavaBeans 2.0//EN'
   'http://java.sun.com/dtd/ejb-jar_2_0.dtd'>

<ejb-jar>
   <enterprise-beans>
      <entity>
         <ejb-name>DemoEntityBean</ejb-name>
         <home>se.jguru.demoEntity.DemoEntityHome</home>
         <remote>se.jguru.demoEntity.DemoEntity</remote>
         <ejb-class>se.jguru.demoEntity.DemoEntity</ejb-class>
         <persistence-type>Container</persistence-type>
         <prim-key-class>java.lang.Integer</prim-key-class>
         <reentrant>False</reentrant>
         <cmp-version>2.x</cmp-version>
         <abstract-schema-name>DemoEntityBean</abstract-schema-name>
```

```
        <cmp-field>
          <field-name>firstName</field-name>
        </cmp-field>
        <cmp-field>
          <field-name>lastName</field-name>
        </cmp-field>
        <cmp-field>
          <field-name>id</field-name>
        </cmp-field>
        <primkey-field>id</primkey-field>

        <query>
          <query-method>
            <method-name>findByFirstName</method-name>
            <method-params>
              <method-param>java.lang.String</method-param>
            </method-params>
          </query-method>
          <ejb-ql>
            SELECT OBJECT(i) FROM DemoEntityTable i
            WHERE i.firstName like '?1%'
          </ejb-ql>
        </query>
        <query>
          <query-method>
            <method-name>findByLastName</method-name>
            <method-params>
              <method-param>java.lang.String</method-param>
            </method-params>
          </query-method>
          <ejb-ql>
            SELECT OBJECT(i) FROM DemoEntityTable i
            WHERE i.lastName like '?1%'
          </ejb-ql>
        </query>
    ...
</ejb-jar>
```

The deployment descriptor provided in Listing 8-17 shows the standard J2EE deployment descriptor for the `DemoEntity` EJB component. The deployment descriptor consists of the Enterprise beans metadata section containing one or more bean deployment descriptors. (This case includes a single entity bean descriptor for the `DemoEntity` session bean.) After the Entity EJB has been given a description and a display name of its own, the following important properties are defined:

- `<ejb-name>` has the same function as a primary key in a database: it uniquely identifies an EJB component within the `ejb-jar.xml` descriptor. This value can be chosen arbitrarily, although it is recommended that you select a name that illustrates which type or function the EJB behind it plays. In this case, the qualified type name of the remote interface has been chosen.

- `<home>` contains the fully qualified type name of the Entity bean's Home interface. This interface must extend `javax.ejb.EJBHome` directly or indirectly.

- `<remote>` contains the fully qualified type name of the Entity bean's Remote interface. This interface must extend `javax.ejb.EJBObject` directly or indirectly.

- `<ejb-class>` contains the fully qualified type name of the Entity bean's implementation class. As we are deploying an Entity EJB, this class must implement `javax.ejb.EntityBean` directly or indirectly.

- `<persistence-type>` defines whether the Entity EJB uses BMP or CMP persistence management.

- `<prim-key-class>` contains the fully qualified type name of the Entity bean's primary key class.

- `<cmp-version>` has the value 1.x if the Entity EJB uses the persistence mechanisms defined in the 1.0 or 1.1 EJB specifications. It contains the value 2.x if the Entity EJB uses the persistence mechanisms from the EJB 2.0 specification.

- `<abstract-schema-name>` contains the name of the logical view used to populate this Entity EJB component. Normally, the abstract schema name is not present in the data source with which this EJB component communicates. Instead, the abstract schema name is mapped to a set of physical tables in the data source from which the state of this EJB component is read. This mapping is frequently done in custom application server descriptors.

- `<cmp-field>` contains the name of a field whose data should be written to persistent state by the EJB container.

- `<primkey-field>` contains the name of one of the `<cmp-field>` definitions that contains the primary key of the Entity EJB component being defined.

- `<query>` contains an EJB-QL query that is used to get the state of the Entity EJB component from its data source. The EJB-QL language is quite similar to the SQL language used by most databases to read and modify data. The QJB-QL language is defined in the EJB 2.0 specification, and it provides a database-independent language for selecting data from the database and inserting it into the fields of an Entity EJB component. Refer to the EJB specification for a thorough walkthrough of the EJB-QL language.

Although the EJB deployment descriptor may seem rather complex, it is nicely described in the EJB 2.0 specification, which may be downloaded from the JavaSoft Web site (`http://www.javasoft.com`). Feel free to examine its structure and details, but don't forget to consult the documentation of your J2EE application server to find the required custom deployment descriptors that are required to convert the JNDI names and logical schema names to values having real-world significance.

Step 6—Compile the EJB Classes

Packaging the EJB classes (shown in Figure 8-26) and deployment descriptors created in steps 1 through 5 is identical to the step shown in "Step 6—Compile and Package Classes and Deployment Descriptors" earlier in this chapter.

> **NOTE** *I will refrain from creating another trivial EJB JavaBean proxy. For examples of how to create Entity EJB components and clients, refer to Chapter 9.*

An item of particular interest is the strict life cycle enforced by the application server that each EJB instance must adhere to. Time flies, so let's study the EJB life cycle.

The EJB Life Cycle

EJB components are given a specific context when they are deployed in an application server. This context is referred to as the *EJB container*, and one of its tasks is maintaining a strict life cycle in all its EJBs. The container maintains the life cycle by calling a set of methods in the EJB, making it cycle through a set of specific states.

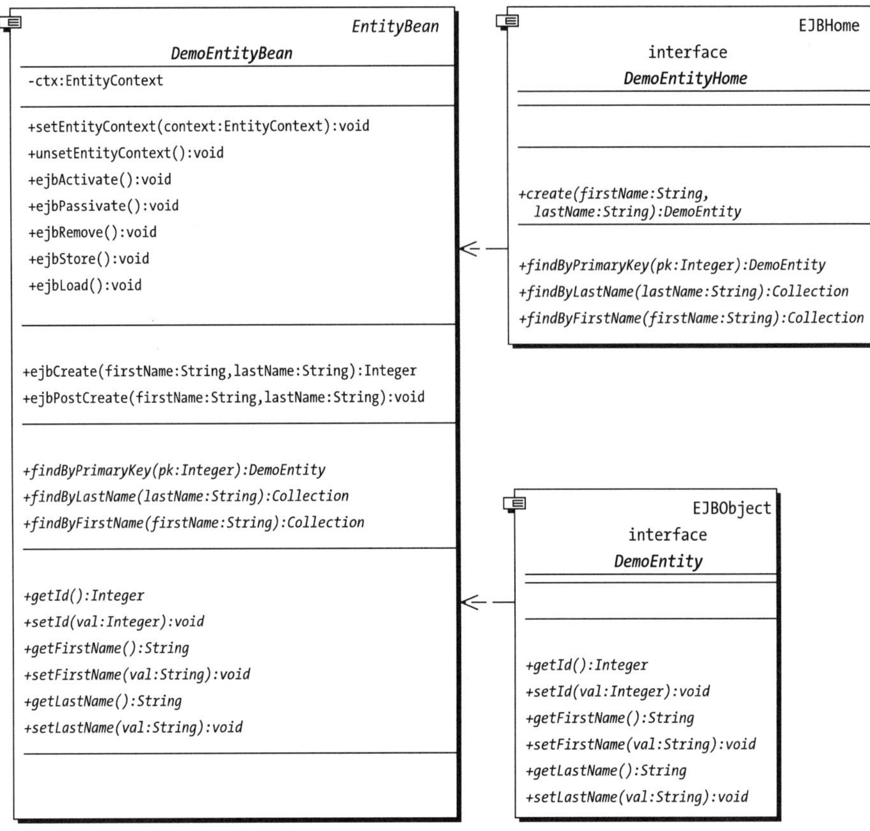

Figure 8-26. The structure of the `DemoEntity` *EJB component types*

The Life Cycle of Session EJBs

Depending on the type of bean, some states may be unreachable or irrelevant to the EJB component. For instance, there are two types of Session EJB component: *stateful* session EJBs that maintain a specific state that associates the EJB component with a session (in its turn associated with a particular user), and *stateless* session EJBs that do not maintain conversational state with a particular user. The state cycle pertaining to session EJBs is illustrated in Figure 8-27.

Before the EJB container has run the `newInstance()` method on the EJB component, it is considered nonexistent. When a business call from an EJB client hits the EJB container, it creates instances of the skeleton and implementation classes, and sets the EJB component in active state. The three methods called by the EJB container to activate a Session EJB are: `create()`, which is called in the Home interface and forces the EJB container to call `newInstance()` if the Bean implementation instance is null, `setSessionContext(SessionContext ctx)` is then called in the Bean implementation class, followed by a call to `ejbCreate()`.

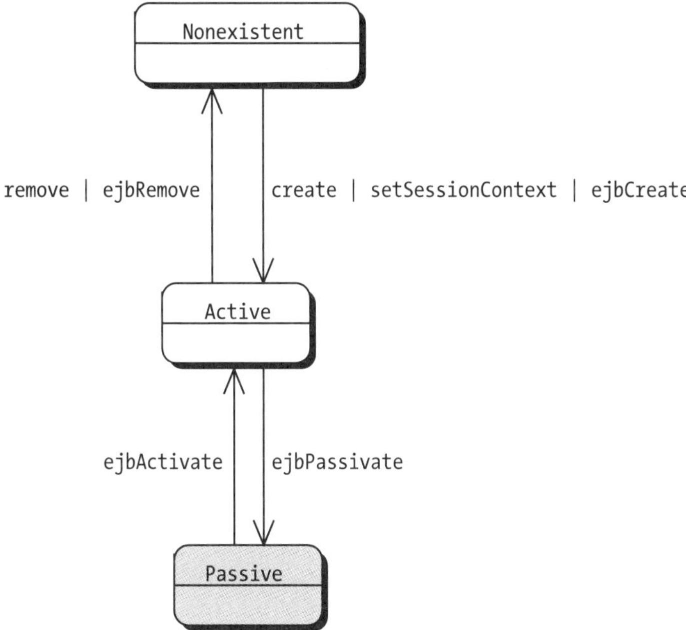

Figure 8-27. The states of a session bean

The passive state is available only to stateful session beans, whereas all session beans may be nonexistent or active. The methods illustrated beside the state transition arrows in Figure 8-27 are called when the EJB component is sent into the receiving state.

The life-cycle methods of a Session EJB are all defined in two places: the Home interface of the EJB component contains its create method declarations, and the Session EJB Remote interface that is implemented by the Bean implementation class contains its other life-cycle methods. For Session EJBs, the Home interface contains only `create` methods. (Refer to "Step 2—Define the `Create` Methods of the Home Interface" earlier in this chapter.

Investigate the `SessionBean` interface in Figure 8-28.

The life-cycle methods can be perceived as event handler methods, because they are invoked when the EJB component receives a state transition event from its container. It is normally quite wise to nullify any internal state variables in a `SessionBean` object in the `ejbPassivate` method.

The `ejbRemove` method is called just before the session EJB component is deleted from memory. It may therefore be used as a destructor or a `finalize()` method: closing any open database or other connections and erasing any lock instances or other dependents. In short, clean out any unwanted or garbage-like state in the `ejbRemove` method.

```
                              javax.ejb.EnterpriseBean
                         interface
                  javax.ejb.SessionBean
-------------------------------------------------------
+ejbActivate():void
+ejbPassivate():void
+ejbRemove():void
+setSessionContext(:javax.ejb.SessionContext):void
```

Figure 8-28. UML diagram of the `SessionBean` *interface, containing life-cycle method definitions for* `SessionBean` *implementation classes. Calling a particular method makes the EJB Bean implementation class change state according to the arrows shown in Figure 8-27.*

The `ejbPassivate` method is invoked before sending the EJB component to passive state (normally by writing its state to a temporary database). Its sibling, `ejbActivate`, is called directly after bringing the session EJB component back from the passive state. Only invoked by the EJB container for stateful session EJB components, you may frequently define the `ejbPassivate` and `ejbActivate` methods with empty method bodies—unless, of course, you need to perform some operations in connection with passivating or activating the component.

The life cycles of Entity EJB components are quite similar to that of session EJB components, although the states are somewhat more complex due to the task of communicating with a data source and synchronizing the internal state from the data source. Let us proceed to study the life cycle of Entity beans.

The Life Cycle of Entity EJB Components

Quite frequently, session EJBs may connect to a data source and execute queries or insert particular data into the database. Properly handling data source connections (including transaction isolation and updating internal state variables) requires a more complex state machine for the EJB component. Evidence of this fact is shown in the Entity EJB life cycle, as shown in Figure 8-29.

The Entity EJB life cycle is, thankfully, identical to both types of Entity EJB components, but the implementation class and deployment descriptors differ quite drastically between Entity beans using bean-managed persistence (BMP) and those using container-managed persistence (CMP). Entity bean components using BMP handle all communication to data sources and synchronization itself, whereas EJBs using CMP delegate all code generation for database synchronization to the EJB container. Although CMP may sound like a relief to the developer, the deployment descriptor hacking and rehacking time tends to equalize the time consumption and practicality. In plain English: although CMP may look deceptively simple to implement in Java code, you may find that the time spent hacking deployment descriptors and struggling with the application server deployment tools is far greater than simply using BMP.

On a more practical note, EJBs using CMP can mainly be applied when the persistent data comes from one table in the database. In fact, one may safely say that a CMP entity bean is a neat object encapsulation of the data in a table row. BMP entity beans are used to encapsulate more complex relational data, such as the one created by a complex SQL statement. The state cycle pertaining to all types of Entity EJB component is illustrated in Figure 8-29.

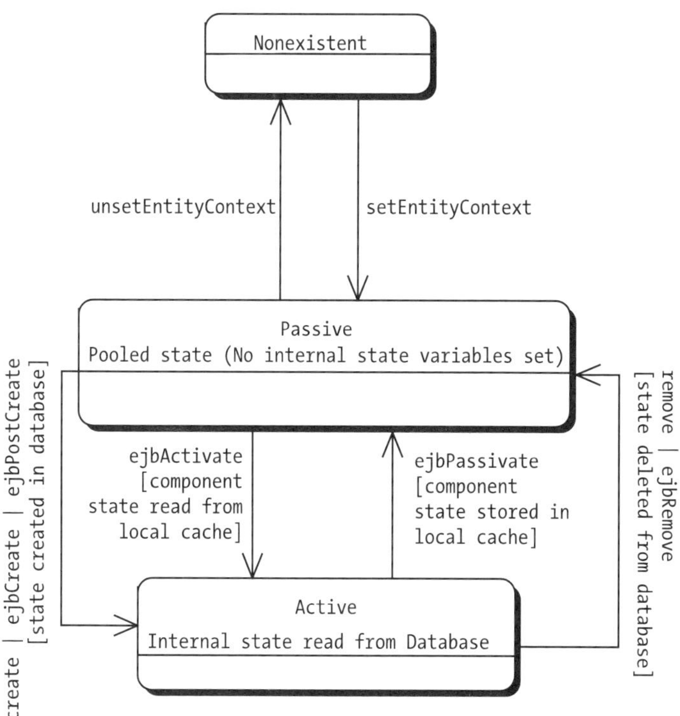

Figure 8-29. UML state diagram for an Entity Enterprise JavaBean. Nonexistent Entity EJB components have null references, and passive Entity EJB components have invalid internal structure. Activating an Entity EJB populates or creates its internal state variables using values from a persistent storage such as a database. Business methods may be called only in active Entity EJBs components.

The life-cycle methods of an Entity EJB component are defined partly in the `javax.ejb.EntityBean` interface and partly in the specific Home interface. The `EntityBean` interface is shown in Figure 8-30; note that the `EntityBean` interface differs from its SessionBean sibling by adding methods ejbLoad/ejbStore (that transfers the state of an EJB to or from the database) and unsetEntityContext (which is used to nullify the bean's reference to its entityContext).

```
javax.ejb.EnterpriseBean
interface
javax.ejb.EntityBean
---
+ejbActivate():void
+ejbLoad():void
+ejbPassivate():void
+ejbRemove():void
+ejbStore():void
+setEntityContext(:javax.ejb.EntityContext):void
+unsetEntityContext():void
```

Figure 8-30. UML diagram of the EntityBean *interface, containing life-cycle method definitions for* EntityBean *implementation classes. Calling a particular method makes the EJB Bean implementation class change state according to the arrows shown in Figure 8-29.*

Whenever an Entity EJB is passivated, its content is stored in the database with which it communicates.

EJB Deployment Descriptors

EJB deployment descriptors control the compilation process required to generate the stub and skeleton classes for the EJB. The code generated by the deployment tool of your application server of choice varies quite drastically with the parameters provided in the deployment descriptor of the EJB. So, what are deployment descriptors? Simply put, a modern deployment descriptor is a well-formed XML document that complies with a particular specification (document type definition (DTD)).

Currently, there are three different standards, the two most modern of which use XML deployment descriptors. Because the old-style, binary deployment descriptors used in EJB specification 1.0 are now obsolete in all major EJB application servers, we will focus on the two modern specification versions: EJB standards 1.1 and 2.0. This walkthrough uses specification 2.0 for all examples, whereas the 1.1 versions of the deployment descriptors are provided in an appendix for compatibility. I warmly recommend using EJB specification version 2.0 over 1.1—

especially if you are planning on using Entity EJBs with CMP—because the specification and Bean class implementation have changed, and for the better.

Note, however, that only parts of the deployment descriptors required to actually deploy an EJB component are standardized. As shown earlier in this chapter under "Step 5—Create the Deployment Descriptors," the standard deployment descriptor must normally be complemented with an application server-specific deployment descriptor to pass the stub/skeleton compilation, and generate a deployable JAR with an EJB component.

When working with EJB components, you are normally required to create two separate standard J2EE deployment descriptors: the `ejb-jar.xml` server-side descriptor for an EJB component and the `application-client.xml` client-side descriptor for an EJB client. If you are planning on running the EJB only within the application server (that is, accessed only by servlets or JSP documents, not by direct clients), you need only the server descriptor.

The ejb-jar.xml Deployment Descriptor

Start by looking at a diagram of a portion of the server-side `ejb-jar.xml` descriptor shown in Figure 8-31. It is rather large—but fear not: most good application servers come with tools that generate both the standard `ejb-jar.xml` descriptor and whatever other nonstandard descriptors are needed to deploy the EJB component. Another point of relief is that the `ejb-jar.xml` has a rather simple structure; if you understand part of the XML tree, you will understand the rest of the deployment descriptor tree without too much trouble.

Because the full DTD for the `ejb-jar.xml` deployment descriptor is rather large, we will examine smaller pieces of it that are logically combined into the complete descriptor. The structure of the descriptor is given by the DTD document, which defines the permitted XML structure as well as the individual order of the elements. Therefore, the general structure of the `ejb-jar.xml` file is as follows:

```
[XML header]
[Global EJB JAR metadata]
[EJB component definitions]
[Relationship definitions]
[Assembly descriptor]
[EJB client JAR definitions]
```

The main bulk of the `ejb-jar.xml` document consists of the EJB component definitions section and their assembly descriptor settings. Let us take a tour through six of the seven sections of the `ejb-jar.xml` descriptor, leaving the relationship definitions to the EJB specification.

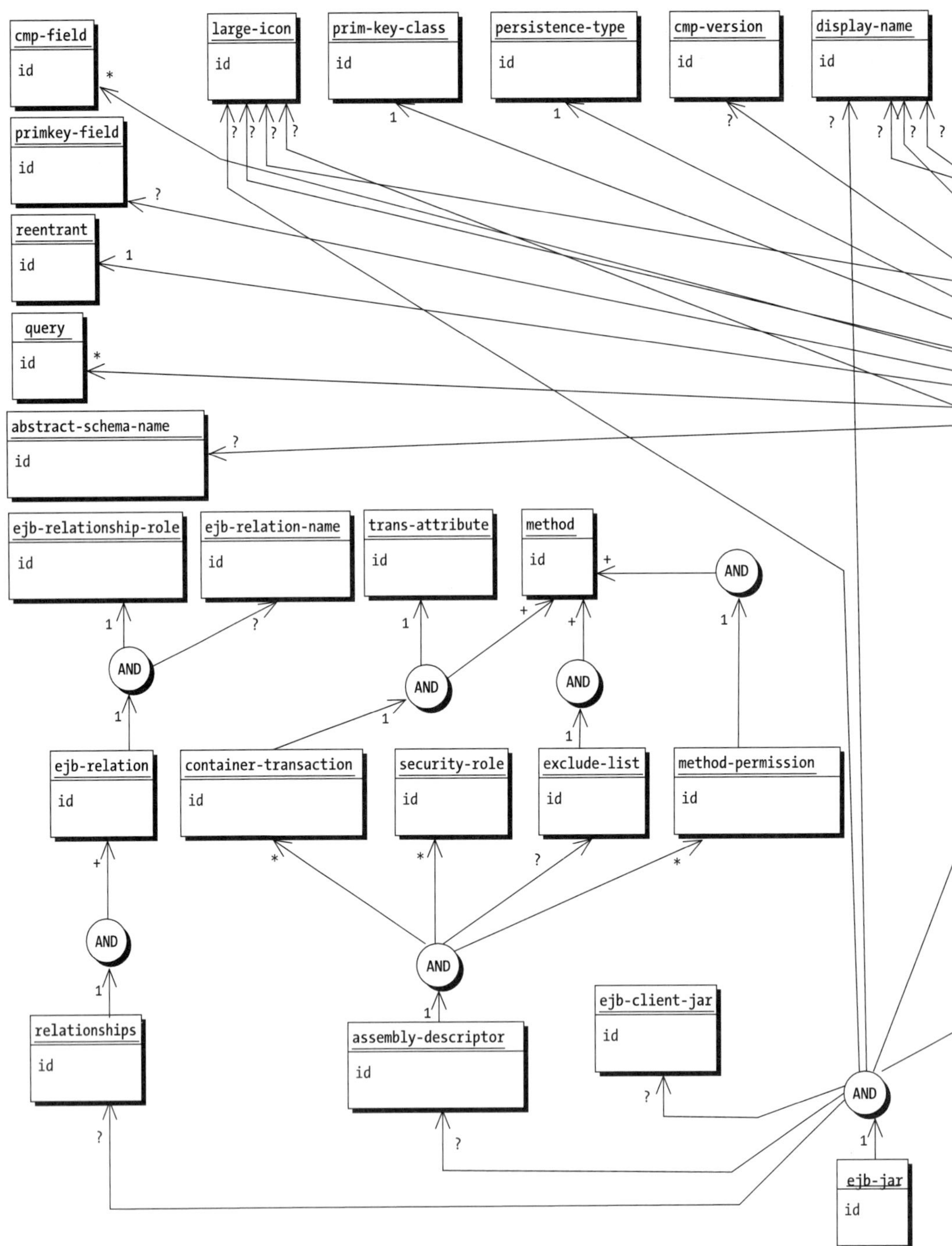

Figure 8-31. Partial structure of the `ejb-jar.xml` *file for EJB specification version 2.0 (PFD 2). All entries are contained within the root* `<ejb-jar>` *element. Although the descriptor specification in its entirety may look overwhelming at first, its simple node structure quickly makes up for the multitude of options. Associations with a * denote cardinality 0..n, the symbol + denotes cardinality 1..n, and the ? symbol denotes cardinality 0..1.*

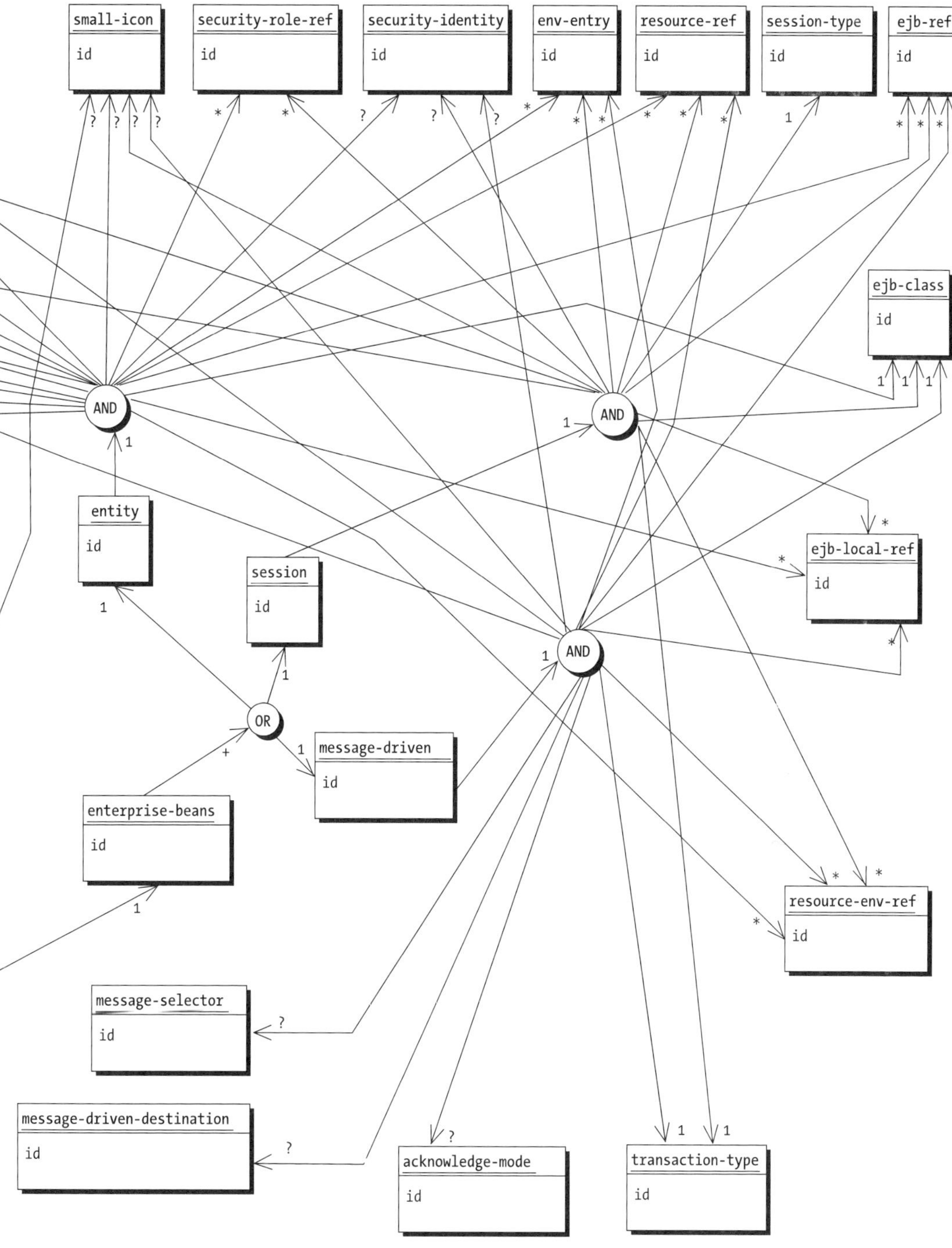

small-icon
id
security-role-ref
id
security-identity
id
env-entry
id
resource-ref
id
session-type
id
ejb-ref
id
ejb-class
id
AND
AND
AND
entity
id
session
id
OR
message-driven
id
ejb-local-ref
id
resource-env-ref
id
enterprise-beans
id
message-selector
id
message-driven-destination
id
acknowledge-mode
id
transaction-type
id

The XML Header

The first part of the ejb-jar.xml file defines the XML standard, as well as its DTD. This is simply bulk text that must be copied as a common header of all ejb-jar.xml files:

```
<?xml version="1.0"?>

<!DOCTYPE ejb-jar PUBLIC
   '-//Sun Microsystems, Inc.//DTD Enterprise JavaBeans 2.0//EN'
   'http://java.sun.com/dtd/ejb-jar_2_0.dtd'>
```

The XML header requires no attention from the programmer. We may therefore simply continue to the real settings of the ejb-jar.xml document.

The Global EJB JAR Metadata

The first section of the deployment descriptor consists of defined attributes that apply to all components of the EJB JAR file. These properties are placed immediately after the opening <ejb-jar> container element, which encloses all configuration text in the ejb-jar.xml document. The ejb-jar DTD defines the structure of the <ejb-jar> element as shown here:

```
<!ELEMENT ejb-jar (description?, display-name?, small-icon?, large-icon?,
   enterprise-beans, relationships?, assembly-descriptor?, ejb-client-jar?)>
```

The bold elements are part of the global EJB JAR metadata section; they are all optional, as indicated by the ? character immediately following each element.

The metadata elements permitted appear in the following list in the order in which they must be entered in the ejb-jar.xml file. Optional elements are marked with [Opt], mandatory ones with [Mand].

- <description> [Opt], holding a human-readable description of the EJB JAR, shown in application server administration tools and deployment tools.

- <display-name> [Opt], which contains a shorter, human-readable identifier of the EJB JAR, shown in administration deployment tools.

- <small-icon> [Opt], which contains the path of a 16×16 pixels GIF or JPEG image that is to be used as an icon for the EJB JAR in application server tools. The image file must be stored within the EJB JAR.

- <large-icon> [Opt], which contains the path of a 32×32 pixels GIF or JPEG image that is to be used as an icon for the EJB JAR in application server tools. The image file must be stored within the EJB JAR.

Although the entire EJB JAR metadata section may be left empty, it is convenient to define at least a display name to prevent the default naming algorithm of each application server from providing a new display name. An example EJB JAR metadata section snippet is shown here:

```
<description>A walkthrough of classes i the EJB version 2.0 API</description>
<display-name>EjbAPIwalkthrough</display-name>
<small-icon>images/ejbJarSmallIcon.gif</small-icon>
<large-icon>images/ejbJarLargeIcon.gif</large-icon>
```

The global EJB metadata section is quite trivial because it contains only four possible entries. However, all other sections of the ejb-jar.xml deployment descriptor are more complex. The next section of the ejb-jar.xml descriptor is the only required part: the EJB component definition section.

The EJB Component Definition Section

The prime task of the ejb-jar.xml deployment descriptor is to define all EJB components. This is done in the EJB component definition section, which has its own DTD specification:

```
<!ELEMENT enterprise-beans (session | entity | message-driven)+>
```

Alas, the Enterprise beans container may contain several entries, with each describing a session, entity, or message-driven bean.

> **NOTE** *This book covers the session and entity beans only, as message-driven beans belong to the J2EE back-end technologies. Message-driven EJB components are tightly coupled with the Java Message Service, which is a J2EE back-end service.*

The <session> and <entity> descriptors are largely similar, although some elements are unique to one of the bean types. Start by examining the DTDs of the two front-end EJB component types. All elements common to both EJB types appear in bold text in Listing 8-18.

Listing 8-18. The session and entity XML element definitions

```
<!ELEMENT session (description?, display-name?, small-icon?, large-icon?, ejb-name,
   home?, remote?, local-home?, local?, ejb-class, session-type, transaction-type,
   env-entry*, ejb-ref*, ejb-local-ref*, security-role-ref*, security-identity?,
   resource-ref*, resource-env-ref*)>
```

and

```
<!ELEMENT entity (description?, display-name?, small-icon?, large-icon?, ejb-name,
   home?, remote?, local-home?, local?, ejb-class, persistence-type, prim-key-class,
   reentrant, cmp-version?, abstract-schema-name?, cmp-field*, primkey-field?,
   env-entry*, ejb-ref*, ejb-local-ref*, security-role-ref*, security-identity?,
   resource-ref*, resource-env-ref*, query*)>
```

Most of the definition fields are common to both EJB types: 17 out of the 19 elements of the session descriptor are used in both bean descriptors. The XML container elements that are unique to the entity bean descriptor configure the communication with the database table wherein its persistent data is stored. Because session EJB components are not persistent, such specification is not required.

Moreover, most of the elements in the specifications above are optional, either with the cardinalities [0..1] or [0..n]. The bare-bones session EJB deployment descriptor is therefore rather manageable:

```
<session>
            <ejb-name>currExchangeBean</ejb-name>
            <home>se.jguru.finance.utils.CurrencyExchangeHome</home>
            <remote>se.jguru.finance.utils.CurrencyExchange</remote>
            <ejb-class>se.jguru.finance.utils.CurrencyExchangeBean</ejb-class>
            <session-type>Stateless</session-type>
            <transaction-type>Container</transaction-type>
</session>
```

Although deployable, this bare-bones session descriptor leaves some room for improvisation by the application server deployment tool; one frequently provides at least a display name and a description as well.

The following sections discuss all 17 descriptor elements that are common to both session and Entity EJBs. The remaining descriptor elements will be described afterwards, in separate sections dedicated to each EJB type.

Trivial Descriptor Elements Common to Session and Entity EJBs

Up to now, all descriptor elements have been of a descriptive nature; if you misspell a word in a `<description>` element, you may offend your old English teacher, but no functionality crashes due to poor linguistic control. However, some of the EJB descriptor elements contain type specifications and filenames that will, if misspelled, thwart the deployment process, and make the application server EJB compiler throw exceptions.

The majority of the Enterprise bean descriptor elements are available to both session and Entity EJB descriptors. I'll walk through them, and provide some skeleton code examples to show the meaning of some of the more complex elements.

The trivial deployment descriptor elements (which do not require a code example, due to their relative simplicity) can be explained straight away. The elements may be optional (marked [Opt]), conditionally optional (marked [Copt]), or mandatory (marked [Mand]), as illustrated in Figure 8-31. These 10 elements are:

- `<description>` [Opt], holding a human-readable description of the EJB component, shown in application server administration tools and deployment tools.

- `<display-name>` [Opt], which contains a shorter, human-readable identifier of the EJB component, shown in administration deployment tools.

- `<small-icon>` [Opt], which contains the path of a 16×16 pixels GIF or JPEG image that is to be used as an icon for the EJB component in application server tools. The image file must be stored within the EJB JAR.

- `<large-icon>` [Opt], which contains the path of a 32×32 pixels GIF or JPEG image that is to be used as an icon for the EJB component in application server tools. The image file must be stored within the EJB JAR.

- `<ejb-name>` [Mand], which is the identifier of the EJB component internally in the descriptor. This value may be arbitrarily chosen, but it must be unique for each component. The `<ejb-name>` is comparable to a primary key in a relational database table.

- `<home>` [Copt], which contains the fully qualified type name of the Home interface of the EJB, such as `se.jguru.games.GameServerHome`. The interface must extend `javax.ejb.EJBHome`. The EJB component must provide type information for at least one of the `<home>`/`<remote>` or `<local-home>`/`<local>` pairs. The `<home>` element is required if the EJB client must be able to connect to the deployed EJB component from a JVM other than the application server's. Thus, if your EJB component must support communication with an application client, the `<home>` element definition is mandatory.

- `<remote>` [Copt], which contains the fully qualified type name of the Remote interface of the EJB, such as `se.jguru.games.GameServer`. The interface must extend `javax.ejb.EJBObject`. The EJB component must provide type information for at least one of the `<home>/<remote>` or `<local-home>/<local>` pairs. The `<remote>` element is required if the EJB client must be able to connect to the deployed EJB component from a JVM other than the application server's. Thus, if your EJB component must support communication with an application client, the `<remote>` element definition is mandatory.

- `<local-home>` [Copt], which contains the fully qualified type name of the `LocalHome` interface of the EJB, such as `se.jguru.games.GameServerLocalHome`. The interface must extend `javax.ejb.EJBLocalHome`. The EJB component must provide type information for at least one of the `<home>/<remote>` or `<local-home>/<local>` pairs. The `<local-home>` element can be used with greater efficiency for EJB clients deployed in the same J2EE application as the EJB bean, such as servlets, JSP documents, and other EJBs. Thus, if your EJB component doesn't need to support communication with an application client, a `<local-home>` element definition reduces the overhead of a network call.

- `<local>` [Copt], which contains the fully qualified type name of the Local interface of the EJB, such as `se.jguru.games.LocalGameServer`. The interface must extend `javax.ejb.EJBLocalObject`. The EJB component must provide type information for at least one of the `<home>/<remote>` or `<local-home>/<local>` pairs. The `<local>` element can be used with greater efficiency for EJB clients deployed in the same J2EE application as the EJB bean, such as servlets, JSP documents, and other EJBs. Thus, if your EJB component doesn't need to support communication with an application client, a `<local>` element definition reduces the overhead of a network call.

- `<ejb-class>` [Mand], which contains the fully qualified type name of the EJB Bean implementation class, such as `se.jguru.games.GameServerBean`. The interface must implement `javax.ejb.SessionBean` if you are implementing a Session EJB, and `javax.ejb.EntityBean` if you are implementing an Entity EJB.

This concludes the walkthrough of the trivial common descriptor elements in the `ejb-jar.xml` deployment descriptor; the other common elements require a smaller skeleton code example to show their function. On to the nontrivial descriptor elements.

Nontrivial Descriptor Elements Common to Session and Entity EJBs

The majority of the nontrivial Enterprise bean descriptor elements that are available to both session and Entity EJB descriptors cannot be declared only in the J2EE standard descriptors. With the exception of environment entry definitions, all nontrivial descriptor elements require additional setup in application server-specific deployment descriptors. I'll walk through all common nontrivial descriptor elements, providing skeleton code examples to show their meaning.

In distributed applications, the application server JNDI context is frequently used as a master Hashtable containing configuration settings of various sorts. The process of binding configuration settings as environment values in the EJB context is similar to the deployment descriptor required to bind values in the servlet context of a Web application.

The trivial deployment descriptor elements (which do not require a code example, due to their relative simplicity) can be explained straight away. The elements may be optional (marked [Opt]), conditionally optional (marked [Copt]), or mandatory (marked [Mand]), as illustrated in Figure 8-31. These seven elements are:

- `<env-entry>` [Opt], which contains a declaration for a variable bound in the context of the EJB component. Each `<env-entry>` element has the DTD structure `<!ELEMENT env-entry (description?, env-entry-name, env-entry-type, env-entry-value?)>`, which defines the required properties for an environment entry variable:

    - `<description>` [Opt], which contains a human-readable description of the variable bound.

    - `<env-entry-name>` [Mand], which contains the variable name of the variable bound, such as `verboseMode`. This is the key where the variable value may be looked up relative to the JNDI context `java:comp/env`. The `<env-entry-name>` must be unique per variable of an EJB component. Similar to normal Java code, you will get an exception if you're trying to declare a variable with the same name as an existing one.

    - `<env-entry-type>` [Mand], which contains the fully qualified type name of the variable bound, such as `java.lang.Boolean`. The types permitted are `Boolean, Byte, Character, Short, Integer, Double, Float, Long,` and `String`—all from the `java.lang` package.

- <env-entry-type> [Opt], which contains the value of the variable bound. The value is used as the single String parameter to the constructor of the type provided in the <env-entry-type> descriptor.

- <ejb-ref> [Opt], which contains a declaration of a reference to another EJB which is accessed from within the code of the EJB component being deployed. Frequently, session EJB components use the services of Entity EJB components to access legacy data. In this case, the session EJB component requires an <ejb-ref> declaration element that ties a home and remote interface combination to a JNDI name bound relative to the local context java:comp/env. Each <ejb-ref> element has the DTD structure <!ELEMENT ejb-ref (description?, ejb-ref-name, ejb-ref-type, home, remote, ejb-link?)>

  - <description> [Opt], which contains a human-readable description of the EJB reference. This description is visible in deployment tools.

  - <ejb-ref-name> [Mand], which contains the variable name of the EJB reference, such as WebPage. This is the key where the EJB home interface may be looked up relative to the JNDI context java:comp/env. The <env-ref-name> must be unique within the Enterprise bean.

  - <env-entry-type> [Mand], which defines which type of EJB is referenced. The value of this entry must be either Entity or Session.

  - <home> [Mand], which contains the fully qualified type name of the home interface for the EJB component reference, such as se.jguru.games.GameHome. The Home interface type must extend javax.ejb.EJBHome.

  - <remote> [Mand], which contains the fully qualified type name of the remote interface for the EJB component reference, such as se.jguru.games.Game. The remote interface type must extend javax.ejb.EJBObject.

  - <ejb-link> [Opt], which contains the <ejb-name> of EJB component which is referenced by this <ejb-link>. If the EJB component referenced is not part of the same ejb-jar.xml file as the EJB component enclosing this ejb-link, the path of the JAR file where the bean is found precedes the <ejb-name>. The path must be given relative to this JAR file. Two examples of valid ejb-link descriptor elements may look like:

    ```
    <ejb-link>AccountBean</ejb-link>
    <ejb-link>../externalServices/securityEJBs.jar#AuditBean</ejb-link>
    ```

- `<ejb-local-ref>` [Opt], which is identical to the `<ejb-ref>` element, except that it contains a reference to a local EJB. The `<home>` and `<remote>` entries in the `<ejb-ref>` has therefore been replaced with `<local-home>` and `<local>` descriptor elements.

- `<security-role-ref>` [Opt], which contains a structure that maps a security role used in the EJB code to a security role defined in the assembly descriptor section of the bean. The DTD structure is `<!ELEMENT security-role-ref (description?, role-name, role-link?)>`

  - `<description>` [Opt] contains a human-readable description of the security role reference. This description is visible in deployment tools.

  - `<role-name>` [Mand] contains the role name of the security role used within the EJB Bean implementation class, such as `standardUserRole`. The value of the `<role-name>` container can be verified in the Bean implementation class by calling the `EJBContext.isCallerInRole(String roleName)` method.

  - `<role-link>` [Opt] contains the name of a `<security-role>` entry defined within the `<assembly-descriptor>` section of this deployment descriptor.

- `<security-identity>` [Opt] defines whether the caller's or a fixed run-as identity should be used when executing the methods of the EJB component. This is useful for development or for locking the security identity to that of a particular user. If the security-identity element is not present, the identity defaults to the user's logged-in identity. You therefore need to insert the `<security-identity>` element only when you wish to use a security identity other than the user's own, as demonstrated by an example that locks the user to the `Yoda` identity when executing its methods of the deployed EJB:

```
<security-identity>
  <description>Locking the identity during development.</description>
  <run-as>
    <role-name>Yoda</role-name>
  </run-as>
</security-identity>
```

- `<resource-ref>` [Opt], which encapsulates a reference to an external resource factory, such as a data source, bound in the JNDI context of the EJB component. Frequently, one declares a resource reference element if the EJB component requires an explicit connection to a relational database. The `<resource-ref>` element contains a definition structure of five elements, with two optional elements, as shown by its DTD description: `<!ELEMENT resource-ref (description?, res-ref-name, res-type, res-auth, res-sharing-scope?)>.` The elements are:

  - `<description>` [Opt], which contains a human-readable description of the resource reference. This description will be visible in deployment tools.

  - `<res-ref-name>` [Mand], which contains the identifier name of the resource reference used within the EJB Bean implementation class, such as `QuickDataSource`. The `<res-ref-name>` must be unique within the defined EJB component; it refers to a JNDI context relative `java:comp/env`.

  - `<res-type>` [Mand], which contains the fully qualified type name of the data source, such as `javax.sql.DataSource`.

  - `<res-auth>` [Mand], which specifies if the EJB container or the EJB Bean implementation class authorizes the EJB component with the resource manager. The `<res-auth>` element may contain the values `Application` or `Container`.

  - `<res-sharing-scope>` [Opt], which contains a value indicating whether the resource may be shared. Valid values are `Shareable` (default) and `Unshareable`.

- `<resource-env-ref>` [Opt], which encapsulates a reference to an object managing an external resource factory, such as a JMS queue. The `<resource-env-ref>` element contains a definition structure of three elements illustrated by its DTD description:

```
<!ELEMENT resource-env-ref (description?, resource-env-ref-name,
   resource-env-ref-type)>
```

- The contained elements are:

  - `<description>` [Opt], which contains a human-readable description of the resource environment reference. This description is visible in deployment tools.

- `<resource-env-ref-name>` [Mand], which contains the identifier name of the resource environment reference used within the EJB Bean implementation class, such as `FinanceMessageQueue`. The `<resource-env-ref-name>` must be unique within the defined EJB component, and refers to a JNDI context relative `java:comp/env`.

- `<resource-env-ref-type>` [Mand], which contains the fully qualified type name of the resource returned by the factory bound in the environment.

Having examined the meaning of all descriptor elements common to session and Entity beans for the `ejb-jar.xml` deployment descriptor, the following sections provide a few code examples that relate the nontrivial deployment elements to the code of the EJB component.

Using an <env-entry> Element in the EJB Code

How should you access an environment entry value from within the EJB Bean implementation class? Assume that you have a deployment descriptor entry binding a `String` variable with the value `Lennart` in the EJB context under the key `userName`:

```
<env-entry>
    <description>The user name of the Java architect</description>
    <env-entry-name>userName</env-entry-name>
    <env-entry-type>java.lang.String</env-entry-type>
    <env-entry-value>Lennart</env-entry-value>
</env-entry>
```

Reading the value from an EJB component requires access to the context where it is bound:

```
// Get the initial Context
Context initContext = ...

// Lookup the bound value
// The prefix java:comp/env is particular to the
// environment (EJB Context).
String key = "java:comp/env/userName";
String theUserName = (String) initContext.lookup(key);
```

The internal variable `theUserName` now contains the value Lennart, as provided in the deployment descriptor.

Using an <ejb-ref> Element in the EJB Code

If your EJB component requires the services of another EJB, whose EJBHome interface is called `WebPageHome`, you need to bind an `<ejb-ref>` in the calling EJB's context, like so:

```
<ejb-ref>
   <ejb-ref-name>WebPageHome</ejb-ref-name>
   <ejb-ref-type>Entity</ejb-ref-type>
   <home>se.jguru.webdb.legacyintegration.WebPageHome</home>
   <remote>se.jguru.webdb.legacyintegration.WebPage</remote>
</ejb-ref>
```

The EJB reference can then be accessed within the calling EJB component. Note that the lookup string must be identical to the `<ejb-ref-name>` in the descriptor, with the local context prefix (`java:comp/env`) prepended, as shown in the following code snippet:

```
// Get the initial context
Context ctx = new InitialContext();

// Lookup the WebPageHome in the local Context (java:comp/env)
Object obj = ctx.lookup(java:comp/env/WebPageHome);

// Narrow to the proper type
WebPageHome home = (WebPageHome)
    PortableRemoteObject.narrow(obj, WebPageHome.class);

// Find an instance of the remote interface
WebPage remote = home.findBySomeCriteria(…);
```

Note the three dependencies between the deployment descriptor and the EJB code; the name of the `<ejb-ref>` must match the `lookup()` parameter, and the two types declared in the deployment descriptor must be used in the EJB code.

Using an <ejb-local-ref> Element in the EJB Code

The `<ejb-local-ref>` is almost identical in declaration and usage to the `<ejb-ref>`, with the exception that it can be used only from within the same application server as the server EJB component. The differences between the `<ejb-ref>` and the `<ejb-local-ref>` scenarios have been bolded in the following deployment descriptor and code:

```
<ejb-local-ref>
   <ejb-ref-name>WebPageLocalHome</ejb-ref-name>
   <ejb-ref-type>Entity</ejb-ref-type>
   <local-home>se.jguru.webdb.local.LocalWebPageHome</local-home>
   <local>se.jguru.webdb.local.LocalWebPage</local>
</ejb-local-ref>
```

The EJB reference can then be accessed within the calling EJB component. Note that the lookup string must be identical to the `<ejb-ref-name>` in the descriptor, with the local context prefix (`java:comp/env`) prepended, as shown in the following code snippet:

```
// Get the initial context
Context ctx = new InitialContext();

// Lookup the WebPageHome in the local Context (java:comp/env)
Object obj = ctx.lookup(java:comp/env/WebPageLocalHome);

// Narrow to the proper type—note: no PortableRemoteObject!
WebPageLocalHome home = (WebPageLocalHome) obj;

// Find an instance of the remote interface
LocalWebPage local = home.findBySomeCriteria(...);
```

Remember, a `<local>` can be used only by clients deployed in the same JVM as the server EJB.

Using a <resource-ref> Element in the EJB Code

How should you access a resource reference from within the EJB Bean implementation class? Assume that you have a setup data source communicating with a relational database, bound to the JNDI context under the key `jdbc/TransactionDS`:

```
<resource-ref>
   <res-ref-name>jdbc/TransactionDS</res-ref-name>
   <res-type>javax.sql.DataSource</res-type>
   <res-auth>Container</res-auth>
</resource-ref>
```

The resource reference may be accessed within the calling EJB component using the following code (where the `uid` and `password` variables are assumed to be defined elsewhere):

```
// Get the initial Context
Context ctx = new InitialContext();

// Get the DataSource from the context
String lookupString = "java:comp/env/jdbc/TransactionDS";
DataSource ds = (DataSource) ctx.lookup(lookupString);

// Get a Connection from the DataSource
Connection conn = ds.getConnection(this.uid, this.password);
```

Note that what you have retrieved from the JNDI lookup is a data source reference, which was defined in the `ejb-jar.xml` descriptor file. However, the J2EE standard does not cover the specifics of how to deploy or set up the actual data source in the application server. This is left to the application server vendor, and it is normally done in a custom deployment descriptor.

Having examined the deployment descriptor elements that are common to both session and Entity EJB components, it is now time to move on to the deployment descriptor elements that are specific to session and Entity EJBs.

Session EJB Deployment Elements

The two deployment configuration elements that are specific to session EJB descriptors are straightforward but important because they are both mandatory for all session EJB deployment descriptors. In the following XML DTD of the `<session>` element, the elements in question appear in bold text.

```
<!ELEMENT session (description?, display-name?, small-icon?, large-icon?, ejb-name,
   home?, remote?, local-home?, local?, ejb-class, session-type, transaction-type,
   env-entry*, ejb-ref*, ejb-local-ref*, security-role-ref*, security-identity?,
   resource-ref*, resource-env-ref*)>
```

Next, study the significance of the two remaining descriptor elements, which are specific to session EJB components:

- `<session-type>` [Mand], which describes the type of Session EJB component; valid values are `Stateless` or `Stateful`. Stateful EJB components maintain a session with a user enabling server-side state to be held for that user; this is impossible with stateless EJBs. Refer to the "The Life Cycle of Session EJBs" earlier in this chapter to review the differences in EJB life cycle between stateless and stateful session EJB components.

- `<transaction-type>` [Mand], which determines who manages the transactions of the bean; valid values are `Bean` or `Container`. All methods of an EJB component may execute within a transactional context; the transaction type setting determines if the EJB component or the EJB container should manage the transactions. It is illegal for an EJB bean to call any transaction-handling methods (that is, `begin`, `commit`, or `rollback`) if it is configured to use `Container` transaction management.

Having walked through all descriptor elements for a session EJB, take a look at a few examples for a session EJB descriptor. The first of the following examples describes a stateful session EJB component without any bound values or references. The session EJB uses bean-managed transaction handling, which means that the EJB component must define its `UserTransaction`, and call the `begin`, `commit`, and `rollback` methods internally in its methods.

```
<session>
            <description>Interface to the Transaction Server.</description>
            <display-name>Transaction Query Bean</display-name>
            <ejb-name>transactionQueryBean</ejb-name>
            <home>se.jguru.legacycommunication.TransactionQueryHome</home>
            <remote> se.jguru.legacycommunication.TransactionQuery </remote>
            <ejb-class>
               se.jguru.legacycommunication.TransactionQueryBean
            </ejb-class>
            <session-type>Stateful</session-type>
            <transaction-type>Bean</transaction-type>
</session>
```

Although the preceding deployment descriptor is valid, it is rather simple, not showing most of the complexities involved in creating a real-life session EJB deployment descriptor. The next example is the session EJB descriptor of a small (but real) system that is developed and studied in Chapter 10 and 11.

This deployment descriptor, shown in Listing 8-19, contains these bound environment entries, in addition to the standard type definitions:

- Boolean variable named `verboseMode` with the value false.

- Reference to an Entity EJB with the Home interface `se.jguru.webdb.legacyintegration.ImageHome` and the Remote interface `se.jguru.webdb.legacyintegration.Image`.

- Reference to an Entity EJB with the Home interface `se.jguru.webdb.legacyintegration.WebPageHome` and the Remote interface `se.jguru.webdb.legacyintegration.WebPage`.

- Resource reference to a data source that provides connections to a relational database.

Listing 8-19. The session descriptor of the `LegacyFacadeBean` *EJB component*

```
<session>
   <description>
      This is the Session EJB Facade which hides
      all data mining from the Legacy Tier.
   </description>
   <ejb-name>LegacyFacadeBean</ejb-name>
   <home>se.jguru.webdb.proxy.LegacyFacadeHome</home>
   <remote>se.jguru.webdb.proxy.LegacyFacade</remote>
   <ejb-class>se.jguru.webdb.proxy.LegacyFacadeBean</ejb-class>
   <session-type>Stateless</session-type>
   <transaction-type>Container</transaction-type>

   <env-entry>
      <description>Log verbosity level toggle flag</description>
      <env-entry-name>verboseMode</env-entry-name>
      <env-entry-type>java.lang.Boolean</env-entry-type>
      <env-entry-value>true</env-entry-value>
   </env-entry>

   <ejb-ref>
      <ejb-ref-name>WebPageHome</ejb-ref-name>
      <ejb-ref-type>Entity</ejb-ref-type>
      <home>se.jguru.webdb.legacyintegration.WebPageHome</home>
      <remote>se.jguru.webdb.legacyintegration.WebPage</remote>
   </ejb-ref>
   <ejb-ref>
      <ejb-ref-name>ImageHome</ejb-ref-name>
      <ejb-ref-type>Entity</ejb-ref-type>
      <home>se.jguru.webdb.legacyintegration.ImageHome</home>
      <remote>se.jguru.webdb.legacyintegration.Image</remote>
   </ejb-ref>
```

```
  <resource-ref>
    <description>
      This is the DataSource which connects to the
      relational database where the actual data is stored.
    </description>
    <res-ref-name>localDataSource</res-ref-name>
    <res-type>javax.sql.DataSource</res-type>
    <res-auth>Container</res-auth>
  </resource-ref>
</session>
```

Although not trivial, the session deployment descriptor in Listing 8-19 is realistic for many industrial-strength session EJB descriptors because it contains an environment entry reference, multiple references to other EJB components, and a resource reference.

The remaining unique elements belong to the Entity EJB components, described next.

Entity EJB Deployment Elements

The eight deployment configuration elements specific to Entity EJB descriptors (highlighted in the following DTD element definition) are more complex than their session siblings; the persistence settings of Entity EJBs require much configuration—especially in the case of CMP Entity EJBs. The unique elements covered in this section appear in bold text in the XML DTD of the following `<entity>` element:

```
<!ELEMENT entity (description?, display-name?, small-icon?, large-icon?,
  ejb-name, home?, remote?, local-home?, local?, ejb-class, persistence-type,
  prim-key-class, reentrant, cmp-version?, abstract-schema-name?, cmp-field*,
  primkey-field?, env-entry*, ejb-ref*, ejb-local-ref*, security-role-ref*,
  security-identity?, resource-ref*, resource-env-ref*, query*)>
```

Study the significance of the eight remaining descriptor elements, specific to Entity EJB components:

- `<persistence-type>` [Mand], describes the type of persistence used by the EJB component; valid values are `Bean` and `Container`.

- `<prim-key-class>` [Mand], contains the fully qualified type of the primary key of the Entity EJB, such as `java.lang.String`.

- `<reenrant>` [Mand], defines if the Entity EJB is reentrant or not. Valid values are `True` and `False`.

- `<cmp-version>` [Opt], defines the version of the CMP specification that this Entity EJB uses. Valid values are 1.x and 2.x (default).

- `<abstract-schema-name>` [Opt], defines if the abstract schema where this Entity EJB reads and stores its values. This abstract schema name must be used in the EJB-QL statements that query the abstract database schema for the values with which to populate the internal state of this bean.

- `<cmp-field>` [Opt], defines a field whose value should be managed by the container. The field structure from the DTD is `<!ELEMENT cmp-field (description?, field-name)>`, so a valid `cmp-field` definition is:

```
<cmp-field>
    <description>The balance of this account</description>
    <cmp-field>accountBalance</cmp-field>
</cmp-field>
```

  Each `<cmp-field>` definition maps directly to a pair of abstract getter and setter methods in the EJB Bean implementation class. Therefore, the definition above would require a pair of JavaBean methods:

```
public abstract int getAccountBalance();
public abstract void setAccountBalance(int newBalance);
```

- `<primkey-field>` [Mand], defines the name of the primary key field for this EJB component. The primary key field must be managed by the container; that is, the name of the `<primkey-field>` must be equal to one of the `<cmp-field>` definitions.

- `<query>` [Opt], defines the EJB-QL text for an EJB find or select query. The query structure defines four subelements: `<!ELEMENT query (description?, query-method, result-type-mapping?, ejb-ql)>`. The descriptor elements are:

  - `<description>` [Opt], holding a human-readable description of the query, shown in application server administration tools and deployment tools.

  - `<query-method>` [Mand], defines the `finder` or `select` method that runs the EJB-QL query. The `<query-method>` is in itself a structure with the following DTD:

```
<!ELEMENT query-method (method-name, method-intf?, method-params)>
```

- Thus, a valid example of a <query-method> descriptor element is:

```
<query-method>
   <method-name>findByLastName</method-name>
   <method-intf>Home</method-intf>
   <method-params>
      <method-param>java.lang.String</method-param>
   </method-params>
</query-method>
```

- `<method-name>` [Mand], contains the name of a `finder` or `select` method. An asterisk (*)may be used instead of a name if the EJB-QL applies to all methods.

- `<method-intf>` [Opt], defines which interface or interfaces defines the method in question, or implies all possible interfaces if left empty. Valid values are `Home`, `LocalHome`, `Remote`, and `Local`.

- `<method-params>` [Mand], contains a list of `<method-param>` definitions that has the fully qualified type name of a method parameter.

- `<result-type-mapping>` [Opt], indicates whether the result of a query should be mapped to an `EJBLocalObject` (default) or an `EJBObject`. The latter case is required if the Entity EJB is used remotely by an application client. This is quite unlikely. Valid values are `Local` and `Remote`.

- `<ejb-ql>` [Mand], defines the actual query that selects the bean infrastructure from its data source. An example of an EJB-QL string shows a great similarity with the SQL language of most relational databases. EJB-QL has better constructs to support object-oriented programming structures. Method parameters sent to finders and selectors may be used by the EJB-QL when extracting data from the back end. The first (left-most) parameter of the method is marked in the EJB-QL text with the token `?1`, the second parameter with `?2`, and so on. Of course, exceptions are generated during EJB compilation if the parameter number is greater than the number of defined parameters.

```
<ejb-ql>SELECT object(a) FROM Accounts a WHERE a.balance > 20000</ejb-ql>
<ejb-ql>SELECT object(a) FROM Accounts a WHERE a.ownerName LIKE '?1'</ejb-ql>
```

Having examined all descriptor elements for an Entity EJB, you may take a look at a few Entity EJB descriptor examples. The first example in Listing 8-20 describes a simple Entity EJB component using bean-managed persistence and not using any bound values or references. Similar to a trivial table in a database, the GameMetadataBean uses an Integer for primary key:

Listing 8-20. Small deployment descriptor example for a BMP entity bean

```
<entity>
   <description>Game metadata bean</description>
   <display-name>GameMetadataBean</display-name>
   <ejb-name>GameMetadataBean</ejb-name>
   <local-home>se.jguru.games.GameMetadataHome</local-home>
   <local>se.jguru.games.GameMetadata</local>
   <ejb-class>se.jguru.games.GameMetadataBean</ejb-class>
   <persistence-type>Bean</persistence-type>
   <prim-key-class>java.lang.Integer</prim-key-class>
   <reentrant>False</reentrant>
</entity>
```

The slightly more complex Entity EJB descriptor example in Listing 8-21 illustrates an Entity EJB that uses the CMP mechanism to delegate the management of data source values to the EJB container.

Listing 8-21. Deployment descriptor for a CMP EJB component

```
<entity>
   <ejb-name>ImageBean</ejb-name>
   <home>se.jguru.webdb.legacyintegration.ImageHome</home>
   <remote>se.jguru.webdb.legacyintegration.Image</remote>
   <ejb-class>se.jguru.webdb.legacyintegration.ImageBean</ejb-class>
   <persistence-type>Container</persistence-type>
   <prim-key-class>java.lang.Integer</prim-key-class>
   <reentrant>False</reentrant>
   <cmp-version>2.x</cmp-version>
   <abstract-schema-name>ImageBean</abstract-schema-name>

   <cmp-field>
      <field-name>data</field-name>
   </cmp-field>
   <cmp-field>
      <field-name>mimeType</field-name>
   </cmp-field>
   <cmp-field>
      <field-name>id</field-name>
   </cmp-field>
```

```
    <cmp-field>
        <field-name>fileName</field-name>
    </cmp-field>

    <primkey-field>id</primkey-field>

    <env-entry>
        <description>Log verbosity level toggle flag</description>
        <env-entry-name>verboseMode</env-entry-name>
        <env-entry-type>java.lang.Boolean</env-entry-type>
        <env-entry-value>true</env-entry-value>
    </env-entry>

    <query>
        <query-method>
            <method-name>findByMimeType</method-name>
            <method-params>
                <method-param>java.lang.String</method-param>
            </method-params>
        </query-method>
        <ejb-ql>SELECT OBJECT(i) FROM Images i WHERE i.mimeType like '?1%'</ejb-ql>
    </query>
</entity>
```

The preceding Entity EJB descriptor example shown is rather complex, as is customary with CMP Entity EJBs. (After all, if you delegate a lot of mindless code creation to the container, it is likely to want more instructions about how the code should be manufactured). Most elements in the Entity EJB descriptor are trivial, but the query section deserves a slight elaboration. The `?1` in the EJB-QL text denotes the value of the first method parameter (that is, the String parameter defined for the `findByMimeType` method).

The large component definition section is now examined in detail, and we may move on to the bean's assembly descriptor that defines deployment properties related to security and transactional settings.

The Assembly Descriptor

The optional assembly descriptor section of the `ejb-jar.xml` deployment descriptor contains security-related configuration settings, transactional definitions for beans using container managed transaction management, and a list of methods that should be excluded from invocation. The XML DTD of the assembly-descriptor element reveals a small top structure:

```
<!ELEMENT assembly-descriptor (security-role*, method-permission*,
   container-transaction*, exclude-list?)>
```

The four top XML descriptor elements of the assembly-descriptor are:

- <security-role> [Opt], this element contains an optional description and the name of a security role. A security role is simply a name; it has no implicit privileges. All permissions must be explicitly assigned to it in the method permission section. However, it is important to understand that all security in the J2EE model originates from the <security-role> defined in the assembly descriptor. Refer to the "EJB Security Illustrated" section for an illustrated explanation of EJB security.

  A valid security role definition example is a small structure:

  ```
  <security-role>
     <description>Standard Application User Role</description>
     <role-name>standardUserRole</role-name>
  </security-role>
  ```

- <method-permission> [Opt], the method permission structure grants execute permission on a set of methods to one or more defined security roles. The methods must be defined in the Home or Remote interfaces of the EJB component. If no authorization needs to be checked, the method permission should be defined as unchecked. The XML DTD structure of the <method-permission> deployment descriptor element is:

  ```
  <!ELEMENT method-permission (description?, (role-name+|unchecked), method+)>
  ```

  - <description> [Opt], a human-readable description of this method permission. It is visible in application assembly tools.

  - <role-name> [Mand], the name of a defined security role that should be granted execute privileges for the methods in this method permission structure.

  - <method> [Mand], a method identifier structure that may uniquely pinpoint a method in the Home or Remote interface of an EJB component. The XML DTD of the structure is <!ELEMENT method (description?, ejb-name, method-intf?, method-name, method-params?)>. An example of a valid deployment descriptor element for a method may look like:

```
<method>
   <description>Special create factory</description>
   <ejb-name>LocalTorsionModel</ejb-name>
   <method-intf>LocalHome</method-intf>
   <method-name>create</method-name>
   <method-params>
      <method-param>java.lang.String</method-param>
   </method-params>
</method>
```

Let's examine the detailed descriptions of the descriptor elements of the `<method>` structure.

- `<description>` [Opt], a human-readable description of this method. It is visible in application assembly tools.
- `<ejb-name>` [Mand], the name of a defined EJB component.
- `<method-intf>` [Opt], defines which interface or interfaces defines the method in question, or implies all possible interfaces if left empty. Valid values are `Home`, `LocalHome`, `Remote`, and `Local`.
- `<method-name>` [Mand], contains the name of a `finder` or `select` method. An asterisk (*) may be used instead of a name if the EJB-QL applies to all methods.
- `<method-params>` [Mand], contains a list of `<method-param>` definitions that have the fully qualified type name of a method parameter.

- `<container-transaction>` [Opt], defines how the EJB container should manage transactions for the EJB method invocations. A container transaction element is a structure with the following structure: `<!ELEMENT container-transaction (description?, method+, trans-attribute)>`. You only need to define a container transaction if at least one of your EJBs delegates its transaction management to the container. An example of a valid deployment descriptor element for a container transaction may look like:

```
<container-transaction>
   <description>Standard transaction isolation</description>
   <method>
      <ejb-name>LocalTorsionModel</ejb-name>
      <method-name>*</method-name>
   </method>
   <trans-attribute>Required</trans-attribute>
</container-transaction>
```

Let's examine the detailed descriptions of the descriptor elements of the <method> structure.

- <description> [Opt], a human-readable description of this container transaction. It is visible in application assembly tools.
- <method> [Mand], the name of a defined EJB component. The <method> structure is identical to the one described in the previous <method-permission> descriptor element, so we will not repeat its detailed description here.
- <trans-attribute> [Mand], this descriptor defines how the container should implement the transaction management code within the skeleton and stub classes of the EJB. Valid values are `NotSupported`, `Supports`, `Required`, `RequiresNew`, `Mandatory`, and `Never`. The transactional deployment specifications are simple to understand when illustrated. Refer to the section "EJB Transaction Management Illustrated" for a full explanation of the transactional attributes.

- <exclude-list> [Opt], this descriptor defines a set of methods which cannot be invoked.

The EJB Client JAR Definition Section

The EJB client JAR section contains a single descriptor element, <ejb-client-jar>, which holds the path to an application client connection JAR file. The class files within the application client connection JAR enable an EJB application client to connect to the EJBs deployed within the current EJB JAR.

The structure of the <ejb-client-jar> element is trivial:

```
<ejb-client-jar>../clientJars/AppClientAccess.jar</ejb-client-jar>
```

Let's study two of the seemingly complex deployment structures, which prove to be fairly simple when properly illustrated: EJB security deployment settings and EJB transaction settings.

EJB Security Illustrated

EJB security provides a controlled way to determine if the current caller may or may not invoke a particular method in an EJB component. Although conceptually simple, the EJB component development process model implies a fairly complex, distributed model for access privilege specification. This is well covered in the EJB specification in the "Security Management" section.

However, the specification is poor at illustrating the fairly simple dependencies among the systems, people, and configuration files involved in the access control of an EJB component. As with most computer systems, the individual steps of security configuration and usage may be simple, but, in traditional J2EE configuration style, the number of steps involved convey an illusion of complexity. Therefore, start by establishing a common terminology, which follows the security terms used by the J2EE specification. See Table 8-1 for details.

Table 8-1. Terms Used in the Extended J2EE Security Model

TERM	DESCRIPTION	DEFINED IN	DEFINED BY
User	A security identity having a userID and a password	Application server-specific; not covered in the J2EE specification	Application server administrator
Group	A security principal collecting users and other groups	Application server-specific; not covered in the J2EE specification	Application server administrator
Security role	A security principal collecting users and groups	Standard J2EE deployment descriptor, `ejb-jar.xml`	EJB deployer
Security role reference	A reference to a security role, potentially referenced by the EJB code	Standard J2EE deployment descriptor, `ejb-jar.xml`	EJB developer
Method permission	The privilege to execute a method in an EJB	Standard J2EE deployment descriptor, `ejb-jar.xml`	EJB deployer

Strictly speaking, users and groups are not a standard part of the J2EE specification. They have been added to tie the abstract terms from the J2EE specification to a concrete scenario. The entities of the EJB security structure are associated with one another in a well-defined way, as shown in Figure 8-32.

As shown in Figure 8-32, users may belong to zero or more groups and zero or more security roles, whereas groups may contain users and other groups. Users and groups are defined in a way that is custom to the application server; some application servers use custom deployment descriptors to define users and groups, and other servers rely on the services of the operating system or a third-party authentication product. The reason we include users and groups in

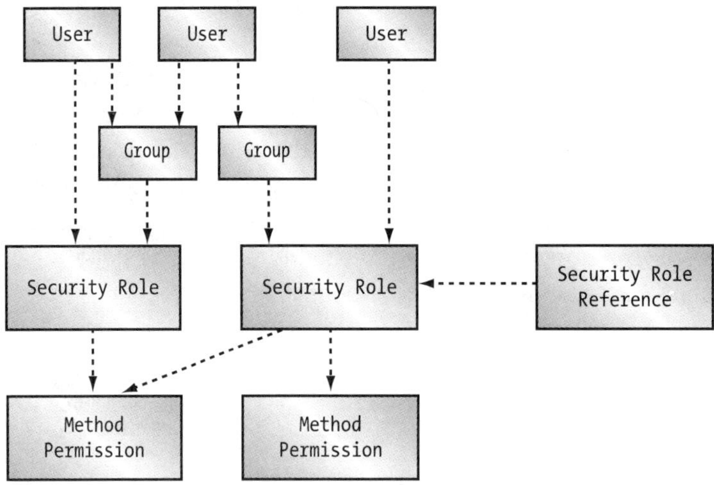

Figure 8-32. The structure of the security entities of a J2EE-compliant application

the J2EE security discussion is one of familiarity; they are common terms that are understood by all programmers.

Security Roles

The J2EE security specification starts with the concept of the security role. A J2EE security role is a logical collection of users and groups, similar to the security roles present in the security systems of many relational databases. For simplicity, I recommend regarding the J2EE security role as a group that collects a set of individual users and groups. Security roles are defined in the assembly descriptor section of the deployment descriptor `ejb-jar.xml`, as illustrated in the section "The Assembly Descriptor." Security roles are therefore global within an EJB JAR, and may be used by all EJB components in the same `<ejb-jar>` structure.

Method Permissions

For each security role, the EJB deployment descriptor may define a set of method permissions, each granting execute access to one or more methods in the EJB component. Therefore, a user or group belonging to a particular security role may execute a method within the EJB only if the security role has been granted access privileges through a method permission.

Security Role References

A security role reference is an alias mapped to a particular security role from an individual EJB. The application developer may want to check security properties from within the EJB code; it therefore requires a mapping between the security role references in the compiled EJB code and the security roles defined in the `ejb-jar.xml` deployment descriptor.

Having understood the concepts behind J2EE security settings, we should examine a small example from a sample application server.

A Short Study in Security

Let's study a short example, taken from the Orion Application Server (OAS), that provides customized deployment descriptor files defining groups and users and mapping groups and users to security roles. Figure 8-33 illustrates the deployment descriptor chain of the OAS.

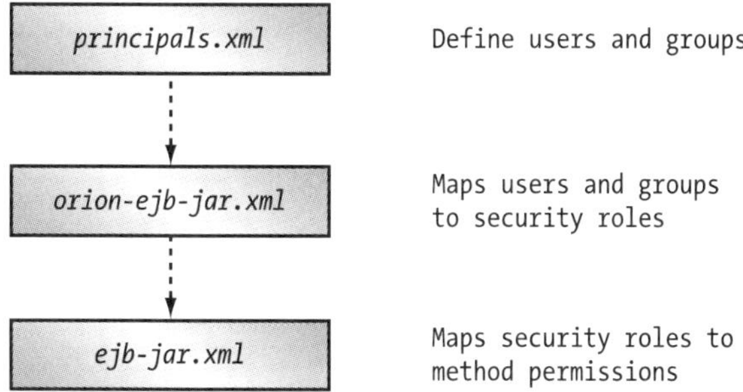

Figure 8-33. The security chain of descriptor files in the Orion Application Server

In our case, the relevant parts of the `principals.xml` descriptor (shown in Listing 8-22) defines the user `obiWan`, with the password `useTheSource`. The user `obiWan` is also defined as a member of the group `defaultApplicationUsers`. The permission privileges shown in italics grants the members of the `defaultApplicationUsers` group Remote Method Invocation (RMI) login permissions, providing access to the JNDI context, among other things.

Listing 8-22. Relevant parts of the `principals.xml` *descriptor*

```
<principals>
<groups>
    <group name="defaultApplicationUsers">
         <description>The default appliation user</description>
         <permission name="rmi:login"/>
         <permission name="com.evermind.server.rmi.RMIPermission"/>
    </group>
</groups>   </groups>
<users>
   <user password="useTheSource"username="obiWan">
      <description>A Jedi-level application user</description>
      <group-membership group="defaultApplicationUsers"/>
   </user>
</users>
```

Having defined the user and group structure we desire, the `orion-ejb-jar.xml` descriptor provides mappings between the application server security principals and the security role named `standardUserRole`. The relevant pieces of the `orion-ejb-jar.xml` file are shown in Listing 8-23.

Listing 8-23. Assembly descriptor of the custom EJB deployment descriptor for the Orion Application Server

```
<orion-ejb-jar deployment-version="1.5.2" deployment-time="e81403c711">
… EJB configuration options and JNDI bindings …
<assembly-descriptor>
   <security-role-mapping name="standardUserRole">
      <group name="defaultApplicationUsers" />
   </security-role-mapping>
</assembly-descriptor>
… other configuration options follow …
</orion-ejb-jar>
```

At last, the `ejb-jar.xml` file contains the definition of the security role `standardUserRole`, and its mapping to the method permission `palindromeServerUserPermission` granting execute privileges for all methods in the EJB with the name `se.jguru.palindromeSrv.PalindromeServer`. Note that the code in the EJB bean may refer to the security role using the security role reference (i.e., alias) `standardUser`, according to the security role reference element defined in the `<session>` description container. See Listing 8-24.

Listing 8-24. The security role mappings defined in the `ejb-jar.xml` *deployment descriptor*

```
<ejb-jar>
   <enterprise-beans>
      <session>
... deployment settings ...
         <ejb-name>se.jguru.palindromeSrv.PalindromeServer</ejb-name>
... deployment settings ...

         <security-role-ref>
            <role-name>standardUser</role-name>
            <description>
               The standard User Role of the palindromeServer
            </description>
            <role-link>standardUserRole</role-link>
         </security-role-ref>
      </session>
   </enterprise-beans>

   <assembly-descriptor>
      <security-role>
         <description>Standard Application User</description>
            <role-name>standardUserRole</role-name>
      </security-role>

      <method-permission>
         <description>palindromeServerUserPermission</description>
         <role-name>standardUserRole</role-name>
         <method>
            <ejb-name>se.jguru.palindromeSrv.PalindromeServer</ejb-name>
            <method-name>*</method-name>
         </method>
      </method-permission>
   </assembly-descriptor>
</ejb-jar>
```

This concludes the example of J2EE EJB security; the only thing remaining to be illustrated from the deployment descriptor odyssey is the transaction management system.

EJB Transaction Management Illustrated

Similar to database legacy systems, it is imperative that a method call on an EJB component not be able to set the J2EE server in an inconsistent state. J2EE servers use transactions to provide an execution environment that protects the internal state from corruption. One may think of a transaction as a bag; if the bag works correctly (that is, has no holes), all its contained items will always be transported together while being isolated from the effects of the environment around the bag. Also, a bag has a very natural scope: it is simple to understand which items are contained inside and which are not. The analog is that all Java statements contained within a transaction either all succeed or all fail while being executed within a particular transaction isolation. The J2EE components that take part in a transaction are part of its scope.

Transactions abide by the atomic, consistent, isolated, durable (ACID) paradigm. The descriptions of each term follow:

- **Atomic**: All statements of a transaction must either execute completely or not at all.

- **Consistent**: The transactional manager ensures that the system is taken from one consistent state to another. The term *commit* describes the process of writing modified data to persistent storage after all methods in a transaction have succeeded, and the term *rollback* describes the process of reverting any modified data to its original state after aborting a transaction. Regardless of whether commit or rollback was executed, all data modified by a transaction is put into its new, modified state or reverted back to the original state.

- **Isolated**: The transaction has its own memory space for local variables ensuring complete isolation from other transactions or other parts of the J2EE server. In short, data affected within a transaction will not be modified by anything but the execution thread driving the transaction.

- **Durable**: Data modified during the transaction must be written to a persistent storage. The effects of a transaction may not be transient; if the J2EE node crashes after committing the transaction, the committed state may be reread after system restart.

The J2EE application server contains a transaction management system that provides transactions compliant with the ACID specification. EJB developers may use the transaction isolation built into the EJB container by defining a `<container-transaction>` specification within the deployment descriptor, as defined in the section "The Assembly Descriptor" earlier in this chapter.

A simple <container-transaction> definition provides a point of origin for our discussion on J2EE transactions. The value of the following bold element <trans-attribute> defines how the transaction should be implemented within the stub/skeleton classes:

```
<container-transaction>
   <description>Standard transaction isolation</description>
   <method>
      <ejb-name>LocalTorsionModel</ejb-name>
      <method-name>*</method-name>
   </method>
   <trans-attribute>Required</trans-attribute>
</container-transaction>
```

Transactions are extremely important in ensuring consistency in a system using multiple legacy data sources or other means of persistent storage. For example, an EJB that modifies data in two data sources, as shown in Figure 8-34, must rely on the support of the J2EE application server system. Otherwise, the state of the system could become corrupt if the execution fails after modifying data in the first data source but failing to make the corresponding alterations to the data in the second data source.

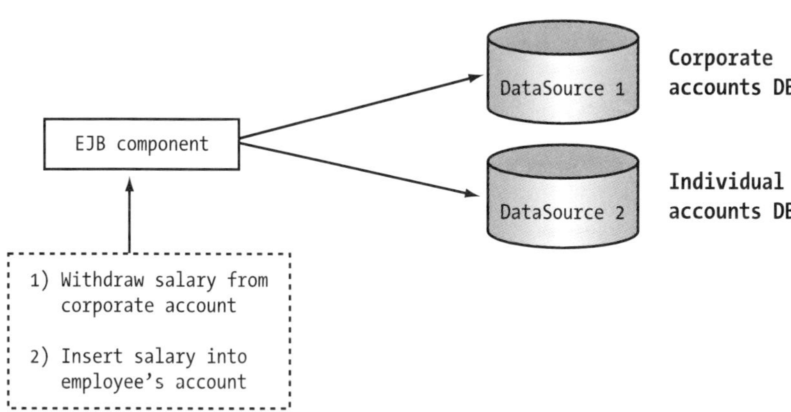

Figure 8-34. The task and structure employed by a particular EJB component, talking to two separate databases storing different bank account types

Consider the disastrous result when the EJB server crashes after deducting money from the corporate account but before adding the corresponding amount in the employee's account. If you are unlucky enough, your whole skiing vacation may have to be canceled due to an unexpected shortage of funds. Transactions are important to increase the reliability of enterprise systems, and EJB components are no exception.

If the transaction is started by the client or programmatically inside the EJB component, the transaction object implements `javax.transaction.UserTransaction`. Although small, the `UserTransaction` interface contains all methods relevant to start, end, and query the state of a transaction, as shown in Figure 8-35.

interface *javax.transaction.UserTransaction*
+begin():void
+commit():void
+getStatus():int
+rollback():void
+setRollbackOnly():void
+setTransactionTimeout(:int):void

Figure 8-35. UML diagram of the `UserTransaction` *interface. Note the* `begin()`, `commit()`, *and* `rollback()` *methods that mark the boundaries of a transaction.*

The skeleton code of a `UserTransaction` is simple, as shown in Listing 8-25.

Listing 8-25. Skeleton code showing how to use a `UserTransaction`

```
UserTransaction trans = myContext.getUserTransaction();
try
{
   // Start the Transaction
   trans.begin();

   ... call all methods which should be part of the transaction ...

   // All went well?
   trans.commit();
}
catch(Exception ex)
{
   // Something went wrong
   trans.rollback();
}
```

Start the `UserTransaction` by invoking the begin method, and end it by either committing or rolling back its effects. If you require more fine-grained control over transactional boundaries than a method, you must create your own transactions according to the formula above. This is known as *client-managed demarcation*, and should generally be avoided, because it prevents the EJB deployer from being able to control the transaction management of the EJB component. The opposite of client-managed demarcations is *container-managed demarcation*, in which the transactional management code is created by the EJB compiler and inserted into the stub and skeleton classes.

> **NOTE** *If you have configured your EJB component to use container-managed demarcation, it is illegal to create a* `UserTransaction` *and call methods in the* `UserTransaction` *interface.*

An EJB component that uses container-managed transaction demarcation may react in six different ways to method calls. These six ways correspond to the six permitted `<trans-attribute>` values provided in the `ejb-jar.xml` deployment descriptor. The text and illustrations in the following section show the effects of container-managed transaction demarcation.

Attribute Types for Container-Managed Transaction Demarcation

The scope of a J2EE transaction denotes all the components that take part in the transaction. The EJB container may manage in six different ways a transaction whose scope consists of at least two components: the client and the EJB component. In this context, *client* may refer to an EJB application client, a component deployed in the Web container (such as a servlet or an JavaBean proxy), or another EJB component.

Each transaction-handling mode is identified by a unique `<trans-attribute>` value, illustrated with descriptions and images. For all images, clients and EJBs having a transactional context are illustrated with solid borders, whereas dashed borders indicate no transactional context. The EJB container relays the method calls, but it is irrelevant with respect to the transactional contexts of the client or EJB.

Never

If the calling client has a transactional context, the EJB component throws a `java.rmi.RemoteException` (if the client was remote) or a `javax.ejb.EJBException` (if the client was local). The transactional context of the EJB component while executing the method in the EJB component is undefined. The effects of the Never `<trans-attribute>` are shown in Figure 8-36.

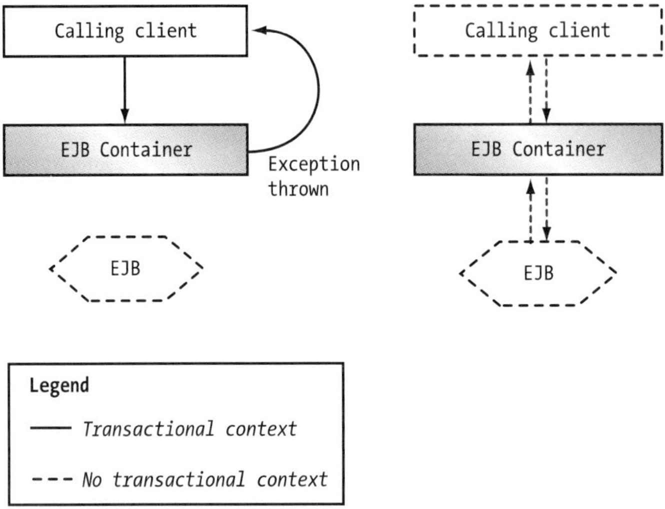

Figure 8-36. The effects of the Never transactional attribute

Mandatory

If the calling client does not have a transactional context, the EJB component throws a `javax.transaction.TransactionRequiredException` (if the client was remote) or a `javax.ejb.TransactionRequiredLocalException` (if the client was local). The effects of the Mandatory `<trans-attribute>` are shown in Figure 8-37.

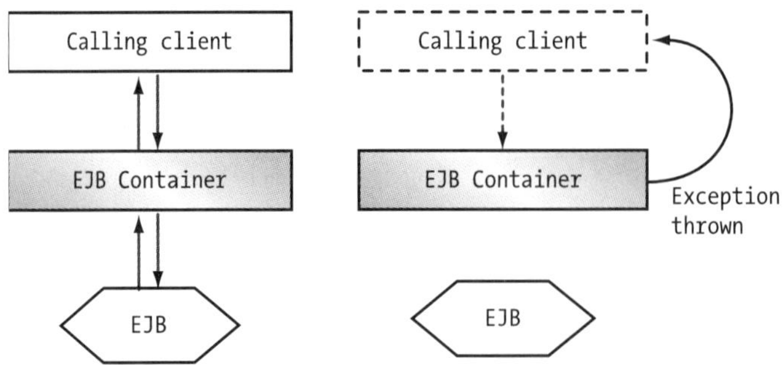

Figure 8-37. The effects of the Mandatory transactional attribute

NotSupported

If the calling client has a transactional context, the EJB component temporarily suspends it while executing the method. The transactional context is not passed to any internal `ResourceManagers` during its execution. The effects of the NotSupported `<trans-attribute>` are shown in Figure 8-38.

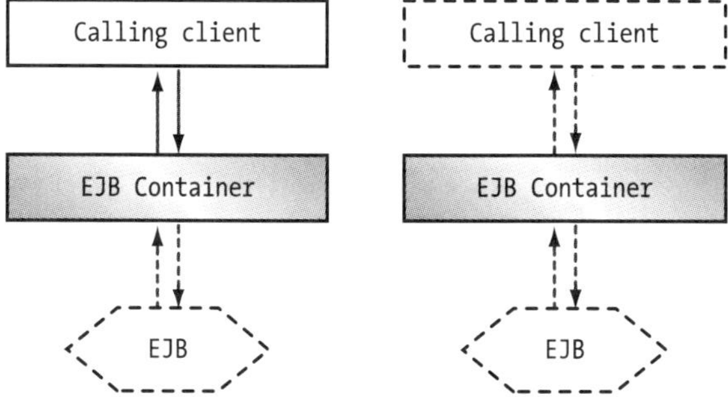

Figure 8-38. The effects of the NotSupported transactional attribute

Required

If the calling client has no transactional context, the EJB container creates one and passes it to the EJB component while executing the method. All resource managers used within the method are enlisted into the transactional context by the container. Should the client have a transactional context, it is used by the EJB component during the method execution. The effects of the Required `<trans-attribute>` are shown in Figure 8-39.

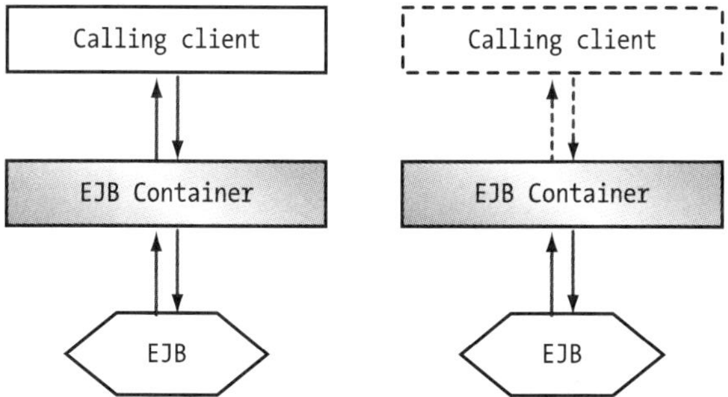

Figure 8-39. The effects of the Required transactional attribute. Note that the EJB component uses the client's transactional context if it exists.

Supports

If the calling client has a transactional context, it is used by the EJB container in the same way as the Required case. If the calling client has no transactional context, the EJB container does not create or use one—in the same manner as the NotSupported case. The effects of the Required `<trans-attribute>` are shown in Figure 8-40.

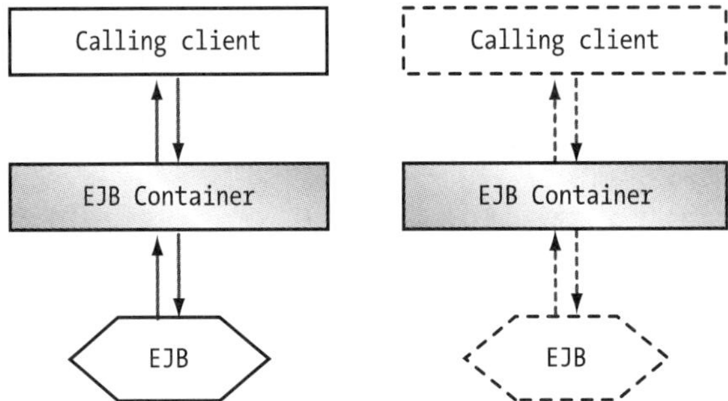

Figure 8-40. The effects of the Supports transactional attribute. Note that the EJB component uses the client's transactional context if it exists.

RequiresNew

The EJB container creates a new transactional context for the EJB component whether or not the calling client has one. Note that this case differs from the Required case, as the EJB component does not use the transactional context of the calling client in any case. The effects of the Required `<trans-attribute>` are shown in Figure 8-41.

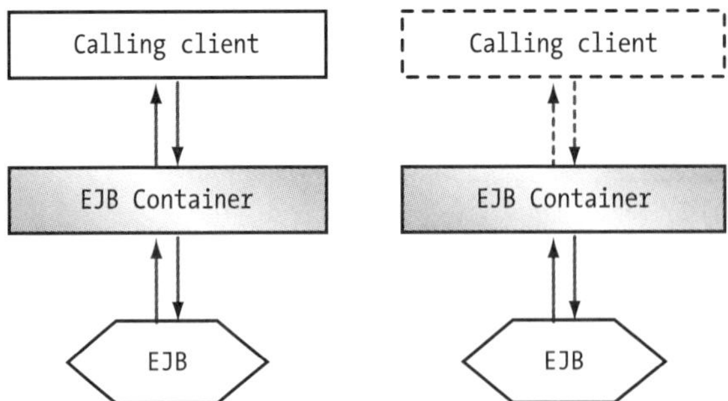

Figure 8-41. The effects of the RequiresNew transactional attribute. Note that the EJB component does not use the client's transactional context. A new transactional context is always created within the container to manage the execution of the EJB methods.

Touring the javax.ejb Package

Most relevant classes used in developing EJB components are found in the `javax.ejb` package. As may be seen from a quick look at the package, all types having to do with EJB component definitions (disregarding the exception types) are interfaces. The interfaces found there are rarely usable outside an application server because most of them require the support of the application server's underlying implementation to return sensible results. The results from calling methods in classes of the `javax.ejb` package may therefore vary a great deal depending on the application server implementation.

Figure 8-42 shows the result of running an application client displaying the result of all nondeprecated methods in the `javax.ejb` package for a stateless session EJB component. The values shown in the right column are converted to strings using the object's own `toString()` method.

> **NOTE** *This section illustrates the classes or interfaces used to produce the result, as well as the other types in the* `javax.ejb` *package relevant to session or Entity EJB components. Therefore, this section will not cover the* `MessageDrivenBean` *and* `MessageDrivenContext` *interfaces.*

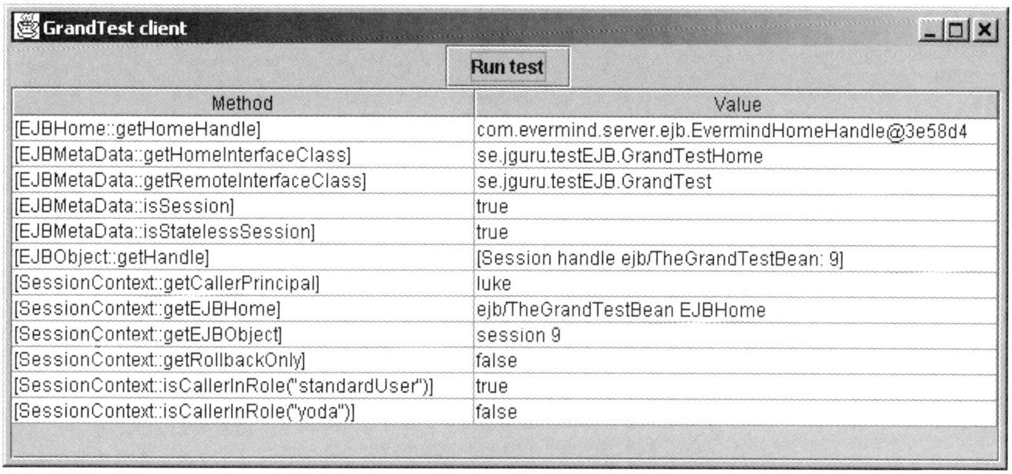

GrandTest client

Run test

Method	Value
[EJBHome::getHomeHandle]	com.evermind.server.ejb.EvermindHomeHandle@3e58d4
[EJBMetaData::getHomeInterfaceClass]	se.jguru.testEJB.GrandTestHome
[EJBMetaData::getRemoteInterfaceClass]	se.jguru.testEJB.GrandTest
[EJBMetaData::isSession]	true
[EJBMetaData::isStatelessSession]	true
[EJBObject::getHandle]	[Session handle ejb/TheGrandTestBean: 9]
[SessionContext::getCallerPrincipal]	luke
[SessionContext::getEJBHome]	ejb/TheGrandTestBean EJBHome
[SessionContext::getEJBObject]	session 9
[SessionContext::getRollbackOnly]	false
[SessionContext::isCallerInRole("standardUser")]	true
[SessionContext::isCallerInRole("yoda")]	false

Figure 8-42. The result of the GrandTest application client shows the class and method name in the left column and values returned from the methods in the right column.

The nonexception classes and interfaces of the `javax.ejb` package fall in one of three categories:

- Interfaces that contain EJB metadata or application server information. These include `EJBContext`, `SessionContext`, `EntityContext`, and `EJBMetaData`.
- Interfaces that define EJB system services (some of these interfaces must be implemented by the EJB component). These include `EJBHome`, `EJBObject`, `EJBLocalHome`, `EJBLocalObject`, `EnterpriseBean`, `EntityBean`, `SessionBean`, `Handle`, and `HomeHandle`.
- EJB service definition interfaces (implemented by the application server and useable by EJB components). These include `EntityContext`, `SessionContext`, and `SessionSynchronization`.

The EJB metadata classes are few and well designed, where each class encapsulates specific information about the EJB component or its context. The main task of these classes is to serve as a reference point wherein all EJB objects may get a reference to their Home or Remote instances, as well as a serializable handler that is frequently used for serialization or passivation.

The system classes contain the life-cycle method definitions of all types of EJB components. The life-cycle definitions are implemented in the bean class, which indicates its EJB type (`EntityBean` or `SessionBean`) according to its implemented interface. As the Home and Remote types are interfaces, they extend their supertypes, `EJBHome` and `EJBObject`. The corresponding local interfaces behave identically; the Home interface of a local EJB component extends the `EJBLocalHome` interface, whereas the Local interface extends `EJBLocalObject`.

The EJBContext Interface

The `EJBContext` is the supertype of all specialized context interfaces, and it is the communications link from the EJB component to the `EJBContainer`. Shown in the UML diagram in Figure 8-43, it is a small class whose methods have undergone a slight transformation from the original EJB 1.0 version. As a result, three methods have been declared deprecated: the `getCallerIdentity()` and `isCallerInRole(Identity)` have been replaced with the `getCallerPrincipal()` and `isCallerInRole(Principal)` methods, and the use of `getEnvironment()` has been deprecated, as we use the JNDI API to query and modify the environment of an EJB component.

All methods of the `EJBContext` interface are callable within the Bean implementation class, and fall in one of the three following categories:

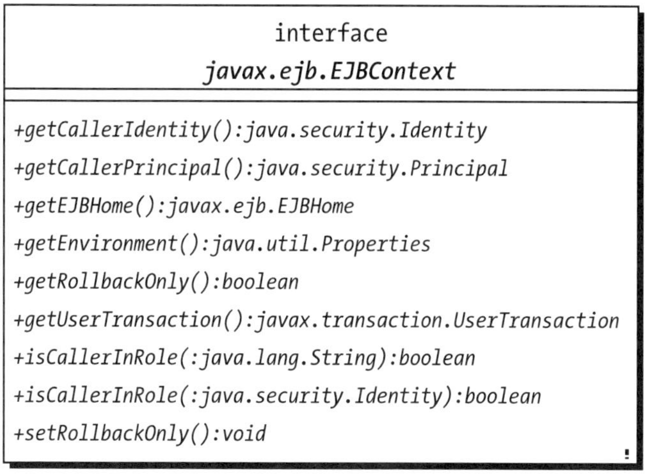

```
interface
javax.ejb.EJBContext
------------------------------------------------------------
+getCallerIdentity():java.security.Identity
+getCallerPrincipal():java.security.Principal
+getEJBHome():javax.ejb.EJBHome
+getEnvironment():java.util.Properties
+getRollbackOnly():boolean
+getUserTransaction():javax.transaction.UserTransaction
+isCallerInRole(:java.lang.String):boolean
+isCallerInRole(:java.security.Identity):boolean
+setRollbackOnly():void
```

Figure 8-43. The `EJBContext` *interface. Note that methods* `getCallerIdentity()`, `getEnvironment()`, *and* `isCallerInRole(Identity)` *are deprecated.*

- The `getCallerPrincipal` and `isCallerInRole` methods retrieve or verify the caller's security principal (translatable to a user ID if the user has logged in to the J2EE security system).

- The `getEJBHome` method returns a reference to the home skeleton of the EJB component, or throws an `IllegalStateException` if the EJB does not have a remote home.

- The `getUserTransaction`, `getRollbackOnly`, and `setRollbackOnly` methods retrieve a `UserTransaction` or information about it from the EJB container. Only session beans with bean-managed transaction demarcation are permitted to call the `getUserTransaction` method; otherwise; it throws an `IllegalStateException`. For similar reasons, only EJB components using container-managed transactions may recommend the container to rollback the transaction by calling the `setRollbackOnly` method.

The other methods of the `EJBContext` interface (`getCallerIdentity`, `isCallerInRole(Identity)`, and `getEnvironment`) are deprecated and should not be used.

The SessionContext Interface

The SessionContext is the abstract type of the reference to the EJBContainer from a session EJB component. As illustrated in its UML diagram in Figure 8-44, the functionality added to that of its superinterface EJBContext is small; a session EJB component may access its Remote EJBObject via its SessionContext.

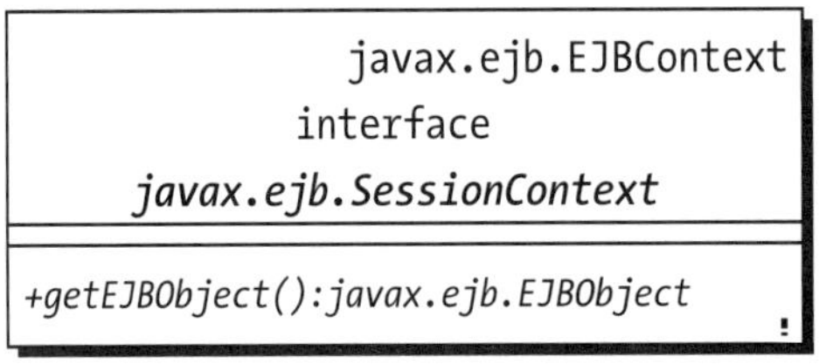

javax.ejb.EJBContext
interface
javax.ejb.SessionContext

+getEJBObject():javax.ejb.EJBObject

Figure 8-44. The SessionContext *interface*

The combined functionality of the methods defined in the SessionContext and EJBContext interfaces is investigated in Listing 8-26, where the getEJBContextData method finds all data that can be dug out of the SessionContext of the surrounding EJB component. The results are stored in a map that is returned to the application client and presented in the form of a JTable. The resulting output is shown in Listing 8-26.

Listing 8-26. The getEJBContextData() *method*

```
public Map getEJBContextData(boolean expandHomeAndEjbObject)
{
    // Buffer all data in the Vector for
    // simple delivery to the client.
    TreeMap map = new TreeMap();

    // Get the data from the Context
    this.append(map, "SessionContext", "getCallerPrincipal",
            this.ctx.getCallerPrincipal().getName());
    this.append(map, "SessionContext", "getRollbackOnly", "" +
            ctx.getRollbackOnly());

    // Get the EJBHome
    EJBHome homeSkeleton = this.ctx.getEJBHome();
    this.append(map, "SessionContext", "getEJBHome", homeSkeleton);
    if(expandHomeAndEjbObject) this.expandEjbHome(map, homeSkeleton);
```

```
    // Get the EJBObject
    EJBObject remoteSkeleton = this.ctx.getEJBObject();
    this.append(map, "SessionContext", "getEJBObject", remoteSkeleton);
    if(expandHomeAndEjbObject) this.expandEjbObject(map, remoteSkeleton);

    // Check authority
    boolean stdUser = this.ctx.isCallerInRole("standardUser");
    boolean yoda = this.ctx.isCallerInRole("yoda");
    this.append(map, "SessionContext", "isCallerInRole(\"standardUser\")", "" +
            stdUser);
    this.append(map, "SessionContext", "isCallerInRole(\"yoda\")", "" + yoda);

    return map;
}
```

The small `append()` helper method (shown in the following code snippet) simply concatenates the data into a string, and puts a new entry into the provided map using the class and package for key and the resulting output of the method call for value.

```
private void append(Map map, String theClass, String theMethod,
                    Object methodCallResult)
{
    map.put("[" + theClass + "::" + theMethod + "]", "" + methodCallResult);
}
```

CAUTION *The specific format of the values bound in the* `EJBContext` *have internal structures that are individual for a particular J2EE application server. You cannot rely on what has been found in the* `SessionContext` *of an EJB deployed in one application server to be usable in the* `SessionContext` *of another J2EE application server.*

The EntityContext Interface

The `EntityContext` is the abstract type of the reference to the `EJBContainer` from an Entity EJB component. As illustrated in its UML diagram in Figure 8-45, the functionality added to that of its superinterface `EJBContext` is slender; an Entity EJB component may access its remote `EJBObject` and its primary key instance via the `EntityContext`.

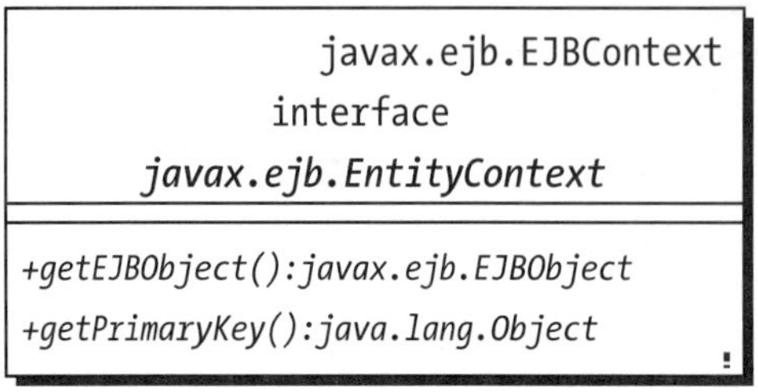

```
                javax.ejb.EJBContext
           interface
    javax.ejb.EntityContext
---------------------------------------
+getEJBObject():javax.ejb.EJBObject
+getPrimaryKey():java.lang.Object
```

Figure 8-45. The `EntityContext` *interface*

Most of the methods of the `EJBContext` interface are inherited by the `EntityContext`, so the code snippet from the earlier section "The SessionContext Interface" could easily be modified to run within an Entity EJB component. Also, the application client producing the output shown in Figure 8-42 will just as easily visualize the properties of an `EntityContext` as those of the `SessionContext`.

The actual implementation of an Entity EJB component that exposes its context properties is therefore left to the code-hungry reader.

The EJBHome Interface

The `EJBHome` is the supertype of all remote home interfaces of the EJB component. As illustrated in the UML diagram of Figure 8-46, the `EJBHome` interface is very small; apart from the remove life-cycle methods, the only two methods available retrieve metadata about the EJB component and a `HomeHandle` that can be used to serialize a reference to the Home interface.

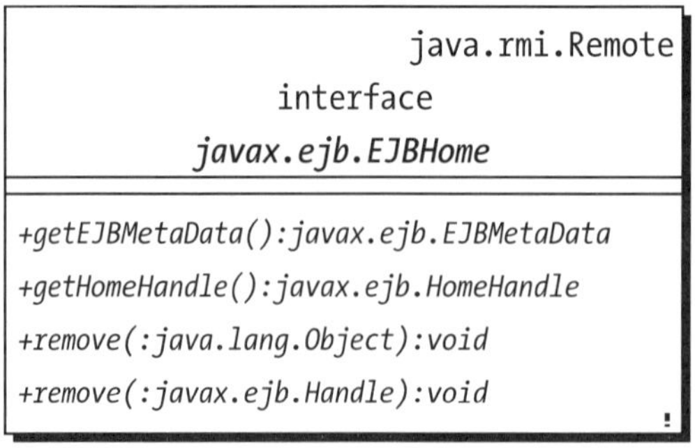

```
                  java.rmi.Remote
           interface
    javax.ejb.EJBHome
---------------------------------------
+getEJBMetaData():javax.ejb.EJBMetaData
+getHomeHandle():javax.ejb.HomeHandle
+remove(:java.lang.Object):void
+remove(:javax.ejb.Handle):void
```

Figure 8-46. The `EJBHome` *interface*

Although one frequently uses the `remove` methods to erase the state of a particular EJB component from the server, the most frequently used methods in the `EJBHome` subclass are the `create` and `find` methods.

The EJBLocalHome Interface

The `EJBHome` is the supertype of all local home interfaces of the EJB component. As illustrated in the UML diagram in Figure 8-47, the `EJBHome` interface is smaller and simpler than its remote sibling.

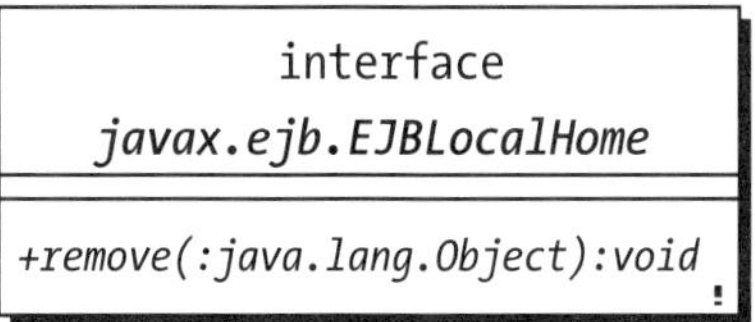

Figure 8-47. The `EJBLocalHome` *interface*

More importantly, the `EJBLocalHome` interface does not extend `java.rmi.Remote`, so it cannot be used remotely and hence is not required to throw `RemoteExceptions` for all its methods. Therefore, the usage of the `EJBLocalHome` is much simpler from a client perspective. Compare it to the following code for invoking the remove method in a remote home:

```
try {
   theEJBHome.remove(anEJB);
}
catch(Exception ex) {
   // Handle the exception...
}
```

with the code of the corresponding LocalHome:

```
theEjbLocalHome.remove(anEJB);
```

Therefore, one should use the LocalHome/Local instead of the Home/Remote when possible.

The EJBLocalObject Interface

The `EJBObject` is the supertype of all local interfaces of the EJB component. As illustrated in the UML diagram in Figure 8-48, the `EJBHome` interface is smaller and simpler than its remote sibling, `EJBObject`.

interface *javax.ejb.EJBLocalObject*
+getEJBLocalHome():javax.ejb.EJBLocalHome *+getPrimaryKey():java.lang.Object* *+remove():void* *+isIdentical(:javax.ejb.EJBLocalObject):boolean*

Figure 8-48. The `EJBLocalHome` *interface*

The `EJBLocalObject` does not extend `java.rmi.Remote`, so the methods exposed by an `EJBLocalObject` cannot be executed from a remote position. In fact, the J2EE application server cannot generate stub and skeleton classes for the `EJBLocalObject` without a Remote instance source. `EJBLocalObjects` are therefore much simpler to use than `EJBObjects`; compare it to the following `EJBLocalObject` code call:

```
anEJB.aLocalMethod();
```

with the code for calling a method in an EJBObject:

```
try
{
   anEjb.aRemoteMethod();
}
catch(RemoteException ex)
{
   // Handle the exception here ...
}
```

From an EJB client's perspective, it is quite convenient and efficient to use `EJBLocalObject` instead of `EJBObject` when possible.

The EnterpriseBean Interface

The `EnterpriseBean` is the supertype of all interfaces that should be implemented by the EJB implementation class (`EntityBean`, `MessageDrivenBean`, and `SessionBean`). The `EnterpriseBean` interface is simply a placeholder without any functionality of its own, as illustrated in the UML diagram in Figure 8-49.

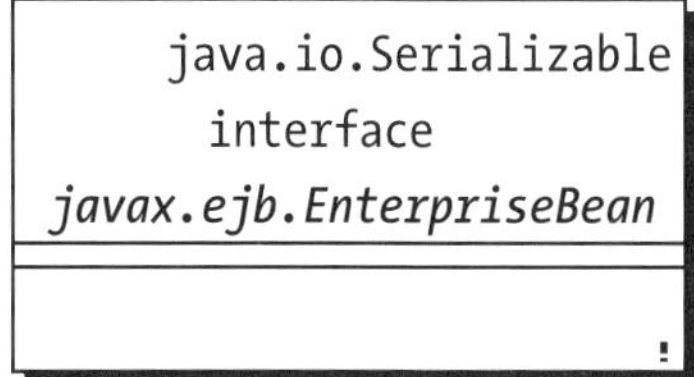

Figure 8-49. The `EnterpriseBean` *interface*

The fact that the EJB Bean implementation class implements—but does not extend—its EJB type specifier is important. As a consequence, your EJB may extend any custom superclass containing functionality common to all EJBs in your application.

> **NOTE** *An example of this code style is provided in the "Refactor2" example of Chapter 11, in which unified logging is provided to all EJB components in the small system through the extension of a common* `EJBRoot` *superclass.*

The SessionBean Interface

The `SessionBean` interface must be implemented by the Bean implementation class of a session EJB component. As illustrated in the UML diagram of Figure 8-50, all life-cycle methods except `create` and `remove` are defined in the `SessionBean` interface.

The skeleton of a `SessionBean` is simple indeed, but it is important to realize which methods in the `SessionBean` interface are used by stateless and which are used only by stateful session EJB components. The comments in the `EmptySkeletonBean` class, shown in Listing 8-27, illustrate which methods are used by the two session EJB variants.

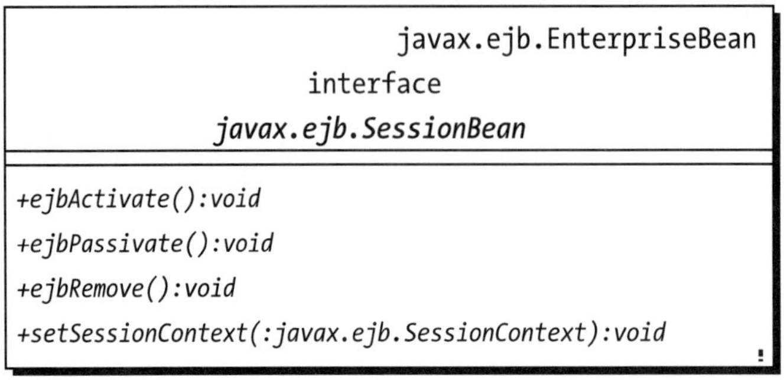

```
javax.ejb.EnterpriseBean
interface
javax.ejb.SessionBean
---
+ejbActivate():void
+ejbPassivate():void
+ejbRemove():void
+setSessionContext(:javax.ejb.SessionContext):void
```

Figure 8-50. The `SessionBean` *interface*

Listing 8-27. The `EmptySkeletonBean` *class*

```
import javax.ejb.*;
public class EmptySkeletonBean implements SessionBean
{
    //
    // Members required by the SessionBean interface;
    // used by all types of SessionBeans.
    //
    protected SessionContext ctx;
    public void setSessionContext(SessionContext context) {
        ctx = context; }

    //
    // Methods required by the SessionBean interface, but only
    // used by Stateful SessionBeans.
    //
    public void ejbActivate() { }
    public void ejbPassivate() { }

    //
    // Methods required by the EJBHome interface
    //
    public void ejbRemove() { }
    public void ejbCreate() throws CreateException { }
}
```

All methods of the `SessionContext` interface are callable within the Bean implementation class, and fall in one of the three following categories.

- The `setSessionContext` method must assign its argument to the internal reference to the `SessionContext` in the EJB. The method is invoked by the EJB container immediately after it has created the EJB instance, so the `SessionContext` variable is always set when other methods in the session EJB lifecycle are called.

- The `ejbActivate` and `ejbPassivate` methods are called by the EJB container following the serialization of the EJB bean instance. Alas, when the J2EE application server runs short of memory and needs to free up resources, the `ejbPassivate` method is called to perform any custom actions before the entire state of the EJB component is serialized. In a similar way, the `ejbActivate` method is called immediately after the bean state has been retrieved from its serialized form by the J2EE application server.

- The `ejbRemove` method mirrors any `remove` methods defined in the Home interface of the EJB component. In this method, you should remove any nonpersistable resources held by the `SessionBean`.

Examples of full `SessionBean` implementations are provided earlier in this chapter as well as Chapter 9.

The EntityBean Interface

The `EntityBean` interface must be implemented by the Bean implementation class of an Entity EJB component. As illustrated in the UML diagram in Figure 8-51, all life-cycle methods except `create` and `remove` are defined in the `EntityBean` interface.

The EJB life-cycle methods defined in the `EntityBean` interface are callback methods that are invoked by the EJB container before (and, sometimes after) a state transition. All methods are provided in pairs—although, of course, the `create` methods are defined in the `EJBHome` interface.

All methods of the `EJBContext` interface are callable within the Bean implementation class, and fall in one of the three following categories.

- The `setEntityContext` and `unsetEntityContext` methods must retrieve or erase the internal reference to the `EntityContext` of the entity bean. The `setEntityContext` method is invoked by the EJB container immediately after creation, so you can be certain that the `EntityContext` variable is set when all other methods in the Entity EJB life cycle are called. The `unsetEntityContext` is consequently called immediately before the J2EE application server sends the EJB implementation class to garbage collection.

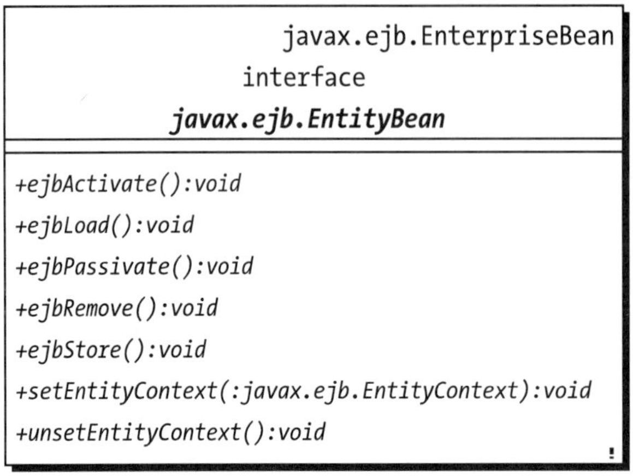

javax.ejb.EnterpriseBean
interface
javax.ejb.EntityBean

+ejbActivate():void
+ejbLoad():void
+ejbPassivate():void
+ejbRemove():void
+ejbStore():void
+setEntityContext(:javax.ejb.EntityContext):void
+unsetEntityContext():void

Figure 8-51. The `EntityBean` *interface*

- The `ejbActivate` and `ejbPassivate` methods are called by the EJB container following the serialization of the EJB bean instance. Alas, when the J2EE application server runs short of memory and needs to free up resources, the `ejbPassivate` method is called to perform any custom actions before the entire state of the EJB component is serialized. In a similar way, the `ejbActivate` method is called immediately after the bean state has been retrieved from its serialized form by the J2EE application server. Although the entity bean maintains a communication channel with a data source, the form of persistence for passivation is entirely defined by the application server and needs not involve the data source at all.

- The `ejbLoad` and `ejbStore` methods are called by the EJB container after loading data from—and before storing data to—the data source with which it communicates. If the `EntityBean` uses bean-managed persistence (BMP), the `ejbStore` and `ejbLoad` methods must perform the actual storage of its state within the data source. If the `EntityBean` uses container-managed persistence (CMP), the `ejbLoad` and `ejbStore` methods are merely used to perform any custom data type configurations required by the bean, as the EJB container performs the actual storing and loading of the EJB state.

Examples of both BMP and CMP entity beans are provided in Chapter 10 and 11.

The EJBMetaData Interface

The `EJBMetaData` interface contains type information for the EJB component, provided by the EJB container. As shown in the UML diagram of Figure 8-52, the `EJBMetaData` interface contains a lot of getter methods.

```
interface
javax.ejb.EJBMetaData

+getEJBHome():javax.ejb.EJBHome
+getHomeInterfaceClass():java.lang.Class
+getPrimaryKeyClass():java.lang.Class
+getRemoteInterfaceClass():java.lang.Class
+isSession():boolean
+isStatelessSession():boolean
```

Figure 8-52. The `EJBMetaData` *interface*

The results of calling the four methods usable by a stateless session EJB in the `EJBMetaData` interface (that is, `getHomeInterfaceClass()`, `getRemoteInterfaceClass()`, `isSession()`, and `isStatelessSession()`) are shown in Figure 8-53. (Figure 8-53 illustrates the part of Figure 8-42 that is relevant for the `EJBMetaData` class.)

Method	Value
[EJBHome::getHomeHandle]	com.evermind.server.ejb.EvermindHomeHandle@3e58d4
[EJBMetaData::getHomeInterfaceClass]	se.jguru.testEJB.GrandTestHome
[EJBMetaData::getRemoteInterfaceClass]	se.jguru.testEJB.GrandTest
[EJBMetaData::isSession]	true
[EJBMetaData::isStatelessSession]	true

Figure 8-53. Resulting output of the map populated by the `expandEjbHome` *method*

The code that extracts the information from the `EJBMetaData` is shown in Listing 8-28. The `EJBMetaData` invocations appear in bold text.

Listing 8-28. The `expandEjbHome()` *method*

```
private void expandEjbHome(Map map, EJBHome homeSkeleton)
{
    try
    {
        // Get the EJBMetaData from the homeSkeleton
        EJBMetaData ejbmd = homeSkeleton.getEJBMetaData();
        String clazz = "EJBMetaData";
        Class homeInterfaceClass = ejbmd.getHomeInterfaceClass();
        Class remoteInterfaceClass = ejbmd.getRemoteInterfaceClass();
        boolean sessionBean = ejbmd.isSession();
        boolean statelessSessionBean = ejbmd.isStatelessSession();

        this.append(map, clazz, "getHomeInterfaceClass",
                    homeInterfaceClass.getName());
        this.append(map, clazz, "getRemoteInterfaceClass",
                    remoteInterfaceClass.getName());
        this.append(map, clazz, "isSession", "" + sessionBean);
        this.append(map, clazz, "isStatelessSession",
                    "" + statelessSessionBean);

        // Get the next aspect of the EJBHome object
        clazz = "EJBHome";
        HomeHandle homeHandle = homeSkeleton.getHomeHandle();
        this.append(map, clazz, "getHomeHandle", "" + homeHandle);
    }
    catch(Exception ex)
    {
        map.put("[GrandTestBean::expandEjbHome]", "Caught exception: "  + ex);
    }
}
```

The `append` method simply formats the class and method names into a string that is used as the key in the `Map.Entry`, where the value is the method result, as shown here:

```
private void append(Map map, String theClass,
                    String theMethod, Object methodCallResult)
{
    map.put("[" + theClass + "::" + theMethod + "]", "" + methodCallResult);
}
```

EJBMetaData provides a quick way to find type information of all classes and interfaces in your EJB component, but you cannot use this information properly to serialize and store an EJBObject for deserialization and consequent use later on. This requires the use of a handle.

The Handle Interface

According to the J2EE JavaDoc, the Handle interface provides an "abstraction of a network reference to an EJB object." In plain English, this means that you may serialize a handle of an EJBObject for later deserialization and use. A handle is a persistent and robust reference to an EJB object. Its API interface is indeed minimal, as illustrated in the UML diagram shown in Figure 8-54.

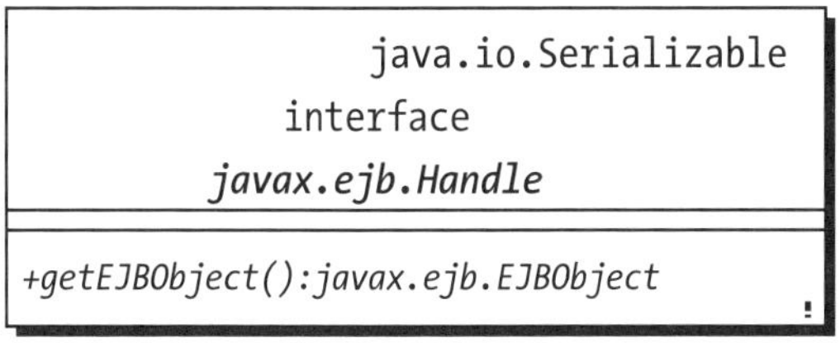

```
java.io.Serializable
interface
javax.ejb.Handle
---
+getEJBObject():javax.ejb.EJBObject
```

Figure 8-54. The Handle *interface*

CAUTION *A handle contains a serialized version of a reference to a particular* EJBObject. *The handle structure is highly customized to a particular application server—you cannot use a serialized handle to awaken an* EJBObject *in any other application server (let alone another type of application server!) than the one that created the handle.*

Using the handle of an EJB is simple; the small code snippet in Listing 8-29 (taken from the EJB application client shown in Figure 8-42) writes all serializable values from the map returned to files with the same name as the methods that generated them.

Listing 8-29. The code serializing/saving all serializable objects to files

```
// Loop over the returned map; insert new rows in the table model
for(Iterator it = map.keySet().iterator(); it.hasNext(); )
{
   // Get the next key/value pair
   Object key = it.next();
   Object value = map.get(key);

   // Write any serializable instances to files
   if(value instanceof Serializable)
   {
      // Strip to a sensible file name
      String daKey = (String) key;
      int startIndex = daKey.lastIndexOf(":") + 1;
      this.writeToFile(daKey.substring(startIndex, daKey.length() - 1),
             (Serializable) value);
   }
   ...
```

Of course, the actual writing is performed in the helper method `writeToFile()`. Its code is small and straightforward:

```
protected void writeToFile(String fileName, Serializable ser)
{
    try
    {
        // Get the filename
        File target = new File(fileName);

        // Write the serializable
        ObjectOutputStream oos =
           new ObjectOutputStream(new FileOutputStream(target));
        oos.writeObject(ser);
        oos.flush();
        oos.close();

    }
    catch(Exception ex)
    {
        this.log("Could not write to file: " + ex);
    }
}
```

The following content of the file `getHandle`, which contains the `Handle` instance after serialization, is small and, as noted in the preceding caution, highly specialized for a particular EJB container.

```
¬í__t_([Session handle ejb/TheGrandTestBean: 2]
```

If viewed in an octal display tool, the binary text at the start of the file is exposed with somewhat better clarity; each combination of two lines in the following short listing shows each character in octal as well as ASCII mode.

```
$ od -a -b applications/EjbApp/GrandTestClientArchive/getHandle
0000000   ,   m nul enq   t nul   (   [   S   e   s   s   i   o   n  sp
        254 355 000 005 164 000 050 133 123 145 163 163 151 157 156 040
0000020   h   a   n   d   l   e  sp   e   j   b   /   T   h   e   G   r
        150 141 156 144 154 145 040 145 152 142 057 124 150 145 107 162
0000040   a   n   d   T   e   s   t   B   e   a   n   :  sp   2   ]
        141 156 144 124 145 163 164 102 145 141 156 072 040 062 135
0000057
```

Of course, not only the `EJBObject` may be referenced through its handle. The `EJBHome` instance has a corresponding `HomeHandle`.

The HomeHandle Interface

The `HomeHandle` interface is for the `EJBHome` what the `Handle` is for the `EJBObject`: a persistent and robust reference to an EJBHome. As with the `Handle` interface, the API of the `HomeHandle` interface is minimal, as illustrated in the UML diagram of Figure 8-55.

```
                java.io.Serializable
           interface
      javax.ejb.HomeHandle
-----------------------------------
+getEJBHome():javax.ejb.EJBHome
```

Figure 8-55. The `HomeHandle` *interface*

> **CAUTION** *A* HomeHandle *contains a serialized version of a reference to a particular* EJBHome. *The* HomeHandle *structure is highly customized to a particular application server—you cannot use a serialized* HomeHandle *to reestablish the connection to an* EJBHome *in any other application server (let alone other type of application server!) than the one that created the* HomeHandle.

Using the code provided in the "The Handle Interface" section, a HomeHandle may be serialized. We end up with a file called getHomeHandle (which is the method name used to obtain it) having the following content:

```
¬í__t_1com.evermind.server.ejb.EvermindHomeHandle@409554
```

Running the OD display tool on the getHomeHandle file, we obtain the following octal dump of the getHomeHandle file:

```
$ od -a -b applications/EjbApp/GrandTestClientArchive/getHomeHandle
0000000   ,   m nul enq   t nul   1   c   o   m   .   e   v   e   r   m
        254 355 000 005 164 000 061 143 157 155 056 145 166 145 162 155
0000020   i   n   d   .   s   e   r   v   e   r   .   e   j   b   .   E
        151 156 144 056 163 145 162 166 145 162 056 145 152 142 056 105
0000040   v   e   r   m   i   n   d   H   o   m   e   H   a   n   d   l
        166 145 162 155 151 156 144 110 157 155 145 110 141 156 144 154
0000060   e   @   4   0   9   5   5   4
        145 100 064 060 071 065 065 064
0000070
```

One thing worth noticing about the serialized home handle is that it—for this particular application server—contains a hashcode obtained from the getHashCode() method of the java.lang.Object class. This implies that the HomeHandle is not valid outside the JVM instance where it was created.

The SessionSynchronization Interface

The SessionSynchronization interface is implemented by a stateful session EJB component that should be informed when a transaction starts or ends. The API of the SessionSynchronization interface, shown in Figure 8-56, implies that all parts of a transaction demarcation may be monitored.

```
interface
javax.ejb.SessionSynchronization
+afterBegin():void
+afterCompletion(:boolean):void
+beforeCompletion():void
```

Figure 8-56. The `SessionSynchronization` *interface*

The three methods of the `SessionSynchronization` interface have the following function:

- The `afterBegin` method is invoked by the EJB container immediately after the transaction is started. All statements in the `afterBegin` method therefore execute within transactional context; it is an ideal place to populate internal members with data read from a data source or equivalent.

- The `beforeCompletion` method is invoked by the EJB container immediately before committing the transaction. All statements in the `beforeCompletion` method therefore execute within the transactional context. The `beforeCompletion` method is ideal for saving any modified internal state variables back to the data source from which they were read in the `afterBegin` method. Note that this method will not get called if the transaction is rolled back.

- The `afterCompletion` method is invoked by the EJB container immediately after committing or rolling back the transaction. The argument to the `afterCompletion` method is true if the transaction was committed and false if the transaction was rolled back. The `afterCompletion` method executes completely outside of transactional context.

Although a session EJB component is not required to implement the `SessionSynchronization` interface, it will get informed about changes in transactional context state only if it does. A session EJB component that implements the `SessionSynchronization` interface also receives an extra execution state, in addition to its Nonexistent, Normal, and Passivated states; all method calls performed within the transactional context are isolated from the effects of the ordinary business calls.

The Exception Classes

All the concrete classes in the `javax.ejb` package are exception types thrown by various methods of the EJB API. However, the exception classes may be grouped into two categories, where all the exceptions belonging to a particular group behave identically (except, of course their difference in type names).

Exception classes derived from `EJBException` are `RuntimeExceptions` containing a child exception indicating the root cause of the EJBException, as shown by Figure 8-57. Because `RuntimeExceptions` do not generate compiler errors if not placed within a try block having a corresponding catch block, they provide optimum simplicity during development while still preserving runtime stability in deployment (where, of course, all exceptions are caught). The contained root cause exception is retrieved by a call to the `getCausedByException()`. In other respects, the `EJBException` subclasses (that is, `AccessLocalException`, `NoSuchException`, `NoSuchObjectLocalException`, `TransactionRequiredLocalException`, and `TransactionRolledbackLocalException`) behave like `RuntimeExceptions`.

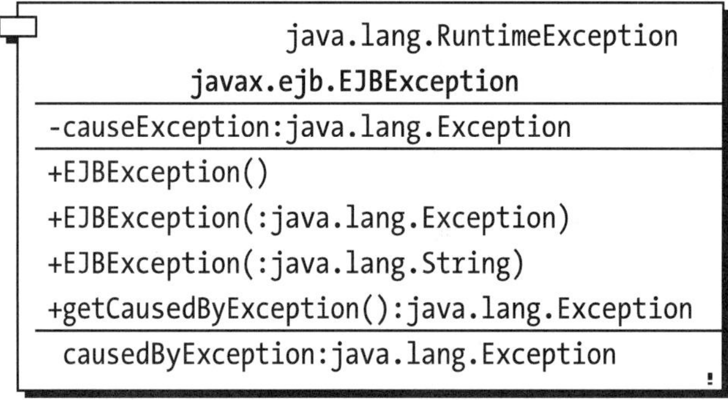

Figure 8-57. The `EJBException` *class contains a root cause exception that may be retrieved by calling* `getCausedByException()`.

The second type of exception classes in the `javax.ejb` package are not derived from `RuntimeException`, and must therefore be placed inside a try block with a corresponding catch block to avoid compiler errors. These exceptions are related to creating, finding, and removing EJB instances: `CreateException` (see Figure 8-58) with its subclass `DuplicateKeyException`, `FinderException` with its subclass `ObjectNotFoundException`, and the `RemoveException`. Their structure is identical to that of the `java.lang.Exception` class.

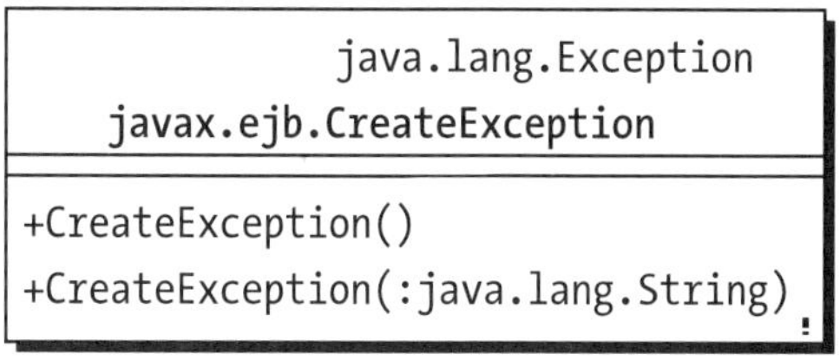

```
java.lang.Exception
javax.ejb.CreateException
+CreateException()
+CreateException(:java.lang.String)
```

Figure 8-58. The structure and usage of the `CreateException` *is identical to those of the* `java.lang.Exception` *class.*

This concludes the tour of the `javax.ejb` package.

CHAPTER 9

Example 1: Centralizing Exchange Rates

IN THE J2EE PROGRAMMING PARADIGM, Enterprise JavaBeans are the glue that binds the server front end with its back end. The "front end" of a server is the part that receives all commands from the user and, after all processing of a command is done, and sends the results back to the user. The "back end" of a server is the part where all data is collected to business and aggregate objects, according to the instructions of the user for the particular task. The back end also hides various complexities that are associated with moving data to and from legacy data sources. Chapters 9 through 11 demonstrate three different scenarios where EJBs are used:

- **Chapter 9**: Direct Java application interaction with the EJB tier using a stateless session EJB server
- **Chapter 10**: Migrating a Web application from old-style servlet-to-database interaction to session EJB proxy operation.
- **Chapter 11**: Continue migration to include aggregate value objects and back-end tier abstraction using Entity EJBs.

We'll start with a small currency exchanger EJB application that illustrates the use of context variables and application EJB clients.

Using a Stateless Session EJB Component

The simplest example of an EJB server is a stateless EJB component whose implementation instances may be switched between clients by the EJB container as needed. Stateless EJB components cannot preserve any state between method calls; in fact, an application server may actively change the implementation object between two incoming calls. In other words, if an EJB client calls two methods in an EJB Remote interface (of a stateless session EJB component) in sequence, the `Bean` instance that generates the response may be different in the two cases.

Figure 9-1 shows a series of three calls between two clients having a reference to a stateless EJB of the same type on the same EJB application server.

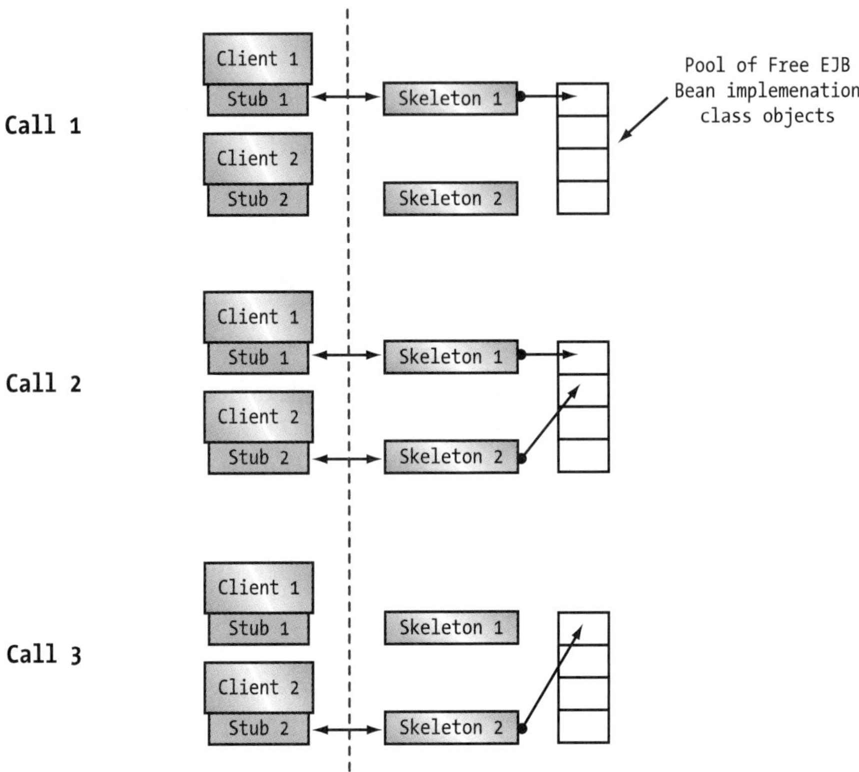

Figure 9-1. A simplified sketch of the sequence diagram for the small system of two clients and a pool of free EJB implementation objects. The EJB container (to the right of the dashed line) manages all assignments of skeleton references to the pool.

The effects of the three calls are described below, with the numbers in the list relating to the call in question.

1. Client 1 invokes a method in its local reference (the instance implementing the EJB Remote interface) of the stateless EJB component. The call is routed to the stub that connects to the appropriate skeleton on the application server. The skeleton acquires a bean implementation object from the pool of free (unused) instances in the application server. As it happens, the object acquired is the first in the pool.

2. Client 2 invokes a method in its local stub reference. The connection procedure is identical to that of client 1; when skeleton 2 retrieves an EJB bean implementation instance from the pool of free objects, it gets a reference to the second implementation object in the pool. After this, both method calls (1 and 2) terminate and return appropriate values, and both skeletons release their reference of the EJB bean implementation object. In the process of releasing the two EJB bean implementation objects, the EJB container may completely wipe their internal state.

3. After a while, client 2 invokes yet another method in its local stub reference. This time, all objects in the pool are free, so skeleton 2 finds itself talking to the first object in the pool of free EJB bean implementation objects. Of course, the skeleton does not really care which object in the free pool it talks to: as long as it *has* a reference to an EJB bean implementation object, all is well.

Stateless EJB components should therefore be used only if all remote methods in the remote API can be called independently of each other. As a result, all methods of a stateless session EJB component work a bit like static methods of a normal Java class; static methods cannot access local data members of the its class, and stateless EJB components should not access local data members in its EJB Bean implementation class, as the actual instance used may be switched by the EJB container as shown in Figure 9-1.

Our small application system consists of a Java application client that communicates with a stateless EJB server. The server manages currency exchange rates and permits users to calculate money from an exchange transaction. Figure 9-2 shows the resulting output of the small client application communicating.

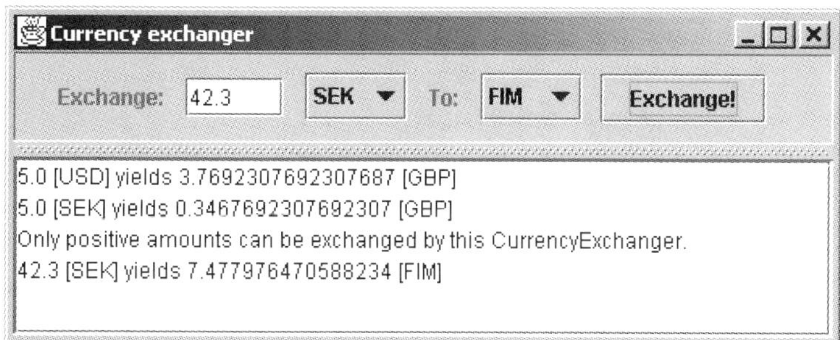

Figure 9-2. The resulting output of a few exhange operations. Note that the system reacts to invalid input data, as shown in row 3 of the output.

The client also presents all known currencies to the user, as shown in Figure 9-3. The list of known currencies is read from the EJB server.

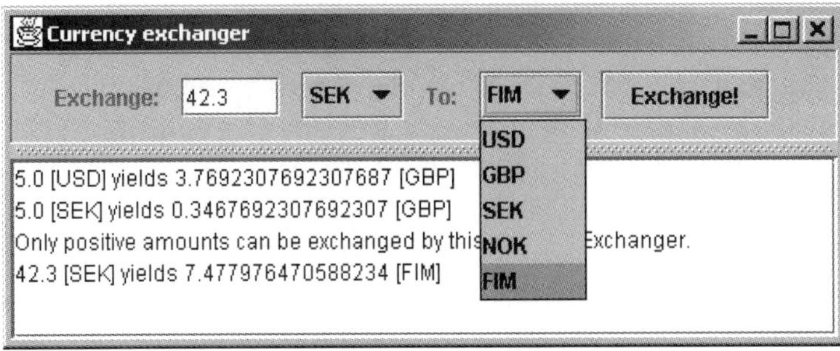

Figure 9-3. The application presents all known currencies to the user in two comboboxes.

The currency exchanger is implemented as a stateless EJB application because the currency converter operation is stateless and does not depend on previous conversions.

Classes of the CurrencyExchangeEJB

This small example requires few classes, but the structures and patterns used are in many ways generic for EJB applications. Figure 9-4 shows the classes deployed on the server.

As shown in Figure 9-4, the only two available business methods of the `CurrencyExchange` component are `getCurrencies()` and `change()`. The former method returns a `Vector` containing the three-letter currency codes of all known currencies to the `CurrencyExchange` EJB component. The latter performs the actual exchange operation, and calculates the amount of money returned in the desired currency.

The application client requires slightly more functionality and information than the EJB server because the client requires information to properly connect to the EJB server and produce a GUI. As shown in Figure 9-5, the `CurrencyExchangeClient` contains most of the functionality, whereas the `EJBUtils` class contains EJB server lookup code to simplify JNDI lookup. The `EJBUtils` class, in turn, uses a very simplified version of the `CommonUtils` class to unify logging.

Start the code review by examining the code of the server-side classes.

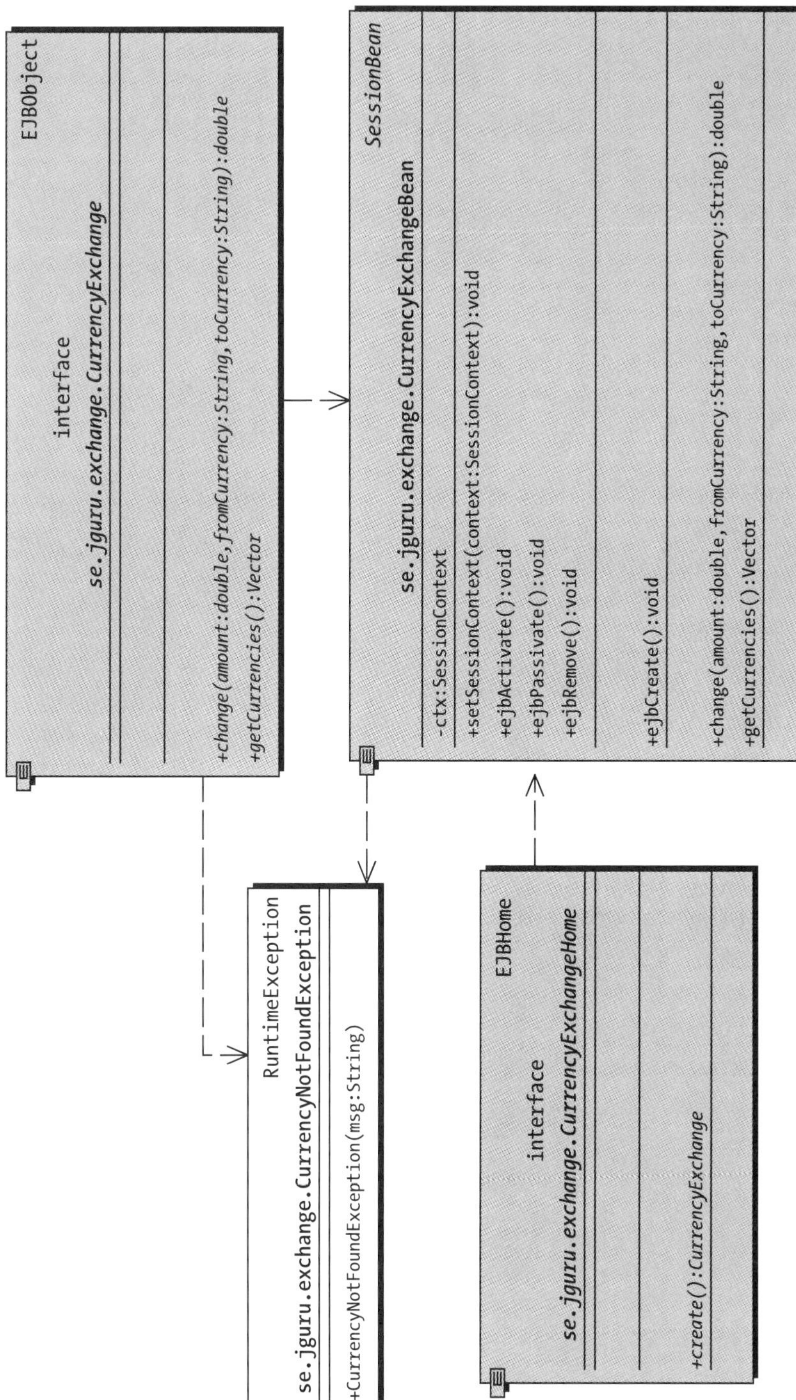

Figure 9-4. The classes (excluding any automatically generated skeletons) deployed in the application server. The classes of the EJB component are shaded.

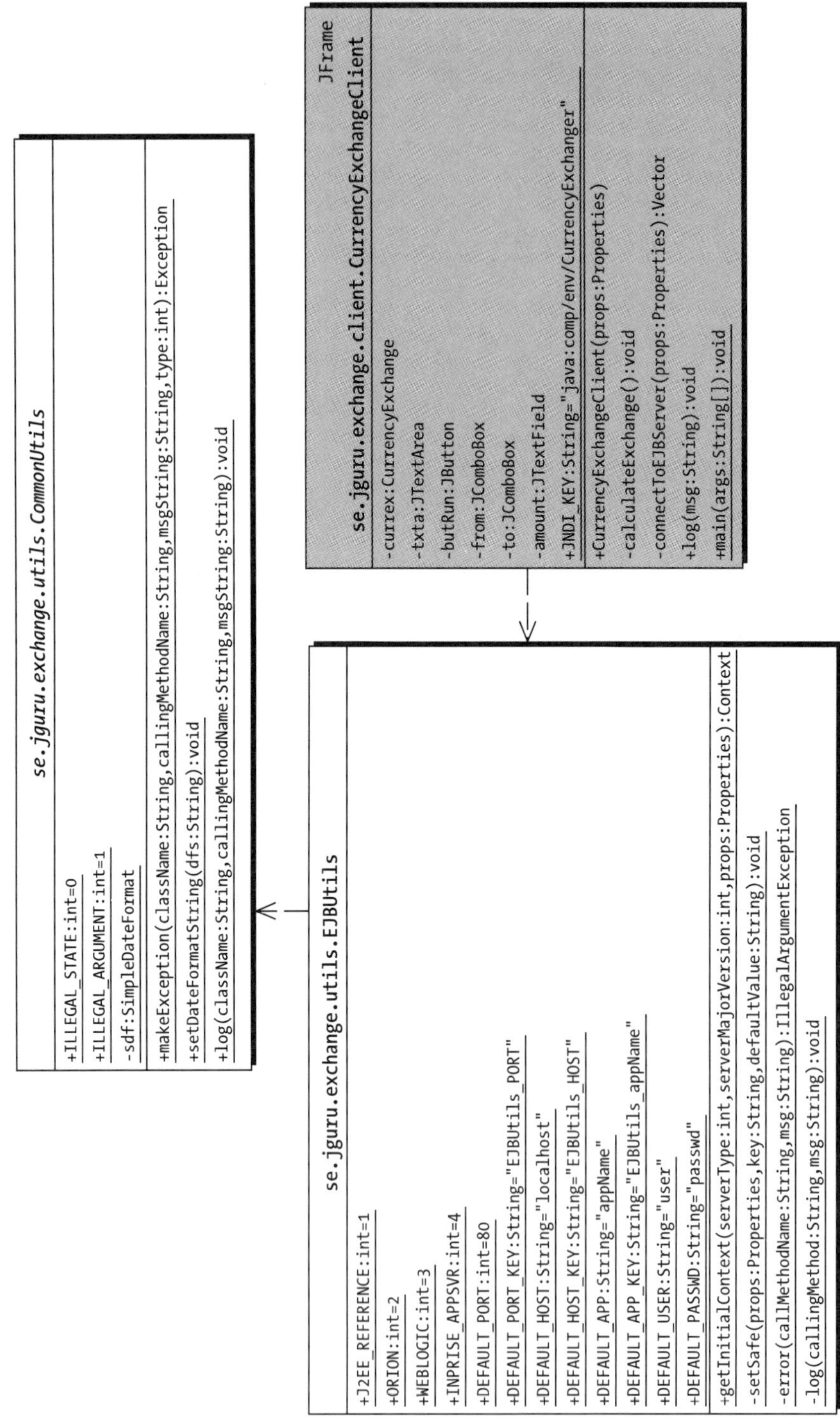

Figure 9-5. Classes (excluding stubs) of the EJB client. Helper classes have white backgrounds, and the actual `CurrencyExchangeClient` *class is shaded.*

The CurrencyExchange Remote Interface

The `CurrencyExchange` interface defines the business methods of the stateless EJB component. As shown in the UML diagram in Figure 9-6, the `CurrencyExchange` EJB component has merely two business methods.

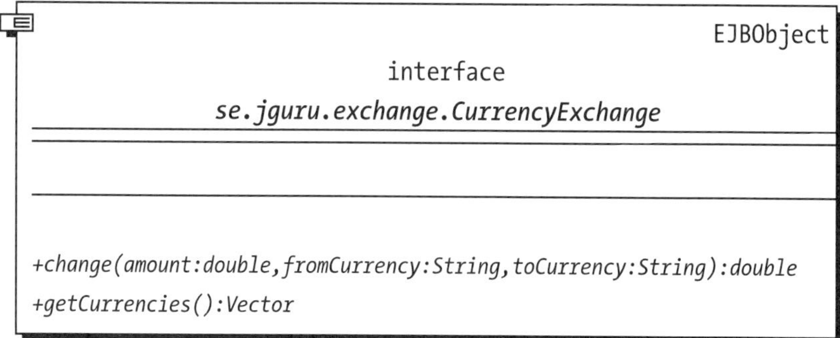

Figure 9-6. The `CurrencyExchange` *interface*

Listing 9-1 contains the code of the `CurrencyExchange` interface. Note the mandatory use of `RemoteException` for all methods, thrown by all remote-enabled methods.

Listing 9-1. The `CurrencyExchange` *interface*

```
/*
 * Copyright (c) 2000,2001 jGuru Europe.
 * All rights reserved.
 */

package se.jguru.exchange;

import javax.ejb.EJBObject;
import java.rmi.RemoteException;
import javax.ejb.EJBException;
import java.util.Vector;
import se.jguru.exchange.CurrencyNotFoundException;
```

```
/**
 * Simple definition of the exchange server remote interface.
 */
public interface CurrencyExchange extends EJBObject
{
    /**
     * Changes the given amount of the currency having the currency code
     * given by the <code>fromCurrency</code> variable, to the currency
     * with the three-letter <code>toCurrency</code> currency code.
     *
     * @return The amount of the resulting currency obtained from the
     *         exchange.
     */
    public double change(double amount, String fromCurrency, String toCurrency)
        throws RemoteException, EJBException, CurrencyNotFoundException;

    /**
     * Retrieves the list of available 3-letter currency codes, corresponding
     * to all known currencies of this CurrencyExchange EJB server.
     *
     * @return A List containing all 3-letter currency codes.
     */
    public Vector getCurrencies() throws RemoteException, EJBException;
}
```

The method definitions are quite simple to understand, but it is important that neither of the implementations in the corresponding EJB Bean implementation class modify any internal state variables. The EJB bean must not care about the method call order.

Let's move on to the extremely simple Home interface.

The CurrencyExchangeHome Interface

For a stateless EJB component, the Home interface shown in Figure 9-7 tends to be extremely simple. Because there is no state to initialize, an empty `create()` method is sufficient. The code in Listing 9-2 is so trivial that no comments have been added to the class.

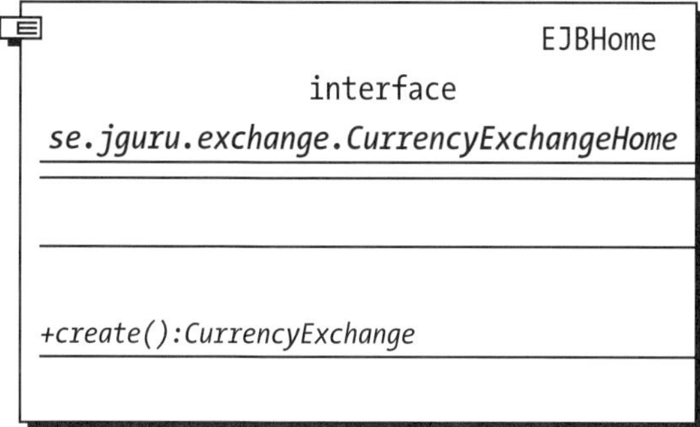

Figure 9-7. The `CurrencyExchangeHome` *interface. Only one* `create()` *method is needed due to the stateless nature of the EJB component.*

Listing 9-2. The `CurrencyExchangeHome` *interface*

```
/*
 * Copyright (c) 2000,2001 jGuru Europe.
 * All rights reserved.
 */

package se.jguru.exchange;

import javax.ejb.EJBHome;
import javax.ejb.CreateException;
import javax.ejb.EJBException;
import java.rmi.RemoteException;

public interface CurrencyExchangeHome extends EJBHome
{
    public CurrencyExchange create()
    throws CreateException, EJBException, RemoteException;
}
```

The only class containing any functionality on the server side is the EJB Bean implementation class, `CurrencyExchangeBean`.

The CurrencyExchangeBean Implementation Class

The EJB implementation class is the operative nexus of any EJB component providing implementation for all business and life-cycle methods. The `CurrencyExchangeBean` shown in Figure 9-8 is no exception. It provides implementation information for all of the EJB component business methods.

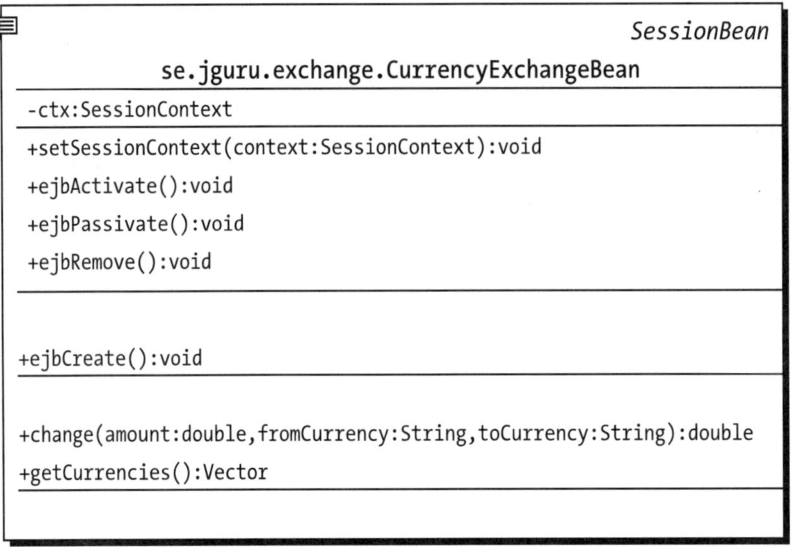

Figure 9-8. The `CurrencyExchangeBean` *implementation class*

Listing 9-3 provides the implementation of the `CurrencyExchangeBean` class.

Listing 9-3. The `CurrencyExchangeBean` *implementation class*

```
/*
 * Copyright (c) 2000,2001 jGuru Europe.
 * All rights reserved.
 */

package se.jguru.exchange;

import javax.ejb.*;
import javax.naming.*;
import java.rmi.RemoteException;

import java.util.*;

/**
 * Stateless exchange server class, showing the use of context
 * lookups and initialization parameters.
 */
```

```
public class CurrencyExchangeBean implements SessionBean
{
    // The SessionContext is unused in this SessionBean
    private SessionContext ctx;

    public void setSessionContext(SessionContext context)
    throws RemoteException, EJBException
    {
        ctx = context;
    }

    //
    // Bean lifecycle methods
    //

    public void ejbActivate()
    {
    }

    public void ejbPassivate()
    {
    }

    public void ejbRemove()
    {
    }

    public void ejbCreate() throws CreateException
    {
    }

    /**
     * Exchanges the amount given from the currency having the fromCurrency
     * currency code to the currency having the toCurrency currency code.
     *
     * @returns the amount in the received currency.
     * @exception CurrencyNotFoundException Thrown if either currency could not
     *            be found.
     */
```

```
public double change(double amount, String fromCurrency, String toCurrency)
    throws CurrencyNotFoundException
{
    try
    {
        // Get the Context of this bean
        Context cx = new InitialContext();

        // Get the exchange rate of the fromCurrency to the reference currency.
        double fromExchangeRate = ((Double)
                    cx.lookup("java:comp/env/" + fromCurrency)).doubleValue();

        // Get the exchange rate of the toCurrency to the reference currency.
        double toExchangeRate = ((Double)
                    cx.lookup("java:comp/env/" + toCurrency)).doubleValue();

        // Find the bank fee percentile, subtracted from the resulting
        // amount in the new currency.
        int feePercent = ((Integer) cx.lookup("java:comp/env/fee")).intValue();

        // Perform the exchange calculation
        return amount * (fromExchangeRate/toExchangeRate)
                      * (1.0 - ((double) feePercent)/100.0);
    }
    catch(Exception ex)
    {
        // Whoops.
        throw new CurrencyNotFoundException("Could not perform exchange: " + ex);
    }
}

/**
 * Retrieves the list of available 3-letter currency codes, corresponding
 * to all known currencies of this CurrencyExchange EJB server.
 *
 * @return A Vector containing all 3-letter currency codes.
 */
public Vector getCurrencies()
{
    try
    {
        // Get the Context
        Context cx = new InitialContext();
```

```
            // Get and parse the string list of known currencies
            String knownCurrencies = (String)
                        cx.lookup("java:comp/env/knowncurrencies");

            // Got a list?
            if(knownCurrencies == null || knownCurrencies.equals(""))
                throw new IllegalStateException("null list of known currencies.");

            // Parse the list.
            Vector toReturn = new Vector();

            StringTokenizer tok = new StringTokenizer(knownCurrencies, ",", false);
            while(tok.hasMoreTokens())
            {
                // Add the token to the list.
                String current = "" + tok.nextToken();
                toReturn.addElement(current);
            }

            // Done. Return the list.
            return toReturn;
        }
        catch(Exception ex)
        {
            // Whoops. Complain.
            System.err.println("[CurrencyExchangeBean::getCurrencies]: Could not "
                + "get the currency list from the Context: " + ex);
        }

        // We should never wind up here.
        return new Vector();
    }
}
```

The `CurrencyExchangeBean` has two main business methods, which use the `InitialContext` and the `SessionBean` environment to find the values of configuration parameters bound in the `InitialContext`.

The lookup prefix `java:comp/env/` provides a reference to the server-side environment of an EJB component. A value bound in the EJB context in the deployment descriptor file under the name `foo` can be accessed in the EJB implementation class under the name `cx.lookup("java:comp/env/foo");`. The `change()` method performs the three following main tasks, in order:

1. Obtaining a reference to the InitialContext of the EJB component using the call to new InitialContext();. This works only if the EJB component runs within an application server; EJB application clients must provide additional information to connect to the InitialContext of a particular application server, as will be shown later.

2. Reading three values from the SessionBean context; the exchange rates for the currencies involved in the transaction and the percentile fee of the bank for performing the transaction.

3. Calculating the result of the exchange operation and returning it to the client.

Much in a similar manner, the getCurrencies() method reads all known currencies as a parameter from the SessionBean context, parses the read value, and returns a Vector containing all currencies found.

Having seen the quite simple code of the stateless SessionBean, all that remains to be understood of the operation of the server-side components is the setting of the context variables in the SessionBean context. The deployment descriptor, ejb-jar.xml, contains all declarations of context variables. The deployment descriptor used in this case is shown in the "The CurrencyExchange EJB Component Deployment Descriptors" section later in this chapter.

The application client using the services of the CurrencyExchange EJB component is quite a bit easier to deploy than the corresponding server-side components. Finding a reference to the InitialContext is a more complex task for a client than it is for a server, so the effort of creating this simple EJB application client is still comparable to the server-side components.

The CurrencyExchangeClient Class

Although the CurrencyExchangeClient class shown in Figure 9-9 may look complex, the portion of the code that communicates with the EJB server-side components is quite small and essentially encapsulated in the two methods connectToEJBSever() and calculateExchange(). All JNDI-specific properties are provided in the main method and used in a delegate class, called EJBUtils, which provides a unified means of retrieving the first InitialContext of the application server.

Take a look at the portions of the CurrencyExchangeClient class that are relevant to the EJB communication, starting with the method connectToEJBServer. See Listing 9-4.

```
                                                   JFrame
   se.jguru.exchange.client.CurrencyExchangeClient
-currex:CurrencyExchange
-txta:JTextArea
-butRun:JButton
-from:JComboBox
-to:JComboBox
-amount:JTextField
+JNDI_KEY:String="java:comp/env/CurrencyExchanger"
+CurrencyExchangeClient(props:Properties)
-calculateExchange():void
-connectToEJBServer(props:Properties):Vector
+log(msg:String):void
+main(args:String[]):void
```

Figure 9-9. The `CurrencyExchangeClient` *class*

Listing 9-4. The `CurrencyExchangeClient` *class*

```
/**
 * Connects to the Application server, using the
 * JNDI connection properties provided.
 *
 * Refer to the EJBUtils class to see the exact properties
 * required to connect to a given application server.
 */
private Vector connectToEJBServer(Properties props)
{
    // Initial context variable
    Context cx = null;

    // Vector of all known currencies
    Vector knownCurrencies = null;

    try
    {
        // Get the InitialContext for an Orion Application Server
        // with the major version 1 given the properties in the
        // props instance.
        cx = EJBUtils.getInitialContext(EJBUtils.ORION, 1, props);
```

```
            // Get the CurrencyExchangeHome instance, and
            // narrow it to its actual class
            Object obj = cx.lookup(JNDI_KEY);
            CurrencyExchangeHome home = (CurrencyExchangeHome)
                PortableRemoteObject.narrow(obj, CurrencyExchangeHome.class);

            // Create the remote EJB reference
            try
            {
                 this.currex = home.create();
            }
            catch(Exception ex)
            {
                this.log("Could not create EJB Home instance: " + ex);
            }

            // Get the list of known currencies
            knownCurrencies = this.currex.getCurrencies();
        }
        catch(NamingException ex)
        {
            this.log("Cannot find the name given in remote Context: " + ex);
        }
        catch(IllegalArgumentException ex)
        {
            this.log("Cannot create initial Context: " + ex);
        }
        catch(RemoteException ex)
        {
            this.log("Could not talk to the server: " + ex);
        }

        // Done. Return.
        return knownCurrencies;
    }
```

The `connectToEJBServer()` method connects to the application server and retrieves a local stub of the `CurrencyExchange` EJB component. The connection and retrieval process consists of the following steps:

1. The `InitialContext` reference is retrieved from the static method `getInitialContext()` in the `EJBUtils` class. The provided parameters define which type of application server is used, and what kind of properties should be used to connect to the EJB server.

2. The CurrencyExchangeHome instance is retrieved from the InitialContext using the standard lookup and narrowing process for all EJB Home objects.

3. The Home interface is used to create a reference to a Remote instance of the EJB component. As shown in the UML visualization of the CurrencyExchangeClient in Figure 9-9, the CurrencyExchange reference is called currex.

4. The getCurrencies method is invoked in the local currex server, to obtain a Vector of all known currencies. This Vector is returned to be used as a model in the JComboBox objects used in the view, as shown in Figure 9-3.

The other relevant method, calculateExchange(), is much more simple than connectToEJBServer(). This is the simple handler method that is invoked whenever the user presses the Exchange! button, and its function is to call the change() method of the CurrencyExchange EJB server. The result of the method is compiled and logged to the display area in the view, as shown in Figure 9-2.

Listing 9-5 contains the code of the calculateExchange() method.

Listing 9-5. The calculateExchange() *method*

```
/**
 * Calculates the exchange rate and amount from a particular
 * exchange operation, and displays the resulting rate on the
 * output textarea.
 */
private void calculateExchange()
{
    // The amount which should be changed.
    double am = 0;

    try
    {
        // Try parsing the text from the textfield into a double
        am = Double.parseDouble(this.amount.getText());

        // We can only handle positive amounts...
        if(am < 0) throw new IllegalArgumentException("Not permitted.");
    }
```

```
        catch(Exception ex)
        {
            // Complain and return.
            this.log("Only positive amounts can be exchanged "
                        + "by this CurrencyExchanger.");
            return;
        }

        // Fire the query to the EJB server
        try
        {
            double gotAmount = this.currex.change(am, "" + from.getSelectedItem(),
                                  "" + to.getSelectedItem());

            // Log the exchange rate.
            this.log("" + am + " [" + from.getSelectedItem() + "] yields "
                + gotAmount + " [" + to.getSelectedItem() + "]");
        }
        catch(Exception ex)
        {
            // complain
            this.log("Error talking to EJB server: " + ex);
        }
    }
```

The `calculateExchange()` method performs three main tasks:

1. It obtains the text from the text field in the GUI and parses that text into a double. If unsuccessful, the client stops the execution in the `calculateExchange` method and prints an error message.

2. Having successfully parsed the double value provided by the user, the `calculateExchange` method invokes the change method in the EJB server, performing the actual calculation.

3. The value returned from the `change` method is formatted into a human-readable string and printed on the standard output log of the client application.

Currently, two mysteries with the `CurrencyExchangeClient` remain: the main method that provides the properties used to retrieve the `InitialContext` of the `CurrencyExchangeClient`, and the implementation of the `EJBUtils.getInitialContext()` method that actually retrieves the `InitialContext` object. Let's start with the main method that defines the properties used to connect.

```
public static void main(String[] args)
{
    // Compile the JNDI connection properties
    Properties props = new Properties();
    props.setProperty(Context.SECURITY_PRINCIPAL, "appClientUser");
    props.setProperty(Context.SECURITY_CREDENTIALS, "whoops");
    props.setProperty(EJBUtils.DEFAULT_HOST_KEY, "localhost");
    props.setProperty(EJBUtils.DEFAULT_APP_KEY, "ExchangeApp");

    new CurrencyExchangeClient(props);
}
```

The Properties object props contain the values that are required to properly connect to the EJB application server. Two of these keys are standardized, provided as constants in the `javax.naming.Context` interface: the `Context.SECURITY_PRINCIPAL` is a string having the value `java.naming.security.principal`, and the `Context.SECURITY_CREDENTIALS` is a string with the value `java.naming.security.credentials`. The last of the properties, `EJBUtils.DEFAULT_HOST_KEY` and `EJBUtils.DEFAULT_APP_KEY`, are constant strings having the values `EJBUtils_HOST` and `EJBUtils_appKey`, respectively. All properties and values defined in the props instance are later used in the `getInitialContext()` method of the `EJBUtils` class to obtain a reference to the `InitialContext` of the chosen application server.

The only important remaining class in the system is the `EJBUtils` class, which is detailed in the next section.

The EJBUtils Class

It is common practice to encapsulate static JNDI lookup and class type information in a utility class. `EJBUtils`, shown in Figure 9-10, is such a utility class, and it has only one purpose in its current form: to simplify retrieval of an `InitialContext` instance.

The only relevant method is the public `getInitialContext()` method that is assisted by the `setSafe()` method. Examine the source code for the `EJBUtils` class in Listing 9-6.

se.jguru.exchange.utils.EJBUtils
+J2EE_REFERENCE:int=1 +ORION:int=2 +WEBLOGIC:int=3 +INPRISE_APPSVR:int=4 +DEFAULT_PORT:int=80 +DEFAULT_PORT_KEY:String="EJBUtils_PORT" +DEFAULT_HOST:String="localhost" +DEFAULT_HOST_KEY:String="EJBUtils_HOST" +DEFAULT_APP:String="appName" +DEFAULT_APP_KEY:String="EJBUtils_appName" +DEFAULT_USER:String="user" +DEFAULT_PASSWD:String="passwd"
+getInitialContext(serverType:int,serverMajorVersion:int,props:Properties):Context -setSafe(props:Properties,key:String,defaultValue:String):void -error(callMethodName:String,msg:String):IllegalArgumentException -log(callingMethod:String,msg:String):void

Figure 9-10. The `EJBUtils` *class*

Listing 9-6. The `EJBUtils` *class*

```
package se.jguru.exchange.utils;

import javax.naming.*;
import java.util.*;
import java.text.SimpleDateFormat;

/**
 * EJB utility class useable by all EJB instances in the
 * system. The purpose of this is to hide the complexities
 * of JNDI property settings (InitialContext factory class,
 * etc. for standalone EJB clients).
 *
 * @author Lennart Jörelid
 */
```

```
public class EJBUtils
{
    // Defined (known) application server types
    public final static int J2EE_REFERENCE = 1;
    public final static int ORION = 2;
    public final static int WEBLOGIC = 3;
    public final static int INPRISE_APPSVR = 4;

    // Default keys and values of frequently used building blocks
    // for constructing the PROVIDER_URL.
    public static final int DEFAULT_PORT = 80;
    public static final String DEFAULT_PORT_KEY = "EJBUtils_PORT";

    public static final String DEFAULT_HOST = "localhost";
    public static final String DEFAULT_HOST_KEY = "EJBUtils_HOST";

    public static final String DEFAULT_APP = "appName";
    public static final String DEFAULT_APP_KEY = "EJBUtils_appName";

    public static final String DEFAULT_USER = "user";
    public static final String DEFAULT_PASSWD = "passwd";

    /**
     * Retrieves the initial context for a particular Application server as indicated.
     *
     * @param serverType Constant indicating which server is used;
     *          determines default property values in the props argument (unless
     *          provided by the client).
     * @param props Populated with properties to indicate the application
     *          server node name and port number. If <code>null</code> is provided,
     *          the call is assumed to come from within the running application
     *          server, as opposed to from a standalone client.
     *
     * @exception java.lang.IllegalArgumentException Thrown if the server
     *             type/majorVersion combination is not supported, or the
     *             properties for connecting were malformed.
     * @exception javax.naming.NamingException Thrown if a Naming
     *             exception was encountered.
     */
    public static Context getInitialContext(int serverType,
           int serverMajorVersion, Properties props)
    throws IllegalArgumentException, NamingException
```

```
{
    // Running within an application server?
    if (props == null) return new InitialContext();

    // Declare the Context to return
    Context initContext = null;

    // Add the default SECURITY_PRINCIPAL and SECURITY_CREDENTIALS
    // if they are not already provided in the Properties
    setSafe(props, Context.SECURITY_PRINCIPAL, DEFAULT_USER);
    setSafe(props, Context.SECURITY_CREDENTIALS, DEFAULT_PASSWD);

    // Add the default PORT, HOST and APP_NAME
    setSafe(props, DEFAULT_HOST_KEY, DEFAULT_HOST);
    setSafe(props, DEFAULT_PORT_KEY, "" + DEFAULT_PORT);
    setSafe(props, DEFAULT_APP_KEY, DEFAULT_APP);

    switch (serverType)
    {
        case ORION:
            {
                // The Orion application server creates its provider
                // URL originating from two properties:
                //
                // 1) hostname
                // 2) application name
               String jndiUrl = "ormi://" + props.getProperty(DEFAULT_HOST_KEY)
                + "/" + props.getProperty(DEFAULT_APP_KEY);

                // We are potentially running as a standalone client
                // Populate props.
                setSafe(props, Context.INITIAL_CONTEXT_FACTORY,
                "com.evermind.server.ApplicationClientInitialContextFactory");
                setSafe(props, Context.PROVIDER_URL, jndiUrl);

                // Done.
                break;
            }
```

```
        case WEBLOGIC:
            {
                // The weblogic application server creates its
                // provider URL originating from two properties:
                // hostname and port.
                String providerUrl = "t3://" + props.getProperty(DEFAULT_HOST_KEY)
                + ":" + props.getProperty(DEFAULT_PORT_KEY);

                // Populate props.
                setSafe(props, Context.INITIAL_CONTEXT_FACTORY,
                "weblogic.jndi.WLInitialContextFactory");
                setSafe(props, Context.PROVIDER_URL, providerUrl);

                // Done.
                break;
            }

        case INPRISE_APPSVR:
            {
                // Populate props.
                setSafe(props, javax.naming.Context.INITIAL_CONTEXT_FACTORY,
                "com.inprise.j2ee.jndi.CtxFactory");
                setSafe(props, javax.naming.Context.URL_PKG_PREFIXES,
                "com.inprise.j2ee");

                // Done.
                break;
            }


        default:
            // Server configuration not supported.
            // Complain.
            throw new java.lang.UnsupportedOperationException("Could "
            + "not support server type : " + serverType
            + "at this time.");
    }

    // Log the contents of Props
    log("getInitialContext", "Creating initialContext using settings: " + props);

    // Create and return the InitialContext
    return new InitialContext(props);
}
```

```
    /**
     * Convenience method to make sure a certain key within a Properties instance
     * has a value - either its existing value or the defaultValue provided.
     *
     * @param props The Properties which to populate
     * @param key   The key that should be verified
     * @param defaultValue The value assigned to the property key, unless
     *              an existing value can be found.
     */
    private static void setSafe(Properties props, String key, String defaultValue)
    throws IllegalArgumentException
    {
        // Check sanity
        if (key == null || key.equals(""))
            throw error("setSafe", "Cannot handle null or empty key.");

        if (defaultValue == null || defaultValue.equals(""))
            throw error("setSafe", "Cannot handle null or empty defaultValue.");

        if (props == null)
            throw error("setSafe", "Cannot handle null Properties.");

        // Sane. Proceed.
        props.setProperty(key, props.getProperty(key, defaultValue));
    }

    /** Local wrapper of the CommonUtils.makeException method */
    private static IllegalArgumentException error(String callMethodName, String msg)
    {
        return (IllegalArgumentException) CommonUtils.makeException("EJBUtils",
        callMethodName, msg, CommonUtils.ILLEGAL_ARGUMENT);
    }

    /** Logs a timestamped message to the standard log stream */
    private static void log(String callingMethod, String msg)
    {
        // Delegate to the CommonUtils log method
        CommonUtils.log("EJBUtils", callingMethod, msg);
    }
}
```

The `EJBUtils` class consists of a number of definitions of constants, in addition to the two relevant methods `setSafe()` and `getInitialContext()`:

- The `setSafe()` method is used to set a property in a Properties object. If the provided key is present in the Properties object, its value is kept as is. Otherwise, it is replaced with the value of the `defaultValue` parameter.

- The `getInitialContext()` method performs two main tasks. First, it makes sure that the props instance contains required standard keys. Second, it populates the application server-specific properties—at the minimum `Context.INITIAL_CONTEXT_FACTORY` and `Context.PROVIDER_URL`—originating from information provided in the props object. When done populating the `InitialContext` properties, the `InitialContext` is created using the properties provided.

The constants are used to avoid typos when addressing keys in the Properties object passed to the `getInitialContext()` as an argument.

The other methods in the `EJBUtils` are utility methods for internal use only; the only class remaining in the small system is therefore the class called `CommonUtils`, which is explained next.

The CommonUtils Class

The supporting class `CommonUtils` contains only one relevant method, `log`, which provides a unified interface to logging in the small J2EE application. See Figure 9-11.

se.jguru.exchange.utils.CommonUtils
+ILLEGAL_STATE:int=0
+ILLEGAL_ARGUMENT:int=1
-sdf:SimpleDateFormat
+makeException(className:String,callingMethodName:String, msgString:String,type:int):Exception
+setDateFormatString(dfs:String):void
+log(className:String,callingMethodName:String,msgString:String):void

Figure 9-11. The `CommonUtils` *class*

Examine the log method in Listing 9-7 to see how the log messages of the EJB application are printed.

Listing 9-7. The log method of the `CommonUtils` *class*

```
/**
 * Logs a message to the standard output stream.
 *
 * @param className The name of the class where this log was called
 * @param callingMethodName The name of the method where this log msg was created.
 * @param msgString The log message
 */
public static void log(String className, String callingMethodName,
String msgString)
{
    // Get a Timestamp
    Date now = new Date();

    // Join the Resulting message string
    String msg = "<" + sdf.format(now) + "> [" + className + "::"
    + callingMethodName + "]: " + msgString;

    // Print to System.out
    System.out.println(msg);
}
```

The log method of the `CommonUtils` class prints a detailed log message to the `System.out` stream, after prepending a timestamp and an exact location where the error occurred. The exact format of a logged message will be something like the following:

```
<16.08:25,687> [EJBUtils::getInitialContext]: Creating initialContext using
settings: {java.naming.provider.url=ormi://localhost/ExchangeApp,
java.naming.factory.initial=com.evermind.server.ApplicationClientInitialContextFactory,
EJBUtils_PORT=80, EJBUtils_appName=ExchangeApp,
java.naming.security.principal=appClientUser, EJBUtils_HOST=localhost,
java.naming.security.credentials=whoops}
```

The `SimpleDateFormat` instance is created in a static initializer block whose statements are executed when the class is loaded into memory. This means that statements in a static code block execute before any objects of the class in question are created. It is therefore illegal to reference anything but static variables (or objects created within the static block) from statements in a static initializer block.

The `SimpleDateFormatter` instance, `sdf`, is a private static member of the `CommonUtils` class, as can be seen in the UML class diagram in Figure 9-11. It may therefore be instantiated within the static initializer block.

```
static
{
    // Set a default SimpleDateFormat instance.
    sdf = new SimpleDateFormat("kk.mm:ss,SSS");
}
```

Having looked at the relevant pieces of the `CommonUtils` class, let's now examine the deployment descriptors used by the `CurrencyExchange` EJB.

The CurrencyExchange EJB Component Deployment Descriptors

Because the stateless `CurrencyExchange` EJB component has many references to variables in its environment, the standard deployment descriptor, `ejb-jar.xml`, is cluttered with the variable definitions. Thankfully, stateless EJB components use the application-specific configuration descriptor relatively little: the main use of this descriptor file is to provide the JNDI name for the Home interface.

Listing 9-8 contains the standard deployment descriptor `ejb-jar.xml` for the `CurrencyExchange` EJB component.

Listing 9-8. The `ejb-jar.xml` *standard deployment descriptor*

```
<?xml version="1.0"?>

<!DOCTYPE ejb-jar PUBLIC
    '-//Sun Microsystems, Inc.//DTD Enterprise JavaBeans 2.0//EN'
    'http://java.sun.com/dtd/ejb-jar_2_0.dtd'>

<ejb-jar>
    <enterprise-beans>
        <session>
            <description>Trivial currency exchange bean which
                        demonstrates the use of context variables.
            </description>
            <ejb-name>CurrencyExchangeBean</ejb-name>
            <home>se.jguru.exchange.CurrencyExchangeHome</home>
            <remote>se.jguru.exchange.CurrencyExchange</remote>
            <ejb-class>se.jguru.exchange.CurrencyExchangeBean</ejb-class>
            <session-type>Stateless</session-type>
            <transaction-type>Container</transaction-type>
```

```
            <env-entry>
                <description>List of all known currencies</description>
                <env-entry-name>knowncurrencies</env-entry-name>
                <env-entry-type>java.lang.String</env-entry-type>
                <env-entry-value>USD,GBP,SEK,NOK,FIM</env-entry-value>
            </env-entry>
            <env-entry>
                <description>Exchange rate for the USD-USD</description>
                <env-entry-name>USD</env-entry-name>
                <env-entry-type>java.lang.Double</env-entry-type>
                <env-entry-value>1.0</env-entry-value>
            </env-entry>
            <env-entry>
                <description>Exchange rate for the GBP-USD</description>
                <env-entry-name>GBP</env-entry-name>
                <env-entry-type>java.lang.Double</env-entry-type>
                <env-entry-value>1.3</env-entry-value>
            </env-entry>
            <env-entry>
                <description>Exchange rate for the SEK-USD</description>
                <env-entry-name>SEK</env-entry-name>
                <env-entry-type>java.lang.Double</env-entry-type>
                <env-entry-value>0.092</env-entry-value>
            </env-entry>
            <env-entry>
                <description>Exchange rate for the NOK-USD</description>
                <env-entry-name>NOK</env-entry-name>
                <env-entry-type>java.lang.Double</env-entry-type>
                <env-entry-value>0.15</env-entry-value>
            </env-entry>
            <env-entry>
                <description>Exchange rate for the FIM-USD</description>
                <env-entry-name>FIM</env-entry-name>
                <env-entry-type>java.lang.Double</env-entry-type>
                <env-entry-value>0.51</env-entry-value>
            </env-entry>
            <env-entry>
              <description>Exchange fee from the bank (percentile)</description>
                <env-entry-name>fee</env-entry-name>
                <env-entry-type>java.lang.Integer</env-entry-type>
                <env-entry-value>2</env-entry-value>
            </env-entry>
        </session>
    </enterprise-beans>
```

```
    <assembly-descriptor>
        <security-role>
            <description>Standard user role</description>
            <role-name>defaultUserRole</role-name>
        </security-role>
        <method-permission>
            <description>Default user security setting</description>
            <role-name>defaultUserRole</role-name>
            <method>
                <ejb-name>CurrencyExchangeBean</ejb-name>
                <method-intf>Home</method-intf>
                <method-name>create</method-name>
            </method>
            <method>
                <ejb-name>CurrencyExchangeBean</ejb-name>
                <method-intf>Remote</method-intf>
                <method-name>change</method-name>
            </method>
            <method>
                <ejb-name>CurrencyExchangeBean</ejb-name>
                <method-intf>Remote</method-intf>
                <method-name>getCurrencies</method-name>
            </method>
        </method-permission>
        <container-transaction>
            <description>Default Transaction Setting</description>
            <method>
                <ejb-name>CurrencyExchangeBean</ejb-name>
                <method-name>*</method-name>
            </method>
            <trans-attribute>Required</trans-attribute>
        </container-transaction>
    </assembly-descriptor>

</ejb-jar>
```

The `ejb-jar.xml` file has three distinct parts that define the session bean, the environment variables it uses, and the assembly descriptor that describes all security roles and transactional requirements on the methods of the session bean EJB component.

The `<session> ... </session>` container element describes basic attributes of the `CurrencyExchange` EJB component (name and concrete types for the Home, Remote, and Bean classes), as well as all environment entries that should be bound to the context of the bean. Each environment entry is defined by the three following properties:

- `<env-entry-name>` provides the variable name of the environment entry. This name should be used when performing a lookup; if the value of the `<env-entry-name>` element is `foo`, the corresponding lookup string is `java:comp/env/foo`.
- `<env-entry-type>` defines the fully qualified java class for which the value should be used in a constructor call. Permitted types are the primitive types and `java.lang.String`.
- `<env-entry-value>` provides the value of the variable.

A Simple Way of Looking at Environment Variables

Environment entries may simply be regarded as a normal variable declaration of the form:

```
<env-entry-type> <env-entry-name> = new <env-entry-type>("<env-entry-value>");
```

Given one of the environment entries in the deployment descriptor (Listing 9-8),

```
<env-entry>
    <description>Exchange rate for the FIM-USD</description>
    <env-entry-name>FIM</env-entry-name>
    <env-entry-type>java.lang.Double</env-entry-type>
    <env-entry-value>0.51</env-entry-value>
</env-entry>
```

the equivalent variable declaration is

```
java.lang.Double FIM = new Double("0.51");
```

All permitted environment variable types may be constructed from a single string constructor parameter.

The last part of the `ejb-jar.xml` file is the `<assembly-descriptor> ... </assembly-descriptor>` element, which defines these three items:

- The `<security-role> ... </security-role>` container element defines a security role named `defaultUserRole`. A security role represents a set of J2EE users or groups that have a particular *privilege set* with the EJB. Each such privilege set grants the right to call a set of methods in the remote and/or Home interfaces of the EJB.
- The `<method-permission> ... </method-permission>` container element defines a privilege set for a particular security role. In our case, the `defaultUserRole` is granted access to three methods: `create()` from the Home interface and the two methods `getCurrencies()` and `change()` from the Remote interface.
- Finally, the `<container-transaction> ... </container-transaction>` container element simply states that all methods of the `CurrencyExchangeBean` component must be executed within a transaction.

Unfortunately, the `ejb-jar.xml` file does not provide all of the required deployment settings; the JNDI name of the `CurrencyExchange` EJB component Home interface, for instance, has not been provided in `ejb-jar.xml`. Let us use the Orion Application Server (OAS) version 1.5.2 (which is one of many application servers that supports the prerelease EJB 2.0 standard) to show an example of an application server-specific deployment descriptor. The DTD of the custom configuration file (`orion-ejb-jar.xml`) for the OAS version 1.5.2 is illustrated in Figure 9-12.

The `orion-ejb-jar.xml` file is largely manufactured automatically by the automatic deployment service in the OAS. As a developer, one needs mainly to add the required JNDI deployment names and any specific security deployment settings.

Listing 9-9 displays the content of the `orion-ejb-jar.xml` file.

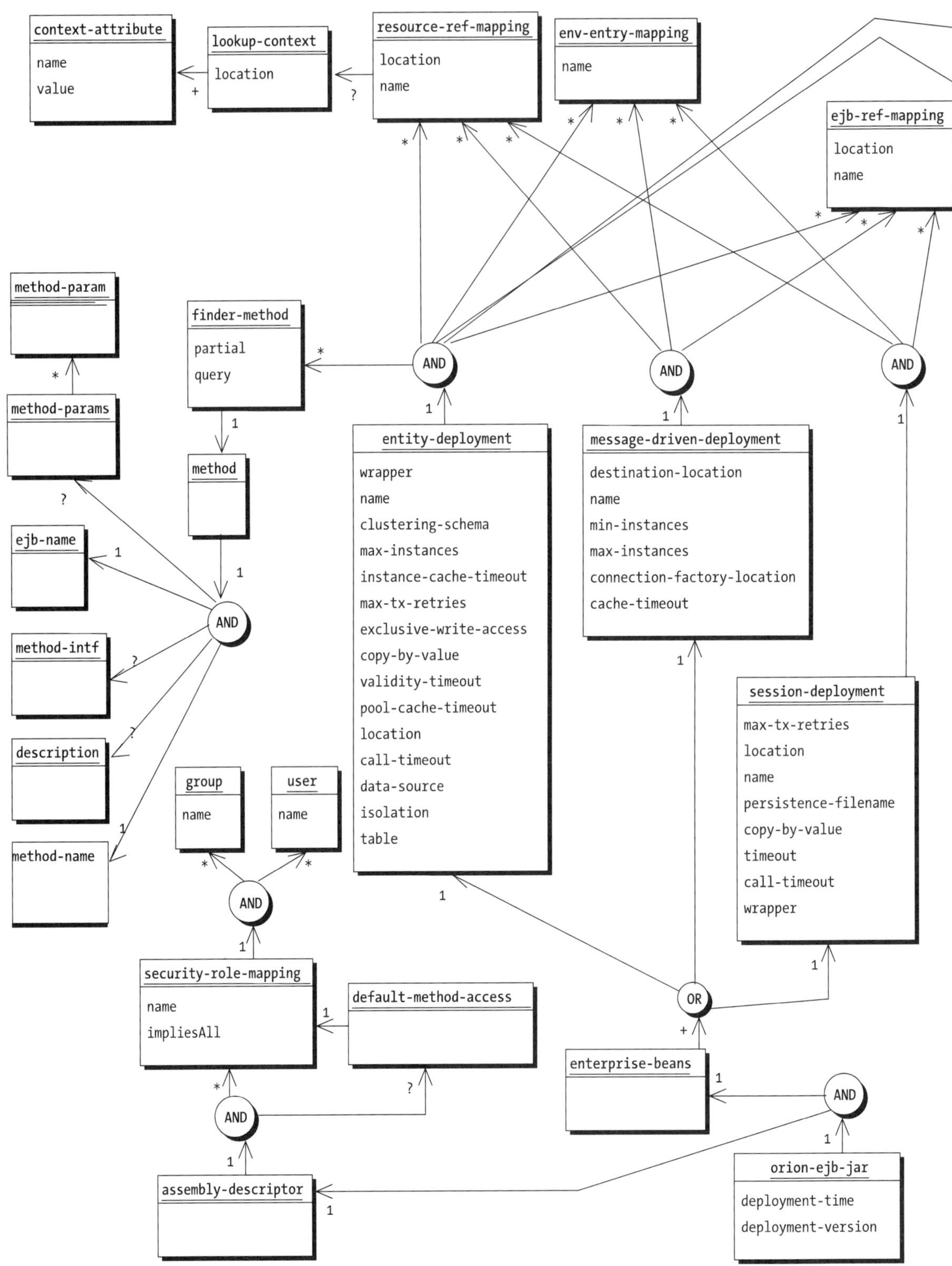

Figure 9-12. XML DTD structure of the `orion-ejb-jar.xml` *configuration file*

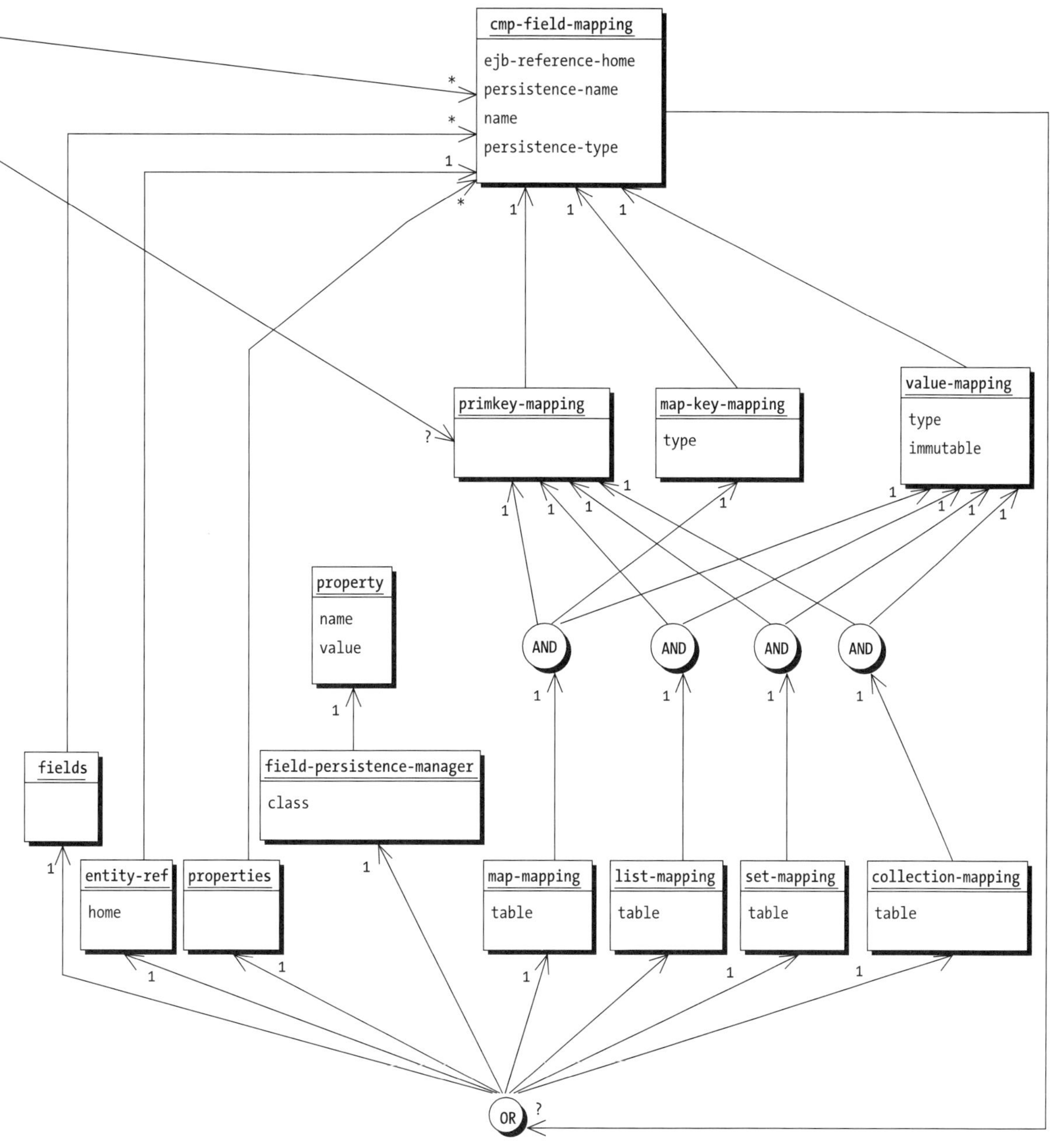
cmp-field-mapping
ejb-reference-home
persistence-name
name
persistence-type
primkey-mapping
map-key-mapping
type
value-mapping
type
immutable
property
name
value
AND
AND
AND
AND
fields
field-persistence-manager
class
entity-ref
home
properties
map-mapping
table
list-mapping
table
set-mapping
table
collection-mapping
table
OR

Listing 9-9. The `orion-ejb-jar.xml` *file*

```
<?xml version="1.0"?>
<!DOCTYPE orion-ejb-jar PUBLIC
     "-//Evermind//DTD Enterprise JavaBeans 1.1 runtime//EN"
     "http://www.orionserver.com/dtds/orion-ejb-jar.dtd">

<orion-ejb-jar deployment-version="1.5.2" deployment-time="e7eec1284d">
     <enterprise-beans>
          <session-deployment name="CurrencyExchangeBean"
                     location="se/jguru/exchange/CurrencyExchangeBean"
                     wrapper="CurrencyExchangeHome_StatelessSessionHomeWrapper21"
                     max-tx-retries="3" cache-timeout="60"
                     persistence-filename="CurrencyExchangeBean" />
     </enterprise-beans>
     <assembly-descriptor>
          <security-role-mapping name="defaultUserRole">
               <group name="standardUsers" />
          </security-role-mapping>
          <default-method-access>
               <security-role-mapping name="&lt;default-ejb-caller-role&gt;">
               </security-role-mapping>
          </default-method-access>
     </assembly-descriptor>
</orion-ejb-jar>
```

The custom deployment descriptor `orion-ejb-jar.xml` defines the specific deployment settings for the `CurrencyExchangeBean` EJB component. Note that the `<ejb-name>` from the `ejb-jar.xml` must match the `name` attribute of a `<session-deployment ... />` element in the `orion-ejb-jar.xml` descriptor file. The two relevant properties defined in the `orion-ejb-jar.xml` are

- The JNDI location of the `CurrencyExchangeHome` interface is set to `se/jguru/exchange/CurrencyExchangeBean`.

- The assembly descriptor of the `CurrencyExchangeBean` maps the security role `defaultUserRole` to the J2EE application server group `standardUsers`. Therefore, all J2EE calls performed by a member of the `standardUsers` group will have the privilege set defined for the `defaultUserRole` on the `CurrencyExchangeBean`.

The custom deployment descriptor has provided a map between the security role defined in the EJB deployment descriptor and a J2EE user or group of users. We have still not defined how to map a principal (that is, combination of a user ID/password or user ID/certificate) to a J2EE user and group that may execute the methods defined in the EJB bean component. As you have already guessed, all these mappings are completely specific to an application server; the J2EE standard has not provided a standard deployment descriptor definition for security mappings.

The OAS provides a deployment descriptor called `principals.xml` that maps a particular user ID/password combination to a J2EE user and assigns the J2EE user to zero or more J2EE groups. Now, only one deployment descriptor is left in the security chain of the OAS; the `orion-application.xml` deployment descriptor provides the privileges settings that grant principals the right to look up objects in the JNDI registry of the application server.

The security chain of the OAS with respect to the involved deployment descriptors of an EJB component is illustrated in Figure 9-13.

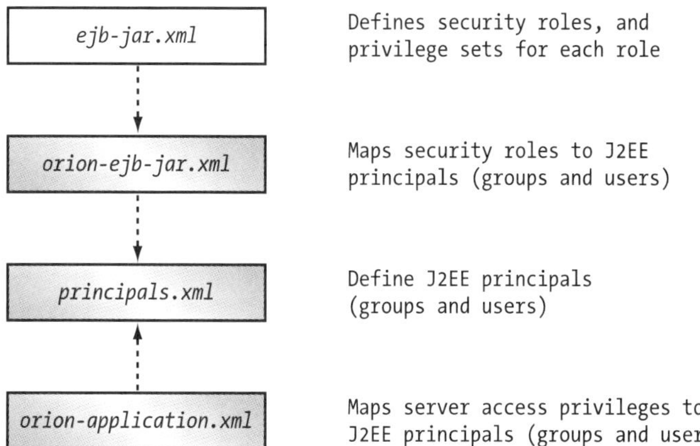

Figure 9-13. The security structure of the descriptors involved in the deployment of an EJB component. Standardized J2EE deployment descriptors have white backgrounds, and OAS-specific deployment descriptors have shaded backgrounds.

A remote application client needs two types of privileges to be able to connect to the OAS and execute remote methods in an EJB server:

- First, the application client must perform a lookup in the JNDI registry of the application server. The J2EE principal used by the application client must therefore be granted RMI connection and JNDI lookup privileges. For the OAS, these privileges are granted in the `orion-application.xml` deployment descriptor.

- Second, the application client must invoke remote methods in the EJB server. The J2EE principal used by the application client must therefore be granted method execute privileges on the EJB server, which means that the J2EE principal must be mapped to a `securityRole` defined in the `ejb-jar.xml` deployment descriptor. For the OAS, this mapping is done in the `orion-ejb-jar.xml` deployment descriptor.

We have already seen how the `defaultUserRole` security role was mapped to the `standardUsers` principal in the `orion-ejb-jar.xml`, but we have not yet seen how the principal `appClientUser` with the password `whoops` was created or mapped to the `standardUsers` group. This is done in the `principals.xml` deployment descriptor. Let's take a look at its code in Listing 9-10.

Listing 9-10. The `principals.xml` *deployment descriptor*

```
<?xml version="1.0"?>
<!DOCTYPE principals PUBLIC
     "//Evermind - Orion Principals//"
     "http://www.orionserver.com/dtds/principals.dtd">

<principals>
     <groups>
          <group name="standardUsers">
               <permission name="rmi:login" />
               <permission name="com.evermind.server.rmi.RMIPermission" />
               <description>StandardUsers for this application</description>
          </group>
     </groups>
     <users>
          <user username="appClientUser" password="whoops">
               <description>Application Client User</description>
               <group-membership group="standardUsers" />
          </user>
     </users>
</principals>
```

The `principals.xml` deployment descriptor defines one user called `appClientUser` with the password `whoops`, and adds the newly defined user to the group `standardUsers`. Also, the `standardUsers` group is granted RMI login privileges in the application server. These privileges are required by the application client to connect to the application server at all.

Simply being able to connect using RMI is not sufficient for an application client because it must still be granted access to perform lookups in the JNDI registry. This configuration setting is done in the `orion-application.xml` deployment descriptor shown in Listing 9-11.

Listing 9-11. The `orion-application.xml` *deployment descriptor. The security settings are shown in bold.*

```
<?xml version="1.0"?>
<!DOCTYPE orion-application PUBLIC
     "-//Evermind//DTD J2EE Application runtime 1.2//EN"
     "http://www.orionserver.com/dtds/orion-application.dtd">

<orion-application deployment-version="1.5.2">
     <ejb-module remote="false" path="exchangeEJBServer" />
     <persistence path="persistence" />
     <principals path="principals.xml" />
     <log>
          <file path="application.log" />
     </log>
     <namespace-access>
          <read-access>
               <namespace-resource root="">
                    <security-role-mapping name="&lt;jndi-user-role&gt;">
                         <group name="administrators" />
                         <group name="standardUsers" />
                    </security-role-mapping>
               </namespace-resource>
          </read-access>
          <write-access>
               <namespace-resource root="">
                    <security-role-mapping name="&lt;jndi-user-role&gt;">
                         <group name="administrators" />
                    </security-role-mapping>
               </namespace-resource>
          </write-access>
     </namespace-access>
</orion-application>
```

The `orion-application.xml` deployment descriptor grants read access in all of the JNDI namespace to any principal belonging to either the administrators group or the `standardUsers` group. Write access in the JNDI registry is granted only to principals belonging in the administrators group. This way, the JNDI registry is effectively rendered read-only to all principals in the `standardUsers` group. This may be a good security precaution, as application clients should generally not be permitted to bind (or rebind) objects in the JNDI registry.

Let's proceed to look at the OAS deployment structure to answer the ever-present question of all application servers: "Where should the different files be deployed?"

Application Server Deployment Structure

The OAS uses two separate directory structures to deploy an application. First, all standard components and deployment descriptor files are deployed in a directory that's normally named `applications`. Each application is deployed in a named directory of its own, with all its contained components deployed in subdirectories. Thus, if you deploy a J2EE application named `ExchangeApp` that contains an EJB component called `exchangeEJBServer`, the `application.xml` deployment descriptor would be found in the `<ORION_HOME>/applications/ExchangeApp/META-INF` directory, and the `ejb-jar.xml` deployment descriptor would be found in the `<ORION_HOME>/applications/ExchangeApp/exchangeEJBServer/META-INF` directory.

Second, custom deployment descriptor files are found in a separate directory structure, normally deployed below the `<ORION_HOME>/application-deployments` directory. Thus, our J2EE application named `ExchangeApp` that contains an EJB component called `exchangeEJBServer` has a custom application configuration file called `orion-application.xml` deployed in `<ORION_HOME>/application-deployments/ExchangeApp` and a custom Web application configuration file called `orion-ejb-jar.xml` deployed in the `<ORION_HOME>/application-deployments/ExchangeApp/exchangeEJBServer` directory. The deployment structure just described is shown in Figure 9-14.

To Package or Not to Package…

The OAS and the WebLogic Application Server (version 6.0 and later) have a nice feature that allows an EJB component to be deployed to and managed by the application server even if it's not packaged in a JAR file. This *EJB development mode* is not unique among application servers, but it is a welcome relief during development to minimize the time consumed by unnecessary repetitive tasks such as packing the compiled files in a JAR and compiling its stubs using proprietary compilation tools. Although the process is very similar for each application server, the time spent learning the eccentricities of yet another stub compiler becomes excessive after relatively few new application servers are learned.

Instead, simply create a top-level directory that mirrors the directory structure of the normal EJB JAR. After you set the output root path of your compiler, all you need to do is simply recompile the code to update the running EJB component—if the application server supports so-called *hot deployment* of EJB components (reloading them in a running EJB container).

The OAS autocompiles any EJB classes found in an application directory, placing all the stub and skeleton classes in a single file called `deployment.cache` in

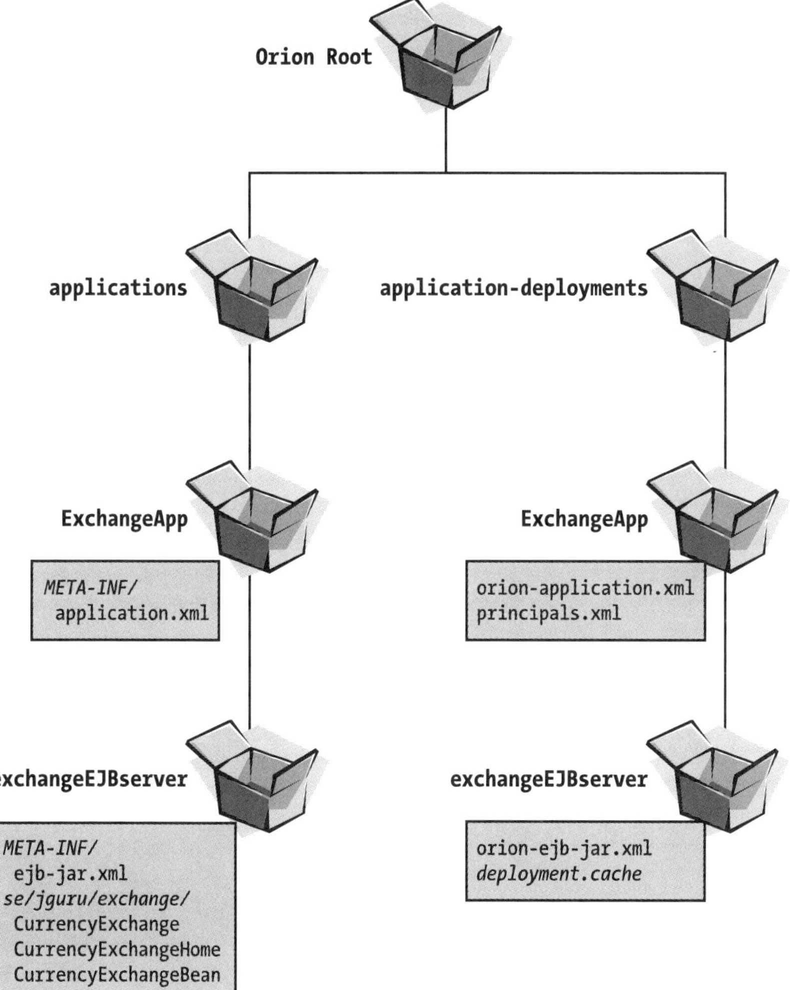

Figure 9-14. The content of the two `ExchangeApp` *application deployment directories in the OAS structure. Note that the only component deployed in the structure shown is the EJB component* `exchangeEJBServer`. *The* `deployment.cache` *file consists of compiled Java bytecode that is read and used by the application server as needed.*

the directory `<ORION_ROOT>/application-deployments/<ApplicationName>/<EJBName>`. As shown in Figure 9-15, the total size of the class files generated by this very simple EJB component are roughly 5KB.

With the server-side deployment completed, let's look at the application client deployment required.

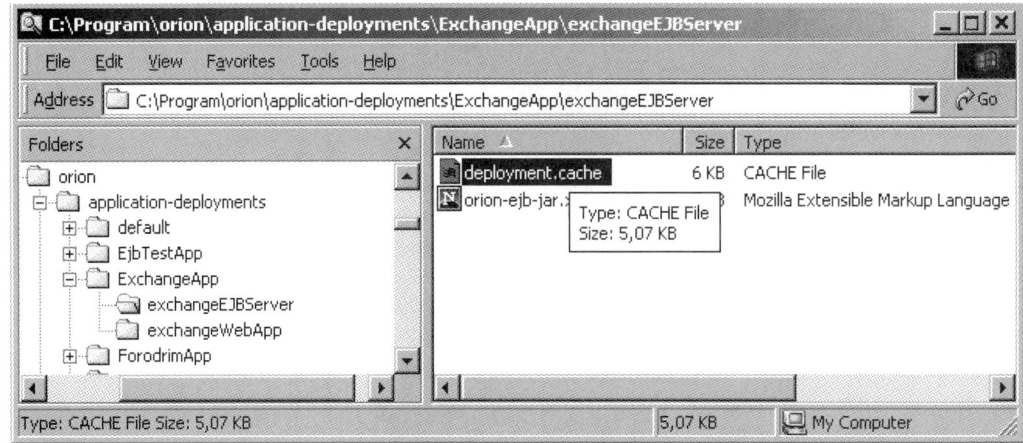

Figure 9-15. The `deployment.cache` *file contains all compiled stub and skeleton classes of the* `CurrencyExchange` *EJB component. Note the custom deployment descriptor* `orion-ejb-jar.xml`*, which is deployed in the same directory.*

Application Client Deployment Structure

The needs of the application client are not as great as those of the corresponding application server components. The client JAR file doesn't need to contain any skeleton-side implementation classes—and, in the case of the OAS, nor any stub implementation classes—so the principal content of the client JAR file is shown in Figure 9-16.

It is imperative that the application client contains all required client libraries so it can connect to the application server in question. These libraries are generally packaged in a JAR file that must be present in the CLASSPATH of the running application client. In the structure shown in Figure 9-16, the libraries are placed in the `lib` directory; simply copy the JAR files from the Orion root directory.

We've already walked through the source code for all of the class files in the implementation section, but the two descriptors `application-client.xml` and `orion-application-client.xml` must be presented. We'll start with the J2EE standard file `application-client.xml`, which is detailed in the next section.

Application Client Deployment Descriptors

The standardized J2EE deployment descriptor for application clients is smaller than the corresponding descriptors for server-side components, such as EJBs or Web applications. However, the application client may use its local JNDI context

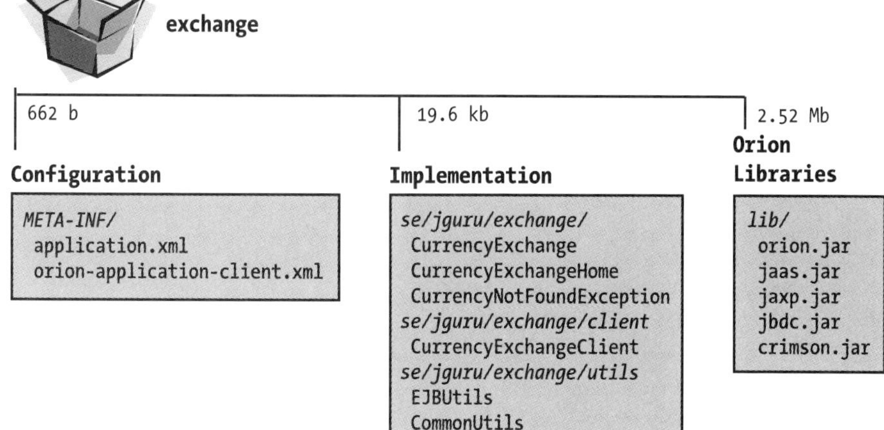

Figure 9-16. Contents of the EJB application client JAR, with the total file sizes of the different file. Note that the library files required to connect to the application server are much larger than the entire application client.

similar to how the server-side components use the JNDI context of the application server. The DTD structure of the `application-client.xml` deployment descriptor is illustrated in Figure 9-17.

In our case, the application client only needs to access the Remote and Home interfaces of the `CurrencyExchange` EJB component. The `application-client.xml` descriptor of the `CurrencyExchange` bean is therefore rather small, as shown in the following code snippet:

```
<?xml version="1.0"?>
<!DOCTYPE application-client PUBLIC
     "-//Sun Microsystems, Inc.//DTD J2EE Application Client 1.2//EN"
     "http://java.sun.com/j2ee/dtds/application-client_1_3.dtd">

<application-client>
     <display-name>The application client</display-name>
     <ejb-ref>
          <ejb-ref-name>CurrencyExchanger</ejb-ref-name>
          <ejb-ref-type>Session</ejb-ref-type>
          <home>se.jguru.exchange.CurrencyExchangeHome</home>
          <remote>se.jguru.exchange.CurrencyExchange</remote>
     </ejb-ref>
</application-client>
```

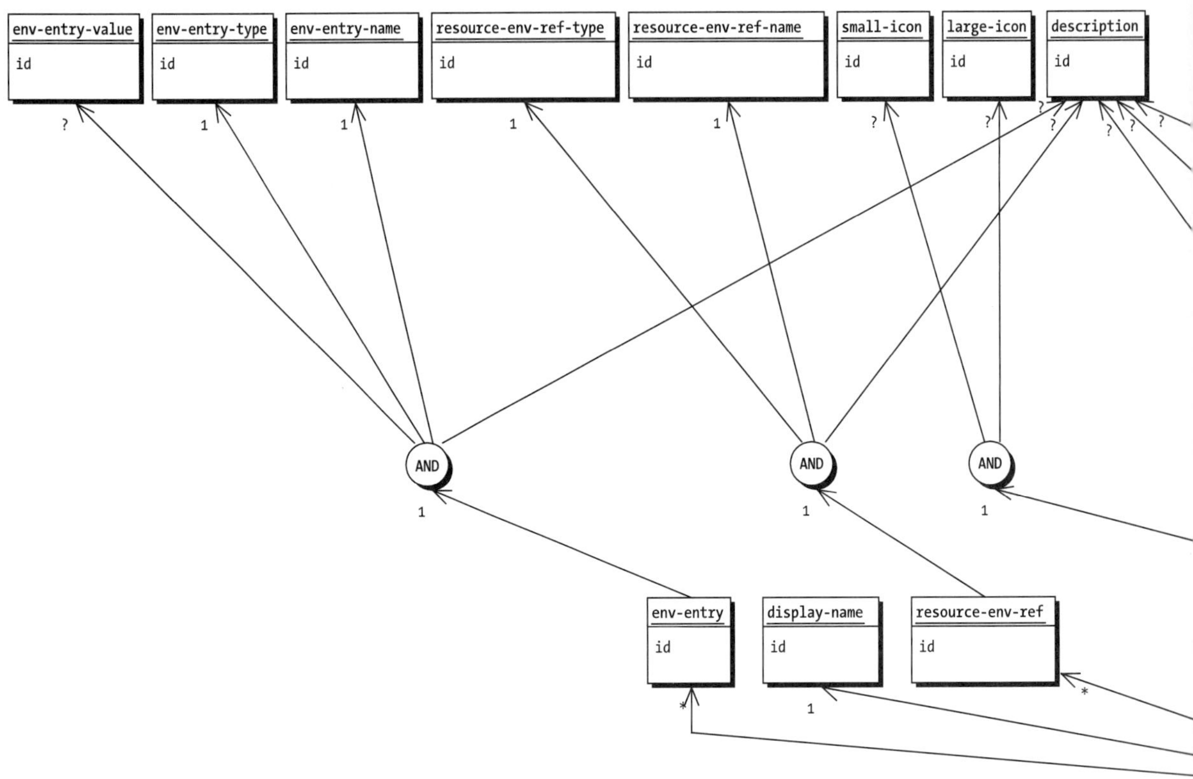

Figure 9-17. The structure of the standard J2EE deployment descriptor `application-client.xml`

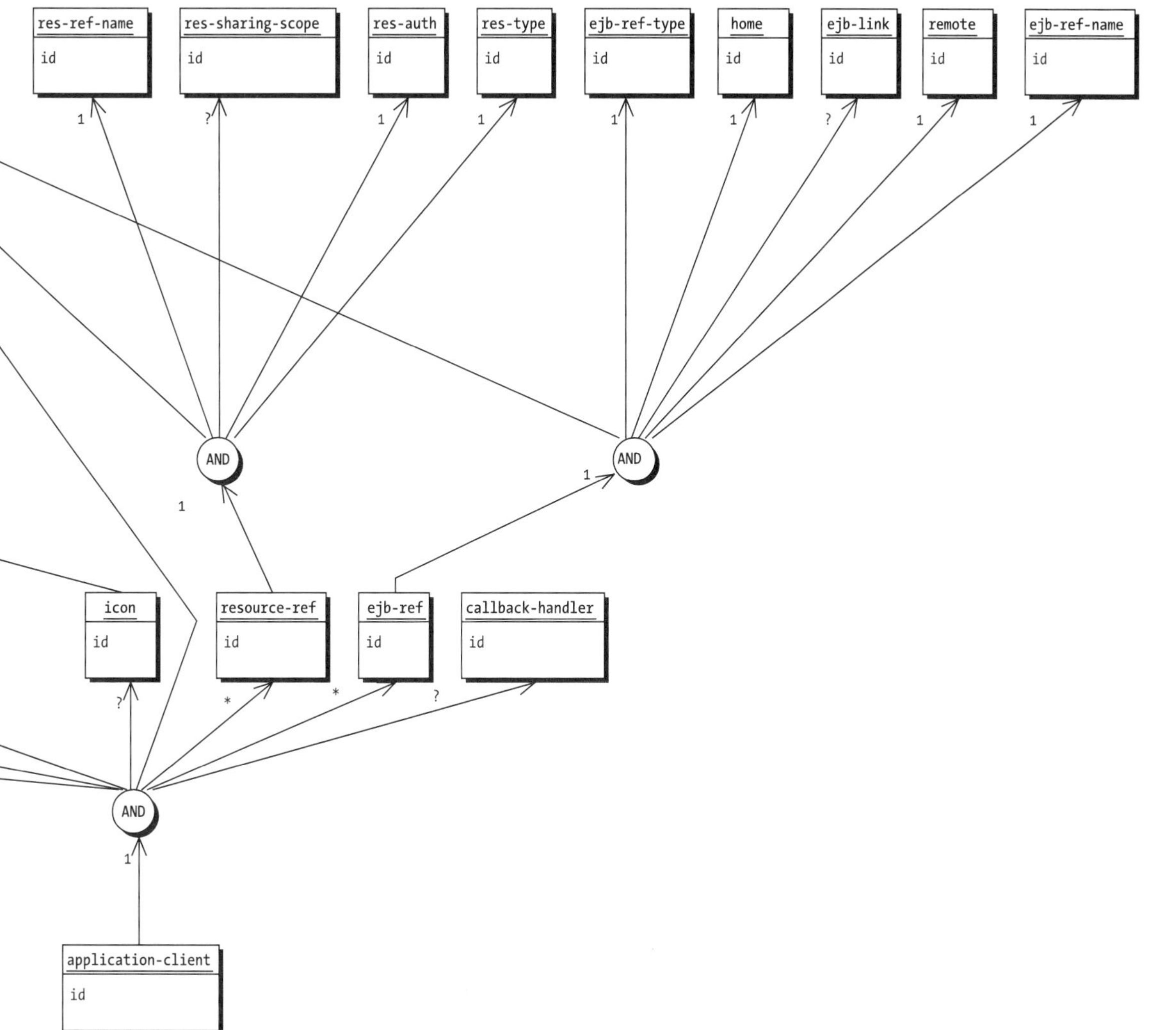
res-ref-name
id
res-sharing-scope
id
res-auth
id
res-type
id
ejb-ref-type
id
home
id
ejb-link
id
remote
id
ejb-ref-name
id
1
?
1
1
1
1
?
1
1
AND
AND
1
1
icon
id
resource-ref
id
ejb-ref
id
callback-handler
id
?
*
*
?
AND
1
application-client
id

The only entry in the application-client.xml defines an EJB reference. However, the CurrencyExchanger EJB reference has not yet been mapped to a real JNDI name. This is done in the custom deployment descriptor, orion-application-client.xml.

Thankfully, the following custom application client deployment descriptor is small and straightforward:

```
<?xml version="1.0"?>
<!DOCTYPE orion-application-client PUBLIC
     "-//Evermind//DTD J2EE Application-client runtime 1.2//EN"
     "http://www.orionserver.com/dtds/orion-application-client.dtd">

<orion-application-client>
       <ejb-ref-mapping name="CurrencyExchanger"
              mapping="se/jguru/exchange/CurrencyExchangeBean" />
</orion-application-client>
```

The CurrencyExchanger EJB reference is mapped to the JNDI name se/jguru/exchange/CurrencyExchangeBean which was used in the application server to bind the Home interface of the CurrencyExchange EJB component. With this last deployment descriptor, we have provided all the deployment descriptors required for the small application.

Don't rush on to the next example without some time for reflection on the example you just walked through.

Reflections on the Centralizing Exchange Rates Example

The centralizing exchange rates example illustrates quite well three facts of life for J2EE Java developers:

> **The actual Java development of distributed EJB components is quite simple, and the time spent actually implementing the business functionality of any component is minimal.** However, it is quite possible to make all classes of a faulty EJB component compile because the relations between method names and types in the Home and Remote interfaces of the EJB component are only loosely related (from a compiler's standpoint) to the corresponding method implementations in the Bean class. Many application servers therefore contain special verifiers that check dependencies between the three types of an EJB component.

The number of deployment descriptors needed by a normal J2EE application is large, and the time spent deploying a correctly compiled J2EE application component is frequently staggering. The saying "code for 5 minutes, deploy for 25 hours" has more truth in it than one would sometimes like to admit. Moreover, the XML text in the deployment descriptors cannot be type checked in the same manner as compilable Java code.

The client libraries that are required to establish a RMI/IIOP connection to the server are currently rather large. The OAS has a fairly small client-side library footprint compared to some of the other application servers with a fair market share. Currently, therefore, deployment of J2EE application clients is limited to PC-like systems. If you want to communicate with more-limited devices (such as PDAs or cell phones), your application must provide a thin client talking to a server-side proxy, normally using HTTP and a Web application proxy.

Despite its small size, the centralizing exchange rates example illustrates all of the steps and considerations that are required to distribute stateless server-side components to a set of clients. Let's move on to a common problem for all J2EE application developers: refactoring an old Web application to a modern architecture for the data tier.

CHAPTER 10

Example 2: Refactoring an Old-Style Web Application

THIS EJB EXAMPLE ILLUSTRATES a fairly common problem: migrating a Web application from old-style servlet-to-database interaction to session EJB proxy operation. This problem, or something quite similar, is frequently encountered by developers who are required to update a first-generation Web application to a more modern architecture.

Many older Web applications have a structure similar to that illustrated by Figure 10-1. Depending on the commands issued by the user, the application's data is read from or written to a back-end database. For our purposes, any database-like legacy server may be substituted for the database in Figure 10-1; the system architecture would not change.

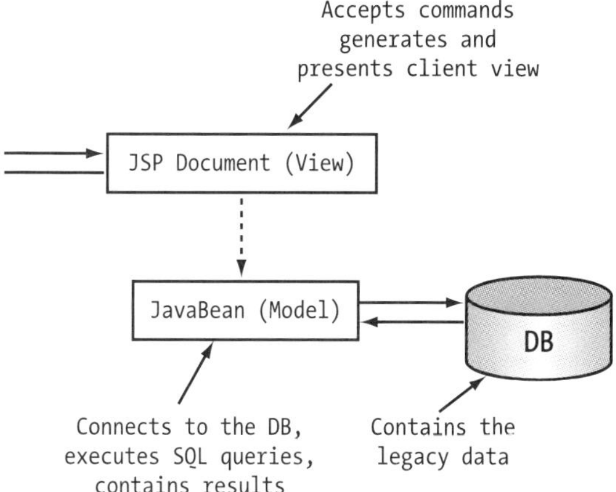

Figure 10-1. Principal structure of many old-style Web applications in which the JSP document View communicates directly with a relational database using its JavaBean model.

Due to its construction, the application illustrated in Figure 10-1 conceals many problems, most of which are hard to discover in the early production phase of the system lifetime (especially if the system is small or has a small number of users). For high-volume systems or systems with great demands on stability, the hidden problems become evident much earlier in the system lifetime. These drawbacks may possibly become too cumbersome for the slim system, which frequently results in a complete redesign of the system.

An alternative to completely redesigning is *refactoring*, wherein the system is migrated to a new design in small steps. The advantage of the small-steps approach is that the system may be continuously improved by a smaller number of people, which limits the total migration costs and increases the system insight of all developers on the migration project. This example demonstrates a small refactoring process by migrating the old-style Web application to an EJB-aware J2EE application.

Before starting the refactoring process, you should take a look at the original system; it is simpler to see the disadvantages of the system and its design in the code. As usual, you should start by taking a look at the resulting output of the system, shown in Figure 10-2.

The View of the Old-Style Web Application

As is customary for any search engine, the resulting output of the JSP document presents all of the matching database hits in its result list. The exact formatting of each result may be simpler than what is normally seen when issuing a real query to an Internet search engine, but it is sufficient for this simple intranet Web application.

Take a look in Listing 10-1 at the JSP document that produces the result list in Figure 10-2.

Figure 10-2. The resulting output of the old-style Web application. The data presented here has been collected from a relational database.

Listing 10-1. The `SearchAndResultsForm.jsp` *document*

```
<%--
     Import all Java classes and Model JavaBeans required for this
     Search and Result presenting JSP document. Note that all request
     Parameters which match a JavaBean property within the dbProxy
     Object are set using the <jsp:setProperty ... /> statement.
--%>
<%@ page import="java.util.*" %>
<jsp:useBean id="dbProxy" scope="session"
     class="se.jguru.webdb.view.DbProxyBean" />
<jsp:setProperty name="dbProxy" property="*" />
```

```
<HTML>
<HEAD>
    <META HTTP-EQUIV="content-type" CONTENT="text/html; charset=ISO-8859-1">
    <TITLE>
    WebSearch
    </TITLE>

    <style>
    <!--
     body {font-family: arial,sans-serif;}
    //-->
    </style>

<%--
     This client-side JavaScript sets the focus to the
     Query <input type="text" name="queryString">
--%>
    <script>
    <!--
     function setfocus() { document.query.queryString.focus(); }
    // -->
    </script>
</HEAD>

<%--
     The onLoad() client-side JavaScript callback method ensures
     That the setFocus() method is called when the page loads in the
     Client browser.
--%>
<BODY body bgcolor=#ffffff text=#000000 link=#0000cc
      vlink=551a8b alink=#ff0000 onLoad=setfocus()>
<center>

    <img align="left" src="silly.jpg">

    <table cellspacing="0" cellpadding="2" bgcolor="#111122" border="0">
    <tr><td>
    <table cellspacing="0" cellpadding="0" bgcolor="#ffffaa" border="0">
    <FORM method="post" name="query">
    <tr align=center valign=middle >
```

```
      <td>
          <H1>Search the Web</H1>
          <br>
      </td>
     </tr>

     <tr align=center valign=middle >
      <td>
<%--
      This is the TextField definition for the text input to the database query
--%>
           <input type=text value="" name="queryString" size=60 maxlength=250>
          <br>
          <input name=subm type=submit value="Find it!">
      </td>
     </tr>
     </FORM>
     </table>
     </td></tr>
     </table>
     </center>


     <%
      if(dbProxy.getResultsFound())
      {

      List urls = dbProxy.getMatchingUrls();
      List data = dbProxy.getDocumentData();

     %>
     <h2><%= "" + urls.size() %> results found:</h2>
     <%

      for(int i = 0; i < urls.size(); i++)
      {
          String currentUrl = "" + urls.get(i);
          String currentData = "" + data.get(i);

          if(currentData.length() > 50)
             currentData = currentData.substring(0,49) + "...";
          int spacePosition = currentData.indexOf(" ", 24);
          if(spacePosition > 40) spacePosition = 25;
     %>
```

```
<!-- List item: <%= i %> -->
<a href="<%= currentUrl %>"><%= currentUrl %></a><br>
<font size=-1>
 <%= currentData.substring(0, spacePosition) %><br>
 <%= currentData.substring(spacePosition) %>
</font>
<br><br>

<%
 }
 }
 else
 {
%>
<h2>
No results found.
</h2>
<% } %>

</BODY>
</HTML>
```

Yuck! The preceding JSP document is as close as you could ever come to code that is impossible to maintain. Some—but not all—of the problems with the monolithic JSP document are listed here:

- The JSP document has a mixture of View and Controller properties, which means that the execution flow cannot be altered in a document separate from the user interface specification. (It is really a Delegate, rather than a View or a Controller.)

- Because the HTML and Java code are mixed, we need a programmer who understands HTML (or a Web designer who can program Java) to modify the document. Most Web designers would have to watch their step while making any alteration to the document, for fear of breaking any Java code.

- It is very hard to read the JSP document and quickly get a good grasp of what it does. Imagine, for instance, that you have to come back and edit it three months after creating it. Unless you have a photographic memory, you would simply have to take the time to read through and understand the document again.

Having seen the sad state of the JSP view, take a quick look at the two classes that build the Web application model: `DbProxyBean` and `DbConnectorPool`.

The Model of the Old-Style Web Application

The JSP document instantiates its JavaBean Model of type `se.jguru.webdb.view.DbProxyBean`. The DbProxyBean, in turn, uses a singleton instance of the `DbConnectorPool` to talk to a relational database. This is required because a new `DbProxyBean` object is created for every new search; if the database connection is opened from within the `DbProxyBean` constructor, each search would be very slow because establishing a database connection is a rather slow process.

The task of the `DbConnectorPool` is to open a set of database connections and hand one of the already opened connections over to the `DbProxyBean` when it calls the `getConnection` method. The same database connection must be returned with the `release` method in the `DbConnectorPool`; otherwise, the pool soon ceases to function.

Figure 10-3 illustrates the static relationship between the JSP View and the two model classes.

DbProxyBean

Start to investigate the nature of the `DbProxyBean`, which is the JavaBean model for the JSP document. The structure of the `DbProxyBean` shown in Listing 10-2 is quite straightforward, as its main function is to make the results of a database query available to the JSP View.

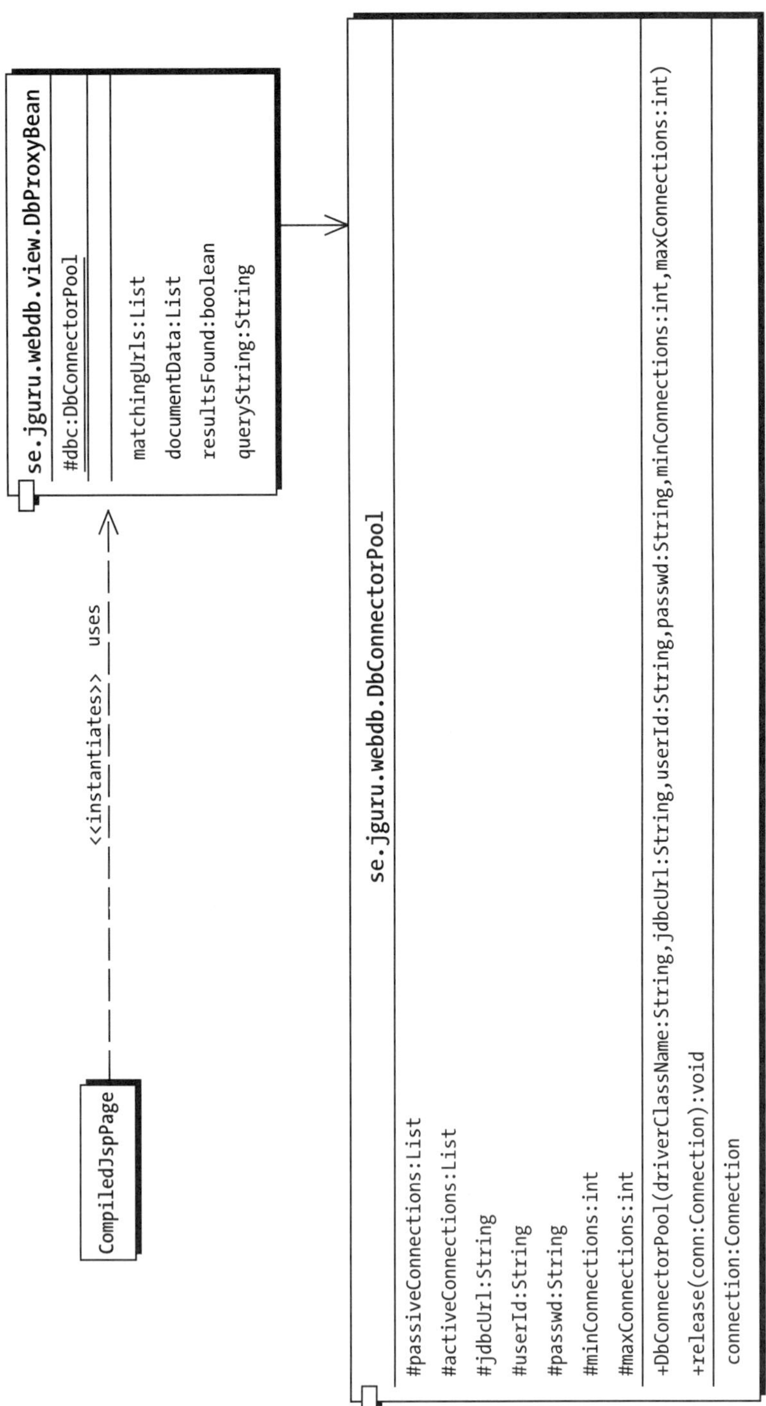

Figure 10-3. UML diagram showing the relational structure of the small Web application. Note that the `dbc` *member of the* `DbProxyBean` *class is static; all instances of the* `DbProxyBean` *share the same* `DbConnectorPool` *object.*

Listing 10-2. The `DbProxyBean` *class*

```
/*
 * Copyright (c) 2000,2001 jGuru Europe.
 * All rights reserved.
 */

package se.jguru.webdb.view;

import se.jguru.webdb.DbConnectorPool;
import java.sql.*;
import java.util.*;

/**
 * The DbProxyBean is a JavaBean proxy class which
 * contains Model data for the JSP document View.
 */
public class DbProxyBean
{
    // The DbConnector pool from which all
    // instances of this DbProxyBean gets
    // its Connections.
    protected static DbConnectorPool dbc;

    static
    {
        // Define values for the DbConnectorPool
        String driver = "interbase.interclient.Driver";
        String jdbcUrl = "jdbc:interbase://localhost/C:/Program/"
                         + "InterBase/InterBase/WEBPAGEDB";
        String userId = "webUser";
        String passwd = "Mellon";
        int minConnections = 5;
        int maxConnections = 10;

        // Create the DbConnectorPool instance.
        dbc = new DbConnectorPool(driver, jdbcUrl, userId,
        passwd, minConnections, maxConnections);
    }

    // The result Lists from the DB query
    private List matchingUrls = null;
    private List documentData = null;
```

```
// Toggle flag to verify if any results
// were found in the DB query.
private boolean resultsFound;

//
// JavaBean getter methods which
// should be used from within
// the JSP view.
//

public List getMatchingUrls()
{
    return this.matchingUrls;
}

public List getDocumentData()
{
    return this.documentData;
}

public boolean getResultsFound()
{
    return this.resultsFound;
}

/**
 * Set the DB query string, execute the query and
 * populate the internal model variables of this
 * JavaBean proxy.
 */
public void setQueryString(String query)
{
    if (query == null) return;

    // Re-create empty result lists
    this.matchingUrls = new ArrayList();
    this.documentData = new ArrayList();

    // Connection from the pool
    Connection conn = null;

    try
    {
        // Get a connection to the Database
        conn = dbc.getConnection();
```

```
        // Create a Statement
        Statement stmnt = conn.createStatement();

        // Fire the query, and check if we got any
        // resulting rows back from the DB
        ResultSet rs = stmnt.executeQuery("select url, data from "
                    + "webpages where data like '%" + query + "%'");
        boolean hasNext = rs.next();

        if (!hasNext)
        {
            // No results were found.
            this.resultsFound = false;
        }
        else
        {
            // Results were found.
            this.resultsFound = true;

            // Create numerical constants for the
            // columns which should be selected.
            int URL = 1;
            int DATA = 2;

            do
            {
                // Get the data from the current
                // row in the ResultSet
                this.matchingUrls.add(rs.getString(URL));
                this.documentData.add(rs.getString(DATA));
            }
            while (rs.next());
        }
    }
    catch (SQLException ex)
    {
        // This should not happen, unless some arcane database error
        // arose. Log it, and bail out.
        System.err.println("[DbProxyBean::setQueryString]: Could not "
        + "perform database query: " + ex);
    }
```

```
            finally
            {
                // Release the connection back to the pool
                dbc.release(conn);
            }
        }
    }
```

The DbProxyBean has three main sections, corresponding to its three main tasks:

Providing constructor parameters to, and creating an instance of the DbConnectorProxy class. This is the first part, including the protected static DbConnectorProxy variable, and the static initializer block. In the static initializer, the DbConnectorProxy object is created, after collecting all attributes required for the constructor.

Declaring all variables holding the state of a database search, including public accessor (getter) methods. All the getters follow the JavaBean naming convention, so all UML tools may quickly identify them as JavaBean properties. This is clear from Figure 10-3, in which the JavaBean properties are provided in the lower compartment of the class icon.

Defining a combined setter and query execution method (setQueryString) that adheres to the JavaBean naming convention. The method orchestrates the database query in a standard JDBC fashion. Note that the actual SQL query is provided as a string in this method, presenting a small portion of the physical view (that is, the names of the database table and its columns where the values are read).

The DbProxyBean is a small class, and it may therefore be seen as a small matter to look after and change for the maintenance phase of the Web application's life cycle. However, it is a poorly designed JSP proxy, especially if the needs of a slightly larger maintenance project are taken into consideration. Some of its problems are as follows:

The combined setter and execution method approach presents difficulties if other setter methods should be added in the future, by adding an extra constraint regarding the execution order of the setters. The combined setter and execution method must be run last of all the setters, and this must be enforced in all JSP View documents that use the particular JavaBean proxy. This effectively prevents all forms of reuse of the JavaBean proxy class.

Hard-coded parameters for the DbConnectionPool implies that a recompilation is required to alter any of the database connection parameters. What happens if the data is moved to another database, or the database administrator chooses to rename the database user?

In its current implementation, the JavaBean proxy must know the physical structure of the database, as the SQL statement is hard-coded into its `setQueryString` method. This is never a good design choice because few (if any) proxies should ever need to know the physical structure of the data it is to contain for the view. Imagine what would happen if the database table was altered for better performance or renamed to match a newly accepted and implemented corporate IS database structure.

DbConnectorPool

At last, we come to the `DbConnectorPool`, an extremely basic implementation of a database connection pool. Its quality and performance cannot compete with any industrial-strength pooling solutions, but it is small and simple to understand. It therefore serves as an adequate reference for our refactoring project. Take a look at its code in Listing 10-3.

Listing 10-3. The `DbConnectorPool` class

```
/*
 * Copyright (c) 2000,2001 jGuru Europe.
 * All rights reserved.
 */

package se.jguru.webdb;

import java.sql.*;
import java.util.*;
import java.io.*;

/**
 * The DbConnectorPool is a trivial implementation of a standalone
 * pool of DB Connections. Although far from industrial-strength, this
 * pool implementation illustrates some of the issues involved in
 * creating a general Resource Pool.
 */
public class DbConnectorPool
{
    // The pool of passive (unused) Connections
    protected List passiveConnections;
    // The pool of active (used) Connections
    protected List activeConnections;
```

```
protected String jdbcUrl;
protected String userId;
protected String passwd;

// Lower limit on the size of the connectionPool.
protected int minConnections;

// Higher limit on the size of the connectionPool.
protected int maxConnections;

/**
 * Connects to a relational DB and opens a pool of
 * database connections, which may be retrieved and
 * returned to the DbConnectorPool.
 *
 * @param driverClassName The class name of the Database driver used
 * @param jdbcUrl The jdbcUrl which we should connect to
 * @param userId The username which should be used in connecting to the DB
 * @param passwrd The password corresponding to the userId in the database.
 * @param minConnections The minimum size of this DbConnectionPool
 * @param maxConnections The maximum size of this DbConnectionPool
 */
public DbConnectorPool(String driverClassName, String jdbcUrl,
String userId, String passwd, int minConnections, int maxConnections)
throws IllegalArgumentException
{
    // Assign internal state
    this.minConnections = minConnections;
    this.maxConnections = maxConnections;
    this.jdbcUrl = jdbcUrl;
    this.userId = userId;
    this.passwd = passwd;

    // Create the pool
    this.activeConnections = Collections.synchronizedList(
        new ArrayList());
    this.passiveConnections = Collections.synchronizedList(
        new ArrayList());

    try
    {
        // Load the database driver class
        Class.forName(driverClassName);
```

```
        // Open minConnections number of connections
        // and add them to the List of Passive (i.e.
        // temporarily unused) Connections.
        for (int i = 0; i < minConnections; i++)
        {
            Connection aNewConnection =
                        DriverManager.getConnection(jdbcUrl, userId, passwd);
            this.passiveConnections.add(aNewConnection);
        }
    }
    catch (Exception ex)
    {
        // Log and re-throw the Exception
        System.err.println("[DbConnectorPool::<constructor>]: Could "
        + "not allocate " + minConnections + " connections to the Database: "
        + ex);

        throw new IllegalArgumentException("" + ex);
    }
}

/**
 * This method seleases the provided DB Connection
 * back to the pool of passive Connections.
 *
 * @param conn The Connection to release (place in the pool
 *        of open but unused Connections). Note that the
 *        conn parameter must reference a Connection previously
 *        received with a call to getConnection() in the same
 *        DbConnectorPool.
 */
public synchronized void release(Connection conn)
throws NullPointerException, IllegalStateException
{
    // Check sanity
    if (conn == null) throw new NullPointerException(
        "[DbConnectorPool::release]: "
        + "Cannot handle null connection argument."
    );

    if (this.passiveConnections.contains(conn))
        throw new IllegalStateException(
            "[DbConnectorPool::release]: The connection "
            + " has already been released."
        );
```

```
        if (!this.activeConnections.contains(conn))
            throw new IllegalStateException(
                   "[DbConnectorPool::release]: The connection "
                   + " is not listed as active in this DbConnectorPool."
        );

        // Sane. Move the Connection to the passive pool
        this.activeConnections.remove(conn);
        this.passiveConnections.add(conn);
    }

    /**
     * Obtains a new connection from the pool, or creates a new one until
     * this.maxConnections number of connections are open. If the maximum
     * number of connections is reached, an IllegalStateException is thrown.
     *
     * @return a new DB Connection.
     * @exception IllegalStateException Thrown if the maximum number of DB
     *            connections from this DbConnectorPool is already active.
     */
    public synchronized Connection getConnection() throws IllegalStateException
    {
        // Check sanity
        if (this.activeConnections.size() >= this.maxConnections)
            throw new IllegalStateException("[DbConnectorPool::getConnection]: "
            + "Cannot create Connection; maximum pool size (" + this.maxConnections
            + ") " + "reached."
            );

        // The connection to return
        Connection conn = null;

        // Any connections left in the passive pool?
        if (this.passiveConnections.size() > 0)
        {
            conn = (Connection)this.passiveConnections.remove(0);
            this.activeConnections.add(conn);
        }
```

```
    else
    {
        try
        {
            // OK to open a new DB Connection.
            conn = DriverManager.getConnection(
                            this.jdbcUrl,
                            this.userId,
                            this.passwd
            );
        }
        catch (SQLException ex)
        {
            // Re-throw the Exception
            throw new IllegalStateException(
                  "[DbConnectorPool::getConnection]: Cannot "
                  + "create a new DbConnection: " + ex
            );
        }

        // Add the new connection to the activeConnections List
        this.activeConnections.add(conn);
    }

    // Done.
    return conn;
}

/*

//
// Unit test main
//

public static void main(String args[]) throws Exception
{
    // Create a test pool
    DbConnectorPool dbc = new DbConnectorPool("interbase.interclient.Driver",
    "jdbc:interbase://localhost/C:/Program/InterBase/InterBase/WEBPAGEDB",
    "webUser", "Mellon!", 5, 10);

    System.out.println("dbc.activeConnections.size():"
           + dbc.activeConnections.size() + ", dbc.passiveConnections.size():"
            + dbc.passiveConnections.size());
```

```
// Fake 8 parallell clients performing a select statement
ArrayList connList = new ArrayList();
ArrayList resultSets = new ArrayList();

for (int i = 0; i < 8; i++)
{
    // Get a connection
    Connection conn = dbc.getConnection();

    // Select data from the WEBPAGES table
    Statement stmnt = conn.createStatement();
        // For a JDBC 2.0 Read-Only ResultSet, use
        // conn.createStatement(ResultSet.TYPE_FORWARD_ONLY,
        // ResultSet.CONCUR_READ_ONLY);
    ResultSet rs = stmnt.executeQuery("select * from WEBPAGES");

    // Store for future reference
    connList.add(conn);
    resultSets.add(rs);
}

// List all results
for (int i = 0; i < resultSets.size(); i++)
{
    // Get the ResultSet
    ResultSet rs = (ResultSet)resultSets.get(i);
    ResultSetMetaData rsmd = rs.getMetaData();

    // Define the current row
    int currentRow = 1;

    while (rs.next())
    {
        StringBuffer rowData = new StringBuffer();
        rowData.append("[RS" + (i + 1) + ":" + currentRow + "]:");

        for (int j = 1; j <= rsmd.getColumnCount(); j++)
        {
            // Get the current cell value, as a String
            String currentCell = rs.getString(j);

            rowData.append(" '");
```

```
                // Truncate if necessary
                if (currentCell.length() > 20)
                    rowData.append(currentCell.substring(0, 20) + "...");
                else
                    rowData.append(currentCell);

                // Close the current cell printout
                rowData.append("'");
            }

            // Bump the current row.
            currentRow++;

            // Printout the current row
            System.out.println(rowData.toString());
        }

        // Done with the ResultSet
        rs.close();
    }

    // Release all Connections
    int theSize = connList.size();
    for (int i = 0; i < theSize; i++)
    {
        Connection conn = (Connection)connList.get(0);
        dbc.release(conn);

        // Remove the connection from the List
        connList.remove(conn);
    }

    System.out.println("dbc.activeConnections.size():"
            + dbc.activeConnections.size()
            + ", dbc.passiveConnections.size():"
            + dbc.passiveConnections.size()
    );
}
*/
}
```

The API of the `DbConnectorPool` is small and simple: it has a constructor that accepts all parameters specifying its mode of operations, a `getConnection` method that retrieves a `java.sql.Connection` from its pool of passive connections, and a release method that returns a connection to the pool. The main method, which provides unit testing for the DbConnectorPool, is currently commented out to indicate that this DbConnectorPool is launched in production (which, in itself, is a sad tribute to the absence of code quality).

The database used to connect to is a small Cloudscape database with the structure shown in Figure 10-4. The data stored in the WebPages table is used as the raw business data of the application.

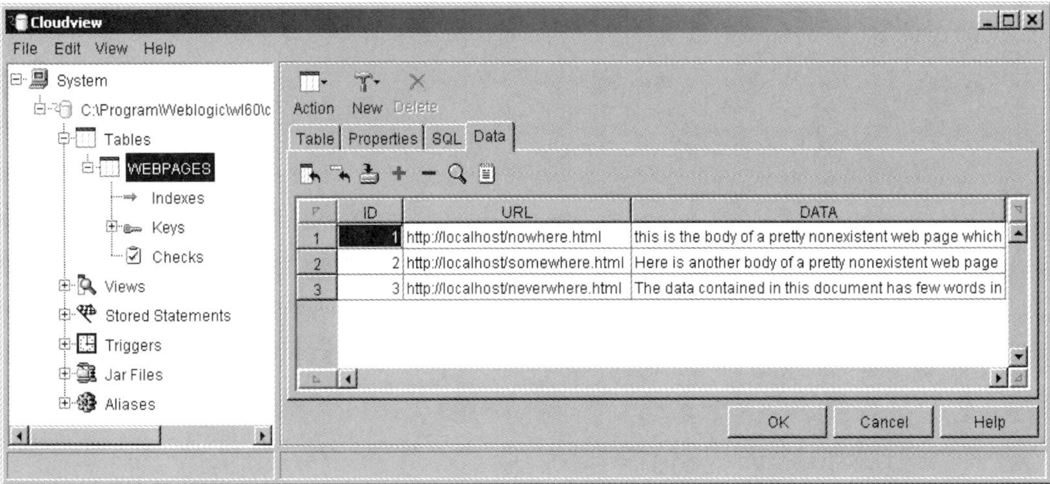

Figure 10-4. The data structure of the WebPages *table. The ID column is the primary key, the URL column contains the URL of a Web page document, and the DATA column contains the Web page document data.*

The call structure of the old-style Web application is shown in Figure 10-5, which shows both the initialization and service calls. Although the figure is greatly simplified, it provides an accurate illustration of the first call to the SearchAndResultForm.jsp document. For all subsequent calls, the DbConnectorPool instance is already present and doesn't need to be created again.

The data in the database is structured to contain a subset of the data in a normal Web search engine, such as Excite or Google. Of course, the database does not contain many documents. (In our case, the structure contains only the three documents seen in the search result list in Figure 10-2.) The purpose of this example is to show the migration process—not to show real Web data.

Enough talk about old-style Web applications! You are ready to start the EJB refactoring of this application by creating a generic EJB facade for the database.

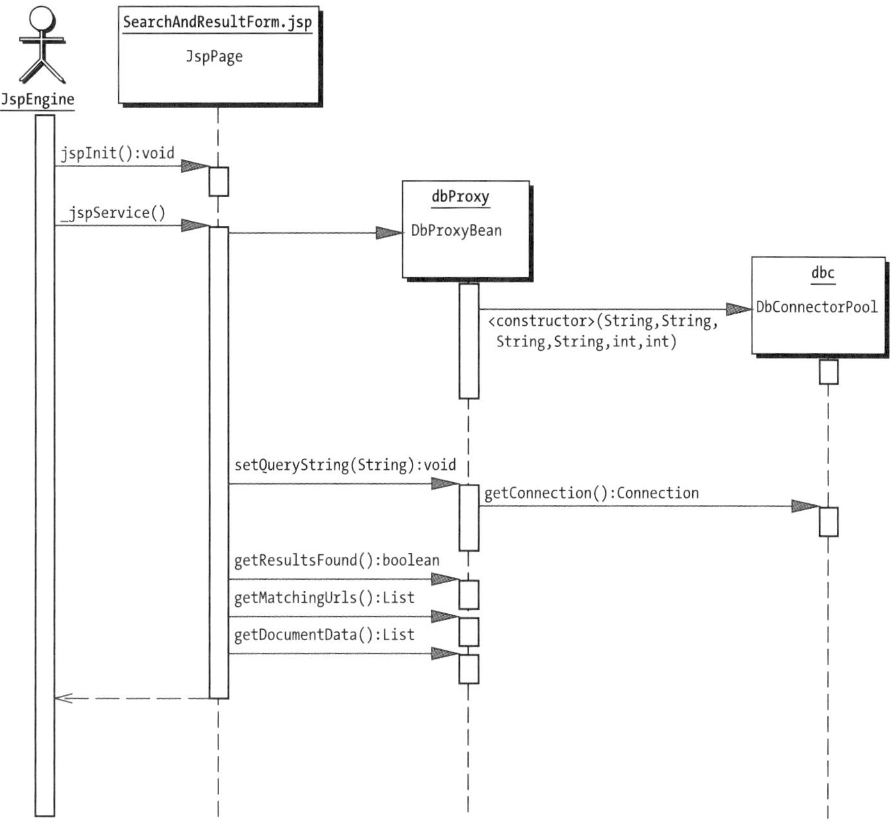

Figure 10-5. The simplified call structure of the old-style Web application

Creating a Generic EJB Facade for the Database

Being able to simplify things is a virtue in systems development. However, what is perceived as the simplest solution for one person is rarely the same for an entire organization or development project. In the eyes of most managers, "simplicity" is often achieved by creating a system that is simple enough that many people may understand and administer.

The database schema of the Web application may change, but the specifics of the new schema and database type won't be known for another two months. However, the refactoring project must start immediately to be able to finish on time. Simplicity therefore dictates that we must hide all of the data regarding the physical view of the database from all View documents.

Choosing to hide all legacy data behind a session EJB facade, we arrive at the system architecture shown in Figure 10-6. As the EJB component must run within an EJB container, the three entities may run on separate computer nodes. Therefore, the different classes are ordered into named tiers.

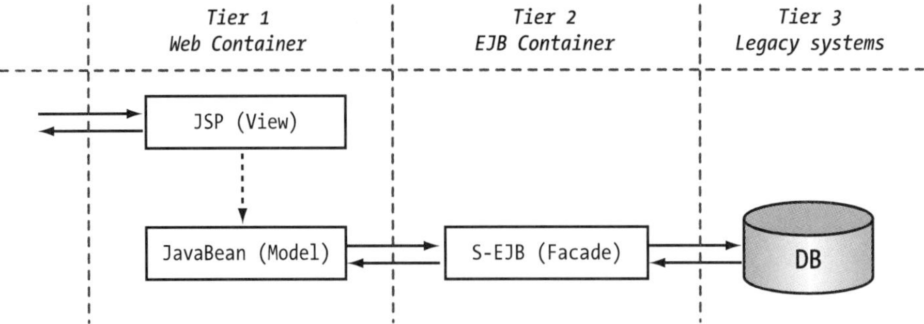

Figure 10-6. An EJB facade has been introduced in the structure to hide all details of the legacy database schema from the JavaBean proxy model.

Although the architecture shown in Figure 10-6 may not be as simple as the one shown in Figure 10-1, the introduction of the EJB facade greatly simplifies the process of gathering data from legacy systems. All JavaBean model proxy objects have a reference to an instance of the Remote interface of the session EJB facade, which exposes a simple API for querying the database. All complexities of connecting to the database and connection pooling are now managed by the EJB container in the application server. The amount of nonreusable code performing resource allocation and deallocation is therefore reduced.

In this step of the refactoring process, the data acquisition from the legacy tier has been changed to better match the needs of a modern enterprise application. Moreover, the old class files may still be present in the Web application so that the system may be reverted to the old model behavior if a problem should arise with the new model. All the new classes work to provide a better proxy structure, so they have been placed in the package `se.jguru.webdb.proxy`. Figure 10-7 shows the types defined in the `se.jguru.webdb.proxy` package.

The first iteration of the refactoring process altered the model proxy structure, adding the types shown in Figure 10-7 to replace the old proxy structure (`DbProxyBean` and `DbConnectorPool`). Each type in the proxy package has a well-defined purpose, which requires a bit of explaining.

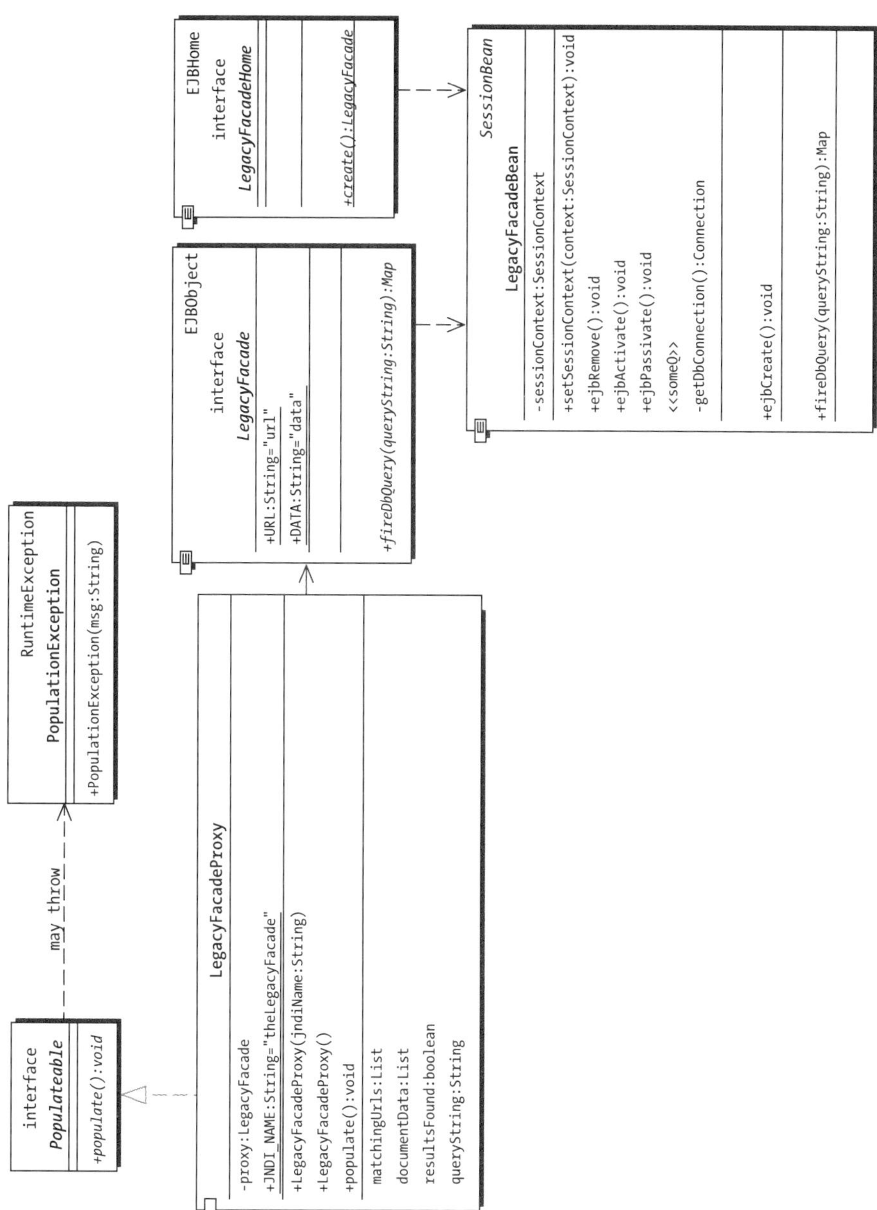

Figure 10-7. The types of the `se.jguru.webdb.proxy` package*. Although six different classes or interfaces are shown here, the only relevant types (containing method definitions, rather than just method declarations) are the* `LegacyFacadeProxy` *and the* `LegacyFacadeBean`*.*

In the next section, study the source code of each of the proxy files in the order in which they were described in Table 10-1.

Table 10-1. Types Used in This Refactoring Example

TYPE NAME	DESCRIPTION
`Populateable`	Interface specifying a standard way (the `populate` method) to populate the internal state of an instance that implements it. The `populate` method is invoked to collect all data from data sources, and process any results retrieved, and so on.
`PopulationException`	Exception thrown by the `populate` method if the population failed. Any message in the `PopulationException` should indicate why the population did not complete successfully.
`LegacyFacadeProxy`	The replacement for the `DbProxyBean` class. This is the JSP JavaBean proxy that acts as the model for the instances running inside the Web container. The `LegacyFacadeProxy` completely replaces `DbProxyBean`, rendering it deprecated.
`LegacyFacade`	The EJB remote interface of the facade proxy. This interface currently defines only one method for querying the database: `fireDbQuery`.
`LegacyFacadeHome`	The EJB Home interface that is used by the `LegacyFacadeProxy` constructor to create an instance of the `LegacyFacade`.
`LegacyFacadeBean`	Implementation class of the `LegacyFacade` EJB component. The `fireDbQuery` method performs the actual querying of the data source, and packages the results in a map.

The Populateable Interface

The purpose of the `Populateable` interface is to introduce a common way to start the population of the state of an object. The usage target of the `Populateable` interface are the JavaBean proxy classes that need a firm structure for populating their state. However, as the `Populateable` interface contains only a normal method definition, any class may use it to retrieve its internal state. The code of the `Populateable` interface is shown in Listing 10-4.

Listing 10-4. The `Populateable` *interface*

```
/*
 * Copyright (c) 2000,2001 jGuru Europe.
 * All rights reserved.
 */

package se.jguru.webdb.proxy;
```

```
/**
 * The Populatable interface specifies a common way to
 * execute any legacy data query, resulting in the
 * population of internal state in the Populateable
 * object.
 *
 * @author Lennart Jörelid
 */
public interface Populateable
{
    /**
     * Populates the internal state of this Populateable,
     * or throws a PopulationException describing why
     * the populate operation failed.
     */
    public void populate() throws PopulationException;
}
```

The PopulationException Class

When any `Populateable` object fails to properly populate its internal state during the execution of the `populate` method, a `PopulationException` is thrown. (See Listing 10-5.) The `PopulationException` indicates to the calling application why the population failed. As the `PopulationException` class extends RuntimeException, the compiler will not generate an error if the programmer does not place the call to populate inside a try block with a corresponding catch.

> **CAUTION** *Although it is convenient during development not to have to catch the myriad exceptions that may arise from a method call, be sure of what you do when defining custom exception types that extend* `RuntimeException`. *As programmers are not forced to catch* `RuntimeException` *(or subtypes thereof) by the compiler, some programmers do not bother to create proper error-handling routines for the custom exception—and system instability may result.*
>
> *On the other hand, if you are certain that a particular exception will not occur when a method is called from a particular object, you may save a lot of mindless coding if you use a* `RuntimeException` *subtype. Designer, know thy programmers, and act upon your instinct.*

Listing 10-5. The `PopulationException` *class*

```
/*
 * Copyright (c) 2000,2001 jGuru Europe.
 * All rights reserved.
 */

package se.jguru.webdb.proxy;

/**
 * Exception type reporting the causes of a failed population
 * of internal state variables.
 *
 * @author Lennart Jörelid
 */
public class PopulationException extends RuntimeException
{
    public PopulationException(String msg)
    {
     super(msg);
    }
}
```

The LegacyFacadeProxy Class

The `LegacyFacadeProxy` class shown in Listing 10-6 is the JavaBean model for the JSP View document. It contains a proxy for the session EJB facade, which implies that the `LegacyFacadeProxy` class must be an EJB client. All details of JNDI lookup are contained within the constructor of the LegacyFacadeProxy class.

Listing 10-6. The `LegacyFacadeProxy` *class*

```
/*
 * Copyright (c) 2000,2001 jGuru Europe.
 * All rights reserved.
 */
package se.jguru.webdb.proxy;

import javax.naming.*;
import javax.rmi.*;
import java.util.*;
```

```
/**
 * This LegacyFacadeProxy is a JavaBean proxy class which
 * contains Model data for the JSP document View. All data
 * is received from the LegacyFacade EJB.
 *
 * @author Lennart Jörelid
 */
public class LegacyFacadeProxy implements Populateable
{
    // The LegacyFacade proxy bean
    private LegacyFacade proxy;

    // The result Lists from the DB query
    private List matchingUrls = null;
    private List documentData = null;

    // Toggle flag to verify if any results
    // were found in the DB query.
    private boolean resultsFound;

    // Properties set by all the setter methods
    // of this proxy
    private String queryString;


    /**
     * Standard JNDI lookup name for the LegacyFacade
     */
    public static final String JNDI_NAME = "theLegacyFacade";

    /**
     * Sets up this LegacyFacadeProxy, originating from the
     * jndiName provided.
     *
     * @param jndiName The lookup string for the LegacyFacadeHome
     *        factory object for the proxy used in this class.
     */
```

```
public LegacyFacadeProxy(String jndiName)
{
 try
 {
    // Get the initial context
    //
    // This client runs within the application server, so we should
    // not be required to submit any initialization parameters to
    // the InitialContext constructor.
    Context ctx = new InitialContext();

    // Lookup the LegacyFacadeHome instance
    Object obj = ctx.lookup(jndiName);

    // Narrow the retrieved object to a LegacyFacadeHome
    LegacyFacadeHome home = (LegacyFacadeHome)
     PortableRemoteObject.narrow(obj, LegacyFacadeHome.class);

    // Create the LegacyFacade instance
    this.proxy = home.create();
 }
 catch(Exception ex)
 {
    // Log and bail out.
    System.err.println("[LegacyFacadeProxy::<constructor>]: Could "
    + "not create a LegacyFacade: " + ex);
 }
}

public LegacyFacadeProxy()
{
 this(JNDI_NAME);
}


//
// JavaBean getter methods which
// should be used from within
// the JSP view.
//
```

```
public List getMatchingUrls()
{
 return this.matchingUrls;
}

public List getDocumentData()
{
 return this.documentData;
}

public boolean getResultsFound()
{
 return this.resultsFound;
}

//
// JavaBean setter methods which
// should be called from within
// the JSP view.
//

public void setQueryString(String queryString)
{
 // Check sanity
 if(queryString == null) return;

 // Set the queryString
 this.queryString = queryString;
}

/**
 * Populates the internal state of this Populateable,
 * or throws a PopulationException describing why
 * the populate operation failed.
 */
public void populate() throws PopulationException
{
 // Check sanity
 if(this.queryString == null)
 throw new PopulationException("Could not populate the internal state "
     + "of the LegacyFacadeProxy. No queryString was supplied.");
```

```
        // Sane. Fire the DB query.
        try
        {
            Map results = this.proxy.fireDbQuery(this.queryString);

            // Assign the results to the internal state of this proxy
            this.documentData = (List) results.get(LegacyFacade.DATA);
            this.matchingUrls = (List) results.get(LegacyFacade.URL);
        }
        catch(Exception ex)
        {
            throw new PopulationException("Could not populate the internal "
             + "state: " + ex);
        }
       }
}
```

The `DbProxyBean` class from the old-style Web application has been replaced entirely by the `LegacyFacadeProxy` class, which is the new JavaBean proxy to use by the JSP View document. The LegacyFacadeProxy design has solved the following set of problems from the old-style Web application by improving the function earlier held by the `DbProxyBean` instance:

- **The `LegacyFacadeProxy` does not contain any knowledge of the physical structure of the database, as the `DbProxyBean` did.** Because no SQL is present in the `LegacyFacadeProxy`, it does not need recompilation whenever the database structure changes.

- **The `LegacyFacadeProxy` holds a reference to a Remote reference object from a session EJB, instead of a direct connection to a relational database.** Because the EJB container managing the proxy may be located on another physical node, the tight coupling between the Web container and the proxy implementation (that is, the business object tier) has been loosened. As a result, overall system flexibility is increased, and performance-enhancing techniques such as clustering may be seamlessly introduced in the system.

- **The `LegacyFacadeProxy` implements `Populateable`, which means that it adheres to a standard API for populating its internal state.** In this case, the implementation calls the `LegacyFacade` instance and receives the results of the RDB query. As a consequence, it is simple to add new setter methods to the `LegacyFacadeProxy` without having to worry about the call order of the setters, as previously discussed.

On the negative side, the `LegacyFacadeProxy` constructor has become much more complex, as all method calls to receive a valid reference to the `LegacyProxy` instance are performed in the constructor. The implementation the `populate` method is considerably more simple than the corresponding `setQueryString` method in the `DbProxyBean` class of the old-style Web application.

The LegacyFacade Remote Interface

The remaining three classes in the `se.jguru.webdb.proxy` package are the Remote, Home, and Bean implementation types for the `LegacyFacade` EJB component. Start with the small Remote interface in Listing 10-7, which holds only one method. Its source code is small enough that it may be presented directly.

Listing 10-7. The `LegacyFacade` *interface*

```
package se.jguru.webdb.proxy;

import java.rmi.*;
import javax.ejb.*;
import java.util.*;

/**
 * Remote interface of the Session EJB facade which
 * encapsulates all database manipulations from the
 * Legacy tier.
 *
 * @author Lennart Jörelid
 */
public interface LegacyFacade extends EJBObject
{
    /**
     * Return map Key constant indicating
     * the entry whose value holds all URLs found.
     */
    public static final String URL = "url";

    /**
     * Return map Key constant indicating
     * the entry whose value holds all
     * webpage data found.
     */
    public static final String DATA = "data";
```

```
    /**
     * Converts the queryString parameter to a
     * well-formed SQL query, and fires the query
     * to the database. The result is packaged as
     * a Map.
     *
     * @param queryString The query string, as
     *        provided by the user.
     *
     * @exception NullPointerException Thrown if the
     *            queryString parameter was null or
     *            empty.
     *
     * @return A Map containing all Lists with the
     *         results of the database query. If the
     *         database query returned no result, null
     *         is returned.
     */
    public Map fireDbQuery(String queryString)
     throws RemoteException, NullPointerException;
}
```

The LegacyFacade EJB remote interface simply contains one method declaration and two constants, to be used as keys in the map returned from the fireDbQuery method. The interface to the LegacyProxy component is therefore the simplest possible, and one method is sufficient for our purposes.

The LegacyFacadeHome Interface

The LegacyFacade EJB Home interface contains one single create method, as seen in Listing 10-8. The LegacyFacade EJB is stateless; because all of its data extraction is done in one method, it does not need to preserve state between method calls. As a consequence, the LegacyFacadeHome doesn't need to support any other create methods than the parameter-less variant.

Listing 10-8. The `LegacyFacadeHome` *interface*

```
package se.jguru.webdb.proxy;

import java.rmi.*;
import javax.ejb.*;

/**
 * Home interface of the LegacyFacade EJB component.
 * @author Lennart Jörelid
 */
public interface LegacyFacadeHome extends EJBHome
{
    public LegacyFacade create() throws RemoteException, CreateException;
}
```

The LegacyFacadeBean Class

The only EJB class that has nontrivial method definitions in this current refactoring iteration is the `LegacyFacadeBean` implementation class. As shown in Figure 10-7, the `LegacyFacadeBean` implements the EJB component version of the method definitions provided in the `LegacyFacade` and `LegacyFacadeHome` interfaces. Apart from the business method and the helper `getConnection` method, the `LegacyFacadeBean` is trivial.

Take a look at the source code of the `LegacyFacadeBean` implementation class in Listing 10-9.

Listing 10-9. The `LegacyFacadeBean` *implementation class*

```
/*
 * Copyright (c) 2000,2001 jGuru Europe.
 * All rights reserved.
 */
package se.jguru.webdb.proxy;

import java.rmi.*;
import javax.ejb.*;
import java.sql.*;
import javax.naming.*;
import javax.sql.*;
import java.util.*;
```

```
/**
 * Implementation class of the LegacyFacade EJB component.
 *
 * @author Lennart Jörelid
 */

public class LegacyFacadeBean implements SessionBean
{
    //
    // Mandatory members for the SessionContext of this bean
    //
    private SessionContext sessionContext;

    public void setSessionContext(SessionContext context)
    {
     sessionContext = context;
    }

    //
    // Life cycle methods for this SessionBean
    //

    public void ejbCreate()
    {
    }

    public void ejbRemove()
    {
    }

    public void ejbActivate()
    {
    }

    public void ejbPassivate()
    {
    }

    /**
     * Converts the queryString parameter to a
     * well-formed SQL query, and fires the query
     * to the database. The result is packaged as
     * a Map.
     *
```

```
 * @param queryString The query string, as
 *        provided by the user.
 *
 * @exception NullPointerException Thrown if the
 *            queryString parameter was null or
 *            empty.
 *
 * @return A Map containing all Lists with the
 *         results of the database query. If the
 *         database query returned no result, null
 *         is returned.
 */
public Map fireDbQuery(String queryString)
 throws NullPointerException
{
 // Check sanity
 if (queryString == null)
 throw new NullPointerException("[LegacyFacadeBean::fireDbQuery()]: "
     + "Cannot handle null queryString.");

 if(queryString.equalsIgnoreCase("")) return null;

 // Create new result Lists which will hold
 // the answer to the query.
 ArrayList matchingUrls = new ArrayList();
 ArrayList documentData = new ArrayList();
 Map toReturn = new HashMap();

 // Get a Connection from our DataSource
 Connection conn = this.getDbConnection();

 // Check sanity
 if(conn == null) return null;

 try
 {
     // Create a Statement
     Statement stmnt = conn.createStatement();

     // Fire the query, and check if we got any
     // resulting rows back from the DB
     ResultSet rs = stmnt.executeQuery("select url, data from "
      + "webpages where data like '%" + queryString + "%'");
     boolean hasNext = rs.next();
```

```
        if (!hasNext)
        {
         // No results were found.
         return null;
        }
        else
        {
         // Create numerical constants for the
         // columns which should be selected.
         int URL = 1;
         int DATA = 2;

         do
         {
             // Get the data from the current
             // row in the ResultSet
             matchingUrls.add(rs.getString(URL));
             documentData.add(rs.getString(DATA));
         }
         while (rs.next());

         // Pack the results into the Map
         toReturn.put(LegacyFacade.URL, matchingUrls);
         toReturn.put(LegacyFacade.DATA, documentData);

         // Done. Return.
         return toReturn;
        }
    }
    catch (SQLException ex)
    {
        // This should not happen, unless some arcane database error
        // arose. Log it, and bail out.
        System.err.println("[LegacyFacadeBean::fireDbQuery]: Could not "
        + "perform database query: " + ex);
    }
    finally
    {
        try
        {
         // Release the connection back to the pool
         conn.close();
        }
```

```
        catch(Exception ex)
        {
         // This should never happen...
         System.out.println("[LegacyFacadeBean::fireDbQuery]: Could not "
          + "close the DB Connection. Weird.");
        }
    }

    // Whoops.
    return null;
   }

   /**
    *  Retrieves a Connection to the Database, by querying a DataSource
    *  factory within the JNDI context. The EJB container manages the
    *  DataSource factory, providing - among other things - Connection pooling.
    *  Note that the specifics for the DataSource are not provided in
    *  this document - so if the unerlying database is changed, the code
    *  in this method will not need to change.
    *
    * @return A Connection to the DataSource
    */
   private Connection getDbConnection()
   {
    try
    {
        // Get a reference to the InitialContext
        Context ctx = new InitialContext();

        // Get a reference to the DataSource bound in the JNDI registry
        DataSource db = (DataSource) ctx.lookup("java:comp/env/localDataSource");

        // Get and return a connection from the DataSource
        return db.getConnection();
    }
    catch(Exception ex)
    {
        System.out.println("[LegacyFacadeBean::getDbConnection]: Could not "
         + "obtain a Connection: " + ex);
    }

    return null;
   }
}
```

The main difference between the implementation of the database SQL query in the `DbProxyBean` and the `LegacyFacadeBean` is that the latter uses the connection pooling mechanism built into the EJB container. The highlighted code in the `getConnection` method illustrates the process of obtaining a reference to a `ConnectionFactory` instance that produces database connections to a specified database.

> **TIP** *The connection pooling mechanism built into an EJB container is generally a stable and efficient implementation that may be optimized for the application server in question. Whenever you want to use a relational database in your EJB application development, you are wise to use the standard J2EE connection pooling built into the application server instead of creating your own custom DB pooling class.*

In keeping with the traditional configuration file clutter of most J2EE application servers, the business code of the any EJB component is—as was shown in Chapter 8—only a portion of the solution. To complete the refactoring step of the model components, we must now take a look at the `ejb-jar.xml` configuration file, and a few custom configuration files of some known application servers.

The LegacyFacade EJB Component Deployment Descriptor

The communication structure of the `LegacyFacadeBean` class is shown in Figure 10-8. Because the EJB connects to a relational database, it needs a reference to a configured data source. The EJB configuration files must therefore set up specifications, including JNDI bindings for the following items:

- The `LegacyFacade` EJB component
- The data source used by the bean
- The relationship between the `LegacyFacade` and the data source

The three components are configured in the `ejb-jar.xml` and the application server-specific configuration file. The EJB configuration specification contains only definitions for how to describe the EJB component configurations, including its relation to the data source, but neither any actual JNDI name nor the specification for the data source are standardized. Therefore, these entities must be configured in an application server-dependent way.

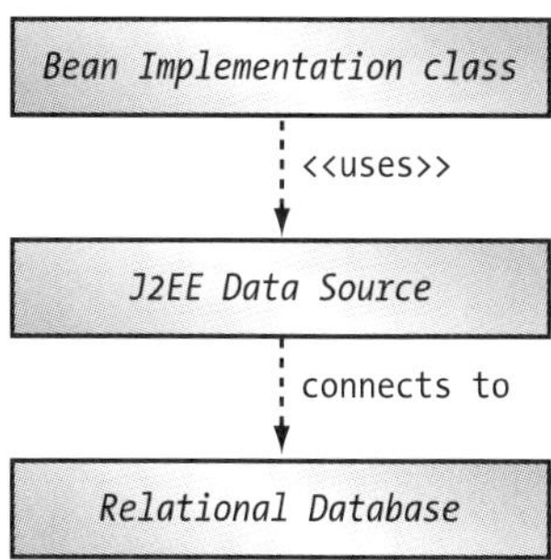

Figure 10-8. The communication between the `LegacyFacadeBean` *object and the database is handled by the EJB container and its data source.*

This example shows the standard `ejb-jar.xml` file and custom configuration settings for two different application servers, which were chosen more or less arbitrarily from the commonly used ones. The application servers used in this example are as follows:

- WebLogic Application Server, version 6.0, using EJB descriptors for the EJB 2.0 specification, and
- Inprise Application Server, version 4.1, using EJB descriptors for the EJB 1.1 specification.

As you shall see, the descriptors for stateful session EJB components have not altered much between the two EJB specifications. Moreover, many application servers use a similar—but not identical—format for describing the nonstandard settings for each EJB component. These nonstandard settings frequently include all JNDI mappings, security specifications, and resource definitions.

Deployment Descriptors for the EJB 2.0 Specification

Aside from the standard `ejb-jar.xml` deployment descriptor file, the WebLogic 6.0 server uses an XML document called `weblogic-ejb-jar.xml` for its nonstandard deployment settings. Both the `ejb-jar.xml` and the `weblogic-ejb-jar.xml` documents are deployed in the `META-INF` directory of the EJB JAR file, as shown in Figure 10-9.

Using the XML DTD for the EJB 2.0 specification, you arrive at the standard `ejb-jar.xml` file shown in Listing 10-10.

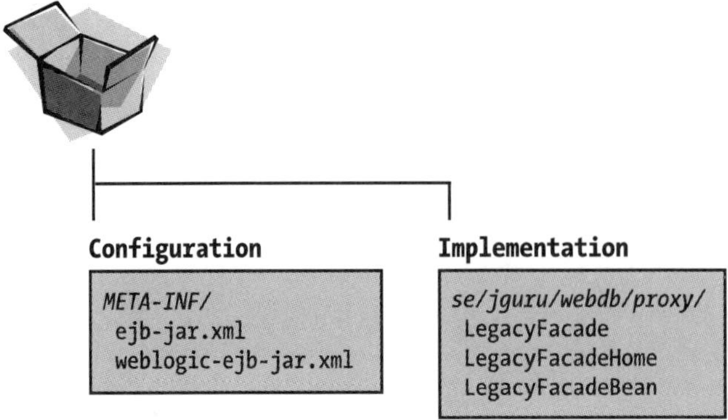

Figure 10-9. The relevant content of the `LegacyFacade` *application directory consists of two groups of files: where the configuration settings are deployed in the* `META-INF` *directory and the class files are deployed in the* `se/jguru/webdb/proxy` *directory.*

Listing 10-10. The `ejb-jar.xml` *deployment descriptor*

```
<?xml version="1.0"?>

<!DOCTYPE ejb-jar PUBLIC
    '-//Sun Microsystems, Inc.//DTD Enterprise JavaBeans 2.0//EN'
    'http://java.sun.com/dtd/ejb-jar_2_0.dtd'>

<ejb-jar>
     <enterprise-beans>
          <session>
               <description>
               This is the Session EJB Facade which hides all
               data mining from the Legacy Tier.
               </description>
               <ejb-name>LegacyFacadeBean</ejb-name>
               <home>se.jguru.webdb.proxy.LegacyFacadeHome</home>
               <remote>se.jguru.webdb.proxy.LegacyFacade</remote>
               <ejb-class>se.jguru.webdb.proxy.LegacyFacadeBean</ejb-class>
               <session-type>Stateful</session-type>
               <transaction-type>Container</transaction-type>
```

```
            <resource-ref>
                <description>
                This is the DataSource which connects to the
                relational database where the actual data is stored.
                </description>
                <res-ref-name>localDataSource</res-ref-name>
                <res-type>javax.sql.DataSource</res-type>
                <res-auth>Container</res-auth>
                 </resource-ref>
        </session>
    </enterprise-beans>

    <assembly-descriptor>
        <container-transaction>
            <method>
                <ejb-name>LegacyFacadeBean</ejb-name>
                <method-name>*</method-name>
            </method>
            <trans-attribute>Required</trans-attribute>
        </container-transaction>
    </assembly-descriptor>

</ejb-jar>
```

The `ejb-jar.xml` file has three distinct parts, defining the session bean, the data source resources it uses, and the transaction requirements on the methods of the session Bean EJB component.

The first part of the `<session> ... </session>` container element describes the basic attributes of the `LegacyFacadeBean` EJB component, such as its name and concrete types for the Home, Remote, and Bean classes. Note that this session EJB component is stateful, which means that the implementation object cannot be altered between method calls, as is the case for a stateless EJB component.

The last subelement of the `<session> ... </session>` container is the `<resource-ref> ... </resource-ref>` element, which declares a data source for use by the session EJB component. The `javax.sql.DataSource` has the logical reference key (similar to a variable name) `localDataSource`, and it is configured to surrender its transaction management to the EJB container. Note that local resources must be obtained through the local environment for the EJB, which is accessed through the JNDI prefix `java:comp/env`. Therefore, the lookup name for the `localDataSource` reference in the EJB Bean implementation class is `java:comp/env/localDataSource`.

The final part of the `ejb-jar.xml` file is the `<assembly-descriptor> ... </assembly-descriptor>` element, which simply states that all methods of the `LegacyFacadeBean` component must be executed within a transaction. Identical to the DataSource, the session EJB component has surrendered its transaction control to the EJB container, so no extra coding is required in the EJB Bean class to manage the required transactions.

The weblogic-ejb-jar.xml deployment descriptor document uses a small subset of its DTD. The main function of the XML document is to specify JNDI bindings for the Home interface of the LegacyFacadeBean and the DataSource used by it.

Listing 10-11 displays the content of the weblogic-ejb-jar.xml.

Listing 10-11. The weblogic-ejb-jar.xml *deployment descriptor*

```
<?xml version="1.0"?>

<!DOCTYPE weblogic-ejb-jar PUBLIC
    '-//BEA Systems, Inc.//DTD WebLogic 6.0.0 EJB//EN'
    'http://www.bea.com/servers/wls600/dtd/weblogic-ejb-jar.dtd'>

<weblogic-ejb-jar>
     <weblogic-enterprise-bean>
          <ejb-name>LegacyFacadeBean</ejb-name>
          <stateful-session-descriptor>
               <stateful-session-cache>
                    <max-beans-in-cache>10</max-beans-in-cache>
               </stateful-session-cache>
          </stateful-session-descriptor>

          <reference-descriptor>
               <resource-description>
                    <res-ref-name>localDataSource</res-ref-name>
                    <jndi-name>legacyDataSource</jndi-name>
               </resource-description>
          </reference-descriptor>

          <jndi-name>theLegacyFacade</jndi-name>

     </weblogic-enterprise-bean>
</weblogic-ejb-jar>
```

The most important task of the weblogic-ejb-jar.xml file is binding the EJB component to a JNDI name in the application server InitialContext. However, the weblogic-ejb-jar.xml file configures three settings:

- The cache of stateful session EJB implementation objects is set to a maximum of ten beans. Therefore, a mere ten parallel connections may be attempted through the stateful EJB component in the WebLogic application server before it needs to swap an active bean to disk.

- The `DataSource` reference `localDataSource` is mapped to the name `legacyDataSource` which is bound in the context.

- Finally, the EJB component Home interface is given a JNDI lookup name, `theLegacyFacade`. Therefore, clients should use this string when acquiring a reference to the Home interface of the EJB component.

The JNDI registry of the WebLogic Application Server is shown in Figure 10-10. The two entries bound in the context are `theLegacyFacade` (which maps to the Home interface of the EJB component) and `legacyDataSource` (which maps to the database factory whose connections maps to the database shown in Figure 10-4).

Figure 10-10. Visualization of the relevant parts of the JNDI registry of the running WebLogic 6.0 Application Server. Note the two bound references, having the lookup names `theLegacyFacade` *and* `legacyDataSource`.

The WebLogic Application Server automatically compiles stub and skeleton classes for all EJB components it finds deployed in its applications directory. The generated stubs and skeletons are found in the `<WebLogic_Root>/tmp_ejb<applicationServerName><port>/<componentName>` directory, as shown in Figure 10-11. Should you want to create a specialized JAR for deployment with an EJB client application, the `*_WLStub` classes are required.

You have now fully deployed the `LegacyFacadeBean` EJB in an EJB 2.0-compliant application server. Before being able to run the WebSearch application, however, we must deploy the Web application structure and required classes, as well as

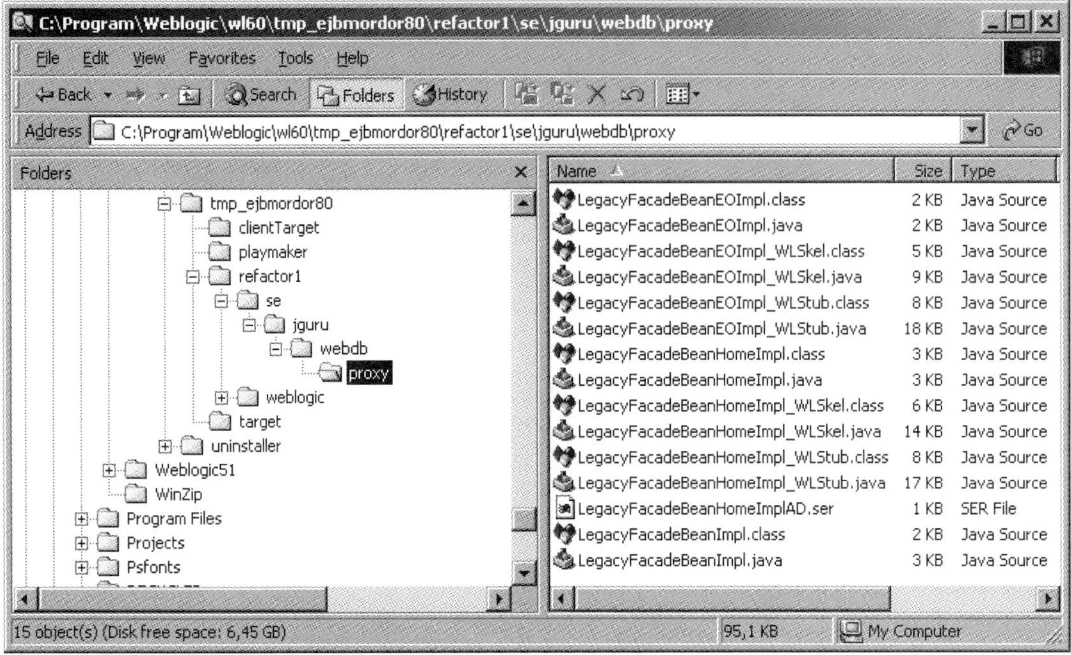

Figure 10-11. The structure of automatically generated skeleton and stub classes in a WebLogic 6.0 Application Server. Note that all generated `.java` *files are kept in this configuration.*

create the `DataSource` factory, bound in the context using the name `legacyDataSource`, as shown in Figure 10-11. These steps cover what you need to do to connect to a database resource reference, bound in the application server JNDI context by the server administrator.

In fact, you could stop describing this example here, as all other configuration settings are unique for a particular application server type. No part of the J2EE specification provides information on how to configure a `DataSource` factory connecting to a database. This is left to the application server vendors.

WebLogic Application Server DataSource Configuration

`DataSource` factory definitions for the JNDI context is unique per application server. The WebLogic Application Server management console provides a simple GUI way of entering this information. Eventually, all information will end up in an XML file called `config.xml`, but the management console gracefully hides the internal structure of the `config.xml` file and presents a user-friendly way to provide the same information. Figure 10-12 shows a `DataSource` definition that maps a JNDI name (`legacyDataSource`) to a particular JDBC `ConnectionPool` (`cloudscapePool`).

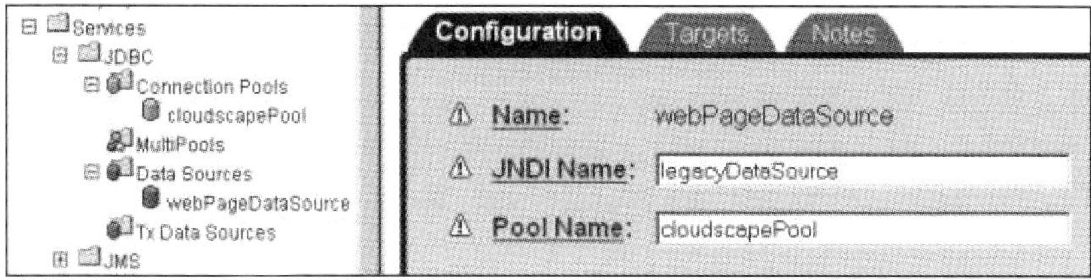

Figure 10-12. The `DataSource` *definition* `webpageDataSource` *maps a particular JDBC* `ConnectionPool` *definition to the JNDI name* `legacyDataSource`.

The `cloudscapePool` entity, shown in the left pane of Figure 10-12, is a `DataSource` factory resource connected to a locally running Cloudscape database containing all legacy data. Figure 10-4 shows the contents of the small database, and Figure 10-13 shows the configuration settings that are required to obtain a JDBC connection to the database.

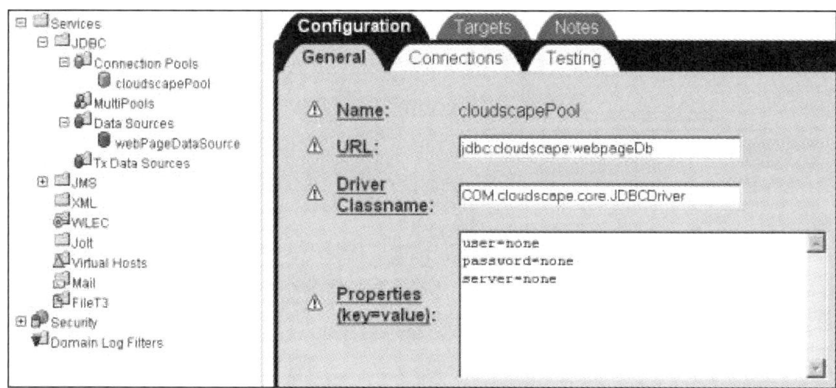

Figure 10-13. The configuration settings for the `cloudscapePool` *provides all of the needed properties to connect to the Cloudscape database holding all data shown in Figure 10-4.*

The configuration and deployment process for application servers running the EJB 1.1 specification is almost identical to the one just described for an EJB 2.0-compliant application server. One must, of course, remember that a great part of EJB deployment is done using proprietary methods and tools; only the structure and content of the `ejb-jar.xml` files are part of the J2EE specification.

Deployment Descriptors for the EJB 1.1 Specification

The Inprise Application Server is used to illustrate deployment of beans that comply to the EJB 1.1 specification. As shown in Chapter 8, the differences between the 1.1 and 2.0 EJB specifications are great for Entity EJB beans using CMP persistence. The `LegacyFacadeBean` is a stateful session EJB component, and the differences between the deployment descriptor files of the Inprise and the WebLogic application servers are therefore relatively minor.

The Inprise Application Server uses two XML documents to describe a deployed EJB component: the standard `ejb-jar.xml` and the Inprise Application Server-specific configuration file `ejb-inprise.xml`. Both the configuration files are deployed in the `META-INF` directory, as shown in Figure 10-14. The class files deployed to the Inprise Application Server are identical to the ones deployed to the WebLogic Application Server.

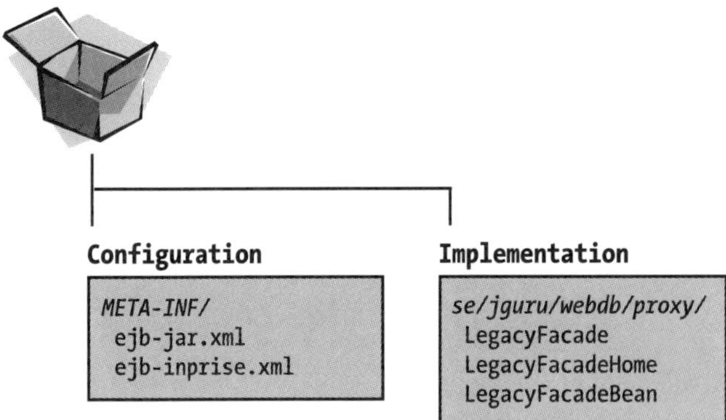

Figure 10-14. The relevant content of the `LegacyFacade.jar` *file consists of two groups of files, where the configuration settings are deployed in the* `META-INF` *directory and the bytecode files are deployed in the* `se/jguru/webdb/proxy` *directory.*

Start with the standard `ejb-jar.xml` file, which contains deployment settings that can be used by any EJB 1.1-compliant application server. Listing 10-12 displays the code for the `ejb-jar.xml` for EJB version 1.1.

Listing 10-12. The standard `ejb-jar.xml` *file*

```
<?xml version="1.0" encoding="Cp1252"?>

<!DOCTYPE ejb-jar PUBLIC
    '-//Sun Microsystems, Inc.//DTD Enterprise JavaBeans 1.1//EN'
    'http://java.sun.com/j2ee/dtds/ejb-jar_1_1.dtd'>

<ejb-jar>
  <enterprise-beans>
    <session>
      <description>
            This is the Session EJB Facade which hides all
            data mining from the Legacy Tier.
      </description>
      <ejb-name>LegacyFacadeBean</ejb-name>
      <home>se.jguru.webdb.proxy.LegacyFacadeHome</home>
      <remote>se.jguru.webdb.proxy.LegacyFacade</remote>
      <ejb-class>se.jguru.webdb.proxy.LegacyFacadeBean</ejb-class>
      <session-type>Stateless</session-type>
      <transaction-type>Container</transaction-type>

<resource-ref>
     <description>
          This is the DataSource which connects to the relational
          database where the actual data is stored.
     </description>
     <res-ref-name>localDataSource</res-ref-name>
     <res-type>javax.sql.DataSource</res-type>
     <res-auth>Container</res-auth>
      </resource-ref>

    </session>
  </enterprise-beans>

     <assembly-descriptor>
          <container-transaction>
               <method>
                    <ejb-name>LegacyFacadeBean</ejb-name>
                    <method-name>*</method-name>
               </method>
               <trans-attribute>Required</trans-attribute>
          </container-transaction>
     </assembly-descriptor>

</ejb-jar>
```

The only difference between the `ejb-jar.xml` for EJB version 2.0 and that of version 1.1 is its `DOCTYPE` definition. This is intentional; standard EJB 1.1 deployment descriptors should be readable by any EJB 2.0-compliant application server. Because the three different sections of the deployment descriptor file (defining the basic attributes for the EJB component, its data source reference, and its assembly descriptor) are identical to the ones presented for the EJB 1.1 case, they will not be covered in detail here.

As always, the `ejb-jar.xml` deployment descriptor needs additional complements to provide deployment descriptor settings for a particular application server. The DTD of the custom configuration file for the Inprise Application Server version 4.1 is illustrated in Figure 10-15.

Our `ejb-inprise.xml` deployment descriptor (shown in Listing 10-13) uses a small subset of the DTD shown in Figure 10-15. The XML document specifies JNDI bindings for the Home interface of the `LegacyFacadeBean` and the data source used by it.

Listing 10-13. The `ejb-inprise.xml` *deployment descriptor*

```
<?xml version="1.0"?>

<!DOCTYPE inprise-specific PUBLIC
   '-//Inprise Corporation//DTD Enterprise JavaBeans 1.1//EN'
   'http://www.borland.com/devsupport/appserver/dtds/ejb-inprise.dtd'>

<inprise-specific>
  <enterprise-beans>
    <session>
      <ejb-name>LegacyFacadeBean</ejb-name>
      <bean-home-name>theLegacyFacade</bean-home-name>
      <timeout>0</timeout>

      <resource-ref>
          <res-ref-name>localDataSource</res-ref-name>
          <jndi-name>legacyDataSource</jndi-name>
          <cmp-resource>True</cmp-resource>
      </resource-ref>

    </session>
  </enterprise-beans>
```

```
  <datasource-definitions>
    <datasource>
      <jndi-name>legacyDataSource</jndi-name>
      <url>jdbc:cloudscape:webpageDb</url>
      <username>none</username>
      <password>none</password>
      <isolation-level>TRANSACTION_SERIALIZABLE</isolation-level>
      <driver-class-name>COM.cloudscape.core.JDBCDriver</driver-class-name>
    </datasource>
  </datasource-definitions>

</inprise-specific>
```

The Inprise-specific configuration file has three distinct definition sections:

- The first part of the `<session> ... </session>` container element defines the JNDI name and session timeout length for the `LegacyFacadeBean` EJB component.

- The second part of the `<session> ... </session>` container element defines a named reference to a resource, known under the JNDI alias `localDataSource` for the `LegacyFacadeBean` EJB. Its reference is a data source whose JNDI name is `legacyDataSource`, and its transactions are managed by the EJB container.

- The `<datasource-definitions > ... </datasource-definitions>` container element defines a named data source that connects to a JDBC database using the `jdbcDriver`, `jdbcUrl`, username, password, and transaction isolation settings provided. Note that the JNDI name of the data source is `legacyDataSource`.

Before you can run the application inside the Inprise Application Server, the stub and skeleton classes of the `LegacyFacadeBean` EJB component must be generated and the application-server specific JAR file deployed.

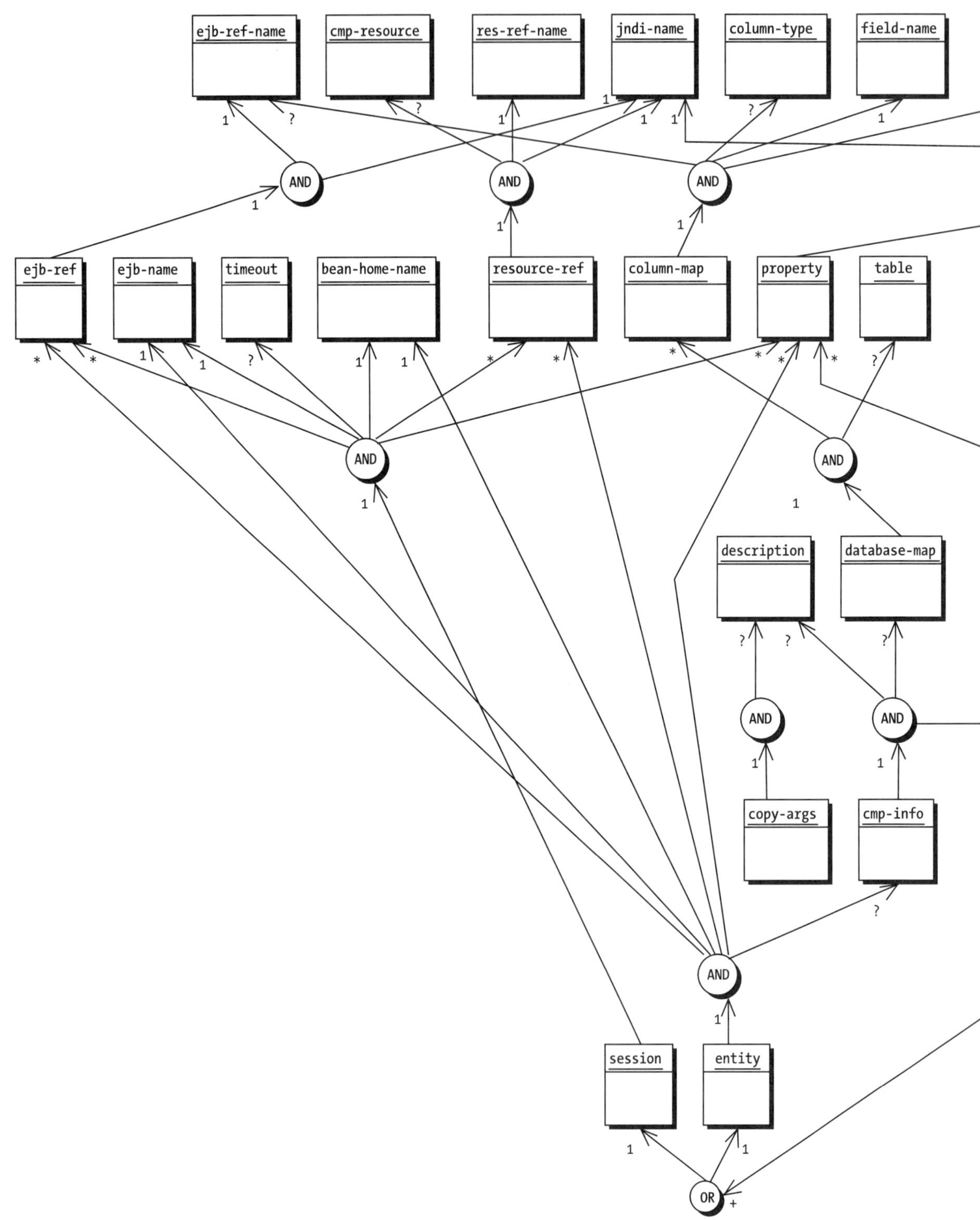

Figure 10-15. Partial XML DTD structure of the `ejb-inprise.xml` configuration file

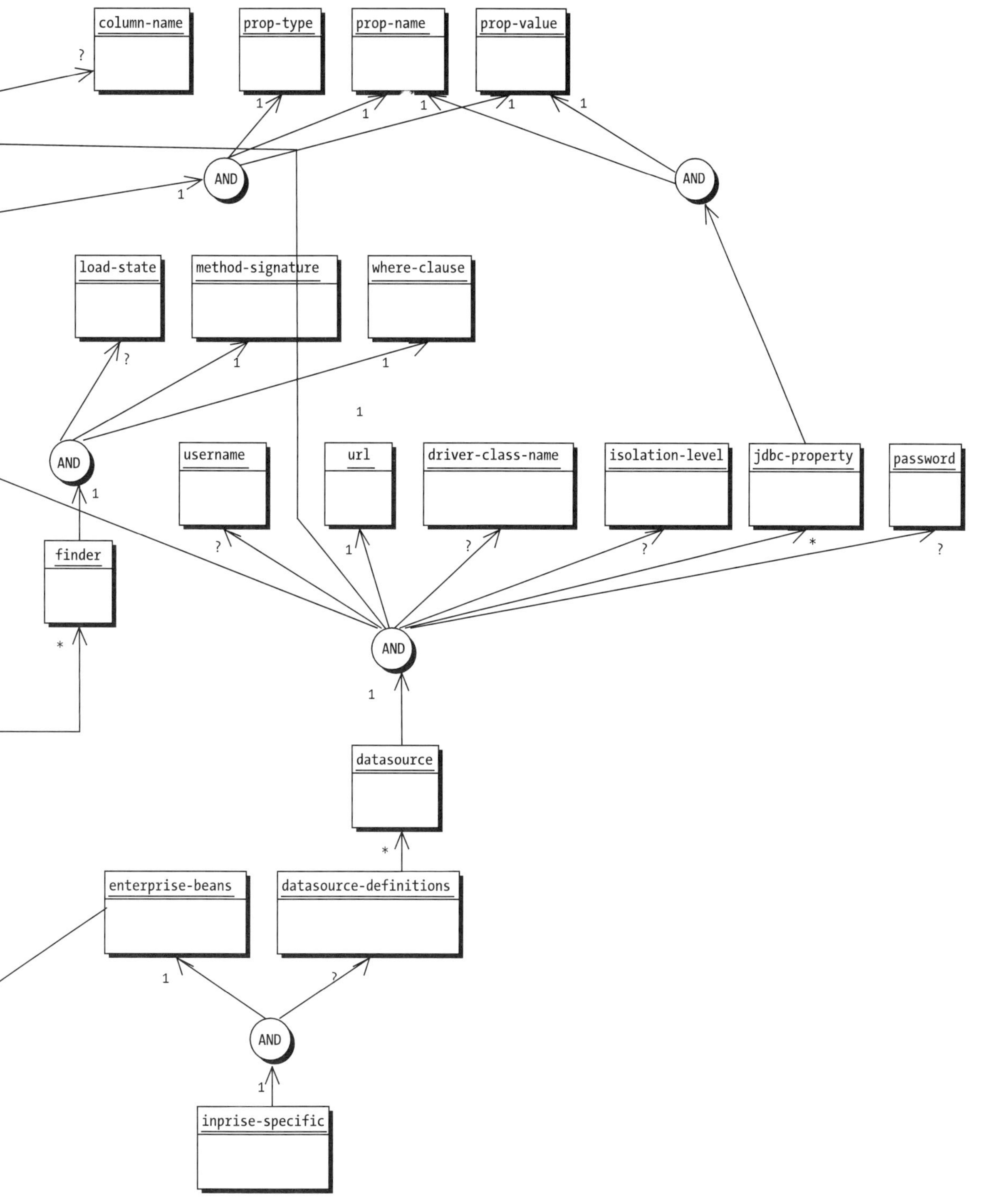
column-name
prop-type
prop-name
prop-value
AND
AND
load-state
method-signature
where-clause
AND
username
url
driver-class-name
isolation-level
jdbc-property
password
finder
AND
datasource
enterprise-beans
datasource-definitions
AND
inprise-specific

Deploying the EJB JAR into the Application Server

The deployment process of the Inprise Application Server is simple, quick, and reliable; using a GUI-enabled wizard, the generic JAR file is introspected, the required stubs and skeleton classes are generated, and the application server-specific JAR file is generated and deployed. The two steps are shown in Figures 10-16 and 10-17.

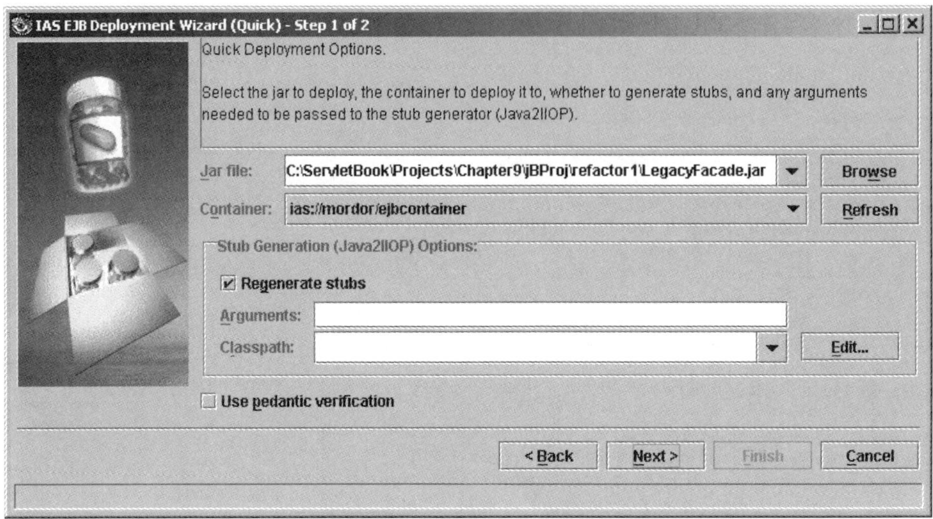

Figure 10-16. The first step of the EJB deployment wizard allows you to choose the JAR containing the bytecode files and XML configuration documents for the EJB component, as well as the EJB container where they should be deployed. Note the Regenerate stubs checkbox.

In the process of deploying the `LegacyFacade` EJB component, the server-specific JAR file has been created and copied to the `<InstallDir>/ejb_jars/ejbcontainer`. Examining the content of the `LegacyFacade.jar` file reveals a series of CORBA stub and skeleton classes (shown in Figure 10-18), which leads to the conclusion that the Inprise Application Server is implemented on top of a CORBA-compliant ORB.

Having examined the deployment process for application servers that are compliant with the EJB 2.0 and EJB 1.1 specifications, we should proceed to deploy the Web application.

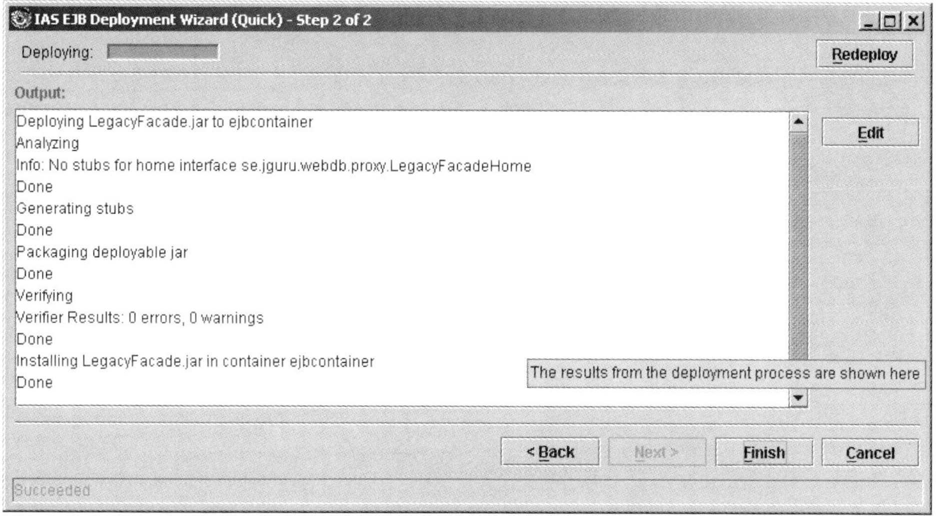

Figure 10-17. The state of the deployment is monitored in the last step of the deployment wizard. As indicated, the stub classes were regenerated, and the resulting JAR was installed into the application server.

Name	Modified	Size	Ratio	Packed	Path
ejb-inprise.xml	2001-06-26 16:19	1 079	52%	516	meta-inf\
ejb-jar.xml	2001-06-26 16:19	1 276	57%	549	meta-inf\
Manifest.mf	2001-06-26 16:19	244	51%	119	meta-inf\
_LegacyFacade_Stub.class	2001-06-28 00:02	3 599	52%	1 743	se\jguru\webdb\proxy\
_LegacyFacadeHome_Stub.class	2001-06-28 00:02	3 947	53%	1 840	se\jguru\webdb\proxy\
LegacyFacade.class	2001-06-26 16:19	524	30%	365	se\jguru\webdb\proxy\
LegacyFacadeBean.class	2001-06-26 16:19	3 692	50%	1 864	se\jguru\webdb\proxy\
LegacyFacadeHelper.class	2001-06-28 00:02	4 587	62%	1 733	se\jguru\webdb\proxy\
LegacyFacadeHolder.class	2001-06-28 00:02	967	53%	450	se\jguru\webdb\proxy\
LegacyFacadeHome.class	2001-06-26 16:19	302	31%	209	se\jguru\webdb\proxy\
LegacyFacadeHomeHelper.class	2001-06-28 00:02	4 663	63%	1 736	se\jguru\webdb\proxy\
LegacyFacadeHomeHolder.class	2001-06-28 00:02	995	54%	454	se\jguru\webdb\proxy\
LegacyFacadeHomeOperations.class	2001-06-28 00:02	357	35%	233	se\jguru\webdb\proxy\
LegacyFacadeHomePOA.class	2001-06-28 00:02	3 871	58%	1 629	se\jguru\webdb\proxy\
LegacyFacadeHomePOAInvokeHandler.class	2001-06-28 00:02	3 106	59%	1 268	se\jguru\webdb\proxy\
LegacyFacadeHomePOATie.class	2001-06-28 00:02	1 660	58%	690	se\jguru\webdb\proxy\
LegacyFacadeOperations.class	2001-06-28 00:02	321	27%	235	se\jguru\webdb\proxy\
LegacyFacadePOA.class	2001-06-28 00:02	3 662	57%	1 562	se\jguru\webdb\proxy\
LegacyFacadePOAInvokeHandler.class	2001-06-28 00:02	3 187	58%	1 347	se\jguru\webdb\proxy\
LegacyFacadePOATie.class	2001-06-28 00:02	1 678	56%	744	se\jguru\webdb\proxy\

Figure 10-18. The content of the application server-specific JAR file for the Inprise Application Server. Note the POA, Holder, and Helper classes, which are typical for CORBA-compliant stubs and skeletons.

The Web Application Deployment Structure

With the EJB component properly deployed into our application server of choice, we need to set up the Web application running the JSP document. Because the JSP document is an EJB client talking to the EJB server component just deployed in the previous section, its needs are slightly different from the ones of the EJB server components.

The deployment structure of the Web application is shown in Figure 10-19.

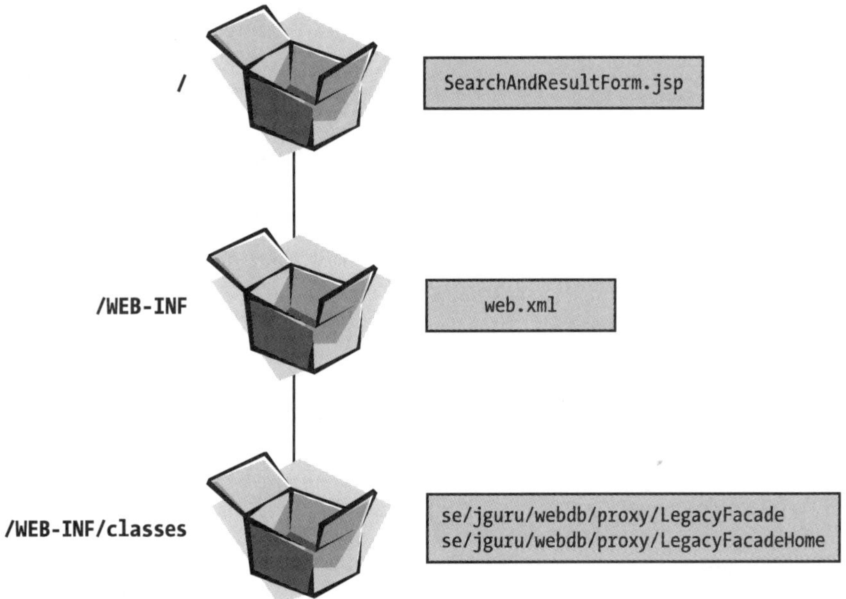

Figure 10-19. Deployment structure of the Web application client (or the WAR file containing the Web application client files). Note that only the Home and Remote interfaces are present in the original structure. Application server-specific JNDI and stub classes are not shown in the image.

The View documents are modified only a little in this first refactoring step. The top two lines of code in the `SearchAndResultsForm.jsp` document must be slightly modified to use the `LegacyFacadeBean` instead of the `dbProxyBean`. When the application server is restarted, the familiar output from Figure 10-4 is shown.

The header of the JSP View document must now make use of the `LegacyFacadeProxy` JavaBean proxy instead of the `DbProxy`, including the call to the `populate` method, as shown here:

```
<%@ page import="java.util.*" %>
<jsp:useBean id="dbProxy" scope="request"
             class="se.jguru.webdb.proxy.LegacyFacadeProxy" />
<jsp:setProperty name="dbProxy" property="*" />
<%
     if(request.getParameter("queryString") != null)
     {
          dbProxy.populate();
     }
%>
```

The rest of the JSP View file may remain unaltered for the time being; however, one should surely clean it up using JSP custom tags instead of all the raw Java code pasted into the JSP document. Porting the Web application to the Struts framework will provide full separation of View and Controller documents. These two porting steps are left as an exercise for the reader; this chapter focused on providing examples for the EJB business object tier, and we don't want to get sidetracked.

CHAPTER 11

Example 3: Entity EJBs for Database Integration

THE DATABASE BACK END we developed in the first refactoring step of the old-style Web application introduced in Chapter 10 is fine for selecting data from the database back end. However, should we wish to modify or update the database content, that refactoring model can be augmented to simplify data alteration and increase flexibility.

One way of providing such augmented data mining is by using Entity EJB components to encapsulate all complex relational database statements. This second step of the refactoring process of the old-style Web application from Chapter 10 contains the following steps:

1. Cleaning up the JNDI tree to comply with the Java naming standards
2. Augmenting the `DataSource` schema to contain images in addition to Web pages
3. Implementing the classes required to manage images in the system (that is, an Image EJB component, an `ImageProxy` class used by the Web tier classes, and a set of servlets managing upload and download of images)
4. Configuring and deploying the Image EJB component and its related servlets and proxy
5. Implementing classes required to manage the Web pages data and metadata in the system. These classes include a Web page EJB component, a `WebPageProxy` bean class used by entities in the Web tier, and a set of views interacting with the `WebPageProxy`.
6. Configuring and deploying the `WebPage` EJB component and its related view documents (JSPs and HTML documents).

Although all actions in the second refactoring step will be described, we focus on the EJB tier and the configuration and design considerations of the interaction between the components of the Web and EJB tiers.

As with all exercises, let's warm up with a simple task: cleaning up the old JNDI structure.

Step 1—JNDI Registry Cleanup

In the first part of the refactoring process covered in Chapter 10, the objects bound in the JNDI registry were merely thrown out in an arbitrary manner. When your J2EE application is small, the disadvantages of a naming registry may not be immediately visible, but you quickly discover them when the application grows.

The JNDI namespace is similar to a library: as its volume grows, it becomes more difficult to remember where to find a particular book unless all librarians adhere to a set of rules. If each librarian uses his or her own set of naming conventions, the library would soon end up in a complete mess: you would have to ask the correct librarian to find a certain book. The same syndrome is true for the JNDI namespace, and so it is imperative that you use the corporate naming standards for all deployment into the JNDI namespace.

Conceptually, a JNDI registry is similar to a namespace containing Java classes. Each JNDI directory (which corresponds to a Java package) may contain two types of entities: other directories and bound objects (which correspond to Java classes). The comparison falters, however, in that Java classes—by definition—have different types, but JNDI bound objects with different names may be of the same type, even if bound in the same JNDI directory.

In the JNDI structure in Figure 11-1, the `se.jguru.webdb.proxy` leaf directory contains objects used by the Web application proxy, and the `se.jguru.webdb.legacyintegration` directory contains the `DataSource` and its business objects (EJB components).

The naming conventions for classes and packages are usable in a JNDI namespace as well. All entries in the JNDI namespace have therefore been placed in a reverse DNS structure, with the packages (JNDI directories) starting with lowercase letters and the actual entity names starting with an uppercase letter.

Although the structure of the JNDI registry is simple to illustrate, the actual binding of objects into the JNDI registry is dependent upon the application server. Remember that the J2EE specification does not include standard JNDI binding tags; this is instead left to the application server providers. Thus, the JNDI configuration is frequently required to be provided in custom deployment descriptors. We will therefore wait with the actual configuration of the JNDI registry until it is time to create the deployment descriptors for the EJB components.

Next, start modifying the database schema as required for the second refactoring step.

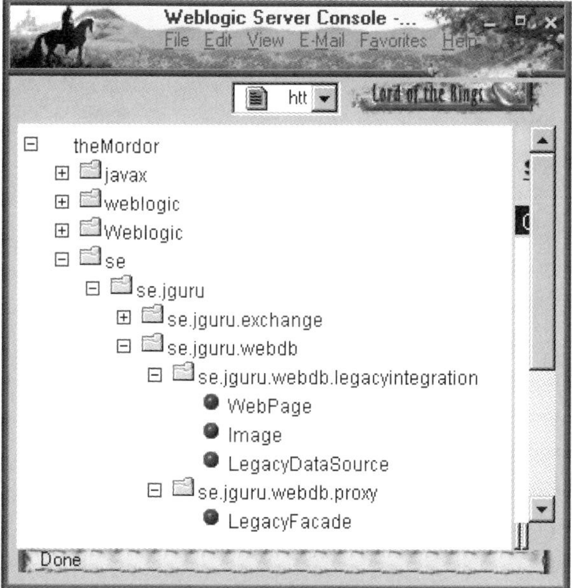

Figure 11-1. The improved and structured JNDI tree of the refactored application provides the directory structure dividing the bound objects into two categories: `se.jguru.webdb.proxy` *and* `se.jguru.webdb.legacyintegration`.

Step 2—DataSource Schema Modification

The `LegacyDataSource` shown in Figure 11-1 provides connections to the legacy database that holds all persistent data. Because we are now required to handle and store all images in the system, we must now provide a table in which image data may be stored (`Images`). The new schema is shown in Figure 11-2.

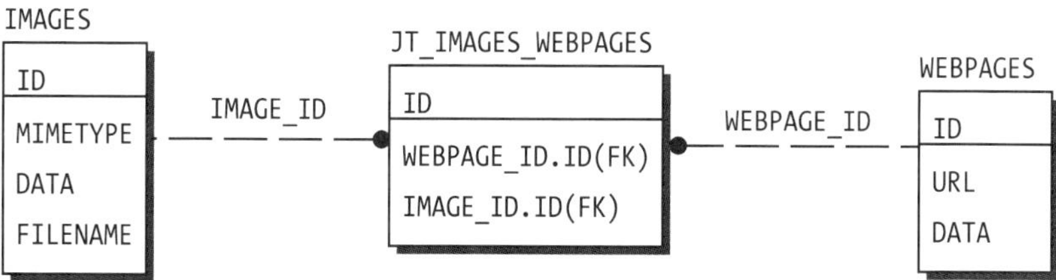

Figure 11-2. The database schema is now modified to include a table storing images and some image metadata known by the Web application in a separate table (`Images`).

Because an image may be included in many Web pages and a Web page may contain several images, the database must be structured to handle a many-to-many relation between images and Web pages. The table `JT_IMAGES_WEBPAGES`, shown in Figure 11-2, contains pairs of foreign keys relating an image to a Web page; this is the way to create a many-to-many relation in a relational database.

For You SQL Aficionados

Although important for the refactoring, the SQL required to generate the schema shown in Figure 11-2 is likely to vary slightly between databases. The database used in this example is the embedded Cloudscape database, which is launched as part of the application server used. Be sure to check the local SQL dialect of your DB handler.

The SQL required to generate the schema shown in Figure 11-3 is straightforward; the `WebPages` table is created from pure SQL standard types. In the following listing, the text in italics is SQL comments, which are not parsed by the database.

```
--
-- Create the WEBPAGES table
--
CREATE TABLE WEBPAGES
(
      ID INT NOT NULL ,
      URL VARCHAR(1024) NOT NULL ,
      DATA VARCHAR(20000) NOT NULL
)
--
-- Add the Primary Key Constraint
--
ALTER TABLE WEBPAGES
   ADD CONSTRAINT WEBPAGEPK Primary Key (ID)
```

The `Images` table in Figure 11-2 looks deceptively simple; it is comparable to the `Webpages` table in complexity. However, the data column that stores the content of an image file has the type `varbinary`, which may not be present in all databases. Be sure to check your database for storage types that may accommodate binary data; this area is still somewhat uncharted territory for the database standardization movement. The Cloudscape database used in this example, defines a type VARBINARY that is used as the SQL type for the column storing the image data:

> **CAUTION** *Be sure to read your database and JDBC driver documentation to find what data types should be used to store binary data within the database.*

> **TIP** *If at all possible, try to use the SQL 3 type BLOB to store binary data such as images or other binary streams. The* `java.sql.Blob` *type encapsulates an SQL BLOB locator that is comparable to a C pointer to byte, which stores the binary data in a compact way within the database. For information on the Blob interface, refer to the J2SE API documentation.*

```
--
-- Create the IMAGES table
--
CREATE TABLE IMAGES
(
      MIMETYPE VARCHAR(30) NOT NULL ,
      DATA VARBINARY(6400000),
      FILENAME VARCHAR(100) NOT NULL ,
      ID INT NOT NULL
)
--
-- Add the Primary Key Constraint
--
ALTER TABLE IMAGES
   ADD CONSTRAINT IMAGES_PK Primary Key (ID)
```

Here, the last table to create is the jumptable relating an `Image` row to a `WebPage` row, implementing a many-to-many relationship in the database:

```
--
-- Create the JT_IMAGES_WEBPAGES jumptable
-- which creates a many-to-many relationship
-- between IMAGES rows and WEBPAGES rows.
--
CREATE TABLE JT_IMAGES_WEBPAGES
(
      WEBPAGE_ID INT NOT NULL ,
      IMAGE_ID INT NOT NULL ,
      ID INT NOT NULL
)
```

```
--
-- Add the Primary Key Constraint
--
ALTER TABLE JT_IMAGES_WEBPAGES
   ADD CONSTRAINT ID Primary Key (ID)


--
-- Add the Foreign Key Constraint which makes
-- the IMAGE_ID column refer to the ID column of
-- the IMAGES table.
--
ALTER TABLE JT_IMAGES_WEBPAGES
   ADD CONSTRAINT IMAGE_ID Foreign Key (IMAGE_ID)
   REFERENCES IMAGES (ID)
--
-- Add the Foreign Key Constraint which makes
-- the WEBPAGE_ID column refer to the ID column of
-- the WEBPAGES table.
--
ALTER TABLE JT_IMAGES_WEBPAGES
   ADD CONSTRAINT WEBPAGE_ID Foreign Key (WEBPAGE_ID)
   REFERENCES WEBPAGES (ID)
```

The small definition of the database schema is thereby complete, and it is time to start implementing the legacy tier classes, starting with the EJB components and servlets pertaining to the `Images` table in Figure 11-3.

Step 3—Implementing the Image Subsystem

The image subsystem of the application provides a means of uploading image documents to the application database, as well as extracting the data from the database and downloading it to a client browser. The user experience of the image subsystem is simple and straightforward: the legacy classes supporting the image subsystem are more complex, as we will shortly discover.

The User Experience of the Image Subsystem

Let's investigate the user's perspective of the image subsystem to familiarize ourselves with it before taking a look at the details. The administrator wanting to upload an image to the system manually starts with the screen shown in Figure 11-3.

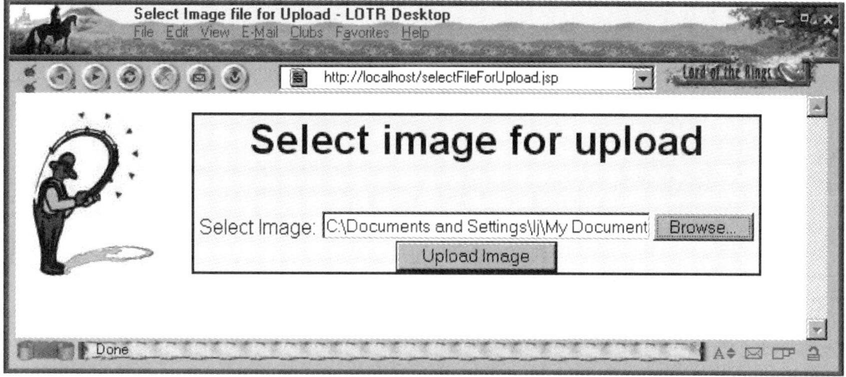

Figure 11-3. The user experience of an Administrator uploading an image to the database

After selecting the image to upload, the administrator clicks on the Upload Image button to commence the upload. The result is shown shortly thereafter; if the upload went well, the image and some of its metadata are presented to the user, as shown in Figure 11-4.

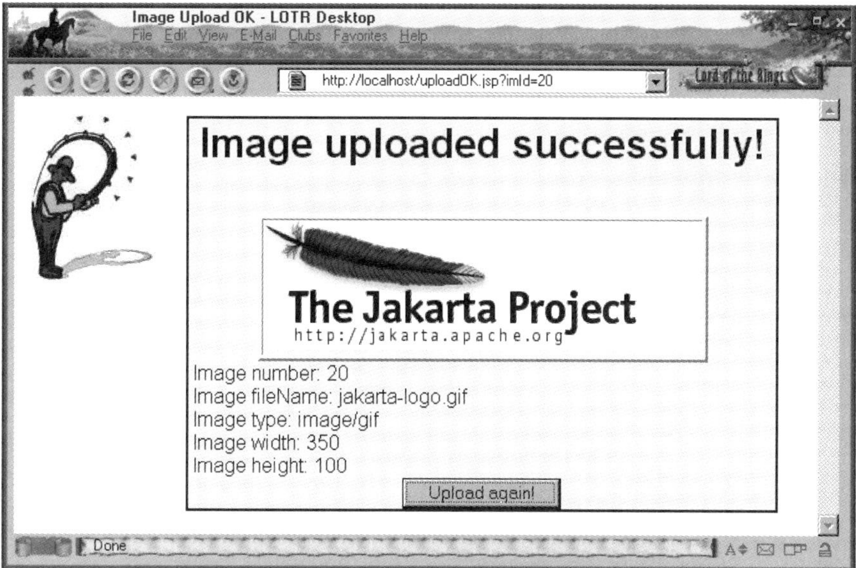

Figure 11-4. The screen shown as a result of a successful image upload. Note the image metadata shown in the lower left corner of the table.

Figure 11-4 shows some metadata of the image just uploaded to the database, as well as the image itself. Note that the image shown in the center of the screen is already stored in the database; its data is extracted from the database and sent to the client browser for display. If the image—for one reason or another—could not be uploaded to the database, the user is instead presented with the screen shown in Figure 11-5.

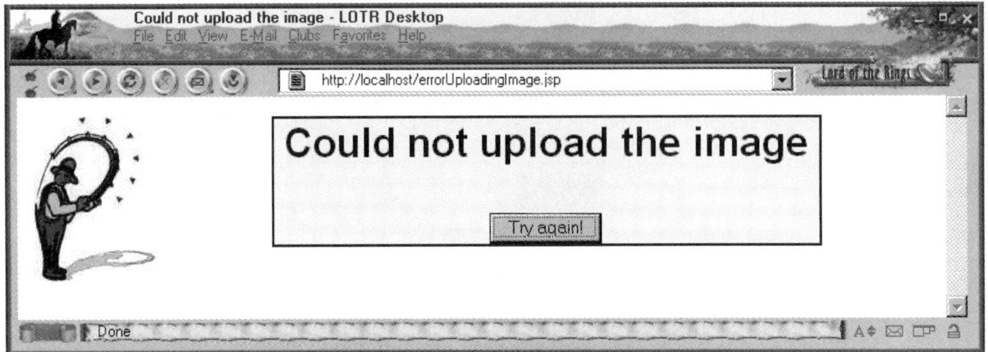

Figure 11-5. The image shown to the user if the image uploading process could not be completed

Different image formats contain its metadata information stored in different ways; in the current implementation of the J2EE application, the width and height of an image can be calculated only from the data content of a GIF image. If an image in another format, such as a JPEG, is uploaded to the database, the confirmation screen does not contain the dimensions of the image. The resulting confirmation view of uploading a progressive JPEG image is shown in Figure 11-6; note that the image dimensions are not presented as they were in Figure 11-4.

The user experience is quite visual for the image subsystem, but the data hidden behind the screens are far from trivial. Let's investigate the class structure of the image subsystem.

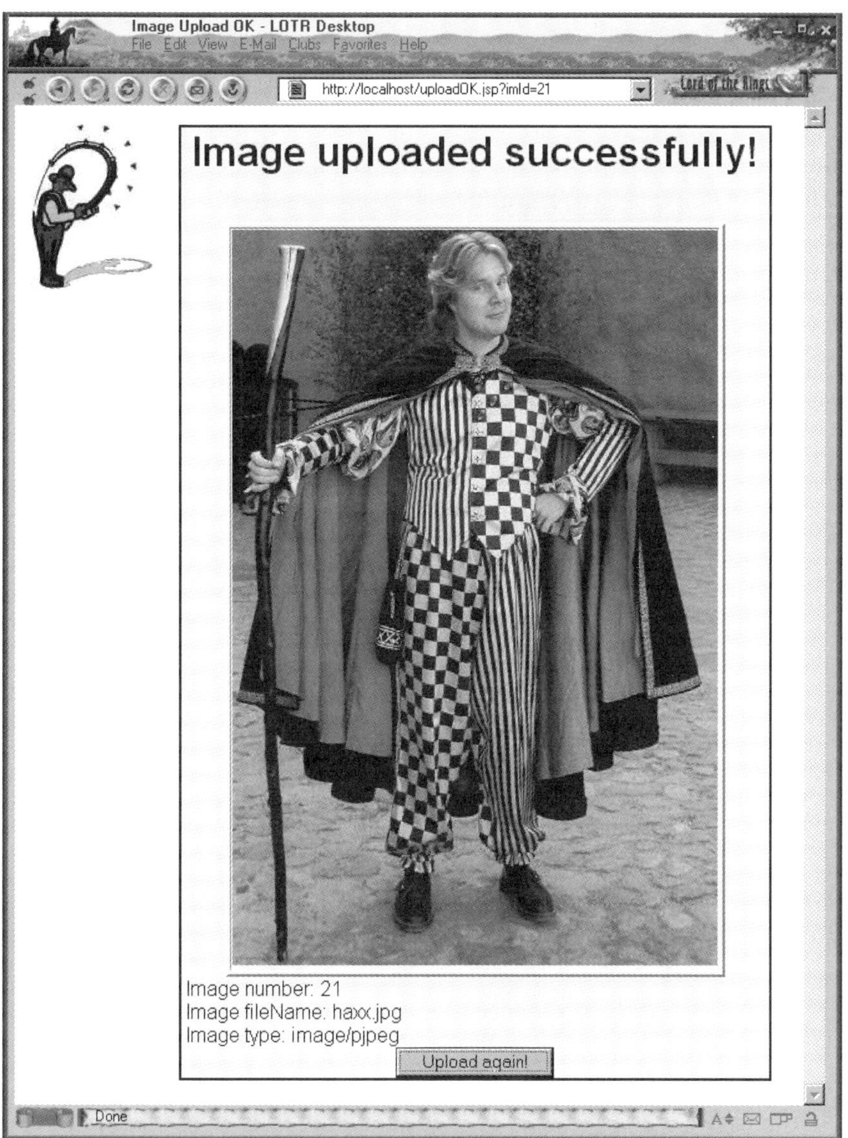

Figure 11-6. The image dimension metadata extraction is not implemented for all image formats. Note the difference between the metadata presented here and in Figure 11-4.

Classes of the Image Subsystem

The image subsystem is small, containing only two servlets: a Web-tier proxy class and an EJB component. As a contrast, the implementation and deployment configuration of the components form a nontrivial net of intertwined settings that must be handled with care. At a glance, the image subsystem is distributed between the Web and EJB containers, as well as a `DataSource` in the legacy tier, as shown in Figure 11-7.

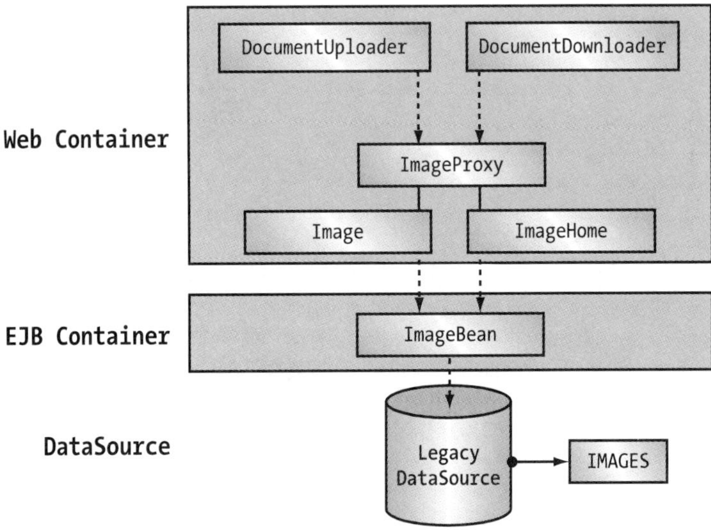

Figure 11-7. Structure of the image subsystem in which the data in the `Images` *table of the* `DataSource` *tier is accessed through the* `ImageBean` *Entity EJB component*

Entity EJBs are the recommended way of encapsulating legacy data in the J2EE programming paradigm. The image subsystem, shown in Figure 11-7, communicates with the legacy `DataSource` layer using an Entity EJB component called `ImageBean`, which provides method definitions corresponding to the two interfaces `Image` and `ImageHome`.

The Remote and Home interfaces of the `ImageBean` EJB component are managed by the `ImageProxy` class that serves as a wrapper and exception handler class. The primary function of the `ImageProxy` class is hiding all usage complexities from its Web clients—instances of the two servlet types `DocumentUploader` and `DocumentDownloader`. The UML visualization in Figure 11-8 shows the structure introduced in Figure 11-7 with fully qualified type names, superclass definitions, and the names of all implemented interfaces. All method details has been left out of Figure 11-8 to make it easier to read.

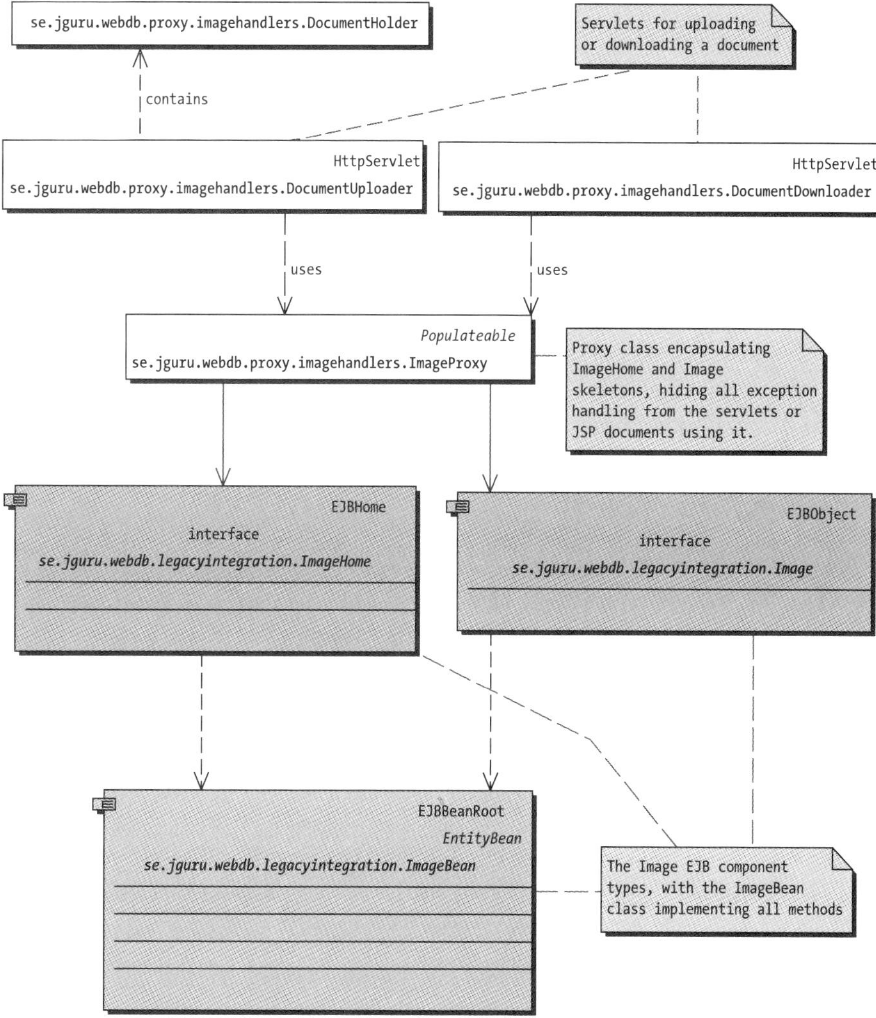

Figure 11-8. Types used in the image subsystem of the `refactor2` *J2EE application*

The shading of the classes indicate where they are deployed in the system; the `ImageBean` object is deployed in the EJB container only; all types with white backgrounds are deployed in the Web container only, and other shaded types (`Image` and `ImageHome`) are deployed in both containers.

The goal of back-end refactoring the J2EE application is to encapsulate each informational atom in the legacy tier (that is, a row in a physical or logical table) into a Java object, frequently called a *business object* because it encapsulates a business entity. When programming for a Java server-side application, it is much easier to use business objects than relational database queries, especially because the exact coupling between the internal data of a business object and the physical structure of a database may be quite complex. Let's start looking into the implementation details of the EJB component.

The Image EJB Component

Figure 11-9 shows all classes used by the Image EJB component, except its primary key class, `java.lang.Integer`. Note that the `EJBBeanRoot` class simply contains some helper methods and variables, common to all EJB components in the system. The image subsystem uses the `EJBBeanRoot` class for convenience and for enforcing a common behavior on all EJB Bean implementation classes. As such, the `EJBBeanRoot` class is not a mandatory part of the EJB pattern; the only requirement of an EJB Bean implementation class is that it implement the `javax.ejb.EnterpriseBean` interface. Developing an entity EJB component, the `ImageBean` class must implement the `javax.ejb.EntityBean` interface, which, in turn, extends `EnterpriseBean`.

Start the study of the `ImageEJB` component system of classes with a look at the two interfaces mirrored by the `ImageBean` class, starting with the remote service interface, `Image`. The method definitions of the `Image` interface expose parts of the service methods implemented in the `ImageBean` implementation class. This is intentional because this EJB class uses the persistence management services of the EJB container. Therefore, one must define an abstract getter/setter method pair per database column, which should be mirrored in the internal state of the Bean implementation class.

However, we're not required to expose all of these accessor methods directly in the service interface, and this is reflected in the `Image` remote interface shown in Listing 11-1.

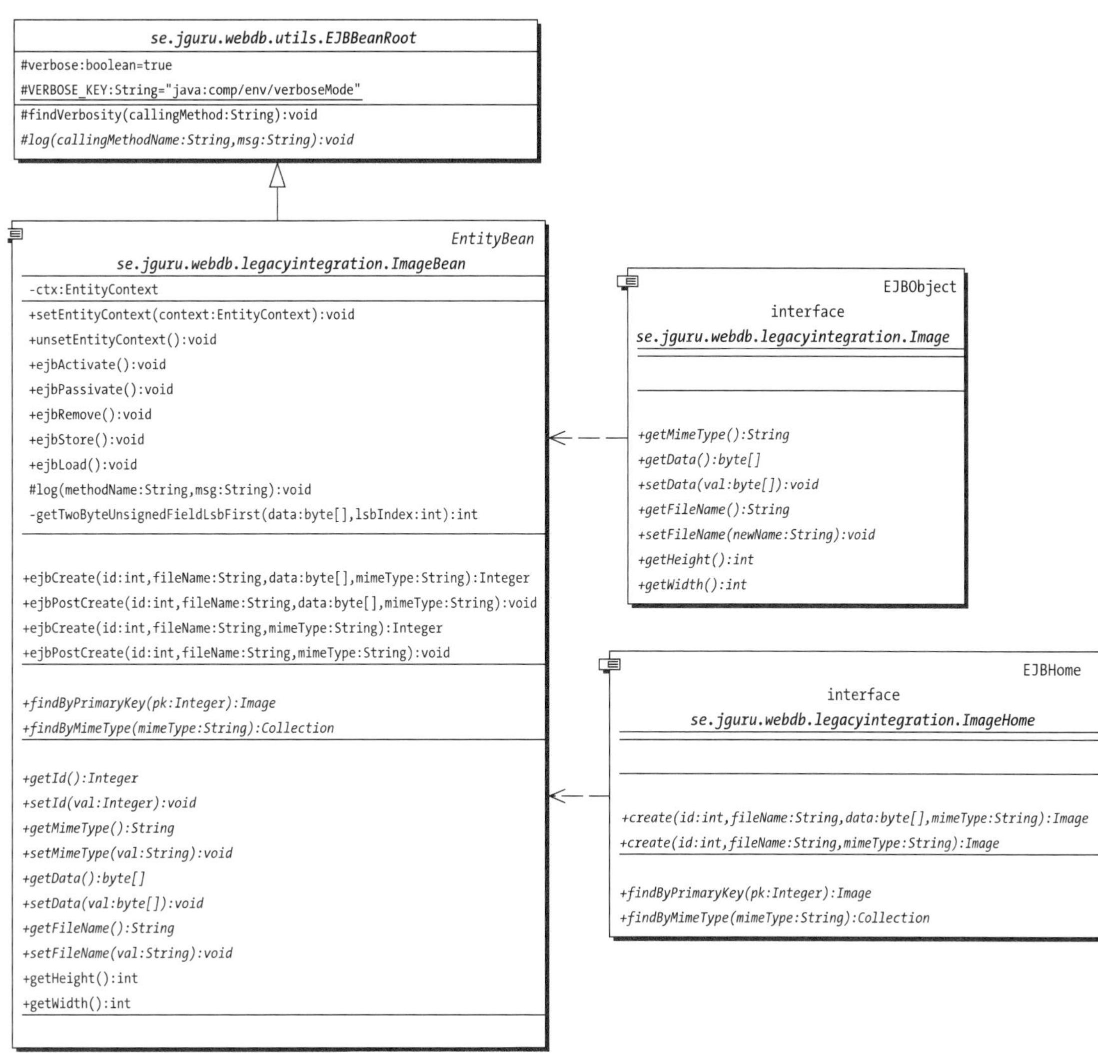

Figure 11-9. Types of the Image EJB component

Listing 11-1. The `Image` *remote interface*

```
/*
 * Copyright (c) 2000,2001 jGuru Europe.
 * All rights reserved.
 */

package se.jguru.webdb.legacyintegration;
```

```
import javax.ejb.EJBObject;
import java.rmi.RemoteException;
import javax.ejb.EJBException;

/**
 * The remote business interface of the Image
 * Entity EJB.
 */
public interface Image extends EJBObject
{
    /**
     * Retrieves the MIME type of this image
     */
    public String getMimeType() throws RemoteException;

    /**
     * Retrieves the data content of this image
     */
    public byte[] getData() throws RemoteException;

    /**
     * Sets the data content of this image
     */
    public void setData(byte[] val) throws RemoteException;

    /**
     * Retrieves the filename of this image
     */
    public String getFileName() throws RemoteException;

    /**
     * Sets the filename of this image
     */
    public void setFileName(String newName) throws RemoteException;

    /**
     * Returns the height of this image, or
     * -1 if the height is unknown.
     */
    public int getHeight() throws RemoteException;

    /**
     * Returns the width of this image, or
     * -1 if the width is unknown.
     */
    public int getWidth() throws RemoteException;
}
```

The service method definitions of the Image EJB component are straightforward and manipulate properties of a stored image file. Some properties, such as height and width, are read-only because they have getter method definitions only.

The Home interface of the Image EJB component contains a set of fewer—but more complex—method definitions. (See Figure 11-4.) The `create` methods simply accept values to all cells in the `Images` table in the database—there is also a test create method which does not actually upload any image data into the database.

Figure 11-10: The ImageHome interface defines all Create and Finder methods.

The Home interface of the Image EJB component contains a set of fewer, but more complex, method definitions. The create methods simply accept values to all cells in the `Images` table in the database. There is also a test `create` method that does not actually upload any image data into the database.

Listing 11-2 contains the code of the `ImageHome` interface.

Listing 11-2. The `ImageHome` *interface*

```
/*
 * Copyright (c) 2000,2001 jGuru Europe.
 * All rights reserved.
 */

package se.jguru.webdb.legacyintegration;
```

```
import javax.ejb.EJBHome;
import javax.ejb.CreateException;
import javax.ejb.EJBException;
import java.rmi.RemoteException;
import javax.ejb.FinderException;
import java.util.Collection;

/**
 * Home interface of the Image Entity EJB.
 */
public interface ImageHome extends EJBHome
{
    /**
     * Default create method for an Image EJB component.
     *
     * @param id The identifier (Primary Key) seed of this ImageBean
     * @param fileName The fileName of the Image
     * @param data The image file data
     * @param mimeType The string MIME type of the file
     */
    public Image create(int id, String fileName, byte[] data, String mimeType)
        throws CreateException, RemoteException;

    /**
     * Default create method for an Image EJB component, in case
     * the data is not received. This create method should be used
     * for TESTING only, to verify the proper workings of the EJB
     * to DataSource communication before actually having a properly
     * working image uploader service.
     *
     * @param id The identifier (Primary Key) seed of this ImageBean
     * @param fileName The fileName of the Image
     * @param mimeType The string MIME type of the file
     */
    public Image create(int id, String fileName, String mimeType)
        throws CreateException, RemoteException;

    /**
     * Standard primary key finder method of this ImageBean.
     *
     * @param pk The primary key of this ImageBean.
     */
    public Image findByPrimaryKey(Integer pk)
        throws FinderException, RemoteException;
```

```
    /**
     * Standard finder method for all images having a particular
     * MIME type.
     *
     * @param mimeType The primary key of this ImageBean.
     */
    public Collection findByMimeType(String mimeType)
        throws RemoteException, FinderException;
}
```

Two things are worth noticing about the method definitions in the Home interface:

- The primary key type of the Entity bean is—as revealed by the argument to the `findByPrimaryKey` method—of type `java.lang.Integer`. Despite this, the `id` argument to both `create` methods is a primitive `int`. This is nothing to worry about: in the corresponding `ejbCreate` methods implemented in the EJB Bean implementation class, we may simply wrap the primitive `int` in an `Integer` object and pass the primary key to the container. However, the conclusion is that we may define any type of `create` method signature, even one without a primary key argument. Occasionally, it may be simpler to permit the database to create the primary key using its facilities to automatically increment counters.

- The `findByMimeType` declaration returns a `Collection` of image instances. All finders capable of returning multiple instances should return a `collection`.

All things considered, the Home interface looks fairly familiar.

EJBBeanRoot and ImageBean

Two classes implement functionality: the `EJBBeanRoot` class and the `ImageBean`. (See Figures 11-11 and 11-12.)

The `EJBBeanRoot` class encapsulates a common logging structure, which may be used in a similar manner by all EJB beans. The only concrete method is `findVerbosity`, which reads a boolean value bound under the key `verboseMode` from the `Context`. If the value read is true, the internal boolean flag verbose is set to `true`, and vice versa. This verbosity flag serves as a hint for the level of verbosity from the system log, invoked by calling the `log` method.

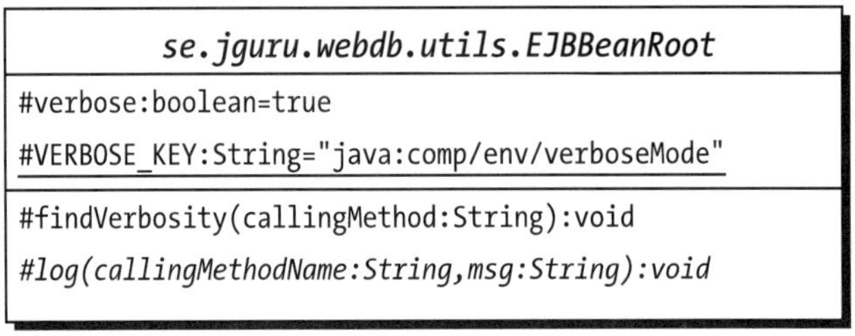

se.jguru.webdb.utils.EJBBeanRoot
#verbose:boolean=true #VERBOSE_KEY:String="java:comp/env/verboseMode"
#findVerbosity(callingMethod:String):void *#log(callingMethodName:String,msg:String):void*

Figure 11-11. The `EJBBeanRoot` *class provides common structures for all EJB Bean implementation classes.*

Listing 11-3 contains the code of the `EJBBeanRoot` class.

Listing 11-3. The `EJBBeanRoot` *class*

```
/*
 * Copyright (c) 2000,2001 jGuru Europe.
 * All rights reserved.
 */
package se.jguru.webdb.utils;

import javax.naming.*;

/**
 * Common properties for all EJB components in the system
 * are collected into this EJBRootBean class. All EJB bean
 * implementation classes should extend this class.
 *
 * @author Lennart Jörelid, jGuru Europe AB
 */
abstract public class EJBBeanRoot
{
    // Log verbosity flag.
    protected boolean verbose = true;

    // JNDI key to use for the verbosity flag lookup in the Context
    protected static final String VERBOSE_KEY = "java:comp/env/verboseMode";

    /**
     * Looks up and sets the internal verbosity toggle flag,
     * as defined in the Context under the VERBOSE_KEY.
     */
    protected void findVerbosity(String callingMethod)
```

```
    {
        // Find out if we are running in verbose mode; this
        // information should be written in our Context.
        try
        {
            // Get the Context
            Context cx = new InitialContext();

            // Find the verbosity reference in our context.
            Boolean runVerbose = (Boolean) cx.lookup(VERBOSE_KEY);

            // Assign our internal verbose flag
            this.verbose = runVerbose.booleanValue();
        }
        catch(Exception ex)
        {
            // Whoops.
            this.log(callingMethod, "Could not find the verboseMode flag "
                + "in the Context. Using verbose mode.");
            this.verbose = true;
        }
    }

    /**
     * Root method for all logging activities in the EJB Bean.
     *
     * @param callingMethodName The name of the method calling this log method.
     * @param msg The logging message.
     */
    abstract protected void log(String callingMethodName, String msg);
}
```

It is important to realize that the `EJBBeanRoot` can be used only by those classes that are deployed within an application server because the parameterless constructor `InitialContext()` used in the `findVerbosity` method can only connect to the context of a local application server. Other coding aspects of the `EJBBeanRoot` class are straightforward.

Let's proceed to the `ImageBean` class, where all service implementations for methods defined in the Remote and Home interfaces reside. (See Figure 11-12.)

When creating a CMP entity bean, all service methods writing data to or reading data from the data source should be left as abstract method definitions. The application server deployment tools will implement all finders, accessor methods, and required internal state variables.

```
                                                        EJBBeanRoot
                                                         EntityBean
          se.jguru.webdb.legacyintegration.ImageBean
---------------------------------------------------------------------
-ctx:EntityContext
---------------------------------------------------------------------
+setEntityContext(context:EntityContext):void
+unsetEntityContext():void
+ejbActivate():void
+ejbPassivate():void
+ejbRemove():void
+ejbStore():void
+ejbLoad():void
#log(methodName:String,msg:String):void
-getTwoByteUnsignedFieldLsbFirst(data:byte[],lsbIndex:int):int
---------------------------------------------------------------------

+ejbCreate(id:int,fileName:String,data:byte[],mimeType:String):Integer
+ejbPostCreate(id:int,fileName:String,data:byte[],mimeType:String):void
+ejbCreate(id:int,fileName:String,mimeType:String):Integer
+ejbPostCreate(id:int,fileName:String,mimeType:String):void
---------------------------------------------------------------------

+findByPrimaryKey(pk:Integer):Image
+findByMimeType(mimeType:String):Collection
---------------------------------------------------------------------

+getId():Integer
+setId(val:Integer):void
+getMimeType():String
+setMimeType(val:String):void
+getData():byte[]
+setData(val:byte[]):void
+getFileName():String
+setFileName(val:String):void
+getHeight():int
+getWidth():int
---------------------------------------------------------------------
```

Figure 11-12. The `ImageBean` *class contains the implementation of all service and* `create` *method definitions in the Home and Remote interfaces.*

The ImageBean class provides several types of methods, listed in Table 11-1 in the order of appearance in the class shown in Figure 11-12.

Table 11-1. Method Descriptions of the Methods in the ImageBean *Class*

CATEGORY	METHOD	DESCRIPTION
EntityContext pattern members	setEntityContext, unsetEntityContext	Container reference for use within the EJB bean implementation class.
Life-cycle methods	ejbActivate, ejbPassivate, ejbRemove, ejbLoad, ejbStore	The life-cycle methods are invoked by the EJB container immediately before (ejbPassivate, ejbRemove, ejbStore) or after (ejbActivate, ejbLoad) making a state transition for the EJB component. Usually the state of the EJB component is read from or written to the data source as part of the state transition. For instance, the ejbActivate and ejbLoad methods usually perform an SQL SELECT call to the database, whereas the ejbPassivate and ejbStore methods perform an SQL UPDATE database call. The ejbRemove method call performs the SQL DELETE, which actually removes the state from persistent storage.
Internal service methods	log, getTwoByteUnsignedFieldLsbFirst	Service methods performing distinct tasks that are needed by other methods in the EJB component. Service methods act as normal private members of any class.
Factory initializer methods	ejbCreate, ejbPostCreate	The ejbCreate data source creational methods provide the instructions to be carried out when initializing the database record saving the persistent state. The data is stored into the database using an SQL INSERT statement.
Data source getter methods	getId, getMimeType, getData, getFileName	The abstract data source getter methods provide the programmatic interface to the database table. The data returned from the getters are read from the database using an SQL SELECT statement.

Table 11-1. Method Descriptions of the Methods in the `ImageBean` *Class (Continued)*

CATEGORY	METHOD	DESCRIPTION
Data source setter methods	`setId`, `setMimeType`, `setData`, `setFileName`	The abstract data source setter methods provide the programmatic interface to the database table. The data provided as arguments to the setter methods is written to the database using an SQL UPDATE statement.
Remote business methods	`getHeight`, `getWidth`	The remote business methods `getHeight` and `getWeight` methods provide calculated information about an image.

Let's now investigate the code of the `ImageBean` class. (See Listing 11-4.) The comments in the listing divide the source code according to the method categories listed in Table 11-1.

Listing 11-4. The `ImageBean` *class*

```
/*
 * Copyright (c) 2000,2001 jGuru Europe.
 * All rights reserved.
 */

package se.jguru.webdb.legacyintegration;

import javax.ejb.*;
import java.rmi.*;
import javax.naming.*;

import se.jguru.webdb.utils.*;

/**
 * Entity bean using CMP (Container Managed Persistence)
 * to read and store its data in a database table row.
 * The Image EJB component also provides some remote
 * business methods to provide additional (calculated)
 * metadata information about the image.
 *
 * @author Lennart Jörelid, jGuru Europe AB
 */
```

```
abstract public class ImageBean extends EJBBeanRoot implements EntityBean
{
    //
    // Entity context pattern.
    //
    private EntityContext ctx;

    public void setEntityContext(EntityContext context) { ctx = context; }
    public void unsetEntityContext() { ctx = null; }

    //
    // End entity context pattern.
    //



    //
    // Abstract CMP method stubs (DataSource setter and getter
    // methods). The application server deployment tools provide
    // the implementation classes for these methods.
    //
    public abstract Integer getId();
    public abstract void setId(Integer val); // Primary key

    public abstract String getMimeType();
    public abstract void setMimeType(String val);

    public abstract byte[] getData();
    public abstract void setData(byte[] val);

    public abstract String getFileName();
    public abstract void setFileName(String val);

    //
    // End Abstract CMP method stubs
    //

    //
    // Remote business methods provinding
    // calculated metadata about the image
    // originating from the data content
    // stored in the database.
    //
```

```
/**
 * Returns the height of a GIF image,
 * wrapped by this bean - or -1 if the
 * height could not be found.
 */
public int getHeight()
{
    // If this is not a GIF image,
    // this implementation does not know
    // how to calculate its size.
    if(!this.getMimeType().equalsIgnoreCase("image/gif"))
    {
        // Log.
        this.log("getHeight", "Cannot determine image Height for "
            + "other image formats than image/gif.");

        // Done.
        return -1;
    }

    byte[] imageData = this.getData();
    if(imageData == null)
    {
        // Log.
        this.log("getHeight", "Found no image data. Returning -1.");

        // Done.
        return -1;
    }

    // Sane. Get the height of this bean.
    //
    // GIF images have their sizes written
    // at bytes location number 8 and 9 in
    // the data stream.
    // Remember that they are written as
    // unsigned bytes - we must compensate
    // for the signed nature of Java.
    return this.getTwoByteUnsignedFieldLsbFirst(imageData, 8);
}

/**
 * Returns the width of a GIF image,
 * wrapped by this bean - or -1 if the
 * height could not be found.
 */
```

```
public int getWidth()
{
    // If this is not a GIF image,
    // this implementation does not know
    // how to calculate its size.
    if(!this.getMimeType().equalsIgnoreCase("image/gif"))
        return -1;

    byte[] imageData = this.getData();
    if(imageData == null)
        return -1;

    // Sane. Get the height of this bean.
    //
    // GIF images have their widths written
    // at bytes location number 6 and 7 in
    // the data stream.
    // Remember that they are written as
    // unsigned bytes - we must compensate
    // for the signed nature of Java.
    return this.getTwoByteUnsignedFieldLsbFirst(imageData, 6);
}

//
// End remote business methods
//

//
// Life cycle methods, called by the EJB
// container to initiate or finalize state
// transitions for the EJB component
//
// This section also contains the factory
// initializer methods, ejbCreate and ejbPostCreate
//

public void ejbActivate()
{
    // Log if verbose to see when ejbActivate is invoked.
    this.log("ejbActivate", "--");
}
```

```
public void ejbPassivate()
{
    // Log if verbose to see when ejbPassivate is invoked.
    this.log("ejbPassivate", "--");
}

public void ejbRemove()
{
    // Log if verbose to see when ejbRemove is invoked.
    this.log("ejbRemove", "--");
}

public void ejbStore()
{
    // Log if verbose to see when ejbStore is invoked.
    this.log("ejbStore", "--");
}

public void ejbLoad()
{
    // Log if verbose to see when ejbLoad is invoked.
    this.log("ejbLoad", "--");
}

public Integer ejbCreate(int id, String fileName, byte[] data, String mimeType)
throws CreateException
{
    // Assign our internal state
    this.setId(new Integer(id));
    this.setFileName(fileName);
    this.setData(data);
    this.setMimeType(mimeType);

    // Log if verbose to see when ejbLoad is invoked.
    this.log("ejbCreate", "Got: id=" + id + ", fileName=" + fileName
        + ", data.length=" + data.length + ", mimeType=" + mimeType);

    // Since this is a CMP bean, the ejbCreate methods
    // must return null - only BMP beans should return
    // their primary keys from the ejbCreate methods.
    return null;
}
```

```
public void ejbPostCreate(int id, String fileName, byte[] data, String mimeType)
{
    // Find out if we are running in verbose mode; this
    // information should be written in our Context.
    this.findVerbosity("ejbPostCreate");
}

public Integer ejbCreate(int id, String fileName, String mimeType)
throws CreateException
{
    // Assign the internal state
    this.setId(new Integer(id));
    this.setFileName(fileName);
    this.setData(new byte[1]);
    this.setMimeType(mimeType);

    // Log if verbose to see when ejbLoad is invoked.
    this.log("ejbCreate", "Got: id=" + id + ", fileName=" + fileName
        + ", mimeType=" + mimeType);

    // Since this is a CMP bean, the ejbCreate methods
    // must return null - only BMP beans should return
    // their primary keys from the ejbCreate methods.
    return null;
}

public void ejbPostCreate(int id, String fileName, String mimeType)
{
    // Find out if we are running in verbose mode; this
    // information should be written in our Context.
    this.findVerbosity("ejbPostCreate");
}

//
// End life cycle methods (including
// factory initializer methods)
//

//
// Private helper methods used internally by
// other methods in the bean.
//
```

```
    /**
     * Encapsulation of the main log method in the CommonUtils class.
     */
    protected void log(String methodName, String msg)
    {
        // Log only if we are running in verbose mode.
        if(verbose) CommonUtils.log("ImageBean", methodName, msg);
    }

    /**
     * Reads two bytes from the data byte array originating from
     * the lsbIndex. Assuming that the bytes are provided in unsigned
     * form, the method converts the results of the two unsigned bytes
     * into an integer.
     */
    private int getTwoByteUnsignedFieldLsbFirst(byte[] data, int lsbIndex)
    {
        // Log
        this.log("getTwoByteUnsignedFieldLsbFirst", "data="
            + data + ", lsbIndex= " + lsbIndex);
        this.log("getTwoByteUnsignedFieldLsbFirst", "data[lsbIndex]="
            + data[lsbIndex] + ", data[lsbIndex + 1]= " + data[lsbIndex + 1]);

        int lsb = (data[lsbIndex] < 0)
                ? 256 + data[lsbIndex]
                : data[lsbIndex];
        int msb = (data[lsbIndex + 1] < 0)
                ? 256 + data[lsbIndex + 1]
                : data[lsbIndex + 1];

        // Log.
        this.log("getTwoByteUnsignedFieldLsbFirst", "lsb = "
                + lsb + ", msb = " + msb);

        // Done.
        return lsb + msb * 256;
    }

    //
    // End private helper methods
    //
}
```

Note that the finder methods defined in the `ImageHome` interface are not mirrored to `ejbFindXXX` methods in the `ImageBean` class. This is characteristic for CMP entity beans: the application server skeleton compiler tool generates the finder methods from EJB-QL definitions in the `ejb-jar.xml` deployment descriptor file, as we will show in the "Step 4—Configuring the Image Subsystem" section. When implementing a CMP entity bean, you need therefore not implement the finder methods in the Bean implementation class code. Simply declare the finders in the Home interface and provide specifications for how to generate the database queries in the deployment descriptor.

The `ejbCreate` methods of an entity bean using CMP has a behavior that may seem peculiar or puzzling at first. An `ejbCreate` method must return the type of the primary key for both types of entity beans (BMP and CMP entity beans); however, according to the EJB specification, CMP entity beans must always return the value `null`. This is for reasons of compatibility: should you wish a BMP Bean implementation class to extend a CMP Bean implementation class, the `ejbCreate` methods must have the same signature. What would happen in that case if the `ejbCreate` method of the CMP Bean implementation class returns `void` instead of `Integer`?

The code bloat of the `ImageBean` class may be significant, but it is indeed manageable. In general, CMP entity beans require little coding but much configuration and deployment setting optimization to minimize the required number of database read and write operations.

The `ImageBean` component is wrapped by an `ImageProxy`, which shields the Web container from any `RemoteExceptions` (and other exceptions caused by the distributed nature of the Image EJB component) raised by the `ImageBean`. Next, we'll investigate the ImageBean proxy.

The ImageBean Proxy Class

When calling methods in EJB remote interfaces from within a Web container, it is important to handle all the exceptions and complexities which may be caused by the distributed nature of the EJB component. These tasks are normally handled by wrapping the EJB object in a proxy class, which has the following primary purposes:

- Encapsulate and hide all code related to JNDI and EJB component lookup. Such statements generally require much exception handling, which makes it cumbersome to use direct calls to EJB components in JSP documents and servlets.

- Translate method names to match the JavaBean naming pattern with setter and getter methods to facilitate use of `<jsp:getProperty ... />` and `<jsp:setProperty ... />` standard actions.

- Condense the data found in a set of EJB remote or other objects into a simple accessor API tailored to the needs of a particular Web page or user story.

In our example, the Image remote interface already follows the JavaBean naming pattern. However, the `ImageBean` proxy performs all tasks in the short list just presented: it simply delegates its method calls to methods with identical names in the EJB remote interface. A UML diagram of the `ImageProxy` class is shown in Figure 11-13.

The `ImageProxy` class provides several types of methods, listed in Table 11-2 in the order of appearance in the class Figure 11-14.

Table 11-2. The Methods of the `ImageProxy` *Class*

CATEGORY	METHOD	DESCRIPTION
Populators	`populate`	Executes an operation (either CREATE, READ, MODIFY or DELETE), which affects the image state.
Operation methods	`createImage`, `readImage`, `modifyImage`, `deleteImage`	Methods affecting the state of an Image EJB object, thereby indirectly modifying the state of the data source where the images are stored.
Internal service methods	`log`, `getImageHome`	Service methods performing distinct tasks that are needed by other methods in the EJB component. Service methods act as normal private members of any class.
JavaBean accessor methods	`getImageData`, `setImageData`, `getId`, `setId`, `getMimeType`, `setMimeType`, `getData`, `setData`, `getFileName`, `setFileName`	These methods call the methods of the Image remote interface to set or get its data. Another important task of these methods is catching any exceptions that may be thrown by the Remote interface.

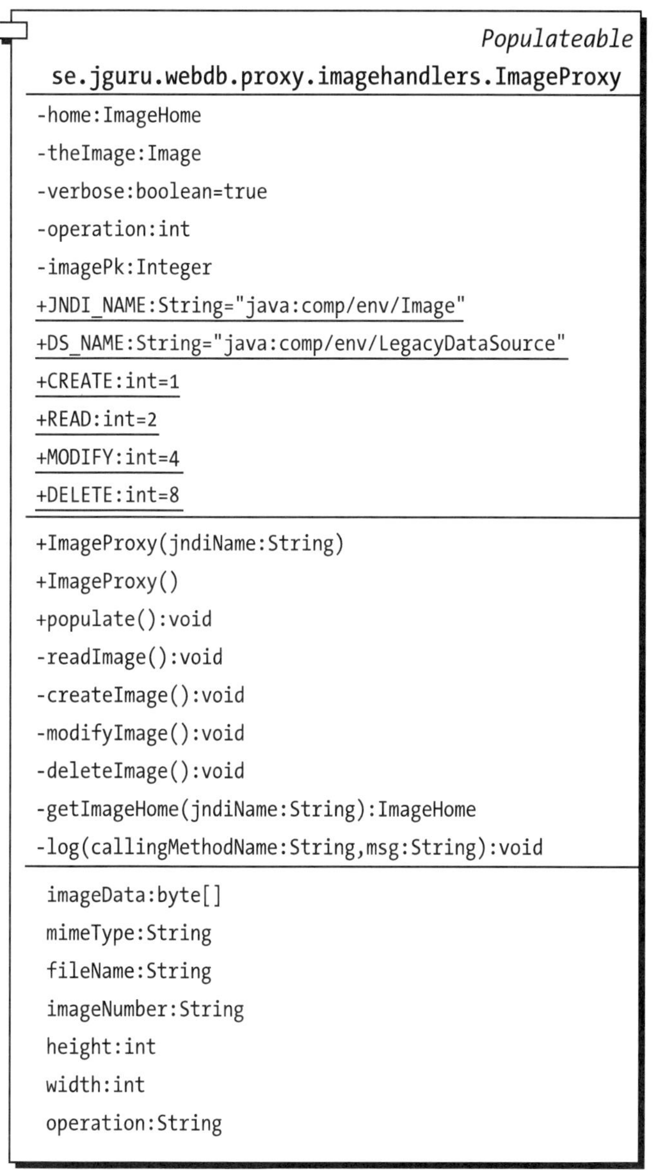

Figure 11-13. The `ImageProxy` *class wraps an* `ImageHome` *and an* `Image` *instance, and provides methods to access the data in the* `Image` *instance.*

The operations recognized by the `ImageProxy` are as follows:

- The CREATE operation generates a new `Image` instance using the data held in the `ImageProxy`. This operation corresponds to creating a new row in the IMAGES tale in the database.

- The READ operation finds an image using the `imageNumber` property that should contain a number identical to that of the primary key for the image that should be retrieved from the database.

- The MODIFY operation alters the `Image` data of an image. Given an image (or an `imageNumber` that may be parsed into the primary key of an image), the data uploaded to the proxy is used to update the persistent storage in the entity EJB.

- The DELETE operation removes an image from persistent storage.

Operations are launched from the `populate()` method, which performs all interactions with the legacy system `DataSource`. The mode of operations when using an `ImageProxy` is therefore identical for all operations, as listed here:

1. Call any of the setter methods to populate the internal state of the `ImageProxy` instance as required. One of the setter methods should be `setOperation`, which indicates which operation should be performed.

2. Call the `populate` method to execute the indicated operation. The populate, in turn, delegates the execution of the operation to `readImage`, `createImage`, `deleteImage`, or `modifyImage` depending on the requested operation.

Let's take a look at the code of the `ImageProxy` class in Listing 11-5.

Listing 11-5. The `ImageProxy` *class*

```
/*
 * Copyright (c) 2000,2001 jGuru Europe.
 * All rights reserved.
 */

package se.jguru.webdb.proxy.imagehandlers;

import javax.naming.*;
import javax.rmi.*;
import java.rmi.RemoteException;
import javax.ejb.CreateException;
import java.sql.*;
import javax.sql.*;
import java.util.*;
```

```
import se.jguru.webdb.legacyintegration.*;
import se.jguru.webdb.proxy.Populateable;
import se.jguru.webdb.proxy.PopulationException;
import se.jguru.webdb.utils.CommonUtils;

/**
 * ImageProxy JavaBean which communicates with
 * an Image EJB component - for uploading/creating
 * as well as downloading data.
 *
 * @author Lennart Jörelid, jGuru Europe AB
 */
public class ImageProxy implements Populateable
{
    // The Home interface for the Image
    private ImageHome home;

    // The Remote interface for the Image
    private Image theImage;

    // Toggle flag for logging verbosity
    private boolean verbose = true;

    // The operation selected
    private int operation;

    // Primary key for the Image to find.
    private Integer imagePk;

    // The data of the image.
    private byte[] imageData;

    // The MimeType of the image
    private String fileName;

    // The mimeType of the image
    private String mimeType;

    /** JNDI lookup name for the ImageHome in the context. */
    public static final String JNDI_NAME = "java:comp/env/Image";

    /** JNDI lookup name for the DataSource. */
    public static final String DS_NAME = "java:comp/env/LegacyDataSource";
```

```
public static final int CREATE = 1;
public static final int READ = 2;
public static final int MODIFY = 4;
public static final int DELETE = 8;

/**
 * Sets up this ImageProxy, originating from the
 * jndiName provided.
 *
 * @param jndiName The lookup string for the ImageProxyHome.
 */
public ImageProxy(String jndiName)
{
    // Create the home
    this.home = this.getImageHome(jndiName);
}

public ImageProxy()
{
    this(JNDI_NAME);
}

//
// JavaBean getter methods which
// should be used from within
// the JSP view.
//

public byte[] getImageData()
{
    try
    {
        return this.theImage.getData();
    }
    catch (RemoteException ex)
    {
        this.log("getImageData", "Could not get image data due to a "
        + "broken connection: " + ex);
    }

    return null;
}
```

```
public String getMimeType()
{
    try
    {
        return this.theImage.getMimeType();
    }
    catch (RemoteException ex)
    {
        this.log("getMimeType", "Could not get the MimeType due to a "
        + "broken connection: " + ex);
    }

    return null;
}

public String getFileName()
{
    try
    {
        return this.theImage.getFileName();
    }
    catch (RemoteException ex)
    {
        this.log("getMimeType", "Could not get the FileName due to a "
        + "broken connection: " + ex);
    }

    return null;
}

public String getImageNumber()
{
    // Check sanity.
    if(this.theImage == null)
    {
        // Not good.
        this.log("getImageNumber", "theImage EJB component is NULL.");

        if(this.imagePk == null)
        {
            this.log("getImageNumber", "this.imagePK is also NULL. "
            + "Insane state; bailing out.");
```

```
                return "" + 1;
            }
            else
            {

                this.log("getImageNumber", "Using local PK ["
                    + this.imagePk + "]");
                return "" + this.imagePk;
            }
        }

        try
        {
            this.log("getImageNumber",
                    "Using image EJB PK ["
                     + this.theImage.getPrimaryKey() + "]");
            return "" + this.theImage.getPrimaryKey();
        }
        catch (RemoteException ex)
        {
            this.log("getImageNumber", "Could not get the ImageNumber due to a "
            + "broken connection: " + ex);
        }

        return null;
    }

    public int getHeight()
    {
        try
        {
            return this.theImage.getHeight();
        }
        catch (RemoteException ex)
        {
            this.log("getHeight", "Could not get the image height due to a "
            + "broken connection: " + ex);
        }

        return -1;
    }
```

```
public int getWidth()
{
    try
    {
        return this.theImage.getWidth();
    }
    catch (RemoteException ex)
    {
        this.log("getWidth", "Could not get the image width due to a "
        + "broken connection: " + ex);
    }

    return -1;
}

//
// JavaBean setter methods which
// should be called from within
// the JSP view.
//

public void setImageNumber(String imagePk)
{
    if (imagePk == null) return;

    this.log("setImageNumber", "imagePk=" + imagePk);

    // Convert to the Primary Key of the Image
    this.imagePk = new Integer(imagePk);
}

public void setImageData(byte[] imageData)
{
    this.imageData = imageData;
}

public void setMimeType(String mimeType)
{
    this.mimeType = mimeType;
}

public void setFileName(String fileName)
{
    this.fileName = fileName;
}
```

```
public void setOperation(String operationId)
{
    // Get an int from the operationId
    int op = READ;

    try
    {
        // Get the operation id
        op = Integer.parseInt(operationId);
    }
    catch (Exception ex)
    {
        // We will use the default FIND
        // operation anyway. Simply log.
        this.log("setOperation", "operationId '" + operationId + "' could "
        + "not be parsed into a number. Using READ operation.");
    }

    // Assign to the internal data.
    this.operation = op;
}

//
// End JavaBean setter methods
//


/**
 * Populates the internal state of this Populateable,
 * or throws a PopulationException describing why
 * the populate operation failed.
 */
public void populate() throws PopulationException
{
    this.log("populate", "Operation=" + this.operation);

    switch (this.operation)
    {
        case READ:
            // This is the default operation; get an image from the DataSource.
            this.readImage();
            break;
```

```
        case CREATE:
            // Write the image to the DataSource
            this.createImage();
            break;

        case MODIFY:
            // Re-write the image to the DataSource
            this.modifyImage();
            break;

        case DELETE:
            // Re-rite the image to the DataSource
            this.deleteImage();
            break;

        default:
            // Unknown operation
            throw new PopulationException("[ImageProxy::populate]: Could not "
           + "populate the Image proxy: Unknown operation " + this.operation);
    }

    // Nullify our internal state
    /*
    this.imageData = null;
    this.mimeType = null;
    this.fileName = null;
    */
}

/**
 * Reads an image from the DataSource, given its primary
 * key (imageNumber).
 */
private void readImage()
{
    // Check sanity
    if(this.imagePk == null)
    {
       this.log("readImage", "NULL primary key. Cannot proceed with lookup.");
        return;
    }
```

```
        try
        {
            // Verify that the home exists
            if(this.home == null)
            {
                this.log("readImage", "NULL home. Recreating.");
                this.home = this.getImageHome(this.JNDI_NAME);
            }
            else this.log("readImage", "this.home exists: " + this.home);

            // Get the Image from the context
            this.log("readImage", "Getting image EJB for pk=" + this.imagePk);
            this.theImage = this.home.findByPrimaryKey(this.imagePk);
            this.log("readImage", "All Done. PK=" + this.imagePk
                + ", data.length=" + this.theImage.getData().length);
        }
        catch (Exception ex)
        {
            this.log("readImage",
                     "Could not read image from the DataSource: " + ex);
        }
    }

    /**
     * Creates an image originating from the current internal
     * state variables.
     */
    private void createImage()
    throws IllegalStateException
    {
        // Check sanity
        if (this.imageData == null)
            throw new IllegalStateException("Cannot write empty Image.");
        if (this.mimeType == null || this.mimeType.equals(""))
            throw new IllegalStateException("Cannot write undefined "
                     + "Image Mime Type.");
        if (this.fileName == null || this.fileName.equals(""))
            this.fileName = "Unnamed [" + mimeType + "] Image.";

        // Sane. Get the next available PK number
        try
        {
            // Get the initial context
            Context ctx = new InitialContext();
            this.log("createImage", "Got Context: " + ctx);
```

```
        // Get a connection
        DataSource ds = (DataSource) ctx.lookup(DS_NAME);
        Connection conn = ds.getConnection();
        this.log("createImage", "Got conn: " + conn);

        // Find the maximum Image number PK of the IMAGES table.
        Statement stmnt = conn.createStatement();
        ResultSet rs = stmnt.executeQuery("select max(ID) from IMAGES");

        if (!rs.next())
            throw new IllegalStateException("Could not find "
                        + "maximum imageNumber.");

        int imageNumber = rs.getInt(1);
        rs.close();
        conn.close();

        this.log("createImage", "Got imageNumber: " + imageNumber
            + ", using: " + (imageNumber + 1));

        this.log("createImage", "fileName=" + this.fileName
            + "; imageData.length=" + this.imageData.length
            + "; mimeType=" + this.mimeType
            + "; home=" + this.home);

        // Create the home if required
        if(this.home == null) this.home = this.getImageHome(JNDI_NAME);

        // Create the image instance
        this.theImage = this.home.create(imageNumber + 1, this.fileName,
                    this.imageData, this.mimeType);

        // Log.
        this.log("createImage", "Made image: " + this.theImage
              + ", pK=" + this.theImage.getPrimaryKey());

        // Set the image primary key
        this.setImageNumber("" +  this.theImage.getPrimaryKey());
    }
    catch (SQLException ex)
    {
        this.log("createImage", "Could not write to the DataSource: " + ex);
    }
```

```
        catch (RemoteException ex)
        {
            this.log("createImage", "Encountered a broken connection: " + ex);
        }
        catch (CreateException ex)
        {
            this.log("createImage", "Could not create the Image: " + ex);
        }
        catch (NamingException ex)
        {
            this.log("createImage", "Could not create the Image: " + ex);
        }
        catch(Exception ex)
        {
            this.log("createImage", "Could not create the Image: " + ex);
        }
    }

    /**
     * Modifies the Data and FileName of the Image
     * currently loaded, if the two variables are
     * non-null.
     */
    private void modifyImage()
    {
        try
        {
            // Check sanity
            if(this.imagePk == null)
            {
                this.log("modifyImage", "NULL primary key. "
                                + "Cannot proceed with lookup.");
                return;
            }

            // Verify that the home exists
            if(this.home == null)
            {
                this.log("modifyImage", "NULL home. Recreating.");
                this.home = this.getImageHome(this.JNDI_NAME);
            }
            else this.log("modifyImage", "this.home exists: " + this.home);

            // Get the image with the provided PK
            this.theImage = this.home.findByPrimaryKey(this.imagePk);
```

```
            // Write all non-null properties to the image
            if (this.imageData != null) this.theImage.setData(this.imageData);
            if (this.fileName != null) this.theImage.setFileName(this.fileName);
        }
        catch (Exception ex)
        {
            this.log("modifyImage", "Could not modify the image: " + ex);
        }
    }

    /**
     * Deletes the image with the provided key from the
     * database.
     */
    private void deleteImage()
    {
        // First, read the image
        if(this.theImage == null)
        {
            // Does the imageNumber (PK) exist?
            if(this.imagePk == null)
            {
                // Insane state -
                this.log("deleteImage", "no image to delete, and "
                    + "no imagePk found. Bailing out.");
                return;
            }

            // At least, we have an image number.
            // Re-read the image.
            this.log("deleteImage", "Re-reading image with PK=" + this.imagePk);
            this.readImage();
        }

        try
        {
             // Now, delete the image
             this.theImage.remove();
        }
        catch(Exception ex)
        {
            this.log("deleteImage", "Could not remove the image: " + ex);
        }
    }
```

```
    /**
     * Looks up and retrieves the Home interface of the Image EJB component.
     */
    private ImageHome getImageHome(String jndiName)
    {
        try
        {
            // Get the initial context
            //
            // This client runs within the application server, so we should
            // not be required to submit any initialization parameters to
            // the InitialContext constructor.
            Context ctx = new InitialContext();

            // Lookup the ImageHome instance
            this.log("getImageHome", "Looking up: " + jndiName);
            Object obj = ctx.lookup(jndiName);
            this.log("getImageHome", "Found obj: " + obj);

            // Narrow the retrieved object to a ImageHome
            ImageHome home = (ImageHome)
                        PortableRemoteObject.narrow(obj, ImageHome.class);
            this.log("getImageHome", "Found home: " + home);

            // Done. Return.
            return home;
        }
        catch (Exception ex)
        {
            // Log and bail out.
            this.log("getImageHome", "Could not create an ImageHome: " + ex);
            this.log("getImageHome", "jndiName: " + jndiName);
        }

        // This should never happen...
        this.log("getImageHome", "Returning null.");
        return null;
    }

    /** Logs a message to the standard log stream. */
    private void log(String callingMethodName, String msg)
    {
        if (verbose) CommonUtils.log("ImageProxy", callingMethodName, msg);
    }
}
```

The `ImageProxy` class provides data to the two servlets uploading images from the user and downloading images to a client browser. Let's investigate these last code parts of the image subsystem.

The DocumentDownloader Servlet

You need a simple means of accessing the images stored in the database and wrapped in an Image EJB component. The small `DocumentDownloader` servlet shown in Figure 11-4 provides just such simple access to Web container documents (such as HTML or JSP documents).

HttpServlet se.jguru.webdb.proxy.imagehandlers.DocumentDownloader
+IMAGE_ID_KEY:String="imId"
+service(request:HttpServletRequest,response:HttpServletResponse):void

Figure 11-14. The `DocumentDownloader` *servlet downloads and shows the image having the primary key given by a request parameter with the name* `imId`.

As shown in Figure 11-14, the `DocumentDownloader` is a small servlet indeed; its only method is `service` that locates and downloads the data of an image stored within the database. The image number (that is, primary key) should be provided as a request parameter with the key "imId".

Listing 11-6 contains the source code of the `DocumentDownloader`.

Listing 11-6. The `DocumentDownloader` *servlet*

```
/*
 * Copyright (c) 2000,2001 jGuru Europe.
 * All rights reserved.
 */

package se.jguru.webdb.proxy.imagehandlers;

import javax.servlet.*;
import javax.servlet.http.*;
import javax.naming.*;
import javax.rmi.*;
import java.io.*;
import java.util.*;
```

```
import se.jguru.webdb.legacyintegration.*;
import se.jguru.webdb.utils.*;
import se.jguru.webdb.proxy.imagehandlers.ImageProxy;

/**
 * Servlet which proxies downloading/showing an image file upon
 * request by the client browser.
 *
 * @author Lennart Jörelid, lj@jguru.se
 */
public class DocumentDownloader extends HttpServlet
{
    public static final String IMAGE_ID_KEY = "imId";

    /**
     * Process the request, and send back the image
     * data with the proper content type.
     */
    public void service(HttpServletRequest request, HttpServletResponse response)
    throws ServletException, IOException
    {
        // Get a session
        HttpSession sess = request.getSession(true);
        if(sess.isNew() ||
                sess.getAttribute( DocumentUploader.IMAGE_PROXY_KEY ) == null)
            sess.setAttribute(DocumentUploader.IMAGE_PROXY_KEY, new ImageProxy());

        // Get the current ImageProxy
        ImageProxy prx = (ImageProxy)
                sess.getAttribute( DocumentUploader.IMAGE_PROXY_KEY );

        // Get the image PK
        String imagePk = request.getParameter(IMAGE_ID_KEY);
        if(imagePk == null) imagePk = "1";

        prx.setImageNumber(imagePk);
        prx.setOperation("" + ImageProxy.READ);
        prx.populate();

        // Get the image data
        byte[] imageData = prx.getImageData();
```

```
        // Set the content type of the response
        response.setContentType( prx.getMimeType() );

        // Write the imageData to the response
        ServletOutputStream out = response.getOutputStream();
        out.write(imageData);
        out.flush();
    }
}
```

The DocumentDownloader provides raw image data to the browser, so we must use a ServletOutputStream rather than a Reader to output the data. The DocumentDownloader is trivial because all data is simply retrieved from the populated ImageProxy object.

As the DocumentUploader servlet must parse uploaded binary data, it requires more infrastructure than its downloader sibling.

The DocumentUploader Servlet

The DocumentUploader servlet handles the uploading of images encoded in HTTP multipart format. (Refer to http://www.w3c.org or Chapter 3 for an explanation of multipart encoding.) The task consists of cutting the binary uploaded image data from the containing HTTP text, creating an ImageProxy, and uploading the image data into it for further delivery into the database. The structure of the DocumentUploader servlet is therefore more complex than the DocumentDownloader servlet, as shown in Figure 11-15.

The DocumentUploader servlet can only be called using the HTTP POST method, as binary data gets garbled when converted back and forth to a string. The doPost method performs the following five tasks for each uploaded image:

1. It creates or retrieves the ImageProxy from the HttpSession.

2. It then acquires the ServletInputStream and splices the multipart encoded data into its parts. Because obtaining the ServletInputStream prevents using any of the Request.getParameter methods, a getValue method duplicating its function is provided in the DocumentUploader servlet.

3. The "document" part is sent to the getPart method, which parses the information about the uploaded image file and separates out the binary image data. After packaging all parsed data in a DocumentHolder object, the data is returned.

```
                                                        HttpServlet
        se.jguru.webdb.proxy.imagehandlers.DocumentUploader
-------------------------------------------------------------------
-errorPage:String=null
-allOKPage:String=null
-noDocumentPage:String=null
-SPLICED_PARTS:String="splicedParts"
-DOCUMENT_NAME:String="document"
+IMAGE_PROXY_KEY:String="imProxy"
-------------------------------------------------------------------
+init(conf:ServletConfig):void
+doPost(request:HttpServletRequest,response:HttpServletResponse):void
#spliceMultipartData(request:HttpServletRequest):List
#getPart(nameKey:String,splicedData:List):DocumentHolder
-getValue(nameKey:String,splicedData:List):byte[]
#getContentType(data:byte[]):String
#getOrigPath(data:byte[],returnFileNameOnly:boolean):String
-indexOf(source:byte[],key:byte[],startIndex:int):int
```

Figure 11-15. The `DocumentUploader` *servlet splices the uploaded image data from the surrounding HTTP text.*

4. The `ImageProxy` created in step 1 is populated with the data from the `DocumentHolder` from step 3, and the image is created.

5. If all went well, the execution is redirected to the `allOkPage`, and the result of the image upload is shown. If an error was encountered, execution is resumed at the `errorPage`. Both the `allOkPage` and the `errorPage` values are provided as initialization parameters to the servlet.

The code of the `DocumentUploader` servlet is complex because all operations must take place on a binary basis. Although some parts of the `ServletInputStream` contains text, the image part contains only binary information, and the methods performing document lexing and parsing must therefore be created by hand.

Despite the programming transpiration associated with implementing simple generic binary parsing methods, the `DocumentUploader` servlet code is fairly straightforward as you can see from Listing 11-7.

Listing 11-7. The `DocumentUploader` *servlet*

```
/*
 * Copyright (c) 2000,2001 jGuru Europe.
 * All rights reserved.
 */

package se.jguru.webdb.proxy.imagehandlers;

import javax.servlet.*;
import javax.servlet.http.*;
import java.util.*;
import java.io.*;

import se.jguru.webdb.proxy.imagehandlers.ImageProxy;

/**
 * The document uploader servlet
 *
 * @author Lennart Jörelid, jGuru Europe AB
 */
public class DocumentUploader extends HttpServlet
{
    // Redirection pages, where to send the
    // user after the potential document upload.
    // These data are global for all calls.
    private String errorPage = null;
    private String allOKPage = null;
    private String noDocumentPage = null;

    // Keys to use when binding session parameters and
    // controlling splicing.
    private static final String SPLICED_PARTS = "splicedParts";
    private static final String DOCUMENT_NAME = "document";

    // Define the key where to bind the ImageProxy bean
    // in the HttpSession.
    public static final String IMAGE_PROXY_KEY = "imProxy";
```

```
// Standard init
public void init(ServletConfig conf) throws ServletException
{
    // Read the redirection parameters for pages
    // to redirect the user to after the document upload.
    this.errorPage = conf.getInitParameter("ERROR_PAGE");
    this.noDocumentPage = conf.getInitParameter("NO_DOCUMENT_PAGE");
    this.allOKPage = conf.getInitParameter("ALL_OK_PAGE");

    // Revert to default redirection values in case
    // no parameter was provided.
    if (this.errorPage == null)
        this.errorPage = "/upload/uploadError.html";
    if (this.noDocumentPage == null)
        this.noDocumentPage = "/upload/noDocument.html";
    if (this.allOKPage == null)
        this.allOKPage = "/upload/noDocument.html";
}

/**
 * Main uploader method, which will handle all types of documents.
 * Since uploaded documents may be binary in nature, we have to use
 * Stream classes, rather than Reader classes to handle the
 * uploaded document.
 */
public void doPost(HttpServletRequest request,
HttpServletResponse response)
throws ServletException, IOException
{
    try
    {
        // Switch on buffering
        // System.out.println("Orig. buffer size = "
        //                       + response.getBufferSize());
        if(response.getBufferSize() < 8000) response.setBufferSize(8000);
       // System.out.println("New buffer size = " + response.getBufferSize());

        // Get or create the HttpSession, and
        // bind or retrieve the ImageProxy bean to it.
        HttpSession sess = request.getSession(true);
        if(sess.getAttribute(IMAGE_PROXY_KEY) == null)
            sess.setAttribute(IMAGE_PROXY_KEY, new ImageProxy());
        ImageProxy prx = (ImageProxy)sess.getAttribute(IMAGE_PROXY_KEY);
```

```
        // Splice the multipart data from the request,
        // and bind it in the session.
        List splicedData = this.spliceMultipartData(request);

        /*  // Take away this comment to see the 100 first bytes of each
            // found data segment; useful for debugging.
        for(int i = 0; i < splicedData.size(); i++)
        {
            String current = new String((byte[]) splicedData.get(i));
            System.out.println("[" + i + "]: "
                    + current.substring(0,Math.min(100, current.length())));
        }
        */

        // Get the uploaded document.
        DocumentHolder doc = this.getPart(DOCUMENT_NAME, splicedData);

        // Upload the document to the database
        prx.setFileName(doc.getOrigDocumentPath());
        prx.setImageData(doc.getData());
        prx.setMimeType(doc.getContentType());

        // Get the operation requested
        String op = "" + ImageProxy.CREATE;
        try
        {
            byte[] opParam = this.getValue("op",splicedData);
            if(opParam != null) op = new String(opParam);
        }
        catch(Exception ex)
        {
            // Running with default CREATE operation
        }
        prx.setOperation(op);

        // Fire!
        prx.populate();

        // All went well.
        // Redirect to the OK page.
        response.sendRedirect(this.allOKPage + "?imId="
                              + prx.getImageNumber());
    }
```

```
        catch (Exception ex)
        {
            // Error in the upload process...
            // redirect to the ERROR_PAGE.
            System.out.println("Encountered exception: " + ex);
            response.sendRedirect(this.errorPage);
        }
    }

    /**
     * Splices a multipart encoded form data input stream, returning
     * a List of all form parts, minus the multipart separator token.
     * The last element in the list *is* the separator token.
     *
     * @param request The HttpServletRequest of the Servlet.
     * @exception if the Content-Type is not "multipart/form-data"
     */
    protected List spliceMultipartData(HttpServletRequest request)
    throws IllegalArgumentException
    {
        // Get HttpServletRequest metadata. The validity of the
        // contentLength data is crucial, as we will use it to
        // create the byte[] data holder.
        String type = request.getContentType();
        int contentLength = request.getContentLength();

        // Declare data holder variables.
        // allData will contain the data and metadata of the
        // uploaded document.
        DataInputStream in = null;
        byte[] allData = null;

        // Check sanity.
        if (!type.startsWith("multipart/form-data"))
            throw new IllegalArgumentException
            ("Cannot parse anything but 'multipart/form-data'");

        if (contentLength == 0) throw new IllegalArgumentException
            ("Null content data length. Aborting.");
        try
        {
            // Get the input stream from the HTTP request.
            in = new DataInputStream(request.getInputStream());
            allData = new byte[contentLength];
```

```
        // Read all raw data,
        // in 1k large chunks.
        for (int bytesRead = 0;
        bytesRead != contentLength;
        bytesRead += in.read(allData, bytesRead, 1024))
        {
            // Comment out this line if you want to monitor
            // the progress of the loading.
            System.out.println("Got " + bytesRead + " bytes.");
        }
    }
    catch (Exception ex)
    {
        System.out.println("Aborting splice operation: " + ex);
        return null;
    }

    // Find the separator key, which is included in the
    // content type string. An example of such a MIME string is
    //
    // multipart/form-data; boundary=This_is_a_separator
    //
    // Isolate the text after the "=" character, to find the
    // multipart MIME separator.
    String separator = "--" +
    type.substring(type.indexOf("=") + 1, type.length());
    byte[] key = separator.getBytes();

    // Declare the return value, and the helper index
    // List, which stores all indices in allData where
    // the separator is found.
    ArrayList allPieces = new ArrayList();
    ArrayList indices = new ArrayList();

    // Find all occurrences of the separator key within
    // the source array.
    for (int currentIndex = 0; currentIndex < allData.length; )
    {
        int tmp = this.indexOf(allData, key, currentIndex);
        if (tmp == -1) break;

        // Append the found index to the indices List
        indices.add(new Integer(tmp));
```

```
        // Move pointer
        currentIndex += tmp + 1;
    }

    int startIndex = 0;
    for (int i = 0; i < indices.size(); i++)
    {
        //
        // Extract the part of allData between indices
        // startIndex and indices.get(i) [which holds the
        // next index of the separator].
        //
        // In short, extract the next document part of the
        // uploaded multipart document.
        //
        int separatorIndex = ((Integer)indices.get(i)).intValue();
        int partLength = separatorIndex - startIndex;
        if (partLength < 1) continue;

        // Copy the bytes from allData to part
        byte[] part = new byte[partLength];
        System.arraycopy(allData, startIndex, part, 0, part.length);

        // Add the newly extracted part to the allPieces List
        allPieces.add(part);

        // Move startIndex pointer
        startIndex = separatorIndex + key.length;
    }

    // Handle the last array index, i.e. the bytes
    // between the last found instance of the separator
    // and the end of the allData array.
    if (indices.size() != 0)
    {
        int lastSeparatorIndex = ((Integer)
        indices.get(indices.size() - 1)).intValue();
        byte[] lastPart = new byte[
        allData.length - lastSeparatorIndex - key.length];
        System.arraycopy(allData, lastSeparatorIndex + key.length,
        lastPart, 0, lastPart.length);
        allPieces.add(lastPart);
    }
```

```
        // Finally, add the separator as the last element of the
        // allPieces List.
        allPieces.add(key);

        // Done.
        return allPieces;
    }

    /**
     * Retrieves the part of a multipart uploaded data stream
     * that has the provided nameKey.
     *
     * @return The data of the multipart data container having
     *           the provided name, or <pre>null</pre> if no such
     *           mulipart data exists.
     */
    protected DocumentHolder getPart(String nameKey, List splicedData)
    {
        // Define internal state tokens
        String tmpKey = "name=";
        byte[] key = tmpKey.getBytes();

        String endToken = "\"";
        byte[] end = endToken.getBytes();

        String newLineToken = "\n";
        byte[] newLine = newLineToken.getBytes();

        String contentTypeToken = "Content-Type";
        byte[] contentType = contentTypeToken.getBytes();

        //
        // Iterate over all multiparts to find the one whose name
        // matches the provided nameKey
        //
        for (Iterator it = splicedData.iterator(); it.hasNext(); )
        {
            // Check sanity with the extracted part.
            byte[] data = (byte[]) it.next();
            int startIndex = this.indexOf(data, key, 0);
            if (startIndex == -1) continue;

            // Extract the name of the current multipart
            startIndex += 1 + key.length;
            int endIndex = this.indexOf(data, end, startIndex);
```

```
            byte[] name = new byte[endIndex - startIndex];
            System.arraycopy(data, startIndex, name, 0, name.length);
            String tmpName = new String(name);

            // Is this the part we are looking for?
            if (tmpName.equals(nameKey))
            {
                // System.out.println("Data: " + new String(data));

                // Find the start index of the return data
                int cntType = this.indexOf(data, contentType, endIndex);
                int nextRow = this.indexOf(data, newLine, cntType);
                nextRow = this.indexOf(data, newLine, nextRow + 1);

                // Declare and populate return data
                byte[] documentData = new byte[data.length - nextRow - 1];
                System.arraycopy(data, nextRow + 1, documentData,
                0, documentData.length);

                // This should be an uploaded document,
                // so we can safely create a DocumentHolder to
                // return.

                return new DocumentHolder(documentData,
                this.getContentType(data),
                this.getOrigPath(data, true));
            }
        }

        // No documents found.
        return null;
    }

   /**
    * Replacement for the request.getParameter() method,
    * which cannot be used as we get/read the ServletInputStream
    */
    private byte[] getValue(String nameKey, List splicedData)
    {
         // Define internal state tokens
        String tmpKey = "name=";
        byte[] key = tmpKey.getBytes();

        String endToken = "\"";
        byte[] end = endToken.getBytes();
```

```
String newLineToken = "\n";
byte[] newLine = newLineToken.getBytes();

String contentTypeToken = "Content-Type";
byte[] contentType = contentTypeToken.getBytes();

//
// Iterate over all multiparts to find the one whose name
// matches the provided nameKey
//
for (Iterator it = splicedData.iterator(); it.hasNext(); )
{
    // Check sanity with the extracted part.
    byte[] data = (byte[]) it.next();
    int startIndex = this.indexOf(data, key, 0);
    if (startIndex == -1) continue;

    // Extract the name of the current multipart
    startIndex += 1 + key.length;
    int endIndex = this.indexOf(data, end, startIndex);

    byte[] name = new byte[endIndex - startIndex];
    System.arraycopy(data, startIndex, name, 0, name.length);
    String tmpName = new String(name);

    // Is this the part we are looking for?
    if (tmpName.equals(nameKey))
    {
        // System.out.println("nameKey: " + nameKey
        // + ", RawData: " + new String(data));

        // After the two "\n"'s the data starts.
        int nl1 = this.indexOf(data, newLine, endIndex);
        int nl2 = this.indexOf(data, newLine, nl1 + 1);

        // Find the index of the separator
        byte[] separator = (byte[])
               splicedData.get(splicedData.size() - 1);
        int separatorIndex = this.indexOf(data, separator, nl2 + 1);
```

```
                // Declare and populate return data, while
                // cutting out the commencing and trailing "\n"
                byte[] spliceValue = new byte[separatorIndex - nl2 - 3];
                System.arraycopy(data, nl2 + 1, spliceValue,
                0, spliceValue.length);

                return spliceValue;

            }
        }

        return null;
    }

    /**
     * Retrieves the content type information from the byte[] data
     * that is assumed to contain the multipart content.
     *
     * @return the Content-Type of the provided multipart document
     *             typecast to a String.
     */
    protected String getContentType(byte[] data)
    {
        // Define the constants for parsing the
        // incoming data byte array.
        String contentTypeToken = "Content-Type:";
        byte[] contentType = contentTypeToken.getBytes();

        String newLineToken = "\n";
        byte[] newLine = newLineToken.getBytes();

        // Find the string of bytes between the contentTypeToken and
        // the newLineToken. Typecast to a String, and trim away
        // starting and trailing whitespace.
        int offset = this.indexOf(data, contentType, 0) + contentType.length;
        int end = this.indexOf(data, newLine, offset);

        // Construct the return String from the bytes between the
        // starting and ending indices.
        String toReturn = new String(data, offset, (end - offset));

        System.out.println("[getContentType]: Returning content type: '"
                + toReturn.trim() + "'");
```

```
        return "" + toReturn.trim();
    }

    /**
     * Finds the original path of the document, as provided
     * by the client browser in the multipart metadata
     */
    protected String getOrigPath(byte[] data, boolean returnFileNameOnly)
    {
        // Find the original path of the document, as provided
        // by the client browser in the multipart metadata
        String fileNameToken = "filename=";
        byte[] fileName = fileNameToken.getBytes();

        String quotationToken = "\"";
        byte[] quotation = quotationToken.getBytes();

        int tmp = this.indexOf(data, fileName, 0);
        int start = this.indexOf(data, quotation, tmp);
        int end = this.indexOf(data, quotation, (start + 1));

        String origPath = new String(data, start + 1, (end - start - 1));
        System.out.println("[getOrigPath]: origPath='" + origPath + "'");
        if(!returnFileNameOnly)
        {
            return origPath;
        }

        // Strip off all but the fileName
        File tmpFile = new File(origPath);
       System.out.println("[getOrigPath]: returning='" + tmpFile.getName() + "'");
        return tmpFile.getName();
    }

    /**
     * Find the index of the first occurrence of key within
     * source, starting from startIndex.
     *
     * @return -1 if none found.
     */
```

```
    private int indexOf(byte[] source, byte[] key, int startIndex)
    {
        // Check sanity.
        if (source == null) throw new NullPointerException
            ("Cannot handle null source.");
        if (key == null) throw new NullPointerException
            ("Cannot handle null key.");
        if (startIndex >= source.length) return -1;
        if (key.length > source.length) return -1;

        // Handle insane argument
        if (startIndex < 0) startIndex = 0;

        // Start finding the desired (key) bytes within the
        // source byte array. Return the first index of a complete
        // match.
        outer :
        for (int i = startIndex; i < (source.length - key.length); i++)
        {
            // Skip as many irrelevant bytes as possible
            if (source[i] != key[0]) continue;

            // Found a match?
            for (int j = 1; j < key.length; j++)
            {
                // Still a match?
                if (source[i + j] != key[j])
                {
                    i += j;
                    continue outer;
                }
            }

            // Found the separator.
            // Return the index of its start
            // within source.
            return i;
        }

        // No match found.
        return -1;
    }

}
```

Phew! The doPost method controls the main execution flow, and the helper methods in the DocumentUploader simply performs the binary housekeeping. The problem with having to handle binary data using the ServletInputStream is that you cannot afterwards use any methods that manipulate the request. One such method is the RequestDispatcher.forward(request, response) method; so the sendRedirect method is used instead to make the browser redirect properly to the allOkPage.

Having developed all the relevant classes of the image subsystem, you must configure the system for deployment in the application server. The only two classes remaining are the trivial DocumentHolder class that stores data about an uploaded document, and the CommonUtils class, which has the main log method. The UML diagram of the DocumentHolder class shown in Figure 11-16.

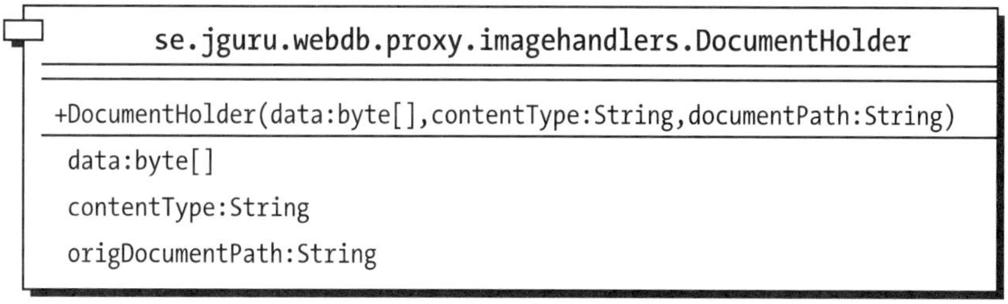

se.jguru.webdb.proxy.imagehandlers.DocumentHolder
+DocumentHolder(data:byte[],contentType:String,documentPath:String)
data:byte[] contentType:String origDocumentPath:String

Figure 11-16. The DocumentHolder *storage class contains three readable JavaBean properties and the constructor that sets the internal members.*

The CommonUtils class contains utility methods and constants usable by all classes in the system, whether deployed in the Web container or the EJB container. The only method used by the classes in the image subsystem is the main log method. Its code appears in Listing 11-8.

Listing 11-8. The log method of the CommonUtils *class*

```
/**
 * Logs a message to the standard output stream.
 *
 * @param className The name of the class where this log was called
 * @param callingMethodName The name of the method
 *                          where this log msg was created.
 * @param msgString The log message
 */
public static void log(String className, String callingMethodName,
String msgString)
{
    // Get a Timestamp
    Date now = new Date();
```

```
        // Create a formatter for the Date
        SimpleDateFormat sdf = new SimpleDateFormat("hh.mm:ss,SSS");

        // Join the Resulting message string
        String msg = "<" + sdf.format(now) + "> [" + className + "::"
        + callingMethodName + "]: " + msgString;

        // Print to System.out
        System.out.println(msg);
    }
```

The log method adds information to trace the origin of the log message, as well as a timestamp when the call was made. Although slightly cleaned up, the code is true to the call order in the `DocumentDownloader` servlet.

```
ImageProxy prx = new ImageProxy();
prx.setImageNumber(imagePk);
prx.setOperation("" + ImageProxy.READ);
prx.populate();
```

The log stream shown in Listing 11-9 is generated by the first lookup of an image resource by the `DocumentDownloader` servlet, as a direct result of this code snippet. The log shows that the EJB container seems rather inefficient when finding and activating the Image EJB component, as it calls `ejbLoad` and `ejbStore` multiple times instead of just once. Depending on the implementation of the EJB container (which may well collect all database calls to a batch to be executed as a unit behind the scenes), the resulting performance may be good or bad.

Listing 11-9. Snippet of the log stream from the deployed `ImageProxy` *and Image EJB components*

```
<03.18:00,339> [ImageProxy::getImageHome]: Looking up: java:comp/env/Image
<03.18:00,429> [ImageProxy::getImageHome]: Found obj:➥
               ClusterableRemoteRef(10.0.0.14 [10.0.0.14])
<03.18:00,449> [ImageProxy::getImageHome]: Found home:➥
               ClusterableRemoteRef(10.0.0.14 [10.0.0.14])
<03.18:00,459> [ImageProxy::setImageNumber]: imagePk=21
<03.18:00,459> [ImageProxy::populate]: Operation=2
<03.18:00,459> [ImageProxy::readImage]: this.home exists:➥
               ClusterableRemoteRef(10.0.0.14 [10.0.0.14])
<03.18:00,459> [ImageProxy::readImage]: Getting image EJB for pk=21
<03.18:00,680> [ImageBean::ejbActivate]: --
<03.18:00,680> [ImageBean::ejbLoad]: --
<03.18:00,690> [ImageBean::ejbStore]: --
```

```
<03.18:00,780> [ImageBean::ejbLoad]: --
<03.18:00,810> [ImageBean::ejbStore]: --
<03.18:00,850> [ImageProxy::readImage]: All Done. PK=21, data.length=58369
<03.18:00,850> [ImageBean::ejbLoad]: --
<03.18:00,860> [ImageBean::ejbStore]: --
<03.18:00,860> [ImageBean::ejbLoad]: --
<03.18:00,870> [ImageBean::ejbStore]: --
```

In traditional J2EE server-side deployment, the configuration phase of the system deployment may well take as long as the development of the application subsystem. However, for the image subsystem, deployment configuration comes in a slightly simpler form, mainly due to its small number of classes.

Step 4—Configuring the Image Subsystem

XML deployment descriptor documents are the standard way to configure a J2EE server, including its deployed components. The image subsystem is split into a Web application part in which the Web context of the servlets is configured, and an EJB part in which the context of the `ImageBean` EJB component is configured. The full system therefore requires quite a few deployment descriptors:

- The Web application needs the standard J2EE `web.xml` and the application server-specific deployment descriptor. The WebLogic Application Server uses a custom Web deployment descriptor called `weblogic.xml`.

- The EJB server needs the standard J2EE `ejb-jar.xml` and the application server-specific deployment descriptor. The WebLogic Application Server uses the custom descriptor `weblogic-ejb-jar.xml` and an arbitrarily named special deployment descriptor to define the CMP settings. In this example, the CMP descriptor is called `weblogic-imageBean-cmp.xml`.

- Should we wish to create an enterprise archive file, we will also need to define the `application.xml` deployment descriptor to define the WAR and JAR files to the application.

Properly creating the three important standard deployment descriptors may be a trifle complex; configuring the (minimum of) two custom deployment descriptors are equally important and adds additional complexity to the system. We will focus our detailed study on the deployment descriptors for the EJB container, and we'll be slightly more brief in the study of the deployment descriptors for the Web container.

Relatively few classes are deployed into the EJB container as part of the image subsystem. Figure 11-17 shows the content of the generic EJB JAR, with the custom deployment descriptors (but no stub or skeleton files) for the WebLogic Application Server added.

ejb-jar.xml	meta-inf\
Manifest.mf	meta-inf\
weblogic-ejb-jar.xml	meta-inf\
weblogic-imageBean-cmp.xml	meta-inf\
Image.class	se\jguru\webdb\legacyintegration\
ImageBean.class	se\jguru\webdb\legacyintegration\
ImageHome.class	se\jguru\webdb\legacyintegration\
Populateable.class	se\jguru\webdb\proxy\
PopulationException.class	se\jguru\webdb\proxy\
CommonUtils.class	se\jguru\webdb\utils\
EJBBeanRoot.class	se\jguru\webdb\utils\

Figure 11-17. The structure of the EJB JAR file, including the two custom WebLogic deployment descriptors `weblogic-ejb-jar.xml` *and* `weblogic-imageBean-cmp.xml`

The responsibilities of each deployment descriptor found in Figure 11-17 is shown in Figure 11-18.

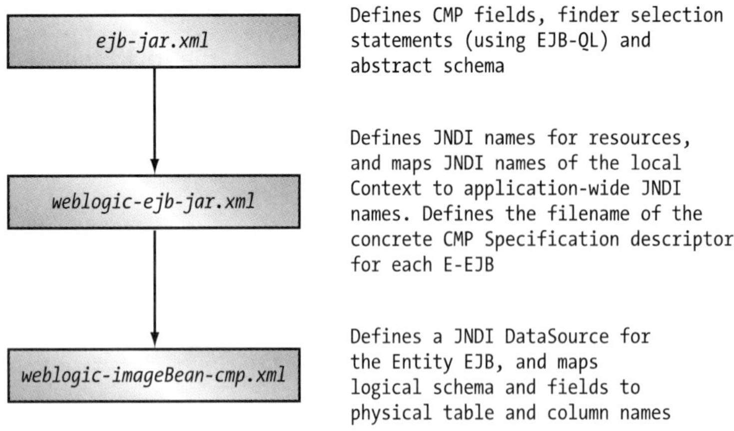

Figure 11-18. The responsibilities of each of the EJB related deployment descriptors

Start the deployment descriptor parade by examining the only standard descriptor in Figure 11-17, `ejb-jar.xml`, as shown in Listing 11-10.

Listing 11-10. The `ejb-jar.xml` *deployment descriptor*

```
<?xml version="1.0"?>

<!DOCTYPE ejb-jar PUBLIC
    '-//Sun Microsystems, Inc.//DTD Enterprise JavaBeans 2.0//EN'
    'http://java.sun.com/dtd/ejb-jar_2_0.dtd'>

<ejb-jar>
     <enterprise-beans>
          <entity>
               <ejb-name>ImageBean</ejb-name>
               <home>se.jguru.webdb.legacyintegration.ImageHome</home>
               <remote>se.jguru.webdb.legacyintegration.Image</remote>

               <ejb-class>se.jguru.webdb.legacyintegration.ImageBean</ejb-class>   1
               <persistence-type>Container</persistence-type>
               <prim-key-class>java.lang.Integer</prim-key-class>
               <reentrant>False</reentrant>
               <cmp-version>2.x</cmp-version>
               <abstract-schema-name>ImageBean</abstract-schema-name>

               <cmp-field>
                    <field-name>data</field-name>
               </cmp-field>

               <cmp-field>
                    <field-name>mimeType</field-name>   2
               </cmp-field>
               <cmp-field>
                    <field-name>id</field-name>
               </cmp-field>
               <cmp-field>
                    <field-name>fileName</field-name>
               </cmp-field>


               <primkey-field>id</primkey-field>   3
```

```
            <env-entry>
                <description>Log verbosity level toggle flag</description>
                <env-entry-name>verboseMode</env-entry-name>
                <env-entry-type>java.lang.Boolean</env-entry-type>          4
                <env-entry-value>true</env-entry-value>
            </env-entry>

            <query>
                <query-method>
                    <method-name>findByMimeType</method-name>
                    <method-params>
                        <method-param>java.lang.String</method-param>
                    </method-params>                                        5
                </query-method>
                <ejb-ql>WHERE mimeType LIKE '?1%'</ejb-ql>
            </query>
        </entity>
    </enterprise-beans>

    <assembly-descriptor>
        <container-transaction>
            <method>

                <ejb-name>ImageBean</ejb-name>                              6
                <method-name>*</method-name>
            </method>
            <trans-attribute>Required</trans-attribute>
        </container-transaction>
    </assembly-descriptor>

</ejb-jar>
```

The `ejb-jar.xml` descriptor has six sections configuring different aspects of the entity EJB component. The number of the section correlates to the following list, which describes the settings.

1. **Type and persistence definitions**: These are the standard type definitions of the EJB component, providing class information for the Remote, Home, EJB implementation, and Primary Key types. However, for CMP Entity EJB components, you have to provide the EJB CMP specification used by the bean because the CMP contract was altered quite a bit with the advent of the EJB 2.0 specification. Note, also, that the deployment descriptor provides a name for the abstract schema used by the bean. You may think of the abstract schema name as the name of a view in a relational database: the abstract schema permits all EJB components to use a logical name for a `DataSource` table, rather than requiring knowledge of the physical table name in a database.

2. **Persistence field definitions**: Each field name defines a logical column in the abstract schema, and each such column requires the definition of a public abstract JavaBean setter and getter method in the EJB Bean implementation class. In other words, given a CMP field definition in the deployment descriptor with the field name `xyz`, the two required abstract method definitions in the EJB bean implementation class are `public abstract void setXyz(Type anXyz);` and `public abstract Type getXyz();`.

3. **Primary key definition**: One of the persistence fields must be the primary key of the Entity EJB component. The `<primkey-field>` container element must refer to a persistence field defined in step 2.

4. **Context variable definitions**: The `ImageBean` uses its `Context` explicitly only to read a parameter indicating its level of logging verbosity. The parameter read is defined here; in the EJB code, the actual lookup is performed in the `findVerbosity` method of the `EJBBeanRoot` class, and the lookup string is found as the value of the `EJBBeanRoot.VERBOSE_KEY` constant. This definition binds a boolean object with the value `true` into the `Context` under the JNDI name `verboseMode`.

> **TIP** *Remember that values bound in the environment of an EJB (that is, defined inside its* `<entity>...</entity>` *or* `<session>...</session>` *container element) are located by using the prefix for the local bean component environment,* `java:comp/env`*. A local environment entry with the name* `xyz` *in the descriptor file may be accessed from within its bean component using the JNDI lookup string* `java:comp/env/xyz`.

5. **CMP finder definitions**: The Bean implementation classes of CMP entity beans should not implement the finder methods defined in the Home interface. With the exception of the mandatory `findByPrimaryKey` method, which is automatically implemented by the application server EJB compiler tools, all finder methods must therefore be defined in the deployment descriptor using the EJB-QL language. EJB-QL is similar in syntax and semantics to the Structured Query Language used by most databases, with a few adoptions to handle the nature of EJB components.

   This finder method definition selects all `ImageBean`s whose value in the `mimeType` persistent field type is similar to the first argument (`?1`) of the finder method. The actual SQL SELECT method created from the finder method definition above is similar to:

   ```
   SELECT data, mimeType, id, fileName
   FROM ImageBean
   WHERE mimeType LIKE '?1%'
   ```

6. **Assembly descriptor definitions**: The assembly descriptor of this Entity EJB component tells the EJB container to execute all methods within a transaction.

The `ejb-jar.xml` file of the CMP 2.0 specification defines all the settings pertaining to the logical schema, field definitions, and finder query methods. However, the EJB 2.0 specification does not provide any information about how to connect a logical schema and fields to actual relational database tables and columns or their equivalents in the object database world. That part of the implementation is left up to application server vendors. As illustrated in Figure 11-8, the WebLogic Application Server uses a special deployment descriptor (called `weblogic-imageBean-cmp.xml` in this example) to provide such concrete specifications.

Let's continue by investigating the `weblogic-imageBean-cmp.xml` deployment descriptor to find the way that the WebLogic Application Server maps abstract schemas and field names to concrete tables in a data source. The DTD is illustrated in

Figure 11-19. For a detailed description of all elements and their functions, refer to documentation for the BEA WebLogic server.

The content of the deployment descriptor in our example is shown in Listing 11-11.

Listing 11-11. The `weblogic-rdbms-jar.xml` *deployment descriptor*

```
<!DOCTYPE weblogic-rdbms-jar PUBLIC
   '-//BEA Systems, Inc.//DTD WebLogic 6.0.0 EJB RDBMS Persistence//EN'
   'http://www.bea.com/servers/wls600/dtd/weblogic-rdbms20-persistence-600.dtd'>
<weblogic-rdbms-jar>
  <weblogic-rdbms-bean>
    <ejb-name>ImageBean</ejb-name>
    <data-source-name>
        se/jguru/webdb/legacyintegration/LegacyDataSource
    </data-source-name>
    <table-name>Images</table-name>

    <field-map>
      <cmp-field>id</cmp-field>
      <dbms-column>id</dbms-column>
    </field-map>
    <field-map>
      <cmp-field>mimeType</cmp-field>
      <dbms-column>mimetype</dbms-column>
    </field-map>
    <field-map>
      <cmp-field>data</cmp-field>
      <dbms-column>data</dbms-column>
    </field-map>
    <field-map>
      <cmp-field>fileName</cmp-field>
      <dbms-column>filename</dbms-column>
    </field-map>
  </weblogic-rdbms-bean>
</weblogic-rdbms-jar>
```

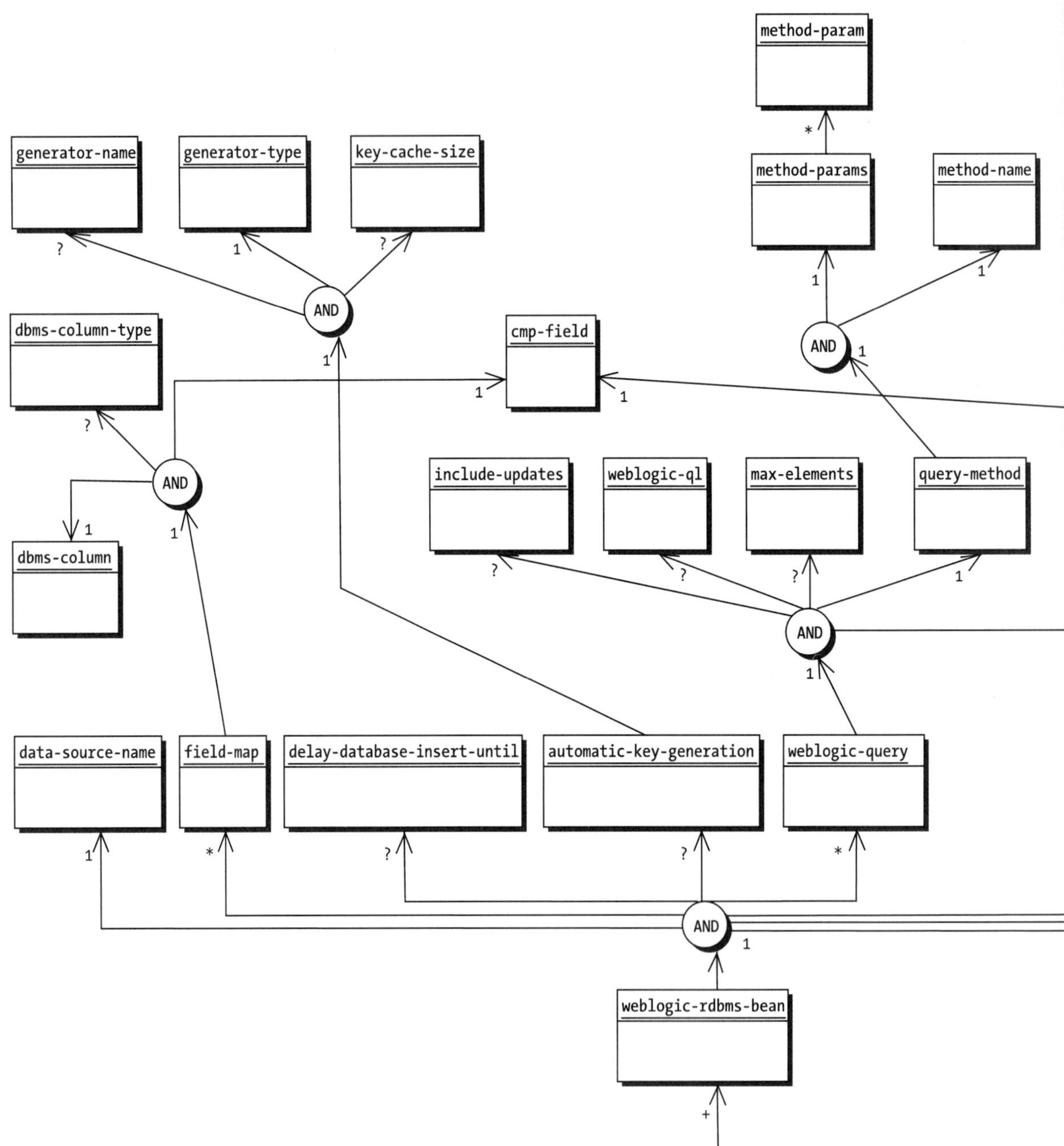

Figure 11-19. The DTD schema of the WebLogic RDBMS-20 persistence deployment descriptor

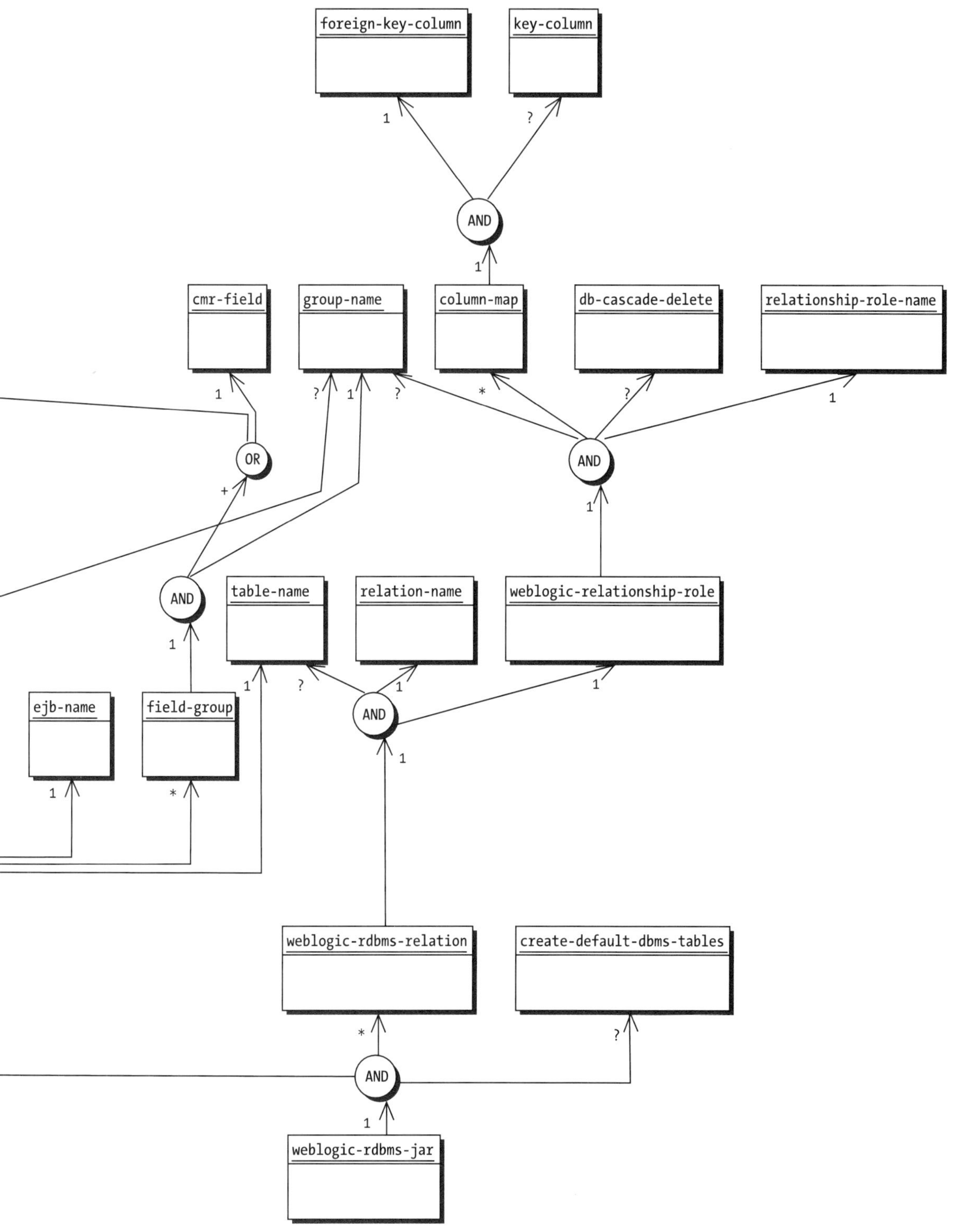
foreign-key-column
key-column
1
?
AND
1
cmr-field
group-name
column-map
db-cascade-delete
relationship-role-name
1
?
1
?
*
?
1
OR
AND
+
1
AND
table-name
relation-name
weblogic-relationship-role
1
1
?
1
1
ejb-name
field-group
AND
1
1
*
weblogic-rdbms-relation
create-default-dbms-tables
*
?
AND
1
weblogic-rdbms-jar

This definition file is a really straightforward mapping between abstract schema name, data source JDNI name and SQL table name. The first section connects a logical `<ejb-name>` to this definition, and provides the data source JNDI name required to find the table with the provided `<table-name>`. The rest of the file contains field maps that relate a given `cmp` field name defined in the `ejb-jar.xml` file to a unique column in the table.

One question remains: How does the application server know which file to search to find the mapping between abstract schema and data source/table name? This information is provided in the second custom EJB deployment descriptor, `weblogic-ejb-jar.xml`. Let's take a look at its contents in Listing 11-12.

Listing 11-12. The `weblogic-ejb-jar.xml` *deployment descriptor*

```
<?xml version="1.0"?>
<!DOCTYPE weblogic-ejb-jar PUBLIC
   '-//BEA Systems, Inc.//DTD WebLogic 6.0.0 EJB//EN'
   'http://www.bea.com/servers/wls600/dtd/weblogic-ejb-jar.dtd'>

<weblogic-ejb-jar>
     <weblogic-enterprise-bean>
          <ejb-name>ImageBean</ejb-name>
          <entity-descriptor>
               <entity-cache>
                    <max-beans-in-cache>1000</max-beans-in-cache>
               </entity-cache>

               <persistence>
                    <persistence-type>
                         <type-identifier>WebLogic_CMP_RDBMS</type-identifier>
                         <type-version>6.0</type-version>
                         <type-storage>
                         META-INF/weblogic-imageBean-cmp.xml
                         </type-storage>
                    </persistence-type>
                    <persistence-use>
                         <type-identifier>WebLogic_CMP_RDBMS</type-identifier>
                         <type-version>6.0</type-version>
                    </persistence-use>
               </persistence>
          </entity-descriptor>

          <jndi-name>se/jguru/webdb/legacyintegration/Image</jndi-name>
     </weblogic-enterprise-bean>
</weblogic-ejb-jar>
```

A quick look through the `weblogic-ejb-jar.xml` file reveals that it defines three things for the `ImageBean` EJB component:

- It limits the amount of bean instances available in cache to 1,000.
- It informs the container that the file `META-INF/weblogic-imageBean-cmp.xml` has a CMP specification and tells the container to use this file for the mapping of abstract schema in the Entity EJB component to concrete database tables.
- It defines the JNDI name for the `ImageBean` component.

In all, these three deployment descriptors may seem like a mouthful, but consider that the largest of them all is the portable standard definition. Although the first Entity EJB components you develop and deploy using the EJB 2.0 specification may cause the occasional occurrence of foul language and deployment error messages, the better part of the deployment descriptor is now portable between application servers.

As larger parts of the required deployment descriptors become portable between EJB servers, you actually get to achieving server-side componentware. Should you want to change application servers, a good part of the EJB porting work is simply rewriting or re-creating the required deployment descriptors.

You are now finished configuring the components that should be deployed in the EJB container. The only part left before being able to test the functionality of the image subsystem is writing the deployment descriptors for the components deployed in the Web application.

Configuring the Web Application

Generally speaking, J2EE Web applications have deployment descriptors that are slightly less complex than their EJB siblings. This is partly due to the fact that most settings for the Web application components are defined in the standard `web.xml` deployment descriptor. As we shall see, this is not the case for all settings in the Web application.

The structure of the Web application is shown in Figure 11-20. Note that the classes contained in the `/WEB-INF/classes` structure are loaded into the `CLASSPATH` of the application server and are thereby accessible from all files in the Web application. However, for production deployment, the files should likely be packaged in a JAR that is deployed in the `/WEB-INF/lib` directory of the Web application instead.

The responsibilities of the two descriptors found in the Web application are shown in Figure 11-21.

Name	Size	Path
errorUploadingImage.jsp	1 202	imageSubsystemWebApp\
selectFileForUpload.jsp	1 251	imageSubsystemWebApp\
silly.jpg	2 987	imageSubsystemWebApp\
testImage.jsp	179	imageSubsystemWebApp\
uploadOK.jsp	2 299	imageSubsystemWebApp\
welcome.jsp	156	imageSubsystemWebApp\
web.xml	2 220	imageSubsystemWebApp\WEB-INF\
weblogic.xml	757	imageSubsystemWebApp\WEB-INF\
Image.class	473	imageSubsystemWebApp\WEB-INF\classes\se\jguru\webdb\legacyintegration\
ImageHome.class	662	imageSubsystemWebApp\WEB-INF\classes\se\jguru\webdb\legacyintegration\
Populateable.class	220	imageSubsystemWebApp\WEB-INF\classes\se\jguru\webdb\proxy\
PopulationException.class	394	imageSubsystemWebApp\WEB-INF\classes\se\jguru\webdb\proxy\
DocumentDownloader.class	2 068	imageSubsystemWebApp\WEB-INF\classes\se\jguru\webdb\proxy\imagehandlers\
DocumentHolder.class	839	imageSubsystemWebApp\WEB-INF\classes\se\jguru\webdb\proxy\imagehandlers\
DocumentUploader.class	9 355	imageSubsystemWebApp\WEB-INF\classes\se\jguru\webdb\proxy\imagehandlers\
ImageProxy.class	9 872	imageSubsystemWebApp\WEB-INF\classes\se\jguru\webdb\proxy\imagehandlers\
CommonUtils.class	2 024	imageSubsystemWebApp\WEB-INF\classes\se\jguru\webdb\utils\

Figure 11-20. All files required by the Web application of the image subsystem. Note the two deployment descriptors `web.xml` *and* `weblogic.xml`, *which are required to fully configure the Web application.*

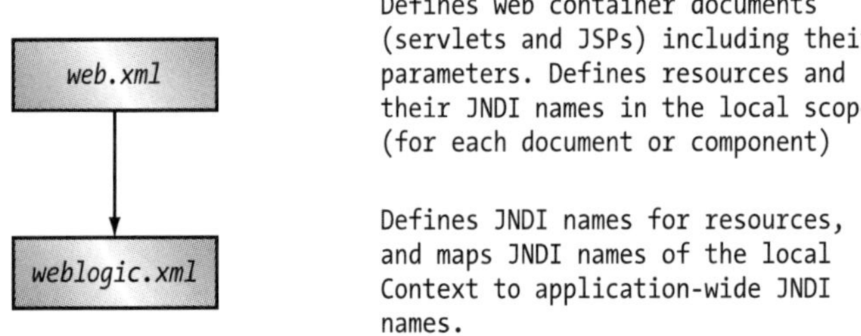

web.xml
Defines web container documents (servlets and JSPs) including their parameters. Defines resources and their JNDI names in the local scope (for each document or component)
weblogic.xml
Defines JNDI names for resources, and maps JNDI names of the local Context to application-wide JNDI names.

Figure 11-21. Responsibilities of the two deployment descriptors for the J2EE Web application deployed in a WebLogic Application Server

Take a look at the `web.xml` deployment descriptor in Listing 11-13 to get a feeling for the Web application used by the image subsystem.

Listing 11-13. The `web.xml` *deployment descriptor*

```
<?xml version="1.0" ?>
<!DOCTYPE web-app PUBLIC
   "-//Sun Microsystems, Inc.//DTD Web Application 1.2//EN"
   "http://java.sun.com/j2ee/dtds/web-app_2_2.dtd">
<web-app>
     <display-name>TheRefactor2WebApp</display-name>
     <description>Web database refactored in step 2</description>
```

```
<servlet>
    <servlet-name>uploaderServlet</servlet-name>
    <servlet-class>
      se.jguru.webdb.proxy.imagehandlers.DocumentUploader
    </servlet-class>

    <init-param>
        <param-name>ERROR_PAGE</param-name>
        <param-value>/errorUploadingImage.jsp</param-value>
    </init-param>

    <init-param>
        <param-name>ALL_OK_PAGE</param-name>
        <param-value>/uploadOK.jsp</param-value>
    </init-param>
</servlet>

<servlet>
    <servlet-name>imageDownloaderServlet</servlet-name>
    <servlet-class>
       se.jguru.webdb.proxy.imagehandlers.DocumentDownloader
    </servlet-class>
</servlet>

<servlet-mapping>
    <servlet-name>uploaderServlet</servlet-name>
    <url-pattern>uploadImage</url-pattern>
</servlet-mapping>

<servlet-mapping>
    <servlet-name>imageDownloaderServlet</servlet-name>
    <url-pattern>showImage</url-pattern>
</servlet-mapping>

<welcome-file-list>
    <welcome-file>index.jsp</welcome-file>
</welcome-file-list>

<resource-ref>
    <res-ref-name>LegacyDataSource</res-ref-name>
    <res-type>javax.sql.DataSource</res-type>
    <res-auth>Container</res-auth>
</resource-ref>
```

```
        <login-config>
            <auth-method>BASIC</auth-method>
        </login-config>

        <env-entry>
            <env-entry-name>verboseMode</env-entry-name>
            <env-entry-value>true</env-entry-value>
            <env-entry-type>java.lang.Boolean</env-entry-type>
        </env-entry>

        <ejb-ref>
            <description>EJB reference to the Image</description>
            <ejb-ref-name>Image</ejb-ref-name>
            <ejb-ref-type>Entity</ejb-ref-type>
            <home>se.jguru.webdb.legacyintegration.ImageHome</home>
            <remote>se.jguru.webdb.legacyintegration.Image</remote>
        </ejb-ref>
</web-app>
```

The top half of the `web.xml` document simply configures the two servlets `DocumentUploader` and `DocumentDownloader` and binds them to the URL patterns `uploadImage` and `showImage`, respectively. The lower half of the deployment descriptor document has three interesting configuration settings, and these configuration settings may be described in separate steps:

1. The `<resource-ref>...</resource-ref>` container element holds a reference to a data source factory resource, which produces JDBC connections talking to a database. The JNDI name to which the data source is bound in the local context is `LegacyDataSource`. Can you remember how to create the JNDI lookup string that is required to access the `LegacyDataSource`?

2. The `<env-entry>...</env-entry>` container element defines a boolean variable with the value `true`, and binds it in the local context under the name `verboseMode`.

3. The `<ejb-ref>...</ejb-ref>` element specifies an EJB client-side component and binds it to the JNDI name `Images` in the local context. Moreover, the Home and Remote interface types of the EJB component are specified, but not the EJB Bean implementation class, because the Web application is a client of the EJB component simply using its services.

The components defined in these three steps of the deployment descriptor lack a full JNDI name to the actual objects bound in the context of the application server. According to the settings in the `web.xml` deployment descriptor, two resources are available for access by all documents internal to the Web application, under the local JNDI names `Image` and `LegacyDataSource`. However, no information has been provided that maps the local JNDI names in the `web.xml` document to actual JNDI keys of the application server. This information must be supplied in the custom deployment descriptor of the application server (`weblogic.xml` in our case).

The `weblogic.xml` deployment descriptor is short and to the point for our application. It simply defines the two mappings of local JNDI aliases to real JDNI names; the `LegacyDataSource` local JNDI alias is mapped to the `se/jguru/webdb/legacyintegration/LegacyDataSource` JNDI name, and the local JNDI alias image to the actual name `se/jguru/webdb/legacyintegration/Image`.

Here's the content of the `weblogic.xml` deployment descriptor:

```
<!DOCTYPE weblogic-web-app PUBLIC
   "-//BEA Systems, Inc.//DTD Web Application 6.0//EN"
   "http://www.bea.com/servers/wls600/dtd/weblogic-web-jar.dtd">
<weblogic-web-app>
     <reference-descriptor>
          <resource-description>
               <res-ref-name>LegacyDataSource</res-ref-name>
               <jndi-name>
                  se/jguru/webdb/legacyintegration/LegacyDataSource
               </jndi-name>
          </resource-description>

          <ejb-reference-description>
               <ejb-ref-name>Image</ejb-ref-name>
               <jndi-name>se/jguru/webdb/legacyintegration/Image</jndi-name>
          </ejb-reference-description>
     </reference-descriptor>
</weblogic-web-app>
```

As shown in Figure 11-22, the JNDI names provided in the `weblogic.xml` document are matched to two bound objects in the JNDI registry.

Why, you may ask, do we need the custom configuration document at all? Why not simply provide actual JNDI registry keys in the `web.xml` deployment descriptor? The answer is that the `web.xml` deployment descriptor is a document that is created by the application developers who create the servlets, JSPs, or other resources of the Web application—but they don't need to know anything about the real settings of the JNDI registry in the server intended for production deployment. Just consider the case when you purchase a third-party server-side component with the intent of deploying it in your local application server.

The component developer does not know the structure of your JNDI registry, but it may require some services that you have created and bound there. A server administrator (application deployer) must therefore provide the mapping between resources required by the component and the actual JNDI registry lookup names in your central JNDI server. The place to provide this mapping is the custom deployment descriptor—in our case, `weblogic.xml`.

Having completely developed and deployed all components for the image subsystem residing in the Web and EJB containers, we may now run the application to upload and download images to and from the database. The image EJB component uses a very simple data access structure, simple enough that CMP services may be used to access the data in the database. Some—but far from all—business objects have an equally simple back-end structure, so we had better examine a BMP EJB component and how to make the two EJB components interact. Let's move on to the `WebPage` BMP EJB component.

Step 5—Implementing the WebPage Search System Classes

Although the database schema shown in Figure 11-2 is very small, the two business objects used in this application contain a lot of code. Granted, the image subsystem is a trifle complex due to the binary nature of the documents handled, but its legacy database operations are quite simple: only reading or writing data handled in the J2EE server into a persistent storage. The `WebPage` EJB component has the opposite problem; it has simple data but slightly more complex relations in the database. We therefore implement it using bean-managed persistence (BMP).

First, let's take a look at the user experience of the refactored Web application to see how the new database searching facilities should look.

The User Experience of the WebPage Search System

The system view of the Web application has been augmented with image information, provided by the image subsystem. The resulting new output is shown in Figure 11-22; when the user searches the Web, the application displays a list of matching Web pages including links to the images found within each document.

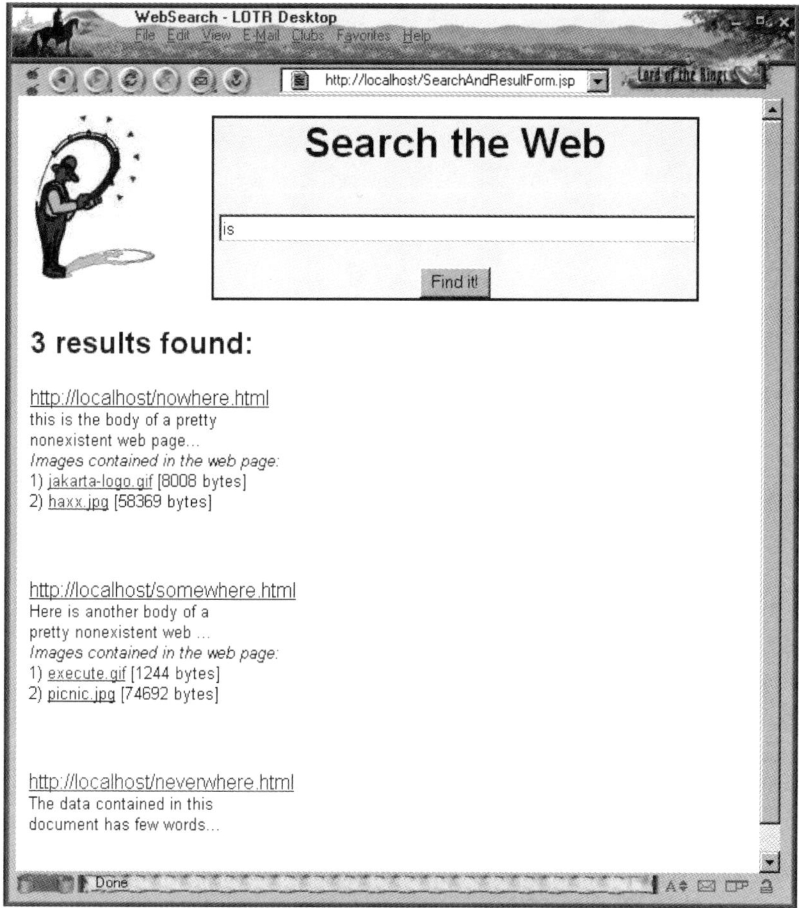

Figure 11-22. The resulting output of the application view. Note the image information regarding each Web page, and the corresponding links.

When the user clicks on one of the image links in the listing, the image is simply displayed as shown in Figure 11-23.

The `WebPage` search system uses the image subsystem from above to handle and show its images. However, the lookup and searching mechanism of the `WebPage` search system is re-made from the first refactoring step of the application.

The user experience is quite visual and trivial for the `WebPage` search subsystem, but the data structures and relationships used behind the screens are far from trivial. Investigate the class structure of the `WebPage` search subsystem.

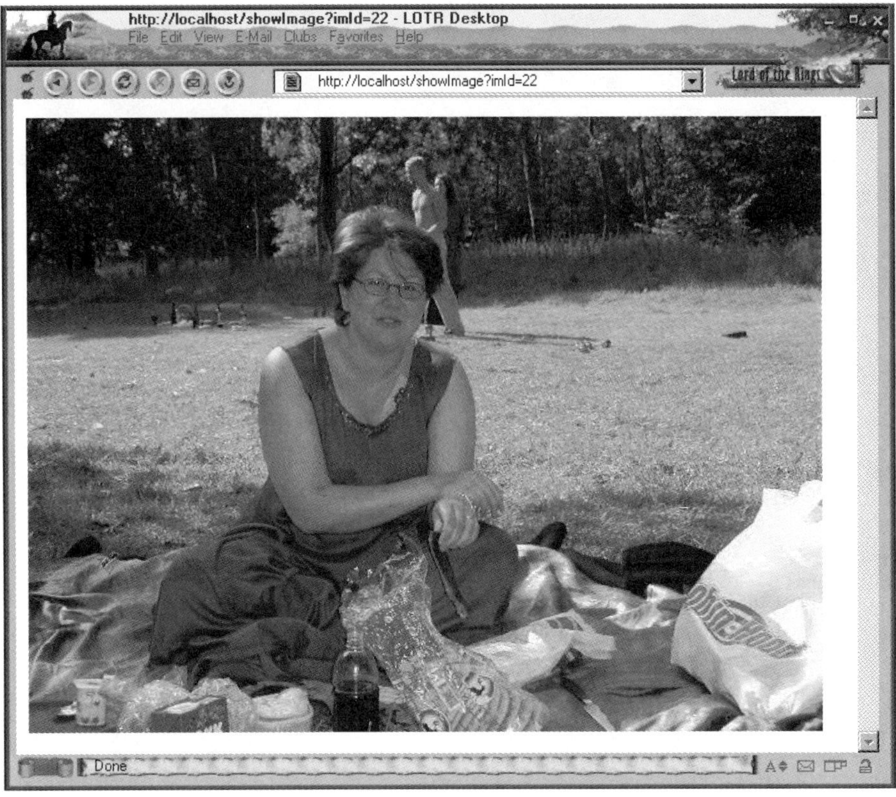

Figure 11-23. When clicking on one of the image links in the listing, the `DocumentDownloader` *servlet extracts the image data from the database and delivers it to the client browser.*

Classes of the WebPage Search Subsystem

The structure of the `WebPage` search subsystem has now been refactored to closely match most industrial-strength scalable J2EE applications. Of course, this example has none of the stability-enhancing mechanisms that an industrial-strength J2EE application requires, but the structure is in place even if the supporting mechanisms are not.

Moreover, because the application developed here would perform mainly database read operations if it were deployed in a production environment, its structure would likely be adopted for speed and not maintainability. However, the database search application serves its purpose well because it illustrates the structure and mechanics of EJB components and their interaction with other J2EE server-side elements. In other words, this example is realistic in its structure but not in its specifics.

Figure 11-24 shows the structure of the `WebPage` search subsystem, with the components shown in their respective deployment containers.

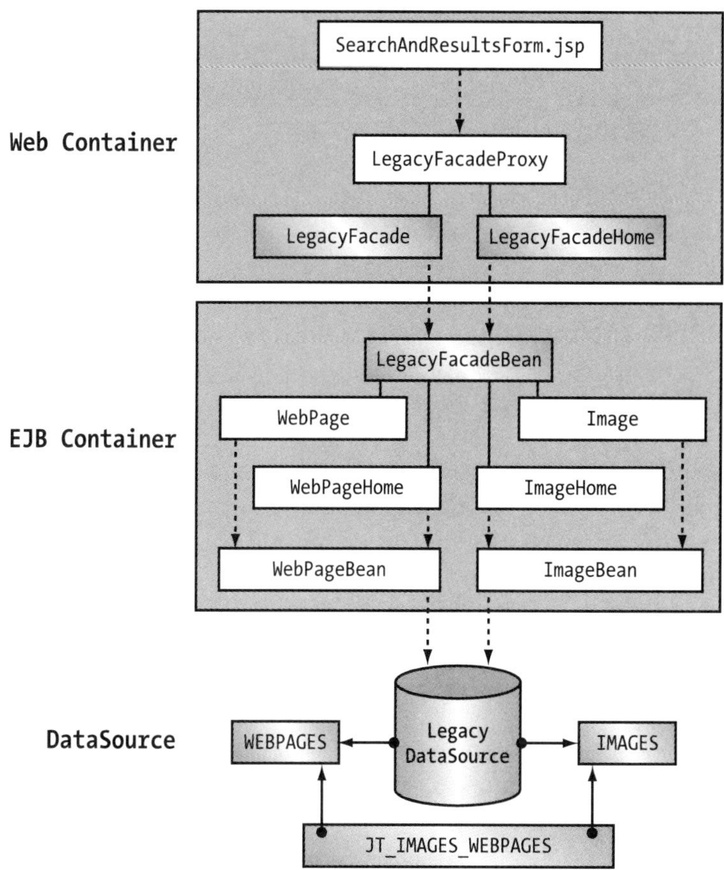

Figure 11-24. The structure of the `WebPage` *search subsystem. The shaded EJB facade component is a session bean, whereas the other EJB components deployed within the EJB container are Entity EJBs.*

Although the system may look complex, the structure is as simple as normally permitted in a real J2EE application system. In fact, as shown in Figure 11-24, the entire system consists of only five components, three of which are simply modified from the first step of the refactoring process. The components are:

- The JSP view, `SearchAndResultsForm.jsp`, interacts with the user and accepts the search string that is used to query the database. The view also joins the data to show the results list illustrated in Figure 11-23. The `SearchAndResultsForm.jsp` is slightly modified from the first step of the refactoring process to properly handle the extra image data provided by the current business objects.

- The JavaBean proxy, LegacyFacadeProxy, wraps an EJB facade component and presents its service methods to the View document in a simple and usable form. Another important task performed by the LegacyFacadeProxy is to shield the view from all forms of programmatic exception handling as a result of the distributed nature of its contained EJB facade. The LegacyFacadeProxy has been greatly modified (that is, simplified) from the first step of the refactoring process, because its LegacyFacade component uses business objects (Entity EJBs) in this second step of the refactoring process.

- The EJB facade bean, LegacyFacade, serves as a portal to the EJB container and the business objects within. If at all possible, it is wise to make each remote business method in the LegacyFacade interface accept all required parameters to complete an operation on the legacy data. This should generally not pose a problem; the LegacyFacadeProxy may be populated over a series of several method calls, only invoking a method in the LegacyFacade when all required parameters are received from the user. The session EJB facade may therefore generally be stateless, which saves much memory resources compared to the stateful variant. The LegacyFacade has been much simplified compared to its structure from the first step of the refactoring process due to the introduction of the WebPage BMP EJB component.

- The Image Entity EJB component is simply the image subsystem CMP EJB component developed in "The Image EJB Component" section. The Image CMP EJB component wraps legacy data from the IMAGES table in the database.

- The WebPage Entity EJB component is the only completely new component in this step of the refactoring process. Similar to the Image Entity EJB, the WebPage EJB component wraps data from a table in the legacy database, but the relations used in the database by the WebPage EJB component are more complex than the ones used by the Image Entity EJB component. Therefore, the WebPageBean class uses BMP to access the data in the database.

The structure of the components deployed in the EJB container is shown in the UML diagram in Figure 11-25. The only relationship between the two EJB components is a one-sided association: each Web page may contain several images so the WebPageBean class has a list that contains the primary keys of all the Image EJBs it is related to.

The EJB components in the se.jguru.webdb.legacyintegration package are business objects (that is, they encapsulate business data from a legacy DataSource). Of the three classes shown in Figure 11-25, we have already studied the EJBBeanRoot and the ImageBean components in detail. Let's proceed to take a look at the code of the WebPageBean EJB component.

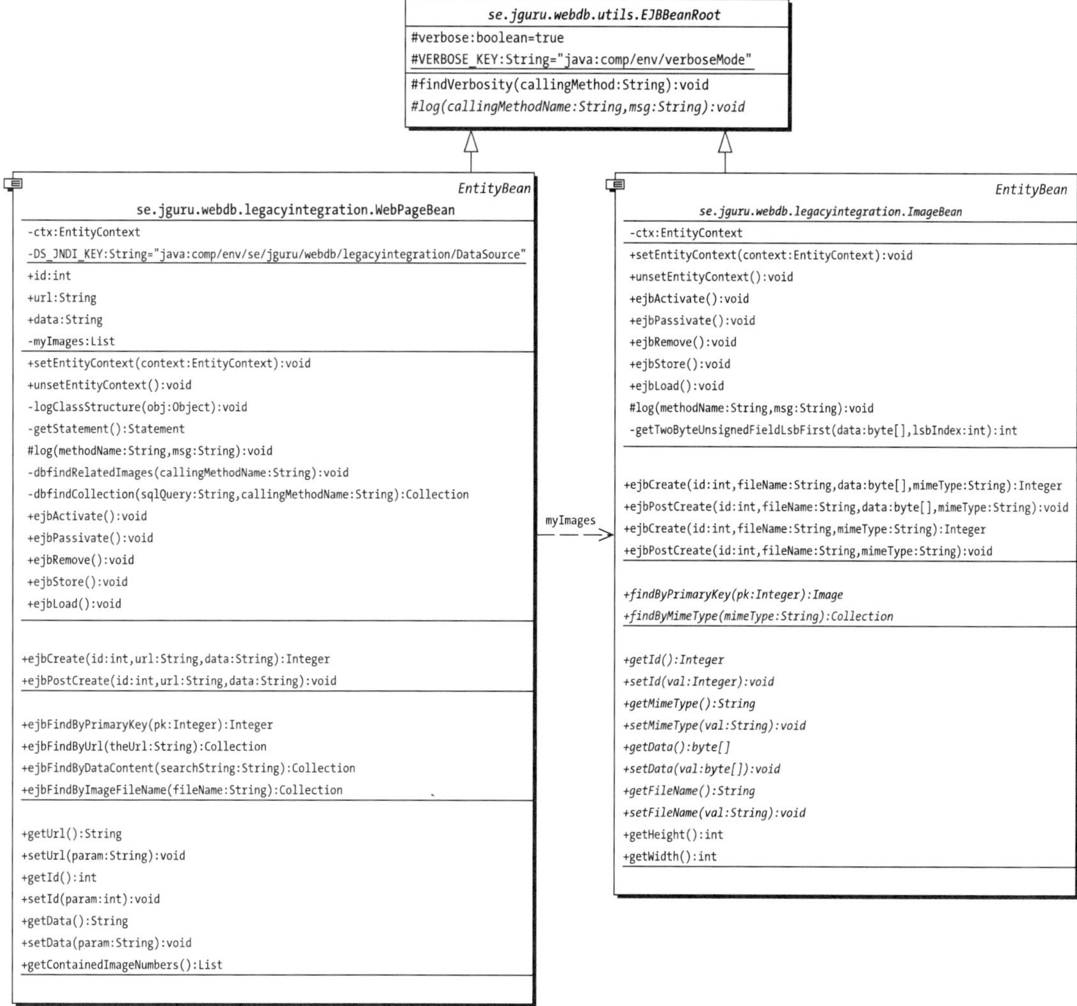

Figure 11-25. The entity beans encapsulating the data in the `Images` *and* `WebPages` *tables. The* `ImageBean` *EJB component uses CMP and the WebPageBean component uses BMP.*

The WebPage EJB Component

Similar in structure to the Image EJB component, the `WebPage` EJB component extends the common superclass `EJBBeanRoot` to provide a unified interface to component logging and verbosity. With the exception of the EJB component primary key class, `java.lang.Integer`, all required types of the `WebPage` EJB component are shown in Figure 11-26.

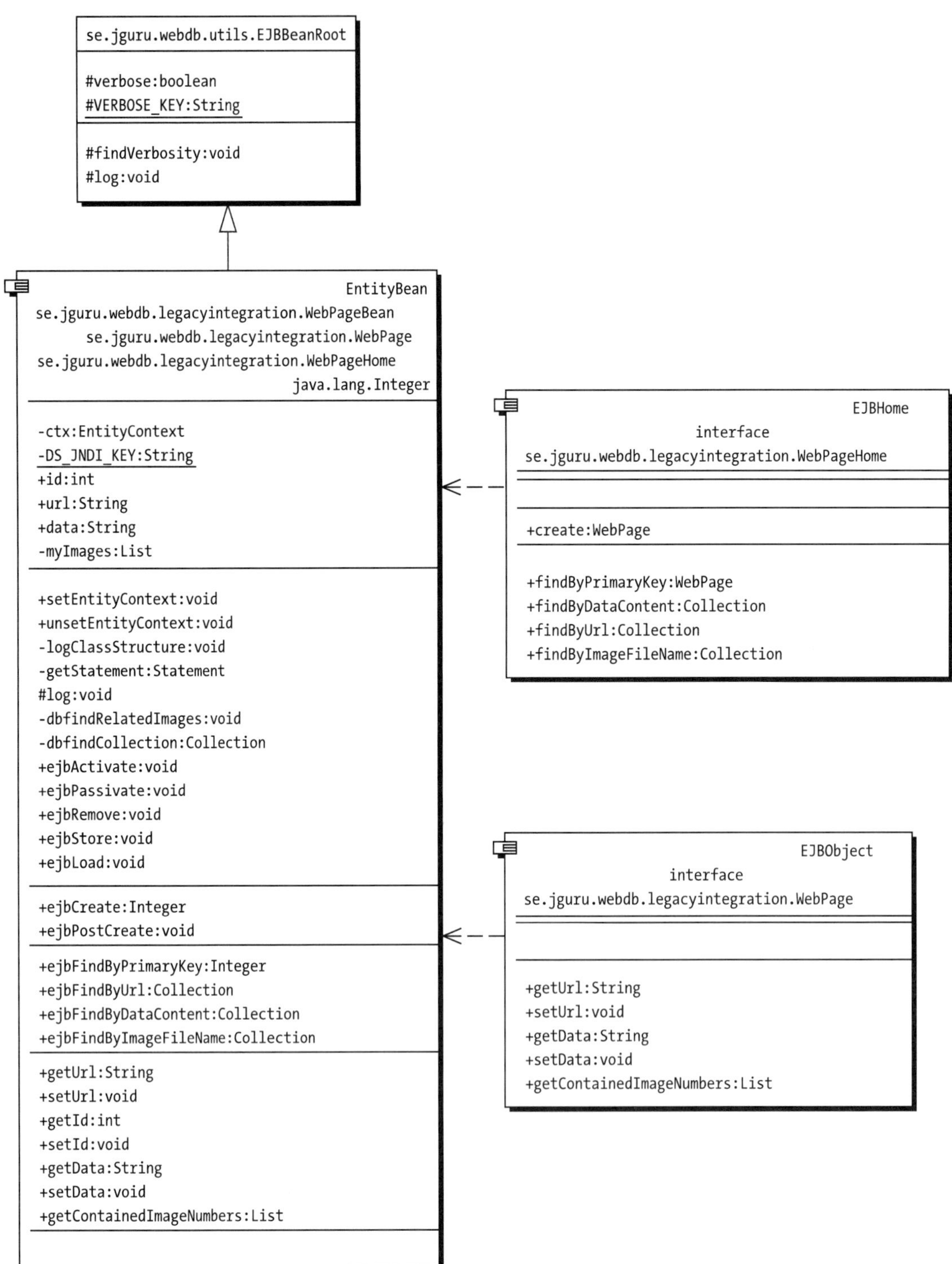

Figure 11-26. Types of the `WebPage` *EJB component*

The relative simplicity of EJB components using CMP is nowhere to be found for BMP Entity EJBs. In fact, the purpose of EJB components managing their own persistence is to attain the highest level of controls over how data is stored in and read from the data source. The question of when the data should be accessed or modified is completely left to be decided by the EJB container.

Let's start the study of the `WebPage` EJB component by examining its two service interfaces: `WebPage` and `WebPageHome`. The remote business interface of the EJB component, WebPage, provides a simple API to access and modify the internal state of the bean. See Listing 11-14.

Listing 11-14. The `WebPage` *component*

```
/*
 * Copyright (c) 2000,2001 jGuru Europe.
 * All rights reserved.
 */

package se.jguru.webdb.legacyintegration;

import javax.ejb.EJBObject;
import java.rmi.RemoteException;
import javax.ejb.EJBException;
import java.util.List;

/**
 * Remote business interface of a simple WebPage document and metadata
 * wrapper, which presents the URL and the DATA (HTML content) of a
 * particular Web Page.
 *
 * @author Lennart Jörelid, lj@jguru.se
 */
public interface WebPage extends EJBObject
{
    /**
     * Gets the URL of this WebPage.
     */
    public String getUrl() throws RemoteException, EJBException;

    /**
     * Sets the URL of this WebPage.
     */
    public void setUrl(String param) throws RemoteException, EJBException;
```

```
    /**
     * Retrieves the HTML document content of this Web Page.
     */
    public String getData() throws RemoteException, EJBException;

    /**
     * Sets the HTML document content of this Web Page.
     */
    public void setData(String param) throws RemoteException, EJBException;

    /**
     * Finds the primary keys of all Images related to (contained within)
     * this WebPage.
     *
     * @return A list populated with Integer objects - which are the
     *         primary keys of the Images contained within this
     *         WebPage. If no images are found in this WebPage, the
     *         return list is empty.
     */
    public List getContainedImageNumbers() throws RemoteException;
}
```

Most of the method declarations in the `WebPage` interface simply access a JavaBean property contained in the `WebPageBean` class. The values of each of those JavaBean properties are read from the `WEBPAGES` table in the database schema shown in Figure 11-2. The `getContainedImageNumbers` method, in contrast, returns a list with values retrieved from a select statement spanning an SQL table relation.

A BMP EJB component may, of course, use much more powerful SQL and/or computational relations to retrieve the responses returned by the methods in the Remote interface. In our simple example, however, we focus on understanding, developing, and deploying the EJB components rather than manipulating database schema.

The `WebPageHome` interface has a simple structure, similar to most Home interfaces of Entity EJB components, as shown in Figure 11-27.

The observant reader has already noted that the three finder methods that return collections simply return all `WebPage` EJB components whose respective internal state fields match the given finder criteria. Because these finders may return multiple `WebPage` instances, the return type of the finder methods in question must be a `java.util.Collection`.

Listing 11-15 displays the content of the `WebPageHome` source code file.

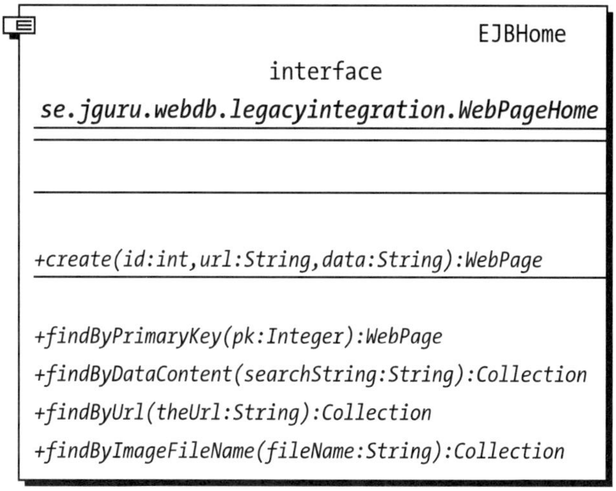

```
                                          EJBHome
                      interface
 se.jguru.webdb.legacyintegration.WebPageHome
-----------------------------------------------
-----------------------------------------------

+create(id:int,url:String,data:String):WebPage
-----------------------------------------------
+findByPrimaryKey(pk:Integer):WebPage
+findByDataContent(searchString:String):Collection
+findByUrl(theUrl:String):Collection
+findByImageFileName(fileName:String):Collection
```

Figure 11-27. The Home interface of the `WebPage` *EJB component*

Listing 11-15. The `WebPageHome` *file*

```
/*
 * Copyright (c) 2000,2001 jGuru Europe.
 * All rights reserved.
 */

package se.jguru.webdb.legacyintegration;

import javax.ejb.EJBObject;
import java.rmi.RemoteException;
import javax.ejb.EJBException;
import java.util.List;

/**
 * Remote business interface of a simple WebPage document and metadata
 * wrapper, which presents the URL and the DATA (HTML content) of a
 * particular Web Page.
 *
 * @author Lennart Jörelid, lj@jguru.se
 */
public interface WebPage extends EJBObject
{
    /**
     * Gets the URL of this WebPage.
     */
```

```
    public String getUrl() throws RemoteException, EJBException;

    /**
     * Sets the URL of this WebPage.
     */
    public void setUrl(String param) throws RemoteException, EJBException;

    /**
     * Retrieves the HTML document content of this Web Page.
     */
    public String getData() throws RemoteException, EJBException;

    /**
     * Sets the HTML document content of this Web Page.
     */
    public void setData(String param) throws RemoteException, EJBException;

    /**
     * Finds the primary keys of all Images related to (contained within)
     * this WebPage.
     *
     * @return A list populated with Integer objects - which are the
     *         primary keys of the Images contained within this
     *         WebPage. If no images are found in this WebPage, the
     *         return list is empty.
     */
    public List getContainedImageNumbers() throws RemoteException;
}
```

As is the case with all EJB components, the EJB implementation class provides method implementations to the contract raised by the Home and the Remote interfaces. The `WebPage` EJB component is no exception, but, because the component uses BMP, it is unshielded from all the detailed method calls required by the data source to obtain and use the `Connection`, `Statement`, and `ResultSet` instances required for proper database communication.

Frequently, the data structures of the Bean implementation classes of Entity EJB components are very simple; for CMP EJB components, it may even be trivial. The `WebPage` EMB component is no exception with respect to its primary data structure, as shown in Figure 11-28. The Bean implementation class has only three internal data fields: `id`, `data`, and `url`.

When creating a BMP entity bean, all internal data fields that should be handled automatically by the EJB container when passivating or activating the EJB component must have public visibility. This is imperative to remember, as the EJB container cannot access private fields for serialization and storage. Thankfully,

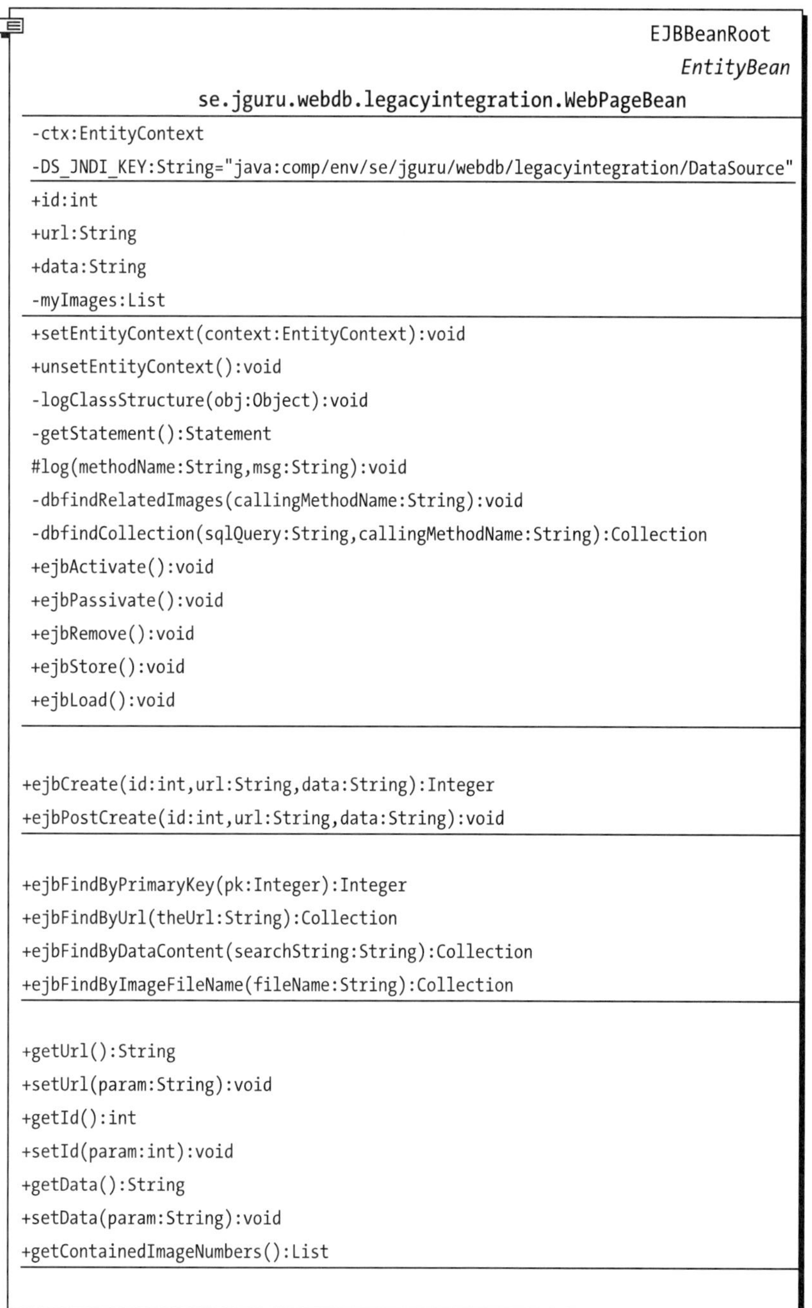

Figure 11-28. Structure of the `WebPageBean` *class. Note that private data fields cannot be serialized by the EJB container; the* `myImages` *list must therefore be nullified before passivation and re-created after activation.*

most application server compilation tools remind you of any mistakes with field visibility during the compilation process required to create the application-server specific EJB JAR file containing your bean.

The WebPageBean class provides several types of members, listed in Table 11-3 in the order of appearance in the class shown in Figure 11-28.

Table 11-3. Methods of the WebPageBean *Class*

CATEGORY	MEMBER	DESCRIPTION
EntityContext pattern members	ctx, setEntityContext, unsetEntityContext	Container reference for the EJB component. The primary key of an entity EJB component may always be found from the EntityContext.
Internal data fields	id, url, data, myImages	Fields storing the internal state of this EJB component. All serializable public fields may be handled by the container before passivating the EJB bean component. The myImages field must therefore be set to null when calling ejbPassivate.
Life-cycle methods	EjbActivate, ejbPassivate, ejbRemove, ejbLoad, ejbStore	The life-cycle methods are invoked by the EJB container immediately before (ejbPassivate, ejbRemove, ejbStore) or after (ejbActivate, ejbLoad) making a state transition for the EJB component. Usually the state of the EJB component is read from or written to the data source as part of the state transition. For instance, the ejbActivate and ejbLoad methods usually perform an SQL SELECT call to the database, whereas the ejbPassivate and ejbStore methods perform an SQL UPDATE database call. The ejbRemove method call performs the SQL DELETE that actually removes the state from persistent storage.
Internal service methods	getStatement, log, dbfindRelatedImages, dbfindCollection	Service methods performing distinct tasks that are needed by other methods in the EJB component. Service methods act as normal private members of any class.
Factory initializer methods	ejbCreate, ejbPostCreate	The ejbCreate data source creational methods provide the instructions to be carried out when initializing the database record saving the persistent state. The data is stored into the data source using an SQL INSERT statement, which must be manufactured by hand because this is a BMP EJB component.

Table 11-3. Methods of the `WebPageBean` *Class (Continued)*

CATEGORY	MEMBER	DESCRIPTION
Entity finder methods	`ejbFindByPrimaryKey`, `ejbFindByUrl`, `ejbFindByDataContent`, `ejbFindByImageFileName`	The `ejbFindXXX` methods perform a SQL SELECT statement on the data source to find the state of EJB bean class. The only mandatory finder method is `ejbFindByPrimaryKey`; other finders may be added as needed.
Data source getter methods	`getId`, `getUrl`, `getData`, `getContainedImageNumbers`	The getter methods provide the programmatic interface to the state held by this EJB component. Unlike CMP EJB components, the getters of a BMP entity bean must be concrete, and therefore frequently simply return the value of a public member.
Data source setter methods	`setId`, `setUrl`, `setData`	The setter methods provide the programmatic interface to the state held by this EJB component. Unlike CMP EJB components, the setters of a BMP entity bean must be concrete, and therefore frequently simply assign the value of a public member.

Because the application server compilation tools do not add internal structure members to the custom application server-generated classes, all BMP entity EJB components must be concrete. This means that the full details of the JDBC database call structure must be handled by the developer; although not complex in itself, the potential for typos and errors related to the text in the unverifiable SQL statements is higher for BMP beans than for their CMP siblings.

Let's look a the code of the `WebPageBean` class in Listing 11-16.

Listing 11-16. The `WebPageBean` *class*

```
/*
 * Copyright (c) 2000,2001 jGuru Europe.
 * All rights reserved.
 */

package se.jguru.webdb.legacyintegration;

import javax.ejb.*;
import javax.rmi.*;
import javax.naming.*;
import java.sql.*;
```

```
import java.util.*;
import javax.sql.*;
import java.rmi.RemoteException;
import se.jguru.webdb.utils.*;

/**
 * This is the Entity bean wrapping the data of
 * a web page table row. This entity EJB uses
 * Bean managed persistence, thereby forcing us
 * to handle connections to the database ourselves.
 *
 *
 * @ejbHome <{se.jguru.webdb.legacyintegration.WebPageHome}>
 * @ejbRemote <{se.jguru.webdb.legacyintegration.WebPage}>
 * @ejbPrimaryKey <{Integer}>
 * @ejbDontSynchronizeNames
 */
public class WebPageBean extends EJBBeanRoot implements EntityBean
{
    //
    // Entity context pattern.
    //
    private EntityContext ctx;

    public void setEntityContext(EntityContext context) { ctx = context; }
    public void unsetEntityContext() { ctx = null; }

    //
    // End entity context pattern.
    //

    // JNDI key to lookup the DataSource of the database.
    private static final String DS_JNDI_KEY =
        "java:comp/env/se/jguru/webdb/legacyintegration/DataSource";

    /** Primary key */
    public int id;

    /** URL of this WebPage */
    public String url;

    /** Content of this WebPage */
    public String data;
```

```
/**
 * The Primary Key values of all images
 * found on this WebPage
 */
private List myImages;

//
// Private helper methods, used by
// methods in the EJB bean
//

/**
 * Helper method which connects to the DataSource of this
 * Entity EJB, and retrieves a Statement.
 */
private Statement getStatement()
{
    try
    {
         // Get the initialContext
        Context cx = new InitialContext();

        // Find the DataSource
        DataSource ds = (DataSource) cx.lookup(DS_JNDI_KEY);

        // Get a connection to the DataSource
        Connection conn = ds.getConnection();

        // Return the Statement
        return conn.createStatement();
    }
    catch(Exception ex)
    {
        // Whoops. Complain.
        this.log("getResultSet", "Error getting a Statement from "
            + "the DataSource: " + ex);
    }

    // If the DataSource is properly configured,
    // we should not wind up here.
    return null;
}
```

```
/**
 * Encapsulation of the main log method in the CommonUtils class.
 */
protected void log(String methodName, String msg)
{
    // Log only if we are running in verbose mode.
    if(verbose) CommonUtils.log("WebPageBean", methodName, msg);
}

/**
 * Finds all images related to/referenced by this WebPage,
 * and populates the myImages list with their primary keys.
 */
private void dbfindRelatedImages(String callingMethodName)
{
    Connection conn = null;

    // Re-find all the remote images
    // related to this web page
    try
    {
        // Find the Primary Keys of all the images
        // related to this webpage
        String sqlQuery = "select IMAGE_ID, WEBPAGE_ID "
            + "from JT_IMAGES_WEBPAGES "
            + "where WEBPAGE_ID = "
            + ((Integer) ctx.getPrimaryKey()).intValue() ;

        // Log.
        this.log("dbFindRelatedImages -> " + callingMethodName,
            "Sending SQL query: " + sqlQuery);

        // Fire the SQL query to the DataSource, and
        // receive the ResultSet.
        ResultSet rs = this.getStatement().executeQuery(sqlQuery);

        // Get the parent Connection of the ResultSet
        conn = rs.getStatement().getConnection();

        // Copy the results to the internal list
        this.myImages = Collections.synchronizedList(new ArrayList());
```

```
            while(rs.next())
            {
                // Add the image PK to the internal list
                Integer thePk = new Integer(rs.getInt(1));
                this.myImages.add(thePk);

                // Log.
                 this.log("dbFindRelatedImages -> " + callingMethodName,
                     "Adding PK: " + thePk);
            }

            // All set up.
            // Close the ResultSet.
            rs.close();
        }
        catch(Exception ex)
        {
            // Whoops.
            this.log("findRelatedImages -> " + callingMethodName,
                        "Could not populate the images ID list: " + ex);

            // Re-create the list
            if(this.myImages == null) this.myImages = new ArrayList();
        }
        finally
        {
            try
            {
                // Close the DataSource connection
                 if(conn != null) conn.close();
            }
            catch(Exception ex)
            {
                // Whoops.
                this.log("findRelatedImages -> " + callingMethodName, "Could not "
                + "close the DataSource connection: " + ex);
            }
        }
    }

    /**
     * Helper method to find all the primary keys of WebPage EJBs which may
     * be found in the DataSource using the provided sqlQuery.
     */
```

```
private Collection dbfindCollection(String sqlQuery, String callingMethodName)
    throws FinderException
{
    Connection conn = null;
    List toReturn = Collections.synchronizedList(new ArrayList());

    try
    {
        // Fire the SQL query to the DataSource, and
        // receive the ResultSet.
        ResultSet rs = this.getStatement().executeQuery(sqlQuery);

        // Get the parent Connection of the ResultSet
        conn = rs.getStatement().getConnection();

        while(rs.next())
        {
            // Add the found primary key to the return collection
            toReturn.add(new Integer(rs.getInt(1)));
        }

        // Close the ResultSet.
        rs.close();

        // Done.
        return toReturn;
    }
    catch(Exception ex)
    {
        // Whoops.
        this.log("dbfindCollection -> " + callingMethodName,
            "Could not find the Collection of Primary Keys: " + ex);
        throw new FinderException("Could not find the Collection "
                    + "of Primary Keys: " + ex);
    }
    finally
    {
        try
        {
            // Close the DataSource connection
             if(conn != null) conn.close();
        }
```

```
        catch(Exception ex)
        {
            // Whoops.
             this.log("dbfindCollection -> " + callingMethodName,
                      "Could not close the DataSource connection: " + ex);
        }
    }
}

//
// End private helper methods
//

//
// Life cycle methods, called by the EJB
// container to initiate or finalize state
// transitions for the EJB component
//

/**
 * During activation, we must re-populate the list of
 * primary keys of the Images contained within (related
 * to) this WebPage.
 */
public void ejbActivate()
{
    // Find and map all Images related to this
    // web page.
    this.dbfindRelatedImages("ejbActivate");
}

/**
 * Before passivating, we should nullify the List of images
 * held by this WebPage.
 */
public void ejbPassivate()
{
    // Simply garbage collect the list of image PK,
    // to refrain from serializing it.
    this.myImages = null;
}
```

```
/**
 * When removing a webpage, we should make sure that we
 * also delete all references to it from the JT_IMAGES_WEBPAGES
 * table, to keep referential integrity.
 */
public void ejbRemove()
{
    Connection conn = null;

    // When removing this WebPage, we should also remove
    // all of its related rows in the JT_IMAGES_WEBPAGES table,
    // where Images are linked to this webpage.
    try
    {
        String sqlQuery = "delete from JT_IMAGES_WEBPAGES "
            + "where WEBPAGE_ID = " + this.getId();

        // Get a Statement
        Statement stmnt = this.getStatement();

        // Get hold of the parent Connection
        conn = stmnt.getConnection();

        // Delete the proper rows from JT_IMAGES_WEBPAGES
        int rowsAffected = stmnt.executeUpdate(sqlQuery);

        // Log the amount of rows deleted
        this.log("ejbRemove", "Deleted " + rowsAffected
            + " references to images before removing myself.");

        // All went well.
        // Close the statement, and open a new one,
        // to remove ourselves from the Database
        stmnt.close();

        // Renew the statement
        stmnt = this.getStatement();
        conn = stmnt.getConnection();

        // Create another SQL query, which deletes
        // the underlying record of this WebPageBean.
        sqlQuery = "delete from WEBPAGES "
            + "where ID = " + this.getId();
```

```
            // Execute the statement
            rowsAffected = stmnt.executeUpdate(sqlQuery);

            // Log the amount of rows deleted.
            this.log("ejbRemove", "Deleted " + rowsAffected
                + " references to WEBPAGES when removing myself.");

            // All went well.
            conn.commit();
        }
        catch(Exception ex)
        {
             // Whoops.
             this.log("ejbRemove", "Could not "
                + "perform pre-removal cleanup: " + ex);
        }
        finally
        {
            // Close the connection
            try
            {
                // Close the DataSource connection
                 if(conn != null) conn.close();
            }
            catch(Exception ex)
            {
                // Whoops.
                 this.log("ejbPassivate", "Could not "
                + "close the DataSource connection: " + ex);
            }
        }
    }

    /**
     * Saves the internal state of this Entity bean in the database.
     */
    public void ejbStore()
    {
        Connection conn = null;

        try
        {
            // Get the Statement
            Statement stmnt = this.getStatement();
            conn = stmnt.getConnection();
```

```
        // Define the SQL query to fire
        //
        String sqlQuery = "update WEBPAGES "
            + "set URL = '" + this.getUrl() + "', DATA = '" + this.getData()
            + "' where ID=" + this.getId();

        // Log.
        this.log("ejbStore", "Sending: " + sqlQuery);

        // Fire the query
        int rowsAffected = stmnt.executeUpdate(sqlQuery);

        // Log.
        this.log("ejbStore", "Saved myself affecting " + rowsAffected
            + " rows.");

        // All went well.
    }
    catch(Exception ex)
    {
         // Whoops.
         this.log("ejbStore", "Could not "
            + "store bean state: " + ex);

         // Rollback.
         try
         {
            this.log("ejbStore", "Rolling back transaction.");
               // Uncomment this if the DataSource does not use autocommit
               // conn.rollback();
         }
         catch(SQLException e)
         {
            // Could not rollback the transaction...
            this.log("ejbStore", "Could not rollback after failing to "
                + "store my state to the DB. Check that the DB server "
                + "is still running: " + e);
         }
    }
```

```
    finally
    {
        // Close the connection
        try
        {
            // Close the DataSource connection
             if(conn != null) conn.close();
        }
        catch(Exception ex)
        {
            // Whoops.
             this.log("ejbStore", "Could not "
            + "close the DataSource connection: " + ex);
        }
    }
}

/**
 * Loads the bean state from the DataSource
 */
public void ejbLoad()
{
    Connection conn = null;

    try
    {
        // Get the primary key from the EntityContext, and
        // assign it to the internal state of this bean.
        this.id = ((Integer) ctx.getPrimaryKey()).intValue();

        // Find the internal state data of this EJB component
        String sqlQuery = "select ID, URL, DATA "
            + "from WEBPAGES "
            + "where ID = " + this.getId();

        // Fire the SQL query to the DataSource, and
        // receive the ResultSet.
        ResultSet rs = this.getStatement().executeQuery(sqlQuery);

        // Get the parent Connection of the ResultSet
        conn = rs.getStatement().getConnection();
```

```
            if(!rs.next())
                throw new IllegalArgumentException("EJB with id " + this.id
                + " not found.");
            else
            {
                // Assign our internal state variables from the
                // ResultSet excavated from the DataSource
                this.url = rs.getString(2);
                this.data = rs.getString(3);
            }

            // All set up.
            // Close the ResultSet.
            rs.close();
        }
        catch(Exception ex)
        {
            // Whoops.
            this.log("ejbLoad", "Could not load the EJB state: " + ex);
        }
        finally
        {
            try
            {
                // Close the DataSource connection
                 if(conn != null) conn.close();
            }
            catch(Exception ex)
            {
                // Whoops.
                 this.log("ejbLoad", "Could not close the DataSource "
                                  + "connection: " + ex);
            }
        }
    }

    /**
     * Creates this Entity, including the DataSource storage.
     */
    public Integer ejbCreate(int id, String url, String data)
        throws CreateException
    {
        // Find our verbosity
        this.findVerbosity("ejbCreate");
```

```
 // Assign our internal state variables
this.id = id;
this.url = url;
this.data = data;

Connection conn = null;

 try
 {
     // Get the Statement
     Statement stmnt = this.getStatement();

     // Define the SQL query to fire
     String sqlQuery = "insert into WEBPAGES (id, url, data) "
         + " values (" + id + ", '" + url + "', '" + data + "')";

     // Fire the query
     int rowsAffected = stmnt.executeUpdate(sqlQuery);

     // Log.
     this.log("ejbCreate", "Created myself affecting " + rowsAffected
         + " rows.");

     // All went well.
     // Uncomment this if the DataSource does not use autocommit
     // conn.commit();
 }
 catch(Exception ex)
 {
      // Whoops.
      this.log("ejbCreate", "Could not "
         + "create bean state: " + ex);

      // Rollback.
      try
      {
         this.log("ejbCreate", "Rolling back transaction.");
            // Uncomment this if the DataSource does not use autocommit
            // conn.rollback();
      }
```

```
            catch(SQLException e)
            {
               // Could not rollback the transaction...
               this.log("ejbCreate", "Could not rollback after failing to "
                  + "insert my state to the DB. Check that the DB server "
                  + "is still running: " + e);
            }
        }
        finally
        {
            // Close the connection
            try
            {
               // Close the DataSource connection
                if(conn != null) conn.close();
            }
            catch(Exception ex)
            {
               // Whoops.
                this.log("ejbCreate", "Could not "
               + "close the DataSource connection: " + ex);
            }
        }

        // At last, return the primary key of this instance.
        // This is required for Entity EJBs using Bean-Managed
        // Persistence (BMP).
        return new Integer(id);
    }

    public void ejbPostCreate(int id, String url, String data)
    {
        // Find all images related to this WebPage
        // and map their Primary Key fields into
        // the myImages List.
        this.dbfindRelatedImages("ejbPostCreate");
     }

    //
    // Finder methods
    //

    /**
     * Finds the EJB Entity from the provided Primary Key.
     */
```

```
public Integer ejbFindByPrimaryKey(Integer pk)
    throws FinderException
{
     Connection conn = null;

    try
    {
        // Find the internal state data of this EJB component
        String sqlQuery = "select ID, URL, DATA "
            + "from WEBPAGES "
            + "where ID = " + pk.intValue();

        // Fire the SQL query to the DataSource, and
        // receive the ResultSet.
        ResultSet rs = this.getStatement().executeQuery(sqlQuery);

        // Get the parent Connection of the ResultSet
        conn = rs.getStatement().getConnection();

        if(!rs.next())
            throw new IllegalArgumentException("EJB with id " + pk.intValue()
            + " not found.");
        else
        {
            // Assign our internal state variables from the
            // ResultSet excavated from the DataSource
            this.id = pk.intValue();
            this.url = rs.getString(2);
            this.data = rs.getString(3);
        }

        // All set up.
        // Close the ResultSet.
        rs.close();
    }
    catch(Exception ex)
    {
        // Whoops.
       this.log("ejbFindByPrimaryKey", "Could not load the EJB state: " + ex);
        throw new FinderException("Could not load the EJB state: " + ex);
    }
```

```
    finally
    {
        try
        {
            // Close the DataSource connection
             if(conn != null) conn.close();
        }
        catch(Exception ex)
        {
            // Whoops.
             this.log("ejbFindByPrimaryKey",
                       "Could not close the DataSource connection: " + ex);
        }
    }

    // Return the primary key of the entity found.
    return pk;
}

/**
 * Finds all the primary keys of the Web Pages with the provided URL.
 */
public Collection ejbFindByUrl(String theUrl)
    throws FinderException
{
    // Create the SQL query
    String sqlQuery = "select ID "
        + "from WEBPAGES "
        + "where URL like '" + theUrl + "'";

     // Delegate the call
    return this.dbfindCollection(sqlQuery, "ejbFindByUrl");
 }

/**
 * Finds a list of WebPage entities which contains the
 * search string in the HTML data content.
 *
 * @param searchString The string which should be found
 *        in the WebPage data to include it in the return
 *        collection of this EJB component.
 */
```

```
public Collection ejbFindByDataContent(String searchString)
    throws FinderException
{
    // Create the SQL query
    String sqlQuery = "select ID "
        + "from WEBPAGES "
        + "where DATA like '%" + searchString + "%'";

    // Delegate the call
    return this.dbfindCollection(sqlQuery, "ejbFindByDataContent");
}


/**
 * Finds all the primary keys of the Web Pages related to
 * the images with the given file name.
 */
public Collection ejbFindByImageFileName(String fileName)
    throws FinderException
{
    // Compile the sqlQuery
    String sqlQuery = "select distinct jt_images_webpages.webpage_id "
        + "from jt_images_webpages, images "
        + "where images.id in "
        + " (select images.id from images "
        + "  where images.filename like '%" + fileName + "%')";

    // Fire and return
    return this.dbfindCollection(sqlQuery, "ejbFindByImageFileName");
}

//
// End finder methods
//

//
// Remote business methods, defined in the remote interface.
//

public String getUrl(){ return url; }
public void setUrl(String param){ this.url = param; }

public int getId(){ return id; }
public void setId(int param){ this.id = param; }
```

```
    public String getData(){ return data; }
    public void setData(String param){ this.data = param; }

    /**
     * Finds the primary keys of all Images related to (contained within)
     * this WebPage.
     *
     * @return A list populated with Integer objects - which are the
     *         primary keys of the Images contained within this
     *         WebPage. If no images are found in this WebPage, the
     *         return list is empty.
     */
    public List getContainedImageNumbers()
    {
        // Re-read internal state?
        if(this.myImages == null)
        {
            this.log("getContainedImageNumbers", "Re-reading the List of "
                + "contained images. (Internal list was null).");

            // Find my related images.
            this.dbfindRelatedImages("getContainedImageNumbers");
        }

        // Done. Return.
        return this.myImages;
    }

    //
    // End remote business methods.
    //
}
```

Although each method in the `WebPageBean` class is fairly simple if studied separately, the sheer mass of the component implementation occasionally makes for interesting reading of the compiler error log. Of course, SQL exceptions generated in the data source as a result of a misspelled table or column name cannot be caught by the Java compiler during compile time. Unit and load testing of all Entity EJB components—particularly those using BMP—is therefore very important to avoid system failures in a production environment.

Most life-cycle methods in the Bean implementation class of a BMP EJB component have a similar structure. Indeed, all of the life-cycle methods of the `WebPageBean` look alike, the structure being as follows:

```
Get the database Connection
Get the database Statement
Compile the SQL query to be fired to the Statement
Fire the SQL query and retrieve the results
Check that the results were OK, and that
      no exceptions were raised by the DataSource
Return the desired value
```

The structure is so strict that a special method, `getStatement`, has been created to perform the two first steps of the method template.

In the `WebPageBean` class shown in Listing 11-16, the only method that retrieves data from a database table other than `WEBPAGES` is the private service method `dbfindRelatedImages`, which finds all the primary key numbers of `Images` related to (referenced from) the `WebPage` in question. Note that this method is called from within `ejbActivate` (to re-create the related image data after activation) and potentially from the `getContainedImageNumbers` business method (if the internal list should be null for any reason).

The introduction of the `WebPage` EJB component implies drastic changes in the internal structure of both the `LegacyFacade` session EJB component and the `LegacyFacadeProxy` class used by the JSP view. Thankfully, in both of these cases, the existence of the `LegacyFacadeProxy` facilitates—rather than obfuscates—the structure of the calling class.

The LegacyFacade EJB Component

Many EJB applications use session EJBs as a facade that accesses legacy data through Entity EJB components (or through other means) and creates value object (frequently referred to as *VO* in J2EE reference literature) wrappers holding the data found in the legacy system. This is particularly resource efficient, because legacy resources such as row locks or connections in databases may be released immediately after extracting the data. It is generally a bad design choice to permit references to Remote interfaces of Entity EJBs be handled by Web container entities, such as servlets or JSP documents, unless one can be sure of either of the two statements below:

- The Entity EJB component will be created, used, and immediately released by the servlet or JSP document; or

- The Entity EJB component will be used by only a relatively small number of concurrent users, such as administrators modifying system-wide parameters through an Entity EJB.

As shown in Figure 11-29, both the internal structure of the LegacyFacadeBean class and the method declarations in the LegacyFacade Remote interface have been greatly modified in the second refactoring step. Mostly, legacy data source communication functionality has been moved to the WebPage and Image Entity EJB components, requiring unnecessary code in the LegacyFacadeProxy EJB component to be deleted.

As can be seen in Figure 11-29, the LegacyFacade component may now be converted into a stateless session EJB, because its ejbCreate method does not require any parameters and the findWebPages method returns the full answer to the database query. The state of the bean will be studied further when examining its deployment descriptors in the "Step 6—Configuring the WebPage Search System" section.

The two service interfaces of the LegacyFacade EJB component are trivial enough that it's only necessary to show the method declaration in the Remote interface:

```
/**
 * Find all the WebPages originating from their
 * data content.
 *
 * @return A fully populated List containing
 *         WebPageValueObjects.
 */
public List findWebPages(String searchString)
    throws RemoteException;
```

The Remote service interface currently has only one method definition, reflecting that only one Use Case (finding WebPages containing a certain string value) is currently implemented in the small system. As more Use Cases are implemented in the system, the LegacyFacade Remote interface will require more method declarations.

The EJB Bean implementation class, LegacyFacadeBean, has no internal state variables (none are required in a stateless session EJB component), but two helper methods that are called from within the remote business method. The only interesting thing to note about the LegacyFacade session EJB component is that the data acquired from the Entity EJB components is repackaged into value objects from the package se.jguru.webdb.proxy.valueobjects.

There is one value object for each type of entity handled, as shown in Figure 11-30; the LegacyFacade creates and populates the value objects in the findWebPages method. This is a common task for a stateless session EJB acting as a facade to the legacy business object data.

The code of the two value objects is trivial, but important to the application. Some IDEs therefore have built-in tools for automatic VO class generation. This

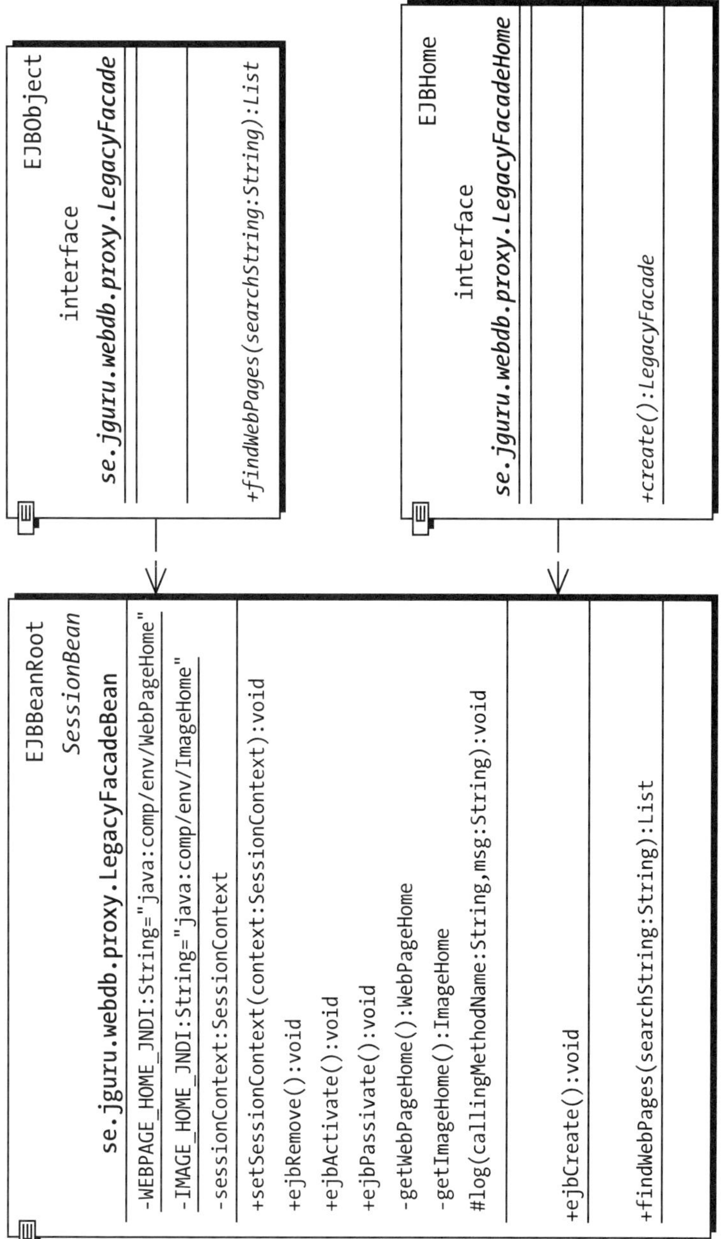

Figure 11-29. Structure of the `LegacyFacade` *session EJB component after refactoring*

is quite convenient, especially for larger Entity classes wherein the amount of mindless creation of getter and setter methods consumes much time. Listing 11-17 shows the code of the two VO classes.

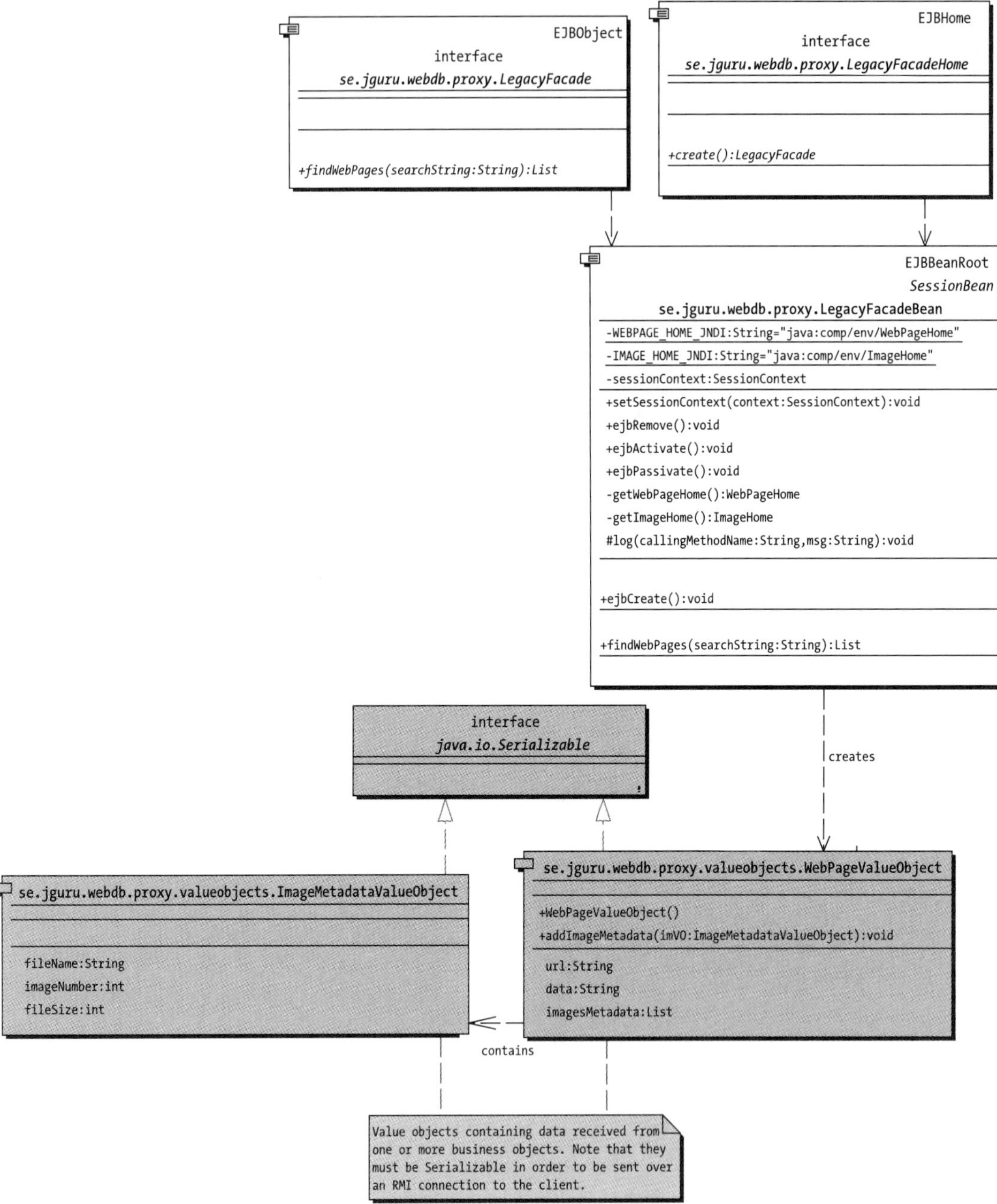

Figure 11-30. The value object classes created by the `LegacyFacadeBean` *component. Note that the internal structure of the value objects mirror that of the Entity EJB components whose data is contained by the VO.*

Listing 11-17. The `ImageMetaDataVallueObject`

```
/*
 * Copyright (c) 2000,2001 jGuru Europe.
 * All rights reserved.
 */

package se.jguru.webdb.proxy.valueobjects;

import java.io.Serializable;

/**
 * Value object carrying the data of a particular Image
 *
 * @author Lennart Jörelid, lj@jguru.se
 */
public class ImageMetadataValueObject implements Serializable
{
    // Internal state variables.
    private String fileName;
    private int imageNumber;
    private int fileSize;

    public String getFileName() { return fileName; }
    public void setFileName(java.lang.String fileName)
    { this.fileName = fileName; }

    public int getImageNumber() { return imageNumber; }
    public void setImageNumber(int imageNumber) { this.imageNumber = imageNumber; }

    public int getFileSize() { return fileSize; }
    public void setFileSize(int size) { this.fileSize = size; }
}
```

The `WebPageValueObject` class is equally trivial.

```
/*
 * Copyright (c) 2000,2001 jGuru Europe.
 * All rights reserved.
 */

package se.jguru.webdb.proxy.valueobjects;
```

```
import java.io.Serializable;
import java.util.List;
import java.util.ArrayList;

/**
 * Value object carrying the data of a particular
 * web page search, i.e. both the list of WebPages
 * and the corresponding list of ImageMetadata.
 *
 * @author Lennart Jörelid, lj@jguru.se
 */
public class WebPageValueObject implements Serializable
{
    // The private members of this value object.
    private String url;
    private String data;
    private List imagesMetadata;

    public WebPageValueObject()
    {
        // Create our internal data structure
        this.imagesMetadata = new ArrayList();
    }

    public String getUrl()
    {
        return url;
    }

    public void setUrl(String url)
    {
        this.url = url;
    }

    public String getData()
    {
        return data;
    }

    public void setData(String data)
    {
        this.data = data;
    }
```

```
    public List getImagesMetadata()
    {
        return imagesMetadata;
    }

    public void addImageMetadata(ImageMetadataValueObject imVO)
    {
        this.imagesMetadata.add(imVO);
    }
}
```

The only class remaining in the `LegacyFacade` component is the actual `LegacyFacadeBean` implementation class. Take a look at the content of the `LegacyFacadeBean.java` file in Listing 11-18.

Listing 11-18. The `LegacyFacadeBean.java` *file*

```
/*
 * Copyright (c) 2000,2001 jGuru Europe.
 * All rights reserved.
 */

package se.jguru.webdb.proxy;

import java.rmi.*;
import javax.rmi.*;
import javax.ejb.*;
import java.sql.*;
import javax.naming.*;
import javax.sql.*;
import java.util.*;

import se.jguru.webdb.utils.*;
import se.jguru.webdb.legacyintegration.*;
import se.jguru.webdb.proxy.valueobjects.*;

/**
 * Implementation class of the LegacyFacade EJB component.
 * In the second refactor step, this LegacyFacade merely
 * relays the communication to the Entity EJB components.
 *
 * @author Lennart Jörelid, lj@jguru.se
 * @version 2.0
*/
```

```
public class LegacyFacadeBean extends EJBBeanRoot implements SessionBean
{
    // Jndi lookup string for the WebPageHome
    private final static String WEBPAGE_HOME_JNDI = "java:comp/env/WebPageHome";

    // Jndi lookup string for the ImageHome
    private final static String IMAGE_HOME_JNDI = "java:comp/env/ImageHome";

    //
    // Mandatory members for the SessionContext of this bean
    //
    private SessionContext sessionContext;

    public void setSessionContext(SessionContext context)
    {
        sessionContext = context;
    }

    //
    // Life cycle methods for this SessionBean
    //


    public void ejbCreate()
    {
        // Find the verbosity
        this.findVerbosity("ejbCreate");

        // Log
        this.log("ejbCreate", "--- Running");
    }

    public void ejbRemove()
    {
        // Log access
        this.log("ejbRemove", "--- Running");
    }

    public void ejbActivate()
    {
        // Log access
        this.log("ejbActivate", "--- Running");
    }
```

```
public void ejbPassivate()
{
    // Log access
    this.log("ejbPassivate", "--- Running");
}

//
// End lifecycle methods
//

//
// Private service methods
//

/** Gets and returns the WegPageHome instance. */
private WebPageHome getWebPageHome()
{
    try
    {
        // Get the initial context
        Context ctx = new InitialContext();

        // Log.
        this.log("getWebPageHome", "Looking up: " + WEBPAGE_HOME_JNDI);

        // Lookup the WebPageHome
        Object obj = ctx.lookup(WEBPAGE_HOME_JNDI);

        // Narrow to the proper type and return
        return (WebPageHome)
               PortableRemoteObject.narrow(obj, WebPageHome.class);
    }
    catch (Exception ex)
    {
        // Whoops.
        this.log("getWebPageHome", "Could not acquire the WebPageHome "
        + "from the Context: " + ex);
    }

    // This should not happen
    this.log("getWebPageHome", "Returning null.");
    return null;
}
```

```
/** Gets and returns the ImageHome instance. */
private ImageHome getImageHome()
{
    try
    {
        // Get the initial context
        Context ctx = new InitialContext();

        // Log.
        this.log("getImageHome", "Looking up: " + IMAGE_HOME_JNDI);

        // Lookup the WebPageHome
        Object obj = ctx.lookup(IMAGE_HOME_JNDI);

        // Narrow to the proper type and return
        return (ImageHome)PortableRemoteObject.narrow(obj, ImageHome.class);
    }
    catch (Exception ex)
    {
        // Whoops.
        this.log("getImageHome", "Could not acquire the ImageHome "
        + "from the Context: " + ex);
    }

    // This should not happen
    this.log("getImageHome", "Returning null.");
    return null;
}

//
// End private service methods
//

//
// Remote business method implementations
//

/**
 * Find all the WebPages originating from their
 * data content.
 */
```

```
public List findWebPages(String searchString)
{
    // Get the WebPageHome
    WebPageHome home = this.getWebPageHome();
    if (home == null)
    {
        // Log.
        this.log("findWebPages", "Got null WebPageHome; bailing out.");
        return new ArrayList();
    }

    // Declare the ImageHome, to be
    // used if any of the web pages
    // contains images.
    ImageHome imHome = this.getImageHome();
    if (imHome == null)
    {
        // Log.
        this.log("findWebPages", "Got null ImageHome; bailing out.");
        return new ArrayList();
    }

    // Define the List to return
    List toReturn = new ArrayList();

    try
    {
        // Get all web pages matching the search
        Collection pages = home.findByDataContent(searchString);

        // Found no pages?
        if (pages.size() == 0)
            return new ArrayList();

        // Pages found. Extract them, and repackage into
        // value objects, so we may release the database
        // connection back to the pool.
        for (Iterator it = pages.iterator(); it.hasNext(); )
        {
            // Get the WebPage
            WebPage current = (WebPage)it.next();
```

```
            // Create a WebPageValueObject and pack all data
            // known by the current instance in that value object.
            // This permits quick closing of the valuable (and
            // slow) database connection.
            WebPageValueObject wpmd = new WebPageValueObject();
            wpmd.setData(current.getData());
            wpmd.setUrl(current.getUrl());

            // Get the List of image PKs held by this page
            List allImages = current.getContainedImageNumbers();

            if (allImages.size() != 0)
            {
                // We have related images; create an
                // ImageMetadataValueObject for each Image,
                // and add it to the WebPageValueObject.
                for (int i = 0; i < allImages.size(); i++)
                {
                    Integer imagePk = (Integer)allImages.get(i);

                    // Find the Image with the given imagePk
                    Image currentImage = imHome.findByPrimaryKey(imagePk);

                    // Create the value object
                    ImageMetadataValueObject imvo =
                                            new ImageMetadataValueObject();
                    imvo.setFileName(currentImage.getFileName());
                    imvo.setImageNumber(imagePk.intValue());

                    byte[] imData = currentImage.getData();
                    int size = (imData == null ? 0 : imData.length);

                    imvo.setFileSize(size);

                    // Add the value object to the WebPageValueObject
                    wpmd.addImageMetadata(imvo);
                }
            }

            // Add the current Value Object
            // to the return List
            toReturn.add(wpmd);
        }
```

```
            // Done.
            return toReturn;
        }
        catch (Exception ex)
        {
            // Whoops
            this.log("findWebPages", "Could not find the web pages: " + ex);
        }

        // Unless an error ocurred, we
        // should not wind up here
        return new ArrayList();
    }


    //
    // End remote business method implementations
    //


    /** Simple logger method. */
    protected void log(String callingMethodName, String msg)
    {
        // Log only if we are running in verbose mode.
        if (verbose) CommonUtils.log("LegacyFacadeBean", callingMethodName, msg);
    }
}
```

Having examined the classes of the `LegacyFacade` EJB component, you may safely conclude that the refactoring has brought a simpler structure to the whole set of component classes. Not only do you have only one single method in the Remote interface, but the need for constructor arguments has also vanished. By revamping the `LegacyFacade` EJB component as a stateless session EJB component, system performance is improved because the application server may reduce the number of instances required for proper operation, which, in turn, reduces the memory consumption of the server as a whole.

The remaining component of the system model is the `LegacyFacadeProxy` class that interacts with the JSP View document.

The LegacyFacadeProxy Class

Restructuring the legacy data tier is important because it implies distinct responsibilities for each part of the system shown in Figure11-25. The JavaBean proxy class, `LegacyFacadeProxy`, illustrated in Figure 11-31 performs two main tasks:

- It hides all exception handling code from the JSP document, shielding it from having to recover from an error in the legacy or business object tier.
- It collects and holds data that can be set or gotten from the JSP views, both before firing a database query through its `LegacyFacade` instance and after receiving the response.

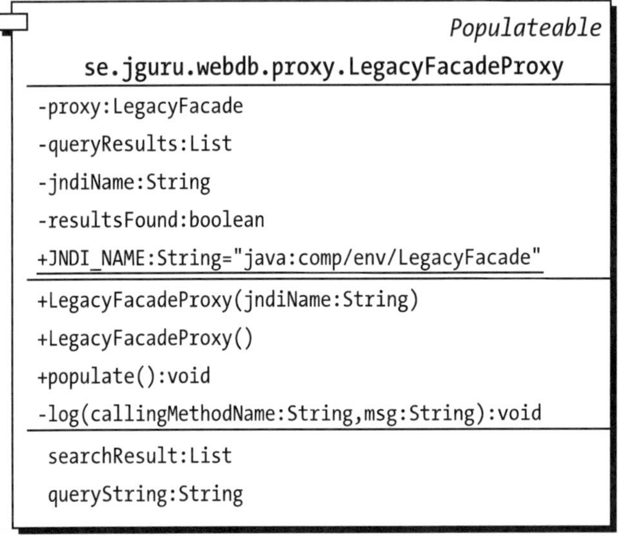

Figure 11-31. The `LegacyFacadeProxy` *class has been reduced in size with the refactoring.*

Any simple properties retrieved from a database query should be mirrored in the JavaBean proxy class, with strict adherence to the JavaBean naming pattern for the accessor methods. That way, any JSP standard actions (`<jsp:getProperty ... />` and `<jsp:setProperty ... />`) may access the JavaBean properties to set or get, and no visible Java code makes the JSP view complex for HTML view developers.

However, for answers that are `Collections`, the simplest solution to keep the JSP view tidy is to create a custom JSP action that unpacks and prints out the relevant parts of the `Collection`. In such cases, simply echo the `Collection` through the JavaBean proxy class.

Listing 11-19 contains the code of the `LegacyFacadeProxy` class.

Listing 11-19. The `LegacyFacadeProxy` *class*

```
/*
 * Copyright (c) 2000,2001 jGuru Europe.
 * All rights reserved.
 */

package se.jguru.webdb.proxy;

import javax.naming.*;
import javax.rmi.*;
import java.util.*;

import se.jguru.webdb.utils.CommonUtils;
import se.jguru.webdb.proxy.valueobjects.*;

/**
 * This LegacyFacadeProxy is a JavaBean proxy class which
 * contains Model data for the JSP document View. All data
 * is received from the LegacyFacade EJB.
 *
 * @author Lennart Jörelid
 */
public class LegacyFacadeProxy implements Populateable
{
    // The LegacyFacade proxy bean
    private LegacyFacade proxy;

    // The resulting List of a query.
    private List queryResults;

    // Toggle flag to verify if any results
    // were found in the DB query.
    private boolean resultsFound;

    // Properties set by all the setter methods
    // of this proxy
    private String queryString;
```

```
/** Standard JNDI lookup name for the LegacyFacade */
public static final String JNDI_NAME = "java:comp/env/LegacyFacade";

/**
 * Sets up this LegacyFacadeProxy, originating from the
 * jndiName provided.
 *
 * @param jndiName The lookup string for the LegacyFacadeHome
 *        factory object for the proxy used in this class.
 */
public LegacyFacadeProxy(String jndiName)
{
    try
    {
        // Get the initial context
        //
        // This client runs within the application server, so we should
        // not be required to submit any initialization parameters to
        // the InitialContext constructor.
        Context ctx = new InitialContext();

        // Lookup the LegacyFacadeHome instance
        this.log("<constructor>", "Looking up: " + jndiName);
        Object obj = ctx.lookup(jndiName);

        // Narrow the retrieved object to a LegacyFacadeHome
        LegacyFacadeHome home = (LegacyFacadeHome)
        PortableRemoteObject.narrow(obj, LegacyFacadeHome.class);

        // Create the LegacyFacade instance
        this.proxy = home.create();
    }
    catch (Exception ex)
    {
        // Log and bail out.
        this.log("<constructor>", "Could "
        + "not create a LegacyFacade: " + ex);
        this.log("<constructor>", "jndiName: " + jndiName);
    }
}
```

```
public LegacyFacadeProxy()
{
    this(JNDI_NAME);
}



//
// JavaBean getter methods which
// should be used from within
// the JSP view.
//

public List getSearchResult()
{
    // Check sanity
    if (this.queryResults == null)
    {
        // log.
        this.log("getSearchResult", "Null queryResults. Returning an "
        + "empty List.");

        return new ArrayList();
    }

    // Log the number of hits returned.
    this.log("getSearchResult", "Found " + this.queryResults.size()
    + " hits.");

    // Return the query results
    return this.queryResults;
}

//
// JavaBean setter methods which
// should be called from within
// the JSP view.
//

public void setQueryString(String queryString)
{
    this.log("setQueryString", "Got " + queryString);

    // Check sanity
    if (queryString == null) return;
```

```
        // Set the queryString
        this.queryString = queryString;
    }


    /**
     * Populates the internal state of this Populateable,
     * or throws a PopulationException describing why
     * the populate operation failed.
     */
    public void populate() throws PopulationException
    {
        // Check sanity
        if (this.queryString == null)
            throw new PopulationException("[LegacyFacadeProxy::populate]: Could "
            + "not populate the internal state of the LegacyFacadeProxy. "
            + "No queryString was supplied.");

        this.log("populate", "(proxy == null): "
        + (proxy == null) + ", queryString: " + queryString);

        if (this.proxy == null)
        {
            // Recreate the proxy
            try
            {
                // Get the initial context
                //
                // This client runs within the application server, so we should
                // not be required to submit any initialization parameters to
                // the InitialContext constructor.
                Context ctx = new InitialContext();

                // Lookup the LegacyFacadeHome instance
                this.log("populate", "Looking up: " + JNDI_NAME);
                Object obj = ctx.lookup(JNDI_NAME);

                // Narrow the retrieved object to a LegacyFacadeHome
                LegacyFacadeHome home = (LegacyFacadeHome)
                PortableRemoteObject.narrow(obj, LegacyFacadeHome.class);

                // Create the LegacyFacade instance
                this.proxy = home.create();
            }
```

```
            catch (Exception ex)
            {
                // Log and bail out.
                this.log("populate", "Could "
                + "not create a LegacyFacade: " + ex);
                this.log("<constructor>", "jndiName: " + JNDI_NAME);
            }

        }

        // Sane. Fire the DB query.
        try
        {
            // Fire the query
            this.queryResults = this.proxy.findWebPages(this.queryString);
            this.log("populate", "Got results size: " + this.queryResults.size());

            // Set the resultsFound flag
            this.resultsFound = (this.queryResults.size() == 0 ? false : true);
        }
        catch (Exception ex)
        {
            throw new PopulationException("Could not populate the internal "
            + "state: " + ex);
        }
    }

    /** Logs a message to the standard log stream. */
    private void log(String callingMethodName, String msg)
    {
        CommonUtils.log("LegacyFacadeProxy", callingMethodName, msg);
    }
}
```

The `LegacyFacadeProxy` is simpler than most JavaBean proxies because we have only one Use Case call method to handle in the `LegacyFacade` interface. Frequently, the JavaBean proxy classes contain quite a lot of information, some of which is vital for the proper operation of the JSP view document.

Frequently, one caches user preference data or configuration parameters in a JavaBean proxy class for quicker access; when binding a JavaBean proxy instance to the user `HttpSession`, all that data may be regarded as permanent during the life of the `HttpSession`.

Having examined the last component of the second refactoring step, all Java code of the system is developed. Before being able to deploy the components into the Web and EJB containers, we must create the required deployment descriptor settings.

Step 6—Configuring the WebPage Search System

When creating the deployment descriptors for the image subsystem, we have already provided all the required XML documents. Of course, we still need to provide the additional settings that are required for the new or updated EJB components, but these settings may simply be added to the existing deployment descriptors, defined earlier in this chapter in "Step 4—Configuring the Image Subsystem".

As a reminder, the full system requires five deployment descriptors, four of which are used by the `WebPage` search system. Furthermore, consider the following points:

- The Web container is described by the standard J2EE `web.xml` and the application server-specific `weblogic.xml` deployment descriptor.
- The EJB container is described by the standard J2EE `ejb-jar.xml` and the application server-specific `weblogic-ejb-jar.xml` deployment descriptor.

The Web application of the `WebPage` search system has been boosted with the client-side types of the new EJB components (`LegacyFacade` and `LegacyFacadeProxy`), as shown in Figure 11-32. Because the JSP documents simply access the `LegacyFacade` JavaBean proxy in addition to the `ImageProxy` (from the image subsystem), the only new descriptor settings in the `web.xml` describe the settings of the new `LegacyFacadeProxy` and `LegacyFacade` components.

Examine the `web.xml` deployment descriptor of the refactored Web application in Listing 11-20. The only new entry altering the deployment descriptor file since it was created in the image subsystem development appears in bold text.

Listing 11-20. The `web.xml` *deployment descriptor of the refactored Web application*

```
<?xml version="1.0" ?>
<!DOCTYPE web-app PUBLIC
   "-//Sun Microsystems, Inc.//DTD Web Application 1.2//EN"
   "http://java.sun.com/j2ee/dtds/web-app_2_2.dtd">
<web-app>
      <display-name>TheRefactor2WebApp</display-name>
      <description>Web database refactored in step 2</description>
```

Name	Size	Path
errorUploadingImage.jsp	1 202	WebPageSearch\
index.html	1 144	WebPageSearch\
index.jsp	1 302	WebPageSearch\
SearchAndResultForm.jsp	3 058	WebPageSearch\
selectFileForUpload.jsp	1 251	WebPageSearch\
silly.jpg	2 987	WebPageSearch\
testImage.jsp	179	WebPageSearch\
uploadOK.jsp	2 299	WebPageSearch\
welcome.jsp	156	WebPageSearch\
web.xml	2 220	WebPageSearch\WEB-INF\
weblogic.xml	757	WebPageSearch\WEB-INF\
Image.class	473	WebPageSearch\WEB-INF\classes\se\jguru\webdb\legacyintegration\
ImageHome.class	662	WebPageSearch\WEB-INF\classes\se\jguru\webdb\legacyintegration\
WebPage.class	457	WebPageSearch\WEB-INF\classes\se\jguru\webdb\legacyintegration\
WebPageHome.class	643	WebPageSearch\WEB-INF\classes\se\jguru\webdb\legacyintegration\
LegacyFacade.class	268	WebPageSearch\WEB-INF\classes\se\jguru\webdb\proxy\
LegacyFacadeHome.class	302	WebPageSearch\WEB-INF\classes\se\jguru\webdb\proxy\
LegacyFacadeProxy.class	4 509	WebPageSearch\WEB-INF\classes\se\jguru\webdb\proxy\
Populateable.class	220	WebPageSearch\WEB-INF\classes\se\jguru\webdb\proxy\
PopulationException.class	394	WebPageSearch\WEB-INF\classes\se\jguru\webdb\proxy\
DocumentDownloader.class	2 068	WebPageSearch\WEB-INF\classes\se\jguru\webdb\proxy\imagehandlers\
DocumentHolder.class	839	WebPageSearch\WEB-INF\classes\se\jguru\webdb\proxy\imagehandlers\
DocumentUploader.class	9 355	WebPageSearch\WEB-INF\classes\se\jguru\webdb\proxy\imagehandlers\
ImageProxy.class	9 872	WebPageSearch\WEB-INF\classes\se\jguru\webdb\proxy\imagehandlers\
ImageMetadataValueObject.cl...	1 064	WebPageSearch\WEB-INF\classes\se\jguru\webdb\proxy\valueobjects\
WebPageValueObject.class	1 306	WebPageSearch\WEB-INF\classes\se\jguru\webdb\proxy\valueobjects\
CommonUtils.class	2 024	WebPageSearch\WEB-INF\classes\se\jguru\webdb\utils\

Figure 11-32. Structure of the `WebPageSearch` *application. Note the package structure, in which all Entity EJB components are placed in the* `legacyintegration` *package, and the proxy classes connecting the JSP view documents to the business objects are placed in (or in a subdirectory to) the proxy directory.*

```
<servlet>
    <servlet-name>uploaderServlet</servlet-name>
    <servlet-class>
        se.jguru.webdb.proxy.imagehandlers.DocumentUploader
    </servlet-class>

    <init-param>
        <param-name>ERROR_PAGE</param-name>
        <param-value>/errorUploadingImage.jsp</param-value>
    </init-param>

    <init-param>
        <param-name>ALL_OK_PAGE</param-name>
        <param-value>/uploadOK.jsp</param-value>
    </init-param>
</servlet>
```

```
<servlet>
    <servlet-name>imageDownloaderServlet</servlet-name>
    <servlet-class>
       se.jguru.webdb.proxy.imagehandlers.DocumentDownloader
    </servlet-class>
</servlet>

<servlet-mapping>
    <servlet-name>uploaderServlet</servlet-name>
    <url-pattern>uploadImage</url-pattern>
</servlet-mapping>

<servlet-mapping>
    <servlet-name>imageDownloaderServlet</servlet-name>
    <url-pattern>showImage</url-pattern>
</servlet-mapping>

<welcome-file-list>
    <welcome-file>index.jsp</welcome-file>
</welcome-file-list>

<resource-ref>
    <res-ref-name>LegacyDataSource</res-ref-name>
    <res-type>javax.sql.DataSource</res-type>
    <res-auth>Container</res-auth>
</resource-ref>

<login-config>
    <auth-method>BASIC</auth-method>
</login-config>

<env-entry>
    <env-entry-name>verboseMode</env-entry-name>
    <env-entry-value>true</env-entry-value>
    <env-entry-type>java.lang.Boolean</env-entry-type>
</env-entry>

<ejb-ref>
    <description>EJB reference to the LegacyFacade</description>
    <ejb-ref-name>LegacyFacade</ejb-ref-name>
    <ejb-ref-type>Session</ejb-ref-type>
    <home>se.jguru.webdb.proxy.LegacyFacadeHome</home>
    <remote>se.jguru.webdb.proxy.LegacyFacade</remote>
</ejb-ref>
```

```
    <ejb-ref>
        <description>EJB reference to the Image</description>
        <ejb-ref-name>Image</ejb-ref-name>
        <ejb-ref-type>Entity</ejb-ref-type>
        <home>se.jguru.webdb.legacyintegration.ImageHome</home>
        <remote>se.jguru.webdb.legacyintegration.Image</remote>
    </ejb-ref>
</web-app>
```

In a similar manner, the custom deployment descriptor `weblogic.xml` has had only one alteration, which is rendered in bold text in Listing 11-21.

Listing 11-21. The `weblogic.xml` *deployment descriptor*

```
<!DOCTYPE weblogic-web-app PUBLIC
  "-//BEA Systems, Inc.//DTD Web Application 6.0//EN"
  "http://www.bea.com/servers/wls600/dtd/weblogic-web-jar.dtd">
<weblogic-web-app>
    <reference-descriptor>
        <resource-description>
            <res-ref-name>LegacyDataSource</res-ref-name>
            <jndi-name>
              se/jguru/webdb/legacyintegration/LegacyDataSource
            </jndi-name>
        </resource-description>
        <ejb-reference-description>
            <ejb-ref-name>LegacyFacade</ejb-ref-name>
            <jndi-name>se/jguru/webdb/proxy/LegacyFacade</jndi-name>
        </ejb-reference-description>
        <ejb-reference-description>
            <ejb-ref-name>Image</ejb-ref-name>
            <jndi-name>se/jguru/webdb/legacyintegration/Image</jndi-name>
        </ejb-reference-description>
    </reference-descriptor>
</weblogic-web-app>
```

Moving your focus to the `refactor2` EJB archive, you see that it has been augmented to accommodate the two server-side EJB components `WebPage` (BMP Entity EJB) and `LegacyFacade` (statcless session EJB), in addition to the Image EJB component already deployed. Figure 11-33 shows the content of the JAR file, in which we only need to add deployment settings to the standard `ejb-jar.xml` and custom `weblogic-ejb-jar.xml` files.

The contents of the `ejb-jar.xml` file are shown in Listing 11-22.

Name	Size	Path
ejb-jar.xml	4 720	refactor2\META-INF\
Manifest.mf	68	refactor2\META-INF\
weblogic-ejb-jar.xml	2 441	refactor2\META-INF\
weblogic-imageBean-cmp.xml	900	refactor2\META-INF\
Image.class	473	refactor2\se\jguru\webdb\legacyintegration\
ImageBean.class	3 989	refactor2\se\jguru\webdb\legacyintegration\
ImageHome.class	662	refactor2\se\jguru\webdb\legacyintegration\
WebPage.class	457	refactor2\se\jguru\webdb\legacyintegration\
WebPageBean.class	10 003	refactor2\se\jguru\webdb\legacyintegration\
WebPageHome.class	643	refactor2\se\jguru\webdb\legacyintegration\
LegacyFacade.class	268	refactor2\se\jguru\webdb\proxy\
LegacyFacadeBean.class	6 083	refactor2\se\jguru\webdb\proxy\
LegacyFacadeHome.class	302	refactor2\se\jguru\webdb\proxy\
Populateable.class	220	refactor2\se\jguru\webdb\proxy\
PopulationException.class	394	refactor2\se\jguru\webdb\proxy\
ImageMetadataValueObject.cl...	1 064	refactor2\se\jguru\webdb\proxy\valueobjects\
WebPageValueObject.class	1 306	refactor2\se\jguru\webdb\proxy\valueobjects\
CommonUtils.class	2 024	refactor2\se\jguru\webdb\utils\
EJBBeanRoot.class	1 107	refactor2\se\jguru\webdb\utils\

Figure 11-33. Contents of the `refactor2.jar` *archive in which all objects being deployed into the EJB container reside*

Listing 11-22. The `ejb-jar.xml` *file*

```
<?xml version="1.0"?>

<!DOCTYPE ejb-jar PUBLIC
   '-//Sun Microsystems, Inc.//DTD Enterprise JavaBeans 2.0//EN'
   'http://java.sun.com/dtd/ejb-jar_2_0.dtd'>

<ejb-jar>
     <enterprise-beans>
          <session>
               <description>
                  This is the Session EJB Facade which hides all data
                  mining from the Legacy Tier.
               </description>
               <ejb-name>LegacyFacadeBean</ejb-name>
               <home>se.jguru.webdb.proxy.LegacyFacadeHome</home>
               <remote>se.jguru.webdb.proxy.LegacyFacade</remote>
               <ejb-class>se.jguru.webdb.proxy.LegacyFacadeBean</ejb-class>
               <session-type>Stateless</session-type>
               <transaction-type>Container</transaction-type>
```

```
        <env-entry>
            <description>Log verbosity level toggle flag</description>
            <env-entry-name>verboseMode</env-entry-name>
            <env-entry-type>java.lang.Boolean</env-entry-type>
            <env-entry-value>true</env-entry-value>
        </env-entry>

        <ejb-ref>
            <ejb-ref-name>WebPageHome</ejb-ref-name>
            <ejb-ref-type>Entity</ejb-ref-type>
            <home>se.jguru.webdb.legacyintegration.WebPageHome</home>
            <remote>se.jguru.webdb.legacyintegration.WebPage</remote>
        </ejb-ref>
        <ejb-ref>
            <ejb-ref-name>ImageHome</ejb-ref-name>
            <ejb-ref-type>Entity</ejb-ref-type>
            <home>se.jguru.webdb.legacyintegration.ImageHome</home>
            <remote>se.jguru.webdb.legacyintegration.Image</remote>
        </ejb-ref>

        <resource-ref>
            <description>
               This is the DataSource which connects to the
               relational database where the actual data is stored.
            </description>
            <res-ref-name>localDataSource</res-ref-name>
            <res-type>javax.sql.DataSource</res-type>
            <res-auth>Container</res-auth>
        </resource-ref>
    </session>
    <entity>
        <ejb-name>ImageBean</ejb-name>
        <home>se.jguru.webdb.legacyintegration.ImageHome</home>
        <remote>se.jguru.webdb.legacyintegration.Image</remote>
        <ejb-class>se.jguru.webdb.legacyintegration.ImageBean</ejb-class>
        <persistence-type>Container</persistence-type>
        <prim-key-class>java.lang.Integer</prim-key-class>
        <reentrant>False</reentrant>
        <cmp-version>2.x</cmp-version>
        <abstract-schema-name>ImageBean</abstract-schema-name>
```

```
        <cmp-field>
            <field-name>data</field-name>
        </cmp-field>
        <cmp-field>
            <field-name>mimeType</field-name>
        </cmp-field>
        <cmp-field>
            <field-name>id</field-name>
        </cmp-field>
        <cmp-field>
            <field-name>fileName</field-name>
        </cmp-field>

        <primkey-field>id</primkey-field>

        <env-entry>
            <description>Log verbosity level toggle flag</description>
            <env-entry-name>verboseMode</env-entry-name>
            <env-entry-type>java.lang.Boolean</env-entry-type>
            <env-entry-value>true</env-entry-value>
        </env-entry>


        <query>
            <query-method>
                <method-name>findByMimeType</method-name>
                <method-params>
                    <method-param>java.lang.String</method-param>
                </method-params>
            </query-method>
            <ejb-ql>
            SELECT OBJECT(i) FROM Images i WHERE i.mimeType like '?1%'
            </ejb-ql>
        </query>
    </entity>
    <entity>
        <ejb-name>WebPageBean</ejb-name>
        <home>se.jguru.webdb.legacyintegration.WebPageHome</home>
        <remote>se.jguru.webdb.legacyintegration.WebPage</remote>
        <ejb-class>se.jguru.webdb.legacyintegration.WebPageBean</ejb-class>
        <persistence-type>Bean</persistence-type>
        <prim-key-class>java.lang.Integer</prim-key-class>
        <reentrant>False</reentrant>
```

```
        <env-entry>
            <description>Log verbosity level toggle flag</description>
            <env-entry-name>verboseMode</env-entry-name>
            <env-entry-type>java.lang.Boolean</env-entry-type>
            <env-entry-value>true</env-entry-value>
        </env-entry>

        <resource-ref>
            <description>
            This is the DataSource which connects to the
            relational database where the actual data is stored.
            </description>
            <res-ref-name>
              se/jguru/webdb/legacyintegration/DataSource
            </res-ref-name>
            <res-type>javax.sql.DataSource</res-type>
            <res-auth>Container</res-auth>
         </resource-ref>

    </entity>
</enterprise-beans>

<assembly-descriptor>
    <container-transaction>
        <method>
            <ejb-name>LegacyFacadeBean</ejb-name>
            <method-name>*</method-name>
        </method>
        <trans-attribute>Required</trans-attribute>
    </container-transaction>

    <container-transaction>
        <method>
            <ejb-name>ImageBean</ejb-name>
            <method-name>*</method-name>
        </method>
        <trans-attribute>Required</trans-attribute>
    </container-transaction>
```

```
        <container-transaction>
            <method>
                <ejb-name>WebPageBean</ejb-name>
                <method-name>*</method-name>
            </method>
            <trans-attribute>Required</trans-attribute>
        </container-transaction>

    </assembly-descriptor>

</ejb-jar>
```

The most interesting part of the `ejb-jar.xml` deployment descriptor document is the settings of the `<session>...</session>` container element that defines the `LegacyFacadeBean`. Because the `LegacyFacadeBean` must access the Home interfaces of both the `WebPage` EJB component and the Image EJB component, two EJB references are bound in the local context environment of the `LegacyFacadeBean`. Each of these two entries have the following form:

```
<ejb-ref>
    <ejb-ref-name>WebPageHome</ejb-ref-name>
    <ejb-ref-type>Entity</ejb-ref-type>
    <home>se.jguru.webdb.legacyintegration.WebPageHome</home>
    <remote>se.jguru.webdb.legacyintegration.WebPage</remote>
</ejb-ref>
```

This straightforward definition simply defines a local context environment entry with the JNDI name `WebPageHome`, which refers to an entity bean whose Home and Remote interfaces have the types provided.

The corresponding setting in the application server-specific deployment settings file defines a relation between the local context JNDI name and the actual JNDI name of the server-side component. Can you find the corresponding name in the main JNDI registry from the listing of the `weblogic-ejb-jar.xml` shown in Listing 11-23?

Listing 11-23. The `weblogic-ejb-jar.xml` *deployment descriptor*

```
<?xml version="1.0"?>

<!DOCTYPE weblogic-ejb-jar PUBLIC
  '-//BEA Systems, Inc.//DTD WebLogic 6.0.0 EJB//EN'
  'http://www.bea.com/servers/wls600/dtd/weblogic-ejb-jar.dtd'>
```

```
<weblogic-ejb-jar>
     <weblogic-enterprise-bean>
          <ejb-name>LegacyFacadeBean</ejb-name>
          <stateful-session-descriptor>
               <stateful-session-cache>
                    <max-beans-in-cache>10</max-beans-in-cache>
               </stateful-session-cache>
          </stateful-session-descriptor>
          <reference-descriptor>
               <resource-description>
                    <res-ref-name>localDataSource</res-ref-name>
                    <jndi-name>
                       se/jguru/webdb/legacyintegration/LegacyDataSource
                    </jndi-name>
               </resource-description>
               <ejb-reference-description>
                    <ejb-ref-name>WebPageHome</ejb-ref-name>
                   <jndi-name>se/jguru/webdb/legacyintegration/WebPage</jndi-name>
               </ejb-reference-description>
               <ejb-reference-description>
                    <ejb-ref-name>ImageHome</ejb-ref-name>
                    <jndi-name>se/jguru/webdb/legacyintegration/Image</jndi-name>
               </ejb-reference-description>
          </reference-descriptor>
          <jndi-name>se/jguru/webdb/proxy/LegacyFacade</jndi-name>
     </weblogic-enterprise-bean>

     <weblogic-enterprise-bean>
          <ejb-name>ImageBean</ejb-name>
          <entity-descriptor>
               <entity-cache>
                    <max-beans-in-cache>1000</max-beans-in-cache>
               </entity-cache>

               <persistence>
                    <persistence-type>
                         <type-identifier>WebLogic_CMP_RDBMS</type-identifier>
                         <type-version>6.0</type-version>
                         <type-storage>
                            META-INF/weblogic-imageBean-cmp.xml
                         </type-storage>
                    </persistence-type>
```

```
                <persistence-use>
                    <type-identifier>WebLogic_CMP_RDBMS</type-identifier>
                    <type-version>6.0</type-version>
                </persistence-use>
            </persistence>
        </entity-descriptor>

        <jndi-name>se/jguru/webdb/legacyintegration/Image</jndi-name>
    </weblogic-enterprise-bean>

    <weblogic-enterprise-bean>
        <ejb-name>WebPageBean</ejb-name>

        <entity-descriptor>
            <entity-cache>
                <max-beans-in-cache>100</max-beans-in-cache>
            </entity-cache>
        </entity-descriptor>

        <reference-descriptor>
            <resource-description>
                <res-ref-name>
                   se/jguru/webdb/legacyintegration/DataSource
                </res-ref-name>
                <jndi-name>
                   se/jguru/webdb/legacyintegration/LegacyDataSource
                </jndi-name>
            </resource-description>
        </reference-descriptor>
        <jndi-name>se/jguru/webdb/legacyintegration/WebPage</jndi-name>
  </weblogic-enterprise-bean>
</weblogic-ejb-jar>
```

The deployment descriptor expo concludes the walkthrough of the rather large Web application refactoring example. Although large, this example shows considerations regarding the development and design of an almost real J2EE application using Web and EJB container components and EJBs of all kinds. The components may be small, but they are treated in a quite realistic way.

Reflections on the Second Refactoring Step

This is a major refactoring step towards a mainstream J2EE application. However, some details have been left as (large but rewarding) exercises for the reader:

- The current image subsystem does not provide a view that permits editing images using the MODIFY operation of the Image EJB component. Provide such an application.

- The current application supports only one type of DB search: finding all Web pages (and related images) for a search string matching text in the `WebPage` data block. Implement other types of DB queries, such as finding all images with a certain MIME type and list their Web pages.

- The data in the database is currently simply hard-coded and without any form of connection to real HTML documents. Create the "grand database populator" class that downloads actual Web page data, parses it, and inserts the Web page data into the database. Of course, any images referenced by a particular Web page must be downloaded and inserted into the database at the same time. (Remember to alter the sources of all images in the HTML document to refer to the newly uploaded images in the database instead of the net URL!)

- Currently, only images have been uploaded to the database using the image subsystem. You may—without altering the system much—create applications that store and retrieve other types of binary document, such as audio files or word processor documents. In a primitive version of this diversified binary document hosting, all binary documents could be treated as images with a different MIME type.

Part V
Appendix

APPENDIX A

The Java 2 Enterprise Edition Reference Implementation Server

THE JAVA 2 ENTERPRISE EDITION (J2EE) reference implementation, which may be downloaded along with the J2EE documentation and APIs from JavaSoft's Web site (`http://java.sun.com/j2ee/download.html`), is a small test environment for your J2EE components. Rather smooth in its graphical user interface–driven administration operations, the J2EE reference implementation server is ideal for testing your J2EE application components, such as servlets, JavaServer Pages (JSP) documents, and Enterprise JavaBean (EJB) components. The J2EE download bundle consists of two files; the smaller file contains the binary installer of the J2EE reference implementation, and the larger contains the J2EE reference documentation. The files are roughly 18.5MB, so be sure *not* to download the J2EE reference implementation over a 28.8 modem (unless, of course, you feel extraordinarily patient). The only dependency of the J2EE is an installed copy of the Java 2 Standard Edition (J2SE); if you have already installed an Integrated Development Environment (IDE) on your computer, you need not install a new copy of the J2SE distribution from JavaSoft.

The J2EE reference implementation server contains five main services:

- Enterprise JavaBean server and container
- HTTP/Web server and container
- HTTPS (HTTP over SSL) Web server and container
- JNDI (COS naming service)
- Authentication service

After installing the J2EE server and documentation, its root structure looks like Figure A-1. Note that a version of the all-Java relational database Cloudscape is deployed as part of the J2EE server.

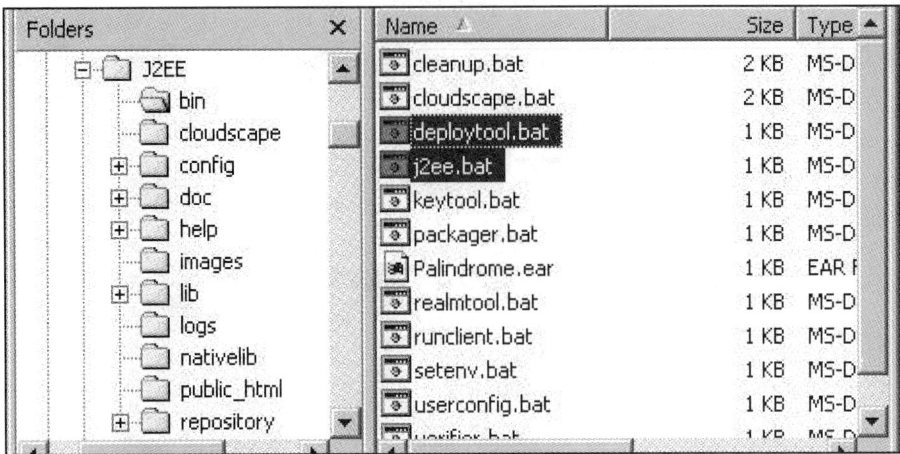

Figure A-1. The J2EE installation root directory contents. The two batch files j2ee.bat *and* deploytool.bat *(or equivalent shell scripts for Unix or other operating systems) are used to launch the J2EE reference implementation server and its component deployment tool, respectively.*

When you develop J2EE applications, you need to include the J2EE API in the classpath of your IDE—or, at least, your compiler. As may be understood from the J2EE installation structure, the required libraries are located in the <J2EE_HOME>/lib directory, as shown in Figure A-2. Usually, you need only add the j2ee.jar library archive to the CLASSPATH environment variable to please your compiler.

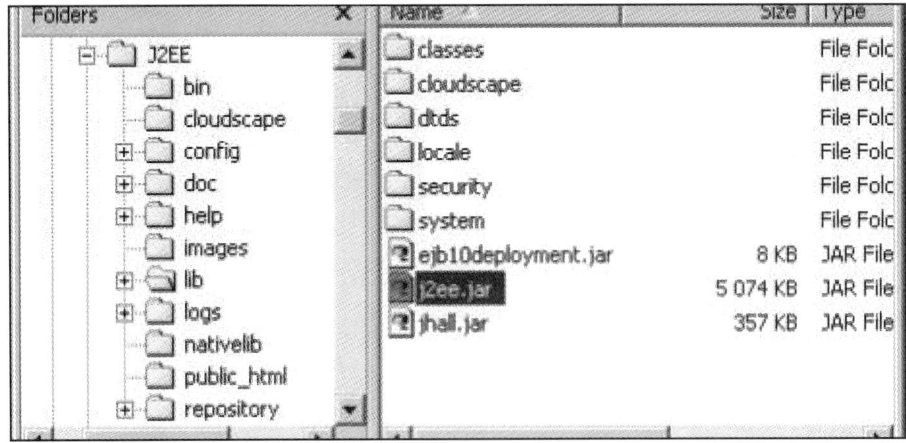

Figure A-2. The content of the root library directory of the J2EE installation. Note that the selected archive, j2ee.jar, *contains all classes required to develop J2EE applications. The* ejb10deployment.jar *archive should only be used if you are deploying EJB components for version 1.0 of the EJB specification (in other words, hopefully never!).*

The Unbearable Lightness of Rebooting...

When developing server-side systems, one is frequently required to reboot the J2EE server (such as after recompiling and redeploying an EJB J2EE component). It is therefore recommended that you slightly modify the startup scripts of the server to be able to start it using a mouse click. For Windows users, I recommend three alterations to the startup scripts:

1. Set the `JAVA_HOME` and `J2EE_HOME` variables in the `setenv.bat` and comment out the call to the `userconfig.bat`. If you have an exceptional amount of settings special to the J2EE server, you may want to place them all in the `userconfig.bat` file instead. Although far from impossible, the likelihood that you will actually require such drastic setup preparations is low.
2. Call the `setenv.bat` file from the top of the `j2ee.bat` start script. Also, you need to alter the actual launch statement, as it contains a minor bug from the installation.
3. Call the `setenv.bat` file from the top of the `deploytool.bat` start script.

Starting out with the first file, `setenv.bat`, it is recommended that you alter its first statements as follows (the bold text sets the paths to the JDK and J2EE root directory):

```
@rem
@rem Set JAVA_HOME and J2EE_HOME before running this script.
rem --> Using HARD-CODED paths to the preferred JDK <--
@rem

set JAVA_HOME=D:\Java\Jdk1.3
set J2EE_HOME=D:\Java\J2EE

@rem first include user-specified definitions.
rem --> Not using personalized userconfig.bat script <--
@rem call %J2EE_HOME%\bin\userconfig.bat
```

The remaining statements, setting environment properties pertaining to directories known to the J2EE server, may remain unaltered. The highlighted path statements in the code sets the `JAVA_HOME` and `J2EE_HOME` variables for the J2EE server.

The `j2ee.bat` script file launches the J2EE reference implementation server by setting the required paths and eventually launching the Java class. Most IDEs have facilities to programmatically launch arbitrary Java programs, such as the J2EE reference server class. You may want to explore your IDE to have it run the J2EE server directly. Should you want to launch the J2EE server from the command-line prompt, I recommend modifying the `j2ee.bat` script as illustrated in the following code. The changes compared to the original `j2ee.bat` script file appear in bold text to simplify locating them:

```
@echo off
rem
rem Set JAVA_HOME and J2EE_HOME before running this script.
rem
rem set JAVA_HOME to the path where you have Java 2 (JDK1.2) installed.
rem
rem set J2EE_HOME to the path where you have installed this package (EJB server).
rem
call setenv.bat

... script is then unmodified down to the actual launch command ...

rem @echo on
%JAVACMD% -Djava.security.policy=%J2EE_HOME%\lib\security\server.policy
              -Dcom.sun.enterprise.home=%J2EE_HOME% -classpath "%CPATH%"
              com.sun.enterprise.server.J2EEServer %1 %2

:END
```

The subtle change in the launch command is that the extra = sign between the –`Djava.security.policy` and its proper setting has been deleted.

Configuring the Server

The J2EE server uses the five following main configuration files, which are placed in the `<J2EE_HOME>/config` directory, to store its configuration settings:

- *auth.properties,* which contains settings for authorization in the J2EE reference implementation server. Essentially, this means security realm definitions, as well as principal and role definitions for the server.

- *default.properties,* which contains Java Database Connectivity (JDBC) driver and `DataSource` configurations for databases used by the J2EE reference implementation server. In the `default.properties` file, you may also find settings that affect all parts of the J2EE server, such as log root directory.

- *ejb.properties,* which contains settings for the EJB container and its controller classes.

- *orb.properties*, which contains configuration settings for the CORBA-compliant Object Request Broker (ORB) running in the J2EE reference implementation server.

- *web.properties*, which contains configuration settings for the Web container and HTTP server integrated into the J2EE reference implementation server.

The five configuration files are illustrated in Figure A-3. The various properties files are sensibly named, so you probably realize what types of settings reside in each file simply by examining their names. To avoid any confusion, I'll elaborate a little on the settings for the J2EE server: There are at least two settings you are likely to want to change before launching for the first time, namely the ports of the Web server and the secure Web server (which may be set to 80 and 443 for the sake of convenience).

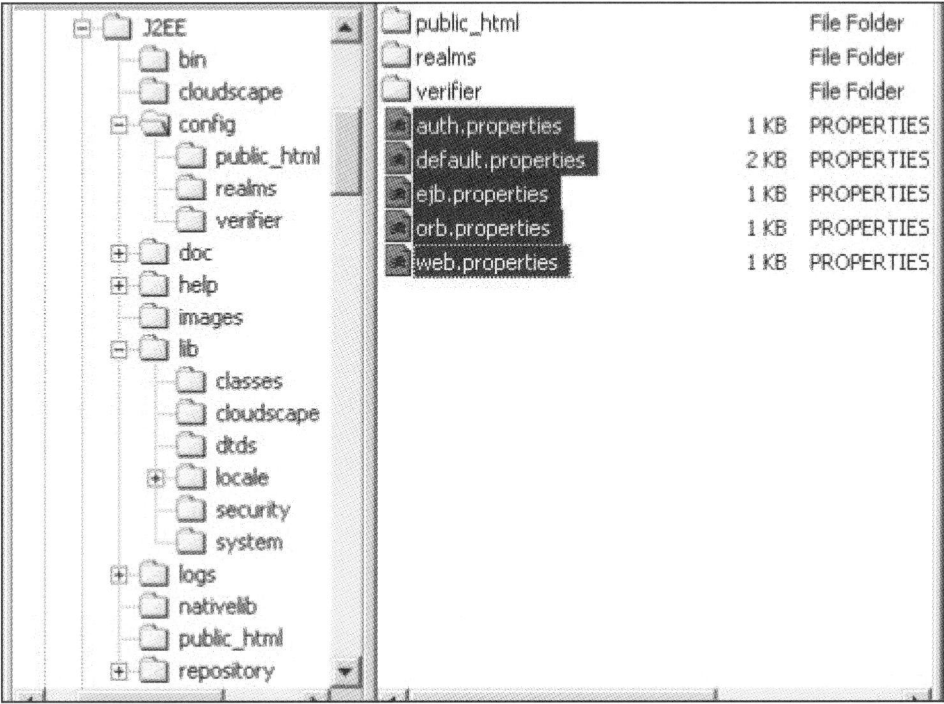

Figure A-3. The primary configuration files of the J2EE reference implementation server. The names of the files reflect the properties contained within each file.

> **TIP** *Before launching the J2EE server for the first time, I recommend altering the default ports for the Web service (in other words, the HTTP server). Change them to match the standard ports of a normal Web server; that way, you won't have to keep entering the port number (8000 by default) of your Web service in your Web browser whenever you want a response from the J2EE Web service.*

Start the overview of the configuration files by taking a look at the `web.properties` file. The files are discussed in order of importance.

The web.properties File

The content of the default `web.properties` file is as follows:

```
http.port=8000
documentroot=public_html/
https.port=7000
keystore.password=changeit
access.log=access.log
error.log=error.log
enable.invoker=false
```

The JavaSoft engineers chose sensible names for all properties in the `web.properties` file, so it is quite simple to understand the significance of each key=value pair.

So how should you modify the default configuration settings? Simple: Change the `http.port` value to the default value for a Web server (80) and the `https.port` similarly to its default value (443). In all, Table A-1 lists the properties of the `web.properties` configuration file.

Table A-1. The Settings of the `web.properties` *File*

PROPERTY KEY	DEFAULT VALUE	DESCRIPTION
`http.port`	8000	Port setting of the Web container listener. Alter this to 80 to avoid typing port numbers for the URLs of your Web browser.
`https.port`	7000	Port setting of the secure Web container listener. Alter this to 443 to avoid typing port numbers for the URLs of your Web browser.
`document_root`	public_html/	Root directory of the Web application (Web site) served from the J2EE application server. The root directory is found in the J2EE install directory (see Figure A-3).

Table A-1. The Settings of the `web.properties` *File (Continued)*

PROPERTY KEY	DEFAULT VALUE	DESCRIPTION
access.log	access.log	Filename of the log file tracing all calls to the Web container of the J2EE server. Understandably, this file grows quickly when the Web container responds to multiple Web access calls. The access.log file is found in the <J2EE_HOME>/<LOG_ROOT>/<HOSTNAME>/web/ directory (the LOG_ROOT directory is set in the default.properties file). The following small snippet illustrates two incoming calls: Request for /index.html on at Wed May 16 22:59:30 GMT+02:00 2001. org.apache.tomcat.core.HttpServletResponseFacade@5ed659 Request for / on at Wed May 16 22:59:30 GMT+02:00 2001. org.apache.tomcat.core.HttpServletResponseFacade@5ed659
error.log	error.log	Filename of the error log file containing all errors generated in the Web container. The error.log file is found in the <J2EE_HOME>/<LOG_ROOT>/<HOSTNAME>/ejb/j2ee directory. All other aspects of the error.log file and setting are similar to those of the access.log file and setting above. If an error message is not found in the error log file specified by the error.log setting, you may well find it in the System.err log, which is specified in the default.properties file.
enable.invoker	false	Enables (if true) or disables (if false) the invoker servlet, which permits calling a servlet using its classname (possibly without mapping it in the web.xml configuration file).
keystore.password	changeit	Password required to alter the <user.home>/.keystore file, which contains certificates used to create an SSL connection for the HTTPS server. <user.home> is the directory returned by the call System.getProperty("user.home");.

After modifying the port settings, the `web.properties` file is ready for normal usage. The resulting configuration file content is as follows:

```
http.port=80
documentroot=public_html/
https.port=443
keystore.password=changeit
access.log=access.log
error.log=error.log
enable.invoker=false
```

Note that you cannot have two servers listening to the same port at any time. The underlying operating system will complain if you try to launch the J2EE server on port 80 if there is another running Web server bound to the default port.

The orb.properties File

The configuration settings for the ORB of the J2EE server are found in the `orb.properties` file. You may wonder what an ORB actually does in a J2EE application server. The answer is that the JNDI naming service of the J2EE server is a CORBA (COS) naming service; whenever you work with the `Context` of a J2EE service, the settings in the `orb.properties` file affect you.

Unlike the `web.properties` file, there is no immediate need to alter the settings in the `orb.properties` file, unless you want to run several naming services on your server node. You will therefore simply take a look at the settings in the `orb.properties` file. Start with its full content:

```
port=1050
host=localhost
serverport=1049
```

Thankfully, there are only three settings in the `orb.properties` file in total, and the settings control the function of the built-in JNDI naming service (see Table A-2).

Table A-2. The `orb.properties` *Settings*

PROPERTY KEY	DEFAULT VALUE	DESCRIPTION
`Port`	`1050`	Port used when resolving JNDI lookups. Specifically, the ORB that runs the JNDI service uses this port. Don't alter this setting unless you are really sure of what you do, or the JNDI will simply stop working.
`Serverport`	`1049`	Serversocket port number of the JNDI server.
`Host`	`localhost`	Host name of the host where the context resides.

The ejb.properties File

The configuration settings for the EJB container are found in the `ejb.properties` file. Although it may be interesting to view the settings, they are rarely in need of alteration for proper operation. The default content of the `ejb.properties` file is as follows:

```
audit.log.file=audit.log
repository.directory=repository
applications.directory=applications
http.port=9191
```

Table A-3 explains the settings found in the `ejb.properties` file.

Table A-3. The Configuration Settings of the `ejb.properties` *File*

PROPERTY KEY	DEFAULT VALUE	DESCRIPTION
repository.directory	repository	Directory name of the EJB repository directory, which contains compiled and precompiled classes and files, for EJB components as well as JSP and servlet components. The repository directory is found in the <J2EE_HOME> directory.
applications.directory	Applications	Name of the subdirectory of the repository where the internal representations of the J2EE applications are stored.
http.port	9191	Port number of the EJB server to download stub classes. This is, for example, the port used by an EJB Home object when it needs to retrieve its corresponding EJB Remote instance.
audit.log.file	audit.log	The name of the audit log file. Note that auditing will not be started unless the *audit* setting in the `auth.properties` file is set to true.

Thankfully, you need not alter any of the settings in the `ejb.properties` configuration file to provide a fully functioning EJB service to your development team.

The default.properties File

The settings in the `default.properties` file are global in the sense that they affect services that may be accessed from multiple containers in the J2EE server. DataSources, for instance, may be used from within the Web container as well as the EJB container. The `default.properties` file therefore contains three main types of information:

- DataSource and XADataSource definitions that consists of a JDBC driver definition, a database connection specification using the JDBC driver, and binding a connection pool of the provided connection specification in the JNDI registry of the application server.

- Resource constraint definitions for conservation of memory and idle client connections, providing definitions that confine the J2EE server process to safe limits (in other words, restricts the amount of resources that may be consumed by the J2EE process).

- Logging definitions providing the names of the main log directory as well as the filenames for the individual logs.

Start the walkthrough of the settings in the `default.properties` file by examining the settings for JDBC drivers and install a new simple DataSource to a new database. Before modifying the configuration file, examine its original content as set by the J2EE installer, as shown in Listing A-1.

Listing A-1. The `default.properties` *configuration file*

```
# JDBC Driver Examples:
# Oracle thin driver:  oracle.jdbc.driver.OracleDriver
# Merant driver:       intersolv.jdbc.sequelink.SequeLinkDriver
# Cloudscape driver:   COM.cloudscape.core.RmiJdbcDriver
#
jdbc.drivers=COM.cloudscape.core.RmiJdbcDriver

# JDBC URL Examples:
# Oracle thin driver:
#      jdbc:oracle:thin:@<host>:<port>:<sid>
# Cloudscape RMI driver:
#      jdbc:cloudscape:rmi:<database>;create=true
# Merant driver:
#      jdbc:sequelink://<host>:<port>/[SQLServer];Database=<database>
#
jdbc.datasources=jdbc/Cloudscape|jdbc:cloudscape:rmi:CloudscapeDB;create=true

passivation.threshold.memory=128000000
idle.resource.threshold=600
user.transaction.jndiname=java:comp/UserTransaction
log.directory=logs
log.output.file=output.log
log.error.file=error.log
log.event.file=event.log
```

```
distributed.transaction.recovery=false
transaction.timeout=0
sessionbean.timeout=0

#
# DataSource configuration for JDBC 2.0 XA drivers only
#
#jdbc20.datasources=jdbc/Merant|jdbc/XAMerant
#xadatasource.0.jndiname=jdbc/XAMerant
#xadatasource.0.classname=com.merant.sequelink.jdbcx.datasource.SequeLinkDataSource
#xadatasource.0.dbuser=<dba user>
#xadatasource.0.dbpassword=<dba password>
#xadatasource.0.prop.url=jdbc:sequelink://<host>:<port>/[Oracle]
#
```

Now start modifying the `default.properties` file to slightly alter the behavior of the J2EE reference implementation server. Your first task is to make data in a relational database available for your J2EE applications. How do you create a new DataSource from a database not yet used by the J2EE server? The process is simple, but involves the four following steps:

1. Copy the JAR file that contains the JDBC driver for your database to the `<J2EE_HOME>/lib/system` directory. By default, that directory has the AllPermission, granting it full access to privileged operations, such as loading a native library (which Type 2 JDBC drivers do).

2. Now, you must include the driver JAR containing the JDBC driver in the `CLASSPATH` environment variable. Although the inclusion may be done in several places, the recommendation from the makers of the J2EE reference implementation is to modify the `<J2EE_HOME>/bin/userconfig.bat` file; by including the classpath to the driver JAR in the `J2EE_CLASSPATH` variable, you also include it into the `CLASSPATH` of the running server. (You must, of course, uncomment the line where the `J2EE_CLASSPATH` variable is set in the `userconfig.bat` file).

3. Append the JDBC driver classname for your database to the `jdbc.drivers` property. Separate driver classes from one another with a colon.

4. Create a DataSource from the JDBC driver using the syntax *<DataSource>*|*<url>* (for example,
   `com/mycorporation/jdbc/HypersonicDbSource|➥`
   `jdbc:HypersonicSQL:hsql://localhost)`

Step 1: Copying the Archive

Now create a DataSource to a Hypersonic database to further illustrate the four preceding steps. The Hypersonic database is a small, open-source database completely written in Java; all its code—including the JDBC driver—is contained in an archive called `hsqldb.jar`. You copy the archive into the system library root directory, as illustrated in Figure A-4.

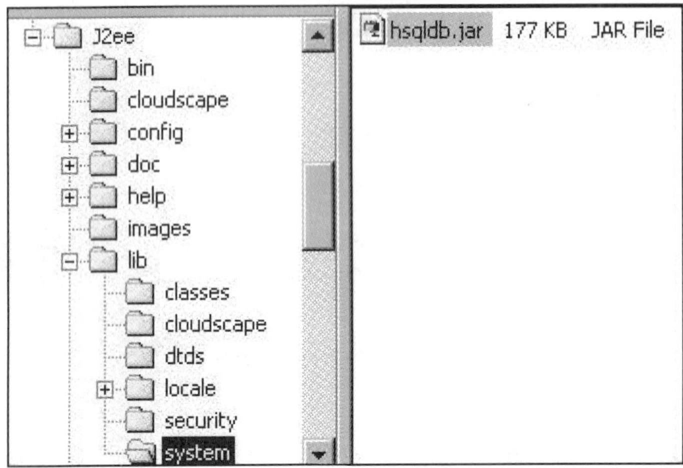

Figure A-4. The placement of the JDBC driver JAR in the J2EE deployment directories

Step 2: Including the Driver JAR

The `<J2EE_HOME>/bin/userconfig.bat` should be modified to include the `hsqldb.jar` file in the `J2EE_CLASSPATH` variable. The relevant parts of the `userconfig.bat` file are as follows:

```
rem J2EE_CLASSPATH is appended to the classpath referenced by the EJB server.
rem J2EE_CLASSPATH must include the location of the JDBC driver classes
rem (except for the Cloudscape driver shipped with this release).
rem Each directory is delimited by a semicolon.
rem
set J2EE_CLASSPATH=C:\Java\J2ee\lib\system\hsqldb.jar
```

Steps 3 and 4: Modifying the default.properties File

Next, modify to the `default.properties` file. After the modification, the two properties `jdbc.drivers` and `jdbc.datasources` are noted as follows:

```
jdbc.drivers=COM.cloudscape.core.RmiJdbcDriver:org.hsqldb.jdbcDriver
jdbc.datasources=jdbc/Cloudscape|jdbc:cloudscape:rmi:CloudscapeDB;create=true➥
      |jdbc/jguru/hyperDB|jdbc:HypersonicSQL:hsql://localhost
```

After performing these four simple steps, a new DataSource has been defined for the J2EE reference implementation application server, to be used as a resource by any deployed J2EE application. The rest of the configuration properties in the `default.properties` file are less complex than the ones involved in setting up a new DataSource. Table A-4 sums them up.

Table A-4. Configuration Properties of the `default.properties` *File*

PROPERTY KEY	DEFAULT VALUE	DESCRIPTION
`passivation.threshold.memory`	128000000	Although the J2EE server is mainly used for testing during the development phase of a project, you are wise to explore the resource conservation settings in the `default.properties` file. The `passivation.threshold.memory` setting controls the minimum memory footprint of the application server when resource passivation sets in. By default, no EJB passivation will take place until the J2EE reference implementation server process reaches 128MB of memory. If you want to test passivation of your EJB components, you are wise to lower the setting so that passivation will occur more often (If your J2EE application is smaller than the passivation.threshold.memory, no passivation will occur.)
`sessionbean.timeout`	0	The `sessionbean.timeout` property defines the default timeout for S-EJB sessions. If an EJB client is idle more than the given amount of seconds, the session times out (invalidates and sends all bound objects to garbage collection). By default, the session never times out (value 0).

Table A-4. Configuration Properties of the `default.properties` *File (Continued)*

PROPERTY KEY	DEFAULT VALUE	DESCRIPTION
`Idle.resource.threshold`	`600`	The maximum number of idle resources permitted before invoking passivation and/or garbage collection.
`log.directory`	`logs`	Name of the root directory where all J2EE server log files are found (`<J2EE_HOME>/logs` in the default case).
`log.output.file`	`output.log`	Name of the default output log file of the J2EE reference implementation server. The file is found in the `<J2EE_HOME>/<log.directory>/<hostname>/ejb/j2ee` directory.
`log.error.file`	`error.log`	Name of the default log file for the error stream of the J2EE reference implementation server. The file is found in the `<J2EE_HOME>/<log.directory>/<hostname>/ejb/j2ee` directory.
`log.event.file`	`event.log`	Name of the default log file for events received by the J2EE reference implementation server. The file is found in the `<J2EE_HOME>/<log.directory>/<hostname>/ejb/j2ee` directory.
`user.transaction.jndiname`	`java:comp/UserTransaction`	Default name of the `UserTransaction` factory, bound in the JNDI context of the J2EE server.
`transaction.timeout`	`0`	Timeout setting for EJB components using container-managed transactions. If the transaction has not completed within the time provided (seconds), the TransactionManager of the application server rolls back the transaction. Using the default setting of 0, transactions never time out.

Table A-4. Configuration Properties of the `default.properties` *File (Continued)*

PROPERTY KEY	DEFAULT VALUE	DESCRIPTION
distributed.transaction.recovery	false	Controls whether the J2EE server `TransactionManager` should try to recover a crashed distributed transaction from an XADataSource spanning multiple databases. If the setting is true, the transaction manager tries to recover any recoverable transactions upon startup.

Let's finish the configuration tour of the J2EE server with a look at the `auth.properties` file.

The auth.properties File

The settings in the `auth.properties` file control the authorization and security settings in the J2EE reference implementation server. The realmtool (found in the `<J2EE_HOME>/bin` directory) manipulates the settings of the `auth.properties` file and all dependent data storages. Although one can certainly use a text editor to alter the contents of the `auth.properties` file, I recommend using the realmtool to add users or groups to the authority structure of the J2EE reference implementation server. The advantage of using the realmtool is that all required modifications, including password hashing, are inserted into their proper files at the same time, preventing the J2EE server from entering illegal configuration states.

The default content of the `auth.properties` file is as follows:

```
realms=default,certificate
realm.default=config/realms/default.properties
realm.certificate=config/realms/certificate.properties
default.principal.name=guest
default.principal.password=guest123
anyone.role.name=ANYONE
audit=false
```

Although the configuration settings in the `auth.properties` file are relatively few, it contains all master security configuration settings. Some settings, such as the default principal and the corresponding password may simply be altered after your preferences using a text editor, but the `realms.*` properties should not be altered by hand. Instead, you should modify the realms settings by running realmtool, which is found in the `<J2EE_HOME>/bin` directory. That way, all realm dependencies required for proper operation of the J2EE reference implementation application server are preserved or properly updated. Table A-5 explains the configuration properties in the `auth.properties` file.

Table A-5. Configuration Properties in the `auth.properties` *File*

PROPERTY KEY	DEFAULT VALUE	DESCRIPTION
`Realms`	`default,certificate`	A listing of all known security realms. The purpose of a security realm is to contain access control lists, mapping users and groups to privileges on resources. An example of the job of a security realm is to restrict access to a JSP document to all users but the ones logged in as Administrator.
`realm.default`	`config/realms/default.properties`	Pinpoints the realm descriptor file for the default realm relative to the `<J2EE_HOME>` directory. The "realm descriptor file" contains a security realm implementation class and a directory definition to the user, group, and password files for a realm may be found. Those required files are *privileges* where the security groups are defined and *keyfile* where users are mapped to encrypted passwords and groups. Both the privileges and keyfile files reside in the `<J2EE_HOME>/<realm.default>/privileges directory`.
`realm.certificate`	`config/realms/certificate.properties`	Pinpoints the realm descriptor file for the certificate realm relative to the `<J2EE_HOME>` directory. The "realm descriptor file" contains a security realm implementation class, and a path to the realm definition files. These realm definition files contain all users, groups and passwords known to the security realm.

Table A-5. Configuration Properties in the `auth.properties` *File*

PROPERTY KEY	DEFAULT VALUE	DESCRIPTION
`default.principal.name`	`guest`	The principal of a user that has not yet authorized himself/herself to the J2EE server. Alter this if you need another default application server principal—it may, for instance, be a good idea to choose the default principal name after an unprivileged user in a backend system.
`default.principal.password`	`guest123`	The password for the default principal. Alter this if you want another standard principal password.
`anyone.role.name`	`ANYONE`	The role of a standard principal.

Having taken a look at the main configuration files of the J2EE reference implementation server, you may launch it to start deploying our J2EE application components. If you did configure the server scripts according to the recommendations in the `web.properties` section previously, you may start the J2EE reference implementation server by a simple double-click on its `j2ee.bat` icon (or, of course, launch normally from the command line).

Deploying J2EE Application Components

The tricky part of most J2EE application development projects is properly deploying the components (particularly Entity EJB components) into the application server. This is mainly an effect of the J2EE 1.2.1 specification because some rather important matters (such as a standardized way to handle EJB component persistence and clear responsibility boundaries between the application server and each container) were left out of the J2EE 1.1 specification.

These matters will be addressed in the J2EE 1.3 specification due out in the latter part of 2001. Application servers that comply with the J2EE 1.1 specification have to compensate for the lack of standards. As a result, large amounts of proprietary configuration settings are used. Learning all those settings and the proprietary deployment tools that tend to follow in their wake is cumbersome work at best.

For the J2EE reference implementation server, you are interested in three different deployment tasks:

1. Creating an application.
2. Deploying a Web component (servlet or JSP document) into the application.
3. Deploying an EJB component (session or Entity EJB; the J2EE reference implementation server does not yet support EJB version 2.0, so message EJBs cannot yet be deployed) into the application.

Take a look at how to perform these tasks.

Creating a J2EE Application

When launching the deployment tool of the J2EE reference implementation server, an empty deployment will appear, as shown in Figure A-5. Note that the only known server is the one running on the localhost node, as shown in the Servers pane to the bottom left. This is the J2EE instance that is covered in this appendix.

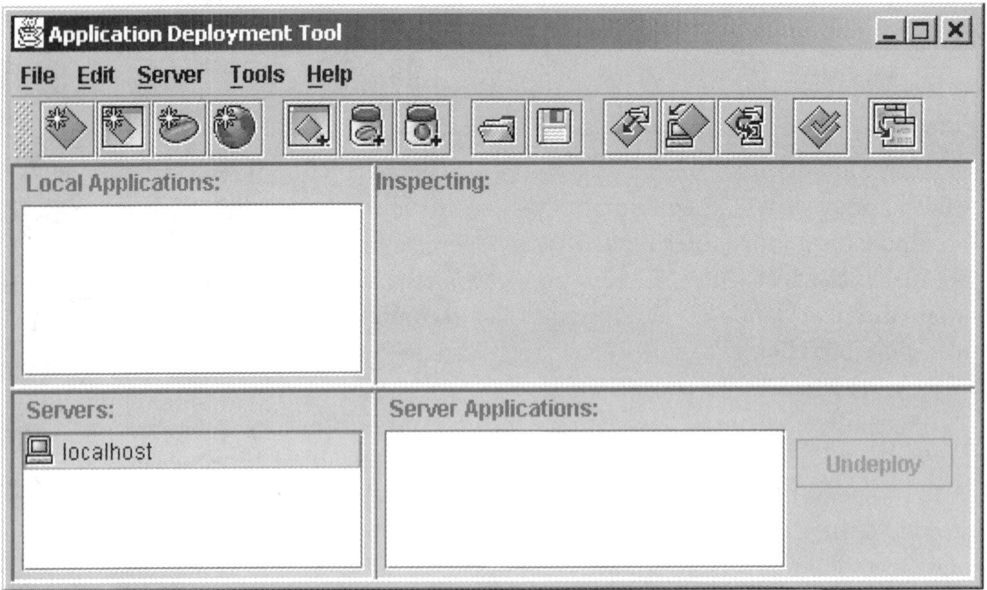

Figure A-5. The main view of the Deploytool GUI. Note that the only server known to the current deployment tool is the J2EE server running on the localhost node.

To create an application, simply select the File | New Application… menu item, as shown in Figure A-6.

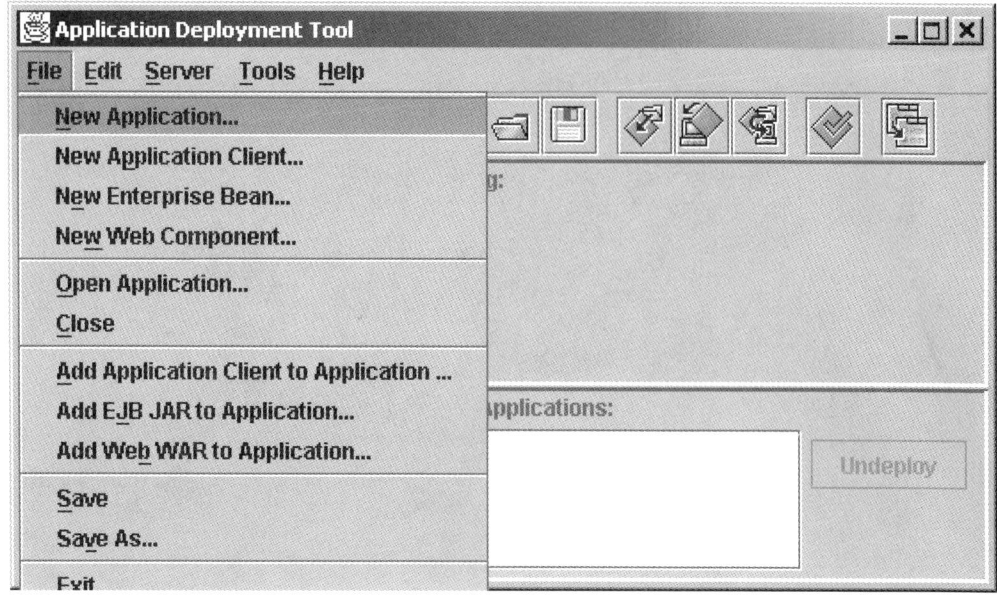

Figure A-6. Create a new application by selecting the File | New Application… menu item.

Complete the selection by providing the data requested by the New Application dialog (see Figure A-7). If you do not browse for another location, the EAR file will appear in your <J2EE_HOME>/bin directory.

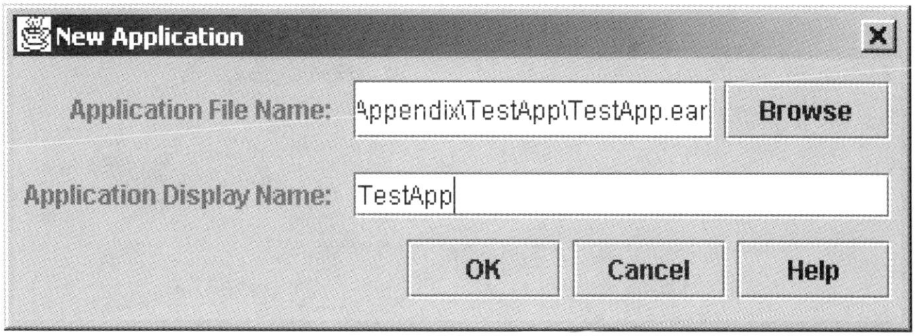

New Application
Application File Name: Appendix\TestApp\TestApp.ear Browse
Application Display Name: TestApp
OK Cancel Help

Figure A-7. Choose an application file name and an application display name for your J2EE application.

When you have created an application, the deploytool main view of the application is altered, as shown in Figure A-8. Note that the application is not yet deployed to the J2EE server; you will need to select Tools | Deploy Application… to actually perform the deployment to the J2EE server.

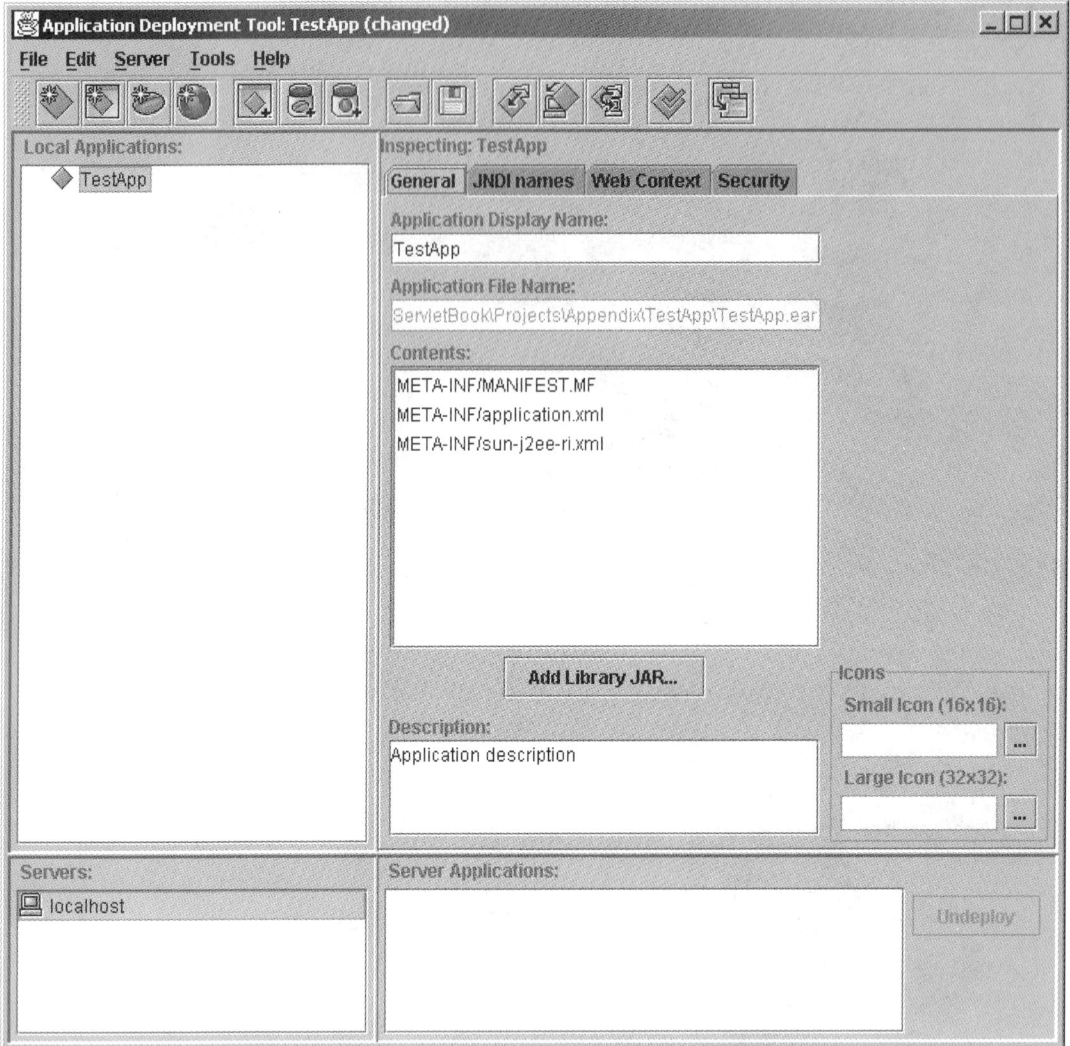

Figure A-8. The main view of an empty J2EE application not yet deployed to the J2EE server (the Server Applications pane in the lower-right corner of the view shows all currently deployed applications).

Deploying an EJB Component JAR to the J2EE Server

Assuming that you have developed an EJB component and packed it into a JAR, you may use the deploytool to simply include your component into an application that may be deployed into the J2EE reference implementation server. You may also originate from the compiled code of the EJB component to create the `ejb-jar.xml` deployment descriptor in a series of wizard-like steps.

I will show both approaches, starting with the simple inclusion of an already compiled and packaged EJB component.

Deploying an EJB JAR

Including an EJB JAR file is the standard procedure if you have purchased an EJB component from a third-party vendor or another development group within your company. For this example, use the palindrome server JAR (containing the Palindrome server EJB component) from Chapter 8. All compiled code, including the `ejb-jar.xml` descriptor, is packed into the file `palindromeServer.jar`. Your task is simply to add the palindromeServer EJB component to the testApplication just created. Simply click on the Add EJB JAR to Application… button marked with an arrow in Figure A-9 and select the archive you want to include from the file system.

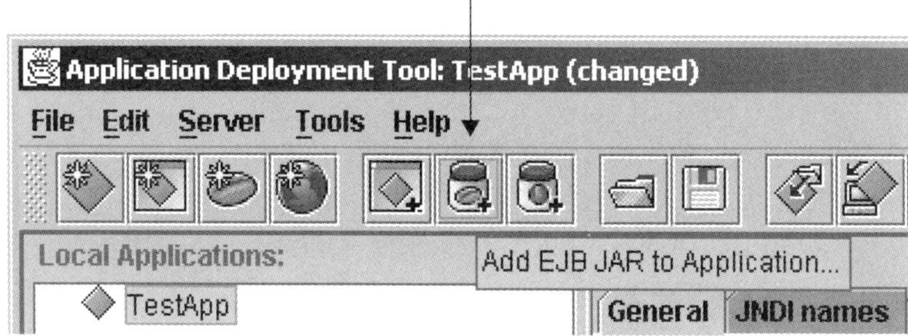

Figure A-9. To include an already prepackaged EJB JAR into the J2EE application, simply click the Add EJB JAR button and select the JAR file.

When the EJB JAR is included in the J2EE application, an EJB archive entry appears in the content tree pane to the left in the deploytool, as shown in Figure A-10. Selecting the archive provides information about its contained EJB components and provides information about the content of the archive.

The only task currently remaining is adding a JNDI name to the Palindrome server EJB component. First study the `ejb-jar.xml` file in Listing A-2, which was shipped with the `PalindromeServer` EJB component. The content of any descriptor file can be shown by the deploytool view by marking the particular descriptor in the contents listing in the bottom-right corner of the deploytool view, and then selecting Tools | Descriptor Viewer….

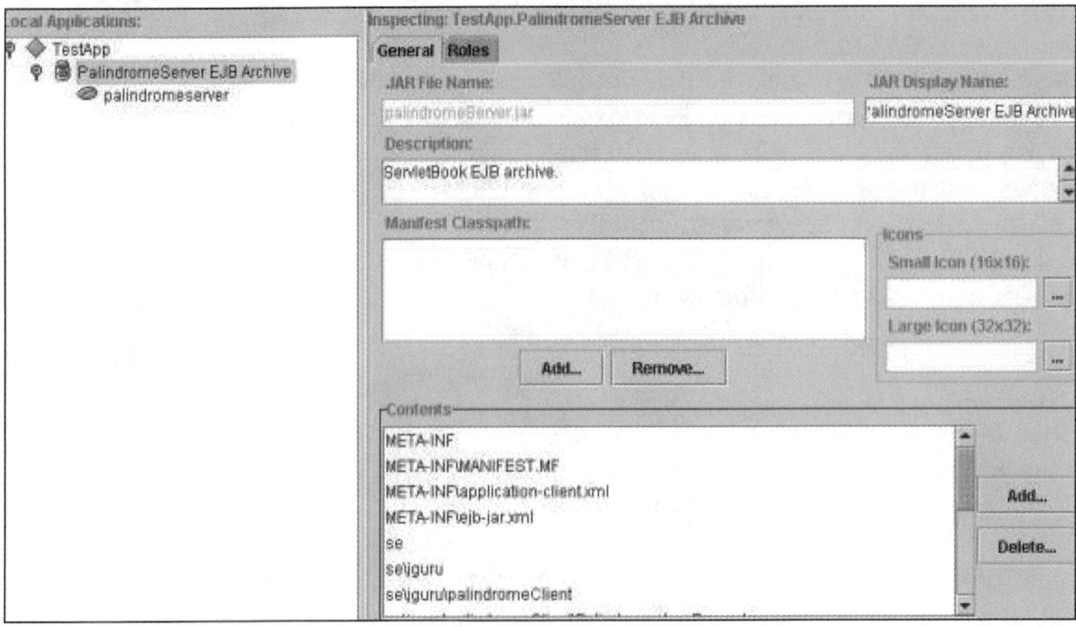

Figure A-10. The view of a deployed EJB archive in the TestApp. Note that the contents of the archive may be altered using the Add… and Delete… buttons to the right of the Contents pane (bottom right).

Listing A-2. The `ejb-jar.xml` *file*

```
<?xml version="1.0" encoding="Cp1252"?>

<!DOCTYPE ejb-jar PUBLIC
   '-//Sun Microsystems, Inc.//DTD Enterprise JavaBeans 1.1//EN'
   'http://java.sun.com/j2ee/dtds/ejb-jar_1_1.dtd'>

<ejb-jar>
  <description>ServletBook EJB archive.</description>
  <display-name>PalindromeServer EJB Archive</display-name>
  <enterprise-beans>
    <session>
      <description>The Palindrome Server.</description>
      <display-name>palindromeserver</display-name>
      <ejb-name>palindromeserver</ejb-name>
      <home>se.jguru.palindromeServer.PalindromeServerHome</home>
      <remote>se.jguru.palindromeServer.PalindromeServer</remote>
      <ejb-class>se.jguru.palindromeServer.PalindromeServerBean</ejb-class>
      <session-type>Stateless</session-type>
      <transaction-type>Container</transaction-type>
```

```
      <ejb-ref>
             <description>The palindromeserver client</description>
             <ejb-ref-name>palindromeServer</ejb-ref-name>
             <ejb-ref-type>Session</ejb-ref-type>
             <home>se.jguru.palindromeServer.PalindromeServerHome</home>
             <remote>se.jguru.palindromeServer.PalindromeServer</remote>
      </ejb-ref>
    </session>
  </enterprise-beans>
  <assembly-descriptor>
    <container-transaction>
      <method>
             <ejb-name>palindromeserver</ejb-name>
             <method-intf>Remote</method-intf>
             <method-name>reverse</method-name>
             <method-params>
               <method-param>java.lang.String</method-param>
             </method-params>
      </method>
      <trans-attribute>Required</trans-attribute>
    </container-transaction>
  </assembly-descriptor>
</ejb-jar>
```

As you can see, the `<display-name>` containers define the text strings shown in the deploytool GUI for both the archive and the EJB component itself. Note that the entries are case sensitive and that the EJB component is called *palindromeserver* internally (from its `<ejb-name>` entry). The palindromeserver EJB component may act as a client to another EJB bean (it has an `<ejb-ref>` entry). Normally, of course, this would be another type of EJB component from which the palindrome server EJB component could gather data or computations. To reduce code bloat in this example, however, the EJB component references another instance of the palindrome server EJB component.

For this exercise, a circular reference from the palindromeserver EJB component to itself has been added to the descriptor file. Note that circular references from EJB components are not permitted according to the specification. The purpose of the exercise is to show how various constructs from `ejb-jar.xml` are shown in the deploytool GUI.

Selecting the EJB component in the left content pane shows the six active panels for each EJB component, where you may tailor the deployment descriptors to your needs before deploying the EJB component to the EJB container of the J2EE reference implementation server.

The General Tab

The General tab (shown in Figure A-11) contains the type definitions for the EJB component; the Home and Remote interfaces are shown to type, as is the Bean implementation class. Because this component was imported from an already existing EJB JAR file, the type definitions are extracted from the `ejb-jar.xml` descriptor and cannot be changed.

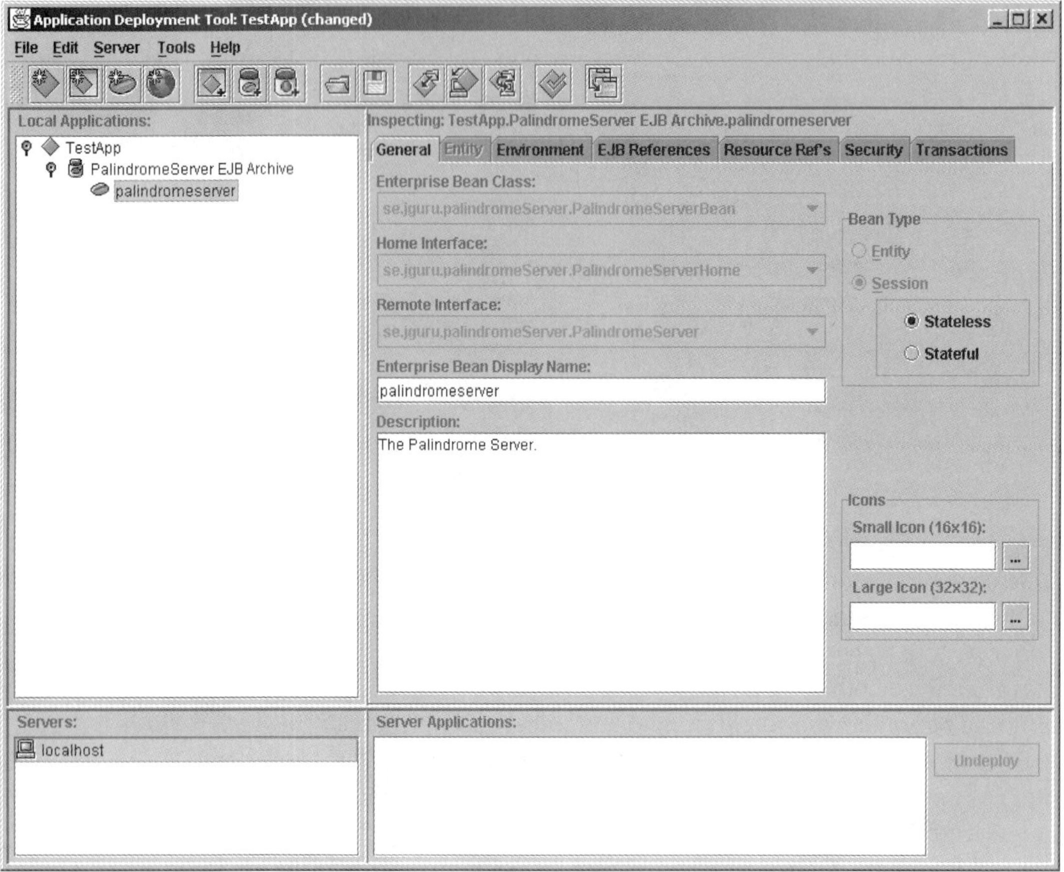

Figure A-11. The General attributes of an EJB component to be deployed into the J2EE reference implementation server

> **NOTE** *Other items and descriptions may be altered as required. For instance, the Bean Type (Stateful or Stateless) may be altered by the application deployer as required, but the bean cannot be altered to an Entity Bean.*

The Environment Tab

The environment settings of each EJB component may be provided or altered in the Environment tab. Simply click the Add button to add an environment reference and the Delete... button to remove it. Figure A-12 shows the types permitted to bind in the EJB environment, according to the EJB specification.

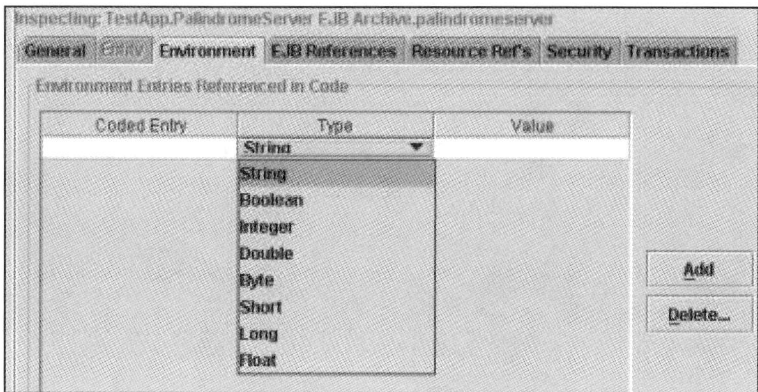

Figure A-12. Types permitted to bind in the environment context of an EJB component. Add a new context reference by clicking the Add button.

The EJB References Tab

The EJB References tab, shown in Figure A-13, contains the information found in the `<ejb-ref>` section of the `ejb-jar.xml` configuration descriptor. The palindromeserver EJB component has a reference (named *palindromeServer* with a capital "S") to another EJB component, whose Home and Remote types are provided. Similar to environment references, you may add or modify EJB references in this tab. Be careful not to alter the Home and Remote values to some value that will give rise to a `ClassCastException` when running the application.

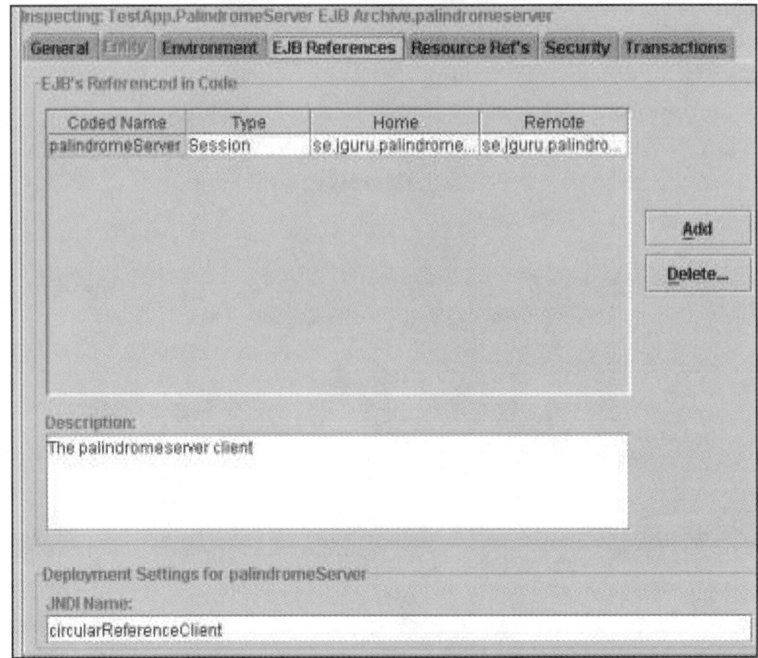

Figure A-13. The EJB References tab of the EJB component deployment. Add new references by clicking the Add button and remove references by clicking the Delete… button.

The Resource Ref's Tab

The Resource Ref's tab contains references to Database, MailSession, or URL resources for the selected EJB component. The data-entry panel adopts itself according to the resource being created. Figure A-14 shows the panel while creating a new DataSource reference for the EJB component. Note that the bottom contains two settings for database user name and password, as well as its JNDI lookup string.

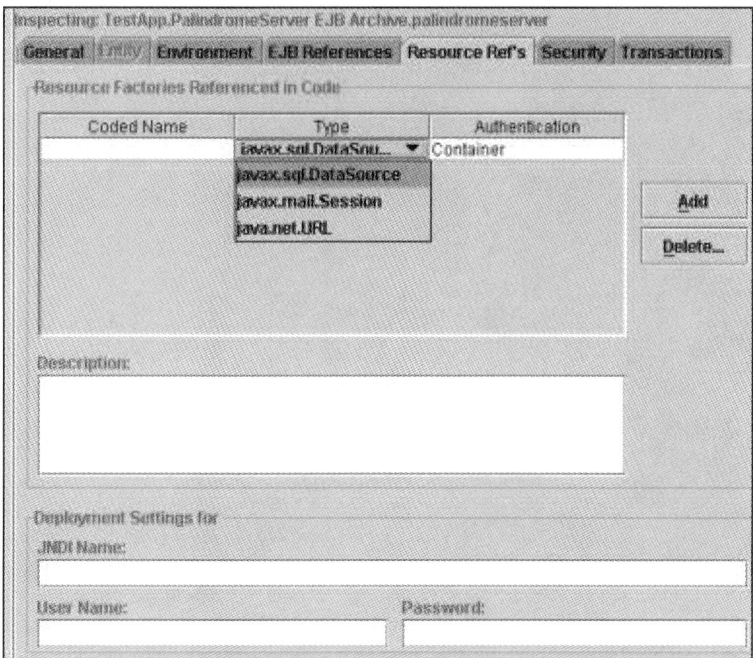

Figure A-14. The Resource reference tab of the J2EE deploytool. Note that the text fields in the bottom adopts after the resource being created so that a mail session resource provides different settings than the DataSource.

The Security Tab

The Security tab enables you to configure method-level permissions for particular J2EE roles. The purpose of this tab is to add roles that may access only a restricted set of methods in the EJB component (such as a standard user) and roles with greater access to the methods in the EJB component (such as an administrator). Figure A-15 shows the Security tab before any roles have been added, and Figure A-16 shows the same tab after adding a role "foo" and assigning permissions to run the `create`, `reverse`, and `isPalindrome` methods. The foo role is known as "bah" in the code.

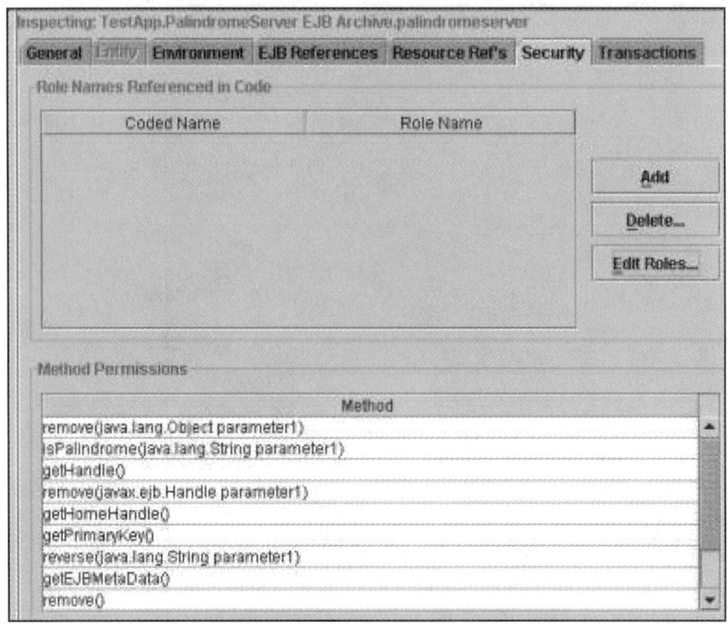

Figure A-15. Security permission tab, when no roles are provided for the EJB component. Thus, all roles are permitted access to all methods of the EJB component.

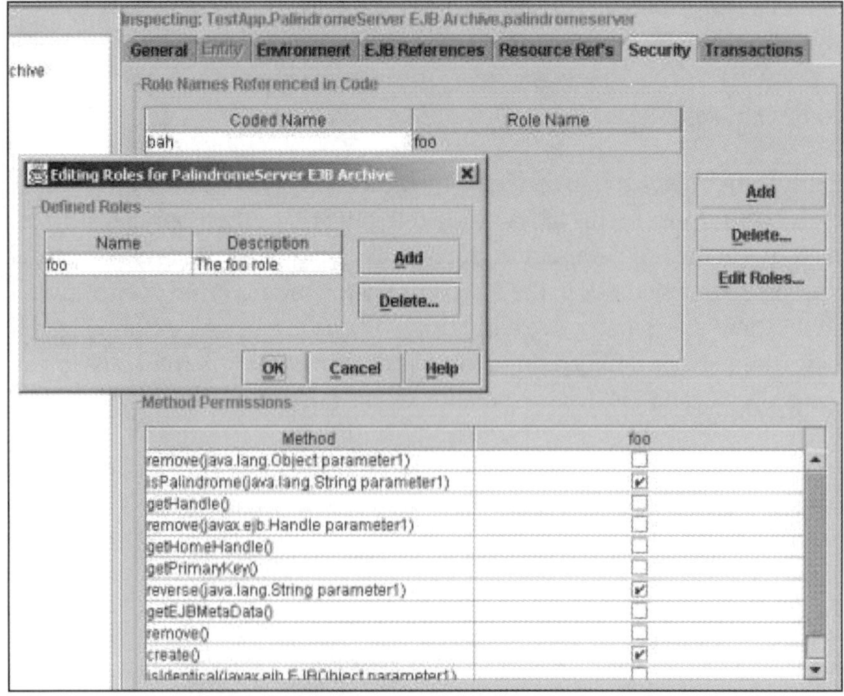

Figure A-16. Security settings applied to the "foo" role on this EJB component. Users that have logged in to the J2EE security realm as a user having the foo role are granted access to three methods: `isPalindrome`*,* `reverse`*, and* `create`*.*

Adding the foo role in the deploytool modifies the `<assembly-descriptor>` of the EJB component to match the settings provided in the deploytool GUI. The snippet altered in the `ejb-jar.xml` file is provided in Listing A-3. As you may well see, the efficiency of entering these descriptor settings by hand is limited relative to that of the deployment tool.

Listing A-3. The assembly descriptor of the `ejb-jar.xml` *file*

```
<assembly-descriptor>
    <security-role>
      <description>The foo role</description>
      <role-name>foo</role-name>
    </security-role>
    <method-permission>
      <role-name>foo</role-name>
      <method>
             <ejb-name>palindromeserver</ejb-name>
             <method-intf>Remote</method-intf>
             <method-name>isPalindrome</method-name>
             <method-params>
               <method-param>java.lang.String</method-param>
             </method-params>
      </method>
      <method>
             <ejb-name>palindromeserver</ejb-name>
             <method-intf>Remote</method-intf>
             <method-name>reverse</method-name>
             <method-params>
               <method-param>java.lang.String</method-param>
             </method-params>
      </method>
      <method>
             <ejb-name>palindromeserver</ejb-name>
             <method-intf>Home</method-intf>
             <method-name>create</method-name>
             <method-params />
      </method>
    </method-permission>

... unaltered portion skipped ...

</assembly-descriptor>
```

The Transactions Tab

The last of the descriptor tabs for the EJB component is the Transactions panel, which provides transaction control over all methods. As can be seen from the descriptor, provided in Listing A-2, and the deploytool in Figure A-17, only the `reverse` method requires a container-managed transaction. The `isPalindrome` method does not support a transaction and is therefore left unwrapped by the EJB container when invoked from an EJB client.

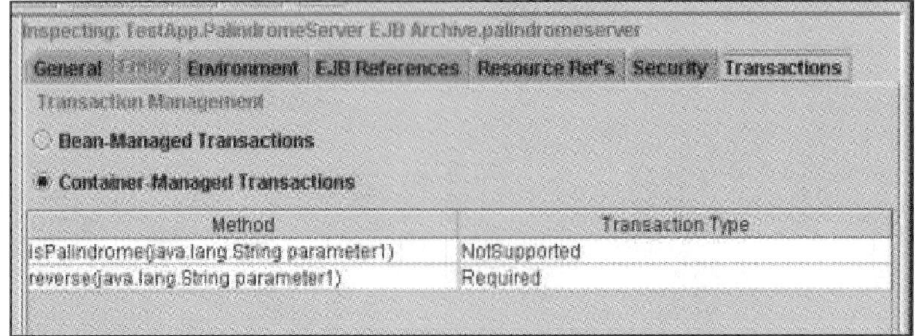

Figure A-17. The transaction tab controls transactional settings for each method in the remote interface of the selected EJB component. Note that the descriptor is set to provide container-managed transaction handling. Should you select the bean-managed variant, you are responsible yourself for starting and committing (or rolling back) the transaction from within the EJB method.

The JNDI Name

The only remaining property of real interest for an EJB component is its JNDI name, which must be used by all EJB clients as the lookup string. Because the JNDI bind name is global to the application, all JNDI names are found when selecting the application in the left content pane and switching to the JNDI tab, as shown in Figure A-18.

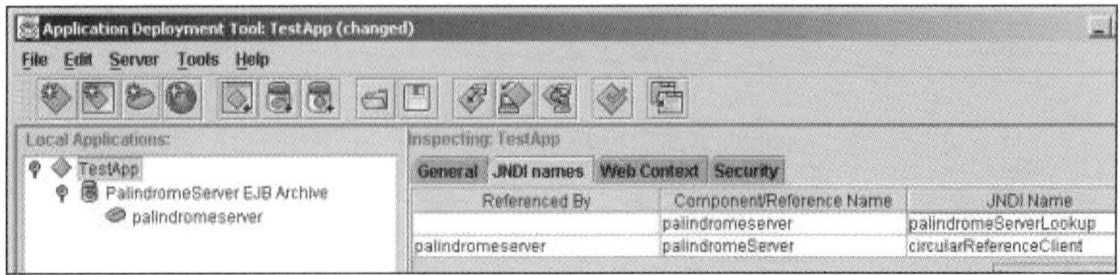

Figure A-18. All application-wide JNDI settings are shown in the JNDI Names tab.

Note that the only non-dependent JNDI name shown in Figure A-18 is `palindromeServerLookup`. The `circularReferenceClient` JNDI name is referenced by the `palindromeserver` EJB component only and cannot be properly used from another EJB client.

Deploying an EJB Component from Its Code

The task to create a new EJB component directly from its code (in other words, not using an existing JAR file where all components are already placed) is both a smoother and a more complex ride than the do-it-yourself way shown in Chapters 8 to 11. It is a smoother creation process because the GUI handles repetitive tasks and makes sure you do not accidentally misspell a relation name, thereby putting the entire EJB component in an illegal state. It is a more complex way of creating your EJB deployment unit because you have to realize which text fields in the view correspond to the XML tags in the `ejb-jar.xml` descriptor file.

Follow these steps to use the deployment wizard for deploying a new EJB component:

1. Press the New Enterprise Bean ... button or select its menu equivalent, File | New Enterprise Bean... (see Figure A-19).

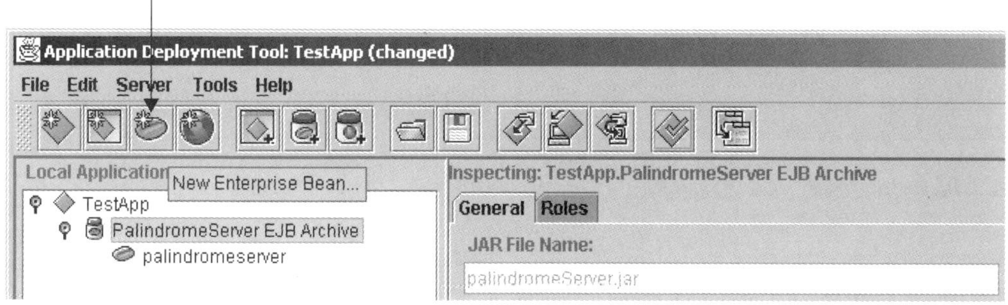

Figure A-19. The New Enterprise Bean... button starts a wizard that will permit deploying a new EJB component originating from its compiled source code.

2. When launching the New Enterprise Bean Wizard, a description splash screen, as shown in Figure A-20, appears. Click the Next... button to start the proper EJB deployment wizard.

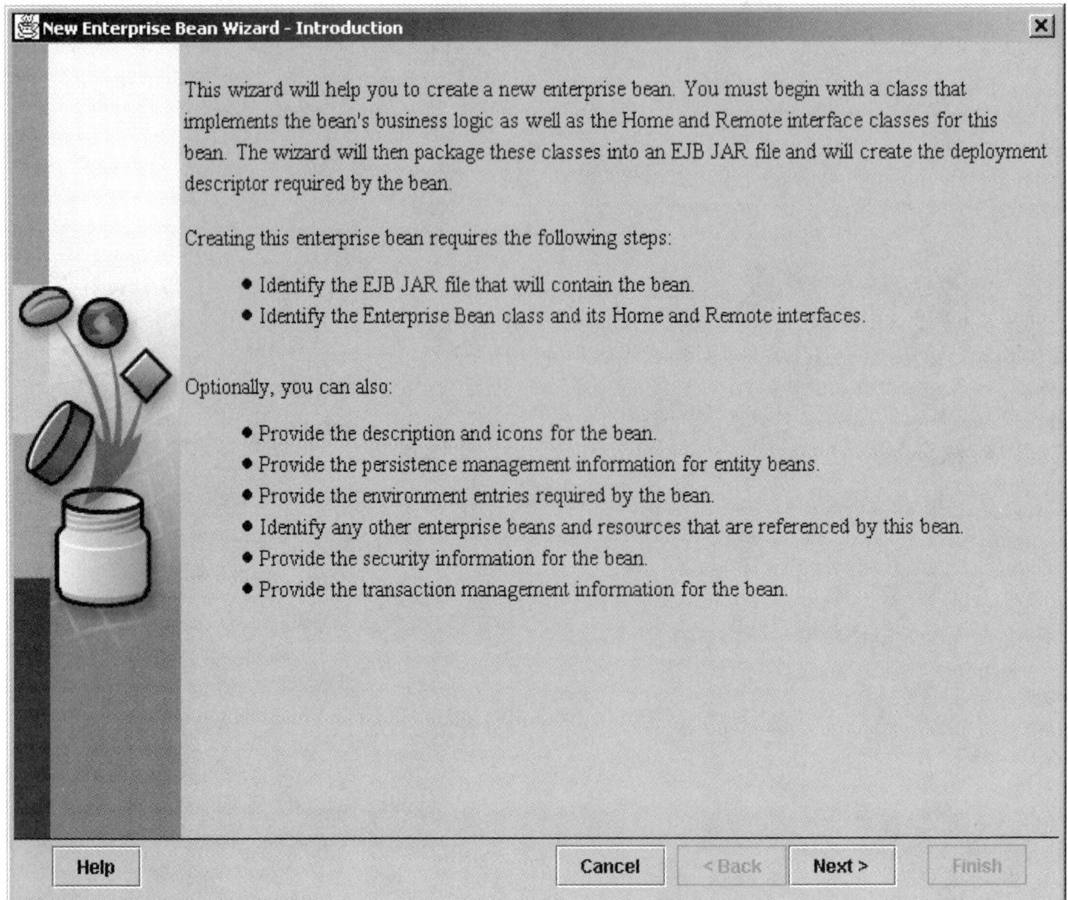

Figure A-20. Introductory splash screen for a new EJB component deployment

3. The first content compilation screen of the deployment wizard (shown in Figure A-21) permits you to include your bytecode files in an existing EJB archive or into a newly created archive. Press the Add… button to add new classes to your EJB archive.

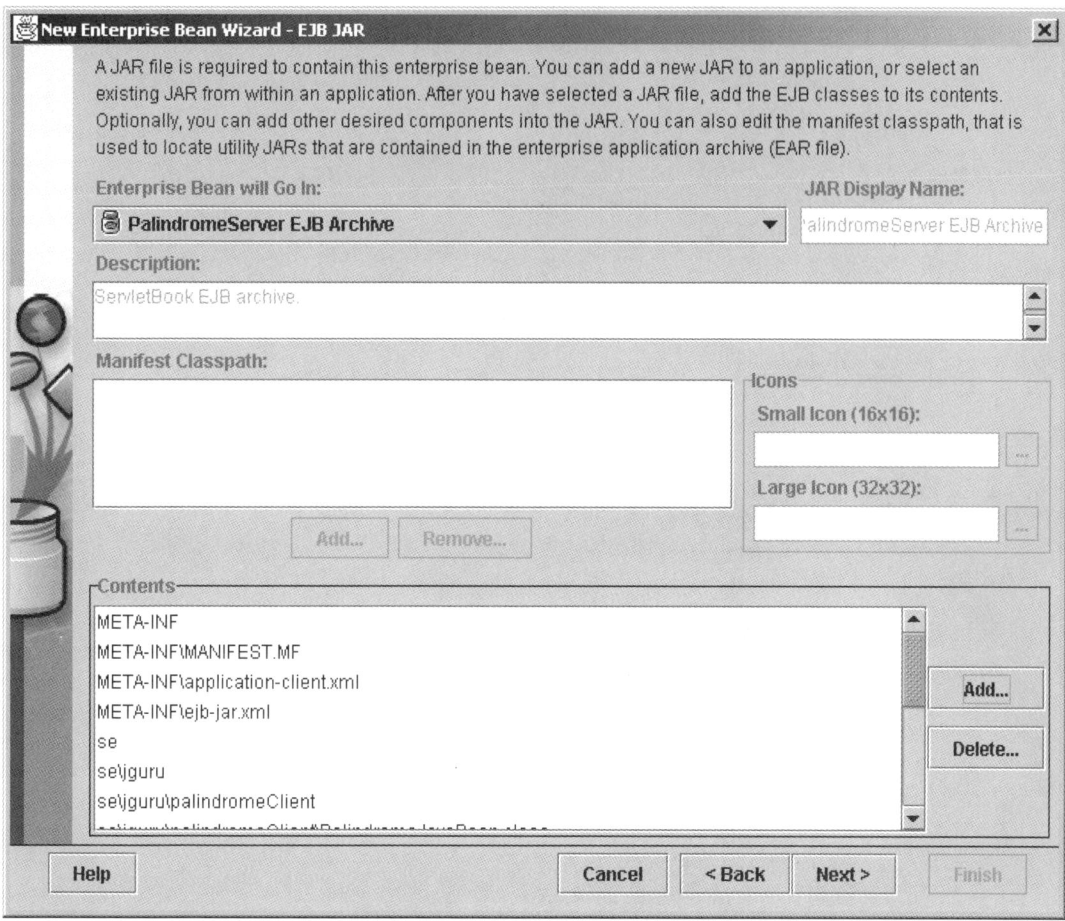

Figure A-21. Add new component classes screen. The Add… button adds new classes to the presently selected EJB component (in other words, the PalindromeServer EJB archive). Switch the combobox ("Enterprise Bean will go in") to the application if you want to create a new EJB archive to deploy instead of adding the components to the currently selected EJB archive.

4. When you press the Add… button inside the Contents pane of the EJB deployment wizard, the Add Files to .JAR dialog (shown in Figure A-22) is shown. After selecting the root directory of the classes you want to include (which is the equivalent of adding a directory to the classpath environment variable), you may select the EJB component classes that you want to include and deploy. The classes you chose in the dialog are included in the Contents pane of the New Enterprise Bean Wizard, as shown in Figure A-23.

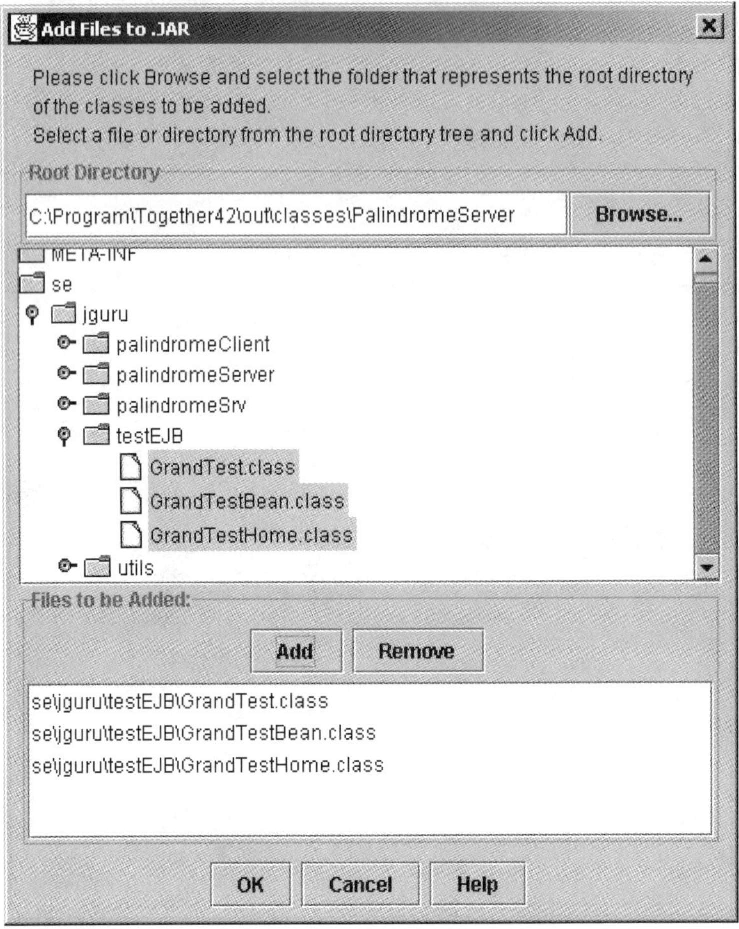

Figure A-22. The Add Files to .JAR dialog in operation. Be sure to set the root path of the EJB (top part of the dialog) before selecting the EJB component classes you want to add to the archive.

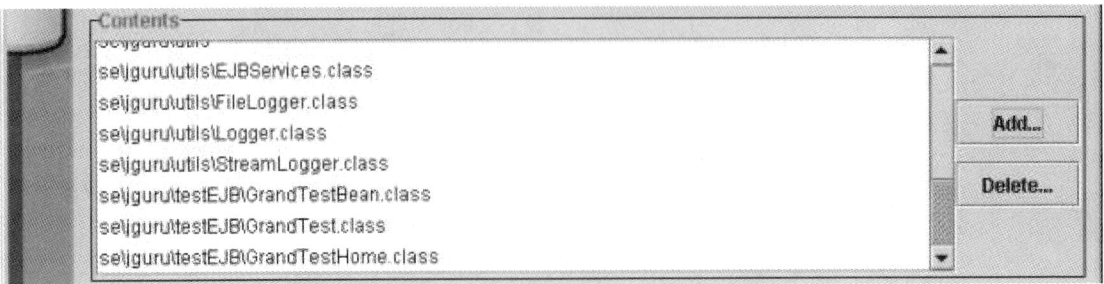

Figure A-23. The Contents list of the EJB JAR after adding the GrandTest EJB component

5. Press the Next button to move a step forward in the wizard. The task at hand is selecting the different parts of the EJB component, as well as providing a display name and an optional description of the EJB bean. As shown in Figure A-24, the task of selecting is a simple one as the wizard presents all available data to the developer in the form of a combobox.

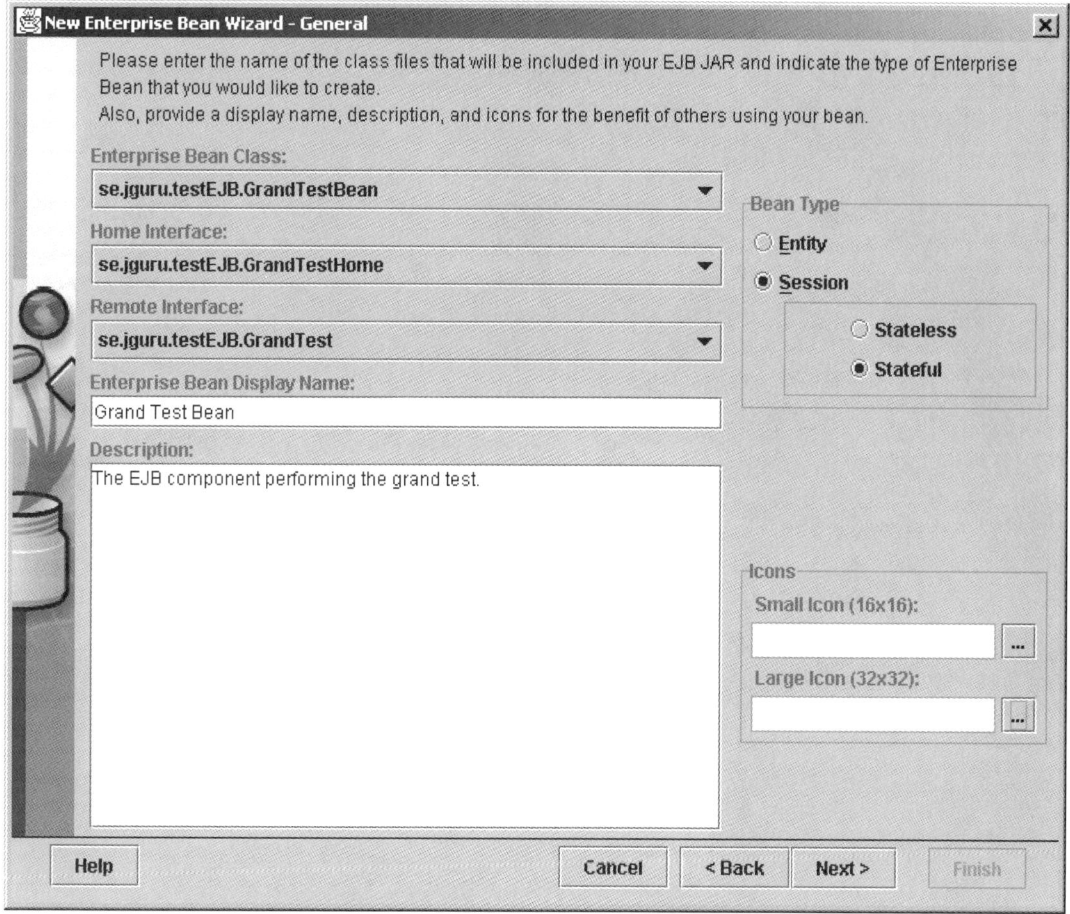

Figure A-24. The general description pane permits selecting the Bean, Home, and Remote types of the EJB component, as well as its state as an entity or session bean. Don't forget inputting a display name and a description for your EJB component. Sensibly selected descriptions and names often prevent much confusion later in a development project.

TIP *Remember to add proper descriptions and names to the EJB component. They are essential to any development project where several developers are involved and generally save huge amounts of money by avoiding confusion in the project.*

6. Press the Next button to arrive at the environment entries pane. If you need to add one or more entries to the EJB environment, simply press the Add button to add a new row to the table. When done, the display of an environment entry is shown in Figure A-25. The wizard applies constraints to the selection to permit to bind only valid (according to the EJB specification) types in the EJB environment, as shown in Figure A-26.

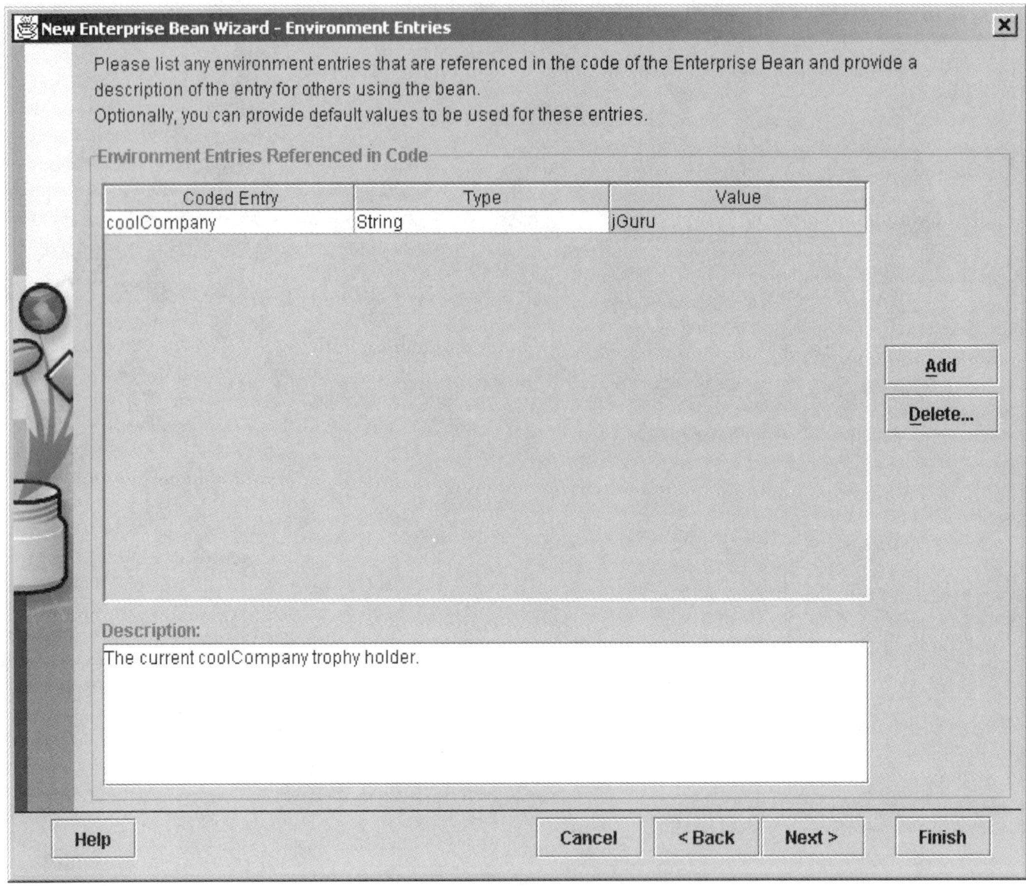

Figure A-25. Adding a new environment entry to the EJB component is done with the Environment Entries pane.

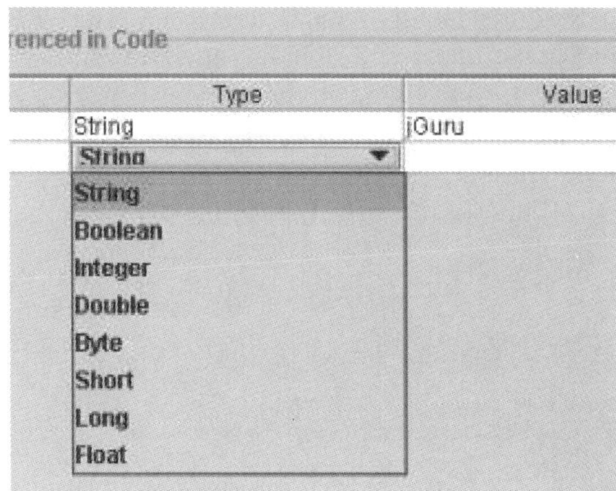

Figure A-26. The dropdown list of the type table assists the developer in binding only types compliant with the EJB specification in the EJB environment.

7. Press the Next button to progress to adding EJB references to the deployed bean. Figure A-27 shows this step. As before, you add a new EJB reference by pressing the Add button and delete it by pressing the Delete button. It is recommended to provide a proper description for each EJB reference and to illustrate its meaning to other developers or deployers.

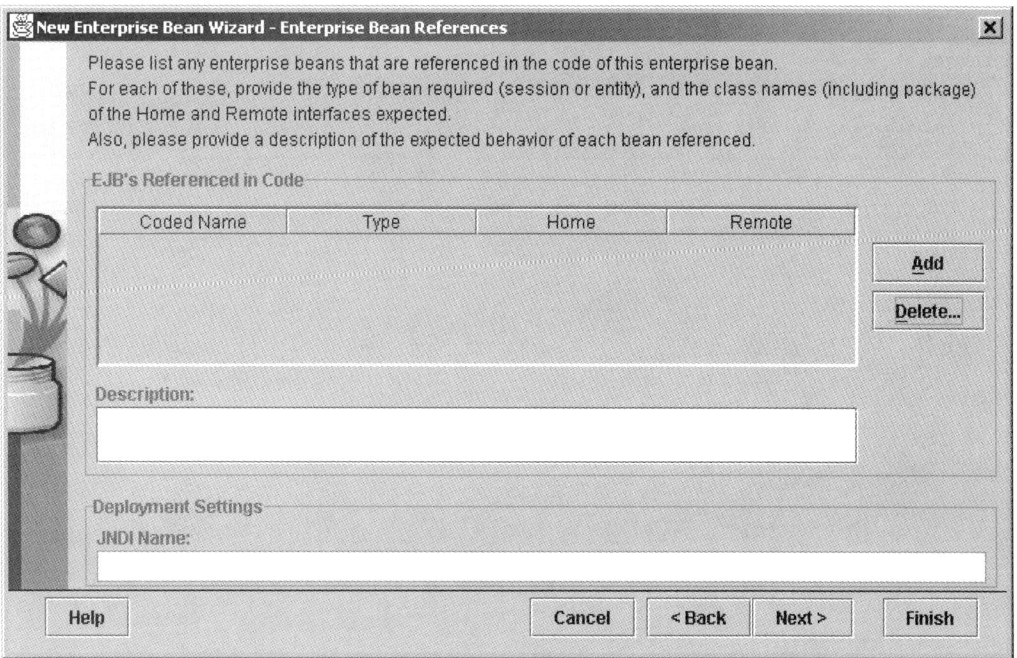

Figure A-27. Adding a new EJB reference to the bean deployed

8. Press Next to move on to the Resource factory pane. This step permits adding resource factories for DataSources, mail Sessions, and URLs. In Figure A-28, a new DataSource with component-managed transactions has been added to the EJB component. Note its deployment settings (userID, JNDI lookup string, and password), which are provided in the bottom of the pane. Figure A-29 shows what types of resources can be added in this step of the wizard.

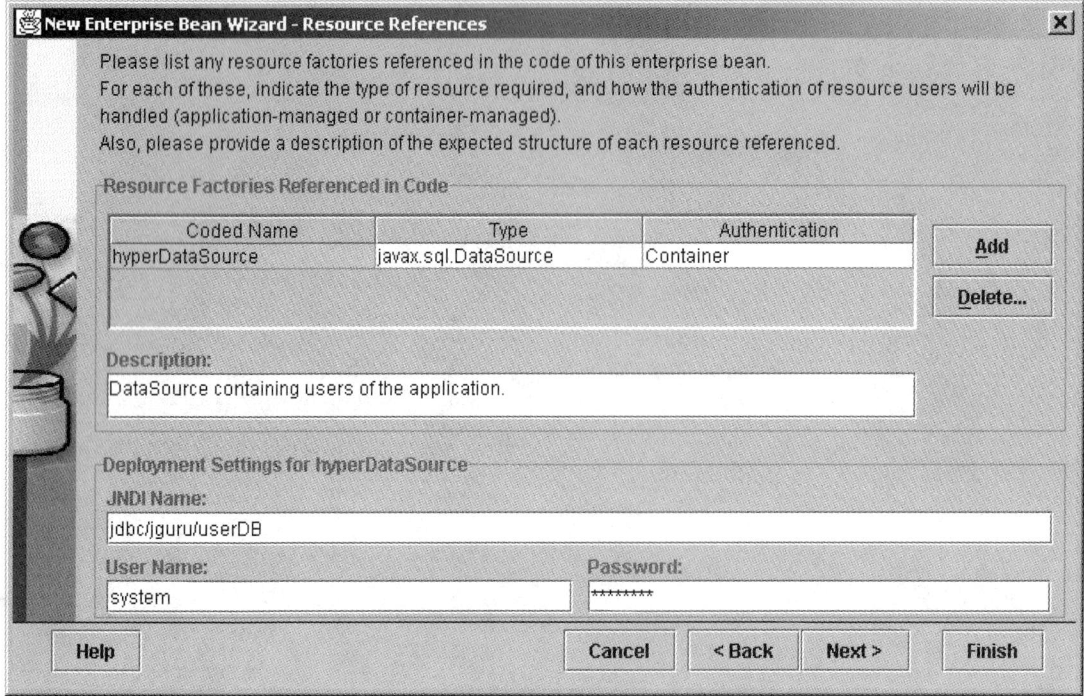

Figure A-28. Adding a new DataSource resource reference to the EJB being deployed

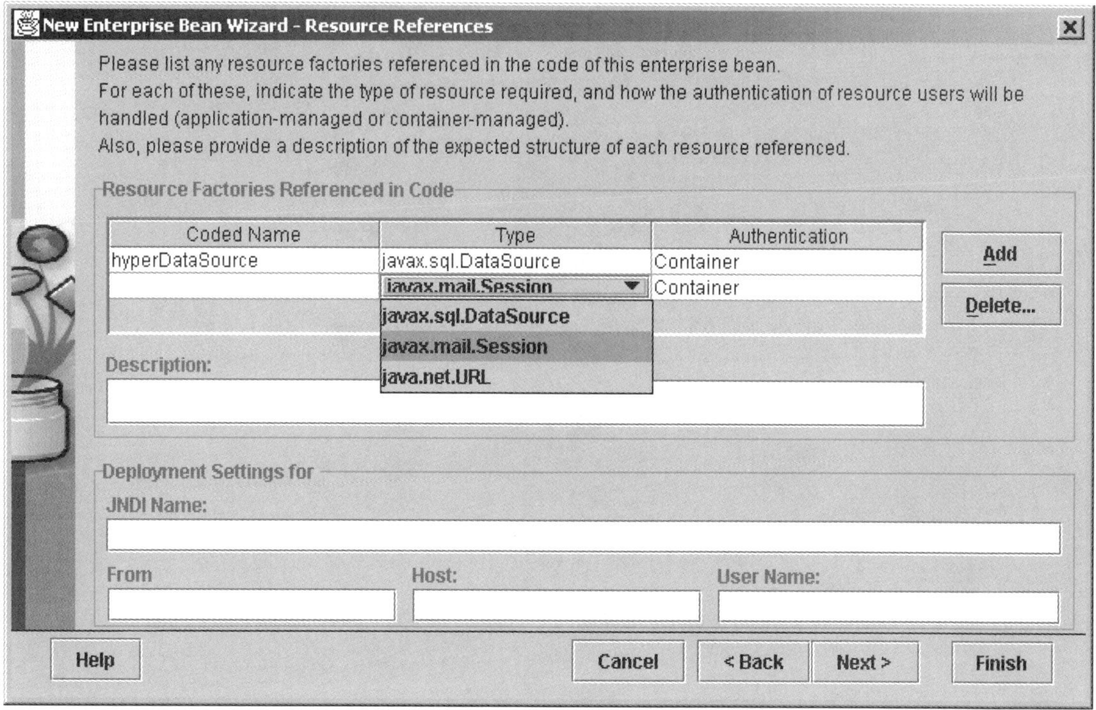

Figure A-29. The resource factory types are constrained to values that comply with the EJB specification. Note that the deployment settings alters depending on the resource factory type.

9. Click Next to move on to the security settings of the EJB component in deployment. Identical to the security settings of an already deployed EJB component (refer to Figures A-15 and A-16 and the discussion around them), you may now restrict usage of any or all methods in the EJB component to users having a particular role, as shown in Figure A-30.

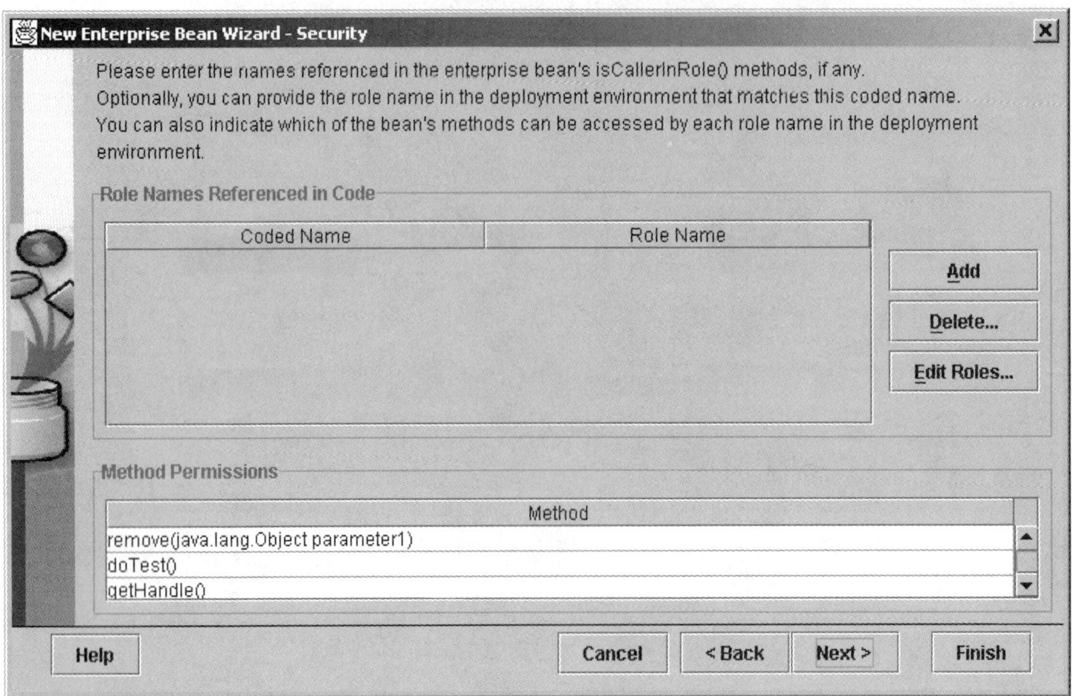

Figure A-30. The security settings of the EJB component being deployed. Similar to the security settings shown in Figures A-15 and A-16, the security settings wizard permits restricting method permissions to specific roles only.

10. Hit the Next button to configure the transaction settings for all methods in the remote interface of the EJB component. For each method in the remote interface, you may choose bean-managed or container-managed state. The permitted settings for container-managed transactions are shown in the dropdown list provided by the wizard, as shown in Figure A-31.

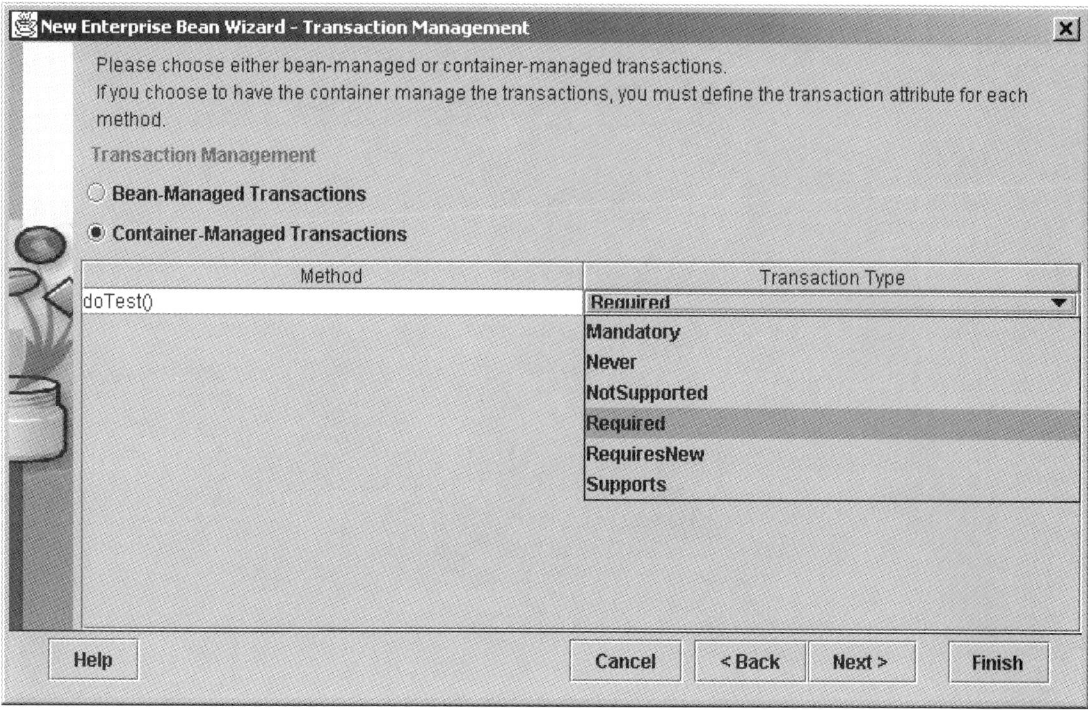

Figure A-31. Transaction setting configuration for each method in the remote interface of the EJB component

11. Click the Next button and move on to the final review screen. Simply verify all settings in the TextArea and press Finish to insert the EJB component into the archive, as shown in Figure A-32.

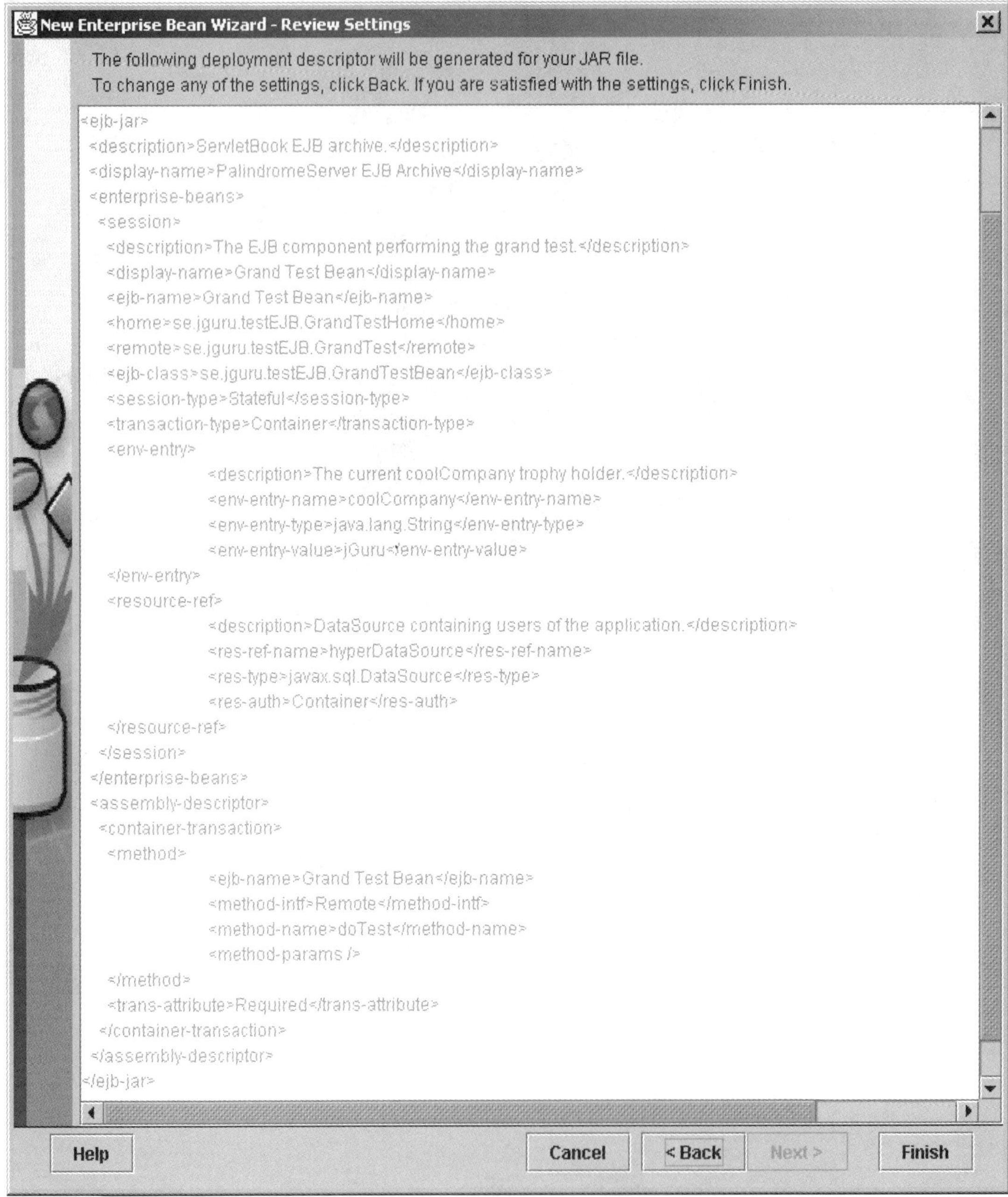

Figure A-32. The final EJB deployment descriptor verification screen shows the current settings of the deployment descriptor for your approval. Press Finish to accept or go Back to edit any of the settings in the descriptor.

If you press the Finish button to accept the EJB component as it is, the deployment editor exits and you are presented with the deployment tool again. Note that the newly created Grand Test Bean is shown as an EJB component in the left content pane (see Figure A-33). Of course, any settings in the Grand Test Bean may be altered in the same manner as any other deployed EJB component—by selecting it in the left application pane and using any of the tabs in the inspector.

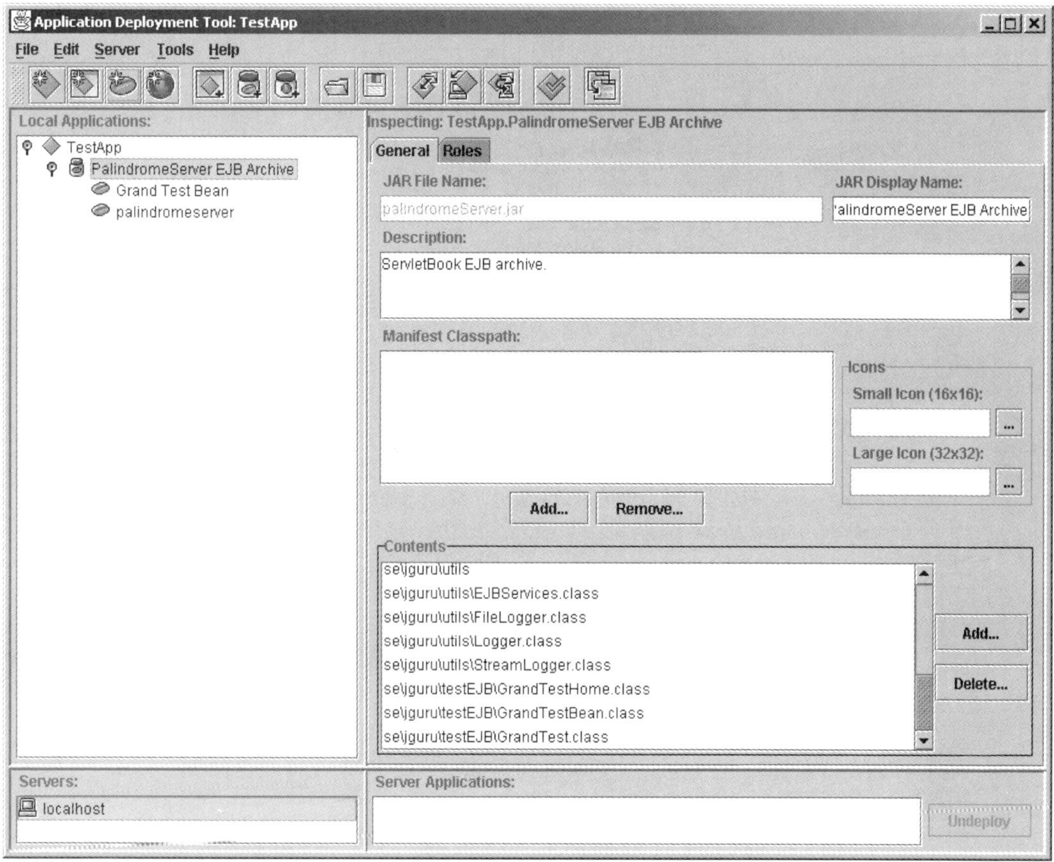

Figure A-33. The result of running the deployment tool. Note that the left content pane shows the display name of the newly added EJB component, and its content classes are shown in the Contents list to the bottom right.

Verifying EJB Component Integrity

A good practice—especially when you are deploying EJB components that have fairly complex descriptor structure and dependent objects—is to run a verifier over your EJB components being deployed into the J2EE server. The verifier performs various tests to ensure that your EJB component is indeed in compliance with the EJB specification and standards. Launch the verifier on a particular archive by selecting it in the leftmost content pane and choosing the Tools | Verifier… menu option, as shown in Figure A-34.

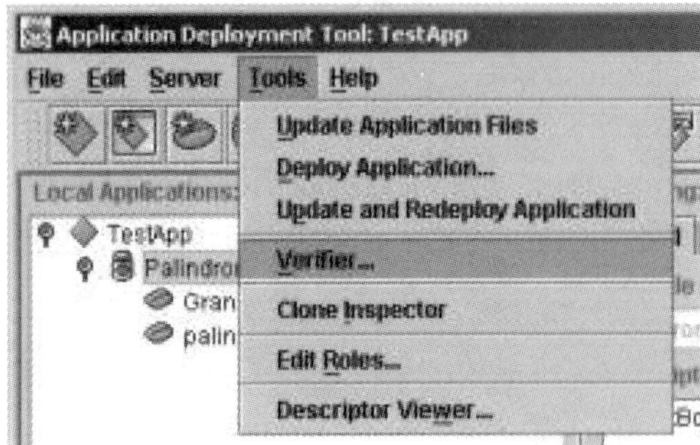

Figure A-34. The Verifier launch menu. Note that you must select the archive that you want to verify before launching the Verifier.

Generally, it is recommended to attend to the warnings and failures found in the Verifier test log. In some special cases, the developer may want to create structures not complying with the EJB test suite. Therefore, one cannot mindlessly use the EJB test suite as a fail proof tool.Afterthought and a bit of experience are always going to be the best asset of any software developer.

1. The detailed description of the warning message in Figure A-35 is shown in the Details area. Read the detailed message to get feedback to re-implement your EJB components before deploying anew to the EJB container.

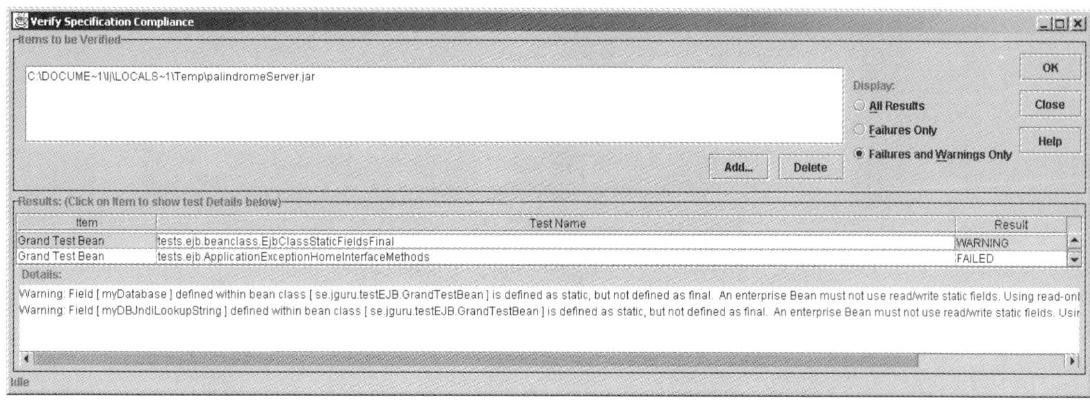

Figure A-35. Verifier status window, displaying a warning (selected) and a failure message from their respective verification tests

2. Deploy the EJB components to the server by selecting the Tools | Deploy Application… menu item as shown in Figure A-36. The first choice you must make in the deployment wizard is choosing whether you want the process to return a client EJB JAR after the deployment (see Figure A-37). Such a client EJB JAR contains the Stub files required to connect to the J2EE reference server, in addition to a J2EE reference implementation specific deployment descriptor. The stub files are named *<BeanName>_Stub.class* (in other words, `GrandTest_Stub.class`) and the J2EE specific deployment descriptor is called `sun-j2ee-ri.xml`.

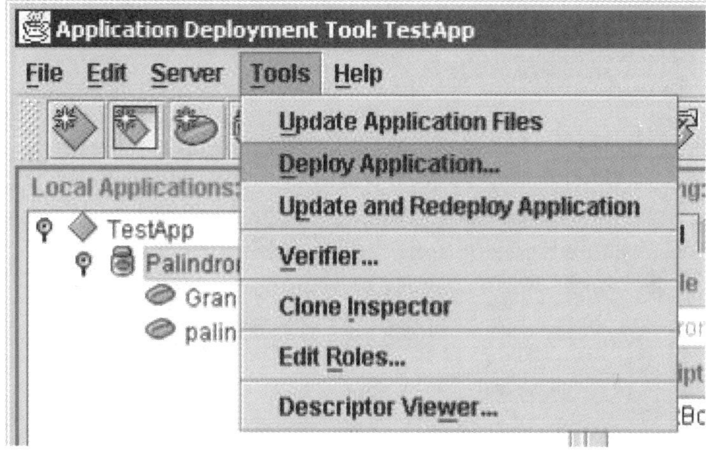

Figure A-36. Deploy the application to the J2EE server by selecting Tools | Deploy Application… (or Tools | Update and Redeploy Application to overwrite an existing application deployment).

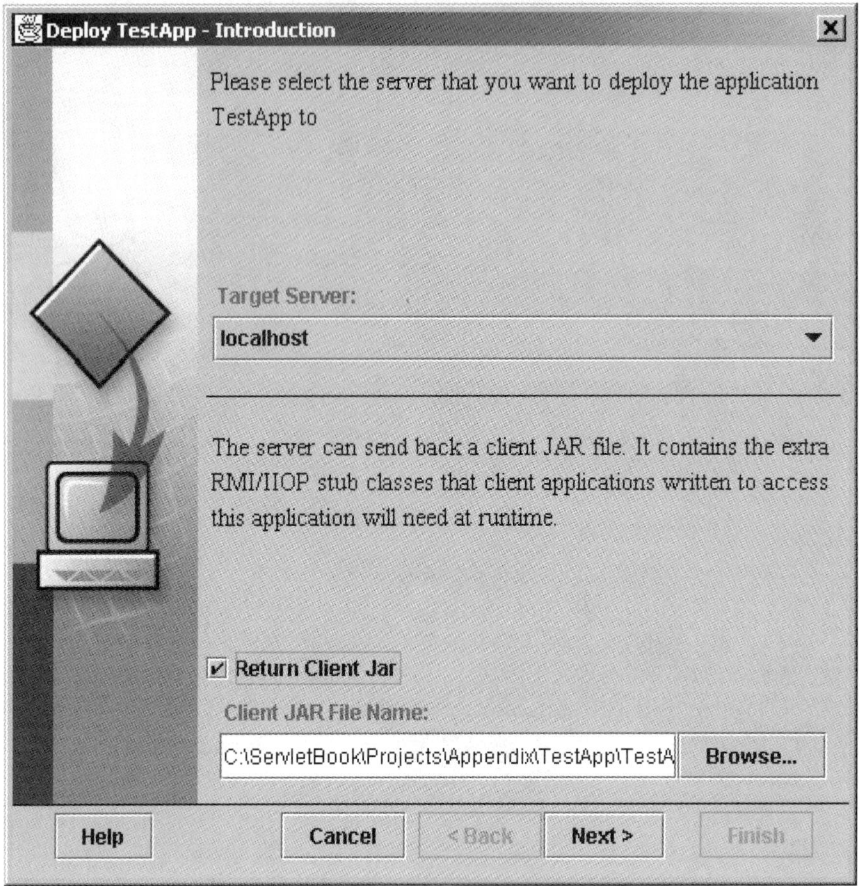

Figure A-37. Select the Return Client Jar option if you want the EJB client Jar to be provided. Such a client JAR contains only the required types to create the EJB client.

3. The next step in the application deployment (shown in Figure A-38) wizard permits editing of the JNDI names for all components in the application, as shown in Figure A-39. When done editing the names of the application, hit the Next and Finish buttons to deploy the EJB archive to the J2EE server. The compilation and deployment progress pane is shown in Figure A-40, and the completed deployment view pane is shown in Figure A-41.

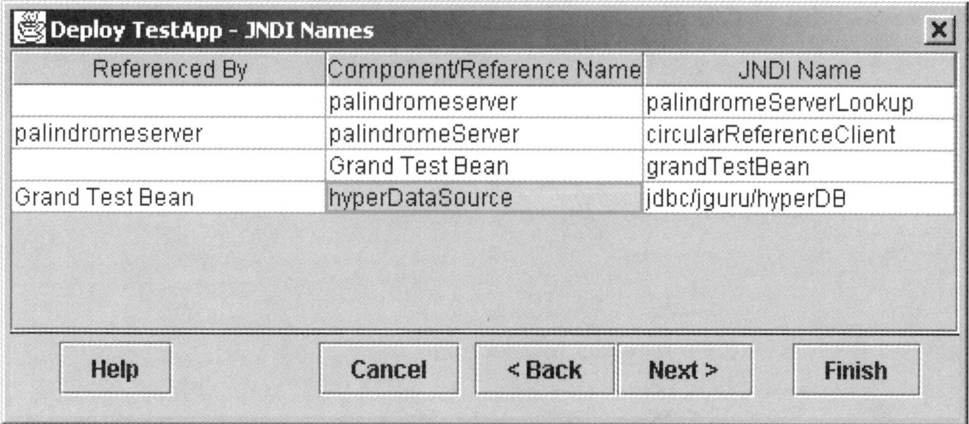

Figure A-38. The JNDI names of all known entities must be specified in the next deployment step. Note that two of the references are specific to the two EJB components within which they are defined.

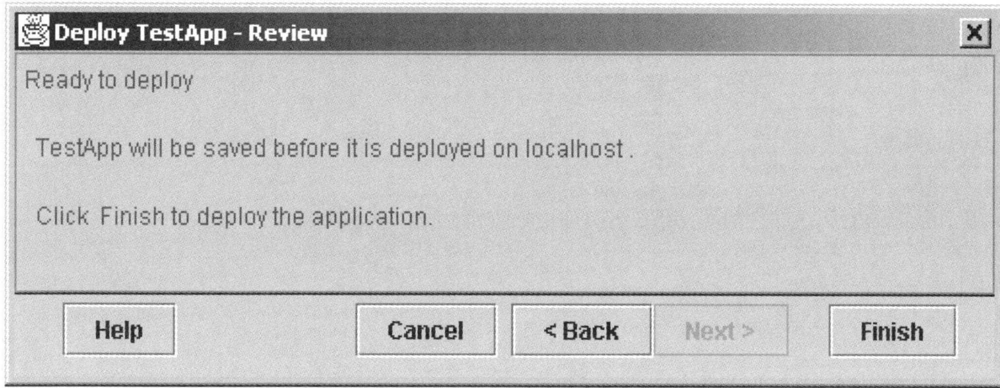

Figure A-39. The final confirmation screen before deploying the archive to the J2EE reference implementation server

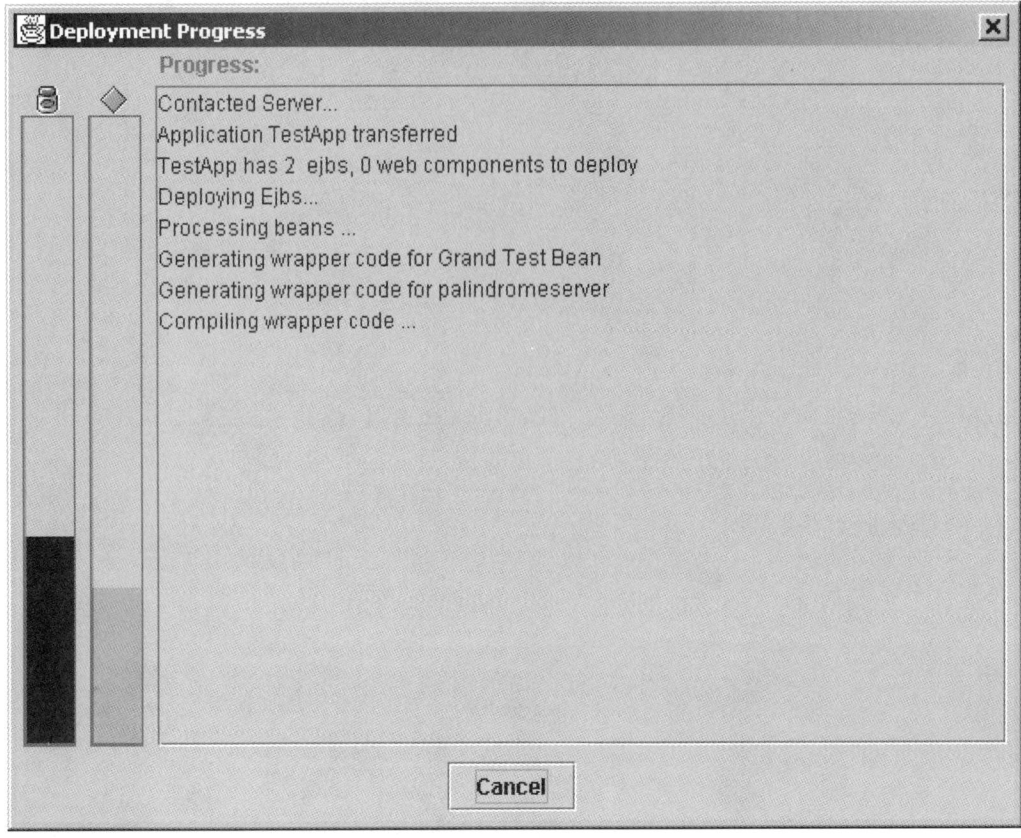

Figure A-40. Progress screen for the compilation and deployment process performed by the deploytool

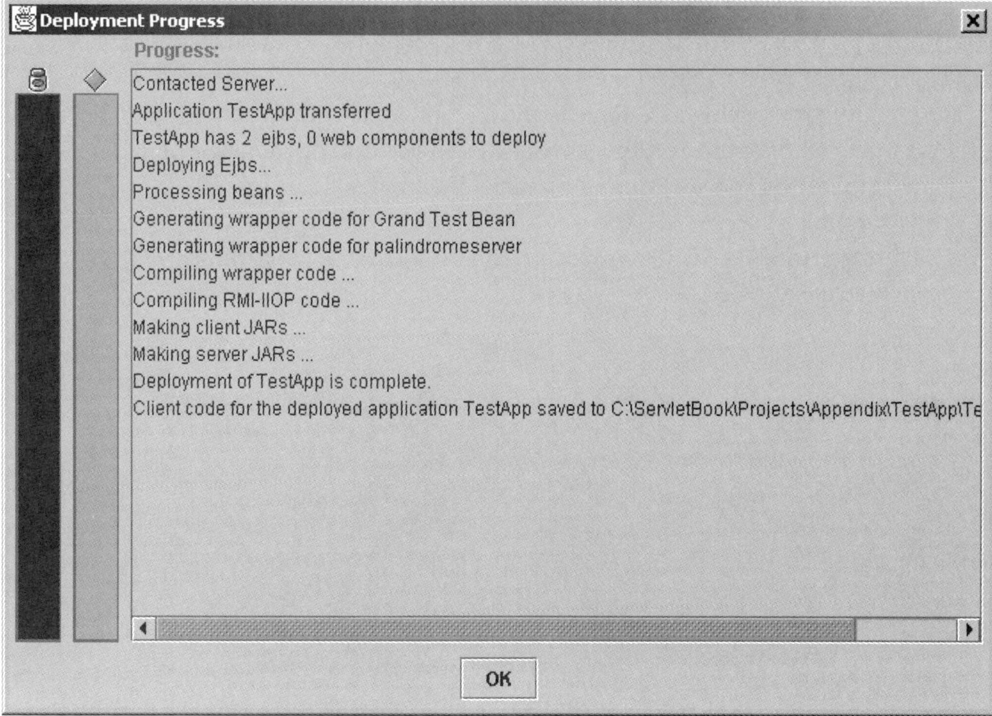

Figure A-41. Resulting view for the completed deployment process

Having added an EJB component to the J2EE reference implementation server, you need to investigate the deployment process for a WAR archive and a Web application (non-packaged) is done.

Adding Web Applications with the J2EE Deployment Tool

Most industrial-strength J2EE applications require that you add not only EJB components but also servlets and/or JSP documents. Thus, the deploytool of the J2EE server contains wizards to deploy Web applications and prepackaged WAR files. Thankfully, few Web applications contain equally complex dependencies to those of EJB components. The deployment process for Web applications is, generally, much simpler than the corresponding EJB deployment process.

> **CAUTION** *The servlet engine in the J2EE reference implementation server is of an elder version than the Apache Tomcat reference implementation. Therefore, you cannot use Servlet 2.3 specific features in the J2EE 1.2.1 server.*

Similar to EJB deployment, Web applications may be deployed into the J2EE server from a prepackaged archive (WAR) or from standalone JSP and class (in other words, bytecode) files.

The process of deploying a WAR file to the J2EE reference implementation server is a rather smooth process, unless your developer team has neglected lots of required application specific property settings. To do so, follow these steps:

1. Press the Add Web WAR to Application… button in the deploytool, as shown in Figure A-42.

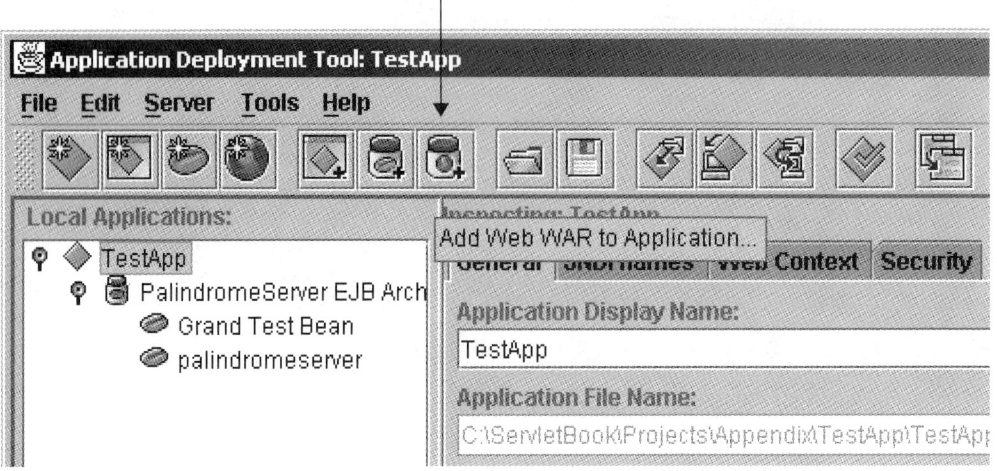

Figure A-42. Adding a prepackaged web archive (WAR) to the application selected

2. Add the Apache Struts Web documentation to the TestApp application. Simply select the WAR file from the file system and select the WAR to include in the TestApp application. The selection dialog is shown in Figure A-43.

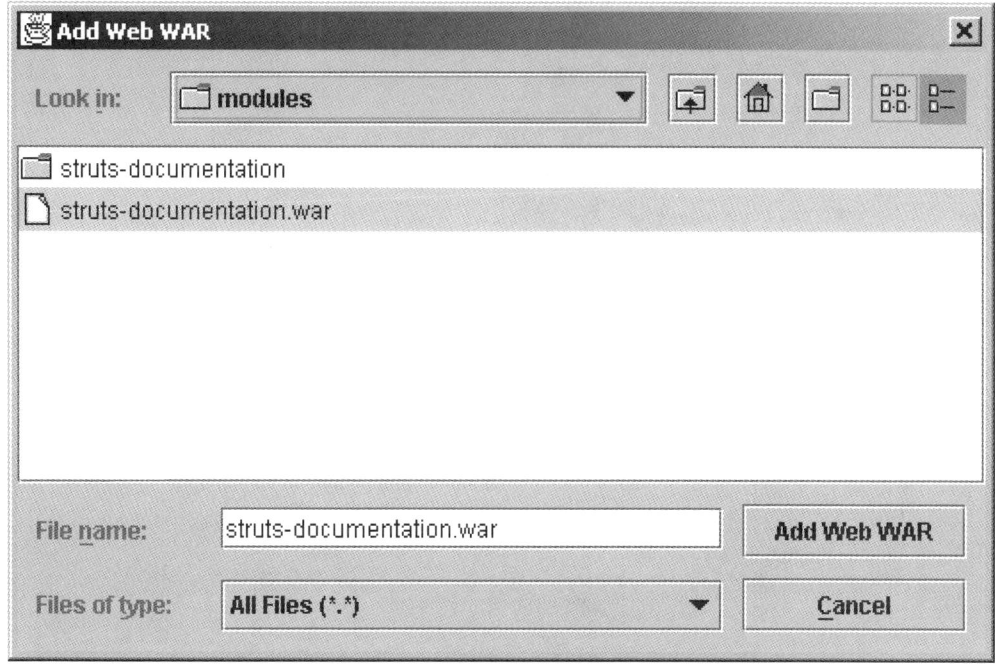

Figure A-43. File selection dialog to pinpoint the WAR file that should be imported

3. Provide a Web application display name—the Struts engineers didn't—and restart the deploytool; the deploytool main view shown in Figure A-44 appears.

   The General definition panel shown in Figure A-44 contains two relevant configuration settings. The first is the MIME Mapping configuration that binds file suffices to outgoing MIME types for the Web application in question. The second is the Contents pane, where a deployer may add files to (or remove files from) the Web application.

NOTE *Most Web applications imported from a WAR file need little or no specific configuration. Of course, two notable exceptions are if you intend to use J2EE security or bind a property in the* `ServletContext` *(Web Container* `Context`. *In the former case, you need to create a security profile (which restricts access to resources to one or more roles). In the latter case, binding values into the Servlet-Context is even simpler than binding values in the EJB Context.*

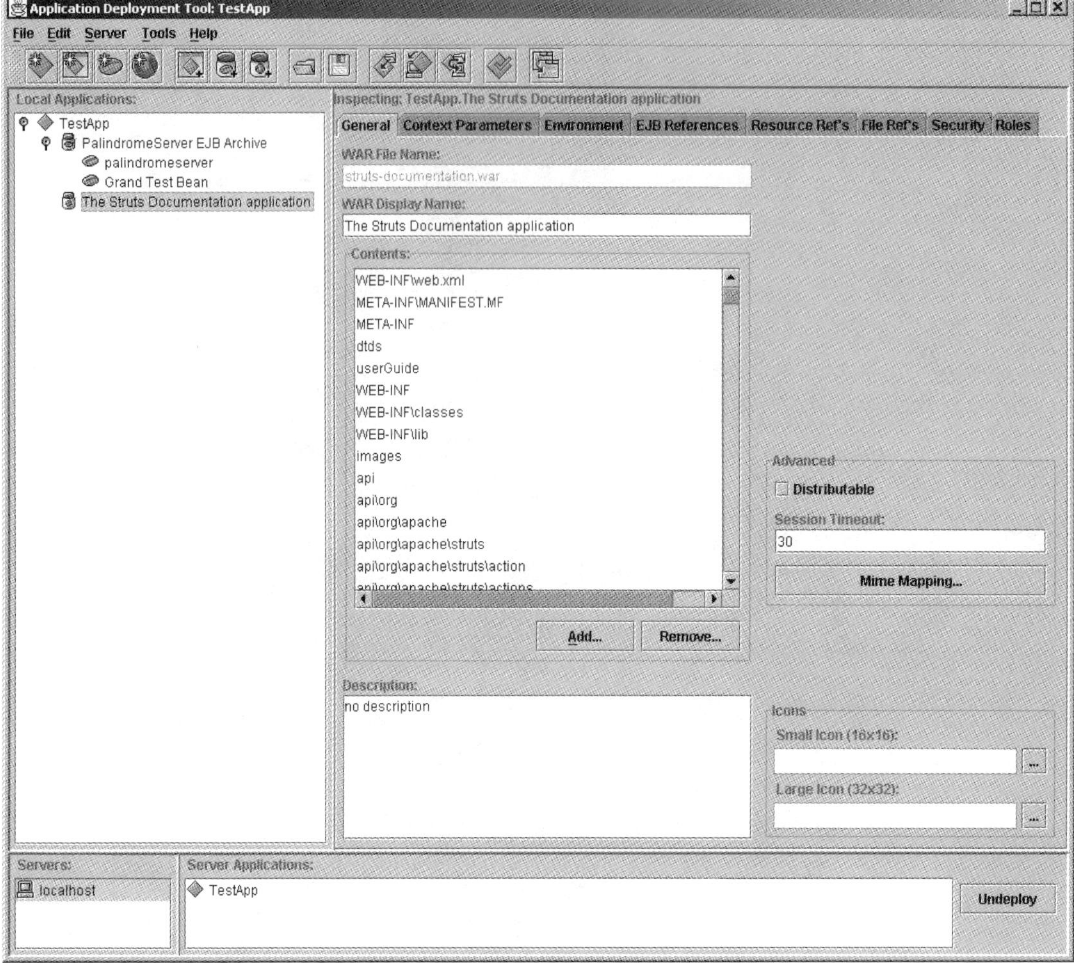

Figure A-44. The deploytool main view after having imported the Struts documentation application

4. To add an entry in the ServletContext of a particular Web application, switch to the Context Parameters tab (illustrated in Figure A-45), and press the Add button. Of course, parameters bound in the ServletContext may be edited or removed while the Context Parameters tab is active.

5. Identical to the Environment entry tab of the EJB container deployment, you may add values to the environment of the Web application if you choose the Environment tab and press the Add button. In a similar fashion to the EJB Environment, the deploytool constrains the types available to the ones permitted by the EJB 1.1 specification. The result of adding an environment variable is shown in Figure A-46.

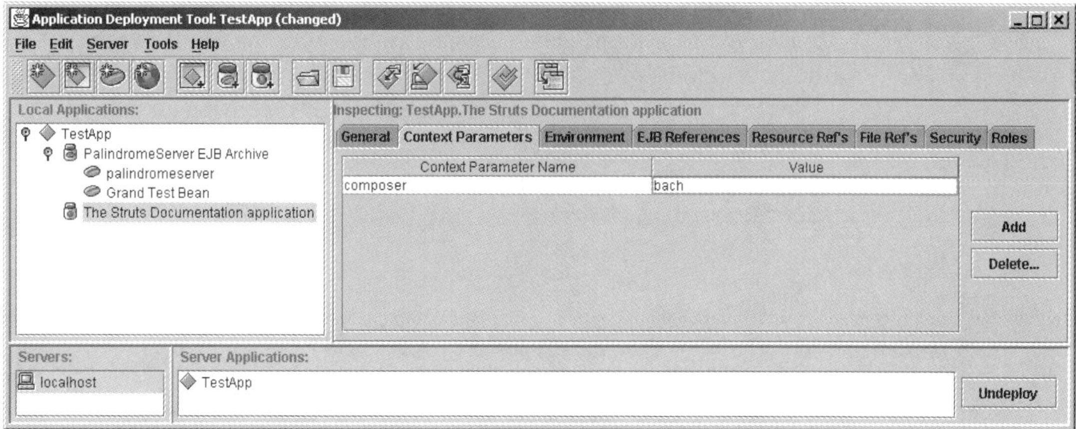

Figure A-45. The Context Parameters pane, where ServletContext entries may be added, edited or deleted

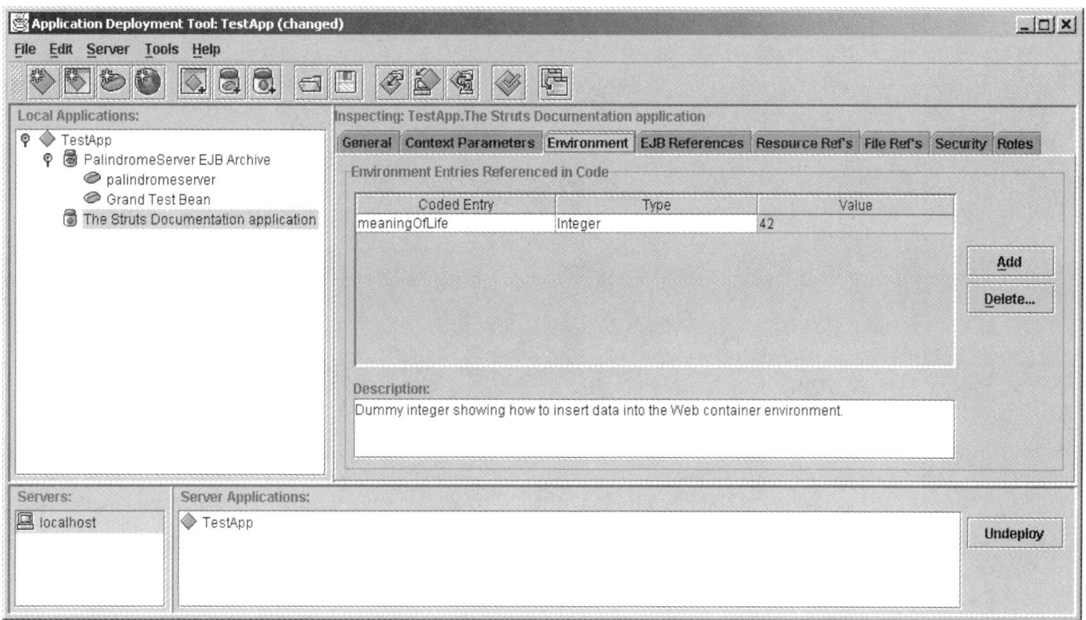

Figure A-46. Adding an environment variable to the Web container environment

6. The Resource Ref's, Security, and Roles tabs are identical to the EJB case shown in the section "Deploying an EJB JAR," but the File Ref's tab deserve a slightly more detailed explanation. As shown in Figure A-47, the File's Ref tab contains definitions for welcome and error pages used by the application, corresponding to the tabs in the `web.xml` descriptor. Thus, you may edit the properties in the File Ref's tab or simply make the alterations to the `web.xml` file in your favorite text editor.

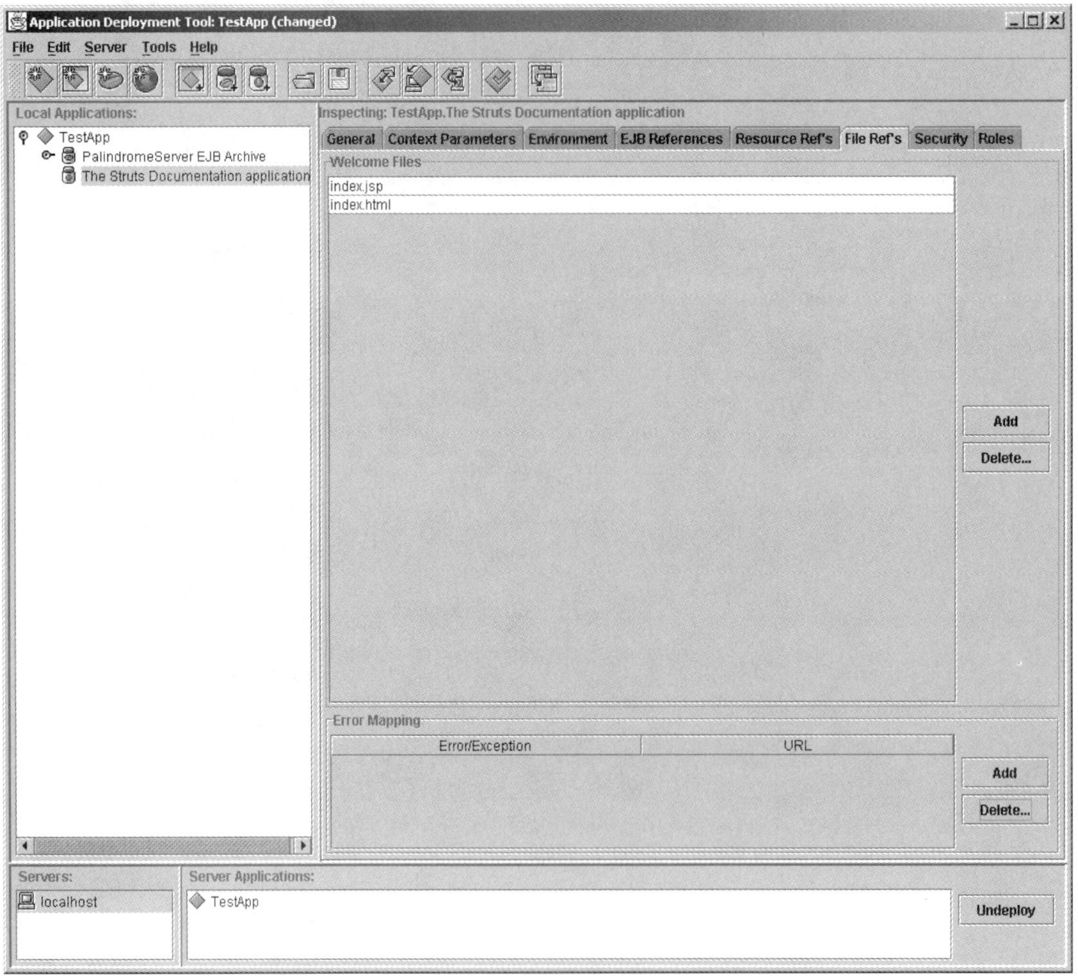

Figure A-47. The File Ref's tab of the deploytool, where setup configuration for welcome pages and error mappings are configured

7. As an alternative to importing a prepackaged Web application, you may create a Web application on the fly by including resources using the New Web Component... wizard, started as shown in Figure A-48.

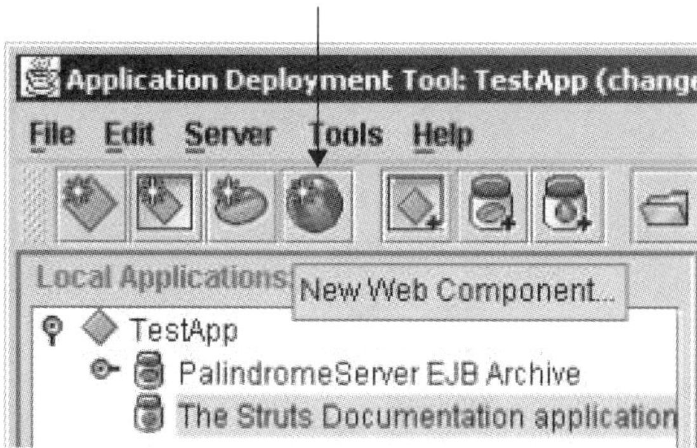

Figure A-48. Start the Web application deployment wizard by pressing the New Web Component button.

8. After launching the new Web Component... wizard, an introductory screen (shown in Figure A-49) lets you know what awaits in the wizard.

9. Click the Next button to open the WAR files General Properties pane (illustrated in Figure A-50), where you may choose a deployment WAR or create a new one. In this case, elect to create a new Web application archive with the display name Test Web Application.

> **TIP** *When in the General Properties pane, try to make a habit of entering good descriptions for your Web application. Descriptions, along with carefully chosen display names, should provide adequate information about a Web application to make a developer realize its purpose without reading through endless system description documents. The description is shown in the bottom-left part of Figure A-50.*

10. You may opt to create one or more MIME types specific for the Web application in question. To do so, press the Mime Mapping... button to pop up the Mime Mappings... dialog as illustrated in Figure A-51. All files requested ending with the suffix `.jguru` will have their Content-Type response header set to `application/x-jguru-launcher`. The browser, in turn, will open the document with whatever application is mapped to the MIME type `x-jguru-launcher`.

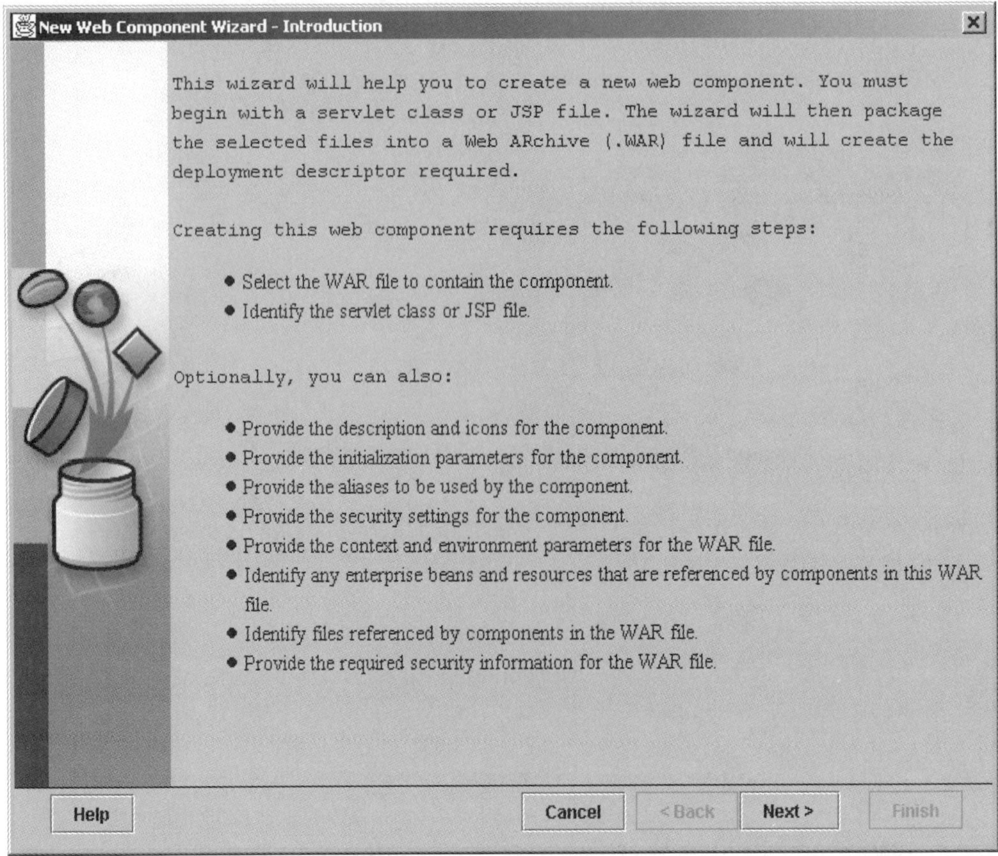

Figure A-49. The start of the add New Web Component Wizard provides a help text describing the steps about to be undertaken.

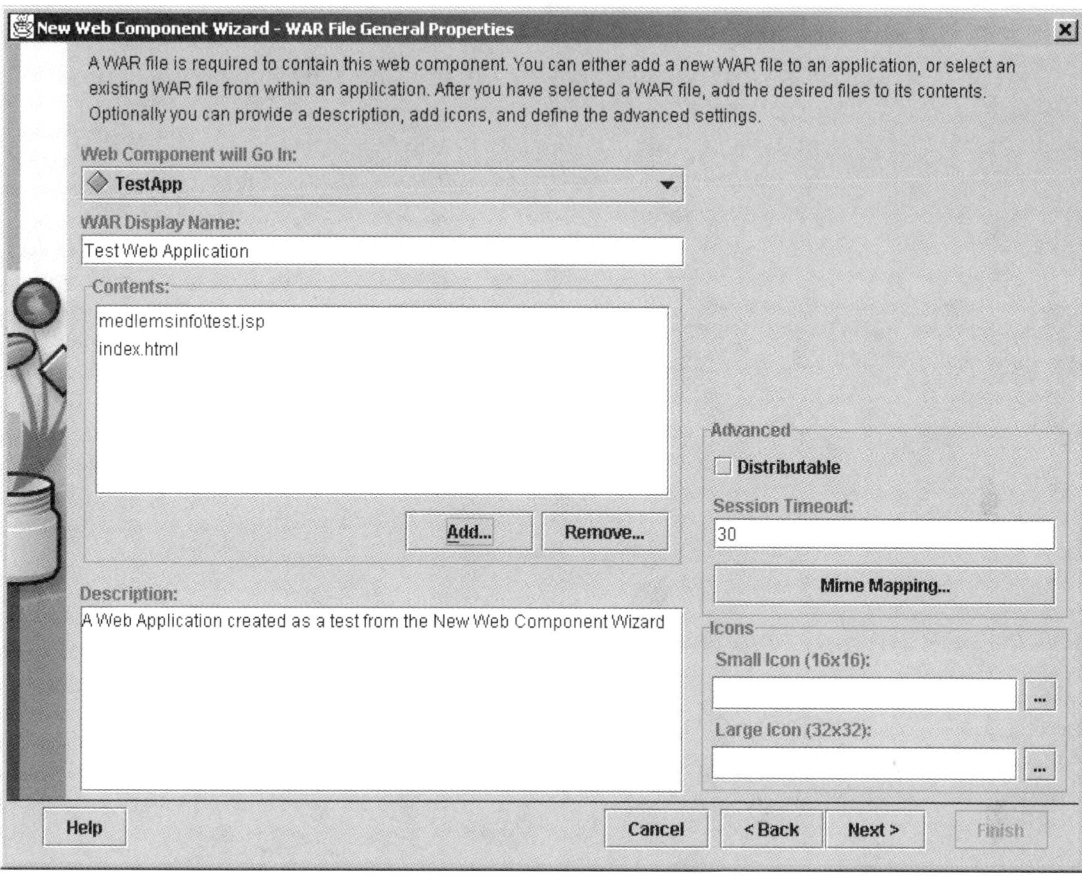

Figure A-50. Adding Web resource to a newly created Web application. Press the Add... button to add new components to the application and the Remove... button to delete selected components. Note that you may also create specific MIME mappings for the application.

Mime Mappings

Extension	Mime Type
.jguru	application/x-jguru-launcher

OK
Cancel
Help
Add
Delete...

Figure A-51. A specific MIME mapping applied to the Web application being created.

11. Press the Next button again to show the Choose Component Type pane (illustrated in Figure A-52), where you may select a Server or JSP document that should be included in the Web Application. If you simply wish to add resources or static HTML documents to the Web Application, you should select the No Web Component option. Press the Next button to move on to the next pane where you may configure your newly included Web component. The Configuration pane is shown in Figure A-53.

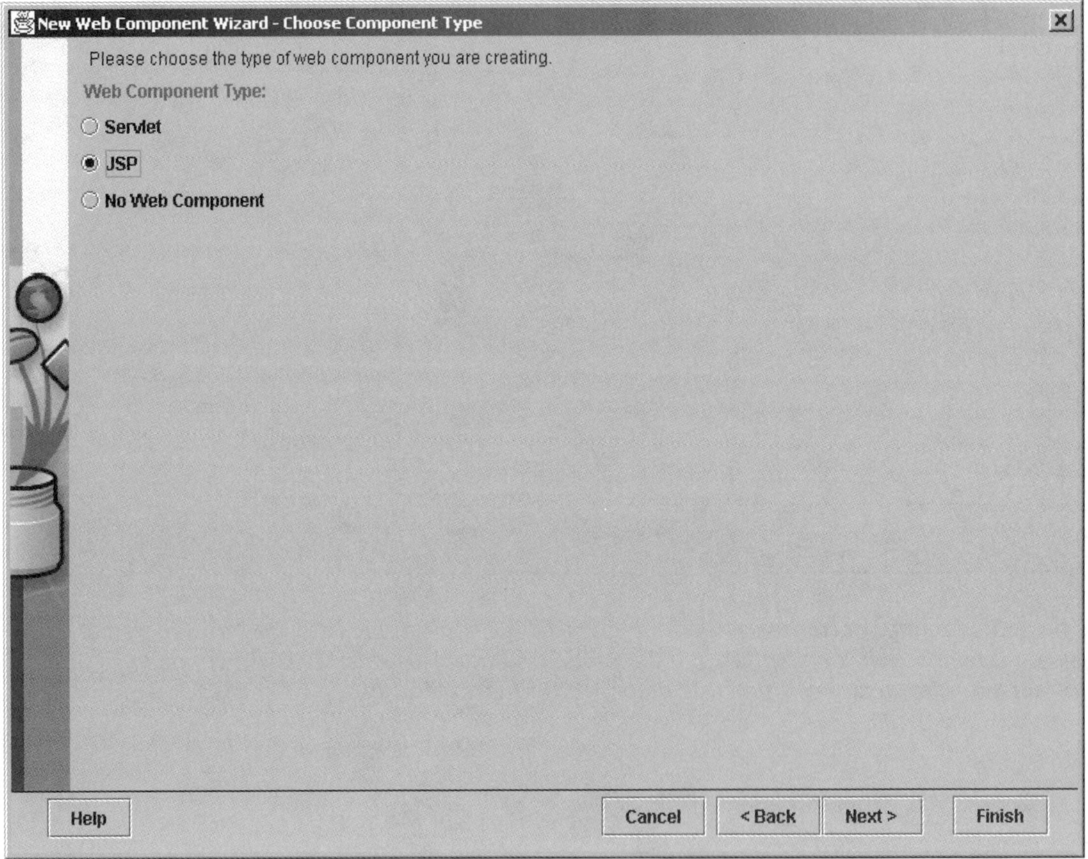

Figure A-52. The Choose Component Type pane permits you to select the type of Web component that should be wrapped in the WAR.

NOTE *The importance of relevant descriptions and sound naming cannot be overly stressed. You will generally save a lot of time in larger projects simply by finding names that pinpoint the function of a particular Web component more exactly—and remember, simplicity is a virtue in its own right. The descriptions shown in Figure A-53 may be suited to illustrate the wizard function and usage in this book, but the industrial-strength application requires more thought on the description texts.*

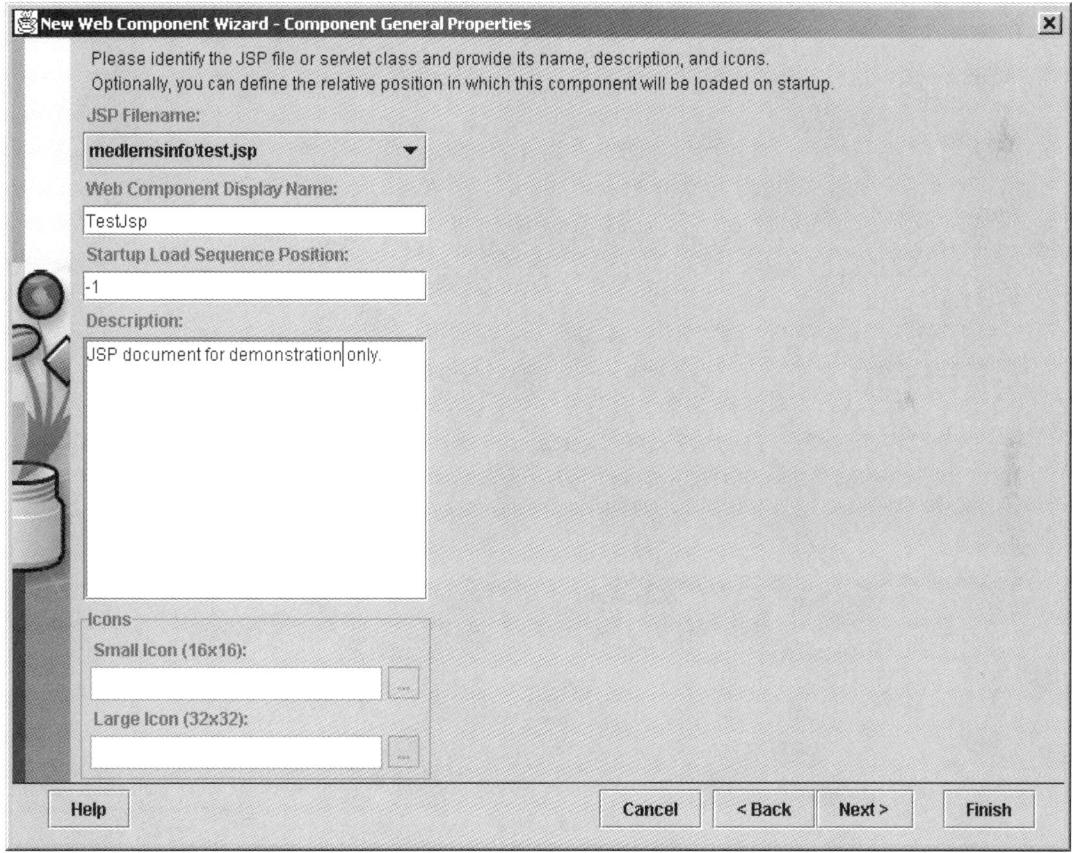

Figure A-53. The Component General Properties pane allows you to select the Web component that should be imported into the Web application being created. Don't forget to use sensibly named and described components.

12. Having configured the Web component, you may want to add initialization parameters to customize its behavior. Click the Next button to show the Component Initialization Parameters screen. Figure A-54 shows that screen and an initialization parameter, named *lookupString* with the value *jdbc/jguru/hyperDB* being added to the JSP document. The pane following the parameter initialization is the Component Aliases pane, where one may supply servlet mapping names (aliases), as illustrated in Figure A-55.

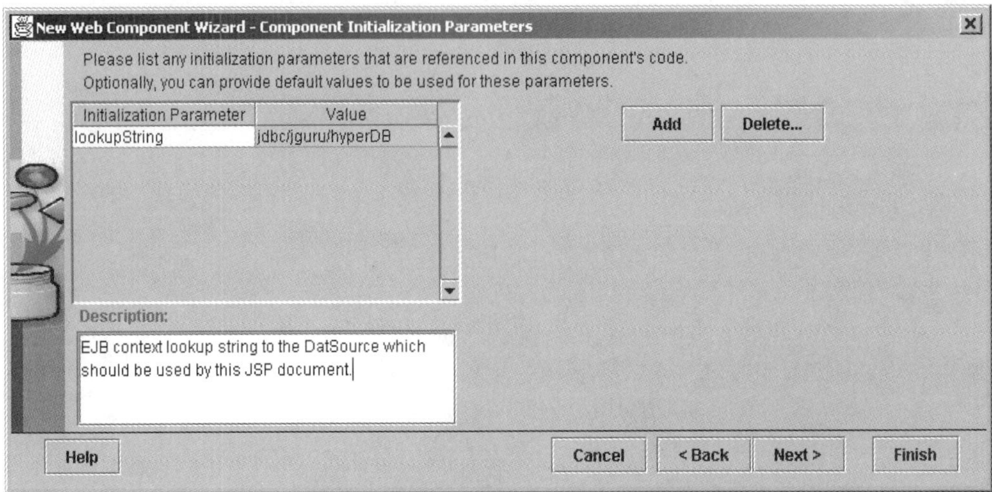

Figure A-54. The Initialization Parameter pane allows you to configure the initialization parameters to the servlet or JSP document. In the case of a servlet, the parameters may be retrieved from its `ServletConfig` *instance* (`getServletConfig().getParameter("lookupString")`).

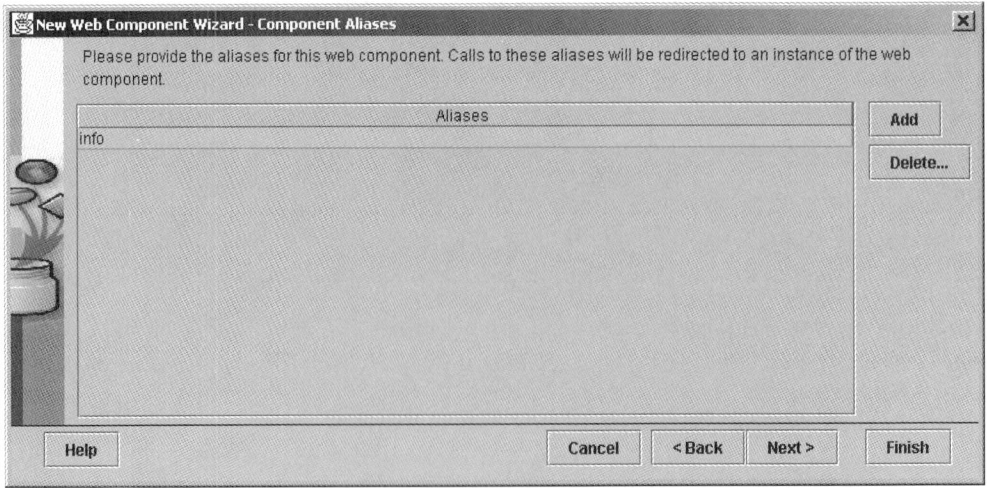

Figure A-55. One may, of course, provide a named alias (map) for the servlet or JSP document inserted into the Web application. In this case, the alias info maps to the `test.jsp` *document that is being deployed (refer to Figure A-53 to see the component definition).*

13. You may now press the Finish button complete the deployment process of the JSP document. Doing so, you find yourself in the main view with the newly created Web application visible in the leftmost content pane. You may now see and edit any configuration parameters for the Web application and its components.

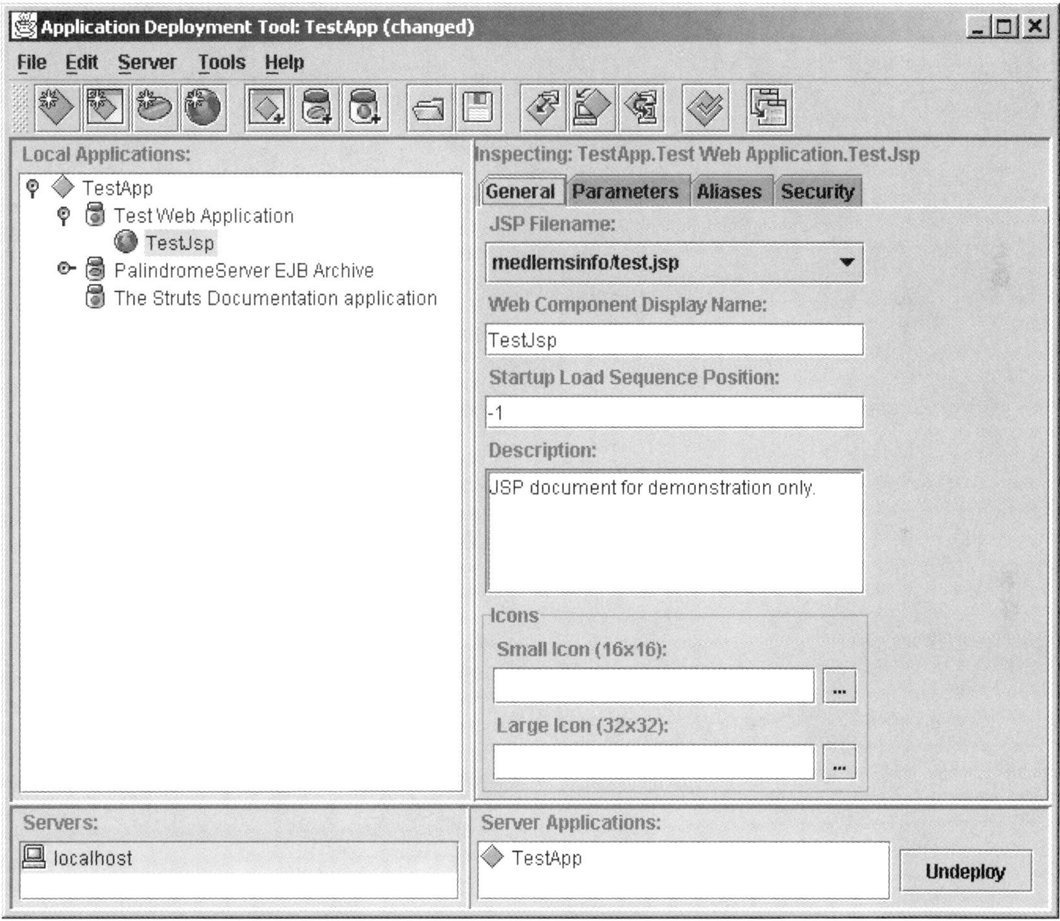

Figure A-56. The newly created Web application is shown in the leftmost content pane. Selecting the JSP component (`TestJsp`) shows its settings and four configuration tabs.

14. So, after a long night of configuring your application in the J2EE reference implementation server, you finally wind up with your finished J2EE application. To deploy it into the server (refer to Figures A-37 to A-41), press the Update and Redeploy Application button, shown in Figure A-57, and wait for the process to complete.

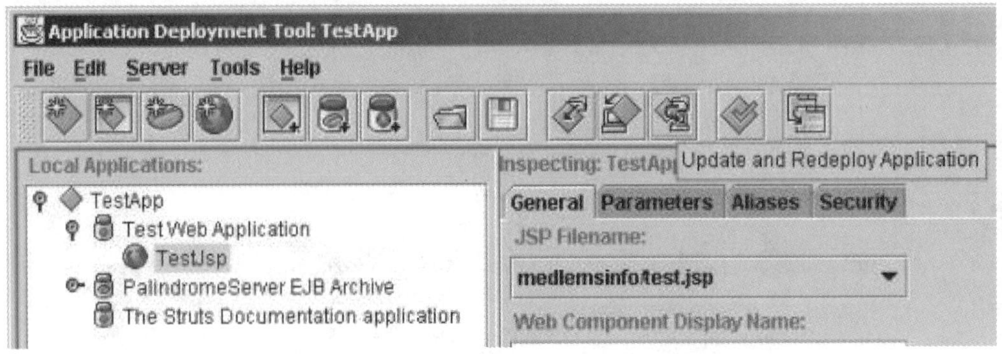

Figure A-57. Press the Update and Redeploy Application button to deploy all its parts to the J2EE server.

Application Deployment in the J2EE 1.3 Reference Implementation Server

The J2EE reference implementation server version 1.3 (J2EEv1.3 RI) and its corresponding administration tools are upgraded from the 1.2.1 version to handle newer versions of the J2EE server-side technologies. The similarities between the J2EE RI server and its deploytool administration application are strong, so the J2EEv1.3 RI server and tools will be introduced simply by highlighting the differences and examining the deployment process of a J2EE application.

> **CAUTION** *At the time of the writing of this book, the J2EE version 1.3 was released in the beta 2 state, so it is possible, however unlikely, that some of the settings for the J2EE reference implementation server may have changed in the release version.*

The services included in the J2EEv1.3 RI server are as follows:

- Web service, using HTTP and HTTPS (in other words, HTTP over SSL), supporting Servlet API version 2.3 and JavaServer Pages API version 1.2
- EJB service supporting Enterprise JavaBeans specification 2.0 and RMI/IIOP
- Java Messaging Service, supporting JMS 1.0.2
- COS naming service, supporting JNDI specification 1.2
- Authentication services, custom to the J2EEv1.3 server

Common legacy APIs supported by all classes deployed within the J2EEv1.3 RI server include the following:

- Java Transaction API version 1.0 enabling uniform transaction handling
- JDBC Standard Extension 2.0 which provides XADataSource connections
- J2EE Connector 1.0 API to facilitate standardized communication with legacy services
- JavaMail version 1.2, which permits sending electronic mail from the legacy Java application
- Java API for XML Parsing (JAXP) version 1.1

Installing the J2EEv1.3 package creates the structure shown in Figure A-58.

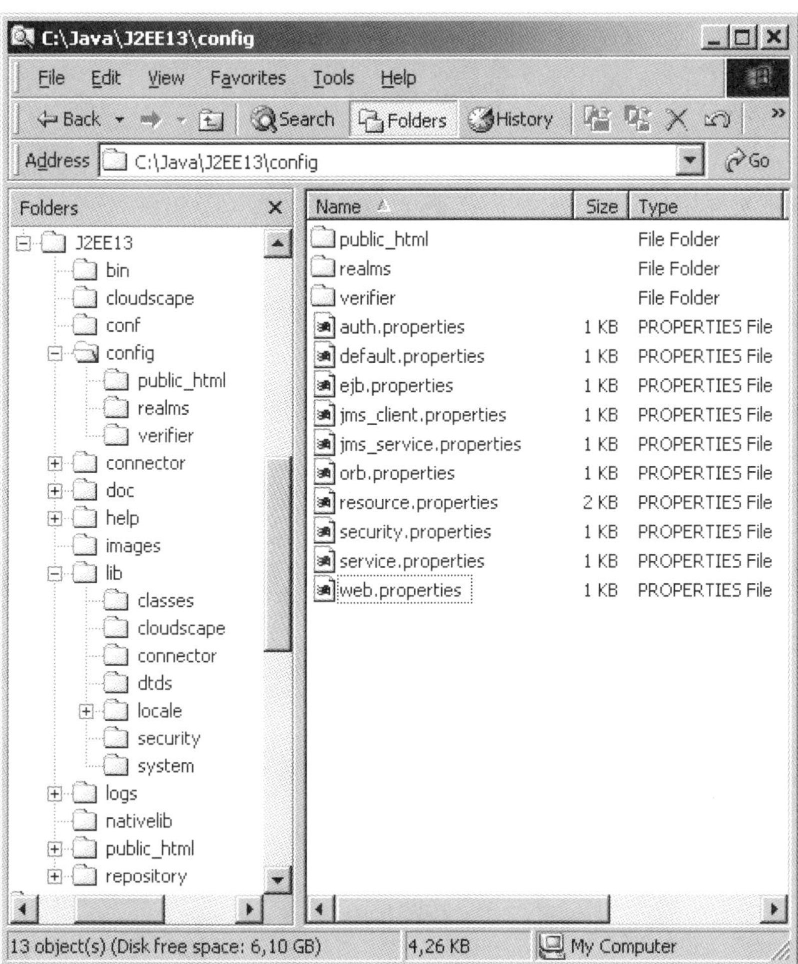

Figure A-58. The deployment structure of the J2EE 1.3 reference implementation server

As shown in Figure A-58, the number of configuration files has grown from five in the J2EE 1.2 RI server to 10 in the J2EE 1.3 RI server. Although some of the configuration files deal with the properties of the Java Message Service (JMS), some of the configuration files described in the "Configuring the Server" section previously have been modified.

Configuring the J2EEv1.3 Server

The J2EEv1.3 server uses 10 main configuration files, placed in the `<J2EE_HOME>/config` directory, to store its configuration settings. These properties files are sensibly named, so you probably realize what types of settings reside in each file simply by examining their names. To avoid any confusion, let's elaborate a little on the settings for the J2EE server; there are at least two settings you are likely to want to change before launching for the first time.

The 10 configuration files (illustrated in Figure A-58) are:

- *auth.properties*, which contains settings for authorization in the J2EEv1.3 RI server. The `auth.properties` file is unaltered from the earlier J2EE RI server version.

- *default.properties*, which has been modified in the 1.3 version of the J2EE RI server. The JDBC driver and DataSource configuration definitions have been moved to the `resource.properties` file. In the `default.properties` file of the J2EEv1.3 RI server, you can only configure properties that affect all parts of the server such as the log root directory, transaction and session timeout, and so forth.

- *ejb.properties*, which contains settings for the EJB container and its controller classes. This properties file contains identical property definitions as the J2EE RI server version 1.2.1, with the addition of one property, `transaction.interoperability`.

- *jms_client.properties*, which is new to the J2EEv1.3 RI server and contains standard type definitions and JNDI properties used by a JMS client to connect to the J2EE service.

- *jms_service.properties*, which is new to the J2EEv1.3 RI server and contains necessary definitions for the JMS server startup process. These definitions include required type specifications, as well as JNDI names and constants used by the JMS server to connect to a persistent storage via JDBC.

- *orb.properties*, which contains configuration settings for the CORBA compliant ORB running in the J2EE reference implementation server. This property file is identical to the J2EE RI server version 1.2.1.

- *resource.properties*, which is new to the J2EEv1.3 RI server and contains JDBC and DataSource definitions, as well as factory and destination definitions for the JMS service.

- *security.properties*, which is new to the J2EEv1.3 RI server and contains property definitions for configuring the security service.

- *service.properties*, which is new to the J2EEv1.3 RI server and contains definitions for the concrete classes used for the JMS service.

- *web.properties*, which contains configuration settings for the Web container and HTTP server integrated into the J2EE reference implementation server. This file is unaltered from the J2EE RI server version 1.2.1.

Although the number of configuration files has grown by a factor of two since the J2EE RI server version 1.2.1, the changes for developers deploying Web and EJB components are minor with respect to the configuration files. The most obvious change is that the JDBC DataSource configuration is done in the `resource.properties` file instead of the `default.properties` file.

Because most of the configuration files have identical (or almost identical) sets of properties in the J2EEv1.3 RI server, let's simply examine the configuration property files that differ from those of the J2EEv1.2.1 RI server.

The configuration settings for the EJB container are found in the `ejb.properties` file. Although it may be interesting to view the settings, they are rarely in need of alteration for proper operation. The default content of the `ejb.properties` file is as follows:

```
jdbcDataSource.0.name=jdbc/Cloudscape
jdbcDataSource.0.url=jdbc:cloudscape:rmi:CloudscapeDB;create=true
jdbcDataSource.1.name=jdbc/DB1
jdbcDataSource.1.url=jdbc:cloudscape:rmi:CloudscapeDB;create=true
jdbcDataSource.2.name=jdbc/DB2
jdbcDataSource.2.url=jdbc:cloudscape:rmi:CloudscapeDB;create=true
jdbcDataSource.3.name=jdbc/EstoreDB
jdbcDataSource.3.url=jdbc:cloudscape:rmi:CloudscapeDB;create=true
jdbcDataSource.4.name=jdbc/InventoryDB
jdbcDataSource.4.url=jdbc:cloudscape:rmi:CloudscapeDB;create=true
jdbcDataSource.5.name=jdbc/cloudscape/webpageDb
jdbcDataSource.5.url=jdbc:cloudscape:rmi://localhost:1099/webpageDb
jdbcDriver.0.name=COM.cloudscape.core.RmiJdbcDriver
```

Setting up a new DataSource in the `resource.properties` file seems fairly trivial; simply add a driver class entry on the form like this:

```
jdbcDriver.X.name=<className>
```

where X is the order number in which the drivers are loaded into memory, and `<className>` is the JDBC driver class of the database for which you want to create a DataSource. Having made sure that the J2EEv1.3 RI server loads the driver you need, simply add the two DataSource entries required:

- `jdbcDataSource.X.url=<jdbcUrl>`, which connects to the database in question
- `jdbcDataSource.X.name=<jndiName>`, where the DataSource will be bound

With regards to Web and EJB component deployment, the `resources.properties` file is the only file new to the 1.3 version of the J2EE RI server. Having added the JDBC drivers and DataSources you need, it is time to deploy an example application.

Deploying J2EE Application Components

Deploying components in the J2EEv1.3 RI server is similar to deploying them in the J2EEv1.2.1 RI server. I will walk through deploying the Image subsystem J2EE application from Chapter 9 because it contains both Web and EJB components holding several references to resource factories and variables in the JNDI local context.

> **NOTE** *Deploying BMP EJB components is simpler than deploying CMP EJBs, so the Image subsystem that contains only a CMP EJB should provide you with the most complex deployment scenario available.*

After modifying the startup shell or batch files as described in the sidebar "The Unbearable Lightness of Rebooting…" earlier in this appendix, start the J2EE server by running the `j2ee.bat` script (or the equivalent shell script on a Unix system). When the console output displays "J2EE server startup complete," you may continue to launch the deploytool of the J2EE RI server. When launched, the start screen of the application deployment tool is slightly modified compared to the 1.2.1 version, as shown in Figure A-59.

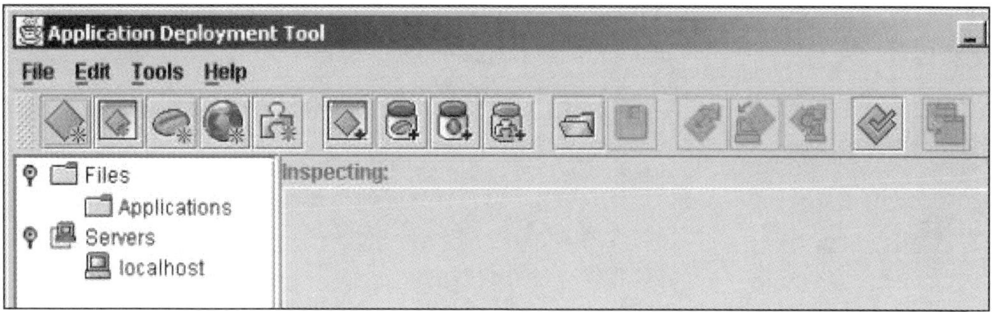

Figure A-59. The startup screen of the deploytool has a slightly modified user interface, compared to its 1.2.1 sibling.

Perform the same three deployment tasks for the J2EEv1.3 RI server as you previously did for the 1.2.1 version:

1. Create an application.
2. Deploy EJB components into the application.
3. Deploy Web components (servlet and JSP documents) into the application.

Deploy the components of the Image subsystems J2EE application developed in Chapter 11 into the J2EE reference implementation server.

Create the J2EE Application

The process to create an EAR (which is the physical manifestation of what the J2EE RI server perceives as an application) is trivial. To do so, follow these steps:

1. Press the New Application ... button or select File | New | Application... as shown in Figure A-60. The New Application dialog box appears (see Figure A-61).
2. After providing the data required to create a new EAR file and give it a display name in the deploytool (or any other proprietary application server deployment tool) GUI, and click OK to close the New Application dialog box.

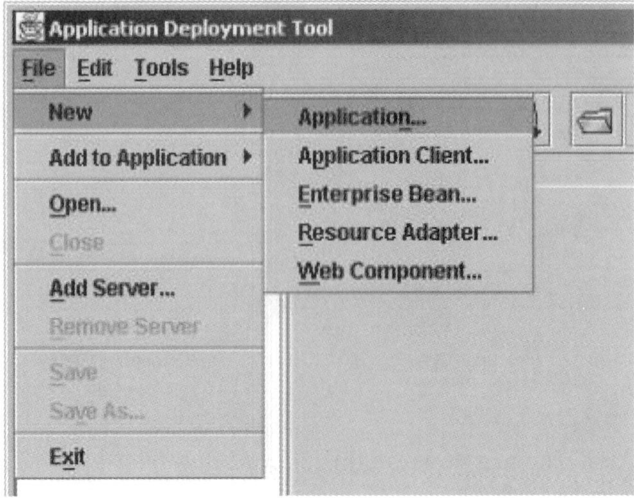

Figure A-60. Creating a new application physically creates an EAR file

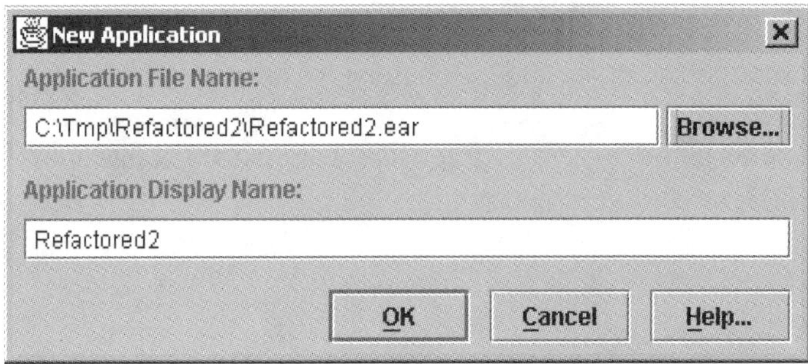

Figure A-61. Provide the location for the EAR file, as well as the DisplayName in the deploytool.

3. You'll return to the deploytool main screen as shown in Figure A-62. The newly created application has been added to the list of known applications, and the deploytool creation process has already provided the two deployment descriptor files required by the J2EE RI server.

The standard `application.xml` descriptor file contains some application template data, but the application server specific deployment descriptor, `sun-j2ee-ri.xml`, holds no configuration data at all.

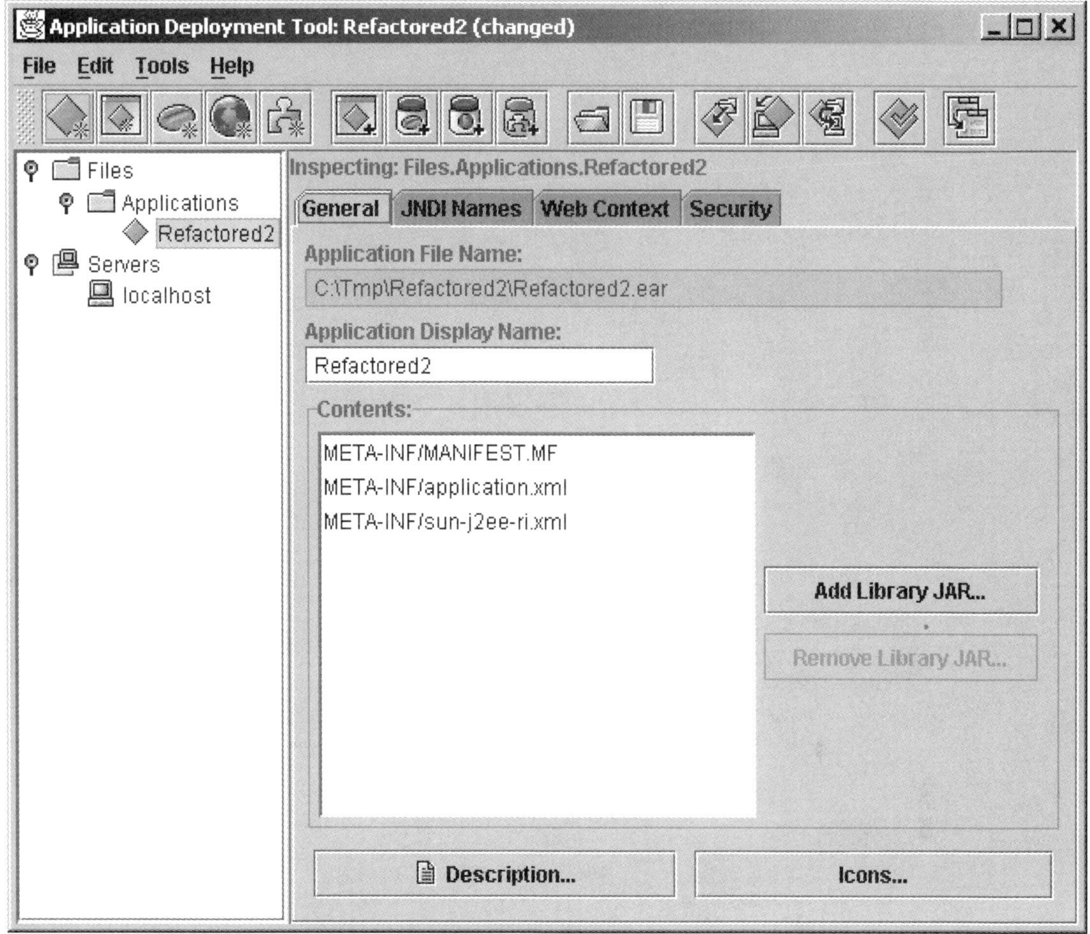

Figure A-62. The verification screen of the deploytool after creating a new application

What's in a Template application.xml File?

The skeleton `application.xml` descriptor is used as a point of origin for the J2EEv1.3 RI server. As shown, the application does not contain any modules (in other words, deployed servlets, JSPs, or EJBs). It has, however, a display-name and a description.

The skeleton `application.xml` file has the following content:

```
<?xml version="1.0" encoding="UTF-8"?>

<!DOCTYPE application PUBLIC '-//Sun Microsystems, Inc.//DTD J2EE Application 1.3//
   EN' 'http://java.sun.com/dtd/application_1_3.dtd'>

<application>
  <display-name>Refactored2</display-name>
  <description>Application description</description>
</application>
```

Adding an EJB Component

It is time to add an EJB component to the Refactored2 J2EE application. Start with the EJB components of the Image subsystem developed as part of the second refactor step example in Chapter 11. To do so, follow these steps:

1. Selecting the File | New | Enterprise Bean … menu item starts the New Enterprise Bean Wizard, as shown in Figure A-63.

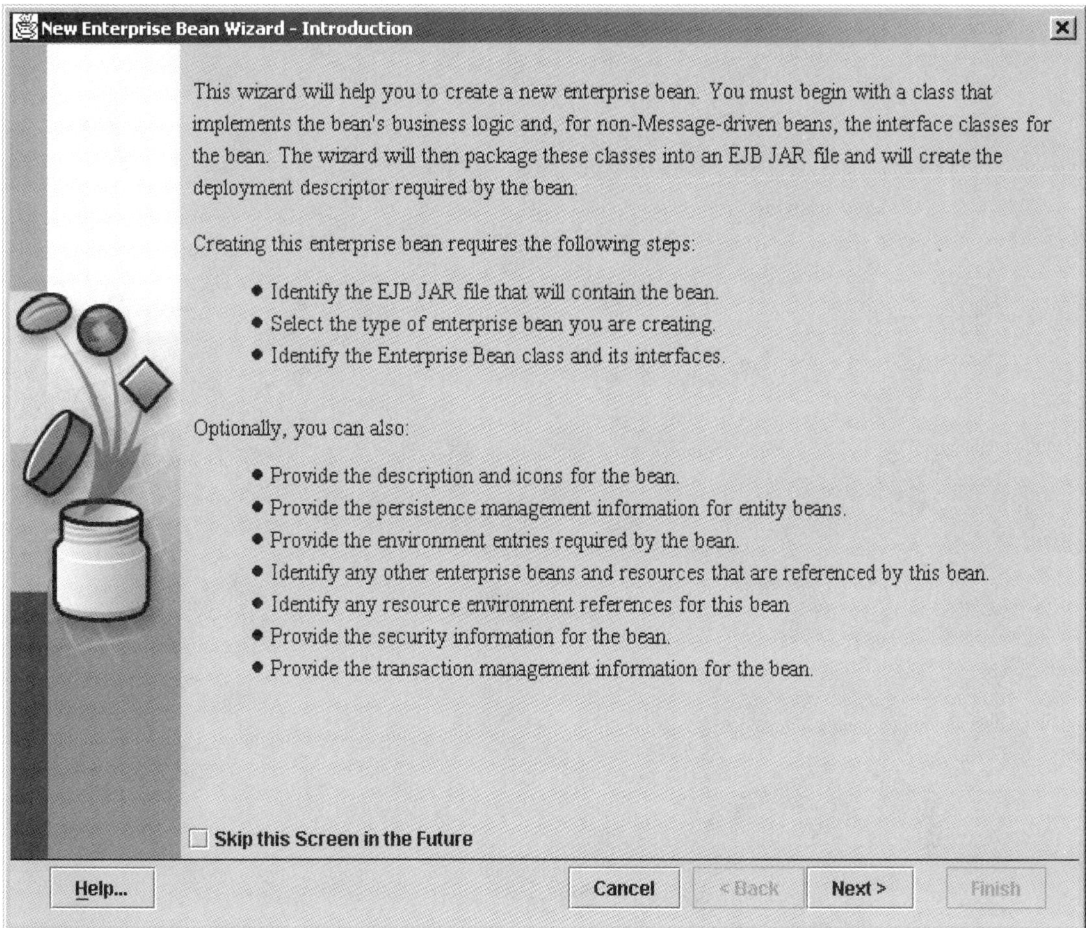

Figure A-63. The Add EJB wizard start screen

2. To dismiss the information screen, press the Next button; if you don't want it displayed the next time you create an EJB component, simply check the Skip the Screen in the Future box before moving to the first definition step of the wizard, as illustrated in Figure A-64.

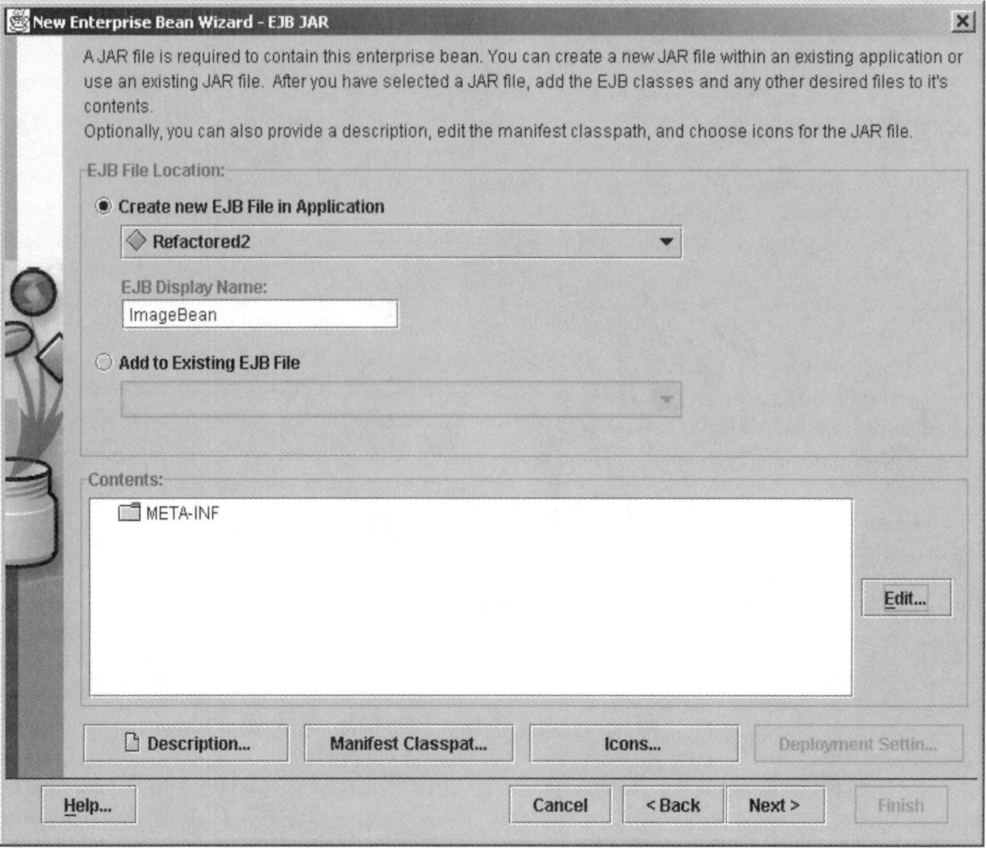

Figure A-64. The first action wizard screen permits entry of basic EJB propereties, such as name and component classes

3. In the first step of the wizard, you should select the application where the EJB component should be deployed and provide a display name.

4. Identify the class files of the EJB component. To do so, launch the Edit Contents of ImageBean dialog by clicking the Edit… button to the right of the Contents list. You may select files from the file system that should be part of the EJB component, as shown in Figure A-65.

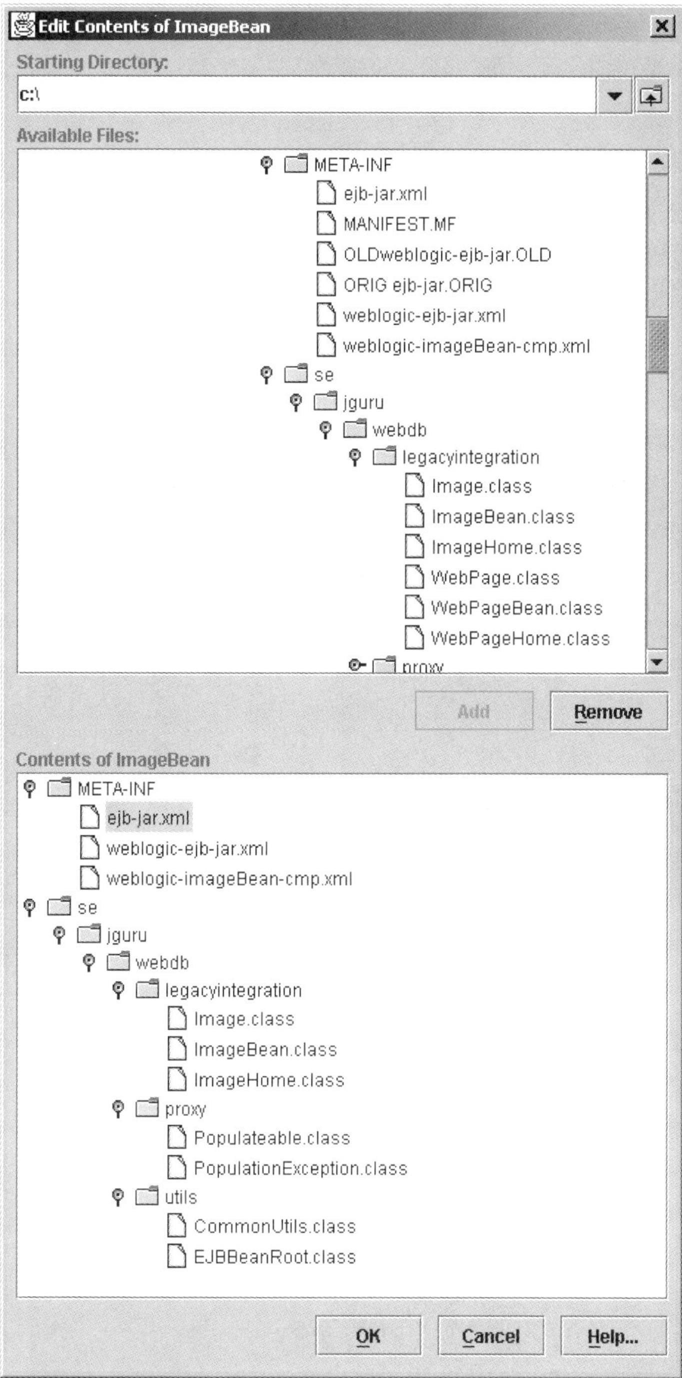

Figure A-65. The files of the EJB component may be selected in this dialog. Simply press the Add button to add a selected file or directory from the topmost file tree to the EJB contents tree below.

5. When done selecting the files the deploytool EJB creation wizard confirms your selection in the Contents tree as shown in Figure A-66. Press the Next button to select the different parts of the EJB component as illustrated in Figure A-67.

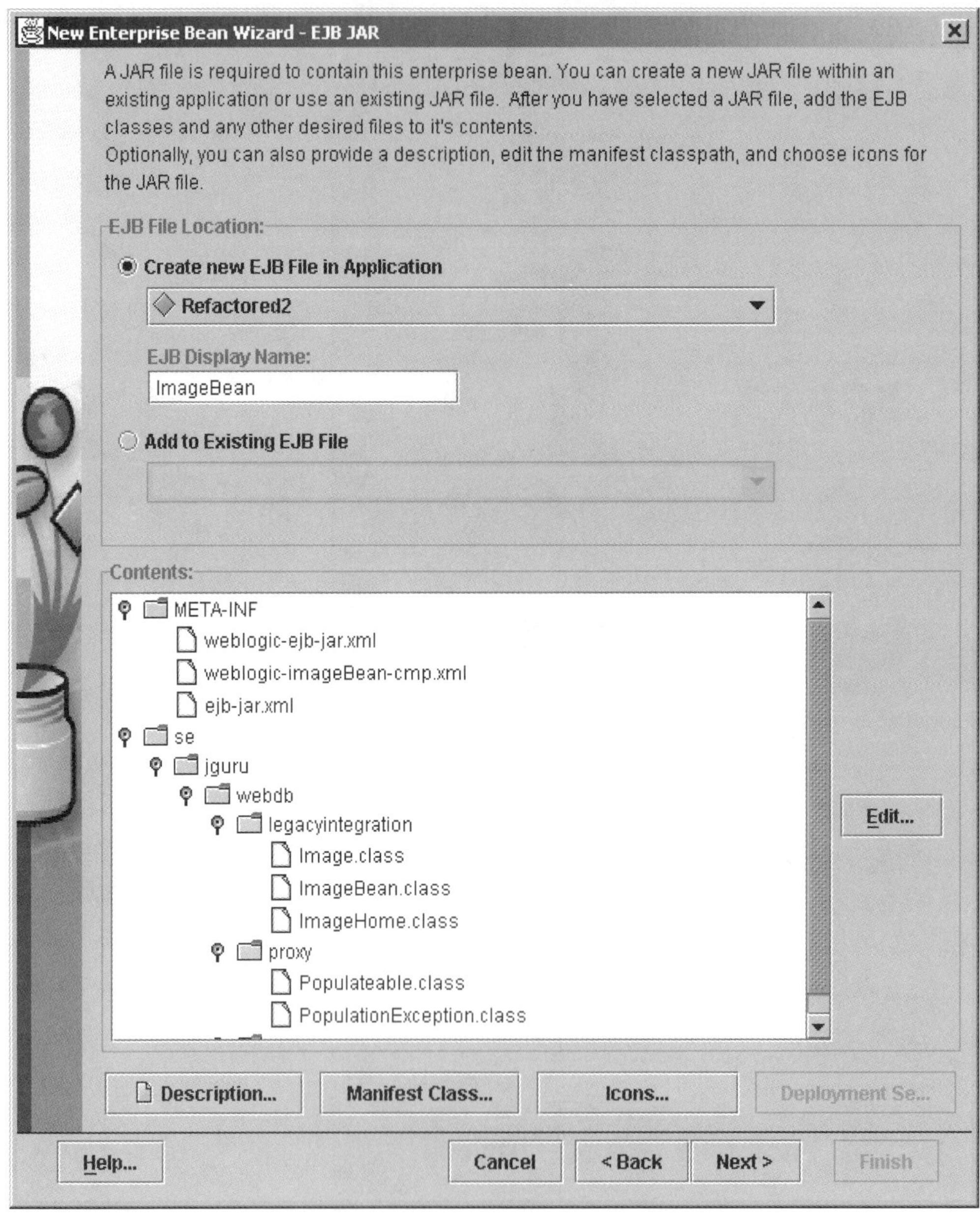

Figure A-66. The Contents tree confirms the contents of the EJB component JAR.

NOTE *Figure A-66 shows that you have kept the custom descriptors from the Weblogic application server, to generate an EJB JAR that may be used in both application servers.*

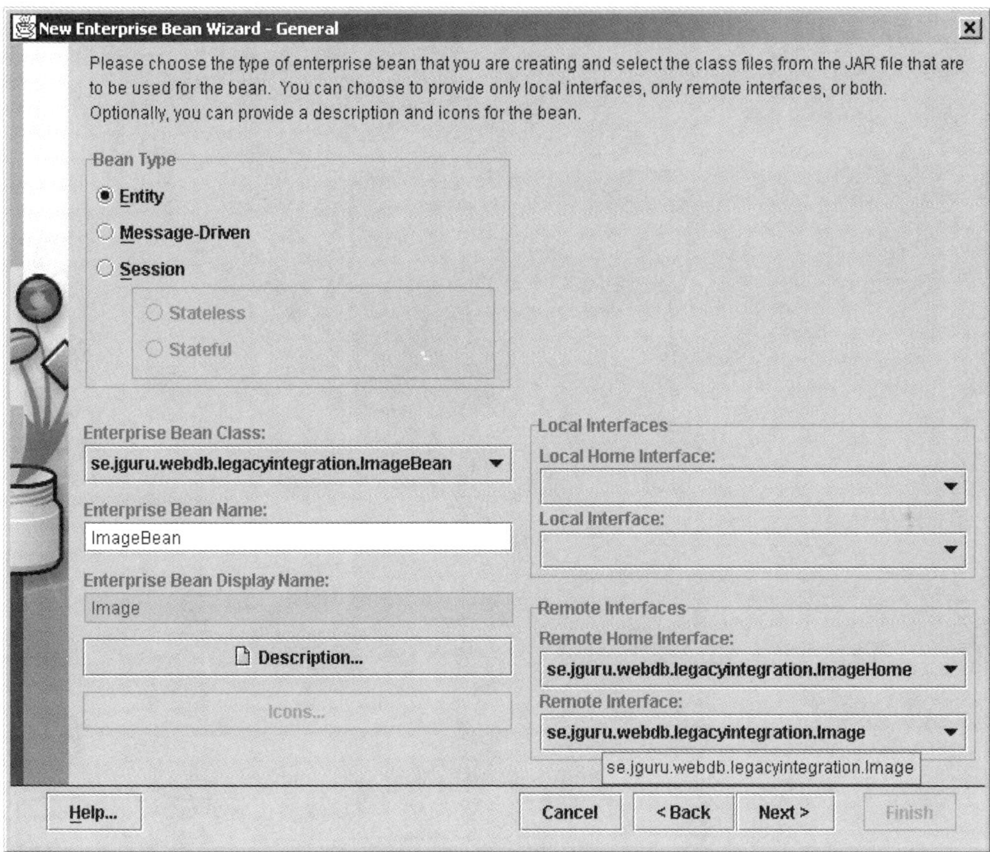

Figure A-67. Selecting the types of the EJB component interfaces and class

Figure A-67 shows the fully populated General pane of the EJB creation wizard. The deploytool uses the same display name as the enterprise bean name.

6. When done selecting the types of the EJB component, press the Next button to continue to set up the persistence properties of the EJB component. As shown in Figure A-68, all available fields in the Entity bean that may be used with the EJB persistence mechanism are shown in the Fields to Be Persisted… list. Select any fields that should be persisted; using EJB 2.0 specification as shown in for the EJB CMP permits you to use EJB-QL in any finder methods.

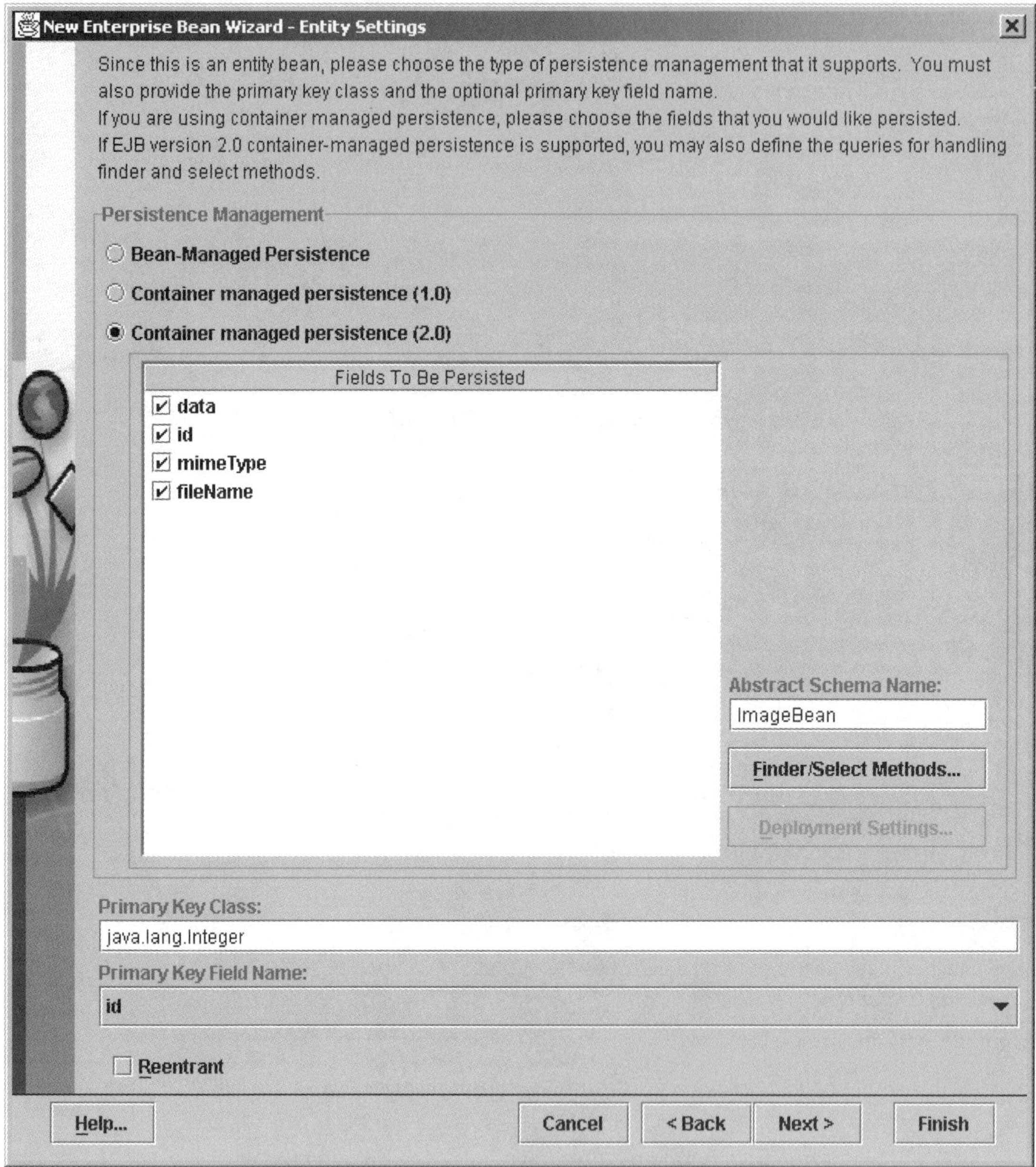

Figure A-68. The entity settings of the EJB component permits selecting the type of persistence used, as well as defining all finders of the EJB component.

7. Specify all finder methods of the EJB component. Remember that this is a CMP EJB component, so all finders are specified in the deployment descriptor—not in the EJB bean implementation class. Press the Finder/Select Methods… button to open the Finder dialog shown in Figure A-69.

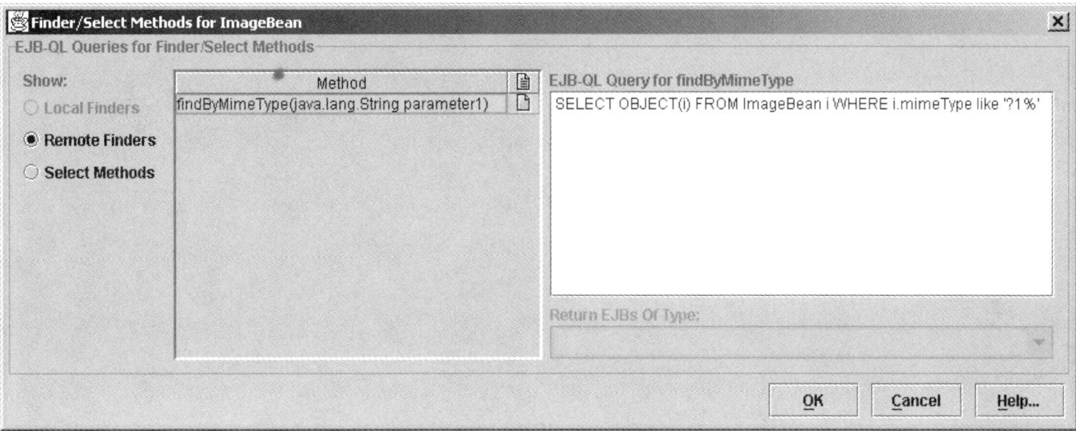

Figure A-69. Specify all the finder methods of the bean using EJB-QL

8. When done specifying all finder methods of the EJB component, close the Finder/Selector method specification dialog and move on in the wizard by pressing the Next button seen to the bottom right of Figure A-68.

9. Specify the transactional settings for all methods in the EJB component. The Transaction Management screen of the EJB creation wizard is shown in Figure A-70. Note that the default value of all the transactional settings is the Required state.

10. Specify the variables set in the environment context of the EJB component. Because the Image EJB component checks the context for a boolean value providing the level of verbosity, define the `verboseMode` parameter in the environment, as shown in Figure A-71.

New Enterprise Bean Wizard - Transaction Management

Please choose whether the bean's transactions are managed by the bean or by the container.
If they are managed by the container, you can also define what level of transaction support is required for each method in each interface.
Optionally, you can provide a description for each method.

Transaction Management

Bean-Managed

Container-Managed

Show:

Local

Local Home

Remote

Remote Home

Method	Transaction Attribute
getData()	Required
getEJBHome()	Required
getFileName()	Required
getHandle()	Required
getHeight()	Required
getMimeType()	Required
getPrimaryKey()	Required
getWidth()	Required
isIdentical(javax.ejb.EJBObject parameter1)	Required
remove()	Required
setData(byte[] parameter1)	Required
setFileName(java.lang.String parameter1)	Required

Help... Cancel < Back Next > Finish

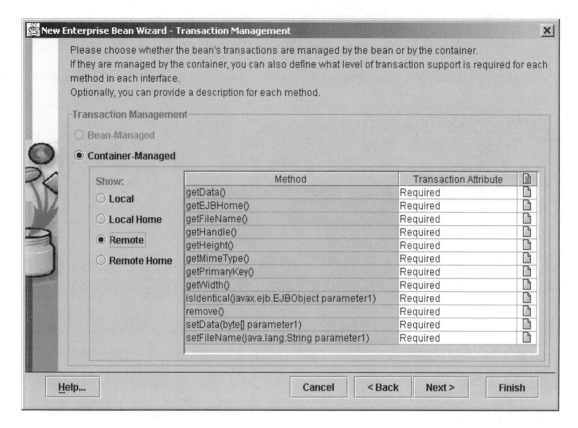

Figure A-70. Specify the transactional settings for all methods of the Remote and Home interfaces.

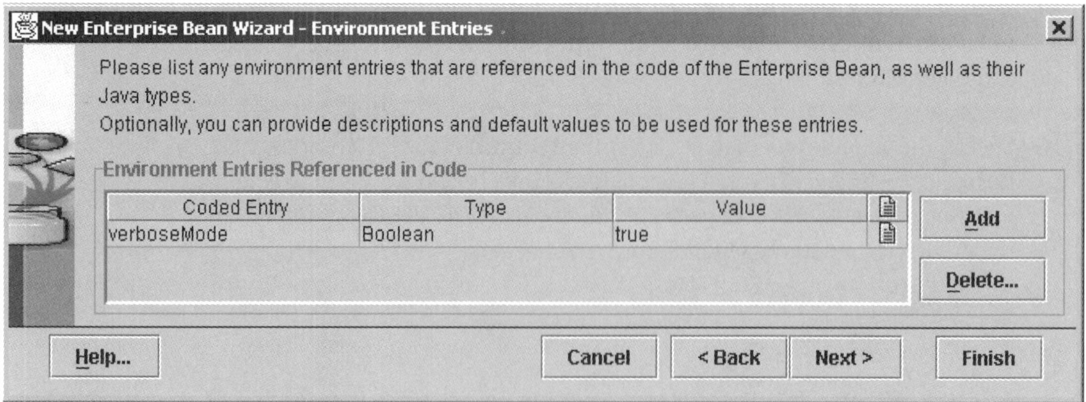

Figure A-71. The boolean flag `verboseMode` *is bound in the environment of the Image EJB.*

11. Press the Next button to continue with defining all EJB references used by the Image bean. Because the Image EJB component does not have any such references, you may simply press Finish to end the configuration process.

    The confirmation screen, shown in Figure A-72, permits you to view the resulting XML descriptor file, possibly moving back in the wizard to alter one or more values.

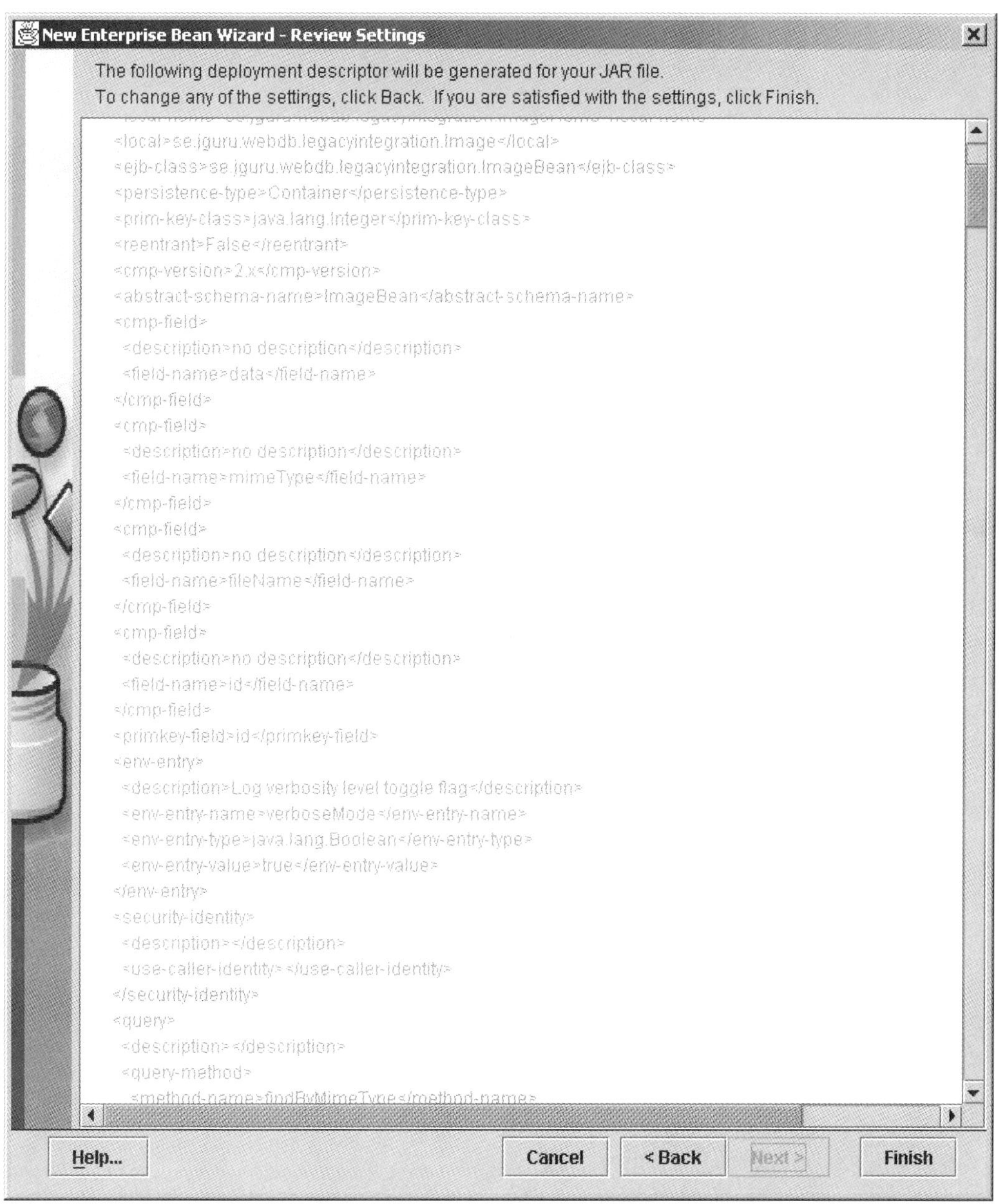

Figure A-72. The confirmation screen shows the XML deployment descriptor.

12. If satisfied with the descriptor content, press the Finish button, to define the new EJB component and display the main result screen, as shown in Figure A-73.

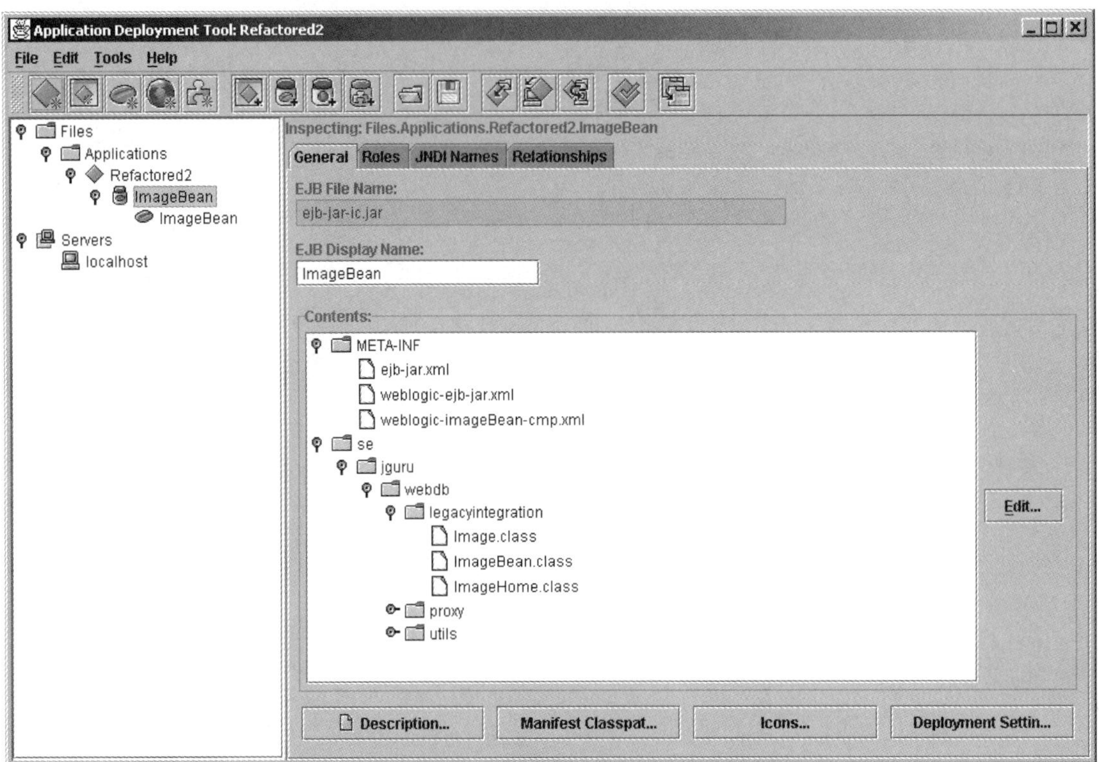

Figure A-73. Confirmation screen informing you about the successful deployment of the ImageBean EJB component

Before deploying the J2EE application Refactored2 to the J2EE reference implementation server, you must tie the Entity EJB component to a DataSource to be used for its persistent properties. Moreover, the DataSource needs to implement (or be wrapped in) an XADataSource. Before you can complete the setup of the ImageBean EJB component, therefore, you must create an XA DataSource mapped to the database where the EJB tables are stored (or will be created in case no tables exist yet).

Creating an XA DataSource

Follow these steps to create an XA DataSource:

1. Select the Tools | Server Configuration… menu item and choose the DataSources | XA tree node in the left pane. The deploytool displays all existing XA-compliant DataSources, as shown in Figure A-74.

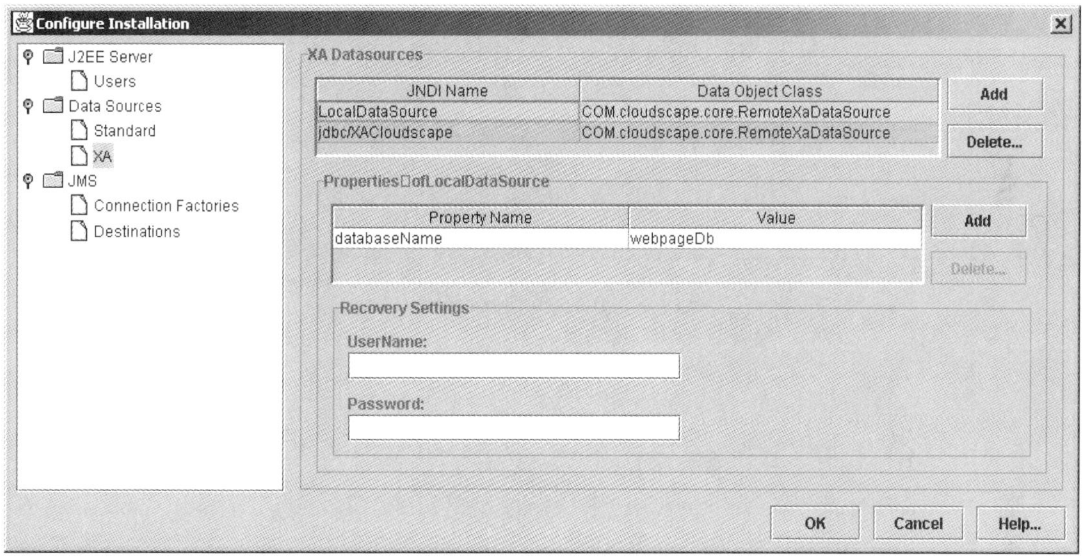

Figure A-74. The XA Datasources installed in the J2EE RI server. The selected DataSource has the JNDI lookup name `LocalDataSource` *and binds a resource of type* `COM.cloudscape.code.RemoteXADataSource`. *Note also that there is no UserName or Password set for this DataSource and that the* `databaseName` *property is set to* `webpageDb`.

The XA DataSource in Figure A-74 cannot create tables for newly deployed EJB components; any XA DataSource that should automatically create tables for newly deployed EJBs must have the `createDatabase` property set to true. This property has been set for the other XA DataSource, as shown in Figure A-75.

2. To add a new XADataSource, simply press the Add button and complete the values in the dialog that pops up.

Because the Image subsystem has a database structure set up, you simply use the `LocalDataSource` to access the data in the table cells. You may now continue with the deployment of the CMP EJB component.

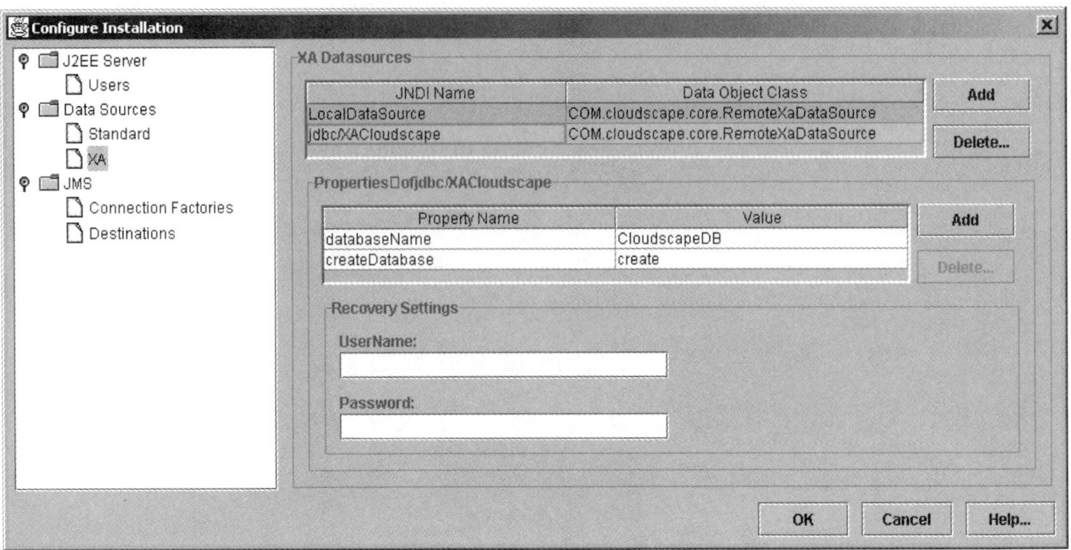

Figure A-75. The `jdbc/XACloudscape` *DataSource may create tables for newly deployed Entity EJBs, as indicated by the* `createDatabase` *property.*

Generating SQL Statements

Although you have provided fairly detailed EJB-QL queries in the `ejb-jar.xml` deployment descriptor, the deployment tool must convert the statements to actual SQL queries to be run in the database of choice. Although the J2EE server is rather good at providing such concrete SQL queries, the deploytool makes an assumption about actual table names that interferes with our current database schema. You must therefore edit the generated SQL statements by hand.

Follow these steps to generate SQL statements:

1. Start with the main screen of the ImageBean EJB component, as shown in Figure A-76. Note that the Entity tab is selected in the right pane.

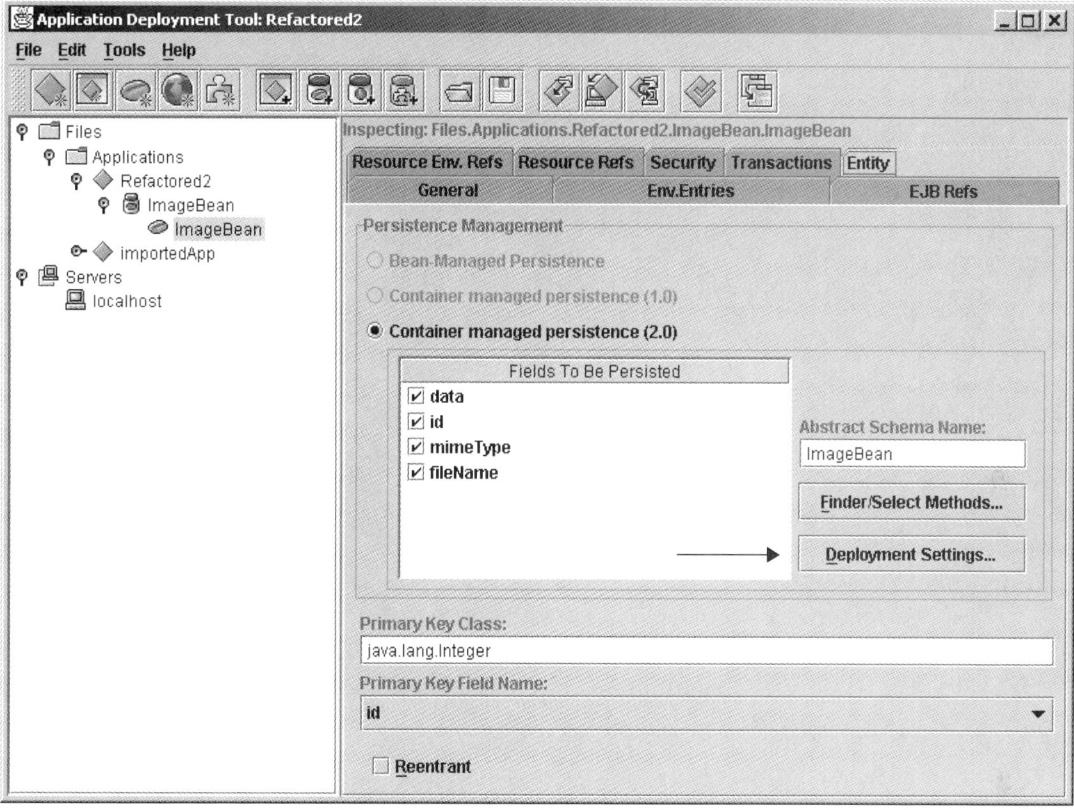

Figure A-76. Main screen of the Entity properties in the ImageBean EJB component

2. The buttons marked in Figure A-76 is used to create the deployment settings of the bean and, thereafter, the concrete SQL statements for the finders of the bean. Press the Deployment Settings… button to launch the dialog that you see in Figure A-77. This dialog permits configuration of the DataSource and concrete SQL statements for the ImageBean.

3. The Database settings of the ImageBean EJB must be set before any SQL statements can be generated, as the JDBC driver of the database is used to acquire concrete SQL types from the EJB-QL select statements. This procedure has the added benefit of always providing correct SQL statements for the database used to persist the bean. Simply press the Database Settings button in the Deployment Settings dialog and provide the JNDI name of the DataSource connected to the database as shown in Figure A-78.

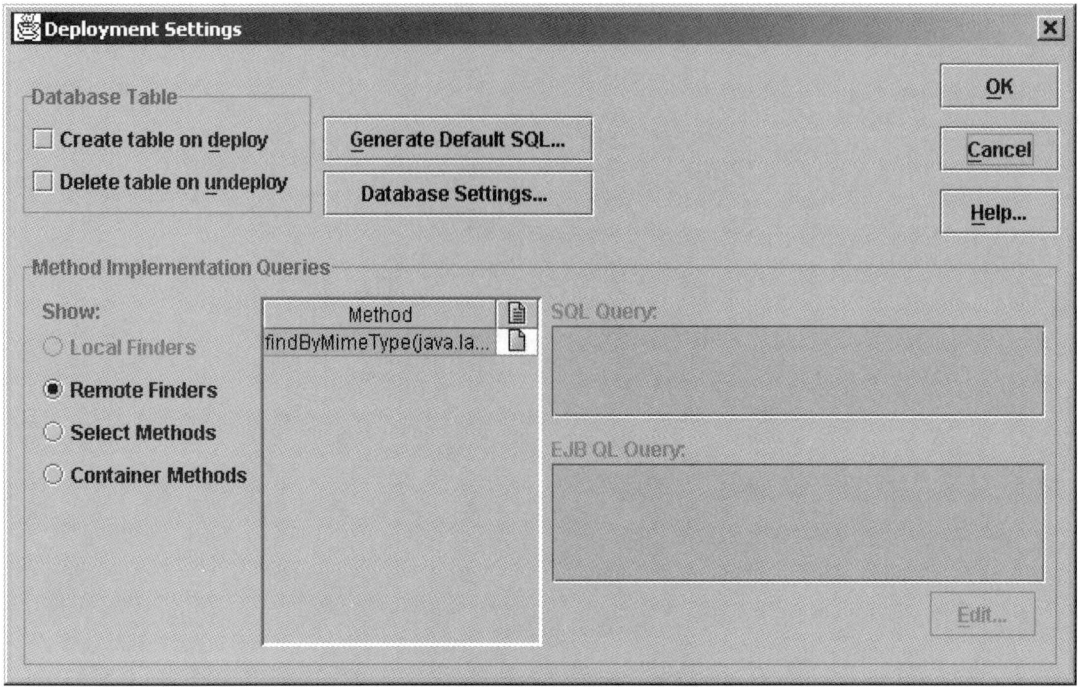

Figure A-77. The Deployment Settings dialog

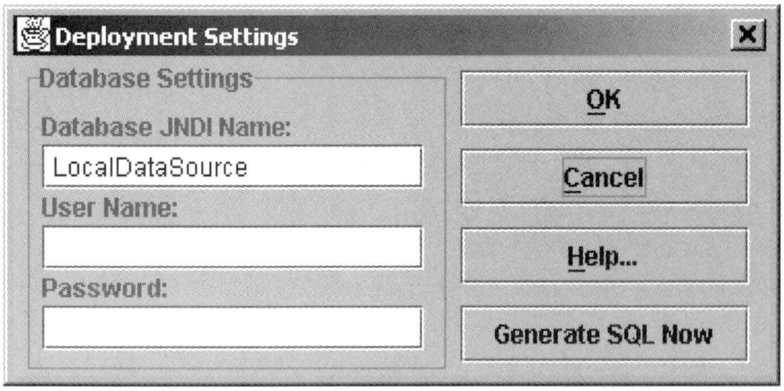

Figure A-78. Use the LocalDataSource to persist all instances of the ImageBean EJB component.

Because you have a table containing data, remember to uncheck the Create Table on Deploy as well as Delete Table on Undeploy checkboxes. Of course, for completely new databases, this may be a desired behavior—each EJB component may treat the database differently.

4. The `LocalDataSource` has been connected to the Cloudscape database, as shown in Figure A-74, so you may select it to talk to the Images table storing the data. To do so, press the Generate SQL Now button and verify that the SQL generated is correct. However, the J2EE RI deploytool assumes that the table name of the generated SQL is `<AbstractSchemaname>Table`. That is, the table name of all generated SQL statements is `ImageBeanTable` in this case—the `AbstractSchema` name is ImageBean, as shown in Figure A-76. Note the default table name in the concrete SQL Query text field shown in Figure A-79.

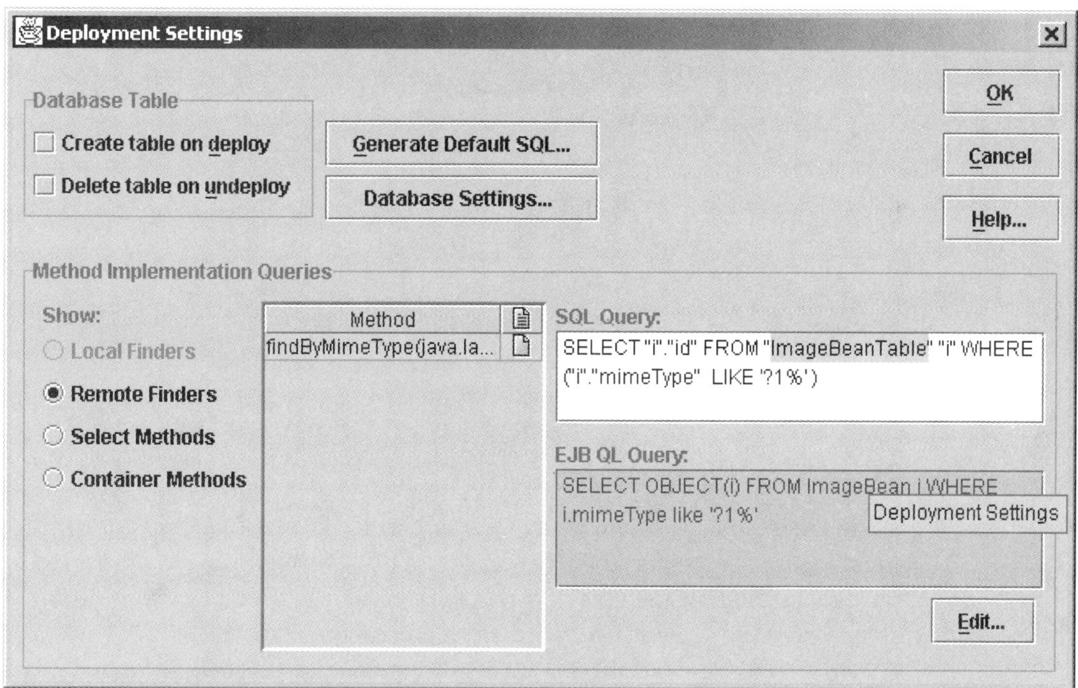

Figure A-79. The name of the table may be changed simply by editing the SQL query generated.

After altering the name of the finder methods, remember to repeat the procedure for all EJB life-cycle methods (known as *container methods* in Figure A-79).

Deploying the CMP EJB Component to the J2EE RI Server

Having generated the SQL for the CMP EJB component, you may now finally deploy the Image subsystem EJB to the J2EE RI server. Simply select the Tools | Deploy menu item to start the deployment process (see Figure A-80).

Figure A-80. Deploy the ImageBean EJB component by clicking the Tools | Deploy menu item.

You may now proceed to deploy the Web application that communicates with the Image EJB component.

Deploying a Web Application to the J2EEv1.3 RI Server

Now that the EJB component of the J2EE application is deployed, it is time to attend to the deployment of J2EE components into the Web container. The Web application of the Image subsystem contains two servlets, requiring some JNDI values as well as a reference to the Image EJB component just deployed. The deployment process for Web components is simpler than that of EJB components, and the J2EEv1.3 RI server has a good deployment GUI.

1. To launch the deployment process, click the File | New | Web Component menu item. The first real entry step in the deployment process is the New Web Component Wizard shown in Figure A-81.

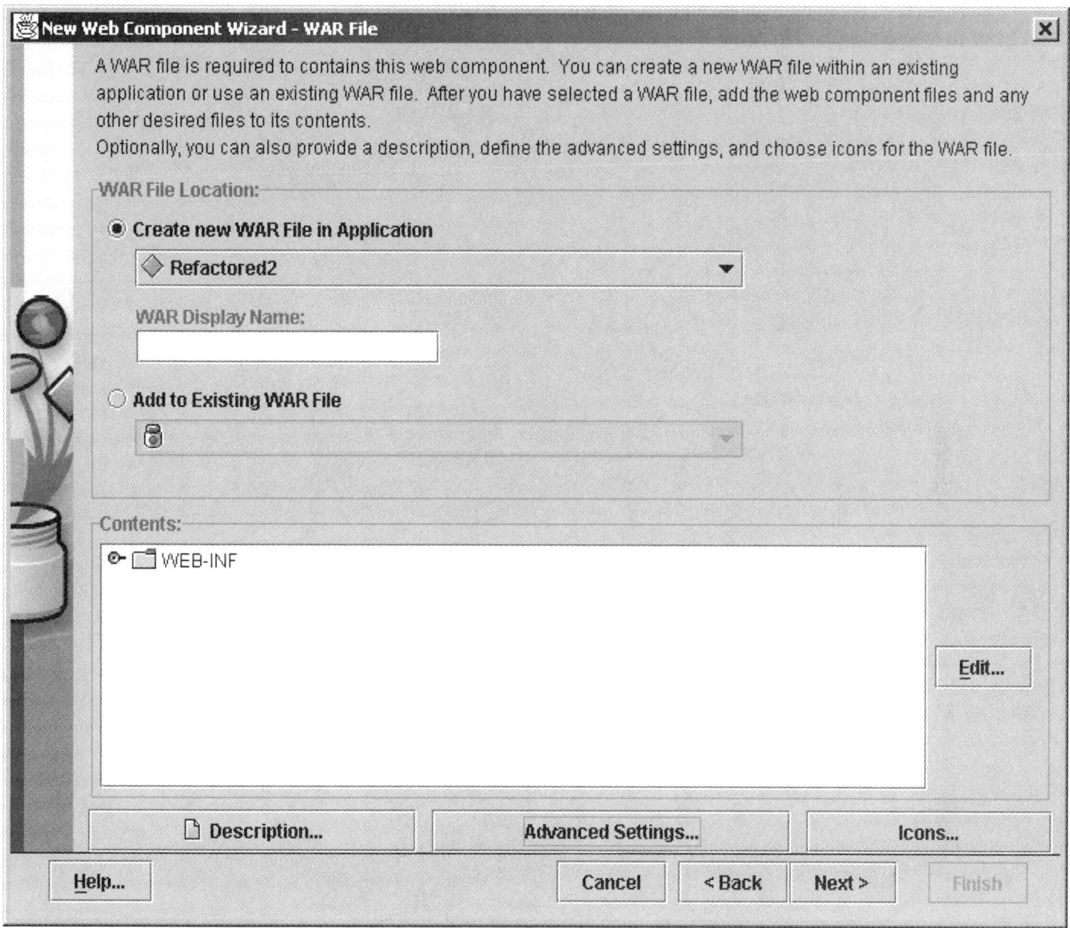

Figure A-81. New Web Component Wizard first screen

2. Press the Edit button shown in Figure A-81 to add content files to the Web application. Be sure to verify that the correct files have been added to the Web application in the Contents tree, as shown in Figure A-82.

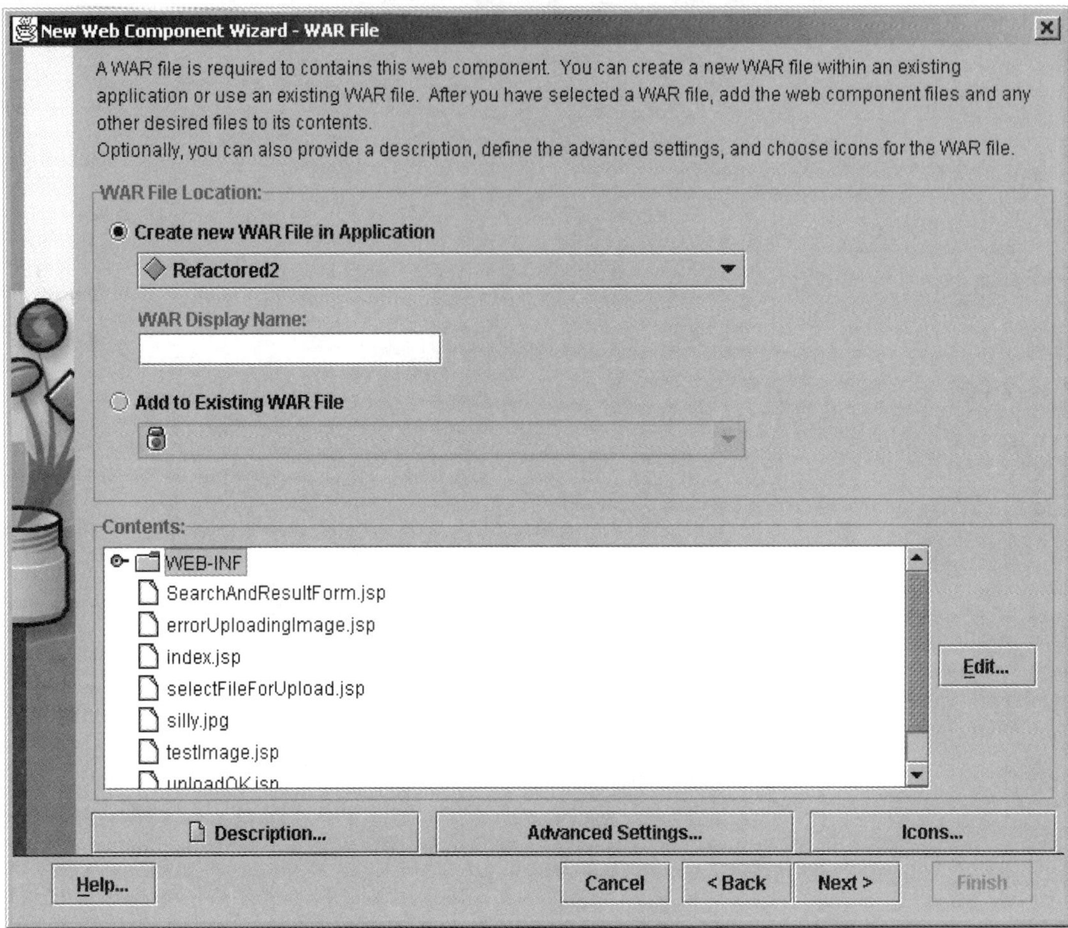

Figure A-82. The Contents tree shows all added files.

3. Press the Next button to present a screen where the user may add a servlet or JSP document to the application. After selecting the servlet alternative and clicking Next again, the New Web Component Wizard presents a General Properties form illustrated in Figure A-83 where you may select the servlet class and enter its component name (which is mirrored as the display name).

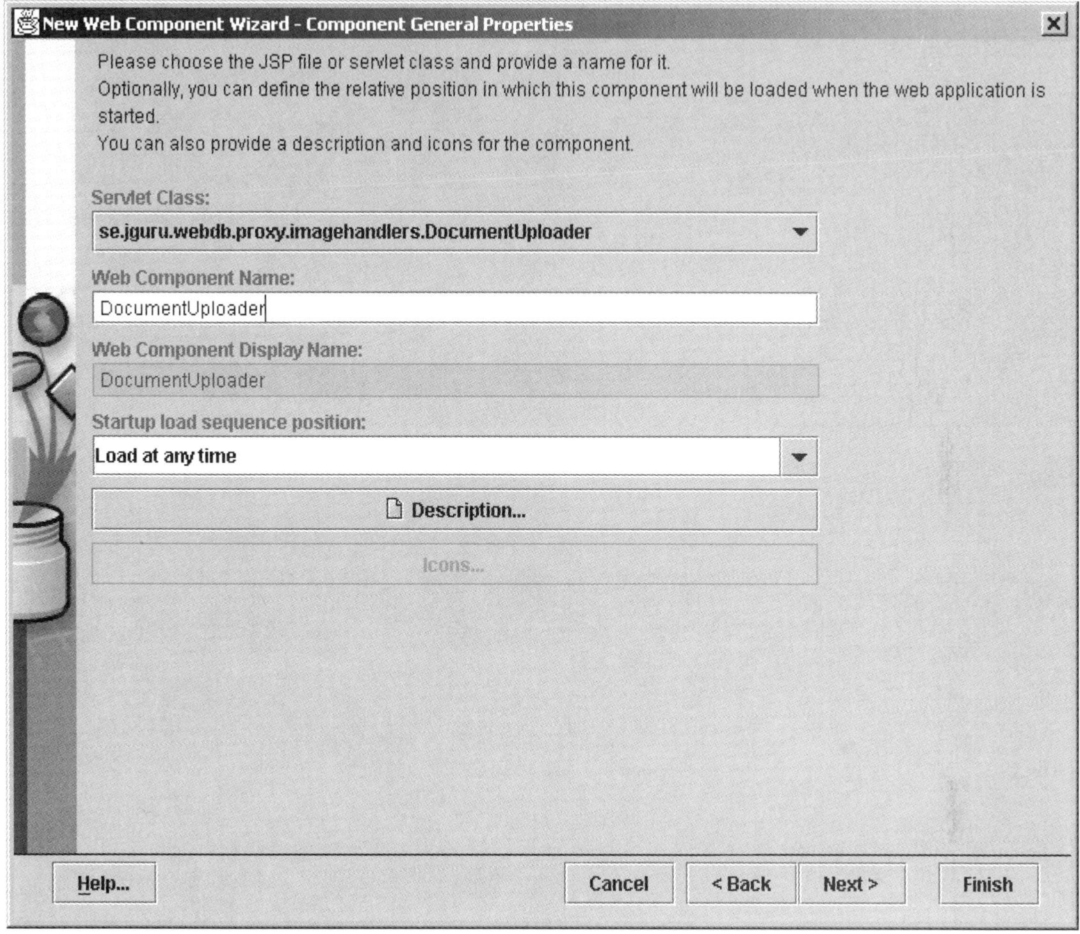

Figure A-83. Select or enter the basic data for the newly added Web component.

4. Click the Next button. The New Web Component Wizard presents a form where initialization parameters for the `DocumentUploader` servlet may be provided. Hit the Add button and fill in the values in the table as shown in Figure A-84.

5. The next screen, Aliases, lets you provide the servlet-mapping for the servlet component. This is somewhat more user-friendly presented as the alias for the servlet, as illustrated in Figure A-85.

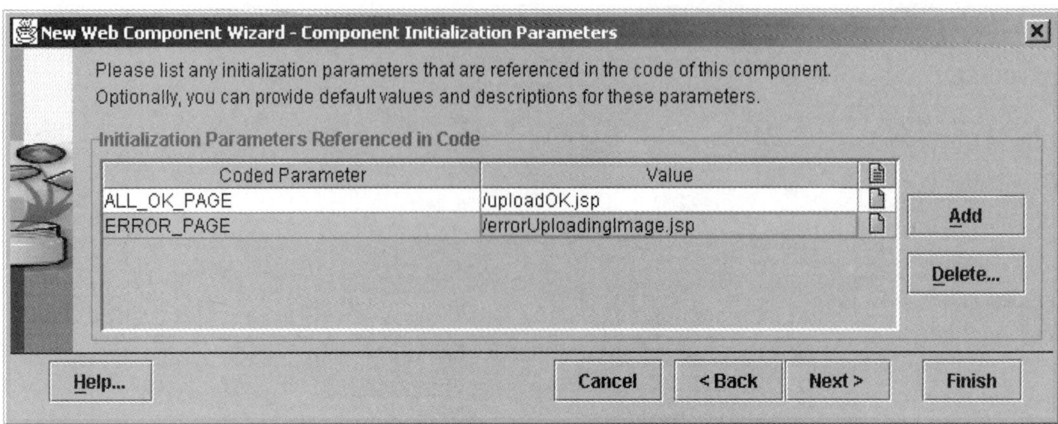

Figure A-84. Provide all initialization parameters for the servlet being deployed.

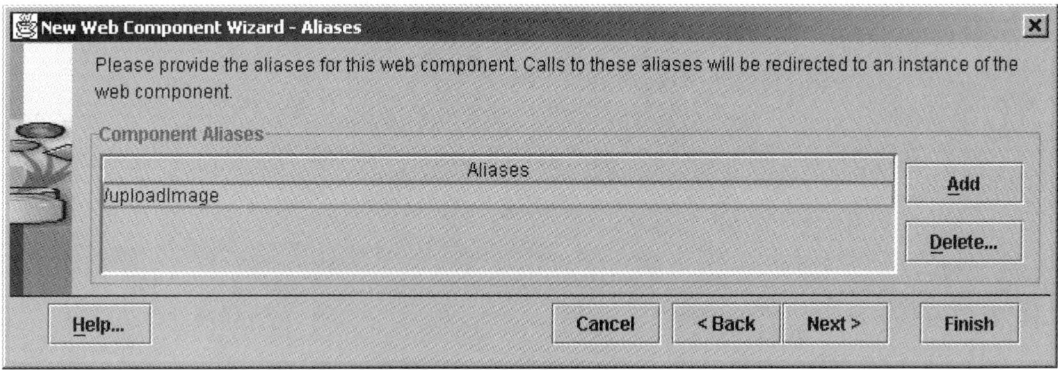

Figure A-85. The `/uploadImage` *servlet mapping will redirect to the* `DocumentUploader` *servlet.*

6. The next deployment wizard screen of relevance permits you to provide all `<env-entry>` elements bound in the local context of the Web application. As shown in Figure A-86, you supply the `verboseMode` boolean flag that controls the level of logging used by the EJB component.

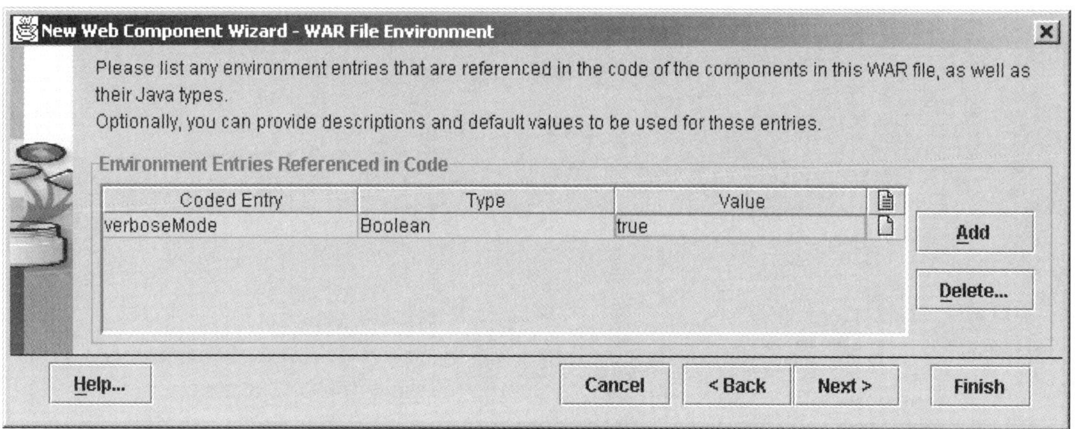

Figure A-86. Add all environment entries used by the servlet.

7. The next relevant step of the deployment wizard adds one or more `<ejb-ref>` entries in the `web.xml` file to grant the servlet a reference to an EJB component. In this case, the `ImageProxy` instance used by the `DocumentUploader` servlet needs to be able to talk to the Image EJB component directly. We must therefore add an `<ejb-ref>` entry to the `web.xml` file, and that reference is added as shown in Figure A-87.

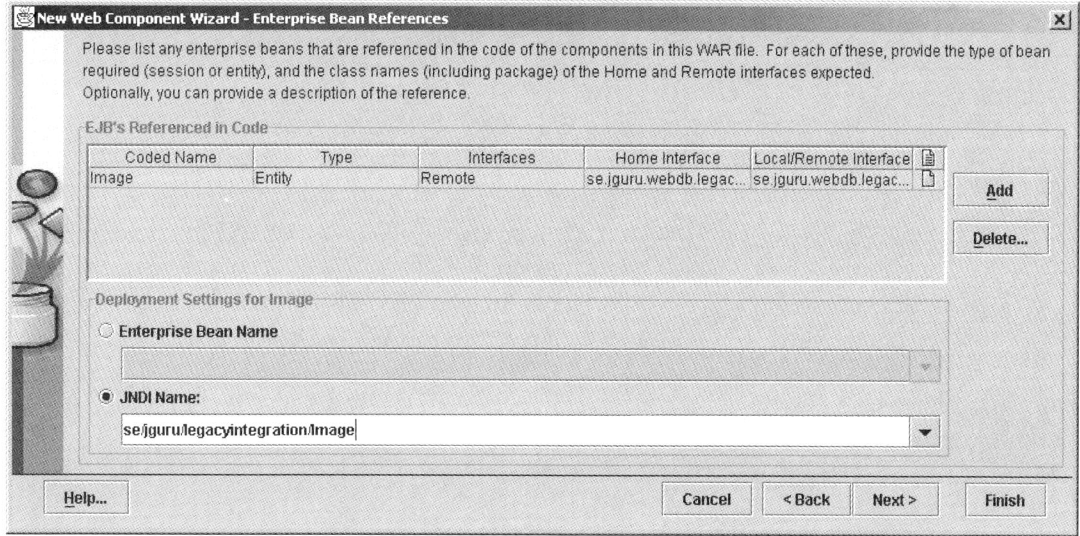

Figure A-87. The Enterprise Beans References screen permits adding an EJB reference (`<ejb-ref>`) to the `web.xml` file.

> **NOTE** *The value in the Coded Name column is the value that should be looked up from within the J2EE component. Referring to the Image EJB component added in Figure A-87, the JNDI lookup string in the servlet code should be* `java:comp/env/Image`*. The* `java:comp/env` *part of the lookup string refers to the local Web application context and the* `Image` *string refers to the key of the EJB component, provided in the Coded Name column.*

The home interface and remote interface column simply contains the values of the home and remote interfaces of the EJB component, but the JNDI name text field in the bottom of the dialog is the actual JNDI name to which `java:comp/env/Image` should be mapped in the registry. In short, the Coded Name used in the servlet component source is mapped to the actual JNDI name where the actual Home interface is bound.

8. Press the Next button to add a reference to a DataSource. The "Resource References" step of the Web Component Deployment Wizard maps a logical (Coded) name to a real JNDI name used by the server. Shown in Figure A-88, the `LegacyDataSource` local context name is a container managed DataSource that is bound in the JNDI registry under the key `se/jguru/legacyintegration/LegacyDataSource`.

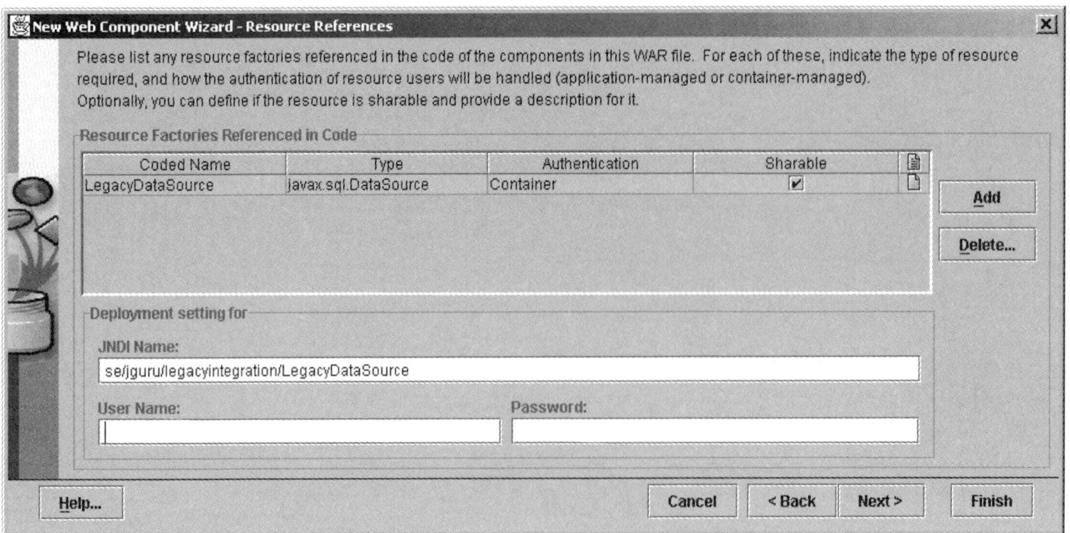

Figure A-88. Adding a resource reference to the Web container. Note the mapping to a real JNDI name in the Deployment Settings section.

9. The File references step of the Web Component Deployment Wizard (shown in Figure A-89) permits adding a welcome file—in this case, the `/selectFileForUpload.jsp` is selected as the welcome file. Should your Web application contain JSP tag libraries, you may add an alias (coded reference) for the real tag library URI provided. Also, if any servlet or JSP document throws a particular exception, the Error mapping list decides which resource should be shown to the client.

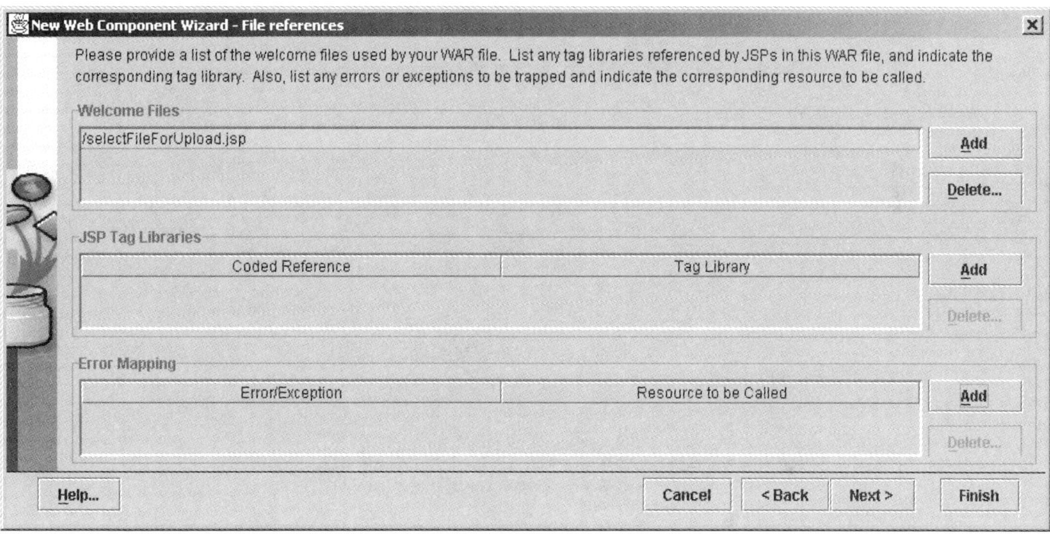

Figure A-89. All file references are added to the Web application in the same step of the Web Application Deployment Wizard.

10. Finally, the `web.xml` deployment descriptor, illustrated in Figure A-90, is shown as a confirmation of your deployment descriptions.

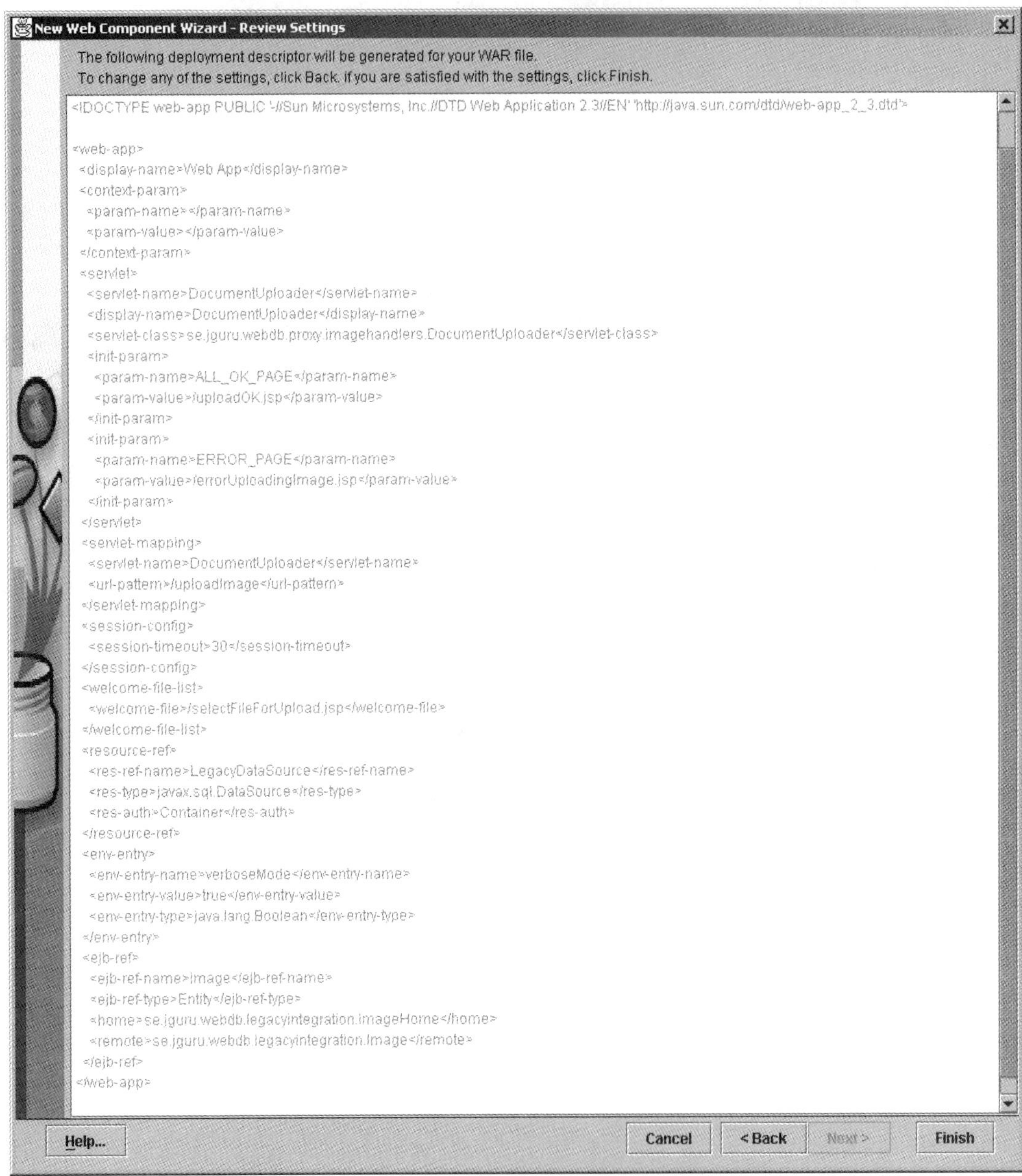
New Web Component Wizard - Review Settings
The following deployment descriptor will be generated for your WAR file.
To change any of the settings, click Back. If you are satisfied with the settings, click Finish.
<!DOCTYPE web-app PUBLIC '-//Sun Microsystems, Inc.//DTD Web Application 2.3//EN' 'http://java.sun.com/dtd/web-app_2_3.dtd'>
<web-app>
<display-name>Web App</display-name>
<context-param>
<param-name></param-name>
<param-value></param-value>
</context-param>
<servlet>
<servlet-name>DocumentUploader</servlet-name>
<display-name>DocumentUploader</display-name>
<servlet-class>se.jguru.webdb.proxy.imagehandlers.DocumentUploader</servlet-class>
<init-param>
<param-name>ALL_OK_PAGE</param-name>
<param-value>/uploadOK.jsp</param-value>
</init-param>
<init-param>
<param-name>ERROR_PAGE</param-name>
<param-value>/errorUploadingImage.jsp</param-value>
</init-param>
</servlet>
<servlet-mapping>
<servlet-name>DocumentUploader</servlet-name>
<url-pattern>/uploadImage</url-pattern>
</servlet-mapping>
<session-config>
<session-timeout>30</session-timeout>
</session-config>
<welcome-file-list>
<welcome-file>/selectFileForUpload.jsp</welcome-file>
</welcome-file-list>
<resource-ref>
<res-ref-name>LegacyDataSource</res-ref-name>
<res-type>javax.sql.DataSource</res-type>
<res-auth>Container</res-auth>
</resource-ref>
<env-entry>
<env-entry-name>verboseMode</env-entry-name>
<env-entry-value>true</env-entry-value>
<env-entry-type>java.lang.Boolean</env-entry-type>
</env-entry>
<ejb-ref>
<ejb-ref-name>Image</ejb-ref-name>
<ejb-ref-type>Entity</ejb-ref-type>
<home>se.jguru.webdb.legacyintegration.ImageHome</home>
<remote>se.jguru.webdb.legacyintegration.Image</remote>
</ejb-ref>
</web-app>
Help...
Cancel
< Back
Next >
Finish

Figure A-90. The deployment confirmation screen shows the `web.xml` *generated by the wizard.*

11. Click the Finish button to return to the deploytool main screen and reveal a fully deployed Web component, as shown in Figure A-91.

12. To deploy the component to the J2EE RI server, simply click the Tools | Deploy menu item.

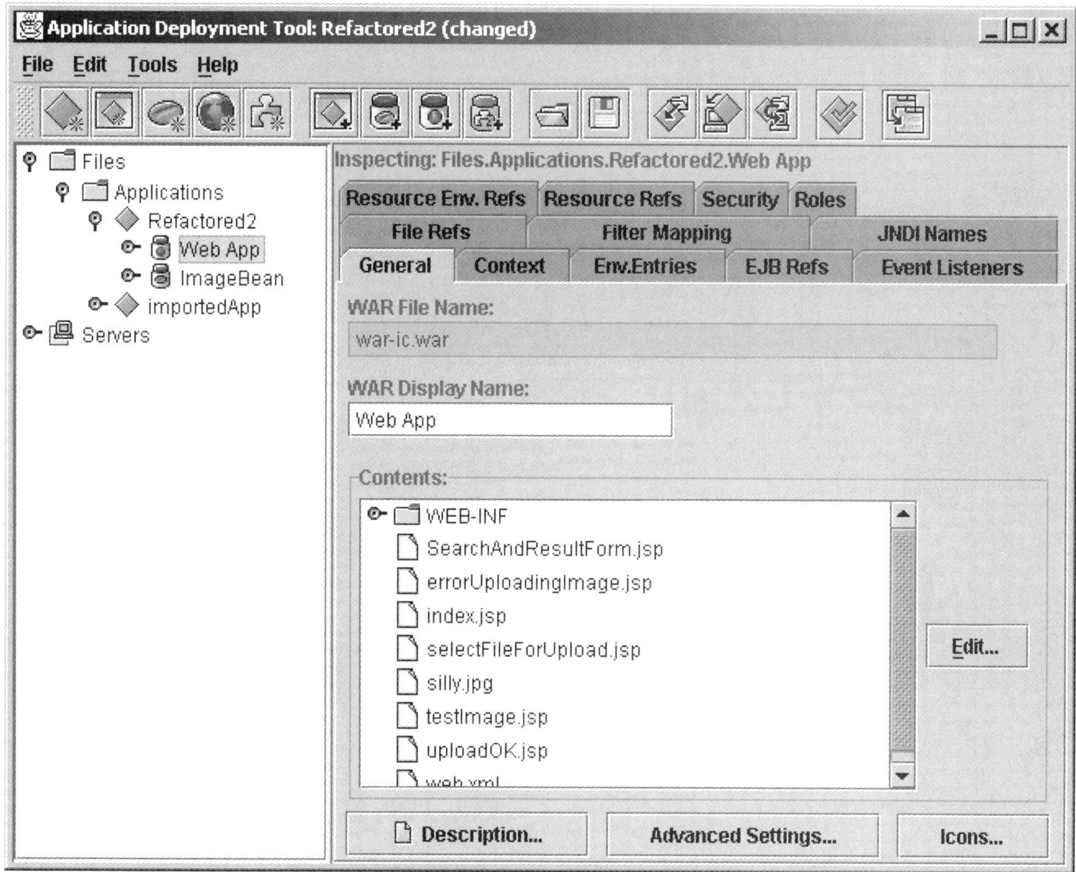

Figure A-91. The main screen of the deploytool shows the newly deployed Web app.

This concludes the walkthrough of the J2EEv1.3 RI deploytool and server. For a more detailed reference description, refer to the downloaded and installed J2EE RI documentation, as well as the J2EE tutorials found on the JavaSoft Web site, `http://www.javasoft.com`.

Index

D

E

F

G

H

J

K

L

M

N

O

S

T

U

V

W

X

books for professionals by professionals™

About Apress

Apress, located in Berkeley, CA, is an innovative publishing company devoted to meeting the needs of existing and potential programming professionals. Simply put, the "A" in Apress stands for the "Author's Press™." Apress' unique author-centric approach to publishing grew from conversations between Dan Appleman and Gary Cornell, authors of best-selling, highly regarded computer books. In 1998, they set out to create a publishing company that emphasized quality above all else, a company with books that would be considered the best in their market. Dan and Gary's vision has resulted in over 30 widely acclaimed titles by some of the industry's leading software professionals.

Do You Have What It Takes to Write for Apress?

Apress is rapidly expanding its publishing program. If you can write and refuse to compromise on the quality of your work, if you believe in doing more than rehashing existing documentation, and if you're looking for opportunities and rewards that go far beyond those offered by traditional publishing houses, we want to hear from you!

Consider these innovations that we offer all of our authors:

- **Top royalties with *no* hidden switch statements**
  Authors typically only receive half of their normal royalty rate on foreign sales. In contrast, Apress' royalty rate remains the same for both foreign and domestic sales.

- **A mechanism for authors to obtain equity in Apress**
  Unlike the software industry, where stock options are essential to motivate and retain software professionals, the publishing industry has adhered to an outdated compensation model based on royalties alone. In the spirit of most software companies, Apress reserves a significant portion of its equity for authors.

- **Serious treatment of the technical review process**
  Each Apress book has a technical reviewing team whose remuneration depends in part on the success of the book since they too receive royalties.

Moreover, through a partnership with Springer-Verlag, one of the world's major publishing houses, Apress has significant venture capital behind it. Thus, we have the resources to produce the highest quality books *and* market them aggressively.

If you fit the model of the Apress author who can write a book that gives the "professional what he or she needs to know™," then please contact one of our Editorial Directors, Gary Cornell (gary_cornell@apress.com), Dan Appleman (dan_appleman@apress.com), Karen Watterson (karen_watterson@apress.com) or Jason Gilmore (jason_gilmore@apress.com) for more information.